EVERYMAN,
I WILL GO WITH THEE,
AND BE THY GUIDE,
IN THY MOST NEED
TO GO BY THY SIDE

MARK TWAIN

COLLECTED
NONFICTION

VOLUME 1

SELECTIONS FROM THE
AUTOBIOGRAPHY, LETTERS,
ESSAYS, AND SPEECHES

WITH AN INTRODUCTION
BY ADAM HOCHSCHILD

EVERYMAN'S LIBRARY
Alfred A. Knopf New York London Toronto

375

THIS IS A BORZOI BOOK
PUBLISHED BY ALFRED A. KNOPF

First included in Everyman's Library, 2016

"The War Prayer," "The United States of Lyncherdom," and "License of the Press" reprinted by arrangement with the Mark Twain Foundation. The letters are reprinted with the permission of the University of California Press from the following volumes:

Mark Twain's Letters, Volume 1: 1853–1866, by Mark Twain. © 1987 by the Mark Twain Foundation. Published by the University of California Press.
Mark Twain's Letters, Volume 3: 1869, by Mark Twain. © 1992 by the Mark Twain Foundation. Published by the University of California Press.
Mark Twain's Letters, Volume 6: 1874–1875, by Mark Twain. © 2002 by the Mark Twain Foundation. Published by the University of California Press.
Miscellaneous Writings: Previously Unpublished Letters, Manuscript Letters, and Literary Manuscripts Available in the Mark Twain Papers, by Mark Twain. © 2001 by the Mark Twain Foundation. Published by the University of California Press.

"Map of Paris," Courtesy of the Mark Twain Project, The Bancroft Library, University of California, Berkeley.

Introduction Copyright © 2016 by Adam Hochschild
Bibliography and Chronology Copyright © 2016 by Everyman's Library
Typography by Peter B. Willberg

The publishers are grateful to the Mark Twain Project for their assistance in the preparation of this two-volume Everyman edition of Mark Twain's collected nonfiction.

www.randomhouse/everymans
www.everymanslibrary.co.uk

ISBN 978-1-101-90770-2 (US)
978-1-84159-375-3 (UK)

A CIP catalogue reference for this book is available from the British Library

Book design by Barbara de Wilde and Carol Devine Carson

Typeset in the UK by Input Data Services, 17 King Square, Bridgwater, Somerset TA6 3DJ
Printed and bound in Germany by GGP Media GmbH, Pössneck

MARK TWAIN

C O N T E N T S

MARK TWAIN

CONTENTS

INTRODUCTION

Some great writers lived lives that seem limited to only a small slice of human experience – Proust, Austen, Dickinson – but they saw far and deep nonetheless. The lives of others – Cervantes, Tolstoy, Dostoevsky – far overflowed what they were able to get between the covers of their books. Mark Twain falls among the overflowers. Even the complete array of his work does not begin to contain the breadth, paradox, and tragedies of his life.

It was a large and restless one that stretched from the era when doctors bled their patients to that of the automobile and the airplane, from the boundless freedom of his childhood (read the passage in these pages about skating on the frozen Mississippi under moonlight, as ice floes break up and separate him from land) to crossing the country by stagecoach, sleeping on top of mailbags, to reach California in the aftermath of the Gold Rush. As a young man, he heard Charles Dickens read *David Copperfield* aloud from a New York stage; as an old one he played miniature golf with Woodrow Wilson. He began as Sam Clemens in the remote riverside town of Hannibal, Missouri; under his pen name of Mark Twain he traveled the world as the most renowned American author of his time, visited or received by princesses and presidents, explorers and emperors, even the admiring Shah of Persia. The young Kipling made a pilgrimage to meet him; Sigmund Freud came to hear him speak. Yet, amid these triumphs, Twain saw his beloved wife and three of his four children die before him.

He denounced the love of money and helped coin the phrase Gilded Age but hobnobbed happily with Andrew Carnegie and other robber barons, vacationed on the 227-foot yacht of one of them, preferred the fanciest of hotels, and lived in a palatial mansion with Tiffany furnishings, a marble-floored entrance hall, and a staff of seven. Hankering badly after still greater wealth, he spent himself deep into debt by investing money, his own and borrowed, in a long string of muddleheaded inventions. The most disastrous was one whose failure could have been predicted by a mechanically-minded teenager: a typesetting machine with eighteen thousand separate parts. Into this hopeless dream the ever-optimistic writer poured the equivalent of well over three million dollars (in early twenty-first-century money). It would take another Twain to get all of this into a novel.

His work, like his life, was of volcanic proportions. It is not without reason that one editor entitled an anthology *Mark Twain in Eruption*. In addition to the more than thirty books he published during his lifetime, Twain wrote thousands of newspaper articles and left behind some fifty notebooks and six hundred unpublished or unfinished manuscripts. Over his seventy-four years, it is estimated, he wrote at least fifty thousand letters, most of which have long since disappeared. The eruptions never ceased. On April 13, 1897, after working on his travelogue, *Following the Equator*, he wrote triumphantly in his notebook, "I finished my book today." Five weeks later came another entry, "Finished the book *again*. Addition of 30,000 words."

On top of all this material, Twain left behind, largely unedited, some half million words of recollections about his life. The more famous he became, the more often people pressed him to write his autobiography. But he claimed that all written memoirs were fraudulent; instead he would create the first truly honest one by *dictating* his, to be published in full only after his death. "If I should talk to the stenographer two hours a day for a hundred years," he declared, "I should still never be able to set down a tenth part of the things which have interested me." Between 1906 and 1909, the year before he died, he made a good start on the hundred years, dictating bountifully in 242 sessions.

Rambling from one corner of his life to another, free-associating, embroidering stories he had once written, mixing fanciful anecdotes, personal experience, and pungent opinions with newspaper clippings and half-finished sketches, Twain's dictated eruptions most resemble a genre that would not be named for nearly another century: blog posts. This mountain of proto-blogging, sometimes with earlier bits of autobiographical writing mixed in, has been repeatedly reshaped by different editors since his death, depending on whether the compiler wanted to present a non-political, avuncular Twain, an auto-biography at manageable length, an all-inclusive colossus, or Twain's life in chronological sequence rather than in the meandering fashion in which he actually recounted it.

The selections in the first portion of this book, pieces that were published in the *North American Review* soon after he dictated them, are only a small part of this gargantuan mountain. But they have a claim to being the most authentic part because – after a $30,000 fee persuaded Twain that not *all* of his auto-biography should be posthumous – they are the only shoulder of the mountain that he himself edited and approved for publication.

One of the great literary memoirs this is not. It digresses wildly, drops famous names, has sentimental patches, and assumes (true for readers then, but not necessarily now) that we already know a good deal about his life. It has pages about billiards and bowling. It could use a careful rewrite. Nonetheless, it yields sudden stretches of great eloquence, like shafts of sun falling on that mountainside, as when he describes child-hood stays on his uncle's farm: "I can call back the solemn twilight and mystery of the deep woods, the earthy smells, the faint odors of the wild flowers, the sheen of rain-washed foliage, the rattling clatter of drops when the wind shook the trees ... the snap-shot glimpses of disturbed wild creatures skurrying through the grass."

Twain had already mined a high point of his life, his years as a steamboat pilot, for what most of us consider his greatest work of nonfiction, *Life on the Mississippi*, but one of the fascina-tions of the dictated autobiography is that we can see in his words some of the sources for his greatest work of fiction, the *Adventures of Huckleberry Finn*. Not just the boyhood figures who were to some degree the models for Huck, Tom Sawyer, and others, but the spirit of that boyhood: the universe of woods, fields, caves, and islands to be explored in an age without supervised after-school activities; the pervasive acceptance of slavery; the small town where everyone knew everyone else's business; the great river coursing past, as ceaseless as the flow of life itself. And in his recollections we can also see Twain's knowledge of the wider world beyond Hannibal: its chicanery, its illusions, and its lust for gain. Without the experience of all this he never could have imagined into being, in his childhood landscape, an outlaw like Huck.

*

The letters that form the next part of this volume give us another cross-section of Twain's life. The selection is again only a small portion of an enormous mass, but the window they provide onto his soul is less mediated and controlled by Twain than the autobiography chapters he saw into print. Through the letters we can feel his thrill at seeing new countries, his enjoyment of his growing fame, and his perpetual grand dreams of making a fortune through a magically successful investment. We see his immense gratitude when his friend the novelist and editor William Dean Howells gives him the greatest gift any writer can give another, which is to mark up a manuscript – in this case *The Adventures of Tom Sawyer*. Twain was startlingly willing to let his wife, Howells, and others prune material out of his writing or select which shorter pieces should be included in a collection, but almost everyone was so in awe of him that he received too little of the tough, intelligent, critical feedback that could have benefited his more ragged and loquacious books.

Nonetheless, he did have another way of testing the effect of his words, integral to sharpening his humor and learning exactly what people responded to. During the course of his lifetime he gave well over five hundred lectures, readings, commencement addresses, or after-dinner speeches, at least 140 of them just on one exhausting, round-the-world, 53,000-mile speaking tour he undertook to pay off his huge debts. "I know a great many secrets about audiences," he says in one letter here, "secrets not to be got out of books, but only acquirable by experience." He learned to speak in a way that would appeal equally to the 25-cent customers in the balconies and those in evening dress in the front-row seats. He was wearied by this endless round of performing, but at the same time reveled in it, noting carefully which lines worked and which didn't, learning the value of a drawl and a calculated pause.

He was a shrewd and interested judge of other performers. His best work all seems born to be read aloud – which usually it was, first to an audience of his wife and daughters and then on stage. It is this side of Twain that the actor Hal Holbrook brought to life by staging constantly changing versions of his one-man show, *Mark Twain Tonight!* on Broadway, on television, on recordings, around the country, and across the world for more than sixty years. This talented imitator of Twain has himself had many imitators.

Above all, the letters let us feel with Twain what lay behind his statement that "the source of all humor is not laughter but sorrow." He feels responsible for the agonizing death of his brother, lethally scalded when a boiler exploded on the steam-boat where Twain had gotten him a job. The blows that would come later in his life help account for the darker tone of the writing from his final decade and a half. The loss from spinal meningitis of his favorite daughter, the twenty-four-year-old Susy, is all the more painful because it comes when he is away from her, in England, finishing up his year-long international lecture tour. "She that had been our wonder and our worship," he calls her. "It is one of the mysteries of our nature that a man, all unprepared, can receive a thunder-stroke like that and live." Some weeks after the news of her death, still deep in mourning, he writes to his friend Rev. Joseph Twichell that "she was my superior in fineness of mind, in the delicacy & subtlety of her intellect ... I know her better now; for I have read her private writings & sounded the deeps of her mind; & I know better, now, the treasure that was mine than I knew it when I had it ... And now she is *dead* – & I can never tell her."

Another daughter, Jean, years later would die horribly on Christmas Eve, while visiting her father, when an epileptic seizure caused her to drown in a bathtub. She was twenty-nine. But perhaps nothing surpassed Twain's grief at the loss of his wife, Livy, in Italy, where they had gone in search of the respite and climate that might have aided her heart disease and difficulty in breathing. One evening he came to her "to say the usual good-night," as he writes Howells, "& she was dead!" To his friend Twichell he describes how he sat with her body for the next twenty hours "till the embalmers came at 5;

& then I saw her no more. In all that night & all that day she never noticed my caressing hand – it seemed strange." It is all the more poignant to read that side-by-side with an early love letter to her, where he speaks of her "eyes that are dearer to me than the light that streams out of the Heavens."

*

The third portion of these pages is a sampling of the newspaper articles, humorous sketches, speeches, diatribes, essays, and pamphlets that flowed from Twain's pen throughout his life. Just because there is a companion Everyman's Library volume of his writing called *The Complete Short Stories*, don't assume that all the pieces in this one are purely nonfiction. More than one of them has some actual event as its kernel, around which Twain then spun a tale at least as tall as anything Tom Sawyer could have invented. "Mark Twain took a democrat's view of fact and fiction," his biographer Ron Powers writes; "he ... let them mingle in his work without prejudice." If he had lived long enough to write for *The New Yorker*, little of his supposed reportage could have gotten past its famed fact-checking department unscathed.

These pieces cover a spectrum of tone from those that seem embarrassingly flat or eccentric today to a few like "A Telephonic Conversation" that can still make us burst into laughter. In them can be found ammunition to supply either side in the famous argument between the critics Van Wyck Brooks and Bernard DeVoto over whether or not this son of the rugged frontier was fatally tamed by his mother, his wife, his wealth, and his long years in the more genteel culture of the East Coast. They show us a Twain who fluctuates between the daringly subversive and the conventional prejudices of his time (about American Indians, for example), and also a Twain who had some decided quirks – a fascination with clairvoyance, for one thing, and the conviction that someone other than Shakespeare wrote those plays.

But these writings also show us something deeper: a man becoming keenly aware of the injustices of his age. From the young Sam Clemens whose father and uncle owned slaves and who even briefly joined a unit of Confederate irregulars (an episode he considerably embellished in "The Private History of a Campaign that Failed"), he grew into the Mark Twain who felt that slavery was America's original sin. *Huckleberry Finn* is surely the most eloquent expression of that feeling in all our literature, a portrait all the more slyly powerful because Huck believes he will be doomed to hell for helping the enslaved Jim – Miss Watson's lawful property – escape down the river toward freedom.

Twain understood, more clearly than most white Americans, that the Civil War had changed too little and that the United States was still a place of lynchings and other horrors for former slaves. One act of generosity by him would reverberate decades after he was dead. Among a number of black students whose studies Twain helped support was one of the first men of color to enter Yale Law School. Twain met him briefly and may have forgotten his name but told the school's dean he would help pay the expenses of "this young man" – who was working odd jobs on the side to make ends meet – until he graduated. The student was Warner T. McGuinn, who became a respected lawyer and a Baltimore city council member, and who, decades later, himself mentored and referred cases to a grateful young black attorney just starting out on his career. *That* lawyer was Thurgood Marshall, who argued the successful Brown v. Board of Education case that ended legal school segregation in America, and who became the first black justice of the United States Supreme Court. We can imagine the smile that would have brought to Twain's face.

As the author aged, he came to see that the racism so intertwined with American slavery took other forms around the world – and it was a world he saw as much or more of than almost any other American writer of his day. As he puts it in one piece here, "I think I have no color prejudices nor caste prejudices nor creed prejudices. All that I care to know is that a man is a human being – that is enough for me; he can't be any worse." While staying in Vienna in the late 1890s, he presciently observed – unlike virtually any foreign journalist of the time – just who were always the first victims of ethnic nationalist demonstrations. "In some cases the Germans [were] the rioters, in others the Czechs," he wrote in *Harper's*, "and in all cases the Jew had to roast, no matter which side he was on."

Although he had spoken as early as 1867 about the harmful impact of American "civilization" on Hawaii and had noticed how brutally Chinese immigrant laborers were treated in California, it was mostly during the last fifteen years of his life that Twain's ire focused on the worldwide drive for colonies, fueled by "the white man's notion that he is less savage than the other savages." When he circled the globe on his lecture tour in 1895 and 1896, he encountered evidence at almost every stop. In Australia he saw how British settlers had displaced and almost exterminated the Aborigines and how they had put South Sea islanders to work in harsh conditions on the sugar plantations. In India he noticed how a white man punched his servant in the face, and sensed the undercurrent among Indians of a desire for self-rule. And his reaction to South Africa was different from that of almost all Americans and Europeans at this time, who saw the territory mainly in terms of the conflict over land and mineral wealth between white Britons and white Afrikaners, or Boers, which would culminate in the Boer War of 1899–1902. Twain, however, felt that the underlying crime had been committed by those who "stole the land from the . . . blacks."

He was appalled when, in the treaty ending the Spanish-American War, the United States acquired a colony of its own by buying the Philippines from Spain, for twenty million dollars. "I am opposed," he declared in an interview, "to having the eagle put its talons on any other land." This didn't stop him, however, from thoroughly enjoying the company of the great imperialists of the age, like the explorer Henry Morton Stanley, the bellicose Kaiser Wilhelm II of Germany, and the young Boer War hero Winston Churchill.

Not surprisingly, Filipino nationalists who had fought for independence from Spain had no wish to see themselves colonized anew by the United States. The brutal Philippine-American War that broke out in 1899 was one of our most shameful: a war of naked conquest that killed at least 200,000 Filipinos and saw American troops use widespread, systematic torture. The war spurred congressional hearings, protest meetings throughout the country, and Twain's most influential work on imperialism, "To the Person Sitting in Darkness." The title alludes to the Gospel according to St. Matthew where "the people which sat in darkness" are those not yet enlightened by Christ's good news; there had been much talk in the air about how it was America's duty to bring Christianity to the backward Filipinos. Millions of Filipinos were already Catholics, but this was ignored. President William McKinley would later say that he wished "to educate the Filipinos, and uplift and civilize and Christianize them."

Against Washington's claim that it was fighting this war on the other side of the world only from the most high-minded of motives (does that sound familiar?) Twain lumped the new American imperial venture with the seizure by Britain, France, Germany and Russia, of territory in Africa and China. This pamphlet was reprinted by many newspapers and magazines, and parts of it were read into the *Congressional Record.* Twain followed it up with "To My Missionary Critics" and several other articles. In Massachusetts, the *Springfield Republican* called him "the most influential anti-imperialist and the most dreaded critic of the sacrosanct person in the White House." In 1901, succeeding the assassinated McKinley, Theodore Roosevelt became that person. When Roosevelt, who ardently craved an American colonial empire, heard a crowd cheering for Twain, he angrily muttered that anti-imperialists like him should be skinned alive.

Soon Twain threw himself into another anti-imperial cause. Artfully outflanking larger European countries, King Leopold II of Belgium had made himself an early beneficiary of the rush for African colonies. He succeeded in having first the United States and then all the major nations of Europe recognize a vast territory in the Congo River basin as belonging to him personally. Once Leopold got his hands on the area, the invention of the inflatable tire sparked a worldwide rubber boom. The king amassed a fortune equal to well over one billion dollars in today's currency by turning much of the Congo's male population into forced laborers to harvest this valuable commodity.

The forced-labor system and the millions of deaths it led to attracted the attention of a brilliant young British journalist, Edmund Dene Morel, who mounted, over this issue, the biggest international human-rights campaign of its time. Morel came to visit Twain in 1904, and persuaded him to make three trips to Washington to lobby President Roosevelt and the State Department to bring pressure on the king, and to write about the Congo. The result was "King Leopold's Soliloquy," which the author's usual publishers found too acid for their taste. Twain gave it, and the royalties from it, to the American branch of Morel's Congo Reform Association, which published it as a pamphlet in 1905. Although the king's soliloquy is of course imaginary, it is based on real events and has quotations from eyewitness testimony. Morel's campaign tools included a slide show of atrocity photographs, some of which Twain printed as well. He has the monarch of his pamphlet rage against "the incorruptible *kodak* ... The only witness I have encountered in my long experience that I couldn't bribe." The writer joined Booker T. Washington in speaking to several protest meetings. "King Leopold's Soliloquy" clearly stung its target; the king's formidable public-relations apparatus issued a forty-seven-page pamphlet entitled "An Answer to Mark Twain."

Remarkably, for decades after Twain died, this whole stream of his writing largely disappeared from new editions of his work. "King Leopold's Soliloquy" and several other attacks on imperialism were not republished until more than half a century after his death. The chief sanitizers of Twain's legacy were his authorized biographer and literary executor, Albert Bigelow Paine, and the author's one surviving child, his daughter Clara, who lived to the age of eighty-eight. They were eager to have the public remember only Twain the humorist, the sage of Hannibal, the kindly white-suited figure with the big mustache and flowing mane of hair. The Twain who had been the strident opponent of colonial conquest they shoved out of sight.

In the various volumes of the writer's speeches, letters, notebooks, and other work that he edited, Paine downplayed, greatly condensed, or simply omitted many of Twain's comments on events like the Philippine War. In his three-volume biography, he never even mentioned that Twain was a vice-president of the Anti-Imperialist League. When Paine edited a collection of the letters, for example, one sentence where Twain had written "I am going to stick close to my desk for a month, now, hoping to write a small book, full of playful and good-natured contempt for the lousy McKinley" ended simply with "hoping to write a small book." Paine's versions of various Twain texts were long accepted as authentic by later editors, who had no idea that they had been bowdlerized. Happily, enough omissions had been discovered and undone by the late 1960s for American opponents of the Vietnam War to be able to use his prophetic work in support of their cause.

All of the Twain pieces in this book, however, are exactly as he wrote them. It is surely testimony to his subversive side that he was in effect censored for so long after his death. In the following pages you will find him utterly unsanitized, in full eruption.

Adam Hochschild

ADAM HOCHSCHILD is a journalist and the author of eight books, including *King Leopold's Ghost*, *Bury the Chains*, and *To End All Wars*. He teaches narrative writing at the Graduate School of Journalism at the University of California, Berkeley.

S E L E C T   B I B L I O G R A P H Y

AUTOBIOGRAPHY

TWAIN, MARK, *Autobiography of Mark Twain*, Vols I–III, University of California Press, Berkeley, 2010, 2013, 2015.

BIOGRAPHY

BURNS, KEN; DUNCAN, DAYTON and WARD, GEOFFREY C., *Mark Twain: An Illustrated Biography*, Alfred A. Knopf, New York, 2001.

EMERSON, EVERETT, *Mark Twain: A Literary Life*, University of Pennsylvania Press, Philadelphia, 2000.

KAPLAN, FRED, *The Singular Mark Twain*, Doubleday, New York, 2003.

LOVING, JEROME, *Mark Twain: The Adventures of Samuel L. Clemens*, University of California Press, Berkeley, 2010.

KATZ, HARRY L. and The Library of Congress, *Mark Twain's America: A Celebration in Words and Images*, Little, Brown and Company, New York, 2014.

POWERS, RON, *Mark Twain, A Life*, Free Press, New York, 2005.

SHELDEN, MICHAEL, *Mark Twain: Man in White*, Random House, New York, 2010.

CRITICISM

BLOOM, HAROLD, ed., *Mark Twain*, Chelsea House Publishers, New York and Philadelphia, 1986.

BUDD, LOUIS J., *Mark Twain: The Contemporary Reviews*, Cambridge University Press, New York, 1999.

MESSENT, PETER, *The Short Works of Mark Twain: A Critical Study*, University of Pennsylvania Press, Philadelphia, 2001.

QUIRK, TOM, *Mark Twain: A Study of the Short Fiction*, Twayne Publishers, New York, 1997.

RAILTON, STEPHEN, *Mark Twain: A Short Introduction*, Blackwell Publishing, Oxford, UK, 2003.

ROBINSON, FORREST G., ed., *The Cambridge Companion to Mark Twain*, Cambridge University Press, New York, 1995.

SCHMITTER, DEAN MORGAN, ed., *Mark Twain: A Collection of Criticism*, McGraw-Hill Book Company, New York, 1974.

ANTHOLOGIES

BUDD, LOUIS J., ed., *Collected Tales, Sketches, Speeches, & Essays, 1852–1890*, The Library of America, New York, 1992; *Collected Tales, Sketches, Speeches, & Essays, 1891–1910*, The Library of America, New York, 1992.

DE VOTO, BERNARD, ed., *The Portable Mark Twain*, Viking, New York, 1946.

NEIDER, CHARLES, ed., *The Selected Letters of Mark Twain*, Cooper Square Press, New York, 1982.

TWAIN, MARK, *Autobiographical Writings*, Penguin Books, New York, 2012.

The Mark Twain Project, University of California Press, Berkeley.

A NOTE ON THE TEXT

Spelling and punctuation of the letters included here follow Clemens's usage. His errors are not emended so long as they may be transcribed intelligibly.

CHRONOLOGY

DATE	AUTHOR'S LIFE	LITERARY CONTEXT
1803		Birth of Emerson.
1811		
1819		Birth of Whitman and Melville. Irving: *The Sketch Book* (to 1820). Scott: *Ivanhoe.*
1821		
1830		Birth of Emily Dickinson.
1832		F. Trollope: *Domestic Manners of the Americans.*
1833		
1834		
1835	Samuel Langhorne Clemens born in Florida, Missouri, sixth of seven children. His father is a country lawyer and merchant.	Tocqueville: *Democracy in America* (I). Browning: *Paracelsus.* Balzac: *Old Goriot.*
1837		Carlyle: *The French Revolution.*
1838		Dickens: *Oliver Twist.*
1839	Family moves to Hannibal, Missouri, a river town on the Mississippi. Death of his sister, Margaret (b. 1830).	Poe: *Tales of the Grotesque and Arabesque.* Stendhal: *The Charterhouse of Parma.* Darwin: *The Voyage of the "Beagle."*
1840		Cooper: *The Pathfinder.*
1841		Emerson: *Essays, First Series.* Thorpe: *The Big Bear of Arkansas.* Cooper: *The Deerslayer.* Dickens: *Barnaby Rudge.*

Louisiana Purchase. Ohio becomes the 17th state to join the Union.
First Mississippi steamboat launched.
Florida Purchase. SS *Savannah* first steam-powered vessel to cross the
Atlantic.

The State of Missouri admitted to the Union as the 24th state. Leads to the
Missouri Compromise: slavery is accepted in the new state but prohibited in
lands north of latitude 36°30' N.
President Andrew Jackson's Indian Removal Act to transfer all Indians to
the west of the Mississippi. The Choctaw Nation is the first to be deported
(1831–3).

Slavery abolished in the British Empire.
The Indian Territory (later to become Oklahoma) reserved by the Federal
government.
Texan Revolution against Mexican rule (to 1836); a republic is declared.
Samuel Colt travels to England to patent his revolver.

Accession of Queen Victoria in Britain. Financial crisis in US (to 1843).
Seminole War in Florida. Osage War: Missouri militia forces out last
remaining Osage Indians. Michigan becomes the 26th state.
The Underground Railway for runaway slaves set up in Ohio. Passage of
the Personal Liberty Laws, impeding enforcement of the Federal Fugitive
Slave Law of 1793. Deportation of Cherokee Nation from Georgia; some
4000 die on the "Trail of Tears" to the Indian Territory. Daguerre–Niepce
method of photography first presented in Paris.
University of Missouri founded. Samuel Cunard wins contract to carry
British Royal Mail to the USA and Canada.

John Tyler becomes US President.

DATE	AUTHOR'S LIFE	LITERARY CONTEXT
1842	Death of his brother, Benjamin (b. 1832).	Dickens tours the US. *American Notes.*
1843		Carlyle: *Past and Present.* Dickens: *Martin Chuzzlewitt* (to 1844). Ruskin: *Modern Painters* (I).
1845		
1846		Melville: *Typee.*
1847	Death of his father.	C. Brontë: *Jane Eyre.* E. Brontë: *Wuthering Heights.* Thackeray: *Vanity Fair* (to 1848).
1848	Sam goes to work as a printer's apprentice.	Lowell: *The Biglow Papers.* Marx and Engels: *The Communist Manifesto.*
1849		Death of Poe. Parkman: *The Oregon Trail.*
1850	His brother Orion, a printer, purchases the *Hannibal Western Union.*	Hawthorne: *The Scarlet Letter.* Dickens: *David Copperfield.*
1851	Working for Orion. Sam's first known published work, "A Gallant Fireman," appears in the paper.	Death of Cooper. Melville: *Moby-Dick.* Hawthorne: *The House of Seven Gables.*
1852		Stowe: *Uncle Tom's Cabin.* Turgenev: *A Sportsman's Notebook.*
1853	Travels to St. Louis, New York, Philadelphia and Washington, working as a jobbing printer (to 1856). Orion moves to Iowa, taking his mother and brother Henry with him.	Thackeray: *The English Humorists* (lectures given in England and the US 1852–3).
1854		Thoreau: *Walden.*
1855		Whitman: *Leaves of Grass.*

CHRONOLOGY

Webster–Ashburton Treaty establishes the northeastern border of the US with British colonies in Canada; US promises co-operation in suppressing the slave trade.
The Oregon Trail – around 900 migrants travel more than 2000 miles from Missouri to settle in Oregon, with increasing numbers to follow during the 1840s.

Texas annexed by the US. James K. Polk becomes US President (to 1849). White Star Line founded.
Mexican War (to 1848). Wilmot Proviso: unsuccessful attempt by northern abolitionists to ban slavery in any territory gained from Mexico. Treaty with Britain establishes 49th Parallel as boundary between Oregon and Canada.
Salt Lake City founded.

Treaty of Guadalupe Hidalgo: US makes huge territorial gains at the end of the war with Mexico, acquiring California, New Mexico and Arizona, and parts of Colarado, Nevada and Utah. Organization of the Free Soil Party. Gold first discovered in California. Year of Revolutions in Europe. Second Republic in France. Franz Josef becomes Austrian Emperor (to 1916). Senator John C. Calhoun's Southern Address against Northern "acts of aggression and encroachment." California Gold Rush underway (to 1855); widespread violence against American Indian tribes leading to catastrophic decline in population.
Compromise of 1850: California admitted to the Union as a free state; Utah and New Mexico established as territories with the right to decide for themselves on the issue of slavery; a tighter Fugitive Slave Bill passed.
Louis Napoleon's *coup d'état* in France leads to re-establishment of Empire in 1852. Great Exhibition in London. Isaac Singer devises continuous stitch sewing machine. *New York Times* founded.

First world trade fair to be held in America opens in New York. Franklin Pierce becomes US President (to 1857). Gadsden Purchase.

Kansas–Nebraska Act effectively repeals the Missouri Compromise. Violent clashes over slavery in Kansas; Kansas–Missouri border troubles (to 1865). Republican party founded.
Obed Hussey invents self-propelled steam engine for plowing.

DATE	AUTHOR'S LIFE	LITERARY CONTEXT
1855 cont.		Longfellow: *The Song of Hiawatha.* Spencer: *The Principles of Psychology.*
1856	Sam writing humorous articles for his brother's new paper, the *Keokuk Daily Post,* under the pseudonym Thomas Jefferson Snodgrass. Moves to Cincinnati in the fall.	Melville: *Piazza Tales.* Flaubert: *Madame Bovary.*
1857	Departs Cincinnati for New Orleans on the *Paul Jones,* piloted by Horace E. Bixby, whom he persuades to train him as a Mississippi River pilot.	Thackeray: *The Virginians* (to 1859). Trollope: *Barchester Towers.* *The Atlantic Monthly* founded.
1858	Younger brother Henry (working with him on the Mississippi as a junior clerk) killed in a steamboat explosion.	
1859	Becomes a licensed river pilot.	Death of Irving. Tennyson: *Idylls of the King.* Dickens: *A Tale of Two Cities.*
1860		Hawthorne: *The Marble Faun.* Emerson: *The Conduct of Life.* Eliot: *The Mill on the Floss.* Collins: *The Woman in White.*
1861	War halts river trade. Enlists briefly in the Confederate Militia. Accompanies Orion to Nevada, where Lincoln has appointed him Secretary. Prospects for gold and silver.	Wendell Holmes: *Elsie Venner.* Dostoevsky: *The House of the Dead.*
1862	Reporter on the *Territorial Enterprise,* Virginia City, Nevada.	Birth of Edith Wharton. Death of Thoreau. Hugo: *Les Misérables.*
1863	Adopts the *nom de plume* "Mark Twain" – the cry of a river boatman taking a sounding of two fathoms (twelve feet).	Longfellow: *Tales of a Wayside Inn.*
1864	Works as a journalist in San Francisco. Forms friendships with the writer Bret Harte, the professional lecturer Artemus Ward and raconteur Jim Gillis.	Death of Hawthorne. Tolstoy: *War and Peace* (to 1869). Verne: *Journey to the Centre of the Earth.*

CHRONOLOGY

James Buchanan becomes US President (to 1861).

Beginning of the Raj: following the Indian Mutiny (1857) the British Crown takes control of India from the East India Company. First transatlantic cable laid.

Darwin publishes *On the Origin of Species*, propounding the theory of evolution. First commercial oil well in US, Titusville, Pennsylvania.

Abraham Lincoln elected US President. Pony Express founded.

Kansas admitted to the Union as a free state. Southern Congress at Montgomery, Alabama; Jefferson Davis elected President of the Confederate States of America. Missouri votes to stay in the Union but the population is divided over the issues. Outbreak of Civil War in US. Western Union completes first transcontinental telegraph line across North America. Apache Wars (to 1900). Italy united under Victor Emmanuel II. Tsar Alexander II emancipates the serfs in Russia.
Battle of Shiloh. Sioux uprising in Minnesota. Bismarck appointed Prime Minister of Prussia.

Lincoln issues Emancipation Proclamation (amendment to constitution passed 1865). Battle of Gettysburg.

US Civil War rages on. Lincoln re-elected President. Massacre of Cheyenne and Arapaho Indians at Sand Creek, Colorado. Karl Marx founds International Workingmen's Association in London. Louis Pasteur establishes connection between bacteria and disease.

DATE	AUTHOR'S LIFE	LITERARY CONTEXT
1865	His short story "Jim Smiley and His Jumping Frog" appears in the *New York Saturday Press* and elsewhere, to great popular acclaim.	Whitman: *Drum Taps.* Carroll: *Alice's Adventures in Wonderland.*
1866	Travels to Hawaii as correspondent of the *Alta California.* Takes up lecturing.	
1867	Becomes the paper's New York correspondent. Delivers first lecture in New York. Publishes his first book, *The Celebrated Jumping Frog of Calaveras County and Other Sketches.* Travels as correspondent to Europe and the Holy Land (June–Nov). Introduced to Olivia (Livy) Langdon in New York (Dec).	Marx: *Das Kapital* (I). Dickens's second American tour (to 1868).
1868	Livy and Twain hear Charles Dickens read. Twain lectures across the US.	Harte: "The Luck of Roaring Camp." Collins: *The Moonstone.*
1869	Publishes *The Innocents Abroad*, a collection of articles written during his recent voyage, which becomes a best-seller. Lecture tour of Midwest.	Harte: "The Outcasts of Poker Flat." Alcott: *Little Women.* Hugo: *L'Homme qui rit.*
1870	Marries Olivia Langdon in Elmira, New York. The couple settle briefly in Buffalo, New York. Writes an early version of *Tom Sawyer* entitled *A Boy's Manuscript.* Birth of son, Langdon.	Death of Dickens. Verne: *Twenty Thousand Leagues Under the Sea.*
1871	The family moves to Hartford, Connecticut, renting a house at Nook Farm. Summers in the 1870s and '80s are spent at Quarry Farm, Elmira, where Twain does much of his writing.	Darwin: *The Descent of Man.*
1872	Publishes *Roughing It.* Birth of daughter, Susy. Langdon contracts diphtheria and dies. First trip to England in the fall. Patents his self-pasting scrapbook, the only one of his inventions to make money.	Wendell Holmes: *The Autocrat at the Breakfast-Table.* Eliot: *Middlemarch.* Hardy: *Under the Greenwood Tree.* Butler: *Erewhon.*

CHRONOLOGY

End of Civil War. Assassination of President Lincoln. Southern Democrat
Andrew Johnson becomes President; favours a policy of Reconstruction
lenient towards the South. Ku Klux Klan founded in Tennessee. Mississippi
first Southern state to adopt a "Black Code" to re-establish white
supremacy.

Civil Rights Bill passed by Congress in spite of presidential veto. Racial
violence in Tennessee and New Orleans. Red Cloud's War in Wyoming
(to 1868).

Increased Republican majority in Congress passes first Reconstruction
Act (again in defiance of presidential veto), placing southern states under
military rule and making readmittance to the Union dependant upon
their acceptance of black suffrage. Building of the first elevated railroad
(New York). Alaska purchased from Russia. British North American Act;
self-governing dominion of Canada established. Dual monarchy of
Austria-Hungary established.

14th Amendment ratified, defining US citizenship to include all those born
or naturalized in the US. (Native Americans, however, were largely
excluded.) Failed impeachment of President Johnson. Gladstone's first
Liberal ministry in Britain (to 1874).

First Pacific Railroad completed, linking East and West coasts. Suez Canal
opens. Ulysses S. Grant becomes US President (to 1877). Elizabeth Cady
Stanton founds National Women's Suffrage Organization.

First African American admitted to Congress. Passage of the 15th
Amendment: "no state shall deprive a citizen of the right to vote on grounds
of race, color, or previous condition of servitude," a promised not fulfilled
for another century. Franco-Prussian War (to 1871).

Fall of Paris; Napoleon III goes into exile; Third Republic in France. Paris
Commune. Wilhelm I of Prussia proclaimed German Emperor. US and
Britain sign Treaty of Washington, settling US–Canadian boundary and
disputes dating from the Civil War. Meeting of Stanley and Livingstone
in Ujiji.

Yellowstone National Park established. President signs amnesty bill for
former Confederates. Grant is re-elected. "Cleveland Massacre' –
Rockefeller's Standard Oil company buys out 22 of its 26 rivals in Cleveland,
Ohio in a first move to achieve national, then multinational domination.

DATE	AUTHOR'S LIFE	LITERARY CONTEXT
1873	Publishes novel, *The Gilded Age*, written with Charles Dudley Warner. Travels with his family to England, Scotland and Ireland. Meets Trollope, Browning, and Spencer. (May–Nov). Returns alone to England for a lecture tour (to Jan 1874).	Tolstoy: *Anna Karenina* (to 1877). Trollope: *The Eustace Diamonds*. Verne: *Around the World in Eighty Days*.
1874	Birth of daughter, Clara. Moves into a mansion he has had built in Hartford, the family home until 1891.	Hugo: *Quatre-vingt-treize*.
1875	Writes *Old Times on the Mississippi* in seven installments for W. D. Havell's *Atlantic Monthly*.	
1876	Publishes *The Adventures of Tom Sawyer*.	Birth of Willa Cather. Henry James: *Roderick Hudson*.
1877	Makes ill-received speech at the 70th birthday dinner for John Greenleaf Whittier.	Turgenev: *Virgin Soil*.
1878	Takes his family to Europe (April). Twain and Joseph Twichell go on a "tramp abroad" through the Black Forest and Swiss Alps. Spends winter in Munich.	James: *Daisy Miller*.
1879	Visits Paris; meets Henry James, Whistler and Darwin. Returns to New York via England (August).	Stevenson: *Travels with a Donkey in the Cévennes*.
1880	Publishes *A Tramp Abroad*. Birth of daughter, Jean.	Maupassant: "Boule de Suif."
1881	*The Prince and the Pauper* (novel) published. Begins to invest in Paige typesetting machine.	James: *The Portrait of a Lady*; *Washington Square*.
1882	Visits the Mississippi with Horace Bixby.	Death of Emerson. Howells: *A Modern Instance*.
1883	Publishes an amended version of *Old Times* as *Life on the Mississippi*.	Riley: *The Old Swimmin'-Hole and 'Leven More Poems*. Stevenson: *Treasure Island*.
1884	*Adventures of Huckleberry Finn* published in London in December (and in the US two months later). Founds publishing company, Charles L. Webster & Co.	

CHRONOLOGY

Colfax Massacre in Louisiana. Panic of 1873 – collapse of a Wall Street banking firm with interests in railroad investment has severe economic repercussions. Conviction of New York political racketeer "Boss" Tweed for corruption. Remington manufacture the first commercial typewriter. First cable car (San Francisco). G. A. Hansen discovers leprosy bacillus.

Disraeli British Prime Minister (to 1880). Impressionists' first exhibition in Paris.

A shortlived Civil Rights Act guarantees equal access, regardless of color, to public transport and recreation, and protects the right to serve on juries.

Great Sioux War (to 1877); US troops defeated at the Battle of Little Bighorn. Colorado becomes US state. Alexander Graham Bell patents the telephone.
Sioux lands officially annexed. Great Railroad Strike put down by militia and federal troops. Disraeli proclaims Queen Victoria Empress of India. Britain annexes the Transvaal. Thomas Edison invents phonograph. Republican Rutherford B. Hayes becomes President after a disputed election, having made a deal with his opponents to lift tough Reconstruction policies in the South. Southern states are free to introduce policies of segregation ("Jim Crow laws"); gradual disenfranchisement of blacks begins.

Zulu War (to 1880).

Gladstone again British Prime Minister (to 1885). First Boer War.

British troops defeated by Boers at Majuba Hill. Britain recognizes Boer Republic of Transvaal.

Chinese Exclusion Act suspends immigration of Chinese laborers.

Brooklyn Bridge opened. Southern Pacific and Northern Pacific transcontinental railroads completed. Supreme Court declares the 1875 Civil Rights Act unconstitutional.
Berlin Conference; the "Scamble for Africa" begins. Merganthaler invents the Linotype machine (first machine installed at the *New York Tribune* in 1886).

DATE	AUTHOR'S LIFE	LITERARY CONTEXT
1885	Webster & Co. publishes the memoirs of Ulysses S. Grant, a useful financial success. Twain pays the expenses of Walter McGuinn, first black student at Yale Law School. Susy begins to write a biography of her father.	Howell: *The Rise of Silas Lapham*. Riley: "Little Orphant Annie." Zola: *Germinal*.
1886	In pursuance of a long campaign to improve copyright protection for authors, appears before a congressional committee on copyright (and again in 1906).	James: *The Bostonians*. Jewett: *A White Heron*. Stevenson: *Dr. Jekyll and Mr. Hyde*; *Kidnapped*.
1887		
1888	Receives an honorary MA from Yale University.	Birth of O'Neill and T. S. Eliot. Kipling: *Plain Tales from the Hills*. Ward: *Robert Elsmere*.
1889	Publishes *A Connecticut Yankee in King Arthur's Court*. Meets Rudyard Kipling in Elmira.	Jerome: *Three Men in a Boat*. Stevenson: *The Master of Ballantrae*.
1890	Death of his mother.	Dickinson: *Poems* (to 1896).
1891	Financial difficulties drive the Clemens family to settle in Europe. They spend the winter of 1891–2 in Berlin.	Death of Melville. Conan Doyle: *The Adventures of Sherlock Holmes*.
1892	Twain dines with Kaiser Wilhelm II.	Death of Whitman and Tennyson. Kipling: *Barrack-Room Ballads*.
1893	Publishes *The $1,000,000 Bank-Note and Other New Stories*. Living in Italy but visiting the US on business.	Kipling: *Many Inventions*.
1894	Twain's publishing company and speculative enterprises, notably the Paige typesetting machine, are bankrupted by the crash of 1893. His health and that of his wife and daughters declines. Family moves to France. *The Tragedy of Pudd'nhead Wilson* published.	Chopin: *Bayou Folk*. Kipling: *The Jungle Book* (I).

CHRONOLOGY

Leopold II of Belgium's personal rule in the Congo Free State (to 1908).
Indian National Congress founded in Bombay. Pasteur successfully uses
rabies vaccine to prevent humans developing the disease after a dog-bite.
Gottlieb Daimler and Wilhelm Maybach patent high-speed internal
combustion engine.

Geronimo signs peace treaty; end of last major Indian war.

Dawes Act enforces assimilation of American Indians by depriving them of
their communal tribal lands in exchange for individual allotments.
Dunlop patents pneumatic tyre.

Large central area of the Indian Territory opened for settlement; major
land rush. Jane Addams and Ellen Gates Starr found Hull House in
Chicago. Cecil Rhodes's British South African Company receives royal
charter and a mandate to colonize further territories. First Kodak camera
using roll film manufactured.
Massacre of Lakota Sioux at Wounded Knee. Fall of Bismarck. Monotype
caster patented.
International Copyright Act.

Ellis Island opens as an immigration station.

Henry Ford and Karl Benz build their first cars. Serious economic
depression in the US. British South African Company invades
Matabeleland; First Matabele War (to 1894).
Dreyfus case begins in France.

DATE	AUTHOR'S LIFE	LITERARY CONTEXT
1895	Returns to the US in May. Embarks on worldwide lecture tour to restore finances (July). Livy and Clara accompany him. Visits Canada, Australia and New Zealand.	Crane: *The Red Badge of Courage.* Dunbar: *Majors and Minors.* Wells: *The Time Machine.* Wilde: *The Importance of Being Earnest.* Hardy: *Jude the Obscure.*
1896	Moves on to Ceylon, India and South Africa, arriving in England in July. Death of his daughter Susy at home in Hartford (August). Clemens family settle in England. Jean diagnosed with epilepsy. *Personal Recollections of Joan of Arc* serialized in *Harper's Magazine.*	Jewett: *The Country of the Pointed Firs.* Beerbohm: *The Works of Max Beerbohm.*
1897	Moves to Vienna where Clara pursues her musical studies and Twain enjoys being lionized. Publishes *How to Tell a Story and Other Essays* and *Following the Equator.* Death of his brother Orion.	Birth of Faulkner. Robinson: *Richard Cory.* Chopin: *A Night in Acadie.* Stoker: *Dracula.* Shaw: *The Devil's Disciple.*
1898	Discharges his debts. "Stirring Times in Austria" appears in *Harper's Magazine.* Working on *What is Man?* and *The Mysterious Stranger* (novel).	Birth of Hemingway. James: *The Turn of the Screw.* Wells: *The War of the Worlds.*
1899	Leaves Vienna (May); audience with Emperor Franz Josef I. Visits Sweden seeking treatment for Jean. "Concerning the Jews," an essay against anti-semitism, published in *Harper's.*	Chopin: *The Awakening.* Norris: *McTeague.* Chekhov: "The Lady with the Dog."
1900	Returns to the US to a national welcome. Lives in New York City. Publishes *The Man That Corrupted Hadleyburg and Other Stories and Essays* and *English As She Is Taught.*	Dreiser: *Sister Carrie.* Freud: *The Interpretation of Dreams.*

CHRONOLOGY

HISTORICAL EVENTS

Cuban War of Independence begins. In Britain, Conservative Lord
Salisbury forms ministry in conjunction with the Liberal Unionists (to 1902).
Jameson Raid on the Transvaal. "Rhodesia" founded. Freud's *Studies in
Hysteria* inaugurates psychoanalysis. First public screening of a film by the
Lumière brothers. Trial of Oscar Wilde.

Plessy v Ferguson: Supreme Court upholds conviction of Homer Plessy for
contravening the Separate Cars Act in Louisiana, endorsing "separate but
equal" policy. Utah becomes 45th state to join the Union. Second Matabele
War (to 1897). Sudan War (to 1899). Anti-semitic Karl Lueger mayor of
Vienna (to 1910). Marconi moves to England to conduct his experiments in
wireless telegraphy.

Klondike gold rush (to 1899). Queen Victoria's Diamond Jubilee.
Destruction of Benin City (West Africa) by the British. Aboriginal peoples in
Australia confined to reserves, strictly controlled by government agencies or
missionaries. Vienna Secession founded. Badeni language ordinances resisted
by German nationalists, leading to riots throughout the Austrian Empire;
Badeni is dismissed and the ordinances are repealed in 1899.

Brief Spanish–American War. By the Treaty of Paris, Spain renounces claim
to Cuba and cedes Puerta Rico and Guam to the US; US purchases the
Philippine Islands from Spain for $20 million. Curtis Act extends Dawes Act
to the "Five Civilized Nations," hitherto exempt; tribal institutions
dismantled. First German Navy Law; arms race with Britain begins. Britain
and France clash in the Sudan (Fashoda incident). Britain granted 99-year
lease on Hong Kong by Chinese government. Assassination of the Empress
Elizabeth (Twain witnesses her funeral in Vienna). Emperor Franz Josef's
Golden Jubilee. Pierre and Marie Curie discover radium. Machine for
magnetic recording of sound patented by V. Poulsen.
Philippine–American War (to 1902). Second Boer War (to 1902). After a
century of expansion the British Empire covers one fifth of the globe, and
is home to one quarter of the world's population. Retrial of Dreyfus and
national outcry in France at his conviction. Scott Joplin's "Maple Leaf
Rag." Death of Johann Strauss II, "the waltz king," in Vienna.

US annexes Hawaii. Britain annexes Transvaal and Orange Free State.
Boxer Rebellion in China. First "direct" election primary tried in
Minneapolis. Texas hurricane kills 8000 – the worst natural disaster in
US history.

DATE	AUTHOR'S LIFE	LITERARY CONTEXT
1901	Moves to Riverdale-on-the-Hudson. Publishes "To the Person Sitting in Darkness" and "To My Missionary Critics" in the *North American Review*. Becomes vice-president of the Anti-Imperialist League.	Washington: *Up From Slavery*. Conan Doyle: *The Hound of the Baskervilles*. Kipling: *Kim*.
1902	*A Double-Barrelled Detective Story*. Awarded an honorary degree by the University of Missouri. Travels to Hannibal, Missouri, for the last time. Livy seriously ill.	Conrad: *Heart of Darkness*; *Typhoon*.
1903	Moves with family to Florence for Livy's health. Harper and Brothers acquires exclusive rights to all of Twain's work. Hartford house sold.	London: *The Call of the Wild*. Dubois: *The Souls of Black Folk*. Butler: *The Way of All Flesh*.
1904	Publishes *Extracts from Adam's Diary*. Begins dictating autobiography. Death of his wife. Family returns to New York.	James: *The Golden Bowl*. O. Henry: *Cabbages and Kings*. London: *The Sea-Wolf*. Conrad: *Nostromo*. Saki: *Reginald*.
1905	*King Leopold's Soliloquy* published. Dines at the White House with President Roosevelt. Banquet at Delmonico's, New York, for his 70th birthday.	Wharton: *The House of Mirth*. Cather: *The Troll Garden*. Shaw: *Man and Superman*; *Major Barbara*.
1906	*Eve's Diary* published. Selected chapters from his autobiography appear in the *North American Review* (to 1907). Resumes dictations. Albert Bigelow Paine moves into Twain's home to begin work as his authorized biographer. *What is Man?* printed anonymously for private distribution.	O. Henry: *The Four Million*. Sinclair: *The Jungle*. London: *White Fang*.
1907	Trip to Bermuda with Joseph Twichell. Visits England to receive an honorary doctorate from Oxford University.	Adams: *The History of Henry Adams*. William James: *Pragmatism*. Conrad: *The Secret Agent*.
1908	Moves to "Stormfield," the house he had commissioned in Redding, Connecticut.	London: *The Iron Heel*. Forster: *A Room with a View*.

CHRONOLOGY

Theodore Roosevelt becomes President after the assassination of William McKinley. First major oil discovery in Texas. Death of Queen Victoria and accession of Edward VII. First Nobel prizes awarded.

Roosevelt embarks on a conservation program to protect wildlife and public land. During his presidency (to 1909) 150 national forests, 51 federal bird reserves and 5 national parks are created. Treaty of Vereeniging ends Boer War. First celebration of Empire Day in Britain. Cuba gains formal independence from the US.

Wright brothers' first successful powered flight. Ford Motor Company set up. Marconi demonstrates wireless communication between Great Britain and the US when President Roosevelt sends a cable to King Edward VII.

Roosevelt wins landslide victory in general election. Panama Canal zone acquired by the US. Russo-Japanese War (to 1905). Congo Reform Association founded by Edmund Dene Morel and Roger Casement.

"Bloody Sunday" in St Petersburg; first Russian Revolution. Moroccan crisis.

Severe anti-Negro riots and martial law in Atlanta. Roosevelt awarded Nobel Peace Prize for negotiating end to the Russo-Japanese War. San Francisco earthquake.

Currency panic; run on banks; J. P. Morgan imports $100 million in gold from Europe to halt crisis. Lenin founds newspaper *The Proletarian* in Geneva. Oklahoma and the Indian Territory combine to become a state. Regular transatlantic radio telegraph service established.
Ford Model T marketed.

DATE	AUTHOR'S LIFE	LITERARY CONTEXT
1909	Holidays in Bermuda. Marriage of Clara. Death of Jean.	Wells: *Tono-Bungay*.
1910	Another trip to Bermuda. Dies at home on April 21. Birth of his only grandchild, Nina. William Dean Howells publishes *My Mark Twain*.	Forster: *Howards End*. Death of Tolstoy, William James and O. Henry.
1911		Wharton: *Ethan Frome*.
1912	Paine's biography published.	
1916	The unfinished *Mysterious Stranger* published, edited by Paine.	Joyce: *A Portrait of the Artist as a Young Man*.
1924	*Mark Twain's Autobiography* (ed. Paine) published.	

CHRONOLOGY

Commercial manufacture of bakelite, the world's first synthetic plastic.
William Howard Taft becomes US President and instigates "Dollar
Diplomacy" to extend US influence.
Culmination of the worst five years of mining disasters (2494 killed) in
American history. Death of Edward VII.

W. C. Handy's revolutionary "Memphis Blues" published. RMS *Titanic*
sinks.

Indian Citizenship Act grants citizenship to all Native Americans born in
the US.

CHAPTERS FROM MY AUTOBIOGRAPHY

NORTH AMERICAN REVIEW
1906–1907

PART I

SEPTEMBER 7, 1906

PREFATORY NOTE – Mr. Clemens began to write his autobiography many years ago, and he continues to add to it day by day. It was his original intention to permit no publication of his memoirs until after his death; but, after leaving "Pier No. 70," he concluded that a considerable portion might now suitably be given to the public. It is that portion, garnered from the quarter-million of words already written, which will appear in this REVIEW during the coming year. No part of the autobiography will be published in book form during the lifetime of the author. – EDITOR N.A.R.

INTRODUCTION

I INTEND THAT this autobiography shall become a model for all future autobiographies when it is published, after my death, and I also intend that it shall be read and admired a good many centuries because of its form and method – a form and method whereby the past and the present are constantly brought face to face, resulting in contrasts which newly fire up the interest all along, like contact of flint with steel. Moreover, this autobiography of mine does not select from my life its showy episodes, but deals mainly in the common experiences which go to make up the life of the average human being, because these episodes are of a sort which he is familiar with in his own life, and in which he sees his own life reflected and set down in print. The usual, conventional autobiographer seems to particularly hunt out those occasions in his career when he came into contact with celebrated persons, whereas his contacts with the uncelebrated were just as interesting to him, and would be to his reader, and were vastly more numerous than his collisions with the famous.

Howells was here yesterday afternoon, and I told him the whole scheme of this autobiography and its apparently systemless system – only apparently systemless, for it is not really that. It is a deliberate system, and the law of the system is that I shall talk about the matter which for the moment interests me, and cast it aside and talk about something else the moment its interest for me is

exhausted. It is a system which follows no charted course and is
not going to follow any such course. It is a system which is a complete and purposed jumble – a course which begins nowhere, follows no specified route, and can never reach an end while I am
alive, for the reason that, if I should talk to the stenographer two
hours a day for a hundred years, I should still never be able to set
down a tenth part of the things which have interested me in my
lifetime. I told Howells that this autobiography of mine would live
a couple of thousand years, without any effort, and would then
take a fresh start and live the rest of the time.

He said he believed it would, and asked me if I meant to make
a library of it.

I said that that was my design; but that, if I should live long
enough, the set of volumes could not be contained merely in a city,
it would require a State, and that there would not be any multi-
billionaire alive, perhaps, at any time during its existence who
would be able to buy a full set, except on the instalment plan.

Howells applauded, and was full of praises and endorsement,
which was wise in him and judicious. If he had manifested a
different spirit, I would have thrown him out of the window. I like
criticism, but it must be my way.

I

Back of the Virginia Clemenses is a dim procession of ancestors
stretching back to Noah's time. According to tradition, some of
them were pirates and slavers in Elizabeth's time. But this is no
discredit to them, for so were Drake and Hawkins and the others.
It was a respectable trade, then, and monarchs were partners in it.
In my time I have had desires to be a pirate myself. The reader –
if he will look deep down in his secret heart, will find – but never
mind what he will find there; I am not writing his Autobiography,
but mine. Later, according to tradition, one of the procession was
Ambassador to Spain in the time of James I, or of Charles I, and
married there and sent down a strain of Spanish blood to warm us
up. Also, according to tradition, this one or another – Geoffrey
Clement, by name – helped to sentence Charles to death.

I have not examined into these traditions myself, partly because

I was indolent, and partly because I was so busy polishing up this end of the line and trying to make it showy; but the other Clemenses claim that they have made the examination and that it stood the test. Therefore I have always taken for granted that I did help Charles out of his troubles, by ancestral proxy. My instincts have persuaded me, too. Whenever we have a strong and persistent and ineradicable instinct, we may be sure that it is not original with us, but inherited – inherited from away back, and hardened and perfected by the petrifying influence of time. Now I have been always and unchangingly bitter against Charles, and I am quite certain that this feeling trickled down to me through the veins of my forebears from the heart of that judge; for it is not my disposition to be bitter against people on my own personal account. I am not bitter against Jeffreys. I ought to be, but I am not. It indicates that my ancestors of James II's time were indifferent to him; I do not know why; I never could make it out; but that is what it indicates. And I have always felt friendly toward Satan. Of course that is ancestral; it must be in the blood, for I could not have originated it.

... And so, by the testimony of instinct, backed by the assertions of Clemenses who said they had examined the records, I have always been obliged to believe that Geoffrey Clement the martyr-maker was an ancestor of mine, and to regard him with favor, and in fact pride. This has not had a good effect upon me, for it has made me vain, and that is a fault. It has made me set myself above people who were less fortunate in their ancestry than I, and has moved me to take them down a peg, upon occasion, and say things to them which hurt them before company.

A case of the kind happened in Berlin several years ago. William Walter Phelps was our Minister at the Emperor's Court, then, and one evening he had me to dinner to meet Count S., a cabinet minister. This nobleman was of long and illustrious descent. Of course I wanted to let out the fact that I had some ancestors, too; but I did not want to pull them out of their graves by the ears, and I never could seem to get the chance to work them in in a way that would look sufficiently casual. I suppose Phelps was in the same difficulty. In fact he looked distraught, now and then – just as a person looks who wants to uncover an ancestor purely by accident, and cannot think of a way that will seem accidental enough. But at last, after dinner, he made a try. He took us about his drawing-room, showing us the pictures, and finally stopped before a rude and ancient engraving. It was a picture of the court that tried Charles I. There was a pyramid of judges in Puritan slouch hats, and below them three bareheaded secretaries seated at a table. Mr. Phelps put his finger upon one of the three, and said with exulting indifference –

"An ancestor of mine."

I put my finger on a judge, and retorted with scathing languidness –

"Ancestor of mine. But it is a small matter. I have others."

It was not noble in me to do it. I have always regretted it since. But it landed him. I wonder how he felt? However, it made no difference in our friendship, which shows that he was fine and high, notwithstanding the humbleness of his origin. And it was also creditable in me, too, that I could overlook it. I made no change in my bearing toward him, but always treated him as an equal.

But it was a hard night for me in one way. Mr. Phelps thought I was the guest of honor, and so did Count S.; but I didn't, for there was nothing in my invitation to indicate it. It was just a friendly offhand note, on a card. By the time dinner was announced Phelps was himself in a state of doubt. Something had to be done; and it was not a handy time for explanations. He tried to get me to go out with him, but I held back; then he tried S., and he also declined. There was another guest, but there was no trouble about him. We finally went out in a pile. There was a decorous plunge for seats, and I got the one at Mr. Phelps's left, the Count captured the one facing Phelps, and the other guest had to take the place of honor, since he could not help himself. We returned to the drawing-room in the original disorder. I had new shoes on, and they were tight. At eleven I was privately crying; I couldn't help it, the pain was so cruel. Conversation had been dead for an hour. S. had been due at the bedside of a dying official ever since half past nine. At last we all rose by one blessed impulse and went down to the street door without explanations – in a pile, and no precedence; and so, parted.

The evening had its defects; still, I got my ancestor in, and was satisfied.

Among the Virginian Clemenses were Jere. (already mentioned), and Sherrard. Jere. Clemens had a wide reputation as a good pistol-shot, and once it enabled him to get on the friendly side of some drummers when they wouldn't have paid any attention to mere smooth words and arguments. He was out stumping the State at the time. The drummers were grouped in front of the stand,

and had been hired by the opposition to drum while he made his speech. When he was ready to begin, he got out his revolver and laid it before him, and said in his soft, silky way –

"I do not wish to hurt anybody, and shall try not to; but I have got just a bullet apiece for those six drums, and if you should want to play on them, don't stand behind them."

Sherrard Clemens was a Republican Congressman from West Virginia in the war days, and then went out to St. Louis, where the James Clemens branch lived, and still lives, and there he became a warm rebel. This was after the war. At the time that he was a Republican I was a rebel; but by the time he had become a rebel I was become (temporarily) a Republican. The Clemenses have always done the best they could to keep the political balances level, no matter how much it might inconvenience them. I did not know what had become of Sherrard Clemens; but once I introduced Senator Hawley to a Republican mass meeting in New England, and then I got a bitter letter from Sherrard from St. Louis. He said that the Republicans of the North – no, the "mudsills of the North" – had swept away the old aristocracy of the South with fire and sword, and it ill became me, an aristocrat by blood, to train with that kind of swine. Did I forget that I was a Lambton?

That was a reference to my mother's side of the house. As I have already said, she was a Lambton – Lambton with a p, for some of the American Lamptons could not spell very well in early times, and so the name suffered at their hands. She was a native of Kentucky, and married my father in Lexington in 1823, when she was twenty years old and he twenty-four. Neither of them had an overplus of property. She brought him two or three negroes, but nothing else, I think. They removed to the remote and secluded village of Jamestown, in the mountain solitudes of east Tennessee. There their first crop of children was born, but as I was of a later vintage I do not remember anything about it. I was postponed – postponed to Missouri. Missouri was an unknown new State and needed attractions.

I think that my eldest brother, Orion, my sisters Pamela and Margaret, and my brother Benjamin were born in Jamestown. There may have been others, but as to that I am not sure. It was a great lift for that little village to have my parents come there. It was hoped that they would stay, so that it would become a city. It was supposed that they would stay. And so there was a boom; but by and by they went away, and prices went down, and it was

many years before Jamestown got another start. I have written
about Jamestown in the "Gilded Age," a book of mine, but it was
from hearsay, not from personal knowledge. My father left a fine
estate behind him in the region round about Jamestown – 75,000
acres.* When he died in 1847 he had owned it about twenty years.
The taxes were almost nothing (five dollars a year for the whole),
and he had always paid them regularly and kept his title perfect.
He had always said that the land would not become valuable in
his time, but that it would be a commodious provision for his children some day. It contained coal, copper, iron and timber, and he
said that in the course of time railways would pierce to that region,
and then the property would be property in fact as well as in name.
It also produced a wild grape of a promising sort. He had sent some
samples to Nicholas Longworth, of Cincinnati, to get his judgment
upon them, and Mr. Longworth had said that they would make as
good wine as his Catawbas. The land contained all these riches;
and also oil, but my father did not know that, and of course in those
early days he would have cared nothing about it if he had known
it. The oil was not discovered until about 1895. I wish I owned a
couple of acres of the land now. In which case I would not be writing Autobiographies for a living. My father's dying charge was,
"Cling to the land and wait; let nothing beguile it away from you."
My mother's favorite cousin, James Lampton, who figures in the
"Gilded Age" as "Colonel Sellers," always said of that land – and
said it with blazing enthusiasm, too, – "There's millions in it –
millions!" It is true that he always said that about everything – and
was always mistaken, too; but this time he was right; which shows
that a man who goes around with a prophecy-gun ought never to
get discouraged; if he will keep up his heart and fire at everything
he sees, he is bound to hit something by and by.

　　Many persons regarded "Colonel Sellers" as a fiction, an invention, an extravagant impossibility, and did me the honor to call
him a "creation"; but they were mistaken. I merely put him on
paper as he was; he was not a person who could be exaggerated.
The incidents which looked most extravagant, both in the book
and on the stage, were not inventions of mine but were facts of his
life; and I was present when they were developed. John T. Raymond's audiences used to come near to dying with laughter over
the turnip-eating scene; but, extravagant as the scene was, it was

---

* Correction. 1906: it was above 100,000, it appears.

faithful to the facts, in all its absurd details. The thing happened in Lampton's own house, and I was present. In fact I was myself the guest who ate the turnips. In the hands of a great actor that piteous scene would have dimmed any manly spectator's eyes with tears, and racked his ribs apart with laughter at the same time. But Raymond was great in humorous portrayal only. In that he was superb, he was wonderful – in a word, great; in all things else he was a pigmy of the pigmies.

The real Colonel Sellers, as I knew him in James Lampton, was a pathetic and beautiful spirit, a manly man, a straight and honorable man, a man with a big, foolish, unselfish heart in his bosom, a man born to be loved; and he was loved by all his friends, and by his family worshipped. It is the right word. To them he was but little less than a god. The real Colonel Sellers was never on the stage. Only half of him was there. Raymond could not play the other half of him; it was above his level. That half was made up of qualities of which Raymond was wholly destitute. For Raymond was not a manly man, he was not an honorable man nor an honest one, he was empty and selfish and vulgar and ignorant and silly, and there was a vacancy in him where his heart should have been. There was only one man who could have played the whole of Colonel Sellers, and that was Frank Mayo.*

It is a world of surprises. They fall, too, where one is least expecting them. When I introduced Sellers into the book, Charles Dudley Warner, who was writing the story with me, proposed a change of Sellers's Christian name. Ten years before, in a remote corner of the West, he had come across a man named Eschol Sellers, and he thought that Eschol was just the right and fitting name for our Sellers, since it was odd and quaint and all that. I liked the idea, but I said that that man might turn up and object. But Warner said it couldn't happen; that he was doubtless dead by this time, a man with a name like that couldn't live long; and be he dead or alive we must have the name, it was exactly the right one and we couldn't do without it. So the change was made. Warner's man was a farmer in a cheap and humble way. When the book had been out a week, a college-bred gentleman of courtly manners and ducal upholstery arrived in Hartford in a sultry state of mind and

* Raymond was playing "Colonel Sellers" in 1876 and along there. About twenty years later Mayo dramatized "Pudd'nhead Wilson" and played the title rôle delightfully.

with a libel suit in his eye, and *his* name was Eschol Sellers! He had
never heard of the other one, and had never been within a thousand miles of him. This damaged aristocrat's programme was
quite definite and businesslike: the American Publishing Company must suppress the edition as far as printed, and change the
name in the plates, or stand a suit for $10,000. He carried away
the Company's promise and many apologies, and we changed the
name back to Colonel Mulberry Sellers, in the plates. Apparently
there is nothing that cannot happen. Even the existence of two
unrelated men wearing the impossible name of Eschol Sellers is a
possible thing.

James Lampton floated, all his days, in a tinted mist of magnificent dreams, and died at last without seeing one of them realized. I saw him last in 1884, when it had been twenty-six years since
I ate the basin of raw turnips and washed them down with a bucket
of water in his house. He was become old and white-headed, but
he entered to me in the same old breezy way of his earlier life, and
he was all there, yet – not a detail wanting: the happy light in his
eye, the abounding hope in his heart, the persuasive tongue, the
miracle-breeding imagination – they were all there; and before
I could turn around he was polishing up his Aladdin's lamp and
flashing the secret riches of the world before me. I said to myself,
"I did not overdraw him by a shade, I set him down as he was; and
he is the same man today. Cable will recognize him." I asked him
to excuse me a moment, and ran into the next room, which was
Cable's; Cable and I were stumping the Union on a reading tour.
I said –

"I am going to leave your door open, so that you can listen.
There is a man in there who is interesting."

I went back and asked Lampton what he was doing now. He
began to tell me of a "small venture" he had begun in New Mexico
through his son; "only a little thing – a mere trifle – partly to amuse
my leisure, partly to keep my capital from lying idle, but mainly to
develop the boy – develop the boy; fortune's wheel is ever revolv-
ing, he may have to work for his living some day – as strange things
have happened in this world. But it's only a little thing – a mere
trifle, as I said."

And so it was – as he began it. But under his deft hands it grew,
and blossomed, and spread – oh, beyond imagination. At the end
of half an hour he finished; finished with the remark, uttered in an
adorably languid manner:

'Yes, it is but a trifle, as things go nowadays – a bagatelle – but amusing. It passes the time. The boy thinks great things of it, but he is young, you know, and imaginative; lacks the experience which comes of handling large affairs, and which tempers the fancy and perfects the judgment. I suppose there's a couple of millions in it, possibly three, but not more, I think; still, for a boy, you know, just starting in life, it is not bad. I should not want him to make a fortune – let that come later. It could turn his head, at his time of life, and in many ways be a damage to him."

Then he said something about his having left his pocket-book lying on the table in the main drawing-room at home, and about its being after banking hours, now, and –

I stopped him, there, and begged him to honor Cable and me by being our guest at the lecture – with as many friends as might be willing to do us the like honor. He accepted. And he thanked me as a prince might who had granted us a grace. The reason I stopped his speech about the tickets was because I saw that he was going to ask me to furnish them to him and let him pay next day; and I knew that if he made the debt he would pay it if he had to pawn his clothes. After a little further chat he shook hands heartily and affectionately, and took his leave. Cable put his head in at the door, and said –

"That was Colonel Sellers."

PART II

SEPTEMBER 21, 1906

2

My experiences as an author began early in 1867. I came to New York from San Francisco in the first month of that year and presently Charles H. Webb, whom I had known in San Francisco as a reporter on *The Bulletin*, and afterward editor of *The Californian*, suggested that I publish a volume of sketches. I had but a slender reputation to publish it on, but I was charmed and excited by the suggestion and quite willing to venture it if some industrious person would save me the trouble of gathering the sketches together.

I was loath to do it myself, for from the beginning of my sojourn in this world there was a persistent vacancy in me where the industry ought to be. ("Ought to was" is better, perhaps, though the most of the authorities differ as to this.)

Webb said I had some reputation in the Atlantic States, but I knew quite well that it must be of a very attenuated sort. What there was of it rested upon the story of "The Jumping Frog." When Artemus Ward passed through California on a lecturing tour, in 1865 or '66, I told him the "Jumping Frog" story, in San Francisco, and he asked me to write it out and send it to his publisher, Carleton, in New York, to be used in padding out a small book which Artemus had prepared for the press and which needed some more stuffing to make it big enough for the price which was to be charged for it.

It reached Carleton in time, but he didn't think much of it, and was not willing to go to the typesetting expense of adding it to the book. He did not put it in the waste-basket, but made Henry Clapp a present of it, and Clapp used it to help out the funeral of his dying literary journal, *The Saturday Press*. "The Jumping Frog" appeared in the last number of that paper, was the most joyous feature of the obsequies, and was at once copied in the newspapers of America and England. It certainly had a wide celebrity, and it still had it at the time that I am speaking of – but I was aware that it was only the frog that was celebrated. It wasn't I. I was still an obscurity.

Webb undertook to collate the sketches. He performed this office, then handed the result to me, and I went to Carleton's establishment with it. I approached a clerk and he bent eagerly over the counter to inquire into my needs; but when he found that I had come to sell a book and not to buy one, his temperature fell sixty degrees, and the old-gold intrenchments in the roof of my mouth contracted three-quarters of an inch and my teeth fell out. I meekly asked the privilege of a word with Mr. Carleton, and was coldly informed that he was in his private office. Discouragements and difficulties followed, but after a while I got by the frontier and entered the holy of holies. Ah, now I remember how I managed it! Webb had made an appointment for me with Carleton; otherwise I never should have gotten over that frontier. Carleton rose and said brusquely and aggressively,

"Well, what can I do for you?"

I reminded him that I was there by appointment to offer him my book for publication. He began to swell, and went on swelling and swelling and swelling until he had reached the dimensions of a god of about the second or third degree. Then the fountains of his great deep were broken up, and for two or three minutes I couldn't see him for the rain. It was words, only words, but they fell so densely that they darkened the atmosphere. Finally he made an imposing sweep with his right hand, which comprehended the whole room and said,

"Books – look at those shelves! Every one of them is loaded with books that are waiting for publication. Do I want any more? Excuse me, I don't. Good morning."

Twenty-one years elapsed before I saw Carleton again. I was then sojourning with my family at the Schweitzerhof, in Luzerne. He called on me, shook hands cordially, and said at once, without any preliminaries,

"I am substantially an obscure person, but I have at least one distinction to my credit of such colossal dimensions that it entitles me to immortality – to wit: I refused a book of yours, and for this I stand without competitor as the prize ass of the nineteenth century."

It was a most handsome apology, and I told him so, and said it was a long-delayed revenge but was sweeter to me than any other that could be devised; that during the lapsed twenty-one years I had in fancy taken his life several times every year, and always in new and increasingly cruel and inhuman ways, but that now I was pacified, appeased, happy, even jubilant; and that thenceforth I should hold him my true and valued friend and never kill him again.

I reported my adventure to Webb, and he bravely said that not all the Carletons in the universe should defeat that book; he would publish it himself on a ten per cent. royalty. And so he did. He brought it out in blue and gold, and made a very pretty little book of it. I think he named it "The Celebrated Jumping Frog of Calaveras County, and Other Sketches," price $1.25. He made the plates and printed and bound the book through a job-printing house, and published it through the American News Company.

In June I sailed in the *Quaker City* Excursion. I returned in November, and in Washington found a letter from Elisha Bliss, of the American Publishing Company of Hartford, offering me five per cent. royalty on a book which should recount the adventures of the Excursion. In lieu of the royalty, I was offered the alternative of ten thousand dollars cash upon delivery of the manuscript. I

consulted A. D. Richardson and he said "take the royalty." I followed his advice and closed with Bliss. By my contract I was to
deliver the manuscript in July of 1868. I wrote the book in San
Francisco and delivered the manuscript within contract time. Bliss
provided a multitude of illustrations for the book, and then
stopped work on it. The contract date for the issue went by, and
there was no explanation of this. Time drifted along and still there
was no explanation. I was lecturing all over the country; and about
thirty times a day, on an average, I was trying to answer this
conundrum:

"When is your book coming out?"

I got tired of inventing new answers to that question, and by
and by I got horribly tired of the question itself. Whoever asked it
became my enemy at once, and I was usually almost eager to make
that appear.

As soon as I was free of the lecture-field I hastened to Hartford
to make inquiries. Bliss said that the fault was not his; that he
wanted to publish the book but the directors of his Company were
staid old fossils and were afraid of it. They had examined the book,
and the majority of them were of the opinion that there were places
in it of a humorous character. Bliss said the house had never published a book that had a suspicion like that attaching to it, and
that the directors were afraid that a departure of this kind would
seriously injure the house's reputation; that he was tied hand and
foot, and was not permitted to carry out his contract. One of the
directors, a Mr. Drake – at least he was the remains of what had
once been a Mr. Drake – invited me to take a ride with him in his
buggy, and I went along. He was a pathetic old relic, and his ways
and his talk were also pathetic. He had a delicate purpose in view
and it took him some time to hearten himself sufficiently to carry
it out, but at last he accomplished it. He explained the house's
difficulty and distress, as Bliss had already explained it. Then he
frankly threw himself and the house upon my mercy and begged
me to take away "The Innocents Abroad" and release the concern
from the contract. I said I wouldn't – and so ended the interview
and the buggy excursion. Then I warned Bliss that he must get to
work or I should make trouble. He acted upon the warning, and
set up the book and I read the proofs. Then there was another long
wait and no explanation. At last toward the end of July (1896,
I think), I lost patience and telegraphed Bliss that if the book was
not on sale in twenty-four hours I should bring suit for damages.

That ended the trouble. Half a dozen copies were bound and placed on sale within the required time. Then the canvassing began, and went briskly forward. In nine months the book took the publishing house out of debt, advanced its stock from twenty-five to two hundred, and left seventy thousand dollars profit to the good. It was Bliss that told me this – but if it was true, it was the first time that he had told the truth in sixty-five years. He was born in 1804.

3

. . . This was in 1849. I was fourteen years old, then. We were still living in Hannibal, Missouri, on the banks of the Mississippi, in the new "frame" house built by my father five years before. That is, some of us lived in the new part, the rest in the old part back of it – the "L." In the autumn my sister gave a party, and invited all the marriageable young people of the village. I was too young for this society, and was too bashful to mingle with young ladies, anyway, therefore I was not invited – at least not for the whole evening. Ten minutes of it was to be my whole share. I was to do the part of a bear in a small fairy play. I was to be disguised all over in a close-fitting brown hairy stuff proper for a bear. About half past ten I was told to go to my room and put on this disguise, and be ready in half an hour. I started, but changed my mind; for I wanted to practise a little, and that room was very small. I crossed over to the large unoccupied house on the corner of Main and Hill streets,* unaware that a dozen of the young people were also going there to dress for their parts. I took the little black slave boy, Sandy, with me, and we selected a roomy and empty chamber on the second floor. We entered it talking, and this gave a couple of half-dressed young ladies an opportunity to take refuge behind a screen undiscovered. Their gowns and things were hanging on hooks behind the door, but I did not see them; it was Sandy that shut the door, but all his heart was in the theatricals, and he was as unlikely to notice them as I was myself.

That was a rickety screen, with many holes in it, but as I did not

* That house still stands.

know there were girls behind it, I was not disturbed by that detail.
If I had known, I could not have undressed in the flood of cruel
moonlight that was pouring in at the curtainless windows; I should
have died of shame. Untroubled by apprehensions, I stripped to
the skin and began my practice. I was full of ambition; I was determined to make a hit; I was burning to establish a reputation as a
bear and get further engagements; so I threw myself into my work
with an abandon that promised great things. I capered back and
forth from one end of the room to the other on all fours, Sandy
applauding with enthusiasm; I walked upright and growled and
snapped and snarled; I stood on my head, I flung handsprings,
I danced a lubberly dance with my paws bent and my imaginary
snout sniffing from side to side; I did everything a bear could do,
and many things which no bear could ever do and no bear with
any dignity would want to do, anyway; and of course I never suspected that I was making a spectacle of myself to any one but
Sandy. At last, standing on my head, I paused in that attitude to
take a minute's rest. There was a moment's silence, then Sandy
spoke up with excited interest and said –

"Marse Sam, has you ever seen a smoked herring?"

"No. What is that?"

"It's a fish."

"Well, what of it? Anything peculiar about it?"

"Yes, suh, you bet you dey is. *Dey eats 'em guts and all!*"

There was a smothered burst of feminine snickers from behind
the screen! All the strength went out of me and I toppled forward
like an undermined tower and brought the screen down with my
weight, burying the young ladies under it. In their fright they discharged a couple of piercing screams – and possibly others, but
I did not wait to count. I snatched my clothes and fled to the dark
hall below, Sandy following. I was dressed in half a minute, and
out the back way. I swore Sandy to eternal silence, then we went
away and hid until the party was over. The ambition was all out
of me. I could not have faced that giddy company after my adventure, for there would be two performers there who knew my secret,
and would be privately laughing at me all the time. I was searched
for but not found, and the bear had to be played by a young gentleman in his civilized clothes. The house was still and everybody
asleep when I finally ventured home. I was very heavy-hearted,
and full of a sense of disgrace. Pinned to my pillow I found a slip
of paper which bore a line that did not lighten my heart, but only

made my face burn. It was written in a laboriously disguised hand, and these were its mocking terms:

"You probably couldn't have played *bear*, but you played *bare* very well – oh, very very well!"

We think boys are rude, unsensitive animals, but it is not so in all cases. Each boy has one or two sensitive spots, and if you can find out where they are located you have only to touch them and you can scorch him as with fire. I suffered miserably over that episode. I expected that the facts would be all over the village in the morning, but it was not so. The secret remained confined to the two girls and Sandy and me. That was some appeasement of my pain, but it was far from sufficient – the main trouble remained: I was under four mocking eyes, and it might as well have been a thousand, for I suspected all girls' eyes of being the ones I so dreaded. During several weeks I could not look any young lady in the face; I dropped my eyes in confusion when any one of them smiled upon me and gave me greeting; and I said to myself, "*That is one of them*," and got quickly away. Of course I was meeting the right girls everywhere, but if they ever let slip any betraying sign I was not bright enough to catch it. When I left Hannibal four years later, the secret was still a secret; I had never guessed those girls out, and was no longer expecting to do it. Nor wanting to, either.

One of the dearest and prettiest girls in the village at the time of my mishap was one whom I will call Mary Wilson, because that was not her name. She was twenty years old; she was dainty and sweet, peach-bloomy and exquisite, gracious and lovely in character, and I stood in awe of her, for she seemed to me to be made out of angel-clay and rightfully unapproachable by an unholy ordinary kind of a boy like me. I probably never suspected her. But –

The scene changes. To Calcutta – forty-seven years later. It was in 1896. I arrived there on my lecturing trip. As I entered the hotel a divine vision passed out of it, clothed in the glory of the Indian sunshine – the Mary Wilson of my long-vanished boyhood! It was a startling thing. Before I could recover from the bewildering shock and speak to her she was gone. I thought maybe I had seen an apparition, but it was not so, she was flesh. She was the granddaughter of the other Mary, the original Mary. That Mary, now a widow, was up-stairs, and presently sent for me. She was old and gray-haired, but she looked young and was very handsome. We sat down and talked. We steeped our thirsty souls in the reviving wine of the past, the beautiful past, the dear and lamented past; we uttered the names that had been silent upon our lips for fifty years, and it was as if they were made of music; with reverent hands we unburied our dead, the mates of our youth, and caressed them with our speech; we searched the dusty chambers of our memories and dragged forth incident after incident, episode after episode, folly after folly, and laughed such good laughs over them, with the tears running down; and finally Mary said suddenly, and without any leading up –

"Tell me! What is the special peculiarity of smoked herrings?"

It seemed a strange question at such a hallowed time as this. And so inconsequential, too. I was a little shocked. And yet I was aware of a stir of some kind away back in the deeps of my memory somewhere. It set me to musing – thinking – searching. Smoked herrings. Smoked herrings. The peculiarity of smo. . . . I glanced up. Her face was grave, but there was a dim and shadowy twinkle in her eye which – All of a sudden I knew! and far away down in the hoary past I heard a remembered voice murmur, "Dey eats 'em guts and all!"

"At – last! I've found one of you, anyway! Who was the other girl?"

But she drew the line there. She wouldn't tell me.

4

. . . But it was on a bench in Washington Square that I saw the most of Louis Stevenson. It was an outing that lasted an hour or more, and was very pleasant and sociable. I had come with him from his house, where I had been paying my respects to his family. His business in the Square was to absorb the sunshine. He was most scantily furnished with flesh, his clothes seemed to fall into hollows as if there might be nothing inside but the frame for a sculptor's statue. His long face and lank hair and dark complexion and musing and melancholy expression seemed to fit these details justly and harmoniously, and the altogether of it seemed especially planned to gather the rays of your observation and focalize them upon Stevenson's special distinction and commanding feature, his splendid eyes. They burned with a smouldering rich fire under the penthouse of his brows, and they made him beautiful.

*

I said I thought he was right about the others, but mistaken as to Bret Harte; in substance I said that Harte was good company and a thin but pleasant talker; that he was always bright, but never brilliant; that in this matter he must not be classed with Thomas Bailey Aldrich, nor must any other man, ancient or modern; that Aldrich was always witty, always brilliant, if there was anybody present capable of striking his flint at the right angle; that Aldrich was as sure and prompt and unfailing as the red-hot iron on the blacksmith's anvil – you had only to hit it competently to make it deliver an explosion of sparks. I added –

"Aldrich has never had his peer for prompt and pithy and witty and humorous sayings. None has equalled him, certainly none has surpassed him, in the felicity of phrasing with which he clothed these children of his fancy. Aldrich was always brilliant, he couldn't help it, he is a fire-opal set round with rose diamonds; when he is not speaking, you know that his dainty fancies are twinkling and glimmering around in him; when he speaks the diamonds flash. Yes, he was always brilliant, he will always be brilliant; he will be brilliant in hell – you will see."

Stevenson, smiling a chuckly smile, "I hope not."

"Well, you will, and he will dim even those ruddy fires and look like a transfigured Adonis backed against a pink sunset."

There on that bench we struck out a new phrase – one or the other of us, I don't remember which – "submerged renown." Variations were discussed: "submerged fame," "submerged reputation," and so on, and a choice was made; "submerged renown" was elected, I believe. This important matter rose out of an incident which had been happening to Stevenson in Albany. While in a book-shop or book-stall there he had noticed a long rank of small books, cheaply but neatly gotten up, and bearing such titles as "Davis's Selected Speeches," "Davis's Selected Poetry," Davis's this and Davis's that and Davis's the other thing; compilations, every one of them, each with a brief, compact, intelligent and useful introductory chapter by this same Davis, whose first name I have forgotten. Stevenson had begun the matter with this question:

"Can you name the American author whose fame and acceptance stretch widest in the States?"

I thought I could, but it did not seem to me that it would be

modest to speak out, in the circumstances. So I diffidently said
nothing. Stevenson noticed, and said –

"Save your delicacy for another time – you are not the one. For
a shilling you can't name the American author of widest note and
popularity in the States. But I can."

Then he went on and told about that Albany incident. He had
inquired of the shopman –

"Who is this Davis?"

The answer was –

"An author whose books have to have freight-trains to carry
them, not baskets. Apparently you have not heard of him?"

Stevenson said no, this was the first time. The man said –

"Nobody has heard of Davis: you may ask all around and you
will see. You never see his name mentioned in print, not even in
advertisement; these things are of no use to Davis, not any more
than they are to the wind and the sea. You never see one of Davis's
books floating on top of the United States, but put on your diving
armor and get yourself lowered away down and down and down
till you strike the dense region, the sunless region of eternal
drudgery and starvation wages – there you'll find them by the million. The man that gets that market, his fortune is made, his bread
and butter are safe, for those people will never go back on him. An
author may have a reputation which is confined to the surface, and
lose it and become pitied, then despised, then forgotten, entirely
forgotten – the frequent steps in a surface reputation. A surface
reputation, however great, is always mortal, and always killable if
you go at it right – with pins and needles, and quiet slow poison,
not with the club and tomahawk. But it is a different matter
with the submerged reputation – down in the deep water; once a
favorite there, always a favorite; once beloved, always beloved;
once respected, always respected, honored, and believed in. For,
what the reviewer says never finds its way down into those placid
deeps; nor the newspaper sneers, nor any breath of the winds of
slander blowing above. Down there they never hear of these
things. Their idol may be painted clay, up there at the surface, and
fade and waste and crumble and blow away, there being much
weather there; but down below he is gold and adamant and
indestructible."

5

This is from this morning's paper:

MARK TWAIN LETTER SOLD
Written to Thomas Nast, it Proposed a Joint Tour.

A Mark Twain autograph letter brought $43 yesterday at the auction by the Merwin-Clayton Company of the library and correspondence of the late Thomas Nast, cartoonist. The letter is nine pages note-paper, is dated Hartford, Nov. 12, 1877, and is addressed to Nast. It reads in part as follows:

HARTFORD, NOV. 12.

MY DEAR NAST: I did not think I should ever stand on a platform again until the time was come for me to say I die innocent. But the same old offers keep arriving that have arriven every year, and been every year declined – $500 for Louisville, $500 for St. Louis, $1,000 gold for two nights in Toronto, half gross proceeds for New York, Boston, Brooklyn, &c. I have declined them all just as usual, though sorely tempted as usual.

Now, I do not decline because I mind talking to an audience, but because (1) travelling alone is so heart-breakingly dreary, and (2) shouldering the whole show is such cheer-killing responsibility.

Therefore I now propose to you what you proposed to me in November, 1867 – ten years ago, (when I was unknown,) viz.; That you should stand on the platform and make pictures, and I stand by you and blackguard the audience. I should enormously enjoy meandering around (to big towns – don't want to go to little ones) with you for company.

The letter includes a schedule of cities and the number of appearances planned for each.

This is as it should be. This is worthy of all praise. I say it myself lest other competent persons should forget to do it. It appears that four of my ancient letters were sold at auction, three of them at twenty-seven dollars, twenty-eight dollars, and twenty-nine dollars respectively, and the one above mentioned at forty-three dollars. There is one very gratifying circumstance about this, to wit: that my literature has more than held its own as regards money value through this stretch of thirty-six years. I judge that the forty-three-dollar letter must have gone at about ten cents a word, whereas if I had written it to-day its market rate would be thirty cents – so I have increased in value two or three hundred per cent. I note another gratifying circumstance – that a letter of General Grant's sold at something short of eighteen dollars. I can't rise to General Grant's lofty place in the estimation of this nation, but it is a deep happiness to me to know that when it comes to epistolary literature he can't sit in the front seat along with me.

This reminds me – nine years ago, when we were living in Tedworth Square, London, a report was cabled to the American journals that I was dying. I was not the one. It was another Clemens, a cousin of mine, – Dr J. Ross Clemens, now of St. Louis – who was due to die but presently escaped, by some chicanery or other characteristic of the tribe of Clemens. The London representatives of the American papers began to flock in, with American cables in their hands, to inquire into my condition. There was nothing the matter with me, and each in his turn was astonished, and disappointed, to find me reading and smoking in my study and worth next to nothing as a text for transatlantic news. One of these men was a gentle and kindly and grave and sympathetic Irishman, who hid his sorrow the best he could, and tried to look glad, and told me that his paper, the *Evening Sun*, had cabled him that it was reported in New York that I was dead. What should he cable in reply? I said –

"Say the report is greatly exaggerated."

He never smiled, but went solemnly away and sent the cable in those words. The remark hit the world pleasantly, and to this day it keeps turning up, now and then, in the newspapers when people have occasion to discount exaggerations.

The next man was also an Irishman. He had his New York cablegram in his hand – from the New York *World* – and he was so evidently trying to get around that cable with invented softnesses and palliations that my curiosity was aroused and I wanted to see what it did really say. So when occasion offered I slipped it out of his hand. It said,

"If Mark Twain dying send five hundred words. If dead send a thousand."

Now that old letter of mine sold yesterday for forty-three dollars. When I am dead it will be worth eighty-six.

PART III

OCTOBER 5, 1906

6

To-morrow will be the thirty-sixth anniversary of our marriage. My wife passed from this life one year and eight months ago, in Florence, Italy, after an unbroken illness of twenty-two months' duration.

I saw her first in the form of an ivory miniature in her brother Charley's stateroom in the steamer "Quaker City," in the Bay of Smyrna, in the summer of 1867, when she was in her twenty-second year. I saw her in the flesh for the first time in New York in the following December. She was slender and beautiful and girlish – and she was both girl and woman. She remained both girl and woman to the last day of her life. Under a grave and gentle exterior burned inextinguishable fires of sympathy, energy, devotion, enthusiasm, and absolutely limitless affection. She was *always* frail in body, and she lived upon her spirit, whose hopefulness and courage were indestructible. Perfect truth, perfect honesty, perfect candor, were qualities of her character which were born with her. Her judgments of people and things were sure and accurate. Her intuitions almost never deceived her. In her judgments of the characters and acts of both friends and strangers, there was always room for charity, and this charity never failed. I have compared and contrasted her with hundreds of persons, and my conviction remains that hers was the most perfect character I have ever met. And I may add that she was the most winningly dignified person I have ever known. Her character and disposition were of the sort that not only invites worship, but commands it. No servant ever left her service who deserved to remain in it. And, as she could choose with a glance of her eye, the servants she selected did in almost all cases deserve to remain, and they *did* remain. She was always cheerful; and she was always able to communicate her cheerfulness to others. During the nine years that we spent in poverty and debt, she was always able to reason me out of my despairs, and find a bright side to the clouds, and make me see it. In all that time, I never knew her to utter a word of regret concerning our altered circumstances, nor did I ever know her children to do the like. For she had taught them, and they drew their fortitude from her. The love which she bestowed upon those whom she loved took the form of worship, and in that form it was returned – returned by relatives, friends and the servants of her household. It was a strange combination which wrought into one individual, so to speak, by marriage – her disposition and character and mine. She poured out her prodigal affections in kisses and caresses, and in a vocabulary of endearments whose profusion was always an astonishment to me. I was born *reserved* as to endearments of speech and caresses, and hers broke upon me as the summer waves break upon Gibraltar. I was reared in that atmosphere of reserve. As I have already said, in another chapter, I never knew a member of my father's family to kiss another member of it except once, and that at a death-bed. And our village was not a kissing community. The kissing and caressing ended with courtship – along with the deadly piano-playing of that day.

She had the heart-free laugh of a girl. It came seldom, but when it broke upon the ear it was as inspiring as music. I heard it for the last time when she had been occupying her sickbed for more than a year, and I made a written note of it at the time – a note not to be repeated.

To-morrow will be the thirty-sixth anniversary. We were married in her father's house in Elmira, New York, and went next day, by special train, to Buffalo, along with the whole Langdon family, and with the Beechers and the Twichells, who had solemnized the marriage. We were to live in Buffalo, where I was to be one of the editors of the Buffalo "Express," and a part owner of the paper. I knew nothing about Buffalo, but I had made my household arrangements there through a friend, by letter. I had instructed him to find a boarding-house of as respectable a character as my light salary as editor would command. We were received at about nine o'clock at the station in Buffalo, and were put into several sleighs and driven all over America, as it seemed to me – for, apparently, we turned all the corners in the town and followed all the streets there were – I scolding freely, and characterizing that friend of mine in very uncomplimentary words for securing a boarding-house that apparently had no definite locality. But there was a conspiracy – and my bride knew of it, but I was in ignorance. Her father, Jervis Langdon, had bought and furnished a new house for us in the fashionable street, Delaware Avenue, and had laid in a cook and housemaids, and a brisk and electric young coachman, an Irishman, Patrick McAleer – and we were being driven all over that city in order that one sleighful of those people could have time to go to the house, and see that the gas was lighted all over it, and a hot supper prepared for the crowd. We arrived at last, and when I entered that fairy place my indignation reached high-water mark, and without any reserve I delivered my opinion to that friend of mine for being so stupid as to put us into a boarding-house whose terms would be far out of my reach. Then Mr. Langdon brought forward a very pretty box and opened it, and took from it a deed of the house. So the comedy ended very pleasantly, and we sat down to supper.

The company departed about midnight, and left us alone in our new quarters. Then Ellen, the cook, came in to get orders for the morning's marketing – and neither of us knew whether beefsteak was sold by the barrel or by the yard. We exposed our ignorance, and Ellen was full of Irish delight over it. Patrick McAleer, that brisk young Irishman, came in to get his orders for next day – and that was our first glimpse of him. . . .

Our first child, Langdon Clemens, was born the 7th of November, 1870, and lived twenty-two months. Susy was born the 19th of March, 1872, and passed from life in the Hartford home, the 18th of August, 1896. With her, when the end came, were Jean and Katy Leary, and John and Ellen (the gardener and his wife). Clara and her mother and I arrived in England from around the world on the 31st of July, and took a house in Guildford. A week later, when Susy, Katy and Jean should have been arriving from America, we got a letter instead.

It explained that Susy was slightly ill – nothing of consequence. But we were disquieted, and began to cable for later news. This was Friday. All day no answer – and the ship to leave Southampton next day, at noon. Clara and her mother began packing, to be ready in case the news should be bad. Finally came a cablegram saying, "Wait for cablegram in the morning." This was not satisfactory – not reassuring. I cabled again, asking that the answer be sent to Southampton, for the day was now closing. I waited in the post-office that night till the doors were closed, toward midnight, in the hope that good news might still come, but there was no message. We sat silent at home till one in the morning, waiting – waiting for we knew not what. Then we took the earliest morning train, and when we reached Southampton the message was there. It said the recovery would be long, but certain. This was a great relief to

me, but not to my wife. She was frightened. She and Clara went
aboard the steamer at once and sailed for America, to nurse Susy.
I remained behind to search for a larger house in Guildford.

That was the 15th of August, 1896. Three days later, when my
wife and Clara were about half-way across the ocean, I was
standing in our dining-room thinking of nothing in particular,
when a cablegram was put into my hand. It said, "Susy was peacefully released to-day."

It is one of the mysteries of our nature that a man, all unprepared, can receive a thunder-stroke like that and live. There is but
one reasonable explanation of it. The intellect is stunned by the
shock, and but gropingly gathers the meaning of the words. The
power to realize their full import is mercifully wanting. The mind
has a dumb sense of vast loss – that is all. It will take mind and
memory months, and possibly years, to gather together the details,
and thus learn and know the whole extent of the loss. A man's
house burns down. The smoking wreckage represents only a
ruined home that was dear through years of use and pleasant associations. By and by, as the days and weeks go on, first he misses
this, then that, then the other thing. And, when he casts about for
it, he finds that it was in that house. Always it is an *essential* – there
was but one of its kind. It cannot be replaced. It was in that house.
It is irrevocably lost. He did not realize that it was an essential
when he had it; he only discovers it now when he finds himself
balked, hampered, by its absence. It will be years before the tale
of lost essentials is complete, and not till then can he truly know
the magnitude of his disaster.

The 18th of August brought me the awful tidings. The mother
and the sister were out there in mid-Atlantic, ignorant of what was
happening; flying to meet this incredible calamity. All that could
be done to protect them from the full force of the shock was done
by relatives and good friends. They went down the Bay and met
the ship at night, but did not show themselves until morning, and
then only to Clara. When she returned to the stateroom she did
not speak, and did not need to. Her mother looked at her and said:
"Susy is dead."

At half past ten o'clock that night, Clara and her mother completed their circuit of the globe, and drew up at Elmira by the same
train and in the same car which had borne them and me Westward
from it one year, one month, and one week before. And again Susy
was there – not waving her welcome in the glare of the lights, as

she had waved her farewell to us thirteen months before, but lying white and fair in her coffin, in the house where she was born.

The last thirteen days of Susy's life were spent in our own house in Hartford, the home of her childhood, and always the dearest place in the earth to her. About her she had faithful old friends – her pastor, Mr. Twichell, who had known her from the cradle, and who had come a long journey to be with her; her uncle and aunt, Mr. and Mrs. Theodore Crane; Patrick, the coachman; Katy, who had begun to serve us when Susy was a child of eight years; John and Ellen, who had been with us many years. Also Jean was there.

At the hour when my wife and Clara set sail for America, Susy was in no danger. Three hours later there came a sudden change for the worse. Meningitis set in, and it was immediately apparent that she was death-struck. That was Saturday, the 15th of August.

"That evening she took food for the last time," (Jean's letter to me). The next morning the brain-fever was raging. She walked the floor a little in her pain and delirium, then succumbed to weakness and returned to her bed. Previously she had found hanging in a closet a gown which she had seen her mother wear. She thought it was her mother, dead, and she kissed it, and cried. About noon she became blind (an effect of the disease) and bewailed it to her uncle.

From Jean's letter I take this sentence, which needs no comment:

"About one in the afternoon Susy spoke for the last time."

It was only one word that she said when she spoke that last time, and it told of her longing. She groped with her hands and found Katy, and caressed her face, and said "Mamma."

How gracious it was that, in that forlorn hour of wreck and ruin, with the night of death closing around her, she should have been granted that beautiful illusion – that the latest vision which rested upon the clouded mirror of her mind should have been the vision of her mother, and the latest emotion she should know in life the joy and peace of that dear imagined presence.

About two o'clock she composed herself as if for sleep, and never moved again. She fell into unconsciousness and so remained two days and five hours, until Tuesday evening at seven minutes past seven, when the release came. She was twenty-four years and five months old.

On the 23d, her mother and her sisters saw her laid to rest – she that had been our wonder and our worship.

In one of her own books I find some verses which I will copy here. Apparently, she always put borrowed matter in quotation marks. These verses lack those marks, and therefore I take them to be her own:

> Love came at dawn, when all the world was fair,
> When crimson glories' bloom and sun were rife;
> Love came at dawn, when hope's wings fanned the air,
> And murmured, "I am life."
>
> Love came at eve, and when the day was done,
> When heart and brain were tired, and slumber pressed;
> Love came at eve, shut out the sinking sun,
> And whispered, "I am rest."

The summer seasons of Susy's childhood were spent at Quarry Farm, on the hills east of Elmira, New York; the other seasons of the year at the home in Hartford. Like other children, she was blithe and happy, fond of play; *un*like the average of children, she was at times much given to retiring within herself, and trying to search out the hidden meanings of the deep things that make the puzzle and pathos of human existence, and in all the ages have baffled the inquirer and mocked him. As a little child aged seven, she was oppressed and perplexed by the maddening repetition of the stock incidents of our race's fleeting sojourn here, just as the same thing has oppressed and perplexed maturer minds from the beginning of time. A myriad of men are born; they labor and sweat and struggle for bread; they squabble and scold and fight; they scramble for little mean advantages over each other; age creeps upon them; infirmities follow; shames and humiliations bring down their prides and their vanities; those they love are taken from them, and the joy of life is turned to aching grief. The burden of pain, care, misery, grows heavier year by year; at length, ambition is dead, pride is dead; vanity is dead; longing for release is in their place. It comes at last – the only unpoisoned gift earth ever had for them – and they vanish from a world where they were of no consequence; where they achieved nothing; where they were a mistake and a failure and a foolishness; there they have left no sign that they have existed – a world which will lament them a day and forget them forever. Then another myriad takes their place, and copies all they did, and goes along the same profitless road, and vanishes as they vanished – to make room for another, and another, and a million other myriads, to follow the same arid path through the same desert, and accomplish what the first myriad, and all the myriads that came after it, accomplished – nothing!

"Mamma, what is it all for?" asked Susy, preliminarily stating the above details in her own halting language, after long brooding over them alone in the privacy of the nursery.

A year later, she was groping her way alone through another sunless bog, but this time she reached a rest for her feet. For a week, her mother had not been able to go to the nursery, evenings, at the child's prayer hour. She spoke of it – was sorry for it, and said she would come to-night, and hoped she could continue to come every night and hear Susy pray, as before. Noticing that the child wished to respond, but was evidently troubled as to how to word her answer, she asked what the difficulty was. Susy explained that Miss Foote (the governess) had been teaching her about the Indians and their religious beliefs, whereby it appeared that they had not only a God, but several. This had set Susy to thinking. As a result of this thinking, she had stopped praying. She qualified this statement – that is, she modified it – saying she did not now pray "in the same way" as she had formerly done. Her mother said:

"Tell me about it, dear."

"Well, mamma, the Indians believed they knew, but now we know they were wrong. By and by, it can turn out that we are wrong. So now I only pray that there may be a God and a Heaven – or something better."

I wrote down this pathetic prayer in its precise wording, at the time, in a record which we kept of the children's sayings, and my reverence for it has grown with the years that have passed over my head since then. Its untaught grace and simplicity are a child's, but the wisdom and the pathos of it are of all the ages that have come and gone since the race of man has lived, and longed, and hoped, and feared, and doubted.

To go back a year – Susy aged seven. Several times her mother said to her:

"There, there, Susy, you mustn't cry over little things."

This furnished Susy a text for thought. She had been breaking her heart over what had seemed vast disasters – a broken toy; a picnic cancelled by thunder and lightning and rain; the mouse that was growing tame and friendly in the nursery caught and killed by the cat – and now came this strange revelation. For some

unaccountable reason, these were not vast calamities. Why? How
is the size of calamities measured? What is the rule? There must
be some way to tell the great ones from the small ones; what is the
law of these proportions? She examined the problem earnestly and
long. She gave it her best thought from time to time, for two or
three days – but it baffled her – defeated her. And at last she gave
up and went to her mother for help.

"Mamma, what is '*little* things'?"

It seemed a simple question – at first. And yet, before the answer
could be put into words, unsuspected and unforeseen difficulties
began to appear. They increased; they multiplied; they brought
about another defeat. The effort to explain came to a standstill.
Then Susy tried to help her mother out – with an instance, an
example, an illustration. The mother was getting ready to go
down-town, and one of her errands was to buy a long-promised
toy-watch for Susy.

"If you forgot the watch, mamma, would that be a little thing?"

She was not concerned about the watch, for she knew it would
not be forgotten. What she was hoping for was that the answer
would unriddle the riddle, and bring rest and peace to her perplexed little mind.

The hope was disappointed, of course – for the reason that the
size of a misfortune is not determinable by an outsider's mea-
surement of it, but only by the measurements applied to it by the
person specially affected by it. The king's lost crown is a vast matter to the king, but of no consequence to the child. The lost toy is
a great matter to the child, but in the king's eyes it is not a thing
to break the heart about. A verdict was reached, but it was based
upon the above model, and Susy was granted leave to measure her
disasters thereafter with her own tape-line.

As a child, Susy had a passionate temper; and it cost her much
remorse and many tears before she learned to govern it, but after
that it was a wholesome salt, and her character was the stronger
and healthier for its presence. It enabled her to be good with dignity; it preserved her not only from being good for vanity's sake,
but from even the appearance of it. In looking back over the long
vanished years, it seems but natural and excusable that I should
dwell with longing affection and preference upon incidents of her
young life which made it beautiful to us, and that I should let its
few small offences go unsummoned and unreproached.

In the summer of 1880, when Susy was just eight years of age, the family were at Quarry Farm, as usual at that season of the year. Hay-cutting time was approaching, and Susy and Clara were counting the hours, for the time was big with a great event for them; they had been promised that they might mount the wagon and ride home from the fields on the summit of the hay mountain. This perilous privilege, so dear to their age and species, had never been granted them before. Their excitement had no bounds. They could talk of nothing but this epoch-making adventure, now. But misfortune overtook Susy on the very morning of the important day. In a sudden outbreak of passion, she corrected Clara – with a shovel, or stick, or something of the sort. At any rate, the offence committed was of a gravity clearly beyond the limit allowed in the nursery. In accordance with the rule and custom of the house, Susy went to her mother to confess, and to help decide upon the size and character of the punishment due. It was quite understood that, as a punishment could have but one rational object and function – to act as a reminder, and warn the transgressor against transgressing in the same way again – the children would know about as well as any how to choose a penalty which would be rememberable and effective. Susy and her mother discussed various punishments, but none of them seemed adequate. This fault was an unusually serious one, and required the setting up of a danger-signal in the memory that would not blow out nor burn out, but remain a fixture there and furnish its saving warning indefinitely. Among the punishments mentioned was deprivation of the hay-wagon ride. It was noticeable that this one hit Susy hard. Finally, in the summing up, the mother named over the list and asked:

"Which one do you think it ought to be, Susy?"

Susy studied, shrank from her duty, and asked:

"Which do you think, mamma?"

"Well, Susy, I would rather leave it to you. *You* make the choice yourself."

It cost Susy a struggle, and much and deep thinking and weighing – but she came out where any one who knew her could have foretold she would.

"Well, mamma, I'll make it the hay-wagon, because you know the other things might not make me remember not to do it again, but if I don't get to ride on the hay-wagon I can remember it easily."

In this world the real penalty, the sharp one, the lasting one, never falls otherwise than on the wrong person. It was not *I* that corrected Clara, but the remembrance of poor Susy's lost hayride still brings *me* a pang – after twenty-six years.

Apparently, Susy was born with humane feelings for the animals, and compassion for their troubles. This enabled her to see a new point in an old story, once, when she was only six years old – a point which had been overlooked by older, and perhaps duller, people for many ages. Her mother told her the moving story of the sale of Joseph by his brethren, the staining of his coat with the blood of the slaughtered kid, and the rest of it. She dwelt upon the inhumanity of the brothers; their cruelty toward their helpless young brother; and the unbrotherly treachery which they prac- tised upon him; for she hoped to teach the child a lesson in gentle pity and mercifulness which she would remember. Apparently, her desire was accomplished, for the tears came into Susy's eyes and she was deeply moved. Then she said:

"Poor little kid!"

A child's frank envy of the privileges and distinctions of its elders is often a delicately flattering attention and the reverse of unwel- come, but sometimes the envy is not placed where the beneficiary is expecting it to be placed. Once, when Susy was seven, she sat breathlessly absorbed in watching a guest of ours adorn herself for a ball. The lady was charmed by this homage; this mute and gentle admiration; and was happy in it. And when her pretty labors were finished, and she stood at last perfect, unimprovable, clothed like Solomon in all his glory, she paused, confident and expectant, to receive from Susy's tongue the tribute that was burning in her eyes. Susy drew an envious little sigh and said:

"I wish *I* could have crooked teeth and spectacles!"

Once, when Susy was six months along in her eighth year, she did something one day in the presence of company, which sub- jected her to criticism and reproof. Afterward, when she was alone with her mother, as was her custom she reflected a little while over the matter. Then she set up what I think – and what the shade of Burns would think – was a quite good philosophical defence.

"Well, mamma, you know I didn't see myself, and so I couldn't know how it looked."

In homes where the near friends and visitors are mainly literary people – lawyers, judges, professors and clergymen – the children's ears become early familiarized with wide vocabularies. It is natural for them to pick up any words that fall in their way; it is natural for them to pick up big and little ones indiscriminately;

it is natural for them to use without fear any word that comes to their net, no matter how formidable it may be as to size. As a result, their talk is a curious and funny musketry clatter of little words, interrupted at intervals by the heavy artillery crash of a word of such imposing sound and size that it seems to shake the ground and rattle the windows. Sometimes the child gets a wrong idea of a word which it has picked up by chance, and attaches to it a meaning which impairs its usefulness – but this does not happen as often as one might expect it would. Indeed, it happens with an infrequency which may be regarded as remarkable. As a child, Susy had good fortune with her large words, and she employed many of them. She made no more than her fair share of mistakes. Once when she thought something very funny was going to happen (but it didn't), she was racked and torn with laughter, by anticipation. But, apparently, she still felt sure of her position, for she said, "If it had happened, I should have been transformed [transported] with glee."

And earlier, when she was a little maid of five years, she informed a visitor that she had been in a church only once, and that was the time when Clara was "crucified" [christened]. . . .

In Heidelberg, when Susy was six, she noticed that the Schloss gardens were populous with snails creeping all about, everywhere. One day she found a new dish on her table and inquired concerning it, and learned that it was made of snails. She was awed and impressed, and said:

"Wild ones, mamma?"

She was thoughtful and considerate of others – an acquired quality, no doubt. No one seems to be born with it. One hot day, at home in Hartford, when she was a little child, her mother borrowed her fan several times (a Japanese one, value five cents), refreshed herself with it a moment or two, then handed it back with a word of thanks. Susy knew her mother would use the fan all the time if she could do it without putting a deprivation upon its owner. She also knew that her mother could not be persuaded to do that. A relief must be devised somehow; Susy devised it. She got five cents out of her money-box and carried it to Patrick, and asked him to take it down-town (a mile and a half) and buy a Japanese fan and bring it home. He did it – and thus thoughtfully and delicately was the exigency met and the mother's comfort secured. It is to the child's credit that she did not save herself expense by bringing down another and more costly kind of fan from up-stairs, but was content to act upon the impression that her mother desired the Japanese kind – content to accomplish the desire and stop with that, without troubling about the wisdom or unwisdom of it.

Sometimes, while she was still a child, her speech fell into quaint and strikingly expressive forms. Once – aged nine or ten – she came to her mother's room, when her sister Jean was a baby, and said Jean was crying in the nursery, and asked if she might ring for the nurse. Her mother asked:

"Is she crying hard?" – meaning cross, ugly.

"Well, no, mamma. It is a weary, lonesome cry."

It is a pleasure to me to recall various incidents which reveal the delicacies of feeling that were so considerable a part of her budding character. Such a revelation came once in a way which, while creditable to her heart, was defective in another direction. She was in her eleventh year then. Her mother had been making the Christmas purchases, and she allowed Susy to see the presents which were for Patrick's children. Among these was a handsome sled for Jimmy, on which a stag was painted; also, in gilt capitals, the word "Deer." Susy was excited and joyous over everything, until she came to this sled. Then she became sober and silent – yet the sled was the choicest of all the gifts. Her mother was surprised, and also disappointed, and said:

"Why, Susy, doesn't it please you? Isn't it fine?"

Susy hesitated, and it was plain that she did not want to say the thing that was in her mind. However, being urged, she brought it haltingly out:

"Well, mamma, it *is* fine, and of course it *did* cost a good deal – but – but – why should that be mentioned?"

Seeing that she was not understood, she reluctantly pointed to that word "Deer." It was her orthography that was at fault, not her heart. She had inherited both from her mother.

PART IV

OCTOBER 19, 1906

When Susy was thirteen, and was a slender little maid with plaited tails of copper-tinged brown hair down her back, and was perhaps the busiest bee in the household hive, by reason of the manifold studies, health exercises and recreations she had to attend to, she secretly, and of her own motion, and out of love, added another task to her labors – the writing of a biography of me. She did this work in her bedroom at night, and kept her record hidden. After a little, the mother discovered it and filched it, and let me see it; then told Susy what she had done, and how pleased I was, and how proud. I remember that time with a deep pleasure. I had had compliments before, but none that touched me like this; none that could approach it for value in my eyes. It has kept that place always since. I have had no compliment, no praise, no tribute from any source, that was so precious to me as this one was and still is. As I read it *now*, after all these many years, it is still a king's message to me, and brings me the same dear surprise it brought me then – with the pathos added, of the thought that the eager and hasty hand that sketched it and scrawled it will not touch mine again – and I feel as the humble and unexpectant must feel when their eyes fall upon the edict that raises them to the ranks of the noble.

Yesterday while I was rummaging in a pile of ancient notebooks of mine which I had not seen for years, I came across a reference to that biography. It is quite evident that several times, at breakfast and dinner, in those long-past days, I was posing for the biography. In fact, I clearly remember that I *was* doing that – and I also remember that Susy detected it. I remember saying a very smart thing, with a good deal of an air, at the breakfast-table one morning, and that Susy observed to her mother privately, a little later, that papa was doing that for the biography.

I cannot bring myself to change any line or word in Susy's sketch of me, but will introduce passages from it now and then just as they came in their quaint simplicity out of her honest heart, which was the beautiful heart of a child. What comes from that source has a charm and grace of its own which may transgress all the recognized laws of literature, if it choose, and yet be literature still, and worthy of hospitality. I shall print the whole of this little biography, before I have done with it – every word, every sentence.

The spelling is frequently desperate, but it was Susy's, and it shall stand. I love it, and cannot profane it. To me, it is gold. To correct it would alloy it, not refine it. It would spoil it. It would take from it its freedom and flexibility and make it stiff and formal. Even when it is most extravagant I am not shocked. It is Susy's spelling, and she was doing the best she could – and nothing could better it for me. . . .

Susy began the biography in 1885, when I was in the fiftieth year of my age, and she just entering the fourteenth of hers. She begins in this way:

> We are a very happy family. We consist of Papa, Mamma, Jean, Clara and me. It is papa I am writing about, and I shall have no trouble in not knowing what to say about him, as he is a *very* striking character.

But wait a minute – I will return to Susy presently.

In the matter of slavish imitation, man is the monkey's superior all the time. The average man is destitute of independence of opinion. He is not interested in contriving an opinion of his own, by study and reflection, but is only anxious to find out what his neighbor's opinion is and slavishly adopt it. A generation ago, I found out that the latest review of a book was pretty sure to be just a reflection of the *earliest* review of it; that whatever the first reviewer found to praise or censure in the book would be repeated in the latest reviewer's report, with nothing fresh added. Therefore more than once I took the precaution of sending my book, in manuscript, to Mr. Howells, when he was editor of the "Atlantic Monthly," so that he could prepare a review of it at leisure. I knew he would say the truth about the book – I also knew that he would find more merit than demerit in it, because I already knew that that was the condition of the book. I allowed no copy of it to go out to the press until after Mr. Howells's notice of it had appeared. That book was always safe. There wasn't a man behind a pen in all America that had the courage to find anything in the book which Mr. Howells had not found – there wasn't a man behind a pen in America that had spirit enough to say a brave and original thing about the book on his own responsibility.

I believe that the trade of critic, in literature, music, and the drama, is the most degraded of all trades, and that it has no real value – certainly no large value. When Charles Dudley Warner and I were about to bring out "The Gilded Age," the editor of the "Daily Graphic" persuaded me to let him have an advance copy, he giving me his word of honor that no notice of it would appear in his paper until after the "Atlantic Monthly" notice should have appeared. This reptile published a review of the book within three days afterward. I could not really complain, because he had only given me his word of honor as security; I ought to have required of him something substantial. I believe his notice did not deal mainly with the merit of the book, or the lack of it, but with my moral attitude toward the public. It was charged that I had used my reputation to play a swindle upon the public; that Mr. Warner had written as much as half of the book, and that I had used my name to float it and give it currency; a currency – so the critic averred – which it could not have acquired without my name, and that this conduct of mine was a grave fraud upon the people. The "Graphic" was not an authority upon any subject whatever. It had a sort of distinction, in that it was the first and only illustrated daily newspaper that the world had seen; but it was without character; it was poorly and cheaply edited; its opinion of a book or of any other work of art was of no consequence. Everybody knew this, yet all the critics in America, one after the other, copied the "Graphic's" criticism, merely changing the phraseology, and left me under that charge of dishonest conduct. Even the great Chicago "Tribune," the most important journal in the Middle West, was not able to invent anything fresh, but adopted the view of the humble "Daily Graphic," dishonesty-charge and all.

However, let it go. It is the will of God that we must have critics, and missionaries, and Congressmen, and humorists, and we must bear the burden. Meantime, I seem to have been drifting into criticism myself. But that is nothing. At the worst, criticism is nothing more than a crime, and I am not unused to that.

What I have been travelling toward all this time is this: the first critic that ever had occasion to describe my personal appearance littered his description with foolish and inexcusable errors whose aggregate furnished the result that I was distinctly and distressingly unhandsome. That description floated around the country in the papers, and was in constant use and wear for a quarter of a century. It seems strange to me that apparently no critic in the country could be found who could look at me and have the courage to take up his pen and destroy that lie. That lie began its course on the Pacific coast, in 1864, and it likened me in personal appearance to Petroleum V. Nasby, who had been out there lecturing. For twenty-five years afterward, no critic could furnish a description of me without fetching in Nasby to help out my portrait. I knew Nasby well, and he was a good fellow, but in my life I have not felt malignant enough about any more than three persons to charge those persons with resembling Nasby. It hurts me to the heart. I was always handsome. Anybody but a critic could have seen it. And it had long been a distress to my family – including Susy – that the critics should go on making this wearisome mistake, year after year, when there was no foundation for it. Even when a critic wanted to be particularly friendly and complimentary to me, he didn't dare to go beyond my clothes. He never ventured beyond that old safe frontier. When he had finished with my clothes he had said all the kind things, the pleasant things, the complimentary things he could risk. Then he dropped back on Nasby.

Yesterday I found this clipping in the pocket of one of those ancient memorandum-books of mine. It is of the date of thirty-nine years ago, and both the paper and the ink are yellow with the bitterness that I felt in that old day when I clipped it out to preserve it and brood over it, and grieve about it. I will copy it here, to wit:

> A correspondent of the Philadelphia "Press," writing of one of Schuyler Colfax's receptions, says of our Washington corre-spondent: "Mark Twain, the delicate humorist, was present; quite a lion, as he deserves to be. Mark is a bachelor, faultless in taste, whose snowy vest is suggestive of endless quarrels with Washington washerwomen; but the heroism of Mark is settled for all time, for such purity and smoothness were never seen before. His lavender gloves might have been stolen from some Turkish harem, so delicate were they in size; but more likely – anything else were more likely than that. In form and feature he bears some resemblance to the immortal Nasby; but whilst Petroleum is brunette to the core, Twain is golden, amber-hued, melting, blonde."

Let us return to Susy's biography now, and get the opinion of one who is unbiassed:

FROM SUSY'S BIOGRAPHY

Papa's appearance has been described many times, but very incorrectly. He has beautiful gray hair, not any too thick or any too long, but just right; a Roman nose, which greatly improves the beauty of his features; kind blue eyes and a small mustache. He has a wonderfully shaped head and profile. He has a very good figure – in short, he is an extrodinarily fine looking man.

All his features are perfect, except that he hasn't extrodinary teeth. His complexion is very fair, and he doesn't ware a beard. He is a very good man and a very funny one. He *has* got a temper, but we all of us have in this family. He is the loveliest man I ever saw or ever hope to see – and oh, so absentminded. He does tell perfectly delightful stories. Clara and I used to sit on each arm of his chair and listen while he told us stories about the pictures on the wall.

I remember the story-telling days vividly. They were a difficult and exacting audience – those little creatures.

Along one side of the library, in the Hartford home, the bookshelves joined the mantelpiece – in fact there were shelves on both sides of the mantelpiece. On these shelves, and on the mantelpiece, stood various ornaments. At one end of the procession was a framed oil-painting of a cat's head, at the other end was a head of a beautiful young girl, life-size – called Emmeline, because she looked just about like that – an impressionist watercolor. Between the one picture and the other there were twelve or fifteen of the bric-à-brac things already mentioned; also an oil-painting by Elihu Vedder, "The Young Medusa." Every now and then the children required me to construct a romance – always impromptu – not a moment's preparation permitted – and into that romance I had to get all that bric-à-brac and the three pictures. I had to start always with the cat and finish with Emmeline. I was never allowed the refreshment of a change, end-for-end. It was not permissible to introduce a bric-à-brac ornament into the story out of its place in the procession.

These bric-à-bracs were never allowed a peaceful day, a reposeful day, a restful Sabbath. In their lives there was no Sabbath, in their lives there was no peace; they knew no existence but a monotonous career of violence and bloodshed. In the course of time, the bric-à-brac and the pictures showed wear. It was because they had had so many and such tumultuous adventures in their romantic careers.

As romancer to the children I had a hard time, even from the beginning. If they brought me a picture, in a magazine, and required me to build a story to it, they would cover the rest of the page with their pudgy hands to keep me from stealing an idea from it. The stories had to come hot from the bat, always. They had to be absolutely original and fresh. Sometimes the children furnished me simply a character or two, or a dozen, and required me to start out at once on that slim basis and deliver those characters up to a vigorous and entertaining life of crime. If they heard of a new trade, or an unfamiliar animal, or anything like that, I was pretty sure to have to deal with those things in the next romance. Once Clara required me to build a sudden tale out of a plumber and a "bawgunstrictor," and I had to do it. She didn't know what a boa-constrictor was, until he developed in the tale – then she was better satisfied with it than ever.

FROM SUSY'S BIOGRAPHY

Papa's favorite game is billiards, and when he is tired and wishes to rest himself he stays up all night and plays billiards, it seems to rest his head. He smokes a great deal almost inces-santly. He has the mind of an author exactly, some of the sim-plest things he cant understand. Our burglar-alarm is often out of order, and papa had been obliged to take the mahogany-room off from the alarm altogether for a time, because the burglar-alarm had been in the habit of ringing even when the mahogany-room was closed. At length he thought that perhaps the burglar-alarm might be in order, and he decided to try and see; accordingly he put it on and then went down and opened the window; consequently the alarm bell rang, it would even if the alarm had been in order. Papa went despairingly upstairs and said to mamma, "Livy the mahogany-room won't go on. I have just opened the window to see."

"Why, Youth," mamma replied "if you've opened the win-dow, why of coarse the alarm will ring!"

"That's what I've opened it for, why I just went down to see if it would ring!"

Mamma tried to explain to papa that when he wanted to go and see whether the alarm would ring while the window was closed he *mustn't* go and open the window – but in vain, papa couldn't understand, and got very impatient with mamma for trying to make him believe an impossible thing true.

This is a frank biographer, and an honest one; she uses no sand-paper on me. I have, to this day, the same dull head in the matter of conundrums and perplexities which Susy had discovered in those long-gone days. Complexities annoy me; they irritate me; then this progressive feeling presently warms into anger. I cannot get far in the reading of the commonest and simplest contract – with its "parties of the first part," and "parties of the second part," and "parties of the third part," – before my temper is all gone. Ashcroft comes up here every day and pathetically tries to make me understand the points of the lawsuit which we are conducting against Henry Butters, Harold Wheeler, and the rest of those Plasmon buccaneers, but daily he has to give it up. It is pitiful to see, when he bends his earnest and appealing eyes upon me and says, after one of his efforts, "Now you *do* understand *that*, don't you?"

I am always obliged to say, "I *don't*, Ashcroft. I wish I could understand it, but I don't. Send for the cat."

In the days which Susy is talking about, a perplexity fell to my lot one day. F. G. Whitmore was my business agent, and he brought me out from town in his buggy. We drove by the *porte-cochère* and toward the stable. Now this was a *single* road, and was like a spoon whose handle stretched from the gate to a great round flower-bed in the neighborhood of the stable. At the approach to the flower-bed the road divided and circumnavigated it, making a loop, which I have likened to the bowl of the spoon. As we neared the loop, I saw that Whitmore was laying his course to port, (I was sitting on the starboard side – the side the house was on), and was going to start around that spoon-bowl on that left-hand side. I said,

"Don't do that, Whitmore; take the right-hand side. Then I shall be next to the house when we get to the door."

He said, "*That* will not happen in *any case*, it doesn't make any difference which way I go around this flower-bed."

I explained to him that he was an ass, but he stuck to his proposition, and I said,

"Go on and try it, and see."

He went on and tried it, and sure enough he fetched me up at the door on the very side that he had said I would be. I was not able to believe it then, and I don't believe it yet.

I said, "Whitmore, that is merely an accident. You can't do it again."

He said he could – and he drove down into the street, fetched around, came back, and actually did it again. I was stupefied, paralyzed, petrified, with these strange results, but they did not convince me. I didn't believe he could do it another time, but he did. He said he could do it all day, and fetch up the same way every time. By that time my temper was gone, and I asked him to go home and apply to the Asylum and I would pay the expenses; I didn't want to see him any more for a week.

I went up-stairs in a rage and started to tell Livy about it, expecting to get her sympathy for me and to breed aversion in her for Whitmore; but she merely burst into peal after peal of laughter, as the tale of my adventure went on, for her head was like Susy's: riddles and complexities had no terrors for it. Her mind and Susy's were analytical; I have tried to make it appear that mine was different. Many and many a time I have told that buggy experiment, hoping against hope that I would some time or other find somebody who would be on my side, but it has never happened. And I am never able to go glibly forward and state the circumstances of that buggy's progress without having to halt and consider, and call up in my mind the spoon-handle, the bowl of the spoon, the buggy and the horse, and my position in the buggy: and the minute I have got that far and try to turn it to the left it goes to ruin; I can't see how it is ever going to fetch me out right when we get to the door. Susy is right in her estimate. I can't understand things.

That burglar-alarm which Susy mentions led a gay and careless life, and had no principles. It was generally out of order at one point or another; and there was plenty of opportunity, because all the windows and doors in the house, from the cellar up to the top floor, were connected with it. However, in its seasons of being out of order it could trouble us for only a very little while: we quickly found out that it was fooling us, and that it was buzzing its blood-curdling alarm merely for its own amusement. Then we would shut it off, and send to New York for the electrician – there not being one in all Hartford in those days. When the repairs were finished we would set the alarm again and reestablish our confidence in it. It never did any real business except upon one single occasion. All the rest of its expensive career was frivolous and without purpose. Just that one time it performed its duty, and its whole duty – gravely, seriously, admirably. It let fly about two o'clock one black and dreary March morning, and I turned out promptly, because I knew that it was not fooling, this time. The bath-room door was on my side of the bed. I stepped in there, turned up the gas, looked at the annunciator, and turned off the alarm – so far as the door indicated was concerned – thus stopping the racket. Then I came back to bed. Mrs. Clemens opened the debate:

"What was it?"

"It was the cellar door."

"Was it a burglar, do you think?"

"Yes," I said, "of course it was. Did you suppose it was a Sunday-school superintendent?"

"No. What do you suppose he wants?"

"I suppose he wants jewelry, but he is not acquainted with the house and he thinks it is in the cellar. I don't like to disappoint a burglar whom I am not acquainted with, and who has done me no harm, but if he had had common sagacity enough to inquire, I could have told him we kept nothing down there but coal and vegetables. Still it may be that he *is* acquainted with the place, and that what he really wants is coal and vegetables. On the whole, I think it is vegetables he is after."

"Are you going down to see?"

"No; I could not be of any assistance. Let him select for himself; I don't know where the things are."

Then she said, "But suppose he comes up to the ground floor!"

"That's all right. We shall know it the minute he opens a door on that floor. It will set off the alarm."

Just then the terrific buzzing broke out again. I said,

"He has arrived. I told you he would. I know all about burglars and their ways. They are systematic people."

I went into the bath-room to see if I was right, and I was. I shut off the dining-room and stopped the buzzing, and came back to bed. My wife said,

"What do you suppose he is after now?"

I said, "I think he has got all the vegetables he wants and is coming up for napkin-rings and odds and ends for the wife and children. They all have families – burglars have – and they are always thoughtful of them, always take a few necessaries of life for themselves, and fill out with tokens of remembrance for the family. In taking them they do not forget us: those very things represent tokens of his remembrance of us, and also of our remembrance of him. We never get them again; the memory of the attention remains embalmed in our hearts."

"Are you going down to see what it is he wants now?"

"No," I said, "I am no more interested than I was before. They are experienced people, – burglars; *they* know what they want; I should be no help to him. I *think* he is after ceramics and

bric-à-brac and such things. If he knows the house he knows that
that is all that he can find on the dining-room floor."

She said, with a strong interest perceptible in her tone, "Suppose he comes up here!"

I said, "It is all right. He will give us notice."

"What shall we do then?"

"Climb out of the window."

She said, a little restively, "Well, what is the use of a burglar-
alarm for us?"

"You have seen, dear heart, that it has been useful up to the
present moment, and I have explained to you how it will be continuously useful after he gets up here."

That was the end of it. He didn't ring any more alarms. Presently I said,

"He is disappointed, I think. He has gone off with the vegetables
and the bric-à-brac, and I think he is dissatisfied."

We went to sleep, and at a quarter before eight in the morning
I was out, and hurrying, for I was to take the 8.29 train for New
York. I found the gas burning brightly – full head – all over the
first floor. My new overcoat was gone; my old umbrella was gone;
my new patent-leather shoes, which I had never worn, were gone.
The large window which opened into the *ombra* at the rear of the
house was standing wide. I passed out through it and tracked the
burglar down the hill through the trees; tracked him without
difficulty, because he had blazed his progress with imitation silver
napkin-rings, and my umbrella, and various other things which he
had disapproved of; and I went back in triumph and proved to my
wife that he *was* a disappointed burglar. I had suspected he would
be, from the start, and from his not coming up to our floor to get
human beings.

Things happened to me that day in New York. I will tell about
them another time.

FROM SUSY'S BIOGRAPHY

Papa has a peculiar gait we like, it seems just to sute him, but
most people do not; he always walks up and down the room
while thinking and between each coarse at meals.

A lady distantly related to us came to visit us once in those days.
She came to stay a week, but all our efforts to make her happy

failed, we could not imagine why, and she got up her anchor and sailed the next morning. We did much guessing, but could not solve the mystery. Later we found out what the trouble was. It was my tramping up and down between the courses. She conceived the idea that I could not stand her society.

That word "Youth," as the reader has perhaps already guessed, was my wife's pet name for me. It was gently satirical, but also affectionate. I had certain mental and material peculiarities and customs proper to a much younger person than I was.

FROM SUSY'S BIOGRAPHY

Papa is very fond of animals particularly of cats, we had a dear little gray kitten once that he named "Lazy" (papa always wears gray to match his hair and eyes) and he would carry him around on his shoulder, it was a mighty pretty sight! the gray cat sound asleep against papa's gray coat and hair. The names that he has given our different cats, are realy remarkably funny, they are namely Stray Kit, Abner, Motley, Fraeulein, Lazy, Bufalo Bill, Cleveland, Sour Mash, and Pestilence and Famine.

At one time when the children were small, we had a very black mother-cat named Satan, and Satan had a small black off-spring named Sin. Pronouns were a difficulty for the children. Little Clara came in one day, her black eyes snapping with indignation, and said,

"Papa, Satan ought to be punished. She is out there at the green-house and there she stays and stays, and his kitten is downstairs crying."

FROM SUSY'S BIOGRAPHY

Papa uses very strong language, but I have an idea not nearly so strong as when he first maried mamma. A lady acquaintance of his is rather apt to interupt what one is saying, and papa told mamma that he thought he should say to the lady's husband "I am glad your wife wasn't present when the Deity said 'Let there be light.' "

It is as I have said before. This is a frank historian. She doesn't cover up one's deficiencies, but gives them an equal showing with one's handsomer qualities. Of course I made the remark which she has quoted – and even at this distant day I am still as much as half persuaded that if that lady had been present when the Creator said, "Let there be light," she would have interrupted Him and we shouldn't ever have got it.

FROM SUSY'S BIOGRAPHY

Papa said the other day, "I am a mugwump and a mugwump is pure from the marrow out. (Papa knows that I am writing this biography of him, and he said this for it.) He doesn't like to go to church at all, why I never understood, until just now, he told us the other day that he couldn't bear to hear any one talk but himself, but that he could listen to himself talk for hours without getting tired, of course he said this in joke, but I've no dought it was founded on truth.

PART V

NOVEMBER 2, 1906

Susy's remark about my strong language troubles me, and I must go back to it. All through the first ten years of my married life I kept a constant and discreet watch upon my tongue while in the house, and went outside and to a distance when circumstances were too much for me and I was obliged to seek relief. I prized my wife's respect and approval above all the rest of the human race's respect and approval. I dreaded the day when she should discover that I was but a whited sepulchre partly freighted with suppressed language. I was so careful, during ten years, that I had not a doubt that my suppressions had been successful. Therefore I was quite as happy in my guilt as I could have been if I had been innocent.

But at last an accident exposed me. I went into the bathroom one morning to make my toilet, and carelessly left the door two or three inches ajar. It was the first time that I had ever failed to take the precaution of closing it tightly. I knew the necessity of being particular about this, because shaving was always a trying ordeal for me, and I could seldom carry it through to a finish without verbal helps. Now this time I was unprotected, but did not suspect it. I had no extraordinary trouble with my razor on this occasion,

and was able to worry through with mere mutterings and growlings of an improper sort, but with nothing noisy or emphatic about
them – no snapping and barking. Then I put on a shirt. My shirts
are an invention of my own. They open in the back, and are but-
toned there – when there are buttons. This time the button was
missing. My temper jumped up several degrees in a moment, and
my remarks rose accordingly, both in loudness and vigor of expression. But I was not troubled, for the bath-room door was a solid
one and I supposed it was firmly closed. I flung up the window and
threw the shirt out. It fell upon the shrubbery where the people on
their way to church could admire it if they wanted to; there was
merely fifty feet of grass between the shirt and the passerby. Still
rumbling and thundering distantly, I put on another shirt. Again
the button was absent. I augmented my language to meet the
emergency, and threw that shirt out of the window. I was too angry
– too insane – to examine the third shirt, but put it furiously on.
Again the button was absent, and that shirt followed its comrades
out of the window. Then I straightened up, gathered my reserves,
and let myself go like a cavalry charge. In the midst of that great
assault, my eye fell upon that gaping door, and I was paralyzed.

It took me a good while to finish my toilet. I extended the time
unnecessarily in trying to make up my mind as to what I would
best do in the circumstances. I tried to hope that Mrs. Clemens
was asleep, but I knew better. I could not escape by the window.
It was narrow, and suited only to shirts. At last I made up my mind
to boldly loaf through the bedroom with the air of a person who
had not been doing anything. I made half the journey successfully.
I did not turn my eyes in her direction, because that would not be
safe. It is very difficult to look as if you have not been doing anything when the facts are the other way, and my confidence in my
performance oozed steadily out of me as I went along. I was aiming
for the left-hand door because it was furthest from my wife. It had
never been opened from the day that the house was built, but it
seemed a blessed refuge for me now. The bed was this one, wherein
I am lying now, and dictating these histories morning after morning with so much serenity. It was this same old elaborately carved
black Venetian bedstead – the most comfortable bedstead that
ever was, with space enough in it for a family, and carved angels
enough surmounting its twisted columns and its headboard and
footboard to bring peace to the sleepers, and pleasant dreams.
I had to stop in the middle of the room. I hadn't the strength to go

on. I believed that I was under accusing eyes – that even the carved angels were inspecting me with an unfriendly gaze. You know how it is when you are convinced that somebody behind you is looking steadily at you. You *have* to turn your face – you can't help it. I turned mine. The bed was placed as it is now, with the foot where the head ought to be. If it had been placed as it should have been, the high headboard would have sheltered me. But the footboard was no sufficient protection, for I could be seen over it. I was exposed. I was wholly without protection. I turned, because I couldn't help it – and my memory of what I saw is still vivid, after all these years.

Against the white pillows I saw the black head – I saw that young and beautiful face; and I saw the gracious eyes with a something in them which I had never seen there before. They were snapping and flashing with indignation. I felt myself crumbling; I felt myself shrinking away to nothing under that accusing gaze. I stood silent under that desolating fire for as much as a minute, I should say – it seemed a very, very long time. Then my wife's lips parted, and from them issued – *my latest bath-room remark.* The language perfect, but the expression velvety, unpractical, apprenticelike, ignorant, inexperienced, comically inadequate, absurdly weak and unsuited to the great language. In my lifetime I had never heard anything so out of tune, so inharmonious, so incongruous, so ill-suited to each other as were those mighty words set to that feeble music. I tried to keep from laughing, for I was a guilty person in deep need of charity and mercy. I tried to keep from bursting, and I succeeded – until she gravely said, "There, now you know how it sounds."

Then I exploded; the air was filled with my fragments, and you could hear them whiz. I said, "Oh Livy, if it sounds like *that* I will never do it again!"

Then she had to laugh herself. Both of us broke into convulsions, and went on laughing until we were physically exhausted and spiritually reconciled.

The children were present at breakfast – Clara aged six and Susy eight – and the mother made a guarded remark about strong language; guarded because she did not wish the children to suspect anything – a guarded remark which censured strong language. Both children broke out in one voice with this comment, "Why, mamma, papa uses it!"

I was astonished. I had supposed that that secret was safe in my own breast, and that its presence had never been suspected. I asked,

"How did you know, you little rascals?"

"Oh," they said, "we often listen over the balusters when you are in the hall explaining things to George."

FROM SUSY'S BIOGRAPHY

One of papa's latest books is "The Prince and the Pauper" and it is unquestionably the best book he has ever written, some people want him to keep to his old style, some gentleman wrote him, "I enjoyed Huckleberry Finn immensely and am glad to see that you have returned to your old style." That enoyed me that enoyed me greatly, because it trobles me [Susy was troubled by that word, and uncertain; she wrote a *u* above it in the proper place, but reconsidered the matter and struck it out] to have so few people know papa, I mean realy know him, they think of Mark Twain as a humorist joking at everything; "And with a mop of reddish brown hair which sorely needs the barbars brush a roman nose, short stubby mustache, a sad careworn face, with maney crow's feet" etc. That is the way people picture papa, I have wanted papa to write a book that would reveal something of his kind sympathetic nature, and "The Prince and the Pauper" partly does it. The book is full of lovely charming ideas, and oh the language! It is *perfect*. I think that one of the most touching scenes in it, is where the pauper is riding on horseback with his nobles in the "recognition procession" and he sees his mother oh and then what followed! How she runs to his side, when she sees him throw up his hand palm outward, and is rudely pushed off by one of the King's officers, and then how the little pauper's consceince troubles him when he remembers the shameful words that were falling from his lips, when she was turned from his side "I know you not woman" and how his grandeurs were stricken valueless, and his pride consumed to ashes. It is a wonderfully beautiful and touching little scene, and papa has described it so wonderfully. I never saw a man with so much variety of feeling as papa has; now the "Prince and the Pauper" is full of touching places; but there is most always a streak of humor in them somewhere. Now in the coronation – in the stirring coronation, just after the little king has got his crown back again papa brings that in about the Seal, where the pauper says he used the Seal "to crack nuts with." Oh it is so funny and nice! Papa very seldom writes a passage without some humor in it somewhere, and I dont think he ever will.

The children always helped their mother to edit my books in manuscript. She would sit on the porch at the farm and read aloud, with her pencil in her hand, and the children would keep an alert and suspicious eye upon her right along, for the belief was well grounded in them that whenever she came across a particularly satisfactory passage she would strike it out. Their suspicions were well founded. The passages which were so satisfactory to them always had an element of strength in them which sorely needed modification or expurgation, and were always sure to get it at their mother's hand. For my own entertainment, and to enjoy the protests of the children, I often abused my editor's innocent confidence. I often interlarded remarks of a studied and felicitously atrocious character purposely to achieve the children's brief delight, and then see the remorseless pencil do its fatal work. I often joined my supplications to the children's for mercy, and strung the argument out and pretended to be in earnest. They were deceived, and so was their mother. It was three against one, and most unfair. But it was very delightful, and I could not resist the temptation. Now and then we gained the victory and there was much rejoicing. Then I privately struck the passage out myself. It had served its purpose. It had furnished three of us with good entertainment, and in being removed from the book by me it was only suffering the fate originally intended for it.

FROM SUSY'S BIOGRAPHY

Papa was born in Missouri. His mother is Grandma Clemens (Jane Lampton Clemens) of Kentucky. Grandpa Clemens was of the F.F.V's of Virginia.

Without doubt it was I that gave Susy that impression. I cannot imagine why, because I was never in my life much impressed by grandeurs which proceed from the accident of birth. I did not get this indifference from my mother. She was always strongly interested in the ancestry of the house. She traced her own line back to the Lambtons of Durham, England – a family which had been occupying broad lands there since Saxon times. I am not sure, but

I think that those Lambtons got along without titles of nobility for eight or nine hundred years, then produced a great man, three-quarters of a century ago, and broke into the peerage. My mother knew all about the Clemenses of Virginia, and loved to aggrandize them to me, but she has long been dead. There has been no one to keep those details fresh in my memory, and they have grown dim.

There was a Jere. Clemens who was a United States Senator, and in his day enjoyed the usual Senatorial fame – a fame which perishes whether it spring from four years' service or forty. After Jere. Clemens's fame as a Senator passed away, he was still remembered for many years on account of another service which he performed. He shot old John Brown's Governor Wise in the hind leg in a duel. However, I am not very clear about this. It may be that Governor Wise shot *him* in the hind leg. However, I don't think it is important. I think that the only thing that is really important is that one of them got shot in the hind leg. It would have been better and nobler and more historical and satisfactory if both of them had got shot in the hind leg – but it is of no use for me to try to recollect history. I never had a historical mind. Let it go. Whichever way it happened I am glad of it, and that is as much enthusiasm as I can get up for a person bearing my name. But I am forgetting the first Clemens – the one that stands furthest back toward the really original *first* Clemens, which was Adam.

FROM SUSY'S BIOGRAPHY

Clara and I are sure that papa played the trick on Grandma, about the whipping, that is related in "The Adventures of Tom Sayer"; "Hand me that switch." The switch hovered in the air, the peril was desperate – "My, look behind you Aunt!" The old lady whirled around and snatched her skirts out of danger. The lad fled on the instant, scrambling up the high board fence and dissapeared over it.

Susy and Clara were quite right about that.
Then Susy says:

And we know papa played "Hookey" all the time. And how readily would papa pretend to be dying so as not to have to go to school!

These revelations and exposures are searching, but they are just. If I am as transparent to other people as I was to Susy, I have wasted much effort in this life.

Grandma couldn't make papa go to school, so she let him go into a printing-office to learn the trade. He did so, and gradually picked up enough education to enable him to do about as well as those who were more studious in early life.

It is noticeable that Susy does not get overheated when she is complimenting me, but maintains a proper judicial and biographical calm. It is noticeable, also, and it is to her credit as a biographer, that she distributes compliment and criticism with a fair and even hand.

My mother had a good deal of trouble with me, but I think she enjoyed it. She had none at all with my brother Henry, who was two years younger than I, and I think that the unbroken monotony of his goodness and truthfulness and obedience would have been a burden to her but for the relief and variety which I furnished in the other direction. I was a tonic. I was valuable to her. I never thought of it before, but now I see it. I never knew Henry to do a vicious thing toward me, or toward any one else – but he frequently did righteous ones that cost me as heavily. It was his duty to report me, when I needed reporting and neglected to do it myself, and he was very faithful in discharging that duty. He is "Sid" in "Tom Sawyer." But Sid was not Henry. Henry was a very much finer and better boy than ever Sid was.

It was Henry who called my mother's attention to the fact that the thread with which she had sewed my collar together to keep me from going in swimming, had changed color. My mother would not have discovered it but for that, and she was manifestly piqued when she recognized that that prominent bit of circumstantial evidence had escaped her sharp eye. That detail probably added a detail to my punishment. It is human. We generally visit our shortcomings on somebody else when there is a possible excuse for it – but no matter, I took it out of Henry. There is always compensation for such as are unjustly used. I often took it out of him – sometimes as an advance payment for something which I hadn't yet done. These were occasions when the opportunity was too strong a temptation, and I had to draw on the future. I did not need to copy this idea from my mother, and probably didn't. Still she wrought upon that principle upon occasion.

If the incident of the broken sugar-bowl is in "Tom Sawyer" – I don't remember whether it is or not – that is an example of it. Henry never stole sugar. He took it openly from the bowl. His mother knew he wouldn't take sugar when she wasn't looking, but she had her doubts about me. Not exactly doubts, either. She knew very well I *would*. One day when she was not present, Henry took sugar from her prized and precious old English sugar-bowl, which was an heirloom in the family – and he managed to break the bowl. It was the first time I had ever had a chance to tell anything on him, and I was inexpressibly glad. I told him I was going to tell on him, but he was not disturbed. When my mother came in and saw the bowl lying on the floor in fragments, she was speechless for a minute. I allowed that silence to work; I judged it would increase the effect. I was waiting for her to ask "Who did that?" – so that I could fetch out my news. But it was an error of calculation. When she got through with her silence she didn't ask anything about it – she merely gave me a crack on the skull with her thimble that I felt all the way down to my heels. Then I broke out with my injured innocence, expecting to make her very sorry that she had punished the wrong one. I expected her to do something remorseful and pathetic. I told her that I was not the one – it was Henry. But there was no upheaval. She said, without emotion, "It's all right. It isn't any matter. You deserve it for something you've done that I didn't know about; and if you haven't done it, why then you deserve it for something that you are going to do, that I sha'n't hear about."

There was a stairway outside the house, which led up to the rear part of the second story. One day Henry was sent on an errand, and he took a tin bucket along. I knew he would have to ascend those stairs, so I went up and locked the door on the inside, and came down into the garden, which had been newly ploughed and was rich in choice firm clods of black mold. I gathered a generous equipment of these, and ambushed him. I waited till he had climbed the stairs and was near the landing and couldn't escape. Then I bombarded him with clods, which he warded off with his tin bucket the best he could, but without much success, for I was a good marksman. The clods smashing against the weather-boarding fetched my mother out to see what was the matter, and I tried to explain that I was amusing Henry. Both of them were after me in a minute, but I knew the way over that high board fence and escaped for that time. After an hour or two, when I ventured back, there was no one around and I thought the incident was closed. But it was not. Henry was ambushing me. With an unusually competent aim for him, he landed a stone on the side of my head which raised a bump there that felt like the Matterhorn. I carried it to my mother straightway for sympathy, but she was not strongly moved. It seemed to be her idea that incidents like this would eventually reform me if I harvested enough of them. So the matter was only educational. I had had a sterner view of it than that, before.

It was not right to give the cat the "Pain-Killer"; I realize it now. I would not repeat it in these days. But in those "Tom Sawyer" days it was a great and sincere satisfaction to me to see Peter perform under its influence – and if actions *do* speak as loud as words, he took as much interest in it as I did. It was a most detestable medicine, Perry Davis's Pain-Killer. Mr. Pavey's negro man, who was a person of good judgment and considerable curiosity, wanted to sample it, and I let him. It was his opinion that it was made of hell-fire.

Those were the cholera days of '49. The people along the Mississippi were paralyzed with fright. Those who could run away, did it. And many died of fright in the flight. Fright killed three persons where the cholera killed one. Those who couldn't flee kept themselves drenched with cholera preventives, and my mother chose Perry Davis's Pain-Killer for me. She was not distressed about herself. She avoided that kind of preventive. But she made me promise to take a teaspoonful of Pain-Killer every day. Originally it was my intention to keep the promise, but at that time I didn't know as much about Pain-Killer as I knew after my first experiment with it. She didn't watch Henry's bottle – she could trust Henry. But she marked my bottle with a pencil, on the label, every day, and examined it to see if the teaspoonful had been removed. The floor was not carpeted. It had cracks in it, and I fed the Pain-Killer to the cracks with very good results – no cholera occurred down below.

It was upon one of these occasions that that friendly cat came waving his tail and supplicating for Pain-Killer – which he got – and then went into those hysterics which ended with his colliding with all the furniture in the room and finally going out of the open window and carrying the flower-pots with him, just in time for my mother to arrive and look over her glasses in petrified astonishment and say, "What in the world is the matter with Peter?"

I don't remember what my explanation was, but if it is recorded in that book it may not be the right one.

Whenever my conduct was of such exaggerated impropriety that my mother's extemporary punishments were inadequate, she saved the matter up for Sunday, and made me go to church Sunday night – which was a penalty sometimes bearable, perhaps, but as a rule it was not, and I avoided it for the sake of my constitution. She would never believe that I had been to church until she had applied her test: she made me tell her what the text was. That was a simple matter, and caused me no trouble. I didn't have to go to church to get a text. I selected one for myself. This worked very well until one time when my text and the one furnished by a neighbor, who had been to church, didn't tally. After that my mother took other methods. I don't know what they were now.

In those days men and boys wore rather long cloaks in the winter-time. They were black, and were lined with very bright and showy Scotch plaids. One winter's night when I was starting to church to square a crime of some kind committed during the week, I hid my cloak near the gate and went off and played with the other boys until church was over. Then I returned home. But in the dark I put the cloak on wrong side out, entered the room, threw the cloak aside, and then stood the usual examination. I got along very well until the temperature of the church was mentioned. My mother said,

"It must have been impossible to keep warm there on such a night."

I didn't see the art of that remark, and was foolish enough to explain that I wore my cloak all the time that I was in church. She asked if I kept it on from church home, too. I didn't see the bearing of that remark. I said that that was what I had done. She said,

"You wore it in church with that red Scotch plaid outside and glaring? Didn't that attract any attention?"

Of course to continue such a dialogue would have been tedious and unprofitable, and I let it go, and took the consequences.

That was about 1849. Tom Nash was a boy of my own age – the postmaster's son. The Mississippi was frozen across, and he and I went skating one night, probably without permission. I cannot see why we should go skating in the night unless without permission, for there could be no considerable amusement to be gotten out of skating at night if nobody was going to object to it. About midnight, when we were more than half a mile out toward the

Illinois shore, we heard some ominous rumbling and grinding and crashing going on between us and the home side of the river, and we knew what it meant – the ice was breaking up. We started for home, pretty badly scared. We flew along at full speed whenever the moonlight sifting down between the clouds enabled us to tell which was ice and which was water. In the pauses we waited; started again whenever there was a good bridge of ice; paused again when we came to naked water and waited in distress until a floating vast cake should bridge that place. It took us an hour to make the trip – a trip which we made in a misery of apprehension all the time. But at last we arrived within a very brief distance of the shore. We waited again; there was another place that needed bridging. All about us the ice was plunging and grinding along and piling itself up in mountains on the shore, and the dangers were increasing, not diminishing. We grew very impatient to get to solid ground, so we started too early and went springing from cake to cake. Tom made a miscalculation, and fell short. He got a bitter bath, but he was so close to shore that he only had to swim a stroke or two – then his feet struck hard bottom and he crawled out. I arrived a little later, without accident. We had been in a drenching perspiration, and Tom's bath was a disaster for him. He took to his bed sick, and had a procession of diseases. The closing one was scarlet-fever, and he came out of it stone deaf. Within a year or two speech departed, of course. But some years later he was taught to talk, after a fashion – one couldn't always make out what it was he was trying to say. Of course he could not modulate his voice, since he couldn't hear himself talk. When he supposed he was talking low and confidentially, you could hear him in Illinois.

Four years ago (1902) I was invited by the University of Missouri to come out there and receive the honorary degree of LL.D. I took that opportunity to spend a week in Hannibal – a city now, a village in my day. It had been fifty-three years since Tom Nash and I had had that adventure. When I was at the railway station ready to leave Hannibal, there was a crowd of citizens there. I saw Tom Nash approaching me across a vacant space, and I walked toward him, for I recognized him at once. He was old and white-headed, but the boy of fifteen was still visible in him. He came up to me, made a trumpet of his hands at my ear, nodded his head toward the citizens and said confidentially – in a yell like a fog-horn –

"Same damned fools, Sam!"

Papa was about twenty years old when he went on the Mississippi as a pilot. Just before he started on his tripp Grandma Clemens asked him to promise her on the Bible not to touch intoxicating liquors or swear, and he said "Yes, mother, I will," and he kept that promise seven years when Grandma released him from it.

Under the inspiring influence of that remark, what a garden of forgotten reforms rises upon my sight!

PART VI

NOVEMBER 16, 1906

Papa made arrangements to read at Vassar College the 1st of May, and I went with him. We went by way of New York City. Mamma went with us to New York and stayed two days to do some shopping. We started Tuesday, at 1/2 past two o'clock in the afternoon, and reached New York about 1/4 past six. Papa went right up to General Grants from the station and mamma and I went to the Everett House. Aunt Clara came to supper with us up in our room. . . .

We and Aunt Clara were going to the theatre right after supper, and we expected papa to take us there and to come home as early as he could. But we got through dinner and he didn't come, and didn't come, and mamma got more perplexed and worried, but at last we thought we would have to go without him. So we put on our things and started down stairs but before we'd goten half down we met papa coming up with a great bunch of roses in his hand. He explained that the reason he was so late was that his watch stopped and he didn't notice and kept thinking it an hour earlier than it really was. The roses he carried were some Col. Fred Grant sent to mamma. We went to the theatre and enjoyed "Adonis" [word illegible] acted very much. We reached home about 1/2 past eleven o'clock and went right to bed. Wednesday morning we got up rather late and had

breakfast about 1/2 past nine o'clock. After breakfast mamma
went out shopping and papa and I went to see papa's agent
about some business matters. After papa had gotten through
talking to Cousin Charlie, [Webster] papa's agent, we went to
get a friend of papa's, Major Pond, to go and see a Dog Show
with us. Then we went to see the dogs with Major Pond and we
had a delightful time seeing so many dogs together; when we
got through seeing the dogs papa thought he would go and see
General Grant and I went with him – this was April 29, 1885.
Papa went up into General Grant's room and he took me with
him, I felt greatly honored and delighted when papa took me
into General Grant's room and let me see the General and Col.
Grant, for General Grant is a man I shall be glad all my life that
I have seen. Papa and General Grant had a long talk together
and papa has written an account of his talk and visit with General Grant for me to put into this biography.

Susy has inserted in this place that account of mine – as
follows:

APRIL 29, 1885.

I called on General Grant and took Susy with me. The General
was looking and feeling far better than he had looked or felt for
some months. He had ventured to work again on his book that
morning – the first time he had done any work for perhaps a
month. This morning's work was his first attempt at dictating,
and it was a thorough success, to his great delight. He had
always said that it would be impossible for him to dictate anything, but I had said that he was noted for clearness of statement,
and as a narrative was simply a statement of consecutive facts,
he was consequently peculiarly qualified and equipped for dictation. This turned out to be true. For he had dictated two hours
that morning to a shorthand writer, had never hesitated for
words, had not repeated himself, and the manuscript when finished needed no revision. The two hours' work was an account
of Appomattox – and this was such an extremely important feature that his book would necessarily have been severely lame
without it. Therefore I had taken a shorthand writer there
before, to see if I could not get him to write at least a few lines

about Appomattox.* But he was at that time not well enough to undertake it. I was aware that of all the hundred versions of Appomattox, not one was really correct. Therefore I was extremely anxious that he should leave behind him the truth. His throat was not distressing him, and his voice was much better and stronger than usual. He was so delighted to have gotten Appomattox accomplished once more in his life – to have gotten the matter off his mind – that he was as talkative as his old self. He received Susy very pleasantly, and then fell to talking about certain matters which he hoped to be able to dictate next day; and he said in substance that, among other things, he wanted to settle once for all a question that had been bandied about from mouth to mouth and from newspaper to newspaper. That question was, "With whom originated the idea of the march to the sea? Was it Grant's, or was it Sherman's idea?" Whether I, or some one else (being anxious to get the important fact settled) asked him with whom the idea originated, I don't remember. But I remember his answer. I shall always remember his answer. General Grant said:

"Neither of us originated the idea of Sherman's march to the sea. The enemy did it."

He went on to say that the enemy, however, necessarily originated a great many of the plans that the general on the opposite side gets the credit for; at the same time that the enemy is doing that, he is laying open other moves which the opposing general sees and takes advantage of. In this case, Sherman had a plan all thought out, of course. He meant to destroy the two remaining railroads in that part of the country, and that would finish up that region. But General Hood did not play the military part that he was expected to play. On the contrary, General Hood made a dive at Chattanooga. This left the march to the sea open to Sherman, and so after sending part of his army to defend and hold what he had acquired in the Chattanooga region, he was perfectly free to proceed, with the rest of it, through Georgia. He saw the opportunity, and he would not have been fit for his place if he had not seized it.

"He wrote me" (the General is speaking) "what his plan was, and I sent him word to go ahead. My staff were opposed to the

* I was his publisher. I was putting his "Personal Memoirs" to press at the time. – S. L. C.

movement." (I think the General said they tried to persuade him to stop Sherman. The chief of his staff, the General said, even went so far as to go to Washington without the General's knowledge and get the ear of the authorities, and he succeeded in arousing their fears to such an extent that they telegraphed General Grant to stop Sherman.)

Then General Grant said, "Out of deference to the Government, I telegraphed Sherman and stopped him twenty-four hours; and then considering that that was deference enough to the Government, I telegraphed him to go ahead again."

I have not tried to give the General's language, but only the general idea of what he said. The thing that mainly struck me was his terse remark that the enemy originated the idea of the march to the sea. It struck me because it was so suggestive of the General's epigrammatic fashion – saying a great deal in a single crisp sentence. (This is my account, and signed "Mark Twain.")

SUSY RESUMES

After papa and General Grant had had their talk, we went back to the hotel where mamma was, and papa told mamma all about his interview with General Grant. Mamma and I had a nice quiet afternoon together.

That pair of devoted comrades were always shutting themselves up together when there was opportunity to have what Susy called "a cozy time." From Susy's nursery days to the end of her life, she and her mother were close friends; intimate friends, passionate adorers of each other. Susy's was a beautiful mind, and it made her an interesting comrade. And with the fine mind she had a heart like her mother's. Susy never had an interest or an occupation which she was not glad to put aside for that something which was in all cases more precious to her – a visit with her mother. Susy died at the right time, the fortunate time of life; the happy age – twenty-four years. At twenty-four, such a girl has seen the best of life – life as a happy dream. After that age the risks begin; responsibility comes, and with it the cares, the sorrows, and the inevitable tragedy. For her mother's sake I would have brought her back from the grave if I could, but I would not have done it for my own.

Then papa went to read in public; there were a great many authors that read, that Thursday afternoon, beside papa; I would have liked to have gone and heard papa read, but papa said he was going to read in Vassar just what he was planning to read in New York, so I stayed at home with mamma.

The next day mamma planned to take the four o'clock car back to Hartford. We rose quite early that morning and went to the Vienna Bakery and took breakfast there. From there we went to a German bookstore and bought some German books for Clara's birthday.

Dear me, the power of association to snatch mouldy dead memories out of their graves and make them walk! That remark about buying foreign books throws a sudden white glare upon the distant past; and I see the long stretch of a New York street with an unearthly vividness, and John Hay walking down it, grave and remorseful. I was walking down it too, that morning, and I overtook Hay and asked him what the trouble was. He turned a lustreless eye upon me and said:

"My case is beyond cure. In the most innocent way in the world I have committed a crime which will never be forgiven by the sufferers, for they will never believe – oh, well, no, I was going to say they would never believe that I did the thing innocently. The truth is they will know that I acted innocently, because they are rational people; but what of that? I never can look them in the face again – nor they me, perhaps."

Hay was a young bachelor, and at that time was on the "Tribune" staff. He explained his trouble in these words, substantially:

"When I was passing along here yesterday morning on my way down-town to the office, I stepped into a bookstore where I am acquainted, and asked if they had anything new from the other side. They handed me a French novel, in the usual yellow paper cover, and I carried it away. I didn't even look at the title of it. It was for recreation reading, and I was on my way to my work. I went mooning and dreaming along, and I think I hadn't gone more than fifty yards when I heard my name called. I stopped, and a private carriage drew up at the sidewalk and I shook hands with the inmates – mother and young daughter, excellent people. They were on their way to the steamer to sail for Paris. The mother said,

" 'I saw that book in your hand and I judged by the look of it that it was a French novel. Is it?'

"I said it was.

"She said, 'Do let me have it, so that my daughter can practise her French on it on the way over.'

"Of course I handed her the book, and we parted. Ten minutes ago I was passing that bookstore again, and I stepped in and fetched away another copy of that book. Here it is. Read the first page of it. That is enough. You will know what the rest is like. I think it must be the foulest book in the French language – one of the foulest, anyway. I would be ashamed to offer it to a harlot – but, oh dear, I gave it to that sweet young girl without shame. Take my advice; don't give away a book until you have examined it."

FROM SUSY'S BIOGRAPHY

Then mamma and I went to do some shopping and papa went to see General Grant. After we had finnished doing our shopping we went home to the hotel together. When we entered our rooms in the hotel we saw on the table a vase full of exquisett red roses. Mamma who is very fond of flowers exclaimed "Oh I wonder who could have sent them." We both looked at the card in the midst of the roses and saw that it was written on in papa's handwriting, it was written in German. 'Liebes Geshchenk on die mamma.' [I am sure I didn't say "on" – that is Susy's spelling, not mine; also I am sure I didn't spell Geschenk so liberally as all that. – S. L. C.] Mamma was delighted. Papa came home and gave mamma her ticket; and after visiting a while with her went to see Major Pond and mamma and I sat down to our lunch. After lunch most of our time was taken up with packing, and at about three o'clock we went to escort mamma to the train. We got on board the train with her and stayed with her about five minutes and then we said good-bye to her and the train started for Hartford. It was the first time I had ever beene away from home without mamma in my life, although I was 13 yrs. old. Papa and I drove back to the hotel and got Major Pond and then went to see the Brooklyn Bridge we went across it to Brooklyn on the cars and then walked back across it from Brooklyn to New York. We enjoyed looking at the beautiful scenery and we could see the bridge moove under the intense heat of the sun. We had a perfectly delightful time, but weer pretty tired when we got back to the hotel.

The next morning we rose early, took our breakfast and took an early train to Poughkeepsie. We had a very pleasant journey to Poughkeepsie. The Hudson was magnificent – shrouded with beautiful mist. When we arived at Poughkeepsie it was raining quite hard; which fact greatly dissapointed me because I very much wanted to see the outside of the buildings of Vassar College and as it rained that would be impossible. It was quite a long drive from the station to Vassar College and papa and I had a nice long time to discuss and laugh over German profanity. One of the German phrases papa particularly enjoys is "O heilige maria Mutter Jesus!" Jean has a German nurse, and this was one of her phrases, there was a time when Jean exclaimed "Ach Gott!" to every trifle, but when mamma found it out she was shocked and instantly put a stop to it.

It brings that pretty little German girl vividly before me – a sweet and innocent and plump little creature with peachy cheeks; a clear-souled little maiden and without offence, notwithstanding her profanities, and she was loaded to the eyebrows with them. She was a mere child. She was not fifteen yet. She was just from Germany, and knew no English. She was always scattering her profanities around, and they were such a satisfaction to me that I never dreamed of such a thing as modifying her. For my own sake, I had no disposition to tell on her. Indeed I took pains to keep her from being found out. I told her to confine her religious exercises to the children's quarters, and urged her to remember that Mrs. Clemens was prejudiced against pieties on week-days. To the children, the little maid's profanities sounded natural and proper and right, because they had been used to that kind of talk in Germany, and they attached no evil importance to it. It grieves me that I have forgotten those vigorous remarks. I long hoarded them in my memory as a treasure. But I remember one of them still, because I heard it so many times. The trial of that little creature's life was the children's hair. She would tug and strain with her comb, accompanying her work with her misplaced pieties. And when finally she was through with her triple job she always fired up and exploded her thanks toward the sky, where they belonged, in this form: "*Gott sei Dank ich bin fertig mit'm Gott verdammtes Haar!*" (I believe I am not quite brave enough to translate it.)

FROM SUSY'S BIOGRAPHY

We at length reached Vassar College and she looked very finely, her buildings and her grounds being very beautiful. We went to the front doore and range the bell. The young girl who came to the doore wished to know who we wanted to see. Evidently we were not expected. Papa told her who we wanted to see and she showed us to the parlor. We waited, no one came; and waited, no one came, still no one came. It was beginning to seem pretty awkward, "Oh well this is a pretty piece of business," papa exclaimed. At length we heard footsteps coming down the long corridor and Miss C, (the lady who had invited papa) came into the room. She greeted papa very pleasantly and they had a nice little chatt together. Soon the lady principal also entered and she was very pleasant and agreable. She showed us to our rooms and said she would send for us when dinner was ready. We went into our rooms, but we had nothing to do for half an hour exept to watch the rain drops as they fell upon the window panes. At last we were called to dinner, and I went down without papa as he never eats anything in the middle of the day. I sat at the table with the lady principal and enjoyed very much seeing all the young girls trooping into the dining-room. After dinner I went around the College with the young ladies and papa stayed in his room and smoked. When it was supper time papa went down and ate supper with us and we had a very delightful supper. After supper the young ladies went to their rooms to dress for the evening. Papa went to his room and I went with the lady principal. At length the guests began to arrive, but papa still remained in his room until called for. Papa read in the chapell. It was the first time I had ever heard him read in my life – that is in public. When he came out on to the stage I remember the people behind me exclaimed "Oh how queer he is! Isn't he funny!" I thought papa was very funny, although I did not think him queer. He read "A Trying Situation" and "The Golden Arm," a ghost story that he heard down South when he was a little boy. "The Golden Arm" papa had told me before, but he had startled me so that I did not much wish to hear it again. But I had resolved this time to be prepared and not to let myself be startled, but still papa did, and very very much; he startled the whole roomful of people and they jumped as one man. The other story was also very funny and interesting and I enjoyed the evening inexpressibly much. After papa had finished reading all went down to the collation in the dining-room and after that there was dancing and singing. Then the guests went away and papa and I went to bed. The next morning we rose early, took an early train for Hartford and reached Hartford at 1/2 past 2 o'clock. We were very glad to get back.

How charitably she treats that ghastly experience! It is a dear and lovely disposition, and a most valuable one, that can brush away indignities and discourtesies and seek and find the pleasanter features of an experience. Susy had that disposition, and it was one of the jewels of her character that had come to her straight from her mother. It is a feature that was left out of me at birth. And, at seventy, I have not yet acquired it. I did not go to Vassar College professionally, but as a guest – as a guest, and gratis. Aunt Clara (now Mrs. John B. Stanchfield) was a graduate of Vassar and it was to please her that I inflicted that journey upon Susy and myself. The invitation had come to me from both the lady mentioned by Susy and the President of the College – a sour old saint who has probably been gathered to his fathers long ago; and I hope they enjoy him; I hope they value his society. I think I can get along without it, in either end of the next world.

We arrived at the College in that soaking rain, and Susy has described, with just a suggestion of dissatisfaction, the sort of reception we got. Susy had to sit in her damp clothes half an hour while we waited in the parlor; then she was taken to a fire-less room and left to wait there again, as she has stated. I do not remember that President's name, and I am sorry. He did not put in an appearance until it was time for me to step upon the platform in front of that great garden of young and lovely blossoms. He caught up with me and advanced upon the platform with me and was going to introduce me. I said in substance:

"You have allowed me to get along without your help thus far, and if you will retire from the platform I will try to do the rest without it."

I did not see him any more, but I detest his memory. Of course my resentment did not extend to the students, and so I had an unforgettable good time talking to them. And I think they had a good time too, for they responded "as one man," to use Susy's unimprovable phrase.

Girls are charming creatures. I shall have to be twice seventy

years old before I change my mind as to that. I am to talk to a
crowd of them this afternoon, students of Barnard College (the
sex's annex to Columbia University), and I think I shall have as
pleasant a time with those lasses as I had with the Vassar girls
twenty-one years ago.

FROM SUSY'S BIOGRAPHY

I stopped in the middle of mamma's early history to tell about
our tripp to Vassar because I was afraid I would forget about it,
now I will go on where I left off. Some time after Miss Emma
Nigh died papa took mamma and little Langdon to Elmira for
the summer. When in Elmira Langdon began to fail but I think
mamma did not know just what was the matter with him.

I was the cause of the child's illness. His mother trusted him to
my care and I took him a long drive in an open barouche for an
airing. It was a raw, cold morning, but he was well wrapped about
with furs and, in the hands of a careful person, no harm would
have come to him. But I soon dropped into a reverie and forgot all
about my charge. The furs fell away and exposed his bare legs. By
and by the coachman noticed this, and I arranged the wraps again,
but it was too late. The child was almost frozen. I hurried home
with him. I was aghast at what I had done, and I feared the consequences. I have alway felt shame for that treacherous morning's
work and have not allowed myself to think of it when I could help
it. I doubt if I had the courage to make confession at that time.
I think it most likely that I have never confessed until now.

FROM SUSY'S BIOGRAPHY

At last it was time for papa to return to Hartford, and Langdon
was real sick at that time, but still mamma decided to go with
him, thinking the journey might do him good. But after they
reached Hartford he became very sick, and his trouble prooved
to be diptheeria. He died about a week after mamma and papa
reached Hartford. He was burried by the side of grandpa at
Elmira, New York. [Susy rests there with them. – S. L. C.] After
that, mamma became very very ill, so ill that there seemed
great danger of death, but with a great deal of good care she
recovered. Some months afterward mamma and papa [and
Susy, who was perhaps fourteen or fifteen months old at the

time. – S. L. C.] went to Europe and stayed for a time in Scot-
land and England. In Scotland mamma and papa became very
well equanted with Dr. John Brown, the author of "Rab and His
Friends," and he mett, but was not so well equanted with, Mr.
Charles Kingsley, Mr. Henry M. Stanley, Sir Thomas Hardy
grandson of the Captain Hardy to whom Nellson said "Kiss me
Hardy," when dying on shipboard, Mr. Henry Irving, Robert
Browning, Sir Charles Dilke, Mr. Charles Reade, Mr. William
Black, Lord Houghton, Frank Buckland, Mr. Tom Hughes,
Anthony Trollope, Tom Hood, son of the poet – and mamma and
papa were quite well equanted with Dr. Macdonald and family,
and papa met Harrison Ainsworth.

I remember all these men very well indeed, except the last one.
I do not recall Ainsworth. By my count, Susy mentions fourteen
men. They are all dead except Sir Charles Dilke.

We met a great many other interesting people, among them
Lewis Carroll, author of the immortal "Alice" – but he was only
interesting to look at, for he was the stillest and shyest full-grown
man I have ever met except "Uncle Remus." Dr. Macdonald and
several other lively talkers were present, and the talk went briskly
on for a couple of hours, but Carroll sat still all the while except
that now and then he answered a question. His answers were brief.
I do not remember that he elaborated any of them.

At a dinner at Smalley's we met Herbert Spencer. At a large
luncheon party at Lord Houghton's we met Sir Arthur Helps, who
was a celebrity of world-wide fame at the time, but is quite forgotten now. Lord Elcho, a large vigorous man, sat at some distance
down the table. He was talking earnestly about Godalming. It was
a deep and flowing and unarticulated rumble, but I got the Godalming pretty clearly every time it broke free of the rumble, and
as all the strength was on the first end of the word it startled me
every time, because it sounded so like swearing. In the middle of
the luncheon Lady Houghton rose, remarked to the guests on her
right and on her left in a matter-of-fact way, "Excuse me, I have
an engagement," and without further ceremony she went off to
meet it. This would have been doubtful etiquette in America. Lord
Houghton told a number of delightful stories. He told them in
French, and I lost nothing of them but the nubs.

PART VII

DECEMBER 7, 1906

I was always heedless. I was born heedless; and therefore I was constantly, and quite unconsciously, committing breaches of the minor proprieties, which brought upon me humiliations which ought to have humiliated me but didn't, because I didn't know anything had happened. But Livy knew; and so the humiliations fell to her share, poor child, who had not earned them and did not deserve them. She always said I was the most difficult child she had. She was very sensitive about me. It distressed her to see me do heedless things which could bring me under criticism, and so she was always watchful and alert to protect me from the kind of transgressions which I have been speaking of.

When I was leaving Hartford for Washington, upon the occasion referred to, she said: "I have written a small warning and put it in a pocket of your dress-vest. When you are dressing to go to the Authors' Reception at the White House you will naturally put your fingers in your vest pockets, according to your custom, and you will find that little note there. Read it carefully, and do as it tells you. I cannot be with you, and so I delegate my sentry duties to this little note. If I should give you the warning by word of mouth, now, it would pass from your head and be forgotten in a few minutes."

It was President Cleveland's first term. I had never seen his wife – the young, the beautiful, the good-hearted, the sympathetic, the fascinating. Sure enough, just as I had finished dressing to go to the White House I found that little note, which I had long ago forgotten. It was a grave little note, a serious little note, like its writer, but it made me laugh. Livy's gentle gravities often produced that effect upon me, where the expert humorist's best joke would have failed, for I do not laugh easily.

When we reached the White House and I was shaking hands with the President, he started to say something, but I interrupted him and said:

"If your Excellency will excuse me, I will come back in a moment; but now I have a very important matter to attend to, and it must be attended to at once."

I turned to Mrs. Cleveland, the young, the beautiful, the fascinating, and gave her my card, on the back of which I had written

"He didn't" – and I asked her to sign her name below those words.
She said: "He didn't? He didn't what?"

"Oh," I said, "never mind. We cannot stop to discuss that now.
This is urgent. Won't you please sign your name?" (I handed her
a fountain-pen.)

"Why," she said, "I cannot commit myself in that way. Who is
it that didn't? – and what is it that he didn't?"

"Oh," I said, "time is flying, flying, flying. Won't you take me
out of my distress and sign your name to it? It's all right. I give you
my word it's all right."

She looked nonplussed; but hesitatingly and mechanically she
took the pen and said:

"I will sign it. I will take the risk. But you must tell me all about
it, right afterward, so that you can be arrested before you get out
of the house in case there should be anything criminal about this."

Then she signed; and I handed her Mrs. Clemens's note, which
was very brief, very simple, and to the point. It said: *"Don't wear
your arctics in the White House."* It made her shout; and at my request
she summoned a messenger and we sent that card at once to the
mail on its way to Mrs. Clemens in Hartford.

When the little Ruth was about a year or a year and a half old,
Mason, an old and valued friend of mine, was consul-general at
Frankfort-on-the-Main. I had known him well in 1867, '68 and '69,
in America, and I and mine had spent a good deal of time with him
and his family in Frankfort in '78. He was a thoroughly competent,
diligent, and conscientious official. Indeed he possessed these
qualities in so large a degree that among American consuls he
might fairly be said to be monumental, for at that time our consu-
lar service was largely – and I think I may say mainly – in the hands
of ignorant, vulgar, and incapable men who had been political
heelers in America, and had been taken care of by transference
to consulates where they could be supported at the Government's
expense instead of being transferred to the poor house, which
would have been cheaper and more patriotic. Mason, in '78, had
been consul-general in Frankfort several years – four, I think. He
had come from Marseilles with a great record. He had been consul
there during thirteen years, and one part of his record was heroic.
There had been a desolating cholera epidemic, and Mason was
the only representative of any foreign country who stayed at his
post and saw it through. And during that time he not only represented his own country, but he represented all the other countries

in Christendom and did their work, and did it well and was praised
for it by them in words of no uncertain sound. This great record
of Mason's had saved him from official decapitation straight along
while Republican Presidents occupied the chair, but now it was
occupied by a Democrat. Mr. Cleveland was not seated in it – he
was not yet inaugurated – before he was deluged with applications
from Democratic politicians desiring the appointment of a thousand or so politically useful Democrats to Mason's place. A year
or two later Mason wrote me and asked me if I couldn't do something to save him from destruction.

I was very anxious to keep him in his place, but at first I could
not think of any way to help him, for I was a mugwump. We, the
mugwumps, a little company made up of the unenslaved of both
parties, the very best men to be found in the two great parties –
that was our idea of it – voted sixty thousand strong for Mr. Cleveland in New York and elected him. Our principles were high, and
very definite. We were not a party; we had no candidates; we had
no axes to grind. Our vote laid upon the man we cast it for no
obligation of any kind. By our rule we could not ask for office; we
could not accept office. When voting, it was our duty to vote for
the best man, regardless of his party name. We had no other creed.
Vote for the best man – that was creed enough.

Such being my situation, I was puzzled to know how to try to
help Mason, and, at the same time, save my mugwump purity
undefiled. It was a delicate place. But presently, out of the ruck of
confusions in my mind, rose a sane thought, clear and bright – to
wit: since it was a mugwump's duty to do his best to put the best
man in office, necessarily it must be a mugwump's duty to try to
keep the best man in when he was already there. My course was easy
now. It might not be quite delicate for a mugwump to approach the
President directly, but I could approach him indirectly, with all
delicacy, since in that case not even courtesy would require him to
take notice of an application which no one could prove had ever
reached him.

Yes, it was easy and simple sailing now. I could lay the matter
before Ruth, in her cradle, and wait for results. I wrote the little
child, and said to her all that I have just been saying about mugwump principles and the limitations which they put upon me.
I explained that it would not be proper for me to apply to her father
in Mr. Mason's behalf, but I detailed to her Mr. Mason's high and
honorable record and suggested that she take the matter in her

own hands and do a patriotic work which I felt some delicacy about venturing upon myself. I asked her to forget that her father was only President of the United States, and her subject and servant; I asked her not to put her application in the form of a command, but to modify it, and give it the fictitious and pleasanter form of a mere request – that it would be no harm to let him gratify himself with the superstition that he was independent and could do as he pleased in the matter. I begged her to put stress, and plenty of it, upon the proposition that to keep Mason in his place would be a benefaction to the nation; to enlarge upon that, and keep still about all other considerations.

In due time I received a letter from the President, written with his own hand, signed by his own hand, acknowledging Ruth's intervention and thanking me for enabling him to save to the country the services of so good and well-tried a servant as Mason, and thanking me, also, for the detailed fulness of Mason's record, which could leave no doubt in any one's mind that Mason was in his right place and ought to be kept there. Mason has remained in the service ever since, and is now consul-general at Paris.

During the time that we were living in Buffalo in '70–'71, Mr. Cleveland was sheriff, but I never happened to make his acquaintance, or even see him. In fact, I suppose I was not even aware of his existence. Fourteen years later, he was become the greatest man in the State. I was not living in the State at the time. He was Governor, and was about to step into the post of President of the United States. At that time I was on the public highway in company with another bandit, George W. Cable. We were robbing the public with readings from our works during four months – and in the course of time we went to Albany to levy tribute, and I said, "We ought to go and pay our respects to the Governor."

So Cable and I went to that majestic Capitol building and stated our errand. We were shown into the Governor's private office, and I saw Mr. Cleveland for the first time. We three stood chatting together. I was born lazy, and I comforted myself by turning the corner of a table into a sort of seat. Presently the Governor said:

"Mr. Clemens, I was a fellow citizen of yours in Buffalo a good many months, a good while ago, and during those months you burst suddenly into a mighty fame, out of a previous long-continued and no doubt proper obscurity – but I was a nobody, and you wouldn't notice me nor have anything to do with me. But now that I have become somebody, you have changed your style, and you come here to shake hands with me and be sociable. How do you explain this kind of conduct?"

"Oh," I said, "it is very simple, your Excellency. In Buffalo you were nothing but a sheriff. I was in society. I couldn't afford to associate with sheriffs. But you are a Governor now, and you are on your way to the Presidency. It is a great difference, and it makes you worth while."

There appeared to be about sixteen doors to that spacious room. From each door a young man now emerged, and the sixteen lined up and moved forward and stood in front of the Governor with an aspect of respectful expectancy in their attitude. No one spoke for a moment. Then the Governor said:

"You are dismissed, gentlemen. Your services are not required. Mr. Clemens is sitting on the bells."

There was a cluster of sixteen bell buttons on the corner of the table; my proportions at that end of me were just right to enable me to cover the whole of that nest, and that is how I came to hatch out those sixteen clerks.

In accordance with the suggestion made in Gilder's letter recently received I have written the following note to ex-President Cleveland upon his sixty-ninth birthday:

HONORED SIR:

Your patriotic virtues have won for you the homage of half the nation and the enmity of the other half. This places your character as a citizen upon a summit as high as Washington's. The verdict is unanimous and unassailable. The votes of both sides are necessary in cases like these, and the votes of the one side are quite as valuable as are the votes of the other. Where the votes are all in a man's favor the verdict is against him. It is sand, and history will wash it away. But the verdict for you is rock, and will stand.

S. L. CLEMENS.

As of date March 18, 1906. ...

In a diary which Mrs. Clemens kept for a little while, a great many years ago, I find various mentions of Mrs. Harriet Beecher Stowe, who was a near neighbor of ours in Hartford, with no fences between. And in those days she made as much use of our grounds as of her own, in pleasant weather. Her mind had decayed, and she was a pathetic figure. She wandered about all the day long in the care of a muscular Irishwoman. Among the colonists of our neighborhood the doors always stood open in pleasant weather. Mrs. Stowe entered them at her own free will, and as she was always softly slippered and generally full of animal spirits, she was able to deal in surprises, and she liked to do it. She would slip up behind a person who was deep in dreams and musings and fetch a war-whoop that would jump that person out of his clothes. And she had other moods. Sometimes we would hear gentle music in the drawing-room and would find her there at the piano singing ancient and melancholy songs with infinitely touching effect.

Her husband, old Professor Stowe, was a picturesque figure. He wore a broad slouch hat. He was a large man, and solemn. His beard was white and thick and hung far down on his breast. The first time our little Susy ever saw him she encountered him on the street near our house and came flying wide-eyed to her mother and said, "Santa Claus has got loose!"

Which reminds me of Rev. Charley Stowe's little boy – a little boy of seven years. I met Rev. Charley crossing his mother's grounds one morning and he told me this little tale. He had been out to Chicago to attend a Convention of Congregational clergymen, and had taken his little boy with him. During the trip he reminded the little chap, every now and then, that he must be on his very best behavior there in Chicago. He said: "We shall be the guests of a clergyman, there will be other guests – clergymen and their wives – and you must be careful to let those people see by your walk and conversation that you are of a godly household. Be very careful about this." The admonition bore fruit. At the first breakfast which they ate in the Chicago clergyman's house he heard his little son say in the meekest and most reverent way to the lady opposite him,

"Please, won't you, for Christ's sake, pass the butter?"

PART VIII

DECEMBER 21, 1906

[*Dictated in 1906.*] In those early days duelling suddenly became a fashion in the new Territory of Nevada, and by 1864 everybody

was anxious to have a chance in the new sport, mainly for the
reason that he was not able to thoroughly respect himself so long
as he had not killed or crippled somebody in a duel or been killed
or crippled in one himself.

At that time I had been serving as city editor on Mr. Goodman's
Virginia City "Enterprise" for a matter of two years. I was twenty-
nine years old. I was ambitious in several ways, but I had entirely
escaped the seductions of that particular craze. I had had no desire
to fight a duel; I had no intention of provoking one. I did not feel
respectable, but I got a certain amount of satisfaction out of feeling
safe. I was ashamed of myself; the rest of the staff were ashamed
of me – but I got along well enough. I had always been accustomed
to feeling ashamed of myself, for one thing or another, so there was
no novelty for me in the situation. I bore it very well. Plunkett was
on the staff; R. M. Daggett was on the staff. These had tried to
get into duels, but for the present had failed, and were waiting.
Goodman was the only one of us who had done anything to shed
credit upon the paper. The rival paper was the Virginia "Union."
Its editor for a little while was Tom Fitch, called the "silver-
tongued orator of Wisconsin" – that was where he came from. He
tuned up his oratory in the editorial columns of the "Union," and
Mr. Goodman invited him out and modified him with a bullet.
I remember the joy of the staff when Goodman's challenge was
accepted by Fitch. We ran late that night, and made much of Joe
Goodman. He was only twenty-four years old; he lacked the wisdom which a person has at twenty-nine, and he was as glad of
being *it* as I was that I wasn't. He chose Major Graves for his
second (that name is not right, but it's close enough; I don't
remember the Major's name). Graves came over to instruct Joe in
the duelling art. He had been a Major under Walker, the "gray-
eyed man of destiny," and had fought all through that remarkable
man's filibustering campaign in Central America. That fact
gauges the Major. To say that a man was a Major under Walker,
and came out of that struggle ennobled by Walker's praise, is to
say that the Major was not merely a brave man but that he was
brave to the very utmost limit of that word. All of Walker's men
were like that. I knew the Gillis family intimately. The father made
the campaign under Walker, and with him one son. They were
in the memorable Plaza fight, and stood it out to the last against
overwhelming odds, as did also all of the Walker men. The son was
killed at the father's side. The father received a bullet through the

eye. The old man – for he was an old man at the time – wore spectacles, and the bullet and one of the glasses went into his skull and
remained there. There were some other sons: Steve, George, and
Jim, very young chaps – the merest lads – who wanted to be in
the Walker expedition, for they had their father's dauntless spirit.
But Walker wouldn't have them; he said it was a serious expedition, and no place for children.

The Major was a majestic creature, with a most stately and
dignified and impressive military bearing, and he was by nature
and training courteous, polite, graceful, winning; and he had that
quality which I think I have encountered in only one other man –
Bob Howland – a mysterious quality which resides in the eye; and
when that eye is turned upon an individual or a squad, in warning,
that is enough. The man that has that eye doesn't need to go
armed; he can move upon an armed desperado and quell him and
take him prisoner without saying a single word. I saw Bob Howland do that, once – a slender, good-natured, amiable, gentle,
kindly little skeleton of a man, with a sweet blue eye that would
win your heart when it smiled upon you, or turn cold and freeze
it, according to the nature of the occasion.

The Major stood Joe up straight; stood Steve Gillis up fifteen
paces away; made Joe turn right side towards Steve, cock his navy
six-shooter – that prodigious weapon – and hold it straight down
against his leg; told him that *that* was the correct position for the
gun – that the position ordinarily in use at Virginia City (that is to
say, the gun straight up in the air, then brought slowly down to
your man) was all wrong. At the word "*One*," you must raise the
gun slowly and steadily to the place on the other man's body that
you desire to convince. Then, after a pause, "*two, three – fire – Stop!*"
At the word "stop," you may fire – but not earlier. You may give
yourself as much time as you please *after* that word. Then, when
you fire, you may advance and go on firing at your leisure and
pleasure, if you can get any pleasure out of it. And, in the meantime, the other man, if he has been properly instructed and is alive
to his privileges, is advancing on *you*, and firing – and it is always
likely that more or less trouble will result.

Naturally, when Joe's revolver had risen to a level it was pointing
at Steve's breast, but the Major said "No, that is not wise. Take all
the risks of getting murdered yourself, but don't run any risk of
murdering the other man. If you survive a duel you want to survive
it in such a way that the memory of it will not linger along with

you through the rest of your life and interfere with your sleep. Aim at your man's leg; not at the knee, not above the knee; for those are dangerous spots. Aim below the knee; cripple him, but leave the rest of him to his mother."

By grace of these truly wise and excellent instructions, Joe tumbled Fitch down next morning with a bullet through his lower leg, which furnished him a permanent limp. And Joe lost nothing but a lock of hair, which he could spare better then than he could now. For when I saw him here in New York a year ago, his crop was gone; he had nothing much left but a fringe, with a dome rising above.

About a year later I got *my* chance. But I was not hunting for it. Goodman went off to San Francisco for a week's holiday, and left me to be chief editor. I had supposed that that was an easy berth, there being nothing to do but write one editorial per day; but I was disappointed in that superstition. I couldn't find anything to write an article about, the first day. Then it occurred to me that inasmuch as it was the 22nd of April, 1864, the next morning would be the three-hundredth anniversary of Shakespeare's birthday – and what better theme could I want than that? I got the Cyclopædia and examined it, and found out who Shakespeare was and what he had done, and I borrowed all that and laid it before a community that couldn't have been better prepared for instruction about Shakespeare than if they had been prepared by art. There wasn't enough of what Shakespeare had done to make an editorial of the necessary length, but I filled it out with what he hadn't done – which in many respects was more important and striking and readable than the handsomest things he had really accomplished. But next day I was in trouble again. There were no more Shakespeares to work up. There was nothing in past history, or in the world's future possibilities, to make an editorial out of, suitable to that community; so there was but one theme left. That theme was Mr. Laird, proprietor of the Virginia "Union." *His* editor had gone off to San Francisco too, and Laird was trying his hand at editing. I woke up Mr. Laird with some courtesies of the kind that were fashionable among newspaper editors in that region, and he came back at me the next day in a most vitriolic way. He was hurt by something I had said about him – some little thing – I don't remember what it was now – probably called him a horse-thief, or one of those little phrases customarily used to describe another editor. They were no doubt just, and accurate, but Laird was a very sensitive creature and he didn't like it. So we expected a challenge from Mr. Laird, because according to the rules – according to the etiquette of duelling as reconstructed and reorganized and improved by the duellists of that region – whenever you said a thing about another person that he didn't like, it wasn't sufficient for him to talk back in the same offensive spirit: etiquette required him to send a challenge; so we waited for a challenge – waited all day. It didn't come. And as the day wore along, hour after hour, and no challenge came, the boys grew depressed. They lost heart. But I was cheerful; I felt better and better all the time. They couldn't understand it, but *I* could understand it. It was my *make* that enabled me to be cheerful when other people were despondent. So then it became necessary for us to waive etiquette and challenge Mr. Laird. When we reached that decision, they began to cheer up, but I began to lose some of my animation. However, in enterprises of this kind you are in the hands of your friends; there is nothing for you to do but to abide by what they consider to be the best course. Daggett wrote a challenge for me, for Daggett had the language – the right language – the convincing language – and I lacked it. Daggett poured out a stream of unsavory epithets upon Mr. Laird, charged with a vigor and venom of a strength calculated to persuade him; and Steve Gillis, my second, carried the challenge and came back to wait for the return. It didn't come. The boys were exasperated, but I kept my temper. Steve carried another challenge, hotter than the other, and we waited again. Nothing came of it. I began to feel quite comfortable. I began to take an interest in the challenges myself. I had not felt any before; but it seemed to me that I was accumulating a great and valuable reputation at no expense, and my delight in this grew and grew, as challenge after challenge was declined, until by midnight I was beginning to think that there was nothing in the world so much to be desired as a chance to fight a duel. So I hurried Daggett up; made him keep on sending challenge after challenge. Oh, well, I over-did it; Laird accepted. I might have known that that would happen – Laird was a man you couldn't depend on.

The boys were jubilant beyond expression. They helped me make my will, which was another discomfort – and I already had enough. Then they took me home. I didn't sleep any – didn't want to sleep. I had plenty of things to think about, and less than four hours to do it in – because five o'clock was the hour appointed for the tragedy, and I should have to use up one hour – beginning at four – in practising with the revolver and finding out which end of it to level at the adversary. At four we went down into a little gorge, about a mile from town, and borrowed a barn door for a mark – borrowed it of a man who was over in California on a visit – and we set the barn door up and stood a fence-rail up against the middle of it, to represent Mr. Laird. But the rail was no proper representative of him, for he was longer than a rail and thinner. Nothing would ever fetch him but a line shot, and then as like as not he would split the bullet – the worst material for duelling purposes that could be imagined. I began on the rail. I couldn't hit the rail; then I tried the barn door; but I couldn't hit the barn door. There was nobody in danger except stragglers around on the flanks of that mark. I was thoroughly discouraged, and I didn't cheer up any when we presently heard pistol-shots over in the next little ravine. I knew what that was – that was Laird's gang out practising him. They would hear my shots, and of course they would come up over the ridge to see what kind of a record I was making – see what their chances were against me. Well, I hadn't any record; and I knew that if Laird came over that ridge and saw my barn door without a scratch on it, he would be as anxious to fight as I was – or as I had been at midnight, before that disastrous acceptance came.

Now just at this moment, a little bird, no bigger than a sparrow, flew along by and lit on a sage-bush about thirty yards away. Steve whipped out his revolver and shot its head off. Oh, he was a marksman – much better than I was. We ran down there to pick up the bird, and just then, sure enough, Mr. Laird and his people came over the ridge, and they joined us. And when Laird's second saw that bird, with its head shot off, he lost color, he faded, and you could see that he was interested. He said:

"Who did that?"

Before I could answer, Steve spoke up and said quite calmly, and in a matter-of-fact way,

"Clemens did it."

The second said, "Why, that is wonderful. How far off was that bird?"

Steve said, "Oh, not far – about thirty yards."

The second said, "Well, that is astonishing shooting. How often can he do that?"

Steve said languidly, "Oh, about four times out of five."

I knew the little rascal was lying, but I didn't say anything. The second said, "Why, that is *amazing* shooting; I supposed he couldn't hit a church."

He was supposing very sagaciously, but I didn't say anything. Well, they said good morning. The second took Mr. Laird home, a little tottery on his legs, and Laird sent back a note in his own hand declining to fight a duel with me on any terms whatever.

Well, my life was saved – saved by that accident. I don't know what the bird thought about that interposition of Providence, but I felt very, very comfortable over it – satisfied and content. Now, we found out, later, that Laird had *hit* his mark four times out of six, right along. If the duel had come off, he would have so filled my skin with bullet-holes that it wouldn't have held my principles.

By breakfast-time the news was all over town that I had sent a challenge and Steve Gillis had carried it. Now that would entitle us to two years apiece in the penitentiary, according to the brand-new law. Judge North sent us no message as coming from himself, but a message *came* from a close friend of his. He said it would be a good idea for us to leave the territory by the first stage-coach. This would sail next morning, at four o'clock – and in the meantime we would be searched for, but not with avidity; and if we were in the Territory after that stage-coach left, we would be the first victims of the new law. Judge North was anxious to have some object-lessons for that law, and he would absolutely keep us in the prison the full two years.

Well, it seemed to me that our society was no longer desirable in Nevada; so we stayed in our quarters and observed proper caution all day – except that once Steve went over to the hotel to attend to another customer of mine. That was a Mr. Cutler. You see Laird was not the only person whom I had tried to reform during my occupancy of the editorial chair. I had looked around and selected several other people, and delivered a new zest of life into them through warm criticism and disapproval – so that when I laid down my editorial pen I had four horse-whippings and two duels owing to me. We didn't care for the horse-whippings; there was no glory in them; they were not worth the trouble of collecting. But honor required that some notice should be taken of that other duel. Mr. Cutler had come up from Carson City, and had sent a man over with a challenge from the hotel. Steve went over to pacify him. Steve weighed only ninety-five pounds, but it was well known throughout the territory that with his fists he could whip anybody that walked on two legs, let his weight and science be what they might. Steve was a Gillis, and when a Gillis confronted a man and had a proposition to make, the proposition always contained business. When Cutler found that Steve was my second he cooled down; he became calm and rational, and was ready to listen. Steve gave him fifteen minutes to get out of the hotel, and half an hour to get out of town or there would be results. So *that* duel went off successfully, because Mr. Cutler immediately left for Carson a convinced and reformed man.

I have never had anything to do with duels since. I thoroughly disapprove of duels. I consider them unwise, and I know they are dangerous. Also, sinful. If a man should challenge me now, I would go to that man and take him kindly and forgivingly by the hand and lead him to a quiet retired spot, and *kill* him.

PART IX

JANUARY 4, 1907

[*Dictated December 13, 1906.*] As regards the coming American monarchy. It was before the Secretary of State had been heard from that the chairman of the banquet said:

"In this time of unrest it is of great satisfaction that such a man as you, Mr. Root, is chief adviser of the President."

Mr. Root then got up and in the most quiet and orderly manner touched off the successor to the San Francisco earthquake. As a result, the several State governments were well shaken up and considerably weakened. Mr. Root was prophesying. He was prophesying, and it seems to me that no shrewder and surer forecasting has been done in this country for a good many years.

He did not say, in so many words, that we are proceeding, in a steady march, toward eventual and unavoidable replacement of the republic by monarchy; but I suppose he was aware that that is the case. He notes the several steps, the customary steps, which in all the ages have led to the consolidation of loose and scattered governmental forces into formidable centralizations of authority; but he stops there, and doesn't add up the sum. He is not unaware that heretofore the sum has been ultimate monarchy, and that the same figures can fairly be depended upon to furnish the same sum whenever and wherever they can be produced, so long as human nature shall remain as it is; but it was not needful that he do the adding, since any one can do it; neither would it have been gracious in him to do it.

In observing the changed conditions which in the course of time have made certain and sure the eventual seizure by the Washington government of a number of State duties and prerogatives which have been betrayed and neglected by the several States, he does not attribute those changes and the vast results which are to flow from them to any thought-out policy of any party or of any body of dreamers or schemers, but properly and rightly attributes them to that stupendous power – *Circumstance* – which moves by laws of its own, regardless of parties and policies, and whose decrees are final, and must be obeyed by all – and will be. The railway is a Circumstance, the steamship is a Circumstance, the telegraph is a Circumstance. They were mere happenings; and to the whole world, the wise and the foolish alike, they were entirely trivial, wholly inconsequential; indeed silly, comical, grotesque. No man, and no party, and no thought-out policy said, "Behold, we will build railways and steamships and telegraphs, and presently you will see the condition and way of life of every man and woman and child in the nation totally changed; unimaginable changes of law and custom will follow, in spite of anything that anybody can do to prevent it."

The changed conditions have come, and Circumstance knows what is following, and will follow. So does Mr. Root. His language is not unclear, it is crystal:

"Our whole life has swung away from the old State centres, and is crystallizing about national centres."

". . . . The old barriers which kept the States as separate communities are completely lost from sight."

". . . . That [State] power of regulation and control is gradually passing into the hands of the national government."

"Sometimes by an assertion of the inter-State commerce power, sometimes by an assertion of the taxing power, the national government is taking up the performance of duties which under the changed conditions the separate States are no longer capable of adequately performing."

"We are urging forward in a development of business and social life which tends more and more to the obliteration of

State lines and the decrease of State power as compared with national power."

"It is useless for the advocates of State rights to inveigh against ... the extension of national authority in the fields of necessary control where the States themselves fail in the performance of their duty."

He is not announcing a policy; he is not forecasting what a party of planners will bring about; he is merely telling what the people will require and compel. And he could have added – which would be perfectly true – that the people will not be moved to it by speculation and cogitation and planning, but by *Circumstance* – that power which arbitrarily compels all their actions, and over which they have not the slightest control.

"*The end is not yet.*"

It is a true word. We are on the march, but at present we are only just getting started.

If the States continue to fail to do their duty as required by the people –

" ... *constructions of the Constitution will be found* to vest the power where it will be exercised – in the national government."

I do not know whether that has a sinister meaning or not, and so I will not enlarge upon it lest I should chance to be in the wrong. It sounds like ship-money come again, but it may not be so intended.

Human nature being what it is, I suppose we must expect to drift into monarchy by and by. It is a saddening thought, but we cannot change our nature: we are all alike, we human beings; and in our blood and bone, and ineradicable, we carry the seeds out of which monarchies and aristocracies are grown: worship of gauds, titles, distinctions, power. We have to worship these things and their possessors, we are all born so, and we cannot help it. We have to be despised by somebody whom we regard as above us, or we are not happy; we have to have somebody to worship and envy, or we cannot be content. In America we manifest this in all the ancient and customary ways. In public we scoff at titles and hereditary privilege, but privately we hanker after them, and when we get a chance we buy them for cash and a daughter. Sometimes we get a good man and worth the price, but we are ready to take him anyway, whether he be ripe or rotten, whether he be clean and decent, or merely a basket of noble and sacred and long-descended offal. And when we get him the whole nation publicly chaffs and scoffs – and privately envies; and also is proud of the honor which has been conferred upon us. We run over our list of titled purchases every now and then, in the newspapers, and discuss them and caress them, and are thankful and happy.

Like all the other nations, we worship money and the possessors of it – they being our aristocracy, and we have to have one. We like to read about rich people in the papers; the papers know it, and they do their best to keep this appetite liberally fed. They even leave out a football bull-fight now and then to get room for all the particulars of how – according to the display heading – "Rich Woman Fell Down Cellar – Not Hurt." The falling down the cellar is of no interest to us when the woman is not rich, but no rich woman can fall down cellar and we not yearn to know all about it and wish it was us.

In a monarchy the people willingly and rejoicingly revere and take pride in their nobilities, and are not humiliated by the reflection that this humble and hearty homage gets no return but contempt. Contempt does not shame them, they are used to it, and they recognize that it is their proper due. We are all made like that. In Europe we easily and quickly learn to take that attitude toward the sovereigns and the aristocracies; moreover, it has been observed that when we get the attitude we go on and exaggerate it, presently becoming more servile than the natives, and vainer of it. The next step is to rail and scoff at republics and democracies. All of which is natural, for we have not ceased to be human beings by becoming Americans, and the human race was always intended to be governed by kingship, not by popular vote.

I suppose we must expect that unavoidable and irresistible Circumstances will gradually take away the powers of the States and concentrate them in the central government, and that the republic will then repeat the history of all time and become a monarchy; but I believe that if we obstruct these encroachments and steadily resist them the monarchy can be postponed for a good while yet.

[*Dictated December 1, 1906.*] An exciting event in our village (Hannibal) was the arrival of the mesmerizer. I think the year was 1850. As to that I am not sure, but I know the month – it was May; that detail has survived the wear of fifty-five years. A pair of connected little incidents of that month have served to keep the memory of it green for me all this time; incidents of no consequence, and not worth embalming, yet my memory has preserved them carefully and flung away things of real value to give them space and make them comfortable. The truth is, a person's memory has no more sense than his conscience, and no appreciation whatever of values and proportions. However, never mind those trifling incidents; my subject is the mesmerizer, now.

He advertised his show, and promised marvels. Admission as usual: 25 cents, children and negroes half price. The village had heard of mesmerism, in a general way, but had not encountered it yet. Not many people attended, the first night, but next day they had so many wonders to tell that everybody's curiosity was fired, and after that for a fortnight the magician had prosperous times. I was fourteen or fifteen years old – the age at which a boy is willing to endure all things, suffer all things, short of death by fire, if thereby he may be conspicuous and show off before the public; and so, when I saw the "subjects" perform their foolish antics on the platform and make the people laugh and shout and admire, I had a burning desire to be a subject myself. Every night, for three nights, I sat in the row of candidates on the platform, and held the magic disk in the palm of my hand, and gazed at it and tried to get sleepy, but it was a failure; I remained wide awake, and had to retire defeated, like the majority. Also, I had to sit there and be gnawed with envy of Hicks, our journeyman; I had to sit there and see him scamper and jump when Simmons the enchanter exclaimed, "See the snake! see the snake!" and hear him say, "My, how beautiful!" in response to the suggestion that he was observing a splendid sunset; and so on – the whole insane business. I couldn't laugh, I couldn't applaud; it filled me with bitterness to have others do it, and to have people make a hero of Hicks, and crowd around him when the show was over, and ask him for more and more particulars of the wonders he had seen in his visions, and manifest in many ways that they were proud to be acquainted with him. Hicks – the idea! I couldn't stand it; I was getting boiled to death in my own bile.

On the fourth night temptation came, and I was not strong enough to resist. When I had gazed at the disk awhile I pretended to be sleepy, and began to nod. Straightway came the professor and made passes over my head and down my body and legs and arms, finishing each pass with a snap of his fingers in the air, to discharge the surplus electricity; then he began to "draw" me with the disk, holding it in his fingers and telling me I could not take my eyes off it, try as I might; so I rose slowly, bent and gazing, and followed that disk all over the place, just as I had seen the others do. Then I was put through the other paces. Upon suggestion I fled from snakes; passed buckets at a fire; became excited over hot steamboat-races; made love to imaginary girls and kissed them; fished from the platform and landed mud-cats that outweighed me – and so on, all the customary marvels. But not in the customary way. I was cautious at first, and watchful, being afraid the professor would discover that I was an impostor and drive me from the platform in disgrace; but as soon as I realized that I was not in danger, I set myself the task of terminating Hicks's usefulness as a subject, and of usurping his place.

It was a sufficiently easy task. Hicks was born honest; I, without that incumbrance – so some people said. Hicks saw what he saw, and reported accordingly; I saw more than was visible, and added to it such details as could help. Hicks had no imagination, I had a double supply. He was born calm, I was born excited. No vision could start a rapture in him, and he was constipated as to language, anyway; but if I saw a vision I emptied the dictionary onto it and lost the remnant of my mind into the bargain.

At the end of my first half-hour Hicks was a thing of the past, a fallen hero, a broken idol, and I knew it and was glad, and said in my heart, Success to crime! Hicks could never have been mesmerized to the point where he could kiss an imaginary girl in public, or a real one either, but I was competent. Whatever Hicks had failed in, I made it a point to succeed in, let the cost be what it might, physically or morally. He had shown several bad defects, and I had made a note of them. For instance, if the magician asked, "What do you see?" and left him to invent a vision for himself, Hicks was dumb and blind, he couldn't see a thing nor say a word, whereas the magician soon found that when it came to seeing visions of a stunning and marketable sort I could get along better without his help than with it. Then there was another thing: Hicks wasn't worth a tallow dip on mute mental suggestion. Whenever Simmons stood behind him and gazed at the back of his skull and tried to drive a mental suggestion into it, Hicks sat with vacant face, and never suspected. If he had been noticing, he could have seen by the rapt faces of the audience that something was going on behind his back that required a response. Inasmuch as I was an impostor I dreaded to have this test put upon me, for I knew the professor would be "willing" me to do something, and as I couldn't know what it was, I should be exposed and denounced. However, when my time came, I took my chance. I perceived by the tense and expectant faces of the people that Simmons was behind me willing me with all his might. I tried my best to imagine what he wanted, but nothing suggested itself. I felt ashamed and miserable, then. I believed that the hour of my disgrace was come, and that in another moment I should go out of that place disgraced. I ought to be ashamed to confess it, but my next thought was, not how I could win the compassion of kindly hearts by going out humbly and in sorrow for my misdoings, but how I could go out most sensationally and spectacularly.

There was a rusty and empty old revolver lying on the table, among the "properties" employed in the performances. On Mayday, two or three weeks before, there had been a celebration by the schools, and I had had a quarrel with a big boy who was the school-bully, and I had not come out of it with credit. That boy was now seated in the middle of the house, half-way down the main aisle. I crept stealthily and impressively toward the table, with a dark and murderous scowl on my face, copied from a popular romance, seized the revolver suddenly, flourished it, shouted the bully's name, jumped off the platform, and made a rush for him and chased him out of the house before the paralyzed people could interfere to save him. There was a storm of applause, and the magician, addressing the house, said, most impressively –

"That you may know how really remarkable this is, and how wonderfully developed a subject we have in this boy, I assure you that without a single spoken word to guide him he has carried out what I mentally commanded him to do, to the minutest detail. I could have stopped him at a moment in his vengeful career by a mere exertion of my will, therefore the poor fellow who has escaped was at no time in danger."

So I was not in disgrace. I returned to the platform a hero, and happier than I have ever been in this world since. As regards mental suggestion, my fears of it were gone. I judged that in case I failed to guess what the professor might be willing me to do, I could count on putting up something that would answer just as well. I was right, and exhibitions of unspoken suggestion became a favorite with the public. Whenever I perceived that I was being willed to do something I got up and did something – anything that occurred to me – and the magician, not being a fool, always ratified it. When people asked me, "How *can* you tell what he is willing you to do?" I said, "It's just as easy," and they always said, admiringly, "Well it beats *me* how you can do it."

Hicks was weak in another detail. When the professor made passes over him and said "his whole body is without sensation now – come forward and test him, ladies and gentlemen," the ladies and gentlemen always complied eagerly, and stuck pins into Hicks, and if they went deep Hicks was sure to wince, then that poor professor would have to explain that Hicks "wasn't sufficiently under the influence." But I didn't wince; I only suffered, and shed tears on the inside. The miseries that a conceited boy will endure to keep up his "reputation"! And so will a conceited man; I know it in my own person, and have seen it in a hundred thousand others. That professor ought to have protected me, and I often hoped he would, when the tests were unusually severe, but he didn't. It may be that he was deceived as well as the others, though I did not believe it nor think it possible. Those were dear good people, but they must have carried simplicity and credulity to the limit. They would stick a pin in my arm and bear on it until they drove it a third of its length in, and then be lost in wonder that by a mere exercise of willpower the professor could turn my arm to iron and make it insensible to pain. Whereas it was not insensible at all; I was suffering agonies of pain.

After that fourth night, that proud night, that triumphant night, I was the only subject. Simmons invited no more candidates to the platform. I performed alone, every night, the rest of the fortnight. In the beginning of the second week I conquered the last doubters. Up to that time a dozen wise old heads, the intellectual aristocracy of the town, had held out, as implacable unbelievers. I was as hurt by this as if I were engaged in some honest occupation. There is nothing surprising about this. Human beings feel dishonor the most, sometimes, when they most deserve it. That handful of over-wise old gentlemen kept on shaking their heads all the first week, and saying they had seen no marvels there that could not have been produced by collusion; and they were pretty vain of their unbelief, too, and liked to show it and air it, and be superior to the ignorant and the gullible. Particularly old Dr. Peake, who was the ring-leader of the irreconcilables, and very formidable; for he was an F.F.V., he was learned, white-haired and venerable, nobly and richly clad in the fashions of an earlier and a courtlier day, he was large and stately, and he not only seemed wise, but was what he seemed, in that regard. He had great influence, and his opinion upon any matter was worth much more than that of any other person in the community. When I conquered him, at last, I knew I was undisputed master of the field; and now, after more than fifty years, I acknowledge, with a few dry old tears, that I rejoiced without shame.

[*Dictated December 2, 1906.*] In 1847 we were living in a large white house on the corner of Hill and Main Streets – a house that still stands, but isn't large now, although it hasn't lost a plank; I saw it a year ago and noticed that shrinkage. My father died in it in March of the year mentioned, but our family did not move out of it until some months afterward. Ours was not the only family in the house, there was another – Dr. Grant's. One day Dr. Grant and Dr. Reyburn argued a matter on the street with sword-canes, and Grant was brought home multifariously punctured. Old Dr. Peake calked the leaks, and came every day for a while, to look after him. The Grants were Virginians, like Peake, and one day when Grant was getting well enough to be on his feet and sit around in the parlor and talk, the conversation fell upon Virginia and old times. I was present, but the group were probably quite unconscious of me, I being only a lad and a negligible quantity. Two of the group – Dr. Peake and Mrs. Crawford, Mrs. Grant's mother – had been of the audience when the Richmond theatre burned down, thirty-six years before, and they talked over the frightful details of that memorable tragedy. These were eye-witnesses, and with their eyes I saw it all with an intolerable vividness: I saw the black smoke rolling and tumbling toward the sky, I saw the flames burst through it and turn red, I heard the shrieks of the despairing, I glimpsed their faces at the windows, caught fitfully through the veiling smoke, I saw them jump to their death, or to mutilation worse than death. The picture is before me yet, and can never fade.

In due course they talked of the colonial mansion of the Peakes, with its stately columns and its spacious grounds, and by odds and ends I picked up a clearly defined idea of the place. I was strongly interested, for I had not before heard of such palatial things from the lips of people who had seen them with their own eyes. One detail, casually dropped, hit my imagination hard. In the wall, by the great front door, there was a round hole as big as a saucer – a British cannon-ball had made it, in the war of the Revolution. It

was breath-taking; it made history real; history had never been real
to me before.

Very well, three or four years later, as already mentioned, I was
king-bee and sole "subject" in the mesmeric show; it was the
beginning of the second week; the performance was half over; just
then the majestic Dr. Peake, with his ruffled bosom and wristbands
and his gold-headed cane, entered, and a deferential citizen
vacated his seat beside the Grants and made the great chief take
it. This happened while I was trying to invent something fresh in
the way of a vision, in response to the professor's remark –

"Concentrate your powers. Look – look attentively. There –
don't you see something? Concentrate – concentrate. Now then –
describe it."

Without suspecting it, Dr. Peake, by entering the place, had
reminded me of the talk of three years before. He had also furnished me capital and was become my confederate, an accomplice
in my frauds. I began on a vision, a vague and dim one (that was
part of the game at the beginning of a vision; it isn't best to see
it too clearly at first, it might look as if you had come loaded
with it). The vision developed, by degrees, and gathered swing,
momentum, energy. It was the Richmond fire. Dr. Peake was cold,
at first, and his fine face had a trace of polite scorn in it; but when
he began to recognize that fire, that expression changed, and his
eyes began to light up. As soon as I saw that, I threw the valves
wide open and turned on all the steam, and gave those people a
supper of fire and horrors that was calculated to last them one
while! They couldn't gasp, when I got through – they were petrified. Dr. Peake had risen, and was standing, – and breathing hard.
He said, in a great voice –

"My doubts are ended. No collusion could produce that miracle. It was totally impossible for him to know those details, yet he
has described them with the clarity of an eyewitness – and with
what unassailable truthfulness God knows I know!"

I saved the colonial mansion for the last night, and solidified and
perpetuated Dr. Peake's conversion with the cannon-ball hole. He
explained to the house that I could never have heard of that small
detail, which differentiated this mansion from all other Virginian
mansions and perfectly identified it, therefore the fact stood
proven that I had *seen* it in my vision. Lawks!

It is curious. When the magician's engagement closed there was
but one person in the village who did not believe in mesmerism,

and I was the one. All the others were converted, but I was to remain an implacable and unpersuadable disbeliever in mesmerism and hypnotism for close upon fifty years. This was because I never would examine them, in after life. I couldn't. The subject revolted me. Perhaps because it brought back to me a passage in my life which for pride's sake I wished to forget; though I thought – or persuaded myself I thought – I should never come across a "proof" which wasn't thin and cheap, and probably had a fraud like me behind it.

The truth is, I did not have to wait long to get tired of my triumphs. Not thirty days, I think. The glory which is built upon a lie soon becomes a most unpleasant incumbrance. No doubt for a while I enjoyed having my exploits told and retold and told again in my presence and wondered over and exclaimed about, but I quite distinctly remember that there presently came a time when the subject was wearisome and odious to me and I could not endure the disgusting discomfort of it. I am well aware that the world-glorified doer of a deed of great and real splendor has just my experience; I know that he deliciously enjoys hearing about it for three or four weeks, and that pretty soon after that he begins to dread the mention of it, and by and by wishes he had been with the damned before he ever thought of doing that deed; I remember how General Sherman used to rage and swear over "When we were Marching through Georgia," which was played at him and sung at him everywhere he went; still, I think I suffered a shade more than the legitimate hero does, he being privileged to soften his misery with the reflection that his glory was at any rate golden and reproachless in its origin, whereas I had no such privilege, there being no possible way to make mine respectable.

How easy it is to make people believe a lie, and how hard it is to undo that work again! Thirty-five years after those evil exploits of mine I visited my old mother, whom I had not seen for ten years; and being moved by what seemed to me a rather noble and perhaps heroic impulse, I thought I would humble myelf and confess my ancient fault. It cost me a great effort to make up my mind; I dreaded the sorrow that would rise in her face, and the shame that would look out of her eyes; but after long and troubled reflection, the sacrifice seemed due and right, and I gathered my resolution together and made the confession.

To my astonishment there were no sentimentalities, no dramatics, no George Washington effects; she was not moved in the least degree; she simply did not believe me, and said so! I was not merely disappointed, I was nettled, to have my costly truthfulness flung out of the market in this placid and confident way when I was expecting to get a profit out of it. I asserted, and reasserted, with rising heat, my statement that every single thing I had done on those long-vanished nights was a lie and a swindle; and when she shook her head tranquilly and said she knew better, I put up my hand and *swore* to it – adding a triumphant "*Now* what do you say?"

It did not affect her at all; it did not budge her the fraction of an inch from her position. If this was hard for me to endure, it did not begin with the blister she put upon the raw when she began to put my sworn oath out of court with *arguments* to prove that I was under a delusion and did not know what I was talking about. Arguments! Arguments to show that a person on a man's outside can know better what is on his inside than he does himself! I had cherished some contempt for arguments before, I have not enlarged my respect for them since. She refused to believe that I had invented my visions myself; she said it was folly: that I was only a child at the time and could not have done it. She cited the Richmond fire and the colonial mansion and said they were quite beyond my capacities. Then I saw my chance! I said she was right – I didn't invent those, I got them from Dr. Peake. Even this great shot did no damage. She said Dr. Peake's evidence was better than mine, and he had said in plain words that it was impossible for me to have heard about those things. Dear, dear, what a grotesque and unthinkable situation: a confessed swindler convicted of honesty and condemned to acquittal by circumstantial evidence furnished by the swindled!

I realized, with shame and with impotent vexation, that I was defeated all along the line. I had but one card left, but it was a formidable one. I played it – and stood from under. It seemed ignoble to demolish her fortress, after she had defended it so valiantly; but the defeated know not mercy. I played that master card. It was the pin-sticking. I said, solemnly –

"I give you my honor, a pin was never stuck into me without causing me cruel pain."

She only said –

"It is thirty-five years. I believe you do think that, *now*, but I was there, and I know better. You never winced."

She was so calm! and I was so far from it, so nearly frantic.

"Oh, my goodness!" I said, "let me *show* you that I am speaking

the truth. Here is my arm; drive a pin into it – drive it to the head
– I shall not wince."

She only shook her gray head and said, with simplicity and conviction –

"You are a man, now, and could dissemble the hurt; but you
were only a child then, and could not have done it."

And so the lie which I played upon her in my youth remained
with her as an unchallengeable truth to the day of her death. Carlyle said "a lie cannot live." It shows that he did not know how to
tell them. If I had taken out a life policy on this one the premiums
would have bankrupted me ages ago.

PART X

JANUARY 18, 1907

[*Dictated March 28, 1906.*] Orion Clemens was born in Jamestown,
Fentress County, Tennessee, in 1825. He was the family's first-
born, and antedated me ten years. Between him and me came a
sister, Margaret, who died, aged ten, in 1837, in that village of
Florida, Missouri, where I was born; and Pamela, mother of
Samuel E. Moffett, who was an invalid all her life and died in the
neighborhood of New York a year ago, aged about seventy-five.
Her character was without blemish, and she was of a most kindly
and gentle disposition. Also there was a brother, Benjamin, who
died in 1848 aged ten or twelve.

Orion's boyhood was spent in that wee little log hamlet of
Jamestown up there among the "knobs" – so called – of East Tennessee. The family migrated to Florida, Missouri, then moved to
Hannibal, Missouri, when Orion was twelve and a half years old.
When he was fifteen or sixteen he was sent to St. Louis and there
he learned the printer's trade. One of his characteristics was
eagerness. He woke with an eagerness about some matter or other
every morning; it consumed him all day; it perished in the night
and he was on fire with a fresh new interest next morning before
he could get his clothes on. He exploited in this way three hundred
and sixty-five red-hot new eagernesses every year of his life. But I
am forgetting another characteristic, a very pronounced one. That
was his deep glooms, his despondencies, his despairs; these had

their place in each and every day along with the eagernesses. Thus his day was divided – no, not divided, mottled – from sunrise to midnight with alternating brilliant sunshine and black cloud. Every day he was the most joyous and hopeful man that ever was, I think, and also every day he was the most miserable man that ever was.

While he was in his apprenticeship in St. Louis, he got well acquainted with Edward Bates, who was afterwards in Mr. Lincoln's first cabinet. Bates was a very fine man, an honorable and upright man, and a distinguished lawyer. He patiently allowed Orion to bring to him each new project; he discussed it with him and extinguished it by argument and irresistible logic – at first. But after a few weeks he found that this labor was not necessary; that he could leave the new project alone and it would extinguish itself the same night. Orion thought he would like to become a lawyer. Mr. Bates encouraged him, and he studied law nearly a week, then of course laid it aside to try something new. He wanted to become an orator. Mr. Bates gave him lessons. Mr. Bates walked the floor reading from an English book aloud and rapidly turning the English into French, and he recommended this exercise to Orion. But as Orion knew no French, he took up that study and wrought at it like a volcano for two or three days; then gave it up. During his apprenticeship in St. Louis he joined a number of churches, one after another, and taught in their Sunday-schools – changing his Sunday-school every time he changed his religion. He was correspondingly erratic in his politics – Whig to-day, Democrat next week, and anything fresh that he could find in the political market the week after. I may remark here that throughout his long life he was always trading religions and enjoying the change of scenery. I will also remark that his sincerity was never doubted; his truthfulness was never doubted; and in matters of business and money his honesty was never questioned. Notwithstanding his forever-recurring caprices and changes, his principles were high, always high, and absolutely unshakable. He was the strangest compound that ever got mixed in a human mould. Such a person as that is given to acting upon impulse and without reflection; that was Orion's way. Everything he did he did with conviction and enthusiasm and with a vainglorious pride in the thing he was doing – and no matter what that thing was, whether good, bad or indifferent, he repented of it every time in sackcloth and ashes before twenty-four hours had sped. Pessimists are born, not made.

Optimists are born, not made. But I think he was the only person I have ever known in whom pessimism and optimism were lodged in exactly equal proportions. Except in the matter of grounded principle, he was as unstable as water. You could dash his spirits with a single word; you could raise them into the sky again with another one. You could break his heart with a word of disapproval; you could make him as happy as an angel with a word of approval. And there was no occasion to put any sense or any vestige of mentality of any kind into these miracles; anything you might say would answer.

He had another conspicuous characteristic, and it was the father of those which I have just spoken of. This was an intense lust for approval. He was so eager to be approved, so girlishly anxious to be approved by anybody and everybody, without discrimination, that he was commonly ready to forsake his notions, opinions and convictions at a moment's notice in order to get the approval of any person who disagreed with them. I wish to be understood as reserving his fundamental principles all the time. He never forsook those to please anybody. Born and reared among slaves and slaveholders, he was yet an abolitionist from his boyhood to his death. He was always truthful; he was always sincere; he was always honest and honorable. But in light matters – matters of small consequence, like religion and politics and such things – he never acquired a conviction that could survive a disapproving remark from a cat.

He was always dreaming; he was a dreamer from birth, and this characteristic got him into trouble now and then.

Once when he was twenty-three or twenty-four years old, and was become a journeyman, he conceived the romantic idea of coming to Hannibal without giving us notice, in order that he might furnish to the family a pleasant surprise. If he had given notice, he would have been informed that we had changed our residence and that that gruff old bass-voiced sailorman, Dr. G., our family physician, was living in the house which we had formerly occupied and that Orion's former room in that house was now occupied by Dr. G.'s two middle-aged maiden sisters. Orion arrived at Hannibal per steamboat in the middle of the night, and started with his customary eagerness on his excursion, his mind all on fire with his romantic project and building and enjoying his surprise in advance. He was always enjoying things in advance; it was the make of him. He never could wait for the event, but must build it out of dream-stuff and enjoy it beforehand – consequently sometimes when the event happened he saw that it was not as good as the one he had invented in his imagination, and so he had lost profit by not keeping the imaginary one and letting the reality go.

When he arrived at the house he went around to the back door and slipped off his boots and crept up-stairs and arrived at the room of those elderly ladies without having wakened any sleepers. He undressed in the dark and got into bed and snuggled up against somebody. He was a little surprised, but not much – for he thought it was our brother Ben. It was winter, and the bed was comfortable, and the supposed Ben added to the comfort – and so he was dropping off to sleep very well satisfied with his progress so far and full of happy dreams of what was going to happen in the morning. But something else was going to happen sooner than that, and it happened now. The maid that was being crowded fumed and fretted and struggled and presently came to a half-waking condition and protested against the crowding. That voice paralyzed Orion. He couldn't move a limb; he couldn't get his breath; and the crowded one discovered his new whiskers and began to scream. This removed the paralysis, and Orion was out of bed and clawing round in the dark for his clothes in a fraction of a second. Both maids began to scream, then, so Orion did not wait to get his whole wardrobe. He started with such parts of it as he could grab. He flew to the head of the stairs and started down, and was paralyzed again at that point, because he saw the faint yellow flame of a candle soaring up the stairs from below and he judged that Dr. G. was behind it, and he was. He had no clothes on to speak of, but no matter, he was well enough fixed for an occasion like this, because he had a butcher-knife in his hand. Orion shouted to him, and this saved his life, for the Doctor recognized his voice. Then in those deep-sea-going bass tones of his that I used to admire so much when I was a little boy, he explained to Orion the change that had been made, told him where to find the Clemens family, and closed with some quite unnecessary advice about posting himself before he undertook another adventure like that – advice which Orion probably never needed again as long as he lived.

One bitter December night, Orion sat up reading until three o'clock in the morning and then, without looking at a clock, sallied forth to call on a young lady. He hammered and hammered at the door; couldn't get any response; didn't understand it. Anybody else would have regarded that as an indication of some kind or other and would have drawn inferences and gone home. But Orion didn't draw inferences, he merely hammered and hammered, and finally the father of the girl appeared at the door in a dressing-gown. He had a candle in his hand and the dressing-gown was all the clothing he had on – except an expression of unwelcome which was so thick and so large that it extended all down his front to his instep and nearly obliterated the dressing-gown. But Orion didn't notice that this was an unpleasant expression. He merely walked in. The old gentleman took him into the parlor, set the candle on a table, and stood. Orion made the usual remarks about the weather and sat down – sat down and talked and talked and went on talking – that old man looking at him vindictively and waiting for his chance – waiting treacherously and malignantly for his chance. Orion had not asked for the young lady. It was not customary. It was understood that a young fellow came to see the girl of the house, not the founder of it. At last Orion got up and made some remark to the effect that probably the young lady was busy and he would go now and call again. That was the old man's chance, and he said with fervency "Why good land, aren't you going to stop to breakfast?"

Orion did not come to Hannibal until two or three years after my father's death. Meantime he remained in St. Louis. He was a journeyman printer and earning wages. Out of his wage he supported my mother and my brother Henry, who was two years younger than I. My sister Pamela helped in this support by taking piano pupils. Thus we got along, but it was pretty hard sledding. I was not one of the burdens, because I was taken from school at once, upon my father's death, and placed in the office of the Hannibal "Courier," as printer's apprentice, and Mr. S., the editor and proprietor of the paper, allowed me the usual emolument of the office of apprentice – that is to say board and clothes, but no money. The clothes consisted of two suits a year, but one of the suits always failed to materialize and the other suit was not purchased so long as Mr. S.'s old clothes held out. I was only about half as big as Mr. S., consequently his shirts gave me the uncomfortable sense of living in a circus tent, and I had to turn up his pants to my ears to make them short enough.

There were two other apprentices. One was Steve Wilkins, seventeen or eighteen years old and a giant. When he was in Mr. S.'s clothes they fitted him as the candle-mould fits the candle – thus he was generally in a suffocated condition, particularly in the summer-time. He was a reckless, hilarious, admirable creature; he had no principles, and was delightful company. At first we three apprentices had to feed in the kitchen with the old slave cook and her very handsome and bright and well-behaved young mulatto daughter. For his own amusement – for he was not generally laboring for other people's amusement – Steve was constantly and persistently and loudly and elaborately making love to that mulatto girl and distressing the life out of her and worrying the old mother to death. She would say, "Now, Marse Steve, Marse Steve, can't you behave yourself?" With encouragement like that, Steve would naturally renew his attentions and emphasize them. It was killingly funny to Ralph and me. And, to speak truly, the old mother's distress about it was merely a pretence. She quite well understood that by the customs of slaveholding communities it was Steve's right to make love to that girl if he wanted to. But the girl's distress was very real. She had a refined nature, and she took all Steve's extravagant love-making in resentful earnest.

We got but little variety in the way of food at that kitchen table, and there wasn't enough of it anyway. So we apprentices used to keep alive by arts of our own – that is to say, we crept into the cellar nearly every night, by a private entrance which we had discovered, and we robbed the cellar of potatoes and onions and such things, and carried them down-town to the printing-office, where we slept on pallets on the floor, and cooked them at the stove and had very good times.

As I have indicated, Mr. S.'s economies were of a pretty close and rigid kind. By and by, when we apprentices were promoted from the basement to the ground floor and allowed to sit at the family table, along with the one journeyman, Harry H., the economies continued. Mrs S. was a bride. She had attained to that distinction very recently, after waiting a good part of a lifetime for it, and she was the right woman in the right place, according to the economics of the place, for she did not trust the sugar-bowl to us, but sweetened our coffee herself. That is, she went through the motions. She didn't really sweeten it. She seemed to put one heaping teaspoonful of brown sugar into each cup, but, according to Steve, that was a deceit. He said she dipped the spoon in the coffee first to make the sugar stick, and then scooped the sugar out of the bowl with the spoon upside down, so that the effect to the eye was a heaped-up spoon, whereas the sugar on it was nothing but a layer. This all seems perfectly true to me, and yet that thing would be so difficult to perform that I suppose it really didn't happen, but was one of Steve's lies.

PART XI

FEBRUARY 1, 1907

[*Dictated March 28th, 1906.*] About 1849 or 1850 Orion severed his connection with the printing-house in St. Louis and came up to Hannibal, and bought a weekly paper called the Hannibal "Journal," together with its plant and its good-will, for the sum of five hundred dollars cash. He borrowed the cash at ten per cent. interest, from an old farmer named Johnson who lived five miles out of town. Then he reduced the subscription price of the paper from two dollars to one dollar. He reduced the rates for advertising in about the same proportion, and thus he created one absolute and unassailable certainty – to wit: that the business would never pay him a single cent of profit. He took me out of the "Courier" office and engaged my services in his own at three dollars and a half a week, which was an extravagant wage, but Orion was always generous, always liberal with everybody except himself. It cost him nothing in my case, for he never was able to pay me a penny as long as I was with him. By the end of the first year he found he must make some economies. The office rent was cheap, but it was not cheap enough. He could not afford to pay rent of any kind, so he moved the whole plant into the house we lived in, and it cramped the dwelling-place cruelly. He kept that paper alive during four years, but I have at this time no idea how he accomplished it. Toward the end of each year he had to turn out and scrape and scratch for the fifty dollars of interest due Mr. Johnson, and that fifty dollars was about the only cash he ever received or paid out, I suppose, while he was proprietor of that newspaper, except for ink and printing-paper. The paper was a dead failure. It had to be that from the start. Finally he handed it over to Mr. Johnson, and went up to Muscatine, Iowa, and acquired a small interest in a weekly newspaper there. It was not a sort of property to marry on – but no matter. He came across a winning and pretty girl who lived in Quincy, Illinois, a few miles below Keokuk, and they became engaged. He was always falling in love with girls, but by some accident or other he had never gone so far as engagement before. And now he achieved nothing but misfortune by it, because he straightway fell in love with a Keokuk girl. He married the Keokuk girl and they began a struggle for life which turned out to be a difficult enterprise, and very unpromising.

To gain a living in Muscatine was plainly impossible, so Orion and his new wife went to Keokuk to live, for she wanted to be near her relatives. He bought a little bit of a job-printing plant – on credit, of course – and at once put prices down to where not even the apprentices could get a living out of it, and this sort of thing went on.

I had not joined the Muscatine migration. Just before that happened (which I think was in 1853) I disappeared one night and fled to St. Louis. There I worked in the composing-room of the "Evening News" for a time, and then started on my travels to see the world. The world was New York City, and there was a little World's Fair there. It had just been opened where the great reservoir afterward was, and where the sumptuous public library is now being built – Fifth Avenue and Forty-second Street. I arrived in New York with two or three dollars in pocket change and a ten-dollar bank-bill concealed in the lining of my coat. I got work at villainous wages in the establishment of John A. Gray and Green in Cliff Street, and I found board in a sufficiently villainous mechanics' boarding-house in Duane Street. The firm paid my wages in wildcat money at its face value, and my week's wage merely sufficed to pay board and lodging. By and by I went to Philadelphia and worked there some months as a "sub" on the "Inquirer" and the "Public Ledger." Finally I made a flying trip to Washington to see the sights there, and in 1854 I went back to the Mississippi Valley, sitting upright in the smoking-car two or three days and nights. When I reached St. Louis I was exhausted. I went to bed on board a steamboat that was bound for Muscatine. I fell asleep at once, with my clothes on, and didn't wake again for thirty-six hours.

... I worked in that little job-office in Keokuk as much as two years, I should say, without ever collecting a cent of wages, for Orion was never able to pay anything – but Dick Higham and I had good times. I don't know what Dick got, but it was probably only uncashable promises.

One day in the midwinter of 1856 or 1857 – I think it was 1856 – I was coming along the main street of Keokuk in the middle of

the forenoon. It was bitter weather – so bitter that that street was
deserted, almost. A light dry snow was blowing here and there on
the ground and on the pavement, swirling this way and that way
and making all sorts of beautiful figures, but very chilly to look at.
The wind blew a piece of paper past me and it lodged against a
wall of a house. Something about the look of it attracted my attention and I gathered it in. It was a fifty-dollar bill, the only one I had
ever seen, and the largest assemblage of money I had ever encountered in one spot. I advertised it in the papers and suffered more
than a thousand dollars' worth of solicitude and fear and distress
during the next few days lest the owner should see the advertisement and come and take my fortune away. As many as four
days went by without an applicant; then I could endure this kind
of misery no longer. I felt sure that another four could not go by
in this safe and secure way. I felt that I must take that money out
of danger. So I bought a ticket for Cincinnati and went to that city.
I worked there several months in the printing-office of Wrightson
and Company. I had been reading Lieutenant Herndon's account
of his explorations of the Amazon and had been mightily attracted
by what he said of coca. I made up my mind that I would go to the
head waters of the Amazon and collect coca and trade in it and
make a fortune. I left for New Orleans in the steamer "Paul Jones"
with this great idea filling my mind. One of the pilots of that boat
was Horace Bixby. Little by little I got acquainted with him, and
pretty soon I was doing a lot of steering for him in his daylight
watches. When I got to New Orleans I inquired about ships leaving
for Pará and discovered that there weren't any, and learned that
there probably wouldn't be any during that century. It had not
occurred to me to inquire about these particulars before leaving
Cincinnati, so there I was. I couldn't get to the Amazon. I had no
friends in New Orleans and no money to speak of. I went to Horace
Bixby and asked him to make a pilot out of me. He said he would
do it for a hundred dollars cash in advance. So I steered for him
up to St. Louis, borrowed the money from my brother-in-law and
closed the bargain. I had acquired this brother-in-law several years
before. This was Mr. William A. Moffett, a merchant, a Virginian
– a fine man in every way. He had married my sister Pamela, and
the Samuel E. Moffett of whom I have been speaking was their
son. Within eighteen months I became a competent pilot, and
I served that office until the Mississippi River traffic was brought
to a standstill by the breaking out of the civil war.

... Meantime Orion had gone down the river and established his little job-printing-office in Keokuk. On account of charging next to nothing for the work done in his job-office, he had almost nothing to do there. He was never able to comprehend that work done on a profitless basis deteriorates and is presently not worth anything, and that customers are then obliged to go where they can get better work, even if they must pay better prices for it. He had plenty of time, and he took up Blackstone again. He also put up a sign which offered his services to the public as a lawyer. He never got a case, in those days, nor even an applicant, although he was quite willing to transact law business for nothing and furnish the stationery himself. He was always liberal that way.

Presently he moved to a wee little hamlet called Alexandria, two or three miles down the river, and he put up that sign there. He got no custom. He was by this time very hard aground. But by this time I was beginning to earn a wage of two hundred and fifty dollars a month as pilot, and so I supported him thenceforth until 1861, when his ancient friend, Edward Bates, then a member of Mr. Lincoln's first cabinet, got him the place of Secretary of the new Territory of Nevada, and Orion and I cleared for that country in the overland stage-coach, I paying the fares, which were pretty heavy, and carrying with me what money I had been able to save – this was eight hundred dollars, I should say – and it was all in silver coin and a good deal of a nuisance because of its weight. And we had another nuisance, which was an Unabridged Dictionary. It weighed about a thousand pounds, and was a ruinous expense, because the stage-coach Company charged for extra baggage by the ounce. We could have kept a family for a time on what that dictionary cost in the way of extra freight – and it wasn't a good dictionary anyway – didn't have any modern words in it – only had obsolete ones that they used to use when Noah Webster was a child.

The Government of the new Territory of Nevada was an interesting menagerie. Governor Nye was an old and seasoned politician from New York – politician, not statesman. He had white hair; he was in fine physical condition; he had a winningly friendly face and deep lustrous brown eyes that could talk as a native language the tongue of every feeling, every passion, every emotion. His eyes could outtalk his tongue, and this is saying a good deal, for he was a very remarkable talker, both in private and on the stump. He was a shrewd man; he generally saw through surfaces and perceived what was going on inside without being suspected of having an eye on the matter.

When grown-up persons indulge in practical jokes, the fact gauges them. They have lived narrow, obscure, and ignorant lives, and at full manhood they still retain and cherish a job-lot of left-over standards and ideals that would have been discarded with their boyhood if they had then moved out into the world and a broader life. There were many practical jokers in the new Territory. I do not take pleasure in exposing this fact, for I liked those people; but what I am saying is true. I wish I could say a kindlier thing about them instead – that they were burglars, or hat-rack thieves, or something like that, that wouldn't be utterly uncomplimentary. I would prefer it, but I can't say those things, they would not be true. These people were practical jokers, and I will not try to disguise it. In other respects they were plenty good-enough people; honest people; reputable and likable. They played practical jokes upon each other with success, and got the admiration and applause and also the envy of the rest of the community. Naturally they were eager to try their arts on big game, and that was what the Governor was. But they were not able to score. They made several efforts, but the Governor defeated these efforts without any trouble and went on smiling his pleasant smile as if nothing had happened. Finally the joker chiefs of Carson City and Virginia City conspired together to see if their combined talent couldn't win a victory, for the jokers were getting into a very uncomfortable place: the people were laughing at them, instead of at their proposed victim. They banded themselves together to the number of ten and invited the Governor to what was a most extraordinary attention in those days – pickled oyster stew and champagne – luxuries very seldom seen in that region, and existing rather as fabrics of the imagination than as facts.

The Governor took me with him. He said disparagingly,

"It's a poor invention. It doesn't deceive. Their idea is to get me drunk and leave me under the table, and from their standpoint this will be very funny. But they don't know me. I am familiar with champagne and have no prejudices against it."

The fate of the joke was not decided until two o'clock in the morning. At that hour the Governor was serene, genial, comfortable, contented, happy and sober, although he was so full that he couldn't laugh without shedding champagne tears. Also, at that hour the last joker joined his comrades under the table, drunk to the last perfection. The Governor remarked,

"This is a dry place, Sam, let's go and get something to drink and go to bed."

The Governor's official menagerie had been drawn from the humblest ranks of his constituents at home – harmless good fellows who had helped in his campaigns, and now they had their reward in petty salaries payable in greenbacks that were worth next to nothing. Those boys had a hard time to make both ends meet. Orion's salary was eighteen hundred dollars a year, and he couldn't even support his dictionary on it. But the Irishwoman who had come out on the Governor's staff charged the menagerie only ten dollars a week apiece for board and lodging. Orion and I were of her boarders and lodgers; and so, on these cheap terms the silver I had brought from home held out very well.

At first I roamed about the country seeking silver, but at the end of '62 or the beginning of '63 when I came up from Aurora to begin a journalistic life on the Virginia City "Enterprise," I was presently sent down to Carson City to report the legislative session. Orion was soon very popular with the members of the legislature, because they found that whereas they couldn't usually trust each other, nor anybody else, they could trust him. He easily held the belt for honesty in that country, but it didn't do him any good in a pecuniary way, because he had no talent for either persuading or scaring legislators. But I was differently situated. I was there every day in the legislature to distribute compliment and censure with evenly balanced justice and spread the same over half a page of the "Enterprise" every morning, consequently I was an influence. I got the legislature to pass a wise and very necessary law requiring every corporation doing business in the Territory to record its charter in full, without skipping a word, in a record to be kept by the Secretary of the Territory – my brother. All the charters were framed in exactly the same words. For this record-service he was authorized to charge forty cents a folio of one hundred words for making the record; also five dollars for furnishing a certificate of each record, and so on. Everybody had a toll-road franchise but no toll-road. But the franchise had to be recorded and paid for. Everybody was a mining corporation, and had to have himself recorded and pay for it. Very well, we prospered. The record-service paid an average of a thousand dollars a month, in gold.

Governor Nye was often absent from the Territory. He liked to run down to San Francisco every little while and enjoy a rest from Territorial civilization. Nobody complained, for he was prodigiously popular. He had been a stage-driver in his early days in New York or New England, and had acquired the habit of remembering names and faces, and of making himself agreeable to his passengers. As a politician this had been valuable to him, and he kept his arts in good condition by practice. By the time he had been Governor a year, he had shaken hands with every human being in the Territory of Nevada, and after that he always knew these people instantly at sight and could call them by name. The whole population, of 20,000 persons, were his personal friends, and he could do anything he chose to do and count upon their being contented with it. Whenever he was absent from the Territory – which was generally – Orion served his office in his place, as Acting Governor, a title which was soon and easily shortened to "Governor." He recklessly built and furnished a house at a cost of twelve thousand dollars, and there was no other house in the sage-brush capital that could approach this property for style and cost.

When Governor Nye's four-year term was drawing to a close, the mystery of why he had ever consented to leave the great State of New York and help inhabit that jack-rabbit desert was solved: he had gone out there in order to become a United States Senator. All that was now necessary was to turn the Territory into a State. He did it without any difficulty. That undeveloped country and that sparse population were not well fitted for the heavy burden of a State Government, but no matter, the people were willing to have the change, and so the Governor's game was made.

Orion's game was made too, apparently, for he was as popular because of his honesty as the Governor was for more substantial reasons; but at the critical moment the inborn capriciousness of his character rose up without warning, and disaster followed.

PART XII
FEBRUARY 15, 1907

ORION CLEMENS — RESUMED

[*Dictated April 5, 1906.*] There were several candidates for all the offices in the gift of the new State of Nevada save two – United States Senator, and Secretary of State. Nye was certain to get a Senatorship, and Orion was so sure to get the Secretaryship that no one but him was named for that office. But he was hit with one of his spasms of virtue on the very day that the Republican party was to make its nominations in the Convention, and refused to go near the Convention. He was urged, but all persuasions failed. He said his presence there would be an unfair and improper influence and that if he was to be nominated the compliment must come to him as a free and unspotted gift. This attitude would have settled his case for him without further effort, but he had another attack of virtue on the same day, that made it absolutely sure. It had been his habit for a great many years to change his religion with his shirt, and his ideas about temperance at the same time. He would be a teetotaler for a while and the champion of the cause; then he would change to the other side for a time. On nomination day he suddenly changed from a friendly attitude toward whiskey – which was the popular attitude – to uncompromising teetotalism, and went absolutely dry. His friends besought and implored, but all in vain. He could not be persuaded to cross the threshold of a saloon. The paper next morning contained the list of chosen nominees. His name was not in it. He had not received a vote.

His rich income ceased when the State government came into power. He was without an occupation. Something had to be done. He put up his sign as attorney-at-law, but he got no clients. It was strange. It was difficult to account for. I cannot account for it – but if I were going to guess at a solution I should guess that by the make of him he would examine both sides of a case so diligently and so conscientiously that when he got through with his argument neither he nor a jury would know which side he was on. I think that his client would find out his make in laying his case before him, and would take warning and withdraw it in time to save himself from probable disaster.

I had taken up my residence in San Francisco about a year

before the time I have just been speaking of. One day I got a tip from Mr. Camp, a bold man who was always making big fortunes in ingenious speculations and losing them again in the course of six months by other speculative ingenuities. Camp told me to buy some shares in the Hale and Norcross. I bought fifty shares at three hundred dollars a share. I bought on a margin, and put up twenty per cent. It exhausted my funds. I wrote Orion and offered him half, and asked him to send his share of the money. I waited and waited. He wrote and said he was going to attend to it. The stock went along up pretty briskly. It went higher and higher. It reached a thousand dollars a share. It climbed to two thousand, then to three thousand; then to twice that figure. The money did not come, but I was not disturbed. By and by that stock took a turn and began to gallop down. Then I wrote urgently. Orion answered that he had sent the money long ago – said he had sent it to the Occidental Hotel. I inquired for it. They said it was not there. To cut a long story short, that stock went on down until it fell below the price I had paid for it. Then it began to eat up the margin, and when at last I got out I was very badly crippled.

When it was too late, I found out what had become of Orion's money. Any other human being would have sent a check, but he sent gold. The hotel clerk put it in the safe and went on vacation, and there it had reposed all this time enjoying its fatal work, no doubt. Another man might have thought to tell me that the money was not in a letter, but was in an express package, but it never occurred to Orion to do that.

Later, Mr. Camp gave me another chance. He agreed to buy our Tennessee land for two hundred thousand dollars, pay a part of the amount in cash and give long notes for the rest. His scheme was to import foreigners from grape-growing and wine-making districts in Europe, settle them on the land, and turn it into a wine-growing country. He knew what Mr. Longworth thought of those Tennessee grapes, and was satisfied. I sent the contracts and things to Orion for his signature, he being one of the three heirs. But they arrived at a bad time – in a doubly bad time, in fact. The temperance virtue was temporarily upon him in strong force, and he wrote and said that he would not be a party to debauching the country with wine. Also he said how could he know whether Mr. Camp was going to deal fairly and honestly with those poor people from Europe or not? – and so, without waiting to find out, he quashed the whole trade, and there it fell, never to be brought to life again. The land, from being suddenly worth two hundred thousand dollars, became as suddenly worth what it was before – nothing, and taxes to pay. I had paid the taxes and the other expenses for some years, but I dropped the Tennessee land there, and have never taken any interest in it since; pecuniarily or otherwise, until yesterday.

I had supposed, until yesterday, that Orion had frittered away the last acre, and indeed that was his own impression. But a gentleman arrived yesterday from Tennessee and brought a map showing that by a correction of the ancient surveys we still own a thousand acres, in a coal district, out of the hundred thousand acres which my father left us when he died in 1847. The gentleman brought a proposition; also he brought a reputable and well-to-do citizen of New York. The proposition was that the Tennesseean gentleman should sell that land; that the New York gentleman should pay all the expenses and fight all the lawsuits, in case any should turn up, and that of such profit as might eventuate the Tennesseean gentleman should take a third, the New-Yorker a third, and Sam Moffett and his sister and I – who are surviving heirs – the remaining third.

This time I hope we shall get rid of the Tennessee land for good and all and never hear of it again.

I came East in January, 1867. Orion remained in Carson City perhaps a year longer. Then he sold his twelve-thousand-dollar house and its furniture for thirty-five hundred in greenbacks at about sixty per cent. discount. He and his wife took passage in the steamer for home in Keokuk. About 1871 or '72 they came to New York. Orion had been trying to make a living in the law ever since he had arrived from the Pacific Coast, but he had secured only two cases. Those he was to try free of charge – but the possible result will never be known, because the parties settled the cases out of court without his help.

Orion got a job as proof-reader on the New York "Evening Post" at ten dollars a week. By and by he came to Hartford and wanted me to get him a place as reporter on a Hartford paper. Here was a chance to try my scheme again, and I did it. I made him go to the Hartford "Evening Post," without any letter of introduction, and propose to scrub and sweep and do all sorts of things for nothing, on the plea that he didn't need money but only needed work, and that that was what he was pining for. Within six weeks he was on the editorial staff of that paper at twenty dollars a week, and he was worth the money. He was presently called for by some other paper at better wages, but I made him go to the "Post" people and tell them about it. They stood the raise and kept him. It was the pleasantest berth he had ever had in his life. It was an easy berth. He was in every way comfortable. But ill-luck came. It was bound to come.

A new Republican daily was to be started in a New England city by a stock company of well-to-do politicians, and they offered him the chief editorship at three thousand a year. He was eager to accept. My beseechings and reasonings went for nothing. I said,

"You are as weak as water. Those people will find it out right away. They will easily see that you have no backbone; that they can deal with you as they would deal with a slave. You may last six months, but not longer. Then they will not dismiss you as they would dismiss a gentleman: they will fling you out as they would fling out an intruding tramp."

It happened just so. Then he and his wife migrated to Keokuk once more. Orion wrote from there that he was not resuming the law; that he thought that what his health needed was the open air, in some sort of outdoor occupation; that his father-in-law had a strip of ground on the river border a mile above Keokuk with some sort of a house on it, and his idea was to buy that place and start a chicken-farm and provide Keokuk with chickens and eggs, and perhaps butter – but I don't know whether you can raise butter on a chicken-farm or not. He said the place could be had for three thousand dollars cash, and I sent the money. He began to raise chickens, and he made a detailed monthly report to me, whereby it appeared that he was able to work off his chickens on the Keokuk people at a dollar and a quarter a pair. But it also appeared that it cost a dollar and sixty cents to raise the pair. This did not seem to discourage Orion, and so I let it go. Meantime he was borrowing a hundred dollars per month of me regularly, month by month. Now to show Orion's stern and rigid business ways – and he really prided himself on his large business capacities – the moment he received the advance of a hundred dollars at the beginning of each month, he always sent me his note for the amount, and with it he sent, *out of that money, three months' interest* on the hundred dollars at six per cent. per annum, these notes being always for three months.

As I say, he always sent a detailed statement of the month's profit and loss on the chickens – at least the month's loss on the chickens – and this detailed statement included the various items of expense

– corn for the chickens, boots for himself, and so on; even car fares, and the weekly contribution of ten cents to help out the missionaries who were trying to damn the Chinese after a plan not satisfactory to those people.

I think the poultry experiment lasted about a year, possibly two years. It had then cost me six thousand dollars.

Orion returned to the law business, and I suppose he remained in that harness off and on for the succeeding quarter of a century, but so far as my knowledge goes he was only a lawyer in name, and had no clients.

My mother died, in her eighty-eighth year, in the summer of 1890. She had saved some money, and she left it to me, because it had come from me. I gave it to Orion and he said, with thanks, that I had supported him long enough and now he was going to relieve me of that burden, and would also hope to pay back some of that expense, and maybe the whole of it. Accordingly, he proceeded to use up that money in building a considerable addition to the house, with the idea of taking boarders and getting rich. We need not dwell upon this venture. It was another of his failures. His wife tried hard to make the scheme succeed, and if anybody could have made it succeed she would have done it. She was a good woman, and was greatly liked. She had a practical side, and she would have made that boarding-house lucrative if circumstances had not been against her.

Orion had other projects for recouping me, but as they always required capital I stayed out of them, and they did not materialize. Once he wanted to start a newspaper. It was a ghastly idea, and I squelched it with a promptness that was almost rude. Then he invented a wood-sawing machine and patched it together himself, and he really sawed wood with it. It was ingenious; it was capable; and it would have made a comfortable little fortune for him; but just at the wrong time Providence interfered again. Orion applied for a patent and found that the same machine had already been patented and had gone into business and was thriving.

Presently the State of New York offered a fifty-thousand-dollar prize for a practical method of navigating the Erie Canal with steam canal-boats. Orion worked at that thing for two or three years, invented and completed a method, and was once more ready to reach out and seize upon imminent wealth when somebody pointed out a defect: his steam canal-boat could not be used in the winter-time; and in the summer-time the commotion its wheels would make in the water would wash away the State of New York on both sides.

Innumerable were Orion's projects for acquiring the means to pay off the debt to me. These projects extended straight through the succeeding thirty years, but in every case they failed. During all those thirty years his well-established honesty kept him in offices of trust where other people's money had to be taken care of, but where no salary was paid. He was treasurer of all the benevolent institutions; he took care of the money and other property of widows and orphans; he never lost a cent for anybody, and never made one for himself. Every time he changed his religion the church of his new faith was glad to get him; made him treasurer at once, and at once he stopped the graft and the leaks in that church. He exhibited a facility in changing his political complexion that was a marvel to the whole community. Once the following curious thing happened, and he wrote me all about it himself.

One morning he was a Republican, and upon invitation he agreed to make a campaign speech at the Republican mass-meeting that night. He prepared the speech. After luncheon he became a Democrat and agreed to write a score of exciting mottoes to be painted upon the transparencies which the Democrats would carry in their torchlight procession that night. He wrote these shouting Democratic mottoes during the afternoon, and they occupied so much of his time that it was night before he had a chance to change his politics again; so he actually made a rousing Republican campaign speech in the open air while his Democratic transparencies passed by in front of him, to the joy of every witness present.

He was a most strange creature – but in spite of his eccentricities he was beloved, all his life, in whatsoever community he lived. And he was also held in high esteem, for at bottom he was a sterling man.

About twenty-five years ago – along there somewhere – I suggested to Orion that he write an autobiography. I asked him to try to tell the straight truth in it; to refrain from exhibiting himself in creditable attitudes exclusively, and to honorably set down all the incidents of his life which he had found interesting to him, including those which were burned into his memory because he was ashamed of them. I said that this had never been done, and that if he could do it his autobiography would be a most valuable piece of literature. I said I was offering him a job which I could not duplicate in my own case, but I would cherish the hope that he might succeed with it. I recognize now that I was trying to saddle upon him an impossibility. I have been dictating this autobiography of mine daily for three months; I have thought of fifteen hundred or two thousand incidents in my life which I am ashamed of, but I have not gotten one of them to consent to go on paper yet. I think that that stock will still be complete and unimpaired when I finish these memoirs, if I ever finish them. I believe that if I should put in all or any of those incidents I should be sure to strike them out when I came to revise this book.

Orion wrote his autobiography and sent it to me. But great was my disappointment; and my vexation, too. In it he was constantly making a hero of himself, exactly as I should have done and am doing now, and he was constantly forgetting to put in the episodes which placed him in an unheroic light. I knew several incidents of his life which were distinctly and painfully unheroic, but when I came across them in his autobiography they had changed color. They had turned themselves inside out, and were things to be intemperately proud of. In my dissatisfaction I destroyed a considerable part of that autobiography. But in what remains there are passages which are interesting, and I shall quote from them here and there and now and then, as I go along.

While we were living in Vienna in 1898 a cablegram came from Keokuk announcing Orion's death. He was seventy-two years old. He had gone down to the kitchen in the early hours of a bitter December morning; he had built the fire, and had then sat down at a table to write something; and there he died, with the pencil in his hand and resting against the paper in the middle of an unfinished word – an indication that his release from the captivity of a long and troubled and pathetic and unprofitable life was mercifully swift and painless.

[*Dictated in 1904.*] A quarter of a century ago I was visiting John Hay at Whitelaw Reid's house in New York, which Hay was occupying for a few months while Reid was absent on a holiday in Europe. Temporarily also, Hay was editing Reid's paper, the New York "Tribune." I remember two incidents of that Sunday visit particularly well. I had known John Hay a good many years, I had known him when he was an obscure young editorial writer on the "Tribune" in Horace Greeley's time, earning three or four times the salary he got, considering the high character of the work which came from his pen. In those earlier days he was a picture to look at, for beauty of feature, perfection of form and grace of carriage and movement. He had a charm about him of a sort quite unusual to my Western ignorance and inexperience – a charm of manner, intonation, apparently native and unstudied elocution, and all that – the groundwork of it native, the ease of it, the polish of it, the winning naturalness of it, acquired in Europe where he had been Chargé d'Affaires some time at the Court of Vienna. He was joyous and cordial, a most pleasant comrade. One of the two incidents above referred to as marking that visit was this:

In trading remarks concerning our ages I confessed to forty-two and Hay to forty. Then he asked if I had begun to write my autobiography, and I said I hadn't. He said that I ought to begin at once, and that I had already lost two years. Then he said in substance this:

"At forty a man reaches the top of the hill of life and starts down on the sunset side. The ordinary man, the average man, not to particularize too closely and say the commonplace man, has at that age succeeded or failed; in either case he has lived all of his life that is likely to be worth recording; also in either case the life lived is worth setting down, and cannot fail to be interesting if he comes as near to telling the truth about himself as he can. And he *will* tell the truth in spite of himself, for his facts and his fictions will work loyally together for the protection of the reader; each fact and each fiction will be a dab of paint, each will fall in its right place, and together they will paint his portrait; not the portrait *he* thinks they are painting, but his real portrait, the inside of him, the soul of him, his character. Without intending to lie he will lie all the time; not bluntly, consciously, not dully unconsciously, but half-consciously – consciousness in twilight; a soft and gentle and merciful twilight which makes his general form comely, with his virtuous prominences and projections discernible and his ungracious ones in shadow. His truths will be recognizable as truths, his modifications of facts which would tell against him will go for nothing, the reader will see the fact through the film and know his man.

"There is a subtle devilish something or other about autobiographical composition that defeats all the writer's attempts to paint his portrait *his* way."

Hay meant that he and I were ordinary average commonplace people, and I did not resent my share of the verdict, but nursed my wound in silence. His idea that we had finished our work in life, passed the summit and were westward bound downhill, with me two years ahead of him and neither of us with anything further to do as benefactors to mankind, was all a mistake. I had written four books then, possibly five. I have been drowning the world in literary wisdom ever since, volume after volume; since that day's sun went down he has been the historian of Mr. Lincoln, and his book will never perish; he has been ambassador, brilliant orator, competent and admirable Secretary of State.

PART XIII

MARCH 1, 1907

... As I have said, that vast plot of Tennessee land was held by my father twenty years – intact. When he died in 1847, we began to manage it ourselves. Forty years afterward, we had managed it all away except 10,000 acres, and gotten nothing to remember the sales by. About 1887 – possibly it was earlier – the 10,000 went. My brother found a chance to trade it for a house and lot in the town of Corry, in the oil regions of Pennsylvania. About 1894 he sold this property for $250. That ended the Tennessee Land.

If any penny of cash ever came out of my father's wise investment but that, I have no recollection of it. No, I am overlooking a detail. It furnished me a field for Sellers and a book. Out of my half of the book I got $15,000 or $20,000; out of the play I got $75,000 or $80,000 – just about a dollar an acre. It is curious: I was not alive when my father made the investment, therefore he was not intending any partiality; yet I was the only member of the family that ever profited by it. I shall have occasion to mention this land again, now and then, as I go along, for it influenced our life in one way or another during more than a generation. Whenever things grew dark it rose and put out its hopeful Sellers hand and cheered us up, and said "Do not be afraid – trust in me – wait." It kept us hoping and hoping, during forty years, and forsook us at last. It put our energies to sleep and made visionaries of us – dreamers and indolent. We were always going to be rich next year – no occasion to work. It is good to begin life poor; it is good to begin life rich – these are wholesome; but to begin it *prospectively* rich! The man who has not experienced it cannot imagine the curse of it.

My parents removed to Missouri in the early thirties; I do not remember just when, for I was not born then, and cared nothing for such things. It was a long journey in those days, and must have been a rough and tiresome one. The home was made in the wee village of Florida, in Monroe county, and I was born there in 1835. The village contained a hundred people and I increased the population by one per cent. It is more than the best man in history ever did for any other town. It may not be modest in me to refer to this, but it is true. There is no record of a person doing as much – not even Shakespeare. But I did it for Florida, and it shows that I could have done it for any place – even London, I suppose.

Recently some one in Missouri has sent me a picture of the house I was born in. Heretofore I have always stated that it was a palace, but I shall be more guarded, now.

I remember only one circumstance connected with my life in it. I remember it very well, though I was but two and a half years old at the time. The family packed up everything and started in wagons for Hannibal, on the Mississippi, thirty miles away. Toward night, when they camped and counted up the children, one was missing. I was the one. I had been left behind. Parents ought always to count the children before they start. I was having a good enough time playing by myself until I found that the doors were fastened and that there was a grisly deep silence brooding over the place. I knew, then, that the family were gone, and that they had forgotten me. I was well frightened, and I made all the noise I could, but no one was near and it did no good. I spent the afternoon in captivity and was not rescued until the gloaming had fallen and the place was alive with ghosts.

My brother Henry was six months old at that time. I used to remember his walking into a fire outdoors when he was a week old. It was remarkable in me to remember a thing like that, which occurred when I was so young. And it was still more remarkable that I should cling to the delusion, for thirty years, that I *did* remember it – for of course it never happened; he would not have been able to walk at that age. If I had stopped to reflect, I should not have burdened my memory with that impossible rubbish so long. It is believed by many people that an impression deposited in a child's memory within the first two years of its life cannot remain there five years, but that is an error. The incident of Benvenuto Cellini and the salamander must be accepted as authentic and trustworthy; and then that remarkable and indisputable instance in the experience of Helen Keller – however, I will speak of that at another time. For many years I believed that I remembered helping my grandfather drink his whiskey toddy when I was six weeks old, but I do not tell about that any more, now; I am grown old, and my memory is not as active as it used to be. When I was younger I could remember anything, whether it had happened or not; but my faculties are decaying, now, and soon I shall be so I cannot remember any but the things that happened. It is sad to go to pieces like this, but we all have to do it.

My uncle, John. A. Quarles, was a farmer, and his place was in the country four miles from Florida. He had eight children, and fifteen or twenty negroes, and was also fortunate in other ways. Particularly in his character. I have not come across a better man than he was. I was his guest for two or three months every year, from the fourth year after we removed to Hannibal till I was eleven or twelve years old. I have never consciously used him or his wife in a book, but his farm has come very handy to me in literature, once or twice. In "Huck Finn" and in "Tom Sawyer Detective" I moved it down to Arkansas. It was all of six hundred miles, but it was no trouble, it was not a very large farm; five hundred acres, perhaps, but I could have done it if it had been twice as large. And as for the morality of it, I cared nothing for that; I would move a State if the exigencies of literature required it.

It was a heavenly place for a boy, that farm of my uncle John's. The house was a double log one, with a spacious floor (roofed in) connecting it with the kitchen. In the summer the table was set in the middle of that shady and breezy floor, and the sumptuous meals – well, it makes me cry to think of them. Fried chicken, roast pig, wild and tame turkeys, ducks and geese; venison just killed; squirrels, rabbits, pheasants, partridges, prairie-chickens; biscuits, hot batter cakes, hot buckwheat cakes, hot "wheat bread," hot rolls, hot corn pone; fresh corn boiled on the ear, succotash, butter-beans, string-beans, tomatoes, pease, Irish potatoes, sweet-potatoes; buttermilk, sweet milk, "clabber"; watermelons, muskmelons, cantaloups – all fresh from the garden – apple pie, peach pie, pumpkin pie, apple dumplings, peach cobbler – I can't remember the rest. The way that the things were cooked was perhaps the main splendor – particularly a certain few of the dishes. For instance, the corn bread, the hot biscuits and wheat bread, and the fried chicken. These things have never been properly cooked in the North – in fact, no one there is able to learn the art, so far as my experience goes. The North thinks it knows how to make corn bread, but this is gross superstition. Perhaps no bread in the world is quite as good as Southern corn bread, and perhaps no bread in the world is quite so bad as the Northern imitation of it. The North seldom tries to fry chicken, and this is well; the art cannot be learned north of the line of Mason and Dixon, nor anywhere in Europe. This is not hearsay; it is experience that is speaking. In Europe it is imagined that the custom of serving various kinds of bread blazing hot is "American," but that is too broad a spread; it is custom in the South, but is much less than that in the North. In the North and in Europe hot bread is considered unhealthy. This is probably another fussy superstition, like the European superstition that ice-water is unhealthy. Europe does not need ice-water, and does not drink it; and yet, notwithstanding this, its word for it is better than ours, because it describes it, whereas ours doesn't. Europe calls it "iced" water. Our word describes water made from melted ice – a drink which we have but little acquaintance with.

It seems a pity that the world should throw away so many good things merely because they are unwholesome. I doubt if God has given us any refreshment which, taken in moderation, is unwholesome, except microbes. Yet there are people who strictly deprive themselves of each and every eatable, drinkable and smokable which has in any way acquired a shady reputation. They pay this price for health. And health is all they get for it. How strange it is; it is like paying out your whole fortune for a cow that has gone dry.

The farmhouse stood in the middle of a very large yard, and the yard was fenced on three sides with rails and on the rear side with high palings; against these stood the smokehouse; beyond the palings was the orchard; beyond the orchard were the negro quarter and the tobacco-fields. The front yard was entered over a stile, made of sawed-off logs of graduated heights; I do not remember any gate. In a corner of the front yard were a dozen lofty hickory-trees and a dozen black-walnuts, and in the nutting season riches were to be gathered there.

Down a piece, abreast the house, stood a little log cabin against the rail fence; and there the woody hill fell sharply away, past the barns, the corn-crib, the stables and the tobacco-curing house, to a limpid brook which sang along over its gravelly bed and curved and frisked in and out and here and there and yonder in the deep shade of overhanging foliage and vines – a divine place for wading, and it had swimming-pools, too, which were forbidden to us and therefore much frequented by us. For we were little Christian children, and had early been taught the value of forbidden fruit.

In the little log cabin lived a bedridden white-headed slave woman whom we visited daily, and looked upon with awe, for we believed she was upwards of a thousand years old and had talked with Moses. The younger negroes credited these statistics, and had furnished them to us in good faith. We accommodated all the details which came to us about her; and so we believed that she had lost her health in the long desert trip coming out of Egypt, and had never been able to get it back again. She had a round bald place on the crown of her head, and we used to creep around and gaze at it in reverent silence, and reflect that it was caused by fright through seeing Pharaoh drowned. We called her "Aunt" Hannah, Southern fashion. She was superstitious like the other negroes; also, like them, she was deeply religious. Like them, she had great faith in prayer, and employed it in all ordinary exigencies, but not in cases where a dead certainty of result was urgent. Whenever witches were around she tied up the remnant of her wool in little tufts, with white thread, and this promptly made the witches impotent.

All the negroes were friends of ours, and with those of our own age we were in effect comrades. I say in effect, using the phrase as a modification. We were comrades, and yet not comrades; color and condition interposed a subtle line which both parties were conscious of, and which rendered complete fusion impossible. We had a faithful and affectionate good friend, ally and adviser in "Uncle Dan'l," a middle-aged slave whose head was the best one in the negro quarter, whose sympathies were wide and warm, and whose heart was honest and simple and knew no guile. He has served me well, these many, many years. I have not seen him for more than half a century, and yet spiritually I have had his welcome company a good part of that time, and have staged him in books under his own name and as "Jim," and carted him all around – to Hannibal, down the Mississippi on a raft, and even across the Desert of Sahara in a balloon – and he has endured it all with the patience and friendliness and loyalty which were his birthright. It was on the farm that I got my strong liking for his race and my appreciation of certain of its fine qualities. This feeling and this estimate have stood the test of sixty years and more and have suffered no impairment. The black face is as welcome to me now as it was then.

In my schoolboy days I had no aversion to slavery. I was not
aware that there was anything wrong about it. No one arraigned
it in my hearing; the local papers said nothing against it; the local
pulpit taught us that God approved it, that it was a holy thing, and
that the doubter need only look in the Bible if he wished to settle
his mind – and then the texts were read aloud to us to make the
matter sure; if the slaves themselves had an aversion to slavery they
were wise and said nothing. In Hannibal we seldom saw a slave
misused; on the farm, never.

There was, however, one small incident of my boyhood days
which touched this matter, and it must have meant a good deal to
me or it would not have stayed in my memory, clear and sharp,
vivid and shadowless, all these slow-drifting years. We had a little
slave boy whom we had hired from some one, there in Hannibal.
He was from the Eastern Shore of Maryland, and had been
brought away from his family and his friends, half-way across the
American continent, and sold. He was a cheery spirit, innocent
and gentle, and the noisiest creature that ever was, perhaps. All
day long he was singing, whistling, yelling, whooping, laughing –
it was maddening, devastating, unendurable. At last, one day, I
lost all my temper, and went raging to my mother, and said Sandy
had been singing for an hour without a single break, and I
couldn't stand it, and *wouldn't* she please shut him up. The tears
came into her eyes, and her lip trembled, and she said something
like this –

"Poor thing, when he sings, it shows that he is not remembering,
and that comforts me; but when he is still, I am afraid he is thinking, and I cannot bear it. He will never see his mother again; if he
can sing, I must not hinder it, but be thankful for it. If you were
older, you would understand me; then that friendless child's noise
would make you glad."

It was a simple speech, and made up of small words, but it went
home, and Sandy's noise was not a trouble to me any more. She
never used large words, but she had a natural gift for making small
ones do effective work. She lived to reach the neighborhood of
ninety years, and was capable with her tongue to the last – especially when a meanness or an injustice roused her spirit. She has
come handy to me several times in my books, where she figures as
Tom Sawyer's "Aunt Polly." I fitted her out with a dialect, and
tried to think up other improvements for her, but did not find any.
I used Sandy once, also; it was in "Tom Sawyer"; I tried to get him

to whitewash the fence, but it did not work. I do not remember what name I called him by in the book.

I can see the farm yet, with perfect clearness. I can see all its belongings, all its details; the family room of the house, with a "trundle" bed in one corner and a spinning-wheel in another – a wheel whose rising and falling wail, heard from a distance, was the mournfulest of all sounds to me, and made me homesick and low-spirited, and filled my atmosphere with the wandering spirits of the dead; the vast fireplace, piled high, on winter nights, with flaming hickory logs from whose ends a sugary sap bubbled out but did not go to waste, for we scraped it off and ate it; the lazy cat spread out on the rough hearthstones, the drowsy dogs braced against the jambs and blinking; my aunt in one chimney-corner knitting, my uncle in the other smoking his corn-cob pipe; the slick and carpetless oak floor faintly mirroring the dancing flame-tongues and freckled with black indentations where fire-coals had popped out and died a leisurely death; half a dozen children romp-ing in the background twilight; "split"-bottomed chairs here and there, some with rockers; a cradle – out of service, but waiting, with confidence; in the early cold mornings a snuggle of children, in shirts and chemises, occupying the hearthstone and procrasti-nating – they could not bear to leave that comfortable place and go out on the wind-swept floor-space between the house and kitchen where the general tin basin stood, and wash.

Along outside of the front fence ran the country road; dusty in the summer-time, and a good place for snakes – they liked to lie in it and sun themselves; when they were rattlesnakes or puff adders, we killed them; when they were black snakes, or racers, or belonged to the fabled "hoop" breed, we fled, without shame; when they were "house snakes" or "garters" we carried them home and put them in Aunt Patsy's work-basket for a surprise; for she was prejudiced against snakes, and always when she took the basket in her lap and they began to climb out of it it disordered her mind. She never could seem to get used to them; her opportun-ities went for nothing. And she was always cold toward bats, too, and could not bear them; and yet I think a bat is as friendly a bird as there is. My mother was Aunt Patsy's sister, and had the same wild superstitions. A bat is beautifully soft and silky; I do not know any creature that is pleasanter to the touch, or is more grateful for caressings, if offered in the right spirit. I know all about these coleoptera, because our great cave, three miles below Hannibal, was multitudinously stocked with them, and often I brought them home to amuse my mother with. It was easy to manage if it was a school day, because then I had ostensibly been to school and hadn't any bats. She was not a suspicious person, but full of trust and confidence; and when I said "There's something in my coat pocket for you," she would put her hand in. But she always took it out again, herself; I didn't have to tell her. It was remarkable, the way she couldn't learn to like private bats.

I think she was never in the cave in her life; but everybody else went there. Many excursion parties came, from considerable distances up and down the river to visit the cave. It was miles in extent, and was a tangled wilderness of narrow and lofty clefts and passages. It was an easy place to get lost in; anybody could do it – including the bats. I got lost in it myself, along with a lady, and our last candle burned down to almost nothing before we glimpsed the search-party's lights winding about in the distance.

"Injun Joe" the half-breed got lost in there once, and would have starved to death if the bats had run short. But there was no chance of that; there were myriads of them. He told me all his story. In the book called "Tom Sawyer" I starved him entirely to death in the cave, but that was in the interest of art; it never happened. "General" Gaines, who was our first town drunkard before Jimmy Finn got the place, was lost in there for the space of a week, and finally pushed his handkerchief out of a hole in a hilltop near Saverton, several miles down the river from the cave's mouth, and somebody saw it and dug him out. There is nothing the matter with his statistics, except the handkerchief. I knew him for years, and he hadn't any. But it could have been his nose. That would attract attention.

Beyond the road where the snakes sunned themselves was a dense young thicket, and through it a dim-lighted path led a quarter of a mile; then out of the dimness one emerged abruptly upon a level great prairie which was covered with wild strawberry-plants, vividly starred with prairie pinks, and walled in on all sides by forests. The strawberries were fragrant and fine, and in the season we were generally there in the crisp freshness of the early morning, while the dew-beads still sparkled upon the grass and the woods were ringing with the first songs of the birds.

Down the forest slopes to the left were the swings. They were made of bark stripped from hickory saplings. When they became dry they were dangerous. They usually broke when a child was forty feet in the air, and this was why so many bones had to be mended every year. I had no ill-luck myself, but none of my cousins escaped. There were eight of them, and at one time and another they broke fourteen arms among them. But it cost next to nothing, for the doctor worked by the year – $25 for the whole family. I remember two of the Florida doctors, Chowning and Meredith. They not only tended an entire family for $25 a year, but furnished the medicines themselves. Good measure, too. Only the largest persons could hold a whole dose. Castor-oil was the principal beverage. The dose was half a dipperful, with half a dipperful of New Orleans molasses added to help it down and make it taste good, which it never did. The next standby was calomel; the next, rhubarb; and the next, jalap. Then they bled the patient, and put mustard-plasters on him. It was a dreadful system, and yet the death-rate was not heavy. The calomel was nearly sure to salivate the patient and cost him some of his teeth. There were no dentists. When teeth became touched with decay or were otherwise ailing, the doctor knew of but one thing to do: he fetched his tongs and dragged them out. If the jaw remained, it was not his fault.

Doctors were not called, in cases of ordinary illness; the family's grandmother attended to those. Every old woman was a doctor, and gathered her own medicines in the woods, and knew how to compound doses that would stir the vitals of a cast-iron dog. And then there was the "Indian doctor"; a grave savage, remnant of his tribe, deeply read in the mysteries of nature and the secret properties of herbs; and most backwoodsmen had high faith in his powers and could tell of wonderful cures achieved by him. In Mauritius, away off yonder in the solitudes of the Indian Ocean, there is a person who answers to our Indian doctor of the old times. He is a negro, and has had no teaching as a doctor, yet there is one disease which he is master of and can cure, and the doctors can't. They send for him when they have a case. It is a child's disease of a strange and deadly sort, and the negro cures it with a herb medicine which he makes, himself, from a prescription which has come down to him from his father and grandfather. He will not let any one see it. He keeps the secret of its components to himself, and it is feared that he will die without divulging it; then there will be consternation in Mauritius. I was told these things by the people there, in 1896.

We had the "faith doctor," too, in those early days – a woman. Her specialty was toothache. She was a farmer's old wife, and lived five miles from Hannibal. She would lay her hand on the patient's jaw and say "Believe!" and the cure was prompt. Mrs. Utterback. I remember her very well. Twice I rode out there behind my mother, horseback, and saw the cure performed. My mother was the patient.

Dr. Meredith removed to Hannibal, by and by, and was our family physician there, and saved my life several times. Still, he was a good man and meant well. Let it go.

I was always told that I was a sickly and precarious and tiresome and uncertain child, and lived mainly on allopathic medicines during the first seven years of my life. I asked my mother about this, in her old age – she was in her 88th year – and said:

"I suppose that during all that time you were uneasy about me?"

"Yes, the whole time."

"Afraid I wouldn't live?"

After a reflective pause – ostensibly to think out the facts –

"No – afraid you would."

It sounds like a plagiarism, but it probably wasn't. The country schoolhouse was three miles from my uncle's farm. It stood in a clearing in the woods, and would hold about twenty-five boys and girls. We attended the school with more or less regularity once or twice a week, in summer, walking to it in the cool of the morning by the forest paths, and back in the gloaming at the end of the day. All the pupils brought their dinners in baskets – corn-dodger, buttermilk and other good things – and sat in the shade of the trees at noon and ate them. It is the part of my education which I look back upon with the most satisfaction. My first visit to the school was when I was seven. A strapping girl of fifteen, in the customary sunbonnet and calico dress, asked me if I "used tobacco" – meaning did I chew it. I said, no. It roused her scorn. She reported me to all the crowd, and said –

"Here is a boy seven years old who can't chaw tobacco."

By the looks and comments which this produced, I realized that I was a degraded object; I was cruelly ashamed of myself. I determined to reform. But I only made myself sick; I was not able to learn to chew tobacco. I learned to smoke fairly well, but that did not conciliate anybody, and I remained a poor thing, and characterless. I longed to be respected, but I never was able to rise. Children have but little charity for each other's defects.

As I have said, I spent some part of every year at the farm until I was twelve or thirteen years old. The life which I led there with my cousins was full of charm, and so is the memory of it yet. I can call back the solemn twilight and mystery of the deep woods, the earthy smells, the faint odors of the wild flowers, the sheen of rain-washed foliage, the rattling clatter of drops when the wind shook the trees, the far-off hammering of wood-peckers and the muffled drumming of wood-pheasants in the remoteness of the forest, the snap-shot glimpses of disturbed wild creatures skurrying through the grass, – I can call it all back and make it as real as it ever was, and as blessed. I can call back the prairie, and its loneliness and peace, and a vast hawk hanging motionless in the sky, with his wings spread wide and the blue of the vault showing through the fringe of their end feathers. I can see the woods in their autumn dress, the oaks purple, the hickories washed with gold, the maples and the sumacs luminous with crimson fires, and I can hear the rustle made by the fallen leaves as we ploughed through them. I can see the blue clusters of wild grapes hanging amongst the foliage of the saplings, and I remember the taste of them and the smell. I know how the wild blackberries looked, and how they tasted; and the same with the pawpaws, the hazelnuts and the persimmons; and I can feel the thumping rain, upon my head, of hickory-nuts and walnuts when we were out in the frosty dawn to scramble for them with the pigs, and the gusts of wind loosed them and sent them down. I know the stain of blackberries, and how pretty it is; and I know the stain of walnut hulls, and how little it minds soap and water; also what grudged experience it had of either of them. I know the taste of maple sap, and when to gather it, and how to arrange the troughs and the delivery tubes, and how to boil down the juice, and how to hook the sugar after it is made; also how much better hooked sugar tastes than any that is honestly come by, let bigots say what they will. I know how a prize watermelon looks when it is sunning its fat rotundity among pumpkin-vines and "simblins"; I know how to tell when it is ripe without "plug-ging" it; I know how inviting it looks when it is cooling itself in a tub of water under the bed, waiting; I know how it looks when it lies on the table in the sheltered great floor-space between house and kitchen, and the children gathered for the sacrifice and their mouths watering; I know the crackling sound it makes when the carving-knife enters its end, and I can see the split fly along in front of the blade as the knife cleaves its way to the other end; I can see its halves fall apart and display the rich red meat and the black seeds, and the heart standing up, a luxury fit for the elect; I know how a boy looks, behind a yard-long slice of that melon, and I know how he feels; for I have been there. I know the taste of the watermelon which has been honestly come by, and I know the taste of the watermelon which has been acquired by art. Both taste good, but the experienced know which tastes best. I know the look of green apples and peaches and pears on the trees, and I know how entertaining they are when they are inside of a person. I know how ripe ones look when they are piled in pyramids under the trees, and how pretty they are and how vivid their colors. I know how a frozen apple looks, in a barrel down cellar in the winter-time, and how hard it is to bite, and how the frost makes the teeth ache, and yet how good it is, notwithstanding. I know the disposition of elderly people to select the specked apples for the children, and I once knew ways to beat the game. I know the look of an apple that is roasting and sizzling on a hearth on a winter's evening, and I know the comfort that comes of eating it hot, along with some sugar and a drench of cream. I know the delicate art and mystery of so cracking hickory-nuts and walnuts on a flatiron with a hammer that the kernels will be delivered whole, and I know how the nuts, taken in conjunction with winter apples, cider and doughnuts, make old people's tales and old jokes sound fresh and crisp and enchanting, and juggle an evening away before you know what went with the time. I know the look of Uncle Dan'l's kitchen as it was on privileged nights when I was a child, and I can see the white and black children grouped on the hearth, with the firelight playing on their faces and the shadows flickering upon the walls, clear back toward the cavernous gloom of the rear, and I can hear Uncle Dan'l telling the immortal tales which Uncle Remus Harris was to gather into his books and charm the world with, by and by; and I can feel again the creepy joy which quivered through me when the time for the ghost-story of the "Golden Arm" was reached – and the sense of regret, too, which came over me, for it was always the last story of the evening, and there was nothing between it and the unwelcome bed.

I can remember the bare wooden stairway in my uncle's house, and the turn to the left above the landing, and the rafters and the slanting roof over my bed, and the squares of moonlight on the floor, and the white cold world of snow outside, seen through the curtainless window. I can remember the howling of the wind and the quaking of the house on stormy nights; and how snug and cozy one felt, under the blankets, listening, and how the powdery snow used to sift in, around the sashes, and lie in little ridges on the floor, and make the place look chilly in the morning, and curb the wild desire to get up – in case there was any. I can remember how very dark that room was, in the dark of the moon, and how packed it was with ghostly stillness when one woke up by accident away in the night, and forgotten sins came flocking out of the secret chambers of the memory and wanted a hearing; and how ill chosen the time seemed for this kind of business; and how dismal was the hoo-hooing of the owl and the wailing of the wolf, sent mourning by on the night wind.

I remember the raging of the rain on that roof, summer nights, and how pleasant it was to lie and listen to it, and enjoy the white splendor of the lightning and the majestic booming and crashing of the thunder. It was a very satisfactory room; and there was a lightning-rod which was reachable from the window, an adorable and skittish thing to climb up and down, summer nights, when there were duties on hand of a sort to make privacy desirable.

I remember the 'coon and 'possum hunts, nights, with the negroes, and the long marches through the black gloom of the woods, and the excitement which fired everybody when the distant bay of an experienced dog announced that the game was treed; then the wild scramblings and stumblings through briars and bushes and over roots to get to the spot; then the lighting of a fire and the felling of the tree, the joyful frenzy of the dogs and the negroes, and the weird picture it all made in the red glare – I remember it all well, and the delight that every one got out of it, except the 'coon.

I remember the pigeon seasons, when the birds would come in millions, and cover the trees, and by their weight break down the branches. They were clubbed to death with sticks; guns were not necessary, and were not used. I remember the squirrel hunts, and the prairie-chicken hunts, and the wild-turkey hunts, and all that; and how we turned out, mornings, while it was still dark, to go on these expeditions, and how chilly and dismal it was, and how often I regretted that I was well enough to go. A toot on a tin horn brought twice as many dogs as were needed, and in their happiness they raced and scampered about, and knocked small people down, and made no end of unnecessary noise. At the word, they vanished away toward the woods, and we drifted silently after them in the melancholy gloom. But presently the gray dawn stole over the world, the birds piped up, then the sun rose and poured light and comfort all around, everything was fresh and dewy and fragrant, and life was a boon again. After three hours of tramping we arrived back wholesomely tired, overladen with game, very hungry, and just in time for breakfast.

PART XIV

MARCH 15, 1907

[*Dictated Thursday, December 6, 1906.*]

FROM SUSY'S BIOGRAPHY OF ME

FEB. 27, SUNDAY.

Clara's reputation as a baby was always a fine one, mine exactly the contrary. One often related story concerning her braveness as a baby and her own opinion of this quality of hers is this. Clara and I often got slivers in our hands and when mama took them out with a much dreaded needle, Clara was always very brave, and I very cowardly. One day Clara got one of these slivers in her hand, a very bad one, and while mama was taking it out, Clara stood perfectly still without even wincing; I saw how brave she was and turning to mamma said "Mamma isn't she a brave little thing!" presently mamma had to give the little hand quite a dig with the needle and noticing how perfectly quiet Clara was about it she exclaimed, Why Clara! you *are* a brave little thing! Clara responded "No bodys braver but God!" –

Clara's pious remark is the main detail, and Susy has accurately remembered its phrasing. The three-year-older's wound was of a formidable sort, and not one which the mother's surgery would have been equal to. The flesh of the finger had been burst by a cruel accident. It was the doctor that sewed it up, and to all appearances it was he, and the other independent witnesses, that did the main part of the suffering; each stitch that he took made Clara wince slightly, but it shrivelled the others.

I take pride in Clara's remark, because it shows that although she was only three years old, her fireside teachings were already making her a thinker – a thinker and also an observer of proportions. I am not claiming any credit for this. I furnished to the children worldly knowledge and wisdom, but was not competent to go higher, and so I left their spiritual education in the hands of the mother. A result of this modesty of mine was made manifest to me in a very striking way, some years afterward, when Jean was nine years old. We had recently arrived in Berlin, at the time, and had begun housekeeping in a furnished apartment. One morning at breakfast a vast card arrived – an invitation. To be precise, it was a command from the Emperor of Germany to come to dinner. During several months I had encountered socially, on the Continent, men bearing lofty titles; and all this while Jean was becoming more and more impressed, and awed, and subdued, by these imposing events, for she had not been abroad before, and they were new to her – wonders out of dreamland turned into realities. The imperial card was passed from hand to hand, around the table, and examined with interest; when it reached Jean she exhibited excitement and emotion, but for a time was quite speechless; then she said,

"Why, papa, if it keeps going on like this, pretty soon there won't be anybody left for you to get acquainted with but God."

It was not complimentary to think I was not acquainted in that quarter, but she was young, and the young jump to conclusions without reflection.

Necessarily, I did myself the honor to obey the command of the Emperor Wilhelm II. Prince Heinrich, and six or eight other guests were present. The Emperor did most of the talking, and he talked well, and in faultless English. In both of these conspicuousnesses I was gratified to recognize a resemblance to myself – a very exact resemblance; no, almost exact, but not quite that – a modified exactness, with the advantage in favour of the Emperor. My English, like his, is nearly faultless; like him I talk well; and when I have guests at dinner I prefer to do all the talking myself. It is the best way, and the pleasantest. Also the most profitable for the others.

I was greatly pleased to perceive that his Majesty was familiar with my books, and that his attitude toward them was not uncomplimentary. In the course of his talk he said that my best and most valuable book was "Old Times on the Mississippi." I will refer to that remark again, presently.

An official who was well up in the Foreign Office at that time, and had served under Bismarck for fourteen years, was still occupying his old place under Chancellor Caprivi. Smith, I will call him of whom I am speaking, though that is not his name. He was a special friend of mine, and I greatly enjoyed his society, although in order to have it it was necessary for me to seek it as late as midnight, and not earlier. This was because Government officials of his rank had to work all day, after nine in the morning, and then attend official banquets in the evening; wherefore they were usually unable to get life-restoring fresh air and exercise for their jaded minds and bodies earlier than midnight; then they turned out, in groups of two or three, and gratefully and violently tramped the deserted streets until two in the morning. Smith had been in the Government service, at home and abroad, for more than thirty years, and he was now sixty years old, or close upon it. He could not remember a year in which he had had a vacation of more than a fortnight's length; he was weary all through to the bones and the marrow, now, and was yearning for a holiday of a whole three months – yearning so longingly and so poignantly that he had at last made up his mind to make a desperate cast for it and stand the consequences, whatever they might be. It was against all rules to *ask* for a vacation – quite against all etiquette; the shock of it would paralyze the Chancellery; stern etiquette and usage required another form: the applicant was not privileged to ask for a vacation, he must send in his *resignation*. The chancellor would know that the applicant was not really trying to resign, and didn't want to resign, but was merely trying in this left-handed way to get a vacation.

The night before the Emperor's dinner I helped Smith take his exercise, after midnight, and he was full of his project. He had sent in his resignation that day, and was trembling for the result; and naturally, because it might possibly be that the chancellor would be happy to fill his place with somebody else, in which case he could accept the resignation without comment and without offence. Smith was in a very anxious frame of mind; not that he feared that Caprivi was dissatisfied with him, for he had no such fear; it was the Emperor that he was afraid of; he did not know how he stood with the Emperor. He said that while apparently it was Caprivi who would decide his case, it was in reality the Emperor who would perform that service; that the Emperor kept personal watch upon everything, and that no official sparrow could fall to the ground without his privity and consent; that the resignation would be laid before his Majesty, who would accept it or decline to accept it, according to his pleasure, and that then his pleasure in the matter would be communicated by Caprivi. Smith said he would know his fate the next evening, after the imperial dinner; that when I should escort his Majesty into the large salon contiguous to the dining-room, I would find there about thirty men – Cabinet ministers, admirals, generals and other great officials of the Empire – and that these men would be standing talking together in little separate groups of two or three persons; that the Emperor would move from group to group and say a word to each, sometimes two words, sometimes ten words; and that the length of his speech, whether brief or not so brief, would indicate the exact standing in the Emperor's regard, of the man accosted; and that by observing this thermometer an expert could tell, to half a degree, the state of the imperial weather in each case; that in Berlin, as in the imperial days of Rome, the Emperor was the sun, and that his smile or his frown meant good fortune or disaster to the man upon whom it should fall. Smith suggested that I watch the thermometer while the Emperor went his rounds of the groups; and added that if his Majesty talked four minutes with any person there present, it meant high favor, and that the sun was in the zenith, and cloudless, for that man.

I mentally recorded that four-minute altitude, and resolved to see if any man there on that night stood in sufficient favor to achieve it.

Very well. After the dinner I watched the Emperor while he passed from group to group, and privately I timed him with a watch. Two or three times he came near to reaching the four-minute altitude, but always he fell short a little. The last man he came to was Smith. He put his hand on Smith's shoulder and began to talk to him; and when he finished, the thermometer had scored seven minutes! The company then moved toward the smoking-room, where cigars, beer and anecdotes would be in brisk service until midnight, and as Smith passed me he whispered,

"That settles it. The chancellor will ask me how much of a vacation I want, and I sha'n't be afraid to raise the limit. I shall call for six months."

Smith's dream had been to spend his three months' vacation – in case he got a vacation instead of the other thing – in one of the great capitals of the Continent – a capital whose name I shall suppress, at present. The next day the chancellor asked him how much of a vacation he wanted, and where he desired to spend it. Smith told him. His prayer was granted, and rather more than granted. The chancellor augmented his salary and attached him to the German Embassy of that selected capital, giving him a place of high dignity bearing an imposing title, and with nothing to do except attend banquets of an extraordinary character at the Embassy, once or twice a year. The term of his vacation was not specified; he was to continue it until requested to come back to his work in the Foreign Office. This was in 1891. Eight years later Smith was passing through Vienna, and he called upon me. There had been no interruption of his vacation, as yet, and there was no likelihood that an interruption of it would occur while he should still be among the living.

[*Dictated Monday, December 17, 1906.*] As I have already remarked, "Old Times on the Mississippi" got the Kaiser's best praise. It was after midnight when I reached home; I was usually out until toward midnight, and the pleasure of being out late was poisoned, every night, by the dread of what I must meet at my front door – an indignant face, a resentful face, the face of the *portier*. The *portier* was a tow-headed young German, twenty-two or three years old; and it had been for some time apparent to me that he did not enjoy being hammered out of his sleep, nights, to let me in. He never had a kind word for me, nor a pleasant look. I couldn't understand it, since it was his business to be on watch and let the occupants of the several flats in at any and all hours of the night. I could not see why he so distinctly failed to get reconciled to it.

The fact is, I was ignorantly violating, every night, a custom in which he was commercially interested. I did not suspect this. No one had told me of the custom, and if I had been left to guess it, it would have taken me a very long time to make a success of it. It was a custom which was so well established and so universally recognized, that it had all the force and dignity of law. By authority of this custom, whosoever entered a Berlin house after ten at night must pay a trifling toll to the *portier* for breaking his sleep to let him in. This tax was either two and a half cents or five cents, I don't remember which; but I had never paid it, and didn't know I owed it, and as I had been residing in Berlin several weeks, I was so far in arrears that my presence in the German capital was getting to be a serious disaster to that young fellow.

I arrived from the imperial dinner sorrowful and anxious, made my presence known and prepared myself to wait in patience the tedious minute or two which the *portier* usually allowed himself to keep me tarrying – as a punishment. But this time there was no stage-wait; the door was instantly unlocked, unbolted, unchained and flung wide; and in it appeared the strange and welcome apparition of the *portier's* round face all sunshine and smiles and welcome, in place of the black frowns and hostility that I was expecting. Plainly he had not come out of his bed: he had been waiting for me, watching for me. He began to pour out upon me in the most enthusiastic and energetic way a generous stream of German welcome and homage, meanwhile dragging me excitedly to his small bedroom beside the front door; there he made me bend down over a row of German translations of my books and said,

"There – you wrote them! I have found it out! By God, I did not know it before, and I ask a million pardons! That one there, the 'Old Times on the Mississippi,' is the best book you ever wrote!"

The usual number of those curious accidents which we call co-incidences have fallen to my share in this life, but for pictur-esqueness this one puts all the others in the shade: that a crowned head and a *portier*, the very top of an empire and the very bottom of it, should pass the very same criticism and deliver the very same verdict upon a book of mine – and almost in the same hour and the same breath – is a coincidence which out-coincidences any coincidence which I could have imagined with such powers of imagination as I have been favored with; and I have not been accustomed to regard them as being small or of an inferior quality. It is always a satisfaction to me to remember that whereas I do not know, for sure, what any other nation thinks of any one of my twenty-three volumes, I do at least know for a certainty what one nation of fifty millions thinks of one of them, at any rate; for if the mutual verdict of the top of an empire and the bottom of it does not establish for good and all the judgment of the entire nation concerning that book, then the axiom that we can get a sure estimate of a thing by arriving at a general average of all the opinions involved, is a fallacy.

[*Dictated Monday, February 10, 1907.*] Two months ago (December 6) I was dictating a brief account of a private dinner in Berlin, where the Emperor of Germany was host and I the chief guest. Something happened day before yesterday which moves me to take up that matter again.

At the dinner his Majesty chatted briskly and entertainingly along in easy and flowing English, and now and then he inter-rupted himself to address a remark to me, or to some other indi-vidual of the guests. When the reply had been delivered, he resumed his talk. I noticed that the table etiquette tallied with that which was the law of my house at home when we had guests: that is to say, the guests answered when the host favored them with a remark, and then quieted down and behaved themselves until they got another chance. If I had been in the Emperor's chair and he in mine, I should have felt infinitely comfortable and at home, and should have done a world of talking, and done it well; but I was guest now, and consequently I felt less at home. From old experience, I was familiar with the rules of the game, and familiar with their exercise from the high place of host; but I was not familiar with the trammelled and less satisfactory position of guest, therefore I felt a little strange and out of place. But there was no animosity – no, the Emperor was host, therefore according to my own rule he had a right to do the talking, and it was my honorable duty to intrude no interruptions or other improvements, except upon invitation; and of course it could be *my* turn some day: some day, on some friendly visit of inspection to America, it might be my pleasure and distinction to have him as guest at my table; then I would give him a rest, and a remarkably quiet time.

In one way there was a difference between his table and mine – for instance, atmosphere; the guests stood in awe of him, and naturally they conferred that feeling upon me, for, after all, I am only human, although I regret it. When a guest answered a question he did it with deferential voice and manner; he did not put any emotion into it, and he did not spin it out, but got it out of his system as quickly as he could, and then looked relieved. The Emperor was used to this atmosphere, and it did not chill his blood; maybe it was an inspiration to him, for he was alert, brilliant and full of animation; also he was most gracefully and felicitously complimentary to my books, – and I will remark here that the happy phrasing of a compliment is one of the rarest of human gifts, and the happy delivery of it another. In that other chapter I mentioned the high compliment which he paid to the book, "Old Times on the Mississippi," but there were other; among them some gratifying praise of my description in "A Tramp Abroad" of certain striking phases of German student life. I mention these things here because I shall have occasion to hark back to them presently.

[*Dictated Tuesday, February 12, 1907.*]

* * *

Those stars indicate the long chapter which I dictated yesterday, a chapter which is much too long for magazine purposes, and therefore must wait until this Autobiography shall appear in book form, five years hence, when I am dead: five years according to my calculation, twenty-seven years according to the prediction furnished me a week ago by the latest and most confident of all the palmists who have ever read my future in my hand. The Emperor's dinner, and its beer-and-anecdote appendix, covered six hours of diligent industry, and this accounts for the extraordinary length of that chapter.

A couple of days ago a gentleman called upon me with a message. He had just arrived from Berlin, where he had been acting for our Government in a matter concerning tariff revision, he being a member of the commission appointed by our Government to conduct our share of the affair. Upon the completion of the commission's labors, the Emperor invited the members of it to an audience, and in the course of the conversation he made a reference to me; continuing, he spoke of my chapter on the German language in "A Tramp Abroad," and characterized it by an adjective which is too complimentary for me to repeat here without bringing my modesty under suspicion. Then he paid some compliments to "The Innocents Abroad," and followed these with the remark that my account in one of my books of certain striking phases of German student life was the best and truest that had ever been written. By this I perceive that he remembers that dinner of sixteen years ago, for he said the same thing to me about the student-chapter at that time. Next he said he wished this gentleman to convey two messages to America from him and deliver them – one to the President, the other to me. The wording of the message to me was:

"Convey to Mr. Clemens my kindest regards. Ask him if he remembers that dinner, and ask him why he didn't do any talking."

Why, how could I talk when he was talking? He "held the age," as the poker-clergy say, and two can't talk at the same time with good effect. It reminds me of the man who was reproached by a friend, who said,

"I think it a shame that you have not spoken to your wife for fifteen years. How do you explain it? How do you justify it?"

That poor man said,

"I didn't want to interrupt her."

If the Emperor had been at my table, he would not have suffered from my silence, he would only have suffered from the sorrows of his own solitude. If I were not too old to travel I would go to Berlin and introduce the etiquette of my own table, which tallies with the etiquette observable at other royal tables. I would say, "Invite me again, your Majesty, and give me a chance"; then I would courteously waive rank and do all the talking myself. I thank his Majesty for his kind message, and am proud to have it and glad to express my sincere reciprocation of its sentiments.

[*Dictated January 17, 1906.*] . . . Rev. Joseph T. Harris and I have been visiting General Sickles. Once, twenty or twenty-five years ago, just as Harris was coming out of his gate Sunday morning to walk to his church and preach, a telegram was put into his hand. He read it immediately, and then, in a manner, collapsed. It said: "General Sickles died last night at midnight." [He had been a chaplain under Sickles through the war.]

It wasn't so. But no matter – it was so to Harris at the time. He walked along – walked to the church – but his mind was far away. All his affection and homage and worship of his General had come to the fore. His heart was full of these emotions. He hardly knew where he was. In his pulpit, he stood up and began the service, but with a voice over which he had almost no command. The congregation had never seen him thus moved, before, in his pulpit. They sat there and gazed at him and wondered what was the matter; because he was now reading, in this broken voice and with occasional tears trickling down his face, what to them seemed a quite unemotional chapter – that one about Moses begat Aaron, and Aaron begat Deuteronomy, and Deuteronomy begat St. Peter, and St. Peter begat Cain, and Cain begat Abel – and he was going along with this, and half crying – his voice continually breaking. The congregation left the church that morning without being able to account for this most extraordinary thing – as it seemed to them. That a man who had been a soldier for more than four years, and who had preached in that pulpit so many, many times on really moving subjects, without even the quiver of a lip, should break all down over the Begats, they couldn't understand. But there it is – any one can see how such a mystery as that would arouse the curiosity of those people to the boiling-point.

Harris has had many adventures. He has more adventures in a year than anybody else has in five. One Saturday night he noticed a bottle on his uncle's dressing-bureau. He thought the label said "Hair Restorer," and he took it in his room and gave his head a good drenching and sousing with it and carried it back and thought no more about it. Next morning when he got up his head was a bright green! He sent around everywhere and couldn't get a substitute preacher, so he had to go to his church himself and preach – and he did it. He hadn't a sermon in his barrel – as it happened – of any lightsome character, so he had to preach a very grave one – a very serious one – and it made the matter worse. The gravity of the sermon did not harmonize with the gayety of his head, and the people sat all through it with handkerchiefs stuffed in their mouths to try to keep down their joy. And Harris told me that he was sure he never had seen his congregation – the whole body of his congregation – the *entire* body of his congregation – absorbed in interest in his sermon, from beginning to end, before. Always there had been an aspect of indifference, here and there, or wandering, somewhere; but this time there was nothing of the kind. Those people sat there as if they thought, "Good for this day and train only: we must have all there is of this show, not waste any of it." And he said that when he came down out of the pulpit more people waited to shake him by the hand and tell him what a good sermon it was, than ever before. And it seemed a pity that these people should do these fictions in such a place – right in the church – when it was quite plain they were not interested in the sermon at all; they only wanted to get a near view of his head.

Well, Harris said – no, Harris didn't say, *I* say, that as the days went on and Sunday followed Sunday, the interest in Harris's hair grew and grew; because it didn't stay merely and monotonously green, it took on deeper and deeper shades of green; and then it would change and become reddish, and would go from that to some other color – purplish, yellowish, bluish, and so on – but it was never a solid color. It was always mottled. And each Sunday it was a little more interesting than it was the Sunday before – and Harris's head became famous, and people came from New York, and Boston, and South Carolina, and Japan, and so on, to look. There wasn't seating-capacity for all the people that came while his head was undergoing these various and fascinating mottlings. And it was a good thing in several ways, because the business had been languishing a little, and now a lot of people joined the church so that they could have the show, and it was the beginning of a prosperity for that church which has never diminished in all these years.

PART XV

APRIL 5, 1907

[Dictated October 8, 1906.]

Papa says that if the collera comes here he will take Sour Mash to the mountains.

This remark about the cat is followed by various entries, covering a month, in which Jean, General Grant, the sculptor Gerhardt, Mrs. Candace Wheeler, Miss Dora Wheeler, Mr. Frank Stockton, Mrs. Mary Mapes Dodge, and the widow of General Custer appear and drift in procession across the page, then vanish forever from the Biography; then Susy drops this remark in the wake of the vanished procession:

Sour Mash is a constant source of anxiety, care, and pleasure to papa.

I did, in truth, think a great deal of that old tortoise-shell harlot; but I haven't a doubt that in order to impress Susy I was pretending agonies of solicitude which I didn't honestly feel. Sour Mash never gave me any real anxiety; she was always able to take care of herself, and she was ostentatiously vain of the fact; vain of it to a degree which often made me ashamed of her, much as I esteemed her.

Many persons would like to have the society of cats during the summer vacation in the country, but they deny themselves this pleasure because they think they must either take the cats along when they return to the city, where they would be a trouble and an encumbrance, or leave them in the country, houseless and homeless. These people have no ingenuity, no invention, no wisdom; or it would occur to them to do as I do: rent cats by the month for the summer and return them to their good homes at the end of it. Early last May I rented a kitten of a farmer's wife, by the month; then I got a discount by taking three. They have been good company for about five months now, and are still kittens – at least they have not grown much, and to all intents and purposes are still kittens, and as full of romping energy and enthusiasm as they were in the beginning. This is remarkable. I am an expert in cats, but I have not seen a kitten keep its kittenhood nearly so long before.

These are beautiful creatures – these triplets. Two of them wear the blackest and shiniest and thickest of sealskin vestments all over their bodies except the lower half of their faces and the terminations of their paws. The black masks reach down below the eyes, therefore when the eyes are closed they are not visible; the rest of the face, and the gloves and stockings, are snow white. These markings are just the same on both cats – so exactly the same that when you call one the other is likely to answer, because they cannot tell each other apart. Since the cats are precisely alike, and can't be told apart by any of us, they do not need two names, so they have but one between them. We call both of them Sackcloth, and we call the gray one Ashes. I believe I have never seen such intelligent cats as these before. They are full of the nicest discriminations. When I read German aloud they weep; you can see the tears run down. It shows what pathos there is in the German tongue. I had not noticed before that all German is pathetic, no matter what the subject is nor how it is treated. It was these humble observers that brought the knowledge to me. I have tried all kinds of German on these cats; romance, poetry, philosophy, theology, market reports; and the result has always been the same – the cats sob, and let the tears run down, which shows that all German is pathetic. French is not a familiar tongue to me, and the pronunciation is difficult, and comes out of me encumbered with a Missouri accent; but the cats like it, and when I make impassioned speeches in that language they sit in a row and put up their paws, palm to palm, and frantically give thanks. Hardly any cats are affected by music, but these are; when I sing they go reverently away, showing how deeply they feel it. Sour Mash never cared for these things. She had many noble qualities, but at bottom she was not refined, and cared little or nothing for theology and the arts.

It is a pity to say it, but these cats are not above the grade of human beings, for I know by certain signs that they are not sincere in their exhibitions of emotion, but exhibit them merely to show off and attract attention – conduct which is distinctly human, yet with a difference: they do not know enough to conceal their desire to show off, but the grown human being does. What is ambition? It is only the desire to be conspicuous. The desire for fame is only the desire to be continuously conspicuous and attract attention and be talked about.

These cats are like human beings in another way: when Ashes began to work his fictitious emotions, and show off, the other members of the firm followed suit, in order to be in the fashion. That is the way with human beings; they are afraid to be outside; whatever the fashion happens to be, they conform to it, whether it be a pleasant fashion or the reverse, they lacking the courage to ignore it and go their own way. All human beings would like to dress in loose and comfortable and highly colored and showy garments, and they had their desire until a century ago, when a king, or some other influential ass, introduced sombre hues and discomfort and ugly designs into masculine clothing. The meek public surrendered to the outrage, and by consequence we are in that odious captivity to-day, and are likely to remain in it for a long time to come.

Fortunately the women were not included in the disaster, and so their graces and their beauty still have the enhancing help of delicate fabrics and varied and beautiful colors. Their clothing makes a great opera audience an enchanting spectacle, a delight to the eye and the spirit, a Garden of Eden for charm and color. The men, clothed in dismal black, are scattered here and there and everywhere over the Garden, like so many charred stumps, and they damage the effect, but cannot annihilate it.

In summer we poor creatures have a respite, and may clothe ourselves in white garments; loose, soft, and in some degree shapely; but in the winter – the sombre winter, the depressing winter, the cheerless winter, when white clothes and bright colors are especially needed to brighten our spirits and lift them up – we all conform to the prevailing insanity, and go about in dreary black, each man doing it because the others do it, and not because he wants to. They are really no sincerer than Sackcloth and Ashes. At bottom the Sackcloths do not care to exhibit their emotions when I am performing before them, they only do it because Ashes started it.

I would like to dress in a loose and flowing costume made all of silks and velvets, resplendent with all the stunning dyes of the rainbow, and so would every sane man I have ever known; but none of us dares to venture it. There is such a thing as carrying conspicuousness to the point of discomfort; and if I should appear on Fifth Avenue on a Sunday morning, at church-time, clothed as

I would like to be clothed, the churches would be vacant, and I should have all the congregations tagging after me, to look, and secretly envy, and publicly scoff. It is the way human beings are made; they are always keeping their real feelings shut up inside, and publicly exploiting their fictitious ones.

Next after fine colors, I like plain white. One of my sorrows, when the summer ends, is that I must put off my cheery and comfortable white clothes and enter for the winter into the depressing captivity of the shapeless and degrading black ones. It is mid-October now, and the weather is growing cold up here in the New Hampshire hills, but it will not succeed in freezing me out of these white garments, for here the neighbors are few, and it is only of crowds that I am afraid. I made a brave experiment, the other night, to see how it would feel to shock a crowd with these unseasonable clothes, and also to see how long it might take the crowd to reconcile itself to them and stop looking astonished and outraged. On a stormy evening I made a talk before a full house, in the village, clothed like a ghost, and looking as conspicuously, all solitary and alone on that platform, as any ghost could have looked; and I found, to my gratification, that it took the house less than ten minutes to forget about the ghost and give its attention to the tidings I had brought.

I am nearly seventy-one, and I recognize that my age has given me a good many privileges; valuable privileges; privileges which are not granted to younger persons. Little by little I hope to get together courage enough to wear white clothes all through the winter, in New York. It will be a great satisfaction to me to show off in this way; and perhaps the largest of all the satisfactions will be the knowledge that every scoffer, of my sex, will secretly envy me and wish he dared to follow my lead.

That mention that I have acquired new and great privileges by grace of my age, is not an uncalculated remark. When I passed the seventieth mile-stone, ten months ago, I instantly realized that I had entered a new country and a new atmosphere. To all the public I was become recognizably old, undeniably old; and from that moment everybody assumed a new attitude toward me – the reverent attitude granted by custom to age – and straightway the stream of generous new privileges began to flow in upon me and refresh my life. Since then, I have lived an ideal existence; and I now believe what Choate said last March, and which at the time I didn't credit: that the best of life begins at seventy; for then your

work is done; you know that you have done your best, let the quality of the work be what it may; that you have earned your holiday
– a holiday of peace and contentment – and that thenceforth, to
the setting of your sun, nothing will break it, nothing interrupt it.

[*Dictated January 22, 1907.*] In an earlier chapter I inserted some
verses beginning "Love Came at Dawn" which had been found
among Susy's papers after her death. I was not able to say that they
were hers, but I judged that they might be, for the reason that she
had not enclosed them in quotation marks according to her habit
when storing up treasures gathered from other people. Stedman
was not able to determine the authorship for me, as the verses were
new to him, but the authorship has now been traced. The verses
were written by William Wilfred Campbell, a Canadian poet, and
they form a part of the contents of his book called "Beyond the
Hills of Dream."

The authorship of the beautiful lines which my wife and
I inscribed upon Susy's gravestone was untraceable for a time. We
had found them in a book in India, but had lost the book and with
it the author's name. But in time an application to the editor of
"Notes and Queries" furnished me the author's name, and it has
been added to the verses upon the gravestone.

Last night, at a dinner-party where I was present, Mr. Peter
Dunne Dooley handed to the host several dollars, in satisfaction
of a lost bet. I seemed to see an opportunity to better my condition,
and I invited Dooley, apparently disinterestedly, to come to my
house Friday and play billiards. He accepted, and I judge that
there is going to be a deficit in the Dooley treasury as a result. In
great qualities of the heart and brain, Dooley is gifted beyond all
propriety. He is brilliant; he is an expert with his pen, and he easily
stands at the head of all the satirists of this generation – but he is
going to walk in darkness Friday afternoon. It will be a fraternal
kindness to teach him that with all his light and culture, he does
not know all the valuable things; and it will also be a fraternal kindness to him to complete his education for him – and I shall do this
on Friday, and send him home in that perfected condition.

I possess a billiard secret which can be valuable to the Dooley
sept, after I shall have conferred it upon Dooley – for a consideration. It is a discovery which I made by accident, thirty-eight years
ago, in my father-in-law's house in Elmira. There was a scarred
and battered and ancient billiard-table in the garret, and along
with it a peck of checked and chipped balls, and a rackful of

crooked and headless cues. I played solitaire up there every day with that difficult outfit. The table was not level, but slanted sharply to the southeast; there wasn't a ball that was round, or would complete the journey you started it on, but would always get tired and stop half-way and settle, with a jolty wabble, to a standstill on its chipped side. I tried making counts with four balls, but found it difficult and discouraging, so I added a fifth ball, then a sixth, then a seventh, and kept on adding until at last I had twelve balls on the table and a thirteenth to play with. My game was caroms – caroms solely – caroms plain, or caroms with cushion to help – anything that could furnish a count. In the course of time I found to my astonishment that I was never able to run fifteen, under any circumstances. By huddling the balls advantageously in the beginning, I could now and then coax fourteen out of them, but I couldn't reach fifteen by either luck or skill. Sometimes the balls would get scattered into difficult positions and defeat me in that way; sometimes if I managed to keep them together, I would freeze; and always when I froze, and had to play away from the contact, there was sure to be nothing to play at but a wide and uninhabited vacancy.

One day Mr. Dalton called on my brother-in-law, on a matter of business, and I was asked if I could entertain him awhile, until my brother-in-law should finish an engagement with another gentleman. I said I could, and took him up to the billiard-table. I had played with him many times at the club, and knew that he could play billiards tolerably well – only tolerably well – but not any better than I could. He and I were just a match. He didn't know our table; he didn't know those balls; he didn't know those warped and headless cues; he didn't know the southeastern slant of the table, and how to allow for it. I judged it would be safe and profitable to offer him a bet on my scheme. I emptied the avalanche of thirteen balls on the table and said:

"Take a ball and begin, Mr. Dalton. How many can you run with an outlay like that?"

He said, with the half-affronted air of a mathematician who has been asked how much of the multiplication table he can recite without a break:

"I suppose a million – eight hundred thousand, anyway."

I said "You shall have the privilege of placing the balls to suit yourself, and I want to bet you a dollar that you can't run fifteen."

I will not dwell upon the sequel. At the end of an hour his face

was red, and wet with perspiration; his outer garments lay scattered here and there over the place; he was the angriest man in the
State, and there wasn't a rag or remnant of an injurious adjective
left in him anywhere – and I had all his small change.

When the summer was over, we went home to Hartford, and one
day Mr. George Robertson arrived from Boston with two or three
hours to spare between then and the return train, and as he was a
young gentleman to whom we were in debt for much social pleasure,
it was my duty, and a welcome duty, to make his two or three hours
interesting for him. So I took him up-stairs and set up my billiard
scheme for his comfort. Mine was a good table, in perfect repair; the
cues were in perfect condition; the balls were ivory, and flawless –
but I knew that Mr. Robertson was my prey, just the same, for by
exhaustive tests with this outfit I had found that my limit was thirty-
one. I had proved to my satisfaction that whereas I could not fairly
expect to get more than six or eight or a dozen caroms out of a run,
I could now and then reach twenty and twenty-five, and after a long
procession of failures finally achieve a run of thirty-one; but in no
case had I ever got beyond thirty-one. Robertson's game, as
I knew, was a little better than mine, so I resolved to require him
to make thirty-two. I believed it would entertain him. He was one
of these brisk and hearty and cheery and self-satisfied young fellows who are brimful of confidence, and who plunge with grateful
eagerness into any enterprise that offers a showy test of their
abilities. I emptied the balls on the table, and said,

"Take a cue and a ball, George, and begin. How many caroms
do you think you can make out of that layout?"

He laughed the laugh of the gay and the care-free, as became
his youth and inexperience, and said,

"I can punch caroms out of that bunch a week without a break."

I said "Place the balls to suit yourself, and begin."

Confidence is a necessary thing in billiards, but overconfidence
is bad. George went at his task with much too much lightsomeness
of spirit and disrespect for the situation. On his first shot he scored
three caroms; on his second shot he scored four caroms; and on
his third shot he missed as simple a carom as could be devised. He
was very much astonished, and said he would not have supposed
that careful play could be needed with an acre of bunched balls in
front of a person.

He began again, and played more carefully, but still with too
much lightsomeness; he couldn't seem to learn to take the situation

seriously. He made about a dozen caroms and broke down. He was irritated with himself now, and he thought he caught me laughing. He didn't. I do not laugh publicly at my client when this game is going on; I only do it inside – or save it for after the exhibition is over. But he thought he had caught me laughing, and it increased his irritation. Of course I knew he thought I was laughing privately – for I was experienced; they all think that, and it has a good effect; it sharpens their annoyance and debilitates their play.

He made another trial and failed. Once more he was astonished; once more he was humiliated – and as for his anger, it rose to summer-heat. He arranged the balls again, grouping them carefully, and said he would win this time, or die. When a client reaches this condition, it is a good time to damage his nerve further, and this can always be done by saying some little mocking thing or other that has the outside appearance of a friendly remark – so I employed this art. I suggested that a bet might tauten his nerves, and that I would offer one, but that as I did not want it to be an expense to him, but only a help, I would make it small – a cigar, if he were willing – a cigar that he would fail again; not an expensive one, but a cheap native one, of the Crown Jewel breed, such as is manufactured in Hartford for the clergy. It set him afire all over! I could see the blue flame issue from his eyes. He said,

"Make it a hundred! – and no Connecticut cabbage-leaf product, but Havana, $25 the box!"

I took him up, but said I was sorry to see him do this, because it did not seem to me right or fair for me to rob him under our own roof, when he had been so kind to us. He said, with energy and acrimony:

"You take care of your own pocket, if you'll be so good, and leave me to take care of mine."

And he plunged at the congress of balls with a vindictiveness which was infinitely contenting to me. He scored a failure – and began to undress. I knew it would come to that, for he was in the condition now that Mr. Dooley will be in at about that stage of the contest on Friday afternoon. A clothes rack will be provided for Mr. Dooley to hang his things on as fast as he shall from time to time shed them. George raised his voice four degrees and flung out the challenge –

"Double or quits!"

"Done," I responded, in the gentle and compassionate voice of one who is apparently getting sorrier and sorrier.

There was an hour and a half of straight disaster after that, and if it was a sin to enjoy it, it is no matter – I did enjoy it. It is half a lifetime ago, but I enjoy it yet, every time I think of it. George made failure after failure. His fury increased with each failure as he scored it. With each defeat he flung off one or another rag of his raiment, and every time he started on a fresh inning he made it "double or quits" once more. Twice he reached thirty and broke down; once he reached thirty-one and broke down. These "nears" made him frantic, and I believe I was never so happy in my life, except the time, a few years later, when the Rev. J. H. Twichell and I walked to Boston and he had the celebrated conversation with the hostler at the Inn at Ashford, Connecticut.

At last, when we were notified that Patrick was at the door to drive him to his train, George owed me five thousand cigars at twenty-five cents apiece, and I was so sorry I could have hugged him. But he shouted,

"Give me ten minutes more!" and added stormily, "it's double or quits again, and I'll win out free of debt or owe you ten thousand cigars, and you'll pay the funeral expenses."

He began on his final effort, and I believe that in all my experience among both amateurs and experts, I have never seen a cue so carefully handled in my lifetime as George handled his upon this intensely interesting occasion. He got safely up to twenty-five, and then ceased to breathe. So did I. He labored along, and added a point, another point, still another point, and finally reached thirty-one. He stopped there, and we took a breath. By this time the balls were scattered all down the cushions, about a foot or two apart, and there wasn't a shot in sight anywhere that any man might hope to make. In a burst of anger and confessed defeat, he sent his ball flying around the table at random, and it crotched a ball that was packed against the cushion and sprang across to a ball against the bank on the opposite side, and counted!

His luck had set him free, and he didn't owe me anything. He had used up all his spare time, but we carried his clothes to the carriage, and he dressed on his way to the station, greatly wondered at and admired by the ladies, as he drove along – but he got his train.

I am very fond of Mr. Dooley, and shall await his coming with affectionate and pecuniary interest.

P. S. Saturday. He has been here. Let us not talk about it.

PART XVI

APRIL 19, 1907

[*Dictated January 12th, 1905.*] . . . But I am used to having my statements discounted. My mother began it before I was seven years old. Yet all through my life my facts have had a substratum of truth, and therefore they were not without preciousness. Any person who is familiar with me knows how to strike my average, and therefore knows how to get at the jewel of any fact of mine and dig it out of its blue-clay matrix. My mother knew that art. When I was seven or eight, or ten, or twelve years old – along there – a neighbor said to her,

"Do you ever believe anything that that boy says?"

My mother said,

"He is the well-spring of truth, but you can't bring up the whole well with one bucket" – and she added, "I know his average, therefore he never deceives me. I discount him thirty per cent. for embroidery, and what is left is perfect and priceless truth, without a flaw in it anywhere."

Now to make a jump of forty years, without breaking the connection: that word "embroidery" was used again in my presence and concerning me, when I was fifty years old, one night at Rev. Frank Goodwin's house in Hartford, at a meeting of the Monday Evening Club. The Monday Evening Club still exists. It was founded about forty-five years ago by that theological giant, Rev. Dr. Bushnell, and some comrades of his, men of large intellectual calibre and more or less distinction, local or national. I was admitted to membership in it in the fall of 1871 and was an active member thenceforth until I left Hartford in the summer of 1891. The membership was restricted, in those days, to eighteen – possibly twenty. The meetings began about the 1st of October and were held in the private houses of the members every fortnight thereafter throughout the cold months until the 1st of May. Usually there were a dozen members present – sometimes as many as fifteen. There was an essay and a discussion. The essayists followed each other in alphabetical order through the season. The essayist could choose his own subject and talk twenty minutes on it, from MS. or orally, according to his preference. Then the discussion followed, and each member present was allowed ten minutes in which to express his views. The wives of these people were always present. It was their privilege. It was also their privilege to keep still; they were not allowed to throw any light upon the discussion. After the discussion there was a supper, and talk, and cigars. This supper began at ten o'clock promptly, and the company broke up and went away at midnight. At least they did except upon one occasion. In my recent Birthday speech I remarked upon the fact that I have always bought cheap cigars, and that is true. I have never bought costly ones.

Well, that night at the Club meeting – as I was saying – George, our colored butler, came to me when the supper was nearly over, and I noticed that he was pale. Normally his complexion was a clear black, and very handsome, but now it had modified to old amber. He said:

"Mr. Clemens, what are we going to do? There is not a cigar in the house but those old Wheeling long nines. Can't nobody smoke them but you. They kill at thirty yards. It is too late to telephone – we couldn't get any cigars out from town – what can we do? Ain't it best to say nothing, and let on that we didn't think?"

"No," I said, "that would not be honest. Fetch out the long nines" – which he did.

I had just come across those "long nines" a few days or a week before. I hadn't seen a long nine for years. When I was a cub pilot on the Mississippi in the late '50's, I had had a great affection for them, because they were not only – to my mind – perfect, but you could get a basketful of them for a cent – or a dime, they didn't use cents out there in those days. So when I saw them advertised in Hartford I sent for a thousand at once. They came out to me in badly battered and disreputable-looking old square pasteboard boxes, two hundred in a box. George brought a box, which was caved in on all sides, looking the worst it could, and began to pass them around. The conversation had been brilliantly animated up to that moment – but now a frost fell upon the company. That is to say, not all of a sudden, but the frost fell upon each man as he took up a cigar and held it poised in the air – and there, in the middle, his sentence broke off. That kind of thing went on all around the table, until when George had completed his crime the whole place was full of a thick solemnity and silence.

Those men began to light the cigars. Rev. Dr. Parker was the first man to light. He took three or four heroic whiffs – then gave it up. He got up with the remark that he had to go to the bedside of a sick parishioner. He started out. Rev. Dr. Burton was the next man. He took only one whiff, and followed Parker. He furnished a pretext, and you could see by the sound of his voice that he didn't think much of the pretext, and was vexed with Parker for getting in ahead with a fictitious ailing client. Rev. Mr. Twichell followed, and said he had to go now because he must take the midnight train for Boston. Boston was the first place that occurred to him, I suppose.

It was only a quarter to eleven when they began to distribute pretexts. At ten minutes to eleven all those people were out of the house. When nobody was left but George and me I was cheerful – I had no compunctions of conscience, no griefs of any kind. But George was beyond speech, because he held the honor and credit of the family above his own, and he was ashamed that this smirch had been put upon it. I told him to go to bed and try to sleep it off. I went to bed myself. At breakfast in the morning when George was passing a cup of coffee, I saw it tremble in his hand. I knew by that sign that there was something on his mind. He brought the cup to me and asked impressively,

"Mr. Clemens, how far is it from the front door to the upper gate?"

I said, "It is a hundred and twenty-five steps."

He said, "Mr. Clemens, you can start at the front door and you can go plumb to the upper gate and tread on one of them cigars every time."

It wasn't true in detail, but in essentials it was.

The subject under discussion on the night in question was Dreams. The talk passed from mouth to mouth in the usual serene way.

I do not now remember what form my views concerning dreams took at the time. I don't remember now what my notion about dreams was then, but I do remember telling a dream by way of illustrating some detail of my speech, and I also remember that when I had finished it Rev. Dr. Burton made that doubting remark which contained that word I have already spoken of as having been uttered by my mother, in some such connection, forty or fifty years before. I was probably engaged in trying to make those people believe that now and then, by some accident, or otherwise, a dream which was prophetic turned up in the dreamer's mind. The date of my memorable dream was about the beginning of May, 1858. It was a remarkable dream, and I had been telling it several times every year for more than fifteen years – and now I was telling it again, here in the club.

In 1858 I was a steersman on board the swift and popular New Orleans and St. Louis packet, "Pennsylvania," Captain Klinefelter. I had been lent to Mr. Brown, one of the pilots of the "Pennsylvania," by my owner, Mr. Horace E. Bixby, and I had been steering for Brown about eighteen months, I think. Then in the early days of May, 1858, came a tragic trip – the last trip of that fleet and famous steamboat. I have told all about it in one of my books called "Old Times on the Mississippi." But it is not likely that I told the dream in that book. It is impossible that I can ever have published it, I think, because I never wanted my mother to know about the dream, and she lived several years after I published that volume.

I had found a place on the "Pennsylvania" for my brother Henry, who was two years my junior. It was not a place of profit, it was only a place of promise. He was "mud" clerk. Mud clerks received no salary, but they were in the line of promotion. They could become, presently, third clerk and second clerk, then chief clerk – that is to say, purser. The dream begins when Henry had been mud clerk about three months. We were lying in port at St. Louis. Pilots and steersmen had nothing to do during the three days that the boat lay in port in St. Louis and New Orleans, but the mud clerk had to begin his labors at dawn and continue them into the night, by the light of pine-knot torches. Henry and I, moneyless and unsalaried, had billeted ourselves upon our brother-in-law, Mr. Moffett, as night lodgers while in port. We took our meals on board the boat. No, I mean I lodged at the house, not Henry. He spent the *evenings* at the house, from nine until eleven, then went to the boat to be ready for his early duties. On the night of the dream he started away at eleven, shaking hands with the family, and said good-by according to custom. I may mention that handshaking as a good-by was not merely the custom of that family, but the custom of the region – the custom of Missouri, I may say. In all my life, up to that time, I had never seen one member of the Clemens family kiss another one – except once. When my father lay dying in our home in Hannibal – the 24th of March, 1847 – he put his arm around my sister's neck and drew her down and kissed her, saying "Let me die." I remember that, and I remember the death rattle which swiftly followed those words, which were his last. These good-bys of Henry's were always executed in the family sitting-room on the second floor, and Henry went from that room and downstairs without further ceremony. But this time my mother went with him to the head of the stairs and said good-by *again*. As I remember it she was moved to this by something in Henry's manner, and she remained at the head of the stairs while he descended. When he reached the door he hesitated, and climbed the stairs and shook hands good-by once more.

In the morning, when I awoke I had been dreaming, and the dream was so vivid, so like reality, that it deceived me, and I thought it *was* real. In the dream I had seen Henry a corpse. He lay in a metallic burial-case. He was dressed in a suit of my clothing, and on his breast lay a great bouquet of flowers, mainly white roses, with a red rose in the centre. The casket stood upon a couple of chairs. I dressed, and moved toward that door, thinking I would go in there and look at it, but I changed my mind. I thought I could not yet bear to meet my mother. I thought I would wait awhile and make some preparation for that ordeal. The house was in Locust Street, a little above 13th, and I walked to 14th, and to the middle of the block beyond, before it suddenly flashed upon me that there was nothing real about this – it was only a dream. I can still feel something of the grateful upheaval of joy of that moment, and I can also still feel the remnant of doubt, the suspicion that maybe it *was* real, after all. I returned to the house almost on a run, flew up the stairs two or three steps at a jump, and rushed into that sitting-room – and was made glad again, for there was no casket there.

We made the usual eventless trip to New Orleans – no, it was not eventless, for it was on the way down that I had the fight with Mr. Brown which resulted in his requiring that I be left ashore at New Orleans. In New Orleans I always had a job. It was my privilege to watch the freight-piles from seven in the evening until seven in the morning, and get three dollars for it. It was a three-night job and occurred every thirty-five days. Henry always joined my watch about nine in the evening, when his own duties were ended, and we often walked my rounds and chatted together until midnight. This time we were to part, and so the night before the boat sailed I gave Henry some advice. I said, "In case of disaster to the boat, don't lose your head – leave that unwisdom to the passengers – they are competent – they'll attend to it. But you rush for the hurricane-deck, and astern to one of the life-boats lashed aft the wheel-house, and obey the mate's orders – thus you will be useful.

When the boat is launched, give such help as you can in getting the women and children into it, and be sure you don't try to get into it yourself. It is summer weather, the river is only a mile wide, as a rule, and you can swim that without any trouble." Two or three days afterward the boat's boilers exploded at Ship Island, below Memphis, early one morning – and what happened afterward I have already told in "Old Times on the Mississippi." As related there, I followed the "Pennsylvania" about a day later, on another boat, and we began to get news of the disaster at every port we touched at, and so by the time we reached Memphis we knew all about it.

I found Henry stretched upon a mattress on the floor of a great building, along with thirty or forty other scalded and wounded persons, and was promptly informed, by some indiscreet person, that he had inhaled steam; that his body was badly scalded, and that he would live but a little while; also, I was told that the physicians and nurses were giving their whole attention to persons who had a chance of being saved. They were short-handed in the matter of physicians and nurses; and Henry and such others as were considered to be fatally hurt were receiving only such attention as could be spared, from time to time, from the more urgent cases. But Dr. Peyton, a fine and large-hearted old physician of great reputation in the community, gave me his sympathy and took vigorous hold of the case, and in about a week he had brought Henry around. Dr. Peyton never committed himself with prognostications which might not materialize, but at eleven o'clock one night he told me that Henry was out of danger, and would get well. Then he said, "At midnight these poor fellows lying here and there all over this place will begin to mourn and mutter and lament and make outcries, and if this commotion should disturb Henry it will be bad for him; therefore ask the physician on watch to give him an eighth of a grain of morphine, but this is not to be done unless Henry shall show signs that he is being disturbed."

Oh well, never mind the rest of it. The physicians on watch were young fellows hardly out of the medical college, and they made a mistake – they had no way of measuring the eighth of a grain of morphine, so they guessed at it and gave him a vast quantity heaped on the end of a knife-blade, and the fatal effects were soon apparent. I think he died about dawn, I don't remember as to that. He was carried to the dead-room and I went away for a while to a citizen's house and slept off some of my accumulated fatigue –

and meantime something was happening. The coffins provided for the dead were of unpainted white pine, but in this instance some of the ladies of Memphis had made up a fund of sixty dollars and bought a metallic case, and when I came back and entered the dead-room Henry lay in that open case, and he was dressed in a suit of my clothing. He had borrowed it without my knowledge during our last sojourn in St. Louis; and I recognized instantly that my dream of several weeks before was here exactly reproduced, so far as these details went – and I think I missed one detail; but that one was immediately supplied, for just then an elderly lady entered the place with a large bouquet consisting mainly of white roses, and in the centre of it was a red rose, and she laid it on his breast.

I told the dream there in the Club that night just as I have told it here.

Rev. Dr. Burton swung his leonine head around, focused me with his eye, and said:

"When was it that this happened?"

"In June, '58."

"It is a good many years ago. Have you told it several times since?"

"Yes, I have, a good many times."

"How many?"

"Why, I don't know how many."

"Well, strike an average. How many times a year do you think you have told it?"

"Well, I have told it as many as six times a year, possibly oftener."

"Very well, then you've told it, we'll say, seventy or eighty times since it happened?"

"Yes," I said, "that's a conservative estimate."

"Now then, Mark, a very extraordinary thing happened to me a great many years ago, and I used to tell it a number of times – a good many times – every year, for it was so wonderful that it always astonished the hearer, and that astonishment gave me a distinct pleasure every time. I never suspected that that tale was acquiring any auxiliary advantages through repetition until one day after I had been telling it ten or fifteen years it struck me that either I was getting old, and slow in delivery, or that the tale was longer than it was when it was born. Mark, I diligently and prayerfully examined that tale with this result: that I found that its proportions were now, as nearly as I could make out, one part fact, straight fact, fact pure and undiluted, golden fact, and twenty-four parts embroidery. I never told that tale afterwards – I was never able to tell it again, for I had lost confidence in it, and so the pleasure of telling it was gone, and gone permanently. How much of this tale of yours is embroidery?"

"Well," I said, "I don't know. I don't think any of it is embroidery. I think it is all just as I have stated it, detail by detail."

"Very well," he said, "then it is all right, but I wouldn't tell it any more; because if you keep on, it will begin to collect embroidery sure. The safest thing is to stop now."

That was a great many years ago. And to-day is the first time that I have told that dream since Dr. Burton scared me into fatal doubts about it. No, I don't believe I can say that. I don't believe that I ever really had any doubts whatever concerning the salient points of the dream, for those points are of such a nature that they are *pictures*, and pictures can be remembered, when they are vivid, much better than one can remember remarks and unconcreted facts. Although it has been so many years since I have told that dream, I can see those pictures now just as clearly defined as if they were before me in this room. I have not told the entire dream. There was a good deal more of it. I mean I have not told all that happened in the dream's fulfilment. After the incident in the death-room I may mention one detail, and that is this. When I arrived in St. Louis with the casket it was about eight o'clock in the morning, and I ran to my brother-in-law's place of business; hoping to find him there, but I missed him, for while I was on the way to his office he was on his way from the house to the boat. When I got back to the boat the casket was gone. He had conveyed it out to his house. I hastened thither, and when I arrived the men were just removing the casket from the vehicle to carry it up-stairs. I stopped that procedure, for I did not want my mother to see the dead face, because one side of it was drawn and distorted by the effects of the opium. When I went up-stairs, there stood the two chairs – placed to receive the coffin – just as I had seen them in my dream; and if I had arrived two or three minutes later, the casket would have been resting upon them, precisely as in my dream of several weeks before.

PART XVII

MAY 3, 1907

Sept. 9, '85. – Mamma is teaching Jean a little natural history and is making a little collection of insects for her. But mamma does not allow Jean to kill any insects she only collects those insects that are found dead. Mamma has told us all, perticularly Jean, to bring her all the little dead insects that she finds. The other day as we were all sitting at supper Jean broke into the room and ran triumfantly up to Mamma and presented her with a plate full of dead flies. Mamma thanked Jean very enthusiastically although she with difficulty concealed her amusement. Just then Sour Mash entered the room and Jean believing her hungry asked Mamma for permission to give her the flies. Mamma laughingly consented and the flies almost immediately dissapeared.

[*Monday, October 15, 1906.*] Sour Mash's presence indicates that this adventure occurred at Quarry Farm. Susy's Biography interests itself pretty exclusively with historical facts; where they happen is not a matter of much concern to her. When other historians refer to the Bunker Hill Monument they know it is not necessary to mention that that monument is in Boston. Susy recognizes that when she mentions Sour Mash it is not necessary to localize her. To Susy, Sour Mash is the Bunker Hill Monument of Quarry Farm.

Ordinary cats have some partiality for living flies, but none for dead ones; but Susy does not trouble herself to apologize for Sour Mash's eccentricities of taste. This Biography was for *us*, and Susy knew that nothing that Sour Mash might do could startle us or need explanation, we being aware that she was not an ordinary cat, but moving upon a plane far above the prejudices and superstitions which are law to common catdom.

Once in Hartford the flies were so numerous for a time, and so troublesome, that Mrs. Clemens conceived the idea of paying George* a bounty on all the flies he might kill. The children saw

* The colored butler.

an opportunity here for the acquisition of sudden wealth. They supposed that their mother merely wanted to accumulate dead flies, for some æsthetic or scientific reason or other, and they judged that the more flies she could get the happier she would be; so they went into business with George on a commission. Straightway the dead flies began to arrive in such quantities that Mrs. Clemens was pleased beyond words with the success of her idea. Next, she was astonished that one house could furnish so many. She was paying an extravagantly high bounty, and it presently began to look as if by this addition to our expenses we were now probably living beyond our income. After a few days there was peace and comfort; not a fly was discoverable in the house; there wasn't a straggler left. Still, to Mrs. Clemens's surprise, the dead flies continued to arrive by the plateful, and the bounty expense was as crushing as ever. Then she made inquiry, and found that our innocent little rascals had established a Fly Trust, and had hired all the children in the neighborhood to collect flies on a cheap and unburdensome commission.

Mrs. Clemens's experience in this matter was a new one for her, but the governments of the world had tried it, and wept over it, and discarded it, every half-century since man was created. Any Government could have told her that the best way to increase wolves in America, rabbits in Australia, and snakes in India, is to pay a bounty on their scalps. Then every patriot goes to raising them.

FROM SUSY'S BIOGRAPHY OF ME

Sept. 10, '85. – The other evening Clara and I brought down our new soap buble water and we all blew soap bubles. Papa blew his soap bubles and filled them with tobacco smoke and as the light shone on them they took very beautiful opaline colors. Papa would hold them and then let us catch them in our hand and they felt delightful to the touch the mixture of the smoke and water had a singularly pleasant effect.

It is human life. We are blown upon the world; we float buoyantly upon the summer air a little while, complacently showing off our grace of form and our dainty iridescent colors; then we vanish with a little puff, leaving nothing behind but a memory – and sometimes not even that. I suppose that at those solemn times when we wake in the deeps of the night and reflect, there is not one of us who is not willing to confess that he is really only a soap-bubble, and as little worth the making.

I remember those days of twenty-one years ago, and a certain pathos clings about them. Susy, with her manifold young charms and her iridescent mind, was as lovely a bubble as any we made that day – and as transitory. She passed, as they passed, in her youth and beauty, and nothing of her is left but a heartbreak and a memory. That long-vanished day came vividly back to me a few weeks ago when, for the first time in twenty-one years, I found myself again amusing a child with smoke-charged soap-bubbles.

Susy's next date is November 29th, 1885, the eve of my fiftieth birthday. It seems a good while ago. I must have been rather young for my age then, for I was trying to tame an old-fashioned bicycle nine feet high. It is to me almost unbelievable, at my present stage of life, that there have really been people willing to trust themselves upon a dizzy and unstable altitude like that, and that I was one of them. Twichell and I took lessons every day. He succeeded, and became a master of the art of riding that wild vehicle, but I had no gift in that direction and was never able to stay on mine long enough to get any satisfactory view of the planet. Every time I tried to steal a look at a pretty girl, or any other kind of scenery, that single moment of inattention gave the bicycle the chance it had been waiting for, and I went over the front of it and struck the ground on my head or my back before I had time to realize that something was happening. I didn't always go over the front way; I had other ways, and practised them all; but no matter which way was chosen for me there was always one monotonous result – the bicycle skinned my leg and leaped up into the air and came down on top of me. Sometimes its wires were so sprung by this violent performance that it had the collapsed look of an umbrella that had had a misunderstanding with a cyclone. After each day's practice I arrived at home with my skin hanging in ribbons, from my knees down. I plastered the ribbons on where they belonged, and bound them there with handkerchiefs steeped in Pond's Extract, and was ready for more adventures next day. It was always a surprise to me that I had so much skin, and that it held out so well. There was always plenty, and I soon came to understand that the supply was going to remain sufficient for all my needs. It turned out that I had nine skins, in layers, one on top of the other like the leaves of a book, and some of the doctors said it was quite remarkable.

I was full of enthusiasm over this insane amusement. My teacher was a young German from the bicycle factory, a gentle, kindly, patient creature, with a pathetically grave face. He never smiled; he never made a remark; he always gathered me tenderly up when I plunged off, and helped me on again without a word. When he had been teaching me twice a day for three weeks I introduced a new gymnastic – one that he had never seen before – and so at last a compliment was wrung from him, a thing which I had been risking my life for days to achieve. He gathered me up and said mournfully: "Mr. Clemens, you can fall off a bicycle in more different ways than any person I ever saw before."

A boy's life is not all comedy; much of the tragic enters into it. The drunken tramp – mentioned in "Tom Sawyer" or "Huck Finn" – who was burned up in the village jail, lay upon my conscience a hundred nights afterward and filled them with hideous dreams – dreams in which I saw his appealing face as I had seen it in the pathetic reality, pressed against the window-bars, with the red hell glowing behind him – a face which seemed to say to me, "If you had not give me the matches, this would not have happened; you are responsible for my death." I was *not* responsible for it, for I had meant him no harm, but only good, when I let him have the matches; but no matter, mine was a trained Presbyterian conscience, and knew but the one duty – to hunt and harry its slave upon all pretexts and on all occasions; particularly when there was no sense or reason in it. The tramp – who was to blame – suffered ten minutes; I, who was not to blame, suffered three months.

The shooting down of poor old Smarr in the main street at noonday supplied me with some more dreams; and in them I always saw again the grotesque closing picture – the great family Bible spread open on the profane old man's breast by some thoughtful idiot; and rising and sinking to the labored breathings, and adding the torture of its leaden weight to the dying struggles. We are curiously made. In all the throng of gaping and sympathetic onlookers there was not one with common sense enough to perceive that an anvil would have been in better taste there than the Bible, less open to sarcastic criticism, and swifter in its atrocious work. In my nightmares I gasped and struggled for breath under the crush of that vast book for many a night.

All within the space of a couple of years we had two or three other tragedies, and I had the ill-luck to be too near by on each occasion. There was the slave man who was struck down with a chunk of slag for some small offence; I saw him die. And the young California emigrant who was stabbed with a bowie knife by a drunken comrade: I saw the red life gush from his breast. And the case of the rowdy young Hyde brothers and their harmless old uncle: one of them held the old man down with his knees on his breast while the other one tried repeatedly to kill him with an Allen revolver which wouldn't go off. I happened along just then, of course.

Then there was the case of the young California emigrant who got drunk and proposed to raid the "Welshman's house" all alone one dark and threatening night. This house stood halfway up Holliday's Hill ("Cardiff" Hill), and its sole occupants were a poor but quite respectable widow and her young and blameless daughter. The invading ruffian woke the whole village with his ribald yells and coarse challenges and obscenities. I went up there with a comrade – John Briggs, I think – to look and listen. The figure of the man was dimly visible; the women were on their porch, but not visible in the deep shadow of its roof, but we heard the elder woman's voice. She had loaded an old musket with slugs, and she warned the man that if he stayed where he was while she counted ten it would cost him his life. She began to count, slowly: he began to laugh. He stopped laughing at "six"; then through the deep stillness, in a steady voice, followed the rest of the tale: "seven ... eight ... nine" – a long pause, we holding our breath – "ten!" A red spout of flame gushed out into the night, and the man dropped, with his breast riddled to rags. Then the rain and the thunder burst loose and the waiting town swarmed up the hill in the glare of the lightning like an invasion of ants. Those people saw the rest; I had had my share and was satisfied. I went home to dream, and was not disappointed.

My teaching and training enabled me to see deeper into these tragedies than an ignorant person could have done. I knew what they were for. I tried to disguise it from myself, but down in the secret deeps of my heart I knew – and I *knew* that I knew. They were inventions of Providence to beguile me to a better life. It sounds curiously innocent and conceited, now, but to me there was nothing strange about it; it was quite in accordance with the thoughtful and judicious ways of Providence as I understood them. It would not have surprised me, nor even over-flattered me, if Providence had killed off that whole community in trying to save an asset like me. Educated as I had been, it would have seemed just the thing, and well worth the expense. *Why* Providence should take such an anxious interest in such a property – that idea never entered my head, and there was no one in that simple hamlet who would have dreamed of putting it there. For one thing, no one was equipped with it.

It is quite true I took all the tragedies to myself; and tallied them off, in turn as they happened, saying to myself in each case, with a sigh, "Another one gone – and on my account; this ought to bring me to repentance; His patience will not always endure." And yet privately I believed it would. That is, I believed it in the daytime; but not in the night. With the going down of the sun my faith failed, and the clammy fears gathered about my heart. It was then that I repented. Those were awful nights, nights of despair, nights charged with the bitterness of death. After each tragedy I recognized the warning and repented; repented and begged; begged like a coward, begged like a dog; and not in the interest of those poor people who had been extinguished for my sake, but only in my own interest. It seems selfish, when I look back on it now.

My repentances were very real, very earnest; and after each tragedy they happened every night for a long time. But as a rule they could not stand the daylight. They faded out and shredded away and disappeared in the glad splendor of the sun. They were the creatures of fear and darkness, and they could not live out of their own place. The day gave me cheer and peace, and at night I repented again. In all my boyhood life I am not sure that I ever tried to lead a better life in the daytime – or wanted to. In my age I should never think of wishing to do such a thing. But in my age, as in my youth, night brings me many a deep remorse. I realize that from the cradle up I have been like the rest of the race – never quite sane in the night. When "Injun Joe" died . . . But never mind: in another chapter I have already described what a raging hell of repentance I passed through then. I believe that for months I was as pure as the driven snow. After dark.

It was back in those far-distant days – 1848 or '9 – that Jim Wolf came to us. He was from Shelbyville, a hamlet thirty or forty miles back in the country, and he brought all his native sweetnesses and gentlenesses and simplicities with him. He was approaching seventeen, a grave and slender lad, trustful, honest, a creature to love and cling to. And he was incredibly bashful.

It is to this kind that untoward things happen. My sister gave a "candy-pull" on a winter's night. I was too young to be of the company, and Jim was too diffident. I was sent up to bed early, and Jim followed of his own motion. His room was in the new part of the house, and his window looked out on the roof of the L annex. That roof was six inches deep in snow, and the snow had an ice-crust upon it which was as slick as glass. Out of the comb of the roof projected a short chimney, a common resort for sentimental cats on moonlight nights – and this was a moonlight night. Down at the eaves, below the chimney, a canopy of dead vines spread away to some posts, making a cozy shelter, and after an hour or two the rollicking crowd of young ladies and gentlemen grouped themselves in its shade, with their saucers of liquid and piping-hot candy disposed about them on the frozen ground to cool. There was joyous chaffing and joking and laughter – peal upon peal of it.

About this time a couple of old disreputable tom-cats got up on the chimney and started a heated argument about something; also about this time I gave up trying to get to sleep, and went visiting to Jim's room. He was awake and fuming about the cats and their intolerable yowling. I asked him, mockingly, why he didn't climb out and drive them away. He was nettled, and said over-boldly that for two cents he *would*.

It was a rash remark, and was probably repented of before it was fairly out of his mouth. But it was too late – he was committed. I knew him; and I knew he would rather break his neck than back down, if I egged him on judiciously.

"Oh, of course you would! Who's doubting it?"

It galled him, and he burst out, with sharp irritation –

"Maybe *you* doubt it!"

"I? Oh no, I shouldn't think of such a thing. You are always doing wonderful things. With your mouth."

He was in a passion, now. He snatched on his yarn socks and began to raise the window, saying in a voice unsteady with anger –

"*You* think I dasn't – *you* do! Think what you blame please – *I* don't care what you think. I'll show you!"

The window made him rage; it wouldn't stay up. I said –

"Never mind, I'll hold it."

Indeed, I would have done anything to help. I was only a boy, and was already in a radiant heaven of anticipation. He climbed carefully out, clung to the window-sill until his feet were safely placed, then began to pick his perilous way on all fours along the glassy comb, a foot and a hand on each side of it. I believe I enjoy it now as much as I did then: yet it is a good deal over fifty years ago. The frosty breeze flapped his short shirt about his lean legs; the crystal roof shone like polished marble in the intense glory of the moon; the unconscious cats sat erect upon the chimney, alertly watching each other; lashing their tails and pouring out their hollow grievances; and slowly and cautiously Jim crept on, flapping as he went, the gay and frolicsome young creatures under the vine-canopy unaware, and outraging these solemnities with their misplaced laughter. Every time Jim slipped I had a hope; but always on he crept and disappointed it. At last he was within reaching distance. He paused, raised himself carefully up, measured his distance deliberately, then made a frantic grab at the nearest cat – and missed. Of course he lost his balance. His heels flew up, he struck on his back, and like a rocket he darted down the roof feet first, crashed through the dead vines and landed in a sitting posture in fourteen saucers of red-hot candy, in the midst of all that party – and dressed as *he* was: this lad who could not look a girl in the face with his clothes on. There was a wild scramble and a storm of shrieks, and Jim fled up the stairs, dripping broken crockery all the way.

The incident was ended. But I was not done with it yet, though I supposed I was. Eighteen or twenty years later I arrived in New York from California, and by that time I had failed in all my other undertakings and had stumbled into literature without intending it. This was early in 1867. I was offered a large sum to write something for the "Sunday Mercury," and I answered with the tale of "Jim Wolf and the Cats." I also collected the money for it – twenty-five dollars. It seemed over-pay, but I did not say anything about that, for I was not so scrupulous then as I am now.

A year or two later "Jim Wolf and the Cats" appeared in a Tennessee paper in a new dress – as to spelling; spelling borrowed from Artemus Ward. The appropriator of the tale had a wide reputation in the West, and was exceedingly popular. Deservedly so, I think. He wrote some of the breeziest and funniest things I have ever read, and did his work with distinguished ease and fluency. His name has passed out of my memory.

A couple of years went by; then the original story – my own version – cropped up again and went floating around in the original spelling, and with my name to it. Soon first one paper and then another fell upon me vigorously for "stealing" Jim Wolf and the Cats from the Tennessee man. I got a merciless basting, but I did not mind it. It's all in the game. Besides, I had learned, a good while before that, that it is not wise to keep the fire going under a slander unless you can get some large advantage out of keeping it alive. Few slanders can stand the wear of silence.

But I was not done with Jim and the Cats yet. In 1873 I was lecturing in London, in the Queen's Concert Rooms, Hanover Square, and was living at the Langham Hotel, Portland Place. I had no domestic household, and no official household except George Dolby, lecture-agent, and Charles Warren Stoddard, the California poet, now (1900) Professor of English Literature in the Roman Catholic University, Washington. Ostensibly Stoddard was my private secretary; in reality he was merely my comrade – I hired him in order to have his company. As secretary there was nothing for him to do except to scrap-book the daily reports of the great trial of the Tichborne Claimant for perjury. But he made a sufficient job out of that, for the reports filled six columns a day and he usually postponed the scrap-booking until Sunday; then he had 36 columns to cut out and paste in – a proper labor for Hercules. He did his work well, but if he had been older and feebler it would have killed him once a week. Without doubt he does his literary lectures well, but also without doubt he prepares them fifteen minutes before he is due on his platform and thus gets into them a freshness and sparkle which they might lack if they underwent the staling process of overstudy.

He was good company when he was awake. He was refined, sensitive, charming, gentle, generous, honest himself and unsuspicious of other people's honesty, and I think he was the purest male I have known, in mind and speech. George Dolby was something of a contrast to him, but the two were very friendly and sociable together, nevertheless. Dolby was large and ruddy, full of life and strength and spirits, a tireless and energetic talker, and always overflowing with good-nature and bursting with jollity. It was a choice and satisfactory menagerie, this pensive poet and this gladsome gorilla. An indelicate story was a sharp distress to Stoddard; Dolby told him twenty-five a day. Dolby always came home with us after the lecture, and entertained Stoddard till midnight. Me too. After he left, I walked the floor and talked, and Stoddard went to sleep on the sofa. I hired him for company.

Dolby had been agent for concerts, and theatres, and Charles Dickens and all sorts of shows and "attractions" for many years; he had known the human being in many aspects, and he didn't much believe in him. But the poet did. The waifs and estrays found

a friend in Stoddard: Dolby tried to persuade him that he was dis-
pensing his charities unworthily, but he was never able to succeed.

One night a young American got access to Stoddard at the Concert Rooms and told him a moving tale. He said he was living on
the Surrey side, and for some strange reason his remittances had
failed to arrive from home; he had no money, he was out of employment, and friendless; his girl-wife and his new baby were actually
suffering for food; for the love of heaven could he lend him a sovereign until his remittances should resume? Stoddard was deeply
touched, and gave him a sovereign on my account. Dolby scoffed,
but Stoddard stood his ground. Each told me his story later in the
evening, and I backed Stoddard's judgment. Dolby said we were
women in disguise, and not a sane kind of women, either.

The next week the young man came again. His wife was ill with
the pleurisy, the baby had the bots, or something, I am not sure
of the name of the disease; the doctor and the drugs had eaten up
the money, the poor little family was starving. If Stoddard "in the
kindness of his heart could only spare him another sovereign," etc.,
etc. Stoddard was much moved, and spared him a sovereign for
me. Dolby was outraged. He spoke up and said to the customer –

"Now, young man, you are going to the hotel with us and state
your case to the other member of the family. If you don't make him
believe in you I sha'n't honour this poet's drafts in your interest any
longer, for I don't believe in you myself."

The young man was quite willing. I found no fault in him. On
the contrary, I believed in him at once, and was solicitous to heal
the wounds inflicted by Dolby's too frank incredulity; therefore
I did everything I could think of to cheer him up and entertain him
and make him feel at home and comfortable. I spun many yarns;
among others the tale of Jim Wolf and the Cats. Learning that he
had done something in a small way in literature, I offered to try to
find a market for him in that line. His face lighted joyfully at that,
and he said that if I could only sell a small manuscript to Tom
Hood's Annual for him it would be the happiest event of his sad
life and he would hold me in grateful remembrance always. That
was a most pleasant night for three of us, but Dolby was disgusted
and sarcastic.

Next week the baby died. Meantime I had spoken to Tom Hood
and gained his sympathy. The young man had sent his manuscript
to him, and the very day the child died the money for the MS.
came – three guineas. The young man came with a poor little strip

of crape around his arm and thanked me, and said that nothing could have been more timely than that money, and that his poor little wife was grateful beyond words for the service I had rendered. He wept, and in fact Stoddard and I wept with him, which was but natural. Also Dolby wept. At least he wiped his eyes and wrung out his handkerchief, and sobbed stertorously and made other exaggerated shows of grief. Stoddard and I were ashamed of Dolby, and tried to make the young man understand that he meant no harm, it was only his way. The young man said sadly that he was not minding it, his grief was too deep for other hurts; that he was only thinking of the funeral, and the heavy expenses which –

We cut that short and told him not to trouble about it, leave it all to us; send the bills to Mr. Dolby and –

"Yes," said Dolby, with a mock tremor in his voice, "send them to me, and I will pay them. What, are you going? You must not go alone in your worn and broken condition; Mr. Stoddard and I will go with you. Come, Stoddard. We will comfort the bereaved mamma and get a lock of the baby's hair."

It was shocking. We were ashamed of him again, and said so. But he was not disturbed. He said –

"Oh, I know this kind, the woods are full of them. I'll make this offer: if he will show me his family I will give him twenty pounds. Come!" The young man said he would not remain to be insulted; and he said good-night and took his hat. But Dolby said he would go with him, and stay by him until he found the family. Stoddard went along to soothe the young man and modify Dolby. They drove across the river and all over Southwark, but did not find the family. At last the young man confessed there wasn't any.

The thing he sold to Tom Hood's Annual was "Jim and the Cats." And he did not put my name to it.

So that small tale was sold three times. I am selling it again, now. It is one of the best properties I have come across.

PART XVIII

MAY 17, 1907

[*Dictated December 21, 1906.*] I wish to insert here some pages of Susy's Biography of me in which the biographer does not scatter,

according to her custom, but sticks pretty steadily to a single subject until she has fought it to a finish:

Feb. 27, '86. – Last summer while we were in Elmira an article
came out in the "Christian Union" by name "What ought he to
have done" treating of the government of children, or rather
giving an account of a fathers battle with his little baby boy, by
the mother of the child and put in the form of a question as to
whether the father disciplined the child corectly or not, different
people wrote their opinions of the fathers behavior, and told
what they thought he should have done. Mamma had long
known how to disciplin children, for in fact the bringing up of
children had been one of her specialties for many years. She had
a great many theories, but one of them was, that if a child was
big enough to be nauty, it was big enough to be whipped and
here we all agreed with her. I remember one morning when
Dr. —— came up to the farm he had a long discussion with
mamma, upon the following topic. Mamma gave *this* as illustrative of one important rule for punishing a child. She said we will
suppose the boy has thrown a handkerchief onto the floor, I tell
him to pick it up, he refuses. I tell him again, he refuses. Then
I say you must either pick up the handkerchief or have a whipping. My theory is never to make a child have a whipping and
pick up the handkerchief too. I say "If you do not pick it up,
I must punish you," if he doesn't he gets the whipping, but *I* pick
up the handkerchief, if he does he gets no punishment. I tell him
to do a thing if he disobeys me he is punished for so doing, but
not forced to obey me afterwards.

When Clara and I had been very nauty or were being very
nauty, the nurse would go and call Mamma and she would
appear suddenly and look at us (she had a way of looking at us
when she was displeased as if she could see right through us) till
we were ready to sink through the floor from embarasment, and
total absence of knowing what to say. This look was usually followed with "Clara" or "Susy what do you mean by this? do you
want to come to the bath-room with me?" Then followed the
climax for Clara and I both new only too well what going to the
bath-room meant.

But mamma's first and foremost object was to make the child
understand that he is being punished for *his* sake, and because
the mother so loves him that she cannot allow him to do wrong;

also that it is as hard for her to punish him as for him to be punished and even harder. Mamma never allowed herself to punish us when she was angry with us she never struck us because she was enoyed at us and felt like striking us if we had been nauty and had enoyed her, so that she thought she felt or would show the least bit of temper toward us while punnishing us, she always postponed the punishment until *she* was no more chafed by our behavior. She never humored herself by striking or punishing us because or while she was the least bit enoyed with us.

Our very worst nautinesses were punished by being taken to the bath-room and being whipped by the paper cutter. But after the whipping was over, mamma did not allow us to leave her until we were perfectly happy, and perfectly understood why we had been whipped. I never remember having felt the least bit bitterly toward mamma for punishing me. I always felt I had deserved my punishment, and was much happier for having received it. For after mamma had punished us and shown her displeasure, she showed no signs of further displeasure, but acted as if we had not displeased her in any way.

Ordinary punishments answered very well for Susy. She was a thinker, and would reason out the purpose of them, apply the lesson, and achieve the reform required. But it was much less easy to devise punishments that would reform Clara. This was because she was a philosopher who was always turning her attention to finding something good and satisfactory and entertaining in everything that came her way; consequently it was sometimes pretty discouraging to the troubled mother to find that after all her pains and thought in inventing what she meant to be a severe and reform-compelling punishment, the child had entirely missed the severities through her native disposition to get interest and pleasure out of them as novelties. The mother, in her anxiety to find a penalty that would take sharp hold and do its work effectively, at last resorted, with a sore heart, and with a reproachful conscience, to that punishment which the incorrigible criminal in the penitentiary dreads above all the other punitive miseries which the warden inflicts upon him for his good – solitary confinement in the dark chamber. The grieved and worried mother shut Clara up in a very small clothes-closet and went away and left her there – for fifteen minutes – it was all that the mother-heart could endure. Then she came softly back and listened – listened for the sobs, but there weren't any; there were muffled and inarticulate sounds, but they could not be construed into sobs. The mother waited half an hour longer; by that time she was suffering so intensely with sorrow and compassion for the little prisoner that she was not able to wait any longer for the distressed sounds which she had counted upon to inform her when there had been punishment enough, and the reform accomplished. She opened the closet to set the prisoner free and take her back into her loving favor and forgiveness, but the result was not the one expected. The captive had manufactured a fairy cavern out of the closet, and friendly fairies out of the clothes hanging from the hooks, and was having a most sinful and unrepentant good time, and requested permission to spend the rest of the day there!

FROM SUSY'S BIOGRAPHY OF ME

But Mamma's oppinions and ideas upon the subject of bringing up children has always been more or less of a joke in our family, perticulary since Papa's article in the "Christian Union," and I am sure Clara and I have related the history of our old family paper-cutter, our punishments and privations with rather more pride and triumph than any other sentiment, because of Mamma's way of rearing us.

When the article "What ought he to have done?" came out Mamma read it, and was very much interested in it. And when papa heard that she had read it he went to work and secretly wrote his opinion of what the father ought to have done. He told Aunt Susy, Clara and I, about it but mamma was not to see it or hear any thing about it till it came out. He gave it to Aunt Susy to read, and after Clara and I had gone up to get ready for bed he brought it up for us to read. He told what he thought the father ought to have done by telling what mamma would have done. The article was a beautiful tribute to mamma and every word in it true. But still in writing about mamma he partly forgot that the article was going to be published, I think, and expressed himself more fully than he would do the second time he wrote it; I think the article has done and will do a great deal of good, and I think it would have been perfect for the family and friend's enjoyment, but a little bit too private to have been published as it was. And Papa felt so too, because the very next day or a few days after, he went down to New York to see if he couldn't get it back before it was published but it was too late, and he had to return without it. When the Christian Union reached the farm and papa's article in it all ready and waiting to be read to mamma papa hadn't the courage to show it to her (for he knew she wouldn't like it at all) at first, and he didn't but he might have let it go and never let her see it, but finally he gave his consent to her seeing it, and told Clara and I we could take it to her, which we did, with tardiness, and we all stood around mamma while she read it, all wondering what she would say and think about it.

She was too much surprised, (and pleased privately, too) to say much at first, but as we all expected publicly, (or rather when she remembered that this article was to be read by every one that took the Christian Union) she was rather shocked and a little displeased.

Clara and I had great fun the night papa gave it to us to read and then hide, so mamma couldn't see it, for just as we were in the midst of reading it mamma appeared papa following anxiously and asked why we were not in bed? then a scuffle ensued for we told her it was a secret and tried to hide it; but she chased us wherever we went, till she thought it was time for us to go to bed, then she surendered and left us to tuck it under Clara's matress.

A little while after the article was published letters began to come in to papa crittisizing it, there were some very pleasant ones but a few very disagreable. One of these, the very worst, mamma got hold of and read, to papa's great regret, it was full of the most disagreble things, and so very enoying to papa that he for a time felt he must do something to show the author of it his great displeasure at being so insulted. But he finally decided not to, because he felt the man had some cause for feeling enoyed at, for papa had spoken of him, (he was the baby's father) rather slightingly in his Christian Union Article.

After all this, papa and mamma both wished I think they might never hear or be spoken to on the subject of the Christian Union article, and whenever any has spoken to me and told me "How much they did enjoy my father's article in the Christian Union" I almost laughed in their faces when I remembered what a great variety of oppinions had been expressed upon the subject of the Christian Union article of papa's.

The article was written in July or August and just the other

day papa received quite a bright letter from a gentleman who
has read the C. U. article and gave his opinion of it in these
words.

It is missing. She probably put the letter between the leaves of
the Biography and it got lost out. She threw away the hostile letters, but tried to keep the pleasantest one for her book; surely there
has been no kindlier biographer than this one. Yet to a quite creditable degree she is loyal to the responsibilities of her position as
historian – not eulogist – and honorably gives me a quiet prod now
and then. But how many, many, many she has withheld that I
deserved! I could prize them now; there would be no acid in her
words, and it is loss to me that she did not set them all down. Oh,
Susy, you sweet little biographer, you break my old heart with your
gentle charities!

I think a great deal of her work. Her canvases are on their easels,
and her brush flies about in a care-free and random way, delivering
a dash here, a dash there and another yonder, and one might suppose that there would be no definite result; on the contrary I think
that an intelligent reader of her little book must find that by the
time he has finished it he has somehow accumulated a pretty clear
and nicely shaded idea of the several members of this family –
including Susy herself – and that the random dashes on the canvases have developed into portraits. I feel that my own portrait,
with some of the defects fined down and others left out, is here;
and I am sure that any who knew the mother will recognize her
without difficulty, and will say that the lines are drawn with a just
judgment and a sure hand. Little creature though Susy was, the
penetration which was born in her finds its way to the surface more
than once in these pages.

Before Susy began the Biography she let fall a remark now and
then concerning my character which showed that she had it under
observation. In the Record which we kept of the children's sayings
there is an instance of this. She was twelve years old at the time.
We had established a rule that each member of the family must
bring a fact to breakfast – a fact drawn from a book or from any
other source; any fact would answer. Susy's first contribution was
in substance as follows. Two great exiles and former opponents in
war met in Ephesus – Scipio and Hannibal. Scipio asked Hannibal
to name the greatest general the world had produced.

"Alexander" – and he explained why.

"And the next greatest?"

"Pyrrhus" – and he explained why.

"But where do you place yourself, then?"

"If I had conquered you I would place myself before the others."

Susy's grave comment was –

"That *attracted* me, it was just like papa – he is so frank about his books."

So frank in admiring them, she meant.

[*Thursday, March 28, 1907.*] Some months ago I commented upon a chapter of Susy's Biography wherein she very elaborately discussed an article about the training and disciplining of children, which I had published in the "Christian Union" (this was twenty-one years ago), an article which was full of worshipful praises of Mrs. Clemens as a mother, and which little Clara and Susy, and I had been hiding from this lovely and admirable mother because we knew she would disapprove of public and printed praises of herself. At the time that I was dictating these comments, several months ago, I was trying to call back to my memory some of the details of that article, but I was not able to do it, and I wished I had a copy of the article so that I could see what there was about it which gave it such large interest for Susy.

Yesterday afternoon I elected to walk home from the luncheon at the St. Regis, which is in 55th Street and Fifth Avenue, for it was a fine spring day and I hadn't had a walk for a year or two, and felt the need of exercise. As I walked along down Fifth Avenue the desire to see that "Christian Union" article came into my head again. I had just reached the corner of 42nd Street then, and there was the usual jam of wagons, carriages, and automobiles there. I stopped to let it thin out before trying to cross the street, but a stranger, who didn't require as much room as I do, came racing by and darted into a crack among the vehicles and made the crossing. But on his way past me he thrust a couple of ancient newspaper clippings into my hand, and said,

"There, you don't know me, but I have saved them in my scrap-book for twenty years, and it occurred to me this morning that perhaps you would like to see them, so I was carrying them down-town to mail them, I not expecting to run across you in this accidental way, of course; but I will give them into your own hands now. Good-by!" – and he disappeared among the wagons.

Those scraps which he had put into my hand were ancient

newspaper copies of that "Christian Union" article! It is a handsome instance of mental telegraphy – or if it isn't that, it is a
handsome case of coincidence.

FROM THE BIOGRAPHY

March 14th, '86. – Mr. Laurence Barrette and Mr. and Mrs. Hutton were here a little while ago, and we had a very interesting
visit from them. Papa said Mr. Barette never had acted so well
before when he had seen him, as he did the first night he was
staying with us. And Mrs. —— said she never had seen an actor
on the stage, whom she more wanted to speak with.

Papa has been very much interested of late, in the "Mind
Cure" theory. And in fact so have we all. A young lady in town
has worked wonders, by using the "Mind Cure" upon people;
she is constantly busy now curing peoples deseases in this way
– and curing her own even, which to me seems the most remarkable of all.

A little while past, papa was delighted with the knowledge of
what he thought the best way of curing a cold, which was by
starving it. This starving did work beautifully, and freed him
from a great many severe colds. Now he says it wasn't the starving that helped his colds, but the trust in the starving, the mind
cure connected with the starving.

I shouldn't wonder if we finally became firm believers in
Mind Cure. The next time papa has a cold, I haven't a doubt,
he will send for Miss H—— the young lady who is doctoring in
the "Mind Cure" theory, to cure him of it.

Mamma was over at Mrs. George Warners to lunch the other
day, and Miss H—— was there too. Mamma asked if anything
as natural as near sightedness could be cured she said oh yes just
as well as other deseases.

When mamma came home, she took me into her room, and
told me that perhaps my near-sightedness could be cured by the
"Mind Cure" and that she was going to have me try the treatment any way, there could be no harm in it, and there might be
great good. If her plan succeeds there certainly will be a great
deal in "Mind Cure" to my oppinion, for I am *very* near sighted
and so is mamma, and I never expected there could be any more
cure for it than for blindness, but now I dont know but what
theres a cure for *that.*

It was a disappointment; her near-sightedness remained with her to the end. She was born with it, no doubt; yet, strangely enough, she must have been four years old, and possibly five, before we knew of its existence. It is not easy to understand how that could have happened. I discovered the defect by accident. I was half-way up the hall stairs one day at home, and was leading her by the hand, when I glanced back through the open door of the dining-room and saw what I thought she would recognize as a pretty picture. It was "Stray Kit," the slender, the graceful, the sociable, the beautiful, the incomparable, the cat of cats, the tortoise-shell, curled up as round as a wheel and sound asleep on the fire-red cover of the dining-table, with a brilliant stream of sunlight falling across her. I exclaimed about it, but Susy said she could see nothing there, neither cat nor table-cloth. The distance was so slight – not more than twenty feet, perhaps – that if it had been any other child I should not have credited the statement.

FROM THE BIOGRAPHY

March 14th, '86. – Clara sprained her ankle, a little while ago, by running into a tree, when coasting, and while she was unable to walk with it she played solotaire with cards a great deal. While Clara was sick and papa saw her play solotaire so much, he got very much interested in the game, and finally began to play it himself a little, then Jean took it up, and at last *mamma*, even played it ocasionally; Jean's and papa's love for it rapidly increased, and now Jean brings the cards every night to the table and papa and mamma help her play, and before dinner is at an end, papa has gotten a separate pack of cards, and is playing alone, with great interest. Mamma and Clara next are made subject to the contagious solatair, and there are four solotaireans at the table; while you hear nothing but "Fill up the place" etc. It is dreadful! after supper Clara goes into the library, and gets a little red mahogany table, and placing it under the gas fixture seats herself and begins to play again, then papa follows with another table of the same discription, and they play solatair till bedtime.

We have just had our Prince and Pauper pictures taken; two groups and some little single ones. The groups (the Interview and Lady Jane Grey scene) were pretty good, the lady Jane scene was perfect, just as pretty as it could be, the Interview was not

so good; and two of the little single pictures were very good
indeed, but one was very bad. Yet on the whole we think they
were a success.

Papa has done a great deal in his life I think, that is good, and
very remarkable, but I think if he had had the advantages with
which he could have developed the gifts which he has made no
use of in writing his books, or in any other way for other peoples
pleasure and benefit outside of his own family and intimate
friends, he could have done *more* than he has and a great deal
more even. He is known to the public as a humorist, but he has
much more in him that is earnest than that is humorous. He has
a keen sense of the ludicrous, notices funny stories and incidents
knows how to tell them, to improve upon them, and does not
forget them. He has been through a great many of the funny
adventures related in "Tom Sayer" and in "Huckleberry Finn,"
himself and he lived among just such boys, and in just such villages all the days of his early life. His "Prince and Pauper is his
most orriginal, and best production; it shows the most of any of
his books what kind of pictures are in his mind, usually. Not that
the pictures of England in the 16th Century and the adventures
of a little prince and pauper are the kind of things he mainly
thinks about; but that *that* book, and those pictures represent
the train of thought and imagination he would be likely to be
thinking of to-day, to-morrow, or next day, more nearly than
those given in "Tom Sawyer or "Huckleberry Finn."

Papa can make exceedingly bright jokes, and he enjoys funny
things, and when he is with people he jokes and laughs a great
deal, but still he is more interested in earnest books and earnest
subjects to talk upon, than in humorous ones.

When we are all alone at home, nine times out of ten, he talks
about some very earnest subjects, (with an ocasional joke
thrown in) and he a good deal more often talks upon such subjects than upon the other kind.

He is as much of a Pholosopher as anything I think. I think
he could have done a great deal in this direction if he had studied
while young, for he seems to enjoy reasoning out things, no matter what; in a great many such directions he has greater ability
than in the gifts which have made him famous.

Thus at fourteen she had made up her mind about me, and in
no timorous or uncertain terms had set down her reasons for her

opinion. Fifteen years were to pass before any other critic – except Mr. Howells, I think – was to reutter that daring opinion and print it. Right or wrong, it was a brave position for that little analyzer to take. She never withdrew it afterward, nor modified it. She has spoken of herself as lacking physical courage, and has evinced her admiration of Clara's; but she had moral courage, which is the rarest of human qualities, and she kept it functionable by exercising it. I think that in questions of morals and politics she was usually on my side; but when she was not she had her reasons and maintained her ground. Two years after she passed out of my life I wrote a Philosophy. Of the three persons who have seen the manuscript only one understood it, and all three condemned it. If she could have read it, she also would have condemned it, possibly, – probably, in fact – but she would have understood it. It would have had no difficulties for her on that score; also she would have found a tireless pleasure in analyzing and discussing its problems.

PART XIX

JUNE 7, 1907

FROM SUSY'S BIOGRAPHY OF ME

March 23, '86. – The other day was my birthday, and I had a little birthday party in the evening and papa acted some very funny charades with Mr. Gherhardt, Mr. Jesse Grant (who had come up from New York and was spending the evening with us) and Mr. Frank Warner. One of them was "on his knees" honyssneeze. There were a good many other funny ones, all of which I dont remember. Mr. Grant was very pleasant, and began playing the charades in the most delightful way.

Susy's spelling has defeated me, this time. I cannot make out what "honys-sneeze" stands for. Impromptu charades were almost a nightly pastime of ours, from the children's earliest days – they played in them with me when they were only five or six years old. As they increased in years and practice their love for the sport almost amounted to a passion, and they acted their parts with a steadily increasing ability. At first they required much drilling; but later they were generally ready as soon as the parts were assigned, and they acted them according to their own devices. Their stage facility and absence of constraint and self-consciousness in the "Prince and Pauper" was a result of their charading practice.

At ten and twelve Susy wrote plays, and she and Daisy Warner and Clara played them in the library or up-stairs in the school-room, with only themselves and the servants for audience. They were of a tragic and tremendous sort, and were performed with great energy and earnestness. They were dramatized (freely) from English history, and in them Mary Queen of Scots and Elizabeth had few holidays. The clothes were borrowed from the mother's wardrobe and the gowns were longer than necessary, but that was not regarded as a defect. In one of these plays Jean (three years old, perhaps) was Sir Francis Bacon. She was not dressed for the part, and did not have to say anything, but sat silent and decorous at a tiny table and was kept busy signing death-warrants. It was a really important office, for few entered those plays and got out of them alive.

March 26. – Mamma and Papa have been in New York for two or three days, and Miss Corey has been staying with us. They are coming home to-day at two o'clock.

Papa has just begun to play chess, and he is very fond of it, so he has engaged to play with Mrs. Charles Warner every morning from 10 to 12, he came down to supper last night, full of this pleasant prospect, but evidently with something on his mind. Finally he said to mamma in an appologetical tone, Susy Warner and I have a plan.

"Well" mamma said "what now, I wonder?"

Papa said that Susy Warner and he were going to name the chess men after some of the old bible heroes and then play chess on Sunday.

April 18, '86. – Mamma and papa Clara and Daisy have gone to New York to see the "Mikado." They are coming home to-night at half past seven.

Last winter when Mr. Cable was lecturing with papa, he wrote this letter to him just before he came to visit us.

DEAR UNCLE, – That's one nice thing about me, I never bother any one, to offer me a good thing twice. You dont ask me to stay over Sunday, but then you dont ask me to leave Saturday night, and knowing the nobility of your nature as I do – thank you, I'll stay till Monday morning.

Your's and the dear familie's

. GEORGE W. CABLE.

[*December 22, 1906.*] It seems a prodigious while ago! Two or three nights ago I dined at a friend's house with a score of other men, and at my side was Cable – actually almost an old man, really almost an old man, that once so young chap! 62 years old, frost on his head, seven grandchildren in stock, and a brand-new wife to re-begin life with!

[*Dictated Nov. 19, 1906.*]

Ever since papa and mamma were married, papa has written his books and then taken them to mamma in manuscript and she has expergated them. Papa read "Huckleberry Finn" to us in manuscript just before it came out, and then he would leave parts of it with mamma to expergate, while he went off up to the study to work, and sometimes Clara and I would be sitting with mamma while she was looking the manuscript over, and I remember so well, with what pangs of regret we used to see her turn down the leaves of the pages, which meant that some delightfully dreadful part must be scratched out. And I remember one part pertickularly which was perfectly fascinating it was dreadful, that Clara and I used to delight in, and oh with what dispair we saw mamma turn down the leaf on which it was written, we thought the book would be almost ruined without it. But we gradually came to feel as mamma did.

It would be a pity to replace the vivacity and quaintness and felicity of Susy's innocent free spelling with the dull and petrified uniformities of the spelling-book. Nearly all the grimness is taken out of the "expergating" of my books by the subtle mollification accidentally infused into the word by Susy's modification of the spelling of it.

I remember the special case mentioned by Susy, and can see the group yet – two-thirds of it pleading for the life of the culprit sentence that was so fascinatingly dreadful and the other third of it patiently explaining why the court could not grant the prayer of the pleaders; but I do not remember what the condemned phrase was. It had much company, and they all went to the gallows; but it is possible that that specially dreadful one which gave those little people so much delight was cunningly devised and put into the book for just that function, and not with any hope or expectation that it would get by the "expergator" alive. It is possible, for I had that custom.

Susy's quaint and effective spelling falls quite opportunely into to-day's atmosphere, which is heavy with the rumblings and grumblings and mutterings of the Simplified Spelling Reform. Andrew Carnegie started this storm, a couple of years ago, by moving a simplifying of English orthography, and establishing a fund for the prosecution and maintenance of the crusade. He began gently. He addressed a circular to some hundreds of his friends, asking them to simplify the spelling of a dozen of our badly spelt words – I think they were only words which end with the superfluous *ugh*. He asked that these friends use the suggested spellings in their private correspondence.

By this, one perceives that the beginning was sufficiently quiet and unaggressive.

Next stage: a small committee was appointed, with Brander Matthews for managing director and spokesman. It issued a list of three hundred words, of average silliness as to spelling, and proposed new and sane spellings for these words. The President of the United States, unsolicited, adopted these simplified three hundred officially, and ordered that they be used in the official documents of the Government. It was now remarked, by all the educated and the thoughtful except the clergy that Sheol was to pay. This was most justly and comprehensively descriptive. The indignant British lion rose, with a roar that was heard across the Atlantic, and stood there on his little isle, gazing, red-eyed, out over the glooming seas, snow-flecked with driving spindrift, and lashing his tail – a most scary spectacle to see.

The lion was outraged because we, a nation of children, without any grown-up people among us, with no property in the language, but using it merely by courtesy of its owner the English nation, were trying to defile the sacredness of it by removing from it peculiarities which had been its ornament and which had made it holy and beautiful for ages.

In truth there is a certain sardonic propriety in preserving our orthography, since ours is a mongrel language which started with a child's vocabulary of three hundred words, and now consists of two hundred and twenty-five thousand; the whole lot, with the exception of the original and legitimate three hundred, borrowed, stolen, smouched from every unwatched language under the sun, the spelling of each individual word of the lot locating the source of the theft and preserving the memory of the revered crime.

Why is it that I have intruded into this turmoil and manifested a desire to get our orthography purged of its asininities? Indeed I do not know why I should manifest any interest in the matter, for at bottom I disrespect our orthography most heartily, and as heartily disrespect everything that has been said by anybody in defence of it. Nothing professing to be a defence of our ludicrous spellings has had any basis, so far as my observation goes, except sentimentality. In these "arguments" the term venerable is used instead of mouldy, and hallowed instead of devilish; whereas there is nothing properly venerable or antique about a language which is not yet four hundred years old, and about a jumble of imbecile spellings which were grotesque in the beginning, and which grow more and more grotesque with the flight of the years.

[*Dictated Monday, November 30, 1906.*]

Jean and Papa were walking out past the barn the other day when Jean saw some little newly born baby ducks, she exclaimed as she perceived them "I dont see why God gives us so much ducks when Patrick kills them so."

Susy is mistaken as to the origin of the ducks. They were not a gift, I bought them. I am not finding fault with her, for that would be most unfair. She is remarkably accurate in her statements as a historian, as a rule, and it would not be just to make much of this small slip of hers; besides I think it was a quite natural slip, for by heredity and habit ours was a religious household, and it was a common thing with us whenever anybody did a handsome thing, to give the credit of it to Providence, without examining into the matter. This may be called automatic religion – in fact that is what it is; it is so used to its work that it can do it without your help or even your privity; out of all the facts and statistics that may be placed before it, it will always get the one result, since it has never been taught to seek any other. It is thus the unreflecting cause of much injustice. As we have seen, it betrayed Susy into an injustice toward me. It had to be automatic, for she would have been far from doing me an injustice when in her right mind. It was a dear

little biographer, and she meant me no harm, and I am not censur-
ing her now, but am only desirous of correcting in advance an
erroneous impression which her words would be sure to convey to
a reader's mind. No elaboration of this matter is necessary; it is
sufficient to say *I* provided the ducks.

It was in Hartford. The greensward sloped down-hill from the
house to the sluggish little river that flowed through the grounds,
and Patrick, who was fertile in good ideas, had early conceived the
idea of having home-made ducks for our table. Every morning he
drove them from the stable down to the river, and the children
were always there to see and admire the waddling white procession; they were there again at sunset to see Patrick conduct the
procession back to its lodgings in the stable. But this was not always
a gay and happy holiday show, with joy in it for the witnesses; no,
too frequently there was a tragedy connected with it, and then
there were tears and pain for the children. There was a stranded
log or two in the river, and on these certain families of snapping-
turtles used to congregate and drowse in the sun and give thanks,
in their dumb way, to Providence for benevolence extended to
them. It was but another instance of misplaced credit; it was the
young ducks that those pious reptiles were so thankful for –
whereas they were *my* ducks. I bought the ducks.

When a crop of young ducks, not yet quite old enough for the
table but approaching that age, began to join the procession, and
paddle around in the sluggish water, and give thanks – not to me
– for that privilege, the snapping-turtles would suspend their songs
of praise and slide off the logs and paddle along under the water
and chew the feet of the young ducks. Presently Patrick would
notice that two or three of those little creatures were not moving
about, but were apparently at anchor, and were not looking as
thankful as they had been looking a short time before. He early
found out what that sign meant – a submerged snapping-turtle was
taking his breakfast, and silently singing his gratitude. Every day
or two Patrick would rescue and fetch up a little duck with incomplete legs to stand upon – nothing left of their extremities but
gnawed and bleeding stumps. Then the children said pitying
things and wept – and at dinner we finished the tragedy which
the turtles had begun. Thus, as will be seen – out of season, at
least – it was really the turtles that gave us so much ducks. At my
expense.

Papa has written a new version of "There is a happy land" it is –

> "There is a boarding-house
>   Far, far away,
> Where they have ham and eggs,
>   Three times a day,
> Oh dont those boarders yell
> When they hear the dinner-bell,
> They give that land-lord rats
>   Three times a day."

Again Susy has made a small error. It was not I that wrote the song. I heard Billy Rice sing it in the negro minstrel show, and I brought it home and sang it – with great spirit – for the elevation of the household. The children admired it to the limit, and made me sing it with burdensome frequency. To their minds it was superior to the Battle Hymn of the Republic.

How many years ago that was! Where now is Billy Rice? He was a joy to me, and so were the other stars of the nigger-show – Billy Birch, David Wambold, Backus, and a delightful dozen of their brethren, who made life a pleasure to me forty years ago, and later. Birch, Wambold, and Backus are gone years ago; and with them departed to return no more forever, I suppose, the real nigger-show – the genuine nigger-show, the extravagant nigger-show, – the show which to me had no peer and whose peer has not yet arrived, in my experience. We have the grand opera; and I have witnessed, and greatly enjoyed, the first act of everything which Wagner created, but the effect on me has always been so powerful that one act was quite sufficient; whenever I have witnessed two acts I have gone away physically exhausted; and whenever I have ventured an entire opera the result has been the next thing to sui-cide. But if I could have the nigger-show back again, in its pristine purity and perfection, I should have but little further use for opera. It seems to me that to the elevated mind and the sensitive spirit the hand-organ and the nigger-show are a standard and a summit to whose rarefied altitude the other forms of musical art may not hope to reach.

[*Dictated September 5, 1906.*] It is years since I have examined "The Children's Record." I have turned over a few of its pages this morning. This book is a record in which Mrs. Clemens and I registered some of the sayings and doings of the children, in the long ago, when they were little chaps. Of course, we wrote these things down at the time because they were of momentary interest – things of the passing hour, and of no permanent value – but at this distant day I find that they still possess an interest for me and also a value, because it turns out that they were *registrations of character*. The qualities then revealed by fitful glimpses, in childish acts and speeches, remained as a permanency in the children's characters in the drift of the years, and were always afterwards clearly and definitely recognizable.

There is a masterful streak in Jean that now and then moves her to set my authority aside for a moment and end a losing argument in that prompt and effective fashion. And here in this old book I find evidence that she was just like that before she was quite four years old.

From The Children's Record. Quarry Farm, July 7, 1884. – Yesterday evening our cows (after being inspected and worshipped by Jean from the shed for an hour,) wandered off down into the pasture, and left her bereft. I thought I was going to get back home, now, but that was an error. Jean knew of some more cows, in a field somewhere, and took my hand and led me thitherward. When we turned the corner and took the right-hand road, I saw that we should presently be out of range of call and sight; so I began to argue against continuing the expedition, and Jean began to argue in favor of it – she using English for light skirmishing, and German for "business." I kept up my end with vigor, and demolished her arguments in detail, one after the other, till I judged I had her about cornered. She hesitated a moment, then answered up sharply:

"*Wir werden nichts mehr darüber sprechen!*" (We won't talk any more about it!)

It nearly took my breath away; though I thought I might possibly have misunderstood. I said:

"Why, you little rascal! *Was hast du gesagt?*"

But she said the same words over again, and in the same decided way. I suppose I ought to have been outraged; but I wasn't, I was charmed. And I suppose I ought to have spanked her; but I didn't, I fraternized with the enemy, and we went on and spent half an hour with the cows.

That incident is followed in the "Record" by the following paragraph, which is another instance of a juvenile characteristic maintaining itself into mature age. Susy was persistently and conscientiously truthful throughout her life with the exception of one interruption covering several months, and perhaps a year. This was while she was still a little child. Suddenly – not gradually – she began to lie; not furtively, but frankly, openly, and on a scale quite disproportioned to her size. Her mother was so stunned, so nearly paralyzed for a day or two, that she did not know what to do with the emergency. Reasonings, persuasions, beseechings, all went for nothing; they produced no effect; the lying went tranquilly on. Other remedies were tried, but they failed. There is a tradition that success was finally accomplished by whipping. I think the Record says so, but if it does it is because the Record is incomplete. Whipping was indeed tried, and was faithfully kept up during two or three weeks, but the results were merely temporary; the reforms achieved were discouragingly brief.

Fortunately for Susy, an incident presently occurred which put a complete stop to all the mother's efforts in the direction of reform. This incident was the chance discovery in Darwin of a passage which said that when a child exhibits a sudden and unaccountable disposition to forsake the truth and restrict itself to lying, the explanation must be sought away back in the past; that an ancestor of the child had had the same disease, at the same tender age; that it was irremovable by persuasion or punishment, and that it had ceased as suddenly and as mysteriously as it had come, when it had run its appointed course. I think Mr. Darwin said that nothing was necessary but to leave the matter alone and let the malady have its way and perish by the statute of limitations.

We had confidence in Darwin, and after that day Susy was relieved of our reformatory persecutions. She went on lying without let or hindrance during several months, or a year; then the lying suddenly ceased, and she became as conscientiously and exactingly truthful as she had been before the attack, and she remained so to the end of her life.

The paragraph in the Record to which I have been leading up is in my handwriting, and is of a date so long posterior to the time of the lying malady that she had evidently forgotten that truth-speaking had ever had any difficulties for her.

Mama was speaking of a servant who had been pretty unveracious, but was now "trying to tell the truth." Susy was a good deal surprised, and said she shouldn't think anybody would have to *try* to tell the truth.

In the Record the children's acts and speeches quite definitely define their characters. Susy's indicated the presence of mentality – thought – and they were generally marked by gravity. She was timid, on her physical side, but had an abundance of moral courage. Clara was sturdy, independent, orderly, practical, persistent, plucky – just a little animal, and very satisfactory. Charles Dudley Warner said Susy was made of mind, and Clara of matter.

When Motley, the kitten, died, some one said that the thoughts of the two children need not be inquired into, they could be divined: that Susy was wondering if this was the *end* of Motley, and had his life been worth while; whereas Clara was merely interested in seeing to it that there should be a creditable funeral.

In those days Susy was a dreamer, a thinker, a poet and philosopher, and Clara – well, Clara wasn't. In after-years a passion for music developed the latent spirituality and intellectuality in Clara, and her practicality took second and, in fact, even third place. Jean was from the beginning orderly, steady, diligent, persistent; and remains so. She picked up languages easily, and kept them.

Susy aged eleven, Jean three. – Susy said the other day when she saw Jean bringing a cat to me of her own motion, "Jean has found out already that mamma loves morals and papa loves cats."

It is another of Susy's remorselessly sound verdicts.

As a child, Jean neglected my books. When she was nine years old Will Gillette invited her and the rest of us to a dinner at the Murray Hill Hotel in New York, in order that we might get acquainted with Mrs. Leslie and her daughters. Elsie Leslie was nine years old, and was a great celebrity on the stage. Jean was astonished and awed to see that little slip of a thing sit up at table and take part in the conversation of the grown people, capably and with ease and tranquillity. Poor Jean was obliged to keep still, for the subjects discussed never happened to hit her level, but at last the talk fell within her limit and she had her chance to contribute to it. "Tom Sawyer" was mentioned. Jean spoke gratefully up and said,

"I know who wrote that book – Harriet Beecher Stowe!"

One evening Susy had prayed, Clara was curled up for sleep; she was reminded that it was her turn to pray now. She said "Oh! one's enough," and dropped off to slumber.

Clara five years old. – We were in Germany. The nurse, Rosa, was not allowed to speak to the children otherwise than in German. Clara grew very tired of it; by and by the little creature's patience was exhausted, and she said "Aunt Clara, I wish God had made Rosa in English."

Clara four years old, Susy six. – This morning when Clara discovered that this is my birthday, she was greatly troubled because she had provided no gift for me, and repeated her sorrow several times Finally she went musing to the nursery and presently returned with her newest and dearest treasure, a large toy horse, and said, "You shall have this horse for your birthday, papa."

I accepted it with many thanks. After an hour she was racing up and down the room with the horse, when Susy said,

"Why Clara, you gave that horse to papa, and now you've tooken it again."

Clara. – "I never give it to him for always; I give it to him for his birthday."

In Geneva, in September, I lay abed late one morning, and as Clara was passing through the room I took her on my bed a moment. Then the child went to Clara Spaulding and said,

"Aunt Clara, papa is a good deal of trouble to me."

"Is he? Why?"

"Well, he wants me to get in bed with him, and I can't do that with jelmuls [gentlemen] – I don't like jelmuls anyway."

"What, you don't like gentlemen! Don't you like Uncle Theodore Crane?"

"Oh yes, but he's not a jelmul, he's a friend."

PART XX

JULY 5, 1907

[*Notes on "Innocents Abroad." Dictated in Florence, Italy, April, 1904.*] –
I will begin with a note upon the dedication. I wrote the book in
the months of March and April, 1868, in San Francisco. It was
published in August, 1869. Three years afterward Mr. Goodman,
of Virginia City, Nevada, on whose newspaper I had served ten
years before, came East, and we were walking down Broadway one
day when he said: "How did you come to steal Oliver Wendell
Holmes's dedication and put it in your book?"

I made a careless and inconsequential answer, for I supposed he
was joking. But he assured me that he was in earnest. He said: "I'm
not discussing the question of whether you stole it or didn't – for
that is a question that can be settled in the first bookstore we come
to – I am only asking you *how* you came to steal it, for that is where
my curiosity is focalized."

I couldn't accommodate him with this information, as I hadn't
it in stock. I could have made oath that I had not stolen anything,
therefore my vanity was not hurt nor my spirit troubled. At bottom
I supposed that he had mistaken another book for mine, and was
now getting himself into an untenable place and preparing sorrow
for himself and triumph for me. We entered a bookstore and he
asked for "The Innocents Abroad" and for the dainty little blue
and gold edition of Dr. Oliver Wendell Holmes's poems. He
opened the books, exposed their dedications and said: "Read
them. It is plain that the author of the second one stole the first
one, isn't it?"

I was very much ashamed, and unspeakably astonished. We
continued our walk, but I was not able to throw any gleam of light
upon that original question of his. I could not remember ever having seen Dr. Holmes's dedication. I knew the poems, but the dedication was new to me.

I did not get hold of the key to that secret until months afterward, then it came in a curious way, and yet it was a natural way;
for the natural way provided by nature and the construction of the
human mind for the discovery of a forgotten event is to employ
another forgotten event for its resurrection.

I received a letter from the Rev. Dr. Rising, who had been rector
of the Episcopal church in Virginia City in my time, in which letter

Dr. Rising made reference to certain things which had happened to us in the Sandwich Islands six years before; among things he made casual mention of the Honolulu Hotel's poverty in the matter of literature. At first I did not see the bearing of the remark, it called nothing to my mind. But presently it did – with a flash! There was but one book in Mr. Kirchhof's hotel, and that was the first volume of Dr. Holmes's blue and gold series. I had had a fortnight's chance to get well acquainted with its contents, for I had ridden around the big island (Hawaii) on horseback and had brought back so many saddle boils that if there had been a duty on them it would have bankrupted me to pay it. They kept me in my room, unclothed, and in persistent pain for two weeks, with no company but cigars and the little volume of poems. Of course I read them almost constantly; I read them from beginning to end, then read them backwards, then began in the middle and read them both ways, then read them wrong end first and upside down. In a word, I read the book to rags, and was infinitely grateful to the hand that wrote it.

Here we have an exhibition of what repetition can do, when persisted in daily and hourly over a considerable stretch of time, where one is merely reading for entertainment, without thought or intention of preserving in the memory that which is read. It is a process which in the course of years dries all the juice out of a familiar verse of Scripture, leaving nothing but a sapless husk behind. In that case you at least know the origin of the husk, but in the case in point I apparently preserved the husk but presently forgot whence it came. It lay lost in some dim corner of my memory a year or two, then came forward when I needed a dedication, and was promptly mistaken by me as a child of my own happy fancy.

I was new, I was ignorant, the mysteries of the human mind were a sealed book to me as yet, and I stupidly looked upon myself as a tough and unforgivable criminal. I wrote to Dr. Holmes and told him the whole disgraceful affair, implored him in impassioned language to believe that I had never intended to commit this crime, and was unaware that I had committed it until I was confronted with the awful evidence. I have lost his answer, I could better have afforded to lose an uncle. Of these I had a surplus, many of them of no real value to me, but that letter was beyond price, beyond uncledom, and unsparable. In it Dr. Holmes laughed the kindest and healingest laugh over the whole matter, and at considerable

length and in happy phrase assured me that there was no crime
in unconscious plagiarism; that I committed it every day, that he
committed it every day, that every man alive on the earth who
writes or speaks commits it every day and not merely once or twice
but every time he opens his mouth; that all our phrasings are spir-
itualized shadows cast multitudinously from our readings; that no
happy phrase of ours is ever quite original with us, there is nothing
of our own in it except some slight change born of our temperament, character, environment, teachings and associations; that
this slight change differentiates it from another man's manner of
saying it, stamps it with our special style, and makes it our own
for the time being; all the rest of it being old, moldy, antique, and
smelling of the breath of a thousand generations of them that have
passed it over their teeth before!

   In the thirty-odd years which have come and gone since then,
I have satisfied myself that what Dr. Holmes said was true.

   I wish to make a note upon the preface of the "Innocents." In
the last paragraph of that brief preface, I speak of the proprietors of
the "Daily Alta California" having "waived their rights" in certain
letters which I wrote for that journal while absent on the "Quaker
City" trip. I was young then, I am white-headed now, but the insult
of that word rankles yet, now that I am reading that paragraph for
the first time in many years, reading it for the first time since it was
written, perhaps. There were rights, it is true − such rights as the
strong are able to acquire over the weak and the absent. Early in
'66 George Barnes invited me to resign my reportership on his
paper, the San Francisco "Morning Call," and for some months
thereafter I was without money or work; then I had a pleasant turn
of fortune. The proprietors of the "Sacramento Union," a great
and influential daily journal, sent me to the Sandwich Islands to
write four letters a month at twenty dollars apiece. I was there four
or five months, and returned to find myself about the best known
honest man on the Pacific Coast. Thomas McGuire, proprietor of
several theatres, said that now was the time to make my fortune −
strike while the iron was hot! − break into the lecture field! I did
it. I announced a lecture on the Sandwich Islands, closing the
advertisement with the remark, "Admission one dollar; doors
open at half-past 7, the trouble begins at 8." A true prophecy. The
trouble certainly did begin at 8, when I found myself in front of
the only audience I had ever faced, for the fright which pervaded
me from head to foot was paralyzing. It lasted two minutes and

was as bitter as death, the memory of it is indestructible, but it had its compensations, for it made me immune from timidity before audiences for all time to come. I lectured in all the principal Californian towns and in Nevada, then lectured once or twice more in San Francisco, then retired from the field rich – for me – and laid out a plan to sail Westward from San Francisco, and go around the world. The proprietors of the "Alta" engaged me to write an account of the trip for that paper – fifty letters of a column and a half each, which would be about two thousand words per letter, and the pay to be twenty dollars per letter.

I went East to St. Louis to say good-bye to my mother, and then I was bitten by the prospectus of Captain Duncan of the "Quaker City" excursion, and I ended by joining it. During the trip I wrote and sent the fifty letters; six of them miscarried, and I wrote six new ones to complete my contract. Then I put together a lecture on the trip and delivered it in San Francisco at great and satisfactory pecuniary profit, then I branched out into the country and was aghast at the result: I had been entirely forgotten, I never had people enough in my houses to sit as a jury of inquest on my lost reputation! I inquired into this curious condition of things and found that the thrifty owners of that prodigiously rich "Alta" newspaper had *copyrighted* all those poor little twenty-dollar letters, and had threatened with prosecution any journal which should venture to copy a paragraph from them!

And there I was! I had contracted to furnish a large book, concerning the excursion, to the American Publishing Co. of Hartford, and I supposed I should need all those letters to fill it out with. I was in an uncomfortable situation – that is, if the proprietors of this stealthily acquired copyright should refuse to let me use the letters. That is just what they did; Mr. Mac – something – I have forgotten the rest of his name – said his firm were going to make a book out of the letters in order to get back the thousand dollars which they had paid for them. I said that if they had acted fairly and honorably, and had allowed the country press to use the letters or portions of them, my lecture-skirmish on the coast would have paid me ten thousand dollars, whereas the "Alta" had lost me that amount. Then he offered a compromise: he would publish the book and allow me ten per cent. royalty on it. The compromise did not appeal to me, and I said so. I was now quite unknown outside of San Francisco, the book's sale would be confined to that city, and my royalty would not pay me enough to board me three months;

whereas my Eastern contract, if carried out, could be profitable to me, for I had a sort of reputation on the Atlantic seaboard acquired through the publication of six excursion-letters in the New York "Tribune" and one or two in the "Herald."

In the end Mr. Mac agreed to suppress his book, on certain conditions: in my preface I must thank the "Alta" for waiving its "rights" and granting me permission. I objected to the thanks. I could not with any large degree of sincerity thank the "Alta" for bankrupting my lecture-raid. After considerable debate my point was conceded and the thanks left out.

Noah Brooks was the editor of the "Alta" at the time, a man of sterling character and equipped with a right heart, also a good historian where facts were not essential. In biographical sketches of me written many years afterward (1902), he was quite eloquent in praises of the generosity of the "Alta" people in giving to me without compensation a book which, as history had afterward shown, was worth a fortune. After all the fuss, I did not levy heavily upon the "Alta" letters. I found that they were newspaper matter, not book matter. They had been written here and there and yonder, as opportunity had given me a chance working-moment or two during our feverish flight around about Europe or in the furnace-heat of my stateroom on board the "Quaker City," therefore they were loosely constructed, and needed to have some of the wind and water squeezed out of them. I used several of them – ten or twelve, perhaps. I wrote the rest of "The Innocents Abroad" in sixty days, and I could have added a fortnight's labor with the pen and gotten along without the letters altogether. I was very young in those days, exceedingly young, marvellously young, younger than I am now, younger than I shall ever be again, by hundreds of years. I worked every night from eleven or twelve until broad day in the morning, and as I did two hundred thousand words in the sixty days, the average was more than three thousand words a day – nothing for Sir Walter Scott, nothing for Louis Stevenson, nothing for plenty of other people, but quite handsome for me. In 1897, when we were living in Tedworth Square, London, and I was writing the book called "Following the Equator" my average was eighteen hundred words a day; here in Florence (1904), my average seems to be fourteen hundred words per sitting of four or five hours.*

* With the pen, I mean. This Autobiography is dictated, not written.

I was deducing from the above that I have been slowing down steadily in these thirty-six years, but I perceive that my statistics have a defect: three thousand words in the spring of 1868 when I was working seven or eight or nine hours at a sitting has little or no advantage over the sitting of today, covering half the time and producing half the output. Figures often beguile me, particularly when I have the arranging of them myself; in which case the remark attributed to Disraeli would often apply with justice and force:

"There are three kinds of lies: lies, damned lies, and statistics."

[*Dictated, January 23, 1907.*] – The proverb says that Providence protects children and idiots. This is really true. I know it because I have tested it. It did not protect George through the most of his campaign, but it saved him in his last inning, and the veracity of the proverb stood confirmed.

I have several times been saved by this mysterious interposition, when I was manifestly in extreme peril. It has been common, all my life, for smart people to perceive in me an easy prey for selfish designs, and I have walked without suspicion into the trap set for me, yet have often come out unscathed, against all the likelihoods. More than forty years ago, in San Francisco, the office staff adjourned, upon conclusion of its work at two o'clock in the morning, to a great bowling establishment where there were twelve alleys. I was invited, rather perfunctorily, and as a matter of etiquette – by which I mean that I was invited politely, but not urgently. But when I diffidently declined, with thanks, and explained that I knew nothing about the game, those lively young fellows became at once eager and anxious and urgent to have my society. This flattered me, for I perceived no trap, and I innocently and gratefully accepted their invitation. I was given an alley all to myself. The boys explained the game to me, and they also explained to me that there would be an hour's play, and that the player who scored the fewest ten-strikes in the hour would have to provide oysters and beer for the combination. This disturbed me very seriously, since it promised me bankruptcy, and I was sorry that this detail had been overlooked in the beginning. But my pride would not allow me to back out now, so I stayed in, and did what I could to look satisfied and glad I had come. It is not likely that I looked as contented as I wanted to, but the others looked glad enough to make up for it, for they were quite unable to hide their evil joy. They showed me how to stand, and how to stoop, and how to aim the ball, and how to let fly; and then the game began. The results were astonishing. In my ignorance I delivered the balls in apparently every way except the right one; but no matter – during half an hour I never started a ball down the alley that didn't score a ten-strike, every time, at the other end. The others lost their grip early, and their joy along with it. Now and then one of them got a ten-strike, but the occurrence was so rare that it made no show alongside of my giant score. The boys surrendered at the end of the half-hour, and put on their coats and gathered around me and in courteous, but sufficiently definite, language expressed their opinion of an experience-worn and seasoned expert who would stoop to lying and deception in order to rob kind and well-meaning friends who had put their trust in him under the delusion that he was an honest and honorable person. I was not able to convince them that I had not lied, for now my character was gone, and they refused to attach any value to anything I said. The proprietor of the place stood by for a while saying nothing, then he came to my defence. He said: "It looks like a mystery, gentlemen, but it isn't a mystery after it's explained. That is a *grooved* alley; you've only to start a ball down it any way you please and the groove will do the rest; it will slam the ball against the northeast curve of the head pin every time, and nothing can save the ten from going down."

It was true. The boys made the experiment and they found that there was no art that could send a ball down that alley and fail to score a ten-strike with it. When I had told those boys that I knew nothing about that game I was speaking only the truth; but it was ever thus, all through my life: whenever I have diverged from custom and principle and uttered a truth, the rule has been that the hearer hadn't strength of mind enough to believe it.

A quarter of a century ago I arrived in London to lecture a few weeks under the management of George Dolby, who had conducted the Dickens readings in America five or six years before. He took me to the Albemarle and fed me, and in the course of the dinner he enlarged a good deal, and with great satisfaction, upon his reputation as a player of fifteen-ball pool, and when he learned by my testimony that I had never seen the game played, and knew nothing of the art of pocketing balls, he enlarged more and more, and still more, and kept on enlarging, until I recognized that I was either in the presence of the very father of fifteen-ball pool or in the presence of his most immediate descendant. At the end of the dinner Dolby was eager to introduce me to the game and show me what he could do. We adjourned to the billiard-room and he framed the balls in a flat pyramid and told me to fire at the apex ball and then go on and do what I could toward pocketing the fifteen, after which he would take the cue and show me what a past-master of the game could do with those balls. I did as required. I began with the diffidence proper to my ignorant estate, and when I had finished my inning all the balls were in the pockets and Dolby was burying me under a volcanic irruption of acid sarcasms.

So I was a liar in Dolby's belief. He thought he had been sold, and at a cheap rate; but he divided his sarcasms quite fairly and quite equally between the two of us. He was full of ironical admiration of his childishness and innocence in letting a wandering and characterless and scandalous American load him up with deceptions of so transparent a character that they ought not to have deceived the house cat. On the other hand, he was remorselessly severe upon me for beguiling him, by studied and discreditable artifice, into bragging and boasting about his poor game in the presence of a professional expert disguised in lies and frauds, who could empty more balls in billiard pockets in an hour than he could empty into a basket in a day.

In the matter of fifteen-ball pool I never got Dolby's confidence wholly back, though I got it in other ways, and kept it until his death. I have played that game a number of times since, but that first time was the only time in my life that I have ever pocketed all the fifteen in a single inning.

My unsuspicious nature has made it necessary for Providence to save me from traps a number of times. Thirty years ago, a couple of Elmira bankers invited me to play the game of "Quaker" with them. I had never heard of the game before, and said that if it required intellect, I should not be able to entertain them. But they said it was merely a game of chance, and required no mentality – so I agreed to make a trial of it. They appointed four in the afternoon for the sacrifice. As the place, they chose a ground-floor room with a large window in it. Then they went treacherously around and advertised the "sell" which they were going to play upon me.

I arrived on time, and we began the game – with a large and eager free-list to superintend it. These superintendents were outside, with their noses pressed against the window-pane. The bankers described the game to me. So far as I recollect, the pattern of it was this: they had a pile of Mexican dollars on the table; twelve of them were of even date, fifty of them were of odd dates. The bankers were to separate a coin from the pile and hide it under a hand, and I must guess "odd" or "even." If I guessed correctly, the coin would be mine; if incorrectly, I lost a dollar. The first guess I made was "even," and was right. I guessed again, "even," and took the money. They fed me another one and I guessed "even" again, and took the money. I guessed "even" the fourth time, and took the money. It seemed to me that "even" was a good guess, and I might as well stay by it, which I did. I guessed "even" twelve times, and took the twelve dollars. I was doing as they secretly desired. Their experience of human nature had convinced them that any human being as innocent as my face proclaimed me to be, would repeat his first guess if it won, and would go on repeating it if it should continue to win. It was their belief that an innocent would be almost sure at the beginning to guess "even," and not "odd," and that if an innocent should guess "even" twelve times in succession and win every time, he would go on guessing "even" to the end – so it was their purpose to let me win those twelve even dates and then advance the odd dates, one by one, until I should lose fifty dollars, and furnish those superintendents something to laugh about for a week to come.

But it did not come out in that way; for by the time I had won the twelfth dollar and last even date, I withdrew from the game because it was so one-sided that it was monotonous, and did not entertain me. There was a burst of laughter from the superintendents at the window when I came out of the place, but I did not know what they were laughing at nor whom they were laughing at, and it was a matter of no interest to me anyway. Through that incident I acquired an enviable reputation for smartness and penetration, but it was not my due, for I had not penetrated anything that the cow could not have penetrated.

PART XXI

AUGUST 2, 1907

FROM SUSY'S BIOGRAPHY OF ME

Feb. 12, '86.
Mamma and I have both been very much troubled of late because papa since he has been publishing Gen. Grant's book

has seemed to forget his own books and work entirely, and the other evening as papa and I were promonading up and down the library he told me that he didn't expect to write but one more book, and then he was ready to give up work altogether, die, or do anything, he said that he had written more than he had ever expected to, and the only book that he had been per-tickularly anxious to write was one locked up in the safe down stairs, not yet published.

But this intended future of course will never do, and although papa usually holds to his own opinions and intents with outsid-ers, when mamma realy desires anything and says that it must be, papa allways gives up his plans (at least so far) and does as she says is right (and she is usually right, if she dissagrees with him at all). It was because he knew his great tendency to being convinced by her, that he published without her knowledge that article in the "Christian Union" concerning the government of children. So judging by the proofs of past years, I think that we will be able to persuade papa to go back to work as before, and not leave off writing with the end of his next story. Mamma says that she sometimes feels, and I do too, that she would rather have papa depend on his writing for a living than to have him think of giving it up.

[*Dictated, November 8, 1906.*] I have a defect of a sort which I think is not common; certainly I hope it isn't: it is rare that I can call before my mind's eye the form and face of either friend or enemy. If I should make a list, now, of persons whom I know in America and abroad – say to the number of even an entire thou-sand – it is quite unlikely that I could reproduce five of them in my mind's eye. Of my dearest and most intimate friends, I could name eight whom I have seen and talked with four days ago, but when I try to call them before me they are formless shadows. Jean has been absent, this past eight or ten days, in the country, and I wish I could reproduce her in the mirror of my mind, but I can't do it.

It may be that this defect is not constitutional, but a result of lifelong absence of mind and indolent and inadequate observa-tion. Once or twice in my life it has been an embarrassment to me. Twenty years ago, in the days of Susy's Biography of Me, there was a dispute one morning at the breakfast-table about the color of a neighbor's eyes. I was asked for a verdict, but had to confess that if that valued neighbor and old friend had eyes I was not sure that I had ever seen them. It was then mockingly suggested that perhaps I didn't even know the color of the eyes of my own family, and I was required to shut my own at once and testify. I was able to name the color of Mrs. Clemens's eyes, but was not able to even suggest a color for Jean's, or Clara's, or Susy's.

All this talk is suggested by Susy's remark: "The other evening as papa and I were promonading up and down the library." Down to the bottom of my heart I am thankful that I can see *that* picture! And it is not dim, but stands out clear in the unfaded light of twenty-one years ago. In those days Susy and I used to "promonade" daily up and down the library, with our arms about each other's waists, and deal in intimate communion concerning affairs of State, or the deep questions of human life, or our small personal affairs.

It was quite natural that I should think I had written myself out when I was only fifty years old, for everybody who has ever written has been smitten with that superstition at about that age. Not even yet have I really written myself out. I have merely stopped writing because dictating is pleasanter work, and because dictating has given me a strong aversion to the pen, and because two hours of talking per day is enough, and because – But I am only damaging my mind with this digging around in it for pretexts where no pretext is needed, and where the simple truth is for this one time better than any invention, in this small emergency. I shall never finish my five or six unfinished books, for the reason that by forty years of slavery to the pen I have earned my freedom. I detest the pen and I wouldn't use it again to sign the death warrant of my dearest enemy.

[*Dictated, March 8, 1906.*] For thirty years, I have received an average of a dozen letters a year from strangers who remember me, or whose fathers remember me as boy and young man. But these letters are almost always disappointing. I have not known these strangers nor their fathers. I have not heard of the names they mention; the reminiscences to which they call attention have had no part in my experience; all of which means that these strangers have been mistaking me for somebody else. But at last I have the refreshment, this morning, of a letter from a man who deals in names that were familiar to me in my boyhood. The writer encloses a newspaper clipping which has been wandering through the press for four or five weeks, and he wants to know if Capt.

Tonkray, lately deceased, was (as stated in the clipping) the original of "Huckleberry Finn."

I have replied that "Huckleberry Finn" was Frank F. As this inquirer evidently knew the Hannibal of the forties, he will easily recall Frank. Frank's father was at one time Town Drunkard, an exceedingly well-defined and unofficial office of those days. He succeeded "General" Gaines, and for a time he was sole and only incumbent of the office; but afterward Jimmy Finn proved competency and disputed the place with him, so we had two town drunkards at one time – and it made as much trouble in that village as Christendom experienced in the fourteenth century when there were two Popes at the same time.

In "Huckleberry Finn" I have drawn Frank exactly as he was. He was ignorant, unwashed, insufficiently fed; but he had as good a heart as ever any boy had. His liberties were totally unrestricted. He was the only really independent person – boy or man – in the community, and by consequence he was tranquilly and continuously happy, and was envied by all the rest of us. We liked him; we enjoyed his society. And as his society was forbidden us by our parents, the prohibition trebled and quadrupled its value, and therefore we sought and got more of his society than of any other boy's. I heard, four years ago, that he was Justice of the Peace in a remote village in the State of ———, and was a good citizen and was greatly respected.

During Jimmy Finn's term he (Jimmy) was not exclusive; he was not finical; he was not hypercritical; he was largely and handsomely democratic – and slept in the deserted tan-yard with the hogs. My father tried to reform him once, but did not succeed. My father was not a professional reformer. In him the spirit of reform was spasmodic. It only broke out now and then, with considerable intervals between. Once he tried to reform Injun Joe. That also was a failure. It was a failure, and we boys were glad. For Injun Joe, drunk, was interesting and a benefaction to us, but Injun Joe, sober, was a dreary spectacle. We watched my father's experiments upon him with a good deal of anxiety, but it came out all right and we were satisfied. Injun Joe got drunk oftener than before, and became intolerably interesting.

I think that in "Tom Sawyer" I starved Injun Joe to death in the cave. But that may have been to meet the exigencies of romantic literature. I can't remember now whether the real Injun Joe died in the cave or out of it, but I do remember that the news of his death reached me at a most unhappy time – that is to say, just at bedtime on a summer night when a prodigious storm of thunder and lightning accompanied by a deluging rain that turned the streets and lanes into rivers, caused me to repent and resolve to lead a better life. I can remember those awful thunder-bursts and the white glare of the lightning yet, and the wild lashing of the rain against the window-panes. By my teachings I perfectly well knew what all that wild riot was for – Satan had come to get Injun Joe. I had no shadow of doubt about it. It was the proper thing when a person like Injun Joe was required in the under world, and I should have thought it strange and unaccountable if Satan had come for him in a less impressive way. With every glare of lightning I shrivelled and shrunk together in mortal terror, and in the inter-val of black darkness that followed I poured out my lamentings over my lost condition, and my supplications for just one more chance, with an energy and feeling and sincerity quite foreign to my nature.

But in the morning I saw that it was a false alarm and concluded to resume business at the old stand and wait for another reminder.

The axiom says "History repeats itself." A week or two ago Mr. Blank-Blank dined with us. At dinner he mentioned a cir-cumstance which flashed me back over about sixty years and landed me in that little bedroom on that tempestuous night, and brought to my mind how creditable to me was my conduct through the whole night, and how barren it was of moral spot or fleck dur-ing that entire period: he said Mr. X was sexton, or something, of the Episcopal church in his town, and had been for many years the competent superintendent of all the church's worldly affairs, and was regarded by the whole congregation as a stay, a blessing, a priceless treasure. But he had a couple of defects – not large defects, but they seemed large when flung against the background of his profoundly religious character: he drank a good deal, and he could outswear a brakeman. A movement arose to persuade him to lay aside these vices, and after consulting with his pal, who occupied the same position as himself in the other Episcopal church, and whose defects were duplicates of his own and had inspired regret in the congregation he was serving, they concluded to try for reform – not wholesale, but half at a time. They took the liquor pledge and waited for results. During nine days the results were entirely satisfactory, and they were recipients of many compliments and much congratulation. Then on New-year's eve they had business a mile and a half out of town, just beyond the State line. Everything went well with them that evening in the bar-room of the inn – but at last the celebration of the occasion by those villagers came to be of a burdensome nature. It was a bitter cold night and the multitudinous hot toddies that were circulating began by and by to exert a powerful influence upon the new pro-hibitionists. At last X's friend remarked,

"X, does it occur to you that we are *outside the diocese*?"

That ended reform No. 1. Then they took a chance in reform No. 2. For a while that one prospered, and they got much applause. I now reach the incident which sent me back a matter of sixty years, as I have remarked a while ago.

One morning Mr. Blank-Blank met X on the street and said,

"You have made a gallant struggle against those defects of yours. I am aware that you failed on No. 1, but I am also aware that you are having better luck with No. 2."

"Yes," X said; "No. 2 is all right and sound up to date, and we are full of hope."

Blank-Blank said, "X, of course you have your troubles like other people, but they never show on the outside. I have never seen you when you were not cheerful. Are you always cheerful? Really always cheerful?"

"Well, no," he said, "no, I can't say that I am always cheerful, but – well, you know that kind of a night that comes: *say* – you wake up 'way in the night and the whole world is sunk in gloom and there are storms and earthquakes and all sorts of disasters in the air threatening, and you get cold and clammy; and when that happens to me I recognize how sinful I am and it all goes clear to my heart and wrings it and I have such terrors and terrors! – oh, they are indescribable, those terrors that assail me, and I slip out of bed and get on my knees and pray and pray and promise that I *will* be good, if I can only have another chance. And then, you know, in the morning the sun shines out *so* lovely, and the birds sing and the whole world is so beautiful, and – *b' God, I rally!*"

Now I will quote a brief paragraph from this letter which I have a minute ago spoken of. The writer says:

You no doubt are at a loss to know who I am. I will tell you. In my younger days I was a resident of Hannibal, Mo., and you and I were schoolmates attending Mr. Dawson's school along with Sam and Will Bowen and Andy Fuqua and others whose names I have forgotten. I was then about the smallest boy in school, for my age, and they called me little Aleck for short.

I only dimly remember him, but I knew those other people as well as I knew the town drunkards. I remember Dawson's schoolhouse perfectly. If I wanted to describe it I could save myself the trouble by conveying the description of it to these pages from "Tom Sawyer." I can remember the drowsy and inviting summer sounds that used to float in through the open windows from that distant boy-Paradise, Cardiff Hill (Holliday's Hill), and mingle with the murmurs of the studying pupils and make them the more dreary by the contrast. I remember Andy Fuqua, the oldest pupil – a man of twenty-five. I remember the youngest pupil, Nannie Owsley, a child of seven. I remember George Robards, eighteen or twenty years old, the only pupil who studied Latin. I remember – in some cases vividly, in others vaguely – the rest of the twenty-five boys and girls. I remember Mr. Dawson very well. I remember his boy, Theodore, who was as good as he could be. In fact, he was inordinately good, extravagantly good, offensively good, detestably good – and he had pop-eyes – and I would have drowned him if I had had a chance. In that school we were all about on an equality, and, so far as I remember, the passion of envy had no place in our hearts, except in the case of Arch Fuqua – the other one's brother. Of course we all went barefoot in the summer-time. Arch Fuqua was about my own age – ten or eleven. In the winter we could stand him, because he wore shoes then, and his great gift was hidden from our sight and we were enabled to forget it. But in the summer-time he was a bitterness to us. He was our envy, for he could double back his big toe and let it fly and you could hear it snap thirty yards. There was not another boy in the school that could approach this feat. He had not a rival as regards a physical distinction – except in Theodore Eddy, who could work his ears like a horse. But he was no real rival, because you couldn't hear him work his ears; so all the advantage lay with Arch Fuqua.

I am not done with Dawson's school; I will return to it in a later chapter.

[*Dictated at Hamilton, Bermuda, January 6, 1907.*] "That reminds me." In conversation we are always using that phrase, and seldom or never noticing how large a significance it bears. It stands for a curious and interesting fact, to wit: that sleeping or waking, dreaming or talking, the thoughts which swarm through our heads are almost constantly, almost continuously, accompanied by a like swarm of reminders of incidents and episodes of our past. A man can never know what a large traffic this commerce of association carries on in our minds until he sets out to write his autobiography; he then finds that a thought is seldom born to him that does not immediately remind him of some event, large or small, in his past experience. Quite naturally these remarks remind me of various things, among others this: that sometimes a thought, by the power of association, will bring back to your mind a lost word or a lost name which you have not been able to recover by any other process known to your mental equipment. Yesterday we had an instance of this. Rev. Joseph H. Twichell is with me on this flying trip to Bermuda. He was with me on my last visit to Bermuda, and to-day we were trying to remember when it was. We thought it was somewhere in the neighborhood of thirty years ago, but that was as near as we could get at the date. Twichell said that the landlady in whose boarding-house we sojourned in that ancient time could doubtless furnish us the date, and we must look her up. We wanted to see her, anyway, because she and her blooming daughter of eighteen were the only persons whose acquaintance we had made at that time, for we were travelling under fictitious names, and people who wear aliases are not given to seeking society and bringing themselves under suspicion. But at this point in our talk we encountered an obstruction: we could not recall the landlady's name. We hunted all around through our minds for that name, using all the customary methods of research, but without success; the name was gone from us, apparently permanently. We finally gave the matter up, and fell to talking about something else. The talk wandered from one subject to another, and finally arrived at Twichell's school-days in Hartford – the Hartford of something more than half a century ago – and he mentioned several of his schoolmasters, dwelling with special interest upon the peculiarities of an aged one named Olney. He remarked that Olney, humble village schoolmaster as he was, was yet a man of superior parts, and had published textbooks which had enjoyed a wide currency in America in their day. I said I remembered those books, and had studied Olney's Geography in school when I was a boy. Then Twichell said,

"That reminds me – our landlady's name was a name that was associated with school-books of some kind or other fifty or sixty years ago. I wonder what it was. I believe it began with K."

Association did the rest, and did it instantly. I said,
"Kirkham's Grammar!"

That settled it. Kirkham was the name; and we went out to seek
for the owner of it. There was no trouble about that, for Bermuda
is not large, and is like the earlier Garden of Eden, in that everybody in it knows everybody else, just as it was in the serpent's head-
quarters in Adam's time. We easily found Miss Kirkham – she that
had been the blooming girl of a generation before – and she was
still keeping boarders; but her mother had passed from this life.
She settled the date for us, and did it with certainty, by help of a
couple of uncommon circumstances, events of that ancient time.
She said we had sailed from Bermuda on the 24th of May, 1877,
which was the day on which her only nephew was born – and he
is now thirty years of age. The other unusual circumstance – she
called it an unusual circumstance, and I didn't say anything – was
that on that day the Rev. Mr. Twichell (bearing the assumed name
of Peters) had made a statement to her which she regarded as a
fiction. I remembered the circumstance very well. We had bidden
the young girl good-by and had gone fifty yards, perhaps, when
Twichell said he had forgotten something (I doubted it) and must
go back. When he rejoined me he was silent, and this alarmed me,
because I had not seen an example of it before. He seemed quite
uncomfortable, and I asked him what the trouble was. He said he
had been inspired to give the girl a pleasant surprise, and so had
gone back and said to her –

"That young fellow's name is not Wilkinson – that's Mark
Twain."

She did not lose her mind; she did not exhibit any excitement
at all, but said quite simply, quite tranquilly,

"Tell it to the marines, Mr. Peters – if that should happen to be
your name."

It was very pleasant to meet her again. We were white-headed,
but she was not; in the sweet and unvexed spiritual atmosphere of
the Bermudas one does not achieve gray hairs at forty-eight.

I had a dream last night, and of course it was born of association,
like nearly everything else that drifts into a person's head, asleep or
awake. On board ship, on the passage down, Twichell was talking
about the swiftly developing possibilities of aerial navigation, and
he quoted those striking verses of Tennyson's which forecast a
future when air-borne vessels of war shall meet and fight above the
clouds and redden the earth below with a rain of blood. This

picture of carnage and blood and death reminded me of something which I had read a fortnight ago – statistics of railway accidents compiled by the United States Government, wherein the appalling fact was set forth that on our 200,000 miles of railway we annually kill 10,000 persons outright and injure 80,000. The warships in the air suggested the railway horrors, and three nights afterward the railway horrors suggested my dream. The work of association was going on in my head, unconsciously, all that time. It was an admirable dream, what there was of it.

In it I saw a funeral procession; I saw it from a mountain peak; I saw it crawling along and curving here and there, serpentlike, through a level vast plain. I seemed to see a hundred miles of the procession, but neither the beginning of it nor the end of it was within the limits of my vision. The procession was in ten divisions, each division marked by a sombre flag, and the whole represented ten years of our railway activities in the accident line; each division was composed of 80,000 cripples, and was bearing its own year's 10,000 mutilated corpses to the grave: in the aggregate 800,000 cripples and 100,000 dead, drenched in blood!

PART XXII

[*Dictated, October 10, 1906.*] Susy has named a number of the friends who were assembled at Onteora at the time of our visit, but there were others – among them Laurence Hutton, Charles Dudley Warner, and Carroll Beckwith, and their wives. It was a bright and jolly company. Some of those choice spirits are still with us; the others have passed from this life: Mrs. Clemens, Susy, Mr. Warner, Mary Mapes Dodge, Laurence Hutton, Dean Sage – peace to their ashes! Susy is in error in thinking Mrs. Dodge was not there at that time; we were her guests.

We arrived at nightfall, dreary from a tiresome journey; but the dreariness did not last. Mrs. Dodge had provided a home-made banquet, and the happy company sat down to it, twenty strong, or more. Then the thing happened which always happens at large dinners, and is always exasperating: everybody talked to his elbow-mates and all talked at once, and gradually raised their voices higher, and higher, and higher, in the desperate effort to be heard.

It was like a riot, an insurrection; it was an intolerable volume of noise. Presently I said to the lady next me –

"I will subdue this riot, I will silence this racket. There is only one way to do it, but I know the art. You must tilt your head toward mine and seem to be deeply interested in what I am saying; I will talk in a low voice; then, just because our neighbors won't be able to hear me, they will *want* to hear me. If I mumble long enough – say two minutes – you will see that the dialogues will one after another come to a standstill, and there will be silence, not a sound anywhere but my mumbling."

Then in a very low voice I began:

"When I went out to Chicago, eleven years ago, to witness the Grant festivities, there was a great banquet on the first night, with six hundred ex-soldiers present. The gentleman who sat next me was Mr. X. X. He was very hard of hearing, and he had a habit common to deaf people of shouting his remarks instead of delivering them in an ordinary voice. He would handle his knife and fork in reflective silence for five or six minutes at a time and then suddenly fetch out a shout that would make you jump out of the United States."

By this time the insurrection at Mrs. Dodge's table – at least that part of it in my immediate neighborhood – had died down, and the silence was spreading, couple by couple, down the long table. I went on in a lower and still lower mumble, and most impressively –

"During one of Mr. X. X.'s mute intervals, a man opposite us approached the end of a story which he had been telling his elbow-neighbor. He was speaking in a low voice – there was much noise – I was deeply interested, and straining my ears to catch his words, stretching my neck, holding my breath, to hear, unconscious of everything but the fascinating tale. I heard him say, 'At this point he seized her by her long hair – she shrieking and begging – bent her neck across his knee, and with one awful sweep of the razor – '

"HOW DO YOU LIKE CHICA-A-AGO?!!!"

That was X. X.'s interruption, hearable at thirty miles. By the time I had reached that place in my mumblings Mrs. Dodge's dining-room was so silent, so breathlessly still, that if you had dropped a thought anywhere in it you could have heard it smack the floor. When I delivered that yell the entire dinner company jumped as one person, and punched their heads through the ceiling, damaging it, for it was only lath and plaster, and it all came down on us, and much of it went into the victuals and made them gritty, but no one was hurt. Then I explained why it was that I had played that game, and begged them to take the moral of it home to their hearts and be rational and merciful thenceforth, and cease from screaming in mass, and agree to let one person talk at a time and the rest listen in grateful and unvexed peace. They granted my prayer, and we had a happy time all the rest of the evening; I do not think I have ever had a better time in my life. This was largely because the new terms enabled me to keep the floor – now that I had it – and do all the talking myself. I do like to hear myself talk. Susy has exposed this in her Biography of me.

Dean Sage was a delightful man, yet in one way a terror to his friends, for he loved them so well that he could not refrain from playing practical jokes on them. We have to be pretty deeply in love with a person before we can do him the honor of joking famil- iarly with him. Dean Sage was the best citizen I have known in America. It takes courage to be a good citizen, and he had plenty of it. He allowed no individual and no corporation to infringe his smallest right and escape unpunished. He was very rich, and very generous, and benevolent, and he gave away his money with a prodigal hand; but if an individual or corporation infringed a right of his, to the value of ten cents, he would spend thousands of dol- lars' worth of time and labor and money and persistence on the matter, and would not lower his flag until he had won his battle or lost it.

He and Rev. Mr. Harris had been classmates in college, and to the day of Sage's death they were as fond of each other as an engaged pair. It follows, without saying, that whenever Sage found an opportunity to play a joke upon Harris, Harris was sure to suffer.

Along about 1873 Sage fell a victim to an illness which reduced him to a skeleton, and defied all the efforts of the physicians to cure it. He went to the Adirondacks and took Harris with him. Sage had always been an active man, and he couldn't idle any day wholly away in inanition, but walked every day to the limit of his strength. One day, toward nightfall, the pair came upon a humble log cabin which bore these words painted upon a shingle: "Enter- tainment for Man and Beast." They were obliged to stop there for the night, Sage's strength being exhausted. They entered the cabin and found its owner and sole occupant there, a rugged and sturdy and simple-hearted man of middle age. He cooked supper and placed it before the travellers – salt junk, boiled beans, corn bread and black coffee. Sage's stomach could abide nothing but the most delicate food, therefore this banquet revolted him, and he sat at the table unemployed, while Harris fed ravenously, limitlessly, gratefully; for he had been chaplain in a fighting regiment all through the war, and had kept in perfection the grand and uncritical appetite and splendid physical vigor which those four years of tough fare and activity had furnished him. Sage went supperless to bed, and tossed and writhed all night upon a shuck mattress that was full of attentive and interested corncobs. In the morning Harris was ravenous again, and devoured the odious breakfast as contentedly and as delightedly as he had devoured its twin the night before. Sage sat upon the porch, empty, and contemplated the performance and meditated revenge. Presently he beckoned to the landlord and took him aside and had a confidential talk with him. He said,

"I am the paymaster. What is the bill?"

"Two suppers, fifty cents; two beds, thirty cents; two breakfasts, fifty cents – total, a dollar and thirty cents."

Sage said, "Go back and make out the bill and fetch it to me here on the porch. Make it thirteen dollars."

"Thirteen dollars! Why, it's impossible! I am no robber. I am charging you what I charge everybody. It's a dollar and thirty cents, and that's all it is."

"My man, I've got something to say about this as well as you. It's thirteen dollars. You'll make out your bill for that, and you'll *take* it, too, or you'll not get a cent."

The man was troubled, and said, "I don't understand this. I can't make it out."

"Well, I understand it. I know what I am about. It's thirteen dollars, and I want the bill made out for that. There's no other terms. Get it ready and bring it out here. I will examine it and be outraged. You understand? I will dispute the bill. You must stand to it. You must refuse to take less. I will begin to lose my temper; you must begin to lose yours. I will call you hard names; you must answer with harder ones. I will raise my voice; you must raise yours. You must go into a rage – foam at the mouth, if you can; insert some soap to help it along. Now go along and follow your instructions."

The man played his assigned part, and played it well. He brought the bill and stood waiting for results. Sage's face began to cloud up, his eyes to snap, and his nostrils to inflate like a horse's; then he broke out with –

"*Thirteen dollars!* You mean to say that you charge thirteen dollars for these damned inhuman hospitalities of yours? Are you a professional buccaneer? Is it your custom to – "

The man burst in with spirit: "Now, I don't want any more out of you – that's a plenty. The bill is thirteen dollars and you'll *pay* it – that's all; a couple of characterless adventurers bilking their way through this country and attempting to dictate terms to a gentleman! a gentleman who received you supposing you were gentlemen yourselves, whereas in my opinion hell's full of – "

Sage broke in –

"Not another word of that! – I won't have it. I regard you as the lowest-down thief that ever –"

"Don't you use that word again! By ——, I'll take you by the neck and –"

Harris came rushing out, and just as the two were about to grapple he pushed himself between them and began to implore –

"Oh, Dean, don't, *don't* – now, Mr. Smith, control yourself! Oh, think of your family, Dean! – think what a scandal – "

But they burst out with maledictions, imprecations and all the hard names they could dig out of the rich accumulations of their educated memories, and in the midst of it the man shouted –

"When *gentlemen* come to this house, I treat them *as* gentlemen. When people come to this house with the ordinary appetites of gentlemen, I charge them a dollar and thirty cents for what I furnished you; but when a man brings a hell-fired Famine here that gorges a barrel of pork and four barrels of beans at two sittings – "

Sage broke in, in a voice that was eloquent with remorse and self-reproach, "I never thought of that, and I ask your pardon; I am ashamed of myself and of my friend. Here's your thirteen dollars, and my apologies along with it."

[*Dictated March 12, 1906.*] I have always taken a great interest in other people's duels. One always feels an abiding interest in any heroic thing which has entered into his own experience.

In 1878, fourteen years after my unmaterialized duel, Messieurs Fortu and Gambetta fought a duel which made heroes of both of them in France, but made them rather ridiculous throughout the rest of the world. I was living in Munich that fall and winter, and I was so interested in that funny tragedy that I wrote a long account of it, and it is in one of my books, somewhere – an account which had some inaccuracies in it, but as an exhibition of the *spirit* of that duel, I think it was correct and trustworthy. And when I was living in Vienna, thirty-four years after my ineffectual duel, my interest in that kind of incident was still strong; and I find here among my Autobiographical manuscripts of that day a chapter which I began concerning it, but did not finish. I wanted to finish it, but held it open in the hope that the Italian ambassador, M. Nigra, would find time to furnish me the *full* history of Señor Cavalotti's adventures in that line. But he was a busy man; there was always an interruption before he could get well started; so my hope was never fulfilled. The following is the unfinished chapter:

As concerns duelling. This pastime is as common in Austria to-day as it is in France. But with this difference, that here in the Austrian States the duel is dangerous, while in France it is not. Here it is tragedy, in France it is comedy; here it is a solemnity, there it is monkey-shines; here the duellist risks his life, there he does not even risk his shirt. Here he fights with pistol or sabre, in France with a hairpin – a blunt one. Here the desperately wounded man tries to walk to the hospital; there they paint the scratch so that they can find it again, lay the sufferer on a stretcher, and conduct him off the field with a band of music.

At the end of a French duel the pair hug and kiss and cry, and praise each other's valor; then the surgeons make an examination and pick out the scratched one, and the other one helps him on to the litter and pays his fare; and in return the scratched one treats to champagne and oysters in the evening, and then "the incident is closed," as the French say. It is all polite, and gracious, and pretty, and impressive. At the end of an Austrian duel the antagonist that is alive gravely offers his hand to the other man, utters some phrases of courteous regret, then bids him good-by and goes his way, and that incident also is closed. The French duellist is painstakingly protected from danger, by the rules of the game. His antagonist's weapon cannot reach so far as his body; if he get a scratch it will not be above his elbow. But in Austria the rules of the game do not provide against danger, they carefully provide *for* it, usually. Commonly the combat must be kept up until one of the men is disabled; a non-disabling slash or stab does not retire him.

For a matter of three months I watched the Viennese

journals, and whenever a duel was reported in their telegraphic columns I scrap-booked it. By this record I find that duelling in Austria is not confined to journalists and old maids, as in France, but is indulged in by military men, journalists, students, physicians, lawyers, members of the legislature, and even the Cabinet, the Bench and the police. Duelling is forbidden by law; and so it seems odd to see the makers and administrators of the laws dancing on their work in this way. Some months ago Count Bodeni, at that time Chief of the Government, fought a pistol-duel here in the capital city of the Empire with representative Wolf, and both of those distinguished Christians came near getting turned out of the Church – for the Church as well as the State forbids duelling.

In one case, lately, in Hungary, the police interfered and stopped a duel after the first innings. This was a sabre-duel between the chief of police and the city attorney. Unkind things were said about it by the newspapers. They said the police remembered their duty uncommonly well when their own officials were the parties concerned in duels. But I think the underlings showed good bread-and-butter judgment. If their superiors had carved each other well, the public would have asked, Where were the police? and their places would have been endangered; but custom does not require them to be around where mere unofficial citizens are explaining a thing with sabres.

There was another duel – a double duel – going on in the immediate neighborhood at the time, and in this case the police obeyed custom and did not disturb it. Their bread and butter was not at stake there. In this duel a physician fought a couple of surgeons, and wounded both – one of them lightly, the other seriously. An undertaker wanted to keep people from interfering, but that was quite natural again.

Selecting at random from my record, I next find a duel at Tarnopol between military men. An officer of the Tenth Dragoons charged an officer of the Ninth Dragoons with an offence against the laws of the card-table. There was a defect or a doubt somewhere in the matter, and this had to be examined and passed upon by a Court of Honor. So the case was sent up to Lemberg for this purpose. One would like to know what the defect was, but the newspaper does not say. A man here who has fought many duels and has a graveyard, says that probably the matter in question was as to whether the accusation was true or not; that if the charge was a very grave one – cheating, for instance – proof of its truth would rule the guilty officer out of the field of honor; the Court would not allow a gentleman to fight with such a person. You see what a solemn thing it is; you see how particular they are; any little careless act can lose you your privilege of getting yourself shot, here. The Court seems to have gone into the matter in a searching and careful fashion, for several months elapsed before it reached a decision. It then sanctioned a duel and the accused killed his accuser.

Next I find a duel between a prince and a major; first with pistols – no result satisfactory to either party; then with sabres, and the major badly hurt.

Next, a sabre-duel between journalists – the one a strong man, the other feeble and in poor health. It was brief; the strong one drove his sword through the weak one, and death was immediate.

Next, a duel between a lieutenant and a student of medicine. According to the newspaper report these are the details. The student was in a restaurant one evening: passing along, he halted at a table to speak with some friends; near by sat a dozen military men; the student conceived that one of these was "staring" at him; he asked the officer to step outside and explain. This officer and another one gathered up their caps and sabres and went out with the student. Outside – this is the student's account – the student introduced himself to the offending officer and said, "You seemed to stare at me"; for answer, the officer struck at the student with his fist; the student parried the blow; both officers drew their sabres and attacked the young fellow, and one of them gave him a wound on the left arm; then they withdrew. This was Saturday night. The duel followed on Monday, in the military riding-school – the customary duelling-ground all over Austria, apparently. The weapons were pistols. The duelling terms were somewhat beyond custom in the matter of severity, if I may gather that from the statement that the combat was fought *"unter sehr schweren Bedingungen"* – to wit, "Distance, 15 steps – with 3 steps advance." There was but one exchange of shots. The student was hit. "He put his hand on his breast, his body began to bend slowly forward, then collapsed in death and sank to the ground."

It is pathetic. There are other duels in my list, but I find in each and all of them one and the same ever-recurring defect – the *principals* are never present, but only their sham representatives. The *real* principals in any duel are not the duellists themselves, but their families. They do the mourning, the suffering, theirs is the loss and theirs the misery. They stake all that, the duellist stakes nothing but his life, and that is a trivial thing compared with what his death must cost those whom he leaves behind him. Challenges should not mention the duellist; he has nothing much at stake, and the real vengeance cannot reach him. The challenge should summon the offender's old gray mother, and his young wife and his little children, – these, or any to whom he is a dear and worshipped possession – and should say, "You have done me no harm, but I am the meek slave of a custom which requires me to crush the happiness out of your hearts and condemn you to years of pain and grief, in order that I may wash clean with your tears a stain which has been put upon me by another person."

The logic of it is admirable: a person has robbed me of a penny; I must beggar ten innocent persons to make good my loss. Surely nobody's "honor" is worth all that.

Since the duellist's family are the real principals in a duel, the State ought to compel them to be present at it. Custom, also, ought to be so amended as to require it; and without it no duel ought to be allowed to go on. If that student's unoffending mother had been present and watching the officer through her tears as he raised his pistol, he – why, he would have fired in the air. We know that. For we know how we are all made. Laws ought to be based upon the ascertained facts of our nature. It would be a simple thing to make a duelling law which would stop duelling.

As things are now, the mother is never invited. She submits to this; and without outward complaint, for she, too, is the vassal of custom, and custom requires her to conceal her pain when she learns the disastrous news that her son must go to the duelling-field, and by the powerful force that is lodged in habit and custom she is enabled to obey this trying requirement – a requirement which exacts a miracle of her, and gets it. Last January a neighbor of ours who has a young son in the army was wakened by this youth at three o'clock one morning, and she sat up in bed and listened to his message:

"I have come to tell you something, mother, which will

distress you, but you must be good and brave, and bear it. I have
been affronted by a fellow officer, and we fight at three this afternoon. Lie down and sleep, now, and think no more about it."

She kissed him good night and lay down paralyzed with grief
and fear, but said nothing. But she did not sleep; she prayed and
mourned till the first streak of dawn, then fled to the nearest
church and implored the Virgin for help; and from that church
she went to another and another and another; church after
church, and still church after church, and so spent all the day
until three o'clock on her knees in agony and tears; then dragged
herself home and sat down comfortless and desolate, to count
the minutes, and wait, with an outward show of calm, for what
had been ordained for her – happiness, or endless misery. Presently she heard the clank of a sabre – she had not known before
what music was in that sound! – and her son put his head in
and said:

"X was in the wrong, and he apologized."

So that incident was closed; and for the rest of her life the
mother will always find something pleasant about the clank of
a sabre, no doubt.

In one of my listed duels – however, let it go, there is nothing
particularly striking about it except that the seconds interfered.
And prematurely, too, for neither man was dead. This was certainly irregular. Neither of the men liked it. It was a duel with
cavalry sabres, between an editor and a lieutenant. The editor
walked to the hospital, the lieutenant was carried. In this country an editor who can write well is valuable, but he is not likely
to remain so unless he can handle a sabre with charm.

The following very recent telegram shows that also in France
duels are humanely stopped as soon as they approach the
(French) danger-point:

"*Reuter's Telegram*. – PARIS, *March 5*. – The duel between Col-
onels Henry and Picquart took place this morning in the Riding
School of the Ecole Militaire, the doors of which were strictly
guarded in order to prevent intrusion. The combatants, who
fought with swords, were in position at ten o'clock.

"At the first reengagement Lieutenant-Colonel Henry was
slightly scratched in the fore arm, and just at the same moment
his own blade appeared to touch his adversary's neck. Senator
Rane, who was Colonel Picquart's second, stopped the fight, but
as it was found that his principal had not been touched, the

combat continued. A very sharp encounter ensued, in which Colonel Henry was wounded in the elbow, and the duel terminated."

After which, the stretcher and the band. In lurid contrast with this delicate flirtation, we have this fatal duel of day before yesterday in Italy, where the earnest Austrian duel is in vogue. I knew Cavalotti slightly, and this gives me a sort of personal interest in his duel. I first saw him in Rome several years ago. He was sitting on a block of stone in the Forum, and was writing something in his note-book – a poem or a challenge, or something like that – and the friend who pointed him out to me said, "That is Cavalotti – he has fought thirty duels; do not disturb him." I did not disturb him.

[*May 13, 1907.*] It is a long time ago. Cavalotti – poet, orator, satirist, statesman, patriot – was a great man, and his death was deeply lamented by his countrymen: many monuments to his memory testify to this. In his duels he killed several of his antagonists and disabled the rest. By nature he was a little irascible. Once when the officials of the library of Bologna threw out his books the gentle poet went up there and challenged the whole fifteen! His parliamentary duties were exacting, but he proposed to keep coming up and fighting duels between trains until all those officials had been retired from the activities of life. Although he always chose the sword to fight with, he had never had a lesson with that weapon. When game was called he waited for nothing, but always plunged at his opponent and rained such a storm of wild and original thrusts and whacks upon him that the man was dead or crippled before he could bring his science to bear. But his latest antagonist discarded science, and won. He held his sword straight forward like a lance when Cavalotti made his plunge – with the result that he impaled himself upon it. It entered his mouth and passed out at the back of his neck. Death was instantaneous.

[*Dictated December 20, 1906.*] Six months ago, when I was recalling early days in San Francisco, I broke off at a place where I was about to tell about Captain Osborn's odd adventure at the "What Cheer," or perhaps it was at another cheap feeding-place – the "Miners' Restaurant." It was a place where one could get good food on the cheapest possible terms, and its popularity was great among the multitudes whose purses were light. It was a good place

to go to, to observe mixed humanity. Captain Osborn and Bret
Harte went there one day and took a meal, and in the course of it
Osborn fished up an interesting reminiscence of a dozen years
before and told about it. It was to this effect:

He was a midshipman in the navy when the Californian gold
craze burst upon the world and set it wild with excitement. His
ship made the long journey around the Horn and was approaching
her goal, the Golden Gate, when an accident happened.

"It happened to me," said Osborn. "I fell overboard. There was
a heavy sea running, but no one was much alarmed about me,
because we had on board a newly patented life-saving device
which was believed to be competent to rescue anything that could
fall overboard; from a midshipman to an anchor. Ours was the
only ship that had this device; we were very proud of it, and had
been anxious to give its powers a practical test. This thing was
lashed to the garboard-strake of the main-to'gallant mizzen-yard
amidships, and there was nothing to do but cut the lashings and
heave it over; it would do the rest. One day the cry of 'Man overboard!' brought all hands on deck. Instantly the lashings were cut
and the machine flung joyously over. Damnation, it went to the
bottom like an anvil! By the time that the ship was brought to and
a boat manned, I was become but a bobbing speck on the waves
half a mile astern and losing my strength very fast; but by good luck
there was a common seaman on board who had practical ideas in
his head and hadn't waited to see what the patent machine was
going to do, but had run aft and sprung over after me the moment
the alarm was cried through the ship. I had a good deal of a start
of him, and the seas made his progress slow and difficult, but he
stuck to his work and fought his way to me, and just in the nick of
time he put his saving arms about me when I was about to go down.
He held me up until the boat reached us and rescued us. By that
time I was unconscious; and I was still unconscious when we
arrived at the ship. A dangerous fever followed, and I was delirious
for three days; then I came to myself and at once inquired for my
benefactor, of course. He was gone. We were lying at anchor in
the Bay and every man had deserted to the gold-mines except the
commissioned officers. I found out nothing about my benefactor
but his name – Burton Sanders – a name which I have held in
grateful memory ever since. Every time I have been on the Coast,
these twelve or thirteen years, I have tried to get track of him, but
have never succeeded. I wish I could find him and make him

understand that his brave act has never been forgotten by me. Harte, I would rather see him and take him by the hand than any other man on the planet."

At this stage or a little later there was an interruption. A waiter near by said to another waiter, pointing,

"Take a look at that tramp that's coming in. Ain't that the one that bilked the house, last week, out of ten cents?"

"I believe it is. Let him alone – don't pay any attention to him; wait till we can get a good look at him."

The tramp approached timidly and hesitatingly, with the air of one unsure and apprehensive. The waiters watched him furtively. When he was passing behind Harte's chair one of them said,

"He's the one!" – and they pounced upon him and proposed to turn him over to the police as a bilk. He begged piteously. He confessed his guilt, but said he had been driven to his crime by necessity – that when he had eaten the plate of beans and slipped out without paying for it, it was because he was starving, and hadn't the ten cents to pay for it with. But the waiters would listen to no explanations, no palliations; he must be placed in custody. He brushed his hand across his eyes and said meekly that he would submit, being friendless. Each waiter took him by an arm and faced him about to conduct him away. Then his melancholy eyes fell upon Captain Osborn, and a light of glad and eager recognition flashed from them. He said,

"Weren't you a midshipman once, sir, in the old 'Lancaster'?"

"Yes," said Osborn. "Why?"

"Didn't you fall overboard?"

"Yes, I did. How do you come to know about it?"

"Wasn't there a new patent machine aboard, and didn't they throw it over to save you?"

"Why, yes," said Osborn, laughing gently, "but it didn't do it."

"No, sir, it was a sailor that done it."

"It certainly was. Look here, my man, you are getting distinctly interesting. Were you of our crew?"

"Yes, sir, I was."

"I reckon you may be right. You do certainly know a good deal about that incident. What is your name?"

"Burton Sanders."

The Captain sprang up, excited, and said,

"Give me your hand! Give me both your hands! I'd rather shake them than inherit a fortune!" – and then he cried to the waiters,

"Let him go! – take your hands off! He is my guest, and can have anything and everything this house is able to furnish. I am responsible."

There was a love-feast, then. Captain Osborn ordered it regardless of expense, and he and Harte sat there and listened while the man told stirring adventures of his life and fed himself up to the eyebrows. Then Osborn wanted to be benefactor in his turn, and pay back some of his debt. The man said it could all be paid with ten dollars – that it had been so long since he had owned that amount of money that it would seem a fortune to him, and he should be grateful beyond words if the Captain could spare him that amount. The Captain spared him ten broad twenty-dollar gold pieces, and made him take them in spite of his modest protestations, and gave him his address and said he must never fail to give him notice when he needed grateful service.

Several months later Harte stumbled upon the man in the street. He was most comfortably drunk, and pleasant and chatty. Harte remarked upon the splendidly and movingly dramatic incident of the restaurant, and said,

"How curious and fortunate and happy and interesting it was that you two should come together, after that long separation, and at exactly the right moment to save you from disaster and turn your defeat by the waiters into a victory. A preacher could make a great sermon out of that, for it does look as if the hand of Providence was in it."

The hero's face assumed a sweetly genial expression, and he said,

"Well now, it wasn't Providence this time. I was running the arrangements myself."

"How do you mean?"

"Oh, I hadn't ever seen the gentleman before. I was at the next table, with my back to you the whole time he was telling about it. I saw my chance, and slipped out and fetched the two waiters with me and offered to give them a commission out of what I could get out of the Captain if they would do a quarrel act with me and give me an opening. So, then, after a minute or two I straggled back, and you know the rest of it as well as I do."

PART XXIII
OCTOBER, 1907

[*Dictated March 9, 1906.*] ... I am talking of a time sixty years ago, and upwards. I remember the names of some of those schoolmates, and, by fitful glimpses, even their faces rise dimly before me for a moment – only just long enough to be recognized; then they vanish. I catch glimpses of George Robards, the Latin pupil – slender, pale, studious, bending over his book and absorbed in it, his long straight black hair hanging down below his jaws like a pair of curtains on the sides of his face. I can see him give his head a toss and flirt one of the curtains back around his head – to get it out of his way, apparently; really to show off. In that day it was a great thing among the boys to have hair of so flexible a sort that it could be flung back in that way, with a flirt of the head. George Robards was the envy of us all. For there was no hair among us that was so competent for this exhibition as his – except, perhaps, the yellow locks of Will Bowen and John Robards. My hair was a dense ruck of short curls, and so was my brother Henry's. We tried all kinds of devices to get these crooks straightened out so that they would flirt, but we never succeeded. Sometimes, by soaking our heads and then combing and brushing our hair down tight and flat to our skulls, we could get it straight, temporarily, and this gave us a comforting moment of joy; but the first time we gave it a flirt it all shrivelled into curls again and our happiness was gone.

John Robards was the little brother of George; he was a wee chap with silky golden curtains to his face which dangled to his shoulders and below, and could be flung back ravishingly. When he was twelve years old he crossed the plains with his father amidst the rush of the gold-seekers of '49; and I remember the departure of the cavalcade when it spurred westward. We were all there to see and to envy. And I can still see that proud little chap sailing by on a great horse, with his long locks streaming out behind. We were all on hand to gaze and envy when he returned, two years later, in unimaginable glory – *for he had travelled!* None of us had ever been forty miles from home. But he had crossed the Continent. He had been in the gold-mines, that fairyland of our imagination. And he had done a still more wonderful thing. He had been in ships – in ships on the actual ocean; in ships on three actual oceans. For he had sailed down the Pacific and around the

Horn among icebergs and through snow-storms and wild wintry gales, and had sailed on and turned the corner and flown northward in the trades and up through the blistering equatorial waters – and there in his brown face were the proofs of what he had been through. We would have sold our souls to Satan for the privilege of trading places with him.

I saw him when I was out on that Missouri trip four years ago. He was old then – though not quite so old as I – and the burden of life was upon him. He said his granddaughter, twelve years old, had read my books and would like to see me. It was a pathetic time, for she was a prisoner in her room and marked for death. And John knew that she was passing swiftly away. Twelve years old – just her grandfather's age when he rode away on that great journey with his yellow hair flapping behind him. In her I seemed to see that boy again. It was as if he had come back out of that remote past and was present before me in his golden youth. Her malady was heart disease, and her brief life came to a close a few days later.

Another of those schoolboys was John Garth. He became a prosperous banker and a prominent and valued citizen; and a few years ago he died, rich and honored. *He died.* It is what I have to say about so many of those boys and girls. The widow still lives, and there are grandchildren. In her pantalette days and my barefoot days she was a schoolmate of mine. I saw John's tomb when I made that Missouri visit.

Her father, Mr. Kercheval, had an apprentice in the early days when I was nine years old, and he had also a slave woman who had many merits. But I can't feel very kindly or forgivingly toward either that good apprentice boy or that good slave woman, for they saved my life. One day when I was playing on a loose log which I supposed was attached to a raft – but it wasn't – it tilted me into Bear Creek. And when I had been under water twice and was coming up to make the third and fatal descent my fingers appeared above the water and that slave woman seized them and pulled me out. Within a week I was in again, and that apprentice had to come along just at the wrong time, and he plunged in and dived, pawed around on the bottom and found me, and dragged me out and emptied the water out of me, and I was saved again. I was drowned seven times after that before I learned to swim – once in Bear Creek and six times in the Mississippi. I do not now know who the people were who interfered with the intentions of a Providence wiser than themselves, but I hold a grudge against them yet. When

I told the tale of these remarkable happenings to Rev. Dr. Burton of Hartford, he said he did not believe it. *He slipped on the ice the very next year and sprained his ankle.*

Will Bowen was another schoolmate, and so was his brother, Sam, who was his junior by a couple of years. Before the Civil War broke out, both became St. Louis and New Orleans pilots. Both are dead, long ago.

[*Dictated March 16, 1906.*] We will return to those schoolchildren of sixty years ago. I recall Mary Miller. She was not my first sweetheart, but I think she was the first one that furnished me a broken heart. I fell in love with her when she was eighteen and I was nine, but she scorned me, and I recognized that this was a cold world. I had not noticed that temperature before. I believe I was as miserable as even a grown man could be. But I think that this sorrow did not remain with me long. As I remember it, I soon transferred my worship to Artimisia Briggs, who was a year older than Mary Miller. When I revealed my passion to her she did not scoff at it. She did not make fun of it. She was very kind and gentle about it. But she was also firm, and said she did not want to be pestered by children.

And there was Mary Lacy. She was a schoolmate. But she also was out of my class because of her advanced age. She was pretty wild and determined and independent. But she married, and at once settled down and became in all ways a model matron and was as highly respected as any matron in the town. Four years ago she was still living, and had been married fifty years.

Jimmie McDaniel was another schoolmate. His age and mine about tallied. His father kept the candy-shop and he was the most envied little chap in the town – after Tom Blankenship ("Huck Finn") – for although we never saw him eating candy, we supposed that it was, nevertheless, his ordinary diet. He pretended that he never ate it, and didn't care for it because there was nothing forbidden about it – there was plenty of it and he could have as much of it as he wanted. He was the first human being to whom I ever told a humorous story, so far as I can remember. This was about Jim Wolfe and the cats; and I gave him that tale the morning after that memorable episode. I thought he would laugh his teeth out. I had never been so proud and happy before, and have seldom been so proud and happy since. I saw him four years ago when I was out there. He wore a beard, gray and venerable, that came half-way down to his knees, and yet it was not difficult for me to recognize him. He had been married fifty-four years. He had many children and grandchildren and great-grandchildren, and also even posterity, they all said – thousands – yet the boy to whom I had told the cat story when we were callow juveniles was still present in that cheerful little old man.

Artimisia Briggs got married not long after refusing me. She married Richmond, the stone mason, who was my Methodist Sunday-school teacher in the earliest days, and he had one distinction which I envied him: at some time or other he had hit his thumb with his hammer and the result was a thumb nail which remained permanently twisted and distorted and curved and pointed, like a parrot's beak. I should not consider it an ornament now, I suppose, but it had a fascination for me then, and a vast value, because it was the only one in the town. He was a very kindly and considerate Sunday-school teacher, and patient and compassionate, so he was the favorite teacher with us little chaps. In that school they had slender oblong paste-board blue tickets, each with a verse from the Testament printed on it, and you could get a blue ticket by reciting two verses. By reciting five verses you could get three blue tickets, and you could trade these at the bookcase and borrow a book for a week. I was under Mr. Richmond's spiritual care every now and then for two or three years, and he was never hard upon me. I always recited the same five verses every Sunday. He was always satisfied with the performance. He never seemed to notice that these were the same five foolish virgins that he had been hearing about every Sunday for months. I always got my tickets and exchanged them for a book. They were pretty dreary books, for there was not a bad boy in the entire bookcase. They were *all* good boys and good girls and drearily uninteresting, but they were better society than none, and I was glad to have their company and disapprove of it.

Twenty years ago Mr. Richmond had become possessed of Tom Sawyer's cave in the hills three miles from town, and had made a tourist-resort of it. In 1849 when the gold-seekers were streaming through our little town of Hannibal, many of our grown men got the gold fever, and I think that all the boys had it. On the Saturday holidays in summer-time we used to borrow skiffs whose owners were not present and go down the river three miles to the cave hollow (Missourian for "valley"), and there we staked out claims and pretended to dig gold, panning out half a dollar a day at first; two or three times as much, later, and by and by whole fortunes, as our imaginations became inured to the work. Stupid and unprophetic lads! We were doing this in play and never suspecting. Why, that cave hollow and all the adjacent hills were made of gold! But we did not know it. We took it for dirt. We left its rich secret in its own peaceful possession and grew up in poverty and went wandering about the world struggling for bread – and this because we had not the gift of prophecy. That region was all dirt and rocks to us, yet all it needed was to be ground up and scientifically handled and it was gold. That is to say, the whole region was a cement-mine – and they make the finest kind of Portland cement there now, five thousand barrels a day, with a plant that cost $2,000,000.

For a little while Reuel Gridley attended that school of ours. He was an elderly pupil; he was perhaps twenty-two or twenty-three years old. Then came the Mexican War and he volunteered. A company of infantry was raised in our town and Mr. Hickman, a tall, straight, handsome athlete of twenty-five, was made captain of it and had a sword by his side and a broad yellow stripe down the leg of his gray pants. And when that company marched back and forth through the streets in its smart uniform – which it did several times a day for drill – its evolutions were attended by all the boys whenever the school hours permitted. I can see that marching company yet, and I can almost feel again the consuming desire that I had to join it. But they had no use for boys of twelve and thirteen, and before I had a chance in another war the desire to kill people to whom I had not been introduced had passed away.

I saw the splendid Hickman in his old age. He seemed about the oldest man I had ever seen – an amazing and melancholy contrast with the showy young captain I had seen preparing his warriors for carnage so many, many years before. Hickman is dead – it is the old story. As Susy said, "What is it all for?"

Reuel Gridley went away to the wars and we heard of him no more for fifteen or sixteen years. Then one day in Carson City while I was having a difficulty with an editor on the sidewalk – an editor better built for war than I was – I heard a voice say, "Give him the best you've got, Sam, I'm at your back." It was Reuel Gridley. He said he had not recognized me by my face but by my drawling style of speech.

He went down to the Reese River mines about that time and presently he lost an election bet in his mining camp, and by the terms of it he was obliged to buy a fifty-pound sack of self-raising

flour and carry it through the town, preceded by music, and
deliver it to the winner of the bet. Of course the whole camp was
present and full of fluid and enthusiasm. The winner of the bet put
up the sack at auction for the benefit of the United States Sanitary
Fund, and sold it. The excitement grew and grew. The sack was
sold over and over again for the benefit of the Fund. The news of
it came to Virginia City by telegraph. It produced great enthusiasm, and Reuel Gridley was begged by telegraph to bring the sack
and have an auction in Virginia City. He brought it. An open barouche was provided, also a brass band. The sack was sold over
and over again at Gold Hill, then was brought up to Virginia City
toward night and sold – and sold again, and again, and still again,
netting twenty or thirty thousand dollars for the Sanitary Fund.
Gridley carried it across California and sold it at various towns.
He sold it for large sums in Sacramento and in San Francisco. He
brought it East, sold it in New York and in various other cities,
then carried it out to a great Fair at St. Louis, and went on selling
it; and finally made it up into small cakes and sold those at a dollar
apiece. First and last, the sack of flour which had originally cost
ten dollars, perhaps, netted more than two hundred thousand dollars for the Sanitary Fund. Reuel Gridley has been dead these
many, many years – it is the old story.

In that school were the first Jews I had ever seen. It took me a
good while to get over the awe of it. To my fancy they were clothed
invisibly in the damp and cobwebby mould of antiquity. They carried me back to Egypt, and in imagination I moved among the
Pharaohs and all the shadowy celebrities of that remote age. The
name of the boys was Levin. We had a collective name for them
which was the only really large and handsome witticism that was
ever born in that Congressional district. We called them "Twenty-
two" – and even when the joke was old and had been worn threadbare we always followed it with the explanation, to make sure that
it would be understood, "Twice Levin – twenty-two."

There were other boys whose names remain with me. Irving
Ayres – but no matter, he is dead. Then there was George Butler,
whom I remember as a child of seven wearing a blue leather belt
with a brass buckle, and hated and envied by all the boys on
account of it. He was a nephew of General Ben Butler and fought
gallantly at Ball's Bluff and in several other actions of the Civil
War. He is dead, long and long ago.

Will Bowen (dead long ago), Ed Stevens (dead long ago) and

John Briggs were special mates of mine. John is still living.

In 1845, when I was ten years old, there was an epidemic of measles in the town and it made a most alarming slaughter among the little people. There was a funeral almost daily, and the mothers of the town were nearly demented with fright. My mother was greatly troubled. She worried over Pamela and Henry and me, and took constant and extraordinary pains to keep us from coming into contact with the contagion. But upon reflection I believed that her judgment was at fault. It seemed to me that I could improve upon it if left to my own devices. I cannot remember now whether I was frightened about the measles or not, but I clearly remember that I grew very tired of the suspense I suffered on account of being continually under the threat of death. I remember that I got so weary of it and so anxious to have the matter settled one way or the other, and promptly, that this anxiety spoiled my days and my nights. I had no pleasure in them. I made up my mind to end this suspense and be done with it. Will Bowen was dangerously ill with the measles and I thought I would go down there and catch them. I entered the house by the front way and slipped along through rooms and halls, keeping sharp watch against discovery, and at last I reached Will's bed-chamber in the rear of the house on the second floor and got into it uncaptured. But that was as far as my victory reached. His mother caught me there a moment later and snatched me out of the house and gave me a most competent scolding and drove me away. She was so scared that she could hardly get her words out, and her face was white. I saw that I must manage better next time, and I did. I hung about the lane at the rear of the house and watched through cracks in the fence until I was convinced that the conditions were favorable; then I slipped through the back yard and up the back way and got into the room and into the bed with Will Bowen without being observed. I don't know how long I was in the bed. I only remember that Will Bowen, as society, had no value for me, for he was too sick to even notice that I was there. When I heard his mother coming I covered up my head, but that device was a failure. It was dead summer-time – the cover was nothing more than a limp blanket or sheet, and anybody could see that there were two of us under it. It didn't remain two very long. Mrs. Bowen snatched me out of the bed and conducted me home herself, with a grip on my collar which she never loosened until she delivered me into my mother's hands along with her opinion of that kind of a boy.

It was a good case of measles that resulted. It brought me within a shade of death's door. It brought me to where I no longer took any interest in anything, but, on the contrary, felt a total absence of interest – which was most placid and enchanting. I have never enjoyed anything in my life any more than I enjoyed dying that time. I *was*, in effect, dying. The word had been passed and the family notified to assemble around the bed and see me off. I knew them all. There was no doubtfulness in my vision. They were all crying, but that did not affect me. I took but the vaguest interest in it, and that merely because I was the centre of all this emotional attention and was gratified by it and vain of it.

When Dr. Cunningham had made up his mind that nothing more could be done for me he put bags of hot ashes all over me. He put them on my breast, on my wrists, on my ankles; and so, very much to his astonishment – and doubtless to my regret – he dragged me back into this world and set me going again.

[*Dictated July 26, 1907.*] In an article entitled "England's Ovation to Mark Twain," Sydney Brooks – but never mind that, now.

I was in Oxford by seven o'clock that evening (June 25, 1907), and trying on the scarlet gown which the tailor had been constructing, and found it right – right and surpassingly becoming. At half past ten the next morning we assembled at All Souls College and marched thence, gowned, mortar-boarded and in double file, down a long street to the Sheldonian Theatre, between solid walls of the populace, very much hurrah'd and limitlessly kodak'd. We made a procession of considerable length and distinction and picturesqueness, with the Chancellor, Lord Curzon, late Viceroy of India, in his rich robe of black and gold, in the lead, followed by a pair of trim little boy train-bearers, and the train-bearers followed by the young Prince Arthur of Connaught, who was to be made a D.C.L. The detachment of D.C.L.'s were followed by the Doctors of Science, and these by the Doctors of Literature, and these in turn by the Doctors of Music. Sidney Colvin marched in front of me; I was coupled with Sidney Lee, and Kipling followed us; General Booth, of the Salvation Army, was in the squadron of D.C.L.'s.

Our journey ended, we were halted in a fine old hall whence we could see, through a corridor of some length, the massed audience in the theatre. Here for a little time we moved about and chatted and made acquaintanceships; then the D.C.L.'s were summoned, and they marched through that corridor and the shouting began in the theatre. It would be some time before the Doctors of Literature and of Science would be called for, because each of those D.C.L.'s had to have a couple of Latin speeches made over him before his promotion would be complete – one by the Regius Professor of Civil Law, the other by the Chancellor. After a while I asked Sir William Ramsay if a person might smoke here and not get shot. He said, "Yes," but that whoever did it and got caught would be fined a guinea, and perhaps hanged later. He said he knew of a place where we could accomplish at least as much as half of a smoke before any informers would be likely to chance upon us, and he was ready to show the way to any who might be willing to risk the guinea and the hanging. By request he led the way, and Kipling, Sir Norman Lockyer and I followed. We crossed an unpopulated quadrangle and stood under one of its exits – an archway of massive masonry – and there we lit up and began to take comfort. The photographers soon arrived, but they were courteous and friendly and gave us no trouble, and we gave them none. They grouped us in all sorts of ways and photographed us at their diligent leisure, while we smoked and talked. We were there more than an hour; then we returned to headquarters, happy, content, and greatly refreshed. Presently we filed into the theatre, under a very satisfactory hurrah, and waited in a crimson column, dividing the crowded pit through the middle, until each of us in his turn should be called to stand before the Chancellor and hear our merits set forth in sonorous Latin. Meantime, Kipling and I wrote autographs until some good kind soul interfered in our behalf and procured for us a rest.

I will now save what is left of my modesty by quoting a paragraph from Sydney Brooks's "Ovation."

*   *   *

Let those stars take the place of it for the present. Sydney Brooks has done it well. It makes me proud to read it; as proud as I was in that old day, sixty-two years ago, when I lay dying, the centre of attraction, with one eye piously closed upon the fleeting vanities of this life – an excellent effect – and the other open a crack to observe the tears, the sorrow, the admiration – all for me – all for me!

Ah, that was the proudest moment of my long life – until Oxford!

*   *   *

Most Americans have been to Oxford and will remember what a dream of the Middle Ages it is, with its crooked lanes, its gray and stately piles of ancient architecture and its meditation-breeding air of repose and dignity and unkinship with the noise and fret and hurry and bustle of these modern days. As a dream of the Middle Ages Oxford was not perfect until Pageant day arrived and furnished certain details which had been for generations lacking. These details began to appear at mid-afternoon on the 27th. At that time singles, couples, groups and squadrons of the three thousand five hundred costumed characters who were to take part in the Pageant began to ooze and drip and stream through house doors, all over the old town, and wend toward the meadows outside the walls. Soon the lanes were thronged with costumes which Oxford had from time to time seen and been familiar with in bygone centuries – fashions of dress which marked off centuries as by dates, and mile-stoned them back, and back, and back, until history faded into legend and tradition, when Arthur was a fact and the Round Table a reality. In this rich commingling of quaint and strange and brilliantly colored fashions in dress the dress-changes of Oxford for twelve centuries stood livid and realized to the eye; Oxford as a dream of the Middle Ages was complete now as it had never, in our day, before been complete; at last there was no discord; the mouldering old buildings, and the picturesque throngs drifting past them, were in harmony; soon – astonishingly soon! – the only persons that seemed out of place, and grotesquely and offensively and criminally out of place were such persons as came intruding along clothed in the ugly and odious fashions of the twentieth century; they were a bitterness to the feelings, an insult to the eye.

The make-ups of illustrious historic personages seemed perfect, both as to portraiture and costume; one had no trouble in recognizing them. Also, I was apparently quite easily recognizable myself. The first corner I turned brought me suddenly face to face with Henry VIII, a person whom I had been implacably disliking for sixty years; but when he put out his hand with royal courtliness and grace and said, "Welcome, well-beloved stranger, to my century and to the hospitalities of my realm," my old prejudices vanished away and I forgave him. I think now that Henry the Eighth has been over-abused, and that most of us, if we had been situated as he was, domestically, would not have been able to get along with as limited a graveyard as he forced himself to put up with. I feel now that he was one of the nicest men in history. Personal contact with a king is more effective in removing baleful prejudices than is any amount of argument drawn from tales and histories. If I had a child I would name it Henry the Eighth, regardless of sex.

Do you remember Charles the First? – and his broad slouch with the plume in it? and his slender, tall figure? and his body clothed in velvet doublet with lace sleeves, and his legs in leather, with long rapier at his side and his spurs on his heels? I encountered him at the next corner, and knew him in a moment – knew him as perfectly and as vividly as I should know the Grand Chain in the Mississippi if I should see it from the pilot-house after all these years. He bent his body and gave his hat a sweep that fetched its plume within an inch of the ground, and gave me a welcome that went to my heart. This king has been much maligned; I shall understand him better hereafter, and shall regret him more than I have been in the habit of doing these fifty or sixty years. He did some things in his time, which might better have been left undone, and which cast a shadow upon his name – we all know that, we all concede it – but our error has been in regarding them as crimes and in calling them by that name, whereas I perceive now that they were only indiscretions. At every few steps I met persons of deathless name whom I had never encountered before outside of pictures and statuary and history, and these were most thrilling and charming encounters. I had hand-shakes with Henry the Second, who had not been seen in the Oxford streets for nearly eight hundred years; and with the Fair Rosamond, whom I now believe to have been chaste and blameless, although I had thought differently about it before; and with Shakespeare, one of the pleasantest foreigners I have ever gotten acquainted with; and with Roger Bacon; and with Queen Elizabeth, who talked five minutes and never swore once – a fact which gave me a new and good opinion of her and moved me to forgive her for beheading the Scottish Mary, if she really did it, which I now doubt; and with the quaintly and anciently clad young King Harold Harefoot, of near nine hundred years ago, who came flying by on a bicycle and smoking a pipe, but at once checked up and got off to shake with me; and also I met a bishop who had lost his way because this was the first time he had been inside the walls of Oxford for as much as twelve hundred years or thereabouts. By this time I had grown so used to the obliterated ages and their best-known people that if I had met Adam I should not have been either surprised or embarrassed; and if he had come in a racing automobile and a cloud of dust, with nothing on but his fig-leaf, it would have seemed to me all right and harmonious.

PART XXIV

FROM SUSY'S BIOGRAPHY OF ME [1885–6]

Mamma and papa have returned from Onteora and they have had a delightful visit. Mr. Frank Stockton was down in Virginia and could not reach Onteora in time, so they did not see him, and Mrs. Mary Mapes Dodge was ill and couldn't go to Onteora, but Mrs. General Custer was there, and mamma said that she was a very attractive, sweet appearing woman.

[*Dictated October 9, 1906.*] Onteora was situated high up in the Cats-kill Mountains, in the centre of a far-reaching solitude. I do not mean that the region was wholly uninhabited; there were farm-houses here and there, at generous distances apart. Their occu-pants were descendants of ancestors who had built the houses in Rip Van Winkle's time, or earlier; and those ancestors were not more primitive than were this posterity of theirs. The city people were as foreign and unfamiliar and strange to them as monkeys would have been, and they would have respected the monkeys as much as they respected these elegant summer-resorters. The resorters were a puzzle to them, their ways were so strange and their interests so trivial. They drove the resorters over the moun-tain roads and listened in shamed surprise at their bursts of enthu-siasm over the scenery. The farmers had had that scenery on exhibition from their mountain roosts all their lives, and had never noticed anything remarkable about it. By way of an incident: a pair of these primitives were overheard chatting about the resorters, one day, and in the course of their talk this remark was dropped:

"I was a-drivin' a passel of 'em round about yisterday evenin', quiet ones, you know, still and solemn, and all to wunst they busted out to make your hair lift and I judged hell was to pay. Now what do you reckon it was? It wa'n't anything but jest one of them com-mon damned yaller sunsets."

In those days –

[*Tuesday, October 16, 1906.*] ... Warner is gone. Stockton is gone. I attended both funerals. Warner was a near neighbor, from the autumn of '71 until his death, nineteen years afterward. It is not the privilege of the most of us to have many intimate friends – a dozen is our aggregate – but I think he could count his by the score. It is seldom that a man is so beloved by both sexes and all ages as Warner was. There was a charm about his spirit, and his ways, and his words, that won all that came within the sphere of its influence. Our children adopted him while they were little creatures, and thenceforth, to the end, he was "Cousin Charley" to them. He was "Uncle Charley" to the children of more than one other friend. Mrs. Clemens was very fond of him, and he always called her by her first name – shortened. Warner died, as she died, and as I would die – without premonition, without a moment's warning.

Uncle Remus still lives, and must be over a thousand years old. Indeed, I know that this must be so, because I have seen a new photograph of him in the public prints within the last month or so, and in that picture his aspects are distinctly and strikingly geological, and one can see he is thinking about the mastodons and plesiosaurians that he used to play with when he was young.

It is just a quarter of a century since I have seen Uncle Remus. He visited us in our home in Hartford and was reverently devoured by the big eyes of Susy and Clara, for I made a deep and awful impression upon the little creatures – who knew his book by heart through my nightly declamation of its tales to them – by revealing to them privately that he was the real Uncle Remus whitewashed so that he could come into people's houses the front way.

He was the bashfulest grown person I have ever met. When there were people about he stayed silent, and seemed to suffer until they were gone. But he was lovely, nevertheless; for the sweetness and benignity of the immortal Remus looked out from his eyes, and the graces and sincerities of his character shone in his face.

It may be that Jim Wolf was as bashful as Harris. It hardly seems possible, yet as I look back fifty-six years and consider Jim Wolf, I am almost persuaded that he was. He was our long slim apprentice in my brother's printing-office in Hannibal. He was seventeen, and yet he was as much as four times as bashful as I was, though I was only fourteen. He boarded and slept in the house, but he was always tongue-tied in the presence of my sister, and when even my gentle mother spoke to him he could not answer

save in frightened monosyllables. He would not enter a room
where a girl was; nothing could persuade him to do such a thing.
Once when he was in our small parlor alone, two majestic old
maids entered and seated themselves in such a way that Jim could
not escape without passing by them. He would as soon have
thought of passing by one of Harris's plesiosaurians ninety feet
long. I came in presently, was charmed with the situation, and sat
down in a corner to watch Jim suffer, and enjoy it. My mother
followed a minute later and sat down with the visitors and began
to talk. Jim sat upright in his chair, and during a quarter of an hour
he did not change his position by a shade – neither General Grant
nor a bronze image could have maintained that immovable pose
more successfully. I mean as to body and limbs; with the face there
was a difference. By fleeting revealments of the face I saw that
something was happening – something out of the common. There
would be a sudden twitch of the muscles of the face, an instant
distortion, which in the next instant had passed and left no trace.
These twitches gradually grew in frequency, but no muscle outside
of the face lost any of its rigidity, or betrayed any interest in what
was happening to Jim. I mean if something *was* happening to him,
and I knew perfectly well that that was the case. At last a pair of
tears began to swim slowly down his cheeks amongst the
twitchings, but Jim sat still and let them run; then I saw his right
hand steal along his thigh until half-way to his knee, then take a
vigorous grip upon the cloth.

That was a *wasp* that he was grabbing! A colony of them were
climbing up his legs and prospecting around, and every time he
winced they stabbed him to the hilt – so for a quarter of an hour
one group of excursionists after another climbed up Jim's legs and
resented even the slightest wince or squirm that he indulged himself with, in his misery. When the entertainment had become
nearly unbearable, he conceived the idea of gripping them
between his fingers and putting them out of commission. He succeeded with many of them, but at great cost, for, as he couldn't see
the wasp, he was as likely to take hold of the wrong end of him as
he was the right; then the dying wasp gave him a punch to remember the incident by.

If those ladies had stayed all day, and if all the wasps in Missouri
had come and climbed up Jim's legs, nobody there would ever
have known it but Jim and the wasps and me. There he would have
sat until the ladies left.

When they finally went away we went up-stairs and he took his clothes off, and his legs were a picture to look at. They looked as if they were mailed all over with shirt buttons, each with a single red hole in the centre. The pain was intolerable – no, would have been intolerable, but the pain of the presence of those ladies had been so much harder to bear that the pain of the wasps' stings was quite pleasant and enjoyable by comparison.

Jim never could enjoy wasps. I remember once –

FROM SUSY'S BIOGRAPHY OF ME [1885–6]

Mamma has given me a very pleasant little newspaper scrap about papa, to copy. I will put it here.

[*Thursday, October 11, 1906.*] It was a rather strong compliment; I think I will leave it out. It was from James Redpath.

The chief ingredients of Redpath's make-up were honesty, sincerity, kindliness, and pluck. He wasn't afraid. He was one of Ossawatomie Brown's right-hand men in the bleeding Kansas days; he was all through that struggle. He carried his life in his hands, and from one day to another it wasn't worth the price of a night's lodging. He had a small body of daring men under him, and they were constantly being hunted by the "jayhawkers," who were proslavery Missourians, guerillas, modern free lances.

[*Friday, October 12, 1906.*] ... I can't think of the name of that daredevil guerilla who led the jayhawkers and chased Redpath up and down the country, and, in turn, was chased by Redpath. By grace of the chances of war, the two men never met in the field, though they several times came within an ace of it.

Ten or twelve years later, Redpath was earning his living in Boston as chief of the lecture business in the United States. Fifteen or sixteen years after his Kansas adventures I became a public lecturer, and he was my agent. Along there somewhere was a press dinner, one November night, at the Tremont Hotel in Boston, and I attended it. I sat near the head of the table, with Redpath between me and the chairman; a stranger sat on my other side. I tried several times to talk with the stranger, but he seemed to be out of words and I presently ceased from troubling him. He was manifestly a very shy man, and, moreover, he might have been losing sleep the night before.

The first man called up was Redpath. At the mention of the

name the stranger started, and showed interest. He fixed a fascinated eye on Redpath, and lost not a word of his speech. Redpath told some stirring incidents of his career in Kansas, and said, among other things:

"Three times I came near capturing the gallant jayhawker chief, and once he actually captured *me*, but didn't know me and let me go, because he said he was hot on Redpath's trail and couldn't afford to waste time and rope on inconsequential small fry."

My stranger was called up next, and when Redpath heard his name he, in turn, showed a startled interest. The stranger said, bending a caressing glance upon Redpath and speaking gently – I may even say sweetly:

"You realize that I was that jayhawker chief. I am glad to know you now and take you to my heart and call you friend" – then he added, in a voice that was pathetic with regret, "but if I had only known you then, what tumultuous happiness I should have had in your society! – while it lasted."

The last quarter of a century of my life has been pretty constantly and faithfully devoted to the study of the human race – that is to say, the study of myself, for, in my individual person, I am the entire human race compacted together. I have found that there is no ingredient of the race which I do not possess in either a small way or a large way. When it is small, as compared with the same ingredient in somebody else, there is still enough of it for all the purposes of examination. In my contacts with the species I find no one who possesses a quality which I do not possess. The shades of difference between other people and me serve to make variety and prevent monotony, but that is all; broadly speaking, we are all alike; and so by studying myself carefully and comparing myself with other people, and noting the divergences, I have been enabled to acquire a knowledge of the human race which I perceive is more accurate and more comprehensive than that which has been acquired and revealed by any other member of our species. As a result, my private and concealed opinion of myself is not of a complimentary sort. It follows that my estimate of the human race is the duplicate of my estimate of myself.

I am not proposing to discuss all of the peculiarities of the human race, at this time; I only wish to touch lightly upon one or two of them. To begin with, I wonder why a man should prefer a good billiard-table to a poor one; and why he should prefer straight cues to crooked ones; and why he should prefer round balls to chipped ones; and why he should prefer a level table to one that slants; and why he should prefer responsive cushions to the dull and unresponsive kind. I wonder at these things, because when we examine the matter we find that the essentials involved in billiards are as competently and exhaustively furnished by a bad billiard outfit as they are by the best one. One of the essentials is amusement. Very well, if there is any more amusement to be gotten out of the one outfit than out of the other, the facts are in favor of the bad outfit. The bad outfit will always furnish thirty per cent. more fun for the players and for the spectators than will the good outfit. Another essential of the game is that the outfit shall give the players full opportunity to exercise their best skill, and display it in a way to compel the admiration of the spectators. Very well, the bad outfit is nothing behind the good one in this regard. It is a difficult matter to estimate correctly the eccentricities of chipped balls and a slanting table, and make the right allowance for them and secure a count; the finest kind of skill is required to accomplish the satisfactory result. Another essential of the game is that it shall add to the interest of the game by furnishing opportunities to bet. Very well, in this regard no good outfit can claim any advantage over a bad one. I know, by experience, that a bad outfit is as valuable as the best one; that an outfit that couldn't be sold at auction for seven dollars is just as valuable for all the essentials of the game as an outfit that is worth a thousand.

I acquired some of this learning in Jackass Gulch, California, more than forty years ago. Jackass Gulch had once been a rich and thriving surface-mining camp. By and by its gold deposits were exhausted; then the people began to go away, and the town began to decay, and rapidly; in my time it had disappeared. Where the bank, and the city hall, and the church, and the gambling-dens, and the newspaper office, and the streets of brick blocks had been, was nothing now but a wide and beautiful expanse of green grass, a peaceful and charming solitude. Half a dozen scattered dwellings were still inhabited, and there was still one saloon of a ruined and rickety character struggling for life, but doomed. In its bar was a billiard outfit that was the counterpart of the one in my father-in-law's garret. The balls were chipped, the cloth was darned and patched, the table's surface was undulating, and the cues were headless and had the curve of a parenthesis – but the forlorn remnant of marooned miners played games there, and those games were more entertaining to look at than a circus and a grand opera combined. Nothing but a quite extraordinary skill could score a carom on that table – a skill that required the nicest estimate of force, distance, and how much to allow for the various slants of the table and the other formidable peculiarities and idiosyncrasies furnished by the contradictions of the outfit. Last winter, here in New York, I saw Hoppe and Schaefer and Sutton and the three or four other billiard champions of world-wide fame contend against each other, and certainly the art and science displayed were a wonder to see; yet I saw nothing there in the way of science and art that was more wonderful than shots which I had seen Texas Tom make on the wavy surface of that poor old wreck in the perishing saloon at Jackass Gulch forty years before. Once I saw Texas Tom make a string of seven points on a single inning! – all calculated shots, and not a fluke or a scratch among them. I often saw him make runs of four, but when he made his great string of seven, the boys went wild with enthusiasm and admiration. The joy and the noise exceeded that which the great gathering at Madison Square produced when Sutton scored five hundred points at the eighteen-inch game, on a world-famous night last winter. With practice, that champion could score nineteen or twenty on the Jackass Gulch table; but to start with, Texas Tom would show him miracles that would astonish him; also it might have another handsome result: it might persuade the great experts to discard their own trifling game and bring the Jackass Gulch outfit here and exhibit their skill in a game worth a hundred of the discarded one, for profound and breathless interest, and for displays of almost superhuman skill.

In my experience, games played with a fiendish outfit furnish ecstasies of delight which games played with the other kind cannot match. Twenty-seven years ago my budding little family spent the summer at Bateman's Point, near Newport, Rhode Island. It was a comfortable boarding-place, well stocked with sweet mothers and little children, but the male sex was scarce; however, there was another young fellow besides myself, and he and I had good times – Higgins was his name, but that was not his fault. He was a very pleasant and companionable person. On the premises there was what had once been a bowling-alley. It was a single alley, and it was estimated that it had been out of repair for sixty years – but not the balls, the balls were in good condition; there were forty-one of them, and they ranged in size from a grapefruit up to a lignum-vitae sphere that you could hardly lift. Higgins and I played on that alley day after day. At first, one of us located himself at the bottom end to set up the pins in case anything should happen to them, but nothing happened. The surface of that alley consisted of a rolling stretch of elevations and depressions, and neither of us could, by any art known to us, persuade a ball to stay on the alley until it should accomplish something. Little balls and big, the same thing always happened – the ball left the alley before it was half-way home and went thundering down alongside of it the rest of the way and made the gamekeeper climb out and take care of himself. No matter, we persevered, and were rewarded. We examined the alley, noted and located a lot of its peculiarities, and little by little we learned how to deliver a ball in such a way that it would travel home and knock down a pin or two. By and by we succeeded in improving our game to a point where we were able to get all of the pins with thirty-five balls – so we made it a thirty-five-ball game. If the player did not succeed with thirty-five, he had lost the game. I suppose that all the balls, taken together, weighed five hundred pounds, or maybe a ton – or along there somewhere – but anyway it was hot weather, and by the time that a player had sent thirty-five of them home he was in a drench of perspiration, and physically exhausted.

Next, we started cocked hat – that is to say, a triangle of three pins, the other seven being discarded. In this game we used the three smallest balls and kept on delivering them until we got the three pins down. After a day or two of practice we were able to get the chief pin with an output of four balls, but it cost us a great many deliveries to get the other two; but by and by we succeeded in perfecting our art – at least we perfected it to our limit. We reached a scientific excellence where we could get the three pins down with twelve deliveries of the three small balls, making thirty-six shots to conquer the cocked hat.

Having reached our limit for daylight work, we set up a couple of candles and played at night. As the alley was fifty or sixty feet long, we couldn't see the pins, but the candles indicated their locality. We continued this game until we were able to knock down the invisible pins with thirty-six shots. Having now reached the limit of the candle game, we changed and played it left-handed. We continued the left-handed game until we conquered its limit, which was fifty-four shots. Sometimes we sent down a succession of fifteen balls without getting anything at all. We easily got out of that old alley five times the fun that anybody could have gotten out of the best alley in New York.

One blazing hot day, a modest and courteous officer of the regular army appeared in our den and introduced himself. He was about thirty-five years old, well built and militarily erect and straight, and he was hermetically sealed up in the uniform of that ignorant old day – a uniform made of heavy material, and much properer for January than July. When he saw the venerable alley, and glanced from that to the long procession of shining balls in the trough, his eye lit with desire, and we judged that he was our meat. We politely invited him to take a hand, and he could not conceal his gratitude; though his breeding, and the etiquette of his profession, made him try. We explained the game to him, and said that there were forty-one balls, and that the player was privileged to extend his inning and keep on playing until he had used them all up – repeatedly – and that for every ten-strike he got a prize. We didn't name the prize – it wasn't necessary, as no prize would ever be needed or called for. He started a sarcastic smile, but quenched it according to the etiquette of his profession. He merely remarked that he would like to select a couple of medium balls and one small one, adding that he didn't think he would need the rest.

Then he began, and he was an astonished man. He couldn't get a ball to stay on the alley. When he had fired about fifteen balls and hadn't yet reached the cluster of pins, his annoyance began to show out through his clothes. He wouldn't let it show in his face; but after another fifteen balls he was not able to control his face; he didn't utter a word, but he exuded mute blasphemy from every pore. He asked permission to take off his coat, which was granted; then he turned himself loose, with bitter determination, and although he was only an infantry officer he could have been mistaken for a battery, he got up such a volleying thunder with those balls. Presently he removed his cravat; after a little he took off his vest; and still he went bravely on. Higgins was suffocating. My condition was the same, but it would not be courteous to laugh; it would be better to burst, and we came near it. That officer was good pluck. He stood to his work without uttering a word, and kept the balls going until he had expended the outfit four times, making four times forty-one shots; then he had to give it up, and he did; for he was no longer able to stand without wobbling. He put on his clothes, bade us a courteous good-by, invited us to call at the Fort, and started away. Then he came back, and said,

"What is the prize for the ten-strike?"

We had to confess that we had not selected it yet.

He said, gravely, that he thought there was no occasion for hurry about it.

I believe Bateman's alley was a better one than any other in America, in the matter of the essentials of the game. It compelled skill; it provided opportunity for bets; and if you could get a stranger to do the bowling for you, there was more and wholesomer and delightfuler entertainment to be gotten out of his industries than out of the finest game by the best expert, and played upon the best alley elsewhere in existence.

PART XXV

DECEMBER, 1907

January 11, 1906. Answer to a letter received this morning:

DEAR MRS. H., – I am forever your debtor for reminding me of that curious passage in my life. During the first year or two after it happened, I could not bear to think of it. My pain and shame were so intense, and my sense of having been an imbecile so settled, established and confirmed, that I drove the episode entirely from my mind – and so all these twenty-eight or twenty-nine years I have lived in the conviction that my performance of that time was coarse, vulgar and destitute of humor. But your suggestion that you and your family found humor in it twenty-eight years ago moved me to look into the matter. So I commissioned a Boston typewriter to delve among the Boston papers of that bygone time and send me a copy of it.

It came this morning, and if there is any vulgarity about it I am not able to discover it. If it isn't innocently and ridiculously funny, I am no judge. I will see to it that you get a copy.

Address of Samuel L. Clemens ("Mark Twain")
From a report of the dinner given by the Publishers
of the Atlantic Monthly in honor of the
Seventieth Anniversary of the
Birth of John Greenleaf Whittier, at the

Hotel Brunswick, Boston, December 17, 1877,
as published in the
BOSTON EVENING TRANSCRIPT,
December 18, 1877

Mr. Chairman – This is an occasion peculiarly meet for the digging up of pleasant reminiscences concerning literary folk;
therefore I will drop lightly into history myself. Standing here on
the shore of the Atlantic and contemplating certain of its largest
literary billows, I am reminded of a thing which happened to
me thirteen years ago, when I had just succeeded in stirring up a
little Nevadian literary puddle myself, whose spume-flakes were
beginning to blow thinly Californiawards. I started an inspection tramp through the southern mines of California. I was callow and conceited, and I resolved to try the virtue of my *nom de
guerre.* I very soon had an opportunity. I knocked at a miner's
lonely log cabin in the foothills of the Sierras just at nightfall.
It was snowing at the time. A jaded, melancholy man of fifty,
barefooted, opened the door to me. When he heard my *nom de
guerre* he looked more dejected than before. He let me in – pretty
reluctantly, I thought – and after the customary bacon and
beans, black coffee and hot whiskey, I took a pipe. This sorrowful man had not said three words up to this time. Now he spoke
up and said, in the voice of one who is secretly suffering, "You're
the fourth – I'm going to move." "The fourth what?" said I.
"The fourth littery man that has been here in twenty-four hours
– I'm going to move." "You don't tell me!" said I; "who were
the others?" "Mr. Longfellow, Mr. Emerson and Mr. Oliver
Wendell Holmes – consound the lot!"

You can easily believe I was interested. I supplicated – three
hot whiskeys did the rest – and finally the melancholy miner
began. Said he –

"They came here just at dark yesterday evening, and I let
them in of course. Said they were going to the Yosemite. They
were a rough lot, but that's nothing; everybody looks rough that
travels afoot. Mr. Emerson was a seedy little bit of a chap, red-
headed. Mr. Holmes was as fat as a balloon; he weighed as much
as three hundred, and had double chins all the way down to his
stomach. Mr. Longfellow was built like a prize-fighter. His head
was cropped and bristly, like as if he had a wig made of hair-
brushes. His nose lay straight down his face, like a finger with

the end joint tilted up. They had been drinking, I could see that. And what queer talk they used! Mr. Holmes inspected this cabin, then he took me by the buttonhole, and says he –

> "'Through the deep caves of thought
> I hear a voice that sings,
> Build thee more stately mansions,
> O my soul!'

"Says I, 'I can't afford it, Mr. Holmes, and moreover I don't want to.' Blamed if I liked it pretty well, either, coming from a stranger, that way. However, I started to get out my bacon and beans, when Mr. Emerson came and looked on awhile, and then *he* takes me aside by the buttonhole and says –

> "'Give me agates for my meat;
> Give me cantharids to eat;
> From air and ocean bring me foods,
> From all zones and altitudes.'

"Says I, 'Mr. Emerson, if you'll excuse me, this ain't no hotel.' You see it sort of riled me – I warn't used to the ways of littery swells. But I went on a-sweating over my work, and next comes Mr. Longfellow and buttonholes me, and interrupts me. Says he,

> "'Honor be to Mudjekeewis!
> You shall hear how Pau-Puk-Keewis – '

"But I broke in, and says I, 'Beg your pardon, Mr. Longfellow, if you'll be so kind as to hold your yawp for about five minutes and let me get this grub ready, you'll do me proud.' Well, sir, after they'd filled up I set out the jug. Mr. Holmes looks at it and then he fires up all of a sudden and yells –

> "'Flash out a stream of blood-red wine!
> For I would drink to other days.'

"By George, I was getting kind of worked up. I don't deny it, I was getting kind of worked up. I turns to Mr. Holmes, and says I, 'Looky here, my fat friend, I'm a-running this shanty, and if the court knows herself, you'll take whiskey straight or you'll go dry.' Them's the very words I said to him. Now I don't want to sass such famous littery people, but you see they kind of forced me. There ain't nothing onreasonable 'bout me; I don't mind a passel of guests a-treadin' on my tail three or four times, but when it comes to *standing* on it it's different, 'and if the court knows herself,' I says, 'you'll take whiskey straight or you'll go dry.' Well, between drinks they'd swell around the cabin and strike attitudes and spout; and pretty soon they got out a greasy old deck and went to playing euchre at ten cents a corner – on trust. I began to notice some pretty suspicious things. Mr. Emerson dealt, looked at his hand, shook his head, says –

> " 'I am the doubter and the doubt – '

and ca'mly bunched the hands and went to shuffling for a new layout. Says he –

> " 'They reckon ill who leave me out;
> They know not well the subtle ways I keep.
> I pass and deal *again!*'

Hang'd if he didn't go ahead and do it, too! O, he was a cool one! Well, in about a minute, things were running pretty tight, but all of a sudden I see by Mr. Emerson's eye he judged he had 'em. He had already corralled two tricks and each of the others one. So now he kind of lifts a little in his chair and says –

> " 'I tire of globes and aces! –
> Too long the game is played!'

– and down he fetched a right bower. Mr. Longfellow smiles as sweet as pie and says –

> " 'Thanks, thanks to thee, my worthy friend,
> For the lesson thou hast taught,'

– and blamed if he didn't down with *another* right bower! Emerson claps his hand on his bowie, Longfellow claps his on his revolver, and I went under a bunk. There was going to be trouble; but that monstrous Holmes rose up, wobbling his double chins, and says he, 'Order, gentlemen; the first man that draws, I'll lay down on him and smother him!' All quiet on the Potomac, you bet!

"They were pretty how-come-you-so, by now, and they begun to blow. Emerson says, 'The nobbiest thing I ever wrote was Barbara Frietchie.' Says Longfellow, 'It don't begin with my Biglow Papers.' Says Holmes, 'My Thanatopsis lays over 'em both.' They mighty near ended in a fight. Then they wished they had some more company – and Mr. Emerson pointed to me and says –

> "'Is yonder squalid peasant all
> That this proud nursery could breed?'

He was a-whetting his bowie on his boot – so I let it pass. Well, sir, next they took it into their heads that they would like some music; so they made me stand up and sing 'When Johnny Comes Marching Home' till I dropped – at thirteen minutes past four this morning. That's what I've been through, my friend. When I woke at seven, they were leaving, thank goodness, and Mr. Longfellow had my only boots on, and his'n under his arm. Says I, 'Hold on, there, Evangeline, what are you going to do with *them?*' He says, 'Going to make tracks with 'em; because –

> "'Lives of great men all remind us
> We can make our lives sublime;
> And, departing, leave behind us
> Footprints on the sands of time.'

As I said, Mr. Twain, you are the fourth in twenty-four hours – and I'm going to move; I ain't suited to a littery atmosphere."

I said to the miner, "Why, my dear sir, *these* were not the gracious singers to whom we and the world pay loving reverence and homage; these were impostors."

The miner investigated me with a calm eye for a while; then said he, "Ah! impostors, were they? Are *you?*"

I did not pursue the subject, and since then I have not travelled on my *nom de guerre* enough to hurt. Such was the reminiscence I was moved to contribute, Mr. Chairman. In my enthusiasm I may have exaggerated the details a little, but you will easily forgive me that fault, since I believe it is the first time

I have ever deflected from perpendicular fact on an occasion
like this.

What I have said to Mrs. H. is true. I did suffer during a year or
two from the deep humiliations of that episode. But at last, in 1888,
in Venice, my wife and I came across Mr. and Mrs. A. P. C., of
Concord, Massachusetts, and a friendship began then of the sort
which nothing but death terminates. The C.'s were very bright
people and in every way charming and companionable. We were
together a month or two in Venice and several months in Rome,
afterwards, and one day that lamented break of mine was mentioned. And when I was on the point of lathering those people for
bringing it to my mind when I had gotten the memory of it almost
squelched, I perceived with joy that the C.'s were indignant about
the way that my performance had been received in Boston. They
poured out their opinions most freely and frankly about the frosty
attitude of the people who were present at that performance, and
about the Boston newspapers for the position they had taken in
regard to the matter. That position was that I had been irreverent
beyond belief, beyond imagination. Very well, I had accepted that
as a fact for a year or two, and had been thoroughly miserable
about it whenever I thought of it – which was not frequently, if
I could help it. Whenever I thought of it I wondered how I ever
could have been inspired to do so unholy a thing. Well, the C.'s
comforted me, but they did not persuade me to continue to think
about the unhappy episode. I resisted that. I tried to get it out of
my mind, and let it die, and I succeeded. Until Mrs. H.'s letter
came, it had been a good twenty-five years since I had thought of
that matter; and when she said that the thing was funny I wondered if possibly she might be right. At any rate, my curiosity was
aroused, and I wrote to Boston and got the whole thing copied, as
above set forth.

I vaguely remember some of the details of that gathering – dimly
I can see a hundred people – no, perhaps fifty – shadowy figures
sitting at tables feeding, ghosts now to me, and nameless forever
more. I don't know who they were, but I can very distinctly see,
seated at the grand table and facing the rest of us, Mr. Emerson,
supernaturally grave, unsmiling; Mr. Whittier, grave, lovely, his
beautiful spirit shining out of his face; Mr. Longfellow, with his
silken white hair and his benignant face; Dr. Oliver Wendell
Holmes, flashing smiles and affection and all good-fellowship

everywhere like a rose-diamond whose facets are being turned toward the light first one way and then another – a charming man, and always fascinating, whether he was talking or whether he was sitting still (what *he* would call still, but what would be more or less motion to other people). I can see those figures with entire distinctness across this abyss of time.

One other feature is clear – Willie Winter (for these past thousand years dramatic editor of the "New York Tribune," and still occupying that high post in his old age) was there. He was much younger then than he is now, and he showed it. It was always a pleasure to me to see Willie Winter at a banquet. During a matter of twenty years I was seldom at a banquet where Willie Winter was not also present, and where he did not read a charming poem written for the occasion. He did it this time, and it was up to standard: dainty, happy, choicely phrased, and as good to listen to as music, and sounding exactly as if it was pouring unprepared out of heart and brain.

Now at that point ends all that was pleasurable about that notable celebration of Mr. Whittier's seventieth birthday – because *I* got up at that point and followed Winter, with what I have no doubt I supposed would be the gem of the evening – the gay oration above quoted from the Boston paper. I had written it all out the day before and had perfectly memorized it, and I stood up there at my genial and happy and self-satisfied ease, and began to deliver it. Those majestic guests, that row of venerable and still active volcanoes, listened, as did everybody else in the house, with attentive interest. Well, I delivered myself of – we'll say the first two hundred words of my speech. I was expecting no returns from that part of the speech, but this was not the case as regarded the rest of it. I arrived now at the dialogue: 'The old miner said, "You are the fourth, I'm going to move." "The fourth what?" said I. He answered, "The fourth littery man that has been here in twenty-four hours. I am going to move." "Why, you don't tell me," said I. "Who were the others?" "Mr. Longfellow, Mr. Emerson, Mr. Oliver Wendell Holmes, consound the lot – "'

Now then the house's *attention* continued, but the expression of interest in the faces turned to a sort of black frost. I wondered what the trouble was. I didn't know. I went on, but with difficulty – I struggled along, and entered upon that miner's fearful description of the bogus Emerson, the bogus Holmes, the bogus Longfellow, always hoping – but with a gradually perishing hope – that somebody would laugh, or that somebody would at least smile, but nobody did. I didn't know enough to give it up and sit down, I was too new to public speaking, and so I went on with this awful performance, and carried it clear through to the end, in front of a body of people who seemed turned to stone with horror. It was the sort of expression their faces would have worn if I had been making these remarks about the Deity and the rest of the Trinity; there is no milder way in which to describe the petrified condition and the ghastly expression of those people.

When I sat down it was with a heart which had long ceased to beat. I shall never be as dead again as I was then. I shall never be as miserable again as I was then. I speak now as one who doesn't know what the condition of things may be in the next world, but in this one I shall never be as wretched again as I was then. Howells, who was near me, tried to say a comforting word, but couldn't get beyond a gasp. There was no use – he understood the whole size of the disaster. He had good intentions, but the words froze before they could get out. It was an atmosphere that would freeze anything. If Benvenuto Cellini's salamander had been in that place he would not have survived to be put into Cellini's autobiography. There was a frightful pause. There was an awful silence, a desolating silence. Then the next man on the list had to get up – there was no help for it. That was Bishop – Bishop had just burst handsomely upon the world with a most acceptable novel, which had appeared in the "Atlantic Monthly," a place which would make any novel respectable and any author noteworthy. In this case the novel itself was recognized as being, without extraneous help, respectable. Bishop was away up in the public favor, and he was an object of high interest, consequently there was a sort of national expectancy in the air; we may say our American millions were standing, from Maine to Texas and from Alaska to Florida, holding their breath, their lips parted, their hands ready to applaud when Bishop should get up on that occasion, and for the first time in his life speak in public. It was under these damaging conditions that he got up to "make good," as the vulgar say. I had spoken several times before, and that is the reason why I was able to go on without dying in my tracks, as I ought to have done – but Bishop had had no experience. He was up facing those awful deities – facing those other people, those strangers – facing human beings for the first time in his life, with a speech to utter. No doubt it was well packed away in his memory, no doubt it was fresh and usable, until I had been heard from. I suppose that after that, and under the smothering pall of that dreary silence, it began to waste away and disappear out of his head like the rags breaking from the edge of a fog, and presently there wasn't any fog left. He didn't go on – he didn't last long. It was not many sentences after his first before he began to hesitate, and break, and lose his grip, and totter, and wobble, and at last he slumped down in a limp and mushy pile.

Well, the programme for the occasion was probably not more than one-third finished, but it ended there. Nobody rose. The next man hadn't strength enough to get up, and everybody looked so dazed, so stupefied, paralyzed, it was impossible for anybody to do anything, or even try. Nothing could go on in that strange atmosphere. Howells mournfully, and without words, hitched himself to Bishop and me and supported us out of the room. It was very kind – he was most generous. He towed us tottering away into some room in that building, and we sat down there. I don't know what my remark was now, but I know the nature of it. It was the kind of remark you make when you know that nothing in the world can help your case. But Howells was honest – he had to say the heart-breaking things he did say: that there was no help for this calamity, this shipwreck, this cataclysm; that this was the most disastrous thing that had ever happened in anybody's history – and then he added, "That is, for *you* – and consider what you have done for Bishop. It is bad enough in your case, you deserve to suffer. You have committed this crime, and you deserve to have all you are going to get. But here is an innocent man. Bishop had never done you any harm, and see what you have done to him. He can never hold his head up again. The world can never look upon Bishop as being a live person. He is a corpse."

That is the history of that episode of twenty-eight years ago, which pretty nearly killed me with shame during that first year or two whenever it forced its way into my mind.

Now, then, I take that speech up and examine it. As I said, it arrived this morning, from Boston. I have read it twice, and unless I am an idiot, it hasn't a single defect in it from the first word to the last. It is just as good as good can be. It is smart; it is saturated with humor. There isn't a suggestion of coarseness or vulgarity in it anywhere. What could have been the matter with that house? It is amazing, it is incredible, that they didn't shout with laughter, and those deities the loudest of them all. Could the fault have been with me? Did I lose courage when I saw those great men up there whom I was going to describe in such a strange fashion? If that happened, if I showed doubt, that can account for it, for you can't be successfully funny if you show that you are afraid of it. Well, I can't account for it, but if I had those beloved and revered old literary immortals back here now on the platform at Carnegie Hall I would take that same old speech, deliver it, word for word, and melt them till they'd run all over that stage. Oh, the fault must have been with *me*, it is not in the speech at all.

[*Dictated October 3, 1907.*] In some ways, I was always honest; even from my earliest years I could never bring myself to use money which I had acquired in questionable ways; many a time I tried, but principle was always stronger than desire. Six or eight months ago, Lieutenant-General Nelson A. Miles was given a great dinner-party in New York, and when he and I were chatting together in the drawing-room before going out to dinner he said,

"I've known you as much as thirty years, isn't it?"

I said, "Yes, that's about it, I think."

He mused a moment or two and then said,

"I wonder we didn't meet in Washington in 1867; you were there at that time, weren't you?"

I said, "Yes, but there was a difference; I was not known then; I had not begun to bud – I was an obscurity; but you had been adding to your fine Civil War record; you had just come back from your brilliant Indian campaign in the Far West, and had been rewarded with a brigadier-generalship in the regular army, and everybody was talking about you and praising you. If you had met me, you wouldn't be able to remember it now – unless some unusual circumstance of the meeting had burnt it into your memory. It is forty years ago, and people don't remember nobodies over a stretch of time like that."

I didn't wish to continue the conversation along that line, so I changed the subject. I could have proven to him, without any trouble, that we did meet in Washington in 1867, but I thought it might embarrass one or the other of us, so I didn't do it. I remember the incident very well. This was the way of it:

I had just come back from the Quaker City Excursion, and had made a contract with Bliss of Hartford to write "The Innocents Abroad." I was out of money, and I went down to Washington to see if I could earn enough there to keep me in bread and butter while I should write the book. I came across William Clinton, brother of the astronomer, and together we invented a scheme for our mutual sustenance; we became the fathers and originators of what is a common feature in the newspaper world now – the syndicate. We became the old original first Newspaper Syndicate on the planet; it was on a small scale, but that is usual with untried new enterprises. We had twelve journals on our list; they were all weeklies, all obscure and poor, and all scattered far away among the back settlements. It was a proud thing for those little newspapers to have a Washington correspondence, and a fortunate thing for us that they felt in that way about it. Each of the twelve took two letters a week from us, at a dollar per letter; each of us wrote one letter per week and sent off six duplicates of it to these benefactors, thus acquiring twenty-four dollars a week to live on – which was all we needed, in our cheap and humble quarters.

Clinton was one of the dearest and loveliest human beings I have ever known, and we led a charmed existence together, in a contentment which knew no bounds. Clinton was refined by nature and breeding; he was a gentleman by nature and breeding; he was highly educated; he was of a beautiful spirit; he was pure in heart and speech. He was a Scotchman, and a Presbyterian; a Presbyterian of the old and genuine school, being honest and sincere in his religion, and loving it, and finding serenity and peace in it. He hadn't a vice – unless a large and grateful sympathy with Scotch whiskey may be called by that name. I didn't regard it as a vice, because he was a Scotchman, and Scotch whiskey to a Scotchman is as innocent as milk is to the rest of the human race. In Clinton's case it was a virtue, and not an economical one. Twenty-four dollars a week would really have been riches to us if we hadn't had to support that jug; because of the jug we were always sailing pretty close to the wind, and any tardiness in the arrival of any part of our income was sure to cause us some inconvenience.

I remember a time when a shortage occurred; we had to have three dollars, and we had to have it before the close of the day. I don't know now how we happened to want all that money at one time; I only know we had to have it. Clinton told me to go out and find it – and he said he would also go out and see what he could do. He didn't seem to have any doubt that we would succeed, but I knew that that was his religion working in him; I hadn't the same confidence; I hadn't any idea where to turn to raise all that bullion, and I said so. I think he was ashamed of me, privately, because of my weak faith. He told me to give myself no uneasiness, no concern; and said in a simple, confident, and unquestioning way, "the Lord will provide." I saw that he fully believed the Lord would provide, but it seemed to me that if he had had my experience –

But never mind that; before he was done with me his strong faith had had its influence, and I went forth from the place almost convinced that the Lord really would provide.

I wandered around the streets for an hour, trying to think up some way to get that money, but nothing suggested itself. At last I lounged into the big lobby of the Ebbitt House, which was then a new hotel, and sat down. Presently a dog came loafing along. He paused, glanced up at me and said, with his eyes, "Are you friendly?" I answered, with my eyes, that I was. He gave his tail a grateful little wag and came forward and rested his jaw on my knee and lifted his brown eyes to my face in a winningly affectionate way. He was a lovely creature – as beautiful as a girl, and he was made all of silk and velvet. I stroked his smooth brown head and fondled his drooping ears, and we were a pair of lovers right away. Pretty soon Brigadier-General Miles, the hero of the land, came strolling by in his blue and gold splendors, with everybody's admiring gaze upon him. He saw the dog and stopped, and there was a light in his eye which showed that he had a warm place in his heart for dogs like this gracious creature; then he came forward and patted the dog and said,

"He is very fine – he is a wonder; would you sell him?"

I was greatly moved; it seemed a marvellous thing to me, the way Clinton's prediction had come true. I said,

"Yes."

The General said,

"What do you ask for him?"

"Three dollars."

The General was manifestly surprised. He said,

"Three dollars? Only three dollars? Why, that dog is a most uncommon dog; he can't possibly be worth less than fifty. If he were mine, I wouldn't take a hundred for him. I'm afraid you are not aware of his value. Reconsider your price if you like, I don't wish to wrong you."

But if he had known me he would have known that I was no more capable of wronging him than he was of wronging me. I responded with the same quiet decision as before,

"No – three dollars. That is his price."

"Very well, since you insist upon it," said the General, and he gave me three dollars and led the dog away, and disappeared up-stairs.

In about ten minutes a gentle-faced middle-aged gentleman came along, and began to look around here and there and under tables and everywhere, and I said to him,

"Is it a dog you are looking for?"

His face was sad, before, and troubled; but it lit up gladly now, and he answered,

"Yes – have you seen him?"

"Yes," I said, "he was here a minute ago, and I saw him follow a gentleman away. I think I could find him for you if you would like me to try."

I have seldom seen a person look so grateful – and there was gratitude in his voice, too, when he conceded that he would like me to try. I said I would do it with great pleasure, but that as it might take a little time I hoped he would not mind paying me something for my trouble. He said he would do it most gladly – repeating that phrase "most gladly" – and asked me how much. I said –

"Three dollars."

He looked surprised, and said,

"Dear me, it is nothing! I will pay you ten, quite willingly."

But I said,

"No, three is the price" – and I started for the stairs without waiting for any further argument, for Clinton had said that that was the amount that the Lord would provide, and it seemed to me that it would be sacrilegious to take a penny more than was promised.

I got the number of the General's room from the office-clerk, as I passed by his wicket, and when I reached the room I found the General there caressing his dog, and quite happy. I said,

"I am sorry, but I have to take the dog again."

He seemed very much surprised, and said,

"Take him again? Why, he is my dog; you sold him to me, and at your own price."

"Yes," I said, "it is true – but I have to have him, because the man wants him again."

"What man?"

"The man that owns him; he wasn't my dog."

The General looked even more surprised than before, and for a moment he couldn't seem to find his voice; then he said,

"Do you mean to tell me that you were selling another man's dog – and knew it?"

"Yes, I knew it wasn't my dog."

"Then why did you sell him?"

I said,

"Well, that is a curious question to ask. I sold him because you wanted him. You offered to buy the dog; you can't deny that. I was not anxious to sell him – I had not even thought of selling him, but it seemed to me that if it could be any accommodation to you – "

He broke me off in the middle, and said,

"*Accommodation* to me? It is the most extraordinary spirit of accommodation I have ever heard of – the idea of your selling a dog that didn't belong to you – "

I broke him off there, and said,

"There is no relevancy about this kind of argument; you said yourself that the dog was probably worth a hundred dollars, I only asked you three; was there anything unfair about that? You offered to pay more, you know you did. I only asked you three; you can't deny it."

"Oh, what in the world has that to do with it! The crux of the matter is that you didn't own the dog – can't you see that? You seem to think that there is no impropriety in selling property that isn't yours provided you sell it cheap. Now, then – "

I said,

"Please don't argue about it any more. You can't get around the fact that the price was perfectly fair, perfectly reasonable – considering that I didn't own the dog – and so arguing about it is only a waste of words. I have to have him back again because the man wants him; don't you see that I haven't any choice in the matter? Put yourself in my place. Suppose you had sold a dog that didn't belong to you; suppose you – "

"Oh," he said, "don't muddle my brains any more with your idiotic reasonings! Take him along, and give me a rest."

So I paid back the three dollars and led the dog down-stairs and passed him over to his owner, and collected three for my trouble.

I went away then with a good conscience, because I had acted honorably; I never could have used the three that I sold the dog for, because it was not rightly my own, but the three I got for restoring him to his rightful owner was righteously and properly mine, because I had earned it. That man might never have gotten that dog back at all, if it hadn't been for me. My principles have remained to this day what they were then. I was always honest; I know I can never be otherwise. It is as I said in the beginning – I was never able to persuade myself to use money which I had acquired in questionable ways.

Now, then, that is the tale. Some of it is true.

LETTERS

NEW YORK, X OCT, SATURDAY, 1853

MY DEAR SISTER:

I have not written to any of the family for some time, from the fact, *firstly*, that I didn't know where they were, and *secondly*, because I have been fooling myself with the idea that I was going to leave New York, every day for the last two weeks. I have taken a liking to the abominable place, and every time I get ready to leave, I put it off a day or so, from some unaccountable cause. It is just as hard on my conscience to leave New York as it was *easy* to leave Hannibal. I think I shall get off Tuesday, though.

Edwin Forrest has been playing, for the last sixteen days, at the Broadway Theatre, but I never went to see him till last night. The play was the "Gladiator." I did not like parts of it much, but other portions were really splendid. In the latter part of the last act, where the "Gladiator" (Forrest) dies at his brother's feet, (in all the fierce pleasure of gratified revenge,) after working the latter's revenge, the man's whole soul seems absorbed in the part he is playing; and it is really startling to see him. I am sorry I did not see him play "Damon and Pythias" – the former character being his greatest. He appears in Philadelphia on Monday night.

I have not received a letter from home lately, but got a "*Journal*" the other day, in which I see the office has been sold. I suppose Ma, Orion and Henry are in St. Louis now. If Orion has no other project in his head, he ought to take the contract for getting out some weekly paper, if he cannot get a foremanship. Now, for such a paper as the "*Presbyterian*" (containing about 60,000,) he could get $20 or $25 per week, and he and Henry could easily do the work: – nothing to do but set the type and make up the forms. I mean they could easily do the work if $5.00 for 25,000 (per week) could beat a little work into (no offence to him) Henry's lazy bones! Orion must get Jim. Wolfe a sit. in St. Louis. He can get 20 cents per 1.000. The foreman of Gray's office has taken a great fancy to go to St. Louis, and has got everything out of me that I know about the place, and I shouldn't be surprised if he should go there.

If my letters do not come often, you need not bother yourself about me; for if you have a brother nearly eighteen years of age, who is not able to take care of himself a few miles from home, such a brother is not worth one's thoughts: and if I don't manage to take care of *No. 1.*, be assured you will never know it. I am not afraid, however: I shall ask favors from no one, and endeavor to be, (and *shall* be,) as "independent as a wood-sawyer's clerk."

I never saw such a place for military companies, as New York. Go on the street when you will, you are sure to meet a company in full uniform, with all the usual appendages of drums, fifes, &c. I saw a large company of soldiers of the war of 1812, the other day, with a '76 veteran scattered here and there in the ranks. And when I passed through one of the parks lately, I came upon a company of *boys* on parade. Their uniforms were neat, and their muskets about half the common size. Some of them were not more than seven or eight years of age; but had evidently been well drilled.

Passage to Albany (160 miles) in the finest steamers that ply the Hudson, is now 25 cents – cheap enough, but is generally cheaper than that in the summer.

I want you to write as soon as I tell you where to direct your letter. I would let you know now, if I knew myself. I may perhaps be here a week longer; but I cannot tell. When you write tell me the whereabouts of the family. My love to Mr. Moffett and Ella. Tell Ella I intend to write to her soon, whether she wants me to or not.

TRULY YOUR BROTHER,

SAML. L. CLEMENS

TO ORION AND HENRY CLEMENS
26–?28 OCTOBER 1853, PHILADELPHIA, PA.

PHILADELPHIA, PA. OCT. 26, 1853

MY DEAR BROTHER:

I[t] was at least two weeks before I left New York, that I received my last letter from home: and since then, devil take the word have I heard from any of you. And now, since I think of it, it wasn't a letter, either, but the last number of the "Daily Journal," saying that that paper was sold, and I very naturally supposed from that, that the family had disbanded, and taken up winter quarters in St. Louis. Therefore, I have been writing to Pamela, till I'm tired of it, and have received no answer. I have been wanting for the last two or three weeks, to send Ma some money, but devil take me if I knew where she was, and so the money has slipped out of my pocket somehow or other, but I have a dollar left, and a good deal owing to me, which will be paid next Monday. I shall enclose the dollar in this letter, and you can hand it to her. I know it's a small amount, but then it will buy her a hankerchief, and at the same time serve as a specimen of the kind of stuff we are paid with in Philadelphia. You see it's against the law in Pennsylvania to keep or pass a bill of less denomination than $5. I have only seen two or three bank bills since I have been in the State. On Monday the hands are paid off in sparkling gold, fresh of the Mint; so your dreams are not troubled, with the fear of having doubtful money in your pocket.

I am subbing at the Inquirer office. One man has engaged me to work for him every Sunday till the first of next April, (when I shall return home to take Ma to Ky;) and another has engaged my services for the 24th of next month; and if I want it, I can get subbing *every night* of the week. I go to work at 7 o'clock in the evening, and work till 3 o'clock the next morning. I can go to the theatre and stay till 12 o'clock, and then go to the office, and get work from that till 3 the next morning; when I go to bed, and sleep till 11 o'clock, then get up and loaf the rest of the day. The type is mostly agate and minion, with some bourgeois; and when one gets a good agate take, he is sure to make money. I made $2.50 last Sunday, and was laughed at by all the hands, the poorest of whom sets 11,000 on Sunday; and if I don't set 10,000, at least, next Sunday, I'll give them leave to laugh as much as the[y] want to. Out of the 22 compositors in this office, 12 at least, set 15,000 on Sunday.

Unlike New York, I like this Phila amazingly, and the people in it. There is only one thing that gets my "dander" up – and that is the hands are always *encouraging* me: telling me "it's no use to get discouraged – no use to be down-hearted, for there is more work here than you can do!" "Downhearted," the devil! I have not had a particle of such a feeling since I left Hannibal, more than four months ago. I fancy they'll have to wait some time till they see me downhearted or afraid of starving while I have strength to work and am in a city of 400,000 inhabitants. When I was in Hannibal; before I had scarcely stepped out of the town limits, nothing could have convinced me than I would starve as soon as I got a little way from home.

The grave of Franklin is in Christ Church-yard, cor. of Fifth and

Arch streets. They keep the gates locked, and one can only see the flat slab that lies over his remains and that of his wife; but you cannot see the inscription distinctly enough to read it. This inscription, I believe, reads thus:

> "Benjamin
> and
> Deborah
> Franklin."

I counted 27 cannons (6 pounders) planted in the edge of the side walk in Water st. the other day. They are driven into the ground, about a foot, with the mouth end upwards. A ball is driven fast into the mouth of each, to exclude the water; they look like so many posts. They were put there during the war. I have also seen them planted in this manner, round the old churches, in N.Y.

The Exchange is where the different omnibus lines have their starting or stopping place. That is it is the head-quarters; and from this they radiate to the different parts of the city. Well, as I was going to say, I went to the Exchange, yesterday, and deposited myself in a Fairmount stage, paid my sixpence, or "fip," as these heathen call it, and started. We rolled along till we began to get towards the out-skirts of the city, where the prettiest part of a large city *always* is. We passed a large house, which looked like a public building. It was built entirely of great blocks of red granite. The pillars in front were all finished but one. These pillars were beautiful ornamented fluted columns, considerably larger than a hogshead at the base, and about as high as Caplinger's second story front windows. No marble pillar is as pretty as these sombre red granite ones; and then to see some of them finished and standing, and then the huge blocks lying about of which the other was to be built, it looks so massy; and carries one in imagination, to the ruined piles of ancient Babylon. I despise the infernal bogus brick columns, plastered over with mortar. Marble is the cheapest building stone about Phila. This marble is the most beautiful I ever saw. I[t] takes a very high polish. Some of it is as black as Egypt, with thin streaks of white running through it, and some is a beautiful snowy white; while the most of it is magnificent black, clouded with white.

But I must go on with my trip. We soon passed long rows of houses, (private dwellings) all the work about the doors, stoop, &c.,

of which, was composed of this pretty marble, glittering in the sun, like glass. We arrived at Fairmount, – got out of the stage, and prepared to look around. The hill, (Fairmount) is very high, and on top of it is the great reservoir. After leaving the stage, I passed up the road, till I came to the wire bridge which stretches across the Schuylkill (or Delaware, darned if I know which! – the former, I believe, – but you know, for you are a better scholar than I am). This is the first bridge of the kind I ever saw. Here I saw, a little above, the fine dam, which hold[s] back the water for the use of the Water Works. It forms quite a nice water-fall. Seeing a park at the foot of the hill, I entered – and found it one of the nicest little places about. Fat marble Cupids, in big marble vases, squirted water upward incessantly. Here stands in a kind of mausoleum, (is that proper?) a well executed piece of sculpture, with the inscription – "Erected by the City Council of Philadelphia, to the memory of Peter Graff, the founder and inventor of the Fairmount Water Works." The bust looks toward the dam. It is all of the purest white marble. I passed along the pavement by the pumphouse (I don't know what else to call it) and seeing a door left open by somebody, I went in. I saw immense water-wheels, &c., but if you will get a back-number of the Lady's Book, you will find a better description of the Works, than I can give you. I passed on further, and saw small steamboats, with their signs up – "For Wissahickon and Manayunk – 25 cts." Geo. Lippard, in his "Legends of Washington and his Generals," has rendered the Wissahickon sacred in my eyes, and I shall make that trip, – as well as one to Germantown, soon.

But to proceed, again. Here was a long flight of stairs, leading to the summit of the hill. I went up – of course. But I forgot to say, that at the foot of this hill a pretty white marble Naiad stands on a projecting rock, and this, I must say is the prettiest fountain I have seen lately. A nice half-inch jet of water is thrown straight up ten or twelve feet, and descends in a shower, all over the fair water spirit. Fountains also gush out of the rock at her feet, in every direction. Well, arrived at the top of the hill, I see nothing but a respectable-sized lake, which [looks] rather out of place in its elevated situation. I can't say I saw *nothing* else, either: – for here I had a magnificent view of the city. Tired of this, I passed up Coates streets, 5 or six squares from the hill, and came to the immense (distributin) branch of the Works. It is built of a kind of dirty yellow stone, and in the style of an ancient feudal Castle. Passing on, I took a squint at the "House of Refuge," (of which we used to read at Sunday School), – then I took a look at the marble Girard College, with its long rows of marble pillars – then jumped into a 'bus, and posted back to the Exchange.

There is one fine custom observed in Phila. A gentleman is always expected to hand up a lady's money for her. Yesterday, I sat in the front end of the 'bus, directly under the driver's box – a lady sat opposite me. She handed me her money, which was right. But, Lord! a St. Louis lady would think herself ruined, if she should be so familiar with a stranger. In St. Louis, a man will sit, in the front end of the stage, and see a lady stagger from the far end, to pay her fare. The Phila. 'bus drivers cannot cheat. In the front end of the stage is a thing like an office clock, with figures, from 0 to 40, marked on its face. When the stage starts, the hand of the clock is turned toward the 0. When you get in and pay your fare, the driver strikes a bell, and the hand moves to the fig. 1 – that is, "one fare, and paid for," and there is your receipt, as good as if you had it in your pocket. When a passenger pays his fare and the driver does not strike the bell immediately, he is greeted "Strike that bell, will you?"

I must close now. I intend visiting the Navy Yard, Mint, &c. before I write again. You must write often. You see I have nothing to write interesting to you, while you can write nothing that will not interest me. Don't say my letters are not *long* enough. Tell Jim to write. Tell all the boys where I am, and to write. Jim Robinson, particularly. I wrote to him from N.Y. Tell me all that is going on in H—l.

TRULY YOUR BROTHER

SAM

Philadelphia is rich in Revolutionary associations. I stepped into the State House yesterday to see the sights. In one of the halls, on a pedestal, is the old cracked "Independence Bell," bearing the inscription "Proclaim liberty throughout the land," or something to that effect. It was cast 25 or 30 years before it made this pro- clamation. It was rung for the first time on "Independence Day," when it "proclaimed liberty" by calling the people together to hear the Declaration of Independence read. It is an interesting relic. A small pine bench or pew in this Hall bears this inscription – "Washington, Franklin and Bishop White sat on this Bench." Of course, I "sot down" on it. I would have whittled off a chip, if I had got half a chance. On the pedestal of the statue of Washington, in the same Hall, is a small block of granite, with the inscription – "A piece of the step on which the Secretary's foot rested when he read the Declaration of Independence." Full length portraits of William Penn and Lafayette hang in this Hall. There is another thing which should have a place in this Hall. It is a flag which I saw in New York. It was the personal property of Washington, and was planted on the Battery when the British evacuated New York. After that, it was not used until the laying of the corner stone of the Washington Monument. Then this faded and tattered, though time-honored relic of "the days that tried men's souls," was taken to Washington and unfurled to the breeze at that ceremony. It is said that when the procession reached the Monumental ground in Washington, the flag was unfurled and the announcement made – "This flag belonged to Washington; it proudly waved defiance to the British from the Battery when they evacuated New York; it is here now to display the stars and stripes under which its illustrious owner so nobly fought" – the multitude gazed on it for a moment, and then a shout went up that would have sent the blood from the cheek of a tyrant.

I came here from New York by way of the Camden and Amboy railroad – the same on which the collision occurred some time since. I never thought of this till our train stopped, "all of a sudden," and then began to go backwards like blazes. Then ran back half a mile, and switched off on another track, and stopped; and the next moment a large passenger train came round a bend in the road, and whistled past us like lightning! Ugh! ejaculated I, as I looked to see if Mr. Clemens's bones were all safe. If we had been three seconds later getting off that track, the two locomotives would have come together, and we should no doubt have been helped off. The conductors silenced all questions by not answering them.

S.C.

[*crosswise over the first paragraph:*] Please send this to Henry if he is not in St. Louis

SAM

TO ORION AND MARY E. (MOLLIE) CLEMENS
9 MARCH 1858, ST. LOUIS, MO.

DEAR BROTHER AND SISTER:

I must take advantage of the opportunity now presented to write you, but I shall necessarily be dull, as I feel uncommonly stupid. We have had a hard trip this time. Left Saint Louis three weeks ago on the Pennsylvania. The weather was very cold, and the ice running densely. We got 15 miles below town, landed the boat, and then one pilot, Second Mate and four deck hands took the sounding boat and shoved out in the ice to hunt the channel. They failed to find it, and the ice drifted them ashore. The pilot left the men with the boat and walked back to us, a mile and a half. Then the other pilot and myself, with a larger crew of men started out and met with the same fate. We drifted ashore just below the other boat. Then the fun commenced. We made fast a line 20 fathoms long, to the bow of the yawl, and put the men, (both crews) to it like horses, on the shore. Brown, the pilot, stood in the bow, with an oar, to keep her head out, and I took the tiller. We would start the men, and all would go well till the yawl would bring up on a heavy cake of ice, and then the men would drop like so many ten-pins, while Brown assumed the horizontal in the bottom of the boat. After an hour's hard work we got back, with ice half an inch thick on the oars. Sent back and warped up the other yawl, and then George (the first mentioned pilot,) and myself, took a double crew of fresh men and tried it again. This time we found the channel in less than an hour, and landed on a island till the Pennsylvania came along and took us off. The next day was colder still. I was out in the yawl twice, and then we got through, but the infernal steamboat came near running over us. We went ten miles further, landed, and George and I cleared out again – found the channel first trial, but got caught in the gorge and drifted helplessly down the river. The Ocean Spray came along and started into the ice after us, but although she didn't succeed in her kind intention of taking us aboard, her waves washed us out, and that was all we wanted. We landed on an island, built a big fire and waited for the boat. She started, and ran aground! It commenced raining and sleeting, and a very interesting time we had on that barren sandbar for the next four hours, when the boat got off and took us aboard.

The next day was *terribly* cold. We sounded Hat Island, warped up around a bar and sounded again – but in order to understand our situation you will have to read Dr Kane. It would have been impossible to get back to the boat. But the Maria Denning was aground at the head of the island – they hailed us, – we ran alongside and they hoisted us in and thawed us out. We had then been out in the yawl from 4 o'clock in the morning till half past 9 without being near a fire. There was a thick coating of ice over men, yawl, ropes, and everything else, and we looked like rock-candy statuary.

We got to Saint Louis this morning, after an absence of 3 weeks – that boat generally makes the trip in 2.

Henry was doing little or nothing here, and I sent him to our clerk to work his way for a trip, by measuring woodpiles, counting coal boxes, and other clerkly duties, which he performed satisfactorily. He may go down with us again, for I expect he likes our bill of fare better than that of his boarding house.

I got your letter at Memphis as I went down. That is the best place to write me at. The post office here is always out of my route, somehow or other. Remember the direction: "S.L.C., Steamer Pennsylvania, Care Duval & Algeo, Wharfboat, Memphis." I cannot correspond with a paper, because when one is learning the river, he is not allowed to do or think about anything else.

I am glad to see you in such high spirits about the land, and I hope will remain so, if you never get richer. I seldom venture to think about our landed wealth, for "hope deferred maketh the heart sick."

I *did* intend to *answer* your letter, but I am too lazy and too sleepy, now. We had had a rough time during the last 24 hours working through the ice between Cairo and Saint Louis, and I have had but little rest.

I got here too late to see the funeral of the 10 victims by the burning of the Pacific hotel in 7th street. Ma says there were 10 hearses, with the fire companies (their engines in mourning – firemen in uniform,) – the various benevolent societies in uniform and mourning, and a multitude of citizens and strangers, forming, altogether, a procession of 30,000 persons! One steam fire-engine was drawn by four white horses, with crape festoons on their heads.

Well, I am – just – about – asleep –

YOUR BROTHER

SAM

TO MARY E. (MOLLIE) CLEMENS
18 JUNE 1858, MEMPHIS, TENN.

MEMPHIS, TENN., FRIDAY, JUNE 18TH, 1858

DEAR SISTER MOLLIE:

Long before this reaches you, my poor Henry, – my darling, my pride, my glory, my *all*, will have finished his blameless career, and the light of my life will have gone out in utter darkness. O, God! this is hard to bear. Hardened, hopeless, – aye, lost – lost – lost and ruined sinner as I am – I, even *I*, have humbled myself to the ground and prayed as never man prayed before, that the great God might let this cup pass from me – that he would strike me to the earth, but spare my brother – that he would pour out the fulness of his just wrath upon my wicked head, but have mercy, mercy, mercy upon that unoffending boy. The horrors of three days have swept over me – they have blasted my youth and left me an old man before my time. Mollie, there are grey hairs in my head to-night. For forty-eight hours I labored at the bedside of my poor burned and bruised, but uncomplaining brother, and then the star of my hope went out and left me in the gloom of despair. Then poor wretched me, that was once so proud, was humbled to the very dust – lower than the dust – for the vilest beggar in the streets of Saint Louis could never conceive of a humiliation like mine. Men take me by the hand and *congratulate* me, and call me "**lucky**" because I was not on the Pennsylvania when she blew up! My God forgive them, for they know not what they say.

Mollie you do not understand why I was not on that boat – I will tell you. I left Saint Louis on her, but on the way down, Mr. Brown, the pilot that was killed by the explosion (poor fellow,) quarreled with Henry without cause, while I was steering – Henry started out of the pilothouse – Brown jumped up and collared him – turned him half way around and *struck him in the face!* – and him nearly six feet high – struck my little brother. I was wild from that moment. I left the boat to steer herself, and avenged the insult – and the Captain said I was right – that he would discharge Brown in N. Orleans if he could get another pilot, and would do it in St. Louis anyhow. Of course both of us could not return to St. Louis on the same boat – no pilot could be found, and the Captain sent me to the A. T. Lacey, with orders to her Captain to bring me to Saint Louis. Had another pilot been found, poor Brown would have been the "lucky" man.

I was on the Pennsylvania five minutes before she left N. Orleans, and I must tell you the truth, Mollie – **three hundred** human beings perished by that fearful disaster. Henry was asleep – was blown up – then fell back on the hot boilers, and I suppose that rubbish fell on him, for he is injured internally. He got into the water and swam to shore, and got into the flatboat with the other survivors. He had nothing on but his wet shirt, and he lay there burning up with a southern sun and freezing in the wind till the Kate Frisbee came along. His wounds were not dressed till he got to Memphis, 15 hours after the explosion. He was senseless and motionless for 12 hours after that. But may God bless Memphis, the noblest city on the face of the earth. She has done her duty by these poor afflicted creatures – especially Henry, for he has had five – aye, ten, fifteen, *twenty* times the care and attention that any one else has had. Dr. Peyton, the best physician in Memphis (he is exactly like the portraits of Webster,) sat by him for 36 hours. There are 32 scalded men in that room, and you would know Dr. Peyton better than I can describe him, if you could follow him around and hear each man murmur as he passes – "May the God of Heaven bless you, Doctor!" The ladies have done well, too. Our second Mate, a handsome, noble-hearted young fellow, will die. Yesterday a beautiful girl of 15 stooped timidly down by his side and handed him a pretty bouquet. The poor suffering boy's eyes kindled, his lips quivered out a gentle "God bless you, Miss," and he burst into tears. He made them write he[r] name on a card for him, that he might not forget it.

Pray for me, Mollie, and pray for my poor sinless brother.

YOUR UNFORTUNATE BROTHER,
SAM^L L. CLEMENS

P.S. I got here two days after Henry.

TO JANE LAMPTON CLEMENS
26 OCTOBER 1861, CARSON CITY, NEV. TERR.

CARSON CITY, NEVADA TER., OCTOBER 26, '61

DEAR MOTHER:

You ask me in your last to tell you about the country – tell everything just as it is – no better and no worse – and *do* let nonsense alone. Very well, then, ma, since you wasted a considerable portion of your life in an unprofitable effort to teach me to tell the truth on all occasions, I will repay you by dealing strictly in facts just this once, and by avoiding that "nonsense" for which you seem to entertain a mild sort of horror.

Thus: "Gold Hill" (which is the name of the finest gold bearing quartz ledge in this vicinity,) sells at $5,000 a foot, cash down; "Wildcat" isn't worth 10 cents. And thus: Nevada Territory is fabulously rich in gold, silver, copper, lead, coal, iron, quicksilver, marble, granite, chalk, slate, plaster of Paris (gypsum,) thieves, murderers, desperadoes, ladies, children, lawyers, Christians, gamblers, Indians, Chinamen, Spaniards, sharpers, cuyotes, (pronounced ki-yo-ties,) preachers, poets and jackass-rabbits.

Furthermore: it never rains here, and the dew never falls. No flowers grow here, and no green thing gladdens the eye. The birds that fly over the land carry their provisions with them. Only the crow and the raven tarry with us. Our city lies in the midst of a desert of the purest, most unadulterated and uncompromising sand – in which infernal soil nothing but that fag-end of vegetable creation, "sage-brush," is mean enough to grow. If you will take a liliputian cedar tree for a model, and build a dozen imitations of it with the stiffest article of telegraph wire – set them one foot apart and then try to walk through them – you will understand, (provided the floor is covered twelve inches deep with sand) what it is to travel through a sage-brush desert. When crushed, sage-brush emits an odor which isn't exactly magnolia, and equally isn't exactly polecat, but a sort of compromise between the two. It looks a good deal like grease-wood, and is probably the ugliest plant that was ever conceived of. It is gray in color. On the plains sage-brush and grease-wood grow to about twice the size of common geranium, and, to my thinking, are very good substitutes for that very useless vegetable. Grease-wood is a perfect imitation, in miniature, of the live-oak tree, "barring" the color of it. As to the other fruits and flowers of the country, there ain't any except "Tula," a species of unpoetical rush, that grows on the banks of the Carson, – a RIVER, *ma mere*, twenty yards wide, knee-deep, and so villainously rapid and crooked, that it looks like it had wandered into the country without intending it, and had run about in a bewildered way and got lost in its hurry to get out again before some thirsty man came along and drank it up.

I said we are situated in a flat, sandy desert. True. And

surrounded on all sides by such prodigious mountains that when you stand at a distance from Carson and gaze at them awhile, – until, by mentally measuring them, and comparing them with things of smaller size, you begin to conceive of their grandeur, and next to feel their vastness expanding your soul like a balloon, and ultimately find yourself growing, and swelling, and spreading into a colossus, – I say when this point is reached, you look disdainfully down upon the insignificant village of Carson, reposing like a cheap print away yonder at the foot of the big hills, and in that instant you are seized with a burning desire to stretch forth your hand, put the city in your pocket, and walk off with it.

Now, although we are *surrounded* by sand, the greater part of the town is built upon what was once a very pretty grassy spot; and the streams of pure water that used to poke about it in rural sloth and solitude, now pass through our dusty streets and gladden the hearts of men by reminding them that there is at least something here that hath its prototype among the homes they left behind them.

And up "King's Canon," (please pronounce *can-yon*, after the manner of the natives,) there are ranches, or farms, where they say hay grows; and grass, and beets, and onions, and turnips and other "truck," which cows are fond of – yea, and even potatoes grow there – a vegetable eminently proper for human consumption; also cabbages, peas and beans.

The houses are mostly frame, and unplastered; but "papered" inside with flour-sacks sewed together – with the addition, in favor of the parlor, of a second papering composed of engravings cut from "Harper's Weekly;" so you will easily perceive that the handsomer the "brand" upon the flour-sacks is, and the more spirited the pictures are, the finer the house looks. There are several stone buildings here, and in the course of time, Ma, there will be several more. On account of the dryness of the atmosphere, the shingles on the houses warp until they look very much like they would be glad to turn over, and lie awhile on the other side.

Notwithstanding the extraordinary mixture of folks which I mentioned in the beginning of my letter, one can find as good society, here, of both sexes, as any Christian need desire. Please do not forget that.

Behold, I have spoken the truth concerning this land. And now, for your other questions, which shall be answered tersely, promptly, and to the point: First – "Do I go to church every

Sunday?" Answer – "Scasely." Second – "Have you a Church in
Carson?" We have – a Catholic one – but, to use a fireman's
expression, I believe "they don't run her now." We have also Protestant service nearly every Sabbath in the school house. Third –
"Are there many ladies in Carson?" Multitudes – probably the
handsomest in the world. Fourth – "Are the citizens generally
moral and religious?" Prodigiously so. Fifth – "When my old
friends ask me how you like Nevada, what reply shall I make?" Tell
them I am *delighted* with it. It is the dustiest country on the face of
the earth – but I rather like dust. And the days are very hot – but
you know I am fond of hot days. And the nights are cold – but one
always sleeps well under blankets. And it never rains here – but
I despise a country where rain and mud are fashionable. And there
are no mosquitoes here – but then I can get along without them.
And there are scorpions here – and tarantulas or spiders, as big as
a mouse – but I am passionately fond of spiders. Tell them I never
liked any country so well before – and my word for it, you will tell
them the truth.

Tell aunt Mary that I am sorry she thought I intended to study
law, because to my mind, that is proof positive that her excellent
judgment has erred this time. I do not love the law. And besides,
there are many young lawyers here, and I am too generous to allow
the glare from my lamp of genius to dim the feeble lustre of their
two-penny dips. In a word, you know – I don't want to be the
means of showing them how little the Lord has done for them. And
while on the subject, let me hint to the craft that fees in this Territory are large – and also, that although there is a shining array of
legal talent here, there is still room in the firmament for another
star or so.

While at breakfast this morning I received a telegraphic dispatch worded as follows, and I have delayed my letter in order to
insert it:

China Town, Oct. 26, – 8 a.m.
"DEAR SAM.: – My brother George died this morning at half
past two o'clock – come down.
WM. H. CLAGETT."

I shall go down in the stage at noon and render Billy all the
assistance in my power, in this, his hour of distress. For the present,
good-bye.

S.L.C.

TO JANE LAMPTON CLEMENS
AND PAMELA A. MOFFETT
11 AND 12 APRIL 1863, VIRGINIA CITY, NEV. TERR.

P.S. I have just heard five pistol shots down street – as such things are in my line, I will go and see about it.

P.S. N° 2–5 A. M. – The pistol did its work well – one man – a Jackson County Missourian, shot two of my friends, (police officers,) through the heart – both died within three minutes. Murderer's name is John Campbell.

VIRGINIA, APRIL 11

MY DEAR MOTHER & SISTER

It is very late at night, & I am writing in my room, which is not quite as large or as nice as the one I had at home. My board, washing & lodging cost me seventy-five dollars a month.

I have just received your letter, Ma, from Carson – the one in which you doubt my veracity about the tape worm, and also about statements I made in a letter to you. That's right. I don't recollect what the statements were, but I suppose they were mining statistics. [*in margin:* Ma, write on *whole* letter sheets – is paper scarce in St Louis?] I have just finished writing up my report for the morning paper, and giving the Unreliable a column of advice about how to conduct himself in church, and now I will tell you a few more lies, while my hand is in. For instance, some of the boys made me a present of fifty feet in the East India G & S. M. Company, ten days ago. I was offered ninety-five dollars a foot for it, yesterday, in gold. *I refused it* – not because I think the claim is worth a cent, for I *don't*, but because I had a curiosity to see how high it *would* go, before people find out how worthless it is. Besides, what if one mining claim *does* fool me? – I have got plenty more. I am not in a particular hurry to get rich. I suppose I couldn't well help getting rich here some time or other, whether I wanted to or not. You folks do not believe in Nevada, and I am glad you don't. Just keep on thinking so.

I was at the Gould & Curry mine, the other day, and they had two or three tons of choice rock piled up, which was valued at $20,000 a ton. I gathered up a hat-full, of chunks, on account of their beauty as specimens – they don't let everybody supply themselves so liberally. I send Mr. Moffett a little specimen of it for his cabinet. If you don't know what the white stuff on it is, I must inform you that it is purer silver than minted coin. There is about as much gold in it as there is silver, but it is not visible. I will explain to you some day how to detect it.

I suppose we are on the verge of war now. If Orion assumes jurisdiction over Esmeralda county, California

[*two MS pages (about 800 words) missing*]

of great, dark, timbered chambers, with a lot of shapeless devils flitting about in the distance, with dim candles flickering in the gloom; and then she could look far above her head, to the top of the shaft, and see a faint little square of daylight, apparently no bigger than one of the spots on a chess-board; or if she found nothing cheerful in these things, she could go to the express offices and see them ship two or three thousand pounds of silver bullion away on the coaches every day. I would show her a hundred proofs that in the course of ten years we shall make that blowing California sing almighty small. How I *hate* everything that looks, or tastes, or smells like California! – and how I hate everybody that loves the cursed State! Californians hate Missourians, – consequently I take great pains to let the public know that "Mark Twain" hails from there. I never let an opportunity slip to blow my horn for Missouri – *you bet* – as these rotten, lop-eared, whopper-jawed, jack-legged California abscesses say – *blast* them! But I have struck it now – I *can* show Pamela something cheerful, in reality, when she comes out: we *hang* one of these scabby, putrefied Californians every now and then – she shall see one of them get his neck stretched. I hate those fellows worse than I hate a Chinaman.

O, say, Ma, *who was* that girl – that sweetheart of mine you say got married, and her father gave her husband $100 (so you said, but I suppose you meant $100,000)? It was Emma Roe, wasn't it? What in thunder did I want with *her?* I mean, since she wouldn't have had me if I had asked her to? Let her slide – I don't suppose her life has ever been, is now, or ever will be, any happier than mine.

Remember me to Zeb, and Uncle Jim, and Aunt Ella, and Cousin Bettie, and tell the whole party to stay in St. Louis – it is such a slow, old fogy, easy-going humbug of a town. And don't forget to remember [me] to Mrs Sexton and Margaret – has Margaret recovered from her illness? And be sure to remember me kindly to *our* Margaret at home.

YR$ AFF SAM

TO JANE LAMPTON CLEMENS
AND PAMELA A. MOFFETT
20 JANUARY 1866, SAN FRANCISCO, CALIF.

SAN FRANCISCO, JAN. 20, 1865

MY DEAR MOTHER & SISTER:

Ma's last letter was sent me by Mollie to-day.

I don't know what to write – my life is so uneventful. I wish I was back there piloting up & down the river again. Verily, all is vanity and little worth – save piloting. To think that after writing many an article a man might be excused for thinking tolerably good, those New York people should single out a villainous backwoods sketch to compliment me on! – "Jim Smiley & His Jumping Frog" – a squib which would never have been written but to please Artemus Ward, & then it reached New York too late to appear in his book. But no matter – his book was a wretchedly poor one, generally speaking, & it could be no credit to either of us to appear between its covers. This paragraph is from the New York correspondence of the San Francisco *Alta*:

> Mark Twain's story in the *Saturday Press* of November 18, called "Jim Smiley and his Jumping Frog," has set all New York in a roar, and he may be said to have made his mark. I have been asked fifty times about it and its author, and the papers are copying it far and near. It is voted the best thing of the day. Cannot the *Californian* afford to keep Mark all to itself? It should not let him seintilate so widely without first being filtered through the California press.

The New York publishing house of Carleton & Co gave the sketch to the "Saturday Press" when they found it was too late for the book.

Bret Harte & I have both quit the "Californian." He will write for a Boston paper hereafter, and I for the "New York Weekly Review" – and possibly for the "Saturday Press" sometimes. I am too lazy to write oftener than once a month, though. I sent a sketch by yesterday's steamer which will probably appear in the "Review" along about the middle or latter part of February. If it makes Annie mad I can't help it. If it makes Ma mad I can't help it. I don't mean *them* any offence at all – I am only using them as types of a class – I am merely hitting other people over their shoulders. The Aunt I mention is *not* Aunt Ella or Aunt Betsy Smith – & I think they will see that she bears no resemblance to them.

Though I am generally placed at the head of my breed of scrib-
blers in this part of the country, the place properly belongs to Bret
Harte, I think (late editor of the "Californian") though he denies
it, along with the rest. He wants me to club a lot of old sketches
together with a lot of his, & publish a book together. I wouldn't do
it, only he agrees to take all the trouble. But I want to know
whether we are going to make anything out of it, first, however.
He has written to a New York publisher, & if we are offered a bargain that will pay for a month's labor, we will go to work & prepare
the volume for the press. My labor will not occupy more than 24
hours, because I will only have to take the scissors & slash my old
sketches out of the Enterprise & the Californian – I burned up a
small cart-load of them lately – so *they* are forever ruled out of any
book – but they were not worth republishing.

Understand – all this I am telling you is in confidence – we want
it to go no further – however, it don't make any difference where
you are, I suppose, so far away.

And we have got another secret on hand. We are going to burlesque a book of poems which the publisher, Bancroft, is to issue in
the spring. We know all the tribe of California poets, & understand
their different styles, & I think we can just make them get up &
howl. If Bancroft prints his book in New York in the spring, ours
shall be in press there at the same time, & come out promptly with
his volume. Then you'll hear these poetical asses here tear around
worse than a pack of wildcats. Bancroft's book is to contain a poem
by every poet in California. We shall only burlesque a few of the
prominent ones, but we will introduce each burlesque poem with
a blast of trumpets & some comments that will be eminently worth
reading, no doubt. I am willing enough to go into this thing,
because there will be *fun* in it.

The San Francisco *Examiner* says: That rare humourist, "Mark
Twain," whose fame is rapidly extending all over the country,
informs us that he has commenced the work of writing a book. He
says that it will treat on an entirely new subject, one that has not
been written about heretofore.   We predict that it will be a very
popular book, and make fame and fortune for its gifted author.

The book referred to in that paragraph is a pet notion of mine
– nobody knows what it is going to be about but just myself. Orion
don't know. I am slow & lazy, you know, & the bulk of it will not
be finished under a year. I expect it to make about three hundred
pages, and the last hundred will have to be written in St. Louis,

because the materials for them can only be got there. If I do not
write it to suit me at first I will write it all over again, & so, who
knows? – I may be an old man before I finish it. I have not written
a line in it for three weeks, & may not for three more. I shall only
write when the spirit moves me. I am the Genius of Indolence.

I still write a letter every day for the "Enterprise." Give my love
to everybody.
AFF'LY
SAM. CLEMENS

P.S. Give the enclosed Enterprise letter to Zeb Leavenworth, or
send it to Bill Kribben, Secretary of the Pilot's Association.

That Ajax is the finest Ocean Steamer in America, & one of the
fastest. She will make this trip to the Sandwich Islands & back in
a month, & it generally take[s] a sailing vessel three months. She
had 52 invited guests aboard – the cream of the town – gentleman
& ladies both, & a splendid brass band. I know lots of the guests.
I got an invitation, but I could not accept it, because there would
be no one to write my correspondence while I was gone. But I am
so sorry now. If the Ajax were back I would go – quick! – and throw
up the correspondence. Where could a man catch such another
crowd together?
MARK

TO JANE LAMPTON CLEMENS
AND PAMELA A. MOFFETT
4 MAY 1866, ISLAND OF MAUI, SANDWICH ISLANDS

WAILUKU SUGAR PLANTATION ISLAND OF MAUI,
H. I, MAY 4, 1866

MY DEAR MOTHER & SISTER:

11 o'clock at Night. – This is the infernalest darkest country,
when the moon don't shine; I stumbled & fell over my horse's lariat
a minute ago & hurt my leg, & so I must stay here to-night; I went
to Ulapalakua Plantation (25 miles,) a few days ago, & returned
yesterday afternoon, to Mr. Cornwell's (Waikapu Plantation) &
staid all night (it is 2 miles from here) & came here this evening to
Mr. Peck's, (Honolulu friends of mine), & took tea, & we have been
playing seven-up & whist (plenty of ladies in his family;) but I only

hitched that horse, intending to ride to the further sea-shore, (this is a narrow peninsula in the middle of the island), & stay all night at the Waihee Plantation, 5 miles from here, but as I said, I couldn't even see the horse it was so dark when I came out of Mr. Peck's a while ago, & so I fell & hurt my leg. I got the same leg hurt last week; I said I hadn't got hold of a spirited horse since I had been on the island, & one of the proprietors loaned me a big, vicious colt; he was altogether too spirited; I went to tighten the cinch before mounting him, when he let out with his left & kicked me across a ten-acre lot. A native rubbed & doctored me so well that I was able to stand on my feet in half an hour. It was then half after 4, & I had an appointment to go 7 miles & get a girl & take her to a card party at 5. If I hadn't had a considerable weakness for her she might have gone to the devil under the circumstances, but as it was, I went after her. I got even with the colt; it was a very rough road, but I got there at 5 minutes past 5, & then had to quit, my leg hurt me so. She was ready & her horse was saddled, but we didn't go. But I had a jolly time – played cribbage nearly all night. If I were worth even $5,000 I would try to marry that plantation – but as it is, I resign myself to a long & useful bachelordom as cheerfully as I may.

I had a pleasant time of it at Ulupalakua Plantation. It is 3,000 feet above the level of the sea (in plain sight from here, 25 miles;) two pretty & accomplished girl's in the family & the plantation yields an income of $60,000 a year – chance for some enterprising scrub. I have been clattering around among the plantations for 3 weeks, now, & next week I am going to visit the extinct crater of Mount Haleakala – the largest in the world; it is ten miles to the foot of the mountain; it rises 10,000 feet above the valley; the crater is 29 miles in circumference & 1,000 feet deep. Seen from the summit, the city of St Louis would look like a picture in the bottom of it.

As soon as I get back from Haleakala (pronounced Hally-ekka-lah,) I will sail for Honolulu again & from thence to the Island of Hawaii (pronounced Hah-*wy*-ye,) to see the greatest *active* volcano in the world – that of Kilauea (pronounced Kee-low-*way*-ah). – & from thence back to San Francisco – & then, doubtless, to the States. I have been on this trip 2 months, & it will probably be 2 more before I get back to California.

YRS AFF'Y
SAM

TO MARY E. (MOLLIE) CLEMENS
22 MAY 1866, HONOLULU, SANDWICH ISLANDS

HONOLULU, MAY 22

MY DEAR SISTER:

I have just got back from a sea voyage – from the beautiful island of Maui. I have spent 5 weeks there, riding backwards & forwards among the sugar plantations – looking up the splendid scenery & visiting the lofty crater of Haleakala. It has been a perfect jubilee to me in the way of pleasure. I have not written a single line, & have not once thought of business, or care, or human toil or trouble or sorrow or weariness. Few such months come in a lifetime.

I set sail again, a week hence, for the island of M Hawaii, to see the great active volcano of Kileaua. I shall not get back here for 4 or 5 weeks, & shall not reach San Francisco before the latter part of July. So it is no use to wait for me to go home. Go on yourselves. It is Orion's duty to attend to that land, & after shutting me out of my attempt to sell it (for which I shall never entirely forgive him,) if he lets it be sold for taxes, all his religion will not wipe out the sin. It is no use to quote Scripture to me, Mollie, – I am in poverty & exile now because of Orion's religious scruples. Religion & poverty cannot go together. I am satisfied Orion will eventually save himself, but in doing it he will damn the balance of the family. I want no such religion. He has got a duty to perform by us – will he perform it?

I have crept into the old subject again, & opened the old sore afresh that cankers within me. It has got into many letters to you & I have burned them. But it is no use disguising it – I always feel bitter & malignant when I think of Ma & Pamela grieving at our absence & the land going to the dogs when I could have sold it & been at home now, instead of drifting about the outskirts of the world, battling for bread. If I were in the east, now, I could stop the publication of a piratical book which has stolen some of my sketches.

I saw the American Minister today & he says Edwin McCook, of Colorado Ter. has been appointed to fill his place – so there is an end to *that* project.

It is late – good-bye, Mollie.

YR BRO
SAM

P.S. – Now *please* don't read this to anybody – I am always *afraid* to write to you – you always show my letters.

HONOLULU, JUNE 27, 1866

MY DEAR MOTHER & SISTER:
    I enjoy being in the Sandwich Islands because I don't

[*three-fourths MS page (about 80 words) missing*]

& Gen. Van Valkenburgh, the United States Ministers to China & Japan say that California is proud of Mark Twain, & that some day America will be too, no doubt.

[*four and three-fourths MS pages (about 530 words) missing*]

tub, with a gill of water a day to each man. I got the whole story from the third mate & ten of the sailors. If my account gets to the Sacramento Union first, it will be *published* first all over the United States, France, England, Russia and Germany – all over the world, I may say. You will see it. Mr. Burlingame went with me all the time, & helped me question the men – throwing away invitations to dinner with the princes & foreign dignitaries, & neglecting all sorts of things to accommodate me – & you know I appreciate that kind of thing – especially from *such* a man, who is acknowledged to have no superior in the diplomatic circles of the world, & obtained from China concessions in favor of America which were refused to Sir Frederick Bruce & the Envoys of France & Russia until procured for them by Burlingame himself – which service was duly acknowledged by those dignitaries. He hunted me up as soon as he came here, & has done me a hundred favors since, & says if I will come to China in the first trip of the great mail steamer next January & make his house in Pekin my home, he will afford me facilities that few men can have there for seeing & learning. He will give me letters to the chiefs of the great Mail Steamship Company which will be of service to me in this matter. I expect to do all this, but I expect to go to the States first. – & from China to the Paris World's Fair.

Don't show this letter.

YRS AFFLY

SAM

P.S. The crown Princess of this Kingdom will be buried tomorrow with great ceremony – after that I sail in 2 weeks for California.

TO JANE LAMPTON CLEMENS
AND PAMELA A. MOFFETT
30 JULY, 6, 7, 8, 10, AND 20 AUGUST 1866
SMYRNIOTE EN ROUTE FROM HONOLULU TO SAN FRANCISCO,
AND SAN FRANCISCO, CALIF.

ON BOARD SHIP SMYRNIOTE, AT SEA, JULY 30, 1866

DEAR MOTHER & SISTER:

I write, now, because I must go hard at work as soon as I get to San Francisco, & then I shall have no time for other things – though truth to say I have nothing *now* to write which will be calculated to interest you much. We left the Sandwich Islands 8 or ten days – or 12 days ago – I don't know which, I have been so hard at work until to-day (at least *part* of each day,) that the time has slipped away almost unnoticed.) The first few days we came at a whooping gait – being in the latitude of the "North-East trades," but we soon ran out of them. We used them as long as they lasted – hundreds of miles – & came dead straight north until exactly abreast of San Francisco – precisely straight west of the city in a bee-line – but a *long* bee-line, as we are about two thousand miles at sea – consequently, we are not a hundred yards nearer San Francisco than *you* are. And here we lie becalmed on a glassy sea – we do not move an inch – we throw banana & orange peel overboard & it lies still on the water by the vessel's side. Sometimes the ocean is as dead level as the Mississippi river, & glitters glassily like it was polished – but usually, of course, no matter how calm the weather is, we roll & surge over the grand ground-swell. We amuse ourselves catching vast sea-birds with a hook-&-line, & by tying pieces of tin to the ship's log & sinking them to see how far we can distinguish them under water – 86 feet was the deepest we could see a small piece of tin, but a white plate would show about as far down as the steeple of Dr Bullard's church would reach, I guess. The sea is very dark & blue here. I play whist & euchre at night until the passengers all tire out & go to bed, & then walk the quarter-deck & smoke with the mates & swap lies with them till 2 oclock (as I call it) but "four bells in the middle watch['"] (as they call it.) Get up at 8 in the morning – always the last man, & never quick enough for the first table – & breakfast with servants, children & subordinate officers. This is better than I do in San Francisco, though – always get up at noon, there.

Ever since we got becalmed – 4 5 days – I have been copying the diary of one of the young Fergusons (the two boys who starved & suffered, with 13 others, in an open boat at sea for 43 days, lately, after their ship, the "Hornet," was burned on the equator.) Both these boys, & Capt Mitchell, are passengers with us. I am copying the diary to publish in Harper's Magazine if I have time to fix it up properly when I get to San F.

I suppose, from present appearances, – light winds & calms – that we shall be two or three weeks at sea, yet, – and I hope so – I am in no hurry to go to work.

SUNDAY MORNING, AUG. 5 6

This is rather slow. We still drift, drift, drift along – at intervals a spanking breeze, & then – drift again – hardly move for half a day. But I enjoy it. We have such snowy moonlight, & such gorgeous sunsets. And the ship is so easy – even in a gale, she rolls very little, compared to other vessels – & in this calm we could dance on deck, if we chose. You can walk a crack, so steady is she. Very different from the Ajax. My trunk used to get loose in the stateroom & rip & tear around the place as if it had life in it, & I always had to take my clothes off in bed because I could not stand up & do it.

There is a ship in sight – the first object we have seen since we left Honolulu. We are still 1300 or 1400 miles from land, & so anything like this that varies the vast solitude of the ocean makes all hands light-hearted & cheerful. We think the ship is the "*Comet*," which left Honolulu several hours before we did. She is about twelve miles away, & so we cannot see her hull, but the sailors think it is the Comet because of some peculiarity about her fore-top-gallant-sails. We have watched her all the forenoon.

Afternoon – We had preaching on the quarter-deck by Rev. Mr. Rising, of Virginia City, old friend of mine. Spread a flag on the booby-hatch, which made a very good pulpit, & then ranged the chairs on either side against the bulwarks; last Sunday we had the shadow of the mainsail, but today we were on the opposite tack, close-hauled, & had the sun. I am leader of the choir on this ship, & a sorry lead it is. I hope they will have a better opinion of the music in Heaven than I have down here. If they don't a thunder-bolt will come down & knock the vessel endways.

The other ship *is* the Comet – she is right abreast, 3 miles away, sailing on our course – both of us in a dead calm. With the glasses we can see what we take to be men & women on her decks. I am well acquainted with nearly all her passengers, & being so close seems right sociable.

Monday 7 – I had just gone to bed a little after midnight when the 2^d mate came & roused up the captain & said "The Comet has come round & is standing away on the other tack." I went up immediately, & so did all our passengers, without waiting to dress – men, women & children. There was a perceptible breeze. Pretty soon the other ship swept down upon us with all her sails set, & made a fine show in the luminous star-light. She passed within a hundred yards of us, so we could faintly see persons on her decks. We had two minutes chat with each other, through the medium of hoarse shouting, & then she bore away to windward.

In the morning she was only a little black peg standing out of the glassy sea in the distant horizon – an almost invisible mark in the bright sky. Dead calm. So the ships have stood, all day long – have not moved 100 yards.

Aug. 9 8 – The calm continues. Magnificent weather. The gentlemen have all turned boys. They play boyish games on the poop and quarter-deck: For instance: They lay a knife on the fife-rail of the main-mast – stand off 3 steps, shut one eye, walk up & strike at it with the forefinger; (seldom hit it); also they lay a knife on the deck & walk 7 or 8 steps with eyes close shut, & try to find it. They kneel – place elbows against knees – extend hands in front along the deck – place knife against end of fingers – then clasp hands behind back & bend forward & try to pick up the knife with their teeth & rise up from knees without rolling over or losing their balance. They tie a string to the shrouds – stand with back against it – walk 3 steps (eyes shut) – turn around 3 times and go & put finger on the string; only a military man can do it. If you want to know how perfectly ridiculous a grown man looks performing such absurdities in the presence of ladies, get one to try it.

Afternoon – The calm is no more. There are 3 vessels in sight. It is so sociable to have them hovering about us on this broad waste of waters. It is sunny & pleasant, but blowing hard. Every rag about the ship is spread to the breeze & she is speeding over the sea like a bird. There is a large brig right astern of us with all her canvas set & chasing us at her best. She came up fast while the winds were light, but now it is hard to tell whether she gains or not. We can see the people on the forecastle with the glass. The race is exciting. I am sorry to know that we shall soon have to quit the vessel & go ashore if she keeps up this speed.

Friday, Aug. 10 – We have breezes & calms alternately. The brig is 2 miles to 3 astern, & just stays there. We sail *directly* east – this brings the brig, with all her canvas set, almost in the eye of the sun, when it sets – beautiful. She looks sharply cut & black as coal against a background of fire & in the midst of a sea of blood.

SAN FRANCISCO, AUG. 20

We never saw the Comet again till the 13th, in the morning, 3 miles away. At 3 oclock that afternoon, 25 days out from Honolulu, both ships entered the Golden Gate of San Francisco *side by side*, & 300 yards apart. There was a gale blowing, & both vessels clapped on every stitch of canvas & swept up through the channel & past the fortresses at a magnificent gait.

Under that day's date I find the following terse & irreverent remark:

"Ashore again, & devilish sorry for it."

I have been up to Sacramento & squared accounts with the *Union.* They paid me a great deal more than they promised me. I suppose that means that I gave satisfaction, but they did not say so.

Orion & Mollie are here. They leave for Santa Cruz tomorrow.

I have sent Captain Mitchell's log overland to the N.Y. *Times*, but told them not to put my name to it, because if I get time I am going to write the whole story of the *Hornet* disaster for Harper's Magazine.

Looking over my note-book, I find the following:

"On board ship Emmeline, off Hawaii, Sandwich Islands: Corn-bread brick-bats for dinner today – I wonder what Margaret would think of *such* corn-bread?"

That reminds me that I went to reading your letters a while ago

at dinner, but there was so little cheerful news in them that I lost
my appetite & came away with an empty stomach.

YRS AFF

SAM

TO FRANCIS BRET HARTE
1 MAY 1867, NEW YORK, N.Y.

WESTMINSTER HOTEL, MAY 1, 1867

DEAR BRET —

I take my pen in hand to inform you that I am well & hope these
few line[s] will find you enjoying the same God's blessing.

The book is out, & is handsome. It is full of damnable errors of
grammar & deadly inconsistencies of spelling in the Frog sketch
because I was away & did not read the proofs – but be a friend &
say nothing about these things. When my hurry is over I will send
you an autograph copy to pisen the children with.

I am to lecture in Cooper Institute next Monday night. Pray
for me.

We sail for the Holy Land June 8. Try & write me (to this hotel,)
& it will be forwarded to Paris, where we remain 10 to 15 days.

Regards & best wishes to Mrs Bret & the family.

TRULY YR FRIEND

MARK

TO JANE LAMPTON CLEMENS AND FAMILY
1 JUNE 1867, NEW YORK, N.Y.

WESTMINSTER HOTEL, NEW YORK, JUNE 1

DEAR FOLKS —

I know I ought to write oftener (just got your last,) & more fully,
but I can *not* overcome my repugnance to telling what I am doing
or what I expect to do or propose to do. Then, what have I left to
write about? Manifestly nothing.

It isn't any use for me to talk about the voyage, because I can have no faith in that voyage or any other voyage till the ship is under way. How do I know she will ever sail? My passage is paid, & if the ship sails, I sail in her – but I make no calculations, have bought no cigars, no sea-going clothing, – have made no preparation whatever – shall not pack my trunk till the morning we sail. Yet my hands are full of what I am *going* to do the day *before* we sail – & what isn't done that day will go undone.

All I do know or feel, is, that I am wild with impatience to move – move – *Move!* Half a dozen times I have wished I had sailed long ago in some ship that wasn't going to keep me chained here to chafe for lagging ages while she got ready to go. Curse the endless delays! They always kill me – they make me neglect every duty & then I have a conscience that tears me like a wild beast. I wish I never had to stop *any*where a month. I do more mean things, the moment I get a chance to fold my hands & sit down than ever I can get forgiveness for.

Yes, we are to meet at Mr Beach's next Thursday night, & I suppose we shall have to be gotten up regardless of expense, in swallow-tails, white kids & everything *en régle.*

I am resigned to Rev. Mr. Hutchinson's or anybody's else's supervision. I don't mind it. I am *fixed.* I have got a splendid, immoral, tobacco-smoking, wine-drinking, godless room-mate who is as good & true & right-minded a man as ever lived – a man whose blameless conduct & example will always be an eloquent sermon to all who shall come within their influence. But send on the professional preachers – there are none I like better to converse with – if they ain't narrow minded & bigoted they make good companions.

I asked them to send the N.Y. Weekly to you – no charge. I am not going to write for it – like all other papers that pay one splendidly, it circulates among stupid people & the *canaille.* I have made no arrangement with any New York paper – I will see about that Monday or Tuesday.

Love to all.
Good Bye

YRS AFFY

SAM

NEW YORK, JUNE 7

DEAR FOLKS —

I suppose we shall be many a league at sea tomorrow night, & goodness knows I shall be unspeakably glad of it.

I haven't got *any*thing to write, else I *would* write it. I have just written myself clear out in letters to the *Alta*, & I think they are the stupidest letters that were ever written from New York. Corresponding has been a perfect drag ever since I got to the States. If it continues, abroad, I don't know what the Tribune & Alta folks will think.

I have withdrawn the Sandwich Island book – it would be useless to publish it in these dull publishing times. As for the Frog book, I don't believe that will ever pay anything worth a cent. I published it simply to advertise myself & not with the hope of making anything out of it.

Well, I haven't anything to write, except that I am so tired of staying in one place that I am in a fever to get away. Read my Alta letters – they contain everything I could possibly write to you. Tell Zeb & John Leavenworth to write me – they can get plenty of gossip from Essie & Lou & the pilots.

An importing house sent two cases of exquisite champaign aboard the ship for me to-day – Veuve Cliquot & Lac d'Or. I & my room-mate have set apart every Saturday as a solemn fast-day, wherein we will entertain no light matters or frivolous conversation, but only get drunk. {That is a joke.} His mother & sisters are the best & most home-like people I have yet found in a brownstone front. There is no style about them except in house & furniture.

I wish Orion were going on this voyage, for I believe with so many months of freedom from business cares he could not help but be cheerful & jolly. I often wonder if his law business is going satisfactorily to him, but knowing that the dull season is setting in now (it looked like it had already set in before,) I have felt as if I could almost answer the question myself – which is to say in plain words, I was afraid to ask. I wish I had gone to Washington in the winter instead of going West. I could have gouged an office out of Bill Stewart for him, & that would have atoned for the loss of my home visit. But I am so worthless that it seems to me I never do anything or accomplish anything that lingers in my mind as a pleasant memory. My mind is stored full of unworthy conduct toward Orion & toward you all, & an accusing conscience gives me peace only in excitement & restless moving from place to place. If I could say I had done one thing for any of you that entitled me to your good opinions (I say nothing of your love, for I am sure of *that*, no matter how unworthy of it I may make myself, – from Orion down, you have always given me that, all the days of my life, when God Almighty knows I have seldom deserved it,) I believe I could go home & stay there – & I *know* I would care little for the world's praise or blame. There is no satisfaction in the world's praise, anyhow, & it has no worth to me save in the way of business. I tried to gather up its compliments to send to you, but the work was distasteful & I dropped it.

You observe that under a cheerful exterior I have got a spirit that is angry with me & gives me freely its contempt. I can get away from that at sea, & be tranquil & satisfied – & so, with my parting love & benediction for Orion & all of you, I say good bye & God bless you all – & welcome the winds that wafts a weary soul to the sunny lands of the Mediterranean!

YRS FOREVER

SAM

TO ELISHA BLISS, JR.
2 DECEMBER 1867, WASHINGTON, D.C.

WASHINGTON, DEC. 2, 1867

E. Bliss, Jr. Esq.
  Sec'y American Publishing Co. –
    DEAR SIR:

I only received your favor of Nov. 21st last night, at the rooms of the Tribune Bureau here. It was forwarded from the Tribune office, New York, where it had lain eight or ten days. This will be a sufficient apology for the seeming discourtesy of my silence.

I wrote fifty-two letters for the San Francisco "Alta California" during the Quaker City excursion, about half of which number have been printed, thus far. The "Alta" has few exchanges in the east, and I suppose scarcely any of these letters have been copied on this side of the Rocky Mountains. I could weed them of their chief faults of con[s]truction & inelegancies of expression, & make a volume that would be more acceptable in many respects than any I could now write. When those letters were written my impressions were fresh, but now they have lost that freshness; they were warm then – they are cold, now. I could strike out certain letters, & write new ones wherewith to supply their places. If you think such a book would suit your purpose, please drop me a line, specifying the size & general style of the volume; *when* the matter ought to be ready; whether it should have pictures in it or not; & particularly what your terms with me would be, & what amount of money I might possibly make out of it. The latter clause has a degree of importance for me which is almost beyond my own comprehension. But you understand that, of course.

I have other propositions for a book, but have doubted the propriety of interfering with good newspaper engagements except my way as an author could be demonstrated to be plain before me. But I know Richardson, & learned from him, some months ago, something of an idea of the subscription plan of publishing. If that is your plan invariably, it looks safe.

I am on the N. Y. Tribune staff here as an "occasional," among other things, and a note from you addressed to New York Tribune Bureau, Washington, will find me, without fail.

VERY TRULY &C
SAM. L. CLEMENS

TO JANE LAMPTON CLEMENS
AND PAMELA A. MOFFETT
8 JANUARY 1868, WASHINGTON, D.C.

224 F. STREET, WASH JAN. 8

MY DEAR MOTHER & SISTER:

And so the old Major has been there, has he? I would like mighty well to see him. I was a sort of a benefactor to him, once. I helped to snatch him out when he was about to ride into a Mohammedan Mosque in that queer old Moorish town of Tangier, in Africa. If he had got in, the Moors would have knocked his venerable old head off, for his temerity.

I have just arrived from New York – been there ever since Christmas day, staying at Dan Slote's house – my Quaker City roommate, & having a splendid time. Charlie Langdon, Jack Van Nostrand, & Dan & I, (all Quaker City night-hawks,) had a blow-out at Dan's house & a lively talk over old times. We went through the Holy Land together, & I just laughed till my sides ached, at some of our reminiscences. It was the unholiest gang that ever cavorted through Palestine, but those are the best boys in the world. We needed Moulton badly. I started to make calls, New Year's Day, but I anchored for the day at the first house I came to – Charlie Langdon's sister was there (beautiful girl,) & Miss Alice Hooker, another beautiful girl, a niece of Henry Ward Beecher's. We sent the old folks home early, with instructions not to send the carriage till midnight, & then I just staid there & deviled the life out of those girls. I am going to spend a few days with the Langdon's, in Elmira, New York, as soon as I get time, & a few days at Mrs. Hooker's, in Hartford, Conn., shortly.

Henry Ward Beecher sent for me last Sunday to come over & dine (he lives in Brooklyn, you know,) & I went. Harriet Beecher Stowe was there, & Mrs. & Miss Beecher, Mrs. Hooker & my old Quaker City favorite, Emma Beach. We had a very gay time, if it *was* Sunday. I expect I told more lies than I have told before in a month. We had a tip-top dinner, but nothing to drink but cider. I told Mr. Beecher that no dinner could be perfect without champaign, or at least some kind of Burgundy, & he said that privately he was a good deal of the same opinion, but it wouldn't do to say it loud. I went back, by invitation, after the evening service, & finished the blow-out, & then staid all night at Mr. Beach's. Henry Ward is a brick.

I found out at 10 oclock, last night, that I was to lecture to-morrow evening & the next, & so you must be aware that I have been working like sin all night to get a lecture written. I have finished it, but don't think a very great deal of it. I call it "Frozen Truth." It is a little top-heavy, though, because there is more truth in the title than there is in the lecture. But thunder, I mustn't sit here writing all day, with so much business before me.

Good bye, & kind regards to all.

YRS AFFLY

SAM L. CLEMENS

TO ORION CLEMENS
21 FEBRUARY 1868, WASHINGTON, D.C.

224 F STREET, WASH., FEB. 21

MY DEAR BRO.,

I am glad you do not want the clerkship, for that Patent Office is in such a muddle that there would be no security for the permanency of a place in it. The same remark will apply to all offices here, now, & no doubt will, till the close of the present administration.

Any man who holds a place here, now, stands prepared at all times to vacate it. You are doing, now, exactly what I wanted you to do a year ago.

We chase phantoms half the days of our lives.

It is well if we learn wisdom even then, & save the other half.

I am in for it. I must go on chasing them – until I marry – *then* I am done with literature & all other bosh, – that is, literature wherewith to please the general public.

I shall write to please myself, then. I hope you *will* set type till you complete that invention, for surely government pap must be nauseating food for a *man* – a man whom God has enabled to saw wood & be independent. It really seemed to me a falling from grace, the idea of going back to San Francisco nothing better than a mere postmaster, albeit the public would have thought I came with gilded honors, & in great glory.

I only retain correspondence enough, now, to make a living for myself, & have discarded all else, so that I may have time to spare for the book. Drat the thing, I wish it were done, or that I had no other writing to do.

This is the place to get a poor opinion of everybody in. There isn't one man in Washington, in civil office, who has the brains of Anson Burlingame – & I suppose if China had not seized & saved his great talents to the world, this government would have discarded him when his time was up.

There are more pitiful intellects in this Congress! Oh, geeminy! There are few of them that I find pleasant enough company to visit.

I am most infernally tired of Wash. & its "attractions." To be *busy* is a man's only happiness – & I *am* – otherwise I should die.

YRS. AFF

SAM

LOCKPORT, N.Y., FEB. 27

DEAR FOLKS —

I enclose $20 for Ma (No. 10.) I thought I was getting a little
ahead of her little assessment of $35 a month, but find I am falling
behindhand instead , & have let her go without money. Well, I did
not mean to do it. But you see when people have been getting
ready for months, in a quiet way to get married, they are bound to
grow stingy, & go to saving up money against the awful day when
it is sure to be needed. I am particularly anxious to place myself
in a position where I can carry on my married life in good shape
on my own hook, because I have paddled my own canoe so long that
I could not be satisfied, now, to let anybody help me – & my proposed father-in-law is naturally so liberal that it would be just like
him to want to give us a start in life. But I don't want it that way.
I can start myself. I don't want any help. I can run the institution
without any outside assistance; & I shall have a wife who will stand
by me like a soldier through thick & thin, & never complain. She
is only a little body, but she hasn't her peer in Christendom. I gave
her only a plain gold engagement ring, when fashion imperatively
demands a two hundred dollar diamond one – & told her it was
typical of her future lot – namely, that she would have to flourish
on substantials rather than luxuries. {But you see I *know* the girl
– she don't care anything about luxuries, and although she has a
respectable fortune in jewels, she wears none of any consequence.
One seldom sees a diamond about her.} She is a splendid girl. She
spends no money but her usual year's allowance, & she spends
nearly every cent of that on other people. She will be a good sensible little wife, without any airs about her. I don't make interces-
sion for her beforehand & ask you to love her, for there isn't any
use in that – you couldn't help it if you were to try. In fact, you had
better, in self-defence, take warning by Mrs. Brooks & all of Livy's
other friends, & try to learn to *hate* her – for I warn you that whosoever comes within the fatal influence of her beautiful nature is her
willing slave forevermore. I take my affidavit on that statement.
Her father & mother & brother embrace her & kiss her & pet her
constantly, precisely as if she were a *sweetheart*, instead of a blood
relation. She has unlimited power over her father, & yet she never

uses it except to make him help people who stand in need of help, & lavishes

[*seven lines (about 40 words) missing*]

allowance.

But if I get fairly started on the subject of my bride, I never shall get through – & so I will quit right here. I went to Elmira a little over a week ago, & staid four days & then had to go to New York on business. Now Lockport wants a lecture – shall talk to-night & Monday night, & then I shall go to Hartford, avoiding New York city if possible so as to save time. I will

[*thirteen lines (about 75 words) missing*]

TO OLIVIA L. LANGDON
2 MARCH 1869, ROCHESTER, N.Y.

ROCHESTER, MARCH I

I love you, Livy. That is not what I sat down especially to say; if it were, I might continue to write, now that I am at it, & never stop again. No – I wished to say, *particularly*, Be sure & send my first Geneseo letter (I mean the one *you* first wrote me, to that point,) to Hartford. Do I make myself understood? Don't you see, Livy, I was so bewitched by you, there in Elmira, that I could think of nothing connectedly & collectedly *but* you, & so I forgot to telegraph those Geneseo folks to retain your letter till I came, – & I wrote them from New York, too late – & so *of course* they had no better sense than to send the letter back to Elmira, directed to Mr. Langdon. Now Livy, please don't tear it up, but forward it to me at Hartford, there's a darling.

And the next thing I wish to say, is, please tell Charlie to tell those tailors to make my coat nearly or full three-quarters of an inch higher in the back of the neck than this one. This one gives me the lockjaw every time I look in the glass. The collar is an unmitigated atrocity. I want the collar of the new coat to be five inches higher than the collar of this one. Tell Charlie, please.

In Geneseo yesterday I got your letter of the 25th. And so you are writing me every day? That is right, you dear L little Livy – only, don't you write me or anybody else when you are tired or are hurried by company. I shall write you every chance I get, just the same; & any time that a letter is due from you & it don't come, I shall feel satisfied that you needed rest, or something interfered, & so I shall be content. I am at rest & peace in you now, L my Livy, & I know perfectly well that when no obstacles intervene, you will be sure to write me regularly – but not a great many weeks ago, the failure of one of your letters to arrive when it was expected, would have terrified me.

You have been writing every day, & I only every other day. But my reason was that I had no opportunity to write oftener. I was in Geneseo thirty hours, & *ought* to have been permitted to write from there, but wasn't. Half a dozen young gentlemen, 20 to 25 years of age, received me at the depot with a handsome open sleigh, & drove me to the hotel in style – & then *took possession of my room*, & invited a dozen more in, & ordered cigars, & made themselves entirely happy & contented. But they were hard to entertain, for they took me for a lion, & I had to carry the bulk of the conversation myself, which is a thing that presently grows wearisome. At dinner I begged off from going sleigh-riding, & said I wanted to go to bed in about an hour. After dinner they came up again. Pretty soon I spoke once more of retiring. It produced no effect. Then I rose & said, "Boys, I shall have to bid you a good-afternoon, for I am stupid & sleepy – & you must pardon my bluntness, but I *must* go to bed." Poor fellows, they were stricken speechless – they looked mortified, & went blundering out like a flock of sheep, treading on each other's heels in their confusion. I undressed & went to bed, & *tried* to go to sleep – but again & again my con-science smote me – again & again I saw that picture of their exodus from the room – again & again I thought of how mean & how shameful a return I had made for their well-meant & whole-hearted friendliness to me a stranger within their gates & how pup-pyish it was in me to be angered instead of gladdened by that gush-ing cordiality of youth, a thing which ought to have won me by its very *naivete* & its rare honesty. And then I said to myself, I'll make amends for this – & so got up & dressed & gave the boys *all* of my time till midnight – & also from this noon till I left at four this afternoon. And so, if any man is thoroughly popular with the young people of Geneseo to-day, it is I. We had a full house last night, & a fine success. I just *love* boys of their age with all my heart – & I don't see how I ever could have treated them discourteously. {Yes I do, too. I know the secret of it. I *wanted to read your letter* – &

if they had only just allowed me an hour of privacy for that, I would have been with them heart & hand from that time forth.} Some of those boys came fourteen miles, from a college at Lima, & were splendid young scalawags. The whole tribe came to the hotel after the lecture, & entertained me with vocal & piano music in the parlor, & with cider & whole worlds of tobacco smoke – but *they* drank a little of everything, & made music which you might have heard a mile. I played sedate old gentleman, but never reproved them once, for I couldn't help saying to myself, You'll be all the better men for sowing your wild oats while you are *young* – *I*'ll go your security. They assembled in the street before the hotel, shortly after I had retired, & gave me three terrific cheers – which was rather more honor than I desired. Of course I *half* promised to lecture in Geneseo & *in the middle of August*, at which time they propose to give me a ball & a concert – & I also *half*-promised to spend my summer vacation there – & I have made that *half*-promise in a good many places, (but always with the thought in my mind, "It will depend entirely upon where *Livy* is going to spend her vacation" – for I don't propose to be very far from *you*, my dear, when *vacations* fall to my good fortune.}

Now if you have kept up your letter a day, I ought to find a perfect feast awaiting me at Hartford – & I do hope it is the case. Remember, "148 Asylum street," Livy dear. But since you have a house full of company to entertain, I am a little afraid you won't have time to write, except after your bed-time, – & you must not do that, Livy. If either of us must suffer, let it be me.

Bless you I am glad to be in your apple sauce – or even in your soup, Livy – for it is a sign that I am in your thoughts, & therefore in your heart, the daintiest mansion that ever *I* inhabited, my darling. And I pray that its doors may never be closed against me until one or the other of us shall go forth forever from among the living. You were brave, Livy – it was like you to come out & acknowledge what was in your mind, without adopting one of those false little subterfuges usual in such circumstances & commonly regarded as permissable.

I still look among the faces in my audiences for one like yours – for one that shall give token of a nature like yours – & I still look in vain. And so I grow prouder & prouder of you day by day, & as each new evidence comes that there is none like you in all the world. If ever a man had reason to be grateful to Divine Providence, it is I. And often & often again I sit & think of the wonder, the curious mystery, the *strangeness* of it, that there should be only *one* woman among the hundreds & hundreds of thousands whose features I have critically scanned, & whose characters I have read in their faces – only *one* woman among them all whom I could love with all my whole heart, & that it should be my amazing good fortune to secure that woman's love. And more, that it should be revealed to me in a single *instant* of time, when I first saw you, that you were that woman. It passes my comprehension. I have stated the case truly – & I can swear to it as I have stated it. I have known many, very many estimable & lovely women, but they all betrayed one or more unpleasant qualities – & all this time, twelve long years, I have been growing naturally more & more critical & hard to please, as is the way of old bachelors – but behold, I have found you at last, & in you I can discover *no* blemish. It is strange, it is very strange. The hand of Providence is in it. When I cease to be grateful, deeply grateful to you for your priceless love, my honored Livy, I shall be – dead. Never before, Livy – never before.

I have been reading – I *am* reading – Gulliver's Travels, & am much more charmed with it than I was when I read it last, in boyhood – for now I can see what a scathing satire it is upon the English government; whereas, before, I only gloated over its prodigies & its marvels. Poor Swift – under the placid surface of this simply-worded book flows the full tide of his venom – the turbid sea of his matchless hate. You would not like the volume, Livy – that is, a part of it. Some of it you would. If you would like to read it, though, I will mark it & tear it until it is fit for your eyes – for portions of it are very coarse & indelicate. I am sorry enough that I didn't ask you to let me prepare Don Quixote for your perusal, in the same way. It pains me to think of your reading that book just as it stands. I have thought of it with regret, time & again. If you haven't finished it, Livy, don't do it. You are as pure as snow, & I would have you always so – untainted, untouched even by the impure thoughts of others. You are the purest woman that ever I knew – & your purity is your most uncommon & most precious ornament. Preserve it, Livy. Read nothing that is not *perfectly* pure. I had rather you read fifty "Jumping Frogs" than one Don Quixote. Don Quixote is one of the most exquisite books that was ever written, & to lose it from the world's literature would be as the wresting of a constellation from the symmetry & perfection of the firmament – but neither it nor Shakspeare are proper books for virgins to read until some hand has culled them of their grossness.

No gross speech is ever harmless. "A man cannot handle pitch & escape defilement," saith the proverb. I did not mean to write a sermon, but still I have done it. However, it is good sense, & it was a matter that lay near my heart; & so I am not sorry that it is written.

It is high time you were in bed, Livy – & so if you will put your arms about my neck & kiss me, while I look for a moment into the eyes that are dearer to me than the light that streams out of the Heavens, you may go. And take you these two kisses & place them as I would if I were there – & so Goodnight, & God bless you always, my own darling.

TILL DEATH,

SAM

TO JANE LAMPTON CLEMENS AND FAMILY
4 JUNE 1869, ELMIRA, N.Y.

ELMIRA, JUNE 4

DEAR FOLKS –

Livy sends you her love & loving good wishes, & I send you mine. The last 3 chapters of the book came to-night – we shall read it in the morning & then, thank goodness, we are *done*.

In twelve months (or rather I believe it is fourteen,) I have earned just *eighty dollars* by my pen – two little magazine squibs & one newspaper letter – altogether the idlest, laziest 14 months I ever spent in my life. And in that time my *absolute* & *necessary* expenses have been scorchingly heavy – for I have now less than three thousand six hundred dollars in bank out of the eight or nine thousand I have made during those months, lecturing. My expenses were something frightful during the winter. I feel ashamed of my idleness, & yet I have had really *no* inclination to [do] anything but court Livy. I haven't any other inclination *yet*. I have determined not to work as hard traveling, any more, as I did last winter, & so I have resolved not to lecture outside of the 6 New England States next winter. My western course would easily amount to $10,000 next winter, but I would rather make 2 or 3 thousand in New England than submit again to so much wearing travel. {I *have* promised to talk ten nights for a thousand dollars in the State of New York, provided the places are close together.} But after all, if I get located in a newspaper in a way to suit me, in the meantime, I don't want to lecture *at all* next winter, & probably shan't. I most cordially hate the lecture-field. And, after all, I shudder to think I may never get out of it. In all conversations with Gough, & Anna Dickinson, Nasby, Oliver Wendell Holmes, Wendell Phillips & the other old stagers, I could not observe that *they* ever expected or hoped to get out of the business. *I* don't want to get wedded to it as they are. Livy thinks we can live on a very moderate sum & that we'll not need to lecture. I know very well that *she* can live on a small allowance, but I am not so sure about myself. I can't scare her by reminding her that her father's family expenses are forty thousand dollars a year, because she produces the documents at once to show that precious little of this outlay is on *her* account. But I must not commence writing about Livy, else I shall never stop. There isn't such another little piece of perfection in the world as she is.

My time is become so short, now, that I doubt if I get to California this summer. If I manage to buy into a paper, I think I will visit you a while & not go to Cal at all. I shall know something about it after my next trip to Hartford. We all go there on the 10th – the whole family – to attend a wedding, on the 17th. I am offered an interest [in] a Cleveland paper which would pay me $2,300 to $2,500 a year, & a salary added of $3,000. The salary is fair enough, but the interest is not large enough, & so I must look a little further. The Cleveland folks say they *can* be induced to do a little better by me, & urge me to come out & talk business. But it don't strike me – I feel little or no inclination to go.

I believe I haven't anything else to write, & it is bed-time. I want to write to Orion, but I keep putting it off – I keep putting *every*thing off. Day after day Livy & I are together all day long & until 10 at night, & then I feel dreadfully sleepy. If Orion will bear with me & forgive me I will square up with him yet. I will even let him kiss Livy.

My love to Mollie & Annie & Sammie & Margaret & all. Good-bye.

AFFECTIONATELY,

SAM.

[*new page:*]
P.S. I see that the toast I am appointed to respond to at the New York Press Club dinner to-morrow night is, "When I, twain, shall become one flesh – the future husband the husband of the future." Pretty pointed – & pretty suggestive. But I shan't be there – & as I am only an invited guest & a sort of honorary member (for I never have joined,) I have used my privilege of proposing my own toast & making my own speech upon it in my own way – & have forwarded the manuscript.

TO THE CALIFORNIA PIONEERS
11 OCTOBER 1869, ELMIRA, N.Y.

ELMIRA, OCT. 11, 1869

To the California Pioneers.

GENTLEMEN: Circumstances render it out of my power to take advantage of the invitation extended to me through Mr. Simonton, & be present at your dinner in New York. I regret this very much, for there are several among you whom I would have a right to join hands with on the score of old friendship, & I suppose I would have a sublime general right to shake hands with the rest of you on the score of kinship in Californian ups & downs in search of fortune. If I were to tell some of my experiences, you would recognize Californian blood in me, I fancy. The old, old story would sound familiar, no doubt. I have the usual stock of reminiscences. For instance: I went to Esmeralda early. I purchased largely in the "Wide West," the "Winnemucca," & other fine claims, & was very wealthy. I fared sumptuously on bread when flour was $200 a barrel, & had beans every Sunday when none but bloated aristocrats could afford such grandeur. But I finished by feeding batteries in a quartz-mill at $15 a week, & wishing I was a battery myself & had somebody to feed *me*. My claims in Esmeralda are there yet. I suppose I could be persuaded to sell. I went to the Humboldt District when it was new. I became largely interested in the "Alba Nueva," & other claims with gorgeous names, & was rich again – in prospect. I owned a vast mining property there. I would not have sold out for less than $400,000, at that time – but I will now. Finally I walked home – some 200 miles – partly

for exercise & partly because stage fares were expensive. Next
I entered upon an affluent career in Virginia City, & by a judicious
investment of labor & the capital of friends, became the owner of
about all the worthless wildcat mines there were in that part of the
country. Assessments did the business for me there. There were 117
assessments to one dividend, & the proportion of income to outlay
was a little against me. My financial thermometer went down to
32 Farenheit, & the subscriber was frozen out. I took up extension[s] on the main lead – extensions that reached to British America in one direction & to the Isthmus of Panama in the other – &
I verily believe I would have been a rich man if I had ever found
those infernal extensions. But I didn't. I ran tunnels till I tapped
the Arctic Ocean, & I sunk shafts till I broke through the roof of
perdition, but those extensions turned up missing every time. I am
willing to sell all that property, & throw in the improvements. Perhaps you remember the celebrated "North Ophir?" I bought
that mine. It was very rich in pure silver. You could take it out
in lumps as large as a filbert. But when it was discovered that those
lumps were melted half-dollars, & hardly melted at that, a painful
case of "saltin" was apparent, & the undersigned adjourned to the
poor-house again. I paid assessments on "Hale & Norcross" till
they sold me out, & I had to take in washing for a living – & the
next month that infamous stock went up to $7,000 a foot. I own
millions & millions of feet of affluent silver leads in Nevada – in
fact I own the entire undercrust of that country, nearly, & if Congress would move that State off my property so that I could get at
it, I would be wealthy yet. But no, there she squats – & here am I.
Failing health persuades me to sell. If you know of any one desiring
a permanent investment, I can furnish him one that will have the
virtue of being eternal.

I have been through the Californian mill, with all its "dips,
spurs, & angles, variations, & sinuosities." I have worked there at
all the different trades & professions known to the catalogue. I have
been everything, from a newspaper editor down to cowcatcher on
a locomotive, & I am encouraged to believe that if there had been
a few more occupations to experiment on, I might have made a
dazzling success at last, & found out what mysterious design Providence had in view in creating me.

But you perceive that although I am not a pioneer, I have had
a sufficiently variegated time of it to enable me to talk pioneer like
a native, & feel like a Forty-Niner. Therefore, I cordially welcome

you to your old remembered homes & your long-deserted firesides, & close this screed with the sincere hope that your visit here will be a happy one, & unembittered by the sorrowful surprises that absence & lapse of years are wont to prepare for wanderers; surprises which come in the form of old friends missed from their places; silence where familiar voices should be; the young grown old; change & decay everywhere; home a delusion & a disappointment; strangers at the hearth-stone; sorrow where gladness was; tears for laughter; the melancholy pomp of death where the grace of life had been!

With all good wishes for the Returned Prodigals, & regrets that I cannot partake of a small piece of the fatted calf (rare & no gravy), I am, yours cordially,

MARK TWAIN

TO ORION CLEMENS
15 JULY 1870, ELMIRA, N.Y.

ELMIRA, JULY 15

MY DEAR BRO:

Per contract I must have another 600-page book ready for my publisher Jan. 1, & I only began it to-day. The subject of it is a secret, because I may possibly change it. But as it stands, I propose to do up Nevada & Cal., beginning with the trip across the country in the stage. Have you a memorandum of the route we took – or the names of any of the Stations we stopped at? Do you remember any of the scenes, names, incidents or adventures of the coach trip? – for I remember next to *nothing* about the matter. Jot down a foolscap page of items for me. I wish I could have two days' talk with you.

I suppose I am to get the biggest copyright, this time, ever paid on a subscription book in this country.

Give our love to Mollie. Mr. Langdon is very low.

YR BRO
SAM

ELMIRA, MONDAY

FRIEND BLISS:

Yrs rec'd enclosing check for $703.35. The old "Innocents" holds out handsomely.

I feel confident that House will make a most readable book. Shall write him what you say.

I have MS. enough on hand now, to make (allowing for engravings) about 400 pages of the book – consequently am two-thirds done. I intended to run up to Hartford about the middle of the week & take it along; because it has chapters in it that ought by all means to be in the prospectus; but I find myself so thoroughly interested in my work, now (a thing I have not experienced for months) that I can't bear to lose a single moment of the inspiration. So I will stay here & peg away as long as it lasts. My present idea is to write as much more as I have already written, & then cull from the mass the very best chapters & discard the rest. I am not half as well satisfied with the first part of the book as I am with what I am writing now. When I get it done I want to see the man who will begin to read it & not finish it. If it falls short of the Innocents in any respect I shall lose my guess.

When I was writing the Innocents my daily "stent" was 30 pages of MS & I hardly ever got beyond it; but I have gone over that nearly every day for the last ten. That shows that I am writing with a red-hot interest. Nothing grieves me now – nothing troubles me, bothers me or gets my attention – I don't think of anything but the book, & don't have an hour's unhappiness about anything & don't care two cents whether school keeps or not. It will be a bully book. If I keep up my present lick three weeks more I shall be able & willing to scratch out half of the chapters of the Overland narrative – & shall do it.

You do not mention having received my second batch of MS, sent a week or two ago – about 100 pages.

If you want to issue a prospectus & go right to canvassing, say the word & I will forward some more MS – or send it by hand – special messenger. Whatever chapters you think are unquestionably good, we will retain of course, & so they can go into a prospectus as well one time as another. The book will be done soon, now. I have 1200 pages of MS already written, & am now writing 200 a week – more than that, in fact; during past week wrote 23 one day, then 30, 33, 35, 52, & 65. How's that?

It will be a starchy book, & should be full of snappy pictures – especially pictures worked in with the letter-press. The dedication will be worth the price of the volume – thus:

To the Late Cain,

This Book is Dedicated:

Not on account of respect for his memory, for it merits little respect; not on account of sympathy with him, for his bloody deed placed him without the pale of sympathy, strictly speaking: but out of a mere humane commiseration for him in that it was his misfortune to live in a dark age that knew not the beneficent Insanity Plea.

I think it will do.

YS
CLEMENS

P.S. The reaction is beginning & my stock is looking up. I am getting the bulliest offers for books & almanacs, am flooded with lecture invitations, & one periodical offers me $6,000 cash for 12 articles, of any length & on any subject, treated humorously or otherwise.

TO JAMES REDPATH
8 AUGUST 1871, HARTFORD, CONN.

HARTFORD, TUESDAY, AUG. 8

DEAR REDPATH –

I am different from other women. They have their monthly period once a month, but I have mine once a week, & sometimes oftener. That is to say, my mind changes that often. People who *have* no mind, can easily be steadfast & firm; but when a man is loaded down to the guards with it, as I am, every heavy sea of foreboding, or inclination, or mayhap indolence, shifts his cargo. See?

Therefore, if you will notice, *one* week I am likely to give rigid instructions to confine me to New England; next week, send me to Arizonia; next week, withdraw my name; next week, give you untrameled swing – & the week following, *modify* it. You must try to keep the run of my mind, Redpath – it is your business, being the agent – & it always was too many for me. It appears to me to be one of the finest pieces of mechanism I have ever met with. Now about the West. *This* week I am willing that you should retain all the western engagements you have made, & make as many more as will *cluster* well, pay high prices & not cost too hard travel.

But what I shall want *next* week, is still with God.

Let us not profane the mysteries with soiled hands & prying eyes of sin.

YRS
MARK

P.S. Shall be here 2 weeks – will run up there when Nasby comes.

TO JOSEPH H. AND HARMONY C. TWICHELL
11 JUNE 1874, ELMIRA, N.Y.

ELMIRA, JUNE 11

MY DEAR OLD JOE & HARMONY:

The baby is here & is the great American Giantess – weighing $7\frac{3}{4}$ pounds, & all solid meat. We had to wait a good long time for her, but she was full compensation when she *did* come. The labor pains fooled along during the evening, after a fashion; became more pronounced at midnight & so continued till 7 AM; then *very* severe for 15 minutes, & the trouble was over. Mrs Gleason & Della came up early in the evening & went to bed right away, up stairs, & neither of them were ever called till 15 minutes before the babe was born. Livy don't call for people till she needs them. She waltzed through this ordeal, walking the floor & sewing baby clothes in the bravest possible way. And even I was cool – slept a good part of the time. I *am* ashamed of that, but I couldn't keep my eyes open. And besides, this baby has fooled along so much that I hadn't much confidence in it. It is an admirable child, though, & has intellect. It puts its fingers against its brow & thinks. It was born with a caul, & so of course possesses the gift of second sight. The Modoc was delighted with it, & gave it her doll at once. There is nothing selfish about the Modoc. She is fascinated with the new baby. The Modoc rips & tears around out doors, most of the time, & consequently is as hard as a pine knot & as brown as an Indian. She is bosom friend to all the chickens, ducks, turkeys & guinea hens on the place. Yesterday as she marched along the winding path that leads up the hill through the red clover beds to the summer-house, there was a long procession of these fowls stringing contentedly after her, led by a stately rooster who can look over the Modoc's head. The devotion of these vassals has been purchased with daily largess of Indian meal, & so the Modoc, attended by her body-guard, moves in state wherever she goes.

Susie Crane has built the loveliest study for me, you ever saw. It is octagonal, with a peaked roof, each octagon filled with a spacious window, & it sits perched in complete isolation on top of an elevation that commands leagues of valley & city & retreating ranges of distant blue hills. It is a cosy nest, with just room in it for a sofa & a table & three or four chairs – & when the storms sweep down the remote valley & the lightning flashes above the hills beyond, & the rain beats upon the roof over my head, imagine the luxury of it! It stands 500 feet above the valley & $2\frac{1}{2}$ miles from it.

However, one must not write all day. We send continents of love to you & yours.

AFFECTIONATELY

MARK.

Mrs Gleason's father, whom she worshiped, died the morning of the day she had to come up here to look after Livy.

FROM SAMUEL L. AND OLIVIA L. CLEMENS TO JOHN BROWN
4 SEPTEMBER 1874, ELMIRA, N.Y.

FARMINGTON AVENUE, HARTFORD.
QUARRY FARM, NEAR ELMIRA, N.Y. SEP. 4

DEAR FRIEND:

I have been writing fifty pages of manuscript a day, on an average, for some time, now, on a book, (a story) & consequently have been so wrapped up in it & so dead to everything else, that I have fallen mighty short in letter-writing. But night before last

I discovered that that day's chapter was a failure, in conception, moral, truth to nature & execution – enough blemishes to impair the excellence of almost any chapter – & so, I must burn up the day's work & do it all over again. It was plain that I had worked myself out, pumped myself dry. So I knocked off, & went to playing billiards for a change. I haven't had an idea or fancy for two days now – an excellent time to write to friends who have plenty of ideas & fancies of their own & so will prefer an offering of the heart before those of the head. Day after tomorrow I go to a neighboring city to see a five-act drama of mine brought out, & suggest amendments in it, & would about as soon spend a night in the Spanish Inquisition as sit there & be tortured with all the adverse criticisms I can contrive to imagine the audience is indulging in. But whether the play be successful or not, I hope I shall never feel obliged to see it performed a second time. My interest in my work dies a sudden & violent death when the work is done.

I have invented & patented a pretty good sort of scrap-book (I think,) but I have backed down from letting it be known as mine just at present – for I can't stand being under discussion on a play & a scrap-book at one & the same time! I shall be away two days, & then return & take our tribe to New York, where we shall remain 5 days buying furniture for the new house & then go to Hartford & settle solidly down for the winter. After all that fallow time I ought to be able to go to work again on the book. We shall reach Hartford about the middle of September, I judge.

We have spent the past four months up here on top of a breezy hill six hundred feet high, some few miles from Elmira, N. Y., & overlooking that town, (Elmira is my wife's birth-place, & that of Susie & the new baby). This little summer house on the hill-top (named Quarry Farm because there's a quarry on it,) belongs to my wife's sister, Mrs. Crane. A photographer came up the other day & wanted to make some views, & shall send you the result per this mail. My study is a snug little octagonal den, with a coal-grate, 6 big windows, one little one, & a wide doorway (the latter opening upon the distant town.) On hot days I spread the study wide open, anchor my papers down with brickbats & write in the midst of hurricanes, clothed in the same thin linen we make shirt bosoms of. The study is nearly on the peak of the hill; it is right in front of the little perpendicular wall of rock left where they used to quarry stone. *On* the peak of the hill is an old arbor roofed with bark & covered with vine you call the "American creeper" – its green is already bloodied with red. The study is 30 yards below the old arbor and 100 yards above the dwelling-house – it is remote from *all noise.*

. . . .

The group represents the vine-clad carriageway in front of the farm-house. On the left is Megalopis sitting in the lap of her German nurse-maid. I am sitting behind them. Mrs. Crane is in the center. Mr. Crane next to her. Then Mrs. Clemens & the new baby. Her Irish nurse stands at her back. Then comes the table waitress, a young negro girl, born free. Next to her is Auntie Cord (a fragment of whose history I have just sent to a magazine). She is the cook; was in slavery more than forty years; & the self-satisfied wench, the last of the group, is the little baby's American nurse-maid. In the middle distance my mother-in-law's coachman (up on errand) has taken a position unsolicited to help out the picture. No, that is not true. He was waiting there a minute or two before the photographer came. In the extreme background, under the archway, you glimpse my study.

. . . .

Now isn't the whole thing pleasantly situated?

In the picture of me in the study you glimpse (through the left-hand window) the little rock bluff that rises behind the pond, and the bases of the little trees on top of it. The small square window is over the fireplace; the chimney divides to make room for it. Without the stereoscope it looks like a framed picture. All the study windows have Venetian blinds; they long ago went out of fashion in America but they have not been replaced with anything half as good yet.

The study is built on top of a tumbled rock-heap that has morning-glories climbing about it & a stone stairway leading down through & dividing it.

There now – if you have not time to read all this, turn it over to "Jock" & drag in the Judge to help.

Mrs. Clemens must put in a late picture of Susie – a picture which she maintains is good, but which I think is a slander on the child.

We revisit the Rutland street home many a time in fancy, for we hold every individual in it in happy & grateful memory. Goodbye –

YOUR FRIEND

SAM L. CLEMENS

P.S. I gave the P.O. Department a blast in the papers about sending misdirected letters of mine back to the writers for reshipment, & got a blast in return, through a New York daily, from the New York postmaster. But I notice that misdirected letters *find* me, now, without any unnecessary fooling around.

S.L.C.

TO WILLIAM DEAN HOWELLS
8 DECEMBER 1874, HARTFORD, CONN.

HDFD, DEC. 8

MY DEAR HOWELLS:

It isn't the Atlantic audience that distresses me; for *it* is the only audience that I sit down before in perfect serenity (for the simple reason that it don't require a "humorist" to paint himself stripèd & stand on his head every fifteen minutes.) The trouble was, that I was only bent on "working up an atmosphere" & that is to me a most fidgety & irksome thing sometimes. I avoid it, unsually, but in this case it was absolutely necessary, else every reader would be applying the atmosphere of his own river or sea experiences, & THAT shirt wouldn't fit, you know.

I could have sent this Article 2 a week ago, or more, but I couldn't bring myself to the drudgery of revising & correcting it. I have been at that tedious work 3 hours, now, & by GEORGE but I am glad it is over.

Say – I am as prompt as a clock, if I only know the *day* a thing is wanted – otherwise I am a natural procrastinaturalist. Tell me what day & date you want Nos. 3 & 4, & I will tackle & revise them & they'll be there to the minute.

I could wind up with No. 4, but there are some things more, which I am powerfully moved to write. Which is natural enough, since I am a person who would quit authorizing in a minute to go to piloting, if the madam would stand it. I would rather sink a steamboat than eat, any time.

My wife was afraid to write you – so I said with simplicity, "*I* will give you the language – & ideas." Through the infinite grace of God there has not been such another insurrection in the family before as followed this. However, the letter was written, &

promptly, too – whereas, heretofore she has *remained* afraid to do such things.

With kind regards to Mrs. Howells,

YRS EVER
MARK

TO WILLIAM DEAN HOWELLS
5 JULY 1875, HARTFORD, CONN.

JULY 5

MY DEAR HOWELLS:

I have finished the story & didn't take the chap beyond boyhood. I believe it would be fatal to do it in any shape but autobiographically – like Gil Blas. I perhaps made a mistake in not writing it in the first person. If I went on, now, & took him into manhood, he would just be like all the one-horse men in literature & the reader would conceive a hearty contempt for him. It is *not* a boy's book, at all. It will only be read by adults. It is only written for adults.

Moreover, the book is plenty long enough, as it stands. It is about 900 pages of MS., & may be 1000 when I shall have finished "working up" vague places so it would make from 130 to 150 pages of the Atlantic – about what the Foregone Conclusion made, isn't it?

I would dearly like to see it in the Atlantic, but I doubt if it would pay the publishers to buy the privilege, or me to sell it. Bret Harte has sold his novel (same size as mine, I should say) to Scribner's Monthly for $6,500 (publication to begin in September, I think,) & he gets a royalty of $7\frac{1}{2}$ per cent from Bliss in book form afterward. He gets a royalty of ten per cent on it in England (issued in serial numbers) & the same royalty on it in book form afterward, & is to receive an advance payment of five hundred pounds the day the first No. of the serial appears. If I could do as well, here & there, with mine, it might possibly pay me, but I seriously doubt it – though it is likely I could do better in England than Bret, who is not widely known there.

You see I take a vile, mercenary view of things – but then my household expenses are something almost ghastly.

By & by I shall take a boy of twelve & run him on through life (in the first person) but not Tom Sawyer – he would not be a good character for it.

I wish you would promise to read the MS of Tom Sawyer some time, & see if you don't really decide that I am right in closing with him as a boy – & point out the most glaring defects for me. It is a tremendous favor to ask, & I expect you to refuse, & would be ashamed to expect you to do otherwise. But the thing has been so many months in my mind that it seems a relief to snake it out. I don't know any other person whose judgment I could venture to take fully & entirely. Don't hesitate about saying no, for I know how your time is taxed, & I would have honest need to blush if you said yes.

Osgood & I are "going for" the puppy Gill on infringement of trademark. To win one or two suits of this kind will set literary folks on a firmer bottom. The N. Y. Tribune doesn't own the world – I wish Osgood would sue it for stealing Holmes's poem. Wouldn't it be gorgeous to sue Whitelaw Read for *petty larceny?* I will promise to go into court & swear I think him capable of stealing pea-nuts from a blind pedlar.

Mrs. C. grows stronger. Susie is down with a fever. Kindest regards to you all.

YRS EVER

CLEMENS

TO WILLIAM DEAN HOWELLS
23 NOVEMBER 1875, HARTFORD, CONN.

HARTFORD, NOV. 23/75

MY DEAR HOWELLS:

Herewith is the proof. In spite of myself, how awkwardly I do jumble words together; & how often I do use three words where one would answer – a thing I am always trying to guard against. I shall become as slovenly a writer as Charles Francis Adams if I don't look out. {That is said in jest; because of course I do not seriously fear getting so bad as that. I never *shall* drop so far toward his & Bret Harte's level as to catch myself saying "It must have been wiser to have believed that he might have accomplished it if he could have felt that he would have been supported by those who should have &c., &c., &c."} The reference to Bret Harte reminds me that I often accuse him of being a deliberate imitator of Dickens; & this in turn reminds me that I have charged unconscious plagiarisms upon Charley Warner; & *this* in turn reminds me that I have been delighting my soul for two weeks over a bran new & ingenious way of beginning a novel – & behold, all at once it flashes upon me that *Charley Warner* originated the idea 3 years ago & told me about it! Aha! So much for self-righteousness! I am well repaid. Here are 108 pages of MS, new & clean, lying disgraced in the waste paper basket, & I am beginning the novel over again in an un-stolen way. I would not wonder if I am the worst literary thief in the world, without knowing it.

It is glorious news that you like Tom Sawyer so well. I mean to see to it that your review of it shall have plenty of time to appear before the other notices. Mrs. Clemens decides with you that the book should issue as a book for boys, pure & simple – & so do I. It is surely the correct idea. As to that last chapter, I think of just leaving it off & adding nothing in its place. Something told me that the book was done when I got to that point – & so the strong temptation to put Huck's life at the widow's into detail instead of generalizing it in a paragraph, was resisted. Just send Sawyer to me by Express – I enclose money for it. If it should get lost it will be no great matter.

Company interfered last night, & so "Private Theatricals" goes over till this evening, to be read aloud. Mrs. Clemens is mad, but the story will take *that* all out. This is going to be a splendid winter night for fireside reading, anyway.

I am almost at a dead stand-still with my new story, on account of the misery of having to do it all over again.

We-all send love to you-all.

YRS EVER

MARK

HARTFORD, JAN 18/76

MY DEAR HOWELLS:

Thanks, & ever so many, for the good opinion of Tom Sawyer. Williams has made about 200 rattling pictures for it – some of them very dainty. Poor devil, what a genius he has, & how he does murder it with rum. He takes a book of mine, & without suggestion from anybody builds no end of pictures just from his reading of it.

There [never] was a man in the world so grateful to another as I was to you day before yesterday, when I sat down (in still rather wretched health) to set myself to the dreary & hateful task of making final revision of Tom Sawyer, & discovered, upon opening the package of MS that your pencil marks were scattered all along. This was splendid, & swept away all labor. Instead of *reading* the MS, I simply hunted out the pencil marks & made the emendations which they suggested. I reduced the boy-battle to a curt paragraph; I finally concluded to cut the Sunday-school speech down to the first two sentences, (leaving no suggestion of satire, since the book is to be for boys & girls; I tamed the various obscenities until I judged that [they] no longer carried offense. So, at a single sitting I began & finished a revision which I had supposed would occupy 3 or 4 days & leave me mentally & physically fagged out at the end. I was careful not to inflict the MS upon you until I had thoroughly & painstakingly revised it. Therefore, the only faults left were those that would discover themselves to others, not me – & these you had pointed out.

There was one expression which perhaps you overlooked. When Huck is complaining to Tom of the rigorous system in vogue at the widow's, he says the servants harass him with all manner of compulsory decencies, & he winds up by saying, "and they comb me all to hell." (No exclamation point.) Long ago, when I read that to Mrs. Clemens, she made no comment; another time I created occasion to read that chapter to her aunt & her mother (both sensitive & loyal subjects of the kingdom of heaven, so to speak,) & *they* let it pass. I was glad, for it was the most natural remark in the world for that boy to make (& he had been allowed few privileges of speech in the book); when I saw that you, too, had let it go without protest, I was glad, & afraid, too – afraid you hadn't observed it.

Did you? And did you question the propriety of it? Since the book is now professedly & confessedly a boy's & girl's book, that dern word bothers me some, nights, but it never did until I had ceased to regard the volume as being for adults.

Don't bother to answer *now*, (for you've writing enough to do without allowing me to add to the burden,) but tell me when you see me again.

Which we do hope will be next Saturday or Sunday or Monday. Couldn't you come now & mull over the alterations which you are going to make in your MS, & make them after you [get] back? Wouldn't it *assist* the work, if you dropped out of harness & routine for a day or two & have that sort of revivification which comes of a holiday-forgetfulness of the workshop? I can always work after I've been to your house; & if you will come to mine, now, & hear the club toot their various horns over the exasperating metaphysical question which I mean to lay before them in the disguise of a literary extravaganza, it would just brace you up like a cordial. As for Ward, you [can] fix it easily with him for the next week.

(I feel sort of mean, trying to persuade a man to put down a critical piece of work at a critical time, but yet I am honest in thinking it would not hurt the work nor impair your interest in it to come, under the circumstances.) Mrs. Clemens says, "Maybe the Howellses could come *Monday* if they cannot come Saturday; ask them; it is worth trying." Well, how's that? *Could* you? It would be splendid if you could. Drop me a postal card – I should have a twinge of conscience if I forced you to write a letter, (I am honest about that,) – & if you find you can't make out to come, tell me that you bodies will come the *next* Saturday if the thing be possible, & stay over Sunday.

YRS EVER
MARK.

TO JACOB H. BURROUGH
1 NOVEMBER 1876, HARTFORD, CONN.

HARTFORD NOV. 1/76

MY DEAR BURROUGH
    As you describe me I can picture myself as I was, 22 years ago.

The portrait is correct. You think I have grown some; upon my word there was room for it. You have described a callow fool, a self-sufficient ass, a mere human tumble-bug, stern in air, heaving at his bit of dung & imagining he is re-modeling the world & is entirely capable of doing it right. Ignorance, intolerance, egotism, self-assertion, opaque perception, dense & pitiful chuckle-headedness – & an almost pathetic unconsciousness of it all. That is what I was at 19–20; & that is what the average Southerner is at 60 to-day. Northerners, too, of a certain grade. It is of children like this that voters are made. And such is the primal source of our government! A man hardly knows whether to swear or cry over it.

I think I comprehend their position there – perfect freedom to vote just as you choose, provided you choose to vote as *other people* think – social ostracism, otherwise. The same thing exists here among the Irish. An Irish republican is a pariah among his people. Yet that race find fault with the same spirit in Know-Nothingism.

Fortunately a good deal of experience of men enabled me to choose my residence wisely. I live in the freest corner of the country. There are no social disabilities between me & my democratic personal friends. We break the bread & eat the salt of hospitality freely together & never dream of such a thing as offering impertinent interference in each other's political opinions.

Don't you ever come to New York again & not run up here to see me. I suppose we were away for the summer when you were east; but no matter, you could have telegraphed & found out. We were at Elmira, N. Y., right on your road, & could have given you a good time if you had allowed us the chance.

Yes, Will Bowen & I have exchanged letters now & then for several years, but I suspecte that I made him mad with my last – shortly after you saw him in St Louis, I judge. There is one thing which I can't stand, & *won't* stand, from many people. That is, sham sentimentality – the kind a school-girl puts into her graduating composition; the sort that makes up the Original Poetry column of a country newspaper; the rot that deals in "the happy days of yore," "the sweet yet melancholy past," with its "blighted hopes" & its "vanished dreams" – & all that sort of drivel. Will's were *always* of this stamp. I stood it years. When I get a letter like that from a grown man & he a widower with a family, it gives me the bowel complaint. And I just told Will Bowen so, last summer. I told him to stop being 16 at 40; told him to stop drooling about the sweet yet melancholy past, & take a pill. I said there was but one solitary thing about the past worth remembering, & that was the fact that it *is* the past – can't be restored. Well, I exaggerated some of these truths a little – but only a little – but my idea was to kill his nasty sham sentimentality once & forever, & so make a good fellow of him again. I went to the unheard-of trouble of re-writing the letter & saying the same harsh things softly, so as to sugar-coat the anguish & make it a little more endurable; & I asked him to write & thank me honestly for doing him the best & kindliest favor than any friend ever *had* done him – but he hasn't done it yet. Maybe he will, sometime. I am grateful to God that I got that letter off before he was married (I get that news from you,) else he would just have slobbered all over me & drowned me when that event happened.

I enclose photograph for the young ladies. I will remark that I do not wear seal-skin for grandeur, but because I found, when I used to lecture in the winter, that nothing else was able to keep a man warm sometimes, in these high latitudes. I wish you had sent pictures of yourself & family – I'll trade picture for picture with you, straight through, if you are commercially inclined.

> YOUR OLD FRIEND
> SAM^L L. CLEMENS

TO ORION CLEMENS
23 MARCH 1878, HARTFORD, CONN.

HARTFORD, MCH 23

MY DEAR BRO –

Every man must *learn* his trade – not pick it up. God requires that he learn it by slow & painful processes. The apprentice-hand, in blacksmithing, in medicine, in literature, in *every*thing is a thing that can't be hidden. It always shows.

But happily there is a market for apprentice-work, else the Innocents Abroad would have had no sale. Happily, too, there's a wider market for some sorts of apprentice-literature than there is for the very best of journey-work. This work of yours is exceedingly crude, but its very over-enthusiasms should commend it to the uncritical common herd. I am free to say it is *less* crude than I expected it to be, & considerably better work than I believed you could do.

It is too crude to offer to any prominent periodical, so I shall speak to the N. Y. Weekly people. To publish it in that will be to bury it. Why could not some good genius have sent me to the N. Y. Weekly with my apprentice-sketches?

You should not publish it in book form at all – for this reason: it is only an imitation of Verne, at last – it is not a burlesque. But I think it may be regarded as proof that Verne cannot *be* burlesqued.

In accompanying notes I have suggested that you vastly modify the first visit to hell, & leave out the second visit altogether. Nobody would or ought to print those things.

You are not advanced enough in literature to venture upon a matter requiring so much practice. Let me show you what a man has got to go through:

Nine years ago I mapped out my "Journey in Heaven." I discussed it with literary friends whom I could trust to keep it to themselves. I gave it a deal of thought, from time to time. After a year or more, I wrote it up. It was not a success. Five years ago I wrote it again, altering the plan. That MS is at my elbow now. It was a considerable improvement on the first attempt, but still *it* wouldn't do. Last year & year before I talked frequently with Howells about the subject, & he kept urging me to do it again. So I thought & thought, at odd moments, & at last I struck what I considered to be the right plan! Mind, I never have altered the *ideas*, from the first – the *plan* was the difficulty. When Howells was here last, I laid before him the whole story without referring to my MS., & he said: "You *have* got it, sure, this time. But drop the idea of making mere magazine stuff of it. Don't waste it. Print it by itself – publish it first in England – ask Dean Stanley to endorse it, which will draw *some* of the teeth of the religious press, & then reprint in America."

I doubt my ability to get Dean Stanley to do anything of the sort, but I shall do the rest – & this is all a *secret*, which you must not divulge.

Now look here – I have tried, all these years, to think of some way of "doing" hell, too – & have always had to give it up. Hell, in my book, will not occupy five pages of MS, I judge – it will be only covert hints, I suppose, & quickly dropped. I may end by not even referring to it. And mind you, in my opinion you will find that *you* can't write up hell so it will stand printing.

Neither Howells nor I believe in hell or the divinity of the Savior – but no matter, the Savior is none the less a sacred Personage &

a man should have no desire or disposition to refer to him lightly, profanely, or otherwise than with the profoundest reverence. The only safe thing is not to introduce him or refer to him at all, I suspect.

I have entirely re-written one book 3 (perhaps 4) times, changing the plan every time – 1200 pages of MS wasted & burned – & shall tackle it again, one of these years & may succeed at last. Therefore you need not expect to get *your* book right the first time.

Go to work & re-vamp or re-write it. God only exhibits his thunder-&-lightning at intervals, & so they always command attention. These are God's adjectives. You thunder-&-lighten too much; the reader ceases to get under the bed, by & by.

Mr. Perkins will send you & Ma your checks when we are gone. But don't write him, ever, except a single line in case he forgets the checks – for the man is driven to death with work.

I see you are already half promising yourself a money-return for your book. In my experience, previously counted chickens never *do* hatch. How many of mine I have counted! – & never a one of them but failed! It is much better to hedge disappointment by not counting. Unexpected money is a delight. The same sum is a bitterness when you expected more.

My time in America is growing mighty short. Perhaps we can manage in this way:

Imprimis, if the N. Y. Weekly people know that you are my brother, they will turn that fact into an advertisement – a thing of value to *them*, but not to you & me. This must be prevented. I will write them a note to say you have a friend near Keokuk, *Charles S. Miller*, who has a MS for sale which you think is a pretty clever travesty on Verne; & if they want it they might write to him in your care. Then if any correspondence ensues between you & them, let *Mollie* write for *you* & sign your name – your own handwriting representing Miller's.

Keep yourself out of sight till you make a strike on your own merits – there is no other way to get a fair verdict upon your merits.

Later – I've written the note to Smith, & with nothing in it which he can use as an advertisement.

I'm called – Good-bye – love to you both. We leave here next Wednesday for Elmira; we leave there Apl 9 or 10 – & sail 11th.

YR BRO

SAM

[enclosure, first 6 pages (about 60 percent) missing:]

billion is replaced once every 30 years, & that therefore about 100,000 people die daily – & here is the same guess on page 267.

279 The story is sufficient in itself – there should be no comments, humorous or otherwise.

281 The descriptive language is generally too strong, & too much of it.

289–90 Too vivid.

Curious again – all this about hell, when I was led to write an exhaustive account of heaven some weeks ago – an account which I gave to Howells by word of mouth some time ago & which he repeatedly urged me to put upon paper. – which I did, & he thinks well of it.

300 This is simply offensive.

310 Chaffy talk does not seem to come properly from old Biblical people.

311 "Next came 100 people who looked *like* they had just been, &c"

That wretched Missourianism occurs in every chapter. You mean, "AS IF."

Finally. I think the Nomad marriage, religion, & the events in the church are not good enough or interesting enough to retain.

I think all of the second visit to hell should come out, & that the first visit should be modified into delicate & convincing satire.

Moreover, one should not call Verne harsh names. His crime should be sarcastically *suggested*, rather than *told*.

Once more – Franklin did not need to fast 4 years, or at all.

I still don't quite understand how the Eskimo came to be imprisoned in that hammock in the cigar boat – I thought he traveled on the backs of those ichthiosauri.

TO WILLIAM DEAN HOWELLS
4 MAY 1878, FRANKFURT ON THE MAIN, GERMANY

MAY 4
FRANKFORT ON THE MAIN

ENGLISCHER HOF. FRANKFURT A/M.

MY DEAR HOWELLS – I only propose to write a single line to

say we are still around. Ah, I have such a deep, grateful, unutterable sense of being "out of it all." I think I foretaste some of the advantage of being dead. Some of the joy of it. I don't read any newspapers or care for them. When people tell me England has declared war, I drop the subject, feeling that it is none of my business; when they tell me Mrs. Tilton has confessed & Mr. B. denied, I say both of them have done that before, therefore let the worn stub of the Plymouth white-wash brush be brought out once more, & let the faithful spit on their hands & get to work again regardless of me – for I am out of it all.

We had 2 almost devilish weeks at sea (& I tell you Bayard Taylor is a really lovable man – which you already knew); then we staid a week in the beautiful, the *very* beautiful city of Hamburg; & since then we have been fooling along, 4 hours per day by rail, with a courier, spending the other 20 in hotels whose enormous bedchambers & private parlors are an overpowering marvel to me. Day before yesterday, in Cassel, we had a love of a bedroom 31 feet long, & a parlor with 2 sofas, 12 chairs, a writing desk & 4 tables scattered around here & there in it. Made of red silk, too, by George.

The times & times I wish you were along! *You* could throw some fun into the journey; whereas I go on, day by day, in a smileless state of solemn admiration.

What a paradise this land is! What clean clothes, what good faces, what tranquil contentment, what prosperity, what genuine freedom, what superb government! And I am so happy, for I am responsible for none of it. I am only here to enjoy.

How charmed I am when I overhear a German word which I understand!

With love from us 2 to you 2.

MARK

P.S. – We are not taking six days to go from Hamburg to Heidelberg because we prefer it. Quite the contrary. Mrs. Clemens picked up a dreadful cold & sore throat on board ship & still keeps them in stock – so she could only travel 4 hours a day. She wanted to dive straight through, but I had different notions about the wisdom of it. I found that 4 hours a day was the best she could do. Before I forget it, our permanent address is Care Messrs. Koester & Co., Bankers, Heidelberg. We go there tomorrow.

Poor Susie! From the day we reached German soil, we have required Rosa to speak German to the children – which they hate with all their souls. The other morning, in Hanover, Susie came to me (from Rosa, in the nursery,) & said, in halting syllables, "Papa, wie viel Uhr ist es?" – then turned, with pathos in her big eyes, & said, "Mamma, I wish Rosa was made in English."

TO WILLIAM DEAN HOWELLS
30 JANUARY 1879, MUNICH, GERMANY

1A KARLSSTRASSE, 2E STOCK, MUNICH, JAN. 30

MY DEAR HOWELLS –

It took a great burden off my heart this morning when your letter arrived & I found my 2 articles had not been lost *in transitu.* I was to going to write today & ask about them. Ordinarily I should trouble myself but little about the loss of 2 articles, for the loss could not rob me of the chief thing, i.e., the pleasure the writing them had afforded me, – but when a body is yoked down to the grinding out of a 600-page 8-vo. book, to lose a chapter is like losing a child. I was not at all sure that I should use both of those chapters in my book, but to *have them around,* in case of need, would give that added comfort which comes of having a life-preserver handy in a ship which *might* go down though nobody is expecting such a thing. But you speak so kindly of them that I shall probably venture to use them both. I have destroyed such lots of MS written for this book! And I suppose there are such lots left which ought to be destroyed. If it should be, it *shall* be, – that is certain. I have rung in that fragrant account of the Limberger cheese & the coffin-box full of guns. Had I better leave that out? Give me your plain, square advice, for I propose to follow it. The back of my big job is broken, now, for the book is rather more than half done; so from this out I can tear up MS without a pang.

You sent me 2 copies of the *first* slip of Pitcairn, but no copy of the remaining half of the article. However, I have mailed one first-slip to Chatto & Windus & asked them to send me one of their second-slips, in exchange.

I wish I *could* give those sharp satires on European life which you mention, but of course a man can't write successful satire except he be in a calm judicial good-humor – whereas I *hate* travel, & I *hate* hotels, & I *hate* the opera, & I *hate* the Old Masters – in truth I don't ever seem to be in a good enough humor with ANYthing to *satirize* it; no, I want to stand up before it & *curse* it, & foam at the mouth, – or take a club & pound it to rags & pulp. I have got in two or three chapters about Wagner's Operas, & managed to do it without showing temper – but the strain of another such effort would burst me. (Mind, whatever I say about the book is a *secret*; – my publisher shall know little or nothing about the book till he gets the MS, for I can't trust his tongue – I am trusting *nobody* but you & Twichell. I like mighty well to tell my plans & swap opinions about them, but I don't like them to get around.) I have exposed the German language in two or three chapters, & have shown what I consider to be the needed improvements in it. I mean to describe a German newspaper, but not satirically – simply in a plain matter of fact way. I wrote the chapter satirically, but found that a plain statement was rather the better satire. In my book I allow it to appear, – casually & without stress, – that I am over here to make the tour of Europe *on foot*. I am in pedestrian costume, as a general thing, & *start* on pedestrian tours, but mount the first conveyance that offers, making but slight explanation or excuse, & endeavoring to seem unconscious that this is not legitimate pedestrianizing. My second object here is to become a German scholar; my third, to study Art, & learn to paint. I have a notion to put a few hideous pen & ink sketches of my own in my book, & explain their merits & defects in the technical language of art. But I shall not put many in – better artists shall do nineteen-twentieths of the illustrating. I have made a pedestrian trip up the Neckar to Heilbronn, with muslin-wound hat, leathern leggings, sun-umbrella, alpenstock, &c – *by rail*, – with my agent, – I employ an agent on a salary, & he does the real work when any is to be done, though I appropriate his emotions to myself & do his marvelling for him – & in yesterday's chapter we have started back to Heidelberg on a raft, & are having a good time. The raft is mine, since I have chartered it, & I shall pick up useful passengers here & there to tell me the legends of the ruined castles, & other things – perhaps the Captain who brought the news of the Pitcairn revolution. I have invented quite a nice little legend for Dilsberg Castle, & maybe that is the only one I *shall* invent – don't know.

I want to make a book which people will *read*, – & I shall make it profitable reading in spots – in spots merely *because* there's not much material for a larger amount. And as soon as it is off my hands I shall take up Wakeman & Heaven at once.

Confound that February number, I wish it would fetch along the Lady of the Aroostook, for we are pretty impatient to see her again. All right, tell me about the Pacific coast trip – I wish we were going with you.

So Aldrich is gone – but he won't go to Egypt if this plague continues to spread. I sent him a paragraph from a German paper the other day: Scientist discovered a Roman vessel near Regensburg of a sort which has long been supposed to have been used to burn fragrant herbs in during cremation of corpses, but there was no proof. He set this one on the stove one day, & presently it began to send out a sweet perfume – resumed its office after a vacation of 1500 years. Thought Aldrich could do a sonnet on it.

Write me here, to above address – for even if the plague drives us away, we shall see to it that our letters follow us all right this time.

With our loves to you & yours –

YRS EVER
MARK.

We missed Mead in Florence – he arrived from Paris right after we left. F.

[*remainder in pencil:*]
over

P.S. Are you in the new house?

Père Jacomo is here & has called twice, but I was out both times, Mrs. C was out once & lying down in undress uniform the other time & had to excuse herself. He has never come near us since. I have written to Venice to ask for his address (he didn't leave us any) & am hoping to get it.

Bay Clemens came within an ace of dying, last week – a mighty close shave. She is about well, now.

TO OLIVIA L. CLEMENS
11 NOVEMBER 1879 2ND OF 2, CHICAGO, ILL.

CHICAGO, NOV. 11, PALMER HOUSE

LIVY DARLING,

I am getting a trifle leg-weary. Dʳ Jackson called & dragged me out of bed at noon, yesterday, & then went off. I went down stairs &

was introduced to some scores of people, & among them an elderly
German gentleman named Raster, who said his wife owed her life
to me – hurt in the Chicago fire & lay menaced with death a long
time, but the Innocents Abroad kept her mind in a cheerful attitude, & so, with the doctor's help for the body she pulled through
– she had said yesterday morning, "Mark Twain is here, that more
interests me than Grant & all the others." There was something
very hearty & simple & winning about this German gentleman, &
when he asked me to drive with him & home & give his wife a
surprise I said all right, & we jumped into a hack & drove there &
had a pipe & a bottle of Rhein wine & a cordial fifteen-minute visit
with madam. Then they drove me to D.ʳ Jackson's & I had an
hour's visit with Mrs. Jackson. Started to walk down Michigan
Avenue, got a few steps on my way & met an erect, soldierly looking
young gentleman who offered his hand, said "Mr. Clemens,
I believe – I wish to introduce myself – you were pointed out to me
yesterday as I was driving down street – my name is Grant."
      "Col. Fred. Grant?"
      "Yes. My house is not ten steps away, & I would like you to come
& have a talk & a pipe, & let me introduce my wife."
      So we turned back & entered the house next to Jackson's &
talked something more than an hour and smoked many pipes
& had a sociable good time. His wife is very gentle & intelligent &
pretty, & they have a cunning little girl nearly as big as Bay but
only 3 years old. They wanted me to come in & spend an evening,
after the banquet, with them & Gen. Grant after this grand pow-
wow is over, but I said I was going home Friday. Then they asked
me to come Friday afternoon, when they & the General will
receive a few friends, & I said I would. Col. Grant said he & Gen.
Sherman used the Innocents Abroad as their guide book when
they were on their travels.
      I stepped in next door & took D.ʳ Jackson to the hotel & we
played billiards from 7 till 10.30 PM & then went to a beer mill to
meet some twenty Chicago journalists – talked, sang songs & made
speeches till 6 o'clock this morning. Nobody got in the least degree
"under the influence," & we had a pleasant time. Read & a while
in bed, slept till 11, shaved, went to breakfast at noon, & by mistake
got into the servants' hall. However, I remained there & breakfasted with twenty or thirty male & female servants, though I had
a table to myself.
      A temporary structure, clothed & canopied with flags, had been

erected at the hotel front, & connected with the second story windows of a drawing room. It was for Gen. Grant to stand on & review the procession. Sixteen persons, besides reporters, had tickets for this place, & a seventeenth was issued for me. I was there, looking down on the packed & struggling crowd when Gen. Grant came forward & was saluted by the cheers of the multitude & the waving of ladies' handkerchiefs – for the windows & roofs of all neighboring buildings were massed full of life. Gen. Grant bowed to the people two or three times, then approached my side of the platform & the mayor pulled me forward & introduced me. It was dreadfully conspicuous. The General said a word or so – I replied, & then said, "But I'll step back, General, I don't want to interrupt your speech."

"But I'm not going to make any – stay where you are – I'll get you to make it for me."

Gen. Sherman came on the platform wearing the uniform of a full General, & you should have heard the cheers. Gen. Logan was going to introduce me, but I didn't want any more conspicuousness.

When the head of the procession passed it was grand to see Sheridan, in his military cloak & his plumed chapeau, sitting as erect & rigid as a statue on his immense black horse – by far the most martial figure I ever saw. And the crowd roared again.

It was chilly, & Gen. Deems lent me his overcoat until night. He came a few minutes ago – 5.45 P.M., & got it, but brought Gen. Willard, who lent me his for the rest of my stay, & will get another for himself when he goes home to dinner. Mine is much too heavy for this warm weather.

I have a seat on the stage at Haverley's Theatre, to-night, where the Army of the Tennessee will receive Gen. Grant, & where Gen. Sherman will make a speech. At midnight I am to attend a meeting of the Owl Club.

I love you ever so much, my darling, & am hoping to get a word from you *yet*.

SAM^L

CHI[C]AGO, NOV. 12/79

Livy darling, it was a great time. There were perhaps thirty people on the stage of the theatre, & I think I never sat elbow-to-elbow with so many historic names before. Grant, Sherman, Sheridan, Schofield, Pope, Logan, Auger, & so on. What an iron man Grant is! He sat facing the house, with his right leg crossed over his left & his right boot-sole tilted up at an angle, & his left hand & arm reposing on the arm of his chair – you note that position? Well, when glowing references were made to *other* grandees on the stage, those grandees always showed a trifle of nervous consciousness – & as these references came frequently, the nervous changes of position & attitude were also frequent. But Grant! – *he* was under a tremendous & ceaseless bombardment of praise & gratulation, but as true as I'm sitting here he never moved a muscle of his body for a single instant, during 30 minutes! You could have played him on a stranger for an effigy. Perhaps he never *would* have moved, but at last a speaker made such a particularly ripping & blood-stirring remark about him that the audience rose & roared & yelled & stamped & clapped an entire minute – Grant sitting as serene as ever – when Gen. Sherman stepped to him, laid his hand affectionately on his shoulder, bent respectfully down & whispered in his ear. Then Grant got up & bowed, & the storm of applause swelled into a hurricane. He sat down, took about the same position & froze to it till by & by there was another of those deafening & protracted roars, when Sherman made him get up & bow again. He broke up his attitude once more – to the extent of something more than a hair's breadth – to indicate me to Sherman when the house was keeping up a determined & persistent call for me, & poor bewildered Sherman, (who did not know me,) was peering abroad over the packed audience for me, not knowing I was only three feet from him & most conspicuously located. (Gen. Sherman was Chairman.)

One of the most illustrious individuals on that stage was "old Abe," the historic war eagle. He stood on his perch – the old savage-eyed rascal – three or four feet behind Gen. Sherman, & as he had been in nearly every battle that was mentioned by the orators his soul was probably stirred pretty often, though he was too proud to let on.

Read Logan's bosh, & try to imagine a burly & magnificent Indian, in General's uniform, striking a heroic attitude & getting that stuff off in the style of a declaiming school-boy.

{———}

Please put the enclosed scraps in the drawer & I will scrap-book them.

I only staid at the Owl Club till 3 this morning & drank little or nothing. Went to sleep without whisky. Ich liebe dich.

SAML

[*in margin:*] Sentinels walked the stage all the evening.

TO OLIVIA L. CLEMENS
14 NOVEMBER 1879, CHICAGO, ILL.

CHICAGO, NOV. 14/79.

A little after 5 in the *morning*.

I've just come to my room. Livy darling, I guess this was the memorable night of my life. By George, I never was so stirred since I was born. I heard four speeches which I can never forget. One by Emory Storrs, one by Gen. Vilas (O, wasn't it wonderful!) one by Gen. Logan (mighty stirring), one by somebody whose name escapes me, & one by that splendid old soul, Col. Bob Ingersoll, – oh, it was just the supremest combination of English words that was ever put together since the world began. My soul, how hand-some he looked, as he stood on that table, in the midst of those 500 shouting men, & poured the molten silver from his lips! Lord, what an organ is human speech when it is played by a master! All these speeches may look dull in print, but how the lightnings glared around them when they were uttered, & how the crowd roared in response! It was a great night, a marvelous night, a memorable night. I am so richly repaid for my journey – & how I did wish with all my whole heart that you were there to be lifted into the very seventh heaven of enthusiasm, as I was. The army songs, the milit-ary music, the crashing applause – Lord bless me, it was unspeakable.

Out of compliment they placed me last in the list – No. 15 – I was to "hold the crowd" – & bless my life I was in awful terror when No. 14 rose at 2 o'clock this morning & killed *all* the enthusiasm by delivering the flattest, insipidest, silliest of all responses to "Woman" that ever a weary multitude listened to. There wasn't a sign of applause & the man ended almost in funereal silence. Then Gen. Sherman (Chairman) announced my toast, & the crowd gave me a good round of applause as I mounted on top of the dinner table, but it was only on account of my name, nothing more, – they were all tired & wretched. They let my first sentence go in silence, till I paused & added "we stand on common ground" – then they burst forth like a hurricane & I saw that I *had* them! From that time on, I stopped at the end of each sentence, & let the tornado of applause & laughter sweep around me. – & when I closed with "And if the child is but the prophecy of the man, there are mighty few will doubt that he succeeded," *I* say it who oughtn't to say it, the house came down with a crash. For two hours & a half, now, I've been shaking hands & listening to congratulations. Gen. Sherman said, "Lord bless you, my boy, I don't know how you do it – it's a secret that's beyond me – but it was great – give me your hand again."

And do you know, Gen. Grant sat through fourteen speeches like a graven image, but I fetched him! I broke him up, utterly! He told me he laughed till the tears came & every bone in his body ached. (And do you know, the biggest part of the success of the speech lay in the fact that the audience *saw* that for once in his life he had been knocked out of his iron serenity.)

Bless your soul, 'twas immense. I never was so proud in my life. Lots & lots of people – hundreds, I might say – told me my speech was the triumph of the evening – which was a lie. Ladies, Tom, Dick & Harry – even the policemen – captured me in the halls & shook hands, & scores of army officers said "We shall always be grateful to you for coming." General Pope came to hunt me up – I was afraid to speak to him on that theatre stage, last night, thinking it might be presumptuous to tackle a man so high up in military history. Gen. Schofield, & other historic men, paid their compliments. Sheridan was ill & could not come, but I'm to go with a General of his staff & see him before I go to Col. Grant's. Gen. Augur – well, I've talked with them *all*, received invitations from them all – from people living everywhere – & as I said before, it's a memorable night. I wouldn't have missed it for anything in the world.

But my sakes, you should have heard Ingersoll's speech on that table! Half an hour ago he ran across me in the crowded halls & put his arms about me & said "Mark, if I live a hundred years, I'll always be grateful for your speech – Lord what a supreme thing it was!" But I told him it wasn't any use to talk, *he* had walked off with the honors of that occasion by something of a majority. Bully boy is Ingersoll – traveled with him in the cars the other day, & you can make up your mind we had a good time.

Of *course* I forgot to go & pay for my hotel car & so secure it, but the army officers told me an hour ago to rest easy, they would go at once, at this unholy hour of the night & compel the railways to do their duty by me, & said "You don't need to *request* the Army of the Tennessee to do your desires – you can *command* its services."

Well, I bummed around that banquet hall from 8 in the evening till 2 in the morning, talking with people & listening to speeches, & I never ate a single bite or took a sup of anything but ice water; so if I seem excited now, it is the intoxication of supreme enthusiasm. By george, it was a grand night, a historical night.

And now it is a quarter past 6 A.M. – so good bye & God bless you & the Bays, my darlings.

SAM^L

Show it to Joe if you want to – I saw some of his friends here.

TO WILLIAM DEAN HOWELLS
17 NOVEMBER 1878, MUNICH, GERMANY

NO. 1A, KARLSTRASSE, 2E STOCK,
MUNICH, NOV. 17.
CARE FRAÜLEIN DAHLWEINER.

MY DEAR HOWELLS –

We arrived here night before last, pretty well fagged: an 8-hour pull from Rome to Florence; a rest there of a day & two nights; then $5\frac{1}{2}$ hours to Bologna; one night's rest; then from noon to 10.30 pm carried us to Trent, in the Austrian Tyrol, where the confounded hotel had not received our message, & so at that miserable hour, in that snowy region, the tribe had to shiver together in fireless rooms while beds were prepared & warmed; then up at 6 in the morning & a noble view of snow-peaks glittering in the rich light of a full moon while the hotel-devils lazily deranged a breakfast for us in the dreary gloom of blinking candles; then a solid 12-hour pull through the loveliest snow-ranges & snow-draped forests – & at 7 pm we hauled up, in drizzle & fog at the domicil which had been engaged for us ten months before. Munich did seem the horriblest place, the most desolate place, the most unendurable place! – & the rooms were *so* small, the conveniences so meagre, & the porcelain stoves so grim, ghastly, dismal, intolerable! So Livy & Clara sat down forlorn, & cried, & I retired to a private place to pray. By & by we all retired to our narrow German beds; & when Livy & I finished talking across the room, it was all decided that we would rest 24 hours, then pay whatever damages were required, & straightway fly to the south of France.

But you see, that was simply fatigue. Next morning the tribe fell in love with the rooms, with the weather, with Munich, & head over heels in love with Fraülein Dahlweiner. We got a larger parlor – an ample one – threw two communicating bedrooms into one, for the children, & now we are entirely comfortable. The only apprehension, now, is that the climate may not be just right for the children – in which case we shall *have* to go to France, but it will be with the sincerest regret.

Now *I* brought the tribe through F from Rome, myself. We never had so little trouble before. The next time anybody has a courier to put out to nurse, I shall not be in the market.

Last night the forlornities had all disappeared; so we gathered around the lamp, after supper, with our beer & my pipe, & in a condition of grateful snugness tackled the new magazines. I read your new story aloud, amid thunders of applause, & we all agreed that Captain Jenness & the old man with the accordion hat are lovely people and most skilfully drawn – & that cabin-boy, too, we like. Of course we are all glad the girl is gone to Venice – for there is no place like Venice. Now I easily understand that the old man couldn't go, because you have a purpose in sending Lyddy by herself; but you could send the old man over in another ship, & we particularly want him along. Suppose you *don't* need him there? What of that? Can't you let him feed the doves? Can't you let him fall in the Canal occasionally? Can't you let his goodnatured purse be a daily prey to guides and beggar-boys? Can't you let the cheerful gondoliers canvas his hat? Can't you let him find peace & rest & fellowship under père Jacopo's kindly wing? (However, you are writing the book, not I, – still, I am one of the people you are writing it for, you understand.) I only want to insist, in a friendly way, that the old man shall shed his sweet influence frequently upon the page – that is all.

The first time we called at the convent, père Jacopo was absent; the next (just at this moment Miss Spaulding spoke up & said something about père Jacopo – there is more in this acting of one mind upon another than people think) time, he was there, & gave us preserved rose-leaves to eat, & talked about you, & Mrs. Howells, & Winnie, & brought out his photographs, & showed us a picture of "the library of your new house," but not so – it was the study in your Cambridge house. He was very sweet & good. He called on us next day; & the day after that we left Venice, after a pleasant sojourn of 3 or 4 weeks. He expects to spend this winter in Munich & will see us often, he said.

Pretty soon I'm going to write something, & when I finish it I shall know whether to put it to itself or in the "Contributor's Club." That "Contributor's Club" was a most happy idea. The idiot does not more unfailingly turn first to the "Drawer" than does the wise man to the "C. C." By the way, *I* think that the man who wrote the paragraph beginning at the bottom of page 643 has said a mighty sound and sensible thing. I wish his suggestion could be adopted.

It is lovely of you to keep that old pipe in such a place of honor.

While it occurs to me, I must tell you Susie's last. She is sorely badgered with dreams; & her stock dream is that she is being eaten up by bears. She is a grave & thoughtful child, as you will remember. Last night she had the usual dream. This morning she stood apart (after telling it,) for some time, looking vacantly at the floor, & absorbed in meditation. At last she looked up, & with the pathos of one who feels he has not been dealt by with even-handed fairness, said, "But mamma, the trouble is, that I am never the *bear*, but always the PERSON." It would not have occurred to me that there might be an advantage, even in a dream, in occasionally being the eater, instead of always the party eaten, but I easily perceived that her point was well taken.

I'm sending to Heidelberg for your letter & Winnie's, & I do hope they haven't been lost. My wife & I send love to you all.

YRS EVER
MARK

TO DAVID WATT BOWSER
20 MARCH 1880, HARTFORD, CONN.

[Don't you let any of this private letter get into print, old fellow.]

FARMINGTON AVENUE, HARTFORD
MARCH 20, 1880.

MY DEAR MASTER BOWSER:

I haven't read the composition, yet – I have only read your letter. I find it isn't wise for ordinary folks to have two interests in their minds at once, else neither of them will get more than a weak & divided attention. This is a marvelously wretched pen, & I will change it.

Would I be a boy again? I will answer:

1. Without any modifying stipulations at all, but just simply be a boy again and start fresh? *NO!*

I have almost always been happy, & usually fortunate. This has been my case, both as boy & man. There is not a cheerfuller person in the world, than I am. I have not the slightest fault to find with my lot. Yet I have no desire to live my life over again. I really am not able to tell why, for I don't know the reasons myself, but that is the way I feel about it.

2. Would I live it over again under certain *conditions?* Certainly I would! The main condition would be that I should emerge from boyhood as a "cub pilot" on a Mississippi boat, & that I should by & by become a pilot, & remain one. The minor conditions would be these: Summer always; the magnolias at Rifle Point always in bloom, so that the dreamy twilight should have the added charm of their perfume; the oleanders on the "coast" always in bloom, likewise; the sugar cane always green – never any "bagasse" burnings; the river always bank-full, so we could run all the chutes – how heavenly that would be! – then in the foot of 63, & in a thousand other places, we should see the thick banks of young willows dipping their leaves into the currentless water, & we could thrash right along against them without any danger of hurting anything; & I would require a new "cut-off" to experiment on, every season – we tried one about a dozen times, one rainy night, & then had to go around, after all – but it was a noble circus while we had it; I should require that there be a dog-watch in the evening, but none in the morning – for a dog-watch in the morning is pure

foolishness; I would rule out the middle watch in the night, except on moonlight nights, because it makes one feel so dreary & low-spirited & forlorn to rouse out of a pleasant sleep at dead midnight & go & perch away up there in the pilot house in the midst of the wide darkness, with apparently nobody alive in the deserted world but him; but the middle watch in summer moonlit nights is a gracious time, especially if the boat steers like a duck, & friends have staid up to keep one company, & sing, & smoke, & spin yarns, and blow the whistle when other boats are met (though I remember that the unpracticed friend from the mainland never blew it right, & consequently always made a little trouble;) & I would have the trips long, & the stays in port short; & my boat should be a big dignified freight boat, with a stately contempt for passenger-hails & a tranquil willingness to "lay up" for fog – being never in a hurry; & her crew should never change, nor ever die; – one such crew I have in mind, & can call their names & see their faces, now: but two decades have done their work upon them, & half are dead, the rest scattered, & the boat's bones are rotting five fathom deep in Madrid Bend. That is the way I would have it all. And in addition, I should require to be notorious among speakers of the English tongue – because I should want to be invited around, a little, you know, & have nice little kindly attentions in cars & ships & other places where such things help out, you see, & keep a body from feeling homesick. And when strangers were introduced I should have them repeat "Mr. Clemens?" doubtfully, & with the rising inflection – & when they were informed that I was the celebrated "Master Pilot of the Mississippi," & immediately took me by the hand & wrung it with effusion, & exclaimed, "O, I know *that* name very well!" I should feel a pleasurable emotion trickling down my spine & know I had not lived in vain.

Yes, under *such* conditions I would most glad[l]y "be a boy" & live this long stretch of time over again – but not under any other conditions, Master Wattie – I mean I wouldn't care to risk re-living my 45 years *without* conditions of a protective nature. It is a hundred to one that in trying to make a better job of the thing on a second trial, I should do worse than I have done this time. I don't wish to take stock in any such risky speculation. If you had reached the threshold of college, would you want to go back & do your schooling all over again?

Do you suppose I shall get any work done to-day if I go gossiping along much longer in this way? Certainly not. Therefore I will stop

– though I had just got down to where I was about to get the hang of this subject, & experience "liberty" in the handling of it, as the preachers say.

No indeed, I have not forgotten your principal at all. She was a very little girl, with a very large spirit, a long memory, a wise head, a great appetite for books, a good mental digestion, with grave ways, & inclined to introspection – an unusual girl. How long ago it was! Another flight backward like this, & I shall begin to realize that I am cheating the cemetery.

YOUR FRIEND & WELL-WISHER

S.L. CLEMENS

P.S. *Now* I have read your composition, & I think it is a very creditable performance. I notice that you use plain, simple language, short words, & brief sentences. That is the way to write English – it is the modern way, & the best way. Stick to it; don't let fluff & flowers & verbosity creep in. When you catch an adjective, kill it. No, I don't mean that, utterly, but kill the most of them – then the rest will be valuable. They weaken when they are close together, they give strength when they are wide apart. An adjective-habit, or a wordy, diffuse, or flowery habit, once fastened upon a person, is as hard to get rid of as any other vice.

I thank you very much for the pleasant things you have said of me.

S.L.C

P.P.S. I have been looking at your report-card, & find it remarkable. Why, I never was marked up 100 in my life, when I was a boy, except for one or two commonplace things, like Good Spelling, & Troublesomeness. You seem to be tolerably slim in the matter of History (5), but you make up for it in the other things. I notice you do not go over 100 in Absence & Tardiness; that is very good indeed; I used to strike 1,000 in those studies, sometimes, when I had my hand in. But between you & me, my boy, I can't seem to have the fullest confidence in that diploma. The teacher's name isn't signed to it; nor your parents'; there haven't *been* 5 months in 1880, yet; & you couldn't carry all that load of "Deportment" at 45, let alone 12. What do you mean by such conduct as those?

ELMIRA, N.Y. AUG. 10

MY DEAR MR. HARRIS:

You can argue *yourself* into the delusion that the principle of life is in the stories themselves & not in their setting; but you will save labor by stopping with that solitary convert, for he is the only intelligent one you will bag. In reality the stories are only alligator pears – one merely eats them for the sake of the salad-dressing. Uncle Remus is most deftly drawn, & is a lovable & delightful creation; he, & the little boy, & their relations with each other, are high & fine literature, & worthy to live, for their own sakes; & certainly the stories are not to be credited with *them*. But enough of this; I seem to be proving to the man that made the multiplication table that twice one are two.

I have been thinking, yesterday & to-day, (plenty of chance to think, as I am abed with lumbago at our little summering farm among the solitudes of the mountain-top,) & I have concluded that I can answer one of your questions with full confidence – thus: Make it a subscription book. Mighty few books that come strictly under the head of *literature* will sell by subscription; but if Uncle Remus won't, the gift of prophecy has departed out of me. When a book *will* sell by subscription, it will sell two or three times as many copies as it would in the trade; & the profit is bulkier because the retail price is greater.

You did not ask me about royalties; still, I will give you a hint, free of charge, which I wish somebody had sold to me for a hundred thousand dollars ten years ago: Make your book at your own expense & pay some publisher ten per cent to sell it for you. On a sale of 50,000 copies this will pay your publisher $15,000, & yourself $35,000 or close upon it. [*But keep these secrets to yourself.*]

You didn't ask me for a subscription-publisher. If you had, I should have recommended Osgood to you. He inaugurates his subscription department with my new book in the fall. I couldn't recommend my former publishers to anybody, except an enemy.

The question which you *did* ask – as to saving all new matter for your new book, instead of first taking the bloom off it in the magazines, etc., I am a little afraid to answer. Osgood can answer that. He will know. You can ask him; or I will, just as you please.

He will arrive from Europe 21ˢᵗ of this month. The fact that you are not offering him the book won't make any difference. There's nothing small about Osgood. He will answer with pleasure, & give his best judgment. Then you can compare it with the opinion of the publisher whom you shall eventually choose, & adopt the suggestion which seems to be soundest.

My idea would be to print *one* yarn in the magazine every 3 months & thus keep before the public & at the same time keep the public unsatisfied; but I wouldn't let them have such generous meals as you have been giving them. For the ficklest people in the world are the public.

Now the doctor has been here & tried to interrupt my yarn about the Golden Arm, but I've got through, anyway.

Of course I *tell it* in the negro dialect – that is necessary; but I have not written it so, for I can't spell it in your matchless way. It is marvelous the way you & Cable spell the negro & creole dialects.

Two grand features are lost in print: the wierd wailing, the rising & falling cadences of the wind, so easily mimicked with one's mouth; & the impressive pauses & eloquent silences, & subdued utterances, toward the end of the yarn (which chain the attention of the children hand & foot, & they sit with parted lips & breathless, to be wrenched limb from limb with the sudden & appalling "YOU got it!") I have so gradually & impressively worked up the last act, with a "grown" audience, as to create a rapt & intense stillness; & then made them jump clear out of their skins, almost, with the final shout. It's a lovely story to tell.

Old Uncle Dan'l, a slave of my uncle's aged 60, used to tell us children yarns every night by the kitchen fire (no other light); & the last yarn demanded, every night, was this one. By this time there was but a ghostly blaze or two flickering about the back-log. We would huddle close about the old man, & begin to shudder with the first familiar words; & under the spell of his impressive delivery we always fell a prey to that climax at the end when the rigid black shape in the twilight sprang at us with a shout.

When you come to glance at the tale you will recollect it – it is as common & familiar as the Tar Baby. Work up the atmosphere with your customary skill & it will "go" in print.

Lumbago seems to make a body garrulous – but you'll forgive it.

TRULY YOURS
S.L. CLEMENS

HARTFORD JAN. 28/82

MY DEAR HOWELLS:

Nobody knows, better than I, that there are times when swearing cannot meet the emergency. How sharply I feel that, at this moment. Not a single profane word has issued from my lips this morning – I have not even had the *impulse* to swear, so wholly ineffectual would swearing have manifestly been, in the circumstances. But I will tell you about it:

About three weeks ago, a sensitive friend, approaching his revelation cautiously, intimated that the N.Y. Tribune was engaged in a kind of crusade against me. This seemed a higher compliment than I deserved; but no matter, it made me very angry. I asked many questions, & gathered, in substance, this: Since Reid's return from Europe, the Tribune had been flinging sneers & brutalities at me with such persistent frequency "as to attract general remark." I was an angered – which is just as good an expression, I take it, as an hungered. Next, I learned that Osgood, among the rest of the "general," was worrying over these constant & pitiless attacks. Next came the testimony of another friend, that the attacks were not merely "frequent," but "almost *daily.*" Reflect upon that: "Almost *daily*" insults, for two months on a stretch. What would you have done?

As for me, I did the thing which was the natural thing for me to do; that is, I set about contriving a plan to accomplish one or the other of two things: 1. Force a peace; or, 2, Get revenge. When I got my plan finished, it pleased me marvelously. It was in six or seven sections, each section to be used in its turn & by itself; the assault to be begun at once with No. 1, & the rest to follow, one after the other, to keep the communications open while I wrote my biography of Reid. I meant to wind up with this latter great work, & then dismiss the subject for good.

Well, ever since then I have worked day & night making notes & collecting & classifying material. I've got collectors at work in England. I went to New York & sat three hours taking evidence while a stenographer set it down. As my labors grew, so also grew my fascination. Malice & malignity faded out of me – or maybe I *drove* them out of me, knowing that a malignant book would hurt

nobody but the fool who wrote it. I got thoroughly in love with this
work; for I saw that I was going to write a book which the very
devils & angels themselves would delight to read, & which would
draw disapproval from nobody but the hero of it, (*and* Mrs.
Clemens, who is bitter against the whole thing.) One part of my
plan was so delicious that I *had* to try my hand on it right away,
just for the luxury of it. I set about it, & sure enough it panned out
to admiration. I wrote that chapter most carefully, & I couldn't
find a fault with it [*It* was not for the biography – no, it belonged
to an immediate & deadlier project.]

Well, five days ago, this thought came into my mind – (from Mrs.
Clemens's): "Wouldn't it be well to make *sure* that the attacks have
been 'almost daily'? – & to also make sure that their number &
character will justify me, in doing what I am proposing to do?"

I at once set a man to work in New York to seek out & copy every
unpleasant reference which had been made to me in the Tribune
from Nov. 1 to date. On my own part I began to watch the current
numbers, for I had subscribed for the paper.

The result arrived from my New York man this morning. O,
what a pitiable wreck of high hopes! The "almost daily" assaults,
for two months, consist of – 1. Adverse criticism of P. & P. from an
enraged idiot in the London Atheneum; 2, Paragraph from some
indignant Englishman in the Pall Mall Gazette who pays me the
vast compliment of gravely rebuking some imaginary ass who has
set me up in the neighborhood of Rabelais; 3, A remark of the Tribune's about the Montreal dinner, touched with an almost invisible
satire; & 4, A remark of the Tribune's about refusal of Canadian
copyright, not complimentary, but not necessarily malicious – &
of course adverse criticism which is not malicious is a thing which
none but fools irritate themselves about.

There – that is the prodigious bugaboo, in its entirety! Can you
conceive of a man's getting himself into a sweat over so diminutive
a provocation? I am sure I can't. What the devil can those friends
of mine have been thinking about, to spread these 3 or 4 harmless
things out into two months of daily sneers & affronts? The whole
offense, boiled down, amounts to just this: *one* uncourteous remark
of the Tribune about my *book* – not me – between Nov. 1 & Dec.
20; & a couple of foreign criticisms (of my *writings*, not me,)
between Nov. 1 & Jan. 26! If I can't stand that amount of friction,
I certainly need reconstruction. Further boiled down, this vast out-
pouring of malice amounts to simply this: *one* jest from the Tribune

(one can make nothing more serious than that out of it.) One jest – & that is all; for the foreign criticisms do not count, they being matters of news, & proper for publication in anybody's newspaper.

And to offset that one jest, the Tribune paid me one compliment, Dec. 23, by publishing my note declining the New York New England dinner, while merely (in the same breath,) *mentioning that* similar letters were read from General Sherman & other men whom we all know to be persons of *real* consequence.

Well, my mountain has brought forth its mouse; & a sufficiently small mouse it is, God knows. And my three weeks' hard work have got to go into the ignominious pigeon-hole. Confound it, I could have earned ten thousand dollars with infinitely less trouble. However, I shouldn't have done it; for I am too lazy, now, in my sere & yellow leaf, to be willing to work for anything but love.

Being now idle once more, I could go to Boston for a day, but House & Koto are coming Monday. They leave again Tuesday. Don't you think you & Mrs Howells could leave the children for a day or two & run down here next Tuesday or Wednesday or Thursday? Don't you think that stepping out of the rut for a moment might be both pleasant & wholesome? Mrs. Clemens & I hope you will feel that way about it & say yes to the proposition. Louis Frèchette is coming to visit us Thursday Feb. 2. If you *can* come, come then, or before, or after – any date will suit us that will suit you.

I kind of envy you people who are permitted for your righteousness' sake, to dwell in a boarding house; not that I should want to *always* live in one, but I should like the change occasionally from this housekeeping slavery to that wild independence. A life of don't-care-a-damn in a boarding house is what I have asked for in many a secret prayer. I shall come by & by & require of you what you have offered me there.

I won't fret you & worry you by insisting & insisting that you & Mrs. Howells come down here, for nothing is quite so utterly hellish as one of these bowelless & implacable insisters – but I shall *yearn* for you just the same.

I wish the godly Osgood would drop in on us a little oftener. All our rooms are finished & habitable, now – & there's rugs enough, you bet! for Mrs. Clemens has been to New York.

YOURS EVER
MARK

QUINCY, ILL, MAY 17/82

Livy darling I am desperately homesick. But I have promised Osgood, & must stick it out; otherwise I would take the train at once & break for home.

I have spent three delightful days in Hannibal, loitering around all day long, examining the old localities & talking with the grey-heads who were boys & girls with me 30 & 40 years ago. It has been a moving time. I spent my nights with John & Helen Garth, three miles from town, in their spacious & beautiful house. They were children with me, & afterwards school-mates. Now they have a daughter 19 or 20 years old. Spent an hour, yesterday, at A. W. Lamb's, who was not married when I saw him last. He married a young lady whom I knew. And now I have been talking with their grown-up sons & daughters. Lieutenant Hickman, the spruce young handsomely-uniformed volunteer of 1846, called on me – a grisly elephantine patriarch of 65, his graces all vanished.

That world which I knew in its blossomy youth is old & bowed & melancholy, now; its soft cheeks are leathery & wrinkled, the fire is gone out in its eyes, & the spring from its step. It will be dust & ashes when I come again. I have been clasping hands with the moribund – & usually they said, "It is for the last time."

Now I am under way again, upon this hideous trip to St Paul, with a heart brimming full of thoughts & images of you & Susie & Bay & the peerless Jean. And so good-night, my love.

SAM

Address, Miss Koto House, Tokio, Japan.

I thank Bay & Susie ever so much for their letters. Jean's Kitty's fall was a good deal of an adventure.

TO WILLIAM DEAN HOWELLS
31 AUGUST 1884, ELMIRA, N.Y.

ELMIRA, AUG 31/84

MY DEAR HOWELLS —

Thank you ever so much for reading that batch of the proof. It was a relief & respite, & I cursed my way through the rest & survived. I was most heavenly glad to get done with it. The sight of a proof-slip is always exasperating to me; but on this book it was maddening.

You see I am trying a new pen. I stood the stylograph as long as I could, & then retired to the pencil. The thing I am trying now is that fountain-pen which is advertised to employ & accommodate itself to any kind of pen. So I selected an ordinary gold pen – a limber one – & sent it to New York & had it cut & fitted to this thing. It goes very well indeed – thus far; but doubtless the devil will be in it by tomorrow.

Mrs. Clemens & I immediately resolved to accept your & Mrs. Howells's invitation for November & be present on your "first night;" but then I remembered that my readings are to begin about Nov. 5; so that spree seems barred. But we shall see. I wish you had to share the affliction of gadding around the country with me; but it couldn't be; it couldn't pay you; & it couldn't easily have been made to pay you. I saw that.

This presidential campaign is too delicious for anything. To see grown men, apparently in their right mind, seriously arguing against a bachelor's fitness for President because he has had private intercourse with a consenting widow! Those grown men know what the bachelor's other alternative was – & tacitly they seem to prefer that to the widow. *Is*n't human nature the most consummate sham & lie that was ever invented? Isn't man a creature to be ashamed of in pretty much all his aspects? Is he really fit for anything but to be stood up on the street corner as a convenience for dogs? Man, "know thyself" – & then thou wilt despise thyself, to a dead moral certainty. Take three quite good specimens – Hawley, Warner, & Charley Clark. Even *I* do not loathe Blaine more than they do; yet Hawley is howling for Blaine, Warner & Clark are eating their daily crow in the paper for him, & all three will vote for him. O Stultification, where is thy sting, O slave where is thy hickory!

I suppose you heard how a marble monument for which St. Gaudens was pecuniarily responsible, burned down in Hartford the other day, uninsured, – for who in the world would ever think of insuring a marble shaft in a cemetery against fire? – & left St. Gaudens out of pocket $15,000. It was a bad day for artists. Gerhardt finished my bust that day, & the work was pronounced admirable by all the kin & friends; but in putting it in plaster (or rather in taking it *out*), next day it got ruined. It was four or five weeks' hard work gone to the dogs. The news flew, & everybody on the farm flocked to the arbor & grouped themselves about the wreck in a profound & moving silence – the farm-help, the colored servants, the German nurse, the children, everybody – a silence interrupted at wide intervals by absent-minded ejaculations wrung from unconscious breasts as the whole size of the disaster gradually worked its way home to the realization of one spirit after another. Some burst out with one thing, some another; the German nurse put up her hands & said, "Oh, Schade! oh, schrecklich!" But Gerhardt said nothing; or almost that. He couldn't word it, I suppose. But he went to work, & by dark had everything thoroughly well under way for a fresh start in the morning, & in three days' time had built a new bust which was a trifle better than the old one – & tomorrow we shall put the finishing touches on it, & it will be about as good a one as nearly anybody could make.

YRS EVER

MARK

If you run across anybody who wants a bust, be sure & recommend Gerhardt on my say-so.

TO WILLIAM DEAN HOWELLS
17 SEPTEMBER 1884 IST OF 2, ELMIRA, N.Y.

ELMIRA, SEPT. 17/84

MY DEAR HOWELLS:

Somehow I can't seem to rest quiet under the idea of your voting for Blaine. I believe you said something about the country & the party. Certainly allegiance to these is well; but as certainly a man's *first* duty is to his own conscience & honor – the party & the country

come second to that, & never first. I don't ask you to vote *at all* –
I only urge you to not soil yourself by voting for Blaine. When you
wrote before, you were able to say the charges against him were
not proven. But you know now that they are proven, & it seems to
me that that bars you & all other honest & honorable men (who
are independently situated) from voting for him.

It is not necessary to vote for Cleveland; the only necessary thing
to do, as I understand it, is that a man shall keep *himself* clean, (by
withholding his vote for an improper man,) even though the party
& the country go to destruction in consequence. It is not *parties* that
make or save countries or that build them to greatness – it is clean
men, clean ordinary citizens, rank & file, the masses. Clean masses
are not made by individuals standing back till the *rest* become
clean.

As I said before, I think a man's first duty is to his own honor;
not to his country & not to his party.

Don't be offended; I mean no offense. I am not so concerned
about the *rest* of the nation, but – well, good-bye.

YS EVER

MARK

TO WILLIAM D. HOWELLS
21 JULY 1885, ELMIRA, N.Y.

ELMIRA, JULY 21, 1885

MY DEAR HOWELLS –

You are really my only author; I am restricted to you; I wouldn't
give a damn for the rest.

I bored through Middlemarch during the past week, with its labored & tedious analyses of feelings & motives, its paltry & tiresome
people, its unexciting & uninteresting story, & its frequent blinding
flashes of single-sentence poetry, philosophy, wit, & what-not, &
nearly died from the overwork. I wouldn't read another of those
books for a farm. I did try to read one other – Daniel Deronda.
I dragged through three chapters, losing flesh all the time, & then
was honest enough to quit, & confess to myself that I haven't *any*
romance-literature appetite, as far as I can see, except for your
books.

But what I started to say, was, that I have just read Part II of Indian Summer, & to my mind there isn't a waste-line in it, or one that could be improved. I read it yesterday, ending with that opinion; & read it again to-day, ending with the same opinion emphasized. I haven't read Part I yet, because that number must have reached Hartford after we left; but we are going to send down town for a copy, & when it comes I am to read both parts aloud to the family. It is a beautiful story, & makes a body laugh all the time, & cry inside, & feel so old & so forlorn; & gives him gracious glimpses of his lost youth that fill him with a measureless regret, & build up in him a cloudy sense of his having been a prince, once, in some enchanted far-off land, & of being an exile now, & desolate – & Lord, no chance to ever get back there again! That is the thing that hurts. Well, you have done it with marvelous facility – & you make all the motives & feelings perfectly clear without analyzing the guts out of them, the way George Eliot does. I can't stand George Eliot, & Hawthorne & those people; I see what they are at, a hundred years before they get to it, & they just tire me to death. And as for The Bostonians, I would rather be damned to John Bunyan's heaven than read that.

YRS EVER
MARK

TO HENRY WARD BEECHER
11 SEPTEMBER 1885, ELMIRA, N.Y.

ELMIRA, N.Y., SEPT. 11/85

MY DEAR MR. BEECHER –

My nephew Webster is in Europe making contracts for the Memoirs. Before he sailed he came to me with a writing, directed to the printers & binders, to this effect:

"Honor no order for a sight or copy of the Memoirs while I am absent, even though it be signed by Mr. Clemens himself."

I gave my permission. There were weighty reasons why I should not only give my permission, but hold it a matter of honor to not dissolve the order or modify it at any time. So I did all of that – said the order should stand undisturbed to the end. If a principal could dissolve his promise as innocently as he can dissolve his

written order unguarded by his promise, I would send you a copy
of the Memoirs instantly. I did not foresee *you*, or I would have
made an exception.

My idea, gained from army men, is that the drunkenness (&
sometimes pretty reckless spreeing, nights,) ceased before he came
east to be Lt. General. [Refer especially to Gen. W^m. B. Franklin.*]
[*written lengthwise in left margin:* *If you could see Franklin & *talk* with
him – then he would unbosom.] It was while Grant was still in the
West that Mr. Lincoln said he wished he could find out what brand
of whisky that fellow used, so he could furnish it to some of the
other generals. Franklin *saw* Grant tumble from his horse drunk,
while reviewing troops in New Orleans. The fall gave him a good
deal of a hurt. He was then on the point of leaving for the Chat-
anooga region. I naturally put "that & that together" when I read
Gen. O. O. Howard's article in the Christian Union 3 or 4 weeks
ago – where he mentions that the new General arrived lame from
a recent accident. [See that article.] And why not write Howard?

Franklin spoke positively of the frequent spreeing. In camp – in
time of war.

Captain Grant was frequently threatened by the Commandant
of his Oregon post with a report to the War Department of his
conduct unless he modified his intemperance. The report would
mean dismissal from the service. At last the report *had* to be made
out; & then, so greatly was the captain beloved, that he was privately informed, & was thus enabled to rush his resignation to
Washington ahead of the report. Did the report *go*, nevertheless?
I don't know. If it did, it is in the War Department now, possibly,
& seeable. I got all this from a regular army man, but I can't name
him to save me.

The only time General Grant ever mentioned liquor to me was
about last April or possibly May. He said:

"If I could only build up my strength! The doctors urge whisky
& champaign; but I can't take them; I can't abide the taste of any
kind of liquor."

Had he made a conquest so complete that even the *taste* of liquor
was become an offense? Or was he so sore over what had been
said about his habit that he wanted to persuade others & likewise
himself that he hadn't even ever *had* any taste for it. It *sounded* like
the latter, but that's no evidence.

He told me in the fall of '84 that there was something the matter
with his throat, & that at the suggestion of his physicians he had

reduced his smoking to one cigar a day. Then he added, in a casual fashion, that he didn't care for *that* one, & seldom smoked it.

I could understand that feeling. He had set out to conquer not the *habit* but the *inclination* – the *desire*. He had gone at the root, not the trunk. It's the *perfect* way & the only true way (I speak from experience.) How I do hate those enemies of the human race who go around enslaving God's free people with PLEDGES – to quit drinking, instead of to quit *wanting* to drink. Any man who will take a pledge ought to be killed – no, flayed alive.

But Sherman & Van Vliet know *everything* concerning Grant; & if you tell them how you want to use the facts, both of them will testify. Regular army men have no concealments about each other; & yet they make their awful statements without shade or color of malice – with a frankness & a child-like naivety, indeed, which is enchanting & stupefying. West Point seems to teach them that, among other priceless things not to be got in any other college in this world. If we talked about our guild-mates as I have heard Sherman, Grant, Van Vliet & others talk about theirs – mates with whom they were on the best possible terms – we could never expect them to speak to us again.

I am reminded, now, of another matter. The day of the funeral I sat an hour over a single drink & several cigars with Van Vliet & Sherman & Senator Sherman; & among other things Gen. Sherman said, with impatient scorn:

"The idea of all this nonsense about Grant not being able to stand rude language & indelicate stories! Why Grant was *full* of humor, & full of the appreciation of it. I have sat with him by the hour listening to Jim Nye's yarns – & I reckon you know the Style of Jim Nye's histories, Clemens. It makes me sick – that newspaper nonsense. Grant was no namby-pamby fool, he was a *man* – all over – rounded & complete."

I wish I had thought of it! I would have said to General Grant: "Put the drunkenness in the Memoirs – & the repentance & reform. Trust the people."

But I will wager there is not a hint in the book. He was sore, there. As much of the book as I have read gives no hint, as far as I recollect.

The sick-room brought out the points of Gen. Grant's character – some of them particularly, to wit:

His patience; his indestructable equability of temper; his exceeding gentleness, kindliness, forbearance, lovingness, charity;

his *loyalty:* to friends, to convictions, to promises, half-promises, infinitesmal fractions & shadows of promises. [There was a requirement of him which I considered an atrocity, an injustice, an outrage; I wanted to implore him to repudiate it; Fred Grant said, "Save your labor, I *know* him; he is in doubt as to whether he made that half-promise or not – & he will give the thing the benefit of the doubt; he will fulfill that half-promise or kill himself trying;" Fred Grant was right – he *did* fulfill it;] his aggravatingly trustful nature; his genuineness, simplicity, modesty, diffidence, self-depreciation, poverty in the quality of vanity – &, in no contradiction of this last, his simple pleasure in the flowers & general ruck sent to him by Tom, Dick & Harry from everywhere – a pleasure that suggested a perennial surprise that he should be the object of so much fine attention – he *was* the most lovable great child in the world; [I mentioned his loyalty: you remember Harrison, the colored body-servant? the whole family hated him, but that did not make any difference, the General always stood at his back, wouldn't allow him to be scolded; always excused his failures & deficiencies with the one unvarying formula, "We are responsible for these things in his race – it is not fair to visit our fault upon them – let him *alone*;" so they did let him alone, under compulsion, until the great heart that was his shield was taken away; then – well they simply couldn't *stand* him, & so they were excusable for determining to discharge him – a thing which they mortally hated to do, & by lucky accident were saved from the necessity of doing;] his toughness as a bargainer when doing business for other people or for his country [witness his "terms" at Donelson, Vicksburg, etc.; Fred Grant told me his father wound up an estate for the widow & orphans of a friend in St. Louis – it took several years; at the end every complication had been straightened out, & the property put upon a prosperous basis; great sums had passed through his hands, & when he handed over the papers there were vouchers to show what had been done with every penny] & his trusting, easy, unexacting fashion when doing business for himself [at that same time he was paying out money in driblets to a man who was running his farm for him – & in his first Presidency he paid every one of those driblets *again* (total, $3,000 F. said,) for he hadn't a scrap of paper to show that he had ever paid them before; in his dealings with me he would *not* listen to terms which would place my money at risk & leave his protected – the thought plainly gave him *pain*, & he put it from him, waved it off with his *hands*, as one does accounts of crushings & mutilations – wouldn't listen, changed the subject]; & his fortitude! He was under sentence of death last spring; he sat thinking, musing, several days – nobody knows what about; then he pulled himself together & set to work to finish that book, a colossal task for a dying man. Presently his hand gave out; fate seemed to have got him checkmated. Dictation was suggested. No, he never could do that; had never tried it; too old to learn, now. By & by – if he could only do Appomattox – well. So he sent for a stenographer, & dictated 9,000 words at a single sitting! – never pausing, never hesitating for a word, never repeating – & in the written-out copy he made hardly a correction. He dictated again, every two or three days – the intervals were intervals of exhaustion & slow recuperation – & at last he was able to tell me that he had written more matter than could be got into the book. I then enlarged the book – had to. Then he lost his voice. He was not quite done yet, however: – there was no end of little plums & spices to be stuck in, here & there; & this work he patiently continued, a few lines a day, with pad & pencil, till far into July, at M^r McGregor. One day he put his pencil aside, & said he was done – there was nothing more to do. If I had been there I could have foretold the shock that struck the world three days later.

Well, I've written all this, & it doesn't seem to amount to anything. But I do want to help, if I only could. I will enclose some scraps from my Autobiography – scraps about Gen. Grant – they may be of some trifle of use, & they may not – they at least verify known traits of his character. My Autobiography is pretty freely dictated, but my idea is to jack-plane it a little before I die, some day or other; I mean the rude construction & rotten grammar. It is the only dictating I ever did, & it was most troublesome & awkward work. You may return it to Hartford.

SINCERELY YOURS
S.L. CLEMENS

TO JEANNETTE L. GILDER
14 MAY 1887, HARTFORD, CONN.

[*in pencil.*] [quite true – but never sent.]

SLC HARTFORD, MAY 14/87

MY DEAR MISS GILDER:

We shall spend the summer at the same old place – the remote farm called "Rest-&-be-Thankful," on top of the hills three miles from Elmira, N.Y. Your other question is harder to answer. It is my habit to keep four or five books in process of erection all the time, & every summer add a few courses of brick to two or three of them; but I cannot forecast which of the two or three it is going to be. It takes seven years to complete a book by this method, but still it is a good method: gives the public a rest. I have [*inserted word and caret canceled*] been accused of "rushing into print" prematurely, moved then to greediness for money; but in truth I have never done that. Do you care for trifles of information? Well, then, "Tom Sawyer" & "The Prince & the Pauper" were each on the stocks two or three years, & "Old times on the Mississippi" eight. One of my unfinished books has been on the stocks sixteen years; another, seventeen. This latter book could have been finished in a day, at any time during the past five years. But as in the first of these two narratives all the action takes place in Noah's ark, & as in the other the action takes place in heaven, there seemed to be no hurry, & so I have not hurried. Tales of stirring adventure in those localities do not need to be rushed to publication lest they get stale by waiting. In twenty-one years, with all my time at my free disposal, I have written & completed only eleven books, whereas with half the labor that a journalist does I could have written sixty in that time. I do not greatly mind being accused of a proclivity for rushing into print, but at the same time I don't believe that the charge is really well founded. Suppose I did write eleven books, have you nothing to be grateful for? Go to – remember the forty-nine which I didn't write.

TRULY YOURS
S.L. CLEMENS

TO WILLIAM DEAN HOWELLS

22 AUGUST 1887, ELMIRA, N.Y.

MY DEAR HOWELLS:

I have my doubts; I suspect that the firm's hands are abundantly full; still I am sending your letter & Mr. Drexel's to Webster.

How stunning are the changes which age makes in a man while he sleeps. When I finished Carlyle's French Revolution in 1871, I was a Girondin; every time I have read it since, I have read it differently – being influenced & changed, little by little, by life & environment (& Taine, & St. Simon): & now I lay the book down once more, & recognize that I am a Sansculotte! – And not a pale, characterless Sansculotte, but a Marat. Carlyle teaches no such gospel: so the change is in *me* – in my vision of the evidences.

People pretend that the Bible means the same to them at 50 that it did at all former milestones in their journey. I wonder how they can lie so. It comes of practice, no doubt. They would not say this of Dickens's or Scott's books. *Nothing* remains the same: when the man goes back to look at the house of his childhood, it has always *shrunk:* there is no instance of such house being as big as the picture in memory & imagination call for. Shrunk how? Why, to its correct dimensions: the *house* hasn't altered; this is the first time it has been in focus.

Well, that's loss. To have house & Bible shrink so, under the disillusioning corrected angle, is loss – for a moment. But there are compensations. You tilt the tube skyward & bring planets & comets & corona-flames a hundred & fifty thousand miles high into the field. Which I see you have done, & found Tolstöi. I can't get *him* in focus yet, but I've got Browning.

But that's neither here nor there; it isn't answering your question – which I will answer now. Yes, I'll have proofs sent you so you can write the introduction. It will be a month or two hence, I think.

If stress of work would allow, I *would* use Mr. Yewell as a pretext, & go & see you – but it won't, & I am sorry.

YS EVER

MARK

OVER

P.S. I bust this open to say that the etching has arrived & is all that Mr. Drexel says about it. I very much thank you & Mr. Yewell both.

TO FRANCES F. CLEVELAND
6 NOVEMBER 1887, HARTFORD, CONN.

HARTFORD, NOV. 6, 1887

MY DEAR MADAM:

I do not know how it is in the White House, but in this house of ours whenever the minor half of the administration tries to run itself without the help of the major half, it gets aground. Last night when I was offered the opportunity to assist you in throwing open the Warner brothers' superb benefaction in Bridgeport to those fortunate women, I naturally appreciated the honor done me, & promptly siezed my chance. I had an engagement, but the circumstances washed it out of my mind. If I had only laid the matter before the major half of the administration on the spot, there would have been no blunder; but I never thought of that. So when I did lay it before her, later, I realized once more that it will not do for the literary fraction of a combination to try to manage affairs which properly belong in the office of the business bulk of it. I suppose the President often acts just like that: goes & makes an impossible promise, & you never find it out until it is next to impossible to break it up & set things straight again. Well, that is just our way, exactly – one half of the administration always busy getting the family into trouble, & the other half busy getting it out again. And so we do seem to be all pretty much alike, after all. The fact is, I had forgotten that we were to have a dinner party on that Bridgeport date – I thought it was the next day: which is a good deal of an improvement for me, because I am more used to being behind a day or two than ahead. But that is just the difference between one end of this kind of an administration & the other end of it, as you have noticed, yourself – the other end does not forget these things. Just so with a funeral: if it is the man's funeral, he is most always there, of course – but that is no credit to him, he wouldn't be there if you depended on *him* to remember about it;

whereas, if on the other hand – but I seem to have got off from my line of argument somehow: never mind about the funeral. Of course I am not meaning to say anything *against* funerals – that is, as occasions – mere occasions – for as diversions I don't think they amount to much. But as I was saying – if you are not busy I will look back & see what it was I was saying.

I don't seem to find the place; but anyway she was as sorry as ever anybody could be that I could not go to Bridgeport, but there was no help for it. And I, I have been not only sorry but very sincerely ashamed of having made an engagement to go without first making sure that I could keep it, & I do not know how to apologize enough for my heedless breach of good manners.

WITH THE SINCEREST RESPECT,
S.L. CLEMENS

Mrs. Grover Cleveland.

TO ANDREW CHATTO
5 DECEMBER 1887, HARTFORD, CONN.

HARTFORD, DEC. 5/87

MY DEAR CHATTO:

Look here, I don't mind paying the tax, but don't you let the Inland Revenue Office send me any more receipts for it, for the postage is something perfectly demoralizing. If they feel obliged to print a receipt on a horse-blanket, why don't they hire a ship & send it over at their own expense?

Wasn't it good that they caught me out with an old book instead of a new one? The tax on a new book would bankrupt a body. It was my purpose to go to England next May & stay the rest of the year, but I've found that tax office out just in time. My new book would issue in March, & they would tax the sale in both countries. Come, we must get up a compromise somehow. You go & work in on the good side of those revenue people & get them to take the profits & give me the tax. Then I will come over & we will divide the swag & have a good time.

I wish you to thank Mr. Christmas for me; but we won't resist. The country that allows me copyright has a right to tax me.

SINCERELY YOURS

S L CLEMENS

TO ORION CLEMENS
29 NOVEMBER 1888, HARTFORD, CONN.

NOV. 29/88

Jesus *Christ* – It is perilous to write to such a man. You can go crazy on less material than anybody that ever lived. What in hell has produced all these maniacal imaginings? You told me you *had* hired an attendant for ma. Now hire one instantly, & stop this nonsense of wearing Mollie & yourself out trying to do that nursing yourselves. Hire the attendant, & tell me her cost so that I can instruct Webster & Co to add it every month to what they already send. Don't fool away any more time about this. And don't write me any more damned rot about "storms," & inability to pay trivial sums of money and – & – hell & dam*nation*! You see I've read only the first page of your letter; I wouldn't read the rest for a million dollars.

YS

SAM

Don't imagine that I have lost my temper because I swear. I swear all day, but I do not lose my temper. And don't imagine that I am on my way to the poorhouse, for I am not; nor that I am uneasy, for I am not; or that I am uncomfortable or unhappy – for *I never am*. I don't know what it *is* to be unhappy or uneasy; & I am not going to try to learn how, at this late day.

SAM

TO ORION CLEMENS
5 JANUARY 1889, HARTFORD, CONN.

HARTFORD, JAN. 5, 89

DEAR ORION:

At 12. 20 this afternoon a line of movable types was spaced & justified by machinery, for the first time in the history of the world! And I was there to see. It was done *automatically* – instantly – perfectly. This is indeed, the first line of movable types that ever *was* perfectly spaced & perfectly justified on this earth.

This was the last function that remained to be tested – & so by long odds the most amazing & extraordinary invention ever born of the brain of man stands completed & perfect. Livy is down stairs celebrating.

But it's a cunning devil, is that machine! – & knows more than any man that ever lived. You shall see. We made the test in this way. We set up a lot of random letters in a stick – three-fourths of a line; then filled out the line with quads representing 14 spaces, each space to be $\frac{35}{1000}$ of an inch thick. Then we threw aside the quads, & put the letters into the machine & formed them into 15 two-letter words, leaving the words separated by two-inch vacancies. Then we started up the machine slowly, by hand, & fastened our eyes on the space-selecting pins. The First pin-block projected its third pin as the first word came traveling along the race-way; second block did the same; but the third block projected its *second* pin!

"Oh, hell! stop the machine – something wrong – it's going to set a $\frac{30}{1000}$ space !"

General consternation. "A foreign substance has got into the spacing-plates." This from the head mathematician.

"Yes, that is the trouble," assented the foreman.

Paige examined. "No – look in, & you can see that there's nothing of the kind." Further examination. "*Now* I know what it is – what it *must* be: one of those plates projects & binds. It's too bad – the first test is a failure." *A pause.* "Well, boys, no use to cry. Get to work – take the machine down. – No – Hold on! don't touch a thing! Go right ahead! We are fools, the machine isn't. The machine knows what it's about. There is a *speck of dirt* on one of those types, & the machine is putting in a thinner space to *allow* for it!"

That was just it. The machine went right ahead, spaced the line, justified it to a hair, & shoved it into the galley complete & perfect! We took it out & examined it with a glass. You could not tell by your eye that the third space was thinner than the others, but the glass & the calipers showed the difference. Paige had always said that the machine would measure invisible particles of dirt & allow for them, but even he had forgotten that vast fact for the moment.

All the witnesses made written record of the immense historical birth – the first justification of a line of movable type by machinery – & also set down the hour & the minute. Nobody had drank anything, & yet everybody seemed drunk. Well – dizzy, stupefied, stunned.

All the other wonderful inventions of the human brain sink pretty nearly into commonplaces contrasted with this awful mechanical miracle. Telephones, telegraphs, locomotives, cotton gins, sewing machines, Babbage, calculators, Jacquard looms, perfecting presses, Arkwright's frames – all mere toys, simplicities! The Paige Compositor marches alone & far in the lead of human inventions.

In two or three weeks we shall work the stiffness out of her joints & have her performing as smoothly & softly as human muscles, & then we shall speak out the big secret & let the world come & gaze.

SAM

{Return me this letter when you have read it.}

TO JOSEPH T. GOODMAN
7 OCTOBER 1889, HARTFORD, CONN.

Private.

HARTFORD, OCT. 7/89

DEAR JOE:

I had a letter from Aleck Badlam day before yesterday, & in answering him I mentioned a matter which I asked him to consider a secret except to you & John M°Comb, as I am not ready yet to get into the newspapers.

I have come near writing you about this matter several times, but it wasn't ripe, & I waited. It is ripe, now. It is a type-setting machine which I undertook to build for the inventor (for a consideration). I have been at it 3 years & 7 months without losing a day, at a cost of $3,000 a month, & in so private a way that Hartford has known nothing about it. Indeed only a dozen men have known of the matter. I have reported progress from time to time to the proprietors of the N.Y. Sun, Herald, Times, World, Harper Brothers & John F. Trow; also the proprietors of the Boston Herald & the Boston Globe. Three years ago I asked all these people to squelch their frantic desire to load up their offices with the Mergenthaler (N.Y. Tribune) machine, & wait for mine & then choose between the two. They have waited – with no very gaudy patience – but still they have waited; & I could prove to them to-day that they have not lost anything by it. But I reserve the proof for the present – except in the case of the N.Y. Herald; I sent an invitation there the other day – a courtesy due a paper which ordered $240,000 worth of our machines long ago when it was still in a crude condition. The Herald has ordered its foreman to come up here next Thursday; but that is the only invitation which will go out for some time yet.

The machine was finished several weeks ago, & has been running ever since in the machine shop. It is a magnificent creature of steel, all of Pratt & Whitney's superbest workmanship, & as nicely adjusted & as accurate as a watch. In construction it is as elaborate & complex as that machine which it ranks *next* to, by every right – Man – & in performance it is as simple & sure.

Anybody can set type on it who can read – & can do it after only 15 minutes' instruction. The operator does not need to leave his seat at the keyboard; for the reason that he is not required to do anything but strike the keys & SET type – merely one function; the spacing, justifying, emptying into the galley, & distributing of dead matter is all done by the machine without anybody's help – four functions.

The ease with which a cub can learn is surprising. Day before yesterday I saw our newest cub set, perfectly space & perfectly justify 2,150 ems of solid nonpareil in an hour & distribute the like amount in the *same* hour – & six hours previously he had never seen the machine or its key-board. It was a good hour's work for 3-year *veterans* on the other type-setting machines to do. We have 3 cubs. The dean of the trio is a school-youth of 18. Yesterday morning he had been an apprentice on the machine 16 working days (8-hour days; & we speeded him to see what he could do in an hour. In the hour he set 5,900 ems solid nonpareil, & the machine perfectly spaced & justified it, & of course distributed the like amount in the same hour. Considering that a good fair compositor sets 700 & distributes 700 in the one hour, this boy did the work of about $8\frac{1}{2}$ compositors in that hour. This fact sends all other type-setting machines a thousand miles to the rear, & the best of them will never be heard of again after we publicly exhibit in New York.

We shall put on 3 more cubs. We have one schoolboy & two compositors, now, & we think of putting on a type writer, a stenographer, & perhaps a shoemaker, to show that no special gifts or training are required with this machine. We shall train these beginners two or three months – or until some one of them gets up to 7,000 an hour – then we will show up in New York & run the machine 24 hours a day 7 days in the week, for several months – to prove that this is a machine which will never get out of order or cause delay, & can stand anything an anvil can stand. You know there is no other type-setting machine that can run two hours on a stretch without causing trouble & delay with its incurable caprices.

We own the whole field – every inch of it – & nothing can dislodge us.

Now then, above is my preachment, & here follows the reason & purpose of it. I want you to run over here, roost over the machine a week & satisfy yourself, & then go to John P. Jones or to whom you please, & sell me a hundred thousand dollars' worth of this property, & take ten per cent in cash or the "property" for your trouble – the latter, if you are wise, because the price I ask is a long way short of the value.

What I call "property" is this. A small part of my ownership consists of a royalty of $500 on every machine marketed under the American patents. My selling-terms are, a permanent royalty of one dollar on every American-marketed machine, for a thousand dollars cash to me in hand paid. We shan't market any fewer than 15,000 machines in 15 years – a return of fifteen thousand dollars for one thousand. A royalty is better than stock, in one way – *it* must be paid, every six months, rain or shine; it is a debt, & must be paid before dividends are declared. By & by, when we become a stock company I shall buy these royalties back for stock if I can get them for anything like reasonable terms.

I have never borrowed a penny to use on the machine, and never sold a penny's worth of the property until the machine was entirely finished & proven by the severest tests to be what she started out to be – perfect, permanent, & occupying the position, as regards all kindred machines, which the City of Paris occupies as regards the canvas-backs of the mercantile marine.

[*some 5 lines (about 30 words) torn away to cancel*]

It is my purpose to sell two hundred dollars of my royalties at the above price during the next two months, & keep the other $300.

Mrs. Clemens begs Mrs. Goodman to come with you, & asks pardon for not writing the message herself – which would be a pathetically-welcome spectacle to me; for I have been her amanuensis for 8 months, now, since her eyes failed her.

YOURS AS ALWAYS

MARK

TO THE HARTFORD GAS COMPANY
12 FEBRUARY 1891, HARTFORD, CONN.

HARTFORD, FEB. 12/91

DEAR SIRS:

Some day you will move me almost to the verge of irritation by your chuckleheaded Goddamned fashion of shutting your God-damned gas off without giving any notice to your Goddamned parishioners. Several times you have come within an ace of smothering half of this household in their beds & blowing up the other half by this idiotic, not to say criminal, custom of yours. And it has happened again to-day. Haven't you a telephone?

YS

S L CLEMENS

[*page 1 missing*]
is so pitiably long.

Your surmise is correct, sharply & exactly so – that I confine myself to life with which I am familiar, when pretending to portray life. But I confined myself to the boy-life out on the Mississippi because that had a peculiar charm for me, & not because I was not familiar with other phases of life. I was a *soldier* two weeks, once, in the beginning of the war, & was hunted like a rat the whole time. Familiar? My splendid Kipling himself hasn't a more burnt-in, hard-baked & unforgetable familiarity with that death-on-the-pale-horse-with-hell-following-after which is a raw soldier's first fortnight in the field & which, without any doubt, is the most tremendous fortnight & the vividest he is ever going to see.

Yes, & I have shoveled silver tailings in a quartz mill a couple of weeks, & acquired the last possibilities of culture in *that* direction. And I've done "pocket-mining" during three months in the one little patch of ground in the whole globe where Nature conceals gold in pockets – or *did*, before we robbed all of those pockets & exhausted, obliterated, annihilated the most curious freak Nature ever indulged in. There are not thirty men left alive who, being told there was a pocket hidden on the broad slope of a mountain would know how to go & find it, or have even the faintest idea of how to set about it – but I am one of the possible 20 or 30 who possess the secret, & I could go & put my hand on that hidden treasure with a most deadly precision.

And I've been a prospector, & know pay rock from poor when I find it – just with a touch of the tongue. And I've been a silver *miner*, & know how to dig & shovel & drill, & put in a blast. And so I know the mines & the miners interiorly as well as Bret Harte knows them exteriorly, & superficially.

And I was a newspaper reporter four years in cities, & so saw the inside of many things; & was reporter in a legislature two sessions & the same in Congress one session & thus learned to know personally the three sample-bodies of the smallest minds & the selfishest souls & the cowardliest hearts that God makes.

And I was some years a Mississippi pilot, & familiarly knew all the different kinds of steamboatmen – a race apart, & not like other folk.

And I was for some years a traveling "jour" printer, & wandered from city to city – & so I know *that* sect familiarly.

And I was a lecturer on the public platform a number of seasons, & was a responder to toasts at all the different kinds of banquets – & so I know a great many secrets about audiences – secrets not to be got out of books, but only acquirable by experience.

And I watched over one dear project of mine five years, spent a fortune on it, & failed to make it go – & the history of that would make a large book in which a million men would see themselves as in a mirror; & they would testify & say, Verily this is not imagination, this fellow has been there – & after would they cast dust upon their heads, cursing & blaspheming.

And I am a publisher, & did pay to one author's widow (General Grant's) the largest copyright checks this world has seen – aggregating more than £80,000 in the first year.

And I have been an author for 20 years & an ass for 55.

Now then: as the most valuable capital, or culture, or education usable in the building of novels is personal experience, I ought to be well equipped for that trade. I surely have the equipment, a wide culture; & all of it real, none of it artificial, for I don't know anything about books. And yet I can't go away from the boyhood period & write novels, because *capital* is not sufficient by itself & I lack the other essential: interest in handling the men & experiences of later times. Yes, & there was another consideration: the boyhood field isn't much or effectively occupied, there's plenty of room: but the other field is crowded, & most competently, too.

TO OLIVIA L. CLEMENS
22 SEPTEMBER 1891, RHONE RIVER, FRANCE

ON THE RHONE BELOW VILLEBOIS,
TUESDAY NOON.

Good morning, sweetheart. Night caught us yesterday where we had to take quarters in a peasant's house which was occupied by the family & a lot of cows & calves – also several rabbits. The latter had a ball, & I was the ball-room; but they were very friendly & didn't bite.

The peasants were mighty kind & hearty, & flew around & did

their best to make us comfortable. This morning I breakfasted on the shore in the open air with two sociable dogs & a cat. Clean cloth, napkin & table furniture, white sugar, a vast hunk of excellent butter, good bread, first class coffee with pure milk, fried fish just caught. Wonderful that so much cleanliness should come out of such a phenomenally dirty house.

An hour ago we ran the Falls of the Rhone, a prodigiously rough & dangerous looking place; shipped a little water but came to no harm. It was one of the most beautiful pieces of piloting & boat-management I ever saw. Our admiral knows his business.

We have had to run ashore for shelter every time it has rained heretofore, but Joseph has been putting in his odd time making a waterproof sunbonnet for the boat, & now we sail along dry although we have many heavy showers this morning.

[*drawing of a boat with a cover and two figures labeled "Joseph" and "Admiral."*]

I'm on the stern seat under shelter & out of sight.

With a world of love to you all & particularly you,

SAML

TO OLIVIA L. CLEMENS
24 AND 25 SEPTEMBER 1891, RHONE RIVER, FRANCE

ON THE RHONE, BELOW VIENNE.

I salute you, my darling. Your telegram saying you had had a letter from the original Prächtel himself, reached me in Lyons last night & was very pleasant news indeed, for it meant a great let-up of your worry.

I was up & shaved before 8 this morning, but we got delayed & didn't sail from Lyons till 10.30 – an hour & a half lost. And we've lost another hour – two of them I guess – since, by an error. We came in sight of Vienne at 2 o'clock, several miles ahead, on a hill, & I proposed to walk down there & let the boat go down there ahead of us. So Joseph & I got out there & struck through a willow swamp there along a dim path, & by & by came out on the steep bank of a slough or inlet or something, & we followed that bank forever & ever trying to get around the head of that slough. Finally I noticed a twig standing up in the water, & by George it had a

distinct & even vigorous quiver to it! I don't know when I have felt
so much like a donkey. On an island! I wanted to drown somebody,
but I hadn't anybody I could spare. However, after another long
tramp we found a lonely native, & he had a scow & soon we were
on the main land – yes, & a blame sight further from Vienne than
we were when we started.

Notes – I make millions of them; & so I get no time to write to
you. If you've got a pad there, please send it post-restante to Avignon. I may not need it but I fear I shall.

I'm straining to make St. Pierre de Boef, but it's going to be a
close fit, I reckon.

P.S. 5 a.m. Next Day (in bed). I hear the villagers beginning to
stir in the streets.

Cover the Child! cover the che-*i*ld! lay on! lay on! *you*'ll make
it! YOU'll make it – and – we – *did* make it! Just by the skin of our
teeth. The gloaming was deep & rich when we struck St. Pierre de
Boef, & it was good dark before we were done climbing crooked
alleys & reached the inn. Did you say you wished you were along,
sweetheart? Don't think of it! A sailor's life is not the life for you;
a life of hardy adventure with rabbits, & indigestibilities, & unimaginable dirt, is not the life for you, my dear. Drop the idea. But it's
the life for me. And for Joseph & the Admiral.

Joseph is perfect. He is at his very best & never was better in his
life. I guess he gets discouraged & feels disliked & in the way when
he is lying around – but here he is perfection, & brim full of useful
alacrities & helps & ingenuities. He dresses & undresses me,
unpacks & packs my things, arranges them handy for me on table
& mantel & washstand – in fact is a gem of a lady's maid; & I am
never allowed to shirk my rubbings either night or morning.

When I woke up an hour ago & heard the clock strike 4, I said
"I seem to have been asleep an immensely long time; I must have
gone to bed mighty early; I wonder what time I *did* go to bed."
And I got up & lit a candle & looked at my watch *to see*. [There –
you are avenged for the incident of Jean helping the boy out with
his rowing.]

Will you or Jean or Clara or Susie or Aunt Sue scrap book these
enclosed rags for me?

TOUJOURS À TOI
SAML

TO OLIVIA L. CLEMENS
25 SEPTEMBER 1891, RHONE RIVER, FRANCE

AFLOAT, FRIDAY, 3 P.M.

Livy darling, we sailed from St. Pierre de Boef six hours ago, & are now approaching Tournon, where we shall not stop, but go on & make Valence, a city of 25,000 people. It's too delicious, floating with the swift current under the awning these superb sunshiny days in deep peace & quietness. Some of these curious old historical towns strongly persuade me, but it is so lovely afloat that I don't stop, but view them from the outside & sail on. We get abundance of grapes & peaches for next to nothing. My, but that inn was suffocating with garlic where we stayed last night! I had to hold my nose as I went up stairs, or I believe I should have fainted.

Little bit of a room, rude board floor unswept, 2 chairs, unpainted white pine table – voila the furniture! Had a good firm bed, solid as a rock, & you could have brained an ox with the bolster.

These six hours have been entirely delightful. I want to do all the rivers of Europe in an open boat in summer weather.

I love you, love you, *love* you, my sweetheart.

SAML

TO OLIVIA L. CLEMENS
28 SEPTEMBER 1891, 1ST OF 2, RHONE RIVER, FRANCE

AFLOAT
2 HOURS BELOW BOURG-ST.-ANDEOL
MONDAY, 11 A.M., SEPT 28

Livy darling, I didn't write yesterday. We left La Voulte in a driving storm of cold rain – couldn't write in it – & at 1 p.m., when we were not thinking of stopping, we saw a picturesque & mighty ruin on a high hill back of a village, & I was siezed with a desire to explore it; so we landed at once & set out with rubbers & umbrella, sending the boat ahead to St. Andéol, & we spent 3 hours clambering about those cloudy heights among those worn & vast & idiotic ruins of a castle built by two crusaders 650 years ago. The work of these asses was full of interest, & we had a good time inspecting, examining & scrutinizing it. All the hills on both sides of the Rhone have peaks & precipices, & each has its gray & wasted pile of mouldy walls & broken towers. The Romans displaced the Gauls, the Visigoths displaced the Romans, the Saracens displaced the Visigoths, the Christians displaced the Saracens, & it was these pious animals who built these strange [*one word canceled*] lairs & cut each other's throats in the name & for the glory of God, & robbed & burned & slew in peace & war; & the pauper & the slave built churches, & the credit of it went to the Bishop who racked the money out of them. These are pathetic shores, & they make one despise the human race.

We came down in an hour by rail, but I couldn't get your telegram till this morning, for it was Sunday & they had shut up the post-office to go to the circus. I went, too. It was all one family – parents & 5 children – performing in the open air to 200 of these enchanted villagers, who contributed coppers when called on. It was a most gay, & strange, & pathetic show. I got up at 7 this morning to see the poor devils cook their poor breakfast & pack up their sordid fineries.

This is a 9 km. current & the wind is with us; we shall make Avignon before 4 o'clock. I saw watermelons & pomegranates for sale at St. Andéol. With a power of love, sweetheart,

                                                              SAML

TO OLIVIA L. CLEMENS
28 SEPTEMBER 1891, 2ND OF 2, AVIGNON, FRANCE

HOTEL D'EUROPE, AVIGNON,
MONDAY, 8 P.M., SEPT. 28

Well, Livy darling, I have been having a perfect feast of letters for an hour, & I thank you & dear Clara with all my heart. It's like hearing from home after a long absence.

It is early to be in bed, but I'm always abed before 9, on this voyage, & up at 7 or a trifle later, every morning. If I ever take such a trip again, I will have myself called at the first tinge of dawn & get to sea as soon after as possible. The early dawn on the water – nothing can be finer, as I know by old Mississippi experience. I did so long for you & Sue yesterday morning – the most superb sunrise! the most marvelous sunrise! & I saw it *all* – from the very faintest suspicion of the coming dawn all the way through to the final explosion of glory. But it had an interest private to itself & not to be found elsewhere in the world; for between me & it, in the far distance eastward, was a silhouetted mountain range in which I had discovered, the previous afternoon, a most noble face upturned to the sky, & mighty form outstretched, which I had named Napoleon Dreaming of Universal Empire – & now, this prodigious face, soft, rich, blue, spirituelle, asleep, tranquil, reposeful, lay *against* that giant conflagration of ruddy & golden splendors all rayed like a wheel with the upstreaming & far-reaching lances of the sun. It made one want to cry for delight, it was so supreme in its unimaginable majesty & beauty.

We had a curious experience to-day. A little after I had sealed & directed my letter to you, in which I said we should make Avignon before 4, *we got lost.* We ceased to encounter any village or ruin mentioned in our particularized & detailed Guide of the Rhone – went drifting along by the hour in a wholly unknown land & on an uncharted river! Confound it, we stopped talking & did nothing but stand up in the boat & search the horizons with the glass & wonder what in the devil had happened. And at last, away yonder at 5 o'clock when some vast towers & fortresses hove in sight we couldn't recognize them for Avignon – yet we know by the broken bridge that it *was* Avignon.

Then we saw what the trouble was – at some time or other we had drifted down the wrong side of an island followed a sluggish branch of the Rhone not frequented in modern times. We lost an hour & a half by it & missed one of the most picturesque & gigantic & history-sodden masses of castellated medieval ruin that Europe can show.

It was dark by the time we had wandered through the town & got the letters & found the hotel – so I went to bed.

We shall leave here at noon tomorrow & float down to Arles, arriving about dark, & there bid good bye to the boat, the river-trip finished. Between Arles & Nimes (& Avignon again), we shall be till Saturday morning – then rail it through on that day to Ouchy, reaching the hotel at 11 at night if the train isn't late.

Next day (Sunday), if you like, go to Basel, & Monday to Berlin. But I shall be at your disposal, to do exactly as you desire & prefer.

With no end of love to all of you & twice as much to you, sweetheart,

SAML

I believe my arm is a trifle better than it was when I started.

SAMUEL L. CLEMENS AND OLIVIA L. CLEMENS TO OLIVIA SUSAN (SUSY) CLEMENS
22 MARCH 1892, MENTON, FRANCE

MENTON, MARCH 22/92

SUSY DEAR—

I have been delighted to note your easy facility with your pen & proud to note also your literary superiorities of one kind & another – clearness of statement, directness, felicity of expression, photographic ability in setting forth an incident, – style – good style – no barnacles on it in the way of retarding, unnecessary words (the shipman scrapes off the barnacles when he wants his racer to go her best gait & straight to the buoy.) You should write a letter every day, long or short – & so ought I, but I don't.

Mamma says, tell Clara yes, she *will* have to write a note if the fan comes back mended.

We couldn't go to Nice to-day – had to give it up, on various accounts – & this was the last chance. I am sorry for Mamma – I wish she could have gone. She got a heavy fall yesterday evening & was pretty stiff & lame this morning, but is working it off trunk-packing.

Joseph is gone to Nice to educate himself in Kodacking – & to get the pictures mounted which Mamma thinks she took here; but I noticed she didn't take the plug out, as a rule. When she did, she took nine pictures on top of each other – composites.

WITH LOTS OF LOVE,
PAPA.

He is a scandalous man, bless him isn't he? Mamma.

TO FREDERICK J. HALL
30 MAY AND 2 JUNE 1893, FLORENCE, ITALY

MAY 30/93

DEAR MR. HALL:

You were to cable me if you sold any machine royalties – so I judge you have not succeeded.

This has depressed me. I have been looking over the past year's letters & statements & am depressed still more.

ADDRESS CARE DREXEL HARJES CO. BANKER PARIS. P.S.

June 2.

The $500 monthly draft which should have left New York May 15 has not arrived, & you do not mention it in your letter of the 19th. The $950 came all right. Perhaps I will cable about the draft if any of the family go to town to-day. The money cannot now reach us in Florence where it is much needed, but we can dip into Mrs. Clemens's letter of credit. We are at a heavy expense, now, in breaking up housekeeping & raking-in old bills.

If the monthly draft can be appointed for a certain day & be always sent on that day without fail, I shall prefer that. We are skimming along like paupers & a day can embarrass us.

I am terribly tired of business. I am by nature and disposition unfitted for it & I want to get out of it. I am standing on the Mount Morris volcano with help from the machine a long ways off – & doubtless a long way further off than the Connecticut Co imagine.

Now here is my idea for getting out.

The firm owes Mrs. Clemens & me – I do not know quite how much, but it is about $170,000 or $175,000, I suppose [I make this guess from the documents here, whose technicalities confuse me horribly.]

The firm owe other sums, but there is stock & cash assets to cover the entire indebtedness & $116,679.20 over. Is that it? In addition we have the L. A. L. plates & copyright, worth more than $130,000 – is that correct?

That is to say, we have property worth about $250,000 above indebtedness, I suppose – or, by one of your estimates, $300,000?

The greater part of the firm's debt to me is in notes paying 6 percent. The rest (the old $70,000 or whatever it is), pays no interest. [*wiggly line drawn in left margin next to the following paragraph:*]

Now then, will Harper, or Appleton, or Putnam give me $200,000 for those debts *and* my two-thirds interest in the firm? (The firm of course taking the Mount Morris & all such obligations off my hands & leaving me clear of all responsibility.)

I don't want much money. I only want first class notes – $200,000-worth of them at 6 per cent, payable *monthly* – yearly notes, renewable annually for 3 years, with $5,000 of the principal payable at the beginning and middle of each year. After that, the notes renewable annually & (perhaps) a larger part of the principal payable semi-annually.

Please advise me & suggest alterations & emendations of the above scheme, for I need that sort of help, being ignorant of business & not able to learn a single detail of it.

Such a deal would make it easy for a big firm to put in a big cash capital & jump L. A. L. up to enormous prosperity. Then your one-third would be a fortune – & I hope to see that day!

I enclose an authority to use with Whitmore in case you have sold any royalties. But if you can't make this deal don't make any. Wait a little & see if you can't make the deal. Do make the deal if you possibly can. And if any presence shall be necessary in order to complete it I will come over, though I hope it can be done without that.

Get me out of business!

And I will be yours forever gratefully,

S.L. CLEMENS

My idea is, that I am offering my 2/3 of L. A. L. & the business for thirty or forty thousand dollars. Is that it?

P.S.S. The new firm could retain my books & reduce them to a 10 per cent royalty.

S.L.C.

TO OLIVIA L. CLEMENS
18 OCTOBER 1893, NEW YORK, N.Y.

THE PLAYERS, 16 GRAMERCY PARK.
OCT. 18/93

Dear dear Sweetheart, I don't seem to get even half a chance to write you, these last two days, & yet there's lots to say.

Apparently everything is at last settled as to the give-away of
L. A. L., and the papers will be signed & the transfer made to-
morrow morning.

Then, a few days later we shall be prepared to talk business with
Walker and Hardy of the Cosmopolitan. Walker's idea is for Hall,
Hardy, himself & me to go into partnership in our "trade" department, make a stock company & publish our books & books to be
taken from the magazine. To-day when I was there the Chief of
the great American News Company happened in & Walker proposed that *he* take some of the stock & become a partner with us.
He confessed that it would be a strong combination, & said he
would go home give it thought.

To get this scheme into shape (if it can be done), will take weeks
& I'll have to stay here & do everything I can to bring it about.
I prodigiously want to accomplish this.

Meantime I have got the best & wisest man in the whole Standard Oil group of multi-millionaires a good deal interested in looking into the type-setter (this is private, don't mention it.) He has
been searching into that thing for three weeks, & yesterday he said
to me, "I find the machine to be all you represented it – I have here
exhaustive reports from my own experts, & I know every detail of
its capacity, its immense value, its construction, cost, history, & all
about its inventor's character. I know that the New York Co & the
Chicago Co are *both* stupid, & that they are unbusinesslike people,
destitute of money and in a hopeless boggle."

Then he told me the scheme he had planned, then said: "If I can
arrange with those people on this basis – it will take several weeks
to find out – I will see to it that they get the money they need. Then
the thing will move right along & your royalties will cease to be
waste paper. I will post you the minute my scheme fails of succeeds.
In the meantime, *you stop walking the floor.* Go off to the country &
try to be gay. You may have to go to walking again, but don't begin
till I tell you my scheme has failed." And he added: "Keep me
posted always as to where you are – for if I need you & can use you
I want to know where to put my hand on you."

If I should even divulge the fact that the Standard oil is merely
talking remotely about going into the type-setter, it would send my
royalties up.

With worlds of love & kisses to you all,

SAML

JAN. 2/95

DEAR MR. ROGERS:

Yours of Dec. 21 has arrived, containing the circular to stockholders & I guess the Co will really quit – there doesn't seem to be any other wise course.

There's one thing which makes it difficult for me to soberly realize that my ten-year dream is actually dissolved; & that is that it reverses my horoscope. The proverb says, "Born lucky, *always* lucky," & I am very superstitious.

As a small boy I was notoriously lucky. It was usual for one or two of our lads (per annum) to get drowned in the Mississippi or in Bear Creek, but I was pulled out in a $\frac{2}{3}$ drowned condition 9 times before I learned to swim, & was considered a cat in disguise. When the "Pennsylvania" blew up & the telegraph reported my brother as fatally injured (with 60 others) but made no mention of me, my uncle said to my mother "it means that Sam was somewhere else, after being on that boat a year & a half – he was born lucky." Yes, I *was* somewhere else. I am so superstitious that I have always been afraid to have business-dealings with certain relatives & friends of mine because they were unlucky people. All my life I have stumbled upon lucky chances of large size, & whenever they were wasted it was because of my own stupidity & carelessness. And so I have felt entirely certain that that machine would turn up trumps eventually. It disappointed me lots of times, but I couldn't shake off the confidence of a life time in my luck.

Well, whatever I get out of the wreckage will be due to good luck, – the good luck of getting you into the scheme – for, but for that, there wouldn't *be* any wreckage, it would be total loss.

I wish you had been in at the beginning. Then we should have had the good luck to step promptly ashore.

Miss Harrison has had a dream which promises me a large bank account, & I want her to go ahead & dream it twice more, so as to make the prediction sure to be fulfilled.

I've got a first-rate subject for a book. It kept me awake all night, & I began it & completed it in my mind. The minute I finish Joan I will take it up.

Love & Happy New Year to you all.

SINCERELY YOURS,
S.L. CLEMENS

TO RUDYARD KIPLING
16 AUGUST 1895, VANCOUVER, CANADA

VANCOUVER, B.C., AUG. 16/95

Dear Kipling. It is reported that you are about to visit India. This has moved me to journey to that far country in order that I may unload from my conscience a debt long due you. Years ago you came from India to Elmira to visit me, as you said at the time. It has always been my purpose to return that visit & that great compliment some day. I shall arrive next January, & you must be ready. I shall come riding my ayah, with his tusks adorned with silver bells & ribbons & escorted by a troop of native howdahs richly clad & mounted upon a herd of wild bungalows; & you must be on hand with a few bottles of ghee, for I shall be thirsty.

TO JOSEPH H. TWICHELL
27 SEPTEMBER 1896, LONDON, ENGLAND

Permanent address:
c/o Chatto & Windus, 111 St. Martin's Lane

LONDON, SEP. 27/96

Through Livy & Katy I have learned, dear old Joe, how loyally you stood poor Susy's friend, & mine, & Livy's: how you came all the way down, twice, from your summer refuge on your merciful errands to bring the peace & comfort of your beloved presence, first to the broken mind of that poor frantic child, & again to the broken heart of her desolate mother. It was like you; like your good great heart, like your matchless & unmatchable self. It was no surprise to me to learn that you staid by Susy long hours, careless of fatigue & heat, it was no surprise to me to learn that you could still the storms that swept her spirit when no other could; for she loved you, revered you, trusted you, & "Uncle Joe" was no empty phrase upon her lips. I am grateful to you, Joe, grateful to the bottom of my heart, which has always been filled with love for you, & respect & admiration; & I would have chosen you out of all the world to take my place at Susy's side & Livy's in those black hours.

Susy was a rare creature; the rarest that has been reared in Hartford this generation. And Livy knew it, & you knew it, & Charley Warner & George, & Harmony & the Hillyers & the Dunhams & the Cheneys & Susy Warner & Lilly, & the Bunces, & Henry Robinson & Dick Burton, & perhaps others. And I also was of the number, but not in the same degree – for she was above my duller comprehension. I merely knew that she was my superior in fineness of mind, in the delicacy & subtlety of her intellect; but to fully measure her I was not competent. I know her better now; for I have read her private writings & sounded the deeps of her mind; & I know better, now, the treasure that was mine than I knew it when I had it. But I have this consolation: that dull as I was, I always knew enough to be proud when she commended me or any of my work – as proud as if Livy had done it herself – & I took it as the accolade from the hand of genius. I see now – as Livy always saw – that she had greatness in her, & she herself was dimly conscious of it.

And now she is *dead* – & I can never tell her.

God bless you Joe – & all your house.

S.L.C.

TO HENRY C. ROBINSON
28 SEPTEMBER 1896, LONDON, ENGLAND

LONDON, SEPT. 28/96

It is as you say, dear old friend, "the pathos of it" – yes, it was a piteous thing – as piteous a tragedy as any the year can furnish. When we started westward upon our long trip at half past ten at night, July 14, 1895, at Elmira, Susy stood on the platform in the blaze of the electric light waving her good-byes to us as the train glided away, her mother throwing back kisses & watching her through her tears. One year, one month, & one week later, Clara

& her mother having exactly completed the circuit of the globe, drew up at that platform at the same hour of the night, in the same train & *in the same car;* & again Susy had come a journey & was near at hand to meet them. She was waiting in the house she was born in, in her coffin.

All the circumstances of this death were pathetic – my brain is worn to rags rehearsing them. Yes, & cursing them – cursing the conception & invention of them. The mere death would have been cruelty enough, without overloading it & emphasizing it with that score of harsh and wanton details. The child was taken away when her mother was within three days of her, & would have given three decades for sight of her.

In my despair & unassuageable misery I upbraid myself for ever parting with her. But there is no use in that. Since it was to happen it would have happened.

WITH LOVE

SLC

TO EMILIE R. ROGERS
26 NOVEMBER 1896, LONDON, ENGLAND

LONDON, NOV. 26/96

For & in behalf of Helen Kellar
  Stone blind & deaf, & formerly dumb.

DEAR MRS ROGERS:

Experience has convinced me that when one wishes to set a hard-worked man at something which he mightn't prefer to be bothered with, it is best to move upon him behind his wife. If she can't convince him it isn't worth while for other people to try.

Mr. Rogers will remember our visit with that astonishing girl at Laurence Hutton's house when she was fourteen years old. Last July, in Boston, when she was 16 she underwent the Harvard examination for admission to Radcliffe College. She passed without a single condition. She was allowed only the same amount of time that is granted to other applicants, & this was shortened in her case by the fact that the question-papers had to be *read* to her. Yet she scored an average of 90 as against an average of 78 on the part of the other applicants.

It won't *do* for America to allow this marvelous child to retire from her studies because of poverty. If she can go on with them she will make a fame that will endure in history for centuries. Along her special lines she is the most extraordinary product of all the ages.

There is danger that she must retire from the struggle for a College degree for lack of support for herself & for Miss Sullivan, (the teacher who has been with her from the start – Mr. Rogers will remember her.) Mrs. Hutton writes to ask me to interest rich Englishmen in her case, & I would gladly try, but my secluded life will not permit it. I see *nobody*. Nobody knows my address. Nothing but the strictest hiding can enable me to write my long book in time.

So I thought of this scheme: Beg you to lay siege to your husband & get him to interest himself and Messrs. John D. & William Rockefeller & the other Standard Oil chiefs in Helen's case; get them to subscribe an annual aggregate of six or seven hundred or a thousand dollars & agree to continue this three or four years, until she has completed her college course. I'm not trying to *limit* their generosity – indeed no, they may pile that Standard Oil Helen Kellar College Fund as high as they please, they have *my* consent.

Mrs. Hutton's idea is to raise a permanent fund the interest upon which shall support Helen & her teacher & put them out of fear of want. I shan't say a word against it, but she will find it a difficult & disheartening job, & meanwhile what is to become of that miraculous girl?

No, for immediate & sound effectiveness, the thing is for you to plead with Mr. Rogers for this hampered wonder of your sex, & send him clothed with plenary powers to plead with the other chiefs – they have spent mountains of money upon the worthiest benevolences, & I think that the same spirit which moved them to put their hands down through their hearts into their pockets in those cases will answer "Here!" when its name is called in this one.

There – I don't need to apologize to you or to H. H. for this appeal that I am making; I know you too well for that.

Good-bye with love to all of you –

S L CLEMENS

Laurence Hutton is on the staff of Harper's Monthly – close by and handy when wanted.

LONDON, JAN. 19/97

DEAR JOE —

Do I want you to write to me? Indeed I do. I do not want other people to write, but I do want you to do it. The others break my heart, but you will not. You have a something divine in you that is not in other men. You have the touch that heals, not lacerates. And you know the secret places of our hearts. You know our life — the outside of it — as the others do — & the inside of it — which they do not. You have seen our whole voyage. You have seen us go to sea, a cloud of sail, & the flag at the peak; & you see us now, chartless, adrift — derelicts; battered, water-logged, our sails a ruck of rags, our pride gone. For it *is* gone. And there is nothing in its place. The vanity of life was all we had, & there is no more vanity left in us. We are even ashamed of that we had; ashamed that we trusted the promises of life & builded high — to come to this!

I did not know that Susy was part *of* us; I did not know that she could go away; I did not know that she could go away, & take our lives with her, yet leave our dull bodies behind. And I did not know what she was. To me she was but treasure in the bank; the amount known, the need to look at it daily, handle it, weigh it, count it, *realize* it, not necessary; & now that I would do it, it is too late; they tell me it is not there, has vanished away in a night, the bank is broken, my fortune is gone, I am a pauper. How am I to comprehend this? How am I to *have* it? Why am I robbed, & who is benefitted?

Ah, well, Susy died at *home*. She had that privilege. Her dying eyes rested upon no thing that was strange to them, but only upon things which they had known & loved always & which had made her young years glad; & she had you & Sue, & Katy, & John & Ellen. This was happy fortune — I am thankful that it was vouchsafed to her. If she had died in another house — well, I think I could not have borne that. To us, our house was not unsentient matter — it had a heart, & a soul, & eyes to see us with; & approvals, & solicitudes, & deep sympathies; it was of us, & we were in its confidence, & lived in its grace & in the peace of its benediction. We never came home from an absence that its face did not light up & speak out its eloquent welcome — & we could not enter it unmoved. And could we now? oh now, in spirit we should enter it unshod.

20th I approve all that Brander Matthews said; & I thank him cordially. You must tell him so for me – & I will tell him again when I see him. I am very glad you sent it to me.

I am trying to add to the "assets" which you estimate so generously. No, I am not. The thought is not in my mind. My purpose is other. I am working, but it is for the sake of the *work* – the "surcease of sorrow" that is found there. I work all the days; & trouble vanishes away when I use that magic. This book will not long stand between it & me, now; but that is no matter, I have many unwritten books to fly to for my preservation; the interval between the finishing of this one & the beginning of the next will not be more than an hour, at most. *Continuances,* I mean; for two of them are already well along – in fact have reached exactly the same stage in their journey: 19,000 words each. The present one will contain 180,000 words – 130,000 are done. *I* am well protected; but Livy! She has nothing in the world to turn to; nothing but housekeeping, & doing things for the children & me. She does not see people, & cannot; books have lost their interest for her. She sits solitary; & all the day, & all the days, wonders how it all happened, & why. We others were always busy with our affairs, but Susy was her comrade – had to be driven from her loving persecutions – sometimes at 1 in the morning. I have done it often. To Livy the persecutions were welcome. It was heaven to her to be plagued like that. But it is ended now. Livy stands so in need of help; & none among us all could help her like you.

Some day you & I will walk again, Joe, & talk. I hope so. We could have *such* talks! We are all grateful to you & Harmony – how grateful it is not given us to say in words. We pay as we can, in love; & in this coin practicing no economy. Good bye, dear old Joe!

MARK

TO FRANCIS E. BLISS
4 NOVEMBER 1897, 2ND OF 2, VIENNA, AUSTRIA

VIENNA, NOV. 4, 1897

DEAR BLISS:

Your cablegram informing me that a letter is in circulation which purports to come from me & which says I have recently made $82,000 & paid all my debts has just reached me, & I have cabled back my regret to you that it is not true. I wrote a letter – a private letter – a short time ago, in which I expressed the belief that I should be out of debt within the next twelvemonth. If you make as much as usual for me out of the book, that belief will crystalize into a fact & I shall be wholly out of debt. I am encoring you now.

It is out of that moderate letter that the Eighty-Two-Thousand-Dollar mare's nest has developed. But why do you worry about the various reports? They do not worry me. They are not unfriendly, & I don't see how they can do any harm. Be patient; you have but a little while to wait; the possible reports are nearly all in. It has been reported that I was seriously ill – it was another man; dying – it was another man; dead – the other man again. It has been reported that I have received a legacy – it was another man; that I am out of debt – it was another man; & now comes this $82,000 – still another man. It has been reported that I am writing books – for publication; I am not doing anything of the kind. It would surprise (& gratify) me if I should be able to get another book ready for the press within the next three years. You can see, yourself, that there isn't anything more to be reported – invention is exhausted. Therefore, don't worry, Bliss – the long night is breaking. As far as I can see, nothing remains to be reported, except that I have become a foreigner. When you hear it, don't you believe it. And don't take the trouble to deny it. Merely just raise the American flag on our house in Hartford, & let it talk.

TRULY YOURS

MARK TWAIN

[*new page*]

P.S. This is not a private letter. I am getting afraid of private letters.

P.S. I perceive that the Herald has stolen your whole canvassing book – a harm ten thousand times more damaging than if you had allowed me to publish the same chapters in the Century.

The New York Journal stood ready to pay for such extracts, & pay well. They applied to me several times – again since I have been in Vienna; & I always referred them to you.

I think you ought to bring suit against the Herald. And put the damage at a good figure.

SLC

TO WILLIAM DEAN HOWELLS

22 JANUARY 1898, VIENNA, AUSTRIA

HOTEL METROPOLE, VIENNA, JAN. 22/98

DEAR HOWELLS —

Look at these ghastly figures. I used to write it "Hartford, *1871*." There was no Susy then — there is no Susy now. And how much lies between — one long lovely stretch of scented fields, & meadows, & shady woodlands; & suddenly Sahara! You speak of the glorious days of that old time & they were. It is my quarrel — that traps like that are set. Susy & Winnie given us, in miserable sport, & then taken away.

About the last time I saw you I described to you the culminating disaster in a book I was going to write (& will yet, when the stroke is further away) — a man's dead daughter brought to him when he had been through all other possible misfortunes — & I said it couldn't be done as it ought to be done except by a man who had lived it — it must be written with the blood out of a man's heart. I could not know, then, how soon I was to be made competent. I have thought of it many a time since. If you were here I think we could cry down each other's necks, as in your dream. For we *are* a pair of old derelicts drifting around, now, with some of our passengers gone & the sunniness of the others in eclipse.

I couldn't get along without work now. I bury myself in it up to the ears. Long hours — 8 & 9 on a stretch, sometimes. And all the days, Sundays included. It isn't all for print, by any means, for much of it fails to suit me; 50,000 words of it in the past year. It was because of the deadness which invaded me when Susy died. But I have made a change lately — into dramatic work — & I find it absorbingly entertaining. I don't know that I can write a play that will play; but no matter, I'll write half a dozen that won't, anyway. Dear me, I didn't know there was such fun in it. I'll write twenty that won't play. I get into immense spirits as soon as my day is fairly started. Of course a good deal of this friskiness comes of my being in sight of land — on the Webster & Co debts, I mean. (*Private.*) We've lived close to the bone & saved every cent we could, & there's no undisputed claim, now, that we can't cash. I have marked this "private" because it is for the friends who are attending to the matter for us in New York to reveal it when they want to & if they want to. There are only two claims which I dispute & which I mean to look into personally before I pay them. But they are small. Both together they amount to only $12,500. I hope you will never get the like of the load saddled onto you that was saddled onto me 3 years ago. And yet there is such a solid pleasure in *paying* the things that I reckon maybe it is worth while to get into that kind of a hobble, after all. Mrs. Clemens gets millions of delight out of it; & the children have never uttered one complaint about the scrimping, from the beginning.

We all send you & all of you our love.

MARK

P.S. I see that I have left out something which I particularly wanted to say. In assuring Mrs. Clemens of your love for her you touched her very deeply, & she has never been more outspokenly grateful for any prized thing which these clouded eighteen months have brought her. She needs all the love she can get, & there is no other support that is so good & so welcome as the love of the old, old friends of the days that are gone.

TO JOSEPH H. TWICHELL
3 FEBRUARY 1898, VIENNA, AUSTRIA

(Private.)

HOTEL METROPOLE, VIENNA, FEB. 3/98

DEAR JOE:

There's that letter that I began so long ago – you see how it is: can't get time to finish anything. I pile up lots of work, nevertheless. There may be idle people in the world, but I'm not one of them.

I say "private" up there because I've got an adventure to tell, & you mustn't let a breath of it get out. First I thought I would lay it up along with a thousand others that I've laid up for the same purpose – to *talk* to you about, but – those others have vanished out of my memory; & that must not happen with this.

The other night I lectured for a Vienna charity; & at the end of it Livy & I were introduced to a princess who is aunt to the heir apparent of the imperial throne – a beautiful lady, with a beautiful spirit, & very cordial in her praises of my books & thanks to me for writing them; & glad to meet me face to face & shake me by the hand – just the kind of princess that adorns a fairy tale & makes it the prettiest tale there is.

Very well, we long ago found out that when you are noticed by supremacies, the correct etiquette is to go within a couple of days & pay your respects in the quite simple form of writing your name in the Visitors' Book kept in the office of the establishment. That is the end of it, & everything is squared up & ship-shape.

So at noon to-day Livy & I drove to the Archducal palace, & got by the sentries all right, & asked the grandly-uniformed portier for the book & said we wished to write our names in it. And he called a servant in livery & was sending us up stairs; & said her Royal Highness was out but would soon be in. Of course Livy said No – no – we only want the book; but he was firm, & said, "You are Americans?"

"Yes."

"Then you are expected – please go up stairs."

"But indeed we are *not* expected – please let us have the book & –"

"Her Royal Highness will be back in a *very* little while – she commanded me to *tell* you so – & you must wait.["]

Well, the soldiers were there close by – there was no use trying to resist – so we followed the servant up; but when he tried to beguile us into a drawing-room, Livy drew the line; she wouldn't go in. And she wouldn't stay up there, either. She said the princess might come in at any moment & catch us, & it would be too infernally ridiculous for anything. So we went down stairs again – to my unspeakable regret. For it was too darling a comedy to spoil. I was hoping & praying the princess *would* come, & catch us up there, & that those other Americans who *were* expected would arrive, & be taken for impostors by the portier, & shot by the sentinels – & then it would all go into the papers, & be cabled all over the world, & make an immense stir & be perfectly lovely. And by that time the princess would discover that *we* were not the right ones, & the Minister of War would be ordered out, & the garrison, & they would come for us, & there would be another prodigious time, & *that* would get cabled too, & – well, Joe, I was in a state of perfect bliss. But happily, oh, so happily, that big portier wouldn't let us out – he was sorry, but he must obey orders – we must go back up stairs & wait. Poor Livy – I couldn't help but enjoy her distress. She said we were in a fix, & how *were* we ever going to explain, if the princess should arrive before the rightful Americans came? We went up stairs again – laid off our wraps, & were conducted through one drawing room & into another, & left alone there & the door closed upon us.

Livy was in a state of mind! She said it was too theatrically ridiculous; & that I would never be able to keep my mouth shut; that I would be sure to let it out & it would get into the papers – & she tried to make me promise – "Promise *what?*" I said – "to be quiet about *this?* Indeed I won't – it's the best thing that ever happened; I'll tell it, & *add* to it; & I wish Joe & Howells were here to make it perfect; I can't make all the rightful blunders myself – it takes all three of us to do full justice to an opportunity like this. I would just like to see Howells get down to his work & explain, & lie, & work his futile & inventionless subterfuges when that princess comes raging in here & wanting to *know*." But Livy could not hear fun – it was not a time to be trying to be funny – we were in a most miserable & shameful situation, & if –

Just then the door spread wide & our princess & 4 more, & 3 little princes flowed in! Our princess, & her sister the Archduchess Marie Therese (mother to the imperial Heir & to the 2 young girl Archduchesses present, & aunt to the 3 little princes) – & we shook hands all around & sat down & had a most sociable good time for half an hour – & by & by it turned out that we *were* the right ones, & had been sent for by a messenger who started too late to catch us at the hotel. We were invited for 2 o'clock, but we beat *that* arrangement by an hour & a half.

Wasn't it a rattling good comedy situation? Seems a kind of pity we were the right ones. It would have been such nuts to see the right ones come, & get fired out, & we chatting along comfortably & nobody suspecting us for impostors.

We all send lots & lots of love.

MARK

TO WILLIAM DEAN HOWELLS

12–13 MAY 1899, VIENNA, AUSTRIA

HOTEL KRANTZ, WIEN, I. NEUER MARKT 6
MAY 12/99

DEAR HOWELLS: (*11 a.m.*)

When Bliss engaged Brander I took it for granted that he had not been able to get you & had therefore followed instructions & got Brander. It was through you that I found out *why* he had commissioned Brander; he did not reveal the reason himself. Then I had a pang which remains a pang yet, & [*one word canceled*] freshly smarts whenever I think of Bliss's stupid uneconomical economy. If I had been there I should have made even his publisher-soul understand that there are honors which are above the reach of computation in dollars – honors of that value at least to one of the partners in the Uniform – & that also *commercially* he was meditating a mistake – a mistake insuring damage for both partners. Damn these human beings; if I had invented them I would go hide my head in a bag. I can't get over the loss of that essay, & that is Mrs. Clemens's feeling about it also. Could you waive rank & let it sum up, as it were, & say the *last* word – as a preface to the closing volume? Do not be offended at the suggestion; I could not make it if your rank were not supreme – if you were not Douglas & above the salt no matter where the salt might be.

Mid-afternoon. Meantime I have answered a part of the accumulation of letters; for we are removing to England and Mrs. Clemens is thrashing around among the milliners & cannot attend to her household duties; & as for the children are concerned they *never* seem to have time to answer anybody's letters but their own, & what they are in the world for I don't know, for they are of no practical value as far as I can see. If I could beget a typewriter – but no, our fertile days are over. – However, I mustn't stop to play now, or I shall never get those helfiard letters answered. (That is not my spelling, but Mrs. Clemens's; I have told her the right way a thousand times, but it does no good, she cannot remember; a person who is not born to spell cannot learn – & in time, association with that kind of people rots one's own spelling.)

4 p.m. I have done 6 letters since; & I did a raft of them yesterday.

Day before yesterday the Harper came, & in the evening I hunted it up & was lying on the sofa, & kept interrupting the

family's repose with laughter & chuckles. Finally Mrs. Clemens
(very late, I thought) asked "What *is* it?"

"Portraits of *you*."

"Where?"

"In Carlsbad. Whether Mrs. March was there or not, *you* were."

Then she let it out that she had already been through the chapter, & had recognised herself. That seems good evidence to me that
Mrs. March is a *type*, going around disguised with a special name;
& she is probably being recognised by lots of Mrs. Marches named
Jones & Smith & so-on. I reckon you had good times writing that
number; it is persistently & devilishly happy & comfortable & easy
& flowing; & exact to the facts in every detail, of outside objects &
inside estimates of them & comments upon them. Your 84 votes
place you where you belong – at the head of the gang; even Jean
will have to concede that.

Game is called – for 5 o'clock tea. (For Mr. & Mrs. Tower, who
are leaving for Russia.) There'll be plenty of Americans, & the
"bad voice" will be largely in evidence. I am getting to where
I can't well stand that infernal voice. There's a beautiful English
girl in the house with a voice like a flute; if she should happen in,
the contrast will be something which a dead person would notice.

7^{15} *p.m.* It's over; 30 nice people & rather creditable to the human
race: Mr. & Mrs. Tower; the new Minister & his wife; the Secretary
of Legation; the Naval (& Military) Attaché; several English ladies;
an Irish lady; a Scotch lady; an English newspaper-heifer (who is
a good soul – a damned good soul, in fact – but wasn't invited &
didn't know it was a private orgy); a particularly nice young Austrian baron who wasn't invited but came & went supposing it was
the usual thing & wondered at the unusually large gathering; two
other Austrians & several Americans who were also in his fix; the
old Baronin Langenau, the only Austrian invited; – the rest were
Americans. It made just a comfortable crowd in our parlor, with
an overflow into Clara's through the folding doors. I don't enjoy
teas, & am daily spared them by Mrs. Clemens, but this was a
pleasant one. I had only one accident. The old Baronin Langenau
is a person I have a strong fondness for, for we violently disagree
on some subjects & as violently agree upon others: for instance,
she is temperance & I am not; she has religious beliefs & feelings
& I have none; (she's a *Methodist!*) she is a democrat & so am I; she
is woman's rights & so am I; she is laborers' rights & approves trade
unions & strikes, & that is me. And so-on. After she was gone an

English lady whom I greatly like, began to talk sharply against her for contributing money, time, labor, & public expression of favor to a strike that is on (for an 11-hour day) in the silk factories of Bohemia – & she caught me unprepared & betrayed me into over-warm argument. I am sorry; for she didn't know anything about the subject, & I did; & one should be gentle with the ignorant, for they are the chosen of God.

[The new minister is a good man, but out of place. The Sec. of Legation is a good man, but out of place. The Attaché is a good man, but out of place. Our government has more talent for displacement than the new White Star ship; & her possible is 17,200 tons.]

May 13, 4 pm. The beautiful English girl & her handsome English husband came up & spent the evening, & she certainly is a bird. English parents – she; born & reared in Roumania & couldn't talk English till she was 8 or 10. She came up clothed like the sunset; & was a delight to look at. (Roumanian costume.)

I was out walking at noon today, in the splendid summer weather, & came dreaming around the corner of a palace, & found myself fenced off by a long leather strap; I traced the strap leftward & found a sweet young lady holding the end of it; I traced it to starboard, then, & found a prodigious dog hitched to that end. [*one word canceled*] He probably thought is was *his* palace, for he had one leg up & was washing it down. I was embarrassed, but those others were not. I waited a second or two, not knowing just what to do, then backed away & pulled out around the Fräulein & departed. She & the string were barring the whole sidewalk. I went a little piece, then stopped to observe. That dog was loaded for bear; & before he had accomplished his relief, a woman, a boy, then a man, then another man, had all been obliged to turn out & deploy around the young lady. They ought to water that dog at home. It would have made a curious picture if I had had a Kodak & courage enough to use it. I felt a good deal of resentment against that girl for making me do all the blushing & embarrassing by myself, there before the public, when by rights it was her place to do it.

Twenty-four young people have gone out to the Semmering to-day (& tomorrow), & Mrs. Clemens & an English lady & old Leschetitzky & his wife have gone to chaperon them. They gave me a chance to go, but there are no snow mountains that I want to look at. Three hours out, three hours back, & sit up all night watching the young people dance; yelling conversationally & being yelled at, conversationally, by new acquaintances, through the deafening

music, about how I like Vienna, & if it's my first visit, & how long
we expect to stay, & did I see the foot-washing, & am I writing a
book about Vienna, & so on. The terms seemed too severe. Snow
mountains are too dear at the price. A frolic in hell itself would not
pay at those figures – when one is chasing up on a 64th birthday.

[A telephone message from the Semmering, waiting for me down
stairs. That is to tell me how lovely it is, I suppose – there's an out-
train in half an hour. "Tell them I am out – then bring me the
message." * * * I was right. So I am still "out" – till that train goes.]

6 p.m. For several years I have been intending to stop writing for
print as soon as I could afford it. At last I can afford it, & have put
the pot-boiler pen away. What I have been wanting was a chance
to write a book without reserves – a book which should take
account of no one's feelings, no one's prejudices, opinions, beliefs,
hopes, illusions, delusions; a book which should say my say, right
out of my heart, in the plainest language & without a limitation of
any sort. I judged that that would be an unimaginable luxury,
heaven on earth. There was no condition but one under which the
writing of such a book could be possible; only one – the consciousness that it would not see print.

It is under way, now, & it *is* a luxury! – an intellectual drunk.
Twice I didn't start it right; & got pretty far in, both times, before
I found it out. But I am sure it is started right this time. It is in tale-
form. I believe I can make it tell what I think of Man, & how he is
constructed, & what a shabby poor ridiculous thing he is, & how
mistaken he is in his estimate of his character & powers & qualities
& his place among the animals.

So far, I think I am succeeding. I let the madam into the secret
day before yesterday, & locked the doors & read to her the opening
chapters. She said –

"It is perfectly horrible – and perfectly beautiful!"

"Within the due limits of modesty, that is what *I* think."

I hope it will take me a year or two to write it, & that it will turn
out to be the right vessel to contain all the ordure I am planning
to dump into it.

YOURS EVER

MARK

We leave in ten days for England, where business calls me. Shall
be there till October – then home to America.

⦃ *Address*: Care Chatto & Windus
⦃   111 St. Martin's Lane, London WC

TO WILLIAM DEAN HOWELLS

25 AND 26 JANUARY 1900, LONDON, ENGLAND

WELLINGTON COURT, KNIGHTSBRIDGE,
JAN. 25, 1900

DEAR HOWELLS:

Yes, the short things will be added to Bliss's Uniform Edition. Harper will issue two volumes of them in the spring. I consented a couple of weeks before their smash. They decline to give them up, now.

If you got half as much as Pond prophecied, be content & praise God – it has not happened to another. But I am sorry he didn't go with you; for it is marvelous to hear him lie. He is good company, cheery & hearty, & his mill is never idle. Your doing a lecture tour was heroic. It was the highest order of grit, & you have a right to be proud of yourself. No amount of applause or money or both could save it from being a hell to a man constituted as you are. It is that even to me, who am made of coarser stuff.

I knew the audiences would come forward & shake hands with you – that one infallible sign of sincere approval. In all my life, wherever it failed me I left the hall sick & ashamed, knowing what it meant.

Privately speaking, this is a sordid & criminal war, & in every way shameful & excuseless. Every day I write (in my head) bitter magazine articles about it, but I have to stop with that. For England must not fall: it would mean an inundation of Russian & German political degradations which would envelop the globe & steep it in a sort of Middle-Age night & slavery which would last till Christ comes again – which I hope he will not do, he made trouble enough before. Even wrong – & she is wrong – England must be upheld. He is an enemy of the human race who shall speak against her now. Why *was* the human race created? Or at least why wasn't something creditable created in place of it. God had His opportunity; He could have made a reputation. But no, He must commit this grotesque folly – a lark which must have cost him a regret or two when He came to think it over & observe effects. For a giddy & unbecoming caprice there has been nothing like it till this war. I talk the war with both sides – always waiting until the other man introduces the topic. Then I say "My head is with the Briton, but my heart & such rags of morals as I have are with the Boer – now we will talk, unembarrassed & without prejudice." And so we discuss, & have no trouble.

JAN. 26.

It was my intention to make some disparaging remarks about the human race; & so I kept this letter open for that purpose, & for the purpose of telling my dream, wherein the Trinity were trying to guess a conundrum propounded by One of Them regarding that premature birth; but I can do better – for I can snip out of the "Times" various samples & side-lights which bring the race down to date, & expose it as of yesterday. If you will notice, there is seldom a telegram in a paper which fails to show up one or more members & beneficiaries of our Civilization as promenading with his shirt-tail up & the rest of his regalia in the wash.

I love to see the holy ones air their smug pieties & admire them & smirk over them, & at the same moment frankly & publicly make water on the pieties of his Boer – confidently expecting the approval of his country & his pulpit, & getting it.

I notice that God is on both sides in this war; thus history repeats itself. But I am the only person who has noticed this; everybody here thinks He is playing the game for this side, & for this side only.

With great love to you all

MARK

TO BRANDER MATTHEWS
4 MAY 1903, RIVERDALE, N.Y.

TELEPHONE 150 KINGSBRIDGE,
N.Y. CITY, MAY 4/03

DEAR BRANDER:

I haven't been out of my bed for 4 weeks, but – well, I have been reading, a good deal, & it occurs to me to ask you to sit down, some time or other when you have 8 or 9 months to spare, & jot me down a certain few literary particulars for my help & elevation. Your time need not be thrown away, for at your further leisure you can make Columbian lectures out of the results & do your students a good turn.

1. Are there in Sir Walter's novels passages done in *good* English – English which is neither slovenly nor involved?

2. Are there passages whose English is not poor & thin & commonplace, but is of a quality above that?

3. Are there passages which burn with real fire – not punk, fox-fire, make-believe?

4. Has he heroes & heroines who are not cads & cadesses?

5. Has he personages whose acts & talk correspond with their characters as described by him?

6. Has he heroes & heroines whom the reader admires? admires, & knows *why?* admires, & is not ashamed of it?

7. Has he funny characters that are funny, & humorous passages that are humorous?

8. Does he ever chain the reader's interest, & make him reluctant to lay the book down?

9. Are there pages where he ceases from posing, ceases from admiring the placid flood & flow of his dilutions, ceases from being artificial, & is for a time, long or short, recognizably sincere & in earnest?

10. Did he know how to write English, & didn't do it because he didn't want to?

11. Did he use the right word only when he couldn't think of another one, or did he run so much to wrong words because he didn't know the right one when he saw it?

12. Can you read him? and keep your respect for him? Of course a person could in *his* day – an era of sentimentality & sloppy romantics – but land! can a body do it to-day?

Brander, I lie here dying, slowly dying, under the blight of Sir Walter. I have read the first volume of Rob Roy, & as far as Chapter XIX of Guy Mannering, & I can no longer hold my head up nor take my nourishment. Lord, it's all so juvenile! so artificial, so shoddy; & *such* wax figures & skeletons & spectres. Interest? Why, it is impossible to feel an interest in these bloodless shams, these milk-&-water humbugs. And oh, the poverty of invention! Not poverty in inventing situations, but poverty in furnishing reasons for them. Sir Walter usually gives himself away when he arranges for a situation – elaborates, & elaborates, & elaborates, till if you live to get to it you don't believe in it when it happens.

I can't find the rest of Rob Roy, I can't stand any more Mannering – I do not know just what to do, but I will reflect, & not quit this great study rashly. He *was* great, in his day, & to his own proper audience; & so was God in Jewish times, for that matter, but why should either of them rank high now? And *do* they – honest, now, *do* they? Dam'd if I believe it.

My, I wish I could see you & Leigh Hunt!

SINCERELY YOURS

S. L. CLEMENS

TO THOMAS F. GATTS
30 MAY 1903, RIVERDALE, N.Y.

NEW YORK CITY, MAY 30/03

THOMAS F. GATTS, ESQ:

Dear Sir: It is indeed a high compliment which you offer me in naming an association after me & in proposing the setting apart of a Mark Twain Day at the great St. Louis Fair, but such compliments are not proper for the living, they are proper & safe for the dead only. I value the impulse which moves you to tender me these honors; I value it as highly as any one can, & am grateful for it, but I should stand in a sort of terror of the honors themselves. So long as we remain alive we are not safe from doing things, which, howsoever righteously & honorably intended, can wreck our repute & extinguish our friendships. I hope that no society will be named for me while I am still alive, for I might at some time or other do something which could cause its members to regret having done me that honor. After I shall have joined the dead I shall follow the custom of those people & be guilty of no conduct that can wound any friend; but until that time shall come I shall be a doubtful quantity, like the rest of our race.

VERY TRULY YOURS

S. L. CLEMENS

TO WILLIAM DEAN HOWELLS
6 JUNE 1904, FLORENCE, ITALY

VILLA DI QUARTO
FLORENCE, JUNE 6/04

DEAR HOWELLS:

Last night at 9.20 I entered Mrs. Clemens's room to say good-night – & she was dead! Tho' no one knew it. She had been cheer-fully talking a moment before. She was sitting up in bed – she had not lain down for months – & Katie & the nurse were supporting her. They supposed she had fainted, & they were holding the oxygen pipe to her mouth, expecting to revive her. I bent over her & looked in her face, & I think I spoke – I was surprised & troubled that she did not notice me. Then we understood, & our hearts broke. How poor we are to-day!

But how thankful I am that her persecutions are ended. I would not call her back if I could.

To-day, treasured in her worn old Testament, I found a dear & gentle letter from you, dated Far Rockaway, Sept. 13, 1896, about our poor Susy's death. I am tired & old; I wish I were with Livy.

I send my love – & hers – to you all.

SLC.

TO JOSEPH H. TWICHELL
8 JUNE 1904, FLORENCE, ITALY

WEDNESDAY AFTERNOON. (CLARA'S BIRTHDAY)
VILLA DI QUARTO, JUNE 8/04

DEAR JOE: We were eager to serve her, all these piteous months. She couldn't devise a plan, however staggering, that we didn't applaud, & do our best to bring it to fruitage. Every day, for weeks & weeks, we went out armed with the enclosed paper, hunting for a villa – to rent for a year, but always with an option to *buy* at a specified figure within the year; & yet, deep down in our unreveal-ing hearts we believed she would never get out of her bed again.

Only last Sunday evening, with death flying toward her, & due in one hour & a quarter, she was full of interest in that matter, &

asked me if I had heard of any more villas for sale. And many a time, these months, she said she wanted a *home* – a house of her own, that she was tired & wanted rest, & could not rest & be in comfort & peace while she was homeless. And now she is at rest, poor worn heart! Joe, she was so lovely, so patient – a murmur at her hard fate; yet – but I *can't* put her sufferings on paper, it breaks my heart to think of them. She sat up in bed 6 months, night & day, & was always in bodily misery, & could get but little sleep, & then only by resting her forehead against a support – think of those lonely nights in the gloom of a taper, with Katy sleeping, & with no company but her fearsome thoughts & her pathetic longings; it makes my heart bleed, it makes me blaspheme, to think of the gratuitous devilishness of it.

How sweet she was in death, how young, how beautiful, how like her girlish self of thirty years ago. Not a gray hair showing. This rejuvenescence was noticeable within 2 hours after death; that was at 11:30; when I went down again (2.30) it was complete; the same at 4, 5, 7, 8 – & so remained the whole of the day till the embalmers came at 5; & then I saw her no more. In all that night & all that day she never noticed my caressing hand – it seemed strange.

She so dreaded death, poor timid little prisoner; for it promised to be by strangulation. Five times in 4 months she went through that choking horror for an hour & more, & came out of it white, haggard, exhausted, & quivering with fright. Then cursing failed me; there was no language bitter enough whereby to curse the cowardly invention of those wanton tortures. But when death came, she did not know it. Nor did we. She was chatting cheerfully, only a minute before. We were all present, I was stooping over her; we saw no change – yet she was gone from us! Why am I required to linger here?

                                                                        SLC

TO JOSEPH H. TWICHELL
18 JUNE 1904, FLORENCE, ITALY

DEAR JOE:

It is 13 days. I am bewildered and must remain so for a time longer. It was so sudden, so unexpected. Imagine a man worth a hundred millions who suddenly finds himself penniless & fifty millions in debt in his old age.

I was richer than any other person in the world, and now I am that pauper without peer. Some day I will tell you about it, not now.

MARK

TO SUSAN L. CRANE
24 SEPTEMBER 1905, DUBLIN, N.H.

DUBLIN, SEPT. 24/05

Susy dear, I have had a lovely dream. Livy, dressed in black, was sitting up in my bed (here) at my right & looking as young & sweet as she used to do when she was in health. She said: "what is the name of your sweet sister?" I said, "Pamela." "Oh, yes, that is it, I thought it was – (naming a name which has escaped me) "Won't you write it down for me?" I reached eagerly for a pen & pad – laid my hands upon both – then said to myself, "It is only a dream," & turned back sorrowfully & there she was, still. The conviction flamed through me that our lamented disaster was a dream, & this a reality. I said, "How blessed it is, how blessed it is, it was all a dream, only a dream!" She only smiled & did not ask what dream I meant, which surprised me. She leaned her head against mine & I kept saying, "I was perfectly sure it was a dream, I never would have believed it wasn't."

I think she said several things, but if so they are gone from my memory. I woke & did not know I had been dreaming. She was gone. I wondered how she could go without my knowing it, but I did not spend any thought upon that, I was too busy thinking of how vivid & real was the dream that we had lost her & how unspeakably blessed it was to find that it was not true & that she was still ours & with us.

S. L. C.

TO WILLIAM DEAN HOWELLS
17 JUNE 1906, DUBLIN, N.H.

DUBLIN, SUNDAY JUNE 17/06

DEAR HOWELLS:

It was wrong to bother you about the story. I only needed to say: "This is Mr. Howell's story, turned into fiction-form" – & then insert the tale "Was it Heaven? – or Hell?" I've done that. In fact that was the *only* right way.

The dictating goes lazily & pleasantly on. (With intervals.) I find that I've been at it, off & on, nearly two hours a day for 155 days, since Jan. 9. To be exact, I've dictated 75 hours in 80 days & loafed [*one word canceled*] 75 days. I've added 60,000 words in the month that I've been here; which indicates that I've dictated during 20 days of that time – 40 hours, at an average of [*one word canceled*] 1,500 words an hour. It's a plenty, & I am satisfied.

There's a good deal of "fat." I've dictated, (from Jan. 9) 210,000 words, & the "fat" adds about 50,000 more.

The "fat" is old pigeon-holed things, of the years gone by, which I or editors didn't das't to print. For instance, I am dumping in the little old book which I read to you in Hartford about 30 years ago, & which you said "publish – & ask Dean Stanley to furnish an introduction; he'll do it." "(Captain Stormfield's Visit to Heaven.") It reads quite to suit me, without altering a word, now that it isn't to see print until I am dead.

To-morrow I mean to dictate a chapter which will get my heirs & assigns burnt alive if they venture to print it this side of 2006 A.D. – which I judge they won't. There'll be lots of such chapters if I live 3 or 4 years longer. The edition of A.D. 2006 will make a stir when it comes out. I shall be hovering around taking notice, along with other dead pals. You are invited.

MARK

P.S.

I think Miss Lyon told you the reason we couldn't send you the Autobiography – there's only one typed copy, & we had to have it for reference, to guard against repetitions. The making of a second copy is now begun; & so, we can presently begin to mail batches of it to you. This book is already perfectly outrageous, in spots, but that's nothing – it's going to be worse by & by if I live beyond my appointed date. I don't care for my other books, now, but I dote on this one as Adam used to dote on a fresh new deformed child after he was 900 years old & wasn't expecting any more surprises. I've written a short Preface. I like the title of it: "Spoken from the Grave." It will prepare the reader for the solemnities within.

I'm in the middle of a history of Bret Harte, but I'll break into that with a newer & hotter interest tomorrow – according to the laws of this book: the newest & hottest interest takes precedence of *anything* I may be talking about. The rest of Bret will be postponed – like Orion. (You didn't see the last of him; he got postponed & pushed ahead several times, by intruding, warmer interests of various kinds.)

Dialogue the other day, over the long-distance, between Miss Lyon & Clara (bad telephone):

Miss L. Your father wants an MS book which is unfinished. In drawer in his study. *(Yells it 3 times.)*

C. Oh, an MS *book?* What's the title? *(Yells it 3 times.)*

L. Has no title. First sentence is, "Tell him to go to hell!" *(Yells it many times.)*

C. Tell him to go . . .?

L. Yes.

C. Go *where?*

L. Go to *hell! (Several times)*

C. I can't get the last word.

L. Oh – *hell!*

C. Can't get it. Spell it.

L. H – e – double – l! HELL! Get it now? Tell – him – to – go – to – HELL!

C. (Shouting.) Tell him to go to hell?

L. That's it. Your father wants it.

[cross-written in the right margin:] You see we might have been hauled to Court by the telephone company.

TO NIKOLAI V. CHAIKOVSKY
28 OR 29 MARCH 1906, NEW YORK, N.Y.

DEAR MR. TCHAYKOFFSKY: I thank you for the honor of the invitation, but I am not able to accept it, because on Thursday evening I shall be presiding at a meeting whose object is to find remunerative work for certain classes of our blind who would gladly support themselves if they had the opportunity.

My sympathies are with the Russian revolution, of course. It goes without saying. I hope it will succeed, and now that I have talked with you I take heart to believe it will. Government by falsified promises, by lies, by treacheries, and by the butcher-knife for the aggrandizement of a single family of drones and its idle and vicious kin has been borne quite long enough in Russia, I should think, and it is to be hoped that the roused nation, now rising in its strength, will presently put an end to it and set up the republic in its place. Some of us, even of the white headed, may live to see the blessed day when Czars and Grand Dukes will be as scarce there as I trust they are in heaven.

MOST SINCERELY YOURS,
MARK TWAIN

TO OLIVER O. HOWARD
PER ISABEL V. LYON
12 JANUARY 1909, REDDING, CONN.

STORMFIELD REDDING CONNECTICUT
JAN 12/09

DEAR GENERAL HOWARD:

You pay me a most gratifying compliment in asking me to preside, & it causes me very real regret that I am obliged to decline, for the object of the meeting appeals strongly to me, since that object is to aid in raising the $500,000 Endowment Fund for Lincoln Memorial University. The Endowment Fund will be the most fitting of all the memorials the country will dedicate to the memory of Lincoln, serving, as it will, to uplift his very own people.

I hope you will meet with complete success, & I am sorry I cannot be there to witness it & help you rejoice. But I am older than people think, nearly twice as old as I used to be; & besides I live away out in the country & never stir from home, except at geological intervals to fill left-over engagements made in Mesozoic Times when I was younger & indiscreeter.

You ought not to say sarcastic things about my "fighting on the other side." General Grant did not act like that. General Grant paid me compliments. He bracketed me with Zenophon – it is there in his memoirs for anybody to read. He said if all the confederate soldiers had followed my example & adopted my military arts he could never have caught enough of them in a bunch to inconvenience the Rebellion. General Grant was a fair man & recognized my worth; but you are prejudiced, & you have hurt my feelings.

But I have an affection for you, anyway.

MARK TWAIN

TO WILLIAM DEAN HOWELLS
18 JANUARY 1909, REDDING, CONN.

STORMFIELD REDDING CONNECTICUT
JAN. 18/09

DEAR HOWELLS:

I *have* to write a line, lazy as I am, to say how your Poe article delights me & charms me; & to add that I am in agreement with substantially all you say about his literature. To me his prose is unreadable – like Jane Austin's. No, there is a difference: I could read his prose on salary, but not Jane's. Jane is entirely impossible. It seems a great pity that they allowed her to die a natural death.

Another thing: you grant that God & circumstances sinned against Poe, but you also grant that he sinned against himself – a thing which he couldn't do & didn't do.

It is lovely up here now. I wish you could come.

YS EVER
MARK

TO CLARA L. CLEMENS
29 DECEMBER 1909, REDDING, CONN.

REDDING CONN.
DEC. 29/09

O, Clara, Clara dear, I am so glad she is out of it & safe – safe!

I am not melancholy; I shall never be melancholy again, I think.

You see, I was in such distress when I came to realize that you were gone far away & no one stood between her & danger but me – & I could die at any moment, & *then* – oh then what would become of her! For she was wilful, you know, & would not have been governable.

You can't imagine what a darling she was, that last two or three days; & how *fine*, & good, & sweet, & noble – & *joyful*, thank Heaven! – & how intellectually brilliant. I had never been acquainted with Jean before. I recognized that.

But I mustn't try to write about her – I can't. I have already poured my heart out with the pen, recording that last day or two. I will send you that – & you must let no one but Ossip read it.

Good-bye. I love you so! And Ossip!

FATHER

TO ELIZABETH WALLACE
26 AND 29 JANUARY 1910, HAMILTON, BERMUDA

STORMFIELD REDDING CONNECTICUT
BERMUDA, JAN. 26/10

DEAR BETSY –

No, revelation – of a valuable sort – does not come through sorrow when one is old. Before 70 the whole satire & swindle of life has been revealed – to all except the wilfully or constitutionally dull. What a silly invention human life is! & how like a glove its silliest religion fits it! & how perfectly our principal God & His Fambly harmonise with the outfit?!

Do I "know more" than I knew before? Oh, *hell* no! There was nothing to learn, (about hereafters & other-such undesirables), there has never *been* anything to learn & know about those insulting mysteries. I am happy – few are so happy – but I get none of this happiness from "knowing more" of the unknowable than I knew before.

Jan. 29 – noon. I intended to be lazy & dictate the rest of this, but my little secretary (Helen Allen, angel-fish) has escaped, & gone bicycling with a schoolmate. I am guest in her parents' house – indefinitely. I never feel a desire to revisit Stormfield. Paine & his wife & little girl are occupying the house for me. The servants like them & will stay with them, I think. I have Claude, best of butlers, valets &-everything-else, with me. He lives at the Hamilton House, but is in close touch with me by telephone and bicycle.

In England Ashcroft committed a forgery in the second degree upon me, & sold for £25 my name (& words which I would not have uttered for a hundred times the money.) Sh–! say nothing about it – we hope to catch him & shut him up in a British prison. It is not a strong hope, for he is smart in covering up his tracks, but we shall get out of it what we can.

He is a reptile – yes, but not so slimy a one as his wife. *She* was intended for an insect – capturable with a fine-tooth comb.

Helen has been gone an hour & a half, & will have to be severely scolded. Did you ever try to scold an angel-fish? I think a person could learn to do it. But he would have to have considerable practice.

GOOD-BYE. AFFECTIONATELY, S L C

[*in Helen S. Allen's hand:*]

Apology. Mr. Clemens wants me to say I am sorry. So I say I am sorry.

HELEN SCHUYLER ALLEN.
SECY

ESSAYS AND
SPEECHES

BLABBING GOVERNMENT
SECRETS!

THE PEOPLE GENERALLY seem to think that the present extra session of the State Legislature was convened for the purpose of transacting this Railroad business, and I hasten from a sense of duty to my fellow-citizens, to correct this wrong impression; their ignorance on this subject shows that they have paid very little attention to the proceedings of the Legislature. – Now this is just the way of it: I didn't like my surname; as for the handles to it, they did very well; *I* wouldn't care if I had twenty more like 'em; but the surname didn't suit; and although the Legislature is not, I believe, accustomed to change people's surnames, I nevertheless wrote to Gov. King, who is a particular friend of mine, requesting him to call the session and make the wished-for alteration, and leaving the selection of the new name to his own refined taste and judgment. Well, the request was granted; the Legislature was convened; my title was altered, shortened, and greatly beautified – and all at a cost of *only a few thousands of dollars to the State!* – these Democratic Legislators work cheap, don't they, Editor?

This new cognomen suits me, and I hope it will meet with favor in the eyes of the inhabitants of this great Union; and if Congress takes the matter up and changes it back the way it was, the villainous President that signs the documents and makes it a law will never get my support – No, sir! not if he's NEVER elected again! As for Queen Victoria and Lord Derby, they may cut up as much as they like – it's none of their business.

Blab – Blab – sounds pretty – makes good jingle – it's just the thing – the Blabs were ancestors of mine, anyhow. The first Blab lived in Adam's time, and had a little falling out with that distinguished gentleman about a tin cup, which both claimed – yes, a *tin cup!* – you needn't giggle either; if you knew as much about the Bible as I do, you'd find that tin cups were tolerably scarce in those days. Well, as I was going to say, they quarreled about the cup; public opinion was in favor of Adam, and Adam got the cup; and ever since that time people haven't thought well of the Blabs; that was right though – they were always a rascally set, and I believe Blab stole the cup; but Adam was no more respectable than Blab – he never had a mother! at least people said so, and folks of that character don't stand very high nowadays. However, if it hadn't been for that little difficulty, a Blab would have been President instead of John Quincy Adams! Despite all these things, the Blabs have been somewhat distinguished, anyhow; honorable mention was made of one of them in a book that was never published, and another one was hung last week for his rascality, and I'm glad of it; for he was a Democrat, and ought to have been hung long ago. I go in for hanging all the Whigs and Democrats, and then the only Blab that ever went unhung would stand a chance – a slim one, too, I reckon, for then that great military hero you mentioned some time since – I believe you call him Ensign Jehiel Stebbings – would step in. It's no go.

W. E. A. B.
September 16, 1852

LETTER FROM CARSON CITY

CARSON, Saturday Night.

EDS. ENTERPRISE: I feel very much as if I had just awakened out of a long sleep. I attribute it to the fact that I have slept the greater part of the time for the last two days and nights. On Wednesday, I sat up all night, in Virginia, in order to be up early enough to take the five o'clock stage on Thursday morning. I was on time. It was a great success. I had a cheerful trip down to Carson, in company with that incessant talker, Joseph T. Goodman. I never saw him flooded with such a flow of spirits before. He restrained his conversation, though, until we had traveled three or four miles, and were just crossing the divide between Silver City and Spring Valley, when he thrust his head out of the dark stage, and allowed a pallid light from the coach lamp to illuminate his features for a moment, after which he returned to darkness again, and sighed and said, "Damn it!" with some asperity. I asked him who he meant it for, and he said, "The weather out there." As we approached Carson, at about half past seven o'clock, he thrust his head out again, and gazed earnestly in the direction of that city – after which he took it in again, with his nose very much frosted. He propped the end of that organ upon the end of his finger, and looked down pensively upon it – which had the effect of making him appear cross-eyed – and remarked, "O, damn it!" with great bitterness. I asked him what he was up to this time, and he said, "The cold, damp fog – it is worse than the weather." This was his last. He never spoke again in my hearing. He went on over the mountains, with a lady fellow-passenger from here. That will stop his clatter, you know, for he seldom speaks in the presence of ladies.

In the evening I felt a mighty inclination to go to a party somewhere. There was to be one at Governor J. Neely Johnson's, and I went there and asked permission to stand around awhile. This was granted in the most hospitable manner, and visions of plain quadrilles soothed my weary soul. I felt particularly comfortable, for if there is one thing more grateful to my feelings than another, it is a new house – a large house, with its ceilings embellished with snowy mouldings; its floors glowing with warm-tinted carpets; with cushioned chairs and sofas to sit on, and a piano to listen to; with fires so arranged that you can see them, and know that there is no humbug about it; with walls garnished with pictures, and

above all, mirrors, wherein you may gaze, and always find something to admire, you know. I have a great regard for a good house,
and a girlish passion for mirrors. Horace Smith, Esq., is also very
fond of mirrors. He came and looked in the glass for an hour, with
me. Finally, it cracked – the night was pretty cold – and Horace
Smith's reflection was split right down the centre. But where his
face had been, the damage was greatest – a hundred cracks con-
verged from his reflected nose, like spokes from the hub of a wagon
wheel. It was the strangest freak the weather has done this Winter.
And yet the parlor seemed very warm and comfortable, too.

About nine o'clock the Unreliable came and asked Gov. Johnson to let him stand on the porch. That creature has got more
impudence than any person I ever saw in my life. Well, he stood
and flattened his nose against the parlor window, and looked hungry and vicious – he always looks that way – until Col. Musser
arrived with some ladies, when he actually fell in their wake and
came swaggering in, looking as if he thought he had been anxiously
expected. He had on my fine kid boots, and my plug hat and my
white kid gloves, (with slices of his prodigious hands grinning
through the bursted seams), and my heavy gold repeater, which
I had been offered thousands and thousands of dollars for, many
and many a time. He took these articles out of my trunk, at Washoe
City, about a month ago, when we went out there to report the
proceedings of the Convention. The Unreliable intruded himself
upon me in his cordial way, and said, "How are you, Mark, old
boy? when d'you come down? It's brilliant, ain't it? Appear to
enjoy themselves, don't they? Lend a fellow two bits, can't you?"
He always winds up his remarks that way. He appears to have an
insatiable craving for two bits.

The music struck up just then, and saved me. The next moment
I was far, far at sea in a plain quadrille. We carried it through with
distinguished success; that is, we got as far as "balance around,"
and "half-a-man-left," when I smelled hot whisky punch, or something of that nature. I tracked the scent through several rooms, and
finally discovered the large bowl from whence it emanated. I found
the omnipresent Unreliable there, also. He set down an empty
goblet, and remarked that he was diligently seeking the gentlemen's dressing room. I would have shown him where it was, but
it occurred to him that the supper table and the punch-bowl ought
not to be left unprotected; wherefore, we staid there and watched
them until the punch entirely evaporated. A servant came in then

to replenish the bowl, and we left the refreshments in his charge. We probably did wrong, but we were anxious to join the hazy dance. The dance was hazier than usual, after that. Sixteen couples on the floor at once, with a few dozen spectators scattered around, is calculated to have that effect in a brilliantly lighted parlor, I believe. Everything seemed to buzz, at any rate. After all the modern dances had been danced several times, the people adjourned to the supper-room. I found my wardrobe out there, as usual, with the Unreliable in it. His old distemper was upon him: he was desperately hungry. I never saw a man eat as much as he did in my life. I have the various items of his supper here in my note-book. First, he ate a plate of sandwiches; then he ate a handsomely iced poundcake; then he gobbled a dish of chicken salad; after which he ate a roast pig; after that, a quantity of blancmange; then he threw in several glasses of punch to fortify his appetite, and finished his monstrous repast with a roast turkey. Dishes of brandy-grapes, and jellies, and such things, and pyramids of fruits, melted away before him as shadows fly at the sun's approach. I am of the opinion that none of his ancestors were present when the five thousand were miraculously fed in the old Scriptural times. I base my opinion upon the twelve baskets of scraps and the little fishes that remained over after that feast. If the Unreliable himself had been there, the provisions would just about have held out, I think.

After supper, the dancing was resumed, and after awhile, the guests indulged in music to a considerable extent. Mrs. J. sang a beautiful Spanish song; Miss R., Miss T., Miss P., and Miss S., sang a lovely duett; Horace Smith, Esq., sang "I'm sitting on the stile, Mary," with a sweetness and tenderness of expression which I have never heard surpassed; Col. Musser sang "From Greenland's Icy Mountains" so fervently that every heart in that assemblage was purified and made better by it; Mrs. T. and Miss C., and Mrs. T. and Mrs. G. sang "Meet me by moonlight alone" charmingly; Judge Dixson sang "O, Charming May" with great vivacity and artistic effect; Joe Winters and Hal Clayton sang the Marseilles Hymn in French, and did it well; Mr. Wasson sang "Call me pet names" with his usual excellence – (Wasson has a cultivated voice, and a refined musical taste, but like Judge Brumfield, he throws so much operatic affectation into his singing that the beauty of his performance is sometimes marred by it – I could not help noticing this fault when Judge Brumfield sang "Rock me to sleep, mother;")

Wm. M. Gillespie sang "Thou hast wounded the spirit that loved thee," gracefully and beautifully, and wept at the recollection of the circumstance which he was singing about. Up to this time I had carefully kept the Unreliable in the back ground, fearful that, under the circumstances, his insanity would take a musical turn; and my prophetic soul was right; he eluded me and planted himself at the piano; when he opened his cavernous mouth and displayed his slanting and scattered teeth, the effect upon that convivial audience was as if the gates of a graveyard, with its crumbling tombstones, had been thrown open in their midst; then he shouted some thing about he "would not live alway" – and if I ever heard anything absurd in my life, that was it. He must have made up that song as he went along. Why, there was no more sense in it, and no more music, than there is in his ordinary conversation. The only thing in the whole wretched performance that redeemed it for a moment, was something about "the few lucid moments that dawn on us here." That was all right; because the "lucid moments" that dawn on that Unreliable are almighty few, I can tell you. I wish one of them would strike him while I am here, and prompt him to return my valuables to me. I doubt if he ever gets lucid enough for that, though. After the Unreliable had finished squawking, I sat down to the piano and sang – however, what I sang is of no consequence to anybody. It was only a graceful little gem from the horse opera.

At about two o'clock in the morning the pleasant party broke up and the crowd of guests distributed themselves around town to their respective homes; and after thinking the fun all over again, I went to bed at four o'clock. So, having been awake forty-eight hours, I slept forty-eight, in order to get even again, which explains the proposition I began this letter with.

Yours, dreamily,

MARK TWAIN.

February 3, 1863

ALL ABOUT THE FASHIONS

"EDRS. GOLDEN ERA – We are all delighted with the 'Letter,' describing the brilliant Ball at Mr. Barron's. I am a Washoe widow, was among the favored few, and went. Sarah Smith skipped me in the toilettes. I suppose I wasn't very stunning, although Brigham & Co. said I looked 'swell,' and that 'Robergh' couldn't get up anything better. Some months ago, when my spouse, now at Reese River, first brought me down from Virginia City to stop in San Francisco, I arrived in the nick of time to attend one of those charming re-unions which are all the rage in the Pacific Metropolis. We have had several soirees since that, but nobody gave any account of them to the papers. It's too bad. Now we are eagerly looking forward to the next soiree, expecting the GOLDEN ERA to tell all about it. One of our boarders says she knows Florence Fane, and means to invite her; but I can't for the life of me get her to tell me the real name of your charming feuilletonist. I hope she'll come. And may-be Mark Twain will stay in town, to be there too. There is some talk of getting up a special gathering in compliment to him. He's such a favorite – stops here for his health – hoping to find out how to cure a cold. I am going to wear a new dress, made precisely after the pattern of one of those sweet Paris Fashion Plates in the *California Magazine*. That Ball Dress in the May number – I think it was – I've kept it in my boudoir ever since. Then if Mark Twain is only there to see; how happy, how happy, I shall be. (I don't mean that for poetry – Like what you put in the GOLDEN ERA.) (To take that license I am free – I write with such facility.) But I have not told you what I wanted. Mark Twain was at our party, last June, and sent the *Territorial Enterprise* an account of the affair. My husband enclosed me the paper in which it appeared. I cut it out and you can copy it. Please do. I've been bothered to death to let everybody see it, and it's dreadfully tattered and torn."

Here it is!

LETTER FROM MARK TWAIN.

ALL ABOUT THE FASHIONS.

SAN FRANCISCO, June 19.

EDS. ENTERPRISE: — I have just received, per Wells-Fargo, the following sweet scented little note, written in a microscopic hand in the center of a delicate sheet of paper – like a wedding invitation or a funeral notice – and I feel it my duty to answer it:

"VIRGINIA, June 16.

"MR. MARK TWAIN: — *Do* tell us something about the fashions. I am dying to know what the ladies of San Francisco are wearing. Do, now, tell us all you know about it, won't you? Pray excuse brevity, for I am in *such* a hurry.

BETTIE.

"P.S. – Please burn this as soon as you have read it."

"*Do* tell us" – and she is in "*such* a hurry." Well, I never knew a girl in my life who could write three consecutive sentences without italicising a word. They can't do it, you know. Now, if I had a wife, and she – however, I don't think I shall have one this week, and it is hardly worth while to borrow trouble.

Bettie, my love, you do me proud. In thus requesting me to fix up the fashions for you in an intelligent manner, you pay a compliment to my critical and observant eye and my varied and extensive information, which a mind less perfectly balanced than mine could scarcely contemplate without excess of vanity. Will I tell you something about the fashions? I will, Bettie – you better bet you bet, Betsey, my darling. I learned those expressions from the Unreliable; like all the phrases which fall from his lips, they are frightfully vulgar – but then they sound rather musical than otherwise.

A happy circumstance has put it in my power to furnish you the fashions from headquarters – as it were, Bettie: I refer to the assemblage of fashion, elegance and loveliness called together in the parlor of the Lick House last night – [a party given by the proprietors on the occasion of my paying up that little balance due on my board bill.] I will give a brief and lucid description of the dresses worn by several of the ladies of my acquaintance who were present. Mrs. B. was arrayed in a superb speckled foulard, with the stripes running fore and aft, and with collets and camails to match; also, a rotonde of Chantilly lace, embroidered with blue and yellow dogs, and birds and things, done in cruel, and edged with a Solferino fringe four inches deep – lovely. Mrs. B. is tall, and graceful and beautiful, and the general effect of her costume was to render her appearance extremely lively.

Miss J. W. wore a charming robe polonais of scarlet ruche a la vieille, with yellow fluted flounces of rich bombazine, fourteen inches wide; low neck and short sleeves; also a Figaro veste of bleached domestic – selvedge edge turned down with a back-stitch, and trimmed with festoons of blue chicoree taffetas – gay? – I reckon not. Her head-dress was the sweetest thing you ever saw: a bunch of stately ostrich plumes – red and white – springing like fountains above each ear, with a crown between, consisting of a single *fleur de soleil*, fresh from the garden – Ah, me! Miss W. looked enchantingly pretty; however, there was nothing unusual about that – I have seen her look so, even in a milder costume.

Mrs. J. B. W. wore a heavy rat-colored brocade silk, studded with large silver stars, and trimmed with organdy; balloon sleeves of nankeen pique, gathered at the wrist, cut bias and hollowed out some at the elbow; also, a bournous of black Honiton lace, scolloped, and embroidered in violent colors with a battle piece representing the taking of Holland by the Dutch; low neck and high-heeled shoes; gloves; palm-leaf fan; hoops; her head-dress consisted of a simple maroon-colored Sontag, with festoons of blue illusion depending from it; upon her bosom reposed a gorgeous bouquet of real sage brush, imported from Washoe. Mrs. W. looked regally handsome. If every article of dress worn by her on this occasion had been multiplied seven times, I do not believe it would have improved her appearance any.

Miss C. wore an elegant *Cheveux de la Reine* (with ruffles and fur-belows trimmed with bands of guipre round the bottom), and a mohair Garibaldi shirt; her unique head-dress was crowned with a graceful *pomme de terre* (Limerick French), and she had her hair done up in papers – greenbacks. The effect was very rich, partly owing to the market value of the material, and partly to the general loveliness of the lady herself.

Miss A. H. wore a splendid Lucia de Lammermoor, trimmed with green baize: also, a cream-colored mantilla-shaped *pardessus*, with a deep gore in the neck, and embellished with a wide greque of taffetas ribbon, and otherwise garnished with ruches, and rad-ishes and things. Her *coiffure* was a simple wreath of sardines on a string. She was lovely to a fault.

Now, what do you think of that effort, Bettie (I wish I knew your other name) for an unsanctified newspaper reporter, devoid of a milliner's education? Doesn't it strike you that there are more brains and fewer oysters in my head than a casual acquaintance with me would lead one to suppose? Ah, well – what I don't know, Bet, is hardly worth the finding out, I can tell you. I could have described the dresses of all the ladies in that party, but I was afraid to meddle with those of strangers, because I might unwittingly get something wrong, and give offense. You see strangers never exercise any charity in matters of this kind – they always get mad at the least inaccuracies of description concerning their apparel, and make themselves disagreeable. But if you will just rig yourself up according to the models I have furnished you, Bets, you'll do, you know – you can weather the circus.

You will naturally wish to be informed as to the most fashionable style of male attire, and I may as well give you an idea of my own personal appearance at the party. I wore one of Mr. Lawlor's shirts, and Mr. Ridgway's vest, and Dr Wayman's coat, and Mr. Camp's hat, and Mr. Paxton's boots, and Jerry Long's white kids, and Judge Gilchrist's cravat, and the Unreliable's brass seal-ring, and Mr. Tollroad McDonald's pantaloons – and if you have an idea that they are anyways short in the legs, do you just climb into them once, sweetness. The balance of my outfit I gathered up indiscriminately from various individuals whose names I have forgotten and have now no means of ascertaining, as I thoughtlessly erased the marks from the different garments this morning. But I looked salubrious, B., if ever a man did.

c. June 21, 1863

HOW TO CURE A COLD

IT IS A good thing, perhaps, to write for the amusement of the public, but it is a far higher and nobler thing to write for their instruction – their profit – their actual and tangible benefit.

The latter is the sole object of this article.

If it prove the means of restoring to health one solitary sufferer among my race – of lighting up once more the fire of hope and joy in his faded eyes – of bringing back to his dead heart again the quick, generous impulses of other days – I shall be amply rewarded for my labor; my soul will be permeated with the sacred delight a Christian feels when he has done a good, unselfish deed.

Having led a pure and blameless life, I am justified in believing that no man who knows me will reject the suggestions I am about to make, out of fear that I am trying to deceive him.

Let the public do itself the honor to read my experience in doctoring a cold, as herein set forth, and then follow in my footsteps.

When the White House was burned in Virginia, I lost my home, my happiness, my constitution and my trunk.

The loss of the two first named articles was a matter of no great consequence, since a home without a mother or a sister, or a distant young female relative in it, to remind you by putting your soiled linen out of sight and taking your boots down off the mantlepiece, that there are those who think about you and care for you, is easily obtained.

And I cared nothing for the loss of my happiness, because, not being a poet, it could not be possible that melancholy would abide with me long.

But to lose a good constitution and a better trunk were serious misfortunes.

I had my Gould and Curry in the latter, you recollect; I may get it back again, though – I came down here this time partly to bully-rag the Company into restoring my stock to me.

On the day of the fire, my constitution succumbed to a severe cold caused by undue exertion in getting ready to do something.

I suffered to no purpose, too, because the plan I was figuring at for the extinguishing of the fire was so elaborate that I never got it completed until the middle of the following week.

The first time I began to sneeze, a friend told me to go and bathe my feet in hot water and go to bed.

I did so.

Shortly afterward, another friend advised me to get up and take a cold shower-bath.

I did that also.

Within the hour, another friend assured me that it was policy to "feed a cold and starve a fever."

I had both.

I thought it best to fill myself up for the cold, and then keep dark and let the fever starve a while.

In a case of this kind, I seldom do things by halves; I ate pretty heartily; I conferred my custom upon a stranger who had just opened his restaurant that morning; he waited near me in respectful silence until I had finished feeding my cold, when he inquired if the people about Virginia were much afflicted with colds?

I told him I thought they were.

He then went out and took in his sign.

I started down toward the office, and on the way encountered another bosom friend, who told me that a quart of salt water, taken warm, would come as near curing a cold as anything in the world.

I hardly thought I had room for it, but I tried it anyhow.

The result was surprising; I must have vomited three-quarters of an hour; I believe I threw up my immortal soul.

Now, as I am giving my experience only for the benefit of those who are troubled with the distemper I am writing about, I feel that they will see the propriety of my cautioning them against following such portions of it as proved inefficient with me – and acting upon this conviction, I warn them against warm salt water.

It may be a good enough remedy, but I think it is too severe. If I had another cold in the head, and there was no course left me but to take either an earthquake or a quart of warm salt water, I would cheerfully take my chances on the earthquake.

After the storm which had been raging in my stomach had subsided, and no more good Samaritans happening along, I went on borrowing handkerchiefs again and blowing them to atoms, as had been my custom in the early stages of my cold, until I came across a lady who had just arrived from over the plains, and who said she had lived in a part of the country where doctors were scarce, and had from necessity acquired considerable skill in the treatment of simple "family complaints."

I knew she must have had much experience, for she appeared to be a hundred and fifty years old.

She mixed a decoction composed of molasses, aquafortis, turpentine, and various other drugs, and instructed me to take a wineglass full of it every fifteen minutes.

I never took but one dose; that was enough; it robbed me of all moral principle, and awoke every unworthy impulse of my nature.

Under its malign influence, my brain conceived miracles of meanness, but my hands were too feeble to execute them; at that time had it not been that my strength had surrendered to a succession of assaults from infallible remedies for my cold, I am satisfied that I would have tried to rob the graveyard.

Like most other people, I often feel mean, and act accordingly, but until I took that medicine I had never reveled in such supernatural depravity and felt proud of it.

At the end of two days, I was ready to go to doctoring again. I took a few more unfailing remedies, and finally drove my cold from my head to my lungs.

I got to coughing incessantly, and my voice fell below Zero; I conversed in a thundering bass two octaves below my natural tone; I could only compass my regular nightly repose by coughing myself down to a state of utter exhaustion, and then the moment I began to talk in my sleep, my discordant voice woke me up again.

My case grew more and more serious every day.

Plain gin was recommended; I took it.

Then gin and molasses; I took that also.

Then gin and onions; I added the onions and took all three.

I detected no particular result, however, except that I had acquired a breath like a buzzard's.

I found I had to travel for my health.

I went to Lake Bigler with my reportorial comrade, Adair Wilson. It is gratifying to me to reflect that we traveled in considerable style; we went in the Pioneer coach, and my friend took all his baggage with him, consisting of two excellent silk handkerchiefs and a daguerreotype of his grandmother.

I had my regular gin and onions along.

Virginia, San Francisco and Sacramento were well represented at the Lake House, and we had a very healthy time of it for a while. We sailed and hunted and fished and danced all day, and I doctored my cough all night.

By managing in this way, I made out to improve every hour in the twenty-four.

But my disease continued to grow worse.

A sheet-bath was recommended. I had never refused a remedy yet, and it seemed poor policy to commence then; therefore I determined to take a sheet-bath, notwithstanding I had no idea what sort of arrangement it was.

It was administered at midnight, and the weather was very frosty. My breast and back were bared, and a sheet (there appeared to be a thousand yards of it) soaked in ice-water, was wound around me until I resembled a swab for a Columbiad.

It is a cruel expedient. When the chilly rag touches one's warm flesh, it makes him start with sudden violence and gasp for breath just as men do in the death agony. It froze the marrow in my bones and stopped the beating of my heart.

I thought my time had come.

Young Wilson said the circumstance reminded him of an anecdote about a negro who was being baptised, and who slipped from the Parson's grasp and came near being drowned; he floundered around, though, and finally rose up out of the water considerably strangled and furiously angry, and started ashore at once, spouting water like a whale, and remarking with great asperity that "One o' dese days, some gen'lman's nigger gwyne to git killed wid jes' sich dam foolishness as dis!"

Then young Wilson laughed at his silly, pointless anecdote, as if he had thought he had done something very smart. I suppose I am not to be affronted every day, though, without resenting it – I coughed my bed-fellow clear out of the house before morning.

Never take a sheet-bath – never. Next to meeting a lady acquaintance, who, for reasons best known to herself, don't see you when she looks at you and don't know you when she does see you, it is the most uncomfortable thing in the world.

It is singular that such a simile as that, happened to occur to me; I haven't thought of that circumstance a dozen times to-day. I used to think she was so pretty, and gentle, and graceful, and considerate, and all that sort of thing.

But I suspect it was all a mistake.

In reality, she is as ugly as a crab; and there is no expression in her countenance, either; she reminds me of one of those dummies in the milliner shops. I know she has got false teeth, and I think one of her eyes is glass. She can never fool me with that French she talks, either; that's Cherokee – I have been among that tribe myself. She has already driven two or three Frenchmen to the verge of suicide with that unchristian gibberish. And that complexion of her's is the dingiest that ever a white woman bore – it is pretty nearly Cherokee itself. It shows out strongest when it is contrasted with her monstrous white sugar-shoveled bonnet; when she gets that on, she looks like a sorrel calf under a new shed. I despise that woman, and I'll never speak to her again. Not unless she speaks to me, anyhow.

But as I was saying, when the sheet-bath failed to cure my cough, a lady friend recommended the application of a mustard plaster to my breast.

I believe that would have cured me effectually, if it had not been for young Wilson.

When I went to bed I put my mustard plaster – which was a very gorgeous one, eighteen inches square – where I could reach it when I was ready for it.

But young Wilson got hungry in the night, and ate it up.

I never saw anybody have such an appetite; I am confident that lunatic would have eaten me if I had been healthy.

After sojourning a week at Lake Bigler, I went to Steamboat Springs, and besides the steam baths, I took a lot of the vilest medicines that were ever concocted. They would have cured me, but I had to go back to Virginia, where, notwithstanding the variety of new remedies I absorbed every day, I managed to aggravate my disease by carelessness and undue exposure.

I finally concluded to visit San Francisco, and the first day I got here a lady at the Lick House told me to drink a quart of whisky every twenty-four hours, and a friend at the Occidental recommended precisely the same course.

Each advised me to take a quart – that makes half a gallon.

I calculate to do it or perish in the attempt.

Now, with the kindest motives in the world, I offer for the consideration of consumptive patients the variegated course of treatment I have lately gone through. Let them try it – if it don't cure them, it can't more than kill them.

September 20, 1863

MISS CLAPP'S SCHOOL

BY AUTHORITY OF an invitation from Hon. Wm. M. Gillespie, member of the House Committee on Colleges and Common Schools, I accompanied that statesman on an unofficial visit to the excellent school of Miss Clapp and Mrs. Cutler, this afternoon. The air was soft and balmy – the sky was cloudless and serene – the odor of flowers floated upon the idle breeze – the glory of the sun descended like a benediction upon mountain and meadow and plain – the wind blew like the very devil, and the day was generally disagreeable.

The school – however, I will mention, first that a charter for an educational institution to be called the Sierra Seminary, was granted to Miss Clapp during the Legislative session of 1861, and a bill will be introduced while the present Assembly is in session, asking an appropriation of $20,000 to aid the enterprise. Such a sum of money could not be more judiciously expended, and I doubt not the bill will pass.

The present school is a credit both to the teachers and the town. It now numbers about forty pupils, I should think, and is well and systematically conducted. The exercises this afternoon were of a character not likely to be unfamiliar to the free American citizen who has a fair recollection of how he used to pass his Friday afternoons in the days of his youth. The tactics have undergone some changes, but these variations are not important. In former times a fellow took his place in the luminous spelling class in the full consciousness that if he spelled cat with a "k," or indulged in any other little orthographical eccentricities of a similar nature, he would be degraded to the foot or sent to his seat; whereas, he keeps his place in the ranks now, in such cases, and his punishment is simply to "'bout face." Johnny Eaves stuck to his first position, to-day, long after the balance of the class had rounded to, but he subsequently succumbed to the word "nape," which he persisted in ravishing of its final vowel. There was nothing irregular about that. Your rightly-constructed schoolboy will spell a multitude of hard words without hesitating once, and then lose his grip and miss fire on the easiest one in the book.

The fashion of reading selections of prose and poetry remains the same; and so does the youthful manner of doing that sort of thing. Some pupils read poetry with graceful ease and correct expression, and others place the rising and falling inflection at measured intervals, as if they had learned the lesson on a "see-saw;" but then they go undulating through a stanza with such an air of unctuous satisfaction, that it is a comfort to be around when they are at it.

> "The boy – stoo-dawn – the bur – ning deck –
> When-sawl – but *him* had fled –
> The flames – that shook – the battle – zreck –
> Shone round – him *o'er* – the dead."

That is the old-fashioned *impressive* style – stately, slow-moving and solemn. It is in vogue yet among scholars of tender age. It always will be. Ever since Mrs. Hemans wrote that verse, it has suited the pleasure of juveniles to emphasize the word "him," and lay atrocious stress upon that other word "o'er," whether she liked it or not; and I am prepared to believe that they will continue this practice unto the end of time, and with the same indifference to Mrs. Hemans' opinions about it, or any body's else.

They sing in school, now-a-days, which is an improvement upon the ancient regime; and they don't catch flies and throw spit-balls at the teacher, as they used to do in my time – which is another improvement, in a general way. Neither do the boys and girls keep a sharp look-out on each other's shortcomings and report the same at headquarters, as was a custom of by-gone centuries. And this reminds me of Gov. Nye's last anecdote, fulminated since the delivery of his message, and consequently not to be found in that document. The company were swapping old school reminiscences, and in due season they got to talking about that extinct species of tell-tales that were once to be found in all minor educational establishments, and who never failed to detect and impartially denounce every infraction of the rules that occurred among their mates. The Governor said that he threw a casual glance at a pretty girl on the next bench one day, and she complained to the teacher – which was entirely characteristic, you know. Says she, "Mister Jones, Warren Nye's looking at me." Whereupon, without a suggestion from anybody, up jumped an infamous, lisping, tow-headed young miscreant, and says he, "Yeth, thir, I *thee* him do it!" I doubt if the old original boy got off that ejaculation with more gusto than the Governor throws into it.

The "compositions" read to-day were as exactly like the

compositions I used to hear read in our school as one baby's nose is exactly like all other babies' noses. I mean the old principal earmarks were all there: the cutting to the bone of the subject with the very first gash, without any preliminary foolishness in the way of a gorgeous introductory; the inevitable and persevering tautology; the brief, monosyllabic sentences (beginning, as a very general thing, with the pronoun "I"); the penchant for presenting rigid, uncompromising facts for the consideration of the hearer, rather than ornamental fancies; the depending for the success of the composition upon its general merits, without tacking artificial aids to the end of it, in the shape of deductions, or conclusions, or claptrap climaxes, albeit their absence sometimes imparts to these essays the semblance of having come to an end before they were finished – of arriving at full speed at a jumping-off place and going suddenly overboard, as it were, leaving a sensation such as one feels when he stumbles without previous warning upon that infernal "To be Continued" in the midst of a thrilling magazine story. I know there are other styles of school compositions, but these are the characteristics of the style which I have in my eye at present. I do not know why this one has particularly suggested itself to my mind, unless the literary effort of one of the boys there to-day left with me an unusually vivid impression. It ran something in this wise:

COMPOSITION.

"I like horses. Where we lived before we came here, we used to have a cutter and horses. We used to ride in it. I like winter. I like snow. I used to have a pony all to myself, where I used to live before I came here. Once it drifted a good deal – very deep – and when it stopped I went out and got in it."

That was all. There was no climax to it, except the spasmodic bow which the tautological little student jerked at the school as he closed his labors.

Two remarkably good compositions were read. Miss P.'s was much the best of these – but aside from its marked literary excellence, it possessed another merit which was peculiarly gratifying to my feelings just at that time. Because it took the conceit out of young Gillespie as completely as perspiration takes the starch out of a shirt-collar. In his insufferable vanity, that feeble member of the House of Representatives had been assuming imposing attitudes, and beaming upon the pupils with an expression of benignant imbecility which was calculated to inspire them with the conviction that there was only one guest of any consequence in the house. Therefore, it was an unspeakable relief to me to see him forced to shed his dignity. Concerning the composition, however. After detailing the countless pleasures which had fallen to her lot during the holidays, the authoress finished with a proviso, in substance as follows – I have forgotten the precise language: "But I have no cheerful reminiscences of Christmas. It was dreary, monotonous and insipid to the last degree. Mr. Gillespie called early, and remained the greater part of the day!" You should have seen the blooming Gillespie wilt when that literary bombshell fell in his camp! The charm of the thing lay in the fact that that last naive sentence was the only suggestion offered in the way of accounting for the dismal character of the occasion. However, to my mind it was sufficient – entirely sufficient.

Since writing the above, I have seen the architectural plans and specifications for Miss Clapp and Mrs. Cutler's proposed "Sierra Seminary" building. It will be a handsome two-story edifice, one hundred feet square, and will accommodate forty "boarders" and any number of pupils beside, who may board elsewhere. Constructed of wood, it will cost $12,000; or of stone, $18,000. Miss Clapp has devoted ten acres of ground to the use and benefit of the institution.

I sat down intending to write a dozen pages of variegated news. I have about accomplished the task – all except the "variegated." I have economised in the matter of current news of the day, considerably more than I purposed to do, for every item of that nature remains stored away in my mind in a very unwritten state, and will afford unnecessarily ample material for another letter. It is useless material, though, I suspect, because, inasmuch as I have failed to incorporate it into this, I fear me I shall not feel industrious enough to weave out of it another letter until it has become too stale to be interesting. Well, never mind – we must learn to take an absorbing delight in educational gossip; nine-tenths of the revenues of the Territory go into the bottomless gullet of that ravenous school fund, you must bear in mind.

MARK TWAIN.
c. January 19, 1864

DOINGS IN NEVADA

CARSON CITY, NEVADA TERRITORY,
January 4, 1864.

Editor T. T. – The concentrated wisdom of Nevada Territory (known unto and respected by the nations of the earth as "Washoe") assembled in convention at Carson recently, and framed a constitution. It was an excellent piece of work in some respects, but it had one or two unfortunate defects which debarred it from assuming to be an immaculate conception. The chief of these was a clause authorizing the taxing of the mines. The people will not stand that. There are some 30,000 gold and silver mining incorporations here, or mines, or claims, or which you please, or all, if it suits you better. Very little of the kind of property thus represented is improved yet, or "developed" as we call it; it will take two or three years to get it in a developed and paying condition, and will require an enormous outlay of capital to accomplish such a result. And until it does begin to pay dividends, the people will not consent that it shall be burdened and hindered by taxation. Therefore, I am satisfied they will refuse to ratify our new constitution on the 19th inst.

It had an amusing feature in it, also. That was the Great Seal of the State. It had snow-capped mountains in it; and tunnels, and shafts, and pickaxes, and quartz-mills, and pack-trains, and mule-teams. These things were good; what there were of them. And it had railroads in it, and telegraphs, and stars, and suspension-bridges, and other romantic fictions foreign to sand and sage-brush. But the richest of it was the motto. It took them thirty days to decide whether it should be "*Volens et Potens*" (which they said meant "Able and Willing"), or "The Union Must and Shall be Preserved." Either would have been presumptuous, and surpassingly absurd just at present. Because we are not able and willing, thus far, to do a great deal more than locate wild-cat mining-claims and reluctantly sell them to confiding strangers at a ruinous sacrifice – of conscience. And if it were left to us to preserve the Union, in case the balance of the country failed in the attempt, I seriously believe we couldn't do it. Possibly, we might make it mighty warm for the Confederacy if it came prowling around here, but ultimately we would have to forsake our high trust, and quit preserving the Union. I am confident of it. And I have thought the matter over a good deal, off and on, as we say in Paris. We have an animal here whose surname is the "jackass rabbit". It is three feet long, has legs like a counting-house stool, ears of monstrous length, and no tail to speak of. It is swifter than a greyhound, and as meek and harmless as an infant. I might mention, also, that it is as handsome as most infants: however, it would be foreign to the subject, and I do not know that a remark of that kind would be popular in all circles. Let it pass, then – I will say nothing about it, though it would be a great comfort to me to do it, if people would consider the source and overlook it. Well, somebody proposed as a substitute for that pictorial Great Seal, a figure of a jackass-rabbit reposing in the shade of his native sage-brush, with the motto "*Volens* enough, but not so d—d *Potens*". Possibly that had something to do with the rejection of one of the proposed mottoes by the Convention.

STATE NOMINATING CONVENTION.

We do not fool away much time in this country. As soon as the Constitution was duly framed and ready for ratification or rejection by the people, a convention to nominate candidates for State offices met at Carson. It finished its labors day before yesterday. The following nominations were made: For Governor, M. N. Mitchell; Lieutenant-Governor, M. S. Thompson; Secretary of State, Orion Clemens; Treasurer, Wm. B. Hickok; Member of Congress, John B. Winters; Superintendant Public Instruction, Rev. A. F. White. Now, that ticket will be elected, but the Constitution won't. In that case, what are we to do with these fellows? We cannot let them starve. They are on our hands, and are entitled to our charity and protection. It is different with them from what it is with other people, because, although the Almighty created them, and used to care for and watch over them, no doubt it was long, long ago, and he may not recollect them now. And I think it is our duty to look after them, and see that they do not suffer. Besides, they all owe me something for traducing and villifying them in the public prints, and thus exciting sympathy for them on the score of persecution, and securing their nomination; and I do not think it right or just that I should be expected to do people favors without being paid for it, merely because those favors failed to produce marketable fruit. No, Sir; I elected those fellows, and I shall take care that I am fairly remunerated for it. Now, if you know any small State, lying around anywhere, that I could get a contract on for the running of it, you will oblige me by mentioning it in your next. You can say that I have all the machinery on hand necessary to the carrying on of a third-rate State; say, also, that it is comparatively new, portions of it never having been used at all; also, that I will part with it on pretty nearly any terms, as my constitution is prostrated, and I am anxious to go into some other business. And say my various State officers are honest and capable – however, don't say that – just leave that out – let us not jest on a serious matter like this. But you might put in a little advertisement for me in the following shape, for instance. And it would be a real kindness to me if you would be so good as to call attention to it in your editorial columns. You see I am a sort of an orphan, away out here, struggling along on my own hook, as it were. My mother lives in St. Louis. She is sixty years of age, and a member of the Presbyterian Church. She takes no pride in being gay; in fact, she don't rush around much in society, now. However, I do not ask any man's sympathy on that account. I was simply going to offer my little advertisement.

FOR SALE OR RENT.

One Governor, entirely new. Attended Sunday-school in his youth, and still remembers it. Never drinks. In other respects, however, his habits are good. As Commander-in-Chief of the Militia, he would be an ornament. Most Governors are.

One Lieutenant-Governor – also new. He has other merits, of minor importance, beside. No objection to going into the country – or elsewhere.

One Secretary of State. An old, experienced hand at the business. Has edited a newspaper, and been Secretary and Governor of Nevada Territory – consequently, is capable; and also consequently, will bear watching, is not bigoted – has no particular set of religious principles – or any other kind.

One small Treasurer – (second-hand). Will make a good officer. Was Treasurer once before, in the States. Took excellent care of the funds – has them yet.

One Member of Congress – new, but smart. Is sometimes called "Old Smarty, from Mud Springs". Has read every newspaper printed in Nevada Territory for two years, and knows all about the war. Would be a good hand to advise the President. Is young, ardent, ambitious, and on it. No objection to traveling, provided his mileage is paid.

One Superintendent of Public Instruction – good as new. Understands all the different systems of teaching, and does not approve of them. It is his laudable boast that he is a self-made man. It has been said of him by his admirers that God Almighty never made such a man. It is probably so. He is the soul of honor, and is willing to take greenbacks at par. No objection to making himself generally useful; can preach, if required.

Also, a large and well-selected assortment of State Legislators, Supreme Judges, Comptrollers, and such gimcracks, handy to have about a State Government, all of which are for sale or rent on the mildest possible terms, as, under present circumstances, they are of no earthly use to the subscriber.

For further particulars, address

MARK TWAIN, Carson, N.T.

OUR CONSTITUTION ILLEGAL.

Now, joking aside, these are all good, honest, capable men, and would reflect credit upon the several positions for which they have been nominated; but then the people are not going to ratify the Constitution; and consequently, they will never get a chance. I am glad that such is the case. In the Legislature, last year, I was wielding the weapon which, under just such circumstances, is mightier than the sword, at the time that the Act authorizing the calling together of a Convention to form a State Constitution was passed; and I know the secret history of that document. It was reported back from the Committee with a lot of blanks in it (for dates, apportionment, and number of members, amount of money appropriated to defray expenses of the Convention, etc.). Both Houses passed the Bill without filling those blanks; it was duly enrolled, brought back, and signed by the presiding officers of the Legislature, and then transmitted – a worthless, meaningless, and intentionally powerless instrument – to Gov. Nye for his signature – at night. And lo! a miracle. When the bill reached the Governor, there was not a solitary blank in it! Who filled them, is – is a great moral question for instance; but the enrolling clerk did not do it at any rate, since the amendments are in an unknown and atrocious handwriting. Therefore, the bill was a fraud; the convention created by it was a fraud; the fruit of the convention was an illegitimate infant constitution and a dead one at that; a State reared upon such a responsibility would be a fraudulent and impotent institution, and the result would be that we should ultimately be kicked back into a territorial condition again on account of it. Wherefore, when men say: "Let our constitution slide for the present", we say Amen.

February 7, 1864

THOSE BLASTED CHILDREN

LICK HOUSE, SAN FRANCISCO, WEDNESDAY, 1863.

EDITORS T. T.: – No. 165 is a pleasant room. It is situated at the head of a long hall, down which, on either side, are similar rooms occupied by sociable bachelors, and here and there one tenanted by an unsociable nurse or so. Charley Creed sleeps in No. 157. He is my time-piece – or, at least, his boots are. If I look down the hall and see Charley's boots still before his door, I know it is early yet, and I may hie me sweetly to bed again. But if those unerring boots are gone, I know it is after eleven o'clock, and time for me to be rising with the lark. This reminds me of the lark of yesterday and last night, which was altogether a different sort of bird from the one I am talking about now. Ah me! Summer girls and summer dresses, and summer scenes at the "Willows", Seal Rock Point, and the grim sea-lions wallowing in the angry surf; glimpses through the haze of stately ships far away at sea; a dash along the smooth beach, and the exhilaration of watching the white waves come surging ashore, and break into seething foam about the startled horse's feet; reveries beside the old wreck, half buried in sand, and compassion for the good ship's fate; home again in a soft twilight, oppressed with the odor of flowers – home again to San Francisco, drunk, perhaps, but not disorderly. Dinner at six, with ladies and gentlemen, dressed with faultless taste and elegance, and all drunk, apparently, but very quiet and well-bred – unaccountably so, under the circumstances, it seemed to my cloudy brain. Many things happened after that, I remember – such as visiting some of their haunts with those dissipated Golden Era fellows, and –

Here come those young savages again – those noisy and inevitable children. God be with them! – or they with him, rather, if it be not asking too much. They are another timepiece of mine. It is two o'clock now; they are invested with their regular lunch, and have come up here to settle it. I will soothe my troubled spirit with a short season of blasphemy, after which I will expose their infamous proceedings with a relentless pen. They have driven me from labor many and many a time; but behold! the hour of retribution is at hand.

That is young Washington Billings, now – a little dog in long flaxen curls and Highland costume.

"Hi, Johnny! look through the keyhole! here's that feller with a long nose, writing again – less stir him up!" [A double kick against the door – a grand infant war-hoop in full chorus – and then a clatter of scampering feet down the echoing corridors.] Ah – one of them has fallen, and hurt himself. I hear the intelligent foreign nurse boxing his ears for it (the parents, Mr. and Mrs. Kerosene, having gone up to Sacramento on the evening boat, and left their offspring properly cared for.)

Here they come again, as soldiers – infantry. I know there are not more than thirty or forty of them, yet they are under no sort of discipline, and they make noise enough for a thousand. Young Oliver Higgins is in command. They assault my works – they try to carry my position by storm – they finally draw off with boistrous cheers, to harrass a handful of skirmishers thrown out by the enemy – a bevy of chambermaids.

Once more they come trooping down the hall. This time as cavalry. They must have captured and disarmed the skirmishers, for half my young ruffians are mounted on broomsticks. They make a reconnoissance in force. They attack my premises in a body, but they achieve nothing approaching a success. I am too strongly intrenched for them.

They invest my stronghold, and lay siege to it – that is to say, they sit down before my camp, and betake themselves to the pastimes of youth. All talking at once, as they do, their conversation is amusing, but not instructive to me.

"Ginn me some o' that you're eat'n." "I won't – you wouldn't lemme play with that dead rat, the peanut-boy give you yesterday." "Well! I don't care; I reckon I know summun't you don't; Oho, Mr. Smarty, 'n' I ain't a goin' to tell you, neither; now, see what you got by it; it's summun't my ma said about your ma, too. I'll tell you, if you'll gimme ever so little o' that, will you? Well." (I imagine from the break in this conversation, while the other besiegers go on talking noisily, that a compromise is being effected.) "There, don't take so much. Now, what'd she say?" "Why, ma told my pa 't if your ma is so mighty rich now she wasn't nobody till she come to Sanf'cisco. That's what she said." "Your ma's a big story-teller, 'n' I'm goin' jes' as straight as I can walk, 'n' tell my ma. You'll see what she'll do." (I foresee a diversion in one or two family circles.) "Flora Low, you quit pulling that doll's legs out, it's mine." "Well, take your old doll, then. I'd thank you to know, Miss Florence Hillyer, 't my pa's Governor, 'n' I can have a thousan' dolls if I want to, 'n' gold ones, too, or silver, or any-thing." (More trouble brewing.) "What do I care for that. I guess my pa could be Governor, too, if he wanted to; but he don't. He owns two hundred feet in the Chollar, 'n' he's got lots more silver mines in Washoe besides. He could fill this house full of silver, clear up to that chandelier, so he could, now, Miss." "You, Bob Miller, you leg go that string – I'll smack you in the eye." "You will, will you? I'd like to see you try it. You jes' hit me if you dare!" "You lay your hands on me, 'n' I will hit you." "Now I've laid my hand on you, why don't you hit?" "Well, I mean, if you lay 'em on me so's to hurt." "Ah-h! you're afraid, that's the reason." "No I ain't, neither, you big fool." (Ah, now they're at it. Discord shall invade the ranks of my foes, and they shall fall by their own hands. It appears from the sound without that two nurses have made a des-cent upon the combatants, and are bearing them from the field. The nurses are abusing each other. One boy proclaims that the other struck him when he wasn't doin' nothin'; and the other boy says he was called a big fool. Both are going right straight, and tell their pa's. Verily, things are going along as comfortably as I could wish, now.) "Sandy Baker, I know what makes your pa's hair kink so; it's 'cause he's a mulatter; I heard my ma say so." "It's a lie!" (Another row, and more skirmishing with the nurses. Truly, happi-ness flows in upon me most bountifully this day.) "Hi, boys! here comes a Chinaman!" (God pity any Chinaman who chances to come in the way of the boys hereabout, for the eye of the law regar-deth him not, and the youth of California in their generation are down upon him.) "Now, boys! grab his clothes basket – take him by the tail!" (There they go, now, like a pack of young demons; they have confiscated the basket, and the dismayed Chinaman is towing half the tribe down the hall by his cue. Rejoice, O my soul, for behold, all things are lovely, etc. – to speak after the manner of the vulgar.) "Oho, Miss Susy Badger, my uncle Tom's goin' across the bay to Oakland, 'n' down to Santa Clara, 'n' Alamedy, 'n' San Leandro, 'n' everywheres – all over the world, 'n' he's goin' to take me with him – he said so." "Humph! that ain't noth'n – I been there. My aunt Mary'd take me to any place I wanted to go, if I wanted her to, but I don't; she's got horses 'n' things – O, ever so many! – millions of 'em; but my ma says it don't look well for little girls to be always gadd'n about. That's why you don't ever see me goin' to places like some girls do. I despise to –" (The end is at hand; the nurses have massed themselves on the left; they move in serried phalanx on my besiegers; they surround them, and capture the last miscreant – horse, foot, and dragoons, munitions of war, and camp equipage. The victory is complete. They are gone – my castle is no longer menaced, and the rover is free. I am here, staunch and true!)

It is a living wonder to me that I haven't scalped some of those children before now. I expect I would have done it, but then I hardly felt well enough acquainted with them. I scarcely ever show them any attention anyhow, unless it is to throw a boot-jack at them or some little nonsense of that kind when I happen to feel playful. I am confident I would have destroyed several of them though, only it might appear as if I were making most too free.

I observe that that young officer of the Pacific Squadron – the one with his nostrils turned up like port-holes – has become a great favorite with half the mothers in the house, by imparting to them much useful information concerning the manner of doctoring children among the South American savages. His brother is brigadier in the Navy. The drab-complexioned youth with the Solferino mustache has corraled the other half with the Japanese treatment. The more I think of it the more I admire it. Now, I am no peanut. I have an idea that I could invent some little remedies that would stir up a commotion among these women, if I chose to try. I always had a good general notion of physic, I believe. It is one of my natural gifts, too, for I have never studied a single day under a regular physician. I will jot down a few items here, just to see how likely I am to succeed.

In the matter of measles, the idea is, to bring it out – bring it to the surface. Take the child and fill it up with saffron tea. Add something to make the patient sleep – say a tablespoonful of arsenic. Don't rock it – it will sleep anyhow.

As far as brain fever is concerned: This is a very dangerous disease, and must be treated with decision and dispatch. In every case where it has proved fatal, the sufferer invariably perished. You must strike at the root of the distemper. Remove the brains; and then – Well, that will be sufficient – that will answer – just remove the brains. This remedy has never been known to fail. It was originated by the lamented J. W. Macbeth, Thane of Cawdor, Scotland, who refers to it thus: "Time was, that when the brains were out, the man would die; but, under different circumstances, I think not; and, all things being equal, I believe you, my boy." Those were his last words.

Concerning worms: Administer a catfish three times a week. Keep the room very quiet; the fish won't bite if there is the least noise.

When you come to fits, take no chances on fits. If the child has them bad, soak it in a barrel of rain-water over night, or a good article of vinegar. If this does not put an end to its troubles, soak it a week. You can't soak a child too much when it has fits.

In cases wherein an infant stammers, remove the under-jaw. In proof of the efficacy of this treatment, I append the following certificate, voluntarily forwarded to me by Mr. Zeb. Leavenworth, of St. Louis, Mo.:

"ST. LOUIS, May 26, 1863.

"MR. MARK TWAIN — DEAR SIR: — Under Providence, I am beholden to you for the salvation of my Johnny. For a matter of three years, that suffering child stuttered to that degree that it was a pain and a sorrow to me to hear him stagger over the sacred name of 'p-p-p-pap'. It troubled me so that I neglected my business; I refused food; I took no pride in my dress, and my hair actually began to fall off. I could not rest; I could not sleep. Morning, noon, and night, I did nothing but moan pitifully, and murmur to myself: 'Hell's fire! what am I going to do about my Johnny?' But in a blessed hour you appeared unto me like an angel from the skies; and without hope of reward, revealed your sovereign remedy – and that very day, I sawed off my Johnny's under-jaw. May Heaven bless you, noble Sir. It afforded instant relief; and my Johnny has never stammered since. I honestly believe he never will again. As to disfigurement, he does seem to look sorter ornery and hog-mouthed, but I am too grateful in having got him effectually saved from that dreadful stuttering, to make much account of small matters. Heaven speed you in your holy work of healing the afflictions of humanity. And if my poor testimony can be of any service to you, do with it as you think will result in the greatest good to our fellow-creatures. Once more, Heaven bless you.

"Zeb. Leavenworth."

Now, that has such a plausible ring about it, that I can hardly keep from believing it myself. I consider it a very fair success.

Regarding Cramps. Take your offspring – let the same be warm and dry at the time – and immerse it in a commodious soup-tureen filled with the best quality of camphene. Place it over a slow fire, and add reasonable quantities of pepper, mustard, horse-radish, saltpetre, strychnine, blue vitriol, aqua fortis, a quart of flour, and eight or ten fresh eggs, stirring it from time to time, to keep up a healthy reaction. Let it simmer fifteen minutes. When your child is done, set the tureen off, and allow the infallible remedy to cool. If this does not confer an entire insensibility to cramps, you must lose no time, for the case is desperate. Take your offspring, and parboil it. The most vindictive cramps cannot survive this treatment; neither can the subject, unless it is endowed with an iron constitution. It is an extreme measure, and I always dislike to resort to it. I never parboil a child until everything else has failed to bring about the desired end.

Well, I think those will do to commence with. I can branch out, you know, when I get more confidence in myself.

O infancy! thou art beautiful, thou art charming, thou art lovely to contemplate! But thoughts like these recall sad memories of the past, of the halcyon days of my childhood, when I was a sweet, prattling innocent, the pet of a dear home-circle, and the pride of the village.

Enough, enough! I must weep, or this bursting heart will break.

MARK TWAIN.

February 21, 1864

WHEREAS

LOVE'S BAKERY! I am satisfied I have found the place now that I have been looking for all this time. I cannot describe to you the sensation of mingled astonishment, gladness, hope, doubt, anxiety, and balmy, blissful emotion that suffused my being and quivered in a succession of streaky thrills down my backbone, as I stood on the corner of Third and Minna streets, last Tuesday, and stared, spell-bound, at those extraordinary words, painted in large, plain letters on a neighboring window-curtain – "LOVE'S BAKERY." "God bless my soul!" said I, "will wonders never cease? – are there to be no limits to man's spirit of invention? – is he to invade the very realms of the immortal, and presume to guide and control the great passions, the impalpable essences, that have hitherto dwelt in the secret chambers of the soul, sacred from all save divine intrusion?"

I read and re-read that remarkable sign with constantly-increasing wonder and interest. There was nothing extraordinary in the appearance of the establishment, and even if it had possessed anything of a supernatural air, it must necessarily have been neutralized by the worldly and substantial look of a pyramid of excellent bread that stood in the window – a sign very inconsistent, it seemed to me, with the character of a place devoted to the high and holy employment of instilling the passion of love into the human heart, although it was certainly in keeping with the atrocious taste which was capable of conferring upon a vice-royalty of heaven itself such an execrable name as "Love's Bakery." Why not Love's Bower, or the Temple of Love, or the Palace of Cupid? – anything – anything in the world would have been less repulsive than such hideous vulgarity of nomenclature as "Love's *Bakery*."

The place seemed very complete, and well supplied with every facility for carrying on the business of creating love successfully. In a window of the second story was a large tin cage with a parrot in it, and near it was a sign bearing the inscription, "Preparatory School for Young Ladies" – that is, of course, a school where they are taught certain things necessary to prepare them for the bakery down below. Not far off is also a "Preparatory School for Young Gentlemen," which is doubtless connected with Love's Bakery too. I saw none of the pupils of either of the schools, but my imagination dwelt upon them with a deep and friendly interest. How irksome, I thought, must this course of instruction be to these tender hearts, so impatient to be baked into a state of perfect love!

Greatly moved by the singular circumstances which surrounded me, I fell into a profound and pleasing reverie. Here, I thought, they take a couple of hopeful hearts in the rough, and work them up, with spices and shortening and sweetening enough to last for a lifetime, and turn them out well kneaded together, baked to a turn, and ready for matrimony, and without having been obliged to undergo a long and harrowing courtship, with the desperate chances attendant thereon, of persevering rivals, unwilling parents, inevitable love-quarrels, and all that sort of thing.

Here, I thought, they will bake you up a couple in moderate circumstances, at short notice and at a cheap rate, and turn them out in good enough shape for the money, perhaps, but nevertheless burnt with the fire of jealousy on one side, and flabby and "duffy" with lukewarmness and indifference on the other, and spotted all over with the salæratus stains of a predisposition to make the conjugal cake bitter and unpalatable for all time to come.

Or they will take an excessively patrician pair, charge them a dozen prices, and deliver them to order in a week, all plastered over with the ghostly vines and flowers of blighted fancies, hopes and yearnings, wrought in chilly ice-work.

Or, perhaps, they will take a brace of youthful, tender hearts, and dish them up in no time, into crisp, delicate "lady-fingers," tempting to contemplate, and suggestive of that serene after-dinner happiness and sociability that come when the gross substantials have been swept from the board and are forgotten in soft dalliance with pastry and ices and sparkling Moselle.

Or maybe they will take two flinty old hearts that have harbored selfishness, envy and all uncharitableness in solitude for half a century, and after a fortnight's roasting, turn them out the hardest kind of hard-tack, invulnerable to all softening influences for evermore.

Here was a revolution far more extended, and destined to be attended by more momentous consequences to the nations of the earth, than any ever projected or accomplished by the greatest of the world's military heroes! Love, the master passion of the human heart, which, since the morning of the creation had shaped the destinies of emperors and beggars alike, and had ruled all men as with a rod of iron, was to be hurled from the seat of power in a single instant, as it were, and brought into subjection to the will of an inspired, a sublimely-gifted baker! By some mysterious magic, by some strange and awful invention, the divine emotion was to be confined within set bounds and limits, controlled, weighed, measured, and doled out to God's creatures in quantities and qualities to suit the purchaser, like vulgar beer and candles!

And in times to come, I thought, the afflicted lover, instead of reading Heuston & Hastings' omnipresent sign and gathering no comfort from it, will read "GO TO LOVE'S BAKERY!" on the deadwalls and telegraph poles, and be saved.

Now I might never have published to the world my discovery of this manufactory of the human affections in a populous thoroughfare of San Francisco, if it had not occurred to me that some account of it would serve as a peculiarly fitting introductory to a story of love and misfortune, which it falls to my lot to relate. And yet even Love's Bakery could afford no help to the sufferers of whom I shall speak, for they do not lack affection for each other, but are the victims of an accumulation of distressing circumstances against which the efforts of that august agent would be powerless.

The facts in the case come to me by letter from a young lady who lives in the beautiful city of San José; she is personally unknown to me, and simply signs herself "Aurelia Maria," which may possibly be a fictitious name. But no matter, the poor girl is almost heartbroken by the misfortunes she has undergone, and so confused by the conflicting counsels of misguided friends and insidious enemies, that she does not know what course to pursue in order to extricate herself from the web of difficulties in which she seems almost hopelessly involved. In this dilemma she turns to me for help, and supplicates for my guidance and instruction with a moving eloquence that would touch the heart of a statue. Hear her sad story:

She says that when she was sixteen years old she met and loved with all the devotion of a passionate nature a young man from New Jersey, named Williamson Breckinridge Caruthers, who was some six years her senior. They were engaged, with the free consent of their friends and relatives, and for a time it seemed as if their career was destined to be characterized by an immunity from sorrow beyond the usual lot of humanity. But at last the tide of fortune turned; young Caruthers became infected with small-pox of the most virulent type, and when he recovered from his illness, his face was pitted like a waffle-mould and his comeliness gone forever. Aurelia thought to break off the engagement at first, but pity for her unfortunate lover caused her to postpone the marriage-day for a season, and give him another trial. The very day before the wedding was to have taken place, Breckinridge, while absorbed in watching the flight of a balloon, walked into a well and fractured one of his legs, and it had to be taken off above the knee. Again Aurelia was moved to break the engagement, but again love triumphed, and she set the day forward and gave him another chance to reform. And again misfortune overtook the unhappy youth. He lost one arm by the premature discharge of a Fourth-of-July cannon, and within three months he got the other pulled out by a carding-machine. Aurelia's heart was almost crushed by these latter calamities. She could not but be deeply grieved to see her lover passing from her by piecemeal, feeling, as she did, that he could not last forever under this disastrous process of reduction, yet knowing of no way to stop its dreadful career, and in her tearful despair she almost regretted, like brokers who hold on and lose, that she had not taken him at first, before he had suffered such an alarming depreciation. Still, her brave soul bore her up, and she resolved to bear with her friend's unnatural disposition yet a little longer. Again the wedding-day approached, and again disappointment overshadowed it: Caruthers fell ill with the erysipelas, and lost the use of one of his eyes entirely. The friends and relatives of the bride, considering that she had already put up with more than could reasonably be expected of her, now came forward and insisted that the match should be broken off; but after waiting awhile, Aurelia, with a generous spirit which did her credit, said she had reflected calmly upon the matter and could not discover that Breckinridge was to blame. So she extended the time once more, and he broke his other leg. It was a sad day for the poor girl when she saw the surgeons reverently bearing away the sack whose uses she had learned by previous experience, and her heart told her the bitter truth that some more of her lover was gone. She felt that the field of her affections was growing more and more circumscribed every day, but once more she frowned down her relatives and renewed her betrothal. Shortly before the time set for the nuptials another disaster occurred. There was but one man scalped by the Owens River Indians last year. That man was Williamson Breckinridge Caruthers, of New Jersey. He was hurrying home with happiness in his heart, when he lost his hair forever, and in that hour of bitterness he almost cursed the mistaken mercy that had spared his head.

At last Aurelia is in serious perplexity as to what she ought to do. She still loves her Breckinridge, she writes, with true womanly feeling – she still loves what is left of him – but her parents are bitterly opposed to the match, because he has no property and is disabled from working, and she has not sufficient means to support both comfortably. "Now, what should she do?" she asks with painful and anxious solicitude.

It is a delicate question; it is one which involves the lifelong happiness of a woman, and that of nearly two-thirds of a man, and I feel that it would be assuming too great a responsibility to do more than make a mere suggestion in the case. How would it do to build to him? If Aurelia can afford the expense, let her furnish her mutilated lover with wooden arms and wooden legs, and a glass eye and a wig, and give him another show; give him ninety days, without grace, and if he does not break his neck in the meantime, marry him and take the chances. It does not seem to me that there is much risk, any way, because if he sticks to his infernal propensity for damaging himself every time he sees a good opportunity, his next experiment is bound to finish him, and then you are all right, you know, married or single. If married, the wooden legs and such other valuables as he may possess, revert to the widow, and you see you sustain no actual loss save the cherished fragment of a noble but most unfortunate husband, who honestly strove to do right, but whose extraordinary instincts were against him. Try it, Maria! I have thought the matter over carefully and well, and it is the only chance I see for you. It would have been a happy conceit on the part of Caruthers if he had started with his neck and broken that first, but since he has seen fit to choose a different policy and string himself out as long as possible, I do not think we ought to upbraid him for it if he has enjoyed it. We must do the best we can under the circumstances, and try not to feel exasperated at him.

October 22, 1864

ANSWERS TO CORRESPONDENTS

DISCARDED LOVER. – "I loved and still love, the beautiful Edwitha Howard, and intended to marry her. Yet during my temporary absence at Benicia, last week, alas! she married Jones. Is my happiness to be thus blasted for life? Have I no redress?"

Of course you have. All the law, written and unwritten, is on your side. The *intention* and not the *act* constitutes crime – in other words, constitutes the *deed*. If you call your bosom friend a fool, and *intend* it for an insult, it *is* an insult; but if you do it playfully, and meaning no insult, it is *not* an insult. If you discharge a pistol *accidentally*, and kill a man, you can go free, for you have done no murder – but if you try to kill a man, and manifestly *intend* to kill him, but fail utterly to do it, the law still holds that the *intention* constituted the crime, and you are guilty of murder. Ergo, if you had married Edwitha *accidentally*, and without really *intending* to do it, you would not actually be married to her at all, because the *act* of marriage could not be complete without the *intention*. And, ergo, in the strict spirit of the law, since you deliberately *intended* to marry Edwitha, and didn't do it, you *are* married to her all the same – because, as I said before, the *intention* constitutes the crime. It is as clear as day that Edwitha is your wife, and your redress lies in taking a club and mutilating Jones with it as much as you can. Any man has a right to protect his own wife from the advances of other men. But you have another alternative – you were married to Edwitha *first*, because of your deliberate intention, and now you can prosecute her for bigamy, in subsequently marrying Jones. But there is another phase in this complicated case: You *intended* to marry Edwitha, and consequently, according to law, she is your wife – there is no getting around that – but she didn't marry you, and if she *never intended* to marry you *you are not her husband*, of course. Ergo, in marrying Jones, she was guilty of bigamy, because she was the wife of another man at the time – which is all very well as far as it goes – but then, don't you see, she had no other *husband* when she married Jones, and consequently she was *not* guilty of bigamy. Now according to this view of the case, Jones married a *spinster*, who was a *widow* at the same time and another man's *wife* at the same time, and yet who had no *husband* and *never had one*, and never had any *intention* of getting married, and therefore, of course, *never had* been married; and by the same reasoning you are a *bachelor*, because you have never been any one's *husband*, and a *married man* because you have a wife living, and to all intents and purposes a *widower*, because you have been deprived of that wife, and a consummate *ass* for going off to Benicia in the first place, while things were so mixed. And by this time I have got myself so tangled up in the intricacies of this extraordinary case that I shall have to give up any further attempt to advise you – I might get confused and fail to make myself understood. I think I could take up the argument where I left off, and by following it closely awhile, perhaps I could prove to your satisfaction, either that you never existed at all, or that you are dead, now, and consequently don't need the faithless Edwitha – I think I could do that, if it would afford you any comfort.

MR. MARK TWAIN – Sir: I wish to call your attention to a matter which has come to my notice frequently, but before doing so, I may remark, *en passant*, that I don't see why your parents should have called you Mark Twain; had they known your *ardent* nature, they would doubtless have named you Water-less Twain. However, *Mark* what I am about to call your attention to, and I do so knowing you to be "capable and honest" in your inquiries after truth, and that you can fathom the mysteries of Love. Now I want to know why, (and this is the object of my enquiry,) a man should proclaim his love in large gilt letters over his door and in his windows. Why does he do so? You may have noticed in the Russ House Block, one door south of the hotel entrance an inscription thus: "I Love Land." Now if this refers to real estate he should not say "love;" he should say "like." Very true, in speaking of one's native soil, we say, "Yes, my native land I love thee," but I am satisfied that even if you could suppose this inscription had any remote reference to a birthplace, it does not mean a ranch or eligibly-situated town site. Why does he do it? why does he?

Yours, without prejudice,
NOMME DE PLUME.

Now, did it never strike this sprightly Frenchman that he could have gone in there and asked the man himself "why he does it," as easily as he could write to me on the subject? But no matter – this is just about the weight of the important questions usually asked of editors and answered in the "Correspondents' Column;" sometimes a man asks how to spell a difficult word – when he might as well have looked in the dictionary; or he asks who discovered America – when he might have consulted history; or he asks who in the mischief Cain's wife was – when a moment's reflection would have satisfied him that nobody knows and nobody cares – at least, except himself. The Frenchman's little joke is good, though, for doubtless "Quarter-less twain," *would* sound like "Waterless twain," if uttered between two powerful brandy punches. But as to why the man in question loves land – I cannot imagine, unless his constitution resembles mine, and he don't love water.

ARABELLA. – No, neither Mr. Dan Setchell nor Mr. Gottschalk are married. Perhaps it will interest you to know that they are both uncommonly anxious to marry, however. And perhaps it will interest you still more to know that in case they do marry, they will doubtless wed females; I hazard this, because, in discussing the question of marrying, they have uniformly expressed a preference for your sex. I answer your inquiries concerning Miss Adelaide Phillips in the order in which they occur, by number, as follows: I. No.   II. Yes.   III. Perhaps.   IV. "Scasely."

PERSECUTED UNFORTUNATE. – You say you owe six months' board, and you have no money to pay it with, and your landlord keeps harassing you about it, and you have made all the excuses and explanations possible, and now you are at a loss what to say to him in future. Well, it is a delicate matter to offer advice in a case like this, but your distress impels me to make a suggestion, at least, since I cannot venture to do more. When he next importunes you, how would it do to take him impressively by the hand and ask, with simulated emotion, "*Monsieur Jean, votre chien, comme se porte-il?*" Doubtless that is very bad French, but you'll find that it will answer just as well as the unadulterated article.

ARTHUR AUGUSTUS. – No, you are wrong; that is the proper way to throw a brickbat or a tomahawk, but it doesn't answer so well for a boquet – you will hurt somebody if you keep it up. Turn your nosegay upside down, take it by the stems, and toss it with an upward sweep – did you ever pitch quoits? – that is the idea. The practice of recklessly heaving immense solid boquets, of the general size and weight of prize cabbages, from the dizzy altitude of the galleries, is dangerous and very reprehensible. Now, night before last, at the Academy of Music, just after Signorina Sconcia had finished that exquisite melody, "The Last Rose of Summer," one of these floral pile-drivers came cleaving down through the atmosphere of applause, and if she hadn't deployed suddenly to the right, it would have driven her into the floor like a shingle-nail. Of course that boquet was well-meant, but how would you have liked to have been the target? A sincere compliment is always grateful to a lady, so long as you don't try to knock her down with it.

AMATEUR SERENADER. – Yes, I will give you some advice, and do it with a good deal of pleasure. I live in a neighborhood which is well stocked with young ladies, and consequently I am excruciatingly sensitive upon the subject of serenading. Sometimes I suffer. In the first place, always tune your instruments before you get within three hundred yards of your destination – this will enable you to take your adored unawares, and create a pleasant surprise by launching out at once upon your music; it astonishes the dogs and cats out of their presence of mind, too, so that if you hurry you can get through before they have a chance to recover and interrupt you; besides, there is nothing captivating in the sounds produced in tuning a lot of melancholy guitars and fiddles, and neither does a group of able-bodied, sentimental young men so engaged look at all dignified. Secondly, clear your throats and do all the coughing you have got to do before you arrive at the seat of war – I have known a young lady to be ruthlessly startled out of her slumbers by such a sudden and direful blowing of noses and "h'm-h'ming" and coughing, that she imagined the house was beleaguered by victims of consumption from the neighboring hospital; do you suppose the music was able to make her happy after that? Thirdly, don't stand right under the porch and howl, but get out in the middle of the street, or better still, on the other side of it – distance lends enchantment to the sound; if you have previously transmitted a hint to the lady that she is going to be serenaded, she will understand who the music is for; besides, if you occupy a neutral position in the middle of the street, may be all the neighbors round will take stock in your serenade and invite you in to take wine with them. Fourthly, don't sing a whole opera through – enough of a thing's enough. Fifthly, don't sing "Lilly Dale" – the profound satisfaction that most of us derive from the reflection that the girl treated of in that song is dead, is constantly marred by the resurrection of the lugubrious ditty itself by your kind of people. Sixthly, don't let your screaming tenor soar an octave above all the balance of the chorus, and remain there setting everybody's teeth on edge for four blocks around; and, above all, don't let him sing a solo; probably there is nothing in the world so suggestive of serene contentment and perfect bliss as the spectacle of a calf chewing a dish-rag, but the nearest approach to it is your reedy tenor, standing apart, in sickly attitude, with head thrown back and eyes uplifted to the moon, piping his distressing solo: now do not pass lightly over this matter, friend, but ponder it with that seriousness which its importance entitles it to. Seventhly, after you have run all the chickens and dogs and cats in the vicinity distracted, and roused them into a frenzy of crowing, and cackling, and yowling, and cat-erwauling, put up your dreadful instruments and go home. Eighthly, as soon as you start, gag your tenor – otherwise he will be letting off a screech every now and then to let the people know he is around; your amateur tenor singer is notoriously the most self-conceited of all God's creatures. Tenthly, don't go serenading at all – it is a wicked, unhappy and seditious practice, and a calamity to all souls that are weary and desire to slumber and be at rest. Eleventhly and lastly, the father of the young lady in the next block says that if you come prowling around his neighborhood again with your infamous scraping and tooting and yelling, he will sally forth and deliver you into the hands of the police. As far as I am concerned myself, I would like to have you come, and come often, but as long as the old man is so prejudiced, perhaps you had better serenade mostly in Oakland, or San José, or around there somewhere.

ST. CLAIR HIGGINS, *Los Angeles*. – "My life is a failure; I have adored, wildly, madly, and she whom I love has turned coldly from me and shed her affections upon another; what would you advise me to do?" You should shed your affections on another, also – or on several, if there are enough to go round. Also, do everything you can to make your former flame unhappy. There is an absurd idea disseminated in novels, that the happier a girl is with another man, the happier it makes the old lover she has blighted. Don't you allow yourself to believe any such nonsense as that. The more cause that girl finds to regret that she did not marry you, the more comfortable you will feel over it. It isn't poetical, but it is mighty sound doctrine.

ARITHMETICUS, *Virginia, Nevada.* – "If it would take a cannon-ball $3\frac{1}{3}$ seconds to travel four miles, and $3\frac{3}{8}$ seconds to travel the next four, and $3\frac{5}{8}$ seconds to travel the next four, and if its rate of progress continued to diminish in the same ratio, how long would it take it to go fifteen hundred millions of miles?" I don't know.

AMBITIOUS LEARNER, *Oakland.* – Yes, you are right – America was not discovered by Alexander Selkirk.

JULIA MARIA. – Fashions? It is out of my line, Maria. How am I to know anything about such mysteries – I that languish alone? Sometimes I am startled into a passing interest in such things, but not often. Now, a few nights ago, I was reading the *Dramatic Chronicle* at the opera, between the acts – reading a poem in it, and reading it after my usual style of ciphering out the merits of poetry, which is to read a line or two near the top, a verse near the bottom and then strike an average, (even professional critics do that) – when – well, it had a curious effect, read as I happened to read it:

> " 'What shall I wear?' asked Addie St. Clair,
>   As she stood by her mirror so young and fair" –

and then I skipped a line or so, while I returned the bow of a strange young lady, who, I observed too late, had intended that courtesy for a ruffian behind me, instead of for myself, and read:

> "The *modiste* replied, 'It were wicked to hide
>   Such peerless perfection that should be your pride' " –

and then I skipped to the climax, to get my average, and read –

> " 'My beautiful bride!' a low voice replied,
>   As handsome Will Vernon appeared at her side,
>   'If you wish from all others my heart to beguile,
>   *Wear a smile* to-night, darling – your own sunny smile.' "

Now there's an airy costume for you! a "sunny smile!" There's a costume, which, for simplicity and picturesqueness, grand-discounts a Georgia major's uniform, which is a shirt-collar and a pair of spurs. But when I came to read the remainder of the poem, it appeared that my new Lady Godiva had other clothes beside her sunny smile, and so – it is not necessary to pursue a subject further which no longer possesses any startling interest. Ask me no questions about fashions, Julia, but use your individual judgment in the matter – "wear your own sunny smile," and such millinery traps and trimmings as may be handy and will be likely to set it off to best advantage.

NOM DE PLUME. – Behold! the Frenchman cometh again, as follows:

"Your courteous attention to my last enquiry induces this acknowledgment of your kindness. I availed myself of your suggestions and made the enquiry of the gentleman, and he told me very frankly that it was – none of my business. So you see we do sometimes have to apply to your correspondence column for correct information, after all. I read in the papers a few days since some remarks upon the grammatical construction of the sentences – *'Sic semper traditoris'* and *'Sic semper traditoribus,'* and I procured a Latin grammar in order to satisfy myself as to the genative, dative and ablative cases of traitors – and while wending my weary way homewards at a late hour of the night, thinking over the matter, and not knowing what moment some cutthroat would knock me over, and, as he escaped, flourishing my watch and portmonaie, exclaim, *'Sic semper tyranis,'* I stumbled over an individual lying on the sidewalk, with a postage stamp pasted on his hat in lieu of a car ticket, and evidently in the *objective case* to the phrase 'how come you so?' As I felt in his pockets to see if his friends had taken care of his money, lest he might be robbed, he exclaimed, tragically, *'Si*(hic) *semper tarantula-juice!'* Not finding the phrase in my grammar, which I examined at once, I thought of your advice and *asked* him what he meant, said he 'I mean jis what I say, and I intend to sti-hic to it.' He was *quarter*less, Twain; when I *sounded* him he hadn't a cent, although he *smelled* strong of a 5-scent shop."

MELTON MOWBRAY, *Dutch Flat.* – This correspondent sends a lot of doggerel, and says it has been regarded as very good in Dutch Flat. I give a specimen verse:

"The Assyrian came down, like a wolf on the fold,

And his cohorts were gleaming in purple and gold;
And the sheen of his spears shone like stars on the sea,
When the blue wave rolls nightly on deep Galilee."

There, that will do. That may be very good Dutch Flat poetry, but it won't do in the metropolis. It is too smooth and blubbery; it reads like buttermilk gurgling from a jug. What the people ought to have, is something spirited – something like "Johnny comes marching home." However, keep on practicing, and you may succeed yet. There is genius in you, but too much blubber.

LAURA MATILDA. – No, Mr. Dan Setchell has never been in the House of Correction. That is to say he never went there by compulsion; he remembers going there once to visit a very dear friend – one of his boyhood's friends – but the visit was merely temporary, and he only staid five or six weeks.

PROFESSIONAL BEGGAR. – No, you are not obliged to take greenbacks at par.

NOTE. – Several letters, chiefly from young ladies and young bachelors, remain over, to be answered next week, want of space precluding the possibility of attending to them at present. I always had an idea that most of the letters written to editors were written by the editors themselves. But I find, now, that I was mistaken.

MORAL STATISTICIAN. – I don't want any of your statistics. I took your whole batch and lit my pipe with it. I hate your kind of people. You are always ciphering out how much a man's health is injured, and how much his intellect is impaired, and how many pitiful dollars and cents he wastes in the course of ninety-two years' indulgence in the fatal practice of smoking; and in the equally fatal practice of drinking coffee; and in playing billiards occasionally; and in taking a glass of wine at dinner, etc., etc., etc. And you are always figuring out how many women have been burned to death because of the dangerous fashion of wearing expansive hoops, etc., etc., etc. You never see but one side of the question. You are blind to the fact that most old men in America smoke and drink coffee, although, according to your theory, they ought to have died young; and that hearty old Englishmen drink wine and survive it, and portly old Dutchmen both drink and smoke freely, and yet grow

older and fatter all the time. And you never try to find out how
much solid comfort, relaxation and enjoyment a man derives from
smoking in the course of a lifetime, (and which is worth ten times
the money he would save by letting it alone,) nor the appalling
aggregate of happiness lost in a lifetime by your kind of people
from *not* smoking. Of course you can save money by denying yourself all these little vicious enjoyments for fifty years, but then what
can you do with it? – what use can you put it to? Money can't save
your infinitesimal soul; all the use that money can be put to is to
purchase comfort and enjoyment in this life – therefore, as you are
an enemy to comfort and enjoyment, where is the use in accumulating cash? It won't do for you to say that you can use it to better
purpose in furnishing a good table, and in charities, and in supporting tract societies, because you know yourself that you people
who have no petty vices are never known to give away a cent, and
that you stint yourselves so in the matter of food that you are
always feeble and hungry. And you never dare to laugh in the daytime for fear some poor wretch, seeing you in a good humor, will
try to borrow a dollar of you; and in church you are always down
on your knees when the contribution box comes around; and you
always pay your debts in greenbacks, and never give the revenue
officers a true statement of your income. Now you know all these
things yourself, don't you? Very well, then, what is the use of your
stringing out your miserable lives to a lean and withered old age?
What is the use of your saving money that is so utterly worthless
to you? In a word, why don't you go off somewhere and die, and
not be always trying to seduce people into becoming as "ornery"
and unloveable as you are yourselves, by your ceaseless and villainous "moral statistics?" Now I don't approve of dissipation, and
I don't indulge in it, either, but I haven't a particle of confidence
in a man who has no redeeming petty vices whatever, and so
I don't want to hear from you any more. I think you are the very
same man who read me a long lecture, last week, about the degrading vice of smoking cigars, and then came back, in my absence,
with your vile, reprehensible fire-proof gloves on, and carried off
my beautiful parlor stove.

SIMON WHEELER, *Sonora.* – The following simple and touching
remarks and accompanying poem have just come to hand from
the rich gold-mining region of Sonora:

To Mr. Mark Twain: The within parson, which I have sot to

poet-try under the name and style of "He Done His Level Best,"
was one among the whitest men I ever see, and it ain't every
man that knowed him that can find it in his heart to say he's glad
the pore cuss is busted and gone home to the States. He was here
in an early day, and he was the handyest man about takin holt
of anything that come along you most ever see, I judge; he was
a cheerful, stirrin cretur, always doin something, and no man
can say he ever see him do anything by halvers. Preachin was
his nateral gait, but he warn't a man to lay back and twidle his
thums because there didn't happen to be nothing doin in his
own espeshial line – no sir, he was a man who would meander
forth and stir up something for hisself. His last acts was to go his
pile on "kings-*and*," (calklatin to fill, but which he didn't fill,)
when there was a "flush" out agin him, and naterally, you see,
he went under. And so, he was cleaned out, as you may say, and
he struck the home-trail, cheerful but flat broke. I knowed this
talonted man in Arkansaw, and if you would print this humbly
tribute to his gorgis abillities, you would greatly obleege his on-
happy friend.

SONORA, Southern Mines, June, 1865.

HE DONE HIS LEVEL BEST.

Was he a mining on the flat –
  He done it with a zest;
Was he a leading of the choir –
  He done his level best.

If he'd a reglar task to do,
  He never took no rest;
Or if twas off-and-on – the same –
  He done his level best.

If he was preachin on his beat,
  He'd tramp from east to west,
And north to south – in cold and heat
  He done his level best.

He'd yank a sinner outen (Hades*)
  And land him with the blest –
Then snatch a prayer 'n waltz in again,
  And do his level best.

He'd cuss and sing and howl and pray,
  And dance and drink and jest,
And lie and steal – all one to him –
  He done his level best.

Whate'er this man was sot to do,
  He done it with a zest:
No matter *what* his contract was,
  HE'D DO HIS LEVEL BEST.

Verily, this man *was* gifted with "gorgis abillities," and it is a happiness to me to embalm the memory of their lustre in these columns. If it were not that the poet crop is unusually large and rank in California this year, I would encourage you to continue writing, Simon – but as it is, perhaps it might be too risky in you to enter against so much opposition.

INQUIRER wishes to know which is the best brand of smoking tobacco, and how it is manufactured. The most popular – mind I do not feel at liberty to give an opinion as to the best, and so I simply say the most popular – smoking tobacco is the miraculous conglomerate they call "Killickinick." It is composed of equal parts of tobacco stems, chopped straw, "old soldiers," fine shavings, oak leaves, dog-fennel, corn-shucks, sun-flower petals, outside leaves of the cabbage plant, and any refuse of any description whatever that costs nothing and will burn. After the ingredients are thoroughly mixed together, they are run through a chopping-machine. The mass is then sprinkled with fragrant Scotch snuff, packed into various seductive shapes, labelled "Genuine Killickinick, from the old original manufactory at Richmond," and sold to consumers at a dollar a pound. The choicest brands contain a double portion of "old soldiers," and sell at a dollar and a half. "Genuine Turkish" tobacco contains a treble quantity of old soldiers, and is worth two or three dollars, according to the amount

* You observe that I have taken the liberty to alter a word for you, Simon – to tone you down a little, as it were. Your language was unnecessarily powerful. M. T.

of service the said "old soldiers" have previously seen. N. B. This article is preferred by the Sultan of Turkey; his picture and autograph are on the label. Take a handful of "Killickinick," crush it as fine as you can, and examine it closely, and you will find that you can make as good an analysis of it as I have done; you must not expect to discover any particles of genuine tobacco by this rough method, however – to do that, it will be necessary to take your specimen to the mint and subject it to a fire-assay. A good article of cheap tobacco is now made of chopped pine-straw and Spanish moss; it contains one "old soldier" to the ton, and is called "Fine Old German Tobacco."

ANNA MARIA says as follows: "We have got such a nice literary society, O! you can't think! It is made up of members of our church, and we meet and read poetry and sketches and essays, and such things – mostly original – in fact, we have got talent enough among ourselves, without having to borrow reading matter from books and newspapers. We met a few evenings since at a dwelling on Howard, between Seventh and Eighth, and ever so many things were read. It was a little dull, though, until a young gentleman, (who is a member of our church, and oh, so gifted!) unrolled a bundle of manuscript and read *such* a funny thing about "Love's Bakery," where they prepare young people for matrimony, and about a young man who was engaged to be married, and who had the small-pox, and the erysipelas, and lost one eye and got both legs broken, and one arm, and got the other arm pulled out by a carding-machine, and finally got so damaged that there was scarcely anything of him left for the young lady to marry. You ought to have been there to hear how well he read it, and how they all laughed. We went right to work and nominated him for the Presidency of the Society, and he only lost it by two votes."

Yes, dear, I remember that "*such* a funny thing" which he read – I wrote it myself, for THE CALIFORNIAN, last October. But as he read it well, I forgive him – I can't bear to hear a good thing read badly. You had better keep an eye on that gifted young man, though, or he will be treating you to Washington's Farewell Address in manuscript the first thing you know – and if *that* should pass unchallenged, nothing in the world could save him from the Presidency.

CHARMING SIMPLICITY.

I once read the following paragraph in a newspaper:

"*Powerful Metaphor.* – A Western editor, speaking of a quill-driving cotemporary, says 'his intellect is so dense that it would take the auger of common sense longer to bore into it than it would to bore through Mont Blanc with a boiled carrot!'"

I have found that man. And I have found him – not in Stockton – not in Congress – not even in the Board of Education – but in the editorial sanctum of the Gold Hill *News*. Hear him:

"BYRON BUSTED. – The most fearful exhibition of literary ignorance – to say nothing of literary judgment – that we have had occasion to notice in many a year, is presented by the San Francisco CALIFORNIAN, a professedly literary journal. It is among the 'Answers to Correspondents.' Lord Byron's magnificent and universally admired verses on the Destruction of Sennacherib, are sent from Dutch Flat to the CALIFORNIAN, and are there not recognized, but denounced as a 'lot of doggerel.' Ye Gods! Perhaps the editor will try to get out of his 'fix' by saying it was all in fun – that it is a Dutch Nix joke! Read the comments:

"'MELTON MOWBRAY, *Dutch Flat.* – This correspondent sends us a lot of doggerel, and says it has been regarded as very good in Dutch Flat. I give a specimen verse:

'The Assyrian came down, like a wolf on the fold,
And his cohorts were gleaming in purple and gold;
And the sheen of his spears shone like stars on the sea,
When the blue wave rolls nightly on deep Galilee.'

"'There, that will do. That may be very good Dutch Flat poetry, but it won't do in the metropolis. It is too smooth and blubbery; it reads like buttermilk gurgling from a jug. What the people should have, is something spirited – something like 'Johnny comes marching home.' However, keep on practicing, and you may succeed yet. There is genius in you, but too much blubber.'"

Come, now, friend, about what style of joke *would* suit your capacity? – because we are anxious to come within the comprehension of all. Try a good old one; for instance: "Jones meets Smith; says

Smith, 'I'm glad it's raining, Jones, because it'll start everything out of the ground.' 'Oh, Lord, I hope not,' says Jones, – 'because then it would start my first wife out!' " How's that? Does that "bore through?"

Since writing the above, I perceive that the *Flag* has fallen into the wake of the *News*, and got sold by the same rather glaring burlesque that disposed of its illustrious predecessor at such an exceedingly cheap rate.

LITERARY CONNOISSEUR asks "Who is the author of these fine lines?

> 'Let dogs delight to bark and bite,
> For God hath made them so!' "

Here is a man gone into ecstasies of admiration over a nursery rhyme! Truly, the wonders of this new position of mine do never cease. The longer I hold it the more I am astonished, and every new applicant for information, who comes to me, leaves me more helplessly stunned than the one who went before him. No, I *don't* know who wrote those "fine lines," but I expect old Wat's-'is-name, who wrote old Watt's hymns, is the heavy gun you are after. However, it may be a bad guess, and if you find it isn't him, why then lay it on Tupper. That is my usual method. It is awkward to betray ignorance. Therefore, when I come across anything in the poetry line, which is particularly mild and aggravating, I always consider it pretty safe to lay it on Tupper. The policy is subject to accidents, of course, but then it works pretty well, and I hit oftener than I miss. A "connoisseur" should never be in doubt about anything. It is ruinous. I will give you a few hints. Attribute all the royal blank verse, with a martial ring to it, to Shakspeare; all the grand ponderous ditto, with a solemn lustre as of holiness about it, to Milton; all the ardent love poetry, tricked out in affluent imagery, to Byron; all the scouring, dashing, descriptive warrior rhymes to Scott; all the sleepy, tiresome, rural stuff, to Thomson and his eternal *Seasons*; all the genial, warm-hearted jolly Scotch poetry, to Burns; all the tender, broken-hearted song-verses to Moore; all the broken-English poetry to Chaucer or Spenser – whichever occurs to you first; all the heroic poetry, about the impossible deeds done before Troy, to Homer; all the nauseating rebellion mush-and-milk about young fellows who have come home to die – just before the battle, mother – to George

F. Root and kindred spirits; all the poetry that everybody admires and appreciates, but nobody ever reads or quotes from, to Dryden, Cowper and Shelley; all the graveyard poetry to Elegy Gray or Wolfe, indiscriminately; all the poetry that you can't understand, to Emerson; all the harmless old platitudes, delivered with a stately and oppressive pretense of originality, to Tupper, and all the "Anonymous" poetry to yourself. Bear these rules in mind, and you will pass muster as a connoisseur; as long as you can talk glibly about the "styles" of authors, you will get as much credit as if you were really acquainted with their works. Throw out a mangled French phrase occasionally, and you will pass for an accomplished man, and a Latin phrase dropped now and then will gain you the reputation of being a learned one. Many a distinguished "connoisseur" in *belles lettres* and classic erudition travels on the same capital I have advanced you in this rather lengthy paragraph. Make a note of that "Anonymous" suggestion – never let a false modesty deter you from "cabbaging" anything you find drifting about without an owner. I shall publish a volume of poems, shortly, over my signature, which became the "children of my fancy" in this unique way.

ETIQUETTICUS, *Monitor Silver Mines.* – "If a lady and gentleman are riding on a mountain trail, should the lady precede the gentleman, or the gentleman precede the lady?" It is not a matter of politeness at all – it is a matter of the heaviest mule. The heavy mule should keep the lower side, so as to brace himself and stop the light one should he lose his footing. But to my notion you are worrying yourself a good deal more than necessary about etiquette, up there in the snow belt. You had better be skirmishing for bunch-grass to feed your mule on, now that the snowy season is nearly ready to set in.

TRUE SON OF THE UNION. – Very well, I will publish the following extract from one of the dailies, since you seem to consider it necessary to your happiness, and since your trembling soul has found in it evidence of lukewarm loyalty on the part of the Collector – but candidly, now, don't you think you are in rather small business? I do, anyhow, though I do not wish to flatter you:

"BATTLE OF BUNKER HILL.

SAN FRANCISCO, June 17, 1865.

Messrs. Editors: Why is it that on this day, the greatest of all in the annals of the rights of man – viz: the Glorious Anniversary of the Battle of Bunker Hill – *our Great Ensign of Freedom does not appear on the Custom House*? Perhaps our worthy Collector is so busy Senator-making that it might have escaped his notice. You will be pleased to assign an excuse for the above official delinquency, and oblige

A NEW ENGLAND MECHANIC."

Why was that published? I think it was simply to gratify a taste for literary pursuits which has suddenly broken out in the system of the artisan from New England; or perhaps he has an idea, somehow or other, in a general way, that it would be a showing of neat and yet not gaudy international politeness for Collectors of ports to hoist their flags in commemoration of British victories, (for the physical triumph was theirs, although we claim all the moral effect of a victory;) or perhaps it struck him that "this day, the greatest of all *in the annals of the rights of man*," (whatever that may mean, for it is a little too deep for me,) was a fine, high-sounding expression, and yearned to get it off in print; or perhaps it occurred to him that "the Glorious Anniversary," and "our Great Ensign of Freedom," being new and startling figures of speech, would probably create something of a sensation if properly marshalled under the leadership of stunning capitals, and so he couldn't resist the temptation to trot them out in grand dress parade before the reading public; or perhaps, finally, he really *did* think the Collector's atrocious conduct partook of the character of a devilish "official delinquency," and imperatively called for explanation or "excuse." And still, after all this elaborate analysis, I am considerably "mixed" as to the actual motive for publishing that thing.

But observe how quibbling and fault-finding breed in a land of newspapers. Yesterday I had the good fortune to intercept the following bitter communication on its way to the office of a cotemporary, and I am happy in being able to afford to the readers of THE CALIFORNIAN the first perusal of it:

Editors of the Flaming Loyalist: What does it mean? The extraordinary conduct of Mr. John Doe, one of the highest Government officials among us, upon the anniversary of the battle of Bunker Hill – that day so inexpressibly dear to every loyal American heart because our patriot forefathers got worsted upon that occasion – is matter of grave suspicion. It was observed (by those who have closely watched Mr. Doe's actions

ever since he has been in office, and who have thought his professions of loyalty lacked the genuine ring,) that this man, *who
has uniformly got drunk, heretofore, upon all the nation's great historical
days, remained thoroughly sober upon the hallowed 17th of June.* Is not
this significant? Was this the pardonable forgetfulness of a loyal
officer, or rather, was it not the deliberate act of a malignant
and a traitorous heart? You will be pleased to assign an excuse
for the above official delinquency, and oblige

A SENTINEL AGRICULTURIST UPON THE
NATIONAL WATCHTOWER.

Now isn't that enough to disgust any man with being an
officeholder? Here is a drudging public servant who has always
served his masters patiently and faithfully, and although there was
nothing in his instructions requiring him to get drunk on national
holidays, yet with an unselfishness, and an enlarged public spirit,
and a gushing patriotism that did him infinite credit, he *did* always
get as drunk as a loon on these occasions – ay, and even upon any
occasion of minor importance when an humble effort on his part
could shed additional lustre upon his country's greatness, never
did he hesitate a moment to go and fill himself full of gin. Now
observe how his splendid services have been appreciated – behold
how quickly the remembrance of them hath passed away – mark
how the tried servant has been rewarded. This grateful officer –
this pure patriot – has been known to get drunk five hundred times
in a year for the honor and glory of his country and his country's
flag, and no man cried "Well done, thou good and faithful servant"
– yet the very first time he ventures to remain sober on a battle
anniversary (exhausted by the wear and tear of previous efforts,
no doubt,) this spying "Agriculturist," who has deserted his onion-
patch to perch himself upon the National Watch-Tower at the risk
of breaking his meddlesome neck, discovers the damning fact that
he is firm on his legs, and sings out: "He don't keep up his lick! –
he's DISLOYAL!"

Oh, stuff! a public officer has a hard enough time of it, at best,
without being constantly hauled over the coals for inconsequential
and insignificant trifles. If you *must* find fault, go and ferret out
something worth while to find fault with – if John Doe or the Collector neglect the actual business they are required by the Government to transact, impeach them. But pray allow them a little
poetical license in the choice of occasions for getting drunk and

hoisting the National flag. If the oriental artisan and the sentinel agriculturalist held the offices of these men, would they ever *attend to anything else* but the flag-flying and gin-soaking outward forms of patriotism and official industry?

SOCRATES MURPHY. – You speak of having given offense to a gentleman at the Opera by *unconsciously* humming an air which the tenor was singing at the time. Now, part of that is a deliberate false-hood. You were not doing it "unconsciously;" no man does such a mean, vulgar, egotistical thing as that unconsciously. You were doing it to "show off;" you wanted the people around you to know you had been to operas before, and to think you were not such an ignorant, self-conceited, supercilious ass as you looked; I can tell you Arizona opera-sharps, any time; you prowl around beer-cellars and listen to some howling-dervish of a Dutchman ex-terminating an Italian air, and then you come into the Academy and prop yourself up against the wall with the stuffy aspect and the imbecile leer of a clothing-store dummy, and go to droning along about half an octave below the tenor, and disgusting every-body in your neighborhood with your beery strains. [N. B. If this rough-shod eloquence of mine touches you on a raw spot occasion-ally, recollect that I am talking for your good, Murphy, and that I am simplifying my language so as to bring it clearly within the margin of your comprehension; it might be gratifying to you to be addressed as if you were an Oxford graduate, but then you wouldn't understand it, you know.] You have got another abomin-able habit, my sage-brush amateur. When one of those Italian footmen in British uniform comes in and sings "O tol de rol! – O, Signo-o-o-ra! – loango – congo – Venezue-e-e-la! whack fol de rol!" (which means "Oh, noble madame, here's one of them dukes from the palace, out here, come to borrow a dollar and a half,") you always stand with expanded eyes and mouth, and one pile-driver uplifted, and your ample hands held apart in front of your face, like a couple of canvas-covered hams, and when he gets almost through, how you do uncork your pent-up enthusiasm and applaud with hoof and palm! You have it pretty much to yourself, and then you look sheepish when you find everybody staring at you. But how very idiotic you do look when something really fine is sung – you generally keep quiet, then. Never mind, though, Murphy, entire audiences do things at the Opera that they have no business to do; for instance, they never let one of those thousand-dollar singers finish – they always break in with their ill-timed applause just as he or she, as the case may be, is preparing to throw all his or her concentrated sweetness into the final strain, and so all that sweetness is lost. Write me again, Murphy – I shall always be happy to hear from you.

ARITHMETICUS, *Virginia, Nevada.* – "I am an enthusiastic student of mathematics, and it is so vexatious to me to find my progress constantly impeded by these mysterious arithmetical technicalities. Now do tell me what the difference is between Geometry and Conchology?"

Here *you* come again, with your diabolical arithmetical conundrums, when I am suffering death with a cold in the head. If you could have seen the expression of ineffable scorn that darkened my countenance a moment ago and was instantly split from the centre in every direction like a fractured looking-glass by my last sneeze, you never would have written that disgraceful question. Conchology is a science which has nothing to do with mathematics; it relates only to shells. At the same time, however, a man who opens oysters for a hotel, or shells a fortified town, or sucks eggs, is not, strictly speaking, a conchologist – a fine stroke of sarcasm, that, but it will be lost on such an intellectual clam as you. Now compare conchology and geometry together, and you will see what the difference is, and your question will be answered. But don't torture me with any more of your ghastly arithmetical horrors (for I do detest figures anyhow,) until you know I am rid of my cold. I feel the bitterest animosity toward you at this moment – bothering me in this way, when I can do nothing but sneeze and quote poetry and snort pocket-handkerchiefs to atoms. If I had you in range of my nose, now, I would blow your brains out.

YOUNG MOTHER. – And so you think a baby is a thing of beauty and a joy forever? Well, the idea is pleasing, but not original – every cow thinks the same of its own calf. Perhaps the cow may not think it so elegantly, but still she thinks it, nevertheless. I honor the cow for it. We all honor this touching maternal instinct wherever we find it, be it in the home of luxury or in the humble cowshed. But really, madam, when I come to examine the matter in all its bearings, I find that the correctness of your assertion does not manifest itself in all cases. A sore-faced baby with a neglected nose cannot be conscientiously regarded as a thing of beauty, and inasmuch as babyhood spans but three short years, no baby is competent to be a joy "forever." It pains me thus to demolish two-thirds of your pretty sentiment in a single sentence, but the position I hold in this chair requires that I shall not permit you to deceive and mislead the public with your plausible figures of speech. I know a female baby aged eighteen months, in this city, which cannot hold out as a "joy" twenty-four hours on a stretch, let alone "forever." And it possesses some of the most remarkable eccentricities of character and appetite that have ever fallen under my notice. I will set down here a statement of this infant's operations, (conceived, planned and carried out by itself, and without suggestion or assistance from its mother or any one else,) during a single day – and what I shall say can be substantiated by the sworn testimony of witnesses. It commenced by eating one dozen large blue-mass pills, box and all; then it fell down a flight of stairs, and arose with a bruised and purple knot on its forehead, after which it proceeded in quest of further refreshment and amusement. It found a glass trinket ornamented with brasswork – mashed up and ate the glass, and then swallowed the brass. Then it drank about twenty or thirty drops of laudanum, and more than a dozen table-spoonsful of strong spirits of camphor. The reason why it took no more laudanum was, because there was no more to take. After this it lay down on its back, and shoved five or six inches of a silver-headed whalebone cane down its throat; got it fast there, and it was all its mother could do to pull the cane out again, without pulling out some of the child with it. Then, being hungry for glass again, it broke up several wine glasses, and fell to eating and swallowing the fragments, not minding a cut or two. Then it ate a quantity of butter, pepper, salt and California matches, actually taking a spoonful of butter, a spoonful of salt, a spoonful of pepper, and three or four lucifer matches, at each mouthful. (I will remark here that this thing of beauty likes painted German lucifers, and eats all she can get of them; but she infinitely prefers California matches – which I regard as a compliment to our home manufactures of more than ordinary value, coming, as it does, from one who is too young to flatter.) Then she washed her head with soap and water, and afterwards ate what soap was left, and drank as much of the suds as she had room for, after which she sallied forth and took the cow familiarly by the tail, and got kicked heels over head. At odd times during the day, when this joy forever happened to have nothing particular on hand, she put in the time by climbing up on places and falling down off them, uniformly damaging herself in the operation. As young as she is, she speaks many words tolerably distinctly, and being plain-spoken in other respects, blunt and to the point, she opens conversation with all strangers, male or female, with the same formula – "How do, Jim?" Not being familiar with the ways of children, it is possible that I have been magnifying into matter of surprise things which may not strike any one who is familiar with infancy as being at all astonishing. However, I cannot believe that such is the case, and so I repeat that my report of this baby's performances is strictly true – and if any one doubts it, I can produce the child. I will further engage that she shall devour anything that is given her, (reserving to myself only the right to exclude anvils,) and fall down from any place to which she may be elevated, (merely stipulating that her preference for alighting on her head shall be respected, and, therefore, that the elevation chosen shall be high enough to enable her to accomplish this to her satisfaction.) But I find I have wandered from my subject – so, without further argument, I will reiterate my conviction that not *all* babies are things of beauty and joys forever.

BLUE-STOCKING, *San Francisco.* – Do I think the writer in the *Golden Era* quoted Burns correctly when he attributed this language to him?

"O, wad the power the gift tae gie us."

No, I don't. I think the proper reading is –

"O, wad some power the giftie gie us."

But how do you know it is Burns? Why don't you wait till you hear from the *Gold Hill News*? Why do you want to rush in ahead of the splendid intellect that discovered as by inspiration that the "Destruction of the Sennacherib" was not written in Dutch Flat?

AGNES ST. CLAIR SMITH. – This correspondent writes as follows: "I suppose you have seen the large oil painting (entitled 'St. Patrick preaching at Tara, A. D. 432,') by J. Harrington, of San Francisco, in the window of the picture store adjoining the Eureka Theatre, on Montgomery street. What do you think of it?"

Yes, I have seen it. I think it is a petrified nightmare. I have not time to elaborate my opinion.

DISCOURAGING.

The fate of Mark Twain's exquisite bit of humor, in which he treats Byron's "Sennacherib" as a communication from a Dutch Flat poet, will teach a lesson to our wits. The next time that Mark gets off a good thing in the same fine vein, he will probably append "a key" to the joke. – *Dramatic Chronicle.*

Ah! but you forget the Gold Hill *News* and the *Flag*. Would they understand the "key" do you think?

YOUNG ACTOR. – This gentleman writes as follows: "I am desperate. *Will* you tell me how I can possibly please the newspaper critics? I have labored conscientiously to achieve this, ever since I made my *début* upon the stage, and I have never yet entirely succeeded in a single instance. Listen: The first night I played after I came among you, I judged by the hearty applause that was frequently showered upon me, that I had made a 'hit' – that my audience were satisfied with me – and I was happy accordingly. I only longed to know if I had been as successful with the critics. The first thing I did in the morning was to send for the papers. I read this: 'Mr. King Lear Macbeth made his first appearance last night, before a large and fashionable audience, as "Lord Blucher," in Bilgewater's great tragedy of *Blood, Hair and the Ground Tore Up.* In the main, his effort may be set down as a success – a very gratifying success. His voice is good, his manner easy and graceful, and his enunciation clear and distinct; his conception of the character he personated was good, and his rendition of it almost perfect. This talented young actor will infallibly climb to a dizzy elevation upon the ladder of histrionic fame, but it rests with himself to say whether this shall be accomplished at an early day or years hence. If the former, then he must at once correct his one great fault – we refer to his habit of throwing extraordinary spirit into passages which do not require it – his habit of *ranting*, to speak plainly. It was this same unfortunate habit which caused him to spoil the noble scene between "Lord Blucher" and "Viscount Cranberry," last night, in that portion of the third act where the latter unjustly accuses the former of attempting to seduce his pure and honored grandmother. His rendition of "Lord Blucher's" observation –

"Speak but another syllable, vile, hell-spawned miscreant, and thou diest the death of a ter-r-raitor!"

was uttered with undue excitement and unseemly asperity – there
was too much rant about it. We trust Mr. Macbeth will consider
the hint we have given him.' That extract, Mr. Twain, was from
the *Morning Thunderbolt*. The *Daily Battering-Ram* gave me many
compliments, but said that in the great scene referred to above,
I gesticulated too wildly and too much – and advised me to be
more circumspect in future, in these matters. I played the same
piece that night, and toned myself down considerably in the matter
of ranting and gesticulation. The next morning neither the *Thunderbolt* or the *Battering-Ram* gave me credit for it, but the one said
my 'Lord Blucher' overdid the pathetic in the scene where his sister died, and the other said I laughed too boisterously in the one
where my servant fell in the dyer's vat and came out as green as a
meadow in Spring-time. The *Daily American Earthquake* said I was
too *tame* in the great scene with the 'Viscount.' I felt a little discouraged, but I made a note of these suggestions and fell to studying
harder than ever. That night I toned down my grief and my mirth,
and worked up my passionate anger and my gesticulation just the
least in the world. I may remark here that I began to perceive a
moderation, both in quantity and quality, of the applause vouchsafed me by the audience. The next morning the papers gave me
no credit for my efforts at improvement, but the *Thunderbolt* said
I was too loving in the scene with my new bride, the *Battering-Ram*
said I was not loving enough, and the *Earthquake* said it was a
masterly performance and never surpassed upon these boards.
I was check-mated. I sat down and considered how I was going to
engineer that love-scene to suit all the critics, until at last I became
stupefied with perplexity. I then went down town, much dejected,
and got drunk. The next day the *Battering-Ram* said I was too spirit-
less in the scene with the 'Viscount,' and remarked sarcastically
that I threatened the 'Viscount's' life with a subdued voice and
manner eminently suited to conversation in a funeral procession.
The *Thunderbolt* said my mirth was too mild in the dyer's vat scene,
and observed that instead of laughing heartily, as it was my place
to do, I smiled as blandly – and as guardedly, apparently – as an
undertaker in the cholera season. These mortuary comparisons
had a very depressing effect upon my spirits, and I turned to the
Earthquake for comfort. That authority said 'Lord Blucher' seemed
to take the death of his idolized sister uncommonly easy, and suggested with exquisite irony that if I would use a toothpick, or pretend to pare my nails, in the death-bed scene, my attractive

indifference would be the perfection of acting. I was almost desperate, but I went to work earnestly again to apply the newspaper hints to my 'Lord Blucher.' I ranted in the 'Viscount' scene (this at home in my private apartments) to suit the *Battering-Ram*, and then toned down considerably, to approach the *Earthquake*'s standard; I worked my grief up strong in the death-bed scene to suit the latter paper, and then modified it a good deal to comply with the *Thunderbolt*'s hint; I laughed boisterously in the dyer's vat scene, in accordance with the suggestion of the *Thunderbolt*, and then toned down toward the *Battering-Ram*'s notion of excellence. That night my audience did not seem to know whether to applaud or not, and the result was that they came as near doing neither one thing nor the other as was possible. The next morning the *Semi-Monthly Literary Bosh* said my rendition of the character of 'Lord Blucher' was faultless – that it was stamped with the seal of inspiration; the *Thunderbolt* said I was an industrious, earnest and aspiring young dramatic student, but I was possessed of only ordinary merit, and could not hope to achieve more than a very moderate degree of success in my profession – and added that my engagement was at an end for the present; the *Battering-Ram* said I was a tolerably good stock-actor, but that the practice of managers in imposing such people as me upon the public as stars, was very reprehensible – and added that my engagement was at an end for the present; the *Earthquake* critic said he had seen worse actors, but not *much* worse – and added that my engagement was at an end for the present. So much for newspapers. The *Monthly Magazine of Literature and Art* (high authority,) remarked as follows: 'Mr. King Lear Macbeth commenced well, but the longer he played, the worse he played. His first performance of "Lord Blucher" in *Blood, Hair and the Ground Tore Up*, may be entered upon the record as a remarkably fine piece of acting – but toward the last he got to making it the most extraordinary exhibition of theatrical lunacy we ever witnessed. In the scene with the "Viscount," which calls for sustained, vigorous, fiery declamation, his manner was an incomprehensible mixture of "fever-heat" and "zero" – to borrow the terms of the thermometer; in the dyer's vat scene he was alternately torn by spasms of mirth and oppressed by melancholy; in the death-bed scene his countenance exhibited profound grief one moment and blank vacancy in the next; in the love scene with his bride – but why particularize? throughout the play he was a mixture – a conglomeration – a miracle of indecision – an aimless, purposeless dramatic lunatic. In a word, his concluding performances of the part of "Lord Blucher" were execrable. We simply assert this, but do not attempt to account for it – we know his first performance was excellence itself, but how that excellence so soon degenerated into the pitiable exhibition of last night, is beyond our ability to determine.' Now, Mr. Twain, you have the facts in this melancholy case – and any suggestion from you as to how I can please these critics will be gratefully received."

I can offer no suggestion, "Young Actor," except that the ordinary run of newspaper criticism will not do to depend upon. If you keep on trying to shape yourself by such models, you will go mad, eventually. Several of the critics you mention probably never saw you play an entire act through in their lives, and it is possible that the balance were no more competent to decide upon the merits of a dramatic performance than of a sermon. Do you note how unconcernedly and how pitilessly they lash you as soon as your engagement is ended? Sometimes those "criticisms" are written and in type before the curtain rises. Don't you remember that the New York *Herald* once came out with a column of criticism upon Edwin Forrest's "Hamlet," when unfortunately the bill had been changed at the last moment, and Mr. Forrest played "Othello" instead of the play criticised? And only lately didn't the same paper publish an elaborate imaginary description of the funeral ceremonies of the late Jacob Little, unaware that the obsequies had been postponed for twenty-four hours? It is vastly funny, your "working yourself up" to suit the *Thunderbolt*, and "toning yourself down" to suit the *Battering-Ram*, and doing all sorts of similarly absurd things to please a lot of "critics" who had probably never seen you play at all, but who threw in a pinch of instruction or censure among their praise merely to give their "notices" a candid, impartial air. Don't bother yourself any more in that way. Pay no attention to the papers, but watch the audience. A silent crowd is damning censure – good, hearty, enthusiastic applause is a sure sign of able acting. It seems you played well at first – I think you had better go back and start over again at the point where you began to instruct yourself from the newspapers. I have often wondered, myself, when reading critiques in the papers, what would become of an actor if he tried to follow all the fearfully conflicting advice they contained.

MARY, *Rincon School.* – Sends a dainty little note, the contents whereof I take pleasure in printing, as follows, (suppressing, of course, certain expressions of kindness and encouragement which she intended for my eye alone): "Please spell and define *gewhilikins* for me."

Geewhillikins is an ejaculation or exclamation, and expresses surprise, astonishment, amazement, delight, admiration, disappointment, deprecation, disgust, sudden conviction, incredulity, joy, sorrow – well, it is capable of expressing pretty nearly any abrupt emotion that flashes through one's heart. For instance, I say to Jones, "Old Grimes is dead!" Jones knowing old Grimes was in good health the last time he heard from him, is surprised, and he naturally exclaims, "Geewhillikins! is that so?" In this case the word simply expresses surprise, mixed with neither joy nor sorrow, Grimes' affairs being nothing to Jones. I meet Morgan, and I say, "Well, I saw Johnson, and he refuses to pay that bill." Johnson exclaims, "Geewhillikins! is that so?" In this case the word expresses astonishment and disappointment, together with a considerable degree of irritation. I meet young Yank, and I observe, "The country is safe now – peace is declared!" Yank swings his hat and shouts, "Geewhillikins! is that so?" – which expresses surprise and extreme delight. I stumble on Thompson, and remark, "There was a tornado in Washoe yesterday which picked up a church in Virginia and blew it to Reed's Station, on the Carson river, eighteen miles away!" Thompson says, "Gee-e-e-*whillikins!*" with a falling inflection and strong emphasis on that portion of the word which I have italicized – thus, with discriminating judgment, imbuing the phrase with the nicest shades of amazement, wonder, and mild incredulity. Stephens, who is carrying home some eggs in his "hind-coat pocket," sits down on them and mashes them – exclaiming, as he rises, gingerly exploring the mucilaginous locality of his misfortune with his hand, "*Gee*whillikins!" – with strong emphasis and falling inflection on the first syllable, and falling inflection on the last syllable also – thus expressing an extremity of grief and unmitigated disgust which no other word in our whole language is capable of conveying. That will do, I suppose – you cannot help understanding my definition, now, and neither will you fail to appreciate the extraordinary comprehensiveness of the word. We will now consider its orthography. You perceive that I spell it with two e's and two l's, which I think is the proper method, though I confess the matter is open to argument. Different people spell it in different ways. Let us give a few examples:

"The horse 'raired' up with a furious neigh,
And over the hills he scoured away!
Mazeppa closed his despairing eye,
And murmured, 'Alas! and must I die!
          'GEE-WHILIKINS!' "

[*Byron's Mazeppa.*

          "Sir Hilary charged at Agincourt –
            Sooth 'twas an awful day!
          And though in that old age of sport
            The rufflers of the camp and court
              Had little time to pray,
          'Tis said Sir Hilary muttered there
          Four syllables by way of prayer:
              'GEE-WHILLIKINS!' "

[*Winthrop Mackworth Praed.*

If the Gold Hill *News* or the *American Flag* say the above excerpts are misquotations, pay no attention to them – they are anything but good authority in matters of this kind. The *Flag* does not spell the word we are speaking of properly, either, in my opinion. I have in my mind a communication which I remember having seen in that paper the morning the result of the presidential election was made known. It possessed something of an exulting tone, and was addressed to a heavy gun among the Copperheads – the editor of the late *Democratic Press*, I think – and read as follows:

"BERIAH BROWN, ESQ. – *Dear Sir:* How are you *now*?
    "Yours, truly,

                        G. WHILLIKINS."

You will have to accept my definition, Mary, for want of a better. As far as the spelling is concerned, you must choose between Mr. Praed and myself on the one hand, and Lord Byron and the *American Flag* on the other, bearing in mind that the two last named authorities disagree, and that neither of them ever knew much about the matter in dispute, anyhow.

ANXIETY. – *S. F.* – Need have no fear of General Halleck. There is no truth in the report that he will compel approaching maternity to take the oath of allegiance. – *Golden Era.*

Another impenetrable conundrum – or, to speak more properly, another fathomless riddle. I shall have to refer to Webster:

"APPROACHING, *ppr.* Drawing nearer; advancing toward."
"MATERNITY, *n.* The character or relation of a mother."

Consequently, "approaching maternity" means the *condition* of being about to become a mother. And according to the profound, the deep, the bottomless expounder who instructs "Anxiety" in my text, General Halleck "will not compel" that *condition* to "take the oath of allegiance." Any numscull could have told that – because how can an insensible, impalpable, invisible *condition* take an oath? That expounder comes as near being a "condition" as anybody, no doubt, but still he cannot take an oath in his character *as* a "condition;" he must take it simply in his character as a man. None but human beings can take the oath of allegiance under our constitution. But didn't you mean that women in the said condition would not be required to take the oath merely *because* they happened to be in that condition? – or didn't you mean that the woman wouldn't have to take it on behalf of her forthcoming progeny? – or didn't you mean that the forthcoming progeny wouldn't be required to take it itself, either before or immediately after it was born? Or, what in the very mischief *did* you mean? – what were you driving at? – what were you trying to ferry across the trackless ocean of your intellect? Now you had better stop this sort of thing, because it is becoming a very serious matter. If you keep it up, you will eventually get some of your subscribers so tangled up that they will seek relief from their troubles and perplexities in the grave of the suicide.

MARK TWAIN. – 'Twas a burning shame to misquote Burns. The wretch who deliberately substituted *italic* for the original would, we verily believe, enjoy martyrdom. Previous thereto his eyes should be stuck full of exclamation points! – *Golden Era.*

Are you wool-gathering, or is it I? I have read that paragraph fourteen or fifteen times, very slowly and carefully, but I can't see that it means anything. Does the point lie in a darkly suggested pun upon "original would" (original *wood?*) – or in the "exclamation *points?*" – or in the bad grammar of the last sentence? – or in – Come, now – explain your ingenious little riddle, and don't go on badgering and bully-ragging people in this mysterious way.

GOLD HILL NEWS. – This old scoundrel calls me an "old humbug from Dutch Nick's." Now this is not fair. It is highly improper for gentlemen of the press to descend to personalities, and I never permit myself to do it. However, as this abandoned outcast evidently meant his remark as complimentary, I take pleasure in so receiving it, in consideration of the fact that the fervent cordiality of his language fully makes up for its want of elegance.

INQUIRER, *Sacramento.* – At your request I have been down and walked under and around and about the grand, gaudy and peculiar

INDEPENDENCE ARCH

which rears its awful form at the conjunction of Montgomery and California streets, and have taken such notes as may enable me to describe it to you and tell you what I think of it. [N. B. I am writing this on Monday, the day preceding the Glorious Fourth.] My friend, I have seen arch-traitors and arch-deacons and architects, and archæologists, and archetypes, and arch-bishops, and, in fact, nearly all kinds of arches, but I give you the word of an honest man that I never saw an arch like this before. I desire to see one more like it and then die. I am the more anxious in this respect because it is not likely that I shall ever get a chance to see one like it in the next world, for something tells me that there is not such an arch as this in any of the seven heavens, and there certainly cannot be anything half as gay in the other place.

I am calling this *one* arch all the time, but in reality it is a cluster of four arches; when you pass up Montgomery street you pass under two of them, and when you pass up California street you pass under the other two. These arches spring from the tops of four huge square wooden pillars which are about fifteen or twenty feet high and painted with dull, dead, blue mud or blue-mass, or something of that kind. Projecting from each face of these sombre columns are bunches of cheap flags adorned with tin spear-heads. The contrast between the dark melancholy blue of the pillars and the gorgeous dyes of the flags is striking and picturesque. The arches reach as high as the eaves of an ordinary three-story house, and they are wide in proportion, the pillars standing nearly the width of the street apart. A flagstaff surmounts each of the pillars. The Montgomery street arches are faced with white canvas, upon which is inscribed the names of the several States in strong black paint; as there is a "slather" of gory red and a "slather" of ghostly white on each side of these black names, a cheerful barber-pole contrast is here presented. The broad tops of the arches are covered (in the barber-pole style, also, which seems to have been the groundwork of this fine conception,) with alternate patches of white and sickly pink cotton, and these patches having a wrinkled and disorderly appearance, remind me unpleasantly of a shirt I "done up" once in the Humboldt country, beyond the Sierras. The general effect of this open, airy, summer-house combination of arches, with its splashes and dashes of blue and red and pink and white, is intensely streaky and stripy; and altogether, if the colossal bird-cage were only "weatherboarded" it would just come up to one's notion of what a grand metropolitan barber-shop ought to be. Or if it were glazed it would be a neat thing in the way of a show-lamp to set up before a Brobdignag theatre. Surmounting the centres of two of the arches – those facing up and down Montgomery street – are large medallion portraits of Lincoln and Washington – daubs – apparently executed in whitewash, mud and brick-dust, with a mop. In these, also, the barber-shop ground-plan is still adhered to with a discriminating and sensitive regard to consistency; Washington is clean-shaved, but he is not done getting shampooed yet; his white hair is foamy with lather, and his countenance bears the expectant aspect of a man who knows that the cleansing shower-bath is about to fall. Good old Father Abe, whose pictured face, heretofore, was always serious, but never unhappy, looks positively worn and dejected and tired out, in the medallion – has exactly the expression of one who has been waiting a long time to get shaved and there are thirteen ahead of him yet. I cannot help admiring how the eternal fitness of things has been preserved in the execution of these portraits. To one who delights in "the unities" of art, could anything be more ravishing than the appropriate appearance and expression of the two countenances, overtopped as they are by sheaves of striped flags and surrounded on all sides by the glaring, tinted bars that symbol the barber's profession? I believe I have nothing left to describe in connection with the two arches which span Montgomery street. However, upon second thought, I forgot to mention that over each of the two sets of portraits stoops a monstrous painted eagle, with wings uplifted over his back, neck stretched forward, beak parted, and eager eye, as if he were on the very point of grabbing a savory morsel of some kind – an imaginary customer of the barber-shop, maybe.

The arch which fronts up California street is faced with white canvas, prominently sewed together in squares, and upon this broad white streak is inscribed in large, plain, black, "horse-type," this inscription:

"HONOR TO THE FOUNDERS AND SAVIOURS
OF THE REPUBLIC."

For some unexplained reason, the "Founders" of the Republic are aggrandized with a capital "F," and the equally meritorious Saviors of it snubbed with a small "s." True, they gave the Saviors a "u" – a letter more than is recommended by Webster's dictionary – but I consider that a lame apology and an illiberal and inadequate compensation for "nipping" their capital S. The centrepiece of this arch consists of an exceedingly happy caricature of the coat-of-arms of California, done in rude imitation of fresco. The female figure is a placid, portly, straight-haired squaw in complete armor, sitting on a recumbent hog, and so absorbed in contemplation of the cobble-stones that she does not observe that she has got her sack of turnips by the wrong end, and that dozens of them are rolling out at the other; neither does she observe that the hog has seized the largest turnip and has got it in his mouth; neither does she observe that her great weight is making it mighty uncomfortable for the hog; she does not notice that she is mashing the breath out of him and making his eyes bulge out with a most agonized expression – nor that it is as much as he can do to hold on to his turnip. There is nothing magnanimous in this picture. Any true-hearted American woman, with the kindly charity and the tenderness that are inseparable from the character, would get up for a minute and give the hog a chance to eat his turnip in peace.

The centre-piece of the opposite arch is a copy of the one just described, except that the woman is a trifle heavier, and of course the distress of the hog is aggravated in a corresponding degree. The motto is –

"MINE EYES HAVE SEEN THE GLORY OF THE
COMING OF THE LORD."

This is an entirely abstract proposition, and does not refer to the surrounding splendors of the situation.

I have now described the arch of which you have heard such glowing accounts (set afloat in the first place by incendiary daily prints, no doubt,) and have thus satisfied your first request. Your second – that I would tell you what I think of it, can be done in a few words. It cost $3,000, and I think it cost a great deal too much, considering the unhappy result attained. I think the taste displayed was very bad – I might even say barbarous, only the tone of some of my preceding paragraphs might lead people to think I was making a pun. If you will notice me you will observe that I never make a pun intentionally – I never do anything like that in cold blood. To proceed – I think the same money expended with better judgment would have procured a set of handsome, graceful arches which could be re-trimmed and used again, perhaps; but I think these can't, as we have no ferry slips now that require gateways resplendent with cheap magnificence; I think the whole affair was gotten up in too great a hurry to be done well – the committee was appointed too late in the day; I suppose the appointing power did not know sooner that the Fourth of July was coming this year; I think the committee did as well as they could under the circumstances, because a member of it told me so, and he could have no object in deceiving me; I think many people considered the cluster of arches, with their Sunday-school-picnic style of ornamentation, pretty, and took a good deal of pride in the same, and therefore I am glad that this article will not be published until the Fourth has come and gone, for I would be sorry that any remarks of mine should mar the pleasure any individual might otherwise take in that truly extraordinary work of art.

Now you have the arches as they looked before the Fourth – the time when the above paragraphs were written. But I must confess – and I don't do it *very* reluctantly – that on the morning of the Fourth they were greatly improved in appearance. One cause was that innumerable small flags had been mounted on the arches, and hid the broad red and pink patchwork covering of the latter from sight, and another that the fiery colors so prevalent about the structure had been pleasantly relieved by the addition of garlands and festoons of evergreens to the embellishments, and the suspension of a champagne basket of other greens and flowers from the centre of it, chandelier fashion. Also, as by this time all Montgomery street was a quivering rainbow of flags, one could not help seeing that the decorations of the arches had to be pretty strong in

coloring to keep up any sort of competition with the brilliant
surroundings.

As I have disparaged this work of art before it had a chance to
put on its best looks, and as I still don't think a great deal of it,
I will act fairly by it, and print the other side of the question, so
that you can form a just estimate of its merits and demerits by comparing the arguments of the prosecution and defence together.
I will re-publish here the opinion entertained of it by the reporter
of the *Alta*, one of its most fanatical, and I may even say, rabid
admirers. I will go further and endorse a portion of what he says,
but not all, by a good deal. I don't endorse the painting "in the
highest style of the decorative art," (although it sounds fine – I may
say eloquent,) nor the "magnificent basket," either:

"The most noticeable feature of the display on this street was the

GRAND TRIUMPHAL ARCH,

at the intersection of California and Montgomery streets,
designed by M. F. Butler, Esq., the architect; erected by A.
Snyder; painted, in the highest style of the decorative art, by
Hopps & Son; and draped and adorned with flags and flowers
by Chas. M. Plum, upholsterer, and A. Barbier, under the management and supervision of a Committee, consisting of John
Sime, W. W. Dodge and M. E. Hughes. This arch was one of
the chief attractions throughout the day and evening. On
Montgomery street, distributed on both north and south sides,
were the names of the thirty-six sovereign States of the Union,
to each one a separate shield, and the names of the leading Generals of the Revolution, side by side with those of the War for
the Union, and on the California street side the names of officers
of the Army and Navy, past and present, the face of the arch on
the east side bearing the words:

'Mine eyes have seen the glory of the coming of the Lord,'

And on the west side –

'Honor to the Founders and Saviors of our Republic.'

The centre of both the arches on Montgomery street were
ornamented with portraits of Washington and Lincoln, and sur-
mounted with flags beautifully and tastefully grouped. The flags
of various nations were also grouped under the base of the

arches at the four corners, and the whole structure was hung with evergreen wreaths and flowers, while a magnificent floral basket hung suspended under the centre of the structure by wreaths depending from the arches. As the procession passed under this arch, the petals of the roses and other flowers were constantly falling upon it in showers as the wreaths swung to and fro in the summer breeze."

Now for my side again. The following blast is from the *Morning Call.* The general felicity of the thing is to be ascribed to the fact that the reporter listened to some remarks of mine used in the course of a private conversation with another man, and turned them to account as a "local item." He is excusable for taking things from me, though, because I used to take little things from him occasionally when I reported with him on the *Call*:

STRAIGHTENING UP. – The likenesses of "Pater Patriæ," and "Salvator Patriæ," on the ornamental (!) barber-shop at the corner of Montgomery and California streets, have been straightened up, and now wear a closer similarity to what might be supposed to represent men of steady habits. While we hold in the most profound veneration the memory of those illustrious men, as well as the day we propose to celebrate, yet we defy any person to look at that triumphal structure, its *blue* pillars and tawdry arches, utterly ignoring architecture and taste – and not laugh.

Now for the other side. The following highly-flavored compliment is also from the *Morning Call,* (same issue as the above extract,) but was written by the chief editor – and editors and reporters will differ in opinion occasionally:

A FINE DISPLAY. – All things promise a fine display to-day, the finest probably that has ever been witnessed in this city. The splendid triumphal arches at the intersection of Montgomery and California streets, will be especial objects of admiration. They were designed by M. F. Butler, Esq., the architect, have been erected under his supervision, and are at once splendid specimens of his artistic skill as well as of the taste of the Committee who chose his designs over all others presented for the occasion. Mr. B. is the pioneer, as well as among the best architects of this State, and this last work, though of a somewhat ephemeral nature, is worthy of the artist who designed and

superintended it, and was properly entrusted to one of our oldest citizens as well as one of the most loyal men of the State.

Now for my side. The following is also from the *Call*, (same issue
as both the above extracts:)

THAT ARCH. – The following bit of satire, from a correspondent, is pretty severe on the anomalous structure our Committee have dignified with the name of triumphal arch:

"The grand Patriotic or Union Arch erected at the corner
of Montgomery and California streets, is a magnificent affair.
I presume it will be retained there for a number of weeks. But
is n't there a very important omission about the structure?
Erected in commemoration of the Nation's birthday and all its
subsequent glories, should not the portrait of the author of the
Declaration of Independence crown one of its beautiful arches?
'76."

Now for the other side once more. The following is from the
Bulletin. The concluding portion of the first sentence is time-worn
and stereotyped, though, and I don't consider that it ought to
count against me. It is always used on such occasions and is never
intended to mean anything:

"The triumphal arch which is now being completed under
the direction of M. F. Butler, architect, at the junction of
Montgomery and California streets, is the most imposing structure of its kind that has ever been erected on this coast. [Here
follows a description of it in dry detail.] The arches are beautifully trimmed with evergreen, and the whole structure is to be
adorned with a profusion of flags representing all nations, with
appropriate mottoes and names of popular Generals scattered
here and there among the Stars and Stripes."

And, finally, for my side again. Having this thing all my own
way I have decided that I am entitled to the closing argument. The
following is from the *American Flag*:

TRIUMPHAL ARCH. – A triumphal arch had been erected at
the intersection of California and Montgomery streets, at a cost
of $3,000. It consisted of four arches, one fronting and spanning
each street, and resting upon four large pillars, thirty feet in
height, painted a dingy blue, festooned with flags of various
nations, and exhibiting upon each side, painted upon shields,

the names, two upon each shield of the heroes of 1776 and 1865, – Grant, Greene; Sheridan, Montgomery; Dahlgren, Decatur; Dupont, Porter, &c. Near the center of each of the arches fronting on Montgomery street, were rather poorly painted portraits, also painted upon a shield, of Washington and Lincoln, surrounded by large spread eagles, and bearing beneath, the initials "W. L;" upon these arches were inscribed upon red and white shields, the names of all the States; the arch facing California street, west, bore the inscription "Honor to the Founders and to the Saviors of the Republic;" and that opposite, "Mine eyes have seen the glory of the coming of the Lord;" and near the center of both was a picture of a female of rather a lugubrious countenance, seated upon a lion couchant, bearing in her left hand a staff, and upon her head something bearing a striking resemblance to the metalic caps worn by the mail-clad warriors of ancient Greece, all of which, we presume, was intended to represent the "Goddess of Liberty victorious over the British Lion," but as we were unable to read the name of the damsel upon the shield which she held in her right hand, we will not be positive on that point. The whole affair was finely decorated with evergreens, flowers, wreaths, flags, etc., and would have been creditably ornamented, had more taste and skill been displayed in the paintings.

The prosecution "rests" here. And the defense will naturally have to "rest" also, because I have given them all the space I intend to. The case may now go to the jury, and while they are out I will give judgment in favor of the plaintiff. I learned that trick from the Washoe judges, long ago. But it stands to reason that when a thing is so frightfully tawdry and devoid of taste that the *Flag* can't stand it, and when a painting is so diabolical that the *Flag* can't admire it, they must be wretched indeed. Such evidence as this is absolutely damning.

STUDENT OF ETIQUETTE. – Asks: "If I step upon one end of a narrow bridge just at the moment that a mad bull rushes upon the other, which of us is entitled to precedence – which should give way and yield the road to the other?"

I decline to answer – leave it to the bull to decide. I am shrouded in doubts upon the subject, but the bull's mind will probably be perfectly clear. At a first glance it would seem that this "Student of Etiquette" is asking a foolish and unnecessary question, inasmuch as it is one which naturally answers itself – yet his inquiry is no more absurd than a dozen I can find any day gravely asked and as gravely answered in the "Correspondents' Column" of literary papers throughout the country. John Smith meets a beautiful girl on the street and falls in love with her, but as he don't know her name, nor her position in society, nor where she lives, nor in fact anything whatever about her, he sits down and writes these particulars to the *Weekly Literary Bushwhacker*, and gravely asks what steps he ought first to take in laying siege to that girl's affections – and is as gravely answered that he must not waylay her when she is out walking alone, nor write her anonymous notes, nor call upon her unendorsed by her friends, but his first move should be to *procure an introduction in due form*. That editor, with a grand flourish of wisdom, would have said: "Give way to the bull!" I, with greater wisdom, scorn to reply at all. If I were in a sarcastic vein, though, I might decide that it was Smith's privilege to butt the bull off the bridge – if he could. Again – John Jones finds a young lady stuck fast in the mud, but never having been introduced to her, he feels a delicacy about pulling her out, and so he goes off, with many misgivings, and writes to the *Diluted Literary Sangaree* about it, craving advice: he is seriously informed that it was not only his privilege, but his duty, to pull the young lady out of the mud, without the formality of an introduction. Inspired wisdom! He too, would have said: "Back down, and let the bull cross first." William Brown writes to the *Weekly Whangdoodle of Literature and Art* that he is madly in love with the divinest of her sex, but unhappily her affections and her hand are already pledged to another – how must he proceed? With supernatural sagacity the editor arrives at the conclusion that it is Brown's duty, as a Christian and gentleman, to go away and let her alone. Marvelous! He, too, would have said: "Waive etiquette, and let the bull have the bridge." However, we will drop the subject for the present. If these editors choose to go on answering foolish questions in the grandiloquent, oracular style that seems to afford them so much satisfaction, I suppose it is no business of mine.

MARY, *Rincon School.* – No, you are mistaken – *bilk* is a good dictionary word. True, the newspapers generally enclose it in quotation marks, (thus: "bilk,") which is the usual sign made use of to denote an illegitimate or slang phrase, but as I said before, the dictionaries recognize the word as good, pure English, nevertheless. I perfectly agree with you, however, that there is not an uglier or more inelegant word in any language, and I appreciate the good taste that ignores its use in polite conversation. For your accommodation and instruction, I have been looking up authorities in the Mercantile Library, and beg leave to offer the result of my labors, as follows:

From Webster's Dictionary, edition of 1828.
BILK, *v. t.* [Goth. *bilaikan*, to mock or deride. This Gothic word appears to be compound, *bi* and *laikan*, to leap or exult.]
To frustrate or disappoint; to deceive or defraud, by non-fulfilment of engagement; as, to *bilk* a creditor.   *Dryden.*
BILKED, *pp.* Disappointed; deceived; defrauded.

From Walker's Dictionary.
BILK, *v. a.* To cheat; to deceive.

From Wright's Universal Pronouncing Dictionary.
BILK. To deceive; to defraud.

From Worcester's Dictionary.
BILK, *v. a.* [Goth. *bi-laikan*, to scoff, to deride.] To cheat; to defraud; to deceive; to elude.
But be sure, says he, don't you *bilk* me.   *Spectator.*

From Spiers and Surenne's French Pronouncing Dictionary.
BILK, V. a. 1. *frustrer;* 2. (argot) *flower* (escroquer, duper).

From Adler's German and English Dictionary.
To BILK, *v. a.* schnellen, prellen, betrügen, im Stiche lassen, (be sonders um die [mit der] Bezahlung); *joc.* einen Husaren machen.

From Seoane's Spanish Dictionary.
To BILK. *va.* Engañar, defraudar, pegarla, chasquear, no pagar lo que se debe.

From Johnson's Dictionary.
To BILK. *v. a.* [derived by Mr. *Lye* from the Gothick *bilaican*.] To cheat; to defraud, by running in debt, and avoiding payment.
Bilk'd stationers for yeomen stood prepared.   *Dryd.*
What comedy, what farce can more delight,
Than grinning hunger, and the pleasing sight
Of your *bilk'd* hopes?   *Dryden.*

From Richardson's Dictionary.

BILK. Mr. Gifford says, "Bilk seems to have become a cant word about this (Ben Jonson's) time, for the use of it is ridiculed by others, as well as Jonson. It is thus *explained* in Cole's *English Dictionary*, 'Bilk, nothing; also to deceive.' " Lye, from the Goth. *Bilaikan*, which properly signifies *insultando illudere*.

To cheat, to defraud, to elude.

Tub. Hee will ha' the last word, though he take *bilke* for't.

Hugh. Bilke? what's that?

Tub. Why nothing, a word signifying nothing; and borrow'd here to express nothing.   *B. Jonson. Tale of a Tub*, Act i. sc. 1.

[He] was then ordered to get into the coach, or behind it, for that he wanted no instructors; but be sure you dog you, says he, don't you *bilk* me.   – *Spectator*, No. 498.

> Patrons in days of yore, like patrons now,
> Expected that the bard should make his bow
> At coming in, and ev'ry now and then
> Hint to the world that they were more than men;
> But, like the patrons of the present day,
> They never *bilk'd* the poet of his pay.
>
> *Churchill. Independence.*

The tabooed word "bilk," then, is more than two hundred years old, for Jonson wrote the "Tale of a Tub" in his old age – say about the year 1630 – and you observe that Mr. Gifford says it "seems to have become a cant word in Jonson's time." It must have risen above its vulgar position and become a legitimate phrase afterwards, though, else it would not have been uniformly printed in dictionaries without protest or explanation, almost from Jonson's time down to our own – for I find it thus printed in the very latest edition of Webster's Unabridged. Still, two centuries of toleration have not been able to make it popular, and I think you had better reflect awhile before you decide to write to Augustus that he is a bilk.

June 3, 10, 17, and 24, July 1 and 8, 1865

ADVICE FOR GOOD LITTLE BOYS

YOU OUGHT NEVER to take anything that don't belong to you – if you can't carry it off.

If you unthinkingly set up a tack in another boy's seat, you ought never to laugh when he sits down on it – unless you can't "hold in."

Good little boys must never tell a lie when the truth will answer just as well. In fact, real good little boys will never tell lies at all – not at all – except in cases of the most urgent necessity.

It is wrong to put a sheepskin under your shirt when you know you are going to get a licking. It is better to retire swiftly to some secret place and weep over your bad conduct until the storm blows over.

You should never do anything wicked and then lay it on your brother, when it is just as convenient to lay it on some other boy.

You ought never to call your aged grandpapa a "rum old file" – except when you want to be unusually funny.

You ought never to knock your little sister down with a club. It is better to use a cat, which is soft. In doing this you must be careful to take the cat by the tail, in such a manner that she cannot scratch you.

June 3, 1865

ADVICE FOR GOOD LITTLE GIRLS

GOOD LITTLE GIRLS ought not to make mouths at their teachers for every trifling offense. This kind of retaliation should only be resorted to under peculiarly aggravating circumstances.

If you have nothing but a rag doll stuffed with saw-dust, while one of your more fortunate little playmates has a costly china one, you should treat her with a show of kindness nevertheless. And you ought not attempt to make a forcible swap with her unless your conscience would justify you in it, and you know you are able to do it.

You ought never to take your little brother's "chawing gum" away from him by main force – it is better to rope him in with the promise of the first two dollars and a half you find floating down the river on a grindstone. In the artless simplicity natural to his time of life, he will regard it as a perfectly fair transaction. In all ages of the world this eminently plausible fiction has lured the obtuse infant to financial ruin and disaster.

If at any time you find it necessary to correct your brother, do not correct him with mud – never on any account throw mud at him, because it will soil his clothes. It is better to scald him a little, for then you attain two desirable results – you secure his immediate attention to the lesson you are inculcating, and at the same time your hot water will have a tendency to remove impurities from his person – and possibly the skin also, in spots.

If your mother tells you to do a thing, it is wrong to reply that you won't. It is better and more becoming to intimate that you will do as she bids you, and then afterwards act quietly in the matter according to the dictates of your better judgment.

You should ever bear in mind that it is to your kind parents that you are indebted for your food, and your nice bed, and your beautiful clothes, and for the privilege of staying home from school when you let on that you are sick. Therefore you ought to respect their little prejudices, and humor their little whims and put up with their little foibles, until they get to crowding you too much.

Good little girls should always show marked deference for the aged. You ought never to "sass" old people – unless they "sass" you first.

June 24, 1865

"MARK TWAIN" ON THE LAUNCH OF THE STEAMER "CAPITAL"

I Get Mr. Muff Nickerson to go with Me and Assist in Reporting the Great Steamboat Launch. He Relates the Interesting History of the Travelling Panoramist.

I WAS JUST starting off to see the launch of the great steamboat *Capital*, on Saturday week, when I came across Mulph, Mulff, Muff, Mumph, Murph, Mumf, Murf, Mumford, Mulford, Murphy Nickerson – (he is well known to the public by all these names, and I cannot say which is the right one) – bound on the same errand. He said that if there was one thing he took more delight in than another, it was a steamboat launch; he would walk miles to see one, any day; he had seen a hundred thousand steamboat launches in his time, and hoped he might live to see a hundred thousand more; he knew all about them; knew everything – *every*thing connected with them – said he "had it all down to a scratch;" he could explain the whole process in minute detail; to the uncultivated eye a steamboat launch presented nothing grand, nothing startling, nothing beautiful, nothing romantic, or awe-inspiring or sublime – but to an optic like his (which saw not the dull outer coating, but the radiant gem it hid from other eyes,) it presented all these – and behold, he had power to lift the veil and display the vision even unto the uninspired. He could do this by word of mouth – by explanation and illustration. Let a man stand by his side, and to him that launch should seem arrayed in the beauty and the glory of enchantment!

This was the man I wanted. I could see that plainly enough. There would be many reporters present at the launch, and the papers would teem with the inevitable old platitudinal trust which this sort of people have compelled to do duty on every occasion like this since Noah launched his ark – but I aspired to higher things. I wanted to write a report which should astonish and delight the whole intellectual world – which should dissect, analyze, and utterly exhaust the subject – which should serve for a model in this species of literature for all time to come. I dropped alongside of Mr. M. M. M. M. M. M. M. M. M. Nickerson, and we went to the launch together.

We set out in a steamer whose decks were crowded with persons of all ages, who were happy in their nervous anxiety to behold the novelty of a steamboat launch. I tried not to pity them, but I could not help whispering to myself, "These poor devils will see nothing but some stupid boards and timbers nailed together – a mere soul-less hulk – sliding into the water!"

As we approached the spot where the launch was to take place, a gentleman from Reese River, by the name of Thompson, came up, with several friends, and said he had been prospecting on the main deck, and had found an object of interest – a bar. This was all very well, and showed him to be a man of parts – but like many another man who produces a favorable impression by an intro-ductory remark replete with wisdom, he followed it up with a vain and unnecessary question – Would we take a drink? This to me! – This to M. M. M., etc., Nickerson!

We proceeded, two-by-two, arm-in-arm, down to the bar in the nether regions, chatting pleasantly and elbowing the restless multi-tude. We took pure, cold, health-giving water, with some other things in it, and clinked our glasses together, and were about to drink, when Smith, of Excelsior, drew forth his handkerchief and wiped away a tear; and then, noticing that the action had excited some attention, he explained it by recounting a most affecting incident in the history of a venerated aunt of his – now deceased – and said that, although long years had passed since the touching event he had narrated, he could never take a drink without think-ing of the kind-hearted old lady.

Mr. Nickerson blew his nose, and said with deep emotion that it gave him a better opinion of human nature to see a man who had had a good aunt, eternally and forever thinking about her.

This episode reminded Jones, of Mud Springs, of a circumstance which happened many years ago in the home of his childhood, and we held our glasses untouched and rested our elbows on the counter, while we listened with rapt attention to his story.

There was something in it about a good natured, stupid man, and this reminded Thompson of Reese River of a person of the same kind whom he had once fallen in with while travelling through the back-settlements of one of the Atlantic States, and we postponed drinking until he should give us the facts in the case. The hero of the tale had unintentionally created some consterna-tion at a camp-meeting by one of his innocent asinine freaks, and this reminded Mr. M. Nickerson of a reminiscence of his temporary sojourn in the interior of Connecticut some months ago, and again our uplifted glasses were stayed on their way to our lips, and we listened attentively to

THE ENTERTAINING HISTORY OF THE SCRIPTURAL PANORAMIST.

[I give the story in Mr. Nickerson's own language.]

There was a fellow travelling around, in that country, (said Mr. Nickerson,) with a moral religious show – a sort of a scriptural panorama – and he hired a wooden-headed old slab to play the piano for him. After the first night's performance, the showman says:

"My friend, you seem to know pretty much all the tunes there are, and you worry along first-rate. But then didn't you notice that sometimes last night the piece you happened to be playing was a little rough on the proprieties so to speak – didn't seem to jibe with the general gait of the picture that was passing at the time, as it were – was a little foreign to the subject, you know – as if you didn't either trump or follow suit, you understand?"

"Well, no," the fellow said; he hadn't noticed, but it might be; he had played along just as it came handy.

So they put it up that the simple old dummy was to keep his eye on the panorama after that, and as soon as a stunning picture was reeled out, he was to fit it to a dot with a piece of music that would help the audience get the idea of the subject, and warm them up like a camp-meeting revival. That sort of thing would corral their sympathies, the showman said.

There was a big audience that night – mostly middle-aged and old people who belonged to the church and took a strong interest in Bible matters, and the balance were pretty much young bucks and heifers – *they* always come out strong on panoramas, you know, because it gives them a chance to taste one another's mugs in the dark.

Well, the showman began to swell himself up for his lecture, and the old mud-dobber tackled the piano and run his fingers up and down once or twice to see that she was all right, and the fellows behind the curtain commenced to grind out the panorama. The showman balanced his weight on his right foot, and propped his hands on his hips, and flung his eye over his shoulder at the scenery, and says:

"Ladies and gentlemen, the painting now before you illustrates the beautiful and touching parable of the Prodigal Son. Observe the happy expression just breaking over the features of the poor suffering youth – so worn and weary with his long march: note also the ecstasy beaming from the uplifted countenance of the aged father, and the joy that sparkles in the eyes of the excited group of youths and maidens and seems ready to burst in a welcoming chorus from their lips. The lesson, my friends, is as solemn and instructive as the story is tender and beautiful."

The mud-dobber was all ready, and the second the speech was finished he struck up:

> "Oh, we'll all get blind drunk
> When Johnny comes marching home!"

Some of the people giggled, and some groaned a little. The showman couldn't say a word. He looked at the piano sharp, but he was all lovely and serene – *he* didn't know there was anything out of gear.

The panorama moved on, and the showman drummed up his grit and started in fresh:

"Ladies and gentlemen, the fine picture now unfolding itself to your gaze exhibits one of the most notable events in Bible History – our Savior and his disciples upon the Sea of Galilee. How grand, how awe inspiring are the reflections which the subject invokes! What sublimity of faith is revealed to us in this lesson from the sacred writings! The Savior rebukes the angry waves, and walks securely upon the bosom of the deep!"

All around the house they were whispering: "Oh, how lovely! how beautiful!" and the orchestra let himself out again:

> "Oh, a life on the ocean wave,
> And a home on the rolling deep!"

There was a good deal of honest snickering turned on this time, and considerable groaning, and one or two old deacons got up and went out. The showman gritted his teeth and cursed the piano man to himself, but the fellow sat there like a knot on a log, and seemed to think he was doing first-rate.

After things got quiet, the showman thought he would make one more stagger at it, any how, though his confidence was beginning to get mighty shaky. The supes started the panorama to grinding along again, and he says:

"Ladies and gentlemen, this exquisite painting illustrates the raising of Lazarus from the dead by our Savior. The subject has been handled with rare ability by the artist, and such touching sweetness and tenderness of expression has he thrown into it, that I have known peculiarly sensitive persons to be even affected to tears by looking at it. Observe the half-confused, half-inquiring look, upon the countenance of the awakening Lazarus. Observe, also, the attitude and expression of the Savior, who takes him gently by the sleeve of his shroud with one hand, while he points with the other toward the distant city."

Before anybody could get off an opinion in the case, the innocent old ass at the piano struck up:

> "Come rise up, William Ri-i-ley,
> And go along with me!"

It was rough on the audience, you bet you. All the solemn old flats got up in a huff to go, and everybody else laughed till the windows rattled.

The showman went down and grabbed the orchestra, and shook him up, and says:

"That lets you out, you know, you chowder-headed old clam! Go to the door-keeper and get your money, and cut your stick! – vamose the ranch! Ladies and gentlemen, circumstances over which I have no control compel me prematurely to dismiss –"

"By George! it was splendid! – come! all hands! let's take a drink!"

It was Phelim O'Flannigan, of San Luis Obispo, who interrupted. I had not seen him before. "What was splendid?" I inquired.

"The launch!"

Our party clinked glasses once more, and drank in respectful silence.

MARK TWAIN.

P.S. – You will excuse me from making a model report of the great launch. I was with Mulf Nickerson, who was going to "explain the whole thing to me as clear as glass," but, you see, they launched the boat with such indecent haste, that we never got a chance to see it. It was a great pity, because Mulph Nickerson understands launches as well as any man.

November 18, 1865

A NEW BIOGRAPHY OF WASHINGTON

THIS DAY, MANY years ago precisely, George Washington was born. How full of significance the thought! Especially to those among us who have had a similar experience, though subsequently; and still more especially to the young, who should take him for a model and faithfully try to be like him, undeterred by the frequency with which the same thing has been attempted by American youths before them and not satisfactorily accomplished. George Washington was the youngest of nine children, eight of whom were the offspring of his uncle and his aunt. As a boy he gave no promise of the greatness he was one day to achieve. He was ignorant of the commonest accomplishments of youth. He could not even lie. But then he never had any of those precious advantages which are within the reach of the humblest of the boys of the present day. Any boy can lie, now. I could lie before I could stand – yet this sort of sprightliness was so common in our family that little notice was taken of it. Young George appears to have had no sagacity whatever. It is related of him that he once chopped down his father's favorite cherry tree, and then didn't know enough to keep dark about it. He came near going to sea, once, as a midshipman; but when his mother represented to him that he must necessarily be absent when he was away from home, and that this must continue to be the case until he got back, the sad truth struck him so forcibly that he ordered his trunk ashore, and quietly but firmly refused to serve in the navy and fight the battles of his king so long as the effect of it would be to discommode his mother. The great rule of his life was, that procrastination was the thief of time, and that we should always do unto others. This is the golden rule. Therefore, he would never discommode his mother.

Young George Washington was actuated in all things, by the highest and purest principles of morality, justice and right. He was a model in every way worthy of the emulation of youth. Young George was always prompt and faithful in the discharge of every duty. It has been said of him, by the historian, that he was always on hand, like a thousand of brick. And well deserved was this noble compliment. The aggregate of the building material specified might have been largely increased – might have been doubled – even without doing full justice to these high qualities in the subject of this sketch. Indeed, it would hardly be possible to express in bricks the exceeding promptness and fidelity of young George Washington. His was a soul whose manifold excellencies were beyond the ken and computation of mathematics, and bricks are, at the least, but an inadequate vehicle for the conveyance of a comprehension of the moral sublimity of a nature so pure as his.

Young George W. was a surveyor in early life – a surveyor of an inland port – a sort of county surveyor; and under a commission from Gov. Dinwiddie, he set out to survey his way four hundred miles through a trackless forest, infested with Indians, to procure the liberation of some English prisoners. The historian says the Indians were the most depraved of their species, and did nothing but lay for white men, whom they killed for the sake of robbing them. Considering that white men only traveled through their country at the rate of one a year, they were probably unable to do what might be termed a land-office business in their line. They did not rob young G. W.; one savage made the attempt, but failed; he fired at the subject of this sketch from behind a tree, but the subject of this sketch immediately snaked him out from behind the tree and took him prisoner.

The long journey failed of success; the French would not give up the prisoners, and Wash went sadly back home again. A regiment was raised to go and make a rescue, and he took command of it. He caught the French out in the rain and tackled them with great intrepidity. He defeated them in ten minutes, and their commander handed in his checks. This was the battle of Great Meadows.

After this, a good while, George Washington became Commander-in-Chief of the American armies, and had an exceedingly dusty time of it all through the Revolution. But every now and then he turned a jack from the bottom and surprised the enemy. He kept up his lick for seven long years, and hazed the British from Harrisburg to Halifax – and America was free! He served two terms as President, and would have been President yet if he had lived – even so did the people honor the Father of his Country. Let the youth of America take his incomparable character for a model and try it one jolt, anyhow. Success is possible – let them remember that – success is possible, though there are chances against it.

I could continue this biography, with profit to the rising generation, but I shall have to drop the subject at present, because of
other matters which must be attended to.

c. February 25, 1866

FEMALE SUFFRAGE

ED. T. T.: – The women of Missouri are bringing a tremendous pressure to bear in an endeavor to secure to themselves the right to vote and hold office. Their petitions to the legislature are scattered abroad, and are filled with signers. Thirty-nine members of the Missouri Legislature have declared in favor of the movement. This thing looks ominous. Through an able spiritual medium I have been permitted to see a Missouri Legislature of five years hence in session. Here is a report of the proceedings:

The P. R. R. Appropriation Bill being the special order for the day, and the hour for its discussion having arrived:

Miss Belcher, of St. Louis, said – Madam Speaker, I call for the special order for to-day.

Madam Speaker. – The clerk will read –

Clerk. – An act supplementary to an Act entitled An Act amendatory of an Act entitled An Act to Appropriate Five millions of dollars in aid of the Pacific Railroad, etc., etc.

Miss Belcher. – Madam Speaker, it is with the keenest pain that I observe the diminishing esteem in which gored dresses are held. It is with pain which these lips are indeed powerless to express. The gored dress of two years ago, Madam, with its long, graceful sweep –

Mr. Jones, of St. Joseph. – Madam Speaker, I rise to a point of order. The lady is not confining herself to the question before the house. What in the nation has these cussed gored dresses and stuff got to do with the great Pacif –

Madam Speaker (amid piping female voices all over the house, shrieking angrily). – Sit down, Sir! Take your seat, Sir, and don't you presume to interrupt again! Go on, Miss Belcher.

Miss Belcher. – I was remarking, Madam, when the un-principled bald-headed outlaw from St. Joseph interrupted me, that it pained me to see the charming and attractive gored dresses we all were once so fond of, going out of fashion. And what, I ask, are we to have in place of it? What is offered to recompense us for its loss? Why, nothing, Madam, but the wretched, slimpsey, new-fangled street-dress, hoopless, shapeless, cut bias, hem-stitched, with the selvedge edge turned down; and all so lank, so short, so cadaverous, and so disgraceful! Excuse these tears. Who can look without emotion upon such a garment? Who can look unmoved upon a dress which exposes feet at every step which may be of dimensions which shrink from inspection? Who can consent to countenance a dress which –

Mr. Slawson, of St. Genevieve. – Madam Speaker, This is absurd. What will such proceedings as these read like in the newspapers? We take up the discussion of a measure of vast consequence – a measure of tremendous financial importance – and a member of the body, totally ignoring the question before the House, launches out into a tirade about womanly apparel! – a matter trivial enough at any time, God knows, but utterly insignificant in presence of so grave a matter as the behests of the Great Pacific Rail –

Madam Speaker. – Consider yourself under arrest, Sir! Sit down, and dare to speak again at your peril! The honorable lady from St. Louis will proceed.

Miss Belcher. – Madam Speaker, I will dismiss the particular section of my subject upon which I was speaking when interrupted by the degraded ruffian from St. Genevieve, and pass to the gist of the matter. I propose, Madam, to prohibit, under heavy penalties, the wearing of the new street-dress, and to restore the discarded gored dress by legislative enactment, and I beg leave to introduce a bill to that end, and without previous notice, if the courtesy of this honorable body will permit it.

Mr. Walker, of Marion. – Madam Speaker, this is an outrage! it is damnable! The Pacific Railroad –

Madam Speaker. – Silence! Plant yourself, Sir! Leave is granted to introduce the Bill. If no objection is made, it will be referred to the Standing Committee on Public Improvements. Reports of Committees are now in order.

Mrs. Baker, of Ralls. – Madam Speaker, the Select Committee of Five, to whom was referred An Act Amendatory of An Act Establishing the Metes and Bounds of School Lands, and to which was added a clause Establishing the Metes and Bounds of Water Privileges, have been unable to agree. The younger members of the committee contend that the added clause is of sufficient latitude to permit of legislation concerning ladies' waterfalls, and they have reported upon that clause alone to the exclusion of all other matters contemplated in the bill. There is no majority report, Madam, and no minority report.

Mr. Bridgewater, of Benton. – There are five women on the committee, ain't there?

Mrs. Baker. – Yes.

Mr. Bilgewater. – Each of 'em made a report by herself, hasn't she?

Mrs. Baker. – Yes, Sir.

Mr. Bilgewater. – Why, certainly. Five women's bound to have five opinions. It's like 'em.

[With the last word the gentleman from Benton darted out at the window, and eleven inkstands followed him.]

The several reports were received and tabled, after considerable discussion. Third reading and final passage of bills being next in order, an Act for Amending the Common School System was taken up, but it was found to be so interlarded with surreptitious clauses for remodeling and establishing fashions for ladies' bonnets, that neither head nor tail could be made of it, and it had to be referred back to the Committee of the Whole again. An Act to Provide Arms for the State Militia was discovered to be so hampered with clauses for the protection of Sewing Societies and Tea Drinkings, that it had to go back to the file also. Every bill on the third reading list was found to be similarly mutilated, until they got down to an Act to Compel Married Gentlemen to be at Home by Nine of the Clock, every evening; an Act to Abolish the Use of Tobacco in any form; and an Act to Abolish the Use of Intoxicating Liquors. These had not been meddled with, and were at once put to vote, and passed over the heads of the male members, who made a gallant fight, but were overcome by heartless and tyrannical numbers.

Mr. Green, of Cape Girardeau, then rose in his place and said, – "I now shake the dust of this House from my feet, and take my eternal leave of it. I never will enter its doors again, to be snubbed and harried by a pack of padded, scraggy, dried-up, snuff-dipping, toothless, old-maids, who –"

He never got any further. A howl went up that shook the building to its foundation, and in the midst of struggling forms, fiery eyes, distorted countenances, and dismembered waterfalls, I saw the daring legislator yield and fall; and when at last he reappeared, and fled toward the door, his shirt-front was in ribbons, his cravat knot under his ear, his face scratched red and white like the national flag, and hardly hair enough left on his head to make a toothbrush.

I shudder now. Is it possible that this revelation of the spirits is a prophecy.

MARK TWAIN
April 7, 1867

MY LATE SENATORIAL
SECRETARYSHIP

I AM NOT a private secretary to a senator any more, now. I held the berth two months in security and in great cheerfulness of spirit, but my bread began to return from over the waters, then – that is to say, my works came back and revealed themselves. I judged it best to resign. The way of it was this. My employer sent for me one morning tolerably early, and, as soon as I had finished inserting some conundrums clandestinely into his last great speech upon finance, I entered the presence. There was something portentous in his appearance. His cravat was untied, his hair was in a state of disorder, and his countenance bore about it the signs of a suppressed storm. He held a package of letters in his tense grasp, and I knew that the dreaded Pacific mail was in. He said:

"I thought you were worthy of confidence."

I said: "Yes, sir."

He said: "I gave you a letter from certain of my constituents in the State of Nevada, asking the establishment of a post office at Baldwin's Ranch, and told you to answer it, as ingeniously as you could, with arguments which should persuade them that there was no real necessity for an office at that place."

I felt easier. "Oh, if that is all, sir, I *did* do that."

"Yes, you *did*. I will read your answer, for your own humiliation:

"'WASHINGTON, NOV. 24, 1867.

"'*Messrs. Smith, Jones, and others.*

"'GENTLEMEN: What the mischief do you suppose you want with a post office at Baldwin's Ranch? It would not do you any good. If any letters came there, you couldn't read them, you know; and, besides, such letters as ought to pass through, with money in them, for other localities, would not be likely to *get* through, you must perceive at once; and that would make trouble for us all. No, don't bother about a post office in your camp. I have your best interests at heart, and feel that it would only be an ornamental folly. What you want is a nice jail, you know – a nice, substantial jail and a free school. These will be a lasting benefit to you. These will make you really contented and happy. I will move in the matter at once.

Very truly, etc.,

"'MARK TWAIN,
"'For James W. Nye, U. S. Senator.'

"That is the way you answered that letter. Those people say they will hang me, if I ever enter that district again; and I am perfectly satisfied they *will*, too."

"Well, sir, I did not know I was doing any harm. I only wanted to convince them."

"Ah. Well, you *did* convince them, I make no manner of doubt. Now, here is another specimen. I gave you a petition from certain gentlemen of Nevada, praying that I would get a bill through Congress incorporating the Methodist Episcopal Church of the State of Nevada. I told you to say, in reply, that the creation of such a law came more properly within the province of the State Legislature; and to endeavor to show them that, in the present feebleness of the religious element in that new commonwealth, the expediency of incorporating the church was questionable. What did you write?

"'WASHINGTON, NOV. 24, 1867.
"'*Rev. John Halifax and others.*

"'GENTLEMEN: You will have to go to the State Legislature about that little speculation of yours – Congress don't know anything about religion. But don't you hurry to go there, either; because this thing you propose to do out in that new country isn't expedient – in fact, it is simply ridiculous. Your religious people there are too feeble, in intellect, in morality, in piety – in everything, pretty much. You had better drop this – you can't make it work. You can't issue stock on an incorporation like that – or if you could, it would only keep you in trouble all the time. The other denominations would abuse it, and "bear" it, and "sell it short," and break it down. They would do with it just as they would with one of your silver mines out there – they would try to make all the world believe it was "wildcat." You ought not to do anything that is calculated to bring a sacred thing into disrepute. You ought to be ashamed of yourselves – that is what *I* think about it. You close your petition with the words: "And we will ever pray." I think you had better – you need to do it. Very truly, etc.,
"'MARK TWAIN,
"'For James W. Nye, U. S. Senator.'

"*That* luminous epistle finishes me with the religious element among my constituents. But that my political murder might be made sure, some evil instinct prompted me to hand you this memorial from the grave company of elders composing the Board of Aldermen of the city of San Francisco, to try your hand upon – a memorial praying that the city's right to the water-lots upon the city front might be established by law of Congress. I told you this was a dangerous matter to move in. I told you to write a non-committal letter to the Aldermen – an ambiguous letter – a letter that should avoid, as far as possible, all real consideration and discussion of the water-lot question. If there is any feeling left in you – any shame – surely this letter you wrote, in obedience to that order, ought to evoke it, when its words fall upon your ears:

"'WASHINGTON, NOV. 27, 1867.

"'*The Hon. Board of Aldermen, etc.*

"'GENTLEMEN: George Washington, the revered Father of his Country, is dead. His long and brilliant career is closed, alas! forever. He was greatly respected in this section of the country, and his untimely decease cast a gloom over the whole community. He died on the 14th day of December, 1799. He passed peacefully away from the scene of his honors and his great achievements, the most lamented hero and the best beloved that ever earth hath yielded unto Death. At such a time as this, *you* speak of water-lots! – what a lot was his!

"'What is fame? Fame is an accident. Sir Isaac Newton discovered an apple falling to the ground – a trivial discovery, truly, and one which a million men had made before him – but his parents were influential, and so they tortured that little circumstance into something wonderful, and, lo! the simple world took up the shout, and, in almost the twinkling of an eye, that man was famous. Treasure these thoughts.

"'Poesy, sweet poesy, who shall estimate what the world owes to thee!

"Mary had a little lamb, its fleece was white as snow –
And everywhere that Mary went, the lamb was sure to go.

"Jack and Gill went up the hill
    To draw a pail of water;
Jack fell down and broke his crown,
    And Gill came tumbling after."

For simplicity, elegance of diction, and freedom from immoral tendencies, I regard those two poems in the light of gems. They are suited to all grades of intelligence, to every sphere of life – to the field, to the nursery, to the guild. Especially should no Board of Aldermen be without them.

"'Venerable fossils! write again. Nothing improves one so much as friendly correspondence. Write again – and if there is anything in this memorial of yours that refers to anything in particular, do not be backward about explaining it. We shall always be happy to hear you chirp.

Very truly, etc.,

"'MARK TWAIN,

"'For James W. Nye, U. S. Senator.'

"That is an atrocious, a ruinous epistle! Distraction!"

"Well, sir, I am really sorry if there is anything wrong about it – but – but – it appears to me to dodge the water-lot question."

"Dodge the mischief! Oh! – but never mind. As long as destruction must come now, let it be complete. Let it be complete – let this last of your performances, which I am about to read, make a finality of it. I am a ruined man. I *had* my misgivings when I gave you the letter from Humboldt, asking that the post route from Indian Gulch to Shakespeare Gap and intermediate points, be changed partly to the old Mormon trail. But I told you it was a delicate question, and warned you to deal with it deftly – to answer it dubiously, and leave them a little in the dark. And your fatal imbecility impelled you to make *this* disastrous reply. I should think you would stop your ears, if you are not dead to all shame:

"'WASHINGTON, NOV. 30, 1867.

"'*Messrs. Perkins, Wagner, et al.*

"'GENTLEMEN: It is a delicate question about this Indian trail, but handled with proper deftness and dubiousness, I doubt not we shall succeed in some measure or otherwise, because the place where the route leaves the Lassen Meadows, over beyond where those two Shawnee chiefs, Dilapidated-Vengeance and Biter-of-the-Clouds, were scalped last winter, this being the favorite direction to some but others preferring something else in consequence of things, the Mormon trail leaving Mosby's at three in the morning, and passing through Jawbone Flat to Blucher, and then down by Jug-Handle, the road passing to the right of it, and naturally leaving it on the right, too, and

Dawson's on the left of the trail where it passes to the left of said Dawson's, and onward thence to Tomahawk, thus making the route cheaper, easier of access to all who can get at it, and compassing all the desirable objects so considered by others, and, therefore, conferring the most good upon the greatest number, and, consequently, I am encouraged to hope we shall. However, I shall be ready, and happy, to afford you still further information upon the subject, from time to time, as you may desire it and the Post Office Department be enabled to furnish it to me.

Very truly, etc.,

"'MARK TWAIN,

"'For James W. Nye, U. S. Senator.'

"There – now, *what* do you think of that?"

"Well, I don't know, sir. It – well, it appears to me – to be dubious enough."

"Du – leave the house! I am a ruined man. Those Humboldt savages never will forgive me for tangling their brains up with this inhuman letter. I have lost the respect of the Methodist Church, the Board of Aldermen –"

"Well, I haven't anything to say about that, because I may have missed it a little in their cases, but I *was* too many for the Baldwin's Ranch people, General!"

"Leave the house! Leave it forever and forever, too!"

I regarded that as a sort of covert intimation that my services could be dispensed with, and so I resigned. I never will be a private secretary to a senator again. You can't please that kind of people. They don't know anything. They can't appreciate a party's efforts.

May 1868

THE NEW CRIME

LEGISLATION NEEDED.

THIS COUNTRY, DURING the last thirty or forty years, has produced some of the most remarkable cases of insanity of which there is any mention in history. For instance, there was the Baldwin case, in Ohio, twenty-two years ago. Baldwin, from his boyhood up, had been of a vindictive, malignant, quarrelsome nature. He put a boy's eye out, once, and never was heard upon any occasion, to utter a regret for it. He did many such things. But at last he did something that was serious. He called at a house just after dark, one evening, knocked, and when the occupant came to the door, shot him dead and then tried to escape but was captured. Two days before, he had wantonly insulted a helpless cripple, and the man he afterward took swift vengeance upon with an assassin bullet, knocked him down. Such was the Baldwin case. The trial was long and exciting; the community was fearfully wrought up. Men said this spiteful, bad-hearted villain had caused grief enough in his time, and now he should satisfy the law. But they were mistaken. Baldwin was insane when he did the deed – they had not thought of that. By the arguments of counsel it was shown that at half-past ten in the morning on the day of the murder, Baldwin became insane, and remained so for eleven hours and a half exactly. This just covered the case comfortably, and he was acquitted. Thus, if an unthinking and excited community had been listened to instead of the arguments of counsel, a poor, crazy creature would have been held to a fearful responsibility for a mere freak of madness. Baldwin went clear, and although his relatives and friends were naturally incensed against the community for their injurious suspicions and remarks, they said let it go for this time, and did not prosecute. The Baldwins were very wealthy. This same Baldwin had momentary fits of insanity twice afterward, and on both occasions killed people he had grudges against. And on both these occasions the circumstances of the killing were so aggravated, and the murders so seemingly heartless and treacherous, that if Baldwin had not been insane he would have been hanged without the shadow of a doubt. As it was, it required all his political and family influence to get him clear in one of the cases, and cost him not less than $10,000 to get clear in the other. One of these men he had notoriously been threatening to kill for twelve years. The poor creature happened, by the merest piece of ill-fortune, to come along a dark alley at the very moment that Baldwin's insanity came upon him, and so he was shot in the back with a gun loaded with slugs. It was exceedingly fortunate for Baldwin that his insanity came on him just when it did.

Take the case of Lynch Hackett, of Pennsylvania. Twice, in public, he attacked a German butcher by the name of Bemis Feldner, with a cane, and both times Feldner whipped him with his fists. Hackett was a vain, wealthy, violent gentleman, who held his blood and family in high esteem and believed that a reverent respect was due his great riches. He brooded over the shame of his chastisement for two weeks, and then, in a momentary fit of insanity armed himself to the teeth, rode into town, waited a couple of hours until he saw Feldner coming down the street with his wife on his arm, and then, as the couple passed the doorway in which he had partially concealed himself, he drove a knife into Feldner's neck, killing him instantly. The widow caught the limp form and eased it to the earth. Both were drenched with blood. Hackett jocosely remarked to her that as a professional butcher's recent wife she could appreciate the artistic neatness of the job that left her in a condition to marry again, in case she wanted to. This remark, and another which he made to a friend, that his position in society made the killing of an obscure citizen simply an "eccentricity" instead of a crime, were shown to be evidences of insanity, and so Hackett escaped punishment. The jury were hardly inclined to accept these as proofs, at first, inasmuch as the prisoner had never been insane before the murder, and under the tranquilizing effect of the butchering had immediately regained his right mind – but when the defence came to show that a third cousin of Hackett's wife's stepfather was insane, and not only insane but had a nose the very counterpart of Hackett's, it was plain that insanity was hereditary in the family and Hackett had come by it by legitimate inheritance. Of course the jury then acquitted him. But it was a merciful providence that Mrs. H.'s people had been afflicted as shown, else Hackett would certainly have been hanged.

However, it is not possible to account all the marvelous cases of insanity that have come under the public notice in the last thirty or forty years. There was the Durgin case in New Jersey three years ago. The servant girl, Bridget Durgin, at dead of night invaded her mistress' bedroom and carved the lady literally to pieces with a knife. Then she dragged the body to the middle of the floor and

beat and banged it with chairs and such things. Next she opened
the feather beds and strewed the contents around, saturated everything with kerosene and set fire to the general wreck. She now took
up the young child of the murdered woman in her blood-smearing
hands, and walked off, through the snow, with no shoes on, to
a neighbor's house a quarter of a mile off, and told a string of
wild, incoherent stories about some men coming and setting fire
to the house; and then she cried piteously, and without seeming
to think there was anything suggestive about the blood upon her
hands, her clothing and the baby, volunteered the remark that
she was afraid those men had murdered her mistress! Afterward,
by her own confession and other testimony, it was proved that
the mistress had always been kind to the girl, consequently there
was no revenge in the murder; and it was also shown that the
girl took nothing away from the burning house, not even her
own shoes, and consequently robbery was not the motive. Now
the reader says, "Here comes that same old plea of insanity
again." But the reader has deceived himself this time. No such
plea was offered in her defence. The judge sentenced her,
nobody persecuted the Governor with petitions for her pardon,
and she was promptly hanged.

There was that youth in Pennsylvania, whose curious confession
was published a year ago. It was simply a conglomeration of incoherent drivel from beginning to end – and so was his lengthy
speech on the scaffold afterward. For a whole year he was haunted
with a desire to disfigure a certain young woman so that no one
would marry her. He did not love her himself, and did not want
to marry her, but he did not want anybody else to do it. He would
not go anywhere with her, and yet was opposed to anybody else's
escorting her. Upon one occasion he declined to go to a wedding
with her, and when she got other company, lay in wait for the
couple by the road, intending to make them go back or kill the
escort. After spending sleepless nights over his ruling desire for a
full year, he at last attempted its execution – that is, attempted to
disfigure the young woman. It was a success. It was permanent. In
trying to shoot her cheek (as she sat at the supper table with her
parents and brothers and sisters) in such a manner as to mar its
comeliness, one of his bullets wandered a little out of the course
and she dropped dead. To the very last moment of his life he
bewailed the ill luck that made her move her face just at the critical
moment. And so he died apparently about half persuaded that

somehow it was chiefly her own fault that she got killed. This idiot was hanged. The plea of insanity was not offered.

The recent case of Lady Mordaunt, in England, had proved beyond cavil that the thing we call common prostitution in America is only insanity in Great Britain. Her husband wanted a divorce, but as her cheerful peculiarities were the offspring of lunacy and consequently she could not be held responsible for them, he had to take her to his bosom again. It is sad to think of a dozen or two of great English lords taking advantage of a poor crazy woman. In this country, if history be worth anything to judge by, the husband would have rented a graveyard and stocked it, and then brought the divorce suit afterward. In which case the jury would have brought *him* in insane, not his wife.

Insanity certainly is on the increase in the world, and crime is dying out. There are no longer any murders – none worth mentioning, at any rate. Formerly, if you killed a man, it was possible that you were insane – but now if you kill a man it is *evidence* that you are a lunatic. In these days, too, if a person of good family and high social standing steals any thing, they call it *kleptomania*, and send him to the lunatic asylum. If a person of high standing squanders his fortune in dissipation and closes his career with strychnine or a bullet, "Temporary Aberration" is what was the trouble with *him*. And finally, as before noted, the list is capped with a new and curious madness in the shape of wholesale adultery.

Is not this insanity plea becoming rather common? Is it not so common that the reader confidently expects to see it offered in every criminal case that comes before the courts? And is it not so cheap, and so common, and often so trivial, that the reader smiles in derision when the newspaper mentions it? And is it not curious to note how very often it wins acquittal for the prisoner? Lately it does not seem possible for a man to so conduct himself, before killing another man, as not to be manifestly insane. If he talks about the stars he is insane. If he appears nervous and uneasy an hour before the killing, he is insane. If he weeps over a great grief, his friends shake their heads and fear that he is "not right." If, an hour after the murder, he seems ill at ease, pre-occupied and excited, he is unquestionably insane.

Really, what we want now, is not laws against crime, but a law against *insanity*. There is where the true evil lies.

And the penalty attached should be imprisonment, not hanging. Then, it might be worth the trouble and expense of trying the Gen.

Coleses, and the Gen. Sickleses and the McFarlands, because juries might lock them up for brief terms, in deference to the majesty of the law; but it is not likely that any of us will ever live to see the murderer of a seducer hanged. Perhaps, if the truth were confessed, few of us *wish* to live that long.

Since I seemed to have wandered into the McFarland case without especially intending to do it, (for my original idea was merely to call attention to how many really crazy people are hanged in these days, and how many that never were crazy a moment in their lives are acquitted of crime on the plea of insanity,) I will venture to suggest – simply as an opinion, and not as an assertion – that the main reason why we shall never succeed in hanging this mean, small villain, McFarland, is, that his real crime did not consist in killing Richardson, but in so conducting himself long before that, as to estrange his wife's affections from himself and drive her to the love and protection of another man. If they would quash this present suit and try him on that, we would get the unreluctant fangs of justice on him sure, if what one good man says against McFarland is worth as much as what another good man says in his favor. We might all consent that he was a criminal in his treatment of his wife at that time, but somehow we hesitate to condemn him to the scaffold for this act of his whereby he inflicted a penalty for a wrong which, down in our secret hearts, we feel is beyond the ability of all law to punish amply and satisfactorily.

No, when a man abuses his wife as McFarland seems to have abused his, any jury would punish him severely, and do it with a relish. But when a man kills the seducer of his wife, a jury cannot be found that will condemn him to suffer for murder. Therefore, it is fair to consider that McFarland's real crime is not in court in New York, now, but is left out of the indictment.

If I seem to have wandered from my subject and thrown in some surplusage, what do I care? With these evidences of a wandering mind present to the reader, am I to be debarred from offering the customary plea of Insanity?

April 16, 1870

WIT-INSPIRATIONS OF THE "TWO-YEAR-OLDS"

ALL INFANTS APPEAR to have an impertinent and disagreeable fashion nowadays of saying "smart" things on most occasions that offer, and especially on occasions when they ought not to be saying anything at all. Judging by the average published specimens of smart sayings, the rising generation of children are little better than idiots. And the parents must surely be but little better than the children, for in most cases they are the publishers of the sunbursts of infantile imbecility which dazzle us from the pages of our periodicals. I may seem to speak with some heat, not to say a suspicion of personal spite; and I do admit that it nettles me to hear about so many gifted infants in these days, and remember that I seldom said anything smart when I was a child. I tried it once or twice, but it was not popular. The family were not expecting brilliant remarks from me, and so they snubbed me sometimes and spanked me the rest. But it makes my flesh creep and my blood run cold to think what might have happened to me if I had dared to utter some of the smart things of this generation's "four-year-olds" where my father could hear me. To have simply skinned me alive and considered his duty at an end would have seemed to him criminal leniency toward one so sinning. He was a stern, unsmiling man, and hated all forms of precocity. If I had said some of the things I have referred to, and said them in his hearing, he would have destroyed me. He would, indeed. He would, provided the opportunity remained with him. But it would not, for I would have had judgment enough to take some strychnine first and say my smart thing afterward. The fair record of my life has been tarnished by just one pun. My father overheard that, and he hunted me over four or five townships seeking to take my life. If I had been full-grown, of course he would have been right; but, child as I was, I could not know how wicked a thing I had done.

I made one of those remarks ordinarily called "smart things" before that, but it was not a pun. Still, it came near causing a serious rupture between my father and myself. My father and mother, my uncle Ephraim and his wife, and one or two others were present, and the conversation turned on a name for me. I was lying there trying some India-rubber rings of various patterns, and endeavoring to make a selection, for I was tired of trying to cut my teeth on people's fingers, and wanted to get hold of something that would enable me to hurry the thing through and get at something else. Did you ever notice what a nuisance it was cutting your teeth on your nurse's finger, or how back-breaking and tiresome it was trying to cut them on your big toe? And did you never get out of patience and wish your teeth were in Jericho long before you got them half cut? To me it seems as if these things happened yesterday. And they did, to some children. But I digress. I was lying there trying the India-rubber rings. I remember looking at the clock and noticing that in an hour and twenty-five minutes I would be two weeks old, and thinking to myself how little I had done to merit the blessings that were so unsparingly lavished upon me. My father said:

"Abraham is a good name. My grandfather was named Abraham."

My mother said:

"Abraham is a good name. Very well. Let us have Abraham for one of his names."

I said:

"Abraham suits the subscriber."

My father frowned, my mother looked pleased; my aunt said:

"What a little darling it is!"

My father said:

"Isaac is a good name, and Jacob is a good name."

My mother assented and said:

"No names are better. Let us add Isaac and Jacob to his names."

I said:

"All right. Isaac and Jacob are good enough for yours truly. Pass me that rattle, if you please. I can't chew India-rubber rings all day."

Not a soul made a memorandum of these sayings of mine, for publication. I saw that, and did it myself, else they would have been utterly lost. So far from meeting with a generous encouragement like other children when developing intellectually, I was now furiously scowled upon by my father; my mother looked grieved and anxious, and even my aunt had about her an expression of seeming to think that maybe I had gone too far. I took a vicious bite out of an India-rubber ring, and covertly broke the rattle over the kitten's head, but said nothing. Presently my father said:

"Samuel is a very excellent name."

I saw that trouble was coming. Nothing could prevent it. I laid down my rattle; over the side of the cradle I dropped my uncle's silver watch, the clothes brush, the toy dog, my tin soldier, the nutmeg grater, and other matters which I was accustomed to examine, and meditate upon, and make pleasant noises with, and bang and batter and break when I needed wholesome entertainment. Then I put on my little frock and my little bonnet, and took my pigmy shoes in one hand and my licorice in the other, and climbed out on the floor. I said to myself, Now, if the worst comes to the worst, I am ready. Then I said aloud, in a firm voice:

"Father, I cannot, cannot wear the name of Samuel."

"My son!"

"Father, I mean it. I cannot."

"Why?"

"Father, I have an invincible antipathy to that name."

"My son, this is unreasonable. Many great and good men have been named Samuel."

"Sir, I have yet to hear of the first instance."

"What! There was Samuel the prophet. Was not he great and good?"

"Not so very."

"My son! With his own voice the Lord called him."

"Yes, sir, and had to call him a couple of times before he would come!"

And then I sallied forth, and that stern old man sallied forth after me. He overtook me at noon the following day, and when the interview was over I had acquired the name of Samuel, and a thrashing, and other useful information; and by means of this compromise my father's wrath was appeased and a misunderstanding bridged over which might have become a permanent rupture if I had chosen to be unreasonable. But just judging by this episode, what *would* my father have done to me if I had ever uttered in his hearing one of the flat, sickly things these "two-year-olds" say in print nowadays? In my opinion there would have been a case of infanticide in our family.

June 1870

THE LATE BENJAMIN FRANKLIN

[Never put off till to-morrow what you can do day after
tomorrow just as well. – B. F.]

THIS PARTY WAS one of those persons whom they call Philosophers. He was twins, being born simultaneously in two different
houses in the city of Boston. These houses remain unto this day,
and have signs upon them worded in accordance with the facts.
The signs are considered well enough to have, though not necessary, because the inhabitants point out the two birth-places to the
stranger anyhow, and sometimes as often as several times in the
same day. The subject of this memoir was of a vicious disposition,
and early prostituted his talents to the invention of maxims and
aphorisms calculated to inflict suffering upon the rising generation
of all subsequent ages. His simplest acts, also, were contrived with
a view to their being held up for the emulation of boys forever –
boys who might otherwise have been happy. It was in this spirit
that he became the son of a soap-boiler; and probably for no other
reason than that the efforts of all future boys who tried to be anything might be looked upon with suspicion unless they were the
sons of soap-boilers. With a malevolence which is without parallel
in history, he would work all day and then sit up nights and let on
to be studying algebra by the light of a smouldering fire, so that all
other boys might have to do that also or else have Benjamin Franklin thrown up to them. Not satisfied with these proceedings, he
had a fashion of living wholly on bread and water, and studying
astronomy at meal time – a thing which has brought affliction to
millions of boys since, whose fathers had read Franklin's pernicious biography.

His maxims were full of animosity toward boys. Nowadays a boy
cannot follow out a single natural instinct without tumbling over
some of those everlasting aphorisms and hearing from Franklin on
the spot. If he buys two cents' worth of peanuts, his father says,
"Remember what Franklin has said, my son, – 'A groat a day's a
penny a year;'" and the comfort is all gone out of those peanuts.
If he wants to spin his top when he is done work, his father quotes,
"Procrastination is the thief of time." If he does a virtuous action,
he never gets anything for it, because "Virtue is its own reward."

And that boy is hounded to death and robbed of his natural rest, because Franklin said once in one of his inspired flights of malignity –

> Early to bed and early to rise
> Make a man healthy and wealthy and wise.

As if it were any object to a boy to be healthy and wealthy and wise on such terms. The sorrow that that maxim has cost me through my parents' experimenting on me with it, tongue cannot tell. The legitimate result is my present state of general debility, indigence, and mental aberration. My parents used to have me up before nine o'clock in the morning, sometimes, when I was a boy. If they had let me take my natural rest, where would I have been now? Keeping store, no doubt, and respected by all.

And what an adroit old adventurer the subject of this memoir was! In order to get a chance to fly his kite on Sunday, he used to hang a key on the string and let on to be fishing for lightning. And a guileless public would go home chirping about the "wisdom" and the "genius" of the hoary Sabbath-breaker. If anybody caught him playing "mumble-peg" by himself, after the age of sixty, he would immediately appear to be ciphering out how the grass grew – as if it was any of his business. My grandfather knew him well, and he says Franklin was always fixed – always ready. If a body, during his old age, happened on him unexpectedly when he was catching flies, or making mud pies, or sliding on a cellar-door, he would immediately look wise, and rip out a maxim, and walk off with his nose in the air and his cap turned wrong side before, trying to appear absent-minded and eccentric. He was a hard lot.

He invented a stove that would smoke your head off in four hours by the clock. One can see the almost devilish satisfaction he took in it, by his giving it his name.

He was always proud of telling how he entered Philadelphia, for the first time, with nothing in the world but two shillings in his pocket and four rolls of bread under his arm. But really, when you come to examine it critically, it was nothing. Anybody could have done it.

To the subject of this memoir belongs the honor of recommending the army to go back to bows and arrows in place of bayonets and muskets. He observed, with his customary force, that the bayonet was very well, under some circumstances, but that he doubted whether it could be used with accuracy at long range.

Benjamin Franklin did a great many notable things for his country, and made her young name to be honored in many lands as the mother of such a son. It is not the idea of this memoir to ignore that or cover it up. No; the simple idea of it is to snub those pretentious maxims of his, which he worked up with a great show of originality out of truisms that had become wearisome platitudes as early as the dispersion from Babel; and also to snub his stove, and his military inspirations, his unseemly endeavor to make himself conspicuous when he entered Philadelphia, and his flying his kite and fooling away his time in all sorts of such ways, when he ought to have been foraging for soap-fat, or constructing candles. I merely desired to do away with somewhat of the prevalent calamitous idea among heads of families that Franklin *acquired* his great genius by working for nothing, studying by moonlight, and getting up in the night instead of waiting till morning like a Christian, and that this programme, rigidly inflicted, will make a Franklin of every father's fool. It is time these gentlemen were finding out that these execrable eccentricities of instinct and conduct are only the *evidences* of genius, not the *creators* of it. I wish I had been the father of my parents long enough to make them comprehend this truth, and thus prepare them to let their son have an easier time of it. When I was a child I had to boil soap, notwithstanding my father was wealthy, and I had to get up early and study geometry at breakfast, and peddle my own poetry, and do everything just as Franklin did, in the solemn hope that I would be a Franklin some day. And here I am.

July 1870

A MEMORY

WHEN I SAY that I never knew my austere father to be enamored of but one poem in all the long half century that he lived, persons who knew him will easily believe me; when I say that I have never composed but one poem in all the long third of a century that I have lived, persons who know me will be sincerely grateful; and finally, when I say that the poem which I composed was not the one which my father was enamored of, persons who may have known us both will not need to have this truth shot into them with a mountain howitzer before they can receive it. My father and I were always on the most distant terms when I was a boy – a sort of armed neutrality, so to speak. At irregular intervals this neutrality was broken, and suffering ensued; but I will be candid enough to say that the breaking and the suffering were always divided up with strict impartiality between us – which is to say, my father did the breaking, and I did the suffering. As a general thing I was a backward, cautious, unadventurous boy; but once I jumped off a two-story stable; another time I gave an elephant a "plug" of tobacco and retired without waiting for an answer; and still another time I pretended to be talking in my sleep, and got off a portion of a very wretched original conundrum in hearing of my father. Let us not pry into the result; it was of no consequence to any one but me.

But the poem I have referred to as attracting my father's attention and achieving his favor was "Hiawatha." Some man who courted a sudden and awful death presented him an early copy, and I never lost faith in my own senses until I saw him sit down and go to reading it in cold blood – saw him open the book, and heard him read these following lines, with the same inflectionless judicial frigidity with which he always read his charge to the jury, or administered an oath to a witness:

> Take your bow, O Hiawatha,
> Take your arrows, jasper-headed,
> Take your war-club, Puggawaugun,
> And your mittens, Minjekahwan,
> And your birch canoe for sailing,
> And the oil of Mishe-Nama.

Presently my father took out of his breast pocket an imposing "Warranty Deed," and fixed his eyes upon it and dropped into meditation. I knew what it was. A Texan lady and gentleman had given my half-brother, Orrin Johnson, a handsome property in a town in the North, in gratitude to him for having saved their lives by an act of brilliant heroism.

By and by my father looked toward me and sighed. Then he said:

"If I had such a son as this poet, here were a subject worthier than the traditions of these Indians."

"If you please, sir, where?"

"In this deed."

"In the – deed?"

"Yes – in this very deed," said my father, throwing it on the table. "There is more poetry, more romance, more sublimity, more splendid imagery hidden away in that homely document than could be found in all the traditions of all the savages that live."

"Indeed, sir? Could I – could I get it out, sir? Could I compose the poem, sir, do you think?"

"You!"

I wilted.

Presently my father's face softened somewhat, and he said:

"Go and try. But mind, curb folly. No poetry at the expense of truth. Keep strictly to the facts."

I said I would, and bowed myself out, and went up stairs.

"Hiawatha" kept droning in my head – and so did my father's remarks about the sublimity and romance hidden in my subject, and also his injunction to beware of wasteful and exuberant fancy. I noticed, just here, that I had heedlessly brought the deed away with me. Now, at this moment came to me one of those rare moods of daring recklessness, such as I referred to a while ago. Without another thought, and in plain defiance of the fact that I knew my father meant me to write the romantic story of my half-brother's adventure and subsequent good fortune, I ventured to heed merely the letter of his remarks and ignore their spirit. I took the stupid "Warranty Deed" itself and chopped it up into Hiawathian blank verse, without altering or leaving out three words, and without transposing six. It required loads of courage to go down stairs and face my father with my performance. I started three or four times before I finally got my pluck to where it would stick. But at last I said I would go down and read it to him if he threw me over the church for it. I stood up to begin, and he told me to come closer.

I edged up a little, but still left as much neutral ground between us as I thought he would stand. Then I began. It would be useless for me to try to tell what conflicting emotions expressed themselves upon his face, nor how they grew more and more intense as I proceeded; nor how a fell darkness descended upon his countenance, and he began to gag and swallow, and his hands began to work and twitch, as I reeled off line after line, with the strength ebbing out of me, and my legs trembling under me:

THE STORY OF A GALLANT DEED.

THIS INDENTURE, made the tenth
    Day of November, in the year
Of our Lord one thousand eight
    Hundred six-and-fifty,

Between JOANNA S. E. GRAY
    And PHILIP GRAY, her husband,
Of Salem City in the State
    Of Texas, of the first part,

And O. B. Johnson, of the town
    Of Austin, ditto, WITNESSETH:
That said party of first part,
    For and in consideration

Of the sum of Twenty Thousand
    Dollars, lawful money of
The U. S. of Americay,
    To them in hand now paid by said

Party of the second part,
    The due receipt whereof is here-
By confessed and acknowledg-ed,
    Have Granted, Bargained, Sold, Remised,

Released and Aliened and Conveyed,
    Confirmed, and by these presents do
Grant and Bargain, Sell, Remise,
    Alien, Release, Convey, and Con-

Firm unto the said aforesaid
    Party of the second part,
And to his heirs and assigns
    Forever and ever, ALL

That certain piece or parcel of
    LAND situate in city of
Dunkirk, county of Chautauqua,
    And likewise furthermore in York State,

Bounded and described, to-wit,
    As follows, herein, namely:
BEGINNING at the distance of
    A hundred two-and-forty feet,

North-half-east, north-east-by-north,
    East-north-east and northerly
Of the northerly line of Mulligan street,
    On the westerly line of Brannigan street,

And running thence due northerly
    On Brannigan street 200 feet,
Thence at right angles westerly,
    North-west-by-west-and-west-half-west,

West-and-by-north, north-west-by-west,
    About –

I kind of dodged, and the boot-jack broke the looking-glass.
I could have waited to see what became of the other missiles if
I had wanted to, but I took no interest in such things.

August 1870

THE NOBLE RED MAN

IN BOOKS HE is tall and tawny, muscular, straight, and of kingly presence; he has a beaked nose and an eagle eye.

His hair is glossy, and as black as the raven's wing; out of its massed richness springs a sheaf of brilliant feathers; in his ears and nose are silver ornaments; on his arms and wrists and ankles are broad silver bands and bracelets; his buckskin hunting suit is gallantly fringed, and the belt and the moccasins wonderfully flowered with colored beads; and when, rainbowed with his war-paint, he stands at full height, with his crimson blanket wrapped about him, his quiver at his back, his bow and tomahawk projecting upward from his folded arms, and his eagle eye gazing at specks against the far horizon which even the paleface's field-glass could scarcely reach, he is a being to fall down and worship.

His language is intensely figurative. He never speaks of the moon, but always of "the eye of the night;" nor of the wind *as* the wind, but as "the whisper of the Great Spirit;" and so forth and so on. His power of condensation is marvellous. In some publications he seldom says anything but "Waugh!" and this, with a page of explanation by the author, reveals a whole world of thought and wisdom that before lay concealed in that one little word.

He is noble. He is true and loyal; not even imminent death can shake his peerless faithfulness. His heart is a well-spring of truth, and of generous impulses, and of knightly magnanimity. With him, gratitude is religion; do him a kindness, and at the end of a lifetime he has not forgotten it. Eat of his bread, or offer him yours, and the bond of hospitality is sealed – a bond which is forever inviolable with him.

He loves the dark-eyed daughter of the forest, the dusky maiden of faultless form and rich attire, the pride of the tribe, the all-beautiful. He talks to her in a low voice, at twilight, of his deeds on the war-path and in the chase, and of the grand achievements of his ancestors; and she listens with downcast eyes, "while a richer hue mantles her dusky cheek."

Such is the Noble Red Man in print. But out on the plains and in the mountains, not being on dress parade, not being gotten up to see company, he is under no obligation to be other than his natural self, and therefore:

He is little, and scrawny, and black, and dirty; and, judged by even the most charitable of our canons of human excellence, is thoroughly pitiful and contemptible. There is nothing in his eye or his nose that is attractive, and if there is anything in his hair that – however, that is a feature which will not bear too close examination. He wears no feathers in his hair, and no ornament or covering on his head. His dull-black, frowsy locks hang straight down to his neck behind, and in front they hang just to his eyes, like a curtain, being cut straight across the forehead, from side to side, and never parted on top. He has no pendants in his ears, and as for his – however, let us not waste time on unimportant particulars, but hurry along. He wears no bracelets on his arms or ankles; his hunting suit is gallantly fringed, but not intentionally; when he does not wear his disgusting rabbit-skin robe, his hunting suit consists wholly of the half of a horse blanket brought over in the Pinta or the Mayflower, and frayed out and fringed by inveterate use. He is not rich enough to possess a belt; he never owned a moccasin or wore a shoe in his life; and truly he is nothing but a poor, filthy, naked scurvy vagabond, whom to exterminate were a charity to the Creator's worthier insects and reptiles which he oppresses. Still, when contact with the white man has given to the Noble Son of the Forest certain cloudy impressions of civilization, and aspirations after a nobler life, he presently appears in public with one boot on and one shoe – shirtless, and wearing ripped and patched and buttonless pants which he holds up with his left hand – his execrable rabbit-skin robe flowing from his shoulders – an old hoop-skirt on, outside of it – a necklace of battered sardine-boxes and oyster-cans reposing on his bare breast – a venerable flint-lock musket in his right hand – a weather-beaten stove-pipe hat on, canted "gallusly" to starboard, and the lid off and hanging by a thread or two; and when he thus appears, and waits patiently around a saloon till he gets a chance to strike a "swell" attitude before a looking-glass, he is a good, fair, desirable subject for extermination if ever there was one.*

There is nothing figurative, or moonshiny, or sentimental about his language. It is very simple and unostentatious, and consists of plain, straightforward lies. His "wisdom" conferred upon an idiot would leave that idiot helpless indeed.

He is ignoble – base and treacherous, and hateful in every way.

* This is not a fancy picture; I have seen it many a time in Nevada, just as it is here limned.

Not even imminent death can startle him into a spasm of virtue. The ruling trait of all savages is a greedy and consuming selfishness, and in our Noble Red Man it is found in its amplest development. His heart is a cesspool of falsehood, of treachery, and of low and devilish instincts. With him, gratitude is an unknown emotion; and when one does him a kindness, it is safest to keep the face toward him, lest the reward be an arrow in the back. To accept of a favor from him is to assume a debt which you can never repay to his satisfaction, though you bankrupt yourself trying. To give him a dinner when he is starving, is to precipitate the whole hungry tribe upon your hospitality, for he will go straight and fetch them, men, women, children, and dogs, and these they will huddle patiently around your door, or flatten their noses against your window, day after day, gazing beseechingly upon every mouthful you take, and unconsciously swallowing when you swallow! The scum of the earth!

And the Noble Son of the Plains becomes a mighty hunter in the due and proper season. That season is the summer, and the prey that a number of the tribes hunt is crickets and grasshoppers! The warriors, old men, women, and children, spread themselves abroad in the plain and drive the hopping creatures before them into a ring of fire. I could describe the feast that then follows, without missing a detail, if I thought the reader would stand it.

All history and honest observation will show that the Red Man is a skulking coward and a windy braggart, who strikes without warning – usually from an ambush or under cover of night, and nearly always bringing a force of about five or six to one against his enemy; kills helpless women and little children, and massacres the men in their beds; and then brags about it as long as he lives, and his son and his grandson and great-grandson after him glorify it among the "heroic deeds of their ancestors." A regiment of Fenians will fill the whole world with the noise of it when they are getting ready to invade Canada; but when the Red Man declares war, the first intimation his friend the white man whom he supped with at twilight has of it, is when the war-whoop rings in his ears and the tomahawk sinks into his brain. In June, seven Indians went to a small station on the Plains where three white men lived, and asked for food; it was given them, and also tobacco. They stayed two hours, eating and smoking and talking, waiting with Indian patience for their customary odds of seven to one to offer, and as soon as it came they seized the opportunity; that is, when two of the men went out, they killed the other the instant he turned his back to do some solicited favor; then they caught his comrades separately, and killed one, but the other escaped.

The Noble Red Man seldom goes prating loving foolishness to a splendidly caparisoned blushing maid at twilight. No; he trades a crippled horse, or a damaged musket, or a dog, a gallon of grasshoppers, and an inefficient old mother for her, and makes her work like an abject slave all the rest of her life to compensate him for the outlay. He never works himself. She builds the habitation, when they use one (it consists in hanging half a dozen rags over the weather side of a sage-brush bush to roost under); gathers and brings home the fuel; takes care of the raw-boned pony when they possess such grandeur; she walks and carries her nursing cubs while he rides. She wears no clothing save the fragrant rabbit-skin robe which her great-grandmother before her wore, and all the "blushing" she does can be removed with soap and a towel, provided it is only four or five weeks old and not caked.

Such is the genuine Noble Aborigine. I did not get him from books, but from personal observation.

By Dr Keim's excellent book it appears that from June, 1868, to October, 1869, the Indians *massacred nearly 200 white persons and ravished over forty women captured in peaceful outlying settlements along the border, or belonging to emigrant trains traversing the settled routes of travel. Children were burned alive in the presence of their parents. Wives were ravished before their husbands' eyes. Husbands were mutilated, tortured, and scalped, and their wives compelled to look on.* These facts and figures are official, and they exhibit the misunderstood Son of the Forest in his true character – as a creature devoid of brave or generous qualities, but cruel, treacherous, and brutal. During the Pi-Ute war the Indians often dug the sinews out of the backs of white men before they were dead. (The sinews are used for bow-strings.) But their favorite mutilations cannot be put into print. Yet it is this same Noble Red Man who is always greeted with a wail of humanitarian sympathy from the Atlantic seaboard whenever he gets into trouble; the maids and matrons throw up their hands in horror at the bloody vengeance wreaked upon him, and the newspapers clamor for a court of inquiry to examine into the conduct of the inhuman officer who inflicted the little pleasantry upon the "poor abused Indian." (They always look at the matter from the abused-Indian point of view, never from that of the bereaved white widow and orphan.) But it is a great and unspeakable comfort to know that, let them be as prompt about it as they may, the inquiry has always got to come *after* the good officer has administered his little admonition.

September 1870

THE APPROACHING EPIDEMIC

ONE CALAMITY TO which the death of Mr. Dickens dooms this country has not awakened the concern to which its gravity entitles it. We refer to the fact that the nation is to be lectured to death and read to death all next winter, by Tom, Dick, and Harry, with poor lamented Dickens for a pretext. All the vagabonds who can spell will afflict the people with "readings" from Pickwick and Copperfield, and all the insignificants who have been ennobled by the notice of the great novelist or transfigured by his smile will make a marketable commodity of it now, and turn the sacred reminiscence to the practical use of procuring bread and butter. The lecture rostrums will fairly swarm with these fortunates. Already the signs of it are perceptible. Behold how the unclean creatures are wending toward the dead lion and gathering to the feast:

"Reminiscences of Dickens." A lecture. By John Smith, who heard him read eight times.

"Remembrances of Charles Dickens." A lecture. By John Jones, who saw him once in a street car and twice in a barber shop.

"Recollections of Mr. Dickens." A lecture. By John Brown, who gained a wide fame by writing deliriously appreciative critiques and rhapsodies upon the great author's public readings; and who shook hands with the great author upon various occasions, and held converse with him several times.

"Readings from Dickens." By John White, who has the great delineator's style and manner perfectly, having attended all his readings in this country and made these things a study, always practising each reading before retiring, and while it was hot from the great delineator's lips. Upon this occasion Mr. W. will exhibit the remains of a cigar which he saw Mr. Dickens smoke. This Relic is kept in a solid silver box made purposely for it.

"Sights and Sounds of the Great Novelist." A popular lecture. By John Gray, who waited on his table all the time he was at the Grand Hotel, New York, and still has in his possession and will exhibit to the audience a fragment of the Last Piece of Bread which the lamented author tasted in this country.

"Heart Treasures of Precious Moments with Literature's Departed Monarch." A lecture. By Miss Serena Amelia Tryphenia McSpadden, who still wears, and will always wear, a glove upon the hand made sacred by the clasp of Dickens. Only Death shall remove it.

"Readings from Dickens." By Mrs. J. O'Hooligan Murphy, who washed for him.

"Familiar Talks with the Great Author." A narrative lecture. By John Thomas, for two weeks his valet in America.

And so forth, and so on. This isn't half the list. The man who has a "Toothpick once used by Charles Dickens" will have to have a hearing; and the man who "once rode in an omnibus with Charles Dickens;" and the lady to whom Charles Dickens "granted the hospitalities of his umbrella during a storm;" and the person who "possesses a hole which once belonged in a handker-chief owned by Charles Dickens." Be patient and long-suffering, good people, for even this does not fill up the measure of what you must endure next winter. There is no creature in all this land who has had any personal relations with the late Mr. Dickens, however slight or trivial, but will shoulder his way to the rostrum and inflict his testimony upon his helpless countrymen. To some people it is fatal to be noticed by greatness.

September 1870

MAP OF PARIS

I PUBLISHED MY "Map of the Fortifications of Paris" in my own paper a fortnight ago, but am obliged to reproduce it in THE GALAXY, to satisfy the extraordinary demand for it which has arisen in military circles throughout the country. General Grant's outspoken commendation originated this demand, and General Sherman's fervent endorsement added fuel to it. The result is that tons of these maps have been fed to the suffering soldiers of our land, but without avail. They hunger still. We will cast THE GALAXY into the breach and stand by and await the effect.

The next Atlantic mail will doubtless bring news of a European frenzy for the map. It is reasonable to expect that the siege of Paris will be suspended till a German translation of it can be forwarded (it is now in preparation), and that the defence of Paris will likewise be suspended to await the reception of the French translation (now progressing under my own hands, and likely to be unique). King William's high praise of the map and Napoleon's frank enthusiasm concerning its execution will ensure its prompt adoption in Europe as the only authoritative and legitimate exposition of the present military situation. It is plain that if the Prussians cannot get into Paris with the facilities afforded by this production of mine they ought to deliver the enterprise into abler hands.

Strangers to me keep insisting that this map does *not* "explain itself." One person came to me with bloodshot eyes and a harassed look about him, and shook the map in my face and said he believed I was some new kind of idiot. I have been abused a good deal by other quick-tempered people like him, who came with similar complaints. Now, therefore, I yield willingly, and for the information of the ignorant will briefly explain the present military situation as illustrated by the map. Part of the Prussian forces, under Prince Frederick William, are now boarding at the "farm-house" in the margin of the map. There is nothing between them and Vincennes but a rail fence in bad repair. Any corporal can see at a glance that they have only to burn it, pull it down, crawl under, climb over, or walk around it, just as the commander-in-chief shall elect. Another portion of the Prussian forces are at Podunk, under Von Moltke. They have nothing to do but float down the river Seine on a raft and scale the walls of Paris. Let the worshippers of that overrated soldier believe in him still, and abide the result – for me, *I* do not believe he will ever think of a raft. At Omaha and the High Bridge are vast masses of Prussian infantry, and it is only fair to say that they are likely to *stay* there, as that figure of a window-sash between them stands for a brewery. Away up out of sight over the top of the map is the fleet of the Prussian navy, ready at any moment to come cavorting down the Erie Canal (unless some new iniquity of an unprincipled Legislature shall put up the tolls and so render it cheaper to walk). To me it looks as if Paris is in a singularly close place. She never was situated before as she is in this map.

MARK TWAIN.

TO THE READER.

The accompanying map explains itself.

The idea of this map is not original with me, but is borrowed from the "Tribune" and the other great metropolitan journals.

I claim no other merit for this production (if I may so call it) than that it is accurate. The main blemish of the city-paper maps of which it is an imitation, is, that in them more attention seems paid to artistic picturesqueness than geographical reliability.

Inasmuch as this is the first time I ever tried to draft and engrave a map, or attempt anything in the line of art at all, the commendations the work has received and the admiration it has excited among the people, have been very grateful to my feelings. And it is touching to reflect that by far the most enthusiastic of these praises have come from people who know nothing at all about art.

By an unimportant oversight I have engraved the map so that it reads wrong end first, except to left-handed people. I forgot that in order to make it right in print it should be drawn and engraved upside down. However, let the student who desires to contemplate the map stand on his head or hold it before her looking-glass. That will bring it right.

The reader will comprehend at a glance that that piece of river with the "High Bridge" over it got left out to one side by reason of a slip of the graving-tool, which rendered it necessary to change the entire course of the river Rhine or else spoil the map. After having spent two days in digging and gouging at the map, I would have changed the course of the Atlantic ocean before I would have lost so much work.

I never had so much trouble with anything in my life as I did with this map. I had heaps of little fortifications scattered all

FORTIFICATIONS OF PARIS.

around Paris, at first, but every now and then my instruments would slip and fetch away whole miles of batteries and leave the vicinity as clean as if the Prussians had been there.

The reader will find it well to frame this map for future reference, so that it may aid in extending popular intelligence and dispelling the wide-spread ignorance of the day.

MARK TWAIN.

OFFICIAL COMMENDATIONS.

It is the only map of the kind I ever saw. U.S. GRANT.

It places the situation in an entirely new light. BISMARCK.

I cannot look upon it without shedding tears.

BRIGHAM YOUNG.

It is very nice, large print. NAPOLEON.

My wife was for years afflicted with freckles, and though everything was done for her relief that could be done, all was in vain. But, sir, since her first glance at your map, they have entirely left her. She has nothing but convulsions now.

J. SMITH.

If I had had this map I could have got out of Metz without any trouble.

BAZAINE.

I have seen a great many maps in my time, but none that this one reminds me of.

TROCHU.

It is but fair to say that in some respects it is a truly remarkable map.

W.T. SHERMAN.

I said to my son Frederick William, "If you could only make a map like that, I would be perfectly willing to see you die – even anxious."

WILLIAM III.
November 1870

ONE OF MANKIND'S BORES

I SUPPOSE THAT if there is one thing in the world more hateful than another to all of us, it is to have to write a letter. A private letter especially. And business letters, to my thinking, are very little pleasanter. Nearly all the enjoyment is taken out of every letter I get by the reflection that it must be answered. And I do so dread the affliction of writing those answers, that often my first and gladdest impulse is to burn my mail before it is opened. For ten years I never felt that sort of dread at all, because I was moving about constantly, from city to city, from State to State, and from country to country, and so I could leave all letters unanswered if I chose, and the writers of them would naturally suppose that I had changed my post-office and missed receiving my correspondence. But I am "cornered" now. I cannot use that form of deception any more. I am anchored, and letters of all kinds come straight to me with deadly precision.

They are letters of all sorts and descriptions, and they treat of everything. I generally read them at breakfast, and right often they kill a day's work by diverting my thoughts and fancies into some new channel, thus breaking up and making confusion of the programme of scribbling I had arranged for my working hours. After breakfast I clear for action, and for an hour try hard to write; but there is no getting back into the old train of thought after such an interruption, and so at last I give it up and put off further effort till next day. One would suppose that I would now answer those letters and get them out of the way; and I suppose one of those model young men we read about, who enter New York barefoot and live to become insolent millionaires, would be sure to do that; but I don't. I never shall be a millionaire, and so I disdain to copy the ways of those men. I did not start right. I made a fatal mistake to begin with, and entered New York with boots on and above forty cents in my pocket. With such an unpropitious beginning, any efforts of mine to acquire great wealth would be frowned upon as illegitimate, and I should be ruthlessly put down as an impostor. And so, as I said before, I decline to follow the lead of those chrysalis Croesuses and answer my correspondents with commercial promptness. I stop work for the day, and leave the new letters stacked up along with those that came the day before, and the day before that, and the day before that, and so on. And by-and-by, the pile grows so large that it begins to distress me, and then I attack it and give full five and sometimes six hours to the assault. And how many of the letters do I answer in that time? Never more than nine; usually only five or six. The correspondence clerk in a great mercantile house would answer a hundred in that many hours. But a man who has spent years in writing for the press cannot reasonably be expected to have such facility with a pen. From old habit he gets to thinking and thinking, patiently puzzling for minutes together over the proper turning of a sentence in an answer to some unimportant private letter, and so the precious time slips away.

It comes natural to me in these latter years to do all manner of composition laboriously and ploddingly, private letters included. Consequently, I do fervently hate letter-writing, and so do all the newspaper and magazine men I am acquainted with.

The above remarks are by way of explanation and apology to parties who have written me about various matters, and whose letters I have neglected to answer. I tried in good faith to answer them – tried every now and then, and always succeeded in clearing off several, but always as surely left the majority of those received each week to lie over till the next. The result was always the same, to wit: the unanswered letters would shortly begin to have a reproachful look about them, next an upbraiding look, and by-and-by an aggressive and insolent aspect; and when it came to that, I always opened the stove door and made an example of them. The return of cheerfulness and the flight of every feeling of distress on account of neglected duty, was immediate and thorough.

I did not answer the letter of the Wisconsin gentleman, who inquired whether imported brads were better than domestic ones, because I did not know what brads were, and did not choose to "let on" to a stranger. I thought it would have looked much better in him, anyhow, to have asked somebody who he knew was in the habit of eating brads, or wearing them, whichever is the proper way of utilizing them.

I did manage to answer the little Kentucky boy who wished to send me his wildcat. I thanked him very kindly and cordially for his donation, and said I was very fond of cats of all descriptions, and told him to do like the little Indiana boy, and forward it to Rev. Mr. Beecher, and I would call and get it some time. I could not bear to check the warm young tide of his generosity, and yet I had no (immediate) use for the insect myself.

I did not answer the young man who wrote me from Tennessee, inquiring "how to become a good reporter and acceptable journalist," chiefly because if one marks out the nice easy method which he knows these kind of inquirers have in their mind's eye, they straightway begin to afflict him with semi-weekly specimens of what they can do, under the thin disguise of a friendly correspondence; and if he marks out the unromantic and unattractive method which he believes in his heart to be the absolutely necessary one, they always write back and call him a "nigger" or a "thief." These people are so illogical.

February 1871

ABOUT BARBERS

ALL THINGS CHANGE except barbers, the ways of barbers, and the surroundings of barbers. These never change. What one experiences in a barber shop the first time he enters one, is what he always experiences in barber shops afterward till the end of his days. I got shaved this morning as usual. A man approached the door from Jones street as I approached it from Main – a thing that always happens. I hurried up, but it was of no use; he entered the door one little step ahead of me, and I followed in on his heels and saw him take the only vacant chair, the one presided over by the best barber. It always happens so. I sat down, hoping that I might fall heir to the chair belonging to the better of the remaining two barbers, for he had already begun combing his man's hair, while his comrade was not yet quite done rubbing up and oiling his customer's locks. I watched the probabilities with strong interest. When I saw that No. 2 was gaining on No. 1, my interest grew to solicitude. When No. 1 stopped a moment to make change on a bath ticket for a new-comer, and lost ground in the race, my solicitude rose to anxiety. When No. 1 caught up again, and both he and his comrade were pulling the towels away and brushing the powder from their customers' cheeks, and it was about an even thing which one would say "Next!" first, my very breath stood still with the suspense. But when, at the final culminating moment, No. 1 stopped to pass a comb a couple of times through his customer's eyebrows, I saw that he had lost the race by a single instant, and I rose indignant and quitted the shop, to keep from falling into the hands of No. 2; for I have none of that enviable firmness that enables a man to look calmly into the eyes of a waiting barber and tell him he will wait for his fellow-barber's chair. I stayed out fifteen minutes, and then went back, hoping for better luck. Of course all the chairs were occupied now, and four men sat waiting, silent, unsociable, distraught, and looking bored, as men always do who are awaiting their turn in a barber's shop. I sat down in one of the iron-armed compartments of an old sofa, and put in the time for a while, reading the framed advertisements of all sorts of quack nostrums for dyeing and coloring the hair. Then I read the greasy names on the private bay rum bottles; read the names and noted the numbers on the private shaving cups in the pigeon-holes; studied the stained and damaged cheap prints on the walls, of

battles, early Presidents, and voluptuous, recumbent sultanas, and
the tiresome and ever-lasting young girl putting her grandfather's
spectacles on; execrated in my heart the cheerful canary and the
distracting parrot that few barber shops are without. Finally,
I searched out the least dilapidated of the last year's illustrated
papers that littered the foul centre table, and conned their
unjustifiable misrepresentations of old forgotten events. At last my
turn came. A voice said "Next!" and I surrendered to – No. 2 of
course. It always happens so. I said meekly that I was in a hurry,
and it affected him as strongly as if he had never heard it. He
shoved up my head and put a napkin under it. He ploughed his
fingers into my collar and fixed a towel there. He explored my hair
with his claws and suggested that it needed trimming. I said I did
not want it trimmed. He explored again and said it was pretty long
for the present style – better have a little taken off; it needed it
behind, especially. I said I had had it cut only a week before. He
yearned over it reflectively a moment, and then asked, with a disparaging manner, who cut it. I came back at him promptly with a
"You did!" I had him there. Then he fell to stirring up his lather
and regarding himself in the glass, stopping now and then to get
close and examine his chin critically or torture a pimple. Then he
lathered one side of my face thoroughly, and was about to lather
the other, when a dog fight attracted his attention, and he ran to
the window and stayed and saw it out, losing two shillings on the
result in bets with the other barbers, a thing which gave me great
satisfaction. He finished lathering, meantime getting the brush
into my mouth only twice, and then began to rub in the suds with
his hand; and as he now had his head turned, discussing the dog
fight with the other barbers, he naturally shovelled considerable
lather into my mouth without knowing it, but I did. He now began
to sharpen his razor on an old suspender, and was delayed a good
deal on account of a controversy about a cheap masquerade ball
he had figured at the night before, in red cambric and bogus
ermine, as some kind of a king. He was so gratified with being
chaffed about some damsel whom he had smitten with his charms,
that he used every means to continue the controversy by pretending to be annoyed at the chaffings of his fellows. This matter
begot more surveyings of himself in the glass, and he put down
his razor and brushed his hair with elaborate care, plastering an
inverted arch of it down on his forehead, accomplishing an accurate "part" behind, and brushing the two wings forward over his

ears with nice exactness. In the mean time the lather was drying on my face, and apparently eating into my vitals. Now he began to shave, digging his fingers into my countenance to stretch the skin, making a handle of my nose now and then, bundling and tumbling my head this way and that as convenience in shaving demanded, and "hawking" and expectorating pleasantly all the while. As long as he was on the tough sides of my face I did not suffer; but when he began to rake, and rip, and tug at my chin, the tears came. I did not mind his getting so close down to me; I did not mind his garlic, because all barbers eat garlic, I suppose; but there was an added something that made me fear that he was decaying inwardly while still alive, and this gave me much concern. He now put his finger into my mouth to assist him in shaving the corners of my upper lip, and it was by this bit of circumstantial evidence that I discovered that a part of his duties in the shop was to clean the kerosene lamps. I had often wondered in an indolent way whether the barbers did that, or whether it was the boss. About this time I was amusing myself trying to guess where he would be most likely to cut me this time, but he got ahead of me and sliced me on the end of the chin before I had got my mind made up. He immediately sharpened his razor – he might have done it before. I do not like a close shave, and would not let him go over me a second time. I tried to get him to put up his razor, dreading that he would make for the side of my chin, my pet tender spot, a place which a razor cannot touch twice without making trouble. But he said he only wanted to just smooth off one little roughness, and in that same moment he slipped his razor along the forbidden ground, and the dreaded pimple-signs of a close shave rose up smarting and answered to the call. Now he soaked his towel in bay rum, and slapped it all over my face nastily; slapped it over as if a human being ever yet washed his face in that way. Then he dried it by slapping with the dry part of the towel, as if a human being ever dried his face in such a fashion; but a barber seldom rubs you like a Christian. Next he poked bay rum into the cut place with his towel, then choked the wound with powdered starch, then soaked it with bay rum again, and would have gone on soaking and powdering it for evermore, no doubt, if I had not rebelled and begged off. He powdered my whole face now, straightened me up and began to plough my hair thoughtfully with his hands and examine his fingers critically. Then he suggested a shampoo, and said my hair needed it badly, very badly. I observed that I had shampooed it myself very thoroughly in the bath yester-day. I "had him" again. He next recommended some of "Smith's Hair Glorifier," and offered to sell me a bottle. I declined. He praised the new perfume, "Jones's Delight of the Toilet," and pro-posed to sell me some of that. I declined again. He tendered me a tooth-wash atrocity of his own invention, and when I declined, offered to trade knives with me. He returned to business after the miscarriage of this last enterprise, sprinkled me all over, legs and all, greased my hair in defiance of my protests against it, rubbed and scrubbed a good deal of it out by the roots, and combed and brushed the rest, parting it behind and plastering the eternal inverted arch of hair down on my forehead, and then, while comb-ing my scant eyebrows and defiling them with pomade, strung out an account of the achievements of a six-ounce black and tan terrier of his till I heard the whistles blow for noon, and knew I was five minutes too late for the train. Then he snatched away the towel, brushed it lightly about my face, passed his comb through my eye-brows once more, and gayly sang out "Next!"

This barber fell down and died of apoplexy two hours later. I am waiting over a day for my revenge – I am going to attend his funeral.

August 1871

LICENSE OF THE PRESS

Hartford Monday Evening Club

... IT (THE PRESS) has scoffed at religion till it has made scoffing popular. It has defended official criminals, on party pretexts, until it has created a United States Senate whose members are incapable of determining what crime against law and the dignity of their own body *is*, they are so morally blind, and it has made light of dishonesty till we have as a result a Congress which contracts to work for a certain sum and then deliberately steals additional wages out of the public pocket and is pained and surprised that anybody should worry about a little thing like that.

I am putting all this odious state of things upon the newspaper, and I believe it belongs there – chiefly, at any rate. It is a free press – a press that is more than free – a press which is licensed to say any infamous thing it chooses about a private or a public man, or advocate any outrageous doctrine it pleases. It is tied in *no* way. The public opinion which *should* hold it in bounds it has itself degraded to its own level. There are laws to protect the freedom of the press's speech, but none that are worth anything to protect the people from the press. A libel suit simply brings the plaintiff before a vast newspaper court to be tried before the law tries him, and reviled and ridiculed without mercy. The touchy Charles Reade can sue English newspapers and get verdicts; he would soon change his tactics here; the papers (backed by a public well taught by themselves) would soon teach him that it is better to suffer any amount of misrepresentation than go into our courts with a libel suit and make himself the laughing stock of the community.

It seems to me that just in the ratio that our newspapers increase, our morals decay. The more newspapers the worse morals. Where we have one newspaper that does good, I think we have fifty that do harm. We *ought* to look upon the establishment of a newspaper of the average pattern in a virtuous village as a calamity.

The difference between the tone and conduct of newspapers today and those of thirty or forty years ago is *very* noteworthy and very sad – I mean the average newspaper (for they had bad ones then, too). In those days the average newspaper was the champion of right and morals, and it dealt conscientiously in the truth. It is not the case now. The other day a reputable New York daily had an editorial defending the salary steal and justifying it on the ground that Congressmen were not paid enough – as if that were an all-sufficient excuse for stealing. That editorial put the matter in a new and perfectly satisfactory light with many a leather-headed reader, without a doubt. It has become a sarcastic proverb that a thing must be true if you saw it in a newspaper. That is the opinion intelligent people have of that lying vehicle in a nutshell. But the trouble is that the stupid people – who constitute the grand over-whelming majority of this and all other nations – *do* believe and *are* moulded and convinced by what they get out of a newspaper, and there is where the harm lies.

Among us, the newspaper is a tremendous power. It can make or mar any man's reputation. It has perfect freedom to call the best man in the land a fraud and a thief, and he is destroyed beyond help. Whether Mr. Colfax is a liar or not can never be ascertained now – but he will rank as one till the day of his death – for the newspapers have so doomed him. Our newspapers – *all* of them, without exception – glorify the "Black Crook" and make it an opu-lent success – they could have killed it dead with one broadside of contemptuous silence if they had wanted to. *Days Doings* and *Police Gazettes* flourish in the land unmolested by the law, because the *virtuous* newspapers long ago nurtured up a public laxity that loves indecency and never cares whether laws are administered or not.

In the newspapers of the West you can use the *editorial voice* in the editorial columns to defend any wretched and injurious dogma you please by paying a dollar a line for it.

Nearly all newspapers foster Rozensweigs and kindred criminals and send victims to them by opening their columns to their advert-isements. You all know that.

In the Foster murder case the New York papers made a weak pretense of upholding the hands of the Governor and urging the people to sustain him in standing firmly by the law; but they printed a whole page of sickly, maudlin appeals to his clemency as a paid advertisement. And I suppose they would have published enough pages of abuse of the Governor to destroy his efficiency as a public official to the end of his term if anybody had come forward and paid them for it – as an advertisement. The newspaper that obstructs the law on a trivial pretext, for money's sake, is a danger-ous enemy to the public weal.

That awful power, the public opinion of a nation, is created in America by a horde of ignorant, self-complacent simpletons who failed at ditching and shoemaking and fetched up in journalism on their way to the poorhouse. I am personally acquainted with hundreds of journalists, and the opinion of the majority of them would not be worth tuppence in private, but when they speak in print it is the *newspaper* that is talking (the pygmy scribe is not visible) and *then* their utterances shake the community like the thunders of prophecy.

I know from personal experience the proneness of journalists to lie. I once started a peculiar and picturesque fashion of lying myself on the Pacific coast, and it is not dead there to this day. Whenever I hear of a shower of blood and frogs combined, in California, or a sea serpent found in some desert, there, or a cave frescoed with diamonds and emeralds (*always* found by an Injun who died before he could finish telling where it was), I say to myself I am the father of this child – I have got to answer for this lie. And habit is everything – to this day I am liable to lie if I don't watch all the time.

The license of the press has scorched every individual of us in our time, I make no doubt. Poor Stanley was a very god, in England, his praises in every man's mouth. But nobody said anything about his lectures – they were charitably quiet on that head, and were content to praise his higher virtues. But our papers tore the poor creature limb from limb and scattered the fragments from Maine to California – merely because he couldn't lecture well. His prodigious achievement in Africa goes for naught – the man is pulled down and utterly destroyed – but *still* the persecution follows him as relentlessly from city to city and from village to village as if he had committed some bloody and detestable crime. Bret Harte was suddenly snatched out of obscurity by our papers and throned in the clouds – all the editors in the land stood out in the inclement weather and adored him through their telescopes and swung their hats till they wore them out and then borrowed more; and the first time his family fell sick, and in his trouble and harassment he ground out a rather flat article in place of another heathen Chinee, that hurrahing host said, "Why, this man's a fraud," and then they began to reach up there for him. And they got him, too, and fetched him down, and walked over him, and rolled him in the mud, and tarred and feathered him, and then set him up for a target and have been heaving dirt at him ever since. The result is that the man has had only just nineteen engagements to lecture this year, and the audience have been so scattering, too, that he has never discharged a sentence yet that hit two people at the same time. The man is ruined – never can get up again. And yet he is a person who has great capabilities, and might have accomplished great things for our literature and for himself if he had had a happier chance. And he made the mistake, too, of doing a pecuniary kindness for a starving beggar of our guild – one of the journalistic shoemaker class – and that beggar made it his business as soon as he got back to San Francisco to publish four columns of exposures of crimes committed by his benefactor, the least of which ought to make any decent man blush. The press that admitted that stuff to its columns had too much license.

In a town in Michigan I declined to dine with an editor who was drunk, and he said, in his paper, that my lecture was profane, indecent, and calculated to encourage intemperance. And yet that man never heard it. It might have reformed him if he had.

A Detroit paper once said that I was in the constant habit of beating my wife and that I still kept this recreation up, although I had crippled her for life and she was no longer able to keep out of my way when I came home in my usual frantic frame of mind. Now scarcely the half of that was true. Perhaps I ought to have sued that man for libel – but I knew better. All the papers in America – with a few creditable exceptions – would have found out then, to *their* satisfaction, that I was a wife beater, and they would have given it a pretty general airing, too.

Why *I* have published vicious libels upon people *myself* – and ought to have been hanged before my time for it, too – if I *do* say it myself, that shouldn't.

But I will not continue these remarks. I have a sort of vague general idea that there is too much liberty of the press in this country, and that through the absence of all wholesome restraint the newspaper has become in a large degree a national *curse*, and will probably damn the Republic yet.

There *are* some excellent virtues in newspapers, some powers that wield vast influences for good; and I could have told all about these things, and glorified them exhaustively – but that would have left you gentlemen nothing to say.

March 31, 1873

FOURTH OF JULY SPEECH
IN LONDON

MR. CHAIRMAN AND ladies and gentlemen: I thank you for the compliment which has just been tendered me, and to show my appreciation of it I will not afflict you with many words. It is pleasant to celebrate in this peaceful way, upon this old mother soil, the anniversary of an experiment which was born of war with this same land so long ago, and wrought out to a successful issue by the devotion of our ancestors. It has taken nearly a hundred years to bring the English and Americans into kindly and mutually appreciative relations, but I believe it has been accomplished at last. It was a great step when the two last misunderstandings were settled by arbitration instead of cannon. It is another great step when England adopts our sewing machines without claiming the invention – as usual. It was another when they imported one of our sleeping cars the other day. And it warmed my heart more than I can tell, yesterday, when I witnessed the spectacle of an Englishman ordering an American sherry cobbler of his own free will and accord – and not only that, but with a great brain and level head, reminding the barkeeper not to forget the strawberries. With a common origin, a common literature, a common religion and common drinks, what is longer needful to the cementing of the two nations together in a permanent bond of brotherhood?

This is an age of progress, and ours is a progressive land. A great and glorious land, too – a land which has developed a Washington, a Franklin, a William M. Tweed, a Longfellow, a Motley, a Jay Gould, a Samuel C. Pomeroy, a recent Congress which has never had its equal – (in some respects) and a United States Army which conquered sixty Indians in eight months by tiring them out – which is much better than uncivilized slaughter, God knows. We have a criminal jury system which is superior to any in the world; and its efficiency is only marred by the difficulty of finding twelve men every day who don't know anything and can't read. And I may observe that we have an insanity plea that would have saved Cain. I think I can say, and say with pride, that we have some legislatures that bring higher prices than any in the world.

I refer with effusion to our railway system, which consents to let us live, though it might do the opposite, being our owners. It only destroyed 3,070 lives last year by collisions, and 27,260 by running over heedless and unnecessary people at crossings. The companies seriously regretted the killing of these 30,000 people, and went so far as to pay for some of them – voluntarily, of course, for the meanest of us would not claim that we possess a court treacherous enough to enforce a law against a railway company. But thank heaven the railway companies are generally disposed to do the right and kindly thing without compulsion. I know of an instance which greatly touched me at the time. After an accident the company sent home the remains of a dear, distant old relative of mine in a basket, with the remark, "Please state what figure you hold him at – and return the basket." Now there couldn't be anything friendlier than that.

But I must not stand here and brag all night. However, you won't mind a body bragging a little about his country on the Fourth of July. It is a fair and legitimate time to fly the eagle. I will say only one more word of brag – and a hopeful one. It is this. We have a form of government which gives each man a fair chance and no favor. With us no individual is born with a right to look down upon his neighbor and hold him in contempt. Let such of us as are not dukes find our consolation in that. And we may find hope for the future in the fact that as unhappy as is the condition of our political morality today, England has risen up out of a far fouler since the days when Charles II ennobled courtesans and all political place was a matter of bargain and sale. Be sure there is hope for us yet.

Footnote. At least the above is the speech which I was *going* to make; but our minister, General Schenck, presided, and after the blessing, got up and made a great long inconceivably dull harangue, and wound up by saying that inasmuch as speech-making did not seem to exhilarate the guests much, all further oratory would be dispensed with, during the evening, and we could just sit and talk privately to our elbow-neighbors and have a good sociable time. It is known that in consequence of that remark forty-four perfected speeches died in the womb. The depression, the gloom, the solemnity that reigned over the banquet from that time forth will be a lasting memory with many that were there. By that one thoughtless remark General Schenck lost forty-four of the best friends he had in England. More than one said that night, "And this is the sort of person that is sent to represent us in a great sister empire!"

July 4, 1873

THE LADIES

I AM PROUD, indeed, of the distinction of being chosen to respond to this especial toast – to "The Ladies" – or to *Woman*, if you please, for that is the preferable term, perhaps; it is certainly the older, and therefore the more entitled to reverence. I have noticed and probably you may have noticed that the Bible, with that plain, blunt honesty which is such a conspicuous characteristic of the Scriptures, is always careful to never even refer to the illustrious mother of all mankind herself as a "lady," but speaks of her as a woman. It is odd but I think you will find that it is so. I am peculiarly proud of this honor, because I think that the toast to women is one which, by right and every rule of gallantry, should take precedence of all others – of the army, the navy, of even royalty itself perhaps, though the latter is not necessary in this day and in this land, for the reason that, tacitly, you do drink a broad general health to *all* good women when you drink the health of the Queen of England and the Princess of Wales.

I have in mind a poem, just now, which is familiar to you all, familiar to everybody. And what an inspiration that was (and how instantly the present toast recalls the verses to all our minds), where the most noble, the most gracious, the purest and sweetest of all poets says:

> Woman! O woman – er –
> Wom –

However, you remember the lines. And you remember *how* feelingly, how daintily, how almost imperceptibly the verses raise up before you, feature by feature, the ideal of a true and perfect woman; and how, as you contemplate the finished marvel, your homage grows into worship of the intellect that could create so fair a thing out of mere breath, mere words.

And you call to mind, now, as I speak, how the poet, with stern fidelity to the history of all humanity, delivers *this* beautiful child of his heart and his brain over to the trials and sorrows that must come to all, sooner or later, that abide in the earth; and how the pathetic story culminates in that apostrophe – so wild, so regretful, so full of mournful retrospection. The lines run thus:

Alas! Alas! – a – alas!
Alas! – alas! –

and so on. I do not remember the rest. But taken altogether, it seems to me that that poem is the noblest tribute to woman *that* human genius has ever brought forth – and I feel that if I were to talk hours I could not do my great theme completer or more graceful justice than I have now done in simply quoting that poet's matchless words.

The phases of the womanly nature are infinite in their variety. Take any type of woman, and you shall find in it something to respect, something to admire, something to love. And you shall find the whole world joining your heart and hand. Who was more patriotic than Joan of Arc? Who was braver? Who has given us a grander instance of self-sacrificing devotion? Ah! you remember, you remember well, what a throb of pain, what a great tidal wave of grief swept over us all when Joan of Arc fell at Waterloo. Who does not sorrow for the loss of Sappho, the sweet singer of Israel? Who among us does not *miss* the gentle ministrations, the softening influence, the humble piety, of Lucretia Borgia?

Who can join in the heartless libel that says woman is extravagant in dress, when he can look back and call to mind our simple and lowly Mother Eve arrayed in her modification of the Highland costume?

Sir, women have been soldiers, women have been painters, women have been poets. As long as language lives, the name of Cleopatra will live. And not because she conquered George III – but because she wrote those divine lines:

Let dogs delight to bark and bite,
For God hath made them so.

The story of the world is adorned with the names of illustrious ones of our own sex – some of them sons of St. Andrew, too – Scott, Bruce, Burns, the warrior Wallace, Ben Nevis, the gifted Ben Lomond, and the great new Scotchman, Ben Disraeli.

Out of the great plains of history tower whole mountain ranges of sublime women – the Queen of Sheba, Josephine, Semiramis, Sairey Gamp; the list is endless. But I will not call the mighty roll – the names rise up in your own memories at the mere suggestion, luminous with the glory of deeds that cannot die, hallowed by the loving worship of the good and the true of all epochs and all climes.

Suffice it for our pride and our honor that we in our day have added to it such names as those of Grace Darling and Florence Nightingale.

Woman is all that she should be – gentle, patient, long-suffering, *trust*ful, unselfish, full of generous impulses. It is her blessed mission to comfort the sorrowing, plead for the erring, encourage the faint of purpose, succor the distressed, uplift the fallen, befriend the friendless – in a word, afford the healing of her sympathies and a home in her heart for all the bruised and persecuted children of misfortune that knock at its hospitable door. And when I say, God bless her, there is none here present who has known the ennobling affection of a wife, or the steadfast devotion of a mother but in his heart will say, Amen!

c. November 1873

THE TEMPERANCE
INSURRECTION

Hartford, U.S., March 12.

TO THE EDITOR.

SIR, – THE WOMEN'S crusade against the rumsellers continues. It began in an Ohio village early in the new year, and has now extended itself eastwardly to the Atlantic seaboard, 600 miles, and westwardly (at a bound, without stopping by the way), to San Francisco, about 2500 miles. It has also scattered itself along down the Ohio and Mississippi rivers southwardly some ten or twelve hundred miles. Indeed, it promises to sweep, eventually, the whole United States, with the exception of the little cluster of commonwealths which we call New England. Puritan New England is sedate, reflective, conservative, and very hard to inflame.

The method of the crusaders is singular. They contemn the use of force in the breaking up of the whisky traffic. They only assemble before a drinking shop, or within it, and sing hymns and pray, hour after hour – and day after day, if necessary – until the publican's business is broken up and he surrenders. This is not force, at least they do not consider it so. After the surrender the crusaders march back to head-quarters and proclaim the victory, and ascribe it to the powers above. They rejoice together awhile, and then go forth again in their strength and conquer another whisky shop with their prayers and hymns and their staying capacity (pardon the rudeness), and spread *that* victory upon the battle-flag of the powers above. In this generous way the crusaders have parted with the credit of not less than three thousand splendid triumphs, which some carping people say they gained their ownselves, without assistance from any quarter. If I am one of these, I am the humblest. If I seem to doubt that prayer is the agent that conquers these rumsellers, I do it honestly, and not in a flippant spirit. If the crusaders were to stay at home and pray for the rumseller and for his adoption of a better way of life, or if the crusaders even assembled together in a church and offered up such a prayer with a united voice, and it accomplished a victory, I would then feel that it was the praying that moved Heaven to do the miracle; for I believe that if the prayer is the agent that brings about the desired result, it cannot be necessary to pray the prayer in any particular place in order to get the ear, or move the grace, of the Deity. When the crusaders go and invest a whisky shop and fall to praying, one suspects that they are praying rather less to the Deity than *at* the rum-man. So I cannot help feeling (after carefully reading the details of the rum sieges) that as much as nine-tenths of the credit of each of the 3000 victories achieved thus far belongs of right to the crusaders themselves, and it grieves me to see them give it away with such spendthrift generosity.

I will not afflict you with statistics, but I desire to say just a word or two about the character of this crusade. The crusaders are young girls and women – not the inferior sort, but the very best in the village communities. The telegraph keeps the newspapers supplied with the progress of the war, and thus the praying infection spreads from town to town, day after day, week after week. When it attacks a community it seems to seize upon almost everybody in it at once. There is a meeting in a church, speeches are made, resolutions are passed, a purse for expenses is made up, a "praying band" is appointed; if it be a large town, half a dozen praying bands, each numbering as many as a hundred women, are appointed, and the working district of each band marked out. Then comes a grand assault in force, all along the line. Every stronghold of rum is invested; first one and then another champion ranges up before the proprietor, and offers up a special petition for him; he has to stand meekly there behind his bar, under the eyes of a great concourse of ladies who are better than he is and are aware of it, and hear all the secret iniquities of his business divulged to the angels above, accompanied by the sharp sting of wishes for his regeneration, which imply an amount of need for it which is in the last degree uncomfortable to him. If he holds out bravely, the crusaders hold out more bravely still – or at least more persistently; though I doubt if the grandeur of the performance would not be considerably heightened if one solitary crusader were to try praying at a hundred rumsellers in a body for a while, and see how it felt to have everybody against her instead of for her. If the man holds out the crusaders camp before his place and keep up the siege till they wear him out. In one case they besieged a rum shop two whole weeks. They built a shed before it and kept up the praying all night and all day long every day of the fortnight, and this in the bitterest winter weather too. They conquered.

You may ask if such an investment and such interference with a man's business (in cases where he is "protected" by a licence) is lawful? By no means. But the whole community being with the crusaders, the authorities have usually been overawed and afraid to execute the laws, the authorities being, in too many cases, mere little politicians, and more given to looking to chances of re-election than fearlessly discharging their duty according to the terms of their official oaths.

Would you consider the conduct of these crusaders justifiable? I do – thoroughly justifiable. They find themselves voiceless in the making of laws and the election of officers to execute them. Born with brains, born in the country, educated, having large interests at stake, they find their tongues tied and their hands fettered, while every ignorant whisky-drinking foreign-born savage in the land may hold office, help to make the laws, degrade the dignity of the former and break the latter at his own sweet will. They see their fathers, husbands, and brothers sit inanely at home and allow the scum of the country to assemble at the "primaries," name the candidates for office from their own vile ranks, and, unrebuked, elect them. They live in the midst of a country where there is no end to the laws and no beginning to the execution of them. And when the laws intended to protect their sons from destruction by intemperance lie torpid and without sign of life year after year, they recognise that here is a matter which interests them person-ally – a matter which comes straight home to them. And since they are allowed to lift no legal voice against the outrageous state of things they suffer under in this regard, I think it is no wonder that their patience has broken down at last, and they have contrived to persuade themselves that they are justifiable in breaking the law of trespass when the laws that should make the trespass needless are allowed by the voters to lie dead and inoperative.

I cannot help glorying in the pluck of these women, sad as it is to see them displaying themselves in these unwomanly ways; sad as it is to see them carrying their grace and their purity into places which should never know their presence; and sadder still as it is to see them trying to save a set of men who, it seems to me, there can be no reasonable object in saving. It does not become us to scoff at the crusaders, remembering what it is they have borne all these years, but it does become us to admire their heroism – a heroism that boldly faces jeers, curses, ribald language, obloquy of every kind and degree – in a word, every manner of thing that pure-hearted, pure-minded women such as these are naturally dread and shrink from, and remains steadfast through it all, undismayed, patient, hopeful, giving no quarter, asking none, determined to conquer, and succeeding. It is the same old superb spirit that animated that other devoted, magnificent, mistaken crusade of six hundred years ago. The sons of such women as these must surely be worth saving from the destroying power of rum.

The present crusade will doubtless do but little work against intemperance that will be really permanent, but it will do what is as much, or even more, to the purpose, I think. I think it will suggest to more than one man that if women could vote they would vote on the side of morality, even if they did vote and speak rather frantically and furiously; and it will also suggest that when the women once made up their minds that it was not good to leave the all-powerful "primaries" in the hands of loafers, thieves, and pernicious little politicians, they would not sit indolently at home as their husbands and brothers do now, but would hoist their praying banners, take the field in force, pray the assembled political scum back to the holes and slums where they belong, and set up some candidates fit for decent human beings to vote for.

I dearly want the women to be raised to the political altitude of the negro, the imported savage, and the pardoned thief, and allowed to vote. It is our last chance, I think. The women will be voting before long, and then if a B. F. Butler can still continue to lord it in Congress; if the highest offices in the land can still continue to be occupied by perjurers and robbers; if another Congress (like the forty-second) consisting of 15 honest men and 296 of the other kind can once more be created, it will at last be time, I fear, to give over trying to save the country by human means, and appeal to Providence. Both the great parties have failed. I wish we might have a woman's party now, and see how that would work. I feel persuaded that in extending the suffrage to women this country could lose absolutely nothing and might gain a great deal. For thirty centuries history has been iterating and reiterating that in a moral fight woman is simply dauntless, and we all know, even with our eyes shut upon Congress and our voters, that from the day that Adam ate of the apple and told on Eve down to the present day, man, in a moral fight, has pretty uniformly shown himself to be an arrant coward.

I will mention casually that while I cannot bring myself to find fault with the women whom we call the crusaders, since I feel that they, being politically fettered, have the natural right of the oppressed to rebel, I have a very different opinion about the clergy-men who have in a multitude of instances attached themselves to the movement, and by voice and act have countenanced and upheld the women in unlawfully trespassing upon whisky mills and interrupting the rumsellers' business. It seems to me that it would better become clergymen to teach their flocks to respect the laws of the land, and urge them to refrain from breaking them. But it is not a new thing for a thoroughly good and well-meaning preacher's soft heart to run away with his soft head.

MARK TWAIN
March 26, 1874

PETITION CONCERNING COPYRIGHT

TO THE HONORABLE THE SENATE AND HOUSE OF
REPRESENTATIVES IN CONGRESS ASSEMBLED:

Whereas, The Constitution guarantees equal rights to all, backed by the Declaration of Independence; and

Whereas, Under our laws, the right of property in real estate is perpetual; and

Whereas, Under our laws, the right of property in the literary result of a citizen's intellectual labor is restricted to forty-two years; and

Whereas, Forty-two years seems an exceedingly just and righteous term, and a sufficiently long one for the retention of property:

Therefore, Your petitioner, having the good of his country solely at heart, humbly prays that "equal rights" and fair and equal treatment may be meted out to all citizens, by the restriction of rights in *all* property, real estate included, to the beneficent term of forty-two years. Then shall all men bless your honorable body and be happy. And for this will your petitioner ever pray.

MARK TWAIN.

A PARAGRAPH NOT ADDED TO THE PETITION.

The charming absurdity of restricting property-rights in books to forty-two years sticks prominently out in the fact that hardly any man's books ever *live* forty-two years, or even the half of it; and so, for the sake of getting a shabby advantage of the heirs of about one Scott or Burns or Milton in a hundred years, the law makers of the "Great" Republic are content to leave that poor little pilfering edict upon the statute books. It is like an emperor lying in wait to rob a phenix's nest, and waiting the necessary century to get the chance.

1875

A LITERARY NIGHTMARE

WILL THE READER please to cast his eye over the following verses, and see if he can discover anything harmful in them?

> "Conductor, when you receive a fare,
> Punch in the presence of the passenjare!
> A blue trip slip for an eight-cent fare,
> A buff trip slip for a six-cent fare,
> A pink trip slip for a three-cent fare,
> Punch in the presence of the passenjare!
>
> CHORUS.
> Punch, brothers! punch with care!
> Punch in the presence of the passenjare!"

I came across these jingling rhymes in a newspaper, a little while ago, and read them a couple of times. They took instant and entire possession of me. All through breakfast they went waltzing through my brain; and when, at last, I rolled up my napkin, I could not tell whether I had eaten anything or not. I had carefully laid out my day's work the day before – a thrilling tragedy in the novel which I am writing. I went to my den to begin my deed of blood. I took up my pen, but all I could get it to say was, "Punch in the presence of the passenjare." I fought hard for an hour, but it was useless. My head kept humming, "A blue trip slip for an eight-cent fare, a buff trip slip for a six-cent fare," and so on and so on, without peace or respite. The day's work was ruined – I could see that plainly enough. I gave up and drifted down town, and presently discovered that my feet were keeping time to that relentless jingle. When I could stand it no longer I altered my step. But it did no good; those rhymes accommodated themselves to the new step and went on harassing me just as before. I returned home, and suffered all the afternoon; suffered all through an unconscious and unrefreshing dinner; suffered, and cried, and jingled all through the evening; went to bed and rolled, tossed, and jingled right along, the same as ever; got up at midnight frantic, and tried to read; but there was nothing visible upon the whirling page except "Punch! punch in the presence of the passenjare." By sunrise I was out of my mind, and everybody marveled and was distressed at the idiotic burden of my ravings, – "Punch! oh, punch! punch in the presence of the passenjare!"

Two days later, on Saturday morning, I arose, a tottering wreck, and went forth to fulfill an engagement with a valued friend, the Rev. Mr.——, to walk to the Talcott Tower, ten miles distant. He stared at me, but asked no questions. We started. Mr.—— talked, talked, talked – as is his wont. I said nothing; I heard nothing. At the end of a mile, Mr.—— said, –

"Mark, are you sick? I never saw a man look so haggard and worn and absent-minded. Say something; do!"

Drearily, without enthusiasm, I said: "Punch, brothers, punch with care! Punch in the presence of the passenjare!"

My friend eyed me blankly, looked perplexed, then said, –

"I do not think I get your drift, Mark. There does not seem to be any relevancy in what you have said, certainly nothing sad; and yet – maybe it was the way you *said* the words – I never heard anything that sounded so pathetic. What is" –

But I heard no more. I was already far away with my pitiless, heart-breaking "blue trip slip for an eight-cent fare, buff trip slip for a six-cent fare, pink trip slip for a three-cent fare; punch in the presence of the passenjare." I do not know what occurred during the other nine miles. However, all of a sudden Mr.—— laid his hand on my shoulder and shouted, –

"Oh, wake up! wake up! wake up! Don't sleep all day! Here we are at the Tower, man! I have talked myself deaf and dumb and blind, and never got a response. Just look at this magnificent autumn landscape! Look at it! look at it! Feast your eyes on it! You have traveled; you have seen boasted landscapes elsewhere. Come, now, deliver an honest opinion. What do you say to this?"

I sighed wearily, and murmured, –

"A buff trip slip for a six-cent fare, a pink trip slip for a three-cent fare, punch in the presence of the passenjare."

Rev. Mr.—— stood there, very grave, full of concern, apparently, and looked long at me; then he said, –

"Mark, there is something about this that I cannot understand. Those are about the same words you said before; there does not seem to be anything in them, and yet they nearly break my heart when you say them. Punch in the – how is it they go?"

I began at the beginning and repeated all the lines. My friend's face lighted with interest. He said, –

"Why, what a captivating jingle it is! It is almost music. It flows along so nicely. I have nearly caught the rhymes myself. Say them over just once more, and then I'll have them, sure."

I said them over. Then Mr.—— said them. He made one little mistake, which I corrected. The next time and the next he got them right. Now a great burden seemed to tumble from my shoulders. That torturing jingle departed out of my brain, and a grateful sense of rest and peace descended upon me. I was light-hearted enough to sing; and I did sing for half an hour, straight along, as we went jogging homeward. Then my freed tongue found blessed speech again, and the pent talk of many a weary hour began to gush and flow. It flowed on and on, joyously, jubilantly, until the fountain was empty and dry. As I wrung my friend's hand at parting, I said, –

"Have n't we had a royal good time! But now I remember, you have n't said a word for two hours. Come, come, out with something!"

The Rev. Mr.—— turned a lacklustre eye upon me, drew a deep sigh, and said, without animation, without apparent consciousness, –

"Punch, brothers, punch with care! Punch in the presence of the passenjare!"

A pang shot through me as I said to myself, "Poor fellow, poor fellow! *he* has got it, now."

I did not see Mr.—— for two or three days after that. Then, on Tuesday evening, he staggered into my presence and sank dejectedly into a seat. He was pale, worn; he was a wreck. He lifted his faded eyes to my face and said, –

"Ah, Mark, it was a ruinous investment that I made in those heartless rhymes. They have ridden me like a nightmare, day and night, hour after hour, to this very moment. Since I saw you I have suffered the torments of the lost. Saturday evening I had a sudden call, by telegraph, and took the night train for Boston. The occasion was the death of a valued old friend who had requested that I should preach his funeral sermon. I took my seat in the cars and set myself to framing the discourse. But I never got beyond the opening paragraph; for then the train started and the car-wheels began their 'clack-clack-clack-clack! clack-clack-clack-clack!' and right away those odious rhymes fitted themselves to that accompaniment. For an hour I sat there and set a syllable of those rhymes to every separate and distinct clack the car-wheels made. Why, I was as fagged out, then, as if I had been chopping wood all day. My skull was splitting with headache. It seemed to me that I must go mad if I sat there any longer; so I undressed and went to bed.

I stretched myself out in my berth, and – well, you know what the result was. The thing went right along, just the same. 'Clack-clack-clack, a blue trip slip, clack-clack-clack; for an eight-cent fare; clack-clack-clack, a buff trip slip, clack-clack-clack, for a six-cent fare, and so on, and so on, and so on – *punch*, in the presence of the passenjare!' Sleep? Not a single wink! I was almost a lunatic when I got to Boston. Don't ask me about the funeral. I did the best I could, but every solemn individual sentence was meshed and tangled and woven in and out with 'Punch, brothers, punch with care, punch in the presence of the passenjare.' And the most distressing thing was that my *delivery* dropped into the undulating rhythm of those pulsing rhymes, and I could actually catch absent-minded people nodding *time* to the swing of it with their stupid heads. And, Mark, you may believe it or not, but before I got through, the entire assemblage were placidly bobbing their heads in solemn unison, mourners, undertaker, and all. The moment I had finished, I fled to the anteroom in a state bordering on frenzy. Of course it would be my luck to find a sorrowing and aged maiden aunt of the deceased there, who had arrived from Springfield too late to get into the church. She began to sob, and said, –

"'Oh, oh, he is gone, he is gone, and I did n't see him before he died!'

"'Yes!' I said, 'he *is* gone, he *is* gone, he *is* gone – oh, *will* this suffering never cease!'

"'*You* loved him, then! Oh, you too loved him!'

"'Loved him! Loved *who*?'

"'Why, my poor George! my poor nephew!'

"'Oh – *him!* Yes – oh, yes, yes. Certainly – certainly. Punch – punch – oh, this misery will kill me!'

"'Bless you! bless you, sir, for these sweet words! *I*, too, suffer in this dear loss. Were you present during his last moments?'

"'Yes! I – *whose* last moments?'

"'*His.* The dear departed's.'

"'Yes! Oh, yes – yes – *yes!* I suppose so, I think so, *I* don't know! Oh, certainly – I was there – *I* was there!'

"'Oh, what a privilege! what a precious privilege! And his last words – oh, tell me, tell me his last words! What did he say?'

'He said – he said – oh, my head, my head, my head! He said – he said – he never said anything but Punch, punch, *punch* in the presence of the passenjare! Oh, leave me, madam! In the name of all that is generous, leave me to my madness, my misery, my despair! – a buff trip slip for a six-cent fare, a pink trip slip for a three-cent fare – endu-rance *can* no fur-ther go! – PUNCH in the presence of the passenjare!' "

My friend's hopeless eyes rested upon mine a pregnant minute, and then he said impressively, –

"Mark, you do not say anything. You do not offer me any hope. But, ah me, it is just as well – it is just as well. You could not do me any good. The time has long gone by when words could comfort me. Something tells me that my tongue is doomed to wag forever to the jigger of that remorseless jingle. There – there it is coming on me again: a blue trip slip for an eight-cent fare, a buff trip slip for a" –

Thus murmuring faint and fainter, my friend sank into a peaceful trance and forgot his sufferings in a blessed respite.

How did I finally save him from the asylum? I took him to a neighboring university and made him discharge the burden of his persecuting rhymes into the eager ears of the poor, unthinking students. How is it with *them*, now? The result is too sad to tell. Why did I write this article? It was for a worthy, even a noble, purpose. It was to warn you, reader, if you should come across those merciless rhymes, to avoid them – avoid them as you would a pestilence!

February 1876

THE OLDEST INHABITANT – THE
WEATHER OF NEW ENGLAND

Seventy-first Annual Dinner, New England Society of New York

> Who can lose it and forget it?
> Who can have it and regret it?
> Be interposer 'twixt us *Twain*.
> *Merchant of Venice*

GENTLEMEN: I REVERENTLY believe that the Maker who made us all, makes everything in New England – but the weather. I don't know who makes that, but I think it must be raw apprentices in the Weather Clerk's factory, who experiment and learn how in New England, for board and clothes, and then are promoted to make weather for countries that require a good article, and will take their custom elsewhere if they don't get it. There is a sumptuous variety about the New England weather that compels the stranger's admiration – and regret. The weather is always doing something there; always attending strictly to business; always getting up new designs and trying them on the people to see how they will go. But it gets through more business in spring than in any other season. In the spring I have counted one hundred and thirty-six different kinds of weather inside of four and twenty hours. It was I that made the fame and fortune of that man that had that marvelous collection of weather on exhibition at the Centennial that so astounded the foreigners. He was going to travel all over the world and get specimens from all the climes. I said, "Don't you do it; you come to New England on a favorable spring day." I told him what we could do, in the way of style, variety, and quantity. Well, he came, and he made his collection in four days. As to variety – why, he confessed that he got hundreds of kinds of weather that he had never heard of before. And as to quantity – well, after he had picked out, and discarded all that was blemished in any way, he not only had weather enough, but weather to spare; weather to hire out; weather to sell; to deposit; weather to invest; weather to give to the poor.

The people of New England are by nature patient and forbearing; but there are some things which they will not stand. Every year they kill a lot of poets for writing about "Beautiful Spring." These are generally casual visitors, who bring their notions of spring from somewhere else, and cannot, of course, know how the natives feel about spring. And so, the first thing they know, the opportunity to inquire how they feel has permanently gone by.

Old Probabilities has a mighty reputation for accurate prophecy, and thoroughly well deserves it. You take up the papers and observe how crisply and confidently he checks off what today's weather is going to be on the Pacific, down South, in the Middle States, in the Wisconsin region; see him sail along in the joy and pride of his power till he gets to New England, and then – see his tail drop. *He* doesn't know what the weather is going to be like in New England. He can't any more tell than he can tell how many Presidents of the United States there's going to be next year. Well, he mulls over it, and by and by he gets out something about like this: Probable nor'-east to sou'-west winds, varying to the southard and westard and eastard and points between; high and low barometer, swapping around from place to place; probable areas of rain, snow, hail, and drought, succeeded or preceded by earthquakes, with thunder and lightning. Then he jots down this postscript from his wandering mind, to cover accidents: "But it is possible that the program may be wholly changed in the meantime."

Yes, one of the brightest gems in the New England weather is the dazzling uncertainty of it. There is only one thing certain about it, you are certain there is going to be plenty of weather – a perfect grand review; but you never can tell which end of the procession is going to move first. You fix up for the drought; you leave your umbrella in the house and sally out with your sprinkling pot, and ten to one you get drowned. You make up your mind that the earthquake is due, you stand from under, and take hold of something to steady yourself, and the first thing you know, you get struck by lightning. These are great disappointments. But they can't be helped. The lightning there is peculiar; it is so convincing! When it strikes a thing, it doesn't leave enough of that thing behind for you to tell whether – well, you'd think it was something valuable, and a Congressman had been there.

And the thunder. When the thunder commences to merely tune up, and scrape, and saw, and key up the instruments for the performance, strangers say, "Why, what awful thunder you have here!" But when the baton is raised and the real concert begins, you'll find that stranger down in the cellar, with his head in the ash barrel.

Now, as to the *size* of the weather in New England – lengthways,

I mean. It is utterly disproportioned to the size of that little country. Half the time, when it is packed as full as it can stick, you will see that New England weather sticking out beyond the edges and projecting around hundreds and hundreds of miles over the neighboring states. She can't hold a tenth part of her weather. You can see cracks all about, where she has strained herself trying to do it.

I could speak volumes about the inhuman perversity of the New England weather, but I will give but a single specimen. I like to hear rain on a tin roof, so I covered part of my roof with tin, with an eye to that luxury. Well, sir, do you think it ever rains on the tin? No, sir; skips it every time.

Mind, in this speech I have been trying merely to do honor to the New England weather – no language could do it justice. But, after all, there are at least one or two things about that weather (or, if you please, effects produced by it) which we residents would not like to part with. If we hadn't our bewitching autumn foliage, we should still have to credit the weather with one feature which compensates for all its bullying vagaries – the ice storm – when a leafless tree is clothed with ice from the bottom to the top – ice that is as bright and clear as crystal; when every bough and twig is strung with ice beads, frozen dewdrops, and the whole tree sparkles, cold and white, like the Shah of Persia's diamond plume. Then the wind waves the branches, and the sun comes out and turns all those myriads of beads and drops to prisms, that glow and burn and flash with all manner of colored fires, which change and change again, with inconceivable rapidity, from blue to red, from red to green, and green to gold – the tree becomes a spraying fountain, a very explosion of dazzling jewels; and it stands there the acme, the climax, the supremest possibility in art or nature, of bewildering, intoxicating, intolerable magnificence! One cannot make the words too strong.

Month after month I lay up my hate and grudge against the New England weather; but when the ice storm comes at last, I say: "There – I forgive you, now – the books are square between us, you don't owe me a cent; go, and sin no more; your little faults and foibles count for nothing – you are the most enchanting weather in the world!"

December 22, 1876

FAREWELL BANQUET FOR BAYARD TAYLOR

Dinner Speech, Delmonico's, New York

MR. CHAIRMAN: I had intended to make an address of some length here tonight, and in fact wrote out an impromptu speech, but have had no time to memorize it. I cannot make a speech on the moment, and therefore being unprepared I am silent and undone. However, I will say this much for the speech that I had written out – that it was a very good one and I gave it away as I had no further use for it, and saw that I could not deliver it. Therefore I will ask the indulgence of the company here to let me retire without speaking. I will make my compliments to our honored friend, Mr. Taylor, but I will make them on board ship where I shall be a fellow passenger.

[The following is the speech Mark Twain had prepared.]

I have been warned – as, no doubt, have all among you that are inexperienced – that a dinner to our Ambassador is an occasion which demands, and even requires, a peculiar caution and delicacy in the handling of the dangerous weapon of speech. I have been warned to avoid all mention of international politics, and all criticisms, however mild, of countries with which we are at peace, lest such utterances embarrass our minister and our government in their dealings with foreign states. In a word, I have been cautioned to talk, but be careful not to say anything. I do not consider this a difficult task.

Now, it has often occurred to me that the conditions under which we live at the present day, with the revelations of geology all about us, viewing, upon the one hand, the majestic configurations of the silurian, oolitic, old red sandstone periods, and, upon the other, the affiliations, and stratifications, and ramifications of the prehistoric, post-pliocene, antepenultimate epochs, we are stricken dumb with amazed surprise, and can only lift up our hands and say with that wise but odious Frenchman: "It was a slip of the tongue, sir, and wholly unintentional – entirely unintentional." It would ill become me, upon an occasion like this, purposely to speak slightingly of a citizen of a country with whom we are at peace – and especially great and gracious France, whom God preserve! The subject, however, is a delicate one, and I will not pursue it.

But – as I was about to remark – cast your eye abroad, sir, for one pregnant moment over the vista which looms before you in the mighty domain of intellectual progression and contemplate the awe-compelling theory of the descent of man! Development, sir! Development! Natural selection! Correlation of the sexes! Spontaneous combustion! – what gulfs and whirlwinds of intellectual stimulus these magic words fling upon the burning canvas of the material universe of soul! Across the chasm of the ages we take the oyster by the hand and call him brother; and back, and still further back, we go, and breathe the germ we cannot see, and know, in him, our truer Adam! And as we stand, dazed, transfixed, exalted, and gaze down the long procession of life, marking how steadily, how symmetrically we have ascended, step by step, to our sublime estate and dignity of humanity – out of one lowly form into a little higher and a little higher forms – adding grace after every change – developing from tadpoles into frogs, frogs into fishes, fishes into birds, birds into reptiles, reptiles into Russians – I beg a million pardons, sir and gentlemen – it was a wholly innocent slip of the tongue, and due only to the excitement of debate – for far be it from me, on such an occasion as this, to cast a seeming slur upon a great nation with which we are at peace – a great and noble and Christian nation – whom God expand!

But, as I was about to remark, I maintain – and nothing can ever drive me from that position – that the contributions of the nineteenth century to science and the industrial arts are – are – but, of course they are. There is no need to dwell upon that. You look at it yourself. Look at steam! Look at the steamboat, look at the railway, look at the steamship! Look at the telegraph, which enables you to flash your thoughts from world to world, ignoring intervening seas. Look at the telephone, which enables you to speak into affection's remote ear the word that cheers, and into the ear of the foe the opinion which you ought not to risk at shorter range. Look at the sewing machine, look at the foghorn, look at the bell punch, look at the book agent. And, more than all, a thousand times, look at the last and greatest, the aerophone, which will enable Moody and Sankey to stand on the tallest summit of the Rocky Mountains and deliver their message to listening America! – and necessarily it will annul and do away with the pernicious custom of taking up a collection. Look at all these things, sir, and say if it is not a far prouder and more precious boon to have been born in the nineteenth century than in any century that went before it. Ah, sir, clothed with the all-sufficient grandeur of citizenship in the nineteenth century, even the wild and arid New Jerseyman might – a mistake, sir, a mistake, and entirely unintentional. Of all the kingdoms, principalities and countries with which it is our privilege to hold peaceful relations, I regard New Jersey as dearest to our admiration, nearest to our heart, the wisest and the purest among the nations. I retire the undiplomatic language, and beg your sympathy and indulgence.

But, as I was about to remark, it has always seemed to me – that is, of course, since I reached a reasoning age – that this much agitated question of future rewards and punishments was one upon which honest and sincere differences of opinion might exist; one individual, with more or less justice, leaning to the radical side of it, whilst another with apparently equal justice, but with infinitely more common sense, more intelligence, more justification, leans to a bitter and remorseless detestation of the pitiless Prince of Perdition – a slip of the tongue, I do sincerely assure you – I beg you to let me withdraw that unintentional slur upon the character of that great and excellent personage with whom and whose country we are upon the closest and warmest terms, and who – it is no use, sir, I will sit down; I don't seem to have any knack at a diplomatic speech. I have probably compromised the country enough for the present.

Nonsense aside, sir, I am most sincerely glad to assist at this public expression of appreciation of Mr. Taylor's character, scholarship, and distinguished literary service. I am sure he was not merely one of the fittest men we had for the place, but the fittest. In so honoring him, our country has conspicuously honored herself.

April 4, 1878

THE BABIES. AS THEY COMFORT US IN OUR SORROWS, LET US NOT FORGET THEM IN OUR FESTIVITIES

Thirteenth Reunion Banquet, Army of the Tennessee, Chicago

I LIKE THAT. We haven't all had the good fortune to be ladies; we haven't all been generals, or poets, or statesmen; but when the toast works down to the babies, we stand on common ground, for we've all been babies. It is a shame that for a thousand years the world's banquets have utterly ignored the baby – as if *he* didn't amount to anything! If you gentlemen will stop and think a minute – if you will go back fifty or a hundred years, to your early married life, and recontemplate your first baby, you will remember that he amounted to a good deal, and even something over. You soldiers all know that when that little fellow arrived at family headquarters, you had to hand in your resignation. He took entire command. You became his lackey – his mere body servant, and you had to stand around, too. He was not a commander who made allowances for time, distance, weather, or anything else – you had to execute his order whether it was possible or not. And there was only one form of marching in his manual of tactics, and that was the double-quick. He treated you with every sort of insolence and disrespect, and the bravest of you didn't dare to say a word.

You could face the death storm at Donelson and Vicksburg, and give back blow for blow; but when he clawed your whiskers, and pulled your hair, and twisted your nose, you had to take it. When the thunders of war were sounding in your ears, you set your face toward the batteries, and advanced with steady tread; but, when he turned on the terrors of his war whoop, you advanced in the other direction – and mighty glad of the chance, too. When he called for soothing syrup, did you venture to throw out any side remarks about certain services being unbecoming an officer and a gentleman? No. You got up and *got* it. When he ordered his pap bottle, and it wasn't warm, did you talk back? Not you. You went to work and *warmed* it. You even descended so far in your menial office as to take a suck at that warm, insipid stuff yourself, just to see if it was right – three parts water to one of milk, a touch of sugar to modify the colic, and a drop of peppermint to kill those infernal hiccups. I can taste that stuff yet.

And how many things you learned, as you went along! Sentimental young folks still take stock in that beautiful old saying that when the baby smiles in his sleep, it is because angels are whispering to him. Very pretty, but too thin – simply wind on the stomach, my friends! If the baby proposed to take a walk at the usual hour – half-past two in the morning – didn't you rise up promptly and remark – with a mental addition which wouldn't improve a Sunday school book *much* – that that was the very thing you were about to propose yourself? Oh, you were under good discipline. And as you went fluttering up and down the room in your undress uniform, you not only prattled undignified baby talk, but even turned up your martial voices and tried to *sing*! – "Rock-a-by baby in the tree top," for instance. And what an affliction for the neighbors, too – for it isn't everybody within a mile around that likes military music at three in the morning. And when you had been keeping this sort of thing up two or three hours, and your little velvet-head intimated that nothing suited him like exercise and noise, and proposed to fight it out on that line if it took all night – what did you do? [When Mark Twain paused, voices shouted: "Go on!"] You simply *went* on till you dropped in the last ditch.

The idea that a *baby* doesn't amount to anything! Why, *one* baby is just a house and front yard full by itself. *One* baby can furnish more business than you and your whole Interior Department can attend to. He is enterprising, irrepressible, brim full of lawless activities. Do what you please, you can't make him stay on the reservation. Sufficient unto the day is one baby – as long as you are in your right mind don't you ever pray for twins. Twins amount to a permanent riot; and there ain't any real difference between triplets and an insurrection.

Yes, it was high time for a toastmaster to recognize the importance of the babies. Think what is in store for the present crop! Fifty years from now we shall all be dead – I trust – and then this flag, if it still survive – and let us hope it may – will be floating over a Republic numbering 200,000,000 souls, according to the settled laws of our increase; our present schooner of State will have grown into a political leviathan – a *Great Eastern* – and the cradled babies of today will be on deck. Let them be well trained, for we are going to leave a big contract on their hands. Among the three or four million cradles now rocking in the land are some which this nation would preserve for ages as sacred things, if we could know which ones they are. In one of these cradles the unconscious Farragut of the future is at this moment *teething* – think of it! – and putting in a world of dead earnest, unarticulated and perfectly justifiable profanity over it, too; in another, the future renowned astronomer is blinking at the shining Milky Way, with but a languid interest – poor little chap! – and wondering what has become of that other one they call the wet nurse; in another the future great historian is lying – and doubtless he will continue to lie until his earthly mission is ended; in another the future President is busying himself with no profounder problem of state than what the mischief has become of his hair so early, and in a mighty array of other cradles there are now some sixty thousand future office-seekers getting ready to furnish him occasion to grapple with that same old problem a second time.

And in still one more cradle, somewhere under the flag, the future illustrious Commander in Chief of the American armies is so little burdened with his approaching grandeurs and responsibilities as to be giving his whole strategic mind, at this moment, to trying to find out some way to get his own big toe into his mouth – an achievement which, meaning no disrespect, the illustrious guest of this evening turned *his* whole attention to some fifty-six years ago. And if the child is but a prophecy of the man, there are mighty few who will doubt that he *succeeded*.

November 13, 1879

A TELEPHONIC CONVERSATION

I CONSIDER THAT a conversation by telephone – when you are simply sitting by and not taking any part in that conversation – is one of the solemnest curiosities of this modern life. Yesterday I was writing a deep article on a sublime philosophical subject while such a conversation was going on in the room. I notice that one can always write best when somebody is talking through a telephone close by. Well, the thing began in this way. A member of our household came in and asked me to have our house put into communication with Mr. Bagley's, down town. I have observed, in many cities, that the sex always shrink from calling up the central office themselves. I don't know why, but they do. So I touched the bell, and this talk ensued: –

   Central Office.   [Gruffly.] Hello!

   I.   Is it the Central Office?

   C. O.   Of course it is. What do you want?

   I.   Will you switch me on to the Bagleys, please?

   C. O.   All right. Just keep your ear to the telephone.

   Then I heard, *k-look, k-look, k'look – klook-klook-klook-look-look!* then a horrible "gritting" of teeth, and finally a piping female voice: Y-e-s? [Rising inflection.] Did you wish to speak to me?

Without answering, I handed the telephone to the applicant, and sat down. Then followed that queerest of all the queer things in this world, – a conversation with only one end to it. You hear questions asked; you don't hear the answer. You hear invitations given; you hear no thanks in return. You have listening pauses of dead silence, followed by apparently irrelevant and unjustifiable exclamations of glad surprise, or sorrow, or dismay. You can't make head or tail of the talk, because you never hear anything that the person at the other end of the wire says. Well, I heard the following remarkable series of observations, all from the one tongue, and all shouted, – for you can't ever persuade the sex to speak gently into a telephone: –

Yes? Why, how did *that* happen?

Pause.

What did you say?

Pause.

Oh, no, I don't think it was.

Pause.

No! Oh, no, I did n't mean *that*. I meant, put it in while it is still boiling, – or just before it *comes* to a boil.

Pause.

WHAT?

Pause.

I turned it over with a back stitch on the selvage edge.

Pause.

Yes, I like that way, too; but I think it's better to baste it on with Valenciennes or bombazine, or something of that sort. It gives it such an air, – and attracts so much notice.

Pause.

It's forty-ninth Deuteronomy, sixty-fourth to ninety-seventh inclusive. I think we ought all to read it often.

Pause.

Perhaps so; I generally use a hair-pin.

Pause.

What did you say? [*Aside*] Children, do be quiet!

Pause.

Oh! B *flat!* Dear me, I thought you said it was the cat!

Pause.

Since *when*?

Pause.

Why, *I* never heard of it.

Pause.

You astound me! It seems utterly impossible!

Pause.

Who did?

Pause.

Good-ness gracious!

Pause.

Well, what *is* this world coming to? Was it right in *church*?

Pause.

And was her *mother* there?

Pause.

Why, Mrs Bagley, I should have died of humiliation! What did they *do*?

Long pause.

I can't be perfectly sure, because I have n't the notes by me; but I think it goes something like this: te-rolly-loll-loll, loll lolly-loll-loll, O tolly-loll-loll-*lee-ly-li-i*-do! And then *repeat*, you know.

Pause.

Yes, I think it *is* very sweet, – and very solemn and impressive, if you get the andantino and the pianissimo right.

Pause.

Oh, gum-drops, gum-drops! But I never allow them to eat striped candy. And of course they *can't*, till they get their teeth, any way.

Pause.

What?

Pause.

Oh, not in the least, – go right on. He's here writing, – it does n't bother *him*.

Pause.

Very well, I 'll come if I can. [*Aside.*] Dear me, how it does tire a person's arm to hold this thing up so long! I wish she'd –

Pause.

Oh, no, not at all; I *like* to talk, – but I'm afraid I'm keeping you from your affairs.

Pause.

Visitors?

Pause.

No, we never use butter on them.

Pause.

Yes, that is a very good way; but all the cook-books say they are very unhealthy when they are out of season. And *he* does n't like them, any way, – especially canned.

Pause.

Oh, I think that is too high for them; we have never paid over fifty cents a bunch.

Pause.

Must you go? Well, *good*-by.

Pause.

Yes, I think so. *Good*-by.

Pause.

Four o'clock, then – I 'll be ready. *Good*-by.

Pause.

Thank you ever so much. *Good*-by.

Pause.

Oh, not at all! – just as fresh – Which? Oh, I'm glad to hear you say that. *Good*-by.

[Hangs up the telephone and says, "Oh, it *does* tire a person's arm so!"]

A man delivers a single brutal "Good-by," and that is the end of it. Not so with the gentle sex, – I say it in their praise; they cannot abide abruptness.

June 1880

REPLY TO A BOSTON GIRL

This note comes to me from the home of culture: –

> DEAR MR——: Your writings interest me very much; but I cannot help wishing you would not place adverbs between the particle and verb in the Infinitive. For example: "to *even* realize," "to *mysteriously* disappear" "to *wholly* do away." You should say, *even* to realize; to disappear mysteriously, etc. "rose up" is another mistake – tautology, you know. Yours truly
>
> A BOSTON GIRL.

I PRINT THE note just as it was written, for one or two reasons: (1.) It flatters a superstition of mine that a person may learn to excel in only such details of an art as take a particularly strong hold upon his native predilections or instincts. (2.) It flatters another superstition of mine that whilst all the details of that art may be of equal importance *he* cannot be made to feel that it is so. Possibly he may be made to *see* it, through argument and illustration; but that will be of small value to him except he *feel* it, also. Culture would be able to make him feel it by and by, no doubt, but never very sharply, I think. Now I have certain instincts, and I wholly lack certain others. (Is that "wholly" in the right place?) For instance, I am dead to adverbs; they cannot excite me. To misplace an adverb is a thing which I am able to do with frozen indifference; it can never give me a pang. But when my young lady puts no point after "Mr.;" when she begins "adverb," "verb," and "particle" with the small letter, and aggrandizes "Infinitive" with a capital; and when she puts no comma after "to mysteriously disappear," etc., I am troubled; and when she begins a sentence with a small letter I even *suffer*. Or I suffer, *even*, – I do not know which it is; but she will, because the adverb is in her line, whereas only those minor matters are in mine. Mark these prophetic words: though this young lady's grammar be as the drifted snow for purity, she will never, never, never learn to punctuate while she lives; this is her demon, the adverb is mine. I thank her, honestly and kindly, for her lesson, but I know thoroughly well that I shall never be able to get it into my head. Mind, I do not say I shall not be able to make it *stay* there; I say and mean that I am not capable of *getting it into* my head. There are subtleties which I cannot master at all, – they confuse me, they mean absolutely nothing to me, – and this adverb plague is one of them.

We all have our limitations in the matter of grammar, I suppose. I have never seen a book which had no grammatical defects in it. This leads me to believe that all people have my infirmity, and are afflicted with an inborn inability to feel or mind certain sorts of grammatical particularities. There are people who were not born to spell; these can never be taught to spell correctly. The enviable ones among them are those who do not take the trouble to care whether they spell well or not, – though in truth these latter are absurdly scarce. I have been a correct speller, always; but it is a low accomplishment, and not a thing to be vain of. Why should one take pride in spelling a word rightly when he knows he is spelling it wrongly? *Though* is the right way to spell "though," but it is not *the* right way to spell it. Do I make myself understood?

Some people were not born to punctuate; these cannot learn the art. They can learn only a rude fashion of it; they cannot attain to its niceties, for these must be *felt*; they cannot be reasoned out. Cast-iron rules will not answer, here, any way; what is one man's comma is another man's colon. One man can't punctuate another man's manuscript any more than one person can make the gestures for another person's speech.

What is known as "dialect" writing looks simple and easy, but it is not. It is exceedingly difficult; it has rarely been done well. A man not born to write dialect cannot learn how to write it correctly. It is a gift. Mr. Harte can write a delightful story; he can *reproduce* Californian scenery so that you see it before you, and hear the sounds and smell the fragrances and feel the influences that go with it and belong to it; he can describe the miner and the gambler perfectly,– as to gait and look and garb; but no human being, living or dead, ever had experience of the dialect which he puts into his people's mouths. Mr. Harte's originality is not questioned; but if it ever shall be, the caviler will have to keep his hands off that dialect, for that *is* original. Mind, I am not objecting to its use; I am not saying its inaccuracy is a fatal blemish. No, it is Mr. Harte's adverb; let him do as he pleases with it; he can no more mend it than I can mine; neither will any but Boston Girls ever be likely to find us out.

Yes, there are things which we cannot learn, and there is no use in fretting about it. I cannot learn adverbs; and what is more I won't. If I try to seat a person at my right hand, I have no trouble, provided I am facing north at the time; but if I am facing south, I get him on my left, sure. As this thing was born in me, and cannot be educated out of me, I do not worry over it or care about it. A gentleman picked me up, last week, and brought me home in his buggy; he drove past the door, and as he approached the circular turn I saw he meant to go around to the left; I was on his left, – that is, I *think* I was, but I have got it all mixed up again in my head; at any rate, I halted him, and asked him to go round the circle the other way. He backed his horse a length or two, put his helm down and "slewed" him to the right, then "came ahead on him," and made the trip. As I got out at the door, he looked puzzled, and asked why I had particularly wanted to pass to the right around the circle. I said, "Because that would bring me next the door coming back, and I would n't have to crowd past your knees." He came near laughing his store teeth out, and said it was all the same whether we drove to the right or to the left in going around the circle; either would bring me back to the house on the side the door was on, since I was on the opposite side when I first approached the circle. I regarded this as false. He was willing to illustrate: so he drove me down to the gate and into the street, turned and drove back past the house, moved leftward around the circle, and brought me back to the door; and as sure as I am sitting here I *was* on the side next the door. I did not believe he could do it again, but he did. He did it eleven times hand running. Was I convinced? No. I was not *capable* of being convinced – *all through*. My sight and intellect (to call it by that name) were convinced, but not my *feeling*. It is simply another case of adverb. It is a piece of dead-corpsy knowledge, which is of no use to me, because I merely *know* it, but do not *understand* it.

The fact is, as the poet has said, we are all fools. The difference is simply in the degree. The mercury in some of the fool-thermometers stands at ten, fifteen, twenty, thirty, and so on; in some it gets up to seventy-five; in some it soars to ninety-nine. I never examine mine, – take no interest in it.

Now as to "rose up." That strikes me as quite a good form; I will use it some more, – that is, when I speak of a person, and wish to signify the full upright position. If I mean less, I will qualify, by saying he rose partly up. It is a form that will answer for the moon sometimes, too. I think it is Bingen on the Rhine who says –

> "The pale moon rose up slowly, and calmly she
>   looked down,
> On the red sands," etc.

But tautology cannot scare me, any way. Conversation would be intolerably stiff and formal without it; and a mild form of it can limber up even printed matter without doing it serious damage. Some folks are so afraid of a little repetition that they make their meaning vague, when they could just as well make it clear, if only their ogre were out of the way.

Talking of Unlearnable Things, would it be genteel, would it be polite, to ask members of this Club to confess what freightage of this sort they carry? Some of the revelations would be curious and instructive, I think. I am acquainted with one member of it who has never been able to learn nine times eight; he always says, "Nine times seven are sixty-three," – then counts the rest on his fingers. He is at home in the balance of the multiplication-table. I am acquainted with another member, who, although he has known for many years that when Monday is the first of the month the following Monday will be the eighth, has never been able to *feel* the fact; so he cannot trust it, but always counts on his fingers, to make sure. I have known people who could spell all words correctly but one. They never could get the upper hand of that one; yet as a rule it was some simple, common affair, such as a cat could spell, if a cat could spell at all. I have a friend who has kept his razors in the top drawer and his strop in the bottom drawer for years; when he wants his razors, he always pulls out the bottom drawer – and swears. Change? Could one imagine he never thought of that? He did change; he has changed a dozen times. It did n't do any good; his afflicted mind was able to keep up with the changes and make the proper mistake every time. I knew a man –

June 1880

DINNER SPEECH IN MONTREAL

Dinner for Mark Twain, Windsor Hotel, Montreal

THAT A BANQUET should be given to me in this ostensibly foreign land and in this great city, and that my ears should be greeted by such complimentary words from such distinguished lips, are eminent surprises to me; and I will not conceal the fact that they are also deeply gratifying. I thank you one and all, gentlemen, for these marks of favor and friendliness; and even if I have not really or sufficiently deserved them, I assure you that I do not any the less keenly enjoy and esteem them on that account.

When a stranger appears abruptly in a country, without any apparent business there, and at an unusual season of the year, the judicious thing for him to do is to explain. This seems peculiarly necessary in my case, on account of a series of unfortunate happenings here, which followed my arrival, and which I suppose the public have felt compelled to connect with that circumstance. I would most gladly explain if I could; but I have nothing for my defense but my bare word; so I simply declare, in all sincerity, and with my hand on my heart, that I never heard of that diamond robbery till I saw it in the morning paper; and I can say with perfect truth that I never saw that box of dynamite till the police came to inquire of me if I had any more of it. These are mere assertions, I grant you, but they come from the lips of one who was never known to utter an untruth, except for practice, and who certainly would not so stultify the traditions of an upright life as to utter one now, in a strange land, and in such a presence as this, when there is nothing to be gained by it and he does not need any practice. I brought with me to this city a friend – a Boston publisher – but, alas, even this does not sufficiently explain these sinister mysteries; if I had brought a Toronto publisher along the case would have been different. But no, possibly not; the burglar took the diamond studs, but left the shirt; only a *reformed* Toronto publisher would have left the shirt.

To continue my explanation, I did not come to Canada to commit crime – this time – but to prevent it. I came here to place myself under the protection of the Canadian law and secure a copyright. I have complied with the requirements of the law; I have followed the instructions of some of the best legal minds in the city, including my own, and so my errand is accomplished, at least so far as any exertions of mine can aid that accomplishment. This is rather a cumbersome way to fence and fortify one's property against the literary buccaneer, it is true; still, if it is effective, it is a great advance upon past conditions, and one to be correspondingly welcomed.

It makes one hope and believe that a day will come when, in the eye of the law, literary property will be as sacred as whiskey, or any other of the necessaries of life. In this age of ours, if you steal another man's label to advertise your own brand of whiskey with, you will be heavily fined and otherwise punished for violating that trademark; if you steal the whiskey without the trademark, you go to jail; but if you could prove that the whiskey was literature, you can steal them both, and the law wouldn't say a word. It grieves me to think how far more profound and reverent a respect the law would have for literature if a body could only get drunk on it. Still the world moves; the interests of literature upon our continent are improving; let us be content and wait.

We have with us here a fellow craftsman, born on our own side of the Atlantic, who has created an epoch in this continent's literary history – an author who has earned and worthily earned and received the vast distinction of being crowned by the Academy of France. This is honor and achievement enough for the cause and the craft for one decade, assuredly.

If one may have the privilege of throwing in a personal impression or two, I may remark that my stay in Montreal and Quebec has been exceedingly pleasant, but the weather has been a good deal of a disappointment. Canada has a reputation for magnificent winter weather, and has a prophet who is bound by every sentiment of honor and duty to furnish it; but the result this time has been a mess of characterless weather, which all right-feeling Canadians are probably ashamed of. Still, only the country is to blame; nobody has a right to blame the prophet, for this wasn't the kind of weather he promised.

Well, never mind, what you lack in weather you make up in the means of grace. This is the first time I was ever in a city where you couldn't throw a brick without breaking a church window. Yet I was told that you were going to build one more. I said the scheme is good, but where are you going to find room? They said, we will build it on top of another church and use an elevator. This shows that the gift of lying is not yet dead in the land.

I suppose one must come in the summer to get the advantages

of the Canadian scenery. A cabman drove me two miles up a perpendicular hill in a sleigh and showed me an admirable snowstorm
from the heights of Quebec. The man was an ass; I could have
seen the snowstorm as well from the hotel window and saved my
money. Still, I may have been the ass myself; there is no telling;
the thing is all mixed up in my mind; but anyway there was an ass
in the party; and I do suppose that wherever a mercenary cabman
and a gifted literary character are gathered together for business,
there is bound to be an ass in the combination somewhere. It has
always been so in my experience; and I have usually been elected,
too. But it is no matter; I would rather be an ass than a cabman,
any time, except in summer-time; then, with my advantages,
I could be both.

I saw the Plains of Abraham, and the spot where the lamented
Wolfe stood when he made the memorable remark that he would
rather be the author of Gray's "Elegy" than take Quebec. But why
did he say so rash a thing? It was because he supposed there was
going to be international copyright. Otherwise there would be no
money in it. I was also shown the spot where Sir William Phipps
stood when he said he would rather take a walk than take two Que-
becs. And he took the walk. I have looked with emotion, here in
your city, upon the monument which makes forever memorable
the spot where Horatio Nelson did not stand when he fell. I have
seen the cab which Champlain employed when he arrived overland at Quebec; I have seen the horse which Jacques Cartier rode
when he discovered Montreal. I have used them both; I will never
do it again. Yes, I have seen all the historical places; the localities
have been pointed out to me where the scenery is warehoused for
the season. My sojourn has been to my moral and intellectual
profit; I have behaved with propriety and discretion; I have
meddled nowhere but in the election. But I am used to voting, for
I live in a town where, if you may judge by local prints, there are
only two conspicuous industries – committing burglaries and
holding elections – and I like to keep my hand in, so I voted a good
deal here.

Where so many of the guests are French, the propriety will be
recognized of my making a portion of my speech in the beautiful
language in order that I may be partly understood. I speak French
with timidity, and not flowingly – except when excited. When
using that language I have often noticed that I have hardly ever
been mistaken for a Frenchman, except, perhaps, by horses; never,

I believe, by people. I had hoped that mere French construction –
with English words – would answer, but this is not the case. I tried
it at a gentleman's house in Quebec, and it would not work. The
maid servant asked, "What would Monsieur?" I said, "Monsieur
So-and-So, is he with himself?" She did not understand that
either. I said, "He will desolate himself when he learns that his
friend American was arrived, and he not with himself to shake him
at the hand." She did not even understand that; I don't know why,
but she didn't and she lost her temper besides. Somebody in the
rear called out, "Qui est donc la?" or words to that effect. She said,
"C'est un fou," and shut the door on me. Perhaps she was right;
but how did she ever find that out? for she had never seen me
before till that moment.

But, as I have already intimated, I will close this oration with a
few sentiments in the French language. I have not ornamented
them, I have not burdened them with flowers or rhetoric, for, to
my mind, that literature is best and most enduring which is characterized by a noble simplicity: J'ai belle bouton d'or de mon oncle,
mais je n'ai pas celui du charpentier. Si vous avez le fromage du
brave menuisier, c'est bon; mais si vous ne l'avez pas, ne se desole
pas, prenez le chapeau de drap noir de son beau frere malade. Tout
a l'heure! Savoir faire! Qu'est ce que vous dit! Pate de fois gras!
Revenons a nos moutons! Pardon, messieurs, pardonnez moi;
essayant a parler la belle langue d'Ollendorf strains me more than
you can possibly imagine. But I mean well, and I've done the best
I could.

December 8, 1881

PLYMOUTH ROCK AND
THE PILGRIMS

First Annual Dinner, New England Society of Philadelphia

I RISE TO protest. I have kept still for years, but really I think there is no sufficient justification for this sort of thing. What do you want to celebrate those people for? – those ancestors of yours, of 1620 – the *Mayflower* tribe, I mean. What do you want to celebrate *them* for? Your pardon; the gentleman at my left assures me that you are not celebrating the Pilgrims themselves, but the landing of the Pilgrims at Plymouth Rock on the 22d of December. So you are celebrating their landing. Why, the other pretext was thin enough, but this is thinner than ever; the other was tissue, tinfoil, fish bladder, but this is gold leaf.

Celebrating their landing! What was there remarkable about it, I would like to know? What can you be thinking of? Why, those Pilgrims had been at sea three or four months. It was the very middle of winter; it was as cold as death off Cape Cod, there. Why shouldn't they come ashore? If they hadn't landed there would be some reason in celebrating the fact. It would have been a case of monumental leatherheadedness which the world would not willingly let die. If it had been *you*, gentlemen, you probably wouldn't have landed, but you have no shadow of right to be celebrating, in your ancestors, gifts which they did not exercise, but only transmitted. Why, to be celebrating the mere landing of the Pilgrims – to be trying to make out that this most natural, and simple, and customary procedure was an extraordinary circumstance – a circumstance to be amazed at and admired, aggrandized and glorified, at orgies like this for two hundred and sixty years – hang it, a horse would have known enough to land; a horse – pardon again; the gentleman on my right assures me that it was not merely the landing of the Pilgrims that we are celebrating, but the Pilgrims themselves. So we have struck an inconsistency here – one says it was the landing, the other says it was the Pilgrims. It is an inconsistency characteristic of your intractable and disputatious tribe, for you never agree about anything but Boston.

Well, then, what do you want to celebrate those Pilgrims for? They were a mighty hard lot – you know it. I grant you, without the slightest unwillingness, that they were a deal more gentle and merciful and just than were the peoples of Europe of that day;

I grant you that they were better than their predecessors. But what of that? – that is nothing. People always progress. You are better than your fathers and grandfathers were (this is the first time I have ever aimed a measureless slander at the departed, for I consider such things improper). Yes, those among you who have not been in the penitentiary, if such there be, are better than your fathers and grandfathers were, but is that any sufficient reason for getting up annual dinners and celebrating you? No, by no means – by no means. Well, I repeat, those Pilgrims were a hard lot. They took good care of themselves, but they abolished everybody else's ancestors. I am a border ruffian from the state of Missouri. I am a Connecticut Yankee by adoption. I have the morals of Missouri and the culture of Connecticut, and that's the combination that makes the perfect man.

But where are my ancestors? Whom shall I celebrate? Where shall I find the raw material? My first American ancestor, gentlemen, was an Indian – an early Indian. Your ancestors skinned him alive, and I am an orphan. Not one drop of my blood flows in that Indian's veins today. I stand here, lone and forlorn, without an ancestor. They skinned him! I do not object to that, if they needed his fur; but alive, gentlemen – alive! They skinned him alive – and before company! That is what rankles. Think how he must have felt; for he was a sensitive Indian and easily embarrassed. If he had been a bird it would have been all right, and no violence done to his feelings, because he would have been considered "dressed." But he was not a bird, gentlemen, he was a man, and probably one of the most undressed men that ever was. I ask you to put yourselves in his place. I ask it as a favor; I ask it as a tardy act of justice; I ask it in the interest of fidelity to the traditions of your ancestors; I ask it that the world may contemplate, with vision unobstructed by disguising swallowtails and white cravats, the spectacle which the true New England Society ought to present. Cease to come to these annual orgies in this hollow modern mockery – the surplus-age of raiment. Come in character; come in the summer grace, come in the unadorned simplicity, come in the free and joyous costume which your sainted ancestors provided for mine.

Later ancestors of mine were the Quakers, William Robinson, Marmaduke Stephenson, *et al.* Your tribe chased them out of the country for their religion's sake; promised them death if they came back, for your ancestors had forsaken the homes they loved, and braved the perils of the sea, the implacable climate, and the savage wilderness, to acquire that highest and most precious of boons, freedom for every man on this broad continent to worship according to the dictates of his own conscience – and they were not going to allow a lot of pestiferous Quakers to interfere with it. Your ancestors broke forever the chains of political slavery, and gave the vote to every man in this wide land, excluding none! – none except those who did not belong to the orthodox church. Your ancestors – yes, they were a hard lot; but, nevertheless, they gave us religious liberty to worship as they required us to worship, and political liberty to vote as the church required; and so I, the bereft one, I, the forlorn one, am here to do my best to help you celebrate them right.

The Quaker woman, Elizabeth Hooton, was an ancestress of mine. Your people were pretty severe with her – you will confess that. But, poor thing! I believe they changed her opinions before she died, and took her into their fold; and so we have every reason to presume that when she died she went to the same place which your ancestors went to. It is a great pity, for she was a good woman. Roger Williams was an ancestor of mine. I don't really remember what your people did with him. But they banished him to Rhode Island, anyway. And then, I believe, recognizing that this was really carrying harshness to an unjustifiable extreme, they took pity on him and burned him. They were a hard lot! All those Salem witches were ancestors of mine. Your people made it tropical for them. Yes, they did; by pressure and the gallows they made such a clean deal with them that there hasn't been a witch and hardly a halter in our family from that day to this, and that is 189 years. The first slave brought into New England out of Africa by your progenitors was an ancestor of mine – for I am of a mixed breed, an infinitely shaded and exquisite mongrel. I'm not one of your sham meerschaums that you can color in a week. No, my complexion is the patient art of eight generations. Well, in my own time, I had acquired a lot of my kin – by purchase, and swapping around, and one way and another – and was getting along very well. Then, with the inborn perversity of your lineage, you got up a war and took them all away from me. And so, again am I bereft, again am I forlorn; no drop of my blood flows in the veins of any living being who is marketable.

Oh my friends, hear me and reform! I seek your good, not mine. You have heard the speeches. Disband these New England societies – nurseries of a system of steadily augmenting laudation and hosannahing, which, if persisted in uncurbed, may some day in the remote future beguile you into prevaricating and bragging. Oh, stop, stop while you are still temperate in your appreciation of your ancestors! Hear me, I beseech you; get up an auction and sell Plymouth Rock! The Pilgrims were a simple and ignorant race. They had never seen any good rocks before, or at least any that were not watched, and so they were excusable for hopping ashore in frantic delight and clapping an iron fence around this one. But you, gentlemen, are educated; you are enlightened; you know that in the rich land of your nativity, opulent New England, overflowing with rocks, this one isn't worth, at the outside, more than thirty-five cents. Therefore, sell it, before it is injured by exposure, or at least throw it open to the patent medicine advertisements, and let it earn its taxes.

Yes, hear your true friend – your only true friend – list to his voice. Disband these societies, hotbeds of vice, of moral decay – perpetuators of ancestral superstition. Here on this board I see water, I see milk, I see the wild and deadly lemonade. These are but steps upon the downward path. Next we shall see tea, then chocolate, then coffee – hotel coffee. A few more years – all too few, I fear – mark my words, we shall have cider! Gentlemen, pause ere it be too late. You are on the broad road which leads to dissipation, physical ruin, moral decay, gory crime and the gallows! I beseech you, I implore you, in the name of your anxious friends, in the name of your suffering families, in the name of your impending widows and orphans, stop ere it be too late. Disband these New England societies, renounce these soul-blistering saturnalia, cease from varnishing the rusty reputations of your long-vanished ancestors – the super-high-moral old ironclads of Cape Cod, the pious buccaneers of Plymouth Rock – go home, and try to learn to behave!

However, chaff and nonsense aside, I think I honor and appreciate your Pilgrim stock as much as you do yourselves, perhaps; and I endorse and adopt a sentiment uttered by a grandfather of mine once – a man of sturdy opinions, of sincere make of mind, and not given to flattery. He said: "People may talk as they like about that Pilgrim stock, but, after all's said and done, it would be pretty hard to improve on those people; and, as for me, I don't mind coming out flat-footed and saying there ain't any way to improve on them – except having them born in Missouri!"

December 22, 1881

ADVICE TO YOUTH

Saturday Morning Club, Boston

BEING TOLD I would be expected to talk here, I inquired what sort of a talk I ought to make. They said it should be something suitable to youth – something didactic, instructive; or something in the nature of good advice. Very well; I have a few things in my mind which I have often longed to say for the instruction of the young; for it is in one's tender early years that such things will best take root and be most enduring, and most valuable. First, then, I will say to you, my young friends – and say it beseechingly, urgingly –.

Always obey your parents, when they are present. This is the best policy in the long run; because if you don't, they will make you. Most parents think they know better than you do; and you can generally make more by humoring that superstition than you can by acting on your own better judgment.

Be respectful to your superiors, if you have any; also to strangers, and sometimes to others. If a person offend you, and you are in doubt as to whether it was intentional or not, do not resort to extreme measures; simply watch your chance and hit him with a brick. That will be sufficient. If you shall find that he had not intended any offense, come out frankly and confess yourself in the wrong when you struck him; acknowledge it like a man, and say you didn't mean to. Yes, always avoid violence; in this age of charity and kindliness, the time has gone by for such things. Leave dynamite to the low and unrefined.

Go to bed early, get up early – this is wise. Some authorities say get up with one thing, some with another. But a lark is really the best thing to get up with. It gives you a splendid reputation with everybody to know that you get up with the lark; and if you get the right kind of a lark, and work at him right, you can easily train him to get up at half-past nine, every time – it is no trick at all.

Now as to the matter of lying. You want to be very careful about lying; otherwise you are nearly sure to get caught. Once caught, you can never again be, in the eyes of the good and the pure, what you were before. Many a young person has injured himself permanently through a single clumsy and ill-finished lie, the result of carelessness born of incomplete training. Some authorities hold that the young ought not to lie at all. That, of course, is putting it rather stronger than necessary; still, while I cannot go quite so far as that, I do maintain, and I believe I am right, that the young ought to be temperate in the use of this great art until practice and experience shall give them that confidence, elegance and precision which alone can make the accomplishment graceful and profitable. Patience, diligence, painstaking attention to detail – these are the requirements; these, in time, will make the student perfect; upon these, and upon these only, may he rely as the sure foundation for future eminence. Think what tedious years of study, thought, practice, experience, went to the equipment of that peerless old master who was able to impose upon the whole world the lofty and sounding maxim that "Truth is mighty and will prevail" – the most majestic compound fracture of fact which any of woman born has yet achieved. For the history of our race, and each individual's experience, are sown thick with evidences that a truth is not hard to kill, and that a lie well told is immortal. There in Boston is a monument to the man who discovered anesthesia; many people are aware, in these latter days, that that man didn't discover it at all, but stole the discovery from another man. Is this truth mighty, and will it prevail? Ah, no, my hearers, the monument is made of hardy material, but the lie it tells will outlast it a million years. An awkward, feeble, leaky lie is a thing which you ought to make it your unceasing study to avoid; such a lie as that has no more real permanence than an average truth. Why, you might as well tell the truth at once and be done with it. A feeble, stupid, preposterous lie will not live two years – except it be a slander upon somebody. It is indestructible, then, of course, but that is no merit of yours. A final word: begin your practice of this gracious and beautiful art early – begin now. If I had begun earlier, I could have learned how.

Never handle firearms carelessly. The sorrow and suffering that have been caused through the innocent but heedless handling of firearms by the young! Only four days ago, right in the next farm-house to the one where I am spending the summer, a mother, old and gray and sweet, one of the loveliest spirits in the land, was sitting at her work, when her young son crept in and got down an old, battered, rusty gun which had not been touched for many years, and was supposed not to be loaded, and pointed it at her, laughing and threatening to shoot. In her fright she ran screaming and pleading toward the door on the other side of the room; but as she passed him he placed the gun almost against her very breast and pulled the trigger! He had supposed it was not loaded. And he was right: it wasn't. So there wasn't any harm done. It is the only case of the kind I ever heard of. Therefore, just the same, don't you meddle with old unloaded firearms; they are the most deadly and unerring things that have ever been created by man. You don't have to take any pains at all, with them; you don't have to have a rest, you don't have to have any sights on the gun, you don't have to take aim, even. No, you just pick out a relative and bang away, and you are sure to get him. A youth who can't hit a cathedral at thirty yards with a Gatling gun in three-quarters of an hour, can take up an old empty musket and bag his mother every time, at a hundred. Think what Waterloo would have been if one of the armies had been boys armed with old rusty muskets supposed not to be loaded, and the other army had been composed of their female relations. The very thought of it makes me shudder.

There are many sorts of books; but good ones are the sort for the young to read. Remember that. They are a great, an inestimable, an unspeakable means of improvement. Therefore be careful in your selection, my young friends; be very careful; confine yourself exclusively to Robertson's *Sermons*, Baxter's *Saint's Rest*, *The Innocents Abroad*, and works of that kind.

But I have said enough. I hope you will treasure up the instructions which I have given you, and make them a guide to your feet and a light to your understanding. Build your character thoughtfully and painstakingly upon these precepts; and by and by, when you have got it built, you will be surprised and gratified to see how nicely and sharply it resembles everybody else's.

April 15, 1882

ON THE DECAY OF
THE ART OF LYING

ESSAY, FOR DISCUSSION, READ AT A MEETING OF THE
HISTORICAL AND ANTIQUARIAN CLUB OF HARTFORD,
AND OFFERED FOR THE THIRTY-DOLLAR PRIZE. NOW
FIRST PUBLISHED.*

OBSERVE, I DO not mean to suggest that the *custom* of lying has
suffered any decay or interruption, – no, for the Lie, as a Virtue,
a Principle, is eternal; the Lie, as a recreation, a solace, a refuge in
time of need, the fourth Grace, the tenth Muse, man's best and
surest friend, is immortal, and cannot perish from the earth while
this Club remains. My complaint simply concerns the decay of the
art of lying. No high-minded man, no man of right feeling, can
contemplate the lumbering and slovenly lying of the present day
without grieving to see a noble art so prostituted. In this veteran
presence I naturally enter upon this theme with diffidence; it is like
an old maid trying to teach nursery matters to the mothers in
Israel. It would not become me to criticize you, gentlemen, who
are nearly all my elders – and my superiors, in this thing – and so,
if I should here and there *seem* to do it, I trust it will in most cases
be more in a spirit of admiration than of fault-finding; indeed if
this finest of the fine arts had everywhere received the attention,
encouragement, and conscientious practice and development
which this Club has devoted to it, I should not need to utter
this lament, or shed a single tear. I do not say this to flatter:
I say it in a spirit of just and appreciative recognition. [It had
been my intention, at this point, to mention names and give
illustrative specimens, but indications observable about me
admonished me to beware of particulars and confine myself to
generalities.]

No fact is more firmly established than that lying is a necessity
of our circumstances, – the deduction that it is then a Virtue goes
without saying. No virtue can reach its highest usefulness without
careful and diligent cultivation, – therefore, it goes without saying,
that this one ought to be taught in the public schools – at the

* Did not take the prize.

fireside – even in the newspapers. What chance has the ignorant, uncultivated liar against the educated expert? What chance have I against Mr. Per – against a lawyer? *Judicious* lying is what the world needs. I sometimes think it were even better and safer not to lie at all than to lie injudiciously. An awkward, unscientific lie is often as ineffectual as the truth.

Now let us see what the philosophers say. Note that venerable proverb: Children and fools *always* speak the truth. The deduction is plain, – adults and wise persons *never* speak it. Parkman, the historian, says, "The principle of truth may itself be carried into an absurdity." In another place in the same chapter he says, "The saying is old that truth should not be spoken at all times; and those whom a sick conscience worries into habitual violation of the maxim are imbeciles and nuisances." It is strong language, but true. None of us could *live* with an habitual truth-teller; but thank goodness none of us has to. An habitual truth-teller is simply an impossible creature; he does not exist; he never has existed. Of course there are people who *think* they never lie, but it is not so, – and this ignorance is one of the very things that shame our so-called civilization. Everybody lies – every day; every hour; awake; asleep; in his dreams; in his joy; in his mourning; if he keeps his tongue still, his hands, his feet, his eyes, his attitude, will convey deception – and purposely. Even in sermons – but that is a platitude.

In a far country where I once lived the ladies used to go around paying calls, under the humane and kindly pretence of wanting to see each other; and when they returned home, they would cry out with a glad voice, saying, "We made sixteen calls and found fourteen of them out," – not meaning that they found out anything against the fourteen, – no, that was only a colloquial phrase to signify that they were not at home, – and their manner of saying it expressed their lively satisfaction in that fact. Now their pretence of wanting to see the fourteen – and the other two whom they had been less lucky with – was that commonest and mildest form of lying which is sufficiently described as a deflection from the truth. Is it justifiable? Most certainly. It is beautiful, it is noble; for its object is, *not* to reap profit, but to convey a pleasure to the sixteen. The iron-souled truth-monger would plainly manifest, or even utter the fact that he did n't want to see those people – and he would be an ass, and inflict a totally unnecessary pain. And next, those ladies in that far country – but never mind, they had a thousand pleasant ways of lying, that grew out of gentle impulses, and were a credit to their intelligence and an honor to their hearts. Let the particulars go.

The men in that far country were liars, every one. Their mere howdy-do was a lie, because *they* did n't care how you did, except they were undertakers. To the ordinary inquirer you lied in return; for you made no conscientious diagnosis of your case, but answered at random, and usually missed it considerably. You lied to the undertaker, and said your health was failing – a wholly commendable lie, since it cost you nothing and pleased the other man. If a stranger called and interrupted you, you said with your hearty tongue, "I'm glad to see you," and said with your heartier soul, "I wish you were with the cannibals and it was dinner time." When he went, you said regretfully, "*Must* you go?" and followed it with a "Call again;" but you did no harm, for you did not deceive anybody nor inflict any hurt, whereas the truth would have made you both unhappy.

I think that all this courteous lying is a sweet and loving art, and should be cultivated. The highest perfection of politeness is only a beautiful edifice, built, from the base to the dome, of graceful and gilded forms of charitable and unselfish lying.

What I bemoan is the growing prevalence of the brutal truth. Let us do what we can to eradicate it. An injurious truth has no merit over an injurious lie. Neither should ever be uttered. The man who speaks an injurious truth lest his soul be not saved if he do otherwise, should reflect that that sort of a soul is not strictly worth saving. The man who tells a lie to help a poor devil out of trouble, is one of whom the angels doubtless say, "Lo, here is an heroic soul who casts his own welfare into jeopardy to succor his neighbor's; let us exalt this magnanimous liar."

An injurious lie is an uncommendable thing; and so, also, and in the same degree, is an injurious truth, – a fact which is recognized by the law of libel.

Among other common lies, we have the *silent* lie, – the deception, which one conveys by simply keeping still and concealing the truth. Many obstinate truth-mongers indulge in this dissipation, imagining that if they *speak* no lie, they lie not at all. In that far country where I once lived, there was a lovely spirit, a lady whose impulses were always high and pure, and whose character answered to them. One day I was there at dinner, and remarked, in a general way, that we are all liars. She was amazed, and said,

"Not *all*?" It was before Pinafore's time, so I did not make the response which would naturally follow in our day, but frankly said, "Yes, *all* – we are all liars; there are no exceptions." She looked almost offended, and said, "Why, do you include *me*?" "Certainly," I said, "I think you even rank as an expert." She said, "Sh – sh! the children!" So the subject was changed in deference to the children's presence, and we went on talking about other things. But as soon as the young people were out of the way, the lady came warmly back to the matter and said, "I have made it the rule of my life to never tell a lie; and I have never departed from it in a single instance." I said, "I don't mean the least harm or disrespect, but really you have been lying like smoke ever since I've been sitting here. It has caused me a good deal of pain, because I am not used to it." She required of me an instance – just a single instance. So I said, –

"Well, here is the unfilled duplicate of the blank which the Oakland hospital people sent to you by the hand of the sick-nurse when she came here to nurse your little nephew through his dangerous illness. This blank asks all manner of questions as to the conduct of that sick-nurse: 'Did she ever sleep on her watch? Did she ever forget to give the medicine?' and so forth and so on. You are warned to be very careful and explicit in your answers, for the welfare of the service requires that the nurses be promptly fined or otherwise punished for derelictions. You told me you were perfectly delighted with that nurse – that she had a thousand perfections and only one fault: you found you never could depend on her wrapping Johnny up half sufficiently while he waited in a chilly chair for her to rearrange the warm bed. You filled up the duplicate of this paper, and sent it back to the hospital by the hand of the nurse. How did you answer this question, – 'Was the nurse at any time guilty of a negligence which was likely to result in the patient's taking cold?' Come – everything is decided by a bet here in California: ten dollars to ten cents you lied when you answered that question." She said, "I didn't; *I left it blank!*" "Just so – you have told a *silent* lie; you have left it to be inferred that you had no fault to find in that matter." She said, "Oh, was that a lie? And how *could* I mention her one single fault, and she so good? – it would have been cruel." I said, "One ought always to lie, when one can do good by it; your impulse was right, but your judgment was crude; this comes of unintelligent practice. Now observe the result of this inexpert deflection of yours. You know

Mr. Jones's Willie is lying very low with scarlet fever; well, your recommendation was so enthusiastic that that girl is there nursing him, and the worn-out family have all been trustingly sound asleep for the last fourteen hours, leaving their darling with full confidence in those fatal hands, because you, like young George Washington, have a reputa –. However, if you are not going to have anything to do, I will come around to-morrow and we'll attend the funeral together, for of course you'll naturally feel a peculiar interest in Willie's case, – as personal a one, in fact, as the undertaker."

But that was all lost. Before I was half-way through she was in a carriage and making thirty miles an hour toward the Jones mansion to save what was left of Willie and tell all she knew about the deadly nurse. All of which was unnecessary, as Willie was n't sick; I had been lying myself. But that same day, all the same, she sent a line to the hospital which filled up the neglected blank, and stated the *facts*, too, in the squarest possible manner.

Now, you see, this lady's fault was *not* in lying, but only in lying injudiciously. She should have told the truth, *there*, and made it up to the nurse with a fraudulent compliment further along in the paper. She could have said, "In one respect this sick-nurse is perfection, – when she is on watch, she never snores." Almost any little pleasant lie would have taken the sting out of that troublesome but necessary expression of the truth.

Lying is universal – we *all* do it; we all *must* do it. Therefore, the wise thing is for us diligently to train ourselves to lie thoughtfully, judiciously; to lie with a good object, and not an evil one; to lie for others' advantage, and not our own; to lie healingly, charitably, humanely, not cruelly, hurtfully, maliciously; to lie gracefully and graciously, not awkwardly and clumsily; to lie firmly, frankly, squarely, with head erect, not haltingly, tortuously, with pusillanimous mien, as being ashamed of our high calling. Then shall we be rid of the rank and pestilent truth that is rotting the land; then shall we be great and good and beautiful, and worthy dwellers in a world where even benign Nature habitually lies, except when she promises execrable weather. Then – But I am but a new and feeble student in this gracious art; I cannot instruct *this* Club.

Joking aside, I think there is much need of wise examination into what sorts of lies are best and wholesomest to be indulged, seeing we *must* all lie and *do* all lie, and what sorts it may be best to avoid,

– and this is a thing which I feel I can confidently put into the hands of this experienced Club, – a ripe body, who may be termed, in this regard, and without undue flattery, Old Masters.

1882

CONCERNING THE
AMERICAN LANGUAGE*

THERE WAS AN Englishman in our compartment, and he complimented me on – on what? But you would never guess. He
complimented me on my English. He said Americans in general
did not speak the English language as correctly as I did. I said I was
obliged to him for his compliment, since I knew he meant it for
one, but that I was not fairly entitled to it, for I did n't speak
English at all, – I only spoke American.

He laughed, and said it was a distinction without a difference.
I said no, the difference was not prodigious, but still it was considerable. We fell into a friendly dispute over the matter. I put my
case as well as I could, and said, –

"The languages were identical several generations ago, but our
changed conditions and the spread of our people far to the south
and far to the west have made many alterations in our pronunciation, and have introduced new words among us and changed the
meanings of many old ones. English people talk through their
noses; we do not. We say *know*, English people say *näo*; we say *cow*,
the Briton says *käow*; we –"

"Oh, come! that is pure Yankee; everybody knows that."

"Yes, it is pure Yankee; that is true. One cannot hear it in America outside of the little corner called New England, which is
Yankee land. The English themselves planted it there, two hundred and fifty years ago, and there it remains; it has never spread.
But England talks through her nose yet; the Londoner and the
backwoods New-Englander pronounce 'know' and 'cow' alike,
and then the Briton unconsciously satirizes himself by making fun
of the Yankee's pronunciation."

We argued this point at some length; nobody won; but no matter, the fact remains, – Englishmen say *näo* and *käow* for "know"
and "cow," and that is what the rustic inhabitant of a very small
section of America does.

"You conferred your *a* upon New England, too, and there it
remains; it has not travelled out of the narrow limits of those six
little States in all these two hundred and fifty years. All England
uses it, New England's small population – say four millions – use

* Being part of a chapter which was crowded out of "A Tramp Abroad." – M.T.

it, but we have forty-five millions who do not use it. You say 'glahs of wawtah,' so does New England; at least, New England says *glahs*. America at large flattens the *a*, and says 'glass of water.' These sounds are pleasanter than yours; you may think they are not right, – well, in English they are *not* right, but in 'American' they are. You say *flahsk*, and *bahsket*, and *jackahss*; we say 'flask,' 'basket,' 'jackass,' – sounding the *a* as it is in 'tallow,' 'fallow,' and so on. Up to as late as 1847 Mr. Webster's Dictionary had the impudence to still pronounce 'basket' *bahsket*, when he knew that outside of his little New England all America shortened the *a* and paid no attention to his English broadening of it. However, it called itself an English Dictionary, so it was proper enough that it should stick to English forms, perhaps. It still calls itself an English Dictionary to-day, but it has quietly ceased to pronounce 'basket' as if it were spelt *bahsket*. In the American language the *h* is respected; the *h* is not dropped or added improperly."

"The same is the case in England, – I mean among the educated classes, of course."

"Yes, that is true; but a nation's language is a very large matter. It is not simply a manner of speech obtaining among the educated handful; the manner obtaining among the vast uneducated multitude must be considered also. Your uneducated masses speak English, you will not deny that; our uneducated masses speak American, – it won't be fair for you to deny that, for you can see, yourself, that when your stableboy says, 'It is n't the 'unting that 'urts the 'orse, but the 'ammer, 'ammer, 'ammer on the 'ard 'ighway,' and our stableboy makes the same remark without suffocating a single *h*, these two people are manifestly talking two different languages. But, if the signs are to be trusted, even your educated classes used to drop the *h*. They say *humble*, now, and *heroic*, and *historic*, etc., but I judge that they used to drop those *h's* because your writers still keep up the fashion of putting *an* before those words, instead of *a*. This is what Mr. Darwin might call a 'rudimentary' sign that that *an* was justifiable once, and useful, – when your educated classes used to say *'umble*, and *'eroic*, and *'istorical*. Correct writers of the American language do not put *an* before those words."

The English gentleman had something to say upon this matter, but never mind what he said, – I'm not arguing his case. I have him at a disadvantage, now. I proceeded: –

"In England you encourage an orator by exclaiming 'H'yaah!

h'yaah!' We pronounce it *heer* in some sections, 'h'*yer*' in others, and so on; but our whites do not say 'h'yaah,' pronouncing the *a*'s like the *a* in *ah*. I have heard English ladies say 'don't you' – making two separate and distinct words of it; your Mr. Bernand has satirized it. But we always say 'dontchu.' This is much better. Your ladies say, 'Oh, it's *o*ful nice!' Ours say, 'Oh, it's *aw*ful nice!' We say, '*Four* hundred,' you say '*For*' – as in the word *or*. Your clergymen speak of 'the Lawd,' ours of 'the Lord'; yours speak of 'the gawds of the heathen,' ours of 'the gods of the heathen.' When you are exhausted, you say you are 'knocked up.' We don't. When you say you will do a thing 'directly,' you mean 'immediately'; in the American language – generally speaking – the word signifies 'after a little.' When you say 'clever,' you mean 'capable'; with us the word used to mean 'accommodating,' but I don't know what it means now. Your word 'stout' means 'fleshy'; our word 'stout' usually means 'strong.' Your words 'gentleman' and 'lady' have a very restricted meaning; with us they include the bar-maid, butcher, burglar, harlot, and horse-thief. You say, 'I have n't *got* any stockings on,' 'I have n't *got* any memory,' 'I have n't *got* any money in my purse'; we usually say, 'I have n't any stockings on,' 'I have n't any memory,' 'I have n't any money in my purse.' You say 'out of window'; we always put in a *the*. If one asks 'How old is that man?' the Briton answers, 'He will be about forty;' in the American language, we should say, 'He *is* about forty.' However, I won't tire you, sir; but if I wanted to, I could pile up differences here until I not only convinced you that English and American are separate languages, but that when I speak my native tongue in its utmost purity an Englishman can't understand me at all."

'I don't wish to flatter you, but it is about all I can do to understand you *now*."

That was a very pretty compliment, and it put us on the pleasantest terms directly, – I use the word in the English sense.

[*Later* –1882. Æsthetes in many of our schools are now begining to teach the pupils to broaden the *a*, and to say "don't you," in the elegant foreign way.]

1882

WOMAN – GOD BLESS HER

Seventy-seventh Annual Dinner, New England Society of New York

THE TOAST INCLUDES the sex, universally: it is to Woman, comprehensively, wheresoever she may be found. Let us consider her ways. First comes the matter of dress. This is a most important consideration, in a subject of this nature, and must be disposed of before we can intelligently proceed to examine the profounder depths of the theme. For text, let us take the dress of two antipodal types – the savage woman of Central Africa, and the cultivated daughter of our high modern civilization. Among the Fans, a great Negro tribe, a woman, when dressed for home, or to go to market, or go out calling, does not wear anything at all but just her complexion. That is all; that is her entire outfit. It is the lightest costume in the world, but is made of the darkest material. It has often been mistaken for mourning. It is the trimmest, and neatest, and gracefulest costume that is now in fashion; it wears well, is fast colors, doesn't show dirt; you don't have to send it downtown to wash, and have some of it come back scorched with the flat-iron, and some of it with the buttons ironed off, and some of it petrified with starch, and some of it chewed by the calf, and some of it rotted with acids, and some of it exchanged for other customers' things that haven't any virtue but holiness, and ten-twelfths of the pieces overcharged for, and the rest of the dozen "mislaid." And it always fits; it is the perfection of a fit. And it is the handiest dress in the whole realm of fashion. It is always ready, always "done up." When you call on a Fan lady and send up your card, the hired girl never says, "Please take a seat, madam is dressing – she will be down in three-quarters of an hour." No, madam is always dressed, always ready to receive; and before you can get the doormat before your eyes, she is in your midst. Then again, the Fan ladies don't go to church to see what each other has got on; and they don't go back home and describe it and slander it.

Such is the dark child of savagery, as to everyday toilette; and thus, curiously enough, she finds a point of contact with the fair daughter of civilization and high fashion – who often has "nothing to wear"; and thus these widely separated types of the sex meet upon common ground. Yes, such is the Fan woman, as she appears in her simple, unostentatious, everyday toilette. But on state occasions she is more dressy. At a banquet, she wears bracelets; at a

lecture she wears earrings and a belt; at a ball she wears stockings
– and with the true feminine fondness for display, she wears them
on her arms; at a funeral she wears a jacket of tar and ashes; at a
wedding the bride who can afford it puts on pantaloons. Thus the
dark child of savagery and the fair daughter of civilization meet
once more upon common ground; and these two touches of nature
make their whole world kin.

Now we will consider the dress of our other type. A large part
of the daughter of civilization is her dress – as it should be. Some
civilized women would lose half their charm without dress; and
some would lose all of it. The daughter of modern civilization,
dressed at her utmost best, is a marvel of exquisite and beautiful
art, and expense. All the lands, all the climes, and all the arts are
laid under tribute to furnish her forth. Her linen is from Belfast,
her robe is from Paris, her lace is from Venice, or Spain, or France;
her feathers are from the remote regions of southern Africa, her
furs from the remoter home of the iceberg and the aurora; her fan
from Japan, her diamonds from Brazil, her bracelets from California, her pearls from Ceylon, her cameos from Rome; she has
gems and trinkets from buried Pompeii; and others that graced
comely Egyptian forms that have been dust and ashes, now, for
forty centuries; her watch is from Geneva, her card case is from
China, her hair is from – from – I don't know where her hair is
from; I never could find out. That is, her other hair – her public
hair, her Sunday hair; I don't mean the hair she goes to bed with.
Why, you ought to know the hair I mean; it's that thing which she
calls a switch, and which resembles a switch as much as it
resembles a brickbat, or a shotgun, or any other thing which you
correct people with. It's that thing which she twists, and then coils
round and round her head, beehive fashion, and then tucks the
end in under the hive and harpoons it with a hairpin. And that
reminds me of a trifle: any time you want to, you can glance around
the carpet of a Pullman car and go and pick up a hairpin; but not
to save your life can you get any woman in that car to acknowledge
that hairpin. Now isn't that strange? But it's true. The woman who
has never swerved from cast iron veracity and fidelity in her whole
life, will, when confronted with this crucial test, deny her hairpin.
She will deny that hairpin before a hundred witnesses. I have
stupidly got into more trouble, and more hot water trying to hunt
up the owner of a hairpin in a Pullman car than by any other
indiscretion of my life.

Well, you see what the daughter of civilization is when she is dressed; and you have seen what the daughter of savagery is when she isn't. Such is Woman, as to costume. I come, now, to consider her in her higher and nobler aspects – as mother, wife, widow, grass widow, mother-in-law, hired girl, telephone operator, telephone helloer, queen, book agent, wet nurse, stepmother, boss, professional fat woman, professional double-headed woman, professional beauty, and so forth and so on.

We will simply discuss these few – let the rest of the sex tarry in Jericho till we come again. First in the list, of right, and first in our gratitude, comes a woman who – why, dear me, I've been talking three-quarters of an hour! I beg a thousand pardons. But you see, yourselves, that I had a large contract. I have accomplished something, anyway: I have introduced my subject; and if I had till next Forefathers' Day, I am satisfied that I could discuss it as adequately and appreciatively as so gracious and noble a theme deserves. But as the matter stands, now, let us finish as we began – and say, without jesting, but with all sincerity, "Woman – God Bless Her!"

December 22, 1882

ON ADAM

Royal Literary and Scientific Society Dinner, Ottawa

I NEVER FEEL wholly at home and equal to the occasion except when I am to respond for the royal family or the President of the United States. But I am full of serenity, courage and confidence then, because I know by experience that I can drink standing and "in silence" just as long as anybody wants me to. Sometimes I have gone on responding to those toasts with mute and diligent enthusiasm until I have become an embarrassment, and people have requested me to sit down and rest myself. But responding by speech is a sore trial to me. The list of toasts being always the same, one is always so apt to forget and say something that has already been said at some other banquet some time or other. For instance, you take the toast to – well, take any toast in the regulation lot, and you won't get far in your speech before you notice that everything you are saying is old; not only old, but stale; and not only stale, but rancid. At any rate, that is my experience. There are gifted men who have the faculty of saying an old thing in a new and happy way – they rub the old Aladdin lamp and bring forth the smoke and thunder, the giants and genii, the pomp and pageantry of all the wide and secret realms of enchantment – and these men are the saviors of the banquet; but for them it must have gone silent, as Carlyle would say, generations ago, and ceased from among the world's occasions and industries. But I cannot borrow their trick; I do not know the mystery of how to rub the old lamp the right way.

And so it has seemed to me that for the behoof of my sort and kind, the toast list ought to be reconstructed. We ought to have some of the old themes knocked out of it and a new one or two inserted in their places. There are plenty of new subjects, if we would only look around. And plenty of old ones, too, that have not been touched. There is Adam, for instance. Who ever talks about Adam at a banquet? All sorts of recent and ephemeral celebrities are held up and glorified on such occasions, but who ever says a good word for Adam? Yet why is he neglected, why is he ignored in this offensive way – can you tell me that? What has he done, that we let banquet after banquet go on, and never give him a lift? Considering what we and the whole world owe him, he ought to be in the list – yes, and he ought to be away up high in the list, too.

He ought to take precedence of the Press; yes, and the Army and Navy; and Literature; and the Day we Celebrate and pretty much everything else. In the United States he ought to be at the very top – he ought to take precedence of the President; and even in the loyalest monarchy he ought at least to come right after the royal family. And be "drunk in silence and standing," too. It is his right; and for one, I propose to stick here and *drink* him in silence and standing till I can't tell a ministering angel from a tax collector. This neglect has been going on too long. You always place Woman at the bottom of the toast list; it is but simple justice to place Adam at the top of it – for if it had not been for the help of these two, where would you and your banquets be? – answer me that. You must excuse me for losing my temper and carrying on in this way; and in truth I would not do it if it were almost anybody but Adam; but I am of a narrow and clannish disposition, and I never can see a relative of mine misused without going into a passion. It is no trick for people with plenty of celebrated kin to keep cool when their folk are misused; but Adam is the only solitary celebrity in our family, and the man that misuses him has got to walk over my dead body – or go around, that is all there is to that. That is the way I feel about Adam. Years ago when I went around trying to collect subscriptions to build a monument to him, there wasn't a man that would give a cent; and generally they lost their temper because I interrupted their business; and they drove me away, and said they didn't care Adam for Adam – and in ninety-nine cases out of a hundred they got the emphasis on the wrong end of the word. Such is the influence of passion on a man's pronunciation. I tried Congress. Congress wouldn't build the monument. They wouldn't sell me the Washington monument, they wouldn't lend it to me temporarily while I could look around for another. I am negotiating for that Bastile yonder by the public square in Montreal, but they say they want to finish it first. Of course that ends the project, because there couldn't be any use of a monument after the man was forgotten. It is a pity, because I thought Adam might have pleasant associations with that building – he must have seen it in his time. But he shall have a monument yet, even if it be only a grateful place in the list of toasts; for to him we owe the two things which are most precious – life, and death. Life, which the young, the hopeful, the undefeated hold above all wealth and all honors; and death, the refuge, the solace, the best and kindliest and most prized friend and benefactor of the erring, the forsaken, the old, and weary, and broken of heart, whose burdens be heavy upon them, and who would lie down and be at rest.

I would like to see the toast list reconstructed, for it seems to me a needed reform; and as a beginning in this direction, if I can meet with a second, I beg to nominate Adam. I am not actuated by family considerations. It is a thing which I would do for any other member of our family, or anybody else's, if I could honestly feel that he deserved it. But I do not. If I seem to be always trying to shove Adam into prominence, I can say sincerely that it is solely because of my admiration of him as a man who was a good citizen at a time when it was difficult to be a good citizen; a good husband at a time when he was not married; a good father at a time when he had to guess his way, having never been young himself; and would have been a good son if he had had the chance. He could have been a governor if he had wanted to; he could have been post-master general, speaker of the House, he could have been anything he chose, if he had been willing to put himself up and stand a canvass. Yet he lived and died a private citizen, without a handle to his name, and he comes down to us as plain simple Adam, and nothing more – a man who could have elected himself Major General Adam or anything else as easy as rolling off a log. I stand up for him on account of his sterling private virtues, as a man and a citizen – as an inventor – inventor of life, and death, and sin, and the fashions – and not because he simply happens to be kin to me.

May 23, 1883

THE CHARACTER OF MAN

CONCERNING MAN — he is too large a subject to be treated as whole; so I will merely discuss a detail or two of him at this time. I desire to contemplate him from this point of view – this premiss: that he was not made for any useful purpose, for the reason that he hasn't served any; that he was most likely not even made *intentionally*; and that his working himself up out of the oyster bed to his present position was probably matter of surprise and regret to the Creator. ... For history, in all climes, all ages and all circumstances, furnishes oceans and continents of proof that of all the creatures that were made he is the most detestable. Of the entire brood he is the only one – the solitary one – that possesses malice. That is the basest of all instincts, passions, vices – the most hateful. That one thing puts him below the rats, the grubs, the trichinæ. He is the only creature that inflicts pain for sport, knowing it to *be* pain. But if the cat knows she is inflicting pain when she plays with the frightened mouse, then we must make an exception here; we must grant that in one detail man is the moral peer of the cat. *All* creatures kill – there seems to be no exception; but of the whole list, man is the only one that kills for fun; he is the only one that kills in malice, the only one that kills for revenge. Also – in all the list he is the only creature that has a nasty mind.

Shall he be extolled for his noble qualities, for his gentleness, his sweetness, his amiability, his lovingness, his courage, his devotion, his patience, his fortitude, his prudence, the various charms and graces of his spirit? The other animals share *all* these with him, yet are free from the blacknesses and rottennesses of his character.

... There are certain sweet-smelling sugar-coated lies current in the world which all politic men have apparently tacitly conspired together to support and perpetuate. One of these is, that there is such a thing in the world as independence: independence of thought, independence of opinion, independence of action. Another is, that the world loves to *see* independence – admires it, applauds it. Another is, that there is such a thing in the world as toleration – in religion, in politics, and such matters; and with it trains that already mentioned auxiliary lie that toleration is admired, and applauded. Out of these trunk-lies spring many branch ones: to-wit, the lie that not all men are slaves; the lie that men are glad when other men succeed; glad when they prosper;

glad to see them reach lofty heights; sorry to see them fall again. And yet other branch-lies: to-wit, that there is heroism in man; that he is not mainly made up of malice and treachery; that he is sometimes not a coward; that there is something about him that ought to be perpetuated – in heaven, or hell, or somewhere. And these other branch-lies, to-wit: that conscience, man's moral medicine chest, is not only created by the Creator, but is put into man ready-charged with the right and only true and authentic correctives of conduct – and the duplicate chest, with the self-same correctives, unchanged, unmodified, distributed to all nations and all epochs. And yet one other branch-lie, to-wit, that I am I, and you are you; that we are units, individuals, and have natures of our own instead of being the tail-end of a tape-worm eternity of ancestors extending in linked procession back – and back – and back – to our source in the monkeys, with this so-called individuality of ours a decayed and rancid mush of inherited instincts and teachings derived, atom by atom, stench by stench, from the entire line of that sorry column, and not so much new and original matter in it as you could balance on a needle point and examine under a microscope. This makes well nigh fantastic the suggestion that there can be such a thing as a personal, original and responsible nature in a man, separable from that in him which is not original, and findable in such quantity as to enable the observer to say, This is a man, not a procession.

... Consider that first mentioned lie: that there is such a thing in the world as independence; that it exists in individuals, that it exists in bodies of men. Surely if anything *is* proven, by whole oceans and continents of evidence, it is that the quality of independence was almost wholly left out of the human race. The scattering exceptions to the rule only emphasize it, light it up, make it glare. The whole population of New England meekly took their turns, for years, in standing up in the railway trains, without so much as a complaint above their breath, till at last these uncounted millions were able to produce exactly one single independent man, who stood to his rights and made the railroad give him a seat. Statistics and the law of probabilities warrant the assumption that it will take New England forty years to breed his fellow. There is a law, with a penalty attached, forbidding trains to occupy the Asylum street crossing more than five minutes at a time. For years people and carriages used to wait there nightly as much as twenty minutes on a stretch while New England trains monopolized that crossing.

I used to hear men use vigorous language about that insolent wrong – but they waited, just the same.

We are discreet sheep; we wait to see how the drove is going, and then go with the drove. We have two opinions: one private, which we are afraid to express; and another one – the one we use – which we force ourselves to wear to please Mrs. Grundy, until habit makes us comfortable in it, and the custom of defending it presently makes us love it, adore it, and forget how pitifully we came by it. Look at in it politics. Look at the candidates whom we loathe, one year, and are afraid to vote against the next; whom we cover with unimaginable filth, one year, and fall down on the public platform and worship, the next – and keep on doing it until the habitual shutting of our eyes to last year's evidences brings us presently to a sincere and stupid belief in this year's.* Look at the tyranny of party – at what is called party allegiance, party loyalty – a snare invented by designing men for selfish purposes – and which turns voters into chattels, slaves, rabbits; and all the while, their masters, and they themselves are shouting rubbish about liberty, independence, freedom of opinion, freedom of speech, honestly unconscious of the fantastic contradiction; and forgetting or ignoring that the fathers and the churches shouted the same blasphemies a generation earlier when they were closing their doors against the hunted slave, beating his handful of humane defenders with Bible-texts and billies, and pocketing the insults and licking the shoes of his Southern master.

If we would learn what the human race really *is*, at bottom, we need only observe it in election times. A Hartford clergyman met me in the street, and spoke of a new nominee – denounced the nomination, in strong, earnest words – words that were refreshing for their independence, their manliness.** He said, "I ought to be proud, perhaps, for this nominee is a relative of mine; on the contrary I am humiliated and disgusted; for I know him intimately – familiarly – and I know that he is an unscrupulous scoundrel, and always has been." You should have seen this clergyman preside at a political meeting forty days later; and urge, and plead, and gush – and you should have heard him paint the character of this same

* Jan. 11/06. It is long ago, but it plainly means Blaine. M.T.
** Jan. 11, '06. I can't remember his name. It began with K, I think. He was one of the American revisers of the New Testament, and was nearly as great a scholar as Hammond Trumbull.

nominee. You would have supposed he was describing the Cid, and Great-heart, and Sir Galahad, and Bayard the Spotless all rolled into one. Was he sincere? Yes – by that time; and therein lies the pathos of it all, the hopelessness of it all. It shows at what trivial cost of effort a man can teach himself a lie, and learn to believe it, when he perceives, by the general drift, that that is the popular thing to do. Does he believe his lie *yet*? Oh, probably not; he has no further use for it. It was but a passing incident; he spared to it the moment that was its due, then hastened back to the serious business of his life.

And what a paltry poor lie is that one which teaches that independence of action and opinion is prized in men, admired, honored, rewarded. When a man leaves a political party, he is treated as if the party owned him – as if he were its bond slave, as most party men plainly are – and had stolen himself, gone off with what was not his own. And he is traduced, derided, despised, held up to public obloquy and loathing. His character is remorselessly assassinated; no means, however vile, are spared to injure his property and his business.

The preacher who casts a vote for conscience' sake, runs the risk of starving. And is rightly served; for he has been teaching a falsity – that men respect and honor independence of thought and action.

Mr. Beecher may be charged with a *crime*, and his whole following will rise as one man, and stand by him to the bitter end; but who so poor to be his friend when he is charge with casting a vote for conscience' sake? Take the editor so charged – take – take anybody.

All the talk about tolerance, in anything or anywhere, is plainly a gentle lie. It does not exist. It is in no man's heart; but it unconsciously and by moss-grown inherited habit, drivels and slabbers from all men's lips. Intolerance is everything for one's self, and nothing for the other person. The mainspring of man's nature is just that – selfishness.

Let us skip the other lies, for brevity's sake. To consider them would prove nothing, except that man is what he is – loving, toward his own, lovable, to his own, – his family, his friends – and otherwise the buzzing, busy, trivial, enemy of his race – who tarries his little day, does his little dirt, commends himself to God, and then goes out into the darkness, to return no more, and send no messages back – selfish even in death.

1885

ON SPEECH-MAKING REFORM

LIKE MANY ANOTHER well-intentioned man, I have made too many speeches. And like other transgressors of this sort, I have from time to time reformed; binding myself, by oath, on New Year's Days, to never make another speech. I found that a new oath holds pretty well; but that when it is become old, and frayed out, and damaged by a dozen annual retyings of its remains, it ceases to be serviceable; any little strain will snap it. So, last New Year's Day I strengthened my reform with a money penalty; and made that penalty so heavy that it has enabled me to remain pure from that day to this. Although I am falling once more now, I think I can behave myself from this out, because the penalty is going to be doubled ten days hence. I see before me and about me the familiar faces of many poor sorrowing fellow sufferers, victims of the passion for speech-making – poor sad-eyed brothers in affliction, who, fast in the grip of this fell, degrading, demoralizing vice, have grown weak with struggling, as the years drifted by, and at last have all but given up hope. To them I say, in this last final obituary of mine, don't give up – don't do it; there is still hope for you. I beseech you, swear one more oath, and back it up with cash. I do not say this to all, of course; for there are some among you who are past reform; some who, being long accustomed to success, and to the delicious intoxication of the applause which follows it, are too wedded to their dissipation to be capable now or hereafter of abandoning it. They have thoroughly learned the deep art of speech-making and they suffer no longer from those misgivings and embarrassments and apprehension which are really the only things which ever make a speech-maker want to reform. They have learned their art by long observation and slowly compacted experience; so now they know, what they did not know at first, that the best and most telling speech is not the actual impromptu one, but the counterfeit of it; they know that that speech is most worth listening to which has been carefully prepared in private and tried on a plaster cast, or an empty chair, or any other appreciative object that will keep quiet, until the speaker has got his matter and his delivery limbered up so that they will seem impromptu to an audience. The expert knows that. A touch of indifferent grammar flung in here and there, apparently at random, has a good effect –

often restores the confidence of a suspicious audience. He arranges these errors in private; for a really random error wouldn't do any good; it would be sure to fall in the wrong place. He also leaves blanks here and there – leaves them where genuine impromptu remarks can be dropped in, of a sort that will add to the natural aspect of the speech without breaking its line of march. At the banquet, he listens to the other speakers, invents happy turns upon remarks of theirs, and sticks these happy turns into his blanks for impromptu use by and by when he shall be called up. When this expert rises to his feet, he looks around over the house with the air of a man who has just been strongly impressed by something. The uninitiated cannot interpret his aspect, but the initiated can.

They know what is coming. When the noise of the clapping and stamping has subsided, this veteran says: "Aware that the hour is late, Mr. Chairman, it was my intention to abide by a purpose which I framed in the beginning of the evening – to simply rise and return my duty and thanks, in case I should be called upon, and then make way for men more able, and who have come with something to say. But, sir, I was so struck by General Smith's remark concerning the proneness of evil to fly upward, that" – etc., etc., etc.; and before you know it he has slidden smoothly along on his compliment to the general, and out of it and into his set speech, and you can't tell, to save you, where it was nor when it was that he made the connection. And that man will soar along, in the most beautiful way, on the wings of a practiced memory; heaving in a little decayed grammar here, and a little wise tautology there, and a little neatly counterfeited embarrassment yonder, and a little finely acted stumbling and stammering for a word – rejecting this word and that, and finally getting the right one, and fetching it out with ripping effect, and with the glad look of a man who has got out of a bad hobble entirely by accident, and wouldn't take a hundred dollars for that accident; and every now and then he will sprinkle you in one of those happy turns on something that has previously been said; and at last, with supreme art, he will catch himself, when in the very act of sitting down, and lean over the table and fire a parting rocket, in the way of an afterthought, which makes everybody stretch his mouth as it goes up, and dims the very stars in heaven when it explodes. And yet that man has been practicing that afterthought and that attitude for about a week.

Well, you can't reform that kind of a man. It's a case of Eli joined to his idols – let him alone. But there is one sort that can be reformed. That is the genuinely impromptu speaker. I mean the man who "didn't expect to be called upon, and isn't prepared"; and yet goes waddling and warbling along, just as if he thought it wasn't any harm to commit a crime so long as it wasn't premeditated. Now and then he says, "but I must not detain you longer"; every little while he says, "Just one word more and I am done" – but at these times he always happens to think of two or three more unnecessary things and so he stops to say them. Now that man has no way of finding out how long his windmill is going. He likes to hear it creak; and so he goes on creaking, and listening to it, and enjoying it, never thinking of the flight of time; and when he comes to sit down at last, and look under his hopper, he is the most surprised person in the house to see what a little bit of a grist he has ground, and how unconscionably long he has been grinding it. As a rule, he finds that he hasn't said anything – a discovery which the unprepared man ought usually to make, and does usually make – and has the added grief of making it at second hand, too.

This is a man who can be reformed. And so can his near relative, who now rises out of my reconstructed past – the man who provisions himself with a single prepared bite, of a sentence or two, and trusts to luck to catch quails and manna as he goes along. This person frequently gets left. You can easily tell when he has finished his prepared bit and begun on the impromptu part. Often the prepared portion has been built during the banquet; it may consist of ten sentences, but it oftener consists of two – oftenest of all, it is but a single sentence; and it has seemed so happy and pat and bright and good that the creator of it, the person that laid it, has been sitting there cackling privately over it and admiring it and petting it and shining it up, and imagining how fine it is going to "go," when, of course, he ought to have been laying another one, and still another one; and maybe a dozen or basketful if it's a fruitful day; yes, and he is thinking that when he comes to hurl that egg at the house there is going to be such an electric explosion of applause that the inspiration of it will fill him instantly with ideas and clothe the ideas in brilliant language, and that an impromptu speech will result which will be infinitely finer than anything he could have deliberately prepared. But there are two damaging things which he is leaving out of the calculation: one is, the historical fact that a man is never called up as soon as he thinks he is going to be called up, and that every speech that is injected into the proceedings ahead of him gives his fires an added chance to cool; and the other thing which he is forgetting is that he can't sit there and keep saying that fine sentence of his over and over to himself, for three-quarters of an hour without by and by getting a trifle tired of it and losing somewhat of confidence in it.

When at last his chance comes and he touches off his pet sentence, it makes him sick to see how shamefacedly and apologetically he has done it; and how compassionate the applause is; and how sorry everybody feels; and then he bitterly thinks what a lie it is to call this a free country where none but the unworthy and the undeserving may swear. And at this point, naked and blind and empty, he wallows off into his *real* impromptu speech; stammers out three or four incredibly flat things, then collapses into his seat, murmuring, "I wish I was in" – he doesn't say where, because he doesn't. The stranger at his left says, "Your opening was very good"; stranger at his right says, "I liked your opening"; man opposite says, "Opening very good indeed – very good"; two or three other people mumble something about his opening. People always feel obliged to pour some healing thing on a crippled man, that way. They mean it for oil; they think it *is* oil; but the sufferer recognizes it for aquafortis.

March 31, 1885

THE PRIVATE HISTORY OF A
CAMPAIGN THAT FAILED

YOU HAVE HEARD from a great many people who did something in the war; is it not fair and right that you listen a little moment to one who started out to do something in it, but didn't? Thousands entered the war, got just a taste of it, and then stepped out again, permanently. These, by their very numbers, are respectable, and are therefore entitled to a sort of voice, – not a loud one, but a modest one; not a boastful one, but an apologetic one. They ought not to be allowed much space among better people – people who did something – I grant that; but they ought at least to be allowed to state why they didn't do anything, and also to explain the process by which they didn't do anything. Surely this kind of light must have a sort of value.

Out West there was a good deal of confusion in men's minds during the first months of the great trouble – a good deal of unsettledness, of leaning first this way, then that, then the other way. It was hard for us to get our bearings. I call to mind an instance of this. I was piloting on the Mississippi when the news came that South Carolina had gone out of the Union on the 20th of December, 1860. My pilot-mate was a New Yorker. He was strong for the Union; so was I. But he would not listen to me with any patience; my loyalty was smirched, to his eye, because my father had owned slaves. I said, in palliation of this dark fact, that I had heard my father say, some years before he died, that slavery was a great wrong, and that he would free the solitary negro he then owned if he could think it right to give away the property of the family when he was so straitened in means. My mate retorted that a mere impulse was nothing – anybody could pretend to a good impulse; and went on decrying my Unionism and libeling my ancestry. A month later the secession atmosphere had considerably thickened on the Lower Mississippi, and I became a rebel; so did he. We were together in New Orleans, the 26th of January, when Louisiana went out of the Union. He did his full share of the rebel shouting, but was bitterly opposed to letting me do mine. He said that I came of bad stock – of a father who had been willing to set slaves free. In the following summer he was piloting a Federal gunboat and shouting for the Union again, and I was in the Confederate army. I held his note for some borrowed money. He was one of the most upright men I ever knew; but he repudiated that note without hesitation, because I was a rebel, and the son of a man who owned slaves.

In that summer – of 1861 – the first wash of the wave of war broke upon the shores of Missouri. Our State was invaded by the Union forces. They took possession of St. Louis, Jefferson Barracks, and some other points. The Governor, Claib Jackson, issued his proclamation calling out fifty thousand militia to repel the invader.

I was visiting in the small town where my boyhood had been spent – Hannibal, Marion County. Several of us got together in a secret place by night and formed ourselves into a military company. One Tom Lyman, a young fellow of a good deal of spirit but of no military experience, was made captain; I was made second lieutenant. We had no first lieutenant; I do not know why; it was long ago. There were fifteen of us. By the advice of an innocent connected with the organization, we called ourselves the Marion Rangers. I do not remember that any one found fault with the name. I did not; I thought it sounded quite well. The young fellow who proposed this title was perhaps a fair sample of the kind of stuff we were made of. He was young, ignorant, good-natured, well-meaning, trivial, full of romance, and given to reading chivalric novels and singing forlorn love-ditties. He had some pathetic little nickel-plated aristocratic instincts, and detested his name, which was Dunlap; detested it, partly because it was nearly as common in that region as Smith, but mainly because it had a plebeian sound to his ear. So he tried to ennoble it by writing it in this way: *d'Unlap.* That contented his eye, but left his ear unsatisfied, for people gave the new name the same old pronunciation – emphasis on the front end of it. He then did the bravest thing that can be imagined, – a thing to make one shiver when one remembers how the world is given to resenting shams and affectations; he began to write his name so: *d'Un Lap.* And he waited patiently through the long storm of mud that was flung at this work of art, and he had his reward at last; for he lived to see that name accepted, and the emphasis put where he wanted it, by people who had known him all his life, and to whom the tribe of Dunlaps had been as familiar as the rain and the sunshine for forty years. So sure of victory at last is the courage that can wait. He said he had found, by consulting some ancient French chronicles, that the name was rightly and originally written d'Un Lap; and said that if it were translated into English it would mean Peterson: *Lap*, Latin or Greek, he said, for stone or rock, same as the French *pierre*, that is to say, Peter; *d'*, of or from; *un*, a or one; hence, d'Un Lap, of or from a stone or a Peter; that is to say, one who is the son of a stone, the son of a Peter – Peterson. Our militia company were not learned, and the explanation confused them; so they called him Peterson Dunlap. He proved useful to us in his way; he named our camps for us, and he generally struck a name that was "no slouch," as the boys said.

That is one sample of us. Another was Ed Stevens, son of the town jeweler, – trim-built, handsome, graceful, neat as a cat; bright, educated, but given over entirely to fun. There was nothing serious in life to him. As far as he was concerned, this military expedition of ours was simply a holiday. I should say that about half of us looked upon it in the same way; not consciously, perhaps, but unconsciously. We did not think; we were not capable of it. As for myself, I was full of unreasoning joy to be done with turning out of bed at midnight and four in the morning, for a while; grateful to have a change, new scenes, new occupations, a new interest. In my thoughts that was as far as I went; I did not go into the details; as a rule one doesn't at twenty-four.

Another sample was Smith, the blacksmith's apprentice. This vast donkey had some pluck, of a slow and sluggish nature, but a soft heart; at one time he would knock a horse down for some impropriety, and at another he would get homesick and cry. However, he had one ultimate credit to his account which some of us hadn't: he stuck to the war, and was killed in battle at last.

Jo Bowers, another sample, was a huge, good-natured, flax-headed lubber; lazy, sentimental, full of harmless brag, a grumbler by nature; an experienced, industrious, ambitious, and often quite picturesque liar, and yet not a successful one, for he had had no intelligent training, but was allowed to come up just any way. This life was serious enough to him, and seldom satisfactory. But he was a good fellow anyway, and the boys all liked him. He was made orderly sergeant; Stevens was made corporal.

These samples will answer – and they are quite fair ones. Well, this herd of cattle started for the war. What could you expect of them? They did as well as they knew how, but really what was justly to be expected of them? Nothing, I should say. That is what they did.

We waited for a dark night, for caution and secrecy were necessary; then, toward midnight, we stole in couples and from various directions to the Griffith place, beyond the town; from that point we set out together on foot. Hannibal lies at the extreme south-eastern corner of Marion County, on the Mississippi River; our objective point was the hamlet of New London, ten miles away, in Ralls County.

The first hour was all fun, all idle nonsense and laughter. But that could not be kept up. The steady trudging came to be like work; the play had somehow oozed out of it; the stillness of the woods and the somberness of the night began to throw a depressing influence over the spirits of the boys, and presently the talking died out and each person shut himself up in his own thoughts. During the last half of the second hour nobody said a word.

Now we approached a log farm-house where, according to report, there was a guard of five Union soldiers. Lyman called a halt; and there, in the deep gloom of the overhanging branches, he began to whisper a plan of assault upon that house, which made the gloom more depressing than it was before. It was a crucial moment; we realized, with a cold suddenness, that here was no jest – we were standing face to face with actual war. We were equal to the occasion. In our response there was no hesitation, no indeci-sion: we said that if Lyman wanted to meddle with those soldiers, he could go ahead and do it; but if he waited for us to follow him, he would wait a long time.

Lyman urged, pleaded, tried to shame us, but it had no effect. Our course was plain, our minds were made up: we would flank the farm-house – go out around. And that is what we did.

We struck into the woods and entered upon a rough time, stum-bling over roots, getting tangled in vines, and torn by briers. At last we reached an open place in a safe region, and sat down, blown and hot, to cool off and nurse our scratches and bruises. Lyman was annoyed, but the rest of us were cheerful; we had flanked the farm-house, we had made our first military movement, and it was a success; we had nothing to fret about, we were feeling just the other way. Horse-play and laughing began again; the expedition was become a holiday frolic once more.

Then we had two more hours of dull trudging and ultimate silence and depression; then, about dawn, we straggled into New London, soiled, heel-blistered, fagged with our little march, and all of us except Stevens in a sour and raspy humor and privately down on the war. We stacked our shabby old shot-guns in Colonel

Ralls's barn, and then went in a body and breakfasted with that veteran of the Mexican war. Afterwards he took us to a distant meadow, and there in the shade of a tree we listened to an old-fashioned speech from him, full of gunpowder and glory, full of that adjective-piling, mixed metaphor, and windy declamation which was regarded as eloquence in that ancient time and that remote region; and then he swore us on the Bible to be faithful to the State of Missouri and drive all invaders from her soil, no matter whence they might come or under what flag they might march. This mixed us considerably, and we could not make out just what service we were embarked in; but Colonel Ralls, the practiced politician and phrase-juggler, was not similarly in doubt; he knew quite clearly that he had invested us in the cause of the Southern Confederacy. He closed the solemnities by belting around me the sword which his neighbor, Colonel Brown, had worn at Buena Vista and Molino del Rey; and he accompanied this act with another impressive blast.

Then we formed in line of battle and marched four miles to a shady and pleasant piece of woods on the border of the far-reaching expanses of a flowery prairie. It was an enchanting region for war – our kind of war.

We pierced the forest about half a mile, and took up a strong position, with some low, rocky, and wooded hills behind us, and a purling, limpid creek in front. Straightway half the command were in swimming, and the other half fishing. The ass with the French name gave this position a romantic title, but it was too long, so the boys shortened and simplified it to Camp Ralls.

We occupied an old maple-sugar camp, whose half-rotted troughs were still propped against the trees. A long corn-crib served for sleeping quarters for the battalion. On our left, half a mile away, was Mason's farm and house; and he was a friend to the cause. Shortly after noon the farmers began to arrive from several directions, with mules and horses for our use, and these they lent us for as long as the war might last, which they judged would be about three months. The animals were of all sizes, all colors, and all breeds. They were mainly young and frisky, and nobody in the command could stay on them long at a time; for we were town boys, and ignorant of horsemanship. The creature that fell to my share was a very small mule, and yet so quick and active that it could throw me without difficulty; and it did this whenever I got on it. Then it would bray – stretching its neck out, laying its ears back, and spreading its jaws till you could see down to its works. It was a disagreeable animal, in every way. If I took it by the bridle and tried to lead it off the grounds, it would sit down and brace back, and no one could budge it. However, I was not entirely destitute of military resources, and I did presently manage to spoil this game; for I had seen many a steamboat aground in my time, and knew a trick or two which even a grounded mule would be obliged to respect. There was a well by the corn-crib; so I substituted thirty fathom of rope for the bridle, and fetched him home with the windlass.

I will anticipate here sufficiently to say that we did learn to ride, after some days' practice, but never well. We could not learn to like our animals; they were not choice ones, and most of them had annoying peculiarities of one kind or another. Stevens's horse would carry him, when he was not noticing, under the huge excrescences which form on the trunks of oak-trees, and wipe him out of the saddle; in this way Stevens got several bad hurts. Sergeant Bowers's horse was very large and tall, with slim, long legs, and looked like a railroad bridge. His size enabled him to reach all about, and as far as he wanted to, with his head; so he was always biting Bowers's legs. On the march, in the sun, Bowers slept a good deal; and as soon as the horse recognized that he was asleep he would reach around and bite him on the leg. His legs were black and blue with bites. This was the only thing that could ever make him swear, but this always did; whenever the horse bit him he always swore, and of course Stevens, who laughed at everything, laughed at this, and would even get into such convulsions over it as to lose his balance and fall off his horse; and then Bowers, already irritated by the pain of the horse-bite, would resent the laughter with hard language, and there would be a quarrel; so that horse made no end of trouble and bad blood in the command.

However, I will get back to where I was – our first afternoon in the sugar-camp. The sugar-troughs came very handy as horse-troughs, and we had plenty of corn to fill them with. I ordered Sergeant Bowers to feed my mule; but he said that if I reckoned he went to war to be dry-nurse to a mule, it wouldn't take me very long to find out my mistake. I believed that this was insubordination, but I was full of uncertainties about everything military, and so I let the thing pass, and went and ordered Smith, the blacksmith's apprentice, to feed the mule; but he merely gave me a large, cold, sarcastic grin, such as an ostensibly seven-year-old horse gives you when you lift his lip and find he is fourteen, and turned his back on me. I then went to the captain, and asked if it was not right and proper and military for me to have an orderly. He said it was, but as there was only one orderly in the corps, it was but right that he himself should have Bowers on his staff. Bowers said he wouldn't serve on anybody's staff; and if anybody thought he could make him, let him try it. So, of course, the thing had to be dropped; there was no other way.

Next, nobody would cook; it was considered a degradation; so we had no dinner. We lazied the rest of the pleasant afternoon away, some dozing under the trees, some smoking cob-pipes and talking sweethearts and war, some playing games. By late supper-time all hands were famished; and to meet the difficulty all hands turned to, on an equal footing, and gathered wood, built fires, and cooked the meal. Afterward everything was smooth for a while; then trouble broke out between the corporal and the sergeant, each claiming to rank the other. Nobody knew which was the higher office; so Lyman had to settle the matter by making the rank of both officers equal. The commander of an ignorant crew like that has many troubles and vexations which probably do not occur in the regular army at all. However, with the song-singing and yarn-spinning around the camp-fire, everything presently became serene again; and by and by we raked the corn down level in one end of the crib, and all went to bed on it, tying a horse to the door, so that he would neigh if any one tried to get in.*

We had some horsemanship drill every forenoon; then, after-noons, we rode off here and there in squads a few miles, and visited the farmers' girls, and had a youthful good time, and got an honest good dinner or supper, and then home again to camp, happy and content.

For a time, life was idly delicious, it was perfect; there was nothing to mar it. Then came some farmers with an alarm one day.

---

* It was always my impression that that was what the horse was there for, and I know that it was also the impression of at least one other of the command, for we talked about it at the time, and admired the military ingenuity of the device; but when I was out West three years ago I was told by Mr. A. G. Fuqua, a member of our company, that the horse was his, that the leaving him tied at the door was a matter of mere forgetfulness, and that to attribute it to intelligent invention was to give him quite too much credit. In support of his position, he called my attention to the suggestive fact that the artifice was not employed again. I had not thought of that before.

They said it was rumored that the enemy were advancing in our direction, from over Hyde's prairie. The result was a sharp stir among us, and general consternation. It was a rude awakening from our pleasant trance. The rumor was but a rumor – nothing definite about it; so, in the confusion, we did not know which way to retreat. Lyman was for not retreating at all, in these uncertain circumstances; but he found that if he tried to maintain that attitude he would fare badly, for the command were in no humor to put up with insubordination. So he yielded the point and called a council of war – to consist of himself and the three other officers; but the privates made such a fuss about being left out, that we had to allow them to be present. I mean we had to allow them to remain, for they were already present, and doing the most of the talking too. The question was, which way to retreat; but all were so flurried that nobody seemed to have even a guess to offer. Except Lyman. He explained in a few calm words, that inasmuch as the enemy were approaching from over Hyde's prairie, our course was simple: all we had to do was not to retreat *toward* him; any other direction would answer our needs perfectly. Everybody saw in a moment how true this was, and how wise; so Lyman got a great many compliments. It was now decided that we should fall back on Mason's farm.

It was after dark by this time, and as we could not know how soon the enemy might arrive, it did not seem best to try to take the horses and things with us; so we only took the guns and ammunition, and started at once. The route was very rough and hilly and rocky, and presently the night grew very black and rain began to fall; so we had a troublesome time of it, struggling and stumbling along in the dark; and soon some person slipped and fell, and then the next person behind stumbled over him and fell, and so did the rest, one after the other; and then Bowers came with the keg of powder in his arms, whilst the command were all mixed together, arms and legs, on the muddy slope; and so he fell, of course, with the keg, and this started the whole detachment down the hill in a body, and they landed in the brook at the bottom in a pile, and each that was undermost pulling the hair and scratching and biting those that were on top of him; and those that were being scratched and bitten scratching and biting the rest in their turn, and all saying they would die before they would ever go to war again if they ever got out of this brook this time, and the invader might rot for all they cared, and the country along with him – and all such talk as that, which was dismal to hear and take part in, in such smothered, low voices, and such a grisly dark place and so wet, and the enemy may be coming any moment.

The keg of powder was lost, and the guns too; so the growling and complaining continued straight along whilst the brigade pawed around the pasty hillside and slopped around in the brook hunting for these things; consequently we lost considerable time at this; and then we heard a sound, and held our breath and listened, and it seemed to be the enemy coming, though it could have been a cow, for it had a cough like a cow; but we did not wait, but left a couple of guns behind and struck out for Mason's again as briskly as we could scramble along in the dark. But we got lost presently among the rugged little ravines, and wasted a deal of time finding the way again, so it was after nine when we reached Mason's stile at last; and then before we could open our mouths to give the countersign, several dogs came bounding over the fence, with great riot and noise, and each of them took a soldier by the slack of his trousers and began to back away with him. We could not shoot the dogs without endangering the persons they were attached to; so we had to look on, helpless, at what was perhaps the most mortifying spectacle of the civil war. There was light enough, and to spare, for the Masons had now run out on the porch with candles in their hands. The old man and his son came and undid the dogs without difficulty, all but Bowers's; but they couldn't undo his dog, they didn't know his combination; he was of the bull kind, and seemed to be set with a Yale time-lock; but they got him loose at last with some scalding water, of which Bowers got his share and returned thanks. Peterson Dunlap afterwards made up a fine name for this engagement, and also for the night march which preceded it, but both have long ago faded out of my memory.

We now went into the house, and they began to ask us a world of questions, whereby it presently came out that we did not know anything concerning who or what we were running from; so the old gentleman made himself very frank, and said we were a curious breed of soldiers, and guessed we could be depended on to end up the war in time, because no government could stand the expense of the shoe-leather we should cost it trying to follow us around. "Marion *Rangers*! good name, b'gosh!" said he. And wanted to know why we hadn't had a picket-guard at the place where the road entered the prairie, and why we hadn't sent out a scouting party to spy out the enemy and bring us an account of his strength, and so on, before jumping up and stampeding out of a strong position upon a mere vague rumor – and so on and so forth, till he made us all feel shabbier than the dogs had done, not half so enthusiastically welcome. So we went to bed shamed and low-spirited; except Stevens. Soon Stevens began to devise a garment for Bowers which could be made to automatically display his battle-scars to the grateful, or conceal them from the envious, according to his occasions; but Bowers was in no humor for this, so there was a fight, and when it was over Stevens had some battle-scars of his own to think about.

Then we got a little sleep. But after all we had gone through, our activities were not over for the night; for about two o'clock in the morning we heard a shout of warning from down the lane, accompanied by a chorus from all the dogs, and in a moment everybody was up and flying around to find out what the alarm was about. The alarmist was a horseman who gave notice that a detachment of Union soldiers was on its way from Hannibal with orders to capture and hang any bands like ours which it could find, and said we had no time to lose. Farmer Mason was in a flurry this time, himself. He hurried us out of the house with all haste, and sent one of his negroes with us to show us where to hide ourselves and our tell-tale guns among the ravines half a mile away. It was raining heavily.

We struck down the lane, then across some rocky pastureland which offered good advantages for stumbling; consequently we were down in the mud most of the time, and every time a man went down he blackguarded the war, and the people that started it, and everybody connected with it, and gave himself the master dose of all for being so foolish as to go into it. At last we reached the wooded mouth of a ravine, and there we huddled ourselves under the streaming trees, and sent the negro back home. It was a dismal and heart-breaking time. We were like to be drowned with the rain, deafened with the howling wind and the booming thunder, and blinded by the lightning. It was indeed a wild night. The drenching we were getting was misery enough, but a deeper misery still was the reflection that the halter might end us before we were a day older. A death of this shameful sort had not occurred to us as being among the possibilities of war. It took the romance all out of the campaign, and turned our dreams of glory into a repulsive nightmare. As for doubting that so barbarous an order had been given, not one of us did that.

The long night wore itself out at last, and then the negro came to us with the news that the alarm had manifestly been a false one, and that breakfast would soon be ready. Straightway we were light-hearted again, and the world was bright, and life as full of hope and promise as ever – for we were young then. How long ago that was! Twenty-four years.

The mongrel child of philology named the night's refuge Camp Devastation, and no soul objected. The Masons gave us a Missouri country breakfast, in Missourian abundance, and we needed it: hot biscuits; hot "wheat bread" prettily criss-crossed in a lattice pattern on top; hot corn pone; fried chicken; bacon, coffee, eggs, milk, buttermilk, etc.; – and the world may be confidently challenged to furnish the equal to such a breakfast, as it is cooked in the South.

We staid several days at Mason's; and after all these years the memory of the dullness, the stillness and lifelessness of that slumberous farm-house still oppresses my spirit as with a sense of the presence of death and mourning. There was nothing to do, nothing to think about; there was no interest in life. The male part of the household were away in the fields all day, the women were busy and out of our sight; there was no sound but the plaintive wailing of a spinning-wheel, forever moaning out from some distant room, – the most lonesome sound in nature, a sound steeped and sodden with homesickness and the emptiness of life. The family went to bed about dark every night, and as we were not invited to intrude any new customs, we naturally followed theirs. Those nights were a hundred years long to youths accustomed to being up till twelve. We lay awake and miserable till that hour every time, and grew old and decrepit waiting through the still eternities for the clock-strikes. This was no place for town boys. So at last it was with something very like joy that we received news that the enemy were on our track again. With a new birth of the old warrior spirit, we sprang to our places in line of battle and fell back on Camp Ralls.

Captain Lyman had taken a hint from Mason's talk, and he now gave orders that our camp should be guarded against surprise by the posting of pickets. I was ordered to place a picket at the forks of the road in Hyde's prairie. Night shut down black and threatening. I told Sergeant Bowers to go out to that place and stay till midnight; and, just as I was expecting, he said he wouldn't do it. I tried to get others to go, but all refused. Some excused themselves on account of the weather; but the rest were frank enough to say they wouldn't go in any kind of weather. This kind of thing sounds odd now, and impossible, but there was no surprise in it at the time. On the contrary, it seemed a perfectly natural thing to do. There were scores of little camps scattered over Missouri where the same thing was happening. These camps were composed of young men who had been born and reared to a sturdy independence, and who did not know what it meant to be ordered around by Tom, Dick, and Harry, whom they had known familiarly all their lives, in the village or on the farm. It is quite within the probabilities that this same thing was happening all over the South. James Redpath recognized the justice of this assumption, and furnished the following instance in support of it. During a short stay in East Tennessee he was in a citizen colonel's tent one day, talking, when a big private appeared at the door, and without salute or other circumlocution said to the colonel:

"Say, Jim, I'm a-goin' home for a few days."

"What for?"

"Well, I hain't b'en there for a right smart while, and I'd like to see how things is comin' on."

"How long are you going to be gone?"

"'Bout two weeks."

"Well, don't be gone longer than that; and get back sooner if you can."

That was all, and the citizen officer resumed his conversation where the private had broken it off. This was in the first months of the war, of course. The camps in our part of Missouri were under Brigadier-General Thomas H. Harris. He was a townsman of ours, a first-rate fellow, and well liked; but we had all familiarly known him as the sole and modest-salaried operator in our telegraph office, where he had to send about one dispatch a week in ordinary times, and two when there was a rush of business; consequently, when he appeared in our midst one day, on the wing, and delivered a military command of some sort, in a large military fashion, nobody was surprised at the response which he got from the assembled soldiery:

"Oh, now, what'll you take to *don't*, Tom Harris!"

It was quite the natural thing. One might justly imagine that we were hopeless material for war. And so we seemed, in our ignorant state; but there were those among us who afterward learned the grim trade; learned to obey like machines; became valuable soldiers; fought all through the war, and came out at the end with excellent records. One of the very boys who refused to go out on picket duty that night, and called me an ass for thinking he would expose himself to danger in such a foolhardy way, had become distinguished for intrepidity before he was a year older.

I did secure my picket that night – not by authority, but by diplomacy. I got Bowers to go, by agreeing to exchange ranks with him for the time being, and go along and stand the watch with him as his subordinate. We staid out there a couple of dreary hours in the pitchy darkness and the rain, with nothing to modify the dreariness but Bowers's monotonous growlings at the war and the weather; then we began to nod, and presently found it next to impossible to stay in the saddle; so we gave up the tedious job, and went back to the camp without waiting for the relief guard. We rode into camp without interruption or objection from anybody, and the enemy could have done the same, for there were no sentries. Everybody was asleep; at midnight there was nobody to send out another picket, so none was sent. We never tried to establish a watch at night again, as far as I remember, but we generally kept a picket out in the daytime.

In that camp the whole command slept on the corn in the big corn-crib; and there was usually a general row before morning, for the place was full of rats, and they would scramble over the boys' bodies and faces, annoying and irritating everybody; and now and then they would bite someone's toe, and the person who owned the toe would start up and magnify his English and begin to throw corn in the dark. The ears were half as heavy as bricks, and when they struck they hurt. The persons struck would respond, and inside of five minutes every man would be locked in a death-grip with his neighbor. There was a grievous deal of blood shed in the corn-crib, but this was all that was spilt while I was in the war. No, that is not quite true. But for one circumstance it would have been all. I will come to that now.

Our scares were frequent. Every few days rumors would come that the enemy were approaching. In these cases we always fell back on some other camp of ours; we never staid where we were. But the rumors always turned out to be false; so at last even we began to grow indifferent to them. One night a negro was sent to our corn-crib with the same old warning: the enemy was hovering in our neighborhood. We all said let him hover. We resolved to stay still and be comfortable. It was a fine warlike resolution, and

no doubt we all felt the stir of it in our veins – for a moment. We
had been having a very jolly time, that was full of horse-play and
school-boy hilarity; but that cooled down now, and presently the
fast-waning fire of forced jokes and forced laughs died out altogether, and the company became silent. Silent and nervous. And
soon uneasy – worried – apprehensive. We had said we would stay,
and we were committed. We could have been persuaded to go, but
there was nobody brave enough to suggest it. An almost noiseless
movement presently began in the dark, by a general but unvoiced
impulse. When the movement was completed, each man knew that
he was not the only person who had crept to the front wall and had
his eye at a crack between the logs. No, we were all there; all there
with our hearts in our throats, and staring out toward the sugar-
troughs where the forest foot-path came through. It was late, and
there was a deep woodsy stillness everywhere. There was a veiled
moonlight, which was only just strong enough to enable us to mark
the general shape of objects. Presently a muffled sound caught our
ears, and we recognized it as the hoof-beats of a horse or horses.
And right away a figure appeared in the forest path; it could have
been made of smoke, its mass had so little sharpness of outline. It
was a man on horseback; and it seemed to me that there were
others behind him. I got hold of a gun in the dark, and pushed it
through a crack between the logs, hardly knowing what I was
doing, I was so dazed with fright. Somebody said "Fire!" I pulled
the trigger. I seemed to see a hundred flashes and hear a hundred
reports, then I saw the man fall down out of the saddle. My first
feeling was of surprised gratification; my first impulse was an
apprentice-sportsman's impulse to run and pick up his game.
Somebody said, hardly audibly, "Good – we've got him! – wait for
the rest." But the rest did not come. We waited – listened – still no
more came. There was not a sound, not the whisper of a leaf; just
perfect stillness; an uncanny kind of stillness, which was all the
more uncanny on account of the damp, earthy, late-night smells
now rising and pervading it. Then, wondering, we crept stealthily
out, and approached the man. When we got to him the moon
revealed him distinctly. He was lying on his back, with his arms
abroad; his mouth was open and his chest heaving with long gasps,
and his white shirt-front was all splashed with blood. The thought
shot through me that I was a murderer; that I had killed a man –
a man who had never done me any harm. That was the coldest
sensation that ever went through my marrow. I was down by him

in a moment, helplessly stroking his forehead; and I would have given anything then – my own life freely – to make him again what he had been five minutes before. And all the boys seemed to be feeling in the same way; they hung over him, full of pitying interest, and tried all they could to help him, and said all sorts of regretful things. They had forgotten all about the enemy; they thought only of this one forlorn unit of the foe. Once my imagination persuaded me that the dying man gave me a reproachful look out of his shadowy eyes, and it seemed to me that I could rather he had stabbed me than done that. He muttered and mumbled like a dreamer in his sleep, about his wife and his child; and I thought with a new despair, "This thing that I have done does not end with him; it falls upon *them* too, and they never did me any harm, any more than he."

In a little while the man was dead. He was killed in war; killed in fair and legitimate war; killed in battle, as you may say; and yet he was as sincerely mourned by the opposing force as if he had been their brother. The boys stood there a half hour sorrowing over him, and recalling the details of the tragedy, and wondering who he might be, and if he were a spy, and saying that if it were to do over again they would not hurt him unless he attacked them first. It soon came out that mine was not the only shot fired; there were five others, – a division of the guilt which was a grateful relief to me, since it in some degree lightened and diminished the burden I was carrying. There were six shots fired at once; but I was not in my right mind at the time, and my heated imagination had magnified my one shot into a volley.

The man was not in uniform, and was not armed. He was a stranger in the country; that was all we ever found out about him. The thought of him got to preying upon me every night; I could not get rid of it. I could not drive it away, the taking of that unoffending life seemed such a wanton thing. And it seemed an epitome of war; that all war must be just that – the killing of strangers against whom you feel no personal animosity; strangers whom, in other circumstances, you would help if you found them in trouble, and who would help you if you needed it. My campaign was spoiled. It seemed to me that I was not rightly equipped for this awful business; that war was intended for men, and I for a child's nurse. I resolved to retire from this avocation of sham soldiership while I could save some remnant of my self-respect. These morbid thoughts clung to me against reason; for at bottom I did not believe I had touched that man. The law of probabilities decreed me guiltless of his blood; for in all my small experience with guns I had never hit anything I had tried to hit, and I knew I had done my best to hit him. Yet there was no solace in the thought. Against a diseased imagination, demonstration goes for nothing.

The rest of my war experience was of a piece with what I have already told of it. We kept monotonously falling back upon one camp or another, and eating up the country. I marvel now at the patience of the farmers and their families. They ought to have shot us; on the contrary, they were as hospitably kind and courteous to us as if we had deserved it. In one of these camps we found Ab Grimes, an Upper Mississippi pilot, who afterwards became famous as a dare-devil rebel spy, whose career bristled with desperate adventures. The look and style of his comrades suggested that they had not come into the war to play, and their deeds made good the conjecture later. They were fine horsemen and good revolver-shots; but their favorite arm was the lasso. Each had one at his pommel, and could snatch a man out of the saddle with it every time, on a full gallop, at any reasonable distance.

In another camp the chief was a fierce and profane old black-smith of sixty, and he had furnished his twenty recruits with gigantic home-made bowie-knives, to be swung with the two hands, like the *machetes* of the Isthmus. It was a grisly spectacle to see that earnest band practicing their murderous cuts and slashes under the eye of that remorseless old fanatic.

The last camp which we fell back upon was in a hollow near the village of Florida, where I was born – in Monroe County. Here we were warned, one day, that a Union colonel was sweeping down on us with a whole regiment at his heels. This looked decidedly serious. Our boys went apart and consulted; then we went back and told the other companies present that the war was a disappointment to us and we were going to disband. They were getting ready, themselves, to fall back on some place or other, and were only waiting for General Tom Harris, who was expected to arrive at any moment; so they tried to persuade us to wait a little while, but the majority of us said no, we were accustomed to falling back, and didn't need any of Tom Harris's help; we could get along perfectly well without him – and save time too. So about half of our fifteen, including myself, mounted and left on the instant; the others yielded to persuasion and staid – staid through the war.

An hour later we met General Harris on the road, with two or three people in his company – his staff, probably, but we could not tell; none of them were in uniform; uniforms had not come into vogue among us yet. Harris ordered us back; but we told him there was a Union colonel coming with a whole regiment in his wake, and it looked as if there was going to be a disturbance; so we had concluded to go home. He raged a little, but it was of no use; our minds were made up. We had done our share; had killed one man, exterminated one army, such as it was; let him go and kill the rest; and that would end the war. I did not see that brisk young general again until last year; then he was wearing white hair and whiskers.

In time I came to know that Union colonel whose coming frightened me out of the war and crippled the Southern cause to that extent – General Grant. I came within a few hours of seeing him when he was as unknown as I was myself; at a time when anybody could have said, "Grant? – Ulysses S. Grant? I do not remember hearing the name before." It seems difficult to realize that there was once a time when such a remark could be rationally made; but there *was*, and I was within a few miles of the place and the occasion too, though proceeding in the other direction.

The thoughtful will not throw this war-paper of mine lightly aside as being valueless. It has this value: it is a not unfair picture of what went on in many and many a militia camp in the first months of the rebellion, when the green recruits were without discipline, without the steadying and heartening influence of trained leaders; when all their circumstances were new and strange, and charged with exaggerated terrors, and before the invaluable experience of actual collision in the field had turned them from rabbits into soldiers. If this side of the picture of that early day has not before been put into history, then history has been to that degree incomplete, for it had and has its rightful place there. There was more Bull Run material scattered through the early camps of this country than exhibited itself at Bull Run. And yet it learned its trade presently, and helped to fight the great battles later. I could have become a soldier myself, if I had waited. I had got part of it learned; I knew more about retreating than the man that invented retreating.

December 1885

THE NEW DYNASTY

Hartford Monday Evening Club

POWER, WHEN LODGED in the hands of man, means oppression
– *insures* oppression: it means oppression *always*: not always consciously, deliberately, purposely; not always severely, or heavily, or
cruelly, or sweepingly; but *oppression*, anyway, and *always*, in one
shape or another. One may say it cannot even lift its hand in kindness but it hurts somebody by the same act whereby it delivers a
benevolence to his neighbor. Power cannot be so righteously
placed that it will neglect to exercise its great specialty, Oppression. Give it to the King of Dahomey, and he will try his new
repeating rifle on the passers-by in the courtyard; and as they fall,
one after another, it hardly occurs to him or to his courtiers that
he is committing an impropriety; give it to the high priest of the
Christian Church in Russia, the Emperor, and with a wave of his
hand he will brush a multitude of young men, nursing mothers,
gray headed patriarchs, gentle young girls, like so many un-
considered flies, into the unimaginable hells of his Siberia, and go
blandly to his breakfast, unconscious that he has committed a bar-
barity; give it to Constantine, or Edward IV, or Peter the Great,
or Richard III, or a hundred other monarchs that might be mentioned, and they slaughter members of their own family, and need
no opiates to help them sleep afterward; give it to Richard II, and
he will win the grateful tears of a multitude of slaves by setting
them free – to gain a vital point – and then laugh in their faces and
tear up their emancipation papers, and promise them a bitterer
and crueler slavery than ever they imagined before, the moment
his point has been gained; give it to the noblesse of the Middle
Ages, and they will claim and seize wandering freedmen as their
serfs; and with a totally unconscious irony will put upon THEM the
burden of proving that they are freedmen and not serfs; give it to
the Church, and she will burn, flay, slay, torture, massacre, ruthlessly – and neither she nor her friends will doubt that she is doing
the best she can for man and God; give it suddenly to the ignorant
masses of the French monarchy, maddened by a thousand years of
unspeakable tyranny, and they will drench the whole land with
blood and make massacre a pastime; give power to whomsoever
you please, and it will oppress; even the horse-car company will
work its men eighteen hours, in Arctic cold or Equatorial heat,

and pay them with starvation; and in expanded or in otherwise modified form, let the horse-car company stand for a thousand other corporations and companies and industries which might be named. Yes, you may follow it straight down, step by step, from the Emperor to the horse-car company, and wherever power resides it is used to oppress.

Now so far as we know or may guess, this has been going on for a million years. Who are the oppressors? The few: the king, the capitalist, and a handful of other overseers and superintendents. Who the oppressed? The many: The nations of the earth; the valuable personages; the workers; they that MAKE the bread that the soft-handed and the idle eat. Why is it right that there is not a fairer division of the spoil all around? BECAUSE LAWS AND CONSTITUTIONS HAVE ORDERED OTHERWISE. Then it follows that if the laws and constitutions should change around and say there SHALL be a more nearly equal division, THAT would have to be recognized as right. That is to confess, then, that in POLITICAL SOCIETIES, IT IS THE PREROGATIVE OF MIGHT TO DETERMINE WHAT IS RIGHT; that it is the prerogative of Might to create Right – and uncreate it, at will. It is to confess that if the banded voters among a laboring kinship of 45,000,000 of persons shall speak out to the other 12,000,000 or 15,000,000 of a nation and command that an existing system of rights and laws be reversed, that existing system has in that moment, in an absolutely clear and clean and legal way, become an obsolete and vanished thing – has utterly ceased to exist, and no creature in all the 15,000,000 is in the least degree privileged to find fault with the act.

We will grant, if you please, that for uncounted ages, the king and the scattering few have oppressed the nations – and have held in their hands the power to say what is right and what is not. Now was that power real, or was it a fiction? Until to-day it was real; but FROM to-day, in THIS country, I take heart of grace to believe, it is forevermore dust and ashes. For a greater than any king has arisen upon this the only soil in this world that is truly sacred to liberty; and you that have eyes to see and ears to hear may catch the sheen of his banners and the tramp of his marching hosts; and men may cavil, and sneer, and make wordy argument – but please God he will mount his throne; and he will stretch out his sceptre, and there will be bread for the hungry, clothing for the naked, and hope in eyes unused to hoping; and the sham nobilities will pass away, and the rightful lord will come to his own.

There was a time for sneering. In all the ages of the world and in all its lands, the huge inert mass of humbler mankind, – compacted crush of poor dull dumb animals, – equipped from its centre to its circumference with unimaginable might, and never suspecting it, has made bread in bitter toil and sweat, all its days for the feeble few to eat, and has impotently raged and wept by turns over its despised households of sore-hearted women and smileless children – and that was a time for sneering. And once in a generation, in all ages and all lands, a little block of this inert mass has stirred, and risen with noise, and said it could no longer endure its oppressions, its degradation, its misery – and then after a few days it has sunk back, vanquished, mute again, and laughed at – and that also was a time for sneers. And in these later decades, single mechanical trades have banded themselves together, and risen hopefully and demanded a better chance in this world's fight; and when it was the bricklayers, the other trades looked on with indifferent eye – it was not their fight; and when this or that or the other trade revolted, the ten millions in the other trades went uninterested about their own affairs – it was not their quarrel; – and that also was a time to sneer – and men did sneer. But when ALL the bricklayers, and all the bookbinders, and all the cooks, and all the barbers, and all the machinists, and all the miners, and blacksmiths, and printers, and hod-carriers, and stevedores, and housepainters, and brakemen, and engineers, and conductors, and factory hands, and horse-car drivers, and all the shop-girls; and all the sewing-women, and all the telegraph operators: in a word, all the myriad of toilers in whom is slumbering the reality of that thing which you call Power, not its age-worn sham and substanceless spectre, – when these rise, call the vast spectacle by any deluding name that will please your ear, but the fact remains, a NATION has risen! And by certain signs you may recognize it. When James Russell Lowell makes his courteous appeal for the little company of American authors before a Committee of the United States Senate – who listen as their predecessors have for sixty years listened to authors' appeals, with something of the indifference due a matter of small weight intruded by a faction inconsequent and few – and sits down and his place is taken by a foreman of a printing office, clad in unpretending gray, who says "I am not here as a printer; I am not here as a brick-layer; or a mason, or a carpenter, or as any other peculiar or particular handicrafts man; but I stand here to represent ALL the trades, ALL the industries, all brethren of ANY calling that labor with their hands for their daily bread and the bread of their wives and their little children, from Maine to the Gulf and from the Atlantic to the Pacific; and when I speak, out of my mouth issues the voice of five millions of men!" – when THAT thunderpeal falls, it is time for the Senatorial lethargy to show sign of life, to show interest, respect – yes, reverence, supple and eager recognition of the master, and to know what might be the King's messenger's commands. And, the Senators realize that indeed such time has come.

The authors had with slender hopefulness indicated what they would like the Congress to do; in the other case, without any insolence of speech or bearing, but reposeful with the clear consciousness of unassailable authority, the five-million-voiced printer DICTATED to the Congress – not anything which it MUST do, but certain things which it must NOT do. And that command will be heeded.

This was the first time in this world, perhaps, that ever a nation did actually and in its own person, not by proxy, speak. And by grace of fortune I was there to hear and see. It seemed to me that all the gauds and shows and spectacles of history somehow lost their splendor in this presence; their tinsel and lacquer and feathers seemed confessed and poor, contrasted with this real blood and flesh of majesty and greatness. And I thought then, and still think, that our country, so wastefully rich in things for her people to be proud of, had here added a thing which transcended all that went before. Here was the nation in person speaking; and its servants, *real* – not masters *called* servants by canting trick of speech – listening. The like could not be seen in any other country, or in any other age.

They whom that printer represented are in truth the nation: and they are still speaking. Have you read their Manifesto of demands? It has a curiously worn and old and threadbare sound. And it is old. It is older than the Scriptures. It is as old as Tyranny – old as Poverty – old as Despair. It is the oldest thing in this world – being as old as the human voice. In one form or another it has wearied the ears of the fortunate and the powerful in all the years of all the ages. And always it seemed the fretful cry of children – the fretful cry of a stranger's children, not one's own – and was not listened to; and did not need to be listened to, since as a matter of course they were crying for the moon, crying for the impossible. So one thought, without listening – without examining. But when *all* the children in a little world cry, one is roused out of his indifference by the mere magnitude of the fact – and he realizes that perhaps something is the matter; and he opens his ears. And what does he hear? Just what he has heard countless times before, as a mere dead formula of words; but now that his attention is awake, he perceives that these words have meaning. And so he – that is, you – do at last listen, do at last con the details of this rag of immemorial antiquity, this Manifesto of Wrongs and Demands, with alert senses. And straightway the thing that springs to your surprised lips when you are confronted by one or two of the things in that list, is the ejaculation, "Is it possible that so plain and manifest a piece of justice as this, is actually lacking to these men, and must be asked for? – has been lacking to them for ages, and the world's fortunate ones did not know it; or, knowing it could be indifferent to it, could endure the shame of it, the inhumanity of it?" And the thought follows in your mind, "Why this is as strange as that a famishing child should want its common right, the breast, and the mother-heart not divine it; or, divining it, turn away indifferent."

Read their Manifesto; read it in a judicial spirit, and ponder it. It impeaches certain of us of high treason against the rightful sovereign of this world; the indictment is found by a competent jury, and in no long time we must stand before the bar of the Republic and answer it. And you will assuredly find counts in it which not any logic of ours can controvert.

Many a time, when I have seen a man abusing a horse, I have wished I knew that horse's language, so that I could whisper in his ear, "Fool, you are master here, if you but knew it. Launch out with your heels!" The working millions, in all the ages, have been horses – were horses; all they needed was a capable leader to organize their strength and tell them how to use it, and they would in that moment be master. They have FOUND that leader somewhere, to-day, and they ARE master – the only time in this world that ever the true king wore the purple; the only time in this world that "By the grace of God, King" was ever uttered when it was not a lie.

And we need not fear this king. All the kings that have ruled the world heretofore were born the protectors and sympathizing friends and supporters of cliques and classes and clans of gilded idlers, selfish pap-hunters, restless schemers, troublers of the State in the interest of their private advantage. But this king is born the enemy of them that scheme and talk and do not work. He will be our permanent shield and defence against the Socialist, the Communist; the Anarchist, the tramp, and the selfish agitator for "reforms" that will beget bread and notoriety for him at cleaner men's expense; he will be our refuge and defence against these, and against all like forms of political disease, pollution, and death.

How will he use his power? *To oppress* – at first. For he is not better than the masters that went before; nor pretends to be. The only difference is, he will oppress the few, they oppressed the many; he will oppress the thousands, they oppressed the millions; but he will imprison nobody, he will massacre, burn, flay, torture, exile nobody, nor work any subject eighteen hours a day, nor starve his family. He will see to it that there is fair play, fair working hours, fair wages: and further than that, when his might has become securely massed and his authority recognized, he will not go, let us hope, and determine also to believe. He will be strenuous, firm, sometimes hard – he *must* be – for a while, till all his craftsmen be gathered into his citadel and his throne established. Until then let us be patient.

It is not long to wait; his day is close at hand: his clans are gathering, they are on their way; his bugles are sounding the call, they are answering; every week that comes and goes, sees ten thousand new crusaders swing into line and add their pulsing footfalls to the thunder-tread of his mighty battalions.

He is the most stupendous product of the highest civilization the world has even seen – and the worthiest and the best; and in no age but this, no land but this, and no lower civilization than this, could he ever have been brought forth. The average of his genuine, practical, valuable knowledge – and knowledge is the truest right divine to power – is an education contrasted with which the education possessed by the kings and nobles who ruled him for a hundred centuries is the untaught twaddle of a nursery, and beneath contempt. The *sum* of his education, as represented in the ten thousand utterly new and delicate and exact handicrafts, and divisions and subdivisions of handicrafts, exercised by his infinite brain and multitudinous members, is a sum of knowledge compared to which the sum of human knowledge in any and all ages of the world previous to the birth-year of the eldest person here present in this room, was as a lake compared to the ocean, the foot-hills compared to the Alps; a sum of knowledge which makes the knowledge of the elder ages seem but ignorance and darkness; even suggests the figure of a landscape lying dim and blurred under the stars, and the same landscape revealed in its infinitude of bloom, color, variety, detail, under the noontide sun. Without his education, he had continued what he was, a slave; with it, he is what he is, a sovereign. His was a weary journey, and long: the constellations have drifted far from the anchorages which they knew in the skies when it began; but at last he is here. He is here, – and he will remain. He is the greatest birth of the greatest age the nations of this world have known. You cannot sneer at him – that time has gone by. He has before him the most righteous work that was ever given into the hand of man to do: and he will do it. Yes, he is here; and the question is not – as it has been heretofore during a thousand ages – What shall we do with him? For the first time in history we are relieved of the necessity of managing his affair for him. He is not a broken dam this time – he is the Flood!

March 22, 1886

OUR CHILDREN

Authors Club Dinner, New York

OUR CHILDREN – yours – and – mine. They seem like little things to talk about – our children, but little things often make up the sum of human life – that's a good sentence. I repeat it, little things often produce great things. Now, to illustrate, take Sir Isaac Newton – I presume some of you have heard of Mr. Newton. Well, once when Sir Isaac Newton – a mere lad – got over into the man's apple orchard – I don't know what he was doing there – I didn't come all the way from Hartford to q-u-e-s-t-i-o-n Mr. Newton's honesty – but when he was there – in the man's orchard – he saw an apple fall and he was a-t-t-racted toward it, and that led to the discovery – not of Mr. Newton – but of the great law of *attraction* and gravitation.

And there was once another great discoverer – I've forgotten his name, and I don't remember what he discovered, but I know it was something very important, and I hope you will all tell your children about it, when you get home. Well, when the great discoverer was once loafin' around down in Virginia, and a-puttin' in his time flirting with Pocahontas – Oh, Captain John Smith, that was the man's name! – and while he and Poca were sitting in Mr. Powhatan's garden, he accidentally put his arm around her and picked something – a simple weed, which proved to be tobacco – and now we find it in every Christian family, shedding its civilizing influence broadcast throughout the whole religious community.

Now there was another great man, I can't think of *his* name either, who used to loaf around, and watch the great chandelier in the cathedral at Pisa, which set him to thinking about the great law of gunpowder, and eventually led to the discovery of the cotton gin.

Now, I don't say this as an inducement for our young men to loaf around like Mr. Newton, and Mr. Galileo, and Captain Smith, but they were once little babies, two days old, and they show what little things have sometimes accomplished.

April 22, 1886

DINNER SPEECH: GENERAL
GRANT'S GRAMMAR

Ninth Annual Reunion Banquet, Army and
Navy Club of Connecticut, Hartford

I WILL DETAIN you with only just a few words – just a few thousand words; and then give place to a better man – if he has been created. Lately a great and honored author, Matthew Arnold, has been finding fault with General Grant's English. That would be fair enough, maybe, if the examples of imperfect English averaged more instances to the page in General Grant's book than they do in Mr. Arnold's criticism upon the book – but they don't. It would be fair enough, maybe, if such instances were commoner in General Grant's book than they are in the works of the average standard author – but they aren't. In truth, General Grant's derelictions in the matter of grammar and construction are not more frequent than are such derelictions in the works of a majority of the professional authors of our time and of all previous times – authors as exclusively and painstakingly trained to the literary trade as was General Grant to the trade of war. This is not a random statement; it is a fact, and easily demonstrable. I have at home a book called *Modern English Literature: Its Blemishes and Defects*, by Henry H. Breen, F.S.A., a countryman of Mr. Arnold. In it I find examples of bad grammar and slovenly English from the pens of Sydney Smith, Sheridan, Hallam, Whately, Carlyle, both Disraelis, Allison, Junius, Blair, Macaulay, Shakespeare, Milton, Gibbon, Southey, Bulwer, Cobbett, Dr. Samuel Johnson, Trench, Lamb, Landor, Smollett, Walpole, Walker (of the dictionary), Christopher North, Kirke White, Mrs. Sigourney, Benjamin Franklin, Sir Walter Scott, and Mr. Lindley Murray, who made the grammar.

In Mr. Arnold's paper on General Grant's book we find a couple of grammatical crimes and more than several examples of very crude and slovenly English – enough of them to easily entitle him to a *lofty* place in that illustrious list of delinquents just named.

The following passage, all by itself, ought to elect him: "Meade suggested to Grant that he might wish to have immediately under him, Sherman, who had been serving with Grant in the West. *He* begged *him* not to hesitate if *he thought* it for the good of the service.

Grant assured *him* that *he* had no thought of moving *him*, and in *his* memoirs, after relating what had passed, *he* adds," etc. To read that passage a couple of times would make a man dizzy; to read it four times would make him drunk. General Grant's grammar is as good as anybody's; but if this were not so, Mr. Breen would brush that inconsequential fact aside and hunt his great book for higher game.

Mr. Breen makes this discriminating remark: "To suppose that because a man is a poet or a historian, he must be correct in his grammar, is to suppose that an architect must be a joiner, or a physician a compounder of medicines." Mr. Breen's point is well taken. If you should climb the mighty Matterhorn to look out over the kingdoms of the earth, it might be a pleasant incident to find strawberries up there. But, great Scott! you don't climb the Matterhorn for strawberries!

I don't think Mr. Arnold was quite wise; for he well knew that that Briton or American was never yet born who could safely assault another man's English; he knew as well as he knows anything, that the man never lived whose English was flawless. Can you believe that Mr. Arnold was immodest enough to imagine himself an exception to this cast iron rule – the sole exception discoverable within the three or four centuries during which the English language proper has been in existence? No, Mr. Arnold did not imagine that; he merely forgot that for a moment he was moving into a glass house, and he had hardly got fairly in before General Fry was shivering the panes over his head.

People may hunt out what microscopic motes they please, but, after all, the fact remains and cannot be dislodged, that General Grant's book is a great, and in its peculiar department unique and unapproachable literary masterpiece. In their line, there is no higher literature than those modest, simple memoirs. Their *style* is at least flawless, and no man can improve upon it; and great books are weighed and measured by their style and matter, not by the trimmings and shadings of their grammar.

There is that about the sun which makes us forget his spots; and when we think of General Grant our pulses quicken and his grammar vanishes; we only remember that this is the simple soldier, who, all untaught of the silken phrase makers, linked words together with an art surpassing the art of the schools, and put into them a something which will still bring to American ears, as long as America shall last, the roll of his vanished drums and the tread of the marching hosts. What do we care for grammar when we think of the man that put together that thunderous phrase: "Unconditional and immediate surrender!" And those others: "I propose to move immediately upon your works!" "I propose to fight it out on this line if it takes all summer!" Mr. Arnold would doubtless claim that that last sentence is not strictly grammatical; and yet it did certainly wake up this nation as a hundred million tons of A No. 1, fourth-proof, hardboiled, hidebound grammar from another mouth couldn't have done. And finally we have that gentler phrase; that one which shows you another true side of the man; shows that in his soldier heart there was room for other than gory war mottoes, and in his tongue the gift to fitly phrase them – "Let us have peace."

April 27, 1887

CONSISTENCY

Hartford Monday Evening Club

WE ARE CONTINUALLY warned to be consistent – by the pulpit, by the newspaper, by our associates. When we depart from consistency, we are reproached for it by these censors. When a man who has been born and brought up a Jew becomes a Christian, the Jews sorrow over it and reproach him for his inconstancy; all his life he has denied the divinity of Christ, but now he makes a lie of all his past; upon him rests the stigma of inconsistency; we can never be sure of him again. We put *in the deadly parallel columns* what he said *formerly* and what he says *now*, and his credit is *gone*. We say, Trust him *not*; we *know* him now; he will change *again*; and possibly *again* and yet *again*; he has no stability.

There are men called life-long Democrats, life-long Republicans. If one of these departs from his allegiance and votes the other ticket, the same thing happens as in the *Jew's* case. The man loses character. He is inconsistent. He is a traitor. His *past* utterances will be double columned with his *present* ones, and he is damned; also despised – even by his *new* political associates, for in theirs, as in *all* men's eyes, inconsistency is a treason and matter for scorn.

These are facts – common, every-day facts; and I have chosen them for that reason; facts known to everybody, facts which no one denies.

What is the most rigorous law of our being? *Growth*. No smallest atom of our moral, mental, or physical structure can stand still a *year*. It grows – it *must* grow; nothing can *prevent* it. It must grow downward *or* upward; it must grow smaller or larger, better or worse – it cannot stand still. In other words, we *change* – and *must* change, constantly, and keep on changing as long as we live. What, then, is the *true* gospel of consistency? *Change*. Who is the *really* consistent man? The man who changes. Since change is the law of his *being*, he cannot *be* consistent if he stick in a rut.

Yet, as the quoted facts show, there are those who would mis-teach us that to stick in a rut *is* consistency – and a *virtue*; and that to climb *out* of the rut is inconsistency – and a *vice*. They will grant you certain things, without murmur or dissent – as things which go without saying; truisms. They will grant that in time the crawling baby *walks* and must not be required to go *on crawling*;

that in time the *youth* has *outgrown* the *child's jacket* and must not
be required to crowd himself *into* it; they grant you that a child's
knowledge is becoming and proper to the *child only* so they grant him
a school and *teach* him, so that he may *change* and *grow*; they grant
you that he must keep *on* learning – through youth and manhood
and straight *on* – he must not be allowed to suppose that the knowledge of *thirty* can be any proper equipment for his *fiftieth* year; they
will grant you that a young man's opinions about mankind and the
universe are *crude*, and sometimes *foolish*, and they would not
dream of requiring him to stick to them the rest of his life, lest by
changing them he bring down upon himself the reproach of *inconsistency*. They will grant you *these*, and everything *else* you can think
of, in the line of progress and change, until you get down to politics
and religion; there they draw the *line*. These must suffer no change.
Once a Presbyterian, *always* a Presbyterian, or you are inconsistent
and a *traitor*; once a Democrat, *always* a Democrat, or you are
inconsistent and a *traitor* – a turncoat.

It is curious logic. Is there but *one* kind of treason? No man
remains the same sort of Presbyterian he was at *first* – the thing is
impossible; time and various *influences modify* his Presbyterianism; it
narrows or it *broadens*, grows *deeper* or *shallower*, but does not stand
still. In some cases it grows so far beyond itself, upward *or* downward, that nothing is really *left of it* but the *name*, and perhaps an
inconsequential *rag* of the original substance, the *bulk* being now
Baptist or Buddhist or something. Well, if he go over to the
Buddhists, he is a traitor. To whom? To what? No man can answer
those questions rationally. Now if he does *not* go over what is he?
Plainly a traitor to *himself*, a traitor to the best and the highest and
the honestest that is *in* him. Which of these treasons is the blackest
one – and the shamefulest? Which is the real and right consistency?
To be consistent to a sham and an empty name, or consistent to
the law of one's *being*, which is *change*, and in this case requires him
to move forward and keep abreast of his best mental and moral
progress, his highest convictions of the right and the true? Suppose
this treason to the name of a church should carry him clear outside
of *all* churches? Is that a blacker treason than to *remain*? So long
as he is loyal to his best *self*, what should he care for *other* loyalties?
It seems to me that a man should secure the *Well done, faithful
servant*, of his own conscience *first* and foremost, and let all other
loyalties go.

I have referred to the fact that when a man retires from his political party he is a *traitor* – that he is so *pronounced* in plain language. *That* is *bold*; so bold as to deceive many into the fancy that it is *true*. Desertion, treason – these are the terms applied. Their *military form* reveals the thought in the man's mind who uses them; to *him* a political party is an *army*. Well, *is* it? Are the two things identical? Do they even *resemble* each other? Necessarily a political party is not an army of conscripts, for *they* are in the ranks by *compulsion*. Then it must be a *regular* army, or an army of volunteers. *Is* it a *regular* army? No, for *these* enlist for a specified and well-understood *term* and can retire without reproach when the term is up. Is it an army of *volunteers* who have *enlisted for the war*, and may righteously be shot if they leave before the war is finished? No, it is not even an army in *that* sense. Those fine military terms are high-sounding, empty *lies* – and are no more rationally applicable to a political party than they would be to an oyster bed. The volunteer soldier comes to the recruiting office and strips himself, and proves that he is so many feet high, and has sufficiently good teeth, and no fingers gone, and is sufficiently sound in body *generally*; he is accepted, but *not* until he has sworn a deep *oath*, or made other solemn form of *promise*, to march under that flag until that war is done or his term of enlistment completed. What is the process when a *voter* joins a *party*? Must he prove that he is sound in *any* way, mind *or* body? Must he prove that *he knows* anything – whatever – is capable *of* anything? Does he take an oath or make a *promise* of any sort? – or doesn't he leave himself entirely *free*? If he were informed by the political boss that if he join it must be forever; that he must be that party's chattel and wear its brass collar the rest of his days, would not that *insult* him? It goes without saying. He would say some rude, unprintable thing and turn his back on that preposterous organization. But the political boss puts *no* conditions upon him at *all*; and his volunteer makes no promises, enlists for no stated *term*. He has in *no sense* become a part of an *army*, he is in no way restrained of his *freedom*. Yet he will presently find that his bosses and his newspapers have *assumed* just the reverse of that; that they have blandly arrogated to themselves an iron-clad military *authority* over him; and within twelve months, if he is an average man, he will have *surrendered* his liberty, and will actually be silly enough to believe that he cannot leave that party, for any cause whatever, without being a shameful *traitor*, a deserter, a legitimately dishonored *man*.

There you have the just measure of that freedom of conscience, freedom of opinion, freedom of speech and action, which we hear so much inflated foolishness about, as being the precious possession of the Republic. Whereas, in *truth*, the surest way for a man to make of himself a target for almost universal scorn, obloquy, slander, and insult is to stop twaddling about these priceless independencies, and attempt to *exercise* one of them. If he is a preacher, half his congregation will clamor for his expulsion, and *will* expel him, except they find it will injure real estate in the neighborhood; if he is a mechanic, he will be discharged, promptly; if he is a lawyer, his clients will take their business elsewhere; if he is a doctor, his own dead will turn against him.

I repeat that the new party member who supposed himself independent will presently find that the party has somehow got a mortgage on his soul, and that within a year he will *recognize* the mortgage, deliver up his liberty, and actually believe he cannot retire from that party from *any* motive, howsoever high and right, in his *own* eyes, without shame and dishonor.

Is it possible for human wickedness to invent a doctrine more infernal and poisonous than this? Is there *imaginable* a baser servitude than it imposes? What slave is so degraded as the slave who is *proud* that he *is* a slave? What is the *essential difference* between a life-long *Democrat* and any other kind of life-long *slave*? Is it less humiliating to dance to the lash of *one* master than *another*?

This atrocious doctrine of allegiance to *party* plays directly into the hands of politicians of the *baser* sort – and doubtless for *that* it was borrowed – or stolen – from the monarchical system. It enables them to foist upon the country officials whom no self-respecting man would *vote* for, if he could but come to understand that loyalty to *himself* is his first and *highest* duty, not loyalty to any *party name*. The wire workers, convention packers, know they are not obliged to put up the *fittest* man for the office, for they know that the docile party will vote for any forked thing they *put up*, even though it do not even strictly *resemble a man*.

I am persuaded – convinced – that this idea of *consistency* – unchanging allegiance to *party* – has lowered the manhood of the whole *nation* – pulled it down and dragged it in the mud. When Mr. Blaine was nominated for the Presidency, I *knew* the man; no, I *judged* I knew him; I don't know him *now*, but at *that* time I *judged* I *knew* him; for my daily paper had been painting him black, and blacker, and blacker *still*, for a series of *years*, during which it had no call to speak anything but the *truth* about him, no call to be *malicious* toward him, no call to be otherwise than just simply and honestly *candid* about him, since he belonged to its *own party* and was not before the nation as a detectable candidate for anything. But within thirty days after the nomination that paper had him all painted up *white* again. *That* is not allegiance to one's best *self*, one's straitest *convictions*; it is allegiance to *party*. Nobody likes to eat a ton of black *paint*, and none but the *master* can make the slave *do* it. Was this paper *alone* at this singular feast? *No*; ten thousand *other* Republican newspapers sat down at the same table and worried down *their* ton apiece; and not any fewer than *100,000* more-or-less-prominent *politicians* sat down all over this country and worried down *their* ton apiece; and after long, long and bitter gagging, some *millions* of the *common* serfdom of the party sat down and worried down *their* ton apiece. *Paint?* It was *dirt*. Enough of it was eaten by the meek Republican party to build a railroad embankment from here to *Japan*; and it pains me to think that a year from now they will probably have to eat it all *over* again.

Well, there was a *lot* of queer feasting done in those days. One *learned in the law* pondered the Mulligan letters and other *frightful* literature, and rendered this impressive verdict: he said the evidence would not *convict* Mr. Blaine in a *court of law*, and so he would *vote* for him. He did not *say* whether the evidences would prove him *innocent* or not. *That* wasn't important.

Now, he knew that this verdict was absolutely inconclusive. He knew that it settled nothing, established nothing whatever, and was wholly valueless as a guide for his action, an answer to his questionings.

He knew that the merciful and righteous barriers raised up by the laws of our humane age for the shelter and protection of the possibly innocent, have often and over again protected and rescued the certainly *guilty*. He knew that in this way many and many a prisoner has gone unchastised from the court when judge and jury and the whole public believed with all their hearts that he was guilty. He knew – all credit not discredit to our age that it is so – that this result is so frequent, so almost commonplace, that the mere failure to satisfy the exacting forms of law and prove a man guilty in a *court*, is a hundred thousand miles from proving him innocent. You see a hiccoughing man wallowing in the gutter at two o'clock in the morning; you think the thing all over and weigh the details of it in your mind as you walk home, and with immeasurable wisdom arrive at the verdict that *you don't know he wasn't a*

Prohibitionist. Of course you don't, and if you stop and think a minute you would realize that you don't know he *was*, either.

Well, a good clergyman who read the Mulligan and other published evidences was not able to *make* up *his* mind, but concluded to take refuge in the verdict rendered by the citizen learned in the *law*; take his intellectual and moral food at second-hand, though he doesn't *rank* as an intellectual infant, unable to chew his own moral and mental nourishment; he decided that an *apparently colored* person who couldn't be proven to be black *in the baffling crosslights of a court of law* was white enough for *him*, he being a little color blind, *anyway*, in matters where the *party* is concerned, and so *he* came reluctantly to the polls, with his redeeming blush on his countenance, and put in his vote.

I met a certain *other* clergyman on the *corner* the day after the nomination. He was very uncompromising. He said: "I *know* Blaine to the *core*; I have known him from boyhood *up*; and I know him to be utterly unprincipled and unscrupulous." Within six weeks after that, this clergyman was at a Republican *mass* meeting in the Opera House, and I think he presided. At *any* rate, he made a speech. If you did not know that the character depicted in it meant Mr. Blaine, you would suppose it meant – well, there isn't anybody down here on the *earth* that you can use as a comparison. It is praise, praise, praise; laudation, laudation, laudation; glorification, glorification, canonization. Conceive of the general crash and upheaval and ripping and tearing and readjustment of things that must have been going on in that man's moral and mental chaos for six weeks! What is any combination of inflammatory rheumatism and St. Vitus's dance to *this*? When the doctrine of allegiance to party can utterly up-end a man's moral constitution and make a temporary *fool* of him *besides*, what excuse are you going to offer for preaching it, teaching it, extending it, perpetuating it? Shall you say, the best good of the country demands allegiance to party? Shall you also say it demands that a man kick his truth and his conscience into the gutter, and become a mouthing lunatic, *besides*? Oh, no! you say; it does not demand *that*. But what if it *produce* that, in *spite* of you? There is no obligation upon a man to do things which he ought *not* to do, when *drunk*, but most men *will* do them, just the same, and so we hear no arguments about obligations in the matter; we only hear men warned to *avoid* the habit of *drinking*; get *rid* of the thing that can betray men into such things.

This is a funny business, all round. The same men who enthusi-astically preach loyal consistency to church and party are always ready and willing and anxious to persuade a Chinaman or an Indian or a Kanaka to desert *his* Church, or a fellow-American to desert *his* party. The man who deserts to them is all that is high and pure and beautiful – apparently; the man who deserts from them is all that is foul and despicable. This is Consistency with a capital C.

With the daintiest and self-complacentest sarcasm the lifelong loyalist scoffs at the Independent – or, as he calls him, with cutting irony, the Mugwump; makes himself too killingly funny for any-thing in this world about him. But – the Mugwump can stand it, for there is a great history at his back, stretching down the centu-ries, and he comes of a mighty ancestry. *He* knows that in the whole history of the race of men no single great and high and beneficent thing was ever done for the souls and bodies, the hearts and the brains, of the children of this world, but a Mugwump started it and Mugwumps carried it to victory. And their names are the stateliest in history: Washington, Garrison, Galileo, Luther, Christ. Loyalty to petrified opinions never yet broke a chain or freed a human soul in *this* world – and never *will.*

To return to the starting point: I am persuaded that the world has been tricked into adopting some false and most pernicious notions about *consistency* – and to such a degree that the average man has turned the rights and *wrongs* of things entirely *around*, and is *proud* to be "consistent," unchanging, immovable, fossilized, where it should be his humiliation that he is so.

December 2, 1887

AMERICAN AUTHORS
AND BRITISH PIRATES

A PRIVATE LETTER AND A PUBLIC POSTSCRIPT.

MY DEAR MATTHEWS:

Come, now, what your cause needs is, that some apparent sufferer shall say a fair word for the other side. That complaint which cannot hunt up a dissenting voice anywhere is out of luck. A thing which is all good or all bad is properly an object of suspicion in this world; we get a sort of impression that it is off its beat; that it belongs in the next world, above or below – climate not suited to it here.

English pirates have hurt me somewhat; how much, I do not know. But, on the other hand, English *law* has helped me vastly. Can any foreign author of books say that about American law? You know he can't.

Look at the matter calmly, reasonably. As I infer, from what you say about your article, your complaint is, that American authors are pirated in England. Well, whose fault is that? It is nobody's but the author's. England furnishes him a perfect remedy; if he does not choose to take advantage of it, let him have self-respect enough to retire to the privacy of his cradle, not sit out on the public curbstone and cry. To-day the American author can go to Canada, spend three days there, and come home with an English and Canadian copyright which is as strong as if it had been built out of railroad iron. If he does not make this trip and do this thing, it is a confession that he does not think his foreign market valuable enough to justify the expense of securing it by the above process. Now it may turn out that that book is presently pirated in London. What then? Why, simply this: the pirate has paid that man a compliment; he has thought more of the book than the man thought of it himself. And doubtless the man is not pecuniarily injured, since the pirate would probably not have offered anything for the book if it had been copyrighted, but would merely have left it in oblivion and unpublished.

I believe, and it stands to reason, that all the American books that are pirated in these latter days in England are of the complimentary sort, and that the piracies work no computable injury to the author's pocket; and I also believe that if this class of books should be copyrighted henceforth, their publication over there would cease, and then all the loss would fall upon the authors, since they wouldn't be any better off, as regards money, than they were before, and would lose their compliment besides.

I think we are not in a good position to throw bricks at the English pirate. We haven't any to spare. We need them to throw at the American Congress; and at the American author, who neglects his great privileges and then tries to hunt up some way to throw the blame upon the only nation in the world that is magnanimous enough to say to him: "While you are the guest of our laws and our flag, you shall not be robbed."

All the books which I have published in the last fifteen years are protected by English copyright. In that time I have suffered pretty heavily in temper and pocket from imperfect copyright laws; but they were American, not English. I have no quarrel over there.

Yours sincerely,

MARK TWAIN.

P. S. (of the feminine sort). I wrote the above (but have concluded not to mail it directly to you) in answer to your letter asking me for facts and statistics concerning English piracies of my books. I had to guess at the probable nature of your NEW PRINCETON article from what you said of it. But I sent out for it this morning, and have read it through. Why, dear, dear distorted mind, I am amazed at you. You stand recorded in the directory, "Brander Matthews, lawyer, 71 Broadway." By your article I half suspected that you were a lawyer, and so I went to the directory to see. It seemed to me that only a lawyer – an old lawyer – a callous, leathery, tough old lawyer – could have the superb pluck to venture into court with such a ragged case as yours is. Why, dear soul, you haven't a leg to stand on, anywhere. I have known you long, and loved you always; but you must let me be frank and say, you haven't a fact that cannot be amply offset by the other side, you haven't an argument that cannot be promptly turned against you.

To start with, you wander a little off to one side of your real case, to tell the world that a couple of reverend British reprobates have been plagiarizing – stealing – from American books. That is a telling fact – if American preachers never steal. But, dear sir, they do. Take this case. E. H. House spends twelve or thirteen years in Japan; becomes exhaustively versed in Japanese affairs; coins these riches into an admirable article, and prints it in the *Atlantic* six

years ago, under the title, "The Martyrdom of an Empire." This
present year, Rev. James King Newton, A. M., "Professor of Modern Languages, Oberlin College," confers upon the literary
museum of the *Bibliotheca Sacra* a crazy-quilt which he wordily
names, "Obligations of the United States to Initiate a Revision of
Treaties between the Western Powers and Japan." This queer
work is made up of rags and scraps of sense and nonsense, sham
and sincerity, theft and butter-mouthed piousness, modesty and
egotism, facts and lies, knowledge and ignorance, first-rate English
and fortieth-rate English, wind and substance, dignity and paltriness, and all through the air about it you seem to catch the soft
clear note of flutes and birds, mingled with the wild weird whoop-
jamboreehoo of the embattled jackass. Now, part of that strange
article is original. The rest of it was "smouched" from House's
Atlantic paper. Will you have a sample?

Atlantic Monthly, May, 1881.	*Bibliotheca Sacra, January, 1887.*
The first effective commercial treaty with Japan was draughted by him in 1858, upon terms which, in general, were not disadvantageous to the unsophisticated people with whom he was dealing.	Mr. Harris made our first commercial treaty in 1858, upon terms which, in general, were reasonable, in an experimental treaty, and not disadvantageous to the unsophisticated people with whom he was dealing.
If he had taken the precaution to insure the absolute expiration of the treaty and its appendages at a proper date, all would have resulted as he desired.	If he had taken the precaution to insure the absolute expiration of the treaty and its appendages at some definite time, all would have resulted according to his honest intention.
The working of the treaty has proved flagrantly injurious to Japan and proportionately favorable to the foreign powers – exceptionally favorable to England, that country having the most extensive trade connection.	The working of the treaties has proved most disastrous to Japan, and proportionately favorable to the western powers; exceptionally so to England, as she has the largest trade connections.

Precisely what this country intended to accomplish by that imposing deed it would be difficult to say. What it did accomplish, etc.	Precisely what our government intended to accomplish by the imposing deed of opening Japan, it would be difficult to say. What it did accomplish, etc.

There you have four samples. I could give you twenty-four more, if they were needed, to show how exactly Mr. Newton can repeat slathers and slathers of another man's literature without ever missing a trick, when the police ain't around. You can get that thing if you would like to look at it. Brer Newton has issued it in pamphlet form, at a Boston admirer's expense; and has printed up in the corner of the cover, "With the Author's Compliments" – meaning House, per'aps.

But then, we are all thieves, and it wasn't worth your while to go out of your way to call particular attention to a couple of reverend British ones.

However, right away you come down to business, and open up your real case. You say: "In 1876, Longfellow" complained that he had been pirated by twenty-two publishers. Did he mean, *after* England had offered him and the rest of us protection, and was standing always ready to make her offer good?

Next, "in 1856, Hawthorne" – some more ancient history. You follow it with more and more and more examples – of ancient history; ancient history, and, properly and righteously, out of court. By no fairness can they be cited in this modern time; by no legitimate pretext can they be summoned to testify in this case of yours. What you are complaining about, what you are making all this trouble about, is a bitter grievance which passed out of this world and into its eternal grave more than fifteen years ago. When I say eternal, I mean, of course, if you will let it alone. Matthews, it is a dead issue – utterly dead, and legally forgotten – and I don't believe that even you can aggravate Parliament into resurrecting it, though you certainly do seem to be doing your level best in that direction.

Now, honestly, as between friend and friend, what could ever have put it into your head to hunt out such a grotesquely barren text for a magazine article? *We* are doing all the pirating in these days; the English used to be in the business, but they dropped out of it long ago. Just look at yourself and your fantastic complaint by the light of allegory. Suppose one of those big Mohammedan slave-dealers in the interior of Africa, lashing his yoked caravan of poor naked creatures through jungle and forest, should turn his grieved attention to us, and between his lashings and thrashings passionately upbraid us with the reminder that "in 1856," and other years and seasons of a hoary and odious antiquity, we used to own our brother human beings, and used to buy them and sell them, lash them, thrash them, break their piteous hearts – and we ought to be ashamed of ourselves, so we ought! What should we answer? What should we say to him? What would *you* say to him concerning so particularly dead an issue as that? – as a lawyer, that is, strictly as a lawyer. I do not know what you would say, but I know what you *could* say. You could say: "Let me take that obsolete case of yours into court; my hand is in, I have been handling one that is just like it – the twin to it, in fact."

In your dozen pages you mention a great many injured American authors, and a great many pirated American books. Now here is a thing which is the exact truth about all of those books and all of those authors: such of the books as were issued before England allowed us copyright, suffered piracy without help; and at the very same time, *five times as many* English books suffered piracy without help on our side of the water. The one fact offsets the other; and the honors are easy – the rascalities, I mean. But, such of those American books as were issued *after* England allowed us copyright, and yet suffered piracy, suffered it by their authors' own fault, not England's, nor anybody else's. Their injuries are of their own creation, and they have no shadow of right to set up a single whimper. Why, I used to furnish a sick child in West Hartford with gratis milk; do you know, that cub's mother wasn't satisfied, but wanted me to come over there and warm it? I may be out in my calculations, but I don't believe England is going to warm the milk for this nursery over here.

Great Scott, what arguments you do set up! John Habberton writes *Helen's Babies*; could have English-copyrighted it; didn't; it was pirated, and he thinks he has something to complain about. What, for instance? – that they didn't warm the milk? He issued other books; took out no foreign copyrights, same as before; is pirated from Canada to Australia, and thinks he has something to complain about, once more. Oh, good land! However, "warned by his early experience, he" – does what? Attempts an evasion of the English law, and gets left. Pardon the slang, it does seem to fit in so handy there. With that attempted evasion in one's mind, the neat bit of sarcasm which Habberton fillips at the morals of "the average British publisher" loses some trifle of its bloom, don't you think?

Consider! Right in the midst of all your and Habberton's discontent and animadversion, you placidly give your cause a deadly stab under the fifth rib, and you don't seem to notice that you have done it at all; you meander right along, fretting the same as before. I refer to this remark of yours – and where you forgot to italicize, I have supplied the defect: "The English courts have held that under certain circumstances prior publication in Great Britain *will give an author copyright in England, whatever his nationality may be.*" How could you set down this great, big, generous fact, this fact which offers its fine and gracious hospitalities, without equivalent or even thank-you, to the swindled scribe of all the climes the sun in his course shines upon – even to you yourself – how could you set it down, and not uncover in its magnificent presence? How could you set it down, and not be smitten with a large and sudden realization of the contrast between its open broad palm and the stingy clinched fist of your own country? How could you look it in the face – that friendly, fresh, wholesome, hearty, welcoming, modern countenance – and go on throwing stale mud over its head at its predecessor, an old kiln-dried, moss-backed, bug-eaten, antediluvian mummy that wasn't doing anything to you, and couldn't if it had wanted to? How could you? You are the very wrong-headedest person in America. I tell it you for your own solace. Why, man, you – well, you are geometrically color-blind; you can't see the proportions of things. And you are injudicious. Don't you know that as long as you've got a goitre that you have to trundle around on a wheelbarrow you can't divert attention from it by throwing bricks at a man that's got a wart on the back of his ear? Those blacklegs in Congress keep us furnished with the prize goitre of the moral and intellectual world, and the thing for you to do is to let the wart-wearers strictly alone.

Well, next you cite another case like Habberton's. "Under certain circumstances," as you have said, the protection of the English law was free to both of these authors. You well know that it was their plain duty to find out what those "circumstances" were. They didn't do it, they exploited some smart ostensibilities instead, and their copyright failed. Those "circumstances" are quite simple and explicit, and quite easy to inform one's self about. It follows, and is a fact, that those sufferers had just themselves to blame, and nobody else.

I wonder what *would* satisfy some people. You are an American, I believe; in fact, I know you are. If you want to copyright a book, here at home, what must you do? This: you must get your title-page printed on a piece of paper; enclose it to the Librarian of Congress; apply to him, in writing, for a copyright; and send him a cash fee. That is what you, personally, have to do; the rest is with your publisher. What do you have to do in order to get the same book copyrighted in England? You are hampered by no bothers, no details of any kind whatever. When you send your manuscript to your English publisher, you tell him the date appointed for the book to issue here, and trust him to bring it out there a day ahead. Isn't that simple enough? No letter to any official; no title-page to any official; no fee to anybody; and yet that book has a copyright on it which the Charleston earthquake couldn't unsettle. "Previous publication" in Great Britain of an American book secures perfect copyright; to "previously publish" all but the tail-end of a book in America, and then "previously publish" that mere tail-end in Great Britain, has what effect? Why, it copyrights that tail-end, of course. Would any person in his right mind imagine that it would copyright any more than that? Mr. Habberton seems to have imagined that it would. Mr. Habberton knows better now.

Let the rest of your instances pass. They are but repetitions. There isn't an instance among your antiquities that has any bearing upon your case, or shadow of right to be cited in it – unless you propose to try a corpse, for crimes committed upon other corpses. Living issue you have none, nor even any spectral semblance of any. Your modern instances convict your clients of not knowing enough to come in when it rains. From your first page to your last one, you do not chance to get your hands on a single argument that isn't a boomerang. And finally, to make your curious work symmetrical and complete, you rest from your pitiless lathering of the bad English publisher, and fall to apologizing to him – and, apparently, to the good one, too, I don't know why: "At bottom, the publishers, good or bad, *are not to blame.*" You are right, for once, perfectly right; they are not to blame – to-day; if they commit a piracy in these days, nine-tenths of the sin belongs with the American author. And since you perceive that they are not to blame, what did you blame them for? If you were going to take it all back, why didn't you take it back earlier, and not write it at all?

Hang it, you are not logical. Do you think that to lather a man all through eleven pages and then tell him he isn't to blame after all, is treating yourself right? Why no, it puts you in such a rickety position. I read it to the cat – well, I never saw a cat carry on so before.

But, of course, somebody or something was to blame. You were in honor bound to make that fact clear, or you couldn't possibly excuse yourself for raising all this dust. Now, I will give any rational man 400,000 guesses, and go bail that he will run short before he has the luck to put his finger on the place where you locate that blame. Now listen – and try to rise to the size of this inspired verdict of yours: "*It is the condition of* THE LAW *which is at fault.*" (*!*) Upon my life, I have never heard anything to begin with the gigantic impudence of that. The cat – but never mind the cat; the cat is dead; a cat can't stand everything. "*The remedy is to* CHANGE THE LAW" – and then you go owling along, just as if there was never anything more serious in this world than the stupefying nonsense you are talking. Change the law? Change it? In what way, pray? A law which gives us absolutely unassailable and indestructible copyright at cost of not a single penny, not a moment of time, not an iota of trouble, not even the bother of *asking* for it! Change it? How are you going to change it? Matthews, I am your friend, and you know it; and that is what makes me say what I do say: you want a change of air, or you'll be in the asylum the first thing you know.

January 1888

YALE COLLEGE SPEECH

Yale Alumni Association Banquet, Hartford

I WAS SINCERELY proud and grateful to be made a Master of Arts by this great and venerable university, and I would have come last June to testify this feeling, as I do now testify it, but that the sudden and unexpected notice of the honor done me found me at a distance from home and unable to discharge that duty and enjoy that privilege.

Along at first, say for the first month or so, I did not quite know how to proceed, because of my not knowing just what authorities and privileges belonged to the title which had been granted me, but after that I consulted some students of Trinity, in Hartford, and they made everything clear to me. It was through them that I found out that my title made me head of the governing body of the university, and lodged in me very broad and severely responsible powers. It is through trying to work these powers up to their maximum of efficiency that I have had such a checkered career this year. I was told that it would be necessary for me to report to you at this time, and of course I comply, though I would have preferred to put it off till I could make a better showing: for indeed I have been so pertinaciously hindered and obstructed at every turn by the faculty that it would be difficult to prove that the university is really in any better shape now than it was when I first took charge. In submitting my report, I am sorry to have to begin with the remark that respect for authority seems to be at a quite low ebb in the college. It is true that this has caused me pain, but it has not discouraged me. By advice, I turned my earliest attention to the Greek department. I told the Greek professor I had concluded to drop the use of the Greek written character, because it was so hard to spell with, and so impossible to read after you get it spelled. Let us draw the curtain there. I saw by what followed that nothing but early neglect saved him from being a very profane man.

I ordered the professor of mathematics to simplify the whole system, because the way it was, I couldn't understand it, and I didn't want things going on in the college in what was practically a clandestine fashion. I told him to drop the conundrum system; it was not suited to the dignity of a college, which should deal in facts, not guesses and suppositions; we didn't want any more cases of *if*

A and B stand at opposite poles of the earth's surface and C at the equator of Jupiter, at what variations of angle will the left limb of the moon appear to these different parties? I said you just let that thing alone; it's plenty time to get in a sweat about it when it happens; as like as not it ain't going to do any harm anyway. His reception of these instructions bordered on insubordination; insomuch that I felt obliged to take his number, and report him.

I found the astronomer of the university gadding around after comets and other such odds and ends – tramps and derelicts of the skies. I told him pretty plainly that we couldn't have that. I told him it was no economy to go on piling up and piling up raw material in the way of new stars and comets and asteroids that we couldn't ever have any use for till we had worked off the old stock. I said if I caught him strawberrying around after any more asteroids, especially, I should have to fire him out. Privately, prejudice got the best of me there, I ought to confess it. At bottom I don't really mind comets so much, but somehow I have always been down on asteroids. There is nothing mature about them; I wouldn't sit up nights, the way that man does, if I could get a basketful of them. He said it was the best line of goods he had; he said he could trade them to Rochester for comets, and trade the comets to Harvard for nebulae, and trade the nebulae to the Smithsonian for flint hatchets. I felt obliged to stop this thing on the spot; I said we couldn't have the university turned into an astronomical junk shop.

And while I was at it I thought I might as well make the reform complete; the astronomer is extraordinarily mutinous; and so with your approval I will transfer him to the law deparment and put one of the law students in his place. A boy will be more biddable, more tractable, also cheaper. It is true he cannot be entrusted with important work at first, but he can comb the skies for nebulae till he gets his hand in. I have other changes in mind, but as they are in the nature of surprises, I judge it politic to leave them unspecified at this time.

February 6, 1889

TO WALT WHITMAN

Hartford, Conn., May 24, 1889.

YOU HAVE LIVED just the seventy years which are greatest in the world's history, and richest in benefit and advancement to its peoples. These seventy years have done much more to widen the interval between man and the other animals than was accomplished by any five centuries which preceded them.

What great births you have witnessed! The steam-press, the steamship, the steel-ship, the railroad, the perfected cotton-gin, the telegraph, the telephone, the phonograph, the photograph, the photogravure, the electrotype, the gaslight, the electric light, the sewing-machine, and the amazing, infinitely varied and innumerable products of coal-tar, those latest and strangest marvels of a marvelous age. And you have seen even greater births than these; for you have seen the application of anæsthesia to surgery-practice, whereby the ancient dominion of pain, which began with the first created life, came to an end in this earth forever; you have seen the slave set free; you have seen monarchy banished from France, and reduced in England to a machine which makes an imposing show of diligence and attention to business, but isn't connected with the works. Yes, you have indeed seen much; but tarry yet awhile, for the greatest is yet to come. Wait thirty years, and *then* look out over the earth! You shall see marvels upon marvels added to these whose nativity you have witnessed; and conspicuous above them you shall see their formidable Result – Man at almost his full stature at last! – and still growing, visibly growing, while you look. In that day, who that hath a throne, or a gilded privilege not attainable by his neighbor, let him procure him slippers and get ready to dance, for there is going to be music. Abide, and see these things! Thirty of us who honor and love you, offer the opportunity. We have among us six hundred years, good and sound, left in the bank of life. Take thirty of them – the richest birthday gift ever offered to poet in this world – and sit down and wait. Wait till you see that great figure appear, and catch the far glint of the sun upon his banner; then you may depart satisfied, as knowing you have seen him for whom the world was made, and that he will proclaim that human wheat is worth more than human tares, and proceed to reorganize human value on that basis.

With best wishes for a happy issue to a grateful undertaking.

1889

ON FOREIGN CRITICS

Dinner for Max O'Rell, Boston

IF I LOOK harried and worn, it is not from an ill conscience. It is from sitting up nights to worry about the foreign critic. He won't concede that we have a civilization – a "real" civilization. Five years ago, he said we had never contributed anything to the betterment of the world. And now comes Sir Lepel Griffin, whom I had not suspected of being in the world at all, and says "there is no country calling itself civilized where one would not rather live than in America, except Russia." That settles it. That is, it settles it for Europe; but it doesn't make me any more comfortable than I was before.

What is a "real" civilization? Nobody can answer that conundrum. They have all tried. Then suppose we try to get at what it is not; and then subtract the what it is not from the general sum, and call the remainder "real" civilization – so as to have a place to stand on while we throw bricks at these people. Let us say, then, in broad terms, that any system which has in it any one of these things, to wit, human slavery, despotic government, inequality, numerous and brutal punishments for crimes, superstition almost universal, ignorance almost universal, and dirt and poverty almost universal – is not a real civilization, and any system which has none of them, is.

If you grant these terms, one may then consider this conundrum: How old is real civilization? The answer is easy and unassailable. A century ago it had not appeared anywhere in the world during a single instant since the world was made. If you grant these terms – and I don't see why it shouldn't be fair, since civilization must surely mean the humanizing of a people, not a class – there is today but one real civilization in the world, and it is not yet thirty years old. We made the trip and hoisted its flag when we disposed of our slavery.

However, there are some partial civilizations scattered around over Europe – pretty lofty civilizations they are, too – but who begot them? What is the seed from which they sprang? Liberty and intelligence. What planted that seed? There are dates and statistics which suggest that it was the American Revolution that planted it. When that revolution began, monarchy had been on trial some thousands of years, over there, and was a distinct and convicted failure, every time. It had never produced anything but a vast, a nearly universal, savagery, with a thin skim of civilization on top, and the main part of that was nickel plate and tinsel. The French, imbruted and impoverished by centuries of oppression and official robbery, were a starving nation clothed in rags, slaves of an aristocracy of smirking dandies clad in unearned silks and velvet. It makes one's cheek burn to read of the laws of the time and realize that they were for human beings; realize that they originated in this world, and not in hell. Germany was unspeakable. In the Scottish lowlands the people lived in styes, and were human swine; in the highlands drunkenness was general, and it hardly smirched a young girl to have a family of her own. In England there was a sham liberty, and not much of that; crime was general; ignorance the same; poverty and misery were widespread; London fed a tenth of her population by charity; the law awarded the death penalty to almost every conceivable offense; what was called medical science by courtesy stood where it had stood for two thousand years; Tom Jones and Squire Western were gentlemen.

The printer's art had been known in Germany and France three and a quarter centuries, and in England three. In all that time there had not been a newspaper in Europe that was worthy the name. Monarchies had no use for that sort of dynamite. When we hoisted the banner of revolution and raised the first genuine shout for human liberty that had ever been heard, this was a newspaperless globe. Eight years later, there were six daily journals in London to proclaim to all the nations the greatest birth this world had ever seen. Who woke that printing press out of its trance of three hundred years? Let us be permitted to consider that we did it. Who summoned the French slaves to rise and set the nation free? We did it. What resulted in England and on the Continent? Crippled liberty took up its bed and walked. From that day to this its march has not halted, and please God it never will. We are called the nation of inventors. And we are. We could still claim that title and wear its loftiest honors, if we had stopped with the first thing we ever invented – which was human liberty. Out of that invention has come the Christian world's great civilization. Without it it was impossible – as the history of all the centuries has proved. Well, then, who invented civilization? Even Sir Lepel Griffin ought to be able to answer that question. It looks easy enough. *We* have contributed nothing! Nothing hurts me like ingratitude.

Yes, the coveted verdict has been persistently withheld from us. Mr. Arnold granted that our whole people – including by especial mention "that immense class, the great bulk of the community," the wage and salary-earners – have liberty, equality, plenty to eat, plenty to wear, comfortable shelter, high pay, abundance of churches, newspapers, libraries, charities, and a good education for everybody's child for nothing. He added, "society seems organized there for their benefit" – benefit of the bulk and mass of the people. Yes, it is conceded that we furnish the greatest good to the greatest number; and so all we lack is a civilization.

Mr. Arnold's indicated civilization would seem to be restricted, by its narrow lines and difficult requirements, to a class – the top class – as in tropical countries snow is restricted to the mountain summits. And from what one may gather from his rather vague and unsure analysis of it, the snow metaphor would seem to fit it in more ways than one. The impression you get of it is, that it is peculiarly hard, and glittering, and bloodless, and unattainable. Now if our bastard were a civilization, it could fairly be figured – by Mr. Arnold's own concessions – by the circulation of the blood, which nourishes and refreshes the whole body alike, delivering its rich streams of life and health impartially to the imperial brain and the meanest extremity.

April 27, 1890

REPLY TO THE EDITOR OF "THE ART OF AUTHORSHIP"

YOUR INQUIRY HAS set me thinking, but, so far, my thought fails to materialise. I mean that, upon consideration, I am not sure that I have methods in composition. I do suppose I have – I suppose I must have – but they somehow refuse to take shape in my mind; their details refuse to separate and submit to classification and description; they remain a jumble – visible, like the fragments of glass when you look in at the wrong end of a kaleidoscope, but still a jumble. If I could turn the whole thing around and look in at the other end, why then the figures would flash into form out of the chaos, and I shouldn't have any more trouble. But my head isn't right for that to-day, apparently. It might have been, maybe, if I had slept last night.

However, let us try guessing. Let us guess that whenever we read a sentence and like it, we unconsciously store it away in our model-chamber; and it goes with the myriad of its fellows to the building, brick by brick, of the eventual edifice which we call our style. And let us guess that whenever we run across other forms – bricks – whose colour, or some other defect, offends us, we unconsciously reject these, and so one never finds them in our edifice. If I have subjected myself to any training processes, and no doubt I have, it must have been in this unconscious or half-conscious fashion. I think it unlikely that deliberate and consciously methodical training is usual with the craft. I think it likely that the training most in use is of this unconscious sort, and is guided and governed and made by-and-by unconsciously systematic, by an automatically-working taste – a taste which selects and rejects without asking you for any help, and patiently and steadily improves itself without troubling you to approve or applaud. Yes, and likely enough when the structure is at last pretty well up, and attracts attention, *you* feel complimented, whereas you didn't build it, and didn't even consciously superintend. Yes; one notices, for instance, that long, involved sentences confuse him, and that he is obliged to re-read them to get the sense. Unconsciously, then, he rejects that brick. Unconsciously he accustoms himself to writing short sentences as a rule. At times he may indulge himself with a long one, but he will make sure that there are no folds in it, no vaguenesses, no parenthetical interruptions of its view as a whole; when he is done with it, it won't be a sea-serpent, with half of its arches under the water, it will be a torchlight procession.

Well, also he will notice in the course of time, as his reading goes on, that the difference between the *almost right* word and the *right* word is really a large matter – 'tis the difference between the lightning-bug and the lightning. After that, of course, that exceedingly important brick, the *exact* word – however, this is running into an essay, and I beg pardon. So I seem to have arrived at this: doubtless I have methods, but they begot themselves, in which case I am only their proprietor, not their father.

1890

AIX-LES-BAINS

CERTAINLY AIX-LES-BAINS is an enchanting place. It is a strong word, but I think the facts justify it. True, there is a rabble of nobilities, big and little, here all the time, and often a king or two, but as these behave quite nicely and also keep mainly to themselves, they are little or no annoyance. And then a king makes the best advertisement there is, and the cheapest. All he costs is a reception at the station by the Mayor and the police in their Sunday uniforms, shop-front decorations along the route from station to hotel, brass band at the hotel, fireworks in the evening, free bath in the morning. This is the whole expense; and in return for it he goes away from here with the broad of his back metaphorically stenciled over with display ads, which shout to all the nations of the earth, assisted by the telegraph:

> Rheumatism routed at Aix-les-Bains!
> Gout admonished, Nerves braced up!
> All Diseases welcomed, and satisfaction
> given, or the money refunded at the door.

We leave nature's noble cliffs and crags undefiled and uninsulted by the advertiser's paint-brush. We use the back of a king, which is better and properer, and more effective, too, for the cliff stays still and few see it, but the king moves across the fields of the world, and is visible from all points like a constellation. We are out of kings this week, but one will be along soon – possibly his Satanic Majesty of Russia. There's a colossus for you! A mysterious and terrible form that towers up into unsearchable space and casts a shadow across the universe like a planet in eclipse. There will be but one absorbing spectacle in this world when we stencil him and start him out.

This is an old valley, this of Aix, both in the history of man and the geological records of its rocks. Its little Lake of Bourget carries the human history back to the lake dwellers, furnishing seven groups of their habitations, and Dr. William Wakefield says in his interesting local guide-book that the mountains round about furnish "geologically, a veritable epitome of the globe." The stratified chapters of the earth's history are clearly and permanently written on the sides of the roaring bulk of the Dent du Chat, but many of the layers of race, religion, and government, which in turn have flourished and perished here between the lake dweller of several thousand years ago and the French Republican of today, are ill-defined and uninforming by comparison. There were several varieties of pagans. They went their way, one after the other, down into night and oblivion, leaving no account of themselves, no memorials. The Romans arrived 2,300 years ago; other parts of France are rich with remembrances of their eight centuries of occupation, but not many are here. Other pagans followed the Romans. By and by Christianity arrived, some 400 years after the time of Christ. The long procession of races, languages, religions, and dynasties demolished each other's monuments and obliterated each other's records – it is man's way always.

As a result, nothing is left of the handiwork of the remoter inhabitants of the region except the constructions of the lake dwellers and some Roman odds and ends. There is part of a small Roman temple, there is part of a Roman bath, there is a graceful and battered Roman arch. It stands on a turfy level over the way from the present great bathhouse, is surrounded by magnolia trees, and is both a picturesque and suggestive object. It has stood there some 1,600 years. Its nearest neighbor, not twenty steps away, is a Catholic church. They are symbols of the two chief eras in the history of Aix. Yes, and of the European world. I judge that the venerable arch is held in reverent esteem by everybody, and that this esteem is its sufficient protection from insult, for it is the only public structure I have yet seen in France which lacks the sign, "It is forbidden to post bills here." Its neighbor, the church, has that sign on more than one of its sides, and other signs, too, forbidding certain other sorts of desecration.

The arch's next nearest neighbor – just at its elbow, like the church – is the telegraph office. So there you have the three great eras bunched together – the era of war, the era of theology, the era of business. You pass under the arch, and the buried Cæsars seem to rise from the dust of the centuries and flit before you; you pass by that old battered church, and are in touch with the middle ages, and with another step you can put down ten francs and shake hands with Oshkosh under the Atlantic.

It is curious to think what changes the last of the three symbols stands for; changes in men's ways and thoughts, changes in material civilization, changes in the Deity – or in men's conception of the Deity, if that is an exacter way of putting it. The second of the symbols arrived in the earth at a time when the Deity's possessions consisted of a small sky freckled with mustard seed stars, and under it a patch of landed estate not so big as the holdings of the Czar today, and all his time was taken up in trying to keep a handful of Jews in some sort of order – exactly the same number of them that the Czar has lately been dealing with in a more abrupt and far less loving and long-suffering way. At a later time – a time within all old men's memories – the Deity was otherwise engaged. He was dreaming his eternities away on his great white throne, steeped in the soft bliss of hymns of praise wafted aloft without ceasing from choirs of ransomed souls, Presbyterians and the rest. This was a Deity proper enough to the size and condition of things, no doubt a provincial Deity with provincial tastes. The change since has been inconceivably vast. His empire has been unimaginably enlarged. Today he is master of a universe made up of myriads upon myriads of gigantic suns, and among them, lost in that limitless sea of light, floats that atom, his earth, which once seemed so good and satisfactory and cost so many days of patient labor to build, a mere cork adrift in the waters of a shoreless Atlantic. This is the business era, and no doubt he is governing his huge empire now, not by dreaming the time away in the buzz of hymning choirs, with occasional explosions of arbitrary power disproportioned to the size of the annoyance, but, by applying laws of a sort proper and necessary to the sane and successful management of a complex and prodigious establishment, and by seeing to it that the exact and constant operation of these laws is not interfered with for the accommodation of any individual or political or religious faction or nation.

Mighty has been the advance of the nations and the liberalization of thought. A result of it is a changed Deity, a Deity of a dignity and sublimity proportioned to the majesty of his office and the magnitude of his empire, a Deity who has been freed from a hundred fretting chains and will in time be freed from the rest by the several ecclesiastical bodies who have these matters in charge. It was, without doubt, a mistake and a step backward when the Presbyterian Synods of America lately decided, by vote, to leave him still embarrassed with the dogma of infant damnation. Situated as we are, we cannot at present know with how much of anxiety he watched the balloting, nor with how much of grieved disappointment he observed the result.

Well, all these eras above spoken of are modern, they are of last week, they are of yesterday, they are of this morning, so to speak.

The springs, the healing waters that gush up from under this hillside village, indeed are ancient; they, indeed, are a genuine antiquity; they antedate all those fresh human matters by processions of centuries; they were born with the fossils of the Dent du Chat, and they have been always limpid and always abundant. They furnished a million gallons a day to wash the lake dwellers with, the same to wash the Cæsars with, no less to wash the Balzac with, and have not diminished on my account. A million gallons a day – for how many days? Figures cannot set forth the number. The delivery, in the aggregate, has amounted to an Atlantic. And there is still an Atlantic down in there. By Dr. Wakefield's calculation that Atlantic is three-quarters of a mile down in the earth. The calculation is based upon the temperature of the water, which is 114° to 117° Fahrenheit, the natural law being that below a certain depth heat augments at the rate of one degree for every sixty feet of descent.

Aix is handsome and handsomely situated, too, on its hill slope, with its stately prospect of mountain range and plain spread out before it and about it. The streets are mainly narrow, and steep, and crooked, and interesting, and offer considerable variety in the way of names; on the corner of one of them you read this: Rue du Puits d'Enfer – pit of Hell street. Some of the sidewalks are only eighteen inches wide; they are for the cats probably. There is a pleasant park, and there are spacious and beautiful grounds connected with the two great pleasure resorts – the Cercle and the Villa des Fleurs. The town consists of big hotels, little hotels, and pensions. The season lasts about six months, beginning with May. When it is at its height there are thousands of visitors here, and in the course of the season as many as 20,000 in the aggregate come and go.

These are not all here for the baths; some come for the gambling facilities and some for the climate. It is a climate where the field strawberry flourishes through the spring, summer, and fall. It is hot in the summer, and hot in earnest; but this is only in the daytime; it is not hot at night. The English season is May and June; they get a good deal of rain then, and they like that. The Americans take July and the French take August. By the 1st of July the open air music and the evening concerts and operas and plays are fairly under way, and from that time onward the rush of pleasure has a steadily increasing boom. It is said that in August the great grounds and the gambling-rooms are crowded all the time and no end of ostensible fun going on.

It is a good place for rest and sleep and general recuperation of forces. The book of Dr. Wakefield says there is something about this atmosphere which is the deadly enemy of insomnia, and I think this must be true, for, if I am any judge, this town is at times the noisiest one in Europe, and yet a body gets more sleep here than he could at home, I don't care where his home is. Now we are living at a most comfortable and satisfactory pension, with a garden of shade trees and flowers and shrubs, and a convincing air of quiet and repose. But just across the little narrow street is the little market square, and at a corner of that is that church that is neighbor to the Roman arch, and that narrow street, and that billiard-table of a market place, and that church are able, on a bet, to turn out more noise to the cubic yard at the wrong time than any other similar combination in the earth or out of it. In the street you have the skull-bursting thunder of the passing hack, a volume of sound not producible by six hacks anywhere else; on the hack is a lunatic with a whip, which he cracks to notify the public to get out of his way. This crack is as keen and sharp and penetrating and ear-splitting as a pistol shot at close range, and the lunatic delivers it in volleys, not single shots. You think you will not be able to live till he gets by, and when he does get by he only leaves a vacancy for the bandit who sells *Le Petit Journal* to fill with his strange and awful yell. He arrives with the early morning and the market people, and there is a dog that arrives at about the same time and barks steadily at nothing till he dies, and they fetch another dog just like him. The bark of this breed is the twin of the whip volley, and stabs like a knife. By and by, what is left of you the church-bell gets. There are many bells, and apparently 6,000 or 7,000 town clocks, and as they are all five minutes apart – probably by law – there are no intervals. Some of them are striking all the time – at least, after you go to bed they are. There is one clock that strikes the hour, and then strikes it over again to see if it was right. Then for evenings and Sundays there is a chime – a chime that starts in pleasantly and musically, then suddenly breaks into a frantic roar, and boom, and crash of warring sounds that make you think Paris is up and the revolution come again. And yet, as I have said, one sleeps here – sleeps like the dead. Once he gets his grip on his sleep neither hack, nor whip, nor news fiend, nor dog, nor bell-cyclone, nor all of them together can wrench it loose or mar its deep and tranquil continuity. Yes, there is indeed something in this air that is death to insomnia.

The buildings of the Cercle and the Villa des Fleurs are huge in size and each has a theater in it and a great restaurant, also conveniences for gambling and general and variegated entertainment. They stand in ornamental grounds of great extent and beauty. The multitudes of fashionable folk sit at refreshment tables in the open air afternoons and listen to the music, and it is there that they mainly go to break the Sabbath.

To get the privilege of entering these grounds and buildings you buy a ticket for a few francs which is good for the whole season. You are then free to go and come at all hours, attend the plays and concerts free, except on special occasions, gamble, buy refreshments, and make yourself symmetrically comfortable.

Nothing could be handier than those two little theaters. The curtain doesn't rise until 8:30. Then between the acts one can idle for half an hour in the other departments of the building, damaging his appetite in the restaurants or his pocket in the baccarat room. The singers and actors are from Paris and their performance is beyond praise.

I was never in a fashionable gambling hell until I came here. I had read several millions of descriptions of such places, but the reality was new to me. I very much wanted to see this animal, especially the now historic game of baccarat, and this was a good place, for Aix ranks next to Monte Carlo for high play and plenty of it. But the result was what I might have expected – the interest of the looker-on perishes with the novelty of the spectacle – that is to say, in a few minutes. A permanent and intense interest is acquirable in baccarat or in any other game, but you have to buy it. You don't get it by standing around looking on.

The baccarat table is covered with green cloth and is marked off in divisions with chalk or something. The banker sits in the middle, the croupier opposite. The customers fill all the chairs at the table, and the rest of the crowd are massed at their backs and leaning over them to deposit chips or gold coins. Constantly money and chips are flung upon the table, and the game seems to consist in the croupier's reaching for those things with a flexible sculling oar and raking them home. It appeared to be a rational enough game for him, and if I could have borrowed his oar I would have staid, but I didn't see where the entertainment of the others came in. This was because I saw without perceiving and observed without understanding. For the widow and the orphan and the others do win money there. Once an old gray mother in Israel or elsewhere pulled out, and I heard her say to her daughter or her granddaughter as they passed me: "There, I've won six louis, and I'm going to quit while I'm ahead." Also there was this statistic. A friend pointed to a young man with the dead stub of a cigar in his mouth, which he kept munching nervously all the time and pitching hundred-dollar chips on the board while two sweet young girls reached down over his shoulders to deposit modest little gold pieces, and said: "He's only funning now; wasting a few hundred to pass the time – waiting for the 'gold room' to open, you know, which won't be till well after midnight – then you'll see him bet! He won £14,000 there last night. They don't bet anything there but big money."

The thing I chiefly missed was the haggard people with the intense eye, the hunted look, the desperate mien, candidates for suicide and the pauper's grave. They are in the descriptions, as a rule, but they were off duty that night. All the gamblers, male and female, old and young, looked abnormally cheerful and prosperous.

However, all the nations were there, clothed richly, and speaking all the languages. Some of the women were painted and were evidently shaky as to character. These items tallied with the descriptions well enough.

The etiquette of the place was difficult to master. In the brilliant and populous halls and corridors you don't smoke, and you wear your hat, no matter how many ladies are in the thick throng of drifting humanity; but the moment you cross the sacred threshold and enter the gambling hell, off the hat must come, and everybody lights his cigar and goes to suffocating the ladies.

But what I came here for, five weeks ago, was the baths. My right arm was disabled with rheumatism. To sit at home in America and guess out the European bath best fitted for a particular ailment or combination of ailments, it is not possible, and it would not be a good idea to experiment in that way, anyhow. There are a great many curative baths on the continent, and some are good for one disease but bad for another. So it is necessary to let a physician name your bath for you. As a rule, Americans go to London to get this advice, and South Americans go to Paris for it. Now and then an economist chooses his bath himself and does a thousand miles of railroading to get to it, and then the local physicians tell him he has come to the wrong place. He sees that he has lost time and money and strength, and almost the minute that he realizes this he loses his temper. I had the rheumatism and was advised to go to Aix, not so much because I had that disease as because I had the promise of certain others. What they were was not explained to me, but they are either in the following menu or I have been sent to the wrong place. Dr. Wakefield's book says:

"We know that the class of maladies benefited by the water and baths at Aix are those due to defect of nutrition, debility of the nervous system, or to a gouty, rheumatic, herpetic, or scrofulous diathesis – all diseases extremely debilitating and requiring a tonic, and not a depressing action of the remedy. This it seems to find here, as recorded experience and daily action can testify. ... According to the line of treatment, followed particularly with due regard to the temperature, the action of the Aix waters can be made sedative, exciting, derivative, or alterative and tonic."

The "Establishment" is the property of France, and all the officers and servants are employés of the French Government. The bath-house is a huge and massive pile of white marble masonry, and looks more like a temple than anything else. It has several floors, and each is full of bath cabinets. There is every kind of bath – for the nose, the ears, the throat, vapor baths, tube baths, swimming baths, and all people's favorite, the douche. It is a good building to get lost in when you are not familiar with it. From early morning until nearly noon people are streaming in and streaming out without halt. The majority come afoot, but great numbers are brought in sedan chairs, a sufficiently ugly contrivance whose cover is a steep little tent made of striped canvas. You see nothing of the patient in this diving-bell as the bearers tramp along, except a glimpse of his ankles bound together and swathed around with blankets or towels to that generous degree that the result suggests a sore piano leg. By attention and practice the pallbearers have got so that they can keep out of step all the time – and they do it. As a consequence their veiled churn goes rocking, tilting, swaying along like a bell-buoy in a ground swell. It makes the oldest sailor sea-sick to look at that spectacle.

The "course" is usually fifteen douche baths and five tub baths. You take the douche three days in succession, then knock off and take a tub. You keep up this distribution through the course. If one course does not cure you, you take another one after an interval. You seek a local physician and he examines your case and prescribes the kind of bath required for it, with various other particulars; then you buy your course tickets and pay for them in advance

– $9. With the tickets you get a memorandum book with your dates and hours all set down in it. The doctor takes you into the bath the first morning and gives some instructions to the two doucheurs who are to handle you through the course. The pour boires are about 10 cents to each of the men for each bath, payable at the end of the course. Also, at the end of the course, you pay three or four francs to the superintendent of your department of the bath house. These are useful particulars to know, and are not to be found in the books. A servant of your hotel carries your towels and sheet to the bath daily and brings them away again. They are the property of the hotel; the French Government doesn't furnish these things.

You meet all kinds of people at a place like this, and if you give them a chance they will submerge you under their experiences, for they are either glad or sorry they came, and they want to spread their feelings out and enjoy them. One of these said to me:

"It's great, these baths. I didn't come here for my health – I only came to find out if there was anything the matter with me. The doctor told me if there was the symptoms would soon appear. After the first douche I had sharp pains in all my muscles. The doctor said it was different varieties of rheumatism, and the best varieties there were, too. After my second bath I had aches in my bones, and skull, and around. The doctor said it was different varieties of neuralgia, and the best in the market – anybody would tell me so. I got many new kinds of pains out of my third douche. These were in my joints. The doctor said it was gout, complicated with heart disease, and encouraged me to go on. Then we had the fourth douche, and I came out on a stretcher that time and fetched with me one vast, diversified, undulating, continental kind of pain, with horizons to it and zones and parallels of latitude and meridians of longitude and isothermal belts and variations of the compass – O, everything tidy and right up to the latest developments, you know. The doctor said it was inflammation of the soul, and just the very thing. Well, I went right on gathering them in – toothache, liver complaint, softening of the brain, nostalgia, bronchitis, osteology, fits, coleoptera, hydrangea, cyclopedia britannica, delirium tre- mens, and a lot of other things that I've got down in my list that I'll show you, and you can keep it if you like and tally off the bric- à-brac as you lay it in.

"The doctor said I was a grand proof of what these baths could do; said I had come here as innocent of disease as a grindstone, and inside of three weeks these baths had sluiced out of me every important ailment known to medical science, along with considerable more that were entirely new and patentable. Why he wanted to exhibit me in his bay window."

There seems to be a good many liars this year. I began to take the baths, and found them most enjoyable; so enjoyable that if I hadn't had a disease I would have borrowed one, just to have a pretext for going on. They took me into a stone-floored basin about fourteen feet square, which had enough strange-looking pipes and things in it to make it look like a torture chamber. The two half-naked men seated me on a pine stool, and kept a couple of warm-water jets as thick as one's wrist playing upon me while they kneaded me, stroked me, twisted me, and applied all the other details of the scientific massage to me for seven or eight minutes. Then they stood me up and played a powerful jet upon me all around for another minute. The cool shower bath came next, and the thing was over. I came out of the bath-house a few minutes later feeling younger and fresher and finer than I have felt since I was a boy. The spring and cheer and delight of this exaltation lasted three hours, and the same uplifting effect has followed the twenty douches which I have taken since.

After my first douche I went to the chemist's on the corner, as per instructions, and asked for half a glass of Challe water. It comes from a spring sixteen miles from here. It was furnished to me, but, perceiving that there was something the matter with it, I offered to wait till they could get some that was fresh, but they said it always smelt that way. They said that the reason that this was so much ranker than the sulphur water of the bath was that this contained thirty-two times as much sulphur as that. It may be true, but in my opinion that water comes from a cemetery, and not a fresh cemetery, either. History says that one of the early Roman Generals lost an army down there somewhere. If he could come back now I think this water would help him find it again. However, I drank the Challe, and have drank it once or twice every day since. I suppose it is all right, but I wish I knew what was the matter with those Romans.

My first baths developed plenty of pain, but the subsequent ones removed almost all of it. I have got back the use of my arm these last few days, and I am going away now.

There are many beautiful drives about Aix, many interesting places to visit, and much pleasure to be found in paddling around the little lake Bourget on the small steamers, but the excursion which satisfied me best was a trip to Annecy and its neighborhood. You go to Annecy in an hour by rail, through a garden land that has not had its equal for beauty, perhaps, since Eden; and certainly Eden was not cultivated as this garden is. The charm and loveliness of the whole region are bewildering. Picturesque rocks, forest-clothed hills, slopes richly bright in the cleanest and greenest grass, fields of grain without fleck or flaw, dainty of color, and as shiny and shimmery as silk, old gray mansions and towers half buried in foliage and sunny eminences, deep chasms with precipitous walls, and a swift stream of pale blue water between, with now and then a tumbling cascade, and always noble mountains in view, with vagrant white clouds curling about their summits.

Then at the end of an hour you come to Annecy and rattle through its old crooked lanes, built solidly up with curious old houses that are a dream of the middle ages, and presently you come to the main object of your trip – Lake Annecy. It is a revelation, it is a miracle. It brings the tears to a body's eyes it is so enchanting. That is to say, it affects you just as all things that you instantly recognize as perfect affect you – perfect music, perfect eloquence, perfect art, perfect joy, perfect grief. It stretches itself out there in the caressing sunlight, and away towards its border of majestic mountains, a crisped and radiant plain of water of the divinest blue that can be imagined. All the blues are there, from the faintest shoal water suggestion of the color, detectable only in the shadow of some overhanging object, all the way through, a little blue and a little bluer still, and again a shade bluer till you strike the deep, rich Mediterranean splendor which breaks the heart in your bosom, it is so beautiful.

And the mountains, as you skim along on the steamboat, how stately their forms, how noble their proportions, how green their velvet slopes, how soft the mottlings of sun and shadow that play about the rocky ramparts that crown them, how opaline the vast upheavals of snow banked against the sky in the remotenesses beyond – Mont Blanc and the others – how shall anybody describe? Why, not even the painter can quite do it, and the most the pen can do is to suggest.

Up the lake there is an old abbey – Talloires – relic of the middle ages. We stopped there; stepped from the sparkling water and the rush and boom and fret and fever of the nineteenth century into the solemnity and the silence and the soft gloom and the brooding mystery of a remote antiquity. The stone step at the water's edge had the traces of a worn-out inscription on it; the wide flight of stone steps that led up to the front door was polished smooth by the passing feet of forgotten centuries, and there was not an unbroken stone among them all. Within the pile was the old square cloister with covered arcade all around it where the monks of the ancient times used to sit and meditate, and now and then welcome to their hospitalities the wandering knight with his tin breeches on, and in the middle of the square court (open to the sky) was a stone well curb, cracked and slick with age and use, and all about it were weeds, and among the weeds moldy brickbats that the Crusaders used to throw at each other. A passage at the further side of the cloister led to another weedy and roofless little inclosure beyond, where there was a ruined wall clothed to the top with masses of ivy and flanking it was a battered and picturesque arch. All over the building there were comfortable rooms and comfortable beds, and clean plank floors with no carpets on them. In one bedroom up-stairs were half a dozen portraits, dimming relics of the vanished centuries – portraits of abbots who used to be as grand as princes in their old day, and very rich and much worshiped and very holy; and in the next room there was a howling chromo and an electric bell. Down stairs there was an ancient wood carving with a Latin word commanding silence, and there was a spang new piano close by. Two elderly French women, with the kindest and honestest and sincerest faces, have the abbey now, and they board and lodge people who are tired of the roar of cities and want to be where the dead silence and serenity and peace of this old nest will heal their blistered spirits and patch up their ragged minds. They fed us well, they slept us well, and I wish I could have staid there a few years and got a solid rest.

November 8, 1891

MENTAL TELEGRAPHY

A MANUSCRIPT WITH A HISTORY

NOTE TO THE EDITOR. – By glancing over the enclosed bundle of rusty old manuscript, you will perceive that I once made a great discovery: the discovery that certain sorts of things which, from the beginning of the world, had always been regarded as merely "curious coincidences" – that is to say, accidents – were no more accidental than is the sending and receiving of a telegram an accident. I made this discovery sixteen or seventeen years ago, and gave it a name – "Mental Telegraphy." It is the same thing around the outer edges of which the Psychical Society of England began to grope (and play with) four or five years ago, and which they named "Telepathy." Within the last two or three years they have penetrated toward the heart of the matter, however, and have found out that mind can act upon mind in a quite detailed and elaborate way over vast stretches of land and water. And they have succeeded in doing, by their great credit and influence, what I could never have done – they have convinced the world that mental telegraphy is not a jest, but a fact, and that it is a thing not rare, but exceedingly common. They have done our age a service – and a very great service, I think.

In this old manuscript you will find mention of an extraordinary experience of mine in the mental telegraphic line, of date about the year 1874 or 1875 – the one concerning the Great Bonanza book. It was this experience that called my attention to the matter under consideration. I began to keep a record, after that, of such experiences of mine as seemed explicable by the theory that minds telegraph thoughts to each other. In 1878 I went to Germany and began to write the book called *A Tramp Abroad*. The bulk of this old batch of manuscript was written at that time and for that book. But I removed it when I came to revise the volume for the press; for I feared that the public would treat the thing as a joke and throw it aside, whereas I was in earnest.

At home, eight or ten years ago, I tried to creep in under shelter of an authority grave enough to protect the article from ridicule – the *North American Review*. But Mr. Metcalf was too wary for me. He said that to treat these mere "coincidences" seriously was a thing which the *Review* couldn't dare to do; that I must put either my name or my *nom de plume* to the article, and thus save the *Review* from harm. But I couldn't consent to that; it would be the surest possible way to defeat my desire that the public should receive the thing seriously, and be willing to stop and give it some fair degree of attention. So I pigeon-holed the MS., because I could not get it published anonymously.

Now see how the world has moved since then. These small experiences of mine, which were too formidable at that time for admission to a grave magazine – if the magazine must allow them to appear as something above and beyond "accidents" and "coincidences" – are trifling and commonplace now, since the flood of light recently cast upon mental telegraphy by the intelligent labors of the Psychical Society. But I think they are worth publishing, just to show what harmless and ordinary matters were considered dangerous and incredible eight or ten years ago.

As I have said, the bulk of this old manuscript was written in 1878; a later part was written from time to time two, three, and four years afterward. The "Postscript" I add to-day.

MAY, '78. – Another of those apparently trifling things has happened to me which puzzle and perplex all men every now and then, keep them thinking an hour or two, and leave their minds barren of explanation or solution at last. Here it is – and it looks inconsequential enough, I am obliged to say. A few days ago I said: "It must be that Frank Millet doesn't know we are in Germany, or he would have written long before this. I have been on the point of dropping him a line at least a dozen times during the past six weeks, but I always decided to wait a day or two longer, and see if we shouldn't hear from him. But now I *will* write." And so I did. I directed the letter to Paris, and thought, "*Now* we shall hear from him before this letter is fifty miles from Heidelberg – it always happens so."

True enough; but *why* should it? That is the puzzling part of it. We are always talking about letters "crossing" each other, for that is one of the very commonest accidents of this life. We call it "accident," but perhaps we misname it. We have the instinct a dozen times a year that the letter we are writing is going to "cross" the other person's letter; and if the reader will rack his memory a little he will recall the fact that this presentiment had strength enough to it to make him cut his letter down to a decided briefness, because it would be a waste of time to write a letter which was going to "cross," and hence be a useless letter. I think that in my experience this instinct has generally come to me in cases where I had put off my letter a good while in the hope that the other person would write.

Yes, as I was saying, I had waited five or six weeks; then I wrote but three lines, because I felt and seemed to know that a letter from Millet would cross mine. And so it did. He wrote the same day that I wrote. The letters crossed each other. His letter went to Berlin, care of the American minister, who sent it to me. In this letter Millet said he had been trying for six weeks to stumble upon somebody who knew my German address, and at last the idea had occurred to him that a letter sent to the care of the embassy at Berlin might possibly find me.

Maybe it was an "accident" that he finally determined to write me at the same moment that I finally determined to write him, but I think not.

With me the most irritating thing has been to wait a tedious time in a purely business matter, hoping that the other party will do the writing, and then sit down and do it myself, perfectly satisfied that that other man is sitting down at the same moment to write a letter which will "cross" mine. And yet one must go on writing, just the same; because if you get up from your table and postpone, that other man will do the same thing, exactly as if you two were harnessed together like the Siamese twins, and must duplicate each other's movements.

Several months before I left home a New York firm did some work about the house for me, and did not make a success of it, as it seemed to me. When the bill came, I wrote and said I wanted the work perfected before I paid. They replied that they were very busy, but that as soon as they could spare the proper man the thing should be done. I waited more than two months, enduring as patiently as possible the companionship of bells which would fire away of their own accord sometimes when nobody was touching them, and at other times wouldn't ring though you struck the button with a sledgehammer. Many a time I got ready to write and then postponed it; but at last I sat down one evening and poured out my grief to the extent of a page or so, and then cut my letter suddenly short, because a strong instinct told me that the firm had begun to move in the matter. When I came down to breakfast next morning the postman had not yet taken my letter away, but the electrical man had been there, done his work, and was gone again!

He had received his orders the previous evening from his employers, and had come up by the night train.

If that was an "accident," it took about three months to get it up in good shape.

One evening last summer I arrived in Washington, registered at the Arlington Hotel, and went to my room. I read and smoked until ten o'clock; then, finding I was not yet sleepy, I thought I would take a breath of fresh air. So I went forth in the rain, and tramped through one street after another in an aimless and enjoyable way. I knew that Mr. O——, a friend of mine, was in town, and I wished I might run across him; but I did not propose to hunt for him at midnight, especially as I did not know where he was stopping. Toward twelve o'clock the streets had become so deserted that I felt lonesome; so I stepped into a cigar shop far up the Avenue, and remained there fifteen minutes, listening to some bummers discussing national politics. Suddenly the spirit of prophecy came upon me, and I said to myself, "Now I will go out at this door, turn to the left, walk ten steps, and meet Mr. O—— face to face." I did it, too! I could not see his face, because he had an umbrella before it, and it was pretty dark anyhow, but he interrupted the man he was walking and talking with, and I recognized his voice and stopped him.

That I should step out there and stumble upon Mr. O—— was nothing, but that I should know beforehand that I was going to do it was a good deal. It is a very curious thing when you come to look at it. I stood far within the cigar shop when I delivered my prophecy; I walked about five steps to the door, opened it, closed it after me, walked down a flight of three steps to the sidewalk, then turned to the left and walked four or five more, and found my man. I repeat that in itself the thing was nothing; but to know it would happen so *beforehand*, wasn't that really curious?

I have criticised absent people so often, and then discovered, to my humiliation, that I was talking with their relatives, that I have grown superstitious about that sort of thing and dropped it. How like an idiot one feels after a blunder like that!

We are always mentioning people, and in that very instant they appear before us. We laugh, and say, "Speak of the devil," and so forth, and there we drop it, considering it an "accident." It is a cheap and convenient way of disposing of a grave and very puzzling mystery. The fact is it does seem to happen too often to be an accident.

Now I come to the oddest thing that ever happened to me. Two or three years ago I was lying in bed, idly musing, one morning – it was the 2d of March – when suddenly a red-hot new idea came whistling down into my camp, and exploded with such comprehensive effectiveness as to sweep the vicinity clean of rubbishy reflections, and fill the air with their dust and flying fragments. This idea, stated in simple phrase, was that the time was ripe and the market ready for a certain book; a book which ought to be written at once; a book which must command attention and be of peculiar interest – to wit, a book about the Nevada silver mines. The "Great Bonanza" was a new wonder then, and everybody was talking about it. It seemed to me that the person best qualified to write this book was Mr. William H. Wright, a journalist of Virginia, Nevada, by whose side I had scribbled many months when I was a reporter there ten or twelve years before. He might be alive still; he might be dead; I could not tell; but I would write him, anyway. I began by merely and modestly suggesting that he make such a book; but my interest grew as I went on, and I ventured to map out what I thought ought to be the plan of the work, he being an old friend, and not given to taking good intentions for ill. I even dealt with details, and suggested the order and sequence which they should follow. I was about to put the manuscript in an envelope, when the thought occurred to me that if this book should be written at my suggestion, and then no publisher happened to want it, I should feel uncomfortable; so I concluded to keep my letter back until I should have secured a publisher. I pigeon-holed my document, and dropped a note to my own publisher, asking him to name a day for a business consultation. He was out of town on a far journey. My note remained unanswered, and at the end of three or four days the whole matter had passed out of my mind. On the 9th of March the postman brought three or four letters, and among them a thick one whose superscription was in a hand which seemed dimly familiar to me. I could not "place" it at first, but presently I succeeded. Then I said to a visiting relative who was present:

"Now I will do a miracle. I will tell you everything this letter contains – date, signature, and all – without breaking the seal. It is from a Mr. Wright, of Virginia, Nevada, and is dated the 2d of March – seven days ago. Mr. Wright proposes to make a book about the silver mines and the Great Bonanza, and asks what I, as a friend, think of the idea. He says his subjects are to be so and so, their order and sequence so and so, and he will close with a history of the chief feature of the book, the Great Bonanza."

I opened the letter, and showed that I had stated the date and the contents correctly. Mr. Wright's letter simply contained what my own letter, written on the same date, contained, and mine still lay in its pigeon-hole, where it had been lying during the seven days since it was written.

There was no clairvoyance about this, if I rightly comprehend what clairvoyance is. I think the clairvoyant professes to actually *see* concealed writing, and read it off word for word. This was not my case. I only seemed to know, and to know absolutely, the contents of the letter in detail and due order, but I had to *word* them myself. I translated them, so to speak, out of Wright's language into my own.

Wright's letter and the one which I had written to him but never sent were in substance the same.

Necessarily this could not come by accident; such elaborate accidents cannot happen. Chance might have duplicated one or two of the details, but she would have broken down on the rest. I could not doubt – there was no tenable reason for doubting – that Mr. Wright's mind and mine had been in close and crystal-clear communication with each other across three thousand miles of mountain and desert on the morning of the 2d of March. I did not consider that both minds *originated* that succession of ideas, but that one mind originated them, and simply telegraphed them to the other. I was curious to know which brain was the telegrapher and which the receiver, so I wrote and asked for particulars. Mr. Wright's reply showed that his mind had done the originating and telegraphing and mine the receiving. Mark that significant thing, now; consider for a moment how many a splendid "original" idea has been unconsciously stolen from a man three thousand miles away! If one should question that this is so, let him look into the cyclopædia and con once more that curious thing in the history of inventions which has puzzled every one so much – that is, the frequency with which the same machine or other contrivance has been invented at the same time by several persons in different quarters of the globe. The world was without an electric telegraph for several thousand years; then Professor Henry, the American, Wheatstone in England, Morse on the sea, and a German in Munich, all invented it at the same time. The discovery of certain ways of applying steam was made in two or three countries in the same year. Is it not possible that inventors are constantly and unwittingly stealing each other's ideas whilst they stand thousands of miles asunder?

Last spring a literary friend of mine,* who lived a hundred miles away, paid me a visit, and in the course of our talk he said he had made a discovery – conceived an entirely new idea – one which certainly had never been used in literature. He told me what it was. I handed him a manuscript, and said he would find substantially the same idea in that – a manuscript which I had written a week before. The idea had been in my mind since the previous November; it had only entered his while I was putting it on paper, a week gone by. He had not yet written his; so he left it unwritten, and gracefully made over all his right and title in the idea to me.

The following statement, which I have clipped from a newspaper, is true. I had the facts from Mr. Howells's lips when the episode was new:

> "A remarkable story of a literary coincidence is told of Mr. Howells's *Atlantic Monthly* serial 'Dr Breen's Practice.' A lady of Rochester, New York, contributed to the magazine, after 'Dr Breen's Practice' was in type, a short story which so much resembled Mr. Howells's that he felt it necessary to call upon her and explain the situation of affairs in order that no charge of plagiarism might be preferred against him. He showed her the proof-sheets of his story, and satisfied her that the similarity between her work and his was one of those strange coincidences which have from time to time occurred in the literary world."

I had read portions of Mr. Howells's story, both in MS. and in proof, before the lady offered her contribution to the magazine.

Here is another case. I clip it from a newspaper:

> "The republication of Miss Alcott's novel *Moods* recalls to a writer in the Boston *Post* a singular coincidence which was brought to light before the book was first published: 'Miss Anna M. Crane, of Baltimore, published *Emily Chester*, a novel which was pronounced a very striking and strong story. A comparison of this book with *Moods* showed that the two writers, though entire strangers to each other, and living hundreds of miles apart, had both chosen the same subject for their novels, had

* W. D. Howells.

followed almost the same line of treatment up to a certain point, where the parallel ceased, and the dénouements were entirely opposite. And even more curious, the leading characters in both books had identically the same names, so that the names in Miss Alcott's novel had to be changed. Then the book was published by Loring.' "

Four or five times within my recollection there has been a lively newspaper war in this country over poems whose authorship was claimed by two or three different people at the same time. There was a war of this kind over "Nothing to Wear," "Beautiful Snow," "Rock Me to Sleep, Mother," and also over one of Mr. Will Carleton's early ballads, I think. These were all blameless cases of unintentional and unwitting mental telegraphy, I judge.

A word more as to Mr. Wright. He had had his book in his mind some time; consequently he, and not I, had originated the idea of it. The subject was entirely foreign to my thoughts; I was wholly absorbed in other things. Yet this friend, whom I had not seen and had hardly thought of for eleven years, was able to shoot his thoughts at me across three thousand miles of country, and fill my head with them, to the exclusion of every other interest, in a single moment. He had begun his letter after finishing his work on the morning paper – a little after three o'clock, he said. When it was three in the morning in Nevada it was about six in Hartford, where I lay awake thinking about nothing in particular; and just about that time his ideas came pouring into my head from across the continent, and I got up and put them on paper, under the impression that they were my own original thoughts.

I have never seen any mesmeric or clairvoyant performances or spiritual manifestations which were in the least degree convincing – a fact which is not of consequence, since my opportunities have been meagre; but I am forced to believe that one human mind (still inhabiting the flesh) can communicate with another, over any sort of a distance, and without any *artificial* preparation of "sympathetic conditions" to act as a transmitting agent. I suppose that when the sympathetic conditions happen to exist the two minds communicate with each other, and that otherwise they don't; and I suppose that if the sympathetic conditions could be kept up right along, the two minds would continue to correspond without limit as to time.

Now there is that curious thing which happens to everybody:

suddenly a succession of thoughts or sensations flocks in upon you, which startles you with the weird idea that you have ages ago experienced just this succession of thoughts or sensations in a previous existence. The previous existence is possible, no doubt, but I am persuaded that the solution of this hoary mystery lies not there, but in the fact that some far-off stranger has been telegraphing his thoughts and sensations into your consciousness, and that he stopped because some counter-current or other obstruction intruded and broke the line of communication. Perhaps they seem repetitions to you because they *are* repetitions, got at second hand from the other man. Possibly Mr. Brown, the "mind-reader," reads other people's minds, possibly he does not; but I know of a surety that I have read another man's mind, and therefore I do not see why Mr. Brown shouldn't do the like also.

I wrote the foregoing about three years ago, in Heidelberg, and laid the manuscript aside, purposing to add to it instances of mind-telegraphing from time to time as they should fall under my experience. Meantime the "crossing" of letters has been so frequent as to become monotonous. However, I have managed to get something useful out of this hint; for now, when I get tired of waiting upon a man whom I very much wish to hear from, I sit down and *compel* him to write, whether he wants to or not; that is to say, I sit down and write him, and then tear my letter up, satisfied that my act has forced him to write me at the same moment. I do not need to mail my letter – the writing it is the only essential thing.

Of course I have grown superstitious about this letter-crossing business – this was natural. We staid awhile in Venice after leaving Heidelberg. One day I was going down the Grand Canal in a gondola, when I heard a shout behind me, and looked around to see what the matter was; a gondola was rapidly following, and the gondolier was making signs to me to stop. I did so, and the pursuing boat ranged up alongside. There was an American lady in it – a resident of Venice. She was in a good deal of distress. She said:

"There's a New York gentleman and his wife at the Hotel Britannia who arrived a week ago, expecting to find news of their son, whom they have heard nothing about during eight months. There was no news. The lady is down sick with despair; the gentleman can't sleep or eat. Their son arrived at San Francisco eight months ago, and announced the fact in a letter to his parents the same day. That is the last trace of him. The parents have been in Europe ever since; but their trip has been spoiled, for they have occupied their time simply in drifting restlessly from place to place, and writing letters everywhere and to everybody, begging for news of their son; but the mystery remains as dense as ever. Now the gentleman wants to stop writing and go to cabling. He wants to cable San Francisco. He has never done it before, because he is afraid of – of he doesn't know what – death of the son, no doubt. But he wants somebody to *advise* him to cable; wants me to do it. Now I simply can't; for if no news came, that mother yonder would die. So I have chased you up in order to get you to support me in urging him to be patient, and put the thing off a week or two longer; it may be the saving of this lady. Come along; let's not lose any time."

So I went along, but I had a programme of my own. When I was introduced to the gentleman I said: "I have some superstitions, but they are worthy of respect. If you will cable San Francisco immediately, you will hear news of your son inside of twenty-four hours. I don't know that you will get the news from San Francisco, but you will get it from somewhere. The only necessary thing is to *cable* – that is all. The news will come within twenty-four hours. Cable Peking, if you prefer; there is no choice in this matter. This delay is all occasioned by your not cabling long ago, when you were first moved to do it."

It seems absurd that this gentleman should have been cheered up by this nonsense, but he was; he brightened up at once, and sent his cablegram; and next day, at noon, when a long letter arrived from his lost son, the man was as grateful to me as if I had really had something to do with the hurrying up of that letter. The son had shipped from San Francisco in a sailing vessel, and his letter was written from the first port he touched at, months afterward.

This incident argues nothing, and is valueless. I insert it only to show how strong is the superstition which "letter-crossing" has bred in me. I was so sure that a cablegram sent to any place, no matter where, would defeat itself by "crossing" the incoming news, that my confidence was able to raise up a hopeless man, and make him cheery and hopeful.

But here are two or three incidents which come strictly under the head of mind-telegraphing. One Monday morning, about a year ago, the mail came in, and I picked up one of the letters and said to a friend: "Without opening this letter I will tell you what it says. It is from Mrs.——, and she says she was in New York last Saturday, and was purposing to run up here in the afternoon train and surprise us, but at the last moment changed her mind and returned westward to her home."

I was right; my details were exactly correct. Yet we had had no suspicion that Mrs.—— was coming to New York, or that she had even a remote intention of visiting us.

I smoke a good deal – that is to say, all the time – so, during seven years, I have tried to keep a box of matches handy, behind a picture on the mantel-piece; but I have had to take it out in trying, because George (colored), who makes the fires and lights the gas, always uses my matches, and never replaces them. Commands and persuasions have gone for nothing with him all these seven years. One day last summer, when our family had been away from home several months, I said to a member of the household:

"Now, with all this long holiday, and nothing in the way to interrupt –"

"I can finish the sentence for you," said the member of the household.

"Do it, then," said I.

"George ought to be able, by practising, to learn to let those matches alone."

It was correctly done. That was what I was going to say. Yet until that moment George and the matches had not been in my mind for three months, and it is plain that the part of the sentence which I uttered offers not the least cue or suggestion of what I was purposing to follow it with.

My mother* is descended from the younger of two English brothers named Lambton, who settled in this country a few generations ago. The tradition goes that the elder of the two eventually fell heir to a certain estate in England (now an earldom), and died right away. This has always been the way with our family. They always die when they could make anything by not doing it. The two Lambtons left plenty of Lambtons behind them; and when at last, about fifty years ago, the English baronetcy was exalted to an earldom, the great tribe of American Lambtons began to bestir themselves – that is, those descended from the elder branch. Ever since that day one or another of these has been fretting his life uselessly away with schemes to get at his "rights." The

* She was still living when this was written.

present "rightful earl" – I mean the American one – used to write me occasionally, and try to interest me in his projected raids upon the title and estates by offering me a share in the latter portion of the spoil; but I have always managed to resist his temptations.

Well, one day last summer I was lying under a tree, thinking about nothing in particular, when an absurd idea flashed into my head, and I said to a member of the household, "Suppose I should live to be ninety-two, and dumb and blind and toothless, and just as I was gasping out what was left of me on my death-bed –"

"Wait, I will finish the sentence," said the member of the household.

"Go on," said I.

"Somebody should rush in with a document, and say, 'All the other heirs are dead, and you are the Earl of Durham!' "

That is truly what I was going to say. Yet until that moment the subject had not entered my mind or been referred to in my hearing for months before. A few years ago this thing would have astounded me, but the like could not much surprise me now, though it happened every week; for I think I *know* now that mind can communicate accurately with mind without the aid of the slow and clumsy vehicle of speech.

This age does seem to have exhausted invention nearly; still, it has one important contract on its hands yet – the invention of the *phrenophone*; that is to say, a method whereby the communicating of mind with mind may be brought under command and reduced to certainty and system. The telegraph and the telephone are going to become too slow and wordy for our needs. We must have the *thought* itself shot into our minds from a distance; then, if we need to put it into words, we can do that tedious work at our leisure. Doubtless the something which conveys our thoughts through the air from brain to brain is a finer and subtler form of electricity, and all we need do is to find out how to capture it and how to force it to do its work, as we have had to do in the case of the electric currents. Before the day of telegraphs neither one of these marvels would have seemed any easier to achieve than the other.

While I am writing this, doubtless somebody on the other side of the globe is writing it too. The question is, am I inspiring him or is he inspiring me? I cannot answer that; but that these thoughts have been passing through somebody else's mind all the time I have been setting them down I have no sort of doubt.

I will close this paper with a remark which I found some time ago in Boswell's *Johnson*:

"Voltaire's *Candide* is wonderfully similar in its plan and conduct to Johnson's *Rasselas*; insomuch that I have heard Johnson say that if they had not been published so closely one after the other that there was not time for imitation, *it would have been in vain to deny that the scheme of that which came latest was taken from the other.*"

The two men were widely separated from each other at the time, and the sea lay between.

POSTSCRIPT.

In the *Atlantic* for June, 1882, Mr. John Fiske refers to the often-quoted Darwin-and-Wallace "coincidence":

"I alluded, just now, to the 'unforeseen circumstance' which led Mr. Darwin in 1859 to break his long silence, and to write and publish the *Origin of Species*. This circumstance served, no less than the extraordinary success of his book, to show how ripe the minds of men had become for entertaining such views as those which Mr. Darwin propounded. In 1858 Mr. Wallace, who was then engaged in studying the natural history of the Malay Archipelago, sent to Mr. Darwin (as to the man most likely to understand him) a paper, in which he sketched the outlines of a theory identical with that upon which Mr. Darwin had so long been at work. The same sequence of observed facts and inferences that had led Mr. Darwin to the discovery of natural selection and its consequences had led Mr. Wallace to the very threshold of the same discovery; but in Mr. Wallace's mind the theory had by no means been wrought out to the same degree of completeness to which it had been wrought in the mind of Mr. Darwin. In the preface to his charming book on Natural Selection, Mr. Wallace, with rare modesty and candor, acknowledges that whatever value his speculations may have had, they have been utterly surpassed in richness and cogency of proof by those of Mr. Darwin. This is no doubt true, and Mr. Wallace has done such good work in further illustration of the theory that he can well afford to rest content with the second place in the first announcement of it.

"The coincidence, however, between Mr. Wallace's conclusions and those of Mr. Darwin was very remarkable. But, after all, coincidences of this sort have not been uncommon in the history of scientific inquiry. Nor is it at all surprising that they should occur now and then, when we remember that a great and pregnant discovery must always be concerned with some question which many of the foremost minds in the world are busy in thinking about. It was so with the discovery of the differential calculus, and again with the discovery of the planet Neptune. It was so with the interpretation of the Egyptian hieroglyphics, and with the establishment of the undulatory theory of light. It was so, to a considerable extent, with the introduction of the new chemistry, with the discovery of the mechanical equivalent of heat, and the whole doctrine of the correlation of forces. It was so with the invention of the electric telegraph and with the discovery of spectrum analysis. And it is not at all strange that it should have been so with the doctrine of the origin of species through natural selection."

He thinks these "coincidences" were apt to happen because the matters from which they sprang were matters which many of the foremost minds in the world were busy thinking about. But perhaps *one* man in each case did the telegraphing to the others. The aberrations which gave Leverrier the idea that there must be a planet of such and such mass and such and such an orbit hidden from sight out yonder in the remote abysses of space were not new; they had been noticed by astronomers for generations. Then why should it happen to occur to three people, widely separated – Leverrier, Mrs. Somerville, and Adams – to suddenly go to worrying about those aberrations all at the same time, and set themselves to work to find out what caused them, and to measure and weigh an invisible planet, and calculate its orbit, and hunt it down and catch it? – a strange project which nobody but they had ever thought of before. If one astronomer had invented that odd and happy project fifty years before, don't you think he would have telegraphed it to several others without knowing it?

But now I come to a puzzler. How is it that *inanimate* objects are able to affect the mind? They seem to do that. However, I wish to throw in a parenthesis first – just a reference to a thing everybody is familiar with – the experience of receiving a clear and particular *answer* to your telegram before your telegram has reached the sender of the answer. That is a case where your telegram has gone straight from your brain to the man it was meant for, far outstripping the wire's slow electricity, and it is an exercise of mental telegraphy which is as common as dining. To return to the influence of inanimate things. In the cases of non-professional clairvoyance examined by the Psychical Society the clairvoyant has usually been blindfolded, then some object which has been touched or worn by a person is placed in his hand; the clairvoyant immediately describes that person, and goes on and gives a history of some event with which the text object has been connected. If the inanimate object is able to affect and inform the clairvoyant's mind, maybe it can do the same when it is working in the interest of mental telegraphy. Once a lady in the West wrote me that her son was coming to New York to remain three weeks, and would pay me a visit if invited, and she gave me his address. I mislaid the letter, and forgot all about the matter till the three weeks were about up. Then a sudden and fiery irruption of remorse burst up in my brain that illuminated all the region round about, and I sat down at once and wrote to the lady and asked for that lost address. But, upon reflection, I judged that the stirring up of my recollection had not been an accident, so I added a postscript to say, never mind, I should get a letter from her son before night. And I did get it; for the letter was already in the town, although not delivered yet. It had influenced me somehow. I have had so many experiences of this sort – a dozen of them at least – that I am nearly persuaded that inanimate objects do not confine their activities to helping the clairvoyant, but do every now and then give the mental telegraphist a lift.

The case of mental telegraphy which I am coming to now comes under I don't exactly know what head. I clipped it from one of our local papers six or eight years ago. I know the details to be right and true, for the story was told to me in the same form by one of the two persons concerned (a clergyman of Hartford) at the time that the curious thing happened:

"A REMARKABLE COINCIDENCE. – Strange coincidences make the most interesting of stories and most curious of studies. Nobody can quite say how they come about, but everybody appreciates the fact when they do come, and it is seldom that any more complete and curious coincidence is recorded of minor importance than the following, which is absolutely true, and occurred in this city:

"At the time of the building of one of the finest residences of Hartford, which is still a very new house, a local firm supplied the wall-paper for certain rooms, contracting both to furnish and to put on the paper. It happened that they did not calculate the size of one room exactly right, and the paper of the design selected for it fell short just half a roll. They asked for delay enough to send on to the manufacturers for what was needed, and were told that there was no especial hurry. It happened that the manufacturer had none on hand, and had destroyed the blocks from which it was printed. They wrote that they had a full list of the dealers to whom they had sold that paper, and that they would write to each of these, and get from some of them a roll. It might involve a delay of a couple of weeks, but they would surely get it.

"In the course of time came a letter saying that, to their great surprise, they could not find a single roll. Such a thing was very unusual, but in this case it had so happened. Accordingly the local firm asked for further time, saying they would write to their own customers who had bought of that pattern, and would get the piece from them. But, to their surprise, this effort also failed. A long time had now elapsed, and there was no use of delaying any longer. They had contracted to paper the room, and their only course was to take off that which was insufficient and put on some other of which there was enough to go around. Accordingly at length a man was sent out to remove the paper. He got his apparatus ready, and was about to begin work, under the direction of the owner of the building, when the latter was for the moment called away. The house was large and very interesting, and so many people had rambled about it that finally admission had been refused by a sign at the door. On the occasion, however, when a gentleman had knocked and asked for leave to look about, the owner, being on the premises, had been sent for to reply to the request in person. That was the call that for the moment delayed the final preparations. The gentleman went to the door and admitted the stranger, saying he would show him about the house, but first must return for a moment to that room to finish his directions there, and he told the curious story about the paper as they went on. They entered the room together, and the first thing the stranger, who lived fifty miles away, said on looking about was, 'Why, I have that very paper on a room in my house, and I have an extra roll of it laid away, which is at your service.' In a few days the wall was papered according to the original contract. Had not the owner been at the house, the

stranger would not have been admitted; had he called a day
later, it would have been too late; had not the facts been almost
accidentally told to him, he would probably have said nothing
of the paper, and so on. The exact fitting of all the circumstances
is something very remarkable, and makes one of those stories
that seem hardly accidental in their nature."

Something that happened the other day brought my hoary MS.
to mind, and that is how I came to dig it out from its dusty pigeon-
hole grave for publication. The thing that happened was a question. A lady asked it: "Have you ever had a vision – when awake?"
I was about to answer promptly, when the last two words of the
question began to grow and spread and swell, and presently they
attained to vast dimensions. She did not know that they were
important; and I did not at first, but I soon saw that they
were putting me on the track of the solution of a mystery which
had perplexed me a good deal. You will see what I mean when
I get down to it. Ever since the English Society for Psychical
Research began its searching investigations of ghost stories,
haunted houses, and apparitions of the living and the dead, I have
read their pamphlets with avidity as fast as they arrived. Now one
of their commonest inquiries of a dreamer or a vision-seer is, "Are
you sure you were awake at the time?" If the man can't say he is
sure he was awake, a doubt falls upon his tale right there. But if he
is positive he was awake, and offers reasonable evidence to sub-
stantiate it, the fact counts largely for the credibility of his story.
It does with the society, and it did with me until that lady asked
me the above question the other day.

The question set me to considering, and brought me to the conclusion that you can be asleep – at least wholly unconscious – for
a time, and not suspect that it has happened, and not have any way
to prove that it *has* happened. A memorable case was in my mind.
About a year ago I was standing on the porch one day, when I saw
a man coming up the walk. He was a stranger, and I hoped he
would ring and carry his business into the house without stopping
to argue with me; he would have to pass the front door to get to
me, and I hoped he wouldn't take the trouble; to help, I tried to
look like a stranger myself – it often works. I was looking straight
at that man; he had got to within ten feet of the door and within
twenty-five feet of me – and suddenly he disappeared. It was as
astounding as if a church should vanish from before your face and

leave nothing behind it but a vacant lot. I was unspeakably delighted. I had seen an apparition at last, with my own eyes, in broad daylight. I made up my mind to write an account of it to the society. I ran to where the spectre had been, to make sure he was playing fair, then I ran to the other end of the porch, scanning the open grounds as I went. No, everything was perfect; he couldn't have escaped without my seeing him; he was an apparition, without the slightest doubt, and I would write him up before he was cold. I ran, hot with excitement, and let myself in with a latch-key. When I stepped into the hall my lungs collapsed and my heart stood still. For there sat that same apparition in a chair, all alone, and as quiet and reposeful as if he had come to stay a year! The shock kept me dumb for a moment or two, then I said, "Did you come in at that door?"

"Yes."

"Did *you* open it, or did you ring?"

"I rang, and the colored man opened it."

I said to myself: "This is astonishing. It takes George all of two minutes to answer the door-bell when he is in a hurry, and I have never seen him in a hurry. How *did* this man stand two minutes at that door, within five steps of me, and I did not see him?"

I should have gone to my grave puzzling over that riddle but for that lady's chance question last week: "Have you ever had a vision – when awake?" It stands explained now. During at least sixty seconds that day I was asleep, or at least totally unconscious, without suspecting it. In that interval the man came to my immediate vicinity, rang, stood there and waited, then entered and closed the door, and I did not see him and did not hear the door slam.

If he had slipped around the house in that interval and gone into the cellar – he had time enough – I should have written him up for the society, and magnified him, and gloated over him, and hurrahed about him, and thirty yoke of oxen could not have pulled the belief out of me that I was of the favored ones of the earth, and had seen a vision – while wide awake.

Now how are you to tell when you are awake? What are you to go by? People bite their fingers to find out. Why, you can do that in a dream.

December 1891

THE CRADLE OF LIBERTY

IT IS A good many years since I was in Switzerland last. In that remote time there was only one ladder railway in the country. That state of things is all changed. There isn't a mountain in Switzerland now that hasn't a ladder railroad or two up its back like suspenders; indeed, some of them are latticed with them, and two years hence all of them will be. In that day the peasant of the high altitudes will have to carry a lantern when he goes visiting in the night to keep from stumbling over railroads that have been built since his last round. And also in that day, if there shall remain a high-altitude peasant whose potato patch hasn't a railroad through it, it will make him as conspicuous as William Tell.

However, there are only two best ways to travel through Switzerland; the first best is afoot, the second best is by open two-horse carriage. One can come from Lucerne to Interlaken over the Brünig by ladder-railroad in an hour or so now, but you can glide smoothly through in a carriage in ten, and have two hours for luncheon at noon. For luncheon, not for rest. There is no fatigue connected with the trip. One arrives fresh in spirit and in person in the evening – no fret in his heart, no grime on his face, no grit in his hair, not a cinder in his eye. This is the right condition of mind and body, the right and due preparation for the solemn event which closes the day – stepping with metaphorically uncovered head into the presence of the most impressive mountain mass that the globe can show – the Jungfrau.

The stranger's first feeling when suddenly confronted by that towering and awful apparition wrapped in its shroud of snow is breath-taking astonishment. It is as if heaven's gates had swung open and exposed the throne.

It is peaceful here and pleasant at Interlaken. Nothing going on – at least nothing but brilliant, life-giving sunshine. There are floods and floods of that. One may properly speak of it as "going on," for it is full of the suggestion of activity; the light pours down with energy, with visible enthusiasm. This is a good atmosphere to be in, morally as well as physically. After trying the political atmosphere of the neighboring monarchies, it is healing and refreshment to breathe an air that has known no taint of slavery for 600 years, and to come among a people whose political history is great and fine, superlatively great and fine, and worthy to be taught in all schools and studied by all races and peoples. For the struggle here throughout the centuries has not been in the interest of any private family or any church, but in the interest of the whole body of the nation and for shelter and protection of all forms of belief. This fact is colossal. If one would realize how colossal it is and of what dignity and majesty let him contrast it with the purposes and objects of the Crusades, the siege of Troy, the Wars of the Roses, and other historic comedies of that sort and size.

Last week I was boating around the Lake of the Four Cantons, and I saw Rütli and Altorf. Rütli is a remote little patch of a meadow, but I do not know how any piece of ground could be holier or better worth crossing oceans and continents to see, since it was there that the great trinity of Switzerland joined hands six centuries ago and swore the oath which set their enslaved and insulted country forever free. And Altorf is also honorable ground and worshipful, since it was there that William, surnamed Tell (which, interpreted, means "the foolish talker," that is to say, the too daring talker), refused to bow to Gessler's hat. Of late years the prying student of history has been delighting himself beyond measure over a wonderful find which he has made – to-wit, that Tell did not shoot the apple from his son's head. To hear the students jubilate, one would suppose that the question of whether Tell shot the apple or didn't was an important matter; whereas it ranks in importance exactly with the question of whether Washington chopped down the cherry tree or didn't. The deeds of Washington the patriot are the essential thing, the cherry-tree incident is of no consequence. To prove that Tell did shoot the apple from his son's head would merely prove that he had better nerve than most men, and was as skillful with a bow as a million more who preceded and followed him, but not a whit more so. But Tell was more and better than a mere marksman, more and better than a mere cool head, he was a type; he stands for Swiss patriotism; in his person was represented a whole people; his spirit was their spirit – the spirit which would bow to none but God – the spirit which said this in words and confirmed it with deeds. There have always been Tells in Switzerland, people who would not bow. There was a sufficiency of them at Rütli, there were plenty of them at Murten, plenty at Granson, there are plenty today. And the first of them all – the very first, earliest banner-bearer of human freedom in this world – was not a man, but a woman, Stauffacher's wife. There she looms, dim and great, through the haze of the centuries, delivering into her husband's charmed ear that gospel of revolt which was to bear fruit in the conspiracy of Rütli and the birth of the first free government the world had ever seen.

THURSDAY, Sept. 10. – From this Victoria Hotel one looks straight across a flat of trifling width to a lofty mountain barrier, which has a gateway in it shaped like an inverted pyramid. Beyond this gateway arises the vast bulk of the Jungfrau, a spotless mass of gleaming snow, into the sky. The gateway in the dark-colored barrier makes a strong frame for the great picture. The somber frame and the glowing snow-pile are startlingly contrasted. It is this frame which concentrates and emphasizes the glory of the Jungfrau and makes it the most engaging, and beguiling, and fascinating spectacle that exists on the earth. There are many mountains of snow that are as lofty as the Jungfrau and as nobly proportioned, but they lack the frame; they stand at large, they are intruded upon and elbowed by neighboring domes and summits, and their grandeur is diminished and fails of effect.

It is a good name, Jungfrau – Virgin. Nothing could be whiter, nothing could be purer, nothing could be saintlier of aspect. At 6 yesterday evening the great intervening barrier, seen through a faint bluish haze, seemed made of air, and substanceless, so soft and rich it was, so shimmering where the wandering lights touched it, and so dim where the shadows lay. Apparently it was dream stuff, a work of the imagination, nothing real about it. The tint was green, slightly varying shades of it, but mainly dark. The sun was down – as far as that barrier was concerned, but not for the Jungfrau, towering into the heavens beyond the gateway. She was a soaring conflagration of blinding white light.

It is said that Fridolin (the holy Fridolin), a saint now, but formerly a missionary, gave the mountain its gracious name. He was an Irishman, son of an Irish King, of whom there were 30,000 reigning in Cork County alone in his time, 1,500 years ago. It got so that they could not make a living, there was so much competition and wages got cut so. Some of them were out of work months at a time, with wife and little children to feed, and not a crust in the place. At last a particularly severe winter fell upon the country, and hundreds of them were reduced to mendicancy and were to be seen day after day in the bitterest weather standing barefoot in the snow, holding out their crowns for alms. Indeed, they would have been obliged to emigrate or starve but for a fortunate idea of Prince Fridolin, who started a labor union, the first one in history, and got the great bulk of them to join it. He thus won the general gratitude and they wanted to make him Emperor – Emperor over them all – Emperor of Cork County; but he said no, walking delegate was good enough for him. For behold, he was modest beyond his years and keen as a whip. To this day in Germany and Switzerland, where St. Fridolin is deeply revered and honored, the peasantry speak of him affectionately as the first walking delegate.

The first walk he took was into France and Germany missionarying – for missionarying was a better thing in those days than it is in ours. All you had to do was to cure the head savage's sick daughter by a "miracle" – a miracle like the miracle of Lourdes in our day, for instance – and immediately that head savage was your convert; he was your convert and filled to the eyes with a new convert's enthusiasm. You could sit down and make yourself easy, now. He would take an ax and convert the rest of the nation himself. Charlemagne was that kind of a walking delegate.

Yes, there were great missionaries in those days, for the methods were sure and the rewards great. We have no such missionaries now, and no such methods.

But to continue the history of the first walking delegate if you are interested. I am interested myself because I have seen his relics at Seckingen, and also the very spot where he worked his greatest miracle – the one which won him his saintship in the Papal Court a few centuries later. To have seen these things makes me feel very near to him, almost like a member of the family, in fact. While wandering about the continent he arrived at the spot on the Rhine which is now occupied by Seckingen, and proposed to settle there, but the people warned him off. He appealed to the King of the Franks, who made him a present of the whole region, people and all. He built a great cloister there for women, and proceeded to teach in it and accumulate more land. There were two wealthy brothers in the neighborhood, Urso and Landulph. Urso died, and Fridolin claimed his estates. Landulph asked for documents and papers. Fridolin had none to show. He said the bequest had been made to him by word of mouth. Landulph suggested that he produce a witness, and said it in a way which he thought was very witty, very sarcastic. This shows that he did not know the walking delegate. Fridolin was not disturbed. He said:

"Appoint your court. I will bring a witness."

The court was created. It consisted of fifteen Counts and Barons. A day was appointed for the trial of the case. On that day the Judges took their seats in state and proclamation was made that the court was ready for business. Five minutes, ten minutes, fifteen minutes passed and yet no Fridolin appeared. Landulph rose and was in the act of claiming judgment by default when a strange clacking sound was heard coming up the stairs. In another moment Fridolin entered at the further door and came walking in a deep hush down the middle aisle with a tall skeleton stalking in his rear.

Amazement and terror sat upon every countenance, for everybody suspected that that skeleton was Urso's. It stopped before the chief judge and raised its bony arm aloft and began to speak while all the assembly shuddered, for they could see the words leak out from between its ribs. It said:

"Brother, why dost thou disturb my blessed rest and withhold by robbery the gift which I gave for the honor of God?"

It seems a strange thing and most irregular, but the verdict was actually given against Landulph on the testimony of this wandering rack-heap of unidentified bones. In our day a skeleton would not be allowed to testify at all; for a skeleton has no moral responsibility, and its word could not rationally be trusted. Most skeletons are not to be believed on oath, and this was probably one of them. However, the incident is valuable as preserving to us a curious sample of the quaint laws of evidence of that remote time – a time so remote, so far back toward the beginning of evolution out of original idiocy that the intellectual difference between a bench of judges and a basket of vegetables was as yet so slight that we may say with all confidence that it didn't really exist.

Sunday – During several afternoons I have been engaged in an interesting and maybe useful piece of work – that is to say, I have been trying to make the mighty Jungfrau earn her living – earn it in a most humble sphere, but on a prodigious scale, on a prodigious scale of necessity, for she couldn't do anything in a small way with her size and style. I have been trying to make her do service as a stupendous dial, and check off the hours as they glide across her pallid face up there against the sky, and tell the time of day to the populations lying within fifty miles of her, and to the people in the moon if they have a good telescope there.

Until late in the afternoon the Jungfrau's aspect is that of a spotless desert of snow set upon edge against the sky. But by midafternoon some elevations, which rise out of the western border of the desert, and whose presence you perhaps had not detected or suspected up to that time, begin to cast black shadows eastward across the gleaming surface. At first there is only one shadow; later there are two. Toward 4 p. m. the other day I was gazing and worshiping, as usual, when I chanced to notice that shadow No. I was beginning to take to itself something of the shape of a human profile. By 4 the back of the head was good, the military cap was pretty good, the nose was bold and strong, the upper lip sharp, but not pretty, and there was a great goatee that shot straight aggressively forward from the chin.

At 4:30 the nose had changed its shape considerably, and the altered slant of the sun had revealed and made conspicuous a huge buttress or barrier of naked rock, which was so located as to answer very well for a shoulder or coat collar to this swarthy and indiscreet sweetheart who had stolen out there right before everybody to pillow his head on the virgin's white breast and whisper soft sentimentalities to her to the sensuous music of crashing ice domes and the boom and thunder of the passing avalanche – music very familiar to his ear, for he has heard it every afternoon at this hour since the day he first came courting this child of the earth, who lives in the sky; and that day is far back – yes, for he was at this pleasant sport before the middle ages drifted by him in the valley; before the Romans marched past; and before the antique and recordless barbarians fished and hunted here and wondered who he might be, and were probably afraid of him; and before primeval man, himself just emerged from his four-footed estate, stepped out upon this plain, first sample of his race, a thousand centuries ago, and cast a glad eye up there, judging he had found a brother human being and consequently something to kill; and before the big saurians wallowed here, still some æons earlier; O, yes, a day so far back that only the eternal sun himself was present to see that first visit; a day so far back that neither tradition nor history was born yet, and a whole weary eternity must come and go before the restless little creature, of whose face this stupendous Shadow-Face was the prophecy, would arrive in the earth and begin his shabby career, and think it a big thing. O, indeed, yes; when you talk about your poor Roman and Egyptian day-before-yesterday antiquities you should choose a time when the hoary Shadow-Face of the Jungfrau is not by. It antedates all antiquities, known or imaginable; for it was here the world itself created the theater of future antiquities. And it is the only witness with a human face that was there to see that marvel, and remains to us a memorial of it.

By 4:40 p. m. the nose of the shadow is perfect and is beautiful. It is black and powerfully marked against the upright canvas of glowing snow and covers hundreds of acres of that resplendent surface.

Meantime shadow No. 2 has been creeping out well to the rear of the face – west of it – and at 5 o'clock has assumed a shape that has rather a poor and rude semblance of a shoe.

Meantime, also, the great Shadow-Face has been gradually changing for twenty minutes, and now, 5 p. m., is become a quite fair portrait of Roscoe Conkling. The likeness is there and is unmistakable. The goatee is shortened now and has an end; formerly it hadn't any, but ran off eastward and arrived nowhere.

By 6 p. m. the face has dissolved and gone, and the goatee has become what looks like the shadow of a tower with a pointed roof; and the shoe has turned into what the printers call a "fist" with a finger pointing.

If I were now imprisoned on a mountain summit a hundred miles northward of this point and was denied a timepiece I could get along well enough from 4 till 6 on clear days, for I could keep track of the time by the changing shapes of these mighty shadows on the Virgin's front, the most stupendous dial I am acquainted with, the oldest clock in the world by a couple of million years.

I suppose I should not have noticed the forms of the shadows if I hadn't the habit of hunting for faces in the clouds and in mountain crags – a sort of amusement which is very entertaining, even when you don't find any, and brilliantly satisfying when you do. I have searched through several bushels of photographs of the Jungfrau here, but found only one with the Face in it, and in this case it was not strictly recognizable as a face, which was evidence that the picture was taken before 4 in the afternoon; and also evidence that all the photographers have persistently overlooked one of the most fascinating features of the Jungfrau show. I say, fascinating, because if you once detect a human face produced on a great plan by unconscious Nature you never get tired of watching it. At first you can't make another person see it all; but after he has made it out once he can't see anything else afterward.

The King of Greece is a man who goes around quietly enough when off duty. One day this summer he was traveling in an ordinary first-class compartment, just in his other suit, the one which he works the realm in when he is at home, and so he was not looking like anybody in particular, but a good deal like everybody in general. By and by a hearty and healthy German-American got in and opened up a frank and interested and sympathetic conversation with him, and asked him a couple of thousand questions about himself, which the King answered good-naturedly, but in a more or less indefinite way as to private particulars.

"Where do you live when you are at home?"

"In Greece."

"Greece! Well, now, that is just astonishing. Born there?"

"Yes."

"Do you speak Greek?"

"Yes."

"Now ain't that strange! I never expected to live to see that. What is your trade? I mean, how do you get your living? What is your line of business?"

"Well, I hardly know how to answer. I am only a kind of foreman, on a salary; and the business – well, it's a very general kind of business."

"Yes, I understand – general jobbing – little of everything – anything that there's money in."

"That's about it, yes."

"Are you traveling for the house now?"

"Well, partly, but not entirely. Of course I do a stroke of business if it falls in the way –"

"Good, I like that in you! That's me, every time. Go on."

"I was only going to say I am off on my vacation, now."

"Well, that's all right, no harm in that; a man works all the better for a little let-up now and then. Not that I've been used to having it myself, for I haven't. I reckon this is my first. I was born in Germany, and when I was a couple of weeks old shipped for America, and I've been there ever since, and that's sixty-four years by the watch. I'm an American in principle and German at heart, and it's the boss combination. Well, how do you get along, as a rule – pretty fair?"

"I've a rather large family –"

"There, that's it – big family and trying to raise them on a salary. Now, what did you go and do that for?"

"Well, I thought –"

"Of course you did. You were young and confident and thought you could branch out and make things go with a whirl, and here you are, you see! But never mind about that, I'm not trying to discourage you. Dear me, I've been just where you are myself. You've got good grit; there's good stuff in you, I can see that. You got a wrong start, that's the whole trouble. But you hold your grip, and we'll see what can be done. Your case ain't half as bad as it might be. You are going to come out all right – I'm bail for that. Boys and girls?"

"My family? Yes, some of them are boys –"

"And the rest girls. It's just as I expected. But that's all right, and it's better so, anyway. What are the boys doing – learning a trade?"

"Well, no – I thought –"

"It's a great mistake; it's the biggest mistake you ever made. You've seen that in your own case. A man ought always to have a trade to fall back on. Now, I was a harness-maker at first. Did that prevent me from becoming one of the biggest brewers in America? O, no, I always had the harness trick to fall back on in rough weather. Now if you had learned how to make harness – however, it's too late now, too late; and it's no good plan to cry over spilt milk. But as to the boys, you see – what's to become of them if anything happens to you?"

"It has been my idea to let the eldest one succeed me –"

"O, come! Suppose the firm don't want him?"

"I hadn't thought of that, but –"

"Now look here, you want to get right down to business and stop dreaming. You are capable of immense things – man, you can make a perfect success in life; all you want is somebody to steady you and boost you along on the right road. Do you own anything in the business?"

"No – not exactly; but if I continue to give satisfaction I suppose I can keep my –"

"Keep your place – yes. Well, don't you depend on anything of the kind. They'll bounce you the minute you get a little old and worked out; they'll do it, sure. Can't you manage somehow to get into the firm – that's the great thing, you know."

"I think it is doubtful, in fact, very doubtful."

"Um – that's bad – yes, and unfair, too. Do you suppose if I should go there and have a talk with your people – look here – do you think you could run a brewery?"

"I have never tried, but I think I could do it after I got a little familiarity with the business."

The German was silent for some time. He did a good deal of thinking and the King waited with curiosity to see what the result was going to be. Finally the German said:

"My mind's made up. You leave that crowd – you'll never amount to anything there. In these old countries they never give a fellow a show. Yes, you come over to America – come to my place in Rochester; bring the family along. You shall have a show in the business and the foremanship besides. George – you said your name was George? – I'll make a man of you, I give you my word. You've never had a chance here, but that's all going to change – by gracious, I'll give you a lift that'll make your hair curl!"

March 6, 1892

PRIVATE HISTORY OF THE "JUMPING FROG" STORY

FIVE OR SIX years ago a lady from Finland asked me to tell her a story in our negro dialect, so that she could get an idea of what that variety of speech was like. I told her one of Hopkinson Smith's negro stories, and gave her a copy of *Harper's Monthly* containing it. She translated it for a Swedish newspaper, but by an oversight named me as the author of it instead of Smith. I was very sorry for that, because I got a good lashing in the Swedish press, which would have fallen to his share but for that mistake; for it was shown that Boccaccio had told that very story, in his curt and meagre fashion, five hundred years before Smith took hold of it and made a good and tellable thing out of it.

I have always been sorry for Smith. But my own turn has come now. A few weeks ago Professor Van Dyke, of Princeton, asked this question:

"Do you know how old your Jumping Frog story is?"

And I answered:

"Yes – forty-five years. The thing happened in Calaveras County in the spring of 1849."

"No; it happened earlier – a couple of thousand years earlier; it is a Greek story."

I was astonished – and hurt. I said:

"I am willing to be a literary thief if it has been so ordained; I am even willing to be caught robbing the ancient dead alongside of Hopkinson Smith, for he is my friend and a good fellow, and I think would be as honest as any one if he could do it without occasioning remark; but I am not willing to antedate his crimes by fifteen hundred years. I must ask you to knock off part of that."

But the professor was not chaffing; he was in earnest and could not abate a century. He named the Greek author, and offered to get the book and send it to me and the college textbook containing the English translation also. I thought I would like the translation best, because Greek makes me tired. January 30th he sent me the English version, and I will presently insert it in this article. It is my Jumping Frog tale in every essential. It is not strung out as I have strung it out, but it is all there.

To me this is very curious and interesting. Curious, for several reasons. For instance:

I heard the story told by a man who was not telling it to his hearers as a thing new to them, but as a thing which *they had witnessed and would remember.* He was a dull person, and ignorant; he had no gift as a story-teller, and no invention; in his mouth this episode was merely history – history and statistics; and the gravest sort of history, too; he was entirely serious, for he was dealing with what to him were austere facts, and they interested him solely because they *were* facts; he was drawing on his memory, not his mind; he saw no humor in his tale, neither did his listeners; neither he nor they ever smiled or laughed; in my time I have not attended a more solemn conference. To him and to his fellow gold-miners there were just two things in the story that were worth considering. One was, the smartness of its hero, Jim Smiley, in taking the stranger in with a loaded frog; and the other was Smiley's deep knowledge of a frog's nature – for he knew (as the narrator asserted and the listeners conceded) that a frog *likes shot* and is always ready to eat it. Those men discussed those two points, and those only. They were hearty in their admiration of them, and none of the party was aware that a first-rate story had been told, in a first-rate way, and that it was brimful of a quality whose presence they never suspected – humor.

Now, then, the interesting question is, *did* the frog episode happen in Angel's Camp in the spring of '49, as told in my hearing that day in the fall of 1865? I am perfectly sure that it did. I am also sure that its duplicate happened in Bœotia a couple of thousand years ago. I think it must be a case of history actually repeating itself, and not a case of a good story floating down the ages and surviving because too good to be allowed to perish.

I would now like to have the reader examine the Greek story and the story told by the dull and solemn Californian, and observe how exactly alike they are in essentials.

[*Translation.*]
THE ATHENIAN AND THE FROG.*

An Athenian once fell in with a Bœotian who was sitting by the road side looking at a frog. Seeing the other approach, the Bœotian said his was a remarkable frog, and asked if he would agree to start a contest of frogs, on condition that he whose frog jumped farthest should receive a large sum of money. The Athenian replied that he would if the other would fetch him a frog,

* Sidgwick, *Greek Prose Composition*, page 116.

for the lake was near. To this he agreed, and when he was gone the Athenian took the frog, and opening its mouth poured some stones into its stomach, so that it did not indeed seem larger than before, but could not jump. The Bœotian soon returned with the other frog, and the contest began. The second frog first was pinched and jumped moderately; then they pinched the Bœotian frog. And he gathered himself for a leap, and used the utmost effort, but he could not move his body the least. So the Athenian departed with the money. When he was gone the Bœotian, wondering what was the matter with the frog, lifted him up and examined him. And being turned upside down, he opened his mouth and vomited out the stones.

And here is the way it happened in California:

FROM "THE CELEBRATED JUMPING FROG OF CALAVERAS COUNTY."

Well, thish-yer Smiley had rat-tarriers, and chicken cocks, and tom-cats, and all them kind of things, till you couldn't rest, and you couldn't fetch nothing for him to bet on but he'd match you. He ketched a frog one day, and took him home, and said he cal'lated to educate him; and so he never done nothing for three months but set in his backyard and learn that frog to jump. And you bet you he *did* learn him, too. He'd give him a little punch behind, and the next minute you'd see that frog whirling in the air like a doughnut – see him turn one summerset, or maybe a couple if he got a good start, and come down flat-footed and all right, like a cat. He got him up so in the matter of ketching flies, and kep' him in practice so constant, that he'd nail a fly every time as fur as he could see him. Smiley said all a frog wanted was education, and he could do 'most anything – and I believe him. Why, I've seen him set Dan'l Webster down here on this floor – Dan'l Webster was the name of the frog – and sing out "Flies, Dan'l, flies!" and quicker'n you could wink he'd spring straight up and snake a fly off'n the counter there, and flop down on the floor ag'in as solid as a gob of mud, and fall to scratching the side of his head with his hind foot as indifferent as if he hadn't no idea he'd been doin' any more'n any frog might do. You never see a frog so modest and straight-for'ard as he was, for all he was so gifted. And when it come to fair and square jumping on a dead level, he could get over more ground at one straddle than any animal of his breed you ever see. Jumping on a dead level was his strong suit, you understand; and when it come to that, Smiley would ante up money on him as long as he had a red. Smiley was monstrous proud of his frog, and well he might be, for fellers that had travelled and been everywheres, all said he laid over any frog that ever *they* see.

Well, Smiley kep' the beast in a little lattice box, and he used to fetch him downtown sometimes and lay for a bet. One day a feller – a stranger in the camp, he was – come acrost him with his box, and says:

"What might it be that you've got in the box?"

And Smiley says, sorter indifferent-like, "It might be a parrot, or it might be a canary, maybe, but it ain't – it's only just a frog."

And the feller took it, and looked at it careful, and turned it round this way and that, and says, "H'm – so 'tis. Well, what's *he* good for?"

"Well," Smiley says, easy and careless, "he's good enough for *one* thing, I should judge – he can outjump any frog in Calaveras County."

The feller took the box again and took another long, particular look, and give it back to Smiley and says very deliberate, "Well," he says, "I don't see no p'ints about that frog that's any better'n any other frog."

"Maybe you don't," Smiley says. "Maybe you understand frogs and maybe you don't understand 'em; maybe you've had experience, and maybe you ain't only a amature, as it were. Anyways, I've got *my* opinion and I'll resk forty dollars that he can outjump any frog in Calaveras County."

And the feller studies a minute and then says, kinder sad like, "Well, I'm only a stranger here, and I ain't got no frog, but if I had a frog I'd bet you."

And then Smiley says: "That's all right – that's all right – if you'll hold my box a minute, I'll go and get you a frog." And so the feller took the box and put up his forty dollars along with Smiley's and set down to wait.

So he set there a good while thinking and thinking to hisself, and then he got the frog out and prized his mouth open and took a teaspoon and filled him full of quail shot – filled him pretty near up to his chin – and set him on the floor. Smiley he went to the swamp and slopped around in the mud for a long time, and finally he ketched a frog and fetched him in and give him to this feller, and says:

"Now, if you're ready, set him alongside of Dan'l, with his forepaws just even with Dan'l's, and I'll give the word." Then he says, "One – two – three – *git!*" and him and the feller touched up the frogs from behind, and the new frog hopped off lively; but Dan'l give a heave, and hysted up his shoulders – so – like a Frenchman, but it warn't no use – he couldn't budge; he was planted as solid as a church, and he couldn't no more stir than if he was anchored out. Smiley was a good deal surprised, and he was disgusted, too, but he didn't have no idea what the matter was, of course.

The feller took the money and started away; and when he was going out at the door, he sorter jerked his thumb over his shoulder – so – at Dan'l, and says again, very deliberate: "Well," he says, "*I* don't see no p'ints about that frog that's any better'n any other frog."

Smiley he stood scratching his head and looking down at Dan'l a long time, and at last he says, "I do wonder what in the nation that frog throw'd off for – I wonder if there ain't something the matter with him – he 'pears to look mighty baggy, somehow." And he ketched Dan'l by the nap of the neck, and hefted him, and says, "Why, blame my cats if he don't weigh five pound!" and turned him upside down and he belched out a double handful of shot. And then he see how it was, and he was the maddest man – he set the frog down and took out after that feller, but he never ketched him.

The resemblances are deliciously exact. There you have the wily Bœotian and the wily Jim Smiley waiting – two thousand years apart – and waiting, each equipped with his frog and "laying" for the stranger. A contest is proposed – for money. The Athenian would take a chance "if the other would fetch him a frog"; the Yankee says: "I'm only a stranger here and I ain't got no frog; but if I had a frog I'd bet you." The wily Bœotian and the wily Californian, with that vast gulf of two thousand years between, retire eagerly and go frogging in the marsh; the Athenian and the Yankee remain behind and work a base advantage, the one with pebbles, the other with shot. Presently the contest began. In the one case "they pinched the Bœotian frog"; in the other, "him and the feller touched up the frogs from behind." The Bœotian frog "gathered himself for a leap" (you can just *see* him!), but "could not move his body in the least"; the Californian frog "give a heave, but it warn't no use – he couldn't budge." In both the ancient and the modern cases the strangers departed with the money. The Bœotian and the Californian wonder what is the matter with their frogs; they lift them and examine; they turn them upside down and out spills the informing ballast.

Yes, the resemblances are curiously exact. I used to tell the story of the Jumping Frog in San Francisco, and presently Artemus Ward came along and wanted it to help fill out a little book which he was about to publish; so I wrote it out and sent it to his publisher, Carleton; but Carleton thought the book had enough matter in it, so he gave the story to Henry Clapp as a present, and Clapp put it in his *Saturday Press*, and it killed that paper with a suddenness that was beyond praise. At least the paper died with that issue, and none but envious people have ever tried to rob me of the honor and credit of killing it. The "Jumping Frog" was the first piece of writing of mine that spread itself through the newspapers and brought me into public notice. Consequently, the *Saturday Press* was a cocoon and I the worm in it; also, I was the gay-colored literary moth which its death set free. This simile has been used before.

Early in '66 the "Jumping Frog" was issued in book form, with other sketches of mine. A year or two later Madame Blanc translated it into French and published it in the *Revue des Deux Mondes*, but the result was not what should have been expected, for the *Revue* struggled along and pulled through, and is alive yet. I think the fault must have been in the translation. I ought to have translated it myself. I think so because I examined into the matter and finally retranslated the sketch from the French back into English, to see what the trouble was; that is, to see just what sort of a focus the French people got upon it. Then the mystery was explained. In French the story is too confused, and chaotic, and unreposeful, and ungrammatical, and insane; consequently it could only cause grief and sickness – it could not kill. A glance at my retranslation will show the reader that this must be true.

[*My Retranslation.*]

THE FROG JUMPING OF THE COUNTY OF CALAVERAS.

Eh bien! this Smiley nourished some terriers à rats, and some cocks of combat, and some cats, and all sort of things; and with his rage of betting one no had more of repose. He trapped one day a frog and him imported with him (*et l'emporta chez lui*) saying that he pretended to make his education. You me believe if you will, but during three months he not has nothing done but to him apprehend to jump (*apprendre à sauter*) in a court retired of her mansion (*de sa maison*). And I you respond that he have succeeded. He him gives a small blow by behind, and the instant after you shall see the frog turn in the air like a grease-biscuit, make one summersault, sometimes two, when she was well started, and re-fall upon his feet like a cat. He him had accomplished in the art of to gobble the flies (*gober des mouches*), and him there exercised continually – so well that a fly at the most far that she appeared was a fly lost. Smiley had custom to say that all which lacked to a frog it was the education, but with the education she could do nearly all – and I him believe. Tenez, I him have seen pose Daniel Webster there upon this plank – Daniel Webster was the name of the frog – and to him sing, "Some flies, Daniel, some flies!" – in a flash of the eye Daniel had bounded and seized a fly here upon the counter, then jumped anew at the earth, where he rested truly to himself scratch the head with his behind-foot, as if he no had not the least idea of his superiority. Never you not have seen frog as modest, as natural, sweet as she was. And when he himself agitated to jump purely and simply upon plain earth, she does more ground in one jump than any beast of his species than you can know.

To jump plain – this was his strong. When he himself agitated for that Smiley multiplied the bets upon her as long as there to him remained a red. It must to know, Smiley was monstrously proud of his frog, and he of it was right, for some men who were traveled, who had all seen, said that they to him would be injurious to him compare to another frog. Smiley guarded Daniel in a little box latticed which he carried bytimes to the village for some bet.

One day an individual stranger at the camp him arrested with his box and him said:

"What is this that you have then shut up there within?"

Smiley said, with an air indifferent:

"That could be a paroquet, or a syringe (*ou un serin*), but this no is nothing of such, it not is but a frog."

The individual it took, it regarded with care, it turned from one side and from the other, then he said:

"*Tiens!* in effect! – At what is she good?"

"My God!" respond Smiley, always with an air disengaged, "she is good for one thing, to my notice, (*à mon avis*), she can batter in jumping (*elle peut batter en sautant*) all frogs of the county of Calaveras."

The individual re-took the box, it examined of new longly, and it rendered to Smiley in saying with an air deliberate:

"*Eh bien!* I no saw not that that frog had nothing of better than each frog." (*Je ne vois pas que cette grenouille ait rien de mieux qu'aucune grenouille*). [If that isn't grammar gone to seed, then I count myself no judge. – M. T.]

"Possible that you not it saw not," said Smiley, "possible that you – you comprehend frogs; possible that you not you there comprehend nothing; possible that you had of the experience, and possible that you not be but an amateur. Of all manner (*De toute manière*) I bet forty dollars that she batter in jumping no matter which frog of the county of Calaveras."

The individual reflected a second, and said like sad:

"I not am but a stranger here, I no have not a frog; but if I of it had one, I would embrace the bet."

"Strong, well!" respond Smiley; "nothing of more facility. If you will hold my box a minute, I go you to search a frog (*j'irai vous chercher*)."

Behold, then, the individual, who guards the box, who puts his forty dollars upon those of Smiley, and who attends (*et qui attend*). He attended enough longtimes, reflecting all solely. And figure you that he takes Daniel, him opens the mouth by force and with a teaspoon him fills with shot of the hunt, even him fills just to the chin, then he him puts by the earth. Smiley during these times was at slopping in a swamp. Finally he trapped (*attrape*) a frog, him carried to that individual, and said:

"Now if you be ready, put him all against Daniel, with their before-feet upon the same line, and I give the signal" – then he added: "One, two, three – advance!"

Him and the individual touched their frogs by behind, and the frog new put to jump smartly, but Daniel himself lifted ponderously, exalted the shoulders thus, like a Frenchman – to what good? he could not budge, he is planted solid like a church, he not advance no more than if one him had put at the anchor.

Smiley was surprised and disgusted, but he not himself doubted not of the turn being intended (*mais il ne se doutait pas du tour bien entendu*). The individual empocketed the silver, himself with it went, and of it himself in going is that he no gives not a jerk of thumb over the shoulder – like that – at the poor Daniel, in saying with his air deliberate – (*L'individu empoche l'argent s'en va et en s'en allant est ce qu'il ne donne pas un coup de pouce par-dessus l'épaule, comme ça, au pauvre Daniel, en disant de son air délibéré.*)

"*Eh bien!* I no see not that that frog has nothing of better than another."

Smiley himself scratched longtimes the head, the eyes fixed upon Daniel, until that which at last he said:

"I me demand how the devil it makes itself that this beast has refused. Is it that she had something? One would believe that she is stuffed."

He grasped Daniel by the skin of the neck, him lifted and said:

"The wolf me bite if he no weigh not five pounds."

He him reversed and the unhappy belched two handfuls of shot (*et le malheureux*, etc.). – When Smiley recognized how it was, he was like mad. He deposited his frog by the earth and ran after that individual, but he not him caught never.

It may be that there are people who can translate better than I can, but I am not acquainted with them.

So ends the private and public history of the jumping frog of Calaveras County, an incident which has this unique feature about it – that it is both old and new, a "chestnut" and not a "chestnut"; for it was original when it happened two thousand years ago, and was again original when it happened in California in our own time.

April 1894

FENIMORE COOPER'S
LITERARY OFFENCES

The Pathfinder and *The Deerslayer* stand at the head of Cooper's novels as artistic creations. There are others of his works which contain parts as perfect as are to be found in these, and scenes even more thrilling. Not one can be compared with either of them as a finished whole.

The defects in both of these tales are comparatively slight. They were pure works of art. – *Prof. Lounsbury.*

The five tales reveal an extraordinary fulness of invention.

... One of the very greatest characters in fiction, "Natty Bumppo." ...

The craft of the woodsman, the tricks of the trapper, all the delicate art of the forest, were familiar to Cooper from his youth up. – *Prof. Brander Matthews.*

Cooper is the greatest artist in the domain of romantic fiction yet produced by America. – *Wilkie Collins.*

IT SEEMS TO me that it was far from right for the Professor of English Literature in Yale, the Professor of English Literature in Columbia, and Wilkie Collins, to deliver opinions on Cooper's literature without having read some of it. It would have been much more decorous to keep silent and let persons talk who have read Cooper.

Cooper's art has some defects. In one place in *Deerslayer*, and in the restricted space of two-thirds of a page, Cooper has scored 114 offences against literary art out of a possible 115. It breaks the record.

There are nineteen rules governing literary art in the domain of romantic fiction – some say twenty-two. In *Deerslayer* Cooper violated eighteen of them. These eighteen require:

1. That a tale shall accomplish something and arrive somewhere. But the *Deerslayer* tale accomplishes nothing and arrives in the air.

2. They require that the episodes of a tale shall be necessary parts of the tale, and shall help to develop it. But as the *Deerslayer* tale is not a tale, and accomplishes nothing and arrives nowhere, the episodes have no rightful place in the work, since there was nothing for them to develop.

3. They require that the personages in a tale shall be alive, except in the case of corpses, and that always the reader shall be able to tell the corpses from the others. But this detail has often been overlooked in the *Deerslayer* tale.

4. They require that the personages in a tale, both dead and alive, shall exhibit a sufficient excuse for being there. But this detail also has been overlooked in the *Deerslayer* tale.

5. They require that when the personages of a tale deal in conversation, the talk shall sound like human talk, and be talk such as human beings would be likely to talk in the given circumstances, and have a discoverable meaning, also a discoverable purpose, and a show of relevancy, and remain in the neighborhood of the subject in hand, and be interesting to the reader, and help out the tale, and stop when the people cannot think of anything more to say. But this requirement has been ignored from the beginning of the *Deerslayer* tale to the end of it.

6. They require that when the author describes the character of a personage in his tale, the conduct and conversation of that personage shall justify said description. But this law gets little or no attention in the *Deerslayer* tale, as "Natty Bumppo's" case will amply prove.

7. They require that when a personage talks like an illustrated, gilt-edged, tree-calf, hand-tooled, seven-dollar Friendship's Offering in the beginning of a paragraph, he shall not talk like a negro minstrel in the end of it. But this rule is flung down and danced upon in the *Deerslayer* tale.

8. They require that crass stupidities shall not be played upon the reader as "the craft of the woodsman, the delicate art of the forest," by either the author or the people in the tale. But this rule is persistently violated in the *Deerslayer* tale.

9. They require that the personages of a tale shall confine themselves to possibilities and let miracles alone; or, if they venture a miracle, the author must so plausibly set it forth as to make it look possible and reasonable. But these rules are not respected in the *Deerslayer* tale.

10. They require that the author shall make the reader feel a deep interest in the personages of his tale and in their fate; and that he shall make the reader love the good people in the tale and hate the bad ones. But the reader of the *Deerslayer* tale dislikes the good people in it, is indifferent to the others, and wishes they would all get drowned together.

11. They require that the characters in a tale shall be so clearly defined that the reader can tell beforehand what each will do in a given emergency. But in the *Deerslayer* tale this rule is vacated.

In addition to these large rules there are some little ones. These require that the author shall

12. *Say* what he is proposing to say, not merely come near it.

13. Use the right word, not its second cousin.

14. Eschew surplusage.

15. Not omit necessary details.

16. Avoid slovenliness of form.

17. Use good grammar.

18. Employ a simple and straightforward style.

Even these seven are coldly and persistently violated in the *Deerslayer* tale.

Cooper's gift in the way of invention was not a rich endowment; but such as it was he liked to work it, he was pleased with the effects, and indeed he did some quite sweet things with it. In his little box of stage properties he kept six or eight cunning devices, tricks, artifices for his savages and woodsmen to deceive and circumvent each other with, and he was never so happy as when he was working these innocent things and seeing them go. A favorite one was to make a moccasined person tread in the tracks of the moccasined enemy, and thus hide his own trail. Cooper wore out barrels and barrels of moccasins in working that trick. Another stage-property that he pulled out of his box pretty frequently was his broken twig. He prized his broken twig above all the rest of his effects, and worked it the hardest. It is a restful chapter in any book of his when somebody doesn't step on a dry twig and alarm all the reds and whites for two hundred yards around. Every time a Cooper person is in peril, and absolute silence is worth four dollars a minute, he is sure to step on a dry twig. There may be a hundred handier things to step on, but that wouldn't satisfy Cooper. Cooper requires him to turn out and find a dry twig; and if he can't do it, go and borrow one. In fact the Leather Stocking Series ought to have been called the Broken Twig Series.

I am sorry there is not room to put in a few dozen instances of the delicate art of the forest, as practiced by Natty Bumppo and some of the other Cooperian experts. Perhaps we may venture two or three samples. Cooper was a sailor – a naval officer; yet he gravely tells us how a vessel, driving toward a lee shore in a gale, is steered for a particular spot by her skipper because he knows of an *undertow* there which will hold her back against the gale and save her. For just pure woodcraft, or sailorcraft, or whatever it is, isn't that neat? For several years Cooper was daily in the society of artillery, and he ought to have noticed that when a cannon ball strikes the ground it either buries itself or skips a hundred feet or so; skips again a hundred feet or so – and so on, till it finally gets tired and rolls. Now in one place he loses some "females" – as he always calls women – in the edge of a wood near a plain at night in a fog, on purpose to give Bumppo a chance to show off the delicate art of the forest before the reader. These mislaid people are hunting for a fort. They hear a cannon-blast, and a cannon-ball presently comes rolling into the wood and stops at their feet. To the females this suggests nothing. The case is very different with the admirable Bumppo. I wish I may never know peace again if he doesn't strike out promptly and *follow the track* of that cannon-ball across the plain through the dense fog and find the fort. Isn't it a daisy? If Cooper had any real knowledge of Nature's ways of doing things, he had a most delicate art in concealing the fact. For instance: one of his acute Indian experts, Chingachgook (pronounced Chicago, I think), has lost the trail of a person he is tracking through the forest. Apparently that trail is hopelessly lost. Neither you nor I could ever have guessed out the way to find it. It was very different with Chicago. Chicago was not stumped for long. He turned a running stream out of its course, and there, in the slush in its old bed, were that person's moccasin-tracks. The current did not wash them away, as it would have done in all other like cases – no, even the eternal laws of Nature have to vacate when Cooper wants to put up a delicate job of woodcraft on the reader.

We must be a little wary when Brander Matthews tells us that Cooper's books "reveal an extraordinary fulness of invention." As a rule, I am quite willing to accept Brander Matthews's literary judgments and applaud his lucid and graceful phrasing of them; but that particular statement needs to be taken with a few tons of salt. Bless your heart, Cooper hadn't any more invention than a horse; and I don't mean a high-class horse, either; I mean a clothes-horse. It would be very difficult to find a really clever "situation" in Cooper's books; and still more difficult to find one of any kind which he has failed to render absurd by his handling of it. Look at the episodes of "the caves;" and at the celebrated scuffle between Magua and those others on the table-land a few days later; and at Hurry Harry's queer water-transit from the castle to the ark; and at Deerslayer's half hour with his first corpse; and at the quarrel between Hurry Harry and Deerslayer later; and at – but choose for yourself; you can't go amiss.

If Cooper had been an observer, his inventive faculty would have worked better, not more interestingly, but more rationally, more plausibly. Cooper's proudest creations in the way of "situations" suffer noticeably from the absence of the observer's protecting gift. Cooper's eye was splendidly inaccurate. Cooper seldom saw anything correctly. He saw nearly all things as through a glass eye, darkly. Of course a man who cannot see the commonest little everyday matters accurately is working at a disadvantage when he is constructing a "situation." In the *Deerslayer* tale Cooper has a stream which is fifty feet wide, where it flows out of a lake; it presently narrows to twenty as it meanders along for no given reason, and yet, when a stream acts like that it ought to be required to explain itself. Fourteen pages later the width of the brook's outlet from the lake has suddenly shrunk thirty feet, and become "the narrowest part of the stream." This shrinkage is not accounted for. The stream has bends in it, a sure indication that it has alluvial banks, and cuts them; yet these bends are only thirty and fifty feet long. If Cooper had been a nice and punctilious observer he would have noticed that the bends were oftener nine hundred feet long than short of it.

Cooper made the exit of that stream fifty feet wide in the first place, for no particular reason; in the second place, he narrowed it to less than twenty to accommodate some Indians. He bends a "sapling" to the form of an arch over this narrow passage, and conceals six Indians in its foliage. They are "laying" for a settler's scow or ark which is coming up the stream on its way to the lake; it is being hauled against the stiff current by a rope whose stationary end is anchored in the lake; its rate of progress cannot be more than a mile an hour. Cooper describes the ark, but pretty obscurely. In the matter of dimensions "it was little more than a modern canal boat." Let us guess, then, that it was about 140 feet long. It was of "greater breadth than common." Let us guess, then, that it was about sixteen feet wide. This leviathan had been prowling down bends which were but a third as long as itself, and scraping between banks where it had only two feet of space to spare on each side. We cannot too much admire this miracle. A low-roofed log dwelling occupies "two-thirds of the ark's length" – a dwelling ninety feet long and sixteen feet wide, let us say – a kind

of vestibule train. The dwelling has two rooms – each forty-five
feet long and sixteen feet wide, let us guess. One of them is the bedroom of the Hutter girls, Judith and Hetty; the other is the parlor,
in the day time, at night it is papa's bed chamber. The ark is arriving at the stream's exit, now, whose width has been reduced to less
than twenty feet to accommodate the Indians – say to eighteen.
There is a foot to spare on each side of the boat. Did the Indians
notice that there was going to be a tight squeeze there? Did
they notice that they could make money by climbing down out of
that arched sapling and just stepping aboard when the ark scraped
by? No; other Indians would have noticed these things, but
Cooper's Indians never notice anything. Cooper thinks they are
marvellous creatures for noticing, but he was almost always in
error about his Indians. There was seldom a sane one among them.

The ark is 140 feet long; the dwelling is 90 feet long. The idea
of the Indians is to drop softly and secretly from the arched sapling
to the dwelling as the ark creeps along under it at the rate of a mile
an hour, and butcher the family. It will take the ark a minute and
a half to pass under. It will take the 90-foot dwelling a minute to
pass under. Now, then, what did the six Indians do? It would take
you thirty years to guess, and even then you would have to give it
up, I believe. Therefore, I will tell you what the Indians did. Their
chief, a person of quite extraordinary intellect for a Cooper
Indian, warily watched the canal boat as it squeezed along under
him, and when he had got his calculations fined down to exactly
the right shade, as he judged, he let go and dropped. And *missed
the house!* That is actually what he did. He missed the house, and
landed in the stern of the scow. It was not much of a fall, yet it
knocked him silly. He lay there unconscious. If the house had been
97 feet long, he would have made the trip. The fault was Cooper's,
not his. The error lay in the construction of the house. Cooper was
no architect.

There still remained in the roost five Indians. The boat has
passed under and is now out of their reach. Let me explain what
the five did – you would not be able to reason it out for yourself.
No. 1 jumped for the boat, but fell in the water astern of it. Then
No. 2 jumped for the boat, but fell in the water still further astern
of it. Then No. 3 jumped for the boat, and fell a good way
astern of it. Then No. 4 jumped for the boat, and fell in the water
away astern. Then even No. 5 made a jump for the boat – for he
was a Cooper Indian. In the matter of intellect, the difference

between a Cooper Indian and the Indian that stands in front of the cigar shop is not spacious. The scow episode is really a sublime burst of invention; but it does not thrill, because the inaccuracy of the details throws a sort of air of fictitiousness and general improbability over it. This comes of Cooper's inadequacy as an observer.

The reader will find some examples of Cooper's high talent for inaccurate observation in the account of the shooting match in *The Pathfinder*. "A common wrought nail was driven lightly into the target, its head having been first touched with paint." The color of the paint is not stated – an important omission, but Cooper deals freely in important omissions. No, after all, it was not an important omission; for this nail head is *a hundred yards* from the marksman and could not be seen by them at that distance no matter what its color might be. How far can the best eyes see a common house fly? A hundred yards? It is quite impossible. Very well, eyes that cannot see a house fly that is a hundred yards away cannot see an ordinary nail head at that distance, for the size of the two objects is the same. It takes a keen eye to see a fly or a nail head at fifty yards – one hundred and fifty feet. Can the reader do it?

The nail was lightly driven, its head painted, and game called. Then the Cooper miracles began. The bullet of the first marksman chipped an edge of the nail head; the next man's bullet drove the nail a little way into the target – and removed all the paint. Haven't the miracles gone far enough now? Not to suit Cooper; for the purpose of this whole scheme is to show off his prodigy, Deerslayer-Hawkeye - Long - Rifle - Leather - Stocking - Pathfinder - Bumppo before the ladies.

> "Be all ready to clench it, boys!" cried out Pathfinder, stepping into his friend's tracks the instant they were vacant. "Never mind a new nail; I can see that, though the paint is gone, and what I can see, I can hit at a hundred yards, though it were only a mosquitoe's eye. Be ready to clench!"
>
> The rifle cracked, the bullet sped its way and the head of the nail was buried in the wood, covered by the piece of flattened lead.

There, you see, is a man who could hunt flies with a rifle, and command a ducal salary in a Wild West show to-day, if we had him back with us.

The recorded feat is certainly surprising, just as it stands; but it is not surprising enough for Cooper. Cooper adds a touch. He has made Pathfinder do this miracle with another man's rifle, and not only that, but Pathfinder did not have even the advantage of load-ing it himself. He had everything against him, and yet he made that impossible shot, and not only made it, but did it with absolute confidence, saying, "Be ready to clench." Now a person like that would have undertaken that same feat with a brickbat, and with Cooper to help he would have achieved it, too.

Pathfinder showed off handsomely that day before the ladies. His very first feat was a thing which no Wild West show can touch. He was standing with the group of marksmen, observing – a hun-dred yards from the target, mind: one Jasper raised his rifle and drove the centre of the bull's-eye. Then the quartermaster fired. The target exhibited no result this time. There was a laugh. "It's a dead miss," said Major Lundie. Pathfinder waited an impressive moment or two, then said in that calm, indifferent, know-it-all way of his, "No, Major – he has covered Jasper's bullet, as will be seen if any one will take the trouble to examine the target."

Wasn't it remarkable! How *could* he see that little pellet fly through the air and enter that distant bullet-hole? Yet that is what he did; for nothing is impossible to a Cooper person. Did any of those people have any deep-seated doubts about this thing? No; for that would imply sanity, and these were all Cooper people.

> The respect for Pathfinder's skill and for his *quickness and accu-racy of sight* (the italics are mine) was so profound and general, that the instant he made this declaration the spectators began to distrust their own opinions, and a dozen rushed to the target in order to ascertain the fact. There, sure enough, it was found that the quartermaster's bullet had gone through the hole made by Jasper's, and that, too, so accurately as to require a minute examination to be certain of the circumstance, which, however, was soon clearly established by discovering one bullet over the other in the stump against which the target was placed.

They made a "minute" examination; but never mind, how could they know that there were two bullets in that hole without digging the latest one out? for neither probe nor eyesight could prove the presence of any more than one bullet. Did they dig? No; as we shall see. It is the Pathfinder's turn now; he steps out before the ladies, takes aim, and fires.

But alas! here is a disappointment; an incredible, an

unimaginable disappointment – for the target's aspect is unchanged; there is nothing there but that same old bullet hole!

"If one dared to hint at such a thing," cried Major Duncan, "I should say that the Pathfinder has also missed the target."

As nobody had missed it yet, the "also" was not necessary; but never mind about that, for the Pathfinder is going to speak.

"No, no, Major," said he, confidently, "that *would* be a risky declaration. I didn't load the piece, and can't say what was in it, but if it was lead, you will find the bullet driving down those of the Quartermaster and Jasper, else is not my name Pathfinder."
A shout from the target announced the truth of this assertion.

Is the miracle sufficient as it stands? Not for Cooper. The Pathfinder speaks again, as he "now slowly advances towards the stage occupied by the females:"

"That's not all, boys, that's not all; if you find the target touched at all, I'll own to a miss. The Quartermaster cut the wood, but you'll find no wood cut by that last messenger."

The miracle is at last complete. He knew – doubtless *saw* – at the distance of a hundred yards – that his bullet had passed into the hole *without fraying the edges*. There were now three bullets in that one hole – three bullets imbedded processionally in the body of the stump back of the target. Everybody knew this – somehow or other – and yet nobody had dug any of them out to make sure. Cooper is not a close observer, but he is interesting. He is certainly always that, no matter what happens. And he is more interesting when he is not noticing what he is about than when he is. This is a considerable merit.

The conversations in the Cooper books have a curious sound in our modern ears. To believe that such talk really ever came out of people's mouths would be to believe that there was a time when time was of no value to a person who thought he had something to say; when it was the custom to spread a two-minute remark out to ten; when a man's mouth was a rolling mill, and busied itself all day long in turning four-foot pigs of thought into thirty-foot bars of conversational railroad iron by attenuation; when subjects were seldom faithfully stuck to, but the talk wandered all around and arrived nowhere; when conversations consisted mainly of irrelevances, with here and there a relevancy, a relevancy with an embarrassed look, as not being able to explain how it got there.

Cooper was certainly not a master in the construction of dialogue. Inaccurate observation defeated him here as it defeated him in so many other enterprises of his. He even failed to notice that the man who talks corrupt English six days in the week must and will talk it on the seventh, and can't help himself. In the *Deerslayer* story he lets Deerslayer talk the showiest kind of book talk sometimes, and at other times the basest of base dialects. For instance, when some one asks him if he has a sweetheart, and if so, where she abides, this is his majestic answer:

> "She's in the forest – hanging from the boughs of the trees, in a soft rain – in the dew on the open grass – the clouds that float about in the blue heavens – the birds that sing in the woods – the sweet springs where I slake my thirst – and in all the other glorious gifts that come from God's Providence!"

And he preceded that, a little before, with this:

> "It consarns me as all things that touches a fri'nd consarns a fri'nd."

And this is another of his remarks:

> "If I was Injin born, now, I might tell of this, or carry in the scalp and boast of the expl'ite afore the whole tribe; or if my inimy had only been a bear" – and so on.

We cannot imagine such a thing as a veteran Scotch Commander-in-Chief comporting himself in the field like a windy melodramatic actor, but Cooper could. On one occasion Alice and Cora were being chased by the French through a fog in the neighborhood of their father's fort:

> "*Point de quartier aux coquins!*" cried an eager pursuer, who seemed to direct the operations of the enemy.
>
> "Stand firm and be ready, my gallant 60ths!" suddenly exclaimed a voice above them; "wait to see the enemy; fire low, and sweep the glacis."
>
> "Father! father!" exclaimed a piercing cry from out the mist; "it is I! Alice! thy own Elsie! spare, O! save your daughters!"
>
> "Hold!" shouted the former speaker, in the awful tones of parental agony, the sound reaching even to the woods, and rolling back in solemn echo. " 'Tis she! God has restored me my

children! Throw open the sally-port; to the field, 6oths, to the field; pull not a trigger, lest ye kill my lambs! Drive off these dogs of France with your steel."

Cooper's word-sense was singularly dull. When a person has a poor ear for music he will flat and sharp right along without knowing it. He keeps near the tune, but it is *not* the tune. When a person has a poor ear for words, the result is a literary flatting and sharping; you perceive what he is intending to say, but you also perceive that he doesn't *say* it. This is Cooper. He was not a word-musician. His ear was satisfied with the *approximate* word. I will furnish some circumstantial evidence in support of this charge. My instances are gathered from half a dozen pages of the tale called *Deerslayer*. He uses "verbal," for "oral"; "precision," for "facility"; "phenomena," for "marvels"; "necessary," for "predetermined"; "unsophisticated," for "primitive"; "preparation," for "expectancy"; "rebuked," for "subdued"; "dependent on," for "resulting from"; "fact," for "condition"; "fact," for "conjecture"; "precaution," for "caution"; "explain," for "determine"; "mortified," for "disappointed"; "meretricious," for "factitious"; "materially," for "considerably"; "decreasing," for "deepening"; "increasing," for "disappearing"; "embedded," for "enclosed"; "treacherous," for "hostile"; "stood," for "stooped"; "softened," for "replaced"; "rejoined," for "remarked"; "situation," for "condition"; "different," for "differing"; "insensible," for "unsentient"; "brevity," for "celerity"; "distrusted," for "suspicious"; "mental imbecility," for "imbecility"; "eyes," for "sight"; "counteracting," for "opposing"; "funeral obsequies," for "obsequies."

There have been daring people in the world who claimed that Cooper could write English, but they are all dead now – all dead but Lounsbury. I don't remember that Lounsbury makes the claim in so many words, still he makes it, for he says that *Deerslayer* is a "pure work of art." Pure, in that connection, means faultless – faultless in all details – and language is a detail. If Mr. Lounsbury had only compared Cooper's English with the English which he writes himself – but it is plain that he didn't; and so it is likely that he imagines until this day that Cooper's is as clean and compact as his own. Now I feel sure, deep down in my heart, that Cooper wrote about the poorest English that exists in our language, and that the English of *Deerslayer* is the very worst that even Cooper ever wrote.

I may be mistaken, but it does seem to me that *Deerslayer* is not a work of art in any sense; it does seem to me that it is destitute of every detail that goes to the making of a work of art; in truth, it seems to me that *Deerslayer* is just simply a literary *delirium tremens*.

A work of art? It has no invention; it has no order, system, sequence, or result; it has no lifelikeness, no thrill, no stir, no seeming of reality; its characters are confusedly drawn, and by their acts and words they prove that they are not the sort of people the author claims that they are; its humor is pathetic; its pathos is funny; its conversations are – oh! indescribable; its love-scenes odious; its English a crime against the language.

Counting these out, what is left is Art. I think we must all admit that.

July 1895

HOW TO TELL A STORY

THE HUMOROUS STORY AN AMERICAN DEVELOPMENT. — ITS
DIFFERENCE FROM COMIC AND WITTY STORIES.

I DO NOT claim that I can tell a story as it ought to be told. I only
claim to know how a story ought to be told, for I have been almost
daily in the company of the most expert story-tellers, for many
years.

There are several kinds of stories, but only one difficult kind –
the humorous. I will talk mainly about that one. The humorous
story is American, the comic story is English, the witty story is
French. The humorous story depends for its effect upon the *manner*
of the telling; the comic story and the witty story upon the *matter*.

The humorous story may be spun out to great length, and may
wander around as much as it pleases, and arrive nowhere in particular; but the comic and witty stories must be brief and end with a
point. The humorous story bubbles gently along, the others burst.

The humorous story is strictly a work of art, – high and delicate
art, – and only an artist can tell it; but no art is necessary in telling the comic and the witty story; anybody can do it. The art of
telling a humorous story – understand, I mean by word of mouth,
not print – was created in America, and has remained at home.

The humorous story is told gravely; the teller does his best to
conceal the fact that he even dimly suspects that there is anything
funny about it; but the teller of the comic story tells you beforehand that it is one of the funniest things he has ever heard, then
tells it with eager delight, and is the first person to laugh when he
gets through. And sometimes, if he has had good success, he is so
glad and happy that he will repeat the "nub" of it and glance
around from face to face, collecting applause, and then repeat it
again. It is a pathetic thing to see.

Very often, of course, the rambling and disjointed humorous
story finishes with a nub, point, snapper, or whatever you like to
call it. Then the listener must be alert, for in many cases the teller
will divert attention from that nub by dropping it in a carefully
casual and indifferent way, with the pretence that he does not
know it is a nub.

Artemus Ward used that trick a good deal; then when the
belated audience presently caught the joke he would look up with
innocent surprise, as if wondering what they had found to laugh

at. Dan Setchell used it before him, Nye and Riley and others use it to-day.

But the teller of the comic story does not slur the nub; he shouts it at you – every time. And when he prints it, in England, France, Germany and Italy, he italicises it, puts some whooping exclamation-points after it, and sometimes explains it in a paren-thesis. All of which is very depressing, and makes one want to renounce joking and lead a better life.

Let me set down an instance of the comic method, using an anecdote which has been popular all over the world for twelve or fifteen hundred years. The teller tells it in this way:

The Wounded Soldier.

In the course of a certain battle a soldier whose leg had been shot off appealed to another soldier who was hurrying by to carry him to the rear, informing him at the same time of the loss which he had sustained; whereupon the generous son of Mars, shoul-dering the unfortunate, proceeded to carry out his desire. The bul-lets and cannon-balls were flying in all directions, and presently one of the latter took the wounded man's head off – without, how-ever, his deliverer being aware of it. In no long time he was hailed by an officer, who said:

"Where are you going with that carcass?"

"To the rear, sir – he's lost his leg!"

"His leg, forsooth?" responded the astonished officer; "you mean his head, you booby."

Whereupon the soldier dispossessed himself of his burden, and stood looking down upon it in great perplexity. At length he said:

"It is true, sir, just as you have said." Then after a pause he added, "*But he* TOLD me IT WAS HIS LEG!!!!!"

Here the narrator bursts into explosion after explosion of thun-derous horse-laughter, repeating that nub from time to time through his gaspings and shriekings and suffocatings.

It takes only a minute and a half to tell that in its comic-story form; and isn't worth the telling, after all. Put into the humorous-story form it takes ten minutes, and is about the funniest thing I have ever listened to – as James Whitcomb Riley tells it.

He tells it in the character of a dull-witted old farmer who has just heard it for the first time, thinks it is unspeakably funny, and is trying to repeat it to a neighbor. But he can't remember it; so he gets it all mixed up and wanders helplessly round and round, putting in tedious details that don't belong in the tale and only retard it; taking them out conscientiously and putting in others that are just as useless; making minor mistakes now and then and stopping to correct them and explain how he came to make them; remembering things which he forgot to put in in their proper place and going back to put them in there; stopping his narrative a good while in order to try to recall the name of the soldier that was hurt, and finally remembering that the soldier's name was not mentioned, and remarking placidly that the name is of no real importance, any way, – better, of course, if one knew it, but not essential, after all, – and so on, and so on, and so on.

The teller is innocent and happy and pleased with himself, and has to stop every little while to hold himself in and keep from laughing outright; and does hold in, but his body quakes in a jelly-like way with interior chuckles; and at the end of the ten minutes the audience have laughed until they are exhausted, and the tears are running down their faces.

The simplicity and innocence and sincerity and unconsciousness of the old farmer are perfectly simulated, and the result is a performance which is thoroughly charming and delicious. This is art – and fine and beautiful, and only a master can compass it; but a machine could tell the other story.

To string incongruities and absurdities together in a wandering and sometimes purposeless way, and seem innocently unaware that they are absurdities, is the basis of the American art, if my position is correct. Another feature is the slurring of the point. A third is the dropping of a studied remark apparently without knowing it, as if one were thinking aloud. The fourth and last is the pause.

Artemus Ward dealt in numbers three and four a good deal. He would begin to tell with great animation something which he seemed to think was wonderful; then lose confidence, and after an apparently absent-minded pause add an incongruous remark in a soliloquizing way; and that was the remark intended to explode the mine – and it did.

For instance, he would say eagerly, excitedly, "I once knew a man in New Zealand who hadn't a tooth in his head" – here his animation would die out; a silent, reflective pause would follow, then he would say dreamily, and as if to himself, "and yet that man could beat a drum better than any man I ever saw."

The pause is an exceedingly important feature in any kind of story, and a frequently recurring feature, too. It is a dainty thing, and delicate, and also uncertain and treacherous; for it must be exactly the right length – no more and no less – or it fails of its purpose and makes trouble. If the pause is too short the impressive point is passed, and the audience have had time to divine that a surprise is intended – and then you can't surprise them, of course.

On the platform I used to tell a negro ghost story that had a pause in front of the snapper on the end, and that pause was the most important thing in the whole story. If I got it the right length precisely, I could spring the finishing ejaculation with effect enough to make some impressible girl deliver a startled little yelp and jump out of her seat – and that was what I was after. This story was called "The Golden Arm," and was told in this fashion. You can practise with it yourself – and mind you look out for the pause and get it right.

The Golden Arm.

Once 'pon a time dey wuz a monsus mean man, en he live 'way out in de prairie all 'lone by hisself, 'cep'n he had a wife. En bimeby she died, en he tuck en toted her way out dah in de prairie en buried her. Well, she had a golden arm – all solid gold, fum de shoulder down. He wuz pow'ful mean – pow'ful; en dat night he couldn't sleep, caze he want dat golden arm so bad.

When it come midnight he couldn't stan' it no mo'; so he git up, he did, en tuck his lantern en shoved out thoo de storm en dug her up en got de golden arm; en he bent his head down 'gin de win', en plowed en plowed en plowed thoo de snow. Den all on a sudden he stop (make a considerable pause here, and look startled, and take a listening attitude) en say: "My *lan'*, what's dat!"

En he listen – en listen – en de win' say (set your teeth together and imitate the wailing and wheezing singsong of the wind), "Bzzz-z-zzz" – en den, way back yonder whah de grave is, he hear a *voice!* – he hear a voice all mix' up in de win' – can't hardly tell 'em 'part – "Bzzz-zzz – W-h-o – g-o-t – m-y – g-o-l-d-e-n *arm*? – zzz – zzz – W-h-o g-o-t m-y g-o-l-d-e-n *arm*?" (You must begin to shiver violently now.)

En he begin to shiver en shake, en say, "Oh, my! *Oh*, my lan'!" en de win' blow de lantern out, en de snow en sleet blow in his face en mos' choke him, en he start a-plowin' knee-deep toward home mos' dead, he so sk'yerd – en pooty soon he hear de voice agin, en (pause) it 'us comin' *after* him! "Bzzz – zzz – zzz – W-h-o – g-o-t – m-y g-o-l-d-e-n – *arm*?"

When he git to de pasture he hear it agin – closter now, en *a-comin'!* – a-comin' back dah in de dark en de storm – (repeat the wind and the voice). When he git to de house he rush up-stairs en jump in de bed en kiver up, head and years, en lay dah shiverin' en shakin' – en den way out dah he hear it *agin!* – en a-*comin'!* En bimeby he hear (pause – awed, listening attitude) – pat – pat – pat – *hit's a-comin' up-stairs!* Den he hear de latch, en he *know* it's in de room!

Den pooty soon he know it's a-*stannin' by de bed!* (Pause.) Den – he know it's a – *bendin' down over him* – en he cain't skasely git his breath! Den – den – he seem to feel someth'n *c-o-l-d*, right down 'most agin his head! (Pause.)

Den de voice say, *right at his year* – "W-h-o – g-o-t – m-y – g-o-l-d-e-n *arm*?" (You must wail it out very plaintively and accusingly; then you stare steadily and impressively into the face of the farthest-gone auditor, – a girl, preferably, – and let that awe-inspiring pause begin to build itself in the deep hush. When it has reached exactly the right length, jump suddenly at that girl and yell, "*You've* got it!"

If you've got the *pause* right, she'll fetch a dear little yelp and spring right out of her shoes. But you *must* get the pause right; and you will find it the most troublesome and aggravating and uncertain thing you ever undertook.)

October 1895

IN MEMORIAM

OLIVIA SUSAN CLEMENS.

DIED AUGUST 18, 1896; AGED 24.

In a fair valley – oh, how long ago, how long ago! –
Where all the broad expanse was clothed in vines
And fruitful fields and meadows starred with flowers,
And clear streams wandered at their idle will,
And still lakes slept, their burnished surfaces
A dream of painted clouds, and soft airs
Went whispering with odorous breath,
And all was peace – in that fair vale,
Shut from the troubled world, a nameless hamlet drowsed.

 Hard by, apart, a temple stood;
And strangers from the outer world
Passing, noted it with tired eyes,
And seeing, saw it not:
A glimpse of its fair form – an answering momentary thrill –
And they passed on, careless and unaware.

They could not know the cunning of its make;
They could not know the secret shut up in its heart;
Only the dwellers of the hamlet knew:
They knew that what seemed brass was gold;
What marble seemed, was ivory;
The glories that enriched the milky surfaces –
The trailing vines, and interwoven flowers,
And tropic birds awing, clothed all in tinted fire –
They knew for what they were, not what they seemed:
Encrustings all of gems, not perishable splendors of the brush.
They knew the secret spot where one must stand –
They knew the surest hour, the proper slant of sun –
To gather in, unmarred, undimmed,
The vision of the fane in all its fairy grace,
A fainting dream against the opal sky.
 And more than this. They knew
That in the temple's inmost place a spirit dwelt,
Made all of light!
 For glimpses of it they had caught

Beyond the curtains when the priests
That served the altar came and went.

   All loved that light and held it dear
That had this partial grace;
But the adoring priests alone who lived
By day and night submerged in its immortal glow
Knew all its power and depth, and could appraise the loss
If it should fade and fail and come no more.

   All this was long ago – so long ago!

The light burned on; and they that worship'd it,
And they that caught its flash at intervals and held it dear,
Contented lived in its secure possession. Ah,
How long ago it was!
            And then when they
Were nothing fearing, and God's peace was in the air,
And none was prophesying harm –
The vast disaster fell:
Where stood the temple when the sun went down,
Was vacant desert when it rose again!

   Ah, yes! 'Tis ages since it chanced!

          So long ago it was,
That from the memory of the hamlet-folk the Light has passed –
They scarce believing, now, that once it was,
Or if believing, yet not missing it,
And reconciled to have it gone.

   Not so the priests! Oh, not so
The stricken ones that served it day and night,
Adoring it, abiding in the healing of its peace:
They stand, yet, where erst they stood
Speechless in that dim morning long ago;
And still they gaze, as then they gazed,
And murmur, "It will come again;
It knows our pain – it knows – it knows –
Ah, surely it will come again."

s.l.c.

LAKE LUCERNE, *August* 18, 1897.

A WORD OF ENCOURAGEMENT
FOR OUR BLUSHING EXILES

... Well, what do you think of our country *now*? And what do you think of the figure she is cutting before the eyes of the world? For one, I am ashamed – (Extract from a long and heated letter from a Voluntary Exile, Member of the American Colony, Paris.)

AND SO YOU are ashamed. I am trying to think out what it can have been that has produced this large attitude of mind and this fine flow of sarcasm. Apparently you are ashamed to look Europe in the face; ashamed of the American name; temporarily ashamed of your nationality. By the light of remarks made to me by an American here in Vienna, I judge that you are ashamed because:

1. We are meddling where we have no business and no right; meddling with the private family matters of a sister nation; intruding upon her sacred right to do as she pleases with her own, unquestioned by anybody.

2. We are doing this under a sham humanitarian pretext.

3. Doing it in order to filch Cuba, the formal and distinct disclaimer in the ultimatum being very, very thin humbug, and easily detectable as such by you and virtuous Europe.

4. And finally you are ashamed of all this because it is new, and base, and brutal, and dishonest; and because Europe, having had no previous experience of such things, is horrified by it and can never respect us nor associate with us any more.

Brutal, base, dishonest? We? Land thieves? Shedders of innocent blood? We? Traitors to our official word? We? Are we going to lose Europe's respect because of this new and dreadful conduct? Russia's, for instance? Is she lying stretched out on her back in Manchuria, with her head among her Siberian prisons and her feet in Port Arthur, trying to read over the fairy tales she told Lord Salisbury, and not able to do it for crying because we are maneuvering to treacherously smouch Cuba from feeble Spain, and because we are ungently shedding innocent Spanish blood?

Is it France's respect that we are going to lose? Is our unchivalric conduct troubling a nation which exists to-day because a brave young girl saved it when its poltroons had lost it – a nation which

deserted her as one man when her day of peril came? Is our treacherous assault upon a weak people distressing a nation which contributed Bartholomew's Day to human history? Is our ruthless
spirit offending the sensibilities of the nation which gave us the
Reign of Terror to read about? Is our unmanly intrusion into the
private affairs of a sister nation shocking the feelings of the people
who sent Maximilian to Mexico? Are our shabby and pusillanimous ways outraging the fastidious people who have sent an innocent man (Dreyfus) to a living hell, taken to their embraces the
slimy guilty one, and submitted to a thousand indignities Emile
Zola – the manliest man in France?

Is it Spain's respect that we are going to lose? Is she sitting sadly
conning her great history and contrasting it with our meddling,
cruel, perfidious one – our shameful history of foreign robberies,
humanitarian shams, and annihilations of weak and unoffending
nations? Is she remembering with pride how she sent Columbus
home in chains; how she sent half of the harmless West Indians
into slavery and the rest to the grave, leaving not one alive; how
she robbed and slaughtered the Inca's gentle race, then beguiled
the Inca into her power with fair promises and burned him at the
stake; how she drenched the New World in blood, and earned and
got the name of The Nation with the Bloody Footprint; how she
drove all the Jews out of Spain in a day, allowing them to sell their
property, but forbidding them to carry any money out of the country; how she roasted heretics by the thousands and thousands in
her public squares, generation after generation, her kings and her
priests looking on as at a holiday show; how her Holy Inquisition
imported hell into the earth; how she was the first to institute it
and the last to give it up – and then only under compulsion; how,
with a spirit unmodified by time, she still tortures her prisoners to-
day; how, with her ancient passion for pain and blood unchanged,
she still crowds the arena with ladies and gentlemen and priests to
see with delight a bull harried and persecuted and a gored horse
dragging his entrails on the ground; and how, with this incredible
character surviving all attempts to civilize it, her Duke of Alva rises
again in the person of General Weyler – to-day the most idolized
personage in Spain – and we see a hundred thousand women and
children shut up in pens and pitilessly starved to death?

Are we indeed going to lose Spain's respect? Is there no way to
avoid this calamity – or this compliment? Are we going to lose her
respect because we have made a promise in our ultimatum which

she thinks we shall break? And meantime is she trying to recall some promise of her own which she has kept?

Is the Professional Official Fibber of Europe really troubled with our morals? Dear Parisian friend, are you taking seriously the daily remark of the newspaper and the orator about "this noble nation with an illustrious history"? That is mere kindness, mere charity for a people in temporary hard luck. The newspaper and the orator do not mean it. They wink when they say it.

And so you are ashamed. Do not be ashamed; there is no occasion for it.

May 24, 1898

MY PLATONIC SWEETHEART

I MET HER first when I was seventeen and she fifteen. It was in a dream. No, I did not meet her; I overtook her. It was in a Missourian village which I had never been in before, and was not in at that time, except dreamwise; in the flesh I was on the Atlantic seaboard ten or twelve hundred miles away. The thing was sudden, and without preparation – after the custom of dreams. There I was, crossing a wooden bridge that had a wooden rail and was untidy with scattered wisps of hay, and there she was, five steps in front of me; half a second previously neither of us was there. This was the exit of the village, which lay immediately behind us. Its last house was the blacksmith-shop; and the peaceful clinking of the hammers – a sound which nearly always seems remote, and is always touched with a spirit of loneliness and a feeling of soft regret for something, you don't know what – was wafted to my ear over my shoulder; in front of us was the winding country road, with woods on one side, and on the other a rail fence, with blackberry vines and hazel bushes crowding its angles; on an upper rail a bluebird, and scurrying toward him along the same rail a fox-squirrel with his tail bent high like a shepherd's crook; beyond the fence a rich field of grain, and far away a farmer in shirt-sleeves and straw hat wading knee-deep through it; no other representative of life, and no noise at all; everywhere a Sabbath stillness.

I remember it all – and the girl, too, and just how she walked, and how she was dressed. In the first moment I was five steps behind her; in the next one I was at her side – without either stepping or gliding; it merely happened; the transfer ignored space. I noticed that, but not with any surprise; it seemed a natural process.

I was at her side. I put my arm around her waist and drew her close to me, for I loved her; and although I did not know her, my behavior seemed to me quite natural and right, and I had no misgivings about it. She showed no surprise, no distress, no displeasure, but put an arm around my waist, and turned up her face to mine with a happy welcome in it, and when I bent down to kiss her she received the kiss as if she was expecting it, and as if it was quite natural for me to offer it and her to take it and have pleasure in it. The affection which I felt for her and which she manifestly felt for me was a quite simple fact; but the quality of it was another

MARK TWAIN

matter. It was not the affection of brother and sister – it was closer than that, more clinging, more endearing, more reverent; and it was not the love of sweethearts, for there was no fire in it. It was somewhere between the two, and was finer than either, and more exquisite, more profoundly contenting. We often experience this strange and gracious thing in our dream-loves; and we remember it as a feature of our childhood-loves, too.

We strolled along, across the bridge and down the road, chatting like the oldest friends. She called me George, and that seemed natural and right, though it was not my name; and I called her Alice, and she did not correct me, though without doubt it was not her name. Everything that happened seemed just natural and to be expected. Once I said, "What a dear little hand it is!" and without any words she laid it gratefully in mine for me to examine it. I did it, remarking upon its littleness, its delicate beauty, and its satin skin, then kissed it; she put it up to her lips without saying anything and kissed it in the same place.

Around a curve of the road, at the end of half a mile, we came to a log house, and entered it and found the table set and everything on it steaming hot – a roast turkey, corn in the ear, butter-beans, and the rest of the usual things – and a cat curled up asleep in a splint-bottomed chair by the fireplace; but no people; just emptiness and silence. She said she would look in the next room if I would wait for her. So I sat down, and she passed through a door, which closed behind her, with a click of the latch. I waited and waited. Then I got up and followed, for I could not any longer bear to have her out of my sight. I passed through the door, and found myself in a strange sort of cemetery, a city of innumerable tombs and monuments stretching far and wide on every hand, and flushed with pink and gold lights flung from the sinking sun. I turned around, and the log house was gone. I ran here and there and yonder down the lanes between the rows of tombs, calling Alice; and presently the night closed down, and I could not find my way. Then I woke, in deep distress over my loss, and was in my bed in Philadelphia. And I was not seventeen, now, but nineteen.

Ten years afterward, in another dream, I found her. I was seventeen again, and she was still fifteen. I was in a grassy place in the twilight deeps of a magnolia forest some miles above Natchez, Mississippi; the trees were snowed over with great blossoms, and the air was loaded with their rich and strenuous fragrance; the ground was high, and through a rift in the wood a burnished patch of the river was visible in the distance. I was sitting on the grass, absorbed in thinking, when an arm was laid around my neck, and there was Alice sitting by my side and looking into my face. A deep and satisfied happiness and an unwordable gratitude rose in me, but with it there was no feeling of surprise; and there was no sense of a time-lapse; the ten years amounted to hardly even a yesterday; indeed, to hardly even a noticeable fraction of it. We dropped in the tranquilest way into affectionate caressings and pettings, and chatted along without a reference to the separation; which was natural, for I think we did not know there had been any that one might measure with either clock or almanac. She called me Jack and I called her Helen, and those seemed the right and proper names, and perhaps neither of us suspected that we had ever borne others; or, if we did suspect it, it was probably not a matter of consequence.

She had been beautiful ten years before; she was just as beautiful still; girlishly young and sweet and innocent, and she was still that now. She had had blue eyes, a hair of flossy gold before; she had black hair now, and dark-brown eyes. I noted these differences, but they did not suggest change; to me she was the same girl she was before, absolutely. It never occurred to me to ask what became of the log house; I doubt if I even thought of it. We were living in a simple and natural and beautiful world where everything that happened was natural and right, and was not perplexed with the unexpected or with any forms of surprise, and so there was no occasion for explanations and no interest attaching to such things.

We had a dear and pleasant time together, and were like a couple of ignorant and contented children. Helen had a summer hat on. She took it off presently and said, "It was in the way; now you can kiss me better." It seemed to me merely a bit of courteous and considerate wisdom, nothing more; and a natural thing for her to think of and do. We went wandering through the woods, and came to a limpid and shallow stream a matter of three yards wide. She said:

"I must not get my feet wet, dear; carry me over."

I took her in my arms and gave her my hat to hold. This was to keep my own feet from getting wet. I did not know why this should have that effect; I merely knew it; and she knew it, too. I crossed the stream, and said I would go on carrying her, because it was so pleasant; and she said it was pleasant to her, too, and wished we had thought of it sooner. It seemed to me a pity that we should have walked so far, both of us on foot, when we could have been having this higher enjoyment; and I spoke of it regretfully, as a something lost which could never be got back. She was troubled about it, too, and said there must be some way to get it back; and she would think. After musing deeply a little while she looked up radiant and proud, and said she had found it.

"Carry me back and start over again."

I can see, now, that that was no solution, but at the time it seemed luminous with intelligence, and I believed that there was not another little head in the world that could have worked out that difficult problem with such swiftness and success. I told her that, and it pleased her; and she said she was glad it all happened, so that I could see how capable she was. After thinking a moment she added that it was "quite atreous." The words seemed to mean something, I do not know why: in fact, it seemed to cover the whole ground and leave nothing more to say; I admired the nice aptness and the flashing felicity of the phrase, and was filled with respect for the marvelous mind that had been able to engender it. I think less of it now. It is a noticeable fact that the intellectual coinage of Dreamland often passes for more there than it would fetch here. Many a time in after years my dream-sweetheart threw off golden sayings which crumbled to ashes under my pencil when I was setting them down in my note-book after breakfast.

I carried her back and started over again; and all the long afternoon I bore her in my arms, miles upon miles, and it never occurred to either of us that there was anything remarkable in a youth like me being able to carry that sweet bundle around half a day without some sense of fatigue or need of rest. There are many dream-worlds, but none is so rightly and reasonably and pleasantly arranged as that one.

After dark we reached a great plantation-house, and it was her home. I carried her in, and the family knew me and I knew them, although we had not met before; and the mother asked me with ill-disguised anxiety how much twelve times fourteen was, and I said a hundred and thirty-five, and she put it down on a piece of paper, saying it was her habit in the process of perfecting her education not to trust important particulars to her memory; and her husband was offering me a chair, but noticed that Helen was asleep, so he said it would be best not to disturb her; and he backed me softly against a wardrobe and said I could stand more easily now; then a negro came in, bowing humbly, with his slouch-hat in his hand, and asked me if I would have my measure taken. The question did not surprise me, but it confused me and worried me, and I said I should like to have advice about it. He started toward the door to call advisers; then he and the family and the lights began to grow dim, and in a few moments the place was pitch dark; but straight-way there came a flood of moonlight and a gust of cold wind, and I found myself crossing a frozen lake, and my arms were empty. The wave of grief that swept through me woke me up, and I was sitting at my desk in the newspaper office in San Francisco, and I noticed by the clock that I had been asleep less than two minutes. And what was of more consequence, I was twenty-nine years old.

That was 1864. The next year and the year after I had mo-mentary glimpses of my dream-sweetheart, but nothing more. These are set down in my note-books under their proper dates, but with no talks nor other particulars added; which is sufficient evidence to me that there were none to add. In both of these instances there was the sudden meeting and recognition, the eager approach, then the instant disappearance, leaving the world empty and of no worth. I remember the two images quite well; in fact, I remember all the images of that spirit, and can bring them before me without help of my note-book. The habit of writing down my dreams of all sorts while they were fresh in my mind, and then studying them and rehearsing them and trying to find out what the source of dreams is, and which of the two or three sepa-rate persons inhabiting us is their architect, has given me a good dream-memory – a thing which is not usual with people, for few drill the dream-memory, and no memory can be kept strong with-out that.

I spent a few months in the Hawaiian Islands in 1866, and in October of that year I delivered my maiden lecture; it was in San Francisco. In the following January I arrived in New York, and had just completed my thirty-first year. In that year I saw my platonic dream-sweetheart again. In this dream I was again standing on the stage of the Opera House in San Francisco, ready to lecture, and with the audience vividly individualized before me in the strong light. I began, spoke a few words, and stopped, cold with fright; for I discovered that I had no subject, no text, nothing to talk about. I choked for a while, then got out a few words, a lame, poor attempt at humor. The house made no response. There was a miserable

pause, then another attempt, and another failure. There were a
few scornful laughs; otherwise the house was silent, unsmilingly
austere, deeply offended. I was consuming with shame. In my distress I tried to work upon its pity. I began to make servile apologies,
mixed with gross and ill-timed flatteries, and to beg and plead for
forgiveness; this was too much, and the people broke into insulting
cries, whistlings, hootings, and cat-calls, and in the midst of this
they rose and began to struggle in a confused mass toward the
door. I stood dazed and helpless, looking out over this spectacle,
and thinking how everybody would be talking about it next day,
and I could not show myself in the streets. When the house was
become wholly empty and still, I sat down on the only chair that
was on the stage and bent my head down on the reading-desk to
shut out the look of that place. Soon that familiar dream-voice
spoke my name, and swept all my troubles away:

"Robert!"

I answered:

"Agnes!"

The next moment we two were lounging up the blossomy gorge
called the Iao Valley, in the Hawaiian Islands. I recognized, without any explanations, that Robert was not my name, but only a
pet name, a common noun, and meant "dear"; and both of us
knew that Agnes was not a name, but only a pet name, a common
noun, whose spirit was affectionate, but not conveyable with
exactness in any but the dream-language. It was about the equivalent of "dear," but the dream-vocabulary shaves meanings finer
and closer than do the world's day-time dictionaries. We did not
know why those words should have those meanings; we had used
words which had no existence in any known language, and had
expected them to be understood, and they were understood. In my
note-books there are several letters from this dream-sweetheart, in
some unknown tongue – presumably dream-tongue – with translations added. I should like to be master of that tongue, then I could
talk in shorthand. Here is one of those letters – the whole of it:

"Rax oha tal."

Translation. – "When you receive this it will remind you that
I long to see your face and touch your hand, for the comfort of it
and the peace."

It is swifter than waking thought; for thought is not thought at
all, but only a vague and formless fog until it is articulated into
words.

We wandered far up the fairy gorge, gathering the beautiful flowers of the ginger-plant and talking affectionate things, and tying and retying each other's ribbons and cravats, which didn't need it; and finally sat down in the shade of a tree and climbed the vine-hung precipices with our eyes, up and up and up toward the sky to where the drifting scarfs of white mist clove them across and left the green summits floating pale and remote, like spectral islands wandering in the deeps of space; and then we descended to earth and talked again.

"How still it is – and soft, and balmy, and reposeful! I could never tire of it. You like it, don't you, Robert?"

"Yes, and I like the whole region – all the islands. Maui. It is a darling island. I have been here before. Have you?"

"Once, but it wasn't an island then."

"What was it?"

"It was a sufa."

I understood. It was the dream-word for "part of a continent."

"What were the people like?"

"They hadn't come yet. There weren't any."

"Do you know, Agnes – that is Haleakala, the dead volcano, over there across the valley; was it here in your friend's time?"

"Yes, but it was burning."

"Do you travel much?"

"I think so. Not here much, but in the stars a good deal."

"Is it pretty there?"

She used a couple of dream-words for "You will go with me some time and you will see." Non-committal, as one perceives now, but I did not notice it then.

A man-of-war-bird lit on her shoulder; I put out my hand and caught it. Its feathers began to fall out, and it turned into a kitten; then the kitten's body began to contract itself to a ball and put out hairy, long legs, and soon it was a tarantula; I was going to keep it, but it turned into a star-fish, and I threw it away. Agnes said it was not worth while to try to keep things; there was no stability about them. I suggested rocks; but she said a rock was like the rest; it wouldn't stay. She picked up a stone, and it turned into a bat and flew away. These curious matters interested me, but that was all; they did not stir my wonder.

While we were sitting there in the Iao gorge talking, a Kanaka came along who was wrinkled and bent and white-headed, and he stopped and talked to us in the native tongue, and we understood him without trouble and answered him in his own speech. He said he was a hundred and thirty years old, and he remembered Captain Cook well, and was present when he was murdered; saw it with his own eyes, and also helped. Then he showed us his gun, which was of strange make, and he said it was his own invention and was to shoot arrows with, though one loaded it with powder and it had a percussion lock. He said it would carry a hundred miles. It seemed a reasonable statement; I had no fault to find with it, and it did not in any way surprise me. He loaded it and fired an arrow aloft, and it darted into the sky and vanished. Then he went his way, saying that the arrow would fall near us in half an hour, and would go many yards into the earth, not minding the rocks.

I took the time, and we waited, reclining upon the mossy slant at the base of a tree, and gazing into the sky. By and by there was a hissing sound, followed by a dull impact, and Agnes uttered a groan. She said, in a series of fainting gasps:

"Take me to your arms – it passed through me – hold me to your heart – I am afraid to die – closer – closer. It is growing dark – I cannot see you. Don't leave me – where are you? You are not gone? You will not leave me? I would not leave you."

Then her spirit passed; she was clay in my arms.

The scene changed in an instant, and I was awake and crossing Bond Street in New York with a friend, and it was snowing hard. We had been talking, and there had been no observable gaps in the conversation. I doubt if I had made any more than two steps while I was asleep. I am satisfied that even the most elaborate and incident-crowded dream is seldom more than a few seconds in length. It would not cost me very much of a strain to believe in Mohammed's seventy-year dream, which began when he knocked his glass over, and ended in time for him to catch it before the water was spilled.

Within a quarter of an hour I was in my quarters, undressed, ready for bed, and was jotting down my dream in my note-book. A striking thing happened now. I finished my notes, and was just going to turn out the gas when I was caught with a most strenuous gape, for it was very late and I was very drowsy. I fell asleep and dreamed again. What now follows occurred while I was asleep; and when I woke again the gape had completed itself, but not long before, I think, for I was still on my feet. I was in Athens – a city which I had not then seen, but I recognized the Parthenon from the pictures, although it had a fresh look and was in perfect repair. I passed by it and climbed a grassy hill toward a palatial sort of mansion which was built of red terra-cotta and had a spacious portico, whose roof was supported by a rank of fluted columns with Corinthian capitals. It was noonday, but I met no one. I passed into the house and entered the first room. It was very large and light, its walls were of polished and richly tinted and veined onyx, and its floor was a pictured pattern in soft colors laid in tiles. I noted the details of the furniture and the ornaments – a thing which I should not have been likely to do when awake – and they took sharp hold and remained in my memory; they are not really dim yet, and this was more than thirty years ago.

There was a person present – Agnes. I was not surprised to see her, but only glad. She was in the simple Greek costume, and her hair and eyes were different as to color from those she had had when she died in the Hawaiian Islands half an hour before, but to me she was exactly her own beautiful little self as I had always known her, and she was still fifteen, and I was seventeen once more. She was sitting on an ivory settee, crocheting something or other, and had her crewels in a shallow willow work-basket in her lap. I sat down by her and we began to chat in the usual way. I remembered her death, but the pain and the grief and the bitterness which had been so sharp and so desolating to me at the moment that it happened had wholly passed from me now, and had left not a scar. I was grateful to have her back, but there was no realizable sense that she had ever been gone, and so it did not occur to me to speak about it, and she made no reference to it herself. It may be that she had often died before, and knew that there was nothing lasting about it, and consequently nothing important enough in it to make conversation out of.

When I think of that house and its belongings, I recognize what a master in taste and drawing and color and arrangement is the dream-artist who resides in us. In my waking hours, when the inferior artist in me is in command, I cannot draw even the simplest picture with a pencil, nor do anything with a brush and colors; I cannot bring before my mind's eye the detailed image of any building known to me except my own house at home; of St. Paul's, St. Peter's, the Eiffel Tower, the Taj, the Capitol at Washington, I can reproduce only portions, partial glimpses; the same with Niagara Falls, the Matterhorn, and other familiar things in nature; I cannot bring before my mind's eye the face or figure of any human being known to me; I have seen my family at breakfast within the past two hours; I cannot bring their images before me, I do not know how they look; before me, as I write, I see a little grove of young trees in the garden; high above them projects the slender lance of a young pine, beyond it is a glimpse of the upper half of a dull-white chimney covered by an A-shaped little roof shingled with brown-red tiles, and half a mile away is a hill-top densely wooded, and the red is cloven by a curved, wide vacancy, which is smooth and grass-clad; I cannot shut my eyes and reproduce that picture as a whole at all, nor any single detail of it except the grassy curve, and that but vaguely and fleetingly.

But my dream-artist can draw anything, and do it perfectly; he can paint with all the colors and all the shades, and do it with delicacy and truth; he can place before me vivid images of palaces, cities, hamlets, hovels, mountains, valleys, lakes, skies, glowing in sunlight or moonlight, or veiled in driving gusts of snow or rain, and he can set before me people who are intensely alive, and who feel, and express their feelings in their faces, and who also talk and laugh, sing and swear. And when I wake I can shut my eyes and bring back those people, and the scenery and the buildings; and not only in general view, but often in nice detail. While Agnes and I sat talking in that grand Athens house, several stately Greeks entered from another part of it, disputing warmly about something or other, and passed us by with courteous recognition; and among them was Socrates. I recognized him by his nose. A moment later the house and Agnes and Athens vanished away, and I was in my quarters in New York again and reaching for my note-book.

In our dreams – I know it! – we do make the journeys we seem to make; we do see the things we seem to see; the people, the horses, the cats, the dogs, the birds, the whales, are real, not chimeras; they are living spirits, not shadows; and they are immortal and indestructible. They go whither they will; they visit all resorts, all points of interest, even the twinkling suns that wander in the wastes of space. That is where those strange mountains are which slide from under our feet while we walk, and where those vast caverns are whose bewildering avenues close behind us and in front when we are lost, and shut us in. We know this because there are no such things here, and they must be there, because there is no other place.

This tale is long enough, and I will close it now. In the

forty-four years that I have known my Dreamland sweetheart, I have seen her once in two years on an average. Mainly these were glimpses, but she was always immediately recognizable, notwithstanding she was so given to repairing herself and getting up doubtful improvements in her hair and eyes. She was always fifteen, and looked it and acted it; and I was always seventeen, and never felt a day older. To me she is a real person, not a fiction, and her sweet and innocent society has been one of the prettiest and pleasantest experiences of my life. I know that to you her talk will not seem of the first intellectual order; but you should hear her in Dreamland – then you would see!

I saw her a week ago, just for a moment. Fifteen, as usual, and I seventeen, instead of going on sixty-three, as I was when I went to sleep. We were in India, and Bombay was in sight; also Windsor Castle, its towers and battlements veiled in a delicate haze, and from it the Thames flowed, curving and winding between its swarded banks, to our feet. I said:

"There is no question about it, England is the most beautiful of all the countries."

Her face lighted with approval, and she said, with that sweet and earnest irrelevance of hers:

"It is, because it is so marginal."

Then she disappeared. It was just as well; she could probably have added nothing to that rounded and perfect statement without damaging its symmetry.

This glimpse of her carries me back to Maui, and that time when I saw her gasp out her young life. That was a terrible thing to me at the time. It was preternaturally vivid; and the pain and the grief and the misery of it to me transcended many sufferings that I have known in waking life. For everything in a dream is more deep and strong and sharp and real than is ever its pale imitation in the unreal life which is ours when we go about awake and clothed with our artificial selves in this vague and dull-tinted artificial world. When we die we shall slough off this cheap intellect, perhaps, and go abroad into Dreamland clothed in our real selves, and aggrandized and enriched by the command over the mysterious mental magician who is here not our slave, but only our guest.

1898

DIPLOMATIC PAY AND CLOTHES

VIENNA, *January 5*. – I find in this morning's papers the statement that the Government of the United States has paid to the two members of the Peace Commission entitled to receive money for their services $100,000 each for their six weeks' work in Paris.

I hope that this is true. I will allow myself the satisfaction of considering that it *is* true, and of treating it as a thing finished and settled.

It is a precedent; and it ought to be a welcome one to our country. A precedent always has a chance to be valuable (as well as the other way); and its best chance to be valuable (or the other way) is when it takes such a striking form as to fix a whole nation's attention upon it. If it come justified out of the discussion which will follow, it will find a career ready and waiting for it.

We realize that the edifice of public justice is built of precedents, from the ground upward; but we do not always realize that all the other details of our civilization are likewise built of precedents. The changes, also, which they undergo, are due to the intrusion of new precedents, which hold their ground against opposition, and keep their place. A precedent may die at birth, or it may live, – it is mainly a matter of luck. If it be imitated once, it has a chance; if twice, a better chance; if three times, it is reaching a point where account must be taken of it; if four, five, or six times, it has probably come to stay – for a whole century, possibly. If a town start a new bow, or a new dance, or a new temperance project, or a new kind of hat, and can get the precedent adopted in the next town, the career of that precedent is begun; and it will be unsafe to bet as to where the end of its journey is going to be. It may not get this start at all, and may have no career; but, if a crown prince introduce the precedent, it will attract vast attention, and its chances for a career are so great as to amount almost to a certainty.

For a long time we have been reaping damage from a couple of disastrous precedents. One is the precedent of shabby pay to public servants standing for the power and dignity of the Republic in foreign lands: the other is a precedent condemning them to exhibit themselves officially in clothes which are not only without grace or dignity, but are a pretty loud and pious rebuke to the vain and frivolous costumes worn by other officials. To our day an American ambassador's official costume remains under the reproach of these defects. At a public function in a European court all foreign representatives except ours wear clothes which in some way distinguish them from the unofficial throng, and mark them as standing for their *countries*. But our representative appears in a plain black swallow-tail, which stands for neither country nor people. It has no nationality. It is found in all countries: it is as international as a night-shirt. It has no particular meaning; but our Government tries to give it one: it tries to make it stand for republican simplicity, modesty, and unpretentiousness. Tries, and without doubt fails; for it is not conceivable that this loud ostentation of simplicity deceives any one. The statue that advertises its modesty with a fig-leaf really brings its modesty under suspicion. Worn officially, our nonconforming swallow-tail is a declaration of ungracious independence in the matter of manners, and is uncourteous. It says to all around: "In Rome we do not choose to do as Rome does; we refuse to respect your tastes and your traditions; we make no sacrifices to any one's customs and prejudices; we yield no jot to the courtesies of life; we prefer our manners, and intrude them here."

That is not the true American spirit, and those clothes misrepresent us. When a foreigner comes among us, and trespasses against our customs and our code of manners, we are offended, and justly so: but our Government commands our ambassadors to wear abroad an official dress which is an offence against foreign manners and customs; and the discredit of it falls upon the nation.

We did not dress our public functionaries in undistinguished raiment before Franklin's time; and the change would not have come if he had been an obscurity. But he was such a colossal figure in the world that whatever he did of an unusual nature attracted the world's attention, and became a precedent. In the case of clothes, the next representative after him, and the next, had to imitate it. After that, the thing was custom; and custom is a petrifaction: nothing but dynamite can dislodge it for a century. We imagine that our queer official costumery was deliberately devised to symbolize our republican simplicity, – a quality which we have never possessed, and are too old to acquire now, if we had any use for it or any leaning toward it. But it is not so; there was nothing deliberate about it; it grew naturally and heedlessly out of the precedent set by Franklin.

If it had been an intentional thing, and based upon a principle, it would not have stopped where it did: we should have applied it further. Instead of clothing our admirals and generals, for courts

martial and other public functions, in superb dress uniforms blazing with color and gold, the Government would put them in
swallow-tails and white cravats, and make them look like ambassadors and lackeys. If I am wrong in making Franklin the father
of our curious official clothes, it is no matter – he will be able to
stand it.

It is my opinion – and I make no charge for the suggestion –
that, whenever we appoint an ambassador or a minister, we ought
to confer upon him the temporary rank of admiral or general, and
allow him to wear the corresponding uniform at public functions
in foreign countries. I would recommend this for the reason that
it is not consonant with the dignity of the United States of America
that her representative should appear upon occasions of state in a
dress which makes him glaringly conspicuous; and that is what his
present undertaker-outfit does when it appears, with its dismal
smudge, in the midst of the butterfly splendors of a Continental
court. It is a most trying position for a shy man, a modest man, a
man accustomed to being like other people. He is the most striking
figure present: there is no hiding from the multitudinous eyes. It
would be funny, if it were not such a cruel spectacle, to see the
hunted creature in his solemn sables scuffling around in that sea
of vivid color, like a mislaid Presbyterian in perdition. We are all
aware that our representative's dress should not compel too much
attention; for anybody but an Indian chief knows that that is a vulgarity. I am saying these things in the interest of our national pride
and dignity. Our representative is the flag. He is the Republic. He
is the United States of America. And when these embodiments
pass by, we do not want them scoffed at: we desire that people shall
be obliged to concede that they are worthily clothed, and politely.

Our Government is oddly inconsistent in this matter of official
dress. When its representative is a civilian who has not been a soldier, it restricts him to the black swallow-tail and white tie; but if
he is a civilian who has been a soldier, it allows him to wear the
uniform of his former rank as an official dress. When Gen. Sickles
was Minister to Spain, he always wore, when on official duty, the
dress uniform of a major-general. When Gen. Grant visited foreign courts, he went handsomely and properly ablaze in the uniform of a full general, and was introduced by diplomatic survivals
of his own Presidential Administration. The latter, by official
necessity, went in the meek and lowly swallow-tail, – a deliciously
sarcastic contrast: the one dress representing the honest and

honorable dignity of the nation; the other, the cheap hypocrisy of the Republican Simplicity tradition. In Paris our present representative can perform his official functions reputably clothed; for he was an officer in the Civil War. In London our late Ambassador was similarly situated; for he, also, was an officer in the Civil War. But Mr. Choate must represent the Great Republic – even at official breakfasts at seven in the morning – in that same old funny swallow-tail.

Our Government's notions about proprieties of costume are indeed very, very odd – as suggested by that last fact. The swallow-tail is recognized the world over as not wearable in the daytime: it is a night-dress, and a night-dress only, – a night-shirt is not more so. Yet, when our representative makes an official visit in the morning, he is obliged by his Government to go in that night-dress. It makes the very cab-horses laugh.

The truth is, that for a while during the present century, and up to something short of forty years ago, we had a lucid interval, and dropped the Republican Simplicity sham, and dressed our foreign representatives in a handsome and becoming official costume. This was discarded by and by, and the swallow-tail substituted. I believe it is not now known which statesman brought about this change; but we all know that, stupid as he was as to diplomatic proprieties in dress, he would not have sent his daughter to a state ball in a corn-shucking costume, nor to a corn-shucking in a state ball costume, to be harshly criticized as an ill-mannered offender against the proprieties of custom in both places. And we know another thing; viz., that he himself would not have wounded the tastes and feelings of a family of mourners by attending a funeral in their house in a costume which was an offence against the dignities and decorum prescribed by tradition and sanctified by custom. Yet that man was so heedless as not to reflect that *all* the social customs of civilized peoples are entitled to respectful observance, and that no man with a right spirit of courtesy in him ever has any disposition to transgress these customs.

There is still another argument for a rational diplomatic dress – a business argument. We are a trading nation; and our representative is our business agent. If he is respected, esteemed, and liked where he is stationed, he can exercise an influence which can extend our trade and forward our prosperity. A considerable number of his business activities have their field in his social relations; and clothes which do not offend against local manners and customs and prejudices are a valuable part of his equipment in this matter, – would be, if Franklin had died earlier.

I have not done with gratis suggestions yet. We made a great and valuable advance when we instituted the office of ambassador. That lofty rank endows its possessor with several times as much influence, consideration, and effectiveness as the rank of minister bestows. For the sake of the country's dignity and for the sake of her advantage commercially, we should have ambassadors, not ministers, at the great courts of the world.

But not at present salaries! No: if we are to maintain present salaries, let us make no more ambassadors; and let us unmake those we have already made. The great position, without the means of respectably maintaining it – there could be no wisdom in that. A foreign representative, to be valuable to his country, must be on good terms with the officials of the capital and with the rest of the influential folk. He must mingle with this society: he cannot sit at home – it is not business, it butters no commercial parsnips. He must attend the dinners, banquets, suppers, balls, receptions, and must *return* these hospitalities. He should return as good as he gets, too, for the sake of the dignity of his country, and for the sake of Business. Have we ever had a minister or an ambassador who could do this on his salary? No – not once, from Franklin's time to ours. Other countries understand the commercial value of properly lining the pockets of their representatives; but apparently our Government has not learned it. England is the most successful trader of the several trading nations; and she takes good care of the watchmen who keep guard in her commercial towers. It has been a long time, now, since we needed to blush for our representatives abroad. It has become custom to send our fittest. We send men of distinction, cultivation, character, – our ablest, our choicest, our best. Then we cripple their efficiency through the meagreness of their pay. Here is a list of salaries for English and American ministers and ambassadors:

CITY.	SALARIES.	
	American.	English.
Paris	$17,500	$45,000
Berlin	17,500	40,000
Vienna	12,000	40,000
Constantinople	10,000	40,000
St. Petersburg	17,500	39,000

| Rome .... | 12,000 | 35,000 |
| Washington .... | | 32,500 |

Sir Julian Pauncefote, the English Ambassador at Washington, has a very fine house besides – at no damage to his salary.

English ambassadors pay no house-rent; they live in palaces owned by England. Our representatives pay house-rent out of their salaries. You can judge by the above figures what kind of houses the United States of America has been used to living in abroad, and what sort of return-entertaining she has done. There is not a salary in our list which would properly house the representative receiving it, and, in addition, pay $3,000 toward his family's bacon and doughnuts, – the strange but economical and customary fare of the American Ambassador's household, except on Sundays, when petrified Boston crackers are added.

The ambassadors and ministers of foreign nations not only have generous salaries, but their Governments provide them with money wherewith to pay a considerable part of their hospitality bills. I believe our Government pays no hospitality bills except those incurred by the navy. Through this concession to the navy, that arm is able to do us credit in foreign parts; and certainly that is well and politic. But why the Government does not think it well and politic that our diplomats should be able to do us like credit abroad, is one of those mysterious inconsistencies which have been puzzling me ever since I stopped trying to understand base-ball, and took up statesmanship as a pastime.

To return to the matter of house-rent. Good houses, properly furnished, in European capitals, are not to be had at small figures. Consequently, our foreign representatives have been accustomed to live in garrets, – sometimes on the roof. Being poor men, it has been the best they could do on the salary which the Government has paid them. How could they adequately return the hospitalities shown them? It was impossible. It would have exhausted the salary in three months. Still, it was their official duty to entertain the influentials after some sort of fashion; and they did the best they could with their limited purse. In return for champagne they furnished lemonade; in return for game they furnished ham; in return for whale they furnished sardines; in return for liquors they furnished condensed milk; in return for the battalion of liveried and powdered flunkeys they furnished the hired girl; in return for the fairy wilderness of sumptuous decorations they draped the stove

with the American flag; in return for the orchestra they furnished
zither and ballads by the family; in return for the ball – but they
didn't return the ball, except in cases where the United States lived
on the roof and had room.

Is this an exaggeration? It can hardly be called that. I saw nearly
the equivalent of it once, a good many years ago. A minister was
trying to create influential friends for a project which might be
worth ten millions a year to the agriculturists of the Republic; and
our Government had furnished him ham and lemonade to persuade the opposition with. The minister did not succeed. He might
not have succeeded if his salary had been what it ought to have
been, – $50,000 or $60,000 a year; – but his chances would have
been very greatly improved. And in any case, he and his dinners
and his country would not have been joked about by the hard-
hearted, and pitied by the compassionate.

Any experienced "drummer" will testify that, when you want
to do business, there is no economy in ham and lemonade. The
drummer takes his country customer to the theatre, the opera, the
circus; dines him, wines him, entertains him all the day and all the
night in luxurious style; and plays upon his human nature in all
seductive ways. For he knows, by old experience, that this is the
best way to get a profitable order out of him. He has his reward.
All Governments except our own play the same policy, with the
same end in view; and they, also, have their reward. But ours
refuses to do business by business ways, and sticks to ham and lemonade. This is the most expensive diet known to the diplomatic
service of the world.

Ours is the only country of first importance that pays its foreign
representatives trifling salaries. If we were poor, we could not find
great fault with these economies, perhaps, – at least one could find
a sort of plausible excuse for them. But we are not poor; and the
excuse fails. As shown above, some of our important diplomatic
representatives receive $12,000; others, $17,500. These salaries are
all ham and lemonade, and unworthy of the flag. When we have
a rich ambassador in London or Paris, he lives as the ambassador
of a country like ours ought to live, and it costs him $100,000 a
year to do it. But why should we allow him to pay that out of his
private pocket? There is nothing fair about it; and the Republic is
no proper subject for any one's charity. In several cases our salaries
of $12,000 should be $50,000; and all of the salaries of $17,500
ought to be $75,000, or $100,000, since we pay no representative's

house-rent. Our State Department realizes the mistake which we are making, and would like to rectify it; but it has not the power.

When a young girl reaches eighteen she is recognized as being a woman. She adds six inches to her skirt, she unplaits her dangling braids and balls her hair on top of her head, she stops sleeping with her little sister and has a room to herself, and becomes in many ways a thundering expense. But she is in society now; and papa has to stand it: there is no avoiding it. Very well. The Great Republic lengthened her skirts last year, balled up her hair, and entered the world's society. This means that, if she would prosper and stand fair with society, she must put aside some of her dearest and darlingest young ways and superstitions, and do as society does. Of course she can decline if she wants to; but this would be unwise. She ought to realize, now that she has "come out," that this is a right and proper time to change a part of her style. She is in Rome; and it has long been granted that when one is in Rome it is good policy to do as Rome does. To advantage Rome? No, – to advantage herself.

If our Government has really paid representatives of ours on the Paris Commission $100,000 apiece for six weeks' work, I feel sure that it is the best cash investment the nation has made in many years. For it seems quite impossible that, with that precedent on the books, the Government will be able to find excuses for continuing its diplomatic salaries at the present mean figure.

MARK TWAIN.

P. S. VIENNA, *January 10.* – I see, by this morning's telegraphic news, that I am not to be the new ambassador here, after all. This – well, I hardly know what to say. I – well, of course I do not care anything about it; but it is at least a surprise. I have for many months been using my influence at Washington to get this diplomatic see expanded into an ambassadorship, with the idea, of course, th— But never mind. Let it go. It is of no consequence. I say it calmly; for I am calm. But at the same time – However, the subject has no interest for me, and never had. I never really intended to take the place, anyway – I made up my mind to it months and months ago, nearly a year. But now, while I am calm, I would like to say this – that, so long as I shall continue to possess an American's proper pride in the honor and dignity of his country, I will not take any ambassadorship in the gift of the flag at a salary short of $75,000 a year. If I shall be charged with wanting to live beyond my country's means, I cannot help it. A country which cannot afford ambassadors' wages should be ashamed to have ambassadors.

Think of a Seventeen-thousand-five-hundred-dollar ambassador! Particularly for *America*. Why, it is the most ludicrous spectacle, the most inconsistent and incongruous spectacle, contrivable by even the most diseased imagination. It is a billionaire in a paper collar, a king in a breechclout, an archangel in a tin halo. And, for pure sham and hypocrisy, the salary is just the match of the ambassador's official clothes, – that boastful advertisement of a Republican Simplicity which manifests itself at home in Fifty-thousand-dollar salaries to insurance presidents and railway lawyers, and in domestic palaces whose fittings and furnishings often transcend in costly display and splendor and richness the fittings and furnishings of the palaces of the sceptred masters of Europe; and which has invented and exported to the Old World the palace-car, the sleeping-car, the tram-car, the electric trolley, the best bicycles, the best motor-cars, the steam-heater, the best and smartest systems of electric calls and telephonic aids to laziness and comfort, the elevator, the private bath-room (hot and cold water on tap), the palace-hotel, with its multifarious conveniences, comforts, shows, and luxuries, the – oh, the list is interminable! In a word, Republican Simplicity found Europe with one shirt to her back, so to speak, as far as *real* luxuries, conveniences, and the comforts of life go, and has clothed her to the chin with the latter. We are the lavishest and showiest and most luxury-loving people on the earth; and at our masthead we fly our one true and honest symbol, the gaudiest flag the world has ever seen. Oh, Republican Simplicity, there are many, many humbugs in the world, but none to which you need take off *your* hat!

M. T.
March 1899

CONCERNING THE JEWS

SOME MONTHS AGO I published a magazine article* descriptive of a remarkable scene in the Imperial Parliament in Vienna. Since then I have received from Jews in America several letters of inquiry. They were difficult letters to answer, for they were not very definite. But at last I have received a definite one. It is from a lawyer, and he really asks the questions which the other writers probably believed they were asking. By help of this text I will do the best I can to publicly answer this correspondent, and also the others – at the same time apologizing for having failed to reply privately. The lawyer's letter reads as follows:

I have read "Stirring Times in Austria." One point in particular is of vital import to not a few thousand people, including myself, being a point about which I have often wanted to address a question to some disinterested person. The show of military force in the Austrian Parliament, which precipitated the riots, was not introduced by any Jew. No Jew was a member of that body. No Jewish question was involved in the Ausgleich or in the language proposition. No Jew was insulting anybody. In short, no Jew was doing any mischief toward anybody whatsoever. In fact, the Jews were the only ones of the nineteen different races in Austria which did not have a party – they are absolutely non-participants. Yet in your article you say that in the rioting which followed, all classes of people were unanimous only on one thing, viz., in being against the Jews. Now will you kindly tell me why, in your judgment, the Jews have thus ever been, and are even now, in these days of supposed intelligence, the butt of baseless, vicious animosities? I dare say that for centuries there has been no more quiet, undisturbing, and well-behaving citizens, as a class, than that same Jew. It seems to me that ignorance and fanaticism cannot alone account for these horrible and unjust persecutions.

Tell me, therefore, from your vantage-point of cold view, what in your mind is the cause. Can American Jews do anything to correct it: either in America or abroad? Will it ever come to an end? Will a Jew be permitted to live honestly, decently, and peaceably like the rest of mankind? What has become of the golden rule?

* See *Harper's Magazine* for March, 1898.

I will begin by saying that if I thought myself prejudiced against the Jew, I should hold it fairest to leave this subject to a person not crippled in that way. But I think I have no such prejudice. A few years ago a Jew observed to me that there was no uncourteous reference to his people in my books, and asked how it happened. It happened because the disposition was lacking. I am quite sure that (bar one) I have no race prejudices, and I think I have no color prejudices nor caste prejudices nor creed prejudices. Indeed, I know it. I can stand any society. All that I care to know is that a man is a human being – that is enough for me; he can't be any worse. I have no special regard for Satan; but I can at least claim that I have no prejudice against him. It may even be that I lean a little his way, on account of his not having a fair show. All religions issue bibles against him, and say the most injurious things about him, but we never hear *his* side. We have none but the evidence for the prosecution, and yet we have rendered the verdict. To my mind, this is irregular. It is un-English; it is un-American; it is French. Without this precedent Dreyfus could not have been condemned. Of course Satan has some kind of a case, it goes without saying. It may be a poor one, but that is nothing; that can be said about any of us. As soon as I can get at the facts I will undertake his rehabilitation myself, if I can find an unpolitic publisher. It is a thing which we ought to be willing to do for any one who is under a cloud. We may not pay him reverence, for that would be indiscreet, but we can at least respect his talents. A person who has for untold centuries maintained the imposing position of spiritual head of four-fifths of the human race, and political head of the whole of it, must be granted the possession of executive abilities of the loftiest order. In his large presence the other popes and politicians shrink to midges for the microscope. I would like to see him. I would rather see him and shake him by the tail than any other member of the European Concert. In the present paper I shall allow myself to use the word Jew as if it stood for both religion and race. It is handy; and besides, that is what the term means to the general world. In the above letter one notes these points:

1. The Jew is a well-behaved citizen.
2. Can ignorance and fanaticism *alone* account for his unjust treatment?
3. Can Jews do anything to improve the situation?
4. The Jews have no party; they are non-participants.
5. Will the persecution ever come to an end?

6. What has become of the golden rule?

Point No. 1. – We must grant proposition No. 1, for several sufficient reasons. The Jew is not a disturber of the peace of any country. Even his enemies will concede that. He is not a loafer, he is not a sot, he is not noisy, he is not a brawler nor a rioter, he is not quarrelsome. In the statistics of crime his presence is conspicuously rare – in all countries. With murder and other crimes of violence he has but little to do: he is a stranger to the hangman. In the police court's daily long roll of "assaults" and "drunk and disorderlies" his name seldom appears. That the Jewish home is a home in the truest sense is a fact which no one will dispute. The family is knitted together by the strongest affections; its members show each other every due respect; and reverence for the elders is an inviolate law of the house. The Jew is not a burden on the charities of the state nor of the city; these could cease from their functions without affecting him. When he is well enough, he works; when he is incapacitated, his own people take care of him. And not in a poor and stingy way, but with a fine and large benevolence. His race is entitled to be called the most benevolent of all the races of men. A Jewish beggar is not impossible, perhaps; such a thing may exist, but there are few men that can say they have seen that spectacle. The Jew has been staged in many uncomplimentary forms, but, so far as I know, no dramatist has done him the injustice to stage him as a beggar. Whenever a Jew has real need to beg, his people save him from the necessity of doing it. The charitable institutions of the Jews are supported by Jewish money, and amply. The Jews make no noise about it; it is done quietly; they do not nag and pester and harass us for contributions; they give us peace, and set us an example – an example which we have not found ourselves able to follow; for by nature we are not free givers, and have to be patiently and persistently hunted down in the interest of the unfortunate.

These facts are all on the credit side of the proposition that the Jew is a good and orderly citizen. Summed up, they certify that he is quiet, peaceable, industrious, unaddicted to high crimes and brutal dispositions; that his family life is commendable; that he is not a burden upon public charities; that he is not a beggar; that in benevolence he is above the reach of competition. These are the very quintessentials of good citizenship. If you can add that he is as honest as the average of his neighbors – But I think that question is affirmatively answered by the fact that he is a successful business

man. The basis of successful business is honesty; a business cannot
thrive where the parties to it cannot trust each other. In the matter
of numbers the Jew counts for little in the overwhelming population of New York; but that his honesty counts for much is guaran-
teed by the fact that the immense wholesale business of Broadway,
from the Battery to Union Square, is substantially in his hands.

I suppose that the most picturesque example in history of a
trader's trust in his fellow-trader was one where it was not Christian trusting Christian, but Christian trusting Jew. That Hessian
Duke who used to sell his subjects to George III. to fight George
Washington with got rich at it; and by-and-by, when the wars
engendered by the French Revolution made his throne too warm
for him, he was obliged to fly the country. He was in a hurry, and
had to leave his earnings behind – $9,000,000. He had to risk the
money with some one without security. He did not select a Christian, but a Jew – a Jew of only modest means, but of high character;
a character so high that it left him lonesome – Rothschild of Frankfort. Thirty years later, when Europe had become quiet and safe
again, the Duke came back from overseas, and the Jew returned
the loan, with interest added.*

---

* Here is another piece of picturesque history; and it reminds us that shabbiness
and dishonesty are not the monopoly of any race or creed, but are merely human.

"Congress has passed a bill to pay $379 56 to Moses Pendergrass, of Libertyville,
Missouri. The story of the reason of this liberality is pathetically interesting, and
shows the sort of pickle that an honest man may get into who undertakes to do an
honest job of work for Uncle Sam. In 1886 Moses Pendergrass put in a bid for the
contract to carry the mail on the route from Knob Lick to Libertyville and
Coffman, thirty miles a day, from July 1, 1887, for one year. He got the postmaster
at Knob Lick to write the letter for him, and while Moses intended that his bid
should be $400, his scribe carelessly made it $4. Moses got the contract, and did
not find out about the mistake until the end of the first quarter, when he got his
first pay. When he found at what rate he was working he was sorely cast down,
and opened communication with the Post Office Department. The department
informed him that he must either carry out his contract or throw it up, and that if
he threw it up his bondsmen would have to pay the government $1459 85 damages.
So Moses carried out his contract, walked thirty miles every week-day for a year,
and carried the mail, and received for his labor $4 – or, to be accurate, $6 84; for,
the route being extended after his bid was accepted, the pay was proportionately
increased. Now, after ten years, a bill was finally passed to pay to Moses the difference between what he earned in that unlucky year and what he received."

The *Sun*, which tells the above story, says that bills were introduced in three or
four Congresses for Moses's relief, and that committees repeatedly investigated
his claim.

The Jew has his other side. He has some discreditable ways, though he has not a monopoly of them, because he cannot get entirely rid of vexatious Christian competition. We have seen that he seldom transgresses the laws against crimes of violence. Indeed, his dealings with courts are almost restricted to matters connected with commerce. He has a reputation for various small forms of cheating, and for practising oppressive usury, and for burning himself out to get the insurance, and for arranging cunning contracts which leave him an exit but lock the other man in, and for smart evasions which find him safe and comfortable just within the strict letter of the law, when court and jury know very well that he has violated the spirit of it. He is a frequent and faithful and capable officer in the civil service, but he is charged with an unpatriotic disinclination to stand by the flag as a soldier – like the Christian Quaker.

Now if you offset these discreditable features by the creditable ones summarized in a preceding paragraph beginning with the words, "These facts are all on the credit side," and strike a balance, what must the verdict be? This, I think: that, the merits and demerits being fairly weighed and measured on both sides, the Christian can claim no superiority over the Jew in the matter of good citizenship.

Yet in all countries, from the dawn of history, the Jew has been persistently and implacably hated, and with frequency persecuted.

Point No. 2. – "Can fanaticism *alone* account for this?"

Years ago I used to think that it was responsible for nearly all of it, but latterly I have come to think that this was an error. Indeed, it is now my conviction that it is responsible for hardly any of it.

In this connection I call to mind Genesis, chapter xlvii.

We have all thoughtfully – or unthoughtfully – read the pathetic story of the years of plenty and the years of famine in Egypt, and

---

It took six Congresses, containing in their persons the compressed virtues of 70,000,000 of people, and cautiously and carefully giving expression to those virtues in the fear of God and the next election, eleven years to find out some way to cheat a fellow-Christian out of about $13 on his honestly executed contract, and out of nearly $300 due him on its enlarged terms. And they succeeded. During the same time they paid out $1,000,000,000 in pensions – a third of it unearned and undeserved. This indicates a splendid all-around competency in theft, for it starts with farthings, and works its industries all the way up to ship-loads. It may be possible that the Jews can beat this, but the man that bets on it is taking chances.

how Joseph, with that opportunity, made a corner in broken
hearts, and the crusts of the poor, and human liberty – a corner
whereby he took a nation's money all away, to the last penny; took
a nation's live-stock all away, to the last hoof; took a nation's land
away, to the last acre; then took the nation itself, buying it for
bread, man by man, woman by woman, child by child, till all were
slaves; a corner which took everything, left nothing; a corner so
stupendous that, by comparison with it, the most gigantic corners
in subsequent history are but baby things, for it dealt in hundreds
of millions of bushels, and its profits were reckonable by
hundreds of millions of dollars, and it was a disaster so crushing
that its effects have not wholly disappeared from Egypt to-day,
more than three thousand years after the event.

Is it presumable that the eye of Egypt was upon Joseph the foreign Jew all this time? I think it likely. Was it friendly? We must
doubt it. Was Joseph establishing a character for his race which
would survive long in Egypt? and in time would his name come to
be familiarly used to express that character – like Shylock's? It is
hardly to be doubted. Let us remember that this was *centuries before
the crucifixion.*

I wish to come down eighteen hundred years later and refer to
a remark made by one of the Latin historians. I read it in a translation many years ago, and it comes back to me now with force. It
was alluding to a time when people were still living who could have
seen the Saviour in the flesh. Christianity was so new that the
people of Rome had hardly heard of it, and had but confused
notions of what it was. The substance of the remark was this: Some
Christians were persecuted in Rome through error, they being
"*mistaken for Jews.*"

The meaning seems plain. These pagans had nothing against
Christians, but they were quite ready to persecute Jews. For some
reason or other they hated a Jew before they even knew what a
Christian was. May I not assume, then, that the persecution of Jews
is a thing which *antedates* Christianity and was not born of Christianity? I think so. What was the origin of the feeling?

When I was a boy, in the back settlements of the Mississippi Valley, where a gracious and beautiful Sunday-school simplicity and
unpracticality prevailed, the "Yankee" (citizen of the New England States) was hated with a splendid energy. But religion had
nothing to do with it. In a trade, the Yankee was held to be about
five times the match of the Westerner. His shrewdness, his insight,

his judgment, his knowledge, his enterprise, and his formidable cleverness in applying these forces were frankly confessed, and most competently cursed.

In the cotton States, after the war, the simple and ignorant negroes made the crops for the white planter on shares. The Jew came down in force, set up shop on the plantation, supplied all the negro's wants on credit, and at the end of the season was proprietor of the negro's share of the present crop and of part of his share of the next one. Before long, the whites detested the Jew, and it is doubtful if the negro loved him.

The Jew is being legislated out of Russia. The reason is not concealed. The movement was instituted because the Christian peasant and villager stood no chance against his commercial abilities. He was always ready to lend money on a crop, and sell vodka and other necessaries of life on credit while the crop was growing. When settlement day came he owned the crop; and next year or year after he owned the farm, like Joseph.

In the dull and ignorant England of John's time everybody got into debt to the Jew. He gathered all lucrative enterprises into his hands; he was the king of commerce; he was ready to be helpful in all profitable ways; he even financed crusades for the rescue of the Sepulchre. To wipe out his account with the nation and restore business to its natural and incompetent channels he had to be banished the realm.

For the like reasons Spain had to banish him four hundred years ago, and Austria about a couple of centuries later.

In all the ages Christian Europe has been obliged to curtail his activities. If he entered upon a mechanical trade, the Christian had to retire from it. If he set up as a doctor, he was the best one, and he took the business. If he exploited agriculture, the other farmers had to get at something else. Since there was no way to successfully compete with him in any vocation, the law had to step in and save the Christian from the poorhouse. Trade after trade was taken away from the Jew by statute till practically none was left. He was forbidden to engage in agriculture; he was forbidden to practise law; he was forbidden to practise medicine, except among Jews; he was forbidden the handicrafts. Even the seats of learning and the schools of science had to be closed against this tremendous antagonist. Still, almost bereft of employments, he found ways to make money, even ways to get rich. Also ways to invest his takings well, for usury was not denied him. In the hard conditions suggested, the Jew without brains could not survive, and the Jew with brains had to keep them in good training and well sharpened up, or starve. Ages of restriction to the one tool which the law was not able to take from him – his brain – have made that tool singularly competent; ages of compulsory disuse of his hands have atrophied them, and he never uses them now. This history has a very, very commercial look, a most sordid and practical commercial look, the business aspect of a Chinese cheap-labor crusade. Religious prejudices may account for one part of it, but not for the other nine.

Protestants have persecuted Catholics, but they did not take their livelihoods away from them. The Catholics have persecuted the Protestants with bloody and awful bitterness, but they never closed agriculture and the handicrafts against them. Why was that? That has the candid look of genuine religious persecution, not a trade-union boycott in a religious disguise.

The Jews are harried and obstructed in Austria and Germany, and lately in France; but England and America give them an open field and yet survive. Scotland offers them an unembarrassed field too, but there are not many takers. There are a few Jews in Glasgow, and one in Aberdeen; but that is because they can't earn enough to get away. The Scotch pay themselves that compliment, but it is authentic.

I feel convinced that the Crucifixion has not much to do with the world's attitude toward the Jew; that the reasons for it are older than that event, as suggested by Egypt's experience and by Rome's regret for having persecuted an unknown quantity called a Christian, under the mistaken impression that she was merely persecuting a Jew. *Merely* a Jew – a skinned eel who was used to it, presumably. I am persuaded that in Russia, Austria, and Germany nine-tenths of the hostility to the Jew comes from the average Christian's inability to compete successfully with the average Jew in business – in either straight business or the questionable sort.

In Berlin, a few years ago, I read a speech which frankly urged the expulsion of the Jews from Germany; and the agitator's *reason* was as frank as his proposition. It was this: *that eighty-five per cent.* of the successful lawyers of Berlin were Jews, and that about the same percentage of the great and lucrative businesses of all sorts in Germany were in the hands of the Jewish race! Isn't it an amazing confession? It was but another way of saying that in a population of 48,000,000, of whom only 500,000 were registered as Jews, eighty-five per cent. of the brains and honesty of the whole was lodged in the Jews. I must insist upon the honesty – it is an essential of successful business, taken by and large. Of course it does not rule out rascals entirely, even among Christians, but it is a good working rule, nevertheless. The speaker's figures may have been inexact, but *the motive of persecution* stands out as clear as day.

The man claimed that in Berlin the banks, the newspapers, the theatres, the great mercantile, shipping, mining, and manufacturing interests, the big army and city contracts, the tramways, and pretty much all other properties of high value, and *also* the small businesses – were in the hands of the Jews. He said the Jew was pushing the Christian to the wall all along the line; that it was all a Christian could do to scrape together a living; and that the Jew *must* be banished, and soon – there was no other way of saving the Christian. Here in Vienna, last autumn, an agitator said that all these disastrous details were true of Austria-Hungary also; and in fierce language he demanded the expulsion of the Jews. When politicians come out without a blush and read the baby act in this frank way, *unrebuked*, it is a very good indication that they have a market back of them, and know where to fish for votes.

You note the crucial point of the mentioned agitation; the argument is that the Christian cannot *compete* with the Jew, and that hence his very bread is in peril. To human beings this is a much more hate-inspiring thing than is any detail connected with religion. With most people, of a necessity, bread and meat take first rank, religion second. I am convinced that the persecution of the Jew is not due in any large degree to religious prejudice.

No, the Jew is a money-getter; and in getting his money he is a very serious obstruction to less capable neighbors who are on the same quest. I think that that is the trouble. In estimating worldly values the Jew is not shallow, but deep. With precocious wisdom he found out in the morning of time that some men worship rank, some worship heroes, some worship power, some worship God, and that over these ideals they dispute and cannot unite – but that they all worship money; so he made it the end and aim of his life to get it. He was at it in Egypt thirty-six centuries ago; he was at it in Rome when that Christian got persecuted by mistake for him; he has been at it ever since. The cost to him has been heavy; his success has made the whole human race his enemy – but it has paid, for it has brought him envy, and that is the only thing which men will sell both soul and body to get. He long ago observed that

MARK TWAIN

a millionaire commands respect, a two-millionaire homage, a multi-millionaire the deepest deeps of adoration. We all know that feeling; we have seen it express itself. We have noticed that when the average man mentions the name of a multi-millionaire he does it with that mixture in his voice of awe and reverence and lust which burns in a Frenchman's eye when it falls on another man's centime.

Point No. 4. – "The Jews have no party; they are non-participants."

Perhaps you have let the secret out and given yourself away. It seems hardly a credit to the race that it is able to say that; or to you, sir, that you can say it without remorse; more, that you should offer it as a plea against maltreatment, injustice, and oppression. Who gives the Jew the right, who gives any race the right, to sit still, in a free country, and let somebody else look after its safety? The oppressed Jew was entitled to all pity in the former times under brutal autocracies, for he was weak and friendless, and had no way to help his case. But he has ways now, and he has had them for a century, but I do not see that he has tried to make serious use of them. When the Revolution set him free in France it was an act of grace – the grace of other people; he does not appear in it as a helper. I do not know that he helped when England set him free. Among the Twelve Sane Men of France who have stepped forward with great Zola at their head to fight (and win, I hope and believe) the battle for the most infamously misused Jew of modern times, do you find a great or rich or illustrious Jew helping? In the United States he was created free in the beginning – he did not need to help, of course. In Austria and Germany and France he has a vote, but of what considerable use is it to him? He doesn't seem to know how to apply it to the best effect. With all his splendid capacities and all his fat wealth he is to-day not politically important in any country. In America, as early as 1854, the ignorant Irish hod-carrier, who had a spirit of his own and a way of exposing it to the weather, made it apparent to all that he must be politically reckoned with; yet fifteen years before that we hardly knew what an Irishman looked like. As an intelligent force, and numerically, he has always been away down, but he has governed the country just the same. It was because he was *organized*. It made his vote valuable – in fact, essential.

You will say the Jew is everywhere numerically feeble. That is nothing to the point – with the Irishman's history for an object-lesson. But I am coming to your numerical feebleness presently. In all parliamentary countries you could no doubt elect Jews to the legislatures – and even *one* member in such a body is sometimes a force which counts. How deeply have you concerned yourselves about this in Austria, France, and Germany? Or even in America, for that matter? You remark that the Jews were not to blame for the riots in this Reichsrath here, and you add with satisfaction that there wasn't one in that body. That is not strictly correct; if it were, would it not be in order for you to explain it and apologize for it, not try to make a merit of it? But I think that the Jew was by no means in as large force there as he ought to have been, with his chances. Austria opens the suffrage to him on fairly liberal terms, and it must surely be his own fault that he is so much in the background politically.

As to your numerical weakness. I mentioned some figures a while ago – 500,000 – as the Jewish population of Germany. I will add some more – 6,000,000 in Russia, 5,000,000 in Austria, 250,000 in the United States. I take them from memory; I read them in the Cyclopædia Britannica ten or twelve years ago. Still, I am entirely sure of them. If those statistics are correct, my argument is not as strong as it ought to be as concerns America, but it still has strength. It is plenty strong enough as concerns Austria, for ten years ago 5,000,000 was nine per cent. of the empire's population. The Irish would govern the Kingdom of Heaven if they had a strength there like that.

I have some suspicions; I got them at second hand, but they have remained with me these ten or twelve years. When I read in the C. B. that the Jewish population of the United States was 250,000, I wrote the editor, and explained to him that I was personally acquainted with more Jews than that in my country, and that his figures were without a doubt a misprint for 25,000,000. I also added that I was personally acquainted with *that* many there; but that was only to raise his confidence in me, for it was not true. His answer miscarried, and I never got it; but I went around talking about the matter; and people told me they had reason to suspect that for business reasons many Jews whose dealings were mainly with the Christians did not report themselves as Jews in the census. It looked plausible; it looks plausible yet. Look at the city of New York; and look at Boston, and Philadelphia, and New Orleans, and Chicago, and Cincinnati, and San Francisco – how your race swarms in those places! – and everywhere else in America, down to the least little village. Read the signs on the marts of commerce and on the shops: Goldstein (gold stone), Edelstein (precious stone), Blumenthal (flower-vale), Rosenthal (rose-vale), Veilchend-uft (violet odor), Singvogel (song-bird), Rosenzweig (rose branch), and all the amazing list of beautiful and enviable names which Prussia and Austria glorified you with so long ago. It is another instance of Europe's coarse and cruel persecution of your race; not that it was coarse and cruel to outfit it with pretty and poetical names like those, but that it was coarse and cruel to make it *pay* for them or else take such hideous and often indecent names that to-day their owners never use them; or, if they do, only on official papers. And it was the many, not the few, who got the odious names, they being too poor to bribe the officials to grant them better ones.

Now why was the race renamed? I have been told that in Prussia it was given to using fictitious names, and often changing them, so as to beat the tax-gatherer, escape military service, and so on; and that finally the idea was hit upon of furnishing all the inmates of a house with *one and the same surname*, and then holding the house responsible right along for those inmates, and accountable for any disappearances that might occur; it made the Jews keep track of *each other*, for self-interest's sake, and saved the government the trouble.*

If that explanation of how the Jews of Prussia came to be renamed is correct, if it is true that they fictitiously registered themselves to gain certain advantages, it may possibly be true that in America they refrain from registering themselves as Jews to fend off the damaging prejudices of the Christian customer. I have no way of knowing whether this notion is well founded or not. There may be other and better ways of explaining why only that poor little 250,000 of our Jews got into the Cyclopædia. I may, of course, be mistaken, but I am strongly of the opinion that we have an immense Jewish population in America.

---

* In Austria the renaming was merely done because the Jews in some newly acquired regions had no surnames, but were mostly named Abraham and Moses, and therefore the tax-gatherer could not tell t'other from which, and was likely to lose his reason over the matter. The renaming was put into the hands of the War Department, and a charming mess the graceless young lieutenants made of it. To them a Jew was of no sort of consequence, and they labelled the race in a way to make the angels weep. As an example, take these two: *Abraham Bellyache* and *Schmul Godbedamned. – Culled from "Namens Studien," by Karl Emil Franzos.*

Point No. 3. – "Can Jews do anything to improve the situation?"

I think so. If I may make a suggestion without seeming to be trying to teach my grandmother how to suck eggs, I will offer it. In our days we have learned the value of combination. We apply it everywhere – in railway systems, in trusts, in trade unions, in Salvation Armies, in minor politics, in major politics, in European Concerts. Whatever our strength may be, big or little, we *organize* it. We have found out that that is the only way to get the most out of it that is in it. We know the weakness of individual sticks, and the strength of the concentrated fagot. Suppose you try a scheme like this, for instance. In England and America put every Jew on the census-book *as* a Jew (in case you have not been doing that). Get up volunteer regiments composed of Jews solely, and, when the drum beats, fall in and go to the front, so as to remove the reproach that you have few Massénas among you, and that you feed on a country but don't like to fight for it. Next, in politics, organize your strength, band together, and deliver the casting vote where you can, and where you can't, compel as good terms as possible. You huddle to yourselves already in all countries, but you huddle to no sufficient purpose, politically speaking. You do not seem to be organized, except for your charities. There you are omnipotent; there you compel your due of recognition – you do not have to beg for it. It shows what you can do when you band together for a definite purpose.

And then from America and England you can encourage your race in Austria, France, and Germany, and materially help it. It was a pathetic tale that was told by a poor Jew in Galicia a fortnight ago during the riots, after he had been raided by the Christian peasantry and despoiled of everything he had. He said his vote was of no value to him, and he wished he could be excused from casting it, for indeed casting it was a sure *damage* to him, since no matter which party he voted for, the other party would come straight and take its revenge out of him. Nine per cent. of the population of the empire, these Jews, and apparently they cannot put a plank into any candidate's platform! If you will send our Irish lads over here I think they will organize your race and change the aspect of the Reichsrath.

You seem to think that the Jews take no hand in politics here, that they are "absolutely non-participants." I am assured by men competent to speak that this is a very large error, that the Jews are exceedingly active in politics all over the empire, but that they scatter their work and their votes among the numerous parties, and thus lose the advantages to be had by concentration. I think that in America they scatter too, but you know more about that than I do.

Speaking of concentration, Dr. Herzl has a clear insight into the value of that. Have you heard of his plan? He wishes to gather the Jews of the world together in Palestine, with a government of their own – under the suzerainty of the Sultan, I suppose. At the convention of Berne, last year, there were delegates from everywhere, and the proposal was received with decided favor. I am not the Sultan, and I am not objecting; but if that concentration of the cunningest brains in the world was going to be made in a free country (bar Scotland), I think it would be politic to stop it. It will not be well to let that race find out its strength. If the horses knew theirs, we should not ride any more.

Point No. 5. – "Will the persecution of the Jews ever come to an end?"

On the score of religion, I think it has already come to an end. On the score of race prejudice and trade, I have the idea that it will continue. That is, here and there in spots about the world, where a barbarous ignorance and a sort of mere animal civilization prevail; but I do not think that elsewhere the Jew need now stand in any fear of being robbed and raided. Among the high civilizations he seems to be very comfortably situated indeed, and to have more than his proportionate share of the prosperities going. It has that look in Vienna. I suppose the race prejudice cannot be removed; but he can stand that; it is no particular matter. By his make and ways he is substantially a foreigner wherever he may be, and even the angels dislike a foreigner. I am using this word foreigner in the German sense – *stranger*. Nearly all of us have an antipathy to a stranger, even of our own nationality. We pile grip-sacks in a vacant seat to keep him from getting it; and a dog goes further, and does as a savage would – challenges him on the spot. The German dictionary seems to make no distinction between a stranger and a foreigner; in its view a stranger *is* a foreigner – a sound position, I think. You will always be by ways and habits and predilections substantially strangers – foreigners – wherever you are, and that will probably keep the race prejudice against you alive.

But you were the favorites of Heaven originally, and your manifold and unfair prosperities convince me that you have crowded

back into that snug place again. Here is an incident that is significant. Last week in Vienna a hailstorm struck the prodigious
Central Cemetery and made wasteful destruction there. In the
Christian part of it, according to the official figures, 621 window-
panes were broken; more than 900 singing-birds were killed; five
great trees and many small ones were torn to shreds and the shreds
scattered far and wide by the wind; the ornamental plants and
other decorations of the graves were ruined, and more than a hundred tomb-lanterns shattered; and it took the cemetery's whole
force of 300 laborers more than three days to clear away the
storm's wreckage. In the report occurs this remark – and in its
italics you can hear it grit its Christian teeth: ". . . . lediglich die
israelitische Abtheilung des Friedhofes vom Hagelwetter *gänzlich
verschont* worden war." Not a hailstone hit the Jewish reservation!
Such nepotism makes me tired.

Point No. 6. – "What has become of the golden rule?"

It exists, it continues to sparkle, and is well taken care of. It is
Exhibit A in the Church's assets, and we pull it out every Sunday
and give it an airing. But you are not permitted to try to smuggle
it into this discussion, where it is irrelevant and would not feel at
home. It is strictly religious furniture, like an acolyte, or a
contribution-plate, or any of those things. It has never been
intruded into business; and Jewish persecution is not a religious
passion, it is a business passion.

To conclude. – If the statistics are right, the Jews constitute but *one
per cent.* of the human race. It suggests a nebulous dim puff of star
dust lost in the blaze of the Milky Way. Properly the Jew ought
hardly to be heard of; but he is heard of, has always been heard
of. He is as prominent on the planet as any other people, and his
commercial importance is extravagantly out of proportion to the
smallness of his bulk. His contributions to the world's list of great
names in literature, science, art, music, finance, medicine, and
abstruse learning are also away out of proportion to the weakness
of his numbers. He has made a marvellous fight in this world, in
all the ages; and has done it with his hands tied behind him. He
could be vain of himself, and be excused for it. The Egyptian, the
Babylonian, and the Persian rose, filled the planet with sound and
splendor, then faded to dream-stuff and passed away; the Greek
and the Roman followed, and made a vast noise, and they are
gone; other peoples have sprung up and held their torch high for
a time, but it burned out, and they sit in twilight now, or have

vanished. The Jew saw them all, beat them all, and is now what he always was, exhibiting no decadence, no infirmities of age, no weakening of his parts, no slowing of his energies, no dulling of his alert and aggressive mind. All things are mortal but the Jew; all other forces pass, but he remains. What is the secret of his immortality?

September 1899

MY BOYHOOD DREAMS

THE DREAMS OF my boyhood? No, they have not been realized. For all who are old, there is something infinitely pathetic about the subject which you have chosen, for in no gray-head's case can it suggest any but one thing – disappointment. Disappointment is its own reason for its pain: the quality or dignity of the hope that failed is a matter aside. The dreamer's valuation of the thing lost – not another man's – is the only standard to measure it by, and his grief for it makes it large and great and fine, and is worthy of our reverence in all cases. We should carefully remember that. There are sixteen hundred million people in the world. Of these there is but a trifling number – in fact, only thirty-eight millions – who can understand why a person should have an ambition to belong to the French army; and why, belonging to it, he should be proud of that; and why, having got down that far, he should want to go on down, down, down till he struck bottom and got on the General Staff; and why, being stripped of his livery, or set free and reinvested with his self-respect by any other quick and thorough process, let it be what it might, he should wish to return to his strange serfage. But no matter: the estimate put upon these things by the fifteen hundred and sixty millions is no proper measure of their value: the proper measure, the just measure, is that which is put upon them by Dreyfus, and is cipherable merely upon the littleness or the vastness of the *disappointment* which their loss cost him.

There you have it: the measure of the magnitude of a dream-failure is the measure of the disappointment the failure cost the dreamer; the value, in others' eyes, of the thing lost, has nothing to do with the matter. With this straightening-out and classification of the dreamer's position to help us, perhaps we can put ourselves in his place and respect his dream – Dreyfus's, and the dreams our friends have cherished and reveal to us. Some that I call to mind, some that have been revealed to me, are curious enough; but we may not smile at them, for they were precious to the dreamers, and their failure has left scars which give them dignity and pathos. With this theme in my mind, dear heads that were brown when they and mine were young together rise old and white before me now, beseeching me to speak for them, and most lovingly will I do it.

Howells, Hay, Aldrich, Matthews, Stockton, Cable, Remus –
how their young hopes and ambitions come flooding back to my
memory now, out of the vague far past, the beautiful past, the
lamented past! I remember it so well – that night we met together
– it was in Boston, and Mr. Fields was there, and Mr. Osgood, and
Ralph Keeler, and Boyle O'Reilly, lost to us now these many years
– and under the seal of confidence revealed to each other what
our boyhood dreams had been: dreams which had not as yet been
blighted, but over which was stealing the gray of the night that
was to come – a night which we prophetically *felt*, and this feeling
oppressed us and made us sad. I remember that Howells's voice
broke twice, and it was only with great difficulty that he was able
to go on; in the end he wept. For he had hoped to be an auctioneer.
He told of his early struggles to climb to his goal, and how at last
he attained to within a single step of the coveted summit. But there
misfortune after misfortune assailed him, and he went down, and
down, and down, until now at last, weary and disheartened, he
had for the present given up the struggle and become editor of the
"Atlantic Monthly." This was in 1830. Seventy years are gone
since, and where now is his dream? It will never be fulfilled. And
it is best so; he is no longer fitted for the position; no one would
take him now; even if he got it, he would not be able to do himself
credit in it, on account of his deliberateness of speech and lack of
trained professional vivacity; he would be put on real estate, and
would have the pain of seeing younger and abler men intrusted
with the furniture and other such goods – goods which draw a
mixed and intellectually low order of customers, who must be
beguiled of their bids by a vulgar and specialized humor and
sparkle, accompanied with antics.

But it is not the thing lost that counts, but only the *disappointment*
the loss brings to the dreamer that had coveted that thing and had
set his heart of hearts upon it, and when we remember this, a great
wave of sorrow for Howells rises in our breasts, and we wish for
his sake that his fate could have been different.

At that time Hay's boyhood dream was not yet past hope of realization, but it was fading, dimming, wasting away, and the wind
of a growing apprehension was blowing cold over the perishing
summer of his life. In the pride of his young ambition he had
aspired to be a steamboat mate; and in fancy saw himself dominat-
ing a forecastle some day on the Mississippi and dictating terms to
roustabouts in high and wounding tones. I look back now, from

this far distance of seventy years, and note with sorrow the stages of that dream's destruction. Hay's history is but Howells's, with differences of detail. Hay climbed high toward his ideal; when success seemed almost sure, his foot upon the very gang-plank, his eye upon the capstan, misfortune came and his fall began. Down – down – down – ever down: Private Secretary to the President; Colonel in the field; Chargé d'Affaires in Paris; Chargé d'Affaires in Vienna; Poet; Editor of the "Tribune"; Biographer of Lincoln; Ambassador to England; and now at last there he lies – Secretary of State, Head of Foreign Affairs. And he has fallen like Lucifer, never to rise again. And his dream – where now is his dream? Gone down in blood and tears with the dream of the auctioneer.

And the young dream of Aldrich – where is that? I remember yet how he sat there that night fondling it, petting it; seeing it recede and ever recede; trying to be reconciled and give it up, but not able yet to bear the thought; for it had been his hope to be a horse-doctor. He, also, climbed high, but, like the others, fell; then fell again, and yet again, and again and again. And now at last he can fall no further. He is old now, he has ceased to struggle, and is only a poet. No one would risk a horse with him now. His dream is over.

Has *any* boyhood dream ever been fulfilled? I must doubt it. Look at Brander Matthews. He wanted to be a cowboy. What is he to-day? Nothing but a professor in a university. Will he ever be a cowboy? It is hardly conceivable.

Look at Stockton. What was Stockton's young dream? He hoped to be a barkeeper. See where *he* has landed.

Is it better with Cable? What was Cable's young dream? To be ring-master in the circus, and swell around and crack the whip. What is he to-day? Nothing but a theologian and novelist.

And Uncle Remus – what was his young dream? To be a buccaneer. Look at him now.

Ah, the dreams of our youth, how beautiful they are, and how perishable! The ruins of these might-have-beens, how pathetic! The heart-secrets that were revealed that night now so long vanished, how they touch me as I give them voice! Those sweet privacies, how they endeared us to each other! We were under oath never to tell any of these things, and I have always kept that oath inviolate when speaking with persons whom I thought not worthy to hear them.

Oh, our lost Youth – God keep its memory green in our hearts!

for Age is upon us, with the indignity of its infirmities, and Death
beckons!

TO THE ABOVE OLD PEOPLE.

Sleep! for the Sun that scores another Day
Against the Tale allotted You to stay,
   Reminding You, is Risen, and now
Serves Notice – ah, ignore it while You may!

The chill Wind blew, and those who stood before
The Tavern murmured, "Having drunk his Score,
   Why tarries He with empty Cup? Behold,
The Wine of Youth once poured, is poured no more.

"Come, leave the Cup, and on the Winter's Snow
Your Summer Garment of Enjoyment throw:
   Your Tide of Life is ebbing fast, and it,
Exhausted once, for You no more shall flow."

While yet the Phantom of false Youth was mine,
I heard a Voice from out the Darkness whine,
   "O Youth, O whither gone? Return,
And bathe my Age in thy reviving Wine."

In this subduing Draught of tender green
And kindly Absinth, with its wimpling Sheen
   Of dusky half-lights, let me drown
The haunting Pathos of the Might-Have-Been.

For every nickeled Joy, marred and brief,
We pay some day its Weight in golden Grief
   Mined from our Hearts. Ah, murmur not –
From this one-sided Bargain dream of no Relief!

The Joy of Life, that streaming through their Veins
Tumultuous swept, falls slack – and wanes
   The Glory in the Eye – and one by one
Life's Pleasures perish and make place for Pains.

Whether one hide in some secluded Nook –
Whether at Liverpool or Sandy Hook –
   'Tis one. Old Age will search him out – and He –
He – He – when ready will know where to look.

From Cradle unto Grave I keep a House
Of Entertainment where may drowse
    Bacilli and kindred Germs – or feed – or breed
Their festering Species in a deep Carouse.

Think – in this battered Caravanserai,
Whose Portals open stand all Night and Day,
    How Microbe after Microbe with his Pomp
Arrives unasked, and comes to stay.

Our ivory Teeth, confessing to the Lust
Of masticating, once, now own Disgust
    Of Clay-plug'd Cavities – full soon our Snags
Are emptied, and our Mouths are filled with Dust.

Our Gums forsake the Teeth and tender grow,
And fat, like over-ripened Figs – we know
    The Sign – the Riggs Disease is ours, and we
Must list this Sorrow, add another Woe;

Our Lungs begin to fail and soon we Cough,
And chilly Streaks play up our Backs, and off
    Our fever'd Foreheads drips an icy Sweat –
We scoffed before, but now we may not scoff.

Some for the Bunions that afflict us prate
Of Plasters unsurpassable, and hate
    To cut a Corn – ah cut, and let the Plaster go,
Nor murmur if the Solace come too late.

Some for the Honors of Old Age, and some
Long for its Respite from the Hum
    And Clash of sordid Strife – O Fools,
The Past should teach them what's to Come:

Lo, for the Honors, cold Neglect instead!
For Respite, disputatious Heirs a Bed
    Of Thorns for them will furnish. Go,
Seek not Here for Peace – but Yonder – with the Dead.

For whether Zal and Rustam heed this Sign,
And even smitten thus, will not repine,
    Let Zal and Rustam shuffle as they may,
The Fine once levied they must Cash the Fine.

O Voices of the Long Ago that were so dear!
Fall'n Silent, now, for many a Mould'ring Year,
   O whither are ye flown? Come back,
And break my Heart, but bless my grieving ear.

Some happy Day my Voice will Silent fall,
And answer not when some that love it call:
   Be glad for Me when this you note – and think
I've found the Voices lost, beyond the Pall.

So let me grateful drain the Magic Bowl
That medicines hurt Minds and on the Soul
   The Healing of its Peace doth lay – if then
Death claim me – Welcome be his Dole!

MARK TWAIN.

SANNA, SWEDEN, *September 15th.*

Private. – If you don't know what Riggs's Disease of the Teeth is, the dentist will tell you. I've had it – and it is more than interesting.

S.L.C.

EDITORIAL NOTE.

Fearing that there might be some mistake, we submitted a proof of this article to the (American) gentlemen named in it, and asked them to correct any errors of detail that might have crept in among the facts. They reply with some asperity that errors cannot creep in among facts where there are no facts for them to creep in among; and that none are discoverable in this article, but only baseless aberrations of a disordered mind. They have no recollection of any such night in Boston, nor elsewhere; and in their opinion there was never any such night. They have *met* Mr. Twain, but have had the prudence not to intrust any privacies to him – particularly under oath; and they think they now see that this prudence was justified, since he has been untrustworthy enough to even betray privacies which had no existence. Further, they think it a strange thing that Mr. Twain, who was never invited to meddle with anybody's boy-hood dreams but his own, has been so gratuitously anxious to see that other people's are placed before the world that he has quite lost his head in his zeal and forgotten to make any mention of his own at all. Provided we insert this explanation, they are willing to let his article pass; otherwise they must require its suppression, in the interest of truth.

P. S. – These replies having left us in some perplexity, and also in some fear lest they might distress Mr. Twain if published without his privity, we judged it but fair to submit them to him and give him an opportunity to defend himself. But he does not seem to be troubled, or even aware that he is in a delicate situation. He merely says:

"Do not worry about those former young people. They can write good literature, but when it comes to speaking the truth, they have not had my training. – MARK TWAIN."

The last sentence seems obscure, and liable to an unfortunate construction. It plainly needs refashioning, but we cannot take the responsibility of doing it.– EDITOR.

January 1900

INTRODUCING WINSTON
S. CHURCHILL

MR. CHURCHILL AND I do not agree on the righteousness of the South African war, but that is of no consequence. There is no place where people all think alike – well, there is heaven; there they do, but let us hope it won't be so always.

For years I have been a self-appointed missionary, and have wrought zealously for my cause – the joining together of America and the motherland in bonds of friendship, esteem and affection – an alliance of the heart which should permanently and beneficently influence the political relations of the two countries. Wherever I have stood before a gathering of Americans or Englishmen, in England, India, Australia or elsewhere, I have urged my mission, and warmed it up with compliments to both countries and pointed out how nearly alike the two peoples are in character and spirit. They ought to be united.

Behold America, the refuge of the homeless, the hunted, the oppressed from everywhere (who can pay ten dollars admission) – anyone except a Chinaman – standing up for human rights everywhere, even helping to make China admit the foreigner when she didn't want him, and to let him in free when she wanted to charge him fifty dollars if he was a harmless Christian or kill him if he was a missionary. And how England, mother of human liberty, uttered that great word, "the slave that sets his foot upon English soil is free" and with her strong hand made that gospel good in every acre of that vast Empire whose dominions girdle the globe; and how unselfishly England has wrought for the open door for all.

And how nobly and piously America also has stood for that same door in all cases where it wasn't her own; and how generous we have been, and how generous England has been in not requiring fancy rates for extinguishing missionaries, the way Germany does, but willing to take produce for them – firecrackers and tea – while Germany has to have territory and cash, and monuments and any other loot that's in reach – and memorial churches, and has thus made true changes of heart and regeneration, and the other details of German trinity so expensive that China won't be able to afford German missionaries any more till she gets in better shape financially; and how self-respectingly England and America have refrained from imitating German bluster, German rapacity, the mailed fist with a burglar's jimmy in it, and the investing mouth above it which alternately chortles bargain counter piety and "no quarter" according to the state of the market; and how nobly (and shamefacedly) we both stood timorously by at Port Arthur and wept sweetly and sympathizingly and shone while France and Germany helped Russia to rob the Japanese; and how gallantly we went to the rescue of poor Cuba, friendless, despairing, borne down by centuries of bitter slavery, and broke off her chains and set her free – with approving England at our back in an attitude toward European powers which did us good service in those days, and we confess it now.

Yes, as a missionary I have sung this song of praise and still sing it; and yet I think that England sinned in getting into a war in South Africa which she could have avoided without loss of credit or dignity – just as I think we have sinned in crowding ourselves into a war in the Philippines on the same terms.

Mr. Churchill will tell you about the war in South Africa, and he is competent – he fought and wrote through it himself. And he made a record there which would be a proud one for a man twice his age. By his father he is English, by his mother he is American – to my mind the blend which makes the perfect man. We are now on the friendliest terms with England. Mainly through my missionary efforts I suppose; and I am glad. We have always been kin: kin in blood, kin in religion, kin in representative government, kin in ideals, kin in just and lofty purposes; and now we are kin in sin, the harmony is complete, the blend is perfect, like Mr. Churchill himself, whom I now have the honor to present to you.

December 12, 1900

TO THE PERSON
SITTING IN DARKNESS

"Christmas will dawn in the United States over a people full of hope and aspiration and good cheer. Such a condition means contentment and happiness. The carping grumbler who may here and there go forth will find few to listen to him. The majority will wonder what is the matter with him and pass on." – *New York Tribune*, on Christmas Eve.

From *The Sun*, of New York:

"The purpose of this article is not to describe the terrible offences against humanity committed in the name of Politics in some of the most notorious East Side districts. *They could not be described, even verbally.* But it is the intention to let the great mass of more or less careless citizens of this beautiful metropolis of the New World get some conception of the havoc and ruin wrought to man, woman and child in the most densely populated and least known section of the city. Name, date and place can be supplied to those of little faith – or to any man who feels himself aggrieved. It is a plain statement of record and observation, written without license and without garnish.

"Imagine, if you can, a section of the city territory completely dominated by one man, without whose permission neither legitimate nor illegitimate business can be conducted; *where illegitimate business is encouraged and legitimate business discouraged;* where the respectable residents have to fasten their doors and windows summer nights and sit in their rooms with asphyxiating air and 100-degree temperature, rather than try to catch the faint whiff of breeze in their natural breathing places, the stoops of their homes; *where naked women dance by night in the streets, and unsexed men prowl like vultures through the darkness on 'business'* not only permitted but encouraged by the police; *where the education of infants begins with the knowledge of prostitution* and the training of little girls is training in the arts of Phryne; where *American* girls brought up with the refinements of *American* homes are imported from small towns up-State, Massachusetts, Connecticut and New Jersey, and kept as virtually prisoners as if they were locked up behind jail bars until they have lost all semblance of womanhood; *where small boys are taught to solicit for the women of disorderly houses;* where there is an organized society of young men *whose sole business in life is to corrupt young girls and turn them over to bawdy houses;* where men walking with their wives along the street are openly insulted; *where children that have adult diseases are the chief patrons of the hospitals and dispensaries;* where it is the rule, rather than the exception, that *murder, rape, robbery and theft go unpunished* – in short where the Premium of the most awful forms of Vice is the Profit of the politicians."

The following news from China appeared in *The Sun*, of New York, on Christmas Eve. The italics are mine:

"The Rev. Mr. Ament, of the American Board of Foreign Missions, has returned from a trip which he made for the purpose of collecting indemnities for damages done by Boxers. *Everywhere he went he compelled the Chinese to pay.* He says that all his native Christians are now provided for. He had 700 of them under his charge, and 300 were killed. He has *collected 300 taels for each* of these murders, and has *compelled full payment for all the property belonging to Christians* that was destroyed. He also assessed *fines* amounting to THIRTEEN TIMES the amount of the indemnity. *This money will be used for the propagation of the Gospel.*

"Mr. Ament declares that the compensation he has collected is *moderate*, when compared with the amount secured by the Catholics, who demand, in addition to money, *head for head.* They collect 500 taels for each murder of a Catholic. In the Wenchiu country, 680 Catholics were killed, and for this the European Catholics here demand 750,000 strings of cash and 680 *heads.*

"In the course of a conversation, Mr. Ament referred to the attitude of the missionaries toward the Chinese. He said:

" 'I deny emphatically that the missionaries are *vindictive*, that they *generally* looted, or that they have done anything *since* the siege that *the circumstances did not demand.* I criticise the Americans. *The soft hand of the Americans is not as good as the mailed fist of the Germans.* If you deal with the Chinese with a soft hand they will take advantage of it.'

"The statement that the French Government will return the loot taken by the French soldiers, is the source of the greatest amusement here. The French soldiers were more systematic looters than the Germans, and it is a fact that to-day *Catholic Christians*, carrying French flags and armed with modern guns, *are looting villages* in the Province of Chili."

By happy luck, we get all these glad tidings on Christmas Eve – just in time to enable us to celebrate the day with proper gaiety and enthusiasm. Our spirits soar, and we find we can even make jokes: Taels I win, Heads you lose.

Our Reverend Ament is the right man in the right place. What we want of our missionaries out there is, not that they shall merely represent in their acts and persons the grace and gentleness and charity and loving kindness of our religion, but that they shall also represent the American spirit. The oldest Americans are the Pawnees. Macallum's History says:

> "When a white Boxer kills a Pawnee and destroys his property, the other Pawnees do not trouble to seek *him* out, they kill any white person that comes along; also, they make some white village pay deceased's heirs the full cash value of deceased, together with full cash value of the property destroyed; they also make the village pay, in addition, *thirteen times* the value of that property into a fund for the dissemination of the Pawnee religion, which they regard as the best of all religions for the softening and humanizing of the heart of man. It is their idea that it is only fair and right that the innocent should be made to suffer for the guilty, and that it is better that ninety and nine innocent should suffer than that one guilty person should escape."

Our Reverend Ament is justifiably jealous of those enterprising Catholics, who not only get big money for each lost convert, but get "head for head" besides. But he should soothe himself with the reflection that the entirety of their exactions are for their own pockets, whereas he, less selfishly, devotes only 300 taels per head to that service, and gives the whole vast thirteen repetitions of the property-indemnity to the service of propagating the Gospel. His magnanimity has won him the approval of his nation, and will get him a monument. Let him be content with these rewards. We all hold him dear for manfully defending his fellow missionaries from exaggerated charges which were beginning to distress us, but which his testimony has so considerably modified that we can now contemplate them without noticeable pain. For now we know that, even before the siege, the missionaries were not "generally" out looting, and that, "since the siege," they have acted quite handsomely, except when "circumstances" crowded them. I am arranging for the monument. Subscriptions for it can be sent to the American Board; designs for it can be sent to me. Designs must allegorically set forth the Thirteen Reduplications of the Indemnity, and the Object for which they were exacted; as Ornaments, the designs must exhibit 680 Heads, so disposed as to give a pleasing and pretty effect; for the Catholics have done nicely, and are entitled to notice in the monument. Mottoes may be suggested, if any shall be discovered that will satisfactorily cover the ground.

Mr. Ament's financial feat of squeezing a thirteen-fold indemnity out of the pauper peasants to square other people's offenses, thus condemning them and their women and innocent little children to inevitable starvation and lingering death, in order that the blood-money so acquired might be "*used for the propagation of the Gospel*," does not flutter my serenity; although the act and the words, taken together, concrete a blasphemy so hideous and so colossal that, without doubt, its mate is not findable in the history of this or of any other age. Yet, if a layman had done that thing and justified it with those words, I should have shuddered, I know. Or, if I had done the thing and said the words myself – however, the thought is unthinkable, irreverent as some imperfectly informed people think me. Sometimes an ordained minister sets out to be blasphemous. When this happens, the layman is out of the running; he stands no chance.

We have Mr. Ament's impassioned assurance that the missionaries are not "vindictive." Let us hope and pray that they will never become so, but will remain in the almost morbidly fair and just and gentle temper which is affording so much satisfaction to their brother and champion to-day.

The following is from the *New York Tribune* of Christmas Eve. It comes from that journal's Tokio correspondent. It has a strange and impudent sound, but the Japanese are but partially civilized as yet. When they become wholly civilized they will not talk so:

"The missionary question, of course, occupies a foremost place in the discussion. It is now felt as essential that the Western Powers take cognizance of the sentiment here, that religious invasions of Oriental countries by powerful Western organizations are tantamount to filibustering expeditions, and should not only be discountenanced, but that stern measures should be adopted for their suppression. The feeling here is that the missionary organizations constitute a constant menace to peaceful international relations."

Shall we? That is, shall we go on conferring our Civilization upon the peoples that sit in darkness, or shall we give those poor things a rest? Shall we bang right ahead in our old-time, loud, pious way, and commit the new century to the game; or shall we sober up and sit down and think it over first? Would it not be prudent to get our Civilization-tools together, and see how much stock is left on hand in the way of Glass Beads and Theology, and Maxim Guns and Hymn Books, and Trade-Gin and Torches of Progress and Enlightenment (patent adjustable ones, good to fire villages with, upon occasion), and balance the books, and arrive at the profit and loss, so that we may intelligently decide whether to continue the business or sell out the property and start a new Civilization Scheme on the proceeds?

Extending the Blessings of Civilization to our Brother who Sits in Darkness has been a good trade and has paid well, on the whole; and there is money in it yet, if carefully worked – but not enough, in my judgment, to make any considerable risk advisable. The People that Sit in Darkness are getting to be too scarce – too scarce and too shy. And such darkness as is now left is really of but an indifferent quality, and not dark enough for the game. The most of those People that Sit in Darkness have been furnished with more light than was good for them or profitable for us. We have been injudicious.

The Blessings-of-Civilization Trust, wisely and cautiously administered, is a Daisy. There is more money in it, more territory, more sovereignty, and other kinds of emolument, than there is in any other game that is played. But Christendom has been playing it badly of late years, and must certainly suffer by it, in my opinion. She has been so eager to get every stake that appeared on the green cloth, that the People who Sit in Darkness have noticed it – they have noticed it, and have begun to show alarm. They have become suspicious of the Blessings of Civilization. More – they have begun to examine them. This is not well. The Blessings of Civilization are all right, and a good commercial property; there could not be a better, in a dim light. In the right kind of a light, and at a proper distance, with the goods a little out of focus, they furnish this desirable exhibit to the Gentlemen who Sit in Darkness:

LOVE,	LAW AND ORDER,
JUSTICE,	LIBERTY,
GENTLENESS,	EQUALITY,
CHRISTIANITY,	HONORABLE DEALING,
PROTECTION TO THE WEAK,	MERCY,
TEMPERANCE,	EDUCATION,

– and so on.

There. Is it good? Sir, it is pie. It will bring into camp any idiot that sits in darkness anywhere. But not if we adulterate it. It is proper to be emphatic upon that point. This brand is strictly for Export – apparently. *Apparently*. Privately and confidentially, it is nothing of the kind. Privately and confidentially, it is merely an outside cover, gay and pretty and attractive, displaying the special patterns of our Civilization which we reserve for Home Consumption, while *inside* the bale is the Actual Thing that the Customer Sitting in Darkness buys with his blood and tears and land and liberty. That Actual Thing is, indeed, Civilization, but it is only for Export. Is there a difference between the two brands? In some of the details, yes.

We all know that the Business is being ruined. The reason is not far to seek. It is because our Mr. McKinley, and Mr. Chamberlain, and the Kaiser, and the Czar and the French have been exporting the Actual Thing *with the outside cover left off*. This is bad for the Game. It shows that these new players of it are not sufficiently acquainted with it.

It is a distress to look on and note the mismoves, they are so strange and so awkward. Mr. Chamberlain manufactures a war out of materials so inadequate and so fanciful that they make the boxes grieve and the gallery laugh, and he tries hard to persuade himself that it isn't purely a private raid for cash, but has a sort of dim, vague respectability about it somewhere, if he could only find the spot; and that, by and by, he can scour the flag clean again after he has finished dragging it through the mud, and make it shine and flash in the vault of heaven once more as it had shone and flashed there a thousand years in the world's respect until he laid his unfaithful hand upon it. It is bad play – bad. For it exposes the Actual Thing to Them that Sit in Darkness, and they say: "What! Christian against Christian? And only for money? Is *this* a case of magnanimity, forbearance, love, gentleness, mercy, protection of the weak – this strange and over-showy onslaught of an elephant upon a nest of field-mice, on the pretext that the mice had squeaked an insolence at him – conduct which 'no self-respecting government could allow to pass unavenged?' as Mr. Chamberlain said. Was that a good pretext in a small case, when it had not been a good pretext in a large one? – for only recently Russia had affronted the elephant three times and survived alive and unsmitten. Is this Civilization and Progress? Is it something better than we already possess? These harryings and burnings and desert-makings in the Transvaal – is this an improvement on our darkness? Is it, perhaps, possible that there are two kinds of Civilization – one for home consumption and one for the heathen market?"

Then They that Sit in Darkness are troubled, and shake their heads; and they read this extract from a letter of a British private, recounting his exploits in one of Methuen's victories, some days before the affair of Magersfontein, and they are troubled again:

"We tore up the hill and into the intrenchments, and the Boers saw we had them; so they dropped their guns and went down on their knees and put up their hands clasped, and begged for mercy. And we gave it them – with *the long spoon*."

The long spoon is the bayonet. See *Lloyd's Weekly*, London, of those days. The same number – and the same column – contained some quite unconscious satire in the form of shocked and bitter upbraidings of the Boers for their brutalities and inhumanities!

Next, to our heavy damage, the Kaiser went to playing the game without first mastering it. He lost a couple of missionaries in a riot in Shantung, and in his account he made an overcharge for them. China had to pay a hundred thousand dollars apiece for them, in money; twelve miles of territory, containing several millions of inhabitants and worth twenty million dollars; and to build a monument, and also a Christian church; whereas the people of China could have been depended upon to remember the missionaries without the help of these expensive memorials. This was all bad play. Bad, because it would not, and could not, and will not now or ever, deceive the Person Sitting in Darkness. He knows that it was an overcharge. He knows that a missionary is like any other man: he is worth merely what you can supply his place for, and no more. He is useful, but so is a doctor, so is a sheriff, so is an editor; but a just Emperor does not charge war-prices for such. A diligent, intelligent, but obscure missionary, and a diligent, intelligent country editor are worth much, and we know it; but they are not worth the earth. We esteem such an editor, and we are sorry to see him go; but, when he goes, we should consider twelve miles of territory, and a church, and a fortune, over-compensation for his loss. I mean, if he was a Chinese editor, and we had to settle for him. It is no proper figure for an editor or a missionary; one can get shop-worn kings for less. It was bad play on the Kaiser's part. It got this property, true; but it *produced the Chinese revolt*, the indignant uprising of China's traduced patriots, the Boxers. The results have been expensive to Germany, and to the other Disseminators of Progress and the Blessings of Civilization.

The Kaiser's claim was paid, yet it was bad play, for it could not fail to have an evil effect upon Persons Sitting in Darkness in China. They would muse upon the event, and be likely to say: "Civilization is gracious and beautiful, for such is its reputation; but can we afford it? There are rich Chinamen, perhaps they could afford it; but this tax is not laid upon them, it is laid upon the peasants of Shantung; it is they that must pay this mighty sum, and their wages are but four cents a day. Is this a better civilization than ours, and holier and higher and nobler? Is not this rapacity? Is not this extortion? Would Germany charge America two hundred thousand dollars for two missionaries, and shake the mailed fist in her face, and send warships, and send soldiers, and say: 'Seize twelve miles of territory, worth twenty millions of dollars, as additional pay for the missionaries; and make those peasants build a monument to the missionaries, and a costly Christian church to remember them by?' And later would Germany say to her soldiers: 'March through America and slay, *giving no quarter*; make the German face there, as has been our Hun-face here, a terror for a thousand years; march through the Great Republic and slay, slay, slay, carving a road for our offended religion through its heart and bowels?' Would Germany do like this to America, to England, to France, to Russia? Or only to China the helpless – imitating the elephant's assault upon the field-mice? Had we better invest in this Civilization – this Civilization which called Napoleon a buccaneer for carrying off Venice's bronze horses, but which steals our ancient astronomical instruments from our walls, and goes looting like common bandits – that is, all the alien soldiers except America's; and (Americans again excepted) storms frightened villages and cables the result to glad journals at home every day: 'Chinese losses, 450 killed; ours, *one officer and two men wounded*. Shall proceed against neighboring village to-morrow, where a *massacre* is reported.' Can we afford Civilization?"

And, next, Russia must go and play the game injudiciously. She affronts England once or twice – with the Person Sitting in Darkness observing and noting; by moral assistance of France and Germany, she robs Japan of her hard-earned spoil, all swimming in Chinese blood – Port Arthur – with the Person again observing and noting; then she seizes Manchuria, raids its villages, and chokes its great river with the swollen corpses of countless massacred peasants – that astonished Person still observing and noting. And perhaps he is saying to himself: "It is yet *another* Civilized Power, with its banner of the Prince of Peace in one hand and its loot-basket and its butcher-knife in the other. Is there no salvation for us but to adopt Civilization and lift ourselves down to its level?"

And by and by comes America, and our Master of the Game plays it badly – plays it as Mr. Chamberlain was playing it in South Africa. It was a mistake to do that; also, it was one which was quite unlooked for in a Master who was playing it so well in Cuba. In Cuba, he was playing the usual and regular *American* game, and it was winning, for there is no way to beat it. The Master, contemplating Cuba, said: "Here is an oppressed and friendless little nation which is willing to fight to be free; we go partners, and put up the strength of seventy million sympathizers and the resources of the United States: play!" Nothing but Europe combined could call that hand: and Europe cannot combine on anything. There, in Cuba, he was following our great traditions in a way which made us very proud of him, and proud of the deep dissatisfaction which his play was provoking in Continental Europe. Moved by a high inspiration, he threw out those stirring words which proclaimed that forcible annexation would be "criminal aggression;" and in that utterance fired another "shot heard round the world." The memory of that fine saying will be outlived by the remembrance of no act of his but one – that he forgot it within the twelvemonth, and its honorable gospel along with it.

For, presently, came the Philippine temptation. It was strong; it was too strong, and he made that bad mistake: he played the European game, the Chamberlain game. It was a pity; it was a great pity, that error; that one grievous error, that irrevocable error. For it was the very place and time to play the American game again. And at no cost. Rich winnings to be gathered in, too; rich and permanent; indestructible; a fortune transmissible forever to the children of the flag. Not land, not money, not dominion – no, something worth many times more than that dross: our share, the spectacle of a nation of long harassed and persecuted slaves set free through our influence; our posterity's share, the golden memory of that fair deed. The game was in our hands. If it had been played according to the American rules, Dewey would have sailed away from Manila as soon as he had destroyed the Spanish fleet – after putting up a sign on shore guaranteeing foreign property and life against damage by the Filipinos, and warning the Powers that interference with the emancipated patriots would be regarded as an act unfriendly to the United States. The Powers cannot combine, in even a bad cause, and the sign would not have been molested.

Dewey could have gone about his affairs elsewhere, and left the competent Filipino army to starve out the little Spanish garrison and send it home, and the Filipino citizens to set up the form of government they might prefer, and deal with the friars and their doubtful acquisitions according to Filipino ideas of fairness and justice – ideas which have since been tested and found to be of as high an order as any that prevail in Europe or America.

But we played the Chamberlain game, and lost the chance to add another Cuba and another honorable deed to our good record.

The more we examine the mistake, the more clearly we perceive that it is going to be bad for the Business. The Person Sitting in Darkness is almost sure to say: "There is something curious about this – curious and unaccountable. There must be two Americas: one that sets the captive free, and one that takes a once-captive's new freedom away from him, and picks a quarrel with him with nothing to found it on; then kills him to get his land."

The truth is, the Person Sitting in Darkness *is* saying things like that; and for the sake of the Business we must persuade him to look at the Philippine matter in another and healthier way. We must arrange his opinions for him. I believe it can be done; for Mr. Chamberlain has arranged England's opinion of the South African matter, and done it most cleverly and successfully. He presented the facts – some of the facts – and showed those confiding people what the facts meant. He did it statistically, which is a good way. He used the formula: "Twice 2 are 14, and 2 from 9 leaves 35." Figures are effective; figures will convince the elect.

Now, my plan is a still bolder one than Mr. Chamberlain's,

though apparently a copy of it. Let us be franker than Mr. Chamberlain; let us audaciously present the whole of the facts, shirking none, then explain them according to Mr. Chamberlain's formula. This daring truthfulness will astonish and dazzle the Person Sitting in Darkness, and he will take the Explanation down before his mental vision has had time to get back into focus. Let us say to him:

"Our case is simple. On the 1st of May, Dewey destroyed the Spanish fleet. This left the Archipelago in the hands of its proper and rightful owners, the Filipino nation. Their army numbered 30,000 men, and they were competent to whip out or starve out the little Spanish garrison; then the people could set up a government of their own devising. Our traditions required that Dewey should now set up his warning sign, and go away. But the Master of the Game happened to think of another plan – the European plan. He acted upon it. This was, to send out an army – ostensibly to help the native patriots put the finishing touch upon their long and plucky struggle for independence, but really to take their land away from them and keep it. That is, in the interest of Progress and Civilization. The plan developed, stage by stage, and quite satisfactorily. We entered into a military alliance with the trusting Filipinos, and they hemmed in Manila on the land side, and by their valuable help the place, with its garrison of 8,000 or 10,000 Spaniards, was captured – a thing which we could not have accomplished unaided at that time. We got their help by – by ingenuity. We knew they were fighting for their independence, and that they had been at it for two years. We knew they supposed that we also were fighting in their worthy cause – just as we had helped the Cubans fight for Cuban independence – and we allowed them to go on thinking so. *Until Manila was ours and we could get along without them.* Then we showed our hand. Of course, they were surprised – that was natural; surprised and disappointed; disappointed and grieved. To them it looked un-American; uncharacteristic; foreign to our established traditions. And this was natural, too; for we were only playing the American Game in public – in private it was the European. It was neatly done, very neatly, and it bewildered them. They could not understand it; for we had been so friendly – so affectionate, even – with those simple-minded patriots! We, our own selves, had brought back out of exile their leader, their hero, their hope, their Washington – Aguinaldo; brought him in a warship, in high honor, under the sacred shelter and hospitality of the flag; brought him back and restored him to his people, and got their moving and eloquent gratitude for it. Yes, we had been so friendly to them, and had heartened them up in so many ways! We had lent them guns and ammunition; advised with them; exchanged pleasant courtesies with them; placed our sick and wounded in their kindly care; entrusted our Spanish prisoners to their humane and honest hands; fought shoulder to shoulder with them against 'the common enemy' (our own phrase); praised their courage, praised their gallantry, praised their mercifulness, praised their fine and honorable conduct; borrowed their trenches, borrowed strong positions which they had previously captured from the Spaniard; petted them, lied to them – officially proclaiming that our land and naval forces came to give them their freedom and displace the bad Spanish Government – fooled them, used them until we needed them no longer; then derided the sucked orange and threw it away. We kept the positions which we had beguiled them of by and by, we moved a force forward and overlapped patriot ground – a clever thought, for we needed trouble, and this would produce it. A Filipino soldier, crossing the ground, where no one had a right to forbid him, was shot by our sentry. The badgered patriots resented this with arms, without waiting to know whether Aguinaldo, who was absent, would approve or not. Aguinaldo did not approve; but that availed nothing. What we wanted, in the interest of Progress and Civilization, was the Archipelago, unencumbered by patriots struggling for independence; and War was what we needed. We clinched our opportunity. It is Mr. Chamberlain's case over again – at least in its motive and intention; and we played the game as adroitly as he played it himself."

At this point in our frank statement of fact to the Person Sitting in Darkness, we should throw in a little trade-taffy about the Blessings of Civilization – for a change, and for the refreshment of his spirit – then go on with our tale:

"We and the patriots having captured Manila, Spain's ownership of the Archipelago and her sovereignty over it were at an end – obliterated – annihilated – not a rag or shred of either remaining behind. It was then that we conceived the divinely humorous idea of *buying* both of these spectres from Spain! [It is quite safe to confess this to the Person Sitting in Darkness, since neither he nor any other sane person will believe it.] In buying those ghosts for twenty millions, we also contracted to take care of the friars and their accumulations. I think we also agreed to propagate leprosy and smallpox, but as to this there is doubt. But it is not important; persons afflicted with the friars do not mind other diseases.

"With our Treaty ratified, Manila subdued, and our Ghosts secured, we had no further use for Aguinaldo and the owners of the Archipelago. We forced a war, and we have been hunting America's guest and ally through the woods and swamps ever since."

At this point in the tale, it will be well to boast a little of our war-work and our heroisms in the field, so as to make our performance look as fine as England's in South Africa; but I believe it will not be best to emphasize this too much. We must be cautious. Of course, we must read the war-telegrams to the Person, in order to keep up our frankness; but we can throw an air of humorousness over them, and that will modify their grim eloquence a little, and their rather indiscreet exhibitions of gory exultation. Before reading to him the following display heads of the dispatches of November 18, 1900, it will be well to practice on them in private first, so as to get the right tang of lightness and gaiety into them:

"ADMINISTRATION WEARY OF PROTRACTED HOSTILITIES!"
"REAL WAR AHEAD FOR FILIPINO REBELS!"*
"WILL SHOW NO MERCY!"
"KITCHENER'S PLAN ADOPTED!"

Kitchener knows how to handle disagreeable people who are fighting for their homes and their liberties, and we must let on that we are merely imitating Kitchener, and have no national interest in the matter, further than to get ourselves admired by the Great Family of Nations, in which august company our Master of the Game has bought a place for us in the back row.

Of course, we must not venture to ignore our General Mac-Arthur's reports – oh, why do they keep on printing those embarrassing things? – we must drop them trippingly from the tongue and take the chances:

"During the last ten months our losses have been 268 killed and 750 wounded; Filipino loss, *three thousand two hundred and twenty-seven killed*, and 694 wounded."

*"Rebels!" Mumble that funny word – don't let the Person catch it distinctly.

We must stand ready to grab the Person Sitting in Darkness, for he will swoon away at this confession, saying: "Good God, those 'niggers' spare their wounded, and the Americans massacre theirs!"

We must bring him to, and coax him and coddle him, and assure him that the ways of Providence are best, and that it would not become us to find fault with them; and then, to show him that we are only imitators, not originators, we must read the following passage from the letter of an American soldier-lad in the Philippines to his mother, published in *Public Opinion*, of Decorah, Iowa, describing the finish of a victorious battle:

"WE NEVER LEFT ONE ALIVE. IF ONE WAS WOUNDED, WE WOULD RUN OUR BAYONETS THROUGH HIM."

Having now laid all the historical facts before the Person Sitting in Darkness, we should bring him to again, and explain them to him. We should say to him:

"They look doubtful, but in reality they are not. There have been lies; yes, but they were told in a good cause. We have been treacherous; but that was only in order that real good might come out of apparent evil. True, we have crushed a deceived and confiding people; we have turned against the weak and the friendless who trusted us; we have stamped out a just and intelligent and well-ordered republic; we have stabbed an ally in the back and slapped the face of a guest; we have bought a Shadow from an enemy that hadn't it to sell; we have robbed a trusting friend of his land and his liberty; we have invited our clean young men to shoulder a discredited musket and do bandit's work under a flag which bandits have been accustomed to fear, not to follow; we have debauched America's honor and blackened her face before the world; but each detail was for the best. We know this. The Head of every State and Sovereignty in Christendom and ninety per cent. of every legislative body in Christendom, including our Congress and our fifty State Legislatures, are members not only of the church, but also of the Blessings-of-Civilization Trust. This world-girdling accumulation of trained morals, high principles, and justice, cannot do an unright thing, an unfair thing, an ungenerous thing, an unclean thing. It knows what it is about. Give yourself no uneasiness; it is all right."

Now then, that will convince the Person. You will see. It will restore the Business. Also, it will elect the Master of the Game to the vacant place in the Trinity of our national gods; and there on their high thrones the Three will sit, age after age, in the people's sight, each bearing the Emblem of his service: Washington, the Sword of the Liberator; Lincoln, the Slave's Broken Chains; the Master, the Chains Repaired.

It will give the Business a splendid new start. You will see.

Everything is prosperous, now; everything is just as we should wish it. We have got the Archipelago, and we shall never give it up. Also, we have every reason to hope that we shall have an opportunity before very long to slip out of our Congressional contract with Cuba and give her something better in the place of it. It is a rich country, and many of us are already beginning to see that the contract was a sentimental mistake. But now – right now – is the best time to do some profitable rehabilitating work – work that will set us up and make us comfortable, and discourage gossip. We cannot conceal from ourselves that, privately, we are a little troubled about our uniform. It is one of our prides; it is acquainted with honor; it is familiar with great deeds and noble; we love it, we revere it; and so this errand it is on makes us uneasy. And our flag – another pride of ours, our chiefest! We have worshipped it so; and when we have seen it in far lands – glimpsing it unexpectedly in that strange sky, waving its welcome and benediction to us – we have caught our breath, and uncovered our heads, and couldn't speak, for a moment, for the thought of what it was to us and the great ideals it stood for. Indeed, we *must* do something about these things; we must not have the flag out there, and the uniform. They are not needed there; we can manage in some other way. England manages, as regards the uniform, and so can we. We have to send soldiers – we can't get out of that – but we can disguise them. It is the way England does in South Africa. Even Mr. Chamberlain himself takes pride in England's honorable uniform, and makes the army down there wear an ugly and odious and appropriate disguise, of yellow stuff such as quarantine flags are made of, and which are hoisted to warn the healthy away from unclean disease and repulsive death. This cloth is called khaki. We could adopt it. It is light, comfortable, grotesque, and deceives the enemy, for he cannot conceive of a soldier being concealed in it.

And as for a flag for the Philippine Province, it is easily managed. We can have a special one – our States do it: we can have just our usual flag, with the white stripes painted black and the stars replaced by the skull and cross-bones.

And we do not need that Civil Commission out there. Having

no powers, it has to invent them, and that kind of work cannot be effectively done by just anybody; an expert is required. Mr. Croker can be spared. We do not want the United States represented there, but only the Game.

By help of these suggested amendments, Progress and Civilization in that country can have a boom, and it will take in the Persons who are Sitting in Darkness, and we can resume Business at the old stand.

February 1901

BATTLE HYMN OF THE REPUBLIC (BROUGHT DOWN TO DATE)

Mine eyes have seen the orgy of the launching of the Sword;
He is searching out the hoardings where the stranger's wealth is
    stored;
He hath loosed his fateful lightnings, and with woe and death has
    scored;
  His lust is marching on.

I have seen him in the watch-fires of a hundred circling camps,
They have builded him an altar in the Eastern dews and damps;
I have read his doomful mission by the dim and flaring lamps –
  His night is marching on.

I have read his bandit gospel writ in burnished rows of steel:
"As ye deal with my pretensions, so with you my wrath shall deal;
Let the faithless son of Freedom crush the patriot with his heel;
  Lo, Greed is marching on!"

We have legalized the strumpet and are guarding her retreat;*
Greed is seeking out commercial souls before his judgment seat;
O, be swift, ye clods, to answer him! be jubilant my feet!
  Our god is marching on!
In a sordid slime harmonious, Greed was born in yonder ditch,
With a longing in his bosom – and for others' goods an itch –
As Christ died to make men holy, let men die to make us rich –
  Our god is marching on.

c. 1901

* In Manila the government has placed a certain industry under the protection of
our flag.

TO MY MISSIONARY CRITICS

BY MARK TWAIN.

I HAVE RECEIVED many newspaper cuttings; also letters from several clergymen; also a note from the Rev. Dr. Judson Smith, Corresponding Secretary of the American Board of Foreign Missions – all of a like tenor; all saying, substantially, what is said in the cutting here copied:

"AN APOLOGY DUE FROM MR. CLEMENS.

"The evidence of the past day or two should induce Mark Twain to make for the amen corner and formulate a prompt apology for his scathing attack on the Rev. Dr. Ament, the veteran Chinese missionary. The assault was based on a Pekin dispatch to the New York *Sun*, which said that Dr. Ament had collected from the Chinese in various places damages thirteen times in excess of actual losses. So Mark Twain charged Mr. Ament with bullyragging, extortion and things. A Pekin dispatch to the *Sun* yesterday, however, explains that the amount collected was not thirteen times the damage sustained, but *one-third in excess of the indemnities*, and that the blunder was due to a cable error in transmission. The 1–3d got converted into 13. Yesterday the Rev. Judson Smith, Secretary of the American Board, received a dispatch from Dr. Ament, calling attention to the cable blunder, and declaring that all the collections which he made were *approved by the Chinese officials*. The fractional amount that was collected in *excess* of actual losses, he explains, is being *used for the support of widows and orphans.*

"So collapses completely – and convulsively – Mark Twain's sensational and ugly bombardment of a missionary whose character and services should have exempted him from such an assault.

"From the charge the underpinning has been knocked out. To Dr. Ament Mr. Clemens has done an injustice which is gross but unintentional. If Mark Twain is the man we take him to be he won't be long in filing a retraction, plus an apology."

I have no prejudice against apologies. I trust I shall never withhold one when it is due; I trust I shall never even have a disposition to do so. These letters and newspaper paragraphs are entitled to my best attention; respect for their writers and for the humane feeling which has prompted their utterances requires this of me. It may be barely possible that, if these requests for an apology had reached me before the 20th of February, I might have had a sort of qualified chance to apologize; but on that day appeared the two little cablegrams referred to in the newspaper cutting copied above – one from the Rev. Dr. Smith to the Rev. Dr. Ament, the other from Dr. Ament to Dr. Smith – and my small chance died then. In my opinion, these cablegrams ought to have been suppressed, for it seems clear that they give Dr. Ament's case entirely away. Still, that is only an opinion, and may be a mistake. It will be best to examine the case from the beginning, by the light of the documents connected with it.

EXHIBIT A.

This is a dispatch from Mr. Chamberlain,* chief of the *Sun*'s correspondence staff in Pekin. It appeared in the *Sun* last Christmas Eve, and in referring to it hereafter I will call it the "C. E. dispatch" for short:

> "The Rev. Mr. Ament, of the American Board of Foreign Missions, has returned from a trip which he made for the purpose of collecting indemnities for damages done by Boxers. Everywhere he went he compelled the Chinese to pay. He says that all his native Christians are now provided for. He had seven hundred of them under his charge, and three hundred were killed. He has collected 300 taels for each of these murders, and has compelled full payment for all the property belonging to Christians that was destroyed. He also assessed fines amounting to thirteen times[†] the amount of the indemnity. This money will be used for the propagation of the Gospel.
>
> "Mr. Ament declares that the compensation he has collected is moderate when compared with the amount secured by the Catholics, who demand, in addition to money, head for head. They collect 500 taels for each murder of a Catholic. In the Wen-Chiu country 680 Catholics were killed, and for this the European Catholics here demand 750,000 strings of cash and 680 heads.
>
> "In the course of a conversation Mr. Ament referred to the

---

* Testimony of the manager of the *Sun*.

† Cable error. For "thirteen times" read "one-third." This correction was made by Dr. Ament in his brief cablegram published Feb. 20, above referred to.

attitude of the missionaries toward the Chinese. He said:

"'I deny emphatically that the missionaries are vindictive, that they generally looted, or that they have done anything since the siege that the circumstances did not demand. I criticise the Americans. The soft hand of the Americans is not as good as the mailed fist of the Germans. If you deal with the Chinese with a soft hand they will take advantage of it.'"

In an article addressed "To the Person Sitting in Darkness," published in the NORTH AMERICAN REVIEW for February, I made some comments upon this C. E. dispatch.

In an Open Letter to me, from the Rev. Dr. Smith, published in the *Tribune* of February 15th, doubt is cast upon the authenticity of the dispatch.

Up to the 20th of February, this doubt was an important factor in the case: Dr. Ament's brief cablegram, published on that date, took the importance all out of it.

In the Open Letter, Dr. Smith quotes this passage from a letter from Dr. Ament, dated November 13th. The italics are mine:

"*This* time I proposed to settle affairs *without the aid of soldiers* or legations."

This cannot mean two things, but only one: that, previously, he *had* collected by armed force.

Also, in the Open Letter, Dr. Smith quotes some praises of Dr. Ament and the Rev. Mr. Tewksbury, furnished by the Rev. Dr. Sheffield, and says:

"Dr. Sheffield is not accustomed to speak thus of *thieves*, or *extortioners*, or *braggarts*."

What can he mean by those vigorous expressions? Can he mean that the first two would be applicable to a missionary who should collect from B, with the "aid of soldiers," indemnities possibly due by A, and upon occasion go out looting?

EXHIBIT B.

Testimony of George Lynch (endorsed as entirely trustworthy by the *Tribune* and the *Herald*), war correspondent in the Cuban and South African wars, and in the march upon Pekin for the rescue of the legations. The italics are mine:

"When the *soldiers* were prohibited from looting, no such

prohibitions seemed to operate with the *missionaries.* For instance, the *Rev. Mr. Tewksbury held a great sale of looted goods, which lasted several days.*

"A day or two after the relief, when looking for a place to sleep in, I met the Rev. Mr. Ament, of the American Board of Foreign Missions. *He told me* he was going to take possession of the house of a wealthy Chinaman who was an old enemy of his, as he had interfered much in the past with his missionary labors in Pekin. A couple of days afterward *he did so,* and held a *great sale of his enemy's effects.* I bought a sable cloak at it for $125, and a couple of statues of Buddha. As the stock became depleted *it was replenished by the efforts of his converts, who were ransacking the houses in the neighborhood.*" – *N. Y. Herald, Feb.* 18.

It is Dr. Smith, not I, who has suggested that persons who act in this way are "thieves and extortioners."

EXHIBIT C.

Sir Robert Hart, in the *Fortnightly Review* for January, 1901. This witness has been for many years the most prominent and important Englishman in China, and bears an irreproachable reputation for moderation, fairness and truth-speaking. In closing a description of the revolting scenes which followed the occupation of Pekin, when the Christian armies (with the proud exception of the American soldiery, let us be thankful for that,) gave themselves up to a ruthless orgy of robbery and spoliation, he says (the italics are mine):

"And even some *missionaries* took such a *leading* part in 'spoiling the Egyptians' for the greater glory of God that a bystander was heard to say: '*For a century to come Chinese converts will consider looting and vengeance Christian virtues!*'"

It is Dr. Smith, not I, who has suggested that persons who act in this way are "thieves and extortioners." According to Mr. Lynch and Mr. Martin (another war correspondent), Dr. Ament helped to spoil several of those Egyptians. Mr. Martin took a photograph of the scene. It was reproduced in the *Herald.* I have it.

EXHIBIT D.

In a brief reply to Dr. Smith's Open Letter to me, I said this in the *Tribune.* I am italicizing several words – for a purpose:

"Whenever he (Dr. Smith) can produce from the Rev. Mr.

Ament an assertion that the *Sun*'s character-blasting dispatch was not authorized *by him*, and whenever Dr. Smith can buttress Mr. Ament's disclaimer with a confession from *Mr. Chamberlain*, the head of the Laffan News Service in China, that that dispatch was a false invention *and unauthorized*, the case against Mr. Ament will fall at once to the ground."

EXHIBIT E.

Brief cablegrams, referred to above, which passed between Dr. Smith and Dr. Ament, and were published on February 20th:

"Ament, Peking: Reported December 24 your collecting thirteen times actual losses; using for propagating the Gospel. Are these statements true? Cable specific answer.   SMITH."

"Statement untrue. Collected 1-3 for church expenses, additional actual damages; now supporting widows and orphans. Publication thirteen times blunder cable. All collections received approval Chinese officials, who are urging further settlements same line.   AMENT."

Only two questions are asked; "specific" answers required; no perilous wanderings among the other details of the unhappy dispatch desired.

EXHIBIT F.

Letter from Dr. Smith to me, dated March 8th. The italics are mine; they tag inaccuracies of statement:

"Permit me to call your attention to the marked paragraphs in the inclosed papers, and to ask you to note their relation to the two conditions named in your letter to the *New York Tribune* of February 15th.

"The first is *Dr. Ament's denial of the truth of the dispatch in the New York 'Sun'* of December 24th, on which your criticisms of him in the NORTH AMERICAN REVIEW of February were founded. The second is a correction by the *'Sun's' special correspondent* in Peking of the dispatch printed in the *Sun* of December 24th.

"Since, as you state in your letter to the *Tribune*, 'the case against Mr. Ament would fall to the ground' *if Mr. Ament denied the truth* of the *Sun*'s first dispatch, and *if the 'Sun's' news agency* in Peking also *declared that dispatch false*, and these two conditions *have thus been fulfilled*, I am sure that upon having these *facts* brought to your attention you will gladly withdraw the criticisms that were *founded on a 'cable blunder.'* "

I think Dr. Smith ought to read me more carefully; then he would not make so many mistakes. Within the narrow space of two paragraphs, totaling eleven lines, he has scored nine departures from fact out of a possible $9\frac{1}{2}$. Now, is that parliamentary? I do not treat him like that. Whenever I quote him, I am particular not to do him the least wrong, or make him say anything he did not say.

(1.) Mr. Ament doesn't "deny the truth of the C. E. dispatch;" he merely changes one of its phrases, without materially changing the meaning, and (immaterially) corrects a cable blunder (which correction I accept). He was asked no question about the other four-fifths of the C. E. dispatch. (2.) I said nothing about "special" correspondents; I named the right and responsible man – Mr. Chamberlain. The "correction" referred to is a repetition of the one I have just accepted, which (immaterially) changes "thirteen times" to "one-third" extra-tax. (3.) I did not say anything about "the *Sun*'s news agency;" I said "Chamberlain." I have every confidence in Mr. Chamberlain, but I am not personally acquainted with the others. (4.) Once more – Mr. Ament didn't "deny the truth" of the C. E. dispatch, but merely made unimportant emendations of a couple of its many details. (5.) I did not say "if Mr. Ament denied the truth" of the C. E. dispatch: I said, if he would assert that the dispatch was not "authorized" *by him*. For example, I did not suppose that the charge that the Catholic missionaries wanted 680 Chinamen beheaded was true; but I did want to know if Dr. Ament personally authorized that statement and the others, as coming from his lips. Another detail: one of my conditions was that Mr. Chamberlain must not stop with confessing that the C. E. was a "false invention," he must also confess that it was "*unauthorized*." Dr. Smith has left out that large detail. (6.) The *Sun*'s news agency did not "declare the C. E. dispatch false," but confined itself to correcting one unimportant detail of its long list – the change of "13 times" to "one-third" extra. (7.) The "two conditions" have not "been fulfilled" – far from it. (8.) Those details labeled "facts" are only fancies. (9.) Finally, my criticisms were by no means confined to that detail of the C. E. dispatch which we now accept as having been a "cable blunder."

Setting to one side these nine departures from fact, I find that what is left of the eleven lines is straight and true. I am not blaming Dr. Smith for these discrepancies – it would not be right, it would not be fair. I make the proper allowances. He has not been a journalist, as I have been – a trade wherein a person is brought to book by the rest of the press so often for divergencies that, by and by, he gets to be almost morbidly afraid to indulge in them. It is so with me. I always have the disposition to tell what is not so; I was born with it; we all have it. But I try not to do it now, because I have found out that it is unsafe. But with the Doctor of course it is different.

I wanted to get at the whole of the facts as regards the C. E. dispatch, and so I wrote to China for them, when I found that the Board was not going to do it. But I am not allowed to wait. It seemed quite within the possibilities that a full detail of the facts might furnish me a chance to make an apology to Mr. Ament – a chance which, I give you my word, I would have honestly used, and not abused. But it is no matter. If the Board is not troubled about the bulk of that lurid dispatch, why should I be? I answered the apology-urging letters of several clergymen with the information that I had written to China for the details, and said I thought it was the only sure way of getting into a position to do fair and full justice to all concerned; but a couple of them replied that it was not a matter that could wait. That is to say, groping your way out of a jungle in the dark with guesses and conjectures is better than a straight march out in the sunlight of fact. It seems a curious idea.

However, those two clergymen were in a large measure right – from their point of view and the Board's; which is, putting it in the form of a couple of questions:

1. *Did Dr. Ament collect the assessed damages and thirteen times over?* The answer is: He did *not*. He collected only *a third* over.

2. *Did he apply the third to the "propagation of the Gospel?"* The answer is this correction: He applied it to "church expenses." Part or all of the outlay, it appears, goes to "supporting widows and orphans." It may be that church expenses and supporting widows and orphans are not part of the machinery for propagating the Gospel. I supposed they were, but it isn't any matter; I prefer this phrasing; it is not so blunt as the other.

In the opinion of the two clergymen and of the Board, these two points are *the only important ones* in the whole C. E. dispatch.

I accept that. Therefore let us throw out the rest of the dispatch as being no longer a part of Dr. Ament's case.

EXHIBIT H.

The two clergymen and the Board are quite content with Dr. Ament's answers upon the two points.

Upon the first point of the two, my own viewpoint may be indicated by a question:

Did Dr. Ament collect from B, (whether by compulsion or simple demand), even so much as a penny in payment for murders or depredations, without knowing, beyond question, that B, and not another, committed the murders or the depredations?

Or, in other words:

Did Dr. Ament ever, by chance or through ignorance, make the innocent pay the debts of the guilty?

In the article entitled "To the Person Sitting in Darkness," I put forward that point in a paragraph taken from Macallum's (imaginary) "History":

EXHIBIT I.

"When a white Boxer kills a Pawnee and destroys his property the other Pawnees do not trouble to seek *him* out; they kill any white person that comes along; also, they make some white village pay deceased's heirs the full cash value of deceased, together with full cash value of the property destroyed; they also make the village pay, in addition, *thirteen times** the value of that property into a fund for the dissemination of the Pawnee religion, which they regard as the best of all religions for the softening and humanizing of the heart of man. It is their idea that it is only fair and right *that the innocent should be made to suffer for the guilty*, and that it is better that ninety and nine innocent should suffer than that one guilty person should escape."

We all know that Dr. Ament did not bring suspected persons into a duly organized court and try them by just and fair Christian and civilized methods, but proclaimed his "conditions," and collected damages from the innocent and the guilty alike, without any court proceedings at all.† That he himself, and not the villagers,

---

* For "thirteen times" read "one-third." – M. T.

† In civilized countries, if a mob destroy property in a town, the damage is paid out of the town treasury, and no tax-payer suffers a disproportionate share of the burden; the mayor is not privileged to distribute the burden according to his private notions, sparing himself and his friends, and fleecing persons he holds a spite against – as in the Orient – and the citizen who is too poor to be a tax-payer pays no part of the fine at all.

made the "conditions," we learn from his letter of November 13th, already quoted from – the one in which he remarked that, upon *that* occasion, he brought no soldiers with him. The italics are mine:

"After our *conditions* were known many villagers came of their own accord and brought their money with them."

Not all, but "many." The Board really believes that those hunted and harried paupers out there were not only willing to strip themselves to pay Boxer damages, whether they owed them or not, but were sentimentally eager to do it. Mr. Ament says, in his letter: "The villagers were extremely grateful because I brought no foreign soldiers, and were glad to settle on the terms proposed." Some of those people know more about theology than they do about human nature. I do not remember encountering even a Christian who was "glad" to pay money he did not owe; and as for a Chinaman doing it, why, dear me, the thing is unthinkable. We have all seen Chinamen, many Chinamen, but not that kind. It is a new kind: an invention of the Board – and "soldiers."

CONCERNING THE COLLECTIONS.

What was the "one-third extra"? Money due? No. Was it a theft, then? Putting aside the "one-third extra," what was the *remainder* of the exacted indemnity, if collected from persons not *known* to owe it, and without Christian and civilized forms of procedure? Was *it* theft, was it robbery? In America it would be that; in Christian Europe it would be that. I have great confidence in Dr. Smith's judgment concerning this detail, and he calls it "theft and extortion" – even in China; for he was talking about the "thirteen times" at the time that he gave it that strong name.* It is his idea that, when you make guilty and innocent villagers pay the appraised damages, and then make them pay thirteen times that, besides, the *thirteen* stand for "theft and extortion."

Then what does *one-third* extra stand for? Will he give that

---

* In his Open Letter, Dr. Smith cites Dr. Ament's letter of November 13th, which contains an account of Dr. Ament's collecting-tour; then Dr. Smith makes this comment: "Nothing is said of securing 'thirteen times' the amount of the losses." Further down, Dr. Smith quotes praises of Dr. Ament and his work (from a letter of the Rev. Dr. Sheffield), and adds this comment: "Dr. Sheffield is not accustomed to speak thus in praise of thieves, or extortioners, or braggarts." The reference is to the "thirteen-times" extra-tax.

one-third a name? Is it Modified Theft and Extortion? Is that it? The girl who was rebuked for having borne an illegitimate child, excused herself by saying, "But it is such a *little* one."

When the "thirteen-times-extra" was alleged, it stood for theft and extortion, in Dr. Smith's eyes, and he was shocked. But when Dr. Ament showed that he had taken only a *third* extra, instead of thirteen-fold, Dr. Smith was relieved, content, happy. I declare I cannot imagine why. That editor – quoted at the head of this article – was happy about it, too. I cannot think why. He thought I ought to "make for the amen corner and formulate a prompt apology." To whom, and for what? It is too deep for me.

To Dr. Smith, the "thirteen-fold-extra" clearly stood for "theft and extortion," and he was right, distinctly right, indisputably right. He manifestly thinks that when it got scaled away down to a mere "one-third," a little thing like that was something other than "theft and extortion." Why? Only the Board knows! I will try to explain this difficult problem, so that the Board can get an idea of it. If a pauper owes me a dollar, and I catch him unprotected and make him pay me fourteen dollars, thirteen of it is "theft and extortion"; if I make him pay only a dollar and thirty-three and a third cents, the thirty-three and a third cents are "theft and extortion" just the same. I will put it in another way, still simpler. If a man owes me one dog – any kind of a dog, the breed is of no consequence – and I – But let it go; the Board would never understand it. It *can't* understand these involved and difficult things.

But *if* the Board could understand, then I could furnish some more instruction – which is this. The one-third, obtained by "theft and extortion," is *tainted money*, and cannot be purified even by defraying "church expenses" and "supporting widows and orphans" with it. It has to be restored to the people it was taken from.

Also, there is another view of these things. By our Christian code of morals and law, the *whole* $1.33 1-3, if taken from a man not formally *proven* to have committed the damage the dollar represents, is "theft and extortion." It cannot be honestly used for any purpose at all. It must be handed back to the man it was taken from.

Is there no way, then, to justify these thefts and extortions and make them clean and fair and honorable? Yes, there is. It can be done; it has been done; it continues to be done – by revising the Ten Commandments and bringing them down to date: for use in pagan lands. For example:

Thou shall not steal – except when it is the custom of the country.

This way out is recognized and *approved* by all the best authorities, including the Board. I will cite witnesses.

The newspaper cutting, above: "Dr. Ament declares that all the collections which he made were approved by the *Chinese* officials." The editor is satisfied.

Dr. Ament's cable to Dr. Smith: "All collections received approval *Chinese* officials." Dr. Ament is satisfied.

Letters from eight clergymen – all to the same effect: Dr. Ament merely did as the *Chinese* do. So they are satisfied.

Mr. Ward, of the Independent.

The Rev. Dr. Washington Gladden.

I have mislaid the letters of these gentlemen and cannot quote their words, but they are of the satisfied.

The Rev. Dr. Smith, in His Open Letter, published in the *Tribune*: "The whole procedure (Dr. Ament's), is in accordance with a custom among the *Chinese*, of holding a village responsible for wrongs suffered in that village, and especially making the head man of the village accountable for wrongs committed there." Dr. Smith is satisfied. Which means that the Board is satisfied.

The "head man"! Why, then, this poor rascal, innocent or guilty, must pay the whole bill, if he cannot squeeze it out of his poor-devil neighbors. But, indeed, he can be depended upon to try, even to the skinning them of their last brass farthing, their last rag of clothing, their last ounce of food. He can be depended upon to get the indemnity out of them, though it cost stripes and blows, blood, tears and flesh.

THE TALE OF THE KING AND HIS TREASURER.

How strange and remote and romantic and Oriental and Arabian-Nighty it all seems – and is. It brings back the old forgotten tales, and we hear the King say to his Treasurer:

"Bring me 30,000 gold tomauns."

"Allah preserve us, Sire! the treasury is empty."

"Do you hear? Bring the money – in ten days. Else, send me your head in a basket."

"I hear and obey."

The Treasurer summons the head men of a hundred villages, and says to one:

"Bring me a hundred gold tomauns." To another, "Bring me

five hundred;" to another, "Bring a thousand. In ten days. Your head is the forfeit."

"Your slaves kiss your feet! Ah, high and mighty lord, be merciful to our hard pressed villagers: they are poor, they are naked, they starve; oh, these impossible sums! even the half —"

"Go! Grind it out of them, crush it out of them, turn the blood of the fathers, the tears of the mothers, the milk of the babes to money – or take the consequences. Have you heard?"

"His will be done, Who is the Fount of love and mercy and compassion, Who layeth this heavy burden upon us by the hand of His anointed servants – blessed be His holy Name! The father shall bleed, the mother shall faint for hunger, the babe shall perish at the dry breast. The chosen of God have commanded: it shall be as they say."

I am not meaning to object to the substitution of pagan customs for Christian, here and there and now and then, when the Christian ones are inconvenient. No; I like it and admire it. I do it myself. And I admire the alertness of the Board in watching out for chances to trade Board morals for Chinese morals, and get the best of the swap; for I cannot endure those people, they are yellow, and I have never considered yellow becoming. I have always been like the Board – perfectly well-meaning, but destitute of the Moral Sense. Now, one of the main reasons why it is so hard to make the Board understand that there is no moral difference between a big filch and a little filch, but only a legal one, is that vacancy in its make-up. Morally, there are no degrees in stealing. The Commandment merely says, "Thou shalt not *steal*," and stops there. It doesn't recognize any difference between stealing a third and stealing thirteen-fold. If I could think of a way to put it before the Board in such a plain and –

THE WATERMELONS.

I have it, now. Many years ago, when I was studying for the gallows, I had a dear comrade, a youth who was not in my line, but still a thoroughly good fellow, though devious. He was preparing to qualify for a place on the Board, for there was going to be a vacancy by superannuation in about five years. This was down South, in the slavery days. It was the nature of the negro then, as now, to steal watermelons. They stole three of the melons of an adoptive brother of mine, the only good ones he had. I suspected three of a neighbor's negroes, but there was no proof: and, besides, the watermelons in those negroes' private patches were all green and small, and not up to indemnity standard. But in the private patches of three other negroes there was a number of competent melons. I consulted with my comrade, the understudy of the Board. He said that if I would approve his arrangements, he would arrange. I said, "Consider me the Board; I approve: arrange." So he took a gun, and went and collected three large melons for my brother-on-the-half-shell, and one over. I was greatly pleased, and asked:

"Who gets the extra one?"

"Widows and orphans."

"A good idea, too. Why didn't you take thirteen?"

"It would have been wrong; a crime, in fact – Theft and Extortion."

"What is the one-third extra – the odd melon – the same?"

It caused him to reflect. But there was no result.

The justice of the peace was a stern man. On the trial, he found fault with the scheme, and required us to explain upon what we based our strange conduct – as he called it. The understudy said:

"On the custom of the niggers. They all do it."

The justice forgot his dignity, and descended to sarcasm:

"Custom of the niggers! Are our morals so inadequate that we have to borrow of niggers?" Then he said to the jury: "Three melons were owing; they were collected from persons not proven to owe them; this is theft. They were collected by compulsion; this is extortion. A melon was added – for the widows and orphans. It was owed by no one. It is another theft, another extortion. Return it whence it came, with the others. It is not permissible, here, to apply to any object goods dishonestly obtained – not even to the feeding of widows and orphans, for that would be to put a shame upon charity and dishonor it."

He said it in open court, before everybody, and to me it did not seem very kind.

A clergyman, in a letter to me, reminds me, with a touch of reproach, that "many of the missionaries are good men, kind-hearted, earnest, devoted to their work." Certainly they are. No one is disputing it. Instead of "many," he could have said "almost all," and still said the truth, no doubt. I know many missionaries; I have met them all about the globe, and have known only one or two who could not fill that bill and answer to that description. "Almost all" comes near to being a proportion and a description

applicable also to lawyers, authors, editors, merchants, manufacturers – in fact to most guilds and vocations. Without a doubt, Dr.
Ament did what he believed to be right, and I concede that when
a man is doing what he believes to be right, there is argument on
his side. I differ with Dr. Ament, but that is only because he got his
training from the Board and I got mine outside. Neither of us is
responsible, altogether.

RECAPITULATION.

But there is no need to sum up. Mr. Ament has acknowledged
the "one-third extra" – no other witness is necessary. The Rev. Dr.
Smith has carefully considered the act and labeled it with a stern
name, and his verdict seems to have no flaw in it. The morals of
the act are Chinese, but are approved by the Board, and by some
of the clergy and some of the newspapers, as being a valuable
improvement upon Christian ones – which leaves me with a closed
mouth, though with a pain in my heart.

IS THE AMERICAN BOARD ON TRIAL?

Do I think that Dr. Ament and certain of his fellow missionaries
are as bad as their conduct? No, I do not. They are the product of
their training; and now that I understand the whole case, and
where they got their ideals, and that they are merely subordinates
and subject to authority, I comprehend that they are rather access-
ories than principals, and that their acts only show faulty heads
curiously trained, not bad hearts. Mainly, as it seems to me, it is
the American Board that is on trial. And again, it is a case of the
head, not of the heart. That it has a heart which has never harbored an evil intention, no one will deny, no one will question;
the Board's history can silence any challenge on that score. The
Board's heart is not in court: it is its head that is on trial.

It is a sufficiently strange head. Its ways baffle comprehension;
its ideas are like no one else's; its methods are novelties to the practical world; its judgments are surprises. When one thinks it is going
to speak and must speak, it is silent; when one thinks it ought to
be silent and must be silent, it speaks. Put your finger where you
think it ought to be, it is not there; put it where you think it ought
not to be, there you find it.

When its servant in China seemed to be charging himself with
amazing things, in a reputable journal, – in a dispatch which was
copied into many other papers – the Board was as silent about it
as any dead man could have been who was informed that his house

was burning over his head. An exchange of cablegrams could have enabled it, within two days, to prove to the world – possibly – that the damaging dispatch had not proceeded from the mouth of its servant; yet it sat silent and asked no questions about the matter.

It was silent during thirty-eight days. Then the dispatch came into prominence again. It chanced that I was the occasion of it. A break in the stillness followed. In what form? An exchange of cablegrams, resulting in proof that the damaging dispatch had not been authorized? No, in the form of an Open Letter by the Corresponding Secretary of the American Board, the Rev. Dr. Smith, in which it was *argued* that Dr. Ament could not have said and done the things set forth in the dispatch.

Surely, this was bad politics. A repudiating telegram would have been worth more than a library of argument.

An extension of the silence would have been better than the Open Letter, I think. I thought so at the time. It seemed to me that mistakes enough had been made and harm enough done. I thought it questionable policy to publish the Letter, for I "did not think it likely that Dr. Ament would disown the dispatch," and I telegraphed that to the Rev. Dr. Smith. Personally, I had nothing against Dr. Ament, and that is my attitude yet.

Once more it was a good time for an extension of the silence. But no; the Board has its own ways, and one of them is to do the unwise thing, when occasion offers. After having waited fifty-six days, it cabled to Dr. Ament. No one can divine why it did so then, instead of fifty-six days earlier.* It got a fatal reply – and was not aware of it. That was that curious confession about the "one-third extra"; its application, not to the "propagation of the Gospel," but only to "church expenses," support of widows and orphans; and, on top of this confession, that other strange one revealing the dizzying fact that our missionaries, who went to China to teach Christian morals and justice, had adopted pagan morals and justice in their place. *That cablegram was dynamite.*

It seems odd that the Board did not see that that revelation made the case far worse than it was before; for there was a saving doubt, before – a doubt which was a Gibraltar for strength, and should have been carefully left undisturbed. Why did the Board allow that

* The cablegram went on the day (Feb. 18) that Mr. George Lynch's account of the looting was published. See "Exhibit B." It seems a pity it did not inquire about the looting and get it denied.

revelation to get into print? Why did the Board not suppress it and keep still? But no; in the Board's opinion, this was once more the time for speech. Hence Dr. Smith's latest letter to me, suggesting that I speak also – a letter which is a good enough letter, barring its nine defects, but is another evidence that the Board's head is not as good as its heart.

A missionary is a man who is pretty nearly all heart, else he would not be in a calling which requires of him such large sacrifices of one kind and another. He is made up of faith, zeal, courage, sentiment, emotion, enthusiasm; and so he is a mixture of poet, devotee and knight-errant. He exiles himself from home and friends and the scenes and associations that are dearest to him; patiently endures discomforts, privations, discouragements; goes with good pluck into dangers which he knows may cost him his life; and when he must suffer death, willingly makes that supreme sacrifice for his cause.

Sometimes the head-piece of that kind of a man can be of an inferior sort, and errors of judgment can result – as we have seen. Then, for his protection, as it seems to me, he ought to have at his back a Board able to know a blunder when it sees one, and prompt to bring him back upon his right course when he strays from it. That is to say, I think the captain of a ship ought to understand navigation. Whether he does or not, he will have to take a captain's share of the blame, if the crew bring the vessel to grief.

MARK TWAIN.

THE UNITED STATES
OF LYNCHERDOM

AND SO MISSOURI has fallen, that great state! Certain of her children have joined the lynchers, and the smirch is upon the rest of us. That handful of her children have given us a character and labeled us with a name, and to the dwellers in the four quarters of the earth we are "lynchers," now, and ever shall be. For the world will not stop and think – it never does, it is not its way; its way is to generalize from a single sample. It will not say, "Those Missourians have been busy eighty years in building an honorable good name for themselves; these hundred lynchers down in the corner of the state are not real Missourians, they are renegades." No, that truth will not enter its mind; it will generalize from the one or two misleading samples and say, "The Missourians are lynchers." It has no reflection, no logic, no sense of proportion. With it, figures go for nothing; to it, figures reveal nothing, it cannot reason upon them rationally; it would say, for instance, that China is being swiftly and surely Christianized, since nine Chinese Christians are being made every day; and it would fail, with him, to notice that the fact that 33,000 pagans are *born* there every day, damages the argument. It would say, "There are a hundred lynchers there, therefore the Missourians are lynchers"; the considerable fact that there are two and a half million Missourians who are *not* lynchers would not affect their verdict.

Oh, Missouri!

The tragedy occurred near Pierce City, down in the southwestern corner of the state. On a Sunday afternoon a young white woman who had started alone from church was found murdered. For there are churches there; in my time religion was more general, more pervasive, in the South than it was in the North, and more virile and earnest, too, I think; I have some reason to believe that this is still the case. The young woman was found murdered. Although it was a region of churches and schools the people rose, lynched three negroes – two of them very aged ones – burned out five negro households, and drove thirty negro families into the woods.

I do not dwell upon the provocation which moved the people to these crimes, for that has nothing to do with the matter; the only question is, does the assassin *take the law into his own hands*? It is very simple, and very just. If the assassin be proved to have usurped the law's prerogative in righting his wrongs, that ends the matter; a thousand provocations are no defense. The Pierce City people had bitter provocation – indeed, as revealed by certain of the particulars, the bitterest of all provocations – but no matter, they took the law into their own hands, when by the terms of their statutes their victim would certainly hang if the law had been allowed to take its course, for there are but few negroes in that region and they are without authority and without influence in overawing juries.

Why has lynching, with various barbaric accompaniments, become a favorite regulator in cases of "the usual crime" – in several parts of the country? Is it because men think a lurid and terrible punishment a more forcible object lesson and a more effective deterrent than a sober and colorless hanging done privately in a jail would be? Surely sane men do not think that. Even the average child should know better. It should know that any strange and much-talked-of event is always followed by imitations, the world being so well supplied with excitable people who only need a little stirring up to make them lose what is left of their heads and do mad things which they would not have thought of ordinarily. It should know that if a man jump off Brooklyn Bridge another will imitate him; that if a person venture down Niagara Whirlpool in a barrel another will imitate him; that if a Jack the Ripper make notoriety by slaughtering women in dark alleys he will be imitated; that if a man attempt a king's life and the newspapers carry the noise of it around the globe, regicides will crop up all around. The child should know that one much-talked-of outrage and murder committed by a negro will upset the disturbed intellects of several other negroes and produce a series of the very tragedies the community would so strenuously wish to prevent; that each of these crimes will produce another series, and year by year steadily increase the tale of these disasters instead of diminishing it; that, in a word, the lynchers are themselves the worst enemies of their women. The child should also know that by a law of our make, communities, as well as individuals, are imitators; and that a much-talked-of lynching will infallibly produce other lynchings here and there and yonder, and that in time these will breed a mania, a fashion; a fashion which will spread wide and wider, year by year, covering state after state, as with an advancing disease. Lynching has reached Colorado, it has reached California, it has reached Indiana – and now Missouri! I may live to see a negro burned in Union Square, New York, with fifty thousand people present, and not a sheriff visible, not a governor, not a constable, not a colonel, not a clergyman, not a law-and-order representative of any sort.

Increase in Lynching. – In 1900 there were eight more cases than in 1899, and probably this year there will be more than there were last year. The year is little more than half gone, and yet there are eighty-eight cases as compared with one hundred and fifteen for all of last year. The four Southern states, Alabama, Georgia, Louisiana, and Mississippi are the worst offenders. Last year there were eight cases in Alabama, sixteen in Georgia, twenty in Louisiana, and twenty in Mississippi – over one-half the total. This year to date there have been nine in Alabama, twelve in Georgia, eleven in Louisiana, and thirteen in Mississippi – again more than one-half the total number in the whole United States. – Chicago *Tribune.*

It must be that the increase comes of the inborn human instinct to imitate – that and man's commonest weakness, his aversion to being unpleasantly conspicuous, pointed at, shunned, as being on the unpopular side. Its other name is Moral Cowardice, and is the commanding feature of the make-up of 9,999 men in the 10,000. I am not offering this as a discovery; privately the dullest of us knows it to be true. History will not allow us to forget or ignore this supreme trait of our character. It persistently and sardonically reminds us that from the beginning of the world no revolt against a public infamy or oppression has ever been begun but by the one daring man in the 10,000, the rest timidly waiting, and slowly and reluctantly joining, under the influence of that man and his fellows from the other ten thousands. The abolitionists remember. Privately the public feeling was with them early, but each man was afraid to speak out until he got some hint that his neighbor was privately feeling as he privately felt himself. Then the boom followed. It always does. It will occur in New York, some day; and even in Pennsylvania.

It has been supposed – and said – that the people at a lynching enjoy the spectacle and are glad of a chance to see it. It cannot be true; all experience is against it. The people in the South are made like the people in the North – the vast majority of whom are right-hearted and compassionate, and would be cruelly pained by such a spectacle – and *would attend it*, and let on to be pleased with it, if the public approval seemed to require it. We are made like that, and we cannot help it. The other animals are not so, but we cannot help that, either. They lack the Moral Sense; we have no way of trading ours off, for a nickel or some other thing above its value. The Moral Sense teaches us what is right, and how to avoid it – when unpopular.

It is thought, as I have said, that a lynching crowd enjoys a lynching. It certainly is not true; it is impossible of belief. It is freely asserted – you have seen it in print many times of late – that the lynching impulse has been misinterpreted; that it is *not* the outcome of a spirit of revenge, but of a "mere atrocious hunger *to look upon human suffering.*" If that were so, the crowds that saw the Windsor Hotel burn down would have enjoyed the horrors that fell under their eyes. Did they? No one will think that of them, no one will make that charge. Many risked their lives to save the men and women who were in peril. Why did they do that? Because *none would disapprove.* There was no restraint; they could follow their natural impulse. Why does a crowd of the same kind of people in Texas, Colorado, Indiana, stand by, smitten to the heart and miserable, and by ostentatious outward signs pretend to enjoy a lynching? Why does it lift no hand or voice in protest? Only because it would be unpopular to do it, I think; each man is afraid of his neighbor's disapproval – a thing which, to the general run of the race, is more dreaded than wounds and death. When there is to be a lynching the people hitch up and come miles to see it, bringing their wives and children. Really to see it? No – they come only because they are afraid to stay at home, lest it be noticed and offensively commented upon. We may believe this, for we all know how *we* feel about such spectacles – also, how we would act under the like pressure. We are not any better nor any braver than anybody else, and we must not try to creep out of it.

A Savonarola can quell and scatter a mob of lynchers with a mere glance of his eye: so can a Merrill* or a Beloat.† For no mob has any sand in the presence of a man known to be splendidly

* Sheriff of Carroll County, Georgia.

† Sheriff, Princeton, Indiana. By that formidable power which lies in an established reputation, for cold pluck they faced lynching mobs and securely held the field against them.

brave. Besides, a lynching mob would *like* to be scattered, for of a certainty there are never ten men in it who would not prefer to be somewhere else – and would be, if they but had the courage to go. When I was a boy I saw a brave gentleman deride and insult a mob and drive it away; and afterward, in Nevada, I saw a noted desperado make two hundred men sit still, with the house burning under them, until he gave them permission to retire. A plucky man can rob a whole passenger train by himself; and the half of a brave man can hold up a stagecoach and strip its occupants.

Then perhaps the remedy for lynchings comes to this: station a brave man in each affected community to encourage, support, and bring to light the deep disapproval of lynching hidden in the secret places of its heart – for it is there, beyond question. Then those communities will find something better to imitate – of course, being human, they must imitate something. Where shall these brave men be found? That is indeed a difficulty; there are not three hundred of them in the earth. If merely *physically* brave men would do, then it were easy; they could be furnished by the cargo. When Hobson called for seven volunteers to go with him to what promised to be certain death, four thousand men responded – the whole fleet, in fact. Because *all the world would approve.* They knew that; but if Hobson's project had been charged with the scoffs and jeers of the friends and associates, whose good opinion and approval the sailors valued, he could not have got his seven.

No, upon reflection, the scheme will not work. There are not enough morally brave men in stock. We are out of moral-courage material; we are in a condition of profound poverty. We have those two sheriffs down South who – but never mind, it is not enough to go around; they have to stay and take care of their own communities.

But if we only *could* have three or four more sheriffs of that great breed! Would it help? I think so. For we are all imitators: other brave sheriffs would follow; to be a dauntless sheriff would come to be recognized as the correct and only thing, and the dreaded disapproval would fall to the share of the other kind; courage in this office would become custom, the absence of it a dishonor, just as courage presently replaces the timidity of the new soldier; then the mobs and the lynchings would disappear, and –

However. It can never be done without some starters, and where are we to get the starters? Advertise? Very well, then, let us advertise.

In the meantime, there is another plan. Let us import American missionaries from China, and send them into the lynching field. With 1,511 of them out there converting two Chinamen apiece per annum against an uphill birth rate of 33,000 pagans per day,* it will take upward of a million years to make the conversions balance the output and bring the Christianizing of the country in sight to the naked eye; therefore, if we can offer our missionaries as rich a field at home at lighter expense and quite satisfactory in the matter of danger, why shouldn't they find it fair and right to come back and give us a trial? The Chinese are universally conceded to be excellent people, honest, honorable, industrious, trustworthy, kind-hearted, and all that – leave them alone, they are plenty good enough just as they are; and besides, almost every convert runs a risk of catching our civilization. We ought to be careful. We ought to think twice before we encourage a risk like that; for, *once civilized, China can never be uncivilized again.* We have not been thinking of that. Very well, we ought to think of it now. Our missionaries will find that we have a field for them – and not only for the 1,511, but for 15,011. Let them look at the following telegram and see if they have anything in China that is more appetizing. It is from Texas:

> The negro was taken to a tree and swung in the air. Wood and fodder were piled beneath his body and a hot fire was made. *Then it was suggested that the man ought not to die too quickly, and he was let down to the ground while a party went to Dexter, about two miles distant, to procure coal oil.* This was thrown on the flames and the work completed.

We implore them to come back and help us in our need. Patriotism imposes this duty on them. Our country is worse off than China; they are our countrymen, their motherland supplicates their aid in this her hour of deep distress. They are competent; our people are not. They are used to scoffs, sneers, revilings, danger; our people are not. They have the martyr spirit; nothing but the martyr spirit can brave a lynching mob, and cow it and scatter it. They can save their country, we beseech them to come home and

---

* These figures are not fanciful; all of them are genuine and authentic. They are from official missionary records in China. See Doctor Morrison's book on his pedestrian journey across China; he quotes them and gives his authorities. For several years he has been the London *Times*'s representative in Peking, and was there through the siege.

do it. We ask them to read that telegram again, and yet again, and picture the scene in their minds, and soberly ponder it; then multiply it by 115, add 88; place the 203 in a row, allowing 600 feet of space for each human torch, so that there may be viewing room around it for 5,000 Christian American men, women, and children, youths and maidens; make it night, for grim effect; have the show in a gradually rising plain, and let the course of the stakes be uphill; the eye can then take in the whole line of twenty-four miles of blood-and-flesh bonfires unbroken, whereas if it occupied level ground the ends of the line would bend down and be hidden from view by the curvature of the earth. All being ready, now, and the darkness opaque, the stillness impressive – for there should be no sound but the soft moaning of the night wind and the muffled sobbing of the sacrifices – let all the far stretch of kerosened pyres be touched off simultaneously and the glare and the shrieks and the agonies burst heavenward to the Throne.

There are more than a million persons present; the light from the fires flushes into vague outline against the night the spires of five thousand churches. O kind missionary, O compassionate missionary, leave China! come home and convert these Christians!

I believe that if anything can stop this epidemic of bloody insanities it is martial personalities that can face mobs without flinching; and as such personalities are developed only by familiarity with danger and by the training and seasoning which come of resisting it, the likeliest place to find them must be among the missionaries who have been under tuition in China during the past year or two. We have abundance of work for them, and for hundreds and thousands more, and the field is daily growing and spreading. Shall we find them? We can try. In 75,000,000 there must be other Merrills and Beloats; and it is the law of our make that each example shall wake up drowsing chevaliers of the same great knighthood and bring them to the front.

August 1901

WHY NOT ABOLISH IT?

WE HAVE MANY good laws. They embody the wisdom and the common sense of the ages. There is one very striking feature about these laws. Let me point it out. Among them –

1. There is not a law which says that if you consent to the robbery of your family, the robber's crime is reduced to a mere impropriety by that consent.

2. There is not a law which says that if you consent to the burning of your father's house, the incendiary's crime is reduced to a mere impropriety by that consent.

3. There is not a law which says that if you consent to let a man starve your mother to death, that man's crime is reduced to a mere impropriety by that consent.

4. There is not a law which says that if you consent to let an assassin cut your throat, the assassin's crime is reduced to a mere impropriety by that consent.

It is strange, but these statements are true. The law does not grant you the tremendous privilege of propagating, inviting, and encouraging crime by your caprice, and of minimizing the responsibility of its perpetrators by the interposition of your royal consent. The law sticks stubbornly to the position that robbers, incendiaries, and murderers are criminals, no matter who are the victims; and it would not concede that they were criminals in a lesser degree in cases where you or your kin were the victims, and you gave your personal consent.

But there is one crime which is more disastrous than all of these put together; more bitter, more cruel, more infamous, more shameful, more insupportable, more far-reaching, more diffusive in its crushing effects, than all of those combined – and over the perpetrator of this one crime the law holds the protecting shield of its mercy and its compassion.

A murder kills the body, but sets it free and ends its cares; it brings grief to the surviving kindred, but it is a grief which time can soften, and even heal. But this other crime, this crime of crimes, kills the mental and spiritual life of its victim, but leaves its body to drag on and on, the symbol and sufferer of a living death, despised of kindred, forsaken of friends; and upon family and friends descends a blight of humiliation which time cannot remove nor forgetfulness ease of its pain.

The law is stern with the assassin, but gentle with the seducer; stern with the murderer of the body, but gentle with the murderer of all that can make life worth the living – honor, self-respect, the esteem of friends, the adoring worship of the sacred home circle, father, mother, and the cradle-mates of the earlier and innocent years. You may drag down into the mud and into enduring misery and shame the trusting and ignorant young flower of this household, and crush the heart of every creature that loves it and lives in the light of its presence; you may murder the spirit and consign to a living death and intolerable wretchedness all these – and if in certain cases you can prove *consent* the law will not deal unkindly with you.

"Consent" necessarily argues previous persuasion. It indicates who the instigator of the trespass was – that is to say, the offender-in-chief. Instead of magnifying his crime, this actually diminishes it, in the eyes of the law. The law establishes an "age of consent" – a limit during which a child of sixteen or seventeen is not privileged to help commit a tremendous and desolating crime against herself and her family; but she is privileged to do it if she is twenty; and in that case the person that persuades her to it is regarded by the law as being substantially guiltless, and it puts upon him no punishment which can be called by that name except sarcastically.

There is *no* age at which the good name of a member of a family ceases to be a part of the *property* of that family – an asset, and worth more than all its bonds and moneys. There is no age at which a member of the family may by consent, and under authority of the law, help a criminal to destroy the family's money and bonds. Then why should there be an age at which a member, by consent, and under connivance of the law, may help a criminal to destroy that far more valuable asset, the family's honor?

There being no age at which the law places the lives of a family in the hands of any member of it to throw away at his whim – including his own life – I see no sound reason why the law should not be consistent – consistently wise – and abolish the age limit in the case of the other and greater crime.

If a man and wife are drowned at sea, and there is no proof as to which died first, the law – in some European countries and in two of our States – decides that it was the wife. She is the weaker vessel. It is usually so in the matter of seduction. She is young, inexperienced, foolish, trustful, persuadable, affectionate; she would harm no one herself, and cannot see why any one should wish to harm her; while as a rule the man is older and stronger than she is, and in every case without exception is a scoundrel. The law protects him now; it seems to me that it ought to protect her, instead.

I think it ought to abolish "consent" – entirely. I think it should say there is *no* age at which consent shall in the least degree modify the seducer's crime or mitigate its punishment. "Consent" means previous persuasion – and there the crime *begins*. It is the first step, and responsible for the whole, for without it there would be no second. I would punish the beginner, the real criminal, and punish him well; society and civilization can be depended upon to punish with a ten thousand times exaggerated and unjust severity his thoughtless victim. If I were a law-maker I should want to make this law quite plain.

I should want it to say nothing about "consent" – I should take the persuasion for granted, and that *persuasion* is what I would punish, along with the resulting infamy. I should say simply that commerce *with a spinster*, of whatever age or condition, should be punished by two years of solitary confinement or five years at hard labor; and let the man take his choice. He has murdered the honor and the happiness of a whole unoffending family, and condemned it to life-long shame and grief, and while he ought to be flayed alive, and the law ought of rights to provide that penalty, I know that no jury would vote it; I could not do it myself, unless mine were the family. And so I would make the penalty as above. A jury would vote that, for the judge would be thoughtful enough to appoint upon it none but fathers of families – families with young girls in them, the treasures of their lives, the light of their homes, the joy of their hearts.

I find the following in this morning's *Herald*. Will you print it?

> Rosie Quinn, who was convicted of murder in the second degree on April 8, for drowning her baby in the lake in Central Park, will be sentenced by Judge Scott to-day in the Criminal Branch of the Supreme Court. Only one sentence, that of life imprisonment, may be imposed, and, although her counsel, Moses A. Sachs, will ask for a new trial, it is not probable it will be granted.
>
> The girl dreads her appearance in the court-room. She spoke of this yesterday with even more horror than that which the idea of a life sentence has aroused in her mind.
>
> She has written to the father of the dead child, but has

received no response. "I don't know what he can be thinking of," is her only comment.

Not even his name has been told to the persons who have approached Rosie Quinn in connection with her trial. She is loyal in this.

For her sisters, who have not been near her since her arrest in November, she displays a surprising thoughtfulness.

"Don't put my sisters' names in the paper," she begged. "I don't want their names used. I didn't even want it known that I had sisters, but it got out somehow." Since her conviction, one of her sisters has called at the prison to caution her against telling their names.

The girl is a most pitiable creature. She seems crazed by the happenings of the last few weeks, and is utterly unable to comprehend the enormity of her crime, or the hopelessness of the doom which is hanging over her. She is like a child, docile, quiet, undemonstrative. She will only say: –

"It was a dear love-affair for me."

Immediately after her sentence persons who have become interested in the girl's sad fate will appeal to Governor Odell in her behalf.

I think many of us will like to sign that petition.

May 2, 1903

"WAS THE WORLD MADE
FOR MAN?"

"Alfred Russell Wallace's revival of the theory that this earth is at the centre of the stellar universe, and is the only habitable globe, has aroused great interest in the world." – *Literary Digest.*

"For ourselves we do thoroughly believe that man, as he lives just here on this tiny earth, is in essence and possibilities the most sublime existence in all the range of non-divine being – the chief love and delight of God." – *Chicago "Interior,"* (Presb.)

I SEEM TO be the only scientist and theologian still remaining to be heard from on this important matter of whether the world was made for man or not. I feel that it is time for me to speak.

I stand almost with the others. They believe the world was made for man, I believe it likely that it was made for man; they think there is proof, astronomical mainly, that it was made for man, I think there is evidence only, not proof, that it was made for him. It is too early, yet, to arrange the verdict, the returns are not all in. When they are all in, I think they will show that the world was made for man; but we must not hurry, we must patiently wait till they are all in.

Now as far as we have got, astronomy is on our side. Mr. Wallace has clearly shown this. He has clearly shown two things: that the world was made for man, and that the universe was made for the world – to stiddy it, you know. The astronomy part is settled, and cannot be challenged.

We come now to the geological part. This is the one where the evidence is not all in, yet. It is coming in, hourly, daily, coming in all the time, but naturally it comes with geological carefulness and deliberation, and we must not be impatient, we must not get excited, we must be calm, and wait. To lose our tranquillity will not hurry geology; nothing hurries geology.

It takes a long time to prepare a world for man, such a thing is not done in a day. Some of the great scientists, carefully ciphering the evidences furnished by geology, have arrived at the conviction that our world is prodigiously old, and they may be right, but Lord Kelvin is not of their opinion. He takes a cautious, conservative view, in order to be on the safe side, and feels sure it is not so old as they think. As Lord Kelvin is the highest authority in science now living, I think we must yield to him and accept his view. He does not concede that the world is more than a hundred million years old. He believes it is that old, but not older. Lyell believed that our race was introduced into the world 31,000 years ago, Herbert Spencer makes it 32,000. Lord Kelvin agrees with Spencer.

Very well. According to these figures it took 99,968,000 years to prepare the world for man, impatient as the Creator doubtless was to see him and admire him. But a large enterprise like this has to be conducted warily, painstakingly, logically. It was foreseen that man would have to have the oyster. Therefore the first preparation was made for the oyster. Very well, you cannot make an oyster out of whole cloth, you must make the oyster's ancestor first. This is not done in a day. You must make a vast variety of invertebrates, to start with – belemnites, trilobites, jebusites, amalekites, and that sort of fry, and put them to soak in a primary sea, and wait and see what will happen. Some will be a disappointment – the belemnites, the ammonites and such; they will be failures, they will die out and become extinct, in the course of the 19,000,000 years covered by the experiment, but all is not lost, for the amalekites will fetch the home-stake; they will develop gradually into encrinites, and stalactites, and blatherskites, and one thing and another as the mighty ages creep on and the Archaean and the Cambrian Periods pile their lofty crags in the primordial seas, and at last the first grand stage in the preparation of the world for man stands completed, the Oyster is done. An oyster has hardly any more reasoning power than a scientist has; and so it is reasonably certain that this one jumped to the conclusion that the nineteen-million years was *a* preparation for *him*; but that would be just like an oyster, which is the most conceited animal there is, except man. And anyway, this one could not know, at that early date, that he was only an incident in a scheme, and that there was some more to the scheme, yet.

The oyster being achieved, the next thing to be arranged for in the preparation of the world for man, was fish. Fish, and coal – to fry it with. So the Old Silurian seas were opened up to breed the fish in, and at the same time the great work of building Old Red Sandstone mountains 80,000 feet high to cold-storage their fossils in was begun. This latter was quite indispensable, for there would be no end of failures again, no end of extinctions – millions of them – and it would be cheaper and less trouble to can them in the rocks than keep tally of them in a book. One does not build the coal beds and 80,000 feet of perpendicular Old Red Sandstone in a brief time – no, it took twenty million years. In the first place, a coal bed is a slow and troublesome and tiresome thing to construct. You have to grow prodigious forests of tree-ferns and reeds and calamites and such things in a marshy region; then you have to sink them under out of sight and let them rot; then you have to turn the streams on them, so as to bury them under several feet of sediment, and the sediment must have time to harden and turn to rock; next you must grow another forest on top, then sink it and put on another layer of sediment and harden it; then more forest and more rock, layer upon layer, three miles deep – ah, indeed it is a sickening slow job to build a coal-measure and do it right!

So the millions of years drag on; and meantime the fish-culture is lazying along and frazzling out in a way to make a person tired. You have developed ten thousand kinds of fishes from the oyster; and come to look, you have raised nothing but fossils, nothing but extinctions. There is nothing left alive and progressive but a ganoid or two and perhaps half a dozen asteroids. Even the cat wouldn't eat such.

Still, it is no great matter; there is plenty of time, yet, and they will develop into something tasty before man is ready for them. Even a ganoid can be depended on for that, when he is not going to be called on for sixty million years.

The Palaeozoic time-limit having now been reached, it was necessary to begin the next stage in the preparation of the world for man, by opening up the Mesozoic Age and instituting some reptiles. For man would need reptiles. Not to eat, but to develop himself from. This being the most important detail of the scheme, a spacious liberality of time was set apart for it – thirty million years. What wonders followed! From the remaining ganoids and asteroids and alkaloids were developed by slow and steady and pains-taking culture those stupendous saurians that used to prowl about the steamy world in those remote ages, with their snaky heads reared forty feet in the air and sixty feet of body and tail racing and thrashing after. All gone, now, alas – all extinct, except the little handful of Arkansawrians left stranded and lonely with us here upon this far-flung verge and fringe of time.

Yes, it took thirty million years and twenty million reptiles to get one that would stick long enough to develop into something else and let the scheme proceed to the next step.

Then the Pterodactyl burst upon the world in all his impressive solemnity and grandeur, and all Nature recognized that the Cainozoic threshold was crossed and a new Period open for business, a new stage begun in the preparation of the globe for man. It may be that the Pterodactyl thought the thirty million years had been intended as a preparation for himself, for there was nothing too foolish for a Pterodactyl to imagine, but he was in error, the preparation was for man. Without doubt the Pterodactyl attracted great attention, for even the least observant could see that there was the making of a bird in him. And so it turned out. Also the makings of a mammal, in time. One thing we have to say to his credit, that in the matter of picturesqueness he was the triumph of his Period; he wore wings and had teeth, and was a starchy and wonderful mixture altogether, a kind of long-distance premonitory symptom of Kipling's marine:

> 'E isn't one o' the reg'lar Line, nor 'e isn't one of the crew,
> 'E's a kind of a giddy harumfrodite – soldier an' sailor too!

From this time onward for nearly another thirty million years the preparation moved briskly. From the Pterodactyl was developed the bird; from the bird the kangaroo, from the kangaroo the other marsupials; from these the mastodon, the megatherium, the giant sloth, the Irish elk, and all that crowd that you make useful and instructive fossils out of – then came the first great Ice Sheet, and they all retreated before it and crossed over the bridge at Behring's strait and wandered around over Europe and Asia and died. All except a few, to carry on the preparation with. Six Glacial Periods with two million years between Periods chased these poor orphans up and down and about the earth, from weather to weather – from tropic swelter at the poles to Arctic frost at the equator and back again and to and fro, they never knowing what kind of weather was going to turn up next; and if ever they settled down anywhere the whole continent suddenly sank under them without the least notice and they had to trade places with the fishes and scramble off to where the seas had been, and scarcely a dry rag on them; and when there was nothing else doing a volcano would let go and fire them out from wherever they had located. They led this unsettled and irritating life for twenty-five million years, half the time afloat, half the time aground, and always wondering what it was all for, they never suspecting, of course, that it was a preparation for man and had to be done just so or it wouldn't be any proper and harmonious place for him when he arrived.

And at last came the monkey, and anybody could see that man wasn't far off, now. And in truth that was so. The monkey went on developing for close upon 5,000,000 years, and then turned into a man – to all appearances.

Such is the history of it. Man has been here 32,000 years. That it took a hundred million years to prepare the world for him is proof that that is what it was done for. I suppose it is. I dunno. If the Eiffel tower were now representing the world's age, the skin of paint on the pinnacle-knob at its summit would represent man's share of that age; and anybody would perceive that that skin was what the tower was built for. I reckon they would, I dunno.

1903

ITALIAN WITHOUT A MASTER

IT IS ALMOST a fortnight now that I am domiciled in a mediæval villa in the country, a mile or two from Florence. I cannot speak the language; I am too old now to learn how, also too busy when I am busy, and too indolent when I am not; wherefore some will imagine that I am having a dull time of it. But it is not so. The "help" are all natives; they talk Italian to me, I answer in English; I do not understand them, they do not understand me, consequently no harm is done, and everybody is satisfied. In order to be just and fair, I throw in an Italian word when I have one, and this has a good influence. I get the word out of the morning paper. I have to use it while it is fresh, for I find that Italian words do not keep in this climate. They fade toward night, and next morning they are gone. But it is no matter; I get a new one out of the paper before breakfast, and thrill the domestics with it while it lasts. I have no dictionary, and I do not want one; I can select my words by the sound, or by orthographic aspect. Many of them have a French or German or English look, and these are the ones I enslave for the day's service. That is, as a rule. Not always. If I find a learnable phrase that has an imposing look and warbles musically along I do not care to know the meaning of it; I pay it out to the first applicant, knowing that if I pronounce it carefully *he* will understand it, and that's enough.

Yesterday's word was *avanti*. It sounds Shakespearian, and probably means Avaunt and quit my sight. To-day I have a whole phrase: *sono dispiacentissimo*. I do not know what it means, but it seems to fit in everywhere and give satisfaction. Although as a rule my words and phrases are good for one day and train only, I have several that stay by me all the time, for some unknown reason, and these come very handy when I get into a long conversation and need things to fire up with in monotonous stretches. One of the best ones is *Dov' è il gatto*. It nearly always produces a pleasant surprise, therefore I save it up for places where I want to express applause or admiration. The fourth word has a French sound, and I think the phrase means "that takes the cake."

During my first week in the deep and dreamy stillness of this woodsy and flowery place I was without news of the outside world, and was well content without it. It had been four weeks since I had seen a newspaper, and this lack seemed to give life a new charm and grace, and to saturate it with a feeling verging upon actual delight. Then came a change that was to be expected: the appetite for news began to rise again, after this invigorating rest. I had to feed it, but I was not willing to let it make me its helpless slave again; I determined to put it on a diet, and a strict and limited one. So I examined an Italian paper, with the idea of feeding it on that, and on that exclusively. On that exclusively, and without help of a dictionary. In this way I should surely be well protected against overloading and indigestion.

A glance at the telegraphic page filled me with encouragement. There were no scare-heads. That was good – supremely good. But there were headings – one-liners and two-liners – and that was good too; for without these, one must do as one does with a German paper – pay out precious time in finding out what an article is about, only to discover, in many cases, that there is nothing in it of interest to you. The headline is a valuable thing.

Necessarily we are all fond of murders, scandals, swindles, robberies, explosions, collisions, and all such things, when we know the people, and when they are neighbors and friends, but when they are strangers we do not get any great pleasure out of them, as a rule. Now the trouble with an American paper is that it has no discrimination; it rakes the whole earth for blood and garbage, and the result is that you are daily overfed and suffer a surfeit. By habit you stow this muck every day, but you come by and by to take no vital interest in it – indeed, you almost get tired of it. As a rule, forty-nine-fiftieths of it concerns strangers only – people away off yonder, a thousand miles, two thousand miles, ten thousand miles from where you are. Why, when you come to think of it, who cares what becomes of those people? I would not give the assassination of one personal friend for a whole massacre of those others. And, to my mind, one relative or neighbor mixed up in a scandal is more interesting than a whole Sodom and Gomorrah of outlanders gone rotten. Give me the home product every time.

Very well. I saw at a glance that the Florentine paper would suit me: five out of six of its scandals and tragedies were local; they were adventures of one's very neighbors, one might almost say one's friends. In the matter of world news there was not too much, but just about enough. I subscribed. I have had no occasion to regret it. Every morning I get all the news I need for the day; sometimes from the headlines, sometimes from the text. I have never had to call for a dictionary yet. I read the paper with ease. Often I do not quite understand, often some of the details escape me, but no matter, I get the idea. I will cut out a passage or two, then you will see how limpid the language is:

The first line means that the Italian sovereigns are coming back – they have been to England. The second line seems to mean that they enlarged the King at the Italian hospital. With a banquet, I suppose. An English banquet has that effect. Further:

Il ritorno dei Sovrani
a Roma

ROMA, 24, ore 22,50. - I Sovrani e le Principessine Reali si attendono a Roma domani alle ore 15,51.

Return of the sovereigns to Rome, you see. Date of the telegram, Rome, November 24, ten minutes before twenty-three o'clock. The telegram seems to say, "The Sovereigns and the Royal Children expect themselves at Rome tomorrow at fifty-one minutes after fifteen o'clock."

I do not know about Italian time, but I judge it begins at midnight and runs through the twenty-four hours without breaking bulk. In the following ad. the theatres open at half past twenty. If these are not matinées, 20.30 must mean 8.30 P.M., by my reckoning.

> **Spettacoli del di 25**
>
> TEATRO DELLA PERGOLA — (Ore 20,30)
>   — Opera : *Bohème.*
> TEATRO ALFIERI. — Compagnia dram-
>   matica Drago — (Ore 20,30) — *La Legge.*
> ALHAMBRA — (Ore 20,30) — Spettacolo
>   variato.
> SALA EDISON — Grandioso spettacolo
>   Cinematografico: *Quo-Vadis?* — Inau-
>   gurazione della Chiesa Russa — In coda
>   al Direttissimo — Vedute di Firenze con
>   gran movimento — America: Trasporto
>   tronchi giganteschi — I ladri in casa del
>   Diavolo — Scene comiche.
> CINEMATOGRAFO — Via Brunelleschi n. 4.
>   — Programma straordinario, *Don Chi-*
>   *sciotte* — Prezzi popolari.

The whole of that is intelligible to me – and sane and rational, too – except the remark about the Inauguration of a Russian Cheese. That one oversizes my hand. Gimme five cards.

This is a four-page paper; and as it is set in long primer leaded and has a page of advertisements, there is no room for the crimes, disasters, and general sweepings of the outside world – thanks be! To-day I find only a single importation of the off-color sort:

> **Una principessa**
> che fugge con un cocchiere
> PARIGI, 24. - Il *Matin* ha da Berlino
> che la principessa Schovenbare-Waldenbure
> scomparve il 9 novembre. Sarebbe partita
> col suo cocchiere.
> La Principessa ha 27 anni.

Twenty-seven years old, and scomparve – scampered – on the 9th November. You see by the added detail that she departed with her coachman. I hope Sarebbe has not made a mistake, but I am afraid the chances are that she has. *Sono dispiacentissimo.*

There are several fires; also a couple of accidents. This is one of them:

> **Grave disgrazia sul Ponte Vecchio**
>
> Stamattina, circa le 7,30, mentre Giuseppe Sciatti, di anni 55, di Casellina e Torri, passava dal Ponte Vecchio, stando seduto sopra un barroccio carico di verdura, perse l' equilibrio e cadde al suolo, rimanendo con la gamba destra sotto una ruota del veicolo.
>
> Lo Sciatti fu subito raccolto da alcuni cittadini, che, per mezzo della pubblica vettura n. 365, lo trasportarono a San Giovanni di Dio.
>
> Ivi il medico di guardia gli riscontrò la frattura della gamba destra e alcune lievi escoriazioni giudicandolo guaribile in 50 giorni salvo complicazioni.

What it seems to say is this: "Serious Disgrace on the Old Old Bridge. This morning about 7.30, Mr. Joseph Sciatti, aged 55, of Casellina and Torri, while standing up in a sitting posture on top of a carico barrow of verdure (foliage? hay? vegetables?), lost his equilibrium and fell on himself, arriving with his left leg under one of the wheels of the vehicle.

"Said Sciatti was suddenly harvested (gathered in?) by several citizens, who by means of public cab No. 365 transported him to St. John of God."

Paragraph No. 3 is a little obscure, but I think it says that the medico set the broken left leg – right enough, since there was nothing the matter with the other one – and that several are encouraged to hope that fifty days will fetch him around in quite giudicandolo-guaribile way, if no complications intervene.

I am sure I hope so myself.

There is a great and peculiar charm about reading news-scraps in a language which you are not acquainted with – the charm that always goes with the mysterious and the uncertain. You can never be absolutely sure of the meaning of anything you read in such circumstances; you are chasing an alert and gamy riddle all the time, and the baffling turns and dodges of the prey make the life of the hunt. A dictionary would spoil it. Sometimes a single word of doubtful purport will cast a veil of dreamy and golden uncertainty over a whole paragraph of cold and practical certainties, and leave steeped in a haunting and adorable mystery an incident which had been vulgar and commonplace but for that benefaction. Would you be wise to draw a dictionary on that gracious word? would you be properly grateful?

After a couple of days' rest I now come back to my subject and seek a case in point. I find it without trouble, in the morning paper; a cablegram from Chicago and Indiana by way of Paris. All the words save one are guessable by a person ignorant of Italian:

> **Revolverate in teatro**
>
> PARIGI, 27. - La *Patrie* ha da Chicago:
> Il guardiano del teatro dell'opera di Wallace (Indiana), avendo voluto espellere uno spettatore che continuava a fumare malgrado il divieto, questo spalleggiato dai suoi amici tirò diversi colpi di rivoltella. Il guardiano rispose. Nacque una scarica generale. Grande panico fra gli spettatori. Nessun ferito.

Translation. – "REVOLVERATION IN THEATRE. *Paris. 27th. La Patrie* has from Chicago: The cop of the theatre of the opera of Wallace, Indiana, had willed to expel a spectator which continued to smoke in spite of the prohibition, who, spalleggiato by his friends, tirò (Fr. *tiré*, Anglice *pulled*) manifold revolver-shots. The cop responded. Result, a general scare; great panic among the spectators. Nobody hurt."

It is bettable that that harmless cataclysm in the theatre of the opera of Wallace, Indiana, excited not a person in Europe but me, and so came near to not being worth cabling to Florence by way of France. But it does excite me. It excites me because I cannot make out, for sure, what it was that moved that spectator to resist the officer. I was gliding along smoothly and without obstruction or accident, until I came to that word spalleggiato, then the bottom fell out. You notice what a rich gloom, what a sombre and pervading mystery, that word sheds all over the whole Wallachian tragedy. That is the charm of the thing, that is the delight of it. This is where you begin, this is where you revel. You can guess and guess, and have all the fun you like; you need not be afraid there will be an end to it; none is possible, for no amount of guessing will ever furnish you a meaning for that word that you can be sure is the right one. All the other words give you hints, by their form, their sound, or their spelling – this one doesn't, this one throws out no hints, this one keeps its secret. If there is even the slightest slight shadow of a hint anywhere, it lies in the very meagerly suggestive fact that spalleggiato carries our word "egg" in its stomach. Well, make the most out of it, and then where are you at? You conjecture that the spectator which was smoking in spite of the prohibition and become reprohibited by the guardians, was "egged on" by his friends, and that it was owing to that evil influence that he initiated the revolveration in theatre that has galloped under the sea and come crashing through the European press without excitng anybody but me. But are you sure, are you dead sure, that that was the way of it? No. Then the uncertainty remains, the mystery abides, and with it the charm. Guess again.

If I had a phrase-book of a really satisfactory sort I would study it, and not give all my free time to undictionarial readngs, but there is no such work on the market. The existing phrase-books are inadequate. They are well enough as far as they go, but when you fall down and skin your leg they don't tell you what to say.

January 2, 1904

SAINT JOAN OF ARC

THE EVIDENCE FURNISHED at the Trials and Rehabilitation sets
forth Joan of Arc's strange and beautiful history in clear and
minute detail. Among all the multitude of biographies that freight
the shelves of the world's libraries, *this is the only one whose validity is
confirmed to us by oath.* It gives us a vivid picture of a career and a
personality of so extraordinary a character that we are helped to
accept them as actualities by the very fact that both are beyond
the inventive reach of fiction. The public part of the career occupied only a mere breath of time – it covered but two years; but
what a career it was! The personality which made it possible is one
to be reverently studied, loved, and marvelled at, but not to be
wholly understood and accounted for by even the most searching
analysis.

In Joan of Arc at the age of sixteen there was no promise of a
romance. She lived in a dull little village on the frontiers of civilization; she had been nowhere and had seen nothing; she knew none
but simple shepherd folk; she had never seen a person of note; she
hardly knew what a soldier looked like; she had never ridden a
horse, nor had a warlike weapon in her hand; she could neither
read nor write: she could spin and sew; she knew her catechism
and her prayers and the fabulous histories of the saints, and this
was all her learning. That was Joan at sixteen. What did she know
of law? of evidence? of courts? of the attorney's trade? of legal procedure? Nothing. Less than nothing. Thus exhaustively equipped
with ignorance, she went before the court at Toul to contest a false-
charge of breach of promise of marriage; she conducted her cause
herself, without any one's help or advice or any one's friendly
sympathy, and won it. She called no witnesses of her own, but

NOTE. – The Official Record of the Trials and Rehabilitation of Joan of Arc is the
most remarkable history that exists in any language; yet there are few people in the
world who can say they have read it: in England and America it has hardly been
heard of.

Three hundred years ago Shakespeare did not know the true story of Joan of
Arc; in his day it was unknown even in France. For four hundred years it existed
rather as a vaguely defined romance than as definite and authentic history. The
true story remained buried in the official archives of France from the Rehabilitation
of 1456 until Quicherat dug it out and gave it to the world two generations ago, in
lucid and understandable modern French. It is a deeply fascinating story. But only
in the Official Trials and Rehabilitation can it be found in its entirety. – M. T.

vanquished the prosecution by using with deadly effectiveness its own testimony. The astonished judge threw the case out of court, and spoke of her as "this marvellous child."

She went to the veteran Commandant of Vaucouleurs and demanded an escort of soldiers, saying she must march to the help of the King of France, since she was commissioned of God to win back his lost kingdom for him and set the crown upon his head. The Commandant said, "What, you? you are only a child." And he advised that she be taken back to her village and have her ears boxed. But she said she must obey God, and would come again, and again, and yet again, and finally she would get the soldiers. She said truly. In time he yielded, after months of delay and refusal, and gave her the soldiers; and took off his sword and gave her that, and said, "Go – and let come what may." She made her long and perilous journey through the enemy's country, and spoke with the King, and convinced him. Then she was summoned before the University of Poitiers to prove that she *was* commissioned of God and not of Satan, and daily during three weeks she sat before that learned congress unafraid, and capably answered their deep questions out of her ignorant but able head and her simple and honest heart; and again she won her case, and with it the wondering admiration of all that august company.

And now, aged seventeen, she was made Commander-in-Chief, with a prince of the royal house and the veteran generals of France for subordinates; and at the head of the first army she had ever seen, she marched to Orleans, carried the commanding fortresses of the enemy by storm in three desperate assaults, and in ten days raised a siege which had defied the might of France for seven months.

After a tedious and insane delay caused by the King's instability of character and the treacherous counsels of his ministers, she got permission to take the field again. She took Jargeau by storm; then Meung; she forced Beaugency to surrender; then – in the open field – she won the memorable victory of Patay against Talbot "the English lion," and broke the back of the Hundred Years' War. It was a campaign which cost but seven weeks of time; yet the political results would have been cheap if the time expended had been fifty years. Patay, that unsung and now long-forgotten battle, was the Moscow of the English power in France; from the blow struck that day it was destined never to recover. It was the beginning of

the end of an alien dominion which had ridden France intermit-
tently for three hundred years.

Then followed the great campaign of the Loire, the capture of
Troyes by assault, and the triumphal march past surrendering
towns and fortresses to Rheims, where Joan put the crown upon
her King's head in the Cathedral, amid wild public rejoicings, and
with her old peasant father there to see these things and believe
his eyes if he could. She had restored the crown and the lost sovereignty; the King was grateful for once in his shabby poor life, and
asked her to name her reward and have it. She asked for nothing
for herself, but begged that the taxes of her native village might be
remitted forever. The prayer was granted, and the promise kept
for three hundred and sixty years. Then it was broken, and remains
broken to-day. France was very poor then, she is very rich now; but
she has been collecting those taxes for more than a hundred years.

Joan asked one other favor: that now that her mission was fulfilled she might be allowed to go back to her village and take up
her humble life again with her mother and the friends of her childhood; for she had no pleasure in the cruelties of war, and the sight
of blood and suffering wrung her heart. Sometimes in battle she
did not draw her sword, lest in the splendid madness of the onset
she might forget herself and take an enemy's life with it. In the
Rouen Trials, one of her quaintest speeches – coming from the
gentle and girlish source it did – was her naïve remark that she had
"never killed any one." Her prayer for leave to go back to the rest
and peace of her village home was not granted.

Then she wanted to march at once upon Paris, take it, and drive
the English out of France. She was hampered in all the ways that
treachery and the King's vacillation could devise, but she forced
her way to Paris at last, and fell badly wounded in a successful
assault upon one of the gates. Of course her men lost heart at once
– she was the only heart they had. They fell back. She begged to
be allowed to remain at the front, saying victory was sure. "I will
take Paris now or die!" she said. But she was removed from the
field by force; the King ordered a retreat, and actually disbanded
his army. In accordance with a beautiful old military custom Joan
devoted her silver armor and hung it up in the Cathedral of St.
Denis. Its great days were over.

Then, by command, she followed the King and his frivolous
court and endured a gilded captivity for a time, as well as her free
spirit could; and whenever inaction became unbearable she

gathered some men together and rode away and assaulted a stronghold and captured it.

At last in a sortie against the enemy, from Compiègne, on the 24th of May (when she was turned eighteen), she was herself captured, after a gallant fight. It was her last battle. She was to follow the drums no more.

Thus ended the briefest epoch-making military career known to history. It lasted only a year and a month, but it found France an English province, and furnishes the reason that France is France to-day and not an English province still. Thirteen months! It was indeed a short career; but in the centuries that have since elapsed five hundred millions of Frenchmen have lived and died blest by the benefactions it conferred; and so long as France shall endure, the mighty debt must grow. And France is grateful; we often hear her say it. Also thrifty: she collects the Domrémy taxes.

Joan was fated to spend the rest of her life behind bolts and bars. She was a prisoner of war, not a criminal, therefore hers was recognized as an honorable captivity. By the rules of war she must be held to ransom, and a fair price could not be refused if offered. John of Luxembourg paid her the just compliment of requiring a prince's ransom for her. In that day that phrase represented a definite sum – 61,125 francs. It was of course supposable that either the King or grateful France, or both, would fly with the money and set their fair young benefactor free. But this did not happen. In five and a half months neither King nor country stirred a hand nor offered a penny. Twice Joan tried to escape. Once by a trick she succeeded for a moment, and locked her jailer in behind her, but she was discovered and caught; in the other case she let herself down from a tower sixty feet high, but her rope was too short, and she got a fall that disabled her and she could not get away.

Finally, Cauchon, Bishop of Beauvais, paid the money and bought Joan – ostensibly for the Church, to be tried for wearing male attire and for other impieties, but really for the English, the enemy into whose hands the poor girl was so piteously anxious not to fall. She was now shut up in the dungeons of the Castle of Rouen and kept in an iron cage with her hands and feet and neck chained to a pillar; and from that time forth during all the months of her imprisonment, till the end, several rough English soldiers stood guard over her night and day – and not outside her room, but in it. It was a dreary and hideous captivity, but it did not conquer her: nothing could break that invincible spirit. From first to last she was a prisoner a year; and she spent the last three months of it on trial for her life before a formidable array of ecclesiastical judges, and disputing the ground with them foot by foot and inch by inch with brilliant generalship and dauntless pluck. The spectacle of that solitary girl, forlorn and friendless, without advocate or adviser, and without the help and guidance of any copy of the charges brought against her or rescript of the complex and voluminous daily proceedings of the court to modify the crushing strain upon her astonishing memory, fighting that long battle serene and undismayed against these colossal odds, stands alone in its pathos and its sublimity; it has nowhere its mate, either in the annals of fact or in the inventions of fiction.

And how fine and great were the things she daily said, how fresh and crisp – and she so worn in body, so starved, and tired, and harried! They run through the whole gamut of feeling and expression – from scorn and defiance, uttered with soldierly fire and frankness, all down the scale to wounded dignity clothed in words of noble pathos; as, when her patience was exhausted by the pestering delvings and gropings and searchings of her persecutors to find out what kind of devil's witchcraft she had employed to rouse the war spirit in her timid soldiers, she burst out with, "What I said was, '*Ride these English down*' – and I did it myself!" and as, when insultingly asked why it was that *her* standard had place at the crowning of the King in the Cathedral of Rheims rather than the standards of the other captains, she uttered that touching speech, *"It had borne the burden, it had earned the honor"* – a phrase which fell from her lips without premeditation, yet whose moving beauty and simple grace it would bankrupt the arts of language to surpass.

Although she was on trial for her life, she was the only witness called on either side; the only witness summoned to testify before a packed jury commissioned with a definite task: to find her guilty, whether she was guilty or not. She must be convicted out of her own mouth, there being no other way to accomplish it. Every advantage that learning has over ignorance, age over youth, experience over inexperience, chicane over artlessness, every trick and trap and gin devisable by malice and the cunning of sharp intellects practised in setting snares for the unwary – all these were employed against her without shame; and when these arts were one by one defeated by the marvellous intuitions of her alert and penetrating mind, Bishop Cauchon stooped to a final baseness which it degrades human speech to describe: a priest who pretended to come from the region of her own home and to be a pitying friend and anxious to help her in her sore need was smuggled into her cell, and he misused his sacred office to steal her confidence; she confided to him the things sealed from revealment by her Voices, and which her prosecutors had tried so long in vain to trick her into betraying. A concealed confederate set it all down and delivered it to Cauchon, who used Joan's secrets, thus obtained, for her ruin.

Throughout the Trials, whatever the foredoomed witness said was twisted from its true meaning when possible, and made to tell against her; and whenever an answer of hers was beyond the reach of twisting it was not allowed to go upon the record. It was upon one of these latter occasions that she uttered that pathetic reproach – to Cauchon: "Ah, you set down everything that is against me, but you will not set down what is for me."

That this untrained young creature's genius for war was wonderful, and her generalship worthy to rank with the ripe products of a tried and trained military experience, we have the sworn testimony of two of her veteran subordinates – one, the Duc d'Alençon, the other the greatest of the French generals of the time, Dunois, Bastard of Orleans; that her genius was as great – possibly even greater – in the subtle warfare of the forum we have for witness the records of the Rouen Trials, that protracted exhibition of intellectual fence maintained with credit against the master-minds of France; that her moral greatness was peer to her intellect we call the Rouen Trials again to witness, with their testimony to a fortitude which patiently and steadfastly endured during twelve weeks the wasting forces of captivity, chains, loneliness, sickness, darkness, hunger, thirst, cold, shame, insult, abuse, broken sleep, treachery, ingratitude, exhausting sieges of cross-examination, the threat of torture, with the rack before her and the executioner standing ready: yet never surrendering, never asking quarter, the frail wreck of her as unconquerable the last day as was her invincible spirit the first.

Great as she was in so many ways, she was perhaps even greatest of all in the lofty things just named – her patient endurance, her steadfastness, her granite fortitude. We may not hope to easily find her mate and twin in these majestic qualities; where we lift our eyes highest we find only a strange and curious contrast – there

in the captive eagle beating his broken wings on the Rock of St.
Helena.

The Trials ended with her condemnation. But as she had conceded nothing, confessed nothing, this was victory for her, defeat
for Cauchon. But his evil resources were not yet exhausted. She
was persuaded to agree to sign a paper of slight import, then by
treachery a paper was substituted which contained a recantation
and a detailed confession of everything which had been charged
against her during the Trials and denied and repudiated by her
persistently during the three months; and this false paper she
ignorantly signed. This was a victory for Cauchon. He followed it
eagerly and pitilessly up by at once setting a trap for her which
she could not escape. When she realized this she gave up the long
struggle, denounced the treason which had been practised against
her, repudiated the false confession, reasserted the truth of the
testimony which she had given in the Trials, and went to her martyrdom with the peace of God in her tired heart, and on her lips
endearing words and loving prayers for the cur she had crowned
and the nation of ingrates she had saved.

When the fires rose about her and she begged for a cross for her
dying lips to kiss, it was not a friend but an enemy, not a Frenchman but an alien, not a comrade in arms but an English soldier,
that answered that pathetic prayer. He broke a stick across his
knee, bound the pieces together in the form of the symbol she so
loved, and gave it her; and his gentle deed is not forgotten, nor
will be.

Twenty-five years afterward the Process of Rehabilitation was
instituted, there being a growing doubt as to the validity of a sovereignty that had been rescued and set upon its feet by a person who
had been proven by the Church to be a witch and a familiar of
evil spirits. Joan's old generals, her secretary, several aged relations
and other villagers of Domrémy, surviving judges and secretaries
of the Rouen and Poitiers Processes – a cloud of witnesses, some
of whom had been her enemies and persecutors, – came and made
oath and testified; and what they said was written down. In that
sworn testimony the moving and beautiful history of Joan of Arc
is laid bare, from her childhood to her martyrdom. From the verdict she rises stainlessly pure, in mind and heart, in speech and
deed and spirit, and will so endure to the end of time.

She is the Wonder of the Ages. And when we consider her origin, her early circumstances, her sex, and that she did all the things upon which her renown rests while she was still a young girl, we recognize that while our race continues she will be also the *Riddle* of the Ages. When we set about accounting for a Napoleon or a Shakespeare or a Raphael or a Wagner or an Edison or other extraordinary person, we understand that the measure of his talent will not explain the whole result, nor even the largest part of it; no, it is the atmosphere in which the talent was cradled that explains; it is the training which it received while it grew, the nurture it got from reading, study, example, the encouragement it gathered from self-recognition and recognition from the outside at each stage of its development: when we know all these details, then we know why the man was ready when his opportunity came. We should expect Edison's surroundings and atmosphere to have the largest share in discovering him to himself and to the world; and we should expect him to live and die undiscovered in a land where an inventor could find no comradeship, no sympathy, no ambition-rousing atmosphere of recognition and applause – Dahomey, for instance. Dahomey could not find an Edison out; in Dahomey an Edison could not find himself out. Broadly speaking, genius is not born with sight, but blind; and it is not itself that opens its eyes, but the subtle influences of a myriad of stimulating exterior circumstances.

We all know this to be not a guess, but a mere commonplace fact, a truism. Lorraine was Joan of Arc's Dahomey. And there the Riddle confronts us. We can understand how she could be born with military genius, with leonine courage, with incomparable fortitude, with a mind which was in several particulars a prodigy – a mind which included among its specialties the lawyer's gift of detecting traps laid by the adversary in cunning and treacherous arrangements of seemingly innocent words, the orator's gift of eloquence, the advocate's gift of presenting a case in clear and compact form, the judge's gift of sorting and weighing evidence, and finally, something recognizable as more than a mere trace of the statesman's gift of understanding a political situation and how to make profitable use of such opportunities as it offers; we can comprehend how she could be born with these great qualities, but we cannot comprehend how they became immediately usable and effective without the developing forces of a sympathetic atmosphere and the training which comes of teaching, study, practice

– years of practice, – and the crowning and perfecting help of a
thousand mistakes. We can understand how the possibilities of the
future perfect peach are all lying hid in the humble bitter-almond,
but we cannot conceive of the peach springing directly from the
almond without the intervening long seasons of patient cultivation
and development. Out of a cattle-pasturing peasant village lost in
the remotenesses of an unvisited wilderness and atrophied with
ages of stupefaction and ignorance we cannot see a Joan of Arc
issue equipped to the last detail for her amazing career and hope
to be able to explain the riddle of it, labor at it as we may.

It is beyond us. All the rules fail in this girl's case. In the world's
history she stands alone – quite alone. Others have been great in
their first public exhibitions of generalship, valor, legal talent, diplomacy, fortitude; but always their previous years and associations
had been in a larger or smaller degree a preparation for these
things. There have been no exceptions to the rule. But Joan was
competent in a law case at sixteen without ever having seen a law-
book or a court-house before; she had no training in soldiership
and no associations with it, yet she was a competent general in her
first campaign; she was brave in her first battle, yet her courage
had had no education – not even the education which a boy's courage gets from never-ceasing reminders that it is not permissible in
a boy to be a coward, but only in a girl; friendless, alone, ignorant,
in the blossom of her youth, she sat week after week, a prisoner in
chains, before her assemblage of judges, enemies hunting her to
her death, the ablest minds in France, and answered them out of an
untaught wisdom which overmatched their learning, baffled their
tricks and treacheries with a native sagacity which compelled their
wonder, and scored every day a victory against these incredible
odds and camped unchallenged on the field. In the history of the
human intellect, untrained, inexperienced, and using only its
birthright equipment of untried capacities, there is nothing which
approaches this. Joan of Arc stands alone, and must continue to
stand alone, by reason of the unfellowed fact that in the things
wherein she was great she was so without shade or suggestion of
help from preparatory teaching, practice, environment, or experience. There is no one to compare her with, none to measure her
by; for all others among the illustrious *grew* towards their high
place in an atmosphere and surroundings which discovered their
gift to them and nourished it and promoted it, intentionally or
unconsciously. There have been other young generals, but they

were not girls; young generals, but they had been soldiers before they were generals: she *began* as a general; she commanded the first army she ever saw; she led it from victory to victory, and never lost a battle with it; there have been young commanders-in-chief, but none so young as she: she is the only soldier in history who has held the supreme command of a nation's armies at the age of seventeen.

Her history has still another feature which sets her apart and leaves her without fellow or competitor: there have been many uninspired prophets, but she was the only one who ever ventured the daring detail of naming, along with a foretold event, the event's precise nature, the special time-limit within which it would occur, and the place – *and scored fulfilment.* At Vaucouleurs she said she must go to the King and be made his general, and break the English power, and crown her sovereign – "at Rheims." It all happened. It was all to happen "next year" – and it did. She foretold her first wound and its character and date a month in advance, and the prophecy was recorded in a public record-book three weeks in advance. She repeated it the morning of the date named, and it was fulfilled before night. At Tours she foretold the limit of her military career – saying it would end in one year from the time of its utterance – and she was right. She foretold her martyrdom – using *that word*, and naming a time three months away – and again she was right. At a time when France seemed hopelessly and permanently in the hands of the English she twice asserted in her prison before her judges that within seven years the English would meet with a mightier disaster than had been the fall of Orleans: it happened within five – the fall of Paris. Other prophecies of hers came true, both as to the event named and the time-limit prescribed.

She was deeply religious, and believed that she had daily speech with angels; that she saw them face to face, and that they counselled her, comforted and heartened her, and brought commands to her direct from God. She had a child-like faith in the heavenly origin of her apparitions and her Voices, and not any threat of any form of death was able to frighten it out of her loyal heart. She was a beautiful and simple and lovable character. In the records of the Trials this comes out in clear and shining detail. She was gentle and winning and affectionate; she loved her home and friends and her village life; she was miserable in the presence of pain and suffering; she was full of compassion: on the field of her most splendid victory she forgot her triumphs to hold in her lap the head of a dying enemy and comfort his passing spirit with pitying words; in an age when it was common to slaughter prisoners she stood dauntless between hers and harm, and saved them alive; she was forgiving, generous, unselfish, magnanimous; she was pure from all spot or stain of baseness. And always she was a *girl*; and dear and worshipful, as is meet for that estate: when she fell wounded, the first time, she was frightened, and cried when she saw her blood gushing from her breast; but she was Joan of Arc! and when presently she found that her generals were sounding the retreat, she staggered to her feet and led the assault again and took that place by storm.

There is no blemish in that rounded and beautiful character.

How strange it is! – that almost invariably the artist remembers only one detail – one minor and meaningless detail of the personality of Joan of Arc: to wit, that she was a peasant girl – and forgets all the rest; and so he paints her as a strapping middle-aged fishwoman, with costume to match, and in her face the spirituality of a ham. He is slave to his one idea, and forgets to observe that the supremely great souls are never lodged in gross bodies. No brawn, no muscle, could endure the work that their bodies must do; they do their miracles by the spirit, which has fifty times the strength and staying power of brawn and muscle. The Napoleons are little, not big; and they work twenty hours in the twenty-four, and come up fresh, while the big soldiers with the little hearts faint around them with fatigue. We know what Joan of Arc was like, without asking – merely by what she did. The artist should paint her *spirit* – then he could not fail to paint her body aright. She would rise before us, then, a vision to win us, not repel: a lithe young slender figure, instinct with "the unbought grace of youth," dear and bonny and lovable, the face beautiful, and transfigured with the light of that lustrous intellect and the fires of that unquenchable spirit.

Taking into account, as I have suggested before, all the circumstances – her origin, youth, sex, illiteracy, early environment, and the obstructing conditions under which she exploited her high gifts and made her conquests in the field and before the courts that tried her for her life, – she is easily and by far the most extraordinary person the human race has ever produced.

December 1904

CONCERNING COPYRIGHT

AN OPEN LETTER TO
THE REGISTER OF COPYRIGHTS

Thorwald Stolberg, Esq.,
  Register of Copyrights,
    Washington, D. C.
Dear Sir:

I have received your excellent summary of the innumerable statutes and substitutes and amendments which a century of Congresses has devised in trying to mete out even-handed justice to the public and the author in the vexed matter of copyright; and, in response to your invitation to the craftsmen of my guild to furnish suggestions for further legislation upon the subject, I beg to submit my share in the unconventional form of

Question and Answer.

Question. How many new American books are copyrighted *annually* in the United States?

Answer. Five or six thousand.

Q. How many have been copyrighted in the last twenty-five years?

A. More than 100,000.

Q. How many altogether in the past 104 years?

A. Doubtless 250,000.

Q. How many of them have survived or will survive the 42-year limit?

A. An average of five per year. Make it ten, to be safe and certain.

Q. Only *ten* a year!

A. That is all. Ten.

Q. Do you actually believe that 249,000 of these books have had no sort of use for a 42-year limit?

A. I can swear to it. They would not have outlived a 20-year limit.

Q. Then where is the use of a 42-year limit?

A. I know of none.

Q. What does it accomplish?

A. Nothing useful, nothing worthy, nothing modest, nothing dignified, nothing honest, so far as I know. An Italian statesman has called it "the Countess Massiglia of legal burlesque." Each year ten venerable copyrights fall in, and the bread of ten persons is taken from them by the Government. This microscopic petty larceny is all that is accomplished.

Q. It does seem a small business.

A. For a big nation – yes. A distinct reversal of the law of the survival of the fittest. It is the assassination of the fittest.

Q. Of course, the lawmakers knew they were arranging a hardship for some persons – all laws do that. But they could not have known how few the number was, do you think?

A. Of course not. Otherwise, they would not have been worrying and suffering over copyright laws for a hundred years. It has cost you, sir, 41 pages of printed notes to merely *outline* the acres of amendments and substitutes they have ground out in a century – *to take the bread out of the mouths of ten authors per year;* usually the ten poorest and most distinguished literary servants of the nation! One book from each of them. It takes a hundred years to hook a thousand books, and by that time eight hundred of them have long ago fallen obsolete and died of inanition.

Q. Certainly there is something most grotesque about this! Is this principle followed elsewhere in our laws?

A. Yes, in the case of the inventors. But in that case it is worth the Government's while. There are a hundred thousand new inventions a year, and a thousand of them are worth seizing at the end of the 17-year limit. But the Government *can't* seize the really great and immensely valuable ones – like the telegraph, the telephone, the air-brake, the Pullman car, and some others, the Shakespeares of the inventor-tribe, so to speak – for the prodigious capital required to carry them on is their protection from competition; their proprietors are not disturbed when the patents perish. Tell me, who are of first importance in the modern nation?

Q. Shall we say the builders of its civilization and promoters of its glory?

A. Yes. Who are they?

Q. Its inventors; the creators of its literature; and the country's defenders on land and sea. Is that correct?

A. I think so. Well, when a soldier retires from the wars, the Government spends $150,000,000 a year upon him and his, and the pension is continued to his widow and orphans. But when it retires a distinguished author's book at the end of 42 years, it takes the book's subsequent profits away from the widow and orphans and gives them – to whom?

Q. To the public.

A. Nothing of the kind!

Q. But it does – the lawmaker will tell you so himself.

A. Who deceived the lawmaker with that limpid falsehood?

Q. Falsehood?

A. That is what it is. And the proof of it lies in this large, and eloquent, and sarcastic fact: that the Government does not give the book to the *public*, it gives it to the *publishers*.

Q. How do you make that out?

A. It is very simple: the publisher *goes on publishing* – there is no law against it – and he takes *all* the profit, both the author's and his own.

Q. Why, it looks like a crime!

A. It doesn't merely look like it, it *is* a crime. A crime perpetrated by a great country, a proud World Power, upon ten poor devils a year. *One book apiece.* The profits on "Uncle Tom's Cabin" continue to-day; nobody but the publishers get them – Mrs. Stowe's share ceased seven years before she died; her daughters receive nothing from the book. Years ago they found themselves no longer able to live in their modest home, and had to move out and find humbler quarters. Washington Irving's poor old adopted daughters fared likewise. Come, does that move you?

Q. Ah, dear me! Well, certainly, there is something wrong about this whole copyright business.

A. Something wrong? Yes, I think so! Something pitifully wrong, pathetically wrong! Consider the nation's attitude toward the Builder of its Material Greatness, toward the Defender of its Homes and its Flag, and (by contrast) toward its Teacher, who is also the Promoter of its Fame and Preserver of it – that Immortal Three! Behold, the spirit of prophecy is upon me, and a picture of a future incident rises upon my sight. You shall share the vision with me: The President sits in state in the White House, with his official family around him; before him stand three groups. In the first group, Edison, Graham Bell, Westinghouse, and other living inventors, and, back of them, dim and vague, the shades of Fulton, Whitney, Morse, Hoe, Howe, Ericsson and others; in the second group stand Dewey, Schley, Miles, Howard, Sickles, Chaffee, together with a private soldier and sailor representing 200,000 fellow-survivors of the bloody field, the sutler's tent and the teamster's camp, and back of these the stately shades of Washington, Paul Jones, Jackson, Taylor, Scott, McClellan, Grant, Sherman, Sheridan, Farragut, Foote, Worden, Sampson and others; in the third group stand three or four living authors, and back of them, with averted faces and ashamed, loom the mighty shades of Emerson, Bancroft, Bryant, Whittier, and behind these, dim and spectral, the shades of Cooper, Judd, Irving, Poe, Hawthorne, Longfellow, Holmes, Lowell, Harriet Beecher Stowe, Parkman and others.

The President Speaks.

"By command of the Nation, whose servant I am, I have summoned you, O illustrious ones! I bring you the message of eighty grateful millions – a message of praise and reward for high service done your country and your flag: from my lips, hear the nation's word! To you, inventors, builders of the land's material greatness, past and present, the people offer homage, worship and imperishable gratitude, with enduring fame for your dead, and untold millions of minted gold for you that survive. To you, defenders of the flag, past and present, creators of the nation's far-shining military glory, the people offer homage, worship and imperishable gratitude, with enduring fame for your dead; and, for you that survive, a hundred and fifty coined millions a year to protect the highest and the humblest of you from want so long as you shall live. To you, historians, poets, creators of ennobling romance, – Teachers – this: you have wrought into enduring form the splendid story of the Great Republic; you have preserved forever from neglect, decay and oblivion the great deeds of the long line of the nation's Builders, Defenders and Preservers; you have diligently and faithfully taught and trained the children of the Republic in lofty political and social ideals, and in that love of country and reverence for the flag which is Patriotism – and without you this would be a Russia to-day, with not an intelligent patriot in it; you have made the American home pure and fragrant and beautiful with your sweet songs and your noble romance-literature; you have carried the American name in honor and esteem to the ends of the earth; in spite of unequal laws which exalt your brother the soldier and inflict upon you an undeserved indignity, you have furnished to your country that great asset, that golden asset, that imperial asset, lacking which no modern State can hold up its head and stand unchallenged in the august company of the sisterhood of Nations – a fine and strong and worthy National Literature! For these inestimable services, the people, by my voice, grant these rewards: to your great dead, as also to you who still live, homage, worship, enduring fame, imper – no, I mean gratitude, just gratitude; gratitude with a 42-year limit, and the poor-house for your widows and children. God abide with you, O illustrious company of the Builders, Defenders and Patriot-Makers of the grateful Republic! Farewell, the incident is closed."

Q. (*After a long and reflective pause.*) Isn't there some right and fair way to remedy this strange and dishonorable condition of things?

A. I think there is.

Q. Suggest it, then.

A Suggestion.

A. In making a 42-year limit, the Government's intention was, to be fair all around. It meant that the ten authors (it supposed the number was greater) should enjoy the profit of their labors a fair and reasonable time; then extinguish the copyright and thus *make the book cheap* – this for the benefit of the public. I repeat, to *insure cheap editions for the public*: now, wasn't that *the* intention? and wasn't it the whole and *only* intention?

Q. It certainly was.

A. Well, that intention has often been defeated. In many a case, the publisher has not lowered the price; in other cases, so many publishers issued editions of the unprotected book that they clogged the market and *killed* the book. And often it was a book that could have survived but for this misfortune. The remedy that I would suggest is this: *that, during the 42d year of the copyright limit, the owner of the copyright shall be obliged to issue an edition of the book at these following rates, to wit: twenty-five cents for each 100,000 words, or less, of its contents, and keep said edition on sale always thereafter, year after year, indefinitely. And if in any year he shall fail to keep such edition on sale during a space of three months, the copyright shall then perish.*

Q. That seems to cover the ground. It meets the Government's sole desire – to *secure a cheap edition for the public.*

A. Why, certainly. It *compels* it. No existing law in any country does that.

Q. You would not put a price upon the publisher's other editions?

A. No; he could make the others as high-priced as he chose.

Q. Would you except books of a certain class?

A. No book occurs to me that could not stand the reduction – I mean a book that promises to live 42 years and upwards. It could not apply to unabridged dictionaries, for they are revised and newly copyrighted every ten or twelve years. It is the one and only book in America whose copyright is *perpetual*.

Q. Your own proposition makes all copyrights perpetual, doesn't it?

A. It does not. It extends the limit indefinitely. But there is still a limit; for in any year after the forty-first that the cheap edition fails, during the space of three months, the copyright dies.

Q. The proposed rate seems excessively cheap. How would the thing work out? About how much of a reduction would it make? Give me an illustration or two.

A. Very well, let me cite my own books – I am on familiar ground there. "Huck Finn" contains 70,000 words; present price $1 50; an edition of it would have to be kept permanently on sale at 25 cents. "Tom Sawyer," 70,000 words, price $1 50; the imagined cheap edition would be 25 cents. Several two-volume books of mine contain a trifle more than 100,000 words per volume; present price $1 75 per volume; the cheap-edition price would be 75 cents per volume – or 75 cents for the complete book if compressed into one volume. My "works," taken together, number 23 volumes; cheapest present price of the set, $36 50. To meet the requirements of copyright-preserving law, I would compress the aggregate contents into 10 volumes of something more than 200,000 words each, and sell the volumes at 75 cents each – or $7 50 for the lot, if a millionaire wanted the whole treasure.

Q. It is a reduction of *four-fifths*, or thereabouts! Would there be any profit?

A. The printer and the binder would get their usual percentage of profit, the middle-man would get his usual commission on sales. The publisher's profit would be very small, mine also would be very small.

Q. Then you are proposing commercial suicide for him and for yourself – is that it?

A. Far from it. I am proposing high commercial prosperity and advantage for him and for me.

Q. How?

A. First of all, the books would remain my children's possession and support, instead of being confiscated by various publishers and issued in cheap form or dear, as they chose, for the support of *their* children.

Q. And secondly?

A. Secondly – let us not overlook the importance of this detail – the cheap edition would advertise our higher-priced editions, and the publisher and my orphans would live on canvasback duck and Cape Cod oysters – not on ham-and-not-enough-of-it, the way certain Government-robbed orphans of my acquaintance are doing now.

Q. Why don't you and your publisher try that cheap edition now, without waiting?

A. Haven't I told you that almost all the profit would go to printer, binder and middle-man? And has this Government ever heard of a publisher who would get out a dirt-cheap edition without being *compelled* to do it? The Government has tried persuasion for many a year, in the interest of the public, and achieved no cheap edition by it: what I am after now is *compulsion.*

Q. Are you guessing at cheap-edition possibilities, or are you speaking from knowledge?

A. From knowledge. Knowledge and experience. I know what it costs to make a book and what it costs to sell it.

Q. If your figures on cheap editions should be challenged by the trade – how then?

A. I could prove my case, and would do it.

Very respectfully,

S. L. CLEMENS (MARK TWAIN).

January 1905

THE CZAR'S SOLILOQUY

After the Czar's morning bath it is his habit to meditate an hour before dressing himself. – *London Times Correspondence.*

[*Viewing himself in the pier glass.*] Naked, what am I? A lank, skinny, spider-legged libel on the image of God! Look at the waxwork head – the face, with the expression of a melon – the projecting ears – the knotted elbows – the dished breast – the knife-edged shins – and then the feet, all beads and joints and bone-sprays, an imitation X-ray photograph! There is nothing imperial about this, nothing imposing, impressive, nothing to invoke awe and reverence. Is it this that a hundred and forty million Russians kiss the dust before and worship? Manifestly not! No one could worship this spectacle, which is Me. Then who is it, what is it, that they worship? Privately, none knows better than I: it is my clothes. Without my clothes I should be as destitute of authority as any other naked person. Nobody could tell me from a parson, a barber, a dude. Then who is the real Emperor of Russia? My clothes. There is no other.

As Teufelsdröckh suggested, what would man be – what would *any* man be – without his clothes? As soon as one stops and thinks over that proposition, one realizes that without his clothes a man would be nothing at all; that the clothes do not merely make the man, the clothes *are* the man; that without them he is a cipher, a vacancy, a nobody, a nothing.

Titles – another artificiality – are a part of his clothing. They and the dry-goods conceal the wearer's inferiority and make him seem great and a wonder, when at bottom there is nothing remarkable about him. They can move a nation to fall on its knees and sincerely worship an Emperor who, without the clothes and the title, would drop to the rank of the cobbler and be swallowed up and lost sight of in the massed multitude of the inconsequentials; an Emperor who, naked in a naked world, would get no notice, excite no remark, and be heedlessly shouldered and jostled like any other uncertified stranger, and perhaps offered a kopek to carry somebody's gripsack; yet an Emperor who, by the sheer might of those artificialities – clothes and a title – can get himself worshipped as a deity by his people, and at his pleasure and unrebuked can exile them, hunt them, harry them, destroy them, just as he would with so many rats if the accident of birth had furnished him a calling better suited to his capacities than empering. It is a stupendous force – that which resides in the all-concealing cloak of clothes and title; they fill the onlooker with awe; they make him tremble; yet he knows that every hereditary regal dignity commemorates a usurpation, a power illegitimately acquired, an authority conveyed and conferred by persons who did not own it. For monarchs have been chosen and elected by aristocracies only: a Nation has never elected one.

There is no power without clothes. It is the power that governs the human race. Strip its chiefs to the skin, and no State could be governed; naked officials could exercise no authority; they would look (and be) like everybody else – commonplace, inconsequential. A policeman in plain clothes is one man; in his uniform he is ten. Clothes and title are the most potent thing, the most formidable influence, in the earth. They move the human race to willing and spontaneous respect for the judge, the general, the admiral, the bishop, the ambassador, the frivolous earl, the idiot duke, the sultan, the king, the emperor. No great title is efficient without clothes to support it. In naked tribes of savages the kings wear some kind of rag or decoration which they make sacred to themselves and allow no one else to wear. The king of the great Fan tribe wears a bit of leopard-skin on his shoulder – it is sacred to royalty; the rest of him is perfectly naked. Without his bit of leopard-skin to awe and impress the people, he would not be able to keep his job.

[*After a silence.*] A curious invention, an unaccountable invention – the human race! The swarming Russian millions have for centuries meekly allowed our Family to rob them, insult them, trample them under foot, while they lived and suffered and died with no purpose and no function but to make that Family comfortable! These people are horses – just that – horses with clothes and a religion. A horse with the strength of a hundred men will let one man beat him, starve him, drive him; the Russian millions allow a mere handful of soldiers to hold them in slavery – and these very soldiers are their own sons and brothers!

A strange thing, when one considers it: to wit, the world applies to Czar and System the same moral axioms that have vogue and acceptance in civilized countries! Because, in civilized countries, it is wrong to remove oppressors otherwise than by process of law, it is held that the same rule applies in Russia, where there is no such thing as law – except for our Family. Laws are merely restraints – they have no other function. In civilized countries they restrain all persons, and restrain them all alike, which is fair and righteous; but in Russia such laws as exist make an exception – our Family. We do as we please; we have done as we pleased for centuries. Our common trade has been crime, our common pastime murder, our common beverage blood – the blood of the nation. Upon our heads lie millions of murders. Yet the pious moralist says it is a crime to assassinate us. We and our uncles are a family of cobras set over a hundred and forty million rabbits, whom we torture and murder and feed upon all our days; yet the moralist urges that to kill us is a crime, not a duty.

It is not for me to say it aloud, but to one on the inside – like me – this is naïvely funny; on its face, illogical. Our Family is above all law; there is no law that can reach us, restrain us, protect the people from us. Therefore, we are outlaws. Outlaws are a proper mark for any one's bullet. Ah! what could our Family do without the moralist? He has always been our stay, our support, our friend; to-day he is our *only* friend. Whenever there has been dark talk of assassination, he has come forward and saved us with his impressive maxim, "Forbear: nothing politically valuable was ever yet achieved by violence." He probably believes it. It is because he has by him no child's book of world-history to teach him that his maxim lacks the backing of statistics. All thrones have been established by violence; no regal tyranny has ever been overthrown except by violence; by violence my fathers set up our throne; by murder, treachery, perjury, torture, banishment and the prison they have held it for four centuries, and by these same arts I hold it to-day. There is no Romanoff of learning and experience but would reverse the maxim and say: "Nothing politically valuable was ever yet achieved *except* by violence." The moralist realizes that today, for the first time in our history, my throne is in real peril and the nation waking up from its immemorial slave-lethargy; but he does not perceive that four deeds of violence are the reason for it: the assassination of the Finland Constitution by my hand; the slaughter, by revolutionary assassins, of Bobrikoff and Plehve; and my massacre of the unoffending innocents the other day. But the blood that flows in my veins – blood informed, trained, educated by its grim heredities, blood alert by its traditions, blood which has been to school four hundred years in the veins of professional assassins, my predecessors – *it* perceives, *it* understands! Those four deeds have set up a commotion in the inert and muddy deeps of the national heart such as no moral suasion could have accomplished; they have aroused hatred and hope in that long-atrophied heart; and, little by little, slowly but surely, that feeling will steal into every breast and possess it. In time, into even the *soldier's* breast – fatal day, day of doom, that! ... By and by, there will be results! How little the academical moralist knows of the tremendous moral force of massacre and assassination! ... Indeed there are going to be results! The nation is in labor; and by and by there will be a mighty birth – PATRIOTISM! To put it in rude, plain, unpalatable words – *true* patriotism, real patriotism: loyalty, not to a Family and a Fiction, but loyalty to the Nation itself!

... There are twenty-five million families in Russia. There is a man-child at every mother's knee. If these were twenty-five million patriotic mothers, they would teach these man-children daily, saying: "Remember this, take it to heart, live by it, die for it if necessary: that our patriotism is medieval, outworn, obsolete; that the modern patriotism, the true patriotism, the only rational patriotism, is *loyalty to the Nation* ALL *the time, loyalty to the Government when it deserves it.*" With twenty-five million taught and trained patriots in the land a generation from now, my successor would think twice before he would butcher a thousand helpless poor petitioners humbly begging for his kindness and justice, as I did the other day.

[*Reflective pause.*] Well, perhaps I have been affected by these depressing newspaper-clippings which I found under my pillow. I will read and ponder them again. [*Reads.*]

POLISH WOMEN KNOUTED.

Reservists' Wives Treated with Awful Brutality – At Least One Killed.

Special Cable to THE NEW YORK TIMES.

BERLIN, Nov. 27. – Infuriated by the unwillingness of the Polish troops to leave their wives and children, the Russian authorities at Kutno, a town on the Polish frontier, have treated the people in a manner almost incredibly cruel.

It is known that *one woman has been knouted to death* and that a number of others have been injured. Fifty persons have been thrown into jail. Some of the prisoners were *tortured into unconsciousness.*

CZAR AS LORD'S ANOINTED.

People Spent Night In Prayer and Fasting Before His Visit to Novgorod.

LONDON TIMES – NEW YORK TIMES.
Special Cablegram.

Copyright, 1904, THE NEW YORK TIMES

LONDON, July 27. – The London Times's Russian correspondents say the following extract from the Petersburger Zeitung, describing the Czar's recent doings at Novgorod, affords a typical instance of the servile adulation which the subjects of the Czar deem it necessary to adopt:

"The blessing of the troops, *who knelt devoutly before his Majesty,* was a pro-

MARK TWAIN

Details of the brutalities are lacking, but it seems that the Cossacks tore the reservists from the arms of their wives and children and then *knouted the women who followed their husbands into the streets.*

In cases where reservists could not be found *their wives were dragged by their hair into the streets and there beaten. The chief official of the district and the Colonel of a regiment are said to have looked on while this was being done.*

A girl who had assisted in distributing Socialist tracts was *treated in an atrocious manner.*

foundly moving spectacle. His Majesty held the sacred ikon aloft and pronounced aloud a blessing in his own name and that of the Empress.

"Thousands *wept with emotion and spiritual ecstasy.* Pupils of girls' schools scattered roses in the path of the monarch.

"People pressed up to the carriage in order to carry away an indelible memory of the *hallowed features of the Lord's Anointed.* Many old people had spent the night in prayer and fasting *in order to be worthy to gaze at his countenance with pure, undefiled souls.*

"The greatest enthusiasm prevails *at the happiness thus vouchsafed to the people.*"

[*Moved.*] How shameful! how pitiful! . . . And how grotesque! . . . To think – it was *I* that did those cruel things . . . There is no escaping the personal responsibility – it was I that did them. And it was I that got that grovelling and awe-smitten worship! *I* – this thing in the mirror – this carrot! With one hand I flogged unoffending women to death and tortured prisoners to unconsciousness; and with the other I held up the fetish toward my fellow deity in heaven and called down His blessing upon my adoring animals whom, and whose forbears, with His holy approval, I and mine have been instructing in the pains of hell for four lagging centuries. It is a picture! To think that this thing in the mirror – this vegetable – is an accepted deity to a mighty nation, an innumerable host, and nobody laughs; and at the same time is a diligent and practical professional devil, and nobody marvels, nobody murmurs about incongruities and inconsistencies! Is the human race a joke? Was it devised and patched together in a dull time when there was nothing important to do? Has it no respect for itself? . . . I think my respect for it is drooping, sinking – and my respect for myself along with it. . . . There is but one restorative – *Clothes!* respect-reviving, spirit-uplifting clothes! heaven's kindliest gift to man, his only protection against finding himself out: they deceive him, they confer dignity upon him; without them he has none. How charitable are clothes, how beneficent, how puissant, how inestimably precious! Mine are able to expand a human cipher into a globe-shadowing portent; they can command the respect of the whole world – including my own, which is fading. I will put them on.

February 2, 1905.

March 1905

THE WAR PRAYER

IT WAS A time of great and exalting excitement. The country was up in arms, the war was on, in every breast burned the holy fire of patriotism; the drums were beating, the bands playing, the toy pistols popping, the bunched firecrackers hissing and spluttering; on every hand and far down the receding and fading spread of roofs and balconies a fluttering wilderness of flags flashed in the sun; daily the young volunteers marched down the wide avenue gay and fine in their new uniforms, the proud fathers and mothers and sisters and sweethearts cheering them with voices choked with happy emotion as they swung by; nightly the packed mass-meetings listened, panting, to patriot oratory which stirred the deepest deeps of their hearts, and which they interrupted at briefest intervals with cyclones of applause, the tears running down their cheeks the while; in the churches the pastors preached devotion to flag and country, and invoked the God of Battles, beseeching His aid in our good cause in outpourings of fervid eloquence which moved every listener. It was indeed a glad and gracious time, and the half dozen rash spirits that ventured to disapprove of the war and cast a doubt upon its righteousness straightway got such a stern and angry warning that for their personal safety's sake they quickly shrank out of sight and offended no more in that way.

Sunday morning came – next day the battalions would leave for the front; the church was filled; the volunteers were there, their young faces alight with martial dreams – visions of the stern advance, the gathering momentum, the rushing charge, the flashing sabres, the flight of the foe, the tumult, the enveloping smoke, the fierce pursuit, the surrender! – then home from the war, bronzed heroes, welcomed, adored, submerged in golden seas of glory! With the volunteers sat their dear ones, proud, happy, and envied by the neighbors and friends who had no sons and brothers to send forth to the field of honor, there to win for the flag, or, failing, die the noblest of noble deaths. The service proceeded; a war-chapter from the Old Testament was read; the first prayer was said; it was followed by an organ-burst that shook the building, and with one impulse the house rose, with glowing eyes and beating hearts and poured out that tremendous invocation –

> God the all-terrible! Thou who ordainest,
> Thunder thy clarion and lightning thy sword!

Then came the "long" prayer. None could remember the like of it for passionate pleading and moving and beautiful language. The burden of its supplication was, that the ever-merciful and benignant Father of us all would watch over our noble young soldiers, and aid, comfort, and encourage them in their patriotic work; bless them, shield them in the day of battle and the hour of peril, bear them in His mighty hand, make them strong and confident, invincible in the bloody on-set, help them to crush the foe, grant to them and to their flag and country imperishable honor and glory –

An aged stranger entered, and moved with slow and noiseless step up the main aisle, his eyes fixed upon the minister, his long body clothed in a robe that reached to his feet, his head bare, his white hair descending in a frothy cataract to his shoulders, his seamy face unnaturally pale, pale even to ghastliness. With all eyes following him and wondering, he made his silent way; without pausing, he ascended to the preacher's side and stood there, waiting. With shut lids the preacher, unconscious of his presence, continued his moving prayer, and at last finished it with the words, uttered in fervent appeal, "Bless our arms, grant us the victory, O Lord our God, Father and Protector of our land and flag!"

The stranger touched his arm, motioned him to step aside – which the startled minister did – and took his place. During some moments he surveyed the spell-bound audience with solemn eyes, in which burned an uncanny light; then in a deep voice he said –

"I come from the Throne – bearing a message from Almighty God!" The words smote the house with a shock; if the stranger perceived it he gave it no attention. "He has heard the prayer of His servant your shepherd, and will grant it if such shall be your desire after I, His messenger, shall have explained to you its import – that is to say, its full import. For it is like unto many of the prayers of men, in that it asks for more than he who utters it is aware of – except he pause and think.

"God's servant and yours has prayed his prayer. Has he paused, and taken thought? Is it one prayer? No, it is two – one uttered, the other not. Both have reached the ear of Him who heareth all supplications, the spoken and the unspoken. Ponder this – keep it in mind. If you would beseech a blessing upon yourself, beware! lest without intent you invoke a curse upon a neighbor at the same time. If you pray for the blessing of rain upon your crop which needs it, by that act you are possibly praying for a curse upon some neighbor's crop which may not need rain and can be injured by it.

"You have heard your servant's prayer – the uttered part of it. I am commissioned of God to put into words the other part of it – that part which the pastor – and also you in your hearts – fervently prayed silently. And ignorantly and unthinkingly? God grant that it was so! You heard these words: 'Grant us the victory, O Lord our God!' That is sufficient. The *whole* of the uttered prayer is compacted into those pregnant words. Elaborations were not necessary. When you have prayed for victory you have prayed for many unmentioned results which follow victory – *must* follow it, cannot help but follow it. Upon the listening spirit of God the Father fell also the unspoken part of the prayer. He commandeth me to put it into words. Listen!

"O Lord, our Father, our young patriots, idols of our hearts, go forth to battle – be Thou near them! With them – in spirit – we also go forth from the sweet peace of our beloved firesides to smite the foe. O Lord, our God, help us to tear their soldiers to bloody shreds with our shells; help us to cover their smiling fields with the pale forms of their patriot dead; help us to drown the thunder of the guns with the shrieks of their wounded, writhing in pain; help us to lay waste their humble homes with a hurricane of fire; help us to wring the hearts of their unoffending widows with unavailing grief; help us to turn them out roofless with their little children to wander unfriended the wastes of their desolated land in rags and hunger and thirst, sport of the sun-flames of summer and the icy winds of winter, broken in spirit, worn with travail, imploring Thee for the refuge of the grave and denied it – for our sakes who adore Thee, Lord, blast their hopes, blight their lives, protract their bitter pilgrimage, make heavy their steps, water their way with their tears, stain the white snow with the blood of their wounded feet! We ask it, in the spirit of love, of Him Who is the Source of Love, and Who is the ever-faithful refuge and friend of all that are sore beset and seek His aid with humble and contrite hearts. Amen."

[*After a pause.*] "Ye have prayed it; if ye still desire it, speak! – The messenger of the Most High waits."

It was believed afterwards, that the man was a lunatic, because there was no sense in what he said.

c. March 10, 1905

CHRISTIAN CITIZENSHIP

IS THERE SUCH a thing as Christian citizenship? No, but it could be created. The process would be quite simple, and not productive of hardship to any one. It will be conceded that every man's first duty is to God; it will also be conceded, and with strong emphasis, that a Christian's first duty is to God. It then follows, as a matter of course, that it is his duty to carry his Christian code of morals to the polls and vote them. Whenever he shall do that, he will not find himself voting for an unclean man, a dishonest man. Whenever a Christian votes, he votes against God or for Him, and he knows this quite well. God is an issue in every election; He is a candidate in the person of every clean nominee on every ticket; His purity and His approval are there, to be voted for or voted against, and no fealty to party can absolve His servant from his higher and more exacting fealty to Him; He takes precedence of party, duty to Him is above every claim of party.

If Christians should vote their duty to God at the polls, they would carry every election, and do it with ease. They would elect every clean candidate in the United States, and defeat every soiled one. Their prodigious power would be quickly realized and recognized, and afterward there would be no unclean candidates upon any ticket, and graft would cease. No church organization can be found in the country that would elect men of foul character to be its shepherd, its treasurer, and superintendent of its Sunday-school. It would be revolted at the idea; it would consider such an election an insult to God. Yet every Christian congregation in the country elects foul men to public office, while quite aware that this also is an open and deliberate insult to God, who can not approve and does not approve the placing of the liberties and the well-being of His children in the hands of infamous men. It is the Christian congregations that are responsible for the filling of our public offices with criminals, for the reason that they could prevent it if they chose to do it. They could prevent it without organizing a league, without framing a platform, without making any speeches or passing any resolutions – in a word, without concert of any kind. They could accomplish it by each individual resolving to vote for God at the polls – that is to say, vote for the candidate whom God would approve. Can a man imagine such a thing as God being a Republican or a Democrat, and voting for a criminal or a blackguard merely because party loyalty required it? Then can we imagine that a man can improve upon God's attitude in this matter, and by help of professional politicians invent a better policy? God has no politics but cleanliness and honesty, and it is good enough for men.

A man's second duty is to his family. There was a time when a clergyman's duty to his family required him to be his congregation's political slave, and vote his congregation's ticket in order to safeguard the food and shelter of his wife and children. But that time has gone by. We have the secret ballot now, and a clergyman can vote for God. He can also plead with his congregation to do the like.

Perhaps. We can not be sure. The congregation would probably inquire whom *he* was going to vote for; and if he stood upon his manhood and answered that they had no Christian right (which is the same as saying no moral right, and, of course, no legal right) to ask the question, it is conceivable – not to say certain – that they would dismiss him, and be much offended at his proposing to be a man as well as a clergyman.

Still, there are clergymen who are so situated as to be able to make the experiment. It would be worth while to try it. If the Christians of America could be persuaded to vote God and a clean ticket, it would bring about a moral revolution that would be incalculably beneficent. It would save the country – a country whose Christians have betrayed it and are destroying it.

The Christians of Connecticut sent Bulkeley to the Senate. They sent to the Legislature the men who elected him. These two crimes they could have prevented; they did not do it, and upon them rest the shame and the responsibility. Only one clergyman remembered his Christian morals and his duty to God, and stood bravely by both. Mr. Smythe is probably an outcast now, but such a man as that can endure ostracism; and such a man as that is likely to possess the treasure of a family that can endure it with him, and be proud to do it. I kiss the hem of his garment.

Four years ago Greater New York had two tickets in the field: one clean, the other dirty, with a single exception; an unspeakable ticket with that lonely exception. One-half of the Christians voted for that foul ticket and against God and the Christian code of morals, putting loyalty to party above loyalty to God and honorable citizenship, and they came within a fraction of electing it; whereas if they had stood by their professed morals they would have buried it out of sight. Christianity was on trial then, it is on trial now. And nothing important is on trial except Christianity.

It was on trial in Philadelphia, and failed; in Pennsylvania and failed; in Rhode Island, and failed; in Connecticut, and failed; in New York, and failed; in Delaware, and failed; in every town and county and State, and was recreant to its trust; it has effusively busied itself with the small matters of charity and benevolence, and has looked on, indifferent while its country was sinking lower and lower in repute and drifting further and further toward moral destruction. It is the one force that can save, and it sits with folded hands. In Greater New York it will presently have an opportunity to elect or defeat some straight, clean, honest men, of the sterling Jerome stamp, and some of the Tammany kind. The Christian vote – and the Christian vote alone – will decide the contest. It, and it alone, is master of the situation, and lord of the result.

September 2, 1905

KING LEOPOLD'S SOLILOQUY

A DEFENSE OF HIS CONGO RULE

"IT IS I"
"Leopold II is the absolute
Master of the whole of the internal and external activity of
the Independent State of the
Congo. The organization of
justice, the army, the industrial
and commercial regimes are established freely by himself. He
would say, and with greater accuracy than did Louis XIV.,
'The State, it is I.' " *Prof. F. Cattier, Brussels University.* "Let
us repeat after so many others what has become a platitude,
the success of the African work is the work of a sole directing
will, without being hampered by the hesitation of timorous
politicians, carried out under his sole responsibility, –
intelligent, thoughtful, con-
scious of the perils and the advantages, discounting with an
admirable prescience the great
results of a near future." *M. Alfred
Poskine in "Bilans Congolais."*

[*Throws down pamphlets which he has been reading. Excitedly combs his
flowing spread of whiskers with his fingers; pounds the table with his fists; lets
off brisk volleys of unsanctified language at brief intervals, repentantly drooping his head, between volleys, and kissing the Louis XI. crucifix hanging from
his neck, accompanying the kisses with mumbled apologies; presently rises,
flushed and perspiring, and walks the floor, gesticulating*]
— —!!— —!! If I had them by the throat! [*Hastily kisses the
crucifix, and mumbles*] In these twenty years I have spent millions
to keep the press of the two hemispheres quiet, and still these
leaks keep on occurring. I have spent other millions on religion
and art, and what do I get for it? Nothing. Not a compliment.
These generosities are studiedly ignored, in print. In print I get
nothing but slanders – and slanders again – and still slanders,
and slanders on top of slanders! Grant them true, what of it?

They are slanders all the same, when uttered against a king.

Miscreants – they are telling *everything*! Oh, everything: how I went pilgriming among the Powers in tears, with my mouth full of Bible and my pelt oozing piety at every pore, and implored them to place the vast and rich and populous Congo Free State in trust in my hands as their agent, so that I might root out slavery and stop the slave raids, and lift up those twenty-five millions of gentle and harmless blacks out of darkness into light, the light of our blessed Redeemer, the light that streams from his holy Word, the light that makes glorious our noble civilization – lift them up and dry their tears and fill their bruised hearts with joy and gratitude – lift them up and make them comprehend that they were no longer outcasts and forsaken, but our very brothers in Christ; how America and thirteen great European states wept in sympathy with me, and were persuaded; how their representatives met in convention in Berlin and made me Head Foreman and Superintendent of the Congo State, and drafted out my powers and limitations, carefully guarding the persons and liberties and properties of the natives against hurt and harm; forbidding whisky traffic and gun traffic; providing courts of justice; making commerce free and fetterless to the merchants and traders of all nations, and welcoming and safe-guarding all missionaries of all creeds and denominations. They have told how I planned and prepared my establishment and selected my horde of officials – "pals" and "pimps" of mine, "unspeakable Belgians" every one – and hoisted my flag, and "took in" a President of the United States, and got him to be the first to recognize it and salute it. Oh, well, let them blackguard me if they like; it is a deep satisfaction to me to remember that I was a shade too smart for that nation that thinks itself so smart. Yes, I certainly did bunco a Yankee – as those people phrase it. Pirate flag? Let them call it so – perhaps it is. All the same, *they were the first to salute it.*

These meddlesome American missionaries! these frank British consuls! these blabbing Belgian-born traitor officials! – those tiresome parrots are always talking, always telling. They have told how for twenty years I have ruled the Congo State not as a trustee of the Powers, an agent, a subordinate, a foreman, but as a sovereign – sovereign over a fruitful domain four times as large as the German Empire – sovereign absolute, irresponsible, above all law; trampling the Berlin-made Congo charter under foot; barring out all foreign traders but myself; restricting commerce to myself, through concessionaires who are my creatures and confederates; seizing and holding the State as my personal property, the whole of its vast revenues as my private "swag" – mine, solely mine – claiming and holding its millions of people as my private property, my serfs, my slaves; their labor mine, with or without wage; the food they raise not their property but mine; the rubber, the ivory and all the other riches of the land mine – mine solely – and gathered for me by the men, the women and the little children under compulsion of lash and bullet, fire, starvation, mutilation and the halter.

These pests! – it is as I say, they have kept back nothing! They have revealed these and yet other details which shame should have kept them silent about, since they were exposures of a king, a sacred personage and immune from reproach, by right of his selection and appointment to his great office by God himself; a king whose acts cannot be criticized without blasphemy, since God has observed them from the beginning and has manifested no dissatisfaction with them, nor shown disapproval of them, nor hampered nor interrupted them in any way. By this sign I recognize his approval of what I have done; his cordial and glad approval, I am sure I may say. Blest, crowned, beatified with this great reward, this golden reward, this unspeakably precious reward, why should I care for men's cursings and revilings of me? [*With a sudden outburst of feeling*] May they toast a million æons in – [*Catches his breath and effusively kisses the crucifix; sorrowfully murmurs, "I shall get myself damned yet, with these indiscretions of speech."*]

Yes, they go on telling everything, these chatterers! They tell how I levy incredibly burdensome taxes upon the natives – taxes which are a pure theft; taxes which they must satisfy by gathering rubber under hard and constantly harder conditions, and by raising and furnishing food supplies gratis – and it all comes out that, when they fall short of their tasks through hunger, sickness, despair, and ceaseless and exhausting labor without rest, and forsake their homes and flee to the woods to escape punishment, my black soldiers, drawn from unfriendly tribes, and instigated and directed by my Belgians, hunt them down and butcher them and burn their villages – reserving some of the girls. They tell it all: how I am wiping a nation of friendless creatures out of existence by every form of murder, for my private pocket's sake. But they never say, although they know it, that I have labored in the cause of religion at the same time and all the time, and have sent missionaries there (of a "convenient stripe," as they phrase it), to teach them the error of their ways and bring them to Him who is all mercy and love, and who is the sleepless guardian and friend of all who suffer. They tell only what is against me, they will not tell what is in my favor.

They tell how England required of me a Commission of Inquiry into Congo atrocities, and how, to quiet that meddling country, with its disagreeable Congo Reform Association, made up of earls and bishops and John Morleys and university grandees and other dudes, more interested in other people's business than in their own, I appointed it. Did it stop their mouths? No, they merely pointed out that it was a commission composed wholly of my "Congo butchers," "the very men whose acts were to be inquired into." They said it was equivalent to appointing a commission of wolves to inquire into depredations committed upon a sheepfold. *Nothing* can satisfy a cursed Englishman!*

And are the fault-finders frank with my private character? They could not be more so if I were a plebeian, a peasant, a mechanic. They remind the world that from the earliest days my house has been chapel and brothel combined, and both industries working full time; that I practised cruelties upon my queen and my daughters, and supplemented them with daily shame and humiliations; that, when my queen lay in the happy refuge of her coffin, and a daughter implored me on her knees to let her look for the last time upon her mother's face, I refused; and that, three years ago, not

---

* Recent information is to the effect that the resident missionaries found the commission as a whole apparently interested to promote reforms. One of its members was a leading Congo official, another an official of the government in Belgium, the third a Swiss jurist. The commission's report will reach the public only through the king, and will be whatever he consents to make it; it is not yet forthcoming, though six months have passed since the investigation was made. There is, however, abundant evidence that horrible abuses were found and conceded, the testimony of missionaries, which had been scouted by the king's defenders, being amply vindicated. One who was present at one hearing of the commission writes: "Men of stone would be moved by the stories that are being unfolded as the commission probes into the awful history of rubber collection." Certain reforms were ordered in the one section visited, but the latest word is that after the commission's departure, conditions soon became worse than before its coming. Very well, then, the king has investigated himself. One stage is achieved. The next one in order is the investigation of conditions in the Congo State *by the Powers responsible for the creation of the Congo State.* The United States is one of these. Such an investigation is advocated by Lyman Abbott, Henry Van Dyke, David Starr Jordan and other prominent citizens in a petition to Congress. – M. T.

being satisfied with the stolen spoils of a whole alien nation, I robbed my own child of her property and appeared by proxy in court, a spectacle to the civilized world, to defend the act and complete the crime. It is as I have said: they are unfair, unjust; they will resurrect and give new currency to such things as those, or to any other things that count against me, but they will not mention any act of mine that is in my favor. I have spent more money on art than any other monarch of my time, and they know it. Do they speak of it, do they tell about it? No, they do not. They prefer to work up what they call "ghastly statistics" into offensive kindergarten object lessons, whose purpose is to make sentimental people shudder, and prejudice them against me. They remark that "if the innocent blood shed in the Congo State by King Leopold were put in buckets and the buckets placed side by side, the line would stretch 2,000 miles; if the skeletons of his ten millions of starved and butchered dead could rise up and march in single file, it would take them seven months and four days to pass a given point; if compacted together in a body, they would occupy more ground than St. Louis covers, World's Fair and all; if they should all clap their bony hands at once, the grisly crash would be heard at a distance of –" Damnation, it makes me tired! And they do similar miracles with the money I have distilled from that blood and put into my pocket. They pile it into Egyptian pyramids; they carpet Saharas with it; they spread it across the sky, and the shadow it casts makes twilight in the earth. And the tears I have caused, the hearts I have broken – oh, nothing can persuade them to let *them* alone!

[*Meditative pause*] Well . . . no matter, I *did* beat the Yankees, anyway! there's comfort in that. [*Reads with mocking smile, the President's Order of Recognition of April 22, 1884*]

" . . . the government of the United States announces its sympathy with and approval of the humane and benevolent purposes of (my Congo scheme), and will order the officers of the United States, both on land and sea, to recognize its flag as the flag of a friendly government."

Possibly the Yankees would like to take that back, now, but they will find that my agents are not over there in America for nothing. But there is no danger; neither nations nor governments can afford to confess a blunder. [*With a contented smile, begins to read from "Report by Rev. W. M. Morrison, American missionary in the Congo Free State"*]

"I furnish herewith some of the many atrocious incidents which have come under my own personal observation; they reveal the *organized system* of plunder and outrage which has been perpetrated and is now being carried on in that unfortunate country by King Leopold of Belgium. I say King Leopold, because he and he *alone* is now responsible, since he is the *absolute sovereign. He styles himself such.* When our government in 1884 laid the foundation of the Congo Free State, by recognizing its flag, little did it know that this concern, parading under the guise of philanthropy, was really King Leopold of Belgium, one of the shrewdest, most heartless and most conscienceless rulers that ever sat on a throne. This is apart from his known corrupt morals, which have made his name and his family a byword in two continents. Our government would most certainly not have recognized that flag had it known that it was really King Leopold individually who was asking for recognition; had it known that it was setting up in the heart of Africa an *absolute monarchy*; had it known that, having put down African slavery in our own country at great cost of blood and money, it was *establishing a worse form of slavery right in Africa.*"

[*With evil joy*] Yes, I certainly was a shade too clever for the Yankees. It hurts; it gravels them. They can't get over it! Puts a shame upon them in another way, too, and a graver way; for they never can rid their records of the reproachful fact that their vain Republic, self-appointed Champion and Promoter of the Liberties of the World, is the only democracy in history that has lent its power and influence to the establishing of an *absolute monarchy*!

[*Contemplating, with an unfriendly eye, a stately pile of pamphlets*] Blister the meddlesome missionaries! They write tons of these things. They seem to be always around, always spying, always eye-witnessing the happenings; and everything they see they commit to paper. They are always prowling from place to place; the natives consider them their only friends; they go to them with their sorrows; they show them their scars and their wounds, inflicted by my soldier police; they hold up the stumps of their arms and lament because their hands have been chopped off, as punishment for not bringing in enough rubber, and as proof to be laid before my officers that the required punishment was well and truly carried out. One of these missionaries saw eighty-one of these hands drying over a fire for transmission to my officials – and of course he must go and set it down and print it. They travel and travel, they spy and spy! And nothing is too trivial for them to print. [*Takes up a pamphlet. Reads a passage from Report of a "Journey made in July, August and September, 1903, by Rev. A. E. Scrivener, a British missionary"*]

"... Soon we began talking, and without any encouragement on my part the natives began the tales I had become so accustomed to. They were living in peace and quietness when the white men came in from the lake with all sorts of requests to do this and that, and they thought it meant slavery. So they attempted to keep the white men out of their country but without avail. The rifles were too much for them. So they submitted and made up their minds to do the best they could under the altered circumstances. First came the command to build houses for the soldiers, and this was done without a murmur. Then they had to feed the soldiers and all the men and women – hangers on – who accompanied them. Then they were told to bring in rubber. This was quite a new thing for them to do. There was rubber in the forest several days away from their home, but that it was worth anything was news to them. A small reward was offered and a rush was made for the rubber. 'What strange white men, to give us cloth and beads for the sap of a wild vine.' They rejoiced in what they thought their good fortune. But soon the reward was reduced until at last they were told to bring in the rubber for nothing. To this they tried to demur; but to their great surprise several were shot by the soldiers, and the rest were told, with many curses and blows, to go at once or more would be killed. Terrified, they began to prepare their food for the fortnight's absence from the village which the collection of rubber entailed. The soldiers discovered them sitting about. 'What, not gone yet?' Bang! bang! bang! and down fell one and another, dead, in the midst of wives and companions. There is a terrible wail and an attempt made to prepare the dead for burial, but this is not allowed. All must go at once to the forest. Without food? Yes, without food. And off the poor wretches had to go without even their tinder boxes to make fires. Many died in the forests of hunger and exposure, and still more from the rifles of the ferocious soldiers in charge of the post. In spite of all their efforts the amount fell off and more and more were killed. I was shown around the place, and the sites of former big chiefs' settlements were pointed out. A careful estimate made the population of, say, seven years ago, to be 2,000 people in and about the post, within a radius of, say, a quarter of a mile. All told, they would not muster 200 now, and there is so much sadness and gloom about them that they are fast decreasing.

"We stayed there all day on Monday and had many talks with the people. On the Sunday some of the boys had told me of some bones which they had seen, so on the Monday I asked to be shown these bones. Lying about on the grass, within a few yards of the house I was occupying, were numbers of human skulls, bones, in some cases complete skeletons. I counted thirty-six skulls, and saw many sets of bones from which the skulls were missing. I called one of the men and asked the meaning of it. 'When the rubber palaver began,' said he, 'the soldiers shot so many we grew tired of burying, and very often we were not allowed to bury; and so just dragged the bodies out into the grass and left them. There are hundreds all around if you would like to see them.' But I had seen more than enough, and was sickened by the stories that came from men and women alike of the awful time they had passed through. The Bulgarian atrocities might be considered as mildness itself when compared with what was done here. How the people submitted I don't know, and even now I wonder as I think of their patience. That some of them managed to run away is some cause for thankfulness. I stayed there two days and the one thing that impressed itself upon me was the collection of rubber. I saw long files of men come in, as at Bongo, with their little baskets under their arms; saw them paid their milk tin full of salt, and the two yards of calico flung to the headmen; saw their trembling timidity, and in fact a great deal that all went to prove the state of terrorism that exists and the virtual slavery in which the people are held."

That is their way; they spy and spy, and run into print with every foolish trifle. And that British consul, Mr. Casement, is just like them. He gets hold of a *diary which had been kept by one of my government officers*, and, although it is a private diary and intended for no eye but its owner's, Mr. Casement is so lacking in delicacy and refinement as to print passages from it. [*Reads a passage from the diary*]

"Each time the corporal goes out to get rubber, cartridges are given him. He must bring back all not used, and for every one used he must bring back a right hand. M. P. told me that sometimes they shot a cartridge at an animal in hunting; they then cut off a hand from a living man. As to the extent to which this is carried on, he informed me that in six months the State on the Mambogo River had used 6,000 cartridges, which means that 6,000 people are killed or mutilated. It means more than 6,000, for the people have told me repeatedly that the soldiers kill the children with the butt of their guns."

When the subtle consul thinks silence will be more effective than words, he employs it. Here he leaves it to be recognized that a thousand killings and mutilations a month is a large output for so small a region as the Mambogo River concession, silently indicating the dimensions of it by accompanying his report with a map of the prodigious Congo State, in which there is not room for so small an object as that river. That silence is intended to say, "If it is a thousand a month in this little corner, imagine the output of the whole vast State!" A gentleman would not descend to these furtivenesses.

Now as to the mutilations. You can't head off a Congo critic and make him stay headed-off; he dodges, and straightway comes back at you from another direction. They are full of slippery arts. When the mutilations (severing hands, unsexing men, etc.) began to stir Europe, we hit upon the idea of excusing them with a retort which we judged would knock them dizzy on that subject for good and all, and leave them nothing more to say; to wit, we boldly laid the custom on the natives, and said we did not invent it, but only followed it. Did it knock them dizzy? did it shut their mouths? Not for an hour. They dodged, and came straight back at us with the remark that "if a Christian king can perceive a saving moral difference between inventing bloody barbarities, and *imitating them from savages*, for charity's sake let him get what comfort he can out of his confession!"

It is most annoying, the way that that consul acts – that spy, that busy-body. [*Takes up pamphlet "Treatment of Women and Children in the Congo State; what Mr. Casement Saw in 1903"*] Hardly two years ago! Intruding that date upon the public was a piece of cold malice. It was intended to weaken the force of my press syndicate's assurances to the public that my severities in the Congo *ceased*, and ceased utterly, *years and years ago*. This man is fond of trifles – revels in them, gloats over them, pets them, fondles them, sets them all down. One doesn't need to drowse through his monotonous report to see that; the mere sub-headings of its chapters prove it. [*Reads*]

"Two hundred and forty persons, *men, women, and children*, compelled to supply government with *one ton* of carefully prepared foodstuffs *per week*, receiving in remuneration, all told, the princely sum of 15s. 10d!"

Very well, it was liberal. It was not much short of a penny a week for each nigger. It suits this consul to belittle it, yet he knows very well that I could have had both the food and the labor for nothing. I can prove it by a thousand instances. [*Reads*]

"Expedition against a village behindhand in its (compulsory) supplies; result, slaughter of sixteen persons; among them three women and a boy of five years. Ten carried off, to be prisoners till ransomed; among them a child, who died during the march."

But he is careful not to explain that we are *obliged* to resort to ransom to collect debts, where the people have nothing to pay with. Families that escape to the woods sell some of their members into slavery and thus provide the ransom. He knows that I would stop this if I could find a less objectionable way to collect their debts ... Mm – here is some more of the consul's delicacy! He reports a conversation he had with some natives:

Q. "How do you know it was the *white* men themselves who ordered these cruel things to be done to you? These things must have been done without the white man's knowledge by the black soldiers."

A. "The white men told their soldiers: 'You only kill *women*; you cannot kill men. You must prove that you kill men.' So then the soldiers when they killed us" (here he stopped and hesitated and then pointing to ... he said:) "then they ... and took them to the white men, who said: 'It is true, you have killed *men*.' "

Q. "You say this is true? Were many of you so treated after being shot?"

All [*shouting out*]: *"Nkoto! Nkoto!"* ("Very many! Very many!")

There was no doubt that these people were not inventing. Their vehemence, their flashing eyes, their excitement, were not simulated.

Of course the critic had to divulge that; he has no self-respect. All his kind reproach me, although they know quite well that I took no pleasure in punishing the men in that particular way, but only did it as a warning to other delinquents. Ordinary punishments are no good with ignorant savages; they make no impression. [*Reads more sub-heads*]

"Devasted region; population reduced from 40,000 to 8,000."

He does not take the trouble to say how it happened. He is fertile in concealments. He hopes his readers and his Congo reformers, of the Lord-Aberdeen-Norbury-John-Morley-Sir-Gilbert-Parker stripe, will think they were all killed. They were not. The great majority of them escaped. They fled to the bush with their families because of the rubber raids, and it was there they died of hunger. Could we help that?

One of my sorrowing critics observes: "Other Christian rulers tax their people, but furnish schools, courts of law, roads, light, water and protection to life and limb in return; King Leopold taxes his stolen nation, but provides *nothing in return but hunger, terror, grief, shame, captivity, mutilation and massacre.*" That is their style! I furnish "nothing!" I send the gospel to the survivors; these censure-mongers know it, but they would rather have their tongues cut out than mention it. I have several times required my raiders to give the dying an opportunity to kiss the sacred emblem; and if they obeyed me I have without doubt been the humble means of saving many souls. None of my traducers have had the fairness to mention this; but let it pass; there is One who has not overlooked it, and that is my solace, that is my consolation.

[*Puts down the Report, takes up a pamphlet, glances along the middle of it*]

This is where the "death-trap" comes in. Meddlesome mission-ary spying around – Rev. W. H. Sheppard. Talks with a black raider of mine after a raid; cozens him into giving away some par-ticulars. The raider remarks:

"I demanded 30 slaves from this side of the stream and 30 from the other side; 2 points of ivory, 2,500 balls of rubber, 13 goats, 10 fowls and 6 dogs, some corn chumy, etc.

'How did the fight come up?' I asked.

'I sent for all their chiefs, sub-chiefs, men and women, to come on a certain day, saying that I was going to finish all the palaver. When they entered these small gates (the walls being made of fences brought from other villages, the high native ones) I demanded all my pay or I would kill them; so they refused to pay me, and I ordered the fence to be closed so they couldn't run away; then we killed them here inside the fence. The panels of the fence fell down and some escaped.'

'How many did you kill?' I asked.

'We killed plenty, will you see some of them?'

That was just what I wanted.

He said: 'I think we have killed between eighty and ninety, and those in the other villages I don't know, I did not go out but sent my people.'

He and I walked out on the plain just near the camp. There were three dead bodies with the flesh carved off from the waist down.

'Why are they carved so, only leaving the bones?' I asked.

'My people ate them,' he answered promptly. He then explained, 'The men who have young children do not eat people, but all the rest ate them.' On the left was a big man, shot in the back and without a head. (All these corpses were nude.)

'Where is the man's head?' I asked.

'Oh, they made a bowl of the forehead to rub up tobacco and diamba in.'

We continued to walk and examine until late in the afternoon, and counted forty-one bodies. The rest had been eaten up by the people.

On returning to the camp, we crossed a young woman, shot in the back of the head, one hand was cut away. I asked why, and Mulunba N'Cusa explained that they always cut off the right hand to give to the State on their return.

'Can you not show me some of the hands?' I asked.

So he conducted us to a framework of sticks, under which was burning a slow fire, and there they were, the right hands – I counted them, eighty-one in all.

There were not less than sixty women (Bena Pianga) prisoners. I saw them.

We all say that we have as fully as possible investigated the whole outrage, and find it was a plan previously made to get all the stuff possible and to catch and kill the poor people in the 'death-trap.' "

Another detail, as we see! – cannibalism. They report cases of it with a most offensive frequency. My traducers do not forget to remark that, inasmuch as I am absolute and with a word can

prevent in the Congo anything I choose to prevent, then whatsoever is done there by my permission is my act, my *personal* act; that
I do it; that the hand of my agent is as truly *my* hand as if it were
attached to my own arm; and so they picture me in my robes of
state, with my crown on my head, munching human flesh, saying
grace, mumbling thanks to Him from whom all good things come.
Dear, dear, when the soft-hearts get hold of a thing like that missionary's contribution they quite lose their tranquility over it.
They speak out profanely and reproach Heaven for allowing such
a fiend to live. Meaning me. They think it irregular. They go
shuddering around, brooding over the reduction of that Congo
population from 25,000,000 to 15,000,000 in the twenty years of
my administration; then they burst out and call me "the King with
Ten Million Murders on his Soul." They call me a "record." The
most of them do not stop with charging merely the 10,000,000
against me. No, they reflect that but for me the population, by natural increase, would now be 30,000,000, so they charge another
5,000,000 against me and make my total death-harvest 15,000,000.
They remark that the man who killed the goose that laid the
golden egg was responsible for the eggs she would subsequently
have laid if she had been let alone. Oh, yes, they call me a "record."
They remark that twice in a generation, in India, the Great Famine destroys 2,000,000 out of a population of 320,000,000, and the
whole world holds up its hands in pity and horror; then they fall
to wondering where the world would find room for its emotions if
I had a chance to trade places with the Great Famine for twenty
years! The idea fires their fancy, and they go on and imagine the
Famine coming in state at the end of the twenty years and prostrat-
ing itself before me, saying: "Teach me, Lord, I perceive that I am
but an apprentice." And next they imagine Death coming, with
his scythe and hour-glass, and begging me to marry his daughter
and reorganize his plant and run the business. For the whole world,
you see! By this time their diseased minds are under full steam,
and they get down their books and expand their labors, with me
for text. They hunt through all biography for my match, working
Attila, Torquemada, Ghengis Khan, Ivan the Terrible, and the
rest of that crowd for all they are worth, and evilly exulting when
they cannot find it. Then they examine the historical earthquakes
and cyclones and blizzards and cataclysms and volcanic eruptions:
verdict, none of them "in it" with me. At last they do really hit it
(as they think), and they close their labors with conceding –

reluctantly – that I have *one* match in history, but only one – the *Flood*. This is intemperate.

But they are always that, when they think of me. They can no more keep quiet when my name is mentioned than can a glass of water control its feelings with a seidlitz powder in its bowels. The bizarre things they can imagine, with me for an inspiration! One Englishman offers to give me the odds of three to one and bet me anything I like, up to 20,000 guineas, that for 2,000,000 years I am going to be the most conspicuous foreigner in hell. The man is so beside himself with anger that he does not perceive that the idea is foolish. Foolish and unbusinesslike: you see, there could be no winner; both of us would be losers, on account of the loss of interest on the stakes; at four or five per cent. compounded, this would amount to – I do not know how much, exactly, but, by the time the term was up and the bet payable, a person could buy hell itself with the accumulation.

Another madman wants to construct a memorial for the perpetuation of my name, out of my 15,000,000 skulls and skeletons, and is full of vindictive enthusiasm over his strange project. He has it all ciphered out and drawn to scale. Out of the skulls he will build a combined monument and mausoleum to me which shall exactly duplicate the Great Pyramid of Cheops, whose base covers thirteen acres, and whose apex is 451 feet above ground. He desires to stuff me and stand me up in the sky on that apex, robed and crowned, with my "pirate flag" in one hand and a butcher-knife and pendant handcuffs in the other. He will build the pyramid in the centre of a depopulated tract, a brooding solitude covered with weeds and the mouldering ruins of burned villages, where the spirits of the starved and murdered dead will voice their laments forever in the whispers of the wandering winds. Radiating from the pyramid, like the spokes of a wheel, there are to be forty grand avenues of approach, each thirty-five miles long, and each fenced on both sides by skulless skeletons standing a yard and a half apart and festooned together in line by short chains stretching from wrist to wrist and attached to tried and true old handcuffs stamped with my private trade-mark, a crucifix and butcher-knife crossed, with motto, "By this sign we prosper;" each osseous fence to consist of 200,000 skeletons on a side, which is 400,000 to each avenue. It is remarked with satisfaction that it aggregates three or four thousand miles (single-ranked) of skeletons, – 15,000,000 all told – and would stretch across America from New York to San Francisco.

It is remarked further, in the hopeful tone of a railroad company forecasting showy extensions of its mileage, that my output is 500,000 corpses a year when my plant is running full time, and that therefore if I am spared ten years longer there will be fresh skulls enough to add 175 feet to the pyramid, making it by a long way the loftiest architectural construction on the earth, and fresh skeletons enough to continue the transcontinental file (on piles) a thousand miles into the Pacific. The cost of gathering the materials from my "widely scattered and innumerable private graveyards," and transporting them, and building the monument and the radiating grand avenues, is duly ciphered out, running into an aggregate of millions of guineas, and then – why then, (— —!! — —!!) this idiot asks me *to furnish the money!* [*Sudden and effusive application of the crucifix*] He reminds me that my yearly income from the Congo is millions of guineas, and that "*only*" 5,000,000 would be required for his enterprise. Every day wild attempts are made upon my purse; they do not affect me, they cost me not a thought. But *this one* – this one troubles me, makes me nervous; for there is no telling what an unhinged creature like this may think of next ... *If he should think of Carnegie* – but I must banish that thought out of my mind! it worries my days; it troubles my sleep. That way lies madness. [*After a pause*] There is no other way – I have got to buy Carnegie.

[*Harassed and muttering, walks the floor a while, then takes to the Consul's chapter-headings again. Reads*]

"Government starved a woman's children to death and killed her sons."

"Butchery of women and children."

"The native has been converted into a being without ambition because without hope."

"Women chained by the neck by rubber sentries."

"Women refuse to bear children because, with a baby to carry, they cannot well run away and hide from the soldiers."

"Statement of a child. 'I, my mother, my grandmother and my sister, we ran away into the bush. A great number of our people were killed by the soldiers ... After that they saw a little bit of my mother's head, and the soldiers ran quickly to where we were and caught my grandmother, my mother, my sister and another little one younger than us. Each wanted my mother for a wife, and argued about it, so they finally decided to kill her.

They shot her through the stomach with a gun and she fell, and
when I saw that I cried very much, because they killed my
grandmother and mother and I was left alone. I saw it all
done!' "

It has a sort of pitiful sound, although they are only blacks. It
carries me back and back into the past, to when my children were
little, and would fly – to the bush, so to speak – when they saw me
coming . . . [*Resumes the reading of chapter-headings*]

"They put a knife through a child's stomach."
"They cut off the hands and brought them to C. D. (white
officer) and spread them out in a row for him to see."
"Captured children left in the bush to die, by the soldiers."
"Friends came to ransom a captured girl; but sentry refused,
saying the white man wanted her because she was young."
"Extract from a native girl's testimony. 'On our way the soldiers saw a little child, and when they went to kill it the child
laughed, so the soldier took the butt of his gun and struck the
child with it and then cut off its head. One day they killed my
half-sister and cut off her head, hands and feet, because she had
bangles on. Then they caught another sister, and sold her to the
W. W. people, and now she is a slave there.' "

The little child laughed! [*A long pause. Musing*] That innocent
creature. Somehow – I wish it had not laughed. [*Reads*]

"Mutilated children."
"Government encouragement of inter-tribal slave-traffic.
The monstrous fines levied upon villages tardy in their supplies
of foodstuffs compel the natives to sell their fellows – and chil-
dren – to other tribes in order to meet the fine."
"A father and mother forced to sell their little boy."
"Widow forced to sell her little girl."

[*Irritated*] Hang the monotonous grumbler, what would he have
me do! Let a widow off merely because she is a widow? He knows
quite well that there is nothing much left, now, *but* widows. I have
nothing against widows, as a class, but business is business, and
I've got to live, haven't I, even if it does cause inconvenience to
somebody here and there? [*Reads*]

"Men intimidated by the torture of their wives and daughters.
(To make the men furnish rubber and supplies and so get their

captured women released from chains and detention.) The sentry explained to me that he caught the women and brought them in (chained together neck to neck) by direction of his employer."

"An agent explained that he was forced to catch women in preference to men, as then the men brought in supplies quicker; but he did not explain how the children deprived of their parents obtained their own food supplies."

"A file of 15 (captured) women."

"Allowing women and children to die of starvation in prison."

[*Musing*] Death from *hunger*. A lingering, long misery that must be. Days and days, and still days and days, the forces of the body failing, dribbling away, little by little – yes, it must be the hardest death of all. And to see food carried by, every day, and you can have none of it! Of course the little children cry for it, and that wrings the mother's heart ... [*A sigh*] Ah, well, it cannot be helped; circumstances make this discipline necessary. [*Reads*]

"The crucifying of sixty women!"

How stupid, how tactless! Christendom's goose flesh will rise with horror at the news. "Profanation of the sacred emblem!" That is what Christendom will shout. Yes, Christendom will buzz. It can hear me charged with half a million murders a year for twenty years and keep its composure, but to profane the Symbol is quite another matter. It will regard this as serious. It will wake up and want to look into my record. Buzz? Indeed it will; I seem to hear the distant hum already ... It was wrong to crucify the women, clearly wrong, manifestly wrong, I can see it now, myself, and am sorry it happened, sincerely sorry. I believe it would have answered just as well to skin them ... [*With a sigh*] But none of us thought of that; one cannot think of everything; after all it is but human to err.

It will make a stir, it surely will, these crucifixions. Persons will begin to ask again, as now and then in times past, how I can hope to win and keep the respect of the human race if I continue to give up my life to murder and pillage. [*Scornfully*] When have they heard me say I wanted the respect of the human race? Do they confuse me with the common herd? do they forget that I am a king? What king has valued the respect of the human race? I mean deep down in his private heart. If they would reflect, they would know that it is impossible that a king should value the respect of the human race. He stands upon an eminence and looks out over the world and sees multitudes of meek human things worshiping the persons, and submitting to the oppressions and exactions, of a dozen human things who are in no way better or finer than themselves – made on just their own pattern, in fact, and out of the same quality of mud. When it *talks*, it is a race of whales; but a king knows it for a race of tadpoles. Its history gives it away. If men were really *men*, how could a Czar be possible? and how could I be possible? But we *are* possible; we are quite safe; and with God's help we shall continue the business at the old stand. It will be found that the race will put up with us, in its docile immemorial way. It may pull a wry face now and then, and make large talk, but it will stay on its knees all the same.

Making large talk is one of its specialties. It works itself up, and froths at the mouth, and just when you think it is going to throw a brick, – it heaves a poem! Lord, what a race it is! [*Reads*]

A CZAR – 1905

"A pasteboard autocrat; a despot out of date;
　A fading planet in the glare of day;
　A flickering candle in the bright sun's ray,
Burnt to the socket; fruit left too late,
　High on a blighted bough, ripe till it's rotten.
　By God forsaken and by time forgotten,
Watching the crumbling edges of his lands,
　A spineless god to whom dumb millions pray,
　From Finland in the West to far Cathay.
Lord of a frost-bound continent he stands,
　Her seeming ruin his dim mind appalls,
And in the frozen stupor of his sleep
　He hears dull thunders, pealing as she falls,
And mighty fragments dropping in the deep."*

It is fine, one is obliged to concede it; it is a great picture, and impressive. The mongrel handles his pen well. Still, with opportunity, I would cruci – flay him ... "A spineless god." It is the Czar to a dot – a god, and spineless; a royal invertebrate, poor lad; softhearted and out of place. "A spineless god *to whom dumb millions pray*." Remorselessly correct; concise, too, and compact – the soul

* B. H. Nadal, in *New York Times*.

and spirit of the human race compressed into half a sentence. On their knees – 140,000,000. On their knees to a little tin deity. Massed together, they would stretch away, and away, and away, across the plains, fading and dimming and failing in a measureless perspective – why, even the telescope's vision could not reach to the final frontier of that continental spread of human servility. Now *why* should a king value the respect of the human race? It is quite unreasonable to expect it. A curious race, certainly! It finds fault with me and with my occupations, and forgets that neither of us could exist an hour without its sanction. It is our confederate and all-powerful protector. It is our bulwark, our friend, our fortress. For this it has our gratitude, our deep and honest gratitude – but not our respect. Let it snivel and fret and grumble if it likes; that is all right; we do not mind that.

[*Turns over leaves of a scrapbook, pausing now and then to read a clipping and make a comment*] The poets – how they do hunt that poor Czar! French, Germans, English, Americans – they all have a bark at him. The finest and capablest of the pack, and the fiercest, are Swilburne (English, I think), and a pair of Americans, Thomas Bailey Eldridge and Colonel Richard Waterson Gilder, of the sentimental periodical called *Century Magazine and Louisville Courier-Journal*. They certainly have uttered some very strong yelps. I can't seem to find them – I must have mislaid them . . . If a poet's bite were as terrible as his bark, why dear me – but it isn't. A wise king minds neither of them; but the poet doesn't know it. It's a case of little dog and lightning express. When the Czar goes thundering by, the poet skips out and rages alongside for a little distance, then returns to his kennel wagging his head with satisfaction, and thinks he has inflicted a memorable scare, whereas nothing has really happened – the Czar didn't know he was around. They never bark at me; I wonder why that is. I suppose my Corruption-Department buys them. That must be it, for certainly I ought to inspire a bark or two; I'm rather choice material, I should say. Why – here *is* a yelp at me. [*Mumbling a poem*]

> ". . . What gives thee holy right to murder hope
> And water ignorance with human blood?
>
> . . .
>
> From what high universe-dividing power
> Draws't thou thy wondrous, ripe brutality?
>
> . . .

O horrible . . . Thou God who seest these things
Help us to blot this terror from the earth."

. . . No, I see it is "To the Czar,"* after all. But there are those
who would say it fits me – and rather snugly, too. "Ripe brutality."
They would say the Czar's isn't ripe yet, but that mine is; and not
merely *ripe* but rotten. Nothing could keep them from saying that;
they would think it smart. "This terror." Let the Czar keep that
name; I am supplied. This long time I have been "the monster";
that was their favorite – the monster of crime. But now I have a
new one. They have found a fossil Dinosaur fifty-seven feet long
and sixteen feet high, and set it up in the museum in New York
and labeled it "Leopold II." But it is no matter, one does not look
for manners in a republic. Um . . . that reminds me; I have never
been caricatured. Could it be that the corsairs of the pencil could
not find an offensive symbol that was big enough and ugly enough
to do my reputation justice? [*After reflection*] There is no other way
– I will buy the Dinosaur. And suppress it. [*Rests himself with some
more chapter-headings. Reads*]

"More mutilation of children." (Hands cut off.)
"Testimony of American Missionaries."
"Evidence of British Missionaries."

It is all the same old thing – tedious repetitions and duplications
of shop-worn episodes; mutilations, murders, massacres, and so
on, and so on, till one gets drowsy over it. Mr. Morel intrudes at
this point, and contributes a comment which he could just as well
have kept to himself – and throws in some italics, of course; these
people can never get along without italics:

"It is one heartrending story of human misery from beginning
to end, and *it is all recent.*"

Meaning 1904 and 1905. I do not see how a person can act so.
This Morel is a king's subject, and reverence for monarchy should
have restrained him from reflecting upon me with that exposure.
This Morel is a reformer; a Congo reformer. That sizes *him* up. He
publishes a sheet in Liverpool called "The West African Mail,"
which is supported by the voluntary contributions of the sap-
headed and the soft-hearted; and every week it steams and reeks

* Louise Morgan Sill, in *Harper's Weekly.*

and festers with up-to-date "Congo atrocities" of the sort detailed in this pile of pamphlets here. I will suppress it. I suppressed a Congo atrocity book there; after it was actually in print; it should not be difficult for me to suppress a newspaper.

[*Studies some photographs of mutilated negroes – throws them down. Sighs*] The kodak has been a sore calamity to us. The most powerful enemy that has confronted us, indeed. In the early years we had no trouble in getting the press to "expose" the tales of the mutilations as slanders, lies, inventions of busy-body American missionaries and exasperated foreigners who had found the "open door" of the Berlin-Congo charter closed against them when they innocently went out there to trade; and by the press's help we got the Christian nations everywhere to turn an irritated and unbelieving ear to those tales and say hard things about the tellers of them. Yes, all things went harmoniously and pleasantly in those good days, and I was looked up to as the benefactor of a down-trodden and friendless people. Then all of a sudden came the crash! That is to say, the incorruptible *kodak* – and all the harmony went to hell! The only witness I have encountered in my long experience that I couldn't bribe. Every Yankee missionary and every interrupted trader sent home and got one; and now – oh, well, the pictures get sneaked around everywhere, in spite of all we can do to ferret them out and suppress them. Ten thousand pulpits and ten thousand presses are saying the good word for me all the time and placidly and convincingly denying the mutilations. Then that trivial little kodak, that a child can carry in its pocket, gets up, uttering never a word, and knocks them dumb!

... What is this fragment? [*Reads*]

"But enough of trying to tally off his crimes! His list is interminable, we should never get to the end of it. His awful shadow lies across his Congo Free State, and under it an unoffending nation of 15,000,000 is withering away and swiftly succumbing to their miseries. It is a land of graves; it is *The* Land of Graves; it is the Congo Free Graveyard. It is a majestic thought: that is, this ghastliest episode in all human history is the work of *one man alone*; one solitary man; just a single individual – Leopold, King of the Belgians. He is personally and solely responsible for all the myriad crimes that have blackened the history of the Congo State. He is *sole* master there; he is absolute. He could have prevented the crimes by his mere command; he could stop them today with a word. He withholds the word. For his pocket's sake.

It seems strange to see a king destroying a nation and laying waste a country for mere sordid money's sake, and solely and only for that. Lust of conquest is royal; kings have always exercised that stately vice; we are used to it, by old habit we condone it, perceiving a certain dignity in it; but *lust of money – lust of shillings – lust of nickels – lust of dirty coin*, not for the nation's enrichment but for *the king's alone –* this is new. It distinctly revolts us, we cannot seem to reconcile ourselves to it, we resent it, we despise it, we say it is shabby, unkingly, out of character. Being democrats we ought to jeer and jest, we ought to rejoice to see the purple dragged in the dirt, but – well, account for it as we may, we don't. We see this awful king, this pitiless and blood-drenched king, this money-crazy king towering toward the sky in a world-solitude of sordid crime, unfellowed and apart from the human race, sole butcher for personal gain findable in all his caste, ancient or modern, pagan or Christian, proper and legitimate target for the scorn of the lowest and the highest, and the execrations of all who hold in cold esteem the oppressor and the coward; and – well, it is a mystery, but *we do not wish to look*; for he is a king, and it hurts us, it troubles us, by ancient and inherited instinct it shames us to see a king degraded to this aspect, and we shrink from hearing the particulars of how it happened. *We shudder* and *turn away* when we come upon them in print."

Why, certainly – *that* is my protection. And you will continue to do it. I know the human race.

WILLIAM DEAN HOWELLS

IS IT TRUE that the sun of a man's mentality touches noon at forty and then begins to wane toward setting? Dr. Osler is charged with saying so. Maybe he said it, maybe he didn't; I don't know which it is. But if he said it, and if it is true, I can point him to a case which proves his rule. Proves it by being an exception to it. To this place I nominate Mr. Howells.

I read his *Venetian Days* about forty years ago. I compare it with his paper on Machiavelli in a late number of *Harper*, and I cannot find that his English has suffered any impairment. For forty years his English has been to me a continual delight and astonishment. In the sustained exhibition of certain great qualities – clearness, compression, verbal exactness, and unforced and seemingly unconscious felicity of phrasing – he is, in my belief, without his peer in the English-writing world. *Sustained*. I intrench myself behind that protecting word. There are others who exhibit those great qualities as greatly as does he, but only by intervalled distributions of rich moonlight, with stretches of veiled and dimmer landscape between; whereas Howells's moon sails cloudless skies all night and all the nights.

In the matter of verbal exactness Mr. Howells has no superior, I suppose. He seems to be almost always able to find that elusive and shifty grain of gold, the *right word*. Others have to put up with approximations, more or less frequently; he has better luck. To me, the others are miners working with the gold-pan – of necessity some of the gold washes over and escapes; whereas, in my fancy, he is quicksilver raiding down a riffle – no grain of the metal stands much chance of eluding him. A powerful agent is the right word: it lights the reader's way and makes it plain; a close approximation to it will answer, and much travelling is done in a well-enough fashion by its help, but we do not welcome it and applaud it and rejoice in it as we do when *the* right one blazes out on us. Whenever we come upon one of those intensely right words in a book or a newspaper the resulting effect is physical as well as spiritual, and electrically prompt: it tingles exquisitely around through the walls of the mouth and tastes as tart and crisp and good as the autumn-butter that creams the sumac-berry. One has no time to examine the word and vote upon its rank and standing, the automatic recognition of its supremacy is so immediate. There is a plenty of acceptable literature which deals largely in approximations, but it may be likened to a fine landscape seen through the rain; the right word would dismiss the rain, then you would see it better. It doesn't rain when Howells is at work.

And where does he get the easy and effortless flow of his speech? and its cadenced and undulating rhythm? and its architectural felicities of construction, its graces of expression, its pemmican quality of compression, and all that? Born to him, no doubt. All in shining good order in the beginning, all extraordinary; and all just as shining, just as extraordinary today, after forty years of diligent wear and tear and use. He passed his fortieth year long and long ago; but I think his English of to-day – his perfect English, I wish to say – can throw down the glove before his English of that antique time and not be afraid.

I will go back to the paper on Machiavelli now, and ask the reader to examine this passage from it which I append. I do not mean, examine it in a bird's-eye way; I mean search it, study it. And, of course, read it aloud. I may be wrong, still it is my conviction that one cannot get out of finely wrought literature all that is in it by reading it mutely:

> Mr. Dyer is rather of the opinion, first luminously suggested by Macaulay, that Machiavelli was in earnest, but must not be judged as a political moralist of our time and race would be judged. He thinks that Machiavelli was in earnest, as none but an idealist can be, and he is the first to imagine him an idealist immersed in realities, who involuntarily transmutes the events under his eye into something like the visionary issues of reverie. The Machiavelli whom he depicts does not cease to be politically a republican and socially a just man because he holds up an atrocious despot like Cæsar Borgia as a mirror for rulers. What Machiavelli beheld round him in Italy was a civic disorder in which there was oppression without statecraft, and revolt without patriotism. When a miscreant like Borgia appeared upon the scene and reduced both tyrants and rebels to an apparent quiescence, he might very well seem to such a dreamer the savior of society whom a certain sort of dreamers are always looking for. Machiavelli was no less honest when he honored the diabolical force of Cæsar Borgia than Carlyle was when at different times he extolled the strong man who destroys liberty in creating order. But Carlyle has only just ceased to be mistaken

for a reformer, while it is still Machiavelli's hard fate to be so trammelled in his material that his name stands for whatever is most malevolent and perfidious in human nature.

You see how easy and flowing it is; how unvexed by ruggednesses, clumsinesses, broken metres; how simple and – so far as you or I can make out – unstudied; how clear, how limpid, how understandable, how unconfused by cross-currents, eddies, undertows; how seemingly unadorned, yet is all adornment, like the lily-of-the-valley; and how compressed, how compact, without a complacency-signal hung out anywhere to call attention to it.

There are twenty-two lines in the quoted passage. After reading it several times aloud, one perceives that a good deal of matter is crowded into that small space. I think it is a model of compactness. When I take its materials apart and work them over and put them together in my way I find I cannot crowd the result back into the same hole, there not being room enough. I find it a case of a woman packing a man's trunk: he can get the things out, but he can't ever get them back again.

The proffered paragraph is a just and fair sample; the rest of the article is as compact as it is; there are no waste words. The sample is just in other ways: limpid, fluent, graceful, and rhythmical as it is, it holds no superiority in these respects over the rest of the essay. Also, the choice phrasing noticeable in the sample is not lonely; there is a plenty of its kin distributed through the other paragraphs. This is claiming much when that kin must face the challenge of a phrase like the one in the middle sentence: "an idealist immersed in realities, who involuntarily transmutes the events under his eye into something like the visionary issues of reverie." With a hundred words to do it with, the literary artisan could catch that airy thought and tie it down and reduce it to a concrete condition, visible, substantial, understandable and all right, like a cabbage; but the artist does it with twenty, and the result is a flower.

The quoted phrase, like a thousand others that have come from the same source, has the quality of certain scraps of verse which take hold of us and stay in our memories, we do not understand why, at first: all the words being the right words, none of them is conspicuous, and so they all seem inconspicuous, therefore we wonder what it is about them that makes their message take hold.

> The mossy marbles rest
> On the lips that he has prest

> In their bloom,
> And the names he loved to hear
> Have been carved for many a year
> On the tomb.

It is like a dreamy strain of moving music, with no sharp notes in it. The words are all "right" words, and all the same size. We do not notice it at first. We get the effect, it goes straight home to us, but we do not know why. It is when the right words are conspicuous that they thunder –

The glory that was Greece and the grandeur that was Rome!

When I go back from Howells old to Howells young I find him arranging and clustering English words well, but not any better than now. He is not more felicitous in concreting abstractions now than he was in translating, then, the visions of the eye of flesh into words that reproduced their forms and colors:

In Venetian streets they give the fallen snow no rest. It is at once shovelled into the canals by hundreds of half-naked *facchini*; and now in St. Mark's Place the music of innumerable shovels smote upon my ear; and I saw the shivering legion of poverty as it engaged the elements in a struggle for the possession of the Piazza. But the snow continued to fall, and through the twilight of the descending flakes all this toil and encounter looked like that weary kind of effort in dreams, when the most determined industry seems only to renew the task. The lofty crest of the bell-tower was hidden in the folds of falling snow, and I could no longer see the golden angel upon its summit. But looked at across the Piazza, the beautiful outline of St. Mark's Church was perfectly pencilled in the air, and the shifting threads of the snowfall were woven into a spell of novel enchantment around the structure that always seemed to me too exquisite in its fantastic loveliness to be anything but the creation of magic. The tender snow had compassionated the beautiful edifice for all the wrongs of time, and so hid the stains and ugliness of decay that it looked as if just from the hand of the builder – or, better said, just from the brain of the architect. There was marvellous freshness in the colors of the mosaics in the great arches of the façade, and all that gracious harmony into which the temple rises, of marble scrolls and leafy exuberance airily supporting the statues of the saints, was a hundred times etherealized by the purity and whiteness of the drifting flakes. The snow lay lightly on the golden globes that tremble like pea-cock-crests above the vast domes, and plumed them with softest white; it robed the saints in ermine; and it danced over all its work, as if exulting in its beauty – beauty which filled me with subtle, selfish yearning to keep such evanescent loveliness for the little-while-longer of my whole life, and with despair to think that even the poor lifeless shadow of it could never be fairly reflected in picture or poem.

Through the wavering snowfall, the Saint Theodore upon one of the granite pillars of the Piazzetta did not show so grim as his wont is, and the winged lion on the other might have been a winged lamb, so gentle and mild he looked by the tender light of the storm. The towers of the island churches loomed faint and far away in the dimness; the sailors in the rigging of the ships that lay in the Basin wrought like phantoms among the shrouds; the gondolas stole in and out of the opaque distance more noise-lessly and dreamily than ever; and a silence, almost palpable, lay upon the mutest city in the world.

The spirit of Venice is there: of a city where Age and Decay, fagged with distributing damage and repulsiveness among the other cities of the planet in accordance with the policy and busi-ness of their profession, come for rest and play between seasons, and treat themselves to the luxury and relaxation of sinking the shop and inventing and squandering charms all about, instead of abolishing such as they find, as is their habit when not on vacation.

In the working season they do business in Boston sometimes, and a character in *The Undiscovered Country* takes accurate note of pathetic effects wrought by them upon the aspects of a street of once dignified and elegant homes whose occupants have moved away and left them a prey to neglect and gradual ruin and progres-sive degradation; a descent which reaches bottom at last, when the street becomes a roost for humble professionals of the faith-cure and fortune-telling sort.

What a queer, melancholy house, what a queer, melancholy street! I don't think I was ever in a street before where quite so many professional ladies, with English surnames, preferred Madam to Mrs. on their door-plates. And the poor old place has such a desperately conscious air of going to the deuce. Every house seems to wince as you go by, and button itself up to the

chin for fear you should find out it had no shirt on, – so to speak.
I don't know what's the reason, but these material tokens of a
social decay afflict me terribly: a tipsy woman isn't dreadfuler
than a haggard old house, that's once been a home, in a street
like this.

Mr. Howells's pictures are not mere stiff, hard, accurate photographs; they are photographs with feeling in them, and sentiment,
photographs taken in a dream, one might say.

As concerns his humor, I will not try to say anything, yet I would
try if I had the words that might approximately reach up to its high
place. I do not think any one else can play with humorous fancies
so gracefully and delicately and deliciously as he does, nor has so
many to play with, nor can come so near making them look as if
they were doing the playing themselves and he was not aware
that they were at it. For they are unobtrusive, and quiet in their
ways, and well conducted. His is a humor which flows softly all
around about and over and through the mesh of the page, pervasive, refreshing, health-giving, and makes no more show and no
more noise than does the circulation of the blood.

There is another thing which is contentingly noticeable in Mr.
Howells's books. That is his "stage directions" – those artifices
which authors employ to throw a kind of human naturalness
around a scene and a conversation, and help the reader to see the
one and get at meanings in the other which might not be perceived
if intrusted unexplained to the bare words of the talk. Some
authors overdo the stage directions, they elaborate them quite
beyond necessity; they spend so much time and take up so much
room in telling us how a person said a thing and how he looked
and acted when he said it that we get tired and vexed and wish he
hadn't said it at all. Other authors' directions are brief enough,
but it is seldom that the brevity contains either wit or information.
Writers of this school go in rags, in the matter of stage directions;
the majority of them have nothing in stock but a cigar, a laugh, a
blush, and a bursting into tears. In their poverty they work these
sorry things to the bone. They say:

"... replied Alfred, flipping the ash from his cigar." (This
explains nothing; it only wastes space.)

"... responded Richard, with a laugh." (There was nothing to
laugh about; there never is. The writer puts it in from habit – automatically; he is paying no attention to his work, or he would see

that there is nothing to laugh at; often, when a remark is unusually and poignantly flat and silly, he tries to deceive the reader by enlarging the stage direction and making Richard break into "frenzies of uncontrollable laughter." This makes the reader sad.)

". . . murmured Gladys, blushing." This poor old shopworn blush is a tiresome thing. We get so we would rather Gladys would fall out of the book and break her neck than do it again. She is always doing it, and usually irrelevantly. Whenever it is her turn to murmur she hangs out her blush; it is the only thing she's got. In a little while we hate her, just as we do Richard.

". . . repeated Evelyn, bursting into tears." This kind keep a book damp all the time. They can't say a thing without crying. They cry so much about nothing that by and by when they have something to cry *about* they have gone dry; they sob, and fetch nothing; we are not moved. We are only glad.

They gravel me, these stale and overworked stage directions, these carbon films that got burnt out long ago and cannot now carry any faintest thread of light. It would be well if they could be relieved from duty and flung out in the literary back yard to rot and disappear along with the discarded and forgotten "steeds" and "halidomes" and similar stage-properties once so dear to our grandfathers. But I am friendly to Mr. Howells's stage directions; more friendly to them than to any one else's, I think. They are done with a competent and discriminating art, and are faithful to the requirements of a stage direction's proper and lawful office, which is to inform. Sometimes they convey a scene and its conditions so well that I believe I could see the scene and get the spirit and meaning of the accompanying dialogue if some one would read merely the stage directions to me and leave out the talk. For instance, a scene like this, from *The Undiscovered Country*:

". . . and she laid her arms with a beseeching gesture on her father's shoulder."

". . . she answered, following his gesture with a glance."

". . . she said, laughing nervously."

". . . she asked, turning swiftly upon him that strange, searching glance."

". . . she answered, vaguely."

". . . she reluctantly admitted."

". . . but her voice died wearily away, and she stood looking into his face with puzzled entreaty."

Mr. Howells does not repeat his forms, and does not need to; he can invent fresh ones without limit. It is mainly the repetition over and over again, by the third-rates, of worn and commonplace and juiceless forms that makes their novels such a weariness and vexation to us, I think. We do not mind one or two deliveries of their wares, but as we turn the pages over and keep on meeting them we presently get tired of them and wish they would do other things for a change:

"... replied Alfred, flipping the ash from his cigar."
"... responded Richard, with a laugh."
"... murmured Gladys, blushing."
"... repeated Evelyn, bursting into tears."
"... replied the Earl, flipping the ash from his cigar."
"... responded the undertaker, with a laugh."
"... murmured the chambermaid, blushing."
"... repeated the burglar, bursting into tears."
"... replied the conductor, flipping the ash from his cigar."
"... responded Arkwright, with a laugh."
"... murmured the chief of police, blushing."
"... repeated the housecat, bursting into tears."

And so on and so on; till at last it ceases to excite. I always notice stage directions, because they fret me and keep me trying to get out of their way, just as the automobiles do. At first; then by and by they become monotonous and I get run over.

Mr. Howells has done much work, and the spirit of it is as beautiful as the make of it. I have held him in admiration and affection so many years that I know by the number of those years that he is old now; but his heart isn't, nor his pen; and years do not count. Let him have plenty of them: there is profit in them for us.

July 1906

OUR GUEST

Society of the Pilgrims Luncheon for Mark Twain, Hotel Savoy, London

PILGRIMS, I DESIRE first to thank those undergraduates of Oxford. When a man has grown so old as I am, when he has reached the verge of seventy-two years, there is nothing that carries him back to the dreamland of his life, to his boyhood, like the recognition of those young hearts up yonder. And so I thank them out of my heart. I desire, too, to thank the Pilgrims of New York also for their kind notice and message which they have cabled over here. Mr. Birrell says he does not know how he got here. But he will be able to get away all right – he has not drunk anything since he came here. I am glad to know about those friends of his – Otway and Chatterton – fresh, new names to me. I am glad of the disposition he has shown to rescue them from the evils of poverty, and if they are still in London, I hope to have a talk with them. For a while I thought he was going to tell us the effect which my books had upon his growing manhood. I thought he was going to tell us how much that effect amounted to, and whether it really made him what he now is, but with the discretion born of Parliamentary experience he dodged that, and we do not know whether he read the books or not. He did that very neatly, I could not do it any better myself.

My books have had effects, and very good ones, too, here and there, and some others not so good. There is no doubt about that. But I remember one monumental instance of it years and years ago. Professor Norton, of Harvard, was over here, and when he came back to Boston I went out with Howells to call on him. Norton was allied in some way by marriage with Darwin. Mr. Norton was very gentle in what he had to say, and almost delicate, and he said: "Mr. Clemens, I have been spending some time with Mr. Darwin in England, and I should like to tell you something connected with that visit. You were the object of it, and I myself would have been very proud of it, but you may not be proud of it. At any rate, I am going to tell you what it was, and to leave you to regard it as you please. Mr. Darwin took me up to his bedroom and pointed out certain things there – pitcher plants, and so on, that he was measuring and watching from day to day – and he said, 'The chambermaid is permitted to do what she pleases in this room, but she must never touch those plants and never touch those books on that table by that candle. With those books I read myself to sleep every night.' Those were your own books." I said, "There is no question to my mind as to whether I should regard that as a compliment or not. I do regard it as a very great compliment, and a very high honor, that that great mind, laboring for the whole human race, should rest itself on my books. I am proud that he should read himself to sleep with them."

Now, I could not keep that to myself – I was so proud of it. As soon as I got home to Hartford I called up my oldest friend – and dearest enemy on occasion – the Rev. Joseph Twichell, my pastor, and I told him about that, and, of course, he was full of interest and venom. Those people who get no compliments like that feel like that. He went off. He did not issue any applause of any kind, and I did not hear of that subject for some time. But when Mr. Darwin passed away from this life, and some time after Darwin's *Life and Letters* came out, the Rev. Mr. Twichell procured an early copy of that work and found something in it which he considered applied to me. He came over to my house – it was snowing, raining, sleeting, but that did not make any difference to Twichell. He produced the book, and turned over and over, until he came to a certain place, when he said, "Here, look at this letter from Mr. Darwin to Sir Joseph Hooker." What Mr. Darwin said – I give you the idea and not the very words – was this: I do not know whether I ought to have devoted my whole life to these drudgeries in natural history and the other sciences or not, for while I may have gained in one way I have lost in another. Once I had a fine perception and appreciation of high literature, but in me that quality is atrophied. "That was the reason," said Mr. Twichell, "he was reading your books."

Mr. Birrell has touched lightly – very lightly, but in not an uncomplimentary way – on my position in this world as a moralist. I am glad to have that recognition, too, because I have suffered since I have been in this town; in the first place, right away, when I came here, from a newsman going around with a great red, highly displayed placard in the place of an apron. He was selling newspapers, and there were two sentences on that placard which would have been all right if they been punctuated; but they ran those two sentences together without a comma or anything, and that would naturally create a wrong impression, because it said, "Mark Twain arrives Ascot Cup stolen." No doubt many a person was misled by those sentences joined together in that unkind way. I have no doubt my character has suffered from it. I suppose I ought to defend my character, but how can I defend it? I can say here and now – and anybody can see by my face that I am sincere, that I speak the truth – that I have never seen that Cup. I have not got the Cup – I did not have a chance to get it. I have always had a good character in that way. I have hardly ever stolen anything, and if I did steal anything I had discretion enough to know about the value of it first. I do not steal things that are likely to get myself into trouble. I do not think any of us do that. I know we all take things – that is to be expected – but really, I have never taken anything, certainly in England, that amounts to any great thing. I do confess that when I was here seven years ago I stole a hat, but that did not amount to anything. It was not a good hat, and was only a clergyman's hat, anyway.

I was at a luncheon party, and Archdeacon Wilberforce was there also. I daresay he is an Archdeacon now – he was a Canon then – and he was serving in the Westminster Battery, if that is the proper term – I do not know, as you mix military and ecclesiastical things together so much. He left the luncheon table before I did. He began this, I did steal his hat, but he began by taking mine. I make that interjection because I would not accuse Archdeacon Wilberforce of stealing my hat – I should not think of it. I confine that phrase to myself. He merely took my hat. And with good judgment, too – it was a better hat than his. He came out before the luncheon was over, and sorted the hats in the hall, and selected one which suited. It happened to be mine. He went off with it. When I came out by and by there was no hat there which would go on my head except his, which was left behind. My head was not the customary size just at that time. I had been receiving a good many very nice and complimentary attentions, and my head was a couple of sizes larger than usual, and his hat just suited me. The bumps and corners were all right intellectually. There were results pleasing to me – possibly so to him. He found out whose hat it was, wrote me saying it was pleasant that all the way home, whenever he met anybody his gravities, his solemnities, his deep thoughts, his eloquent remarks were all snatched up by the people he met, and mistaken for brilliant humorisms.

I had another experience. It was not unpleasing. I was received with a deference which was entirely foreign to my experience by everybody whom I met, so that before I got home I had a much higher opinion of myself than I have ever had before or since. And there is in that very connection an incident which I remember at that old date which is rather melancholy to me, because it shows how a person can deteriorate in a mere seven years. It is seven years ago. I have not that hat now. I was going down Pall Mall, or some other of your big streets, and I recognized that that hat needed ironing. I went into a big shop and passed in my hat, and asked that it might be ironed. They were courteous, very courteous, even courtly. They brought that hat back to me presently very sleek and nice, and I asked how much there was to pay. They replied that they did not charge the clergy anything. I have cherished the delight of that moment from that day to this. It was the first thing I did the other day to go and hunt up that shop and hand in my hat to have it ironed. I said when it came back, "How much to pay?" They said, "Ninepence." In seven years I have acquired all that worldliness, and I am sorry to be back where I was seven years ago.

But now I am chaffing and chaffing and chaffing here, and I hope you will forgive me for that; but when a man stands on the verge of seventy-two you know perfectly well that he never reached that place without knowing what this life is – heartbreaking bereavement. And so our reverence is for our dead. We do not forget them; but our duty is toward the living; and if we can be cheerful, cheerful in spirit, cheerful in speech and in hope, that is a benefit to those who are around us.

My own history includes an incident which will always connect me with England in a pathetic way, for when I arrived here seven years ago with my wife and daughter – we had gone around the globe lecturing to raise money to clear off a debt – my wife and one of my daughters started across the ocean to bring to England our eldest daughter. She was twenty-four years of age and in the bloom of young womanhood, and we were unsuspecting. When my wife and daughter – and my wife has passed from this life since – when they had reached mid-Atlantic, a cablegram – one of those heart-breaking cablegrams which we all in our days have to experience – was put into my hand. It stated that that daughter of ours had gone to her long sleep. And so, as I say, I cannot always be cheerful, and I cannot always be chaffing; I must sometimes lay the cap and bells aside, and recognize that I am of the human race like the rest, and must have my cares and griefs. And, therefore, I noticed what Mr. Birrell said – I was so glad to hear him say it – something that was in the nature of these verses here at the top of this menu.

He lit our life with shafts of sun
   And vanquished pain.
Thus two great nations stand as one
   In honoring Twain.

I am very glad to have those verses. I am very glad and grateful for what Mr. Birrell said in that connection. I have received since I have been here, in this one week, hundreds of letters from all conditions of people in England – men, women, and children – and there is in them compliment, praise, and, above all and better than all, there is in them a note of affection. Praise is well, compliment is well, but affection – that is the last and final and most precious reward that any man can win, whether by character or achievement, and I am very grateful to have that reward. All these letters make me feel that here in England – as in America – when I stand under the English flag, I am not a stranger. I am not an alien, but at home.

June 25, 1907

IS SHAKESPEARE DEAD?

FROM MY AUTOBIOGRAPHY

CHAPTER I

Scattered here and there through the stacks of unpublished manuscript which constitute this formidable Autobiography and Diary of mine, certain chapters will in some distant future be found which deal with "Claimants" – claimants historically notorious: Satan, Claimant; the Golden Calf, Claimant; the Veiled Prophet of Khorassan, Claimant; Louis XVII., Claimant; William Shakespeare, Claimant; Arthur Orton, Claimant; Mary Baker G. Eddy, Claimant – and the rest of them. Eminent Claimants, successful Claimants, defeated Claimants, royal Claimants, pleb Claimants, showy Claimants, shabby Claimants, revered Claimants, despised Claimants, twinkle starlike here and there and yonder through the mists of history and legend and tradition – and oh, all the darling tribe are clothed in mystery and romance, and we read about them with deep interest and discuss them with loving sympathy or with rancorous resentment, according to which side we hitch ourselves to. It has always been so with the human race. There was never a Claimant that couldn't get a hearing, nor one that couldn't accumulate a rapturous following, no matter how flimsy and apparently unauthentic his claim might be. Arthur Orton's claim that he was the lost Tichborne baronet come to life again was as flimsy as Mrs. Eddy's that she wrote *Science and Health* from the direct dictation of the Deity; yet in England near forty years ago Orton had a huge army of devotees and incorrigible adherents, many of whom remained stubbornly unconvinced after their fat god had been proven an impostor and jailed as a perjurer, and to-day Mrs. Eddy's following is not only immense, but is daily augmenting in numbers and enthusiasm. Orton had many fine and educated minds among his adherents, Mrs. Eddy has had the like among hers from the beginning. Her church is as well equipped in those particulars as is any other church. Claimants can always count upon a following, it doesn't matter who they are, nor what they claim, nor whether they come with documents or without. It was always so. Down out of the long-vanished past, across the abyss of the ages, if you listen you can still hear the believing multitudes shouting for Perkin Warbeck and Lambert Simnel.

A friend has sent me a new book, from England – *The Shakespeare Problem Restated* – well restated and closely reasoned; and my fifty years' interest in that matter – asleep for the last three years – is excited once more. It is an interest which was born of Delia Bacon's book – away back in that ancient day – 1857, or maybe 1856. About a year later my pilot-master, Bixby, transferred me from his own steamboat to the *Pennsylvania*, and placed me under the orders and instructions of George Ealer – dead now, these many, many years. I steered for him a good many months – as was the humble duty of the pilot-apprentice: stood a daylight watch and spun the wheel under the severe superintendence and correction of the master. He was a prime chess player and an idolater of Shakespeare. He would play chess with anybody; even with me, and it cost his official dignity something to do that. Also – quite uninvited – he would read Shakespeare to me; not just casually, but by the hour, when it was his watch, and I was steering. He read well, but not profitably for me, because he constantly injected commands into the text. That broke it all up, mixed it all up, tangled it all up – to that degree, in fact, that if we were in a risky and difficult piece of river an ignorant person couldn't have told, sometimes, which observations were Shakespeare's and which were Ealer's. For instance:

What man dare, *I* dare!

Approach thou *what* are you laying in the leads for? what a hell of an idea! like the rugged ease her off a little, ease her off! rugged Russian bear, the armed rhinoceros or the *there* she goes! meet her, meet her! didn't you *know* she'd smell the reef if you crowded it like that? Hyrcan tiger; take any shape but that and my firm nerves she'll be in the *woods* the first you know! stop the starboard! come ahead strong on the larboard! back the starboard! ... *Now* then, you're all right; come ahead on the starboard; straighten up and go 'long, never tremble: or be alive again, and dare me to the desert damnation can't you keep away from that greasy water? pull her down! snatch her! snatch her baldheaded! with thy sword; if trembling I inhabit then, lay in the leads! – no, only the starboard one, leave the other alone, protest me the baby of a girl. Hence horrible shadow! eight bells – that watchman's asleep again, I reckon, go down and call Brown yourself, unreal mockery, hence!

He certainly was a good reader, and splendidly thrilling and stormy and tragic, but it was a damage to me, because I have never since been able to read Shakespeare in a calm and sane way. I cannot rid it of his explosive interlardings, they break in everywhere with their irrelevant "What in hell are you up to *now*! pull her down! more! *more*! – there now, steady as you go," and the other disorganizing interruptions that were always leaping from his mouth. When I read Shakespeare now, I can hear them as plainly as I did in that long-departed time – fifty-one years ago. I never regarded Ealer's readings as educational. Indeed they were a detriment to me.

His contributions to the text seldom improved it, but barring that detail he was a good reader, I can say that much for him. He did not use the book, and did not need to; he knew his Shakespeare as well as Euclid ever knew his multiplication table.

Did he have something to say – this Shakespeare-adoring Mississippi pilot – anent Delia Bacon's book? Yes. And he said it; said it all the time, for months – in the morning watch, the middle watch, the dog watch; and probably kept it going in his sleep. He bought the literature of the dispute as fast as it appeared, and we discussed it all through thirteen hundred miles of river four times traversed in every thirty-five days – the time required by that swift boat to achieve two round trips. We discussed, and discussed, and discussed, and disputed and disputed and disputed; at any rate he did, and I got in a word now and then when he slipped a cog and there was a vacancy. He did his arguing with heat, with energy, with violence; and I did mine with the reserve and moderation of a subordinate who does not like to be flung out of a pilot-house that is perched forty feet above the water. He was fiercely loyal to Shakespeare and cordially scornful of Bacon and of all the pretensions of the Baconians. So was I – at first. And at first he was glad that that was my attitude. There were even indications that he admired it; indications dimmed, it is true, by the distance that lay between the lofty boss-pilotical altitude and my lowly one, yet perceptible to me; perceptible, and translatable into a compliment – compliment coming down from above the snow-line and not well thawed in the transit, and not likely to set anything afire, not even a cub-pilot's self-conceit; still a detectable compliment, and precious.

Naturally it flattered me into being more loyal to Shakespeare – if possible – than I was before, and more prejudiced against Bacon – if possible than I was before. And so we discussed and discussed, both on the same side, and were happy. For a while. Only for a while. Only for a very little while, a very, very, very little while. Then the atmosphere began to change; began to cool off.

A brighter person would have seen what the trouble was, earlier than I did, perhaps, but I saw it early enough for all practical purposes. You see, he was of an argumentative disposition. Therefore it took him but a little time to get tired of arguing with a person who agreed with everything he said and consequently never furnished him a provocative to flare up and show what he could do when it came to clear, cold, hard, rose-cut, hundred-faceted, diamond-flashing reasoning. That was his name for it. It has been applied since, with complacency, as many as several times, in the Bacon-Shakespeare scuffle. On the Shakespeare side.

Then the thing happened which has happened to more persons than to me when principle and personal interest found themselves in opposition to each other and a choice had to be made: I let principle go, and went over to the other side. Not the entire way, but far enough to answer the requirements of the case. That is to say, I took this attitude, to wit: I only *believed* Bacon wrote Shakespeare, whereas I *knew* Shakespeare didn't. Ealer was satisfied with that, and the war broke loose. Study, practice, experience in handling my end of the matter presently enabled me to take my new position almost seriously; a little bit later, utterly seriously; a little later still, lovingly, gratefully, devotedly; finally: fiercely, rabidly, uncompromisingly. After that, I was welded to my faith, I was theoretically ready to die for it, and I looked down with compassion not unmixed with scorn, upon everybody else's faith that didn't tally with mine. That faith, imposed upon me by self-interest in that ancient day, remains my faith to-day, and in it I find comfort, solace, peace, and never-failing joy. You see how curiously theological it is. The "rice Christian" of the Orient goes through the very same steps, when he is after rice and the missionary is after *him*; he goes for rice, and remains to worship.

Ealer did a lot of our "reasoning" – not to say substantially all of it. The slaves of his cult have a passion for calling it by that large name. We others do not call our inductions and deductions and reductions by any name at all. They show for themselves, what they are, and we can with tranquil confidence leave the world to ennoble them with a title of its own choosing.

Now and then when Ealer had to stop to cough, I pulled my induction-talents together and hove the controversial lead myself:

always getting eight feet, eight-and-a-half, often nine, sometimes even quarter-less-twain – as *I* believed; but always "no bottom," as *he* said.

I got the best of him only once. I prepared myself. I wrote out a passage from Shakespeare – it may have been the very one I quoted a while ago, I don't remember – and riddled it with his wild steamboatful interlardings. When an unrisky opportunity offered, one lovely summer day, when we had sounded and buoyed a tangled patch of crossings known as Hell's Half Acre, and were aboard again and he had sneaked the *Pennsylvania* triumphantly through it without once scraping sand, and the *A. T. Lacey* had followed in our wake and got stuck, and he was feeling good, I showed it to him. It amused him. I asked him to fire it off: read it; read it, I diplomatically added, as only he could read dramatic poetry. The compliment touched him where he lived. He did read it; read it with surpassing fire and spirit; read it as it will never be read again; for *he* knew how to put the right music into those thunderous interlardings and make them seem a part of the text, make them sound as if they were bursting from Shakespeare's own soul, each one of them a golden inspiration and not to be left out without damage to the massed and magnificent whole.

I waited a week, to let the incident fade; waited longer; waited until he brought up for reasonings and vituperation my pet position, my pet argument, the one which I was fondest of, the one which I prized far above all others in my ammunition-wagon, to wit: that Shakespeare couldn't have written Shakespeare's works, for the reason that the man who wrote them was limitlessly familiar with the laws, and the law-courts, and law-proceedings, and lawyer-talk, and lawyer-ways – and if Shakespeare was possessed of the infinitely-divided star-dust that constituted this vast wealth, how did he get it, and *where*, and *when*?

"From books."

From books! That was always the idea. I answered as my readings of the champions of my side of the great controversy had taught me to answer: that a man can't handle glibly and easily and comfortably and successfully the *argot* of a trade at which he has not personally served. He will make mistakes; he will not, and cannot, get the trade-phrasings precisely and exactly right; and the moment he departs, by even a shade, from a common trade-form, the reader who has served that trade will know the writer *hasn't*. Ealer would not be convinced; he said a man could learn how to correctly handle the subtleties and mysteries and free-masonries of any trade by careful reading and studying. But when I got him to read again the passage from Shakespeare with the interlardings, he perceived, himself, that books couldn't teach a student a bewildering multitude of pilot-phrases so thoroughly and perfectly that he could talk them off in book and play or conversation and make no mistake that a pilot would not immediately discover. It was a triumph for me. He was silent awhile, and I knew what was happening: he was losing his temper. And I knew he would presently close the session with the same old argument that was always his stay and his support in time of need; the same old argument, the one I couldn't answer – because I dasn't: the argument that I was an ass, and better shut up. He delivered it, and I obeyed.

Oh, dear, how long ago it was – how pathetically long ago! And here am I, old, forsaken, forlorn and alone, arranging to get that argument out of somebody again.

When a man has a passion for Shakespeare, it goes without saying that he keeps company with other standard authors. Ealer always had several high-class books in the pilot-house, and he read the same ones over and over again, and did not care to change to newer and fresher ones. He played well on the flute, and greatly enjoyed hearing himself play. So did I. He had a notion that a flute would keep its health better if you took it apart when it was not standing a watch; and so, when it was not on duty it took its rest, disjointed, on the compass-shelf under the breast-board. When the *Pennsylvania* blew up and became a drifting rack-heap freighted with wounded and dying poor souls (my young brother Henry among them), pilot Brown had the watch below, and was probably asleep and never knew what killed him; but Ealer escaped unhurt. He and his pilot-house were shot up into the air; then they fell, and Ealer sank through the ragged cavern where the hurricane deck and the boiler deck had been, and landed in a nest of ruins on the main deck, on top of one of the unexploded boilers, where he lay prone in a fog of scalding and deadly steam. But not for long. He did not lose his head: long familiarity with danger had taught him to keep it, in any and all emergencies. He held his coat-lapels to his nose with one hand, to keep out the steam, and scrabbled around with the other till he found the joints of his flute, then he took measures to save himself alive, and was successful. I was not on board. I had been put ashore in New Orleans by Captain Klinefelter. The reason – however, I have told all about it in the book called *Old Times on the Mississippi*, and it isn't important anyway, it is so long ago.

CHAPTER II

When I was a Sunday-school scholar something more than sixty years ago, I became interested in Satan, and wanted to find out all I could about him. I began to ask questions, but my class-teacher, Mr. Barclay the stone-mason, was reluctant about answering them, it seemed to me. I was anxious to be praised for turning my thoughts to serious subjects when there wasn't another boy in the village who could be hired to do such a thing. I was greatly interested in the incident of Eve and the serpent, and thought Eve's calmness was perfectly noble. I asked Mr. Barclay if he had ever heard of another woman who, being approached by a serpent, would not excuse herself and break for the nearest timber. He did not answer my question, but rebuked me for inquiring into matters above my age and comprehension. I will say for Mr. Barclay that he was willing to tell me the facts of Satan's history, but he stopped there: he wouldn't allow any discussion of them.

In the course of time we exhausted the facts. There were only five or six of them, you could set them all down on a visiting-card. I was disappointed. I had been meditating a biography, and was grieved to find that there were no materials. I said as much, with the tears running down. Mr. Barclay's sympathy and compassion were aroused, for he was a most kind and gentle-spirited man, and he patted me on the head and cheered me up by saying there was a whole vast ocean of materials! I can still feel the happy thrill which these blessed words shot through me.

Then he began to bail out that ocean's riches for my encouragement and joy. Like this: it was "conjectured" – though not established – that Satan was originally an angel in heaven; that he fell; that he rebelled, and brought on a war; that he was defeated, and banished to perdition. Also, "we have reason to believe" that later he did so-and-so; that "we are warranted in supposing" that at a subsequent time he travelled extensively, seeking whom he might devour; that a couple of centuries afterward, "as tradition instructs us," he took up the cruel trade of tempting people to their ruin, with vast and fearful results; that by-and-by, "as the probabilities seem to indicate," he may have done certain things, he might have done certain other things, he must have done still other things.

And so on and so on. We set down the five known facts by themselves, on a piece of paper, and numbered it "page 1"; then on fifteen hundred other pieces of paper we set down the "conjectures," and "suppositions," and "maybes," and "perhapses," and "doubtlesses," and "rumors," and "guesses," and "probabilities," and "likelihoods," and "we are permitted to thinks," and "we are warranted in believings," and "might have beens," and "could have beens," and "must have beens," and "unquestionablys," and "without a shadow of doubts" – and behold!

Materials? Why, we had enough to build a biography of Shakespeare!

Yet he made me put away my pen; he would not let me write the history of Satan. Why? Because, as he said, he had suspicions; suspicions that my attitude in this matter was not reverent; and that a person must be reverent when writing about the sacred characters. He said any one who spoke flippantly of Satan would be frowned upon by the religious world and also be brought to account.

I assured him, in earnest and sincere words, that he had wholly misconceived my attitude; that I had the highest respect for Satan, and that my reverence for him equalled, and possibly even exceeded, that of any member of any church. I said it wounded me deeply to perceive by his words that he thought I would make fun of Satan, and deride him, laugh at him, scoff at him: whereas in truth I had never thought of such a thing, but had only a warm desire to make fun of those others and laugh at *them.* "What others?" "Why, the Supposers, the Perhapsers, the Might-Have-Beeners, the Could-Have-Beeners, the Must-Have-Beeners, the Without-a-Shadow-of-Doubters, the We-are-Warranted-in-Believingers, and all that funny crop of solemn architects who have taken a good solid foundation of five indisputable and unimportant facts and built upon it a Conjectural Satan thirty miles high."

What did Mr. Barclay do then? Was he disarmed? Was he silenced? No. He was shocked. He was so shocked that he visibly shuddered. He said the Satanic Traditioners and Perhapsers and Conjecturers were *themselves* sacred! As sacred as their work. So sacred that whoso ventured to mock them or make fun of their work, could not afterward enter any respectable house, even by the back door.

How true were his words, and how wise! How fortunate it would

have been for me if I had heeded them. But I was young, I was
but seven years of age, and vain, foolish, and anxious to attract
attention. I wrote the biography, and have never been in a respectable house since.

CHAPTER III

How curious and interesting is the parallel – as far as poverty of
biographical details is concerned – between Satan and Shakespeare. It is wonderful, it is unique, it stands quite alone, there is
nothing resembling it in history, nothing resembling it in romance,
nothing approaching it even in tradition. How sublime is their
position, and how over-topping, how sky-reaching, how supreme
– the two Great Unknowns, the two Illustrious Conjecturabilities!
They are the best-known unknown persons that have ever drawn
breath upon the planet.

For the instruction of the ignorant I will make a list, now, of
those details of Shakespeare's history which are *facts* – verified
facts, established facts, undisputed facts.

FACTS

He was born on the 23d of April, 1564.

Of good farmer-class parents who could not read, could not
write, could not sign their names.

At Stratford, a small back settlement which in that day was
shabby and unclean, and densely illiterate. Of the nineteen
important men charged with the government of the town, thirteen
had to "make their mark" in attesting important documents,
because they could not write their names.

Of the first eighteen years of his life *nothing* is known. They are
a blank.

On the 27th of November (1582) William Shakespeare took out
a license to marry Anne Whateley.

Next day William Shakespeare took out a license to marry Anne
Hathaway. She was eight years his senior.

William Shakespeare married Anne Hathaway. In a hurry. By
grace of a reluctantly-granted dispensation there was but one publication of the banns.

Within six months the first child was born.

About two (blank) years followed, during which period *nothing
at all happened to Shakespeare*, so far as anybody knows.

Then came twins – 1585. February.

Two blank years follow.

Then – 1587 – he makes a ten-year visit to London, leaving the family behind.

Five blank years follow. During this period *nothing happened to him*, as far as anybody actually knows.

Then – 1592 – there is mention of him as an actor.

Next year – 1593 – his name appears in the official list of players.

Next year – 1594 – he played before the queen. A detail of no consequence: other obscurities did it every year of the forty-five of her reign. And remained obscure.

Three pretty full years follow. Full of play-acting. Then

In 1597 he bought New Place, Stratford.

Thirteen or fourteen busy years follow; years in which he accumulated money, and also reputation as actor and manager.

Meantime his name, liberally and variously spelt, had become associated with a number of great plays and poems, as (ostensibly) author of the same.

Some of these, in these years and later, were pirated, but he made no protest. Then – 1610–11 – he returned to Stratford and settled down for good and all, and busied himself in lending money, trading in tithes, trading in land and houses; shirking a debt of forty-one shillings, borrowed by his wife during his long desertion of his family; suing debtors for shillings and coppers; being sued himself for shillings and coppers; and acting as confederate to a neighbor who tried to rob the town of its rights in a certain common, and did not succeed.

He lived five or six years – till 1616 – in the joy of these elevated pursuits. Then he made a will, and signed each of its three pages with his name.

A thoroughgoing business man's will. It named in minute detail every item of property he owned in the world – houses, lands, sword, silver-gilt bowl, and so on – all the way down to his "second-best bed" and its furniture.

It carefully and calculatingly distributed his riches among the members of his family, overlooking no individual of it. Not even his wife: the wife he had been enabled to marry in a hurry by urgent grace of a special dispensation before he was nineteen; the wife whom he had left husbandless so many years; the wife who had had to borrow forty-one shillings in her need, and which the lender was never able to collect of the prosperous husband, but died at last with the money still lacking. No, even this wife was remembered in Shakespeare's will.

He left her that "second-best bed."

And *not another thing*; not even a penny to bless her lucky widowhood with.

It was eminently and conspicuously a business man's will, not a poet's.

It mentioned *not a single book.*

Books were much more precious than swords and silver-gilt bowls and second-best beds in those days, and when a departing person owned one he gave it a high place in his will.

The will mentioned *not a play, not a poem, not an unfinished literary work, not a scrap of manuscript of any kind.*

Many poets have died poor, but this is the only one in history that has died *this* poor; the others all left literary remains behind. Also a book. Maybe two.

If Shakespeare had owned a dog – but we need not go into that: we know he would have mentioned it in his will. If a good dog, Susanna would have got it; if an inferior one his wife would have got a dower interest in it. I wish he had had a dog, just so we could see how painstakingly he would have divided that dog among the family, in his careful business way.

He signed the will in three places.

In earlier years he signed two other official documents.

These five signatures still exist.

There are *no other specimens of his penmanship in existence.* Not a line.

Was he prejudiced against the art? His granddaughter, whom he loved, was eight years old when he died, yet she had had no teaching, he left no provision for her education although he was rich, and in her mature womanhood she couldn't write and couldn't tell her husband's manuscript from anybody else's – she thought it was Shakespeare's.

When Shakespeare died in Stratford *it was not an event.* It made no more stir in England than the death of any other forgotten theatre-actor would have made. Nobody came down from London; there were no lamenting poems, no eulogies, no national tears – there was merely silence, and nothing more. A striking contrast with what happened when Ben Jonson, and Francis Bacon, and Spenser, and Raleigh and the other distinguished literary folk of Shakespeare's time passed from life! No praiseful voice was lifted for the lost Bard of Avon; even Ben Jonson waited seven years before he lifted his.

So far as anybody actually knows and can prove, Shakespeare of Stratford-on-Avon never wrote a play in his life.

So far as anybody knows and can prove, he never wrote a letter to anybody in his life.

So far as any one knows, he received only one letter during his life.

So far as any one *knows and can prove*, Shakespeare of Stratford wrote only one poem during his life. This one is authentic. He did write that one – a fact which stands undisputed; he wrote the whole of it; he wrote the whole of it out of his own head. He commanded that this work of art be engraved upon his tomb, and he was obeyed. There it abides to this day. This is it:

Good friend for Iesus sake forbeare
To digg the dust encloased heare:
Blest be ye man yt spares thes stones
And curst be he yt moves my bones.

In the list as above set down, will be found *every positively known* fact of Shakespeare's life, lean and meagre as the invoice is. Beyond these details we know *not a thing* about him. All the rest of his vast history, as furnished by the biographers, is built up, course upon course, of guesses, inferences, theories, conjectures – an Eiffel Tower of artificialities rising sky-high from a very flat and very thin foundation of inconsequential facts.

CHAPTER IV – CONJECTURES

The historians "suppose" that Shakespeare attended the Free School in Stratford from the time he was seven years old till he was thirteen. There is no *evidence* in existence that he ever went to school at all.

The historians "infer" that he got his Latin in that school – the school which they "suppose" he attended.

They "suppose" his father's declining fortunes made it necessary for him to leave the school they supposed he attended, and get to work and help support his parents and their ten children. But there is no evidence that he ever entered or retired from the school they suppose he attended.

They "suppose" he assisted his father in the butchering business; and that, being only a boy, he didn't have to do full-grown butchering, but only slaughtered calves. Also, that whenever he killed a calf he made a high-flown speech over it. This supposition rests upon the testimony of a man who wasn't there at the time; a man who got it from a man who could have been there, but did not say whether he was or not; and neither of them thought to mention it for decades, and decades, and decades, and two more decades after Shakespeare's death (until old age and mental decay had refreshed and vivified their memories). They hadn't two facts in stock about the long-dead distinguished citizen, but only just the one: he slaughtered calves and broke into oratory while he was at it. Curious. They had only one fact, yet the distinguished citizen had spent twenty-six years in that little town – just half his lifetime. However, rightly viewed, it was the most important fact, indeed almost the only important fact, of Shakespeare's life in Stratford. Rightly viewed. For experience is an author's most valuable asset; experience is the thing that puts the muscle and the breath and the warm blood into the book he writes. Rightly viewed, calf-butchering accounts for *Titus Andronicus*, the only play – ain't it? – that the Stratford Shakespeare ever wrote; and yet it is the only one everybody tries to chouse him out of, the Baconians included.

The historians find themselves "justified in believing" that the young Shakespeare poached upon Sir Thomas Lucy's deer preserves and got haled before that magistrate for it. But there is no shred of respectworthy evidence that anything of the kind happened.

The historians, having argued the thing that *might* have happened into the thing that *did* happen, found no trouble in turning Sir Thomas Lucy into Mr. Justice Shallow. They have long ago convinced the world – on surmise and without trustworthy evidence – that Shallow *is* Sir Thomas.

The next addition to the young Shakespeare's Stratford history comes easy. The historian builds it out of the surmised deer-stealing, and the surmised trial before the magistrate, and the surmised vengeance-prompted satire upon the magistrate in the play: result, the young Shakespeare was a wild, wild, wild, oh *such* a wild young scamp, and that gratuitous slander is established for all time! It is the very way Professor Osborn and I built the colossal skeleton brontosaur that stands fifty-seven feet long and sixteen feet high in the Natural History Museum, the awe and admiration of all the world, the stateliest skeleton that exists on the planet. We had nine bones, and we built the rest of him out of plaster of paris.

We ran short of plaster of paris, or we'd have built a brontosaur that could sit down beside the Stratford Shakespeare and none but an expert could tell which was biggest or contained the most plaster.

Shakespeare pronounced *Venus and Adonis* "the first heir of his invention," apparently implying that it was his first effort at literary composition. He should not have said it. It has been an embarrassment to his historians these many, many years. They have to make him write that graceful and polished and flawless and beautiful poem before he escaped from Stratford and his family – 1586 or '87 – age, twenty-two, or along there; because within the next five years he wrote five great plays, and could not have found time to write another line.

It is sorely embarrassing. If he began to slaughter calves, and poach deer, and rollick around, and learn English, at the earliest likely moment – say at thirteen, when he was supposably wrenched from that school where he was supposably storing up Latin for future literary use – he had his youthful hands full, and much more than full. He must have had to put aside his Warwickshire dialect, which wouldn't be understood in London, and study English very hard. Very hard indeed; incredibly hard, almost, if the result of that labor was to be the smooth and rounded and flexible and letter-perfect English of the *Venus and Adonis* in the space of ten years; and at the same time learn great and fine and unsurpassable literary form.

However, it is "conjectured" that he accomplished all this and more, much more: learned law and its intricacies; and the complex procedure of the law courts; and all about soldiering, and sailoring, and the manners and customs and ways of royal courts and aristocratic society; and likewise accumulated in his one head every kind of knowledge the learned then possessed, and every kind of humble knowledge possessed by the lowly and the ignorant; and added thereto a wider and more intimate knowledge of the world's great literatures, ancient and modern, than was possessed by any other man of his time – for he was going to make brilliant and easy and admiration-compelling use of these splendid treasures the moment he got to London. And according to the surmisers, that is what he did. Yes, although there was no one in Stratford able to teach him these things, and no library in the little village to dig them out of. His father could not read, and even the surmisers surmise that he did not keep a library.

It is surmised by the biographers that the young Shakespeare got his vast knowledge of the law and his familiar and accurate acquaintance with the manners and customs and shop-talk of lawyers through being for a time the *clerk of a Stratford court*; just as a bright lad like me, reared in a village on the banks of the Mississippi, might become perfect in knowledge of the Behring Strait whale-fishery and the shop-talk of the veteran exercisers of that adventure-bristling trade through catching catfish with a "trot-line" Sundays. But the surmise is damaged by the fact that there is no evidence – and not even tradition – that the young Shakespeare was ever clerk of a law court.

It is further surmised that the young Shakespeare accumulated his law-treasures in the first years of his sojourn in London, through "amusing himself" by learning book-law in his garret and by picking up lawyer-talk and the rest of it through loitering about the law-courts and listening. But it is only surmise; there is no *evidence* that he ever did either of those things. They are merely a couple of chunks of plaster of paris.

There is a legend that he got his bread and butter by holding horses in front of the London theatres, mornings and afternoons. Maybe he did. If he did, it seriously shortened his law-study hours and his recreation-time in the courts. In those very days he was writing great plays, and needed all the time he could get. The horse-holding legend ought to be strangled; it too formidably increases the historian's difficulty in accounting for the young Shakespeare's erudition – an erudition which he was acquiring, hunk by hunk and chunk by chunk every day in those strenuous times, and emptying each day's catch into next day's imperishable drama.

He had to acquire a knowledge of war at the same time; and a knowledge of soldier-people and sailor-people and their ways and talk; also a knowledge of some foreign lands and their languages: for he was daily emptying fluent streams of these various knowledges, too, into his dramas. How did he acquire these rich assets?

In the usual way: by surmise. It is *surmised* that he travelled in Italy and Germany and around, and qualified himself to put their scenic and social aspects upon paper; that he perfected himself in French, Italian and Spanish on the road; that he went in Leicester's expedition to the Low Countries, as soldier or sutler or something, for several months or years – or whatever length of time a surmiser needs in his business – and thus became familiar with soldiership and soldier-ways and soldier-talk, and generalship and general-ways and general-talk, and seamanship and sailor-ways and sailor-talk.

Maybe he did all these things, but I would like to know who held the horses in the meantime; and who studied the books in the garret; and who frollicked in the law-courts for recreation. Also, who did the call-boying and the play-acting.

For he became a call-boy; and as early as '93 he became a "vagabond" – the law's ungentle term for an unlisted actor; and in '94 a "regular" and properly and officially listed member of that (in those days) lightly-valued and not much respected profession.

Right soon thereafter he became a stockholder in two theatres, and manager of them. Thenceforward he was a busy and flourishing business man, and was raking in money with both hands for twenty years. Then in a noble frenzy of poetic inspiration he wrote his one poem – his only poem, his darling – and laid him down and died:

> Good friend for Iesus sake forbeare
> To digg the dust encloased heare:
> Blest be ye man yt spares thes stones
> And curst be he yt moves my bones.

He was probably dead when he wrote it. Still, this is only conjecture. We have only circumstantial evidence. Internal evidence.

Shall I set down the rest of the Conjectures which constitute the giant Biography of William Shakespeare? It would strain the Unabridged Dictionary to hold them. He is a Brontosaur: nine bones and six hundred barrels of plaster of paris.

CHAPTER V – "We May Assume"

In the Assuming trade three separate and independent cults are transacting business. Two of these cults are known as the Shakespearites and the Baconians, and I am the other one – the Brontosaurian.

The Shakespearite knows that Shakespeare wrote Shakespeare's Works; the Baconian knows that Francis Bacon wrote them; the Brontosaurian doesn't really know which of them did it, but is quite composedly and contentedly sure that Shakespeare *didn't*, and strongly suspects that Bacon *did*. We all have to do a good deal of assuming, but I am fairly certain that in every case

I can call to mind the Baconian assumers have come out ahead of
the Shakespearites. Both parties handle the same materials, but
the Baconians seem to me to get much more reasonable and
rational and persuasive results out of them than is the case with the
Shakespearites. The Shakespearite conducts his assuming upon a
definite principle, an unchanging and immutable law – which is:
2 and 8 and 7 and 14, added together, make 165. I believe this to
be an error. No matter, you cannot get a habit-sodden Shakespearite to cipher-up his materials upon any other basis. With the
Baconian it is different. If you place before him the above figures
and set him to adding them up, he will never in any case get more
than 45 out of them, and in nine cases out of ten he will get just
the proper 31.

Let me try to illustrate the two systems in a simple and homely
way calculated to bring the idea within the grasp of the ignorant
and unintelligent. We will suppose a case: take a lap-bred, house-
fed, uneducated, inexperienced kitten; take a rugged old Tom
that's scarred from stem to rudder-post with the memorials of
strenuous experience, and is so cultured, so educated, so limitlessly
erudite that one may say of him "all cat-knowledge is his province"; also, take a mouse. Lock the three up in a holeless, crackless,
exitless prison-cell. Wait half an hour, then open the cell, introduce
a Shakespearite and a Baconian, and let them cipher and assume.
The mouse is missing: the question to be decided is, where is it?
You can guess both verdicts beforehand. One verdict will say the
kitten contains the mouse; the other will as certainly say the mouse
is in the tomcat.

The Shakespearite will Reason like this – (that is not my word,
it is his). He will say the kitten *may have been* attending school when
nobody was noticing; therefore *we are warranted in assuming* that it
did so; also, it *could have been* training in a court-clerk's office when
no one was noticing; since that could have happened, *we are justified
in assuming* that it did happen; it *could have studied catology in a garret*
when no one was noticing – therefore it *did*; it *could have* attended
cat-assizes on the shed-roof nights, for recreation, when no one
was noticing, and harvested a knowledge of cat court-forms and
cat lawyer-talk in that way: it *could* have done it, therefore without
a doubt it did; it could have gone soldiering with a war-tribe when
no one was noticing, and learned soldier-wiles and soldier-ways,
and what to do with a mouse when opportunity offers; the plain
inference, therefore is, that that is what it *did*. Since all these

manifold things *could* have occurred, we have *every right to believe* they did occur. These patiently and painstakingly accumulated vast acquirements and competences needed but one thing more – opportunity – to convert themselves into triumphant action. The opportunity came, we have the result; *beyond shadow of question* the mouse is in the kitten.

It is proper to remark that when we of the three cults plant a "*We think we may assume*," we expect it, under careful watering and fertilizing and tending, to grow up into a strong and hardy and weather-defying "*there isn't a shadow of a doubt*" at last – and it usually happens.

We know what the Baconian's verdict would be: "*There is not a rag of evidence that the kitten has had any training, any education, any experience qualifying it for the present occasion, or is indeed equipped for any achievement above lifting such unclaimed milk as comes its way; but there is abundant evidence – unassailable proof, in fact – that the other animal is equipped, to the last detail, with every qualification necessary for the event. Without shadow of doubt the tomcat contains the mouse.*"

CHAPTER VI

When Shakespeare died, in 1616, great literary productions attributed to him as author had been before the London world and in high favor for twenty-four years. Yet his death was not an event. It made no stir, it attracted no attention. Apparently his eminent literary contemporaries did not realize that a celebrated poet had passed from their midst. Perhaps they knew a play-actor of minor rank had disappeared, but did not regard him as the author of his Works. "We are justified in assuming" this.

His death was not even an event in the little town of Stratford. Does this mean that in Stratford he was not regarded as a celebrity of *any* kind?

"We are privileged to assume" – no, we are indeed *obliged* to assume – that such was the case. He had spent the first twenty-two or twenty-three years of his life there, and of course knew everybody and was known by everybody of that day in the town, including the dogs and the cats and the horses. He had spent the last five or six years of his life there, diligently trading in every big and little thing that had money in it; so we are compelled to assume that many of the folk there in those said latter days knew him personally, and the rest by sight and hearsay. But not as a *celebrity*?

Apparently not. For everybody soon forgot to remember any contact with him or any incident connected with him. The dozens of townspeople, still alive, who had known of him or known about him in the first twenty-three years of his life were in the same unremembering condition: if they knew of any incident connected with that period of his life they didn't tell about it. Would they if they had been asked? It is most likely. Were they asked? It is pretty apparent that they were not. Why weren't they? It is a very plausible guess that nobody there or elsewhere was interested to know.

For seven years after Shakespeare's death nobody seems to have been interested in him. Then the quarto was published, and Ben Jonson awoke out of his long indifference and sang a song of praise and put it in the front of the book. Then silence fell *again*.

For sixty years. Then inquiries into Shakespeare's Stratford life began to be made, of Stratfordians. Of Stratfordians who had known Shakespeare or had seen him? No. Then of Stratfordians who had seen people who had known or seen people who had seen Shakespeare? No. Apparently the inquiries were only made of Stratfordians who were not Stratfordians of Shakespeare's day, but later comers; and what they had learned had come to them from persons who had not seen Shakespeare; and what they had learned was not claimed as *fact*, but only as legend – dim and fading and indefinite legend; legend of the calf-slaughtering rank, and not worth remembering either as history or fiction.

Has it ever happened before – or since – that a celebrated person who had spent exactly half of a fairly long life in the village where he was born and reared, was able to slip out of this world and leave that village voiceless and gossipless behind him – utterly voiceless, utterly gossipless? And permanently so? I don't believe it has happened in any case except Shakespeare's. And couldn't and wouldn't have happened in his case if he had been regarded as a celebrity at the time of his death.

When I examine my own case – but let us do that, and see if it will not be recognizable as exhibiting a condition of things quite likely to result, most likely to result, indeed substantially *sure* to result in the case of a celebrated person, a benefactor of the human race. Like me.

My parents brought me to the village of Hannibal, Missouri, on the banks of the Mississippi, when I was two and a half years old. I entered school at five years of age, and drifted from one school to another in the village during nine and a half years. Then my father died, leaving his family in exceedingly straitened circumstances; wherefore my book-education came to a standstill forever, and I became a printer's apprentice, on board and clothes, and when the clothes failed I got a hymn-book in place of them. This for summer wear, probably. I lived in Hannibal fifteen and a half years, altogether, then ran away, according to the custom of persons who are intending to become celebrated. I never lived there afterward. Four years later I became a "cub" on a Mississippi steamboat in the St. Louis and New Orleans trade, and after a year and a half of hard study and hard work the U. S. inspectors rigorously examined me through a couple of long sittings and decided that I knew every inch of the Mississippi – thirteen hundred miles – in the dark and in the day – as well as a baby knows the way to its mother's paps day or night. So they licensed me as a pilot – knighted me, so to speak – and I rose up clothed with authority, a responsible servant of the United States government.

Now then. Shakespeare died young – he was only fifty-two. He had lived in his native village twenty-six years, or about that. He died celebrated (if you believe everything you read in the books). Yet when he died nobody there or elsewhere took any notice of it; and for sixty years afterward no townsman remembered to say anything about him or about his life in Stratford. When the inquirer came at last he got but one fact – no, *legend* – and got that one at second hand, from a person who had only heard it as a rumor, and didn't claim copyright in it as a production of his own. He couldn't, very well, for its date antedated his own birthdate. But necessarily a number of persons were still alive in Stratford who, in the days of their youth, had seen Shakespeare nearly every day in the last five years of his life, and they would have been able to tell that inquirer some first-hand things about him if he had in those last days been a celebrity and therefore a person of interest to the villagers. Why did not the inquirer hunt them up and interview them? Wasn't it worth while? Wasn't the matter of sufficient consequence? Had the inquirer an engagement to see a dog-fight and couldn't spare the time?

It all seems to mean that he never had any literary celebrity, there or elsewhere, and no considerable repute as actor and manager.

Now then, I am away along in life – my seventy-third year being already well behind me – yet *sixteen* of my Hannibal schoolmates are still alive to-day, and can tell – and do tell – inquirers dozens and dozens of incidents of their young lives and mine together; things that happened to us in the morning of life, in the blossom of our youth, in the good days, the dear days, "the days when we went gipsying, a long time ago." Most of them creditable to me, too. One child to whom I paid court when she was five years old and I eight still lives in Hannibal, and she visited me last summer, traversing the necessary ten or twelve hundred miles of railroad without damage to her patience or to her old-young vigor. Another little lassie to whom I paid attention in Hannibal when she was nine years old and I the same, is still alive – in London – and hale and hearty, just as I am. And on the few surviving steamboats – those lingering ghosts and remembrancers of great fleets that plied the big river in the beginning of my water-career – which is exactly as long ago as the whole invoice of the life-years of Shakespeare number – there are still findable two or three river-pilots who saw me do creditable things in those ancient days; and several white-headed engineers; and several roustabouts and mates; and several deck-hands who used to heave the lead for me and send up on the still night air the "six – feet – *scant*!" that made me shudder, and the "*M-a-r-k – twain!*" that took the shudder away, and presently the darling "By the d-e-e-p – four!" that lifted me to heaven for joy. They know about me, and can tell. And so do printers, from St. Louis to New York; and so do newspaper reporters, from Nevada to San Francisco. And so do the police. If Shakespeare had really been celebrated, like me, Stratford could have told things about him; and if my experience goes for anything, they'd have done it.

CHAPTER VII

If I had under my superintendence a controversy appointed to decide whether Shakespeare wrote Shakespeare or not, I believe I would place before the debaters only the one question, *Was Shakespeare ever a practicing lawyer?* and leave everything else out.

It is maintained that the man who wrote the plays was not merely myriad-minded, but also myriad-accomplished: that he not only knew some thousands of things about human life in all its shades and grades, and about the hundred arts and trades and crafts and professions which men busy themselves in, but that he could *talk* about the men and their grades and trades accurately, making no mistakes. Maybe it is so, but have the experts spoken, or is it only Tom, Dick, and Harry? Does the exhibit stand upon wide, and loose, and eloquent generalizing – which is not evidence, and not proof – or upon details, particulars, statistics, illustrations, demonstrations?

Experts of unchallengeable authority have testified definitely as to only one of Shakespeare's multifarious craft-equipments, so far as my recollections of Shakespeare-Bacon talk abide with me – his law-equipment. I do not remember that Wellington or Napoleon ever examined Shakespeare's battles and sieges and strategies, and then decided and established for good and all, that they were militarily flawless; I do not remember that any Nelson, or Drake or Cook ever examined his seamanship and said it showed profound and accurate familiarity with that art; I don't remember that any king or prince or duke has ever testified that Shakespeare was letter-perfect in his handling of royal court-manners and the talk and manners of aristocracies; I don't remember that any illustrious Latinist or Grecian or Frenchman or Spaniard or Italian has proclaimed him a past-master in those languages; I don't remember – well, I don't remember that there is *testimony* – great testimony – imposing testimony – unanswerable and unattackable testimony as to any of Shakespeare's hundred specialties, except one – the law.

Other things change, with time, and the student cannot trace back with certainty the changes that various trades and their processes and technicalities have undergone in the long stretch of a century or two and find out what their processes and technicalities were in those early days, but with the law it is different: it is milestoned and documented all the way back, and the master of that wonderful trade, that complex and intricate trade, that awe-compelling trade, has competent ways of knowing whether Shakespeare-law is good law or not; and whether his law-court procedure is correct or not, and whether his legal shop-talk is the shop-talk of a veteran practitioner or only a machine-made counterfeit of it gathered from books and from occasional loiterings in Westminster.

Richard H. Dana served two years before the mast, and had every experience that falls to the lot of the sailor before the mast of our day. His sailor-talk flows from his pen with the sure touch and the ease and confidence of a person who has *lived* what he is talking about, not gathered it from books and random listenings. Hear him:

Having hove short, cast off the gaskets, and made the bunt of
each sail fast by the jigger, with a man on each yard, at the word
the whole canvas of the ship was loosed, and with the greatest
rapidity possible everything was sheeted home and hoisted up,
the anchor tripped and cat-headed, and the ship under
headway.

Again:

The royal yards were all crossed at once, and royals and sky-
sails set, and, as we had the wind free, the booms were run out,
and all were aloft, active as cats, laying out on the yards and
booms, reeving the studding-sail gear; and sail after sail the captain piled upon her, until she was covered with canvas, her sails
looking like a great white cloud resting upon a black speck.

Once more. A race in the Pacific:

Our antagonist was in her best trim. Being clear of the point,
the breeze became stiff, and the royal-masts bent under our
sails, but we would not take them in until we saw three boys
spring into the rigging of the *California*; then they were all furled
at once, but with orders to our boys to stay aloft at the top-
gallant mast-heads and loose them again at the word. It was my
duty to furl the fore-royal; and while standing by to loose it
again, I had a fine view of the scene. From where I stood, the
two vessels seemed nothing but spars and sails, while their narrow decks, far below, slanting over by the force of the wind aloft,
appeared hardly capable of supporting the great fabrics raised
upon them. The *California* was to windward of us, and had every
advantage; yet, while the breeze was stiff we held our own. As
soon as it began to slacken she ranged a little ahead, and the
order was given to loose the royals. In an instant the gaskets were
off and the bunt dropped. "Sheet home the fore-royal!" –
"Weather sheet's home!" – "Lee sheet's home!" – "Hoist away,
sir!" is bawled from aloft. "Overhaul your clewlines!" shouts the
mate. "Aye-aye, sir, all clear!" – "Taut leech! belay! Well the lee
brace; haul taut to windward!" and the royals are set.

What would the captain of any sailing-vessel of our time say to
that? He would say, "The man that wrote that didn't learn his
trade out of a book, he has *been* there!" But would this same captain
be competent to sit in judgment upon Shakespeare's seamanship

– considering the changes in ships and ship-talk that have necessarily taken place, unrecorded, unremembered, and lost to history
in the last three hundred years? It is my conviction that
Shakespeare's sailor-talk would be Choctaw to him. For instance
– from *The Tempest*:

> *Master.* Boatswain!
> *Boatswain.* Here, master; what cheer?
> *Master.* Good, speak to the mariners: fall to't, yarely, or we
> run ourselves to ground; bestir, bestir!
> (*Enter mariners.*)
> *Boatswain.* Heigh, my hearts! cheerly, cheerly, my hearts!
> yare, yare! Take in the topsail. Tend to the master's whistle ...
> Down with the topmast! yare! lower, lower! Bring her to try wi'
> the main course ... Lay her a-hold, a-hold! Set her two courses.
> Off to sea again; lay her off.

That will do, for the present; let us yare a little, now, for a change.

If a man should write a book and in it make one of his characters
say, "Here, devil, empty the quoins into the standing galley and
the imposing stone into the hell-box; assemble the comps around
the frisket and let them jeff for takes and be quick about it,"
I should recognize a mistake or two in the phrasing, and would
know that the writer was only a printer theoretically, not
practically.

I have been a quartz miner in the silver regions – a pretty hard
life; I know all the palaver of that business: I know all about discovery claims and the subordinate claims; I know all about lodes,
ledges, outcroppings, dips, spurs, angles, shafts, drifts, inclines,
levels, tunnels, air-shafts, "horses," clay casings, granite casings;
quartz mills and their batteries; arastras, and how to charge them
with quicksilver and sulphate of copper; and how to clean them
up, and how to reduce the resulting amalgam in the retorts, and
how to cast the bullion into pigs; and finally I know how to screen
tailings, and also how to hunt for something less robust to do, and
find it. I know the *argot* of the quartz-mining and milling industry
familiarly; and so whenever Bret Harte introduces that industry
into a story, the first time one of his miners opens his mouth
I recognize from his phrasing that Harte got the phrasing by listening – like Shakespeare – I mean the Stratford one – not by
experience. No one can talk the quartz dialect correctly without
learning it with pick and shovel and drill and fuse.

I have been a surface-miner – gold – and I know all its mysteries, and the dialect that belongs with them; and whenever Harte introduces that industry into a story I know by the phrasing of his characters that neither he nor they have ever served that trade.

I have been a "pocket" miner – a sort of gold mining not find-able in any but one little spot in the world, so far as I know. I know how, with horn and water, to find the trail of a pocket and trace it step by step and stage by stage up the mountain to its source, and find the compact little nest of yellow metal reposing in its secret home under the ground. I know the language of that trade, that capricious trade, that fascinating buried-treasure trade, and can catch any writer who tries to use it without having learned it by the sweat of his brow and the labor of his hands.

I know several other trades and the *argot* that goes with them; and whenever a person tries to talk the talk peculiar to any of them without having learned it at its source I can trap him always before he gets far on his road.

And so, as I have already remarked, if I were required to super-intend a Bacon-Shakespeare controversy, I would narrow the mat-ter down to a single question – the only one, so far as the previous controversies have informed me, concerning which illustrious experts of unimpeachable competency have testified: *Was the author of Shakespeare's Works a lawyer?* – a lawyer deeply read and of limit-less experience? I would put aside the guesses, and surmises, and perhapses, and might-have-beens, and could-have-beens, and must-have-beens, and we-are-justified-in-presumings, and the rest of those vague spectres and shadows and indefinitenesses, and stand or fall, win or lose, by the verdict rendered by the jury upon that single question. If the verdict was Yes, I should feel quite con-vinced that the Stratford Shakespeare, the actor, manager, and trader who died so obscure, so forgotten, so destitute of even vil-lage consequence that sixty years afterward no fellow-citizen and friend of his later days remembered to tell anything about him, did not write the Works.

Chapter XIII of *The Shakespeare Problem Restated* bears the head-ing "Shakespeare as a Lawyer," and comprises some fifty pages of expert testimony, with comments thereon, and I will copy the first nine, as being sufficient all by themselves, as it seems to me, to settle the question which I have conceived to be the master-key to the Shakespeare-Bacon puzzle.

CHAPTER VIII – Shakespeare as a Lawyer

The Plays and Poems of Shakespeare supply ample evidence that their author not only had a very extensive and accurate knowledge of law, but that he was well acquainted with the manners and customs of members of the Inns of Court and with legal life generally.

"While novelists and dramatists are constantly making mistakes as to the laws of marriage, of wills, and inheritance, to Shakespeare's law, lavishly as he expounds it, there can neither be demurrer, nor bill of exceptions, nor writ of error." Such was the testimony borne by one of the most distinguished lawyers of the nineteenth century who was raised to the high office of Lord Chief Justice in 1850, and subsequently became Lord Chancellor. Its weight will, doubtless, be more appreciated by lawyers than by laymen, for only lawyers know how impossible it is for those who have not served an apprenticeship to the law to avoid displaying their ignorance if they venture to employ legal terms and to discuss legal doctrines. "There is nothing so dangerous," wrote Lord Campbell, "as for one not of the craft to tamper with our freemasonry." A layman is certain to betray himself by using some expression which a lawyer would never employ. Mr. Sidney Lee himself supplies us with an example of this. He writes (p. 164): "On February 15, 1609, Shakespeare ... obtained judgment from a jury against Addenbroke for the payment of No. 6, and No. 1. 5*s.* 0*d.* costs." Now a lawyer would never have spoken of obtaining "judgment from a jury," for it is the function of a jury not to deliver judgment (which is the prerogative of the court), but to find a verdict on the facts. The error is, indeed, a venial one, but it is just one of those little things which at once enable a lawyer to know if the writer is a layman or "one of the craft."

But when a layman ventures to plunge deeply into legal subjects, he is naturally apt to make an exhibition of his incompetence. "Let a non-professional man, however acute," writes Lord Campbell again, "presume to talk law, or to draw illustrations from legal science in discussing other subjects, and he will speedily fall into laughable absurdity."

And what does the same high authority say about Shakespeare? He had "a deep technical knowledge of the law," and an easy familiarity with "some of the most abstruse proceedings in English jurisprudence." And again: "Whenever he indulges this propensity he uniformly lays down good law." Of *Henry IV.*, Part 2, he says: "If Lord Eldon could be supposed to have written the play, I do not see how he could be chargeable with having forgotten any of his law while writing it." Charles and Mary Cowden Clarke speak of "the marvelous intimacy which he displays with legal terms, his frequent adoption of them in illustration, and his curiously technical knowledge of their form and force." Malone, himself a lawyer, wrote: "His knowledge of legal terms is not merely such as might be acquired by the casual observation of even his all-comprehending mind; it has the appearance of technical skill." Another lawyer and well-known Shakespearean, Richard Grant White, says: "No dramatist of the time, not even Beaumont, who was the younger son of a judge of the Common Pleas, and who after studying in the Inns of Court abandoned law for the drama, used legal phrases with Shakespeare's readiness and exactness. And the significance of this fact is heightened by another, that it is only to the language of the law that he exhibits this inclination. The phrases peculiar to other occupations serve him on rare occasions by way of description, comparison or illustration, generally when something in the scene suggests them, but legal phrases flow from his pen as part of his vocabulary, and parcel of his thought. Take the word 'purchase' for instance, which, in ordinary use, means to acquire by giving value, but applies in law to all legal modes of obtaining property except by inheritance or descent, and in this peculiar sense the word occurs five times in Shakespeare's thirty-four plays, and only in one single instance in the fifty-four plays of Beaumont and Fletcher. It has been suggested that it was in attendance upon the courts in London that he picked up his legal vocabulary. But this supposition not only fails to account for Shakespeare's peculiar freedom and exactness in the use of that phraseology, it does not even place him in the way of learning those terms his use of which is most remarkable, which are not such as he would have heard at ordinary proceedings at *nisi prius*, but such as refer to the tenure or transfer of real property, 'fine and recovery,' 'statutes merchant,' 'purchase,' 'indenture,' 'tenure,' 'double voucher,' 'fee simple,' 'fee farm,' 'remainder,' 'reversion,' 'forfeiture,' etc. This conveyancer's jargon could not have been picked up by hanging round the courts of law in London two hundred and fifty years ago, when suits as to the title of real property were comparatively rare. And beside, Shakespeare uses his law just as freely in his first plays, written in his first London years, as in those produced at a later period. Just as exactly, too; for the correctness and propriety with which these terms are introduced have compelled the admiration of a Chief Justice and a Lord Chancellor."

Senator Davis wrote: "We seem to have something more than a sciolist's temerity of indulgence in the terms of an unfamiliar art. No legal solecisms will be found. The abstrusest elements of the common law are impressed into a disciplined service. Over and over again, where such knowledge is unexampled in writers unlearned in the law, Shakespeare appears in perfect possession of it. In the law of real property, its rules of tenure and descents, its entails, its fines and recoveries, their vouchers and double vouchers, in the procedure of the Courts, the method of bringing writs and arrests, the nature of actions, the rules of pleading, the law of escapes and of contempt of court, in the principles of evidence, both technical and philosophical, in the distinction between the temporal and spiritual tribunals, in the law of attainder and forfeiture, in the requisites of a valid marriage, in the presumption of legitimacy, in the learning of the law of prerogative, in the inalienable character of the Crown, this mastership appears with surprising authority."

To all this testimony (and there is much more which I have not cited) may now be added that of a great lawyer of our own times, *viz.*: Sir James Plaisted Wilde, Q.C. created a Baron of the Exchequer in 1860, promoted to the post of Judge-Ordinary and Judge of the Courts of Probate and Divorce in 1863, and better known to the world as Lord Penzance, to which dignity he was raised in 1869. Lord Penzance, as all lawyers know, and as the late Mr. Inderwick, K.C., has testified, was one of the first legal authorities of his day, famous for his "remarkable grasp of legal principles," and "endowed by nature with a remarkable facility for marshalling facts, and for a clear expression of his views."

Lord Penzance speaks of Shakespeare's "perfect familiarity with not only the principles, axioms, and maxims, but the technicalities of English law, a knowledge so perfect and intimate that he was never incorrect and never at fault ... The mode in which this knowledge was pressed into service on all occasions to express his meaning and illustrate his thoughts, was quite unexampled. He seems to have had a special pleasure in his complete and ready mastership of it in all its branches. As manifested in the plays, this legal knowledge and learning had therefore a special character which places it on a wholly different footing from the rest of the

multifarious knowledge which is exhibited in page after page of
the plays. At every turn and point at which the author required a
metaphor, simile, or illustration, his mind ever turned *first* to the
law. He seems almost to have *thought* in legal phrases, the commonest of legal expressions were ever at the end of his pen in description or illustration. That he should have descanted in lawyer
language when he had a forensic subject in hand, such as Shylock's
bond, was to be expected, but the knowledge of law in 'Shakespeare' was exhibited in a far different manner: it protruded itself
on all occasions, appropriate or inappropriate, and mingled itself
with strains of thought widely divergent from forensic subjects."
Again: "To acquire a perfect familiarity with legal principles, and
an accurate and ready use of the technical terms and phrases not
only of the conveyancer's office but of the pleader's chambers and
the Courts at Westminster, nothing short of employment in some
career involving constant contact with legal questions and general
legal work would be requisite. But a continuous employment
involves the element of time, and time was just what the manager
of two theatres had not at his disposal. In what portion of Shakespeare's (*i.e.* Shakspere's) career would it be possible to point out
that time could be found for the interposition of a legal employment in the chambers or offices of practising lawyers?"

Stratfordians, as is well known, casting about for some possible
explanation of Shakespeare's extraordinary knowledge of law,
have made the suggestion that Shakespeare might, conceivably,
have been a clerk in an attorney's office before he came to London.
Mr. Collier wrote to Lord Campbell to ask his opinion as to the
probability of this being true. His answer was as follows: "You
require us to believe implicitly a fact, of which, if true, positive
and irrefragable evidence in his own handwriting might have been
forthcoming to establish it. Not having been actually enrolled as
an attorney, neither the records of the local court at Stratford nor
of the superior Courts at Westminster would present his name as
being concerned in any suit as an attorney, but it might reasonably
have been expected that there would be deeds or wills witnessed
by him still extant, and after a very diligent search none such can
be discovered."

Upon this Lord Penzance comments: "It cannot be doubted
that Lord Campbell was right in this. No young man could have
been at work in an attorney's office without being called upon continually to act as a witness, and in many other ways leaving traces

of his work and name." There is not a single fact or incident in all that is known of Shakespeare, even by rumor or tradition, which supports this notion of a clerkship. And after much argument and surmise which has been indulged in on this subject, we may, I think, safely put the notion on one side, for no less an authority than Mr. Grant White says finally that the idea of his having been clerk to an attorney has been "blown to pieces."

It is altogether characteristic of Mr. Churton Collins that he, nevertheless, adopts this exploded myth. "That Shakespeare was in early life employed as a clerk in an attorney's office, may be correct. At Stratford there was by royal charter a Court of Record sitting every fortnight, with six attorneys, beside the town clerk, belonging to it, and it is certainly not straining probability to suppose that the young Shakespeare may have had employment in one of them. There is, it is true, no tradition to this effect, but such traditions as we have about Shakespeare's occupation between the time of leaving school and going to London are so loose and baseless that no confidence can be placed in them. It is, to say the least, more probable that he was in an attorney's office than that he was a butcher killing calves 'in a high style,' and making speeches over them."

This is a charming specimen of Stratfordian argument. There is, as we have seen, a very old tradition that Shakespeare was a butcher's apprentice. John Dowdall, who made a tour in Warwickshire in 1693, testifies to it as coming from the old clerk who showed him over the church, and it is unhesitatingly accepted as true by Mr. Halliwell-Phillipps. (Vol. I, p. 11, and see Vol. II, p. 71, 72.) Mr. Sidney Lee sees nothing improbable in it, and it is supported by Aubrey, who must have written his account some time before 1680, when his manuscript was completed. Of the attorney's clerk hypothesis, on the other hand, there is not the faintest vestige of a tradition. It has been evolved out of the fertile imaginations of embarrassed Stratfordians, seeking for some explanation of the Stratford rustic's marvellous acquaintance with law and legal terms and legal life. But Mr. Churton Collins has not the least hesitation in throwing over the tradition which has the warrant of antiquity and setting up in its stead this ridiculous invention, for which not only is there no shred of positive evidence, but which, as Lord Campbell and Lord Penzance point out, is really put out of court by the negative evidence, since "no young man could have been at work in an attorney's office without being called upon continually to act as a witness, and in many other ways leaving traces of his work and name." And as Mr. Edwards further points out, since the day when Lord Campbell's book was published (between forty and fifty years ago), "every old deed or will, to say nothing of other legal papers, dated during the period of William Shakespeare's youth, has been scrutinized over half a dozen shires, and not one signature of the young man has been found."

Moreover, if Shakespeare had served as clerk in an attorney's office it is clear that he must have so served for a considerable period in order to have gained (if indeed it is credible that he could have so gained) his remarkable knowledge of law. Can we then for a moment believe that, if this had been so, tradition would have been absolutely silent on the matter? That Dowdall's old clerk, over eighty years of age, should have never heard of it (though he was sure enough about the butcher's apprentice), and that all the other ancient witnesses should be in similar ignorance!

But such are the methods of Stratfordian controversy. Tradition is to be scouted when it is found inconvenient, but cited as irrefragable truth when it suits the case. Shakespeare of Stratford was the author of the *Plays* and *Poems*, but the author of the *Plays* and *Poems* could not have been a butcher's apprentice. Away, therefore, with tradition. But the author of the *Plays* and *Poems must* have had a very large and a very accurate knowledge of the law. Therefore, Shakespeare of Stratford must have been an attorney's clerk! The method is simplicity itself. By similar reasoning Shakespeare has been made a country schoolmaster, a soldier, a physician, a printer, and a good many other things beside, according to the inclination and the exigencies of the commentator. It would not be in the least surprising to find that he was studying Latin as a schoolmaster and law in an attorney's office at the same time.

However, we must do Mr. Collins the justice of saying that he has fully recognized, what is indeed tolerably obvious, that Shakespeare must have had a sound legal training. "It may, of course, be urged," he writes, "that Shakespeare's knowledge of medicine, and particularly that branch of it which related to morbid psychology, is equally remarkable, and that no one has ever contended that he was a physician. (Here Mr. Collins is wrong; that contention also has been put forward.) It may be urged that his acquaintance with the technicalities of other crafts and callings, notably of marine and military affairs, was also extraordinary, and yet no one has suspected him of being a sailor or a soldier. (Wrong again. Why

even Messrs. Garnett and Gosse 'suspect' that he was a soldier!)
This may be conceded, but the concession hardly furnishes an
analogy. To these and all other subjects he recurs occasionally, and
in season, but with reminiscences of the law his memory, as is
abundantly clear, was simply saturated. In season and out of season now in manifest, now in recondite application, he presses it
into the service of expression and illustration. At least a third of
his myriad metaphors are derived from it. It would indeed be
difficult to find a single act in any of his dramas, nay, in some of
them, a single scene, the diction and imagery of which is not colored by it. Much of his law may have been acquired from three
books easily accessible to him, namely Tottell's *Precedents* (1572),
Pulton's *Statutes* (1578), and Fraunce's *Lawier's Logike* (1588), works
with which he certainly seems to have been familiar; but much of it
could only have come from one who had an intimate acquaintance
with legal proceedings. We quite agree with Mr. Castle that Shakespeare's legal knowledge is not what could have been picked up in
an attorney's office, but could only have been learned by an actual
attendance at the Courts, at a Pleader's Chambers, and on circuit,
or by associating intimately with members of the Bench and Bar."

This is excellent. But what is Mr. Collins' explanation. "Perhaps
the simplest solution of the problem is to accept the hypothesis that
in early life he was in an attorney's office (!), that he there contracted a love for the law which never left him, that as a young man
in London, he continued to study or dabble in it for his amusement, to stroll in leisure hours into the Courts, and to frequent the
society of lawyers. On no other supposition is it possible to explain
the attraction which the law evidently had for him, and his minute
and undeviating accuracy in a subject where no layman who has
indulged in such copious and ostentatious display of legal technicalities has ever yet succeeded in keeping himself from tripping."

A lame conclusion. "No other supposition" indeed! Yes, there
is another, and a very obvious supposition, namely, that Shakespeare was himself a lawyer, well versed in his trade, versed in all
the ways of the courts, and living in close intimacy with judges and
members of the Inns of Court.

One is, of course, thankful that Mr. Collins has appreciated the
fact that Shakespeare must have had a sound legal training, but
I may be forgiven if I do not attach quite so much importance to
his pronouncements on this branch of the subject as to those of
Malone, Lord Campbell, Judge Holmes, Mr. Castle, K.C., Lord

Penzance, Mr. Grant White, and other lawyers, who have expressed their opinion on the matter of Shakespeare's legal acquirements.

Here it may, perhaps, be worth while to quote again from Lord Penzance's book as to the suggestion that Shakespeare had somehow or other managed "to acquire a perfect familiarity with legal principles, and an accurate and ready use of the technical terms and phrases, not only of the conveyancer's office, but of the pleader's chambers and the courts at Westminster." This, as Lord Penzance points out, "would require nothing short of employment in some career involving *constant contact* with legal questions and general legal work." But "in what portion of Shakespeare's career would it be possible to point out that time could be found for the interposition of a legal employment in the chambers or offices of practising lawyers? ... It is beyond doubt that at an early period he was called upon to abandon his attendance at school and assist his father, and was soon after, at the age of sixteen, bound apprentice to a trade. While under the obligation of this bond he could not have pursued any other employment. Then he leaves Stratford and comes to London. He has to provide himself with the means of a livelihood, and this he did in some capacity at the theatre. No one doubts that. The holding of horses is scouted by many, and perhaps with justice, as being unlikely and certainly unproved; but whatever the nature of his employment was at the theatre, there is hardly room for the belief that it could have been other than continuous, for his progress there was so rapid. Ere long he had been taken into the company as an actor, and was soon spoken of as a 'Johannes Factotum.' His rapid accumulation of wealth speaks volumes for the constancy and activity of his services. One fails to see when there could be a break in the current of his life at this period of it, giving room or opportunity for legal or indeed any other employment. 'In 1589,' says Knight, 'we have undeniable evidence that he had not only a casual engagement, was not only a salaried servant, as many players were, but was a shareholder in the company of the Queen's players with other shareholders below him on the list.' This (1589) would be within two years after his arrival in London, which is placed by White and Halliwell-Phillipps about the year 1587. The difficulty in supposing that, starting with a state of ignorance in 1587, when he is supposed to have come to London, he was induced to enter upon a course of most extended study and mental culture, is almost insuperable. Still it was physically possible, provided always that he could have had access to the needful books. But this legal training seems to me to stand on a different footing. It is not only unaccountable and incredible, but it is actually negatived by the known facts of his career." Lord Penzance then refers to the fact that "by 1592 (according to the best authority, Mr. Grant White) several of the plays had been written. *The Comedy of Errors* in 1589, *Love's Labour's Lost* in 1589, *Two Gentlemen of Verona* in 1589 or 1590, and so forth," and then asks, "with this catalogue of dramatic work on hand ... was it possible that he could have taken a leading part in the management and conduct of two theatres, and if Mr. Phillipps is to be relied upon, taken his share in the performances of the provincial tours of his company – and at the same time devoted himself to the study of the law in all its branches so efficiently as to make himself complete master of its principles and practice, and saturate his mind with all its most technical terms?"

I have cited this passage from Lord Penzance's book, because it lay before me, and I had already quoted from it on the matter of Shakespeare's legal knowledge; but other writers have still better set forth the insuperable difficulties, as they seem to me, which beset the idea that Shakespeare might have found time in some unknown period of early life, amid multifarious other occupations, for the study of classics, literature and law, to say nothing of languages and a few other matters. Lord Penzance further asks his readers: "Did you ever meet with or hear of an instance in which a young man in this country gave himself up to legal studies and engaged in legal employments, which is the only way of becoming familiar with the technicalities of practice, unless with the view of practicing in that profession? I do not believe that it would be easy, or indeed possible, to produce an instance in which the law has been seriously studied in all its branches, except as a qualification for practice in the legal profession."

This testimony is so strong, so direct, so authoritative; and so uncheapened, unwatered by guesses, and surmises, and maybe-so's, and might-have-beens, and could-have-beens, and must-have-beens, and the rest of that ton of plaster of paris out of which the biographers have built the colossal brontosaur which goes by the Stratford actor's name, that it quite convinces me that the man who wrote Shakespeare's Works knew all about law and lawyers.

Also, that that man could not have been the Stratford Shakespeare – and *wasn't*.

Who did write these Works, then?

I wish I knew.

CHAPTER IX

Did Francis Bacon write Shakespeare's Works?

Nobody knows.

We cannot say we *know* a thing when that thing has not been proved. *Know* is too strong a word to use when the evidence is not final and absolutely conclusive. We can infer, if we want to, like those slaves ... No, I will not write that word, it is not kind, it is not courteous. The upholders of the Stratford-Shakespeare superstition call *us* the hardest names they can think of, and they keep doing it all the time; very well, if they like to descend to that level, let them do it, but I will not so undignify myself as to follow them. I cannot call them harsh names; the most I can do is to indicate them by terms reflecting my disapproval; and this without malice, without venom.

To resume. What I was about to say, was, those thugs have built their entire superstition upon *inferences*, not upon known and established facts. It is a weak method, and poor, and I am glad to be able to say our side never resorts to it while there is anything else to resort to.

But when we must, we must; and we have now arrived at a place of that sort.

Since the Stratford Shakespeare couldn't have written the Works, we infer that somebody did. Who was it, then? This requires some more inferring.

Ordinarily when an unsigned poem sweeps across the continent like a tidal wave, whose roar and boom and thunder are made up of admiration, delight and applause, a dozen obscure people rise up and claim the authorship. Why a dozen, instead of only one or two? One reason is, because there's a dozen that are recognizably competent to do that poem. Do you remember "Beautiful Snow"? Do you remember "Rock Me to Sleep, Mother, Rock Me to Sleep"? Do you remember "Backward, turn backward, O Time, in thy flight! Make me a child again just for to-night"? I remember them very well. Their authorship was claimed by most of the grown-up people who were alive at the time, and every claimant had one plausible argument in his favor, at least: to wit, he could have done the authoring; he was competent.

Have the Works been claimed by a dozen? They haven't. There was good reason. The world knows there was but one man on the planet at the time who was competent – not a dozen, and not two. A long time ago the dwellers in a far country used now and then to find a procession of prodigious footprints stretching across the plain – footprints that were three miles apart, each footprint a third of a mile long and a furlong deep, and with forests and villages mashed to mush in it. Was there any doubt as to who had made that mighty trail? Were there a dozen claimants? Were there two? No – the people knew who it was that had been along there: there was only one Hercules.

There has been only one Shakespeare. There couldn't be two; certainly there couldn't be two at the same time. It takes ages to bring forth a Shakespeare, and some more ages to match him. This one was not matched before his time; nor during his time; and hasn't been matched since. The prospect of matching him in our time is not bright.

The Baconians claim that the Stratford Shakespeare was not qualified to write the Works, and that Francis Bacon was. They claim that Bacon possessed the stupendous equipment – both natural and acquired – for the miracle; and that no other Englishman of his day possessed the like; or, indeed, anything closely approaching it.

Macaulay, in his Essay, has much to say about the splendor and horizonless magnitude of that equipment. Also, he has synopsized Bacon's history: a thing which cannot be done for the Stratford Shakespeare, for he hasn't any history to synopsize. Bacon's history is open to the world, from his boyhood to his death in old age – a history consisting of known facts, displayed in minute and multitudinous detail; *facts*, not guesses and conjectures and might-have-beens.

Whereby it appears that he was born of a race of statesmen, and had a Lord Chancellor for his father, and a mother who was "distinguished both as a linguist and a theologian: she corresponded in Greek with Bishop Jewell, and translated his *Apologia* from the Latin so correctly that neither he nor Archbishop Parker could suggest a single alteration." It is the atmosphere we are reared in that determines how our inclinations and aspirations shall tend. The atmosphere furnished by the parents to the son in this present

case was an atmosphere saturated with learning; with thinkings
and ponderings upon deep subjects; and with polite culture. It had
its natural effect. Shakespeare of Stratford was reared in a house
which had no use for books, since its owners, his parents, were
without education. This may have had an effect upon the son, but
we do not know, because we have no history of him of an informing
sort. There were but few books anywhere, in that day, and only the
well-to-do and highly educated possessed them, they being almost
confined to the dead languages. "All the valuable books then
extant in all the vernacular dialects of Europe would hardly have
filled a single shelf" – imagine it! The few existing books were in
the Latin tongue mainly. "A person who was ignorant of it was shut
out from all acquaintance – not merely with Cicero and Virgil, but
with the most interesting memoirs, state papers, and pamphlets of
his own time" – a literature necessary to the Stratford lad, for his
fictitious reputation's sake, since the writer of his Works would
begin to use it wholesale and in a most masterly way before the lad
was hardly more than out of his teens and into his twenties.

At fifteen Bacon was sent to the university, and he spent three
years there. Thence he went to Paris in the train of the English
Ambassador, and there he mingled daily with the wise, the cultured, the great, and the aristocracy of fashion, during another
three years. A total of six years spent at the sources of knowledge;
knowledge both of books and of men. The three spent at the university were coeval with the second and last three spent by the little
Stratford lad at Stratford school supposedly, and perhapsedly, and
maybe, and by inference – with nothing to infer from. The second
three of the Baconian six were "presumably" spent by the Stratford lad as apprentice to a butcher. That is, the thugs presume it
– on no evidence of any kind. Which is their way, when they want
a historical fact. Fact and presumption are, for business purposes,
all the same to them. They know the difference, but they also know
how to blink it. They know, too, that while in history-building a
fact is better than a presumption, it doesn't take a presumption
long to bloom into a fact when *they* have the handling of it. They
know by old experience that when they get hold of a presumption-
tadpole he is not going to *stay* tadpole in their history-tank; no, they
know how to develop him into the giant four-legged bullfrog of
fact, and make him sit up on his hams, and puff out his chin, and
look important and insolent and come-to-stay; and assert his genuine simon-pure authenticity with a thundering bellow that will

convince everybody because it is so loud. The thug is aware that loudness convinces sixty persons where reasoning convinces but one. I wouldn't be a thug, not even if – but never mind about that, it has nothing to do with the argument, and it is not noble in spirit besides. If I am better than a thug, is the merit mine? No, it is His. Then to Him be the praise. That is the right spirit.

They "presume" the lad severed his "presumed" connection with the Stratford school to become apprentice to a butcher. They also "presume" that the butcher was his father. They don't know. There is no written record of it, nor any other actual evidence. If it would have helped their case any, they would have apprenticed him to thirty butchers, to fifty butchers, to a wilderness of butchers – all by their patented method "presumption." If it will help their case they will do it yet; and if it will further help it, they will "presume" that all those butchers were his father. And the week after, they will *say* it. Why, it is just like being the past tense of the compound reflexive adverbial incandescent hypodermic irregular accusative Noun of Multitude; which is father to the expression which the grammarians call Verb. It is like a whole ancestry, with only one posterity.

To resume. Next, the young Bacon took up the study of law, and mastered that abstruse science. From that day to the end of his life he was daily in close contact with lawyers and judges; not as a casual onlooker in intervals between holding horses in front of a theatre, but as a practicing lawyer – a great and successful one, a renowned one, a Launcelot of the bar, the most formidable lance in the high brotherhood of the legal Table Round; he lived in the law's atmosphere thenceforth, all his years, and by sheer ability forced his way up its difficult steeps to its supremest summit, the Lord Chancellorship, leaving behind him no fellow craftsman qualified to challenge his divine right to that majestic place.

When we read the praises bestowed by Lord Penzance and the other illustrious experts upon the legal condition and legal aptnesses, brilliances, profundities and felicities so prodigally displayed in the Plays, and try to fit them to the history-less Stratford stage-manager, they sound wild, strange, incredible, ludicrous; but when we put them in the mouth of Bacon they do not sound strange, they seem in their natural and rightful place, they seem at home there. Please turn back and read them again. Attributed to Shakespeare of Stratford they are meaningless, they are inebriate extravagancies – intemperate admirations of the dark side of the moon, so to speak; attributed to Bacon, they are admirations of the golden glories of the moon's front side, the moon at the full – and not intemperate, not overwrought, but sane and right, and justified. "At every turn and point at which the author required a metaphor, simile or illustration, his mind ever turned *first* to the law; he seems almost to have *thought* in legal phrases; the commonest legal phrases, the commonest of legal expressions were ever at the end of his pen." That could happen to no one but a person whose *trade* was the law; it could not happen to a dabbler in it. Veteran mariners fill their conversation with sailor-phrases and draw all their similes from the ship and the sea and the storm, but no mere *passenger* ever does it, be he of Stratford or elsewhere; or could do it with anything resembling accuracy, if he were hardy enough to try. Please read again what Lord Campbell and the other great authorities have said about Bacon when they thought they were saying it about Shakespeare of Stratford.

CHAPTER X – The Rest of the Equipment

The author of the Plays was equipped, beyond every other man of his time, with wisdom, erudition, imagination, capaciousness of mind, grace and majesty of expression. Every one has said it, no one doubts it. Also, he had humor, humor in rich abundance, and always wanting to break out. We have no evidence of any kind that Shakespeare of Stratford possessed any of these gifts or any of these acquirements. The only lines he ever wrote, so far as we know, are substantially barren of them – barren of all of them.

> Good friend for Iesus sake forbeare
> To digg the dust enclosed heare:
> Blest be ye man yt spares thes stones
> And curst be he yt moves my bones.

Ben Jonson says of Bacon, as orator:

> His language, *where he could spare and pass by a jest*, was nobly censorious. No man ever spoke more neatly, more pressly, more weightily, or suffered less emptiness, less idleness, in what he uttered. No member of his speech but consisted of his (its) own graces ... The fear of every man that heard him was lest he should make an end.

From Macaulay:

> He continued to distinguish himself in Parliament, particularly
> by his exertions in favor of one excellent measure on which the
> King's heart was set – the union of England and Scotland. It was
> not difficult for such an intellect to discover many irresistible
> arguments in favor of such a scheme. He conducted the great
> case of the *Post Nati* in the Exchequer Chamber; and the decision
> of the judges – a decision the legality of which may be ques-
> tioned, but the beneficial effect of which must be acknowledged
> – was in a great measure attributed to his dexterous
> management.

Again:

> While actively engaged in the House of Commons and in the
> courts of law, he still found leisure for letters and philosophy.
> The noble treatise on the *Advancement of Learning*, which at a later
> period was expanded into the *De Augmentis*, appeared in 1605.
>
> The *Wisdom of the Ancients*, a work which if it had proceeded
> from any other writer would have been considered as a master-
> piece of wit and learning, was printed in 1609.
>
> In the meantime the *Novum Organum* was slowly proceeding.
> Several distinguished men of learning had been permitted to
> see portions of that extraordinary book, and they spoke with the
> greatest admiration of his genius.
>
> Even Sir Thomas Bodley, after perusing the *Cogitata et Visa*,
> one of the most precious of those scattered leaves out of which
> the great oracular volume was afterward made up, acknow-
> ledged that "in all proposals and plots in that book, Bacon
> showed himself a master workman"; and that "it could not be
> gainsaid but all the treatise over did abound with choice con-
> ceits of the present state of learning, and with worthy contem-
> plations of the means to procure it."
>
> In 1612 a new edition of the *Essays* appeared, with additions
> surpassing the original collection both in bulk and quality.
>
> Nor did these pursuits distract Bacon's attention from a work
> the most arduous, the most glorious, and the most useful that
> even his mighty powers could have achieved, "the reducing and
> recompiling," to use his own phrase, "of the laws of England."

To serve the exacting and laborious offices of Attorney General
and Solicitor General would have satisfied the appetite of any

other man for hard work, but Bacon had to add the vast literary industries just described, to satisfy his. He was a born worker.

The service which he rendered to letters during the last five years of his life, amid ten thousand distractions and vexations, increase the regret with which we think on the many years which he had wasted, to use the words of Sir Thomas Bodley, "on such study as was not worthy such a student."

He commenced a digest of the laws of England, a History of England under the Princes of the House of Tudor, a body of National History, a Philosophical Romance. He made extensive and valuable additions to his Essays. He published the inestimable *Treatise De Argumentis Scientiarum*.

Did these labors of Hercules fill up his time to his contentment, and quiet his appetite for work? Not entirely:

The trifles with which he amused himself in hours of pain and languor bore the mark of his mind. *The best jestbook in the world* is that which he dictated from memory, without referring to any book, on a day on which illness had rendered him incapable of serious study.

Here are some scattered remarks (from Macaulay) which throw light upon Bacon, and seem to indicate – and maybe demonstrate – that he was competent to write the Plays and Poems:

With great minuteness of observation he had an amplitude of comprehension such as has never yet been vouchsafed to any other human being.

The "Essays" contain abundant proofs that no nice feature of character, no peculiarity in the ordering of a house, a garden or a court-masque, could escape the notice of one whose mind was capable of taking in the whole world of knowledge.

His understanding resembled the tent which the fairy Paribanou gave to Prince Ahmed: fold it, and it seemed a toy for the hand of a lady; spread it, and the armies of powerful Sultans might repose beneath its shade.

The knowledge in which Bacon excelled all men was a knowledge of the mutual relations of all departments of knowledge.

In a letter written when he was only thirty-one, to his uncle, Lord Burleigh, he said, "I have taken all knowledge to be my province."

Though Bacon did not arm his philosophy with the weapons of logic, he adorned her profusely with all the richest decorations of rhetoric.

The practical faculty was powerful in Bacon; but not, like his wit, so powerful as occasionally to usurp the place of his reason, and to tyrannize over the whole man.

There are too many places in the Plays where this happens. Poor old dying John of Gaunt volleying second-rate puns at his own name, is a pathetic instance of it. "We may assume" that it is Bacon's fault, but the Stratford Shakespeare has to bear the blame.

No imagination was ever at once so strong and so thoroughly subjugated. It stopped at the first check from good sense.

In truth much of Bacon's life was passed in a visionary world – amid things as strange as any that are described in the "Arabian Tales" ... amid buildings more sumptuous than the palace of Aladdin, fountains more wonderful than the golden water of Parizade, conveyances more rapid than the hippogryph of Ruggiero, arms more formidable than the lance of Astolfo, remedies more efficacious than the balsam of Fierabras. Yet in his magnificent day-dreams there was nothing wild – nothing but what sober reason sanctioned.

Bacon's greatest performance is the first book of the *Novum Organum* ... Every part of it blazes with wit, but with wit which is employed only to illustrate and decorate truth. No book ever made so great a revolution in the mode of thinking, overthrew so many prejudices, introduced so many new opinions.

But what we most admire is the vast capacity of that intellect which, without effort, takes in at once all the domains of science – all the past, the present and the future, all the errors of two thousand years, all the encouraging signs of the passing times, all the bright hopes of the coming age.

He had a wonderful talent for packing thought close and rendering it portable.

His eloquence would alone have entitled him to a high rank in literature.

It is evident that he had each and every one of the mental gifts and each and every one of the acquirements that are so prodigally displayed in the Plays and Poems, and in much higher and richer degree than any other man of his time or of any previous time. He

was a genius without a mate, a prodigy not matable. There was
only one of him; the planet could not produce two of him at one
birth, nor in one age. He could have written anything that is in the
Plays and Poems. He could have written this:

> The cloud-cap'd towers, the gorgeous palaces,
> The solemn temples, the great globe itself,
> Yea, all which it inherit, shall dissolve,
> And, like an insubstantial pageant faded,
> Leave not a rack behind. We are such stuff
> As dreams are made on, and our little life
> Is rounded with a sleep.

Also, he could have written this, but he refrained:

> Good friend for Iesus sake forbeare
> To digg the dust encloased heare:
> Blest be ye man yt spares thes stones
> And curst be ye yt moves my bones.

When a person reads the noble verses about the cloud-cap'd
towers, he ought not to follow it immediately with Good friend for
Iesus sake forbeare, because he will find the transition from great
poetry to poor prose too violent for comfort. It will give him a
shock. You never notice how commonplace and unpoetic gravel
is, until you bite into a layer of it in a pie.

CHAPTER XI

Am I trying to convince anybody that Shakespeare did not write
Shakespeare's Works? Ah, now, what do you take me for? Would
I be so soft as that, after having known the human race familiarly
for nearly seventy-four years? It would grieve me to know that any
one could think so injuriously of me, so uncomplimentarily, so
unadmiringly of me. No-no, I am aware that when even the brightest mind in our world has been trained up from childhood in a
superstition of any kind, it will never be possible for that mind, in
its maturity, to examine sincerely, dispassionately, and conscientiously any evidence or any circumstance which shall seem to cast
a doubt upon the validity of that superstition. I doubt if I could do
it myself. We always get at second hand our notions about systems
of government; and high-tariff and low-tariff; and prohibition and
anti-prohibition; and the holiness of peace and the glories of war;

and codes of honor and codes of morals; and approval of the duel and disapproval of it; and our beliefs concerning the nature of cats; and our ideas as to whether the murder of helpless wild animals is base or is heroic; and our preferences in the matter of religious and political parties; and our acceptance or rejection of the Shakespeares and the Arthur Ortons and the Mrs Eddys. We get them all at second-hand, we reason none of them out for ourselves. It is the way we are made. It is the way we are all made, and we can't help it, we can't change it. And whenever we have been furnished a fetish, and have been taught to believe in it, and love it and worship it, and refrain from examining it, there is no evidence, howsoever clear and strong, that can persuade us to withdraw from it our loyalty and our devotion. In morals, conduct, and beliefs we take the color of our environment and associations, and it is a color that can safely be warranted to wash. Whenever we have been furnished with a tar baby ostensibly stuffed with jewels, and warned that it will be dishonorable and irreverent to disembowel it and test the jewels, we keep our sacrilegious hands off it. We submit, not reluctantly, but rather gladly, for we are privately afraid we should find, upon examination, that the jewels are of the sort that are manufactured at North Adams, Mass.

I haven't any idea that Shakespeare will have to vacate his pedestal this side of the year 2209. Disbelief in him cannot come swiftly, disbelief in a healthy and deeply-loved tar baby has never been known to disintegrate swiftly, it is a very slow process. It took several thousand years to convince our fine race – including every splendid intellect in it – that there is no such thing as a witch; it has taken several thousand years to convince that same fine race – including every splendid intellect in it – that there is no such person as Satan; it has taken several centuries to remove perdition from the Protestant Church's program of postmortem entertainments; it has taken a weary long time to persuade American Presbyterians to give up infant damnation and try to bear it the best they can; and it looks as if their Scotch brethren will still be burning babies in the everlasting fires when Shakespeare comes down from his perch.

We are The Reasoning Race. We can't prove it by the above examples, and we can't prove it by the miraculous "histories" built by those Stratfordolaters out of a hatful of rags and a barrel of sawdust, but there is a plenty of other things we can prove it by, if I could think of them. We are The Reasoning Race, and when we find a vague file of chipmunk-tracks stringing through the dust of Stratford village, we know by our reasoning powers that Hercules has been along there. I feel that our fetish is safe for three centuries yet. The bust, too – there in the Stratford Church. The precious bust, the priceless bust, the calm bust, the serene bust, the emotionless bust, with the dandy moustache, and the putty face, unseamed of care – that face which has looked passionlessly down upon the awed pilgrim for a hundred and fifty years and will still look down upon the awed pilgrim three hundred more, with the deep, deep, deep, subtle, subtle, subtle, expression of a bladder.

CHAPTER XII – Irreverence

One of the most trying defects which I find in these – these – what shall I call them? for I will not apply injurious epithets to them, the way they do to us, such violations of courtesy being repugnant to my nature and my dignity. The furthest I can go in that direction is to call them by names of limited reverence – names merely descriptive, never unkind, never offensive, never tainted by harsh feeling. If *they* would do like this, they would feel better in their hearts. Very well, then – to proceed. One of the most trying defects which I find in these Stratfordolaters, these Shakesperoids, these thugs, these bangalores, these troglodytes, these herumfrodites, these blatherskites, these buccaneers, these bandoleers, is their spirit of irreverence. It is detectable in every utterance of theirs when they are talking about us. I am thankful that in me there is nothing of that spirit. When a thing is sacred to me it is impossible for me to be irreverent toward it. I cannot call to mind a single instance where I have ever been irreverent, except toward the things which were sacred to other people. Am I in the right? I think so. But I ask no one to take my unsupported word; no, look at the dictionary; let the dictionary decide. Here is the definition:

> *Irreverence.* The quality or condition of irreverence toward God and sacred things.

What does the Hindu say? He says it is correct. He says irreverence is lack of respect for Vishnu, and Brahma, and Chrishna, and his other gods, and for his sacred cattle, and for his temples and the things within them. He endorses the definition, you see; and there are 300,000,000 Hindus or their equivalents back of him.

The dictionary had the acute idea that by using the capital G it could restrict irreverence to lack of reverence for *our* Deity and our sacred things, but that ingenious and rather sly idea miscarried: for by the simple process of spelling *his* deities with capitals the Hindu confiscates the definition and restricts it to his own sects, thus making it clearly compulsory upon us to revere *his* gods and *his* sacred things, and nobody's else. We can't say a word, for he has our own dictionary at his back, and its decision is final.

This law, reduced to its simplest terms, is this: 1. Whatever is sacred to the Christian must be held in reverence by everybody else; 2, whatever is sacred to the Hindu must be held in reverence by everybody else; 3, therefore, by consequence, logically, and indisputably, whatever is sacred to *me* must be held in reverence by everybody else.

Now then, what aggravates me is, that these troglodytes and muscovites and bandoleers and buccaneers are *also* trying to crowd in and share the benefit of the law, and compel everybody to revere their Shakespeare and hold him sacred. We can't have that: there's enough of us already. If you go on widening and spreading and inflating the privilege, it will presently come to be conceded that each man's sacred things are the *only* ones, and the rest of the human race will have to be humbly reverent toward them or suffer for it. That can surely happen, and when it happens, the word Irreverence will be regarded as the most meaningless, and foolish, and self-conceited, and insolent, and impudent and dictatorial word in the language. And people will say, "Whose business is it, what gods I worship and what things hold sacred? Who has the right to dictate to my conscience, and where did he get that right?"

We cannot afford to let that calamity come upon us. We must save the word from this destruction. There is but one way to do it, and that is, to stop the spread of the privilege, and strictly confine it to its present limits: that is, to all the Christian sects, to all the Hindu sects, and me. We do not need any more, the stock is watered enough, just as it is.

It would be better if the privilege were limited to me alone. I think so because I am the only sect that knows how to employ it gently, kindly, charitably, dispassionately. The other sects lack the quality of self-restraint. The Catholic Church says the most irreverent things about matters which are sacred to the Protestants, and the Protestant Church retorts in kind about the confessional and other matters which Catholics hold sacred; then both of these irreverencers turn upon Thomas Paine and charge *him* with irreverence. This is all unfortunate, because it makes it difficult for students equipped with only a low grade of mentality to find out what Irreverence really *is*.

It will surely be much better all around if the privilege of regulating the irreverent and keeping them in order shall eventually be withdrawn from all the sects but me. Then there will be no more quarrelling, no more bandying of disrespectful epithets, no more heart burnings.

There will then be nothing sacred involved in this Bacon-Shakespeare controversy except what is sacred to me. That will simplify the whole matter, and trouble will cease. There will be irreverence no longer, because I will not allow it. The first time those criminals charge me with irreverence for calling their Stratford myth an Arthur-Orton-Mary-Baker-Thompson-Eddy-Louis-the-Seventeenth-Veiled-Prophet-of-Khorassan will be the last. Taught by the methods found effective in extinguishing earlier offenders by the Inquisition, of holy memory, I shall know how to quiet them.

CHAPTER XIII

Isn't it odd, when you think of it: that you may list all the celebrated Englishmen, Irishmen, and Scotchmen of modern times, clear back to the first Tudors – a list containing five hundred names, shall we say? – and you can go to the histories, biographies and cyclopedias and learn the particulars of the lives of every one of them. Every one of them except one – the most famous, the most renowned – by far the most illustrious of them all – Shakespeare! You can get the details of the lives of all the celebrated ecclesiastics in the list; all the celebrated tragedians, comedians, singers, dancers, orators, judges, lawyers, poets, dramatists, historians, biographers, editors, inventors, reformers, statesmen, generals, admirals, discoverers, prize-fighters, murderers, pirates, conspirators, horse-jockeys, bunco-steerers, misers, swindlers, explorers, adventurers by land and sea, bankers, financiers, astronomers, naturalists, Claimants, impostors, chemists, biologists, geologists, philologists, college presidents and professors, architects, engineers, painters, sculptors, politicians, agitators, rebels, revolutionists, patriots, demagogues, clowns, cooks, freaks, philosophers, burglars, highwaymen, journalists, physicians, surgeons – you can get the life-histories of all of them but *one*. Just one – the most extraordinary and the most celebrated of them all – Shakespeare!

You may add to the list the thousand celebrated persons furnished by the rest of Christendom in the past four centuries, and you can find out the life-histories of all those people, too. You will then have listed 1500 celebrities, and you can trace the authentic life-histories of the whole of them. Save one – far and away the most colossal prodigy of the entire accumulation – Shakespeare! About him you can find out *nothing*. Nothing of even the slightest importance. Nothing worth the trouble of stowing away in your memory. Nothing that even remotely indicates that he was ever anything more than a distinctly common-place person – a manager, an actor of inferior grade, a small trader in a small village that did not regard him as a person of any consequence, and had forgotten all about him before he was fairly cold in his grave. We can go to the records and find out the life-history of every renowned *race-horse* of modern times – but not Shakespeare's! There are many reasons why, and they have been furnished in cartloads (of guess and conjecture) by those troglodytes; but there is one that is worth all the rest of the reasons put together, and is abundantly sufficient all by itself – *he hadn't any history to record.* There is no way of getting around that deadly fact. And no sane way has yet been discovered of getting around its formidable significance.

Its quite plain significance – to any but those thugs (I do not use the term unkindly) is, that Shakespeare had no prominence while he lived, and none until he had been dead two or three generations. The Plays enjoyed high fame from the beginning; and if he wrote them it seems a pity the world did not find it out. He ought to have explained that he was the author, and not merely a *nom de plume* for another man to hide behind. If he had been less intemperately solicitous about his bones, and more solicitous about his Works, it would have been better for his good name, and a kindness to us. The bones were not important. They will moulder away, they will turn to dust, but the Works will endure until the last sun goes down.

MARK TWAIN.

P.S. *March* 25: About two months ago I was illuminating this Autobiography with some notions of mine concerning the Bacon-Shakespeare controversy, and I then took occasion to air the opinion that the Stratford Shakespeare was a person of no public consequence or celebrity during his lifetime, but was utterly

obscure and unimportant. And not only in great London, but also
in the little village where he was born, where he lived a quarter of
a century, and where he died and was buried. I argued that if he
had been a person of any note at all, aged villagers would have
had much to tell about him many and many a year after his death,
instead of being unable to furnish inquirers a single fact connected
with him. I believed, and I still believe, that if he had been famous,
his notoriety would have lasted as long as mine has lasted in my
native village out in Missouri. It is a good argument, a prodigiously
strong one, and a most formidable one for even the most gifted,
and ingenious, and plausible Stratfordolater to get around or
explain away. To-day a Hannibal *Courier-Post* of recent date has
reached me, with an article in it which reinforces my contention
that a really celebrated person cannot be forgotten in his village
in the short space of sixty years. I will make an extract from it:

> Hannibal, as a city, may have many sins to answer for, but
> ingratitude is not one of them, or reverence for the great men
> she has produced, and as the years go by her greatest son Mark
> Twain, or S. L. Clemens as a few of the unlettered call him,
> grows in the estimation and regard of the residents of the town
> he made famous and the town that made him famous. His name
> is associated with every old building that is torn down to make
> way for the modern structures demanded by a rapidly growing
> city, and with every hill or cave over or through which he might
> by any possibility have roamed, while the many points of inter-
> est which he wove into his stories, such as Holiday Hill, Jack-
> son's Island, or Mark Twain Cave, are now monuments to his
> genius. Hannibal is glad of any opportunity to do him honor as
> he has honored her.
>
> So it has happened that the "old timers" who went to school
> with Mark or were with him on some of his usual escapades have
> been honored with large audiences whenever they were in a
> reminiscent mood and condescended to tell of their intimacy
> with the ordinary boy who came to be a very extraordinary
> humorist and whose every boyish act is now seen to have been
> indicative of what was to come. Like Aunt Beckey and Mrs Cle-
> mens, they can now see that Mark was hardly appreciated when
> he lived here and that the things he did as a boy and was
> whipped for doing were not all bad after all. So they have been
> in no hesitancy about drawing out the bad things he did as well

as the good in their efforts to get a "Mark Twain story," all incidents being viewed in the light of his present fame, until the volume of "Twainiana" is already considerable and growing in proportion as the "old timers" drop away and the stories are retold second and third hand by their descendants. With some seventy-three years young and living in a villa instead of a house he is a fair target, and let him incorporate, copyright, or patent himself as he will, there are some of his "works" that will go swooping up Hannibal chimneys as long as gray-beards gather about the fires and begin with "I've heard father tell" or possibly "Once when I."

The Mrs Clemens referred to is my mother – *was* my mother.

And here is another extract from a Hannibal paper. Of date twenty days ago:

Miss Becca Blankenship died at the home of William Dickason, 408 Rock Street, at 2.30 o'clock yesterday afternoon, aged 72 years. The deceased was a sister of "Huckleberry Finn," one of the famous characters in Mark Twain's *Tom Sawyer*. She had been a member of the Dickason family – the housekeeper – for nearly forty-five years, and was a highly respected lady. For the past eight years she had been an invalid, but was as well cared for by Mr. Dickason and his family as if she had been a near relative. She was a member of the Park Methodist Church and a Christian woman.

I remember her well. I have a picture of her in my mind which was graven there, clear and sharp and vivid, sixty-three years ago. She was at that time nine years old, and I was about eleven. I remember where she stood, and how she looked; and I can still see her bare feet, her bare head, her brown face, and her short tow-linen frock. She was crying. What it was about, I have long ago forgotten. But it was the tears that preserved the picture for me, no doubt. She was a good child, I can say that for her. She knew me nearly seventy years ago. Did she forget me, in the course of time? I think not. If she had lived in Stratford in Shakespeare's time, would she have forgotten him? Yes. For he was never famous during his lifetime, he was utterly obscure in Stratford, and there wouldn't be any occasion to remember him after he had been dead a week.

"Injun Joe," "Jimmy Finn," and "General Gaines" were prominent and very intemperate ne'er-do-weels in Hannibal two generations ago. Plenty of gray-heads there remember them to this day, and can tell you about them. Isn't it curious that two "town-drunkards" and one half-breed loafer should leave behind them, in a remote Missourian village, a fame a hundred times greater and several hundred times more particularized in the matter of definite facts than Shakespeare left behind him in the village where he had lived the half of his lifetime?

MARK TWAIN.

"THE TURNING POINT
OF MY LIFE"

I

If I understand the idea, the *Bazar* invites several of us to write upon the above text. It means the change in my life's course which introduced what must be regarded by me as the most *important* condition of my career. But it also implies – without intention, perhaps – that that turning point was *itself*, individually, the creator of the new condition. This gives it too much distinction, too much prominence, too much credit. It is only the *last* link in a very long chain of turning points commissioned to produce the weighty result; it is not any more important than the humblest of its ten thousand predecessors. Each of the ten thousand did its appointed share, on its appointed date, in forwarding the scheme, and they were all necessary; to have left out any one of them would have defeated the scheme and brought about *some other* result. I know we have a fashion of saying "such and such an event was *the* turning point in my life," but we shouldn't say it. We should merely grant that its place as *last* link in the chain makes it the most *conspicuous* link; in real importance it has no advantage over any one of its predecessors.

Perhaps the most celebrated turning point recorded in history was the crossing of the Rubicon. Suetonius says:

> Coming up with his troops on the banks of the Rubicon, he halted for a while, and, revolving in his mind the importance of the step he was on the point of taking, he turned to those about him and said, "We may still retreat; but if we pass this little bridge, nothing is left for us but to fight it out in arms."

This was a stupendously important moment. And all the incidents, big and little, of Caesar's previous life had been leading up to it, stage by stage, link by link. This was the *last* link – merely the last one, and no bigger than the others; but as we gaze back at it through the inflating mists of our imagination, it looks as big as the orbit of Neptune.

You, the reader, have a *personal* interest in that link, and so have I; so has the rest of the human race. It was one of the links in your life-chain, and it was one of the links in mine. We may wait, now, with bated breath, while Caesar reflects. Your fate and mine are involved in his decision.

While he was thus hesitating, the following incident occurred. A person remarkable for his noble mien and graceful aspect, appeared close at hand, sitting and playing upon a pipe. When not only the shepherds, but a number of soldiers also, flocked to listen to him, and some trumpeters among them, he snatched a trumpet from one of them, ran to the river with it, and sounding the advance with a piercing blast, crossed to the other side. Upon this, Caesar exclaimed, "Let us go whither the omens of the gods and the iniquity of our enemies call us. *The die is cast.*"

So he crossed – and changed the future of the whole human race, for all time. But that stranger was a link in Caesar's life-chain, too; and a necessary one. We don't know his name, we never hear of him again, he was very casual, he acts like an accident; but he was no accident, he was there by compulsion of *his* life-chain, to blow the electrifying blast that was to make up Caesar's mind for him, and thence go piping down the aisles of history forever.

If the stranger hadn't been there! But he *was*. And Caesar crossed. With such results! Such vast events – each a link in the *human race's* life-chain; each event producing the next one, and that one the next one, and so on: the destruction of the republic; the founding of the empire; the breaking up of the empire; the rise of Christianity upon its ruins; the spread of the religion to other lands – and so on: link by link took its appointed place at its appointed time, the discovery of America being one of them; our Revolution another; the inflow of English and other immigrants another; their drift westward (my ancestors among them) another; the settlement of certain of them in Missouri – which resulted in *me*. For I was one of the unavoidable results of the crossing of the Rubicon. If the stranger, with his trumpet blast, had stayed away (which he *couldn't*, for he was an appointed link), Caesar would not have crossed. What would have happened, in that case, we can never guess. We only know that the things that did happen would not have happened. They might have been replaced by equally prodigious things, of course, but their nature and results are beyond our guessing. But the matter that interests me personally is, that I would not be *here*, now, but somewhere else; and probably black – there is no telling. Very well, I am glad he crossed. And very really and thankfully glad, too, though I never cared anything about it before.

II

To me, the most important feature of my life is its literary feature. I have been professionally literary something more than forty years. There have been many turning points in my life, but the one that was the last link in the chain appointed to conduct me to the literary guild is the most *conspicuous* link in that chain. *Because* it was the last one. It was not any more important than its predecessors. All the other links have an inconspicuous look, except the crossing of the Rubicon; but as factors in making me literary they are all of the one size, the crossing of the Rubicon included.

I know how I came to be literary, and I will tell the steps that led up to it and brought it about.

The crossing of the Rubicon was not the first one, it was hardly even a recent one; I should have to go back ages before Caesar's day to find the first one. To save space I will go back only a couple of generations, and start with an incident of my boyhood. When I was twelve and a half years old, my father died. It was in the spring. The summer came, and brought with it an epidemic of measles. For a time, a child died almost every day. The village was paralysed with fright, distress, despair. Children that were not smitten with the disease were imprisoned in their homes to save them from the infection. In the homes there were no cheerful faces, there was no music, there was no singing but of solemn hymns, no voice but of prayer, no romping was allowed, no noise, no laughter, the family moved spectrally about on tiptoe, in a ghostly hush. I was a prisoner. My soul was steeped in this awful dreariness – and in fear. At some time or other every day and every night a sudden shiver shook me to the marrow, and I said to myself, "There, I've got it! and I shall die." Life on these miserable terms was not worth living, and at last I made up my mind to get the disease and have it over, one way or the other. I escaped from the house and went to the house of neighbor where a playmate of mine was very ill with the malady. When the chance offered I crept into his room and got into bed with him. I was discovered by his mother and sent back into captivity. But I had the disease; they could not take that from me. I came near to dying. The whole village was interested, and anxious, and sent for news of me every day; and not only once a day, but several times. Everybody believed I would die; but on the fourteenth day a change came for the worse and they were disappointed.

This was a turning point of my life. (Link number one.) For when I got well my mother closed my school career and apprenticed me to a printer. She was tired of trying to keep me out of mischief, and the adventure of the measles decided her to put me into more masterful hands than hers.

I became a printer, and began to add one link after another to the chain which was to lead me into the literary profession. A long road, but I could not know that; and as I did not know what its goal was, or even that it had one, I was indifferent. Also contented.

A young printer wanders around a good deal, seeking and finding work; and seeking again, when necessity commands. N. B. Necessity is a *Circumstance*; Circumstance is man's master – and when Circumstance commands, he must obey; he may argue the matter – that is his privilege, just as it is the honorable privilege of a falling body to argue with the attraction of gravitation – but it won't do any good, he must *obey*. I wandered for ten years, under the guidance and dictatorship of Circumstance, and finally arrived in a city of Iowa, where I worked several months. Among the books that interested me in those days was one about the Amazon. The traveler told an alluring tale of his long voyage up the great river from Para to the sources of the Madeira, through the heart of an enchanted land, a land wastefully rich in tropical wonders, a romantic land where all the birds and flowers and animals were of the museum varieties, and where the alligator and the crocodile and the monkey seemed as much at home as if they were in the Zoo. Also, he told an astonishing tale about *coca*, a vegetable product of miraculous powers; asserting that it was so nourishing and so strength-giving that the native of the mountains of the Madeira region would tramp up-hill and down all day on a pinch of powdered coca and require no other sustenance.

I was fired with a longing to ascend the Amazon. Also with a longing to open up a trade in coca with all the world. During months I dreamed that dream, and tried to contrive ways to get to Para and spring that splendid enterprise upon an unsuspecting planet. But all in vain. A person may *plan* as much as he wants to, but nothing of consequence is likely to come of it until the magician *Circumstance* steps in and takes the matter off his hands. At last Circumstance came to my help. It was in this way. Circumstance, to help or hurt another man, made him lose a fifty-dollar bill in the street; and to help or hurt me, made me find it. I advertised the find, and left for the Amazon the same day. This was another turning point, another link.

Could Circumstance have ordered another dweller in that town to go to the Amazon and open up a world-trade in coca on a fifty-dollar basis and been obeyed? No, I was the only one. There were other fools there – shoals and shoals of them – but they were not of my kind. I was the only one of my kind.

Circumstance is powerful, but it cannot work alone, it has to have a partner. Its partner is man's *temperament* – his natural disposition. His temperament is not his invention, it is *born* in him, and he has no authority over it, neither is he responsible for its acts. He cannot change it, nothing can change it, nothing can modify it, – except temporarily. But it won't stay modified. It is permanent; like the color of the man's eyes and the shape of his ears. Blue eyes are gray, in certain unusual lights; but they resume their natural color when that stress is removed.

A Circumstance that will coerce one man, will have no effect upon a man of a different temperament. If Circumstance had thrown the bank note in Caesar's way, his temperament would not have made him start for the Amazon. His temperament would have compelled him to do something with the money, but not that. It might have made him advertise the note – and *wait*. We can't tell. Also, it might have made him go to New York and buy into the government; with results that would leave Tweed nothing to learn when it came his turn.

Very well, Circumstance furnished the capital, and my temperament told me what to do with it. Sometimes a temperament is an ass. When that is the case the owner of it is an ass, too, and is going to remain one. Training, experience, association, can temporarily so elevate him that people will think he is a mule, but they will be mistaken. Artificially he *is* a mule, for the time being, but at bottom he is an ass yet, and will remain one.

By temperament I was the kind of person that *does* things. Does them, and reflects afterwards. So I started for the Amazon, without reflecting, and without asking any questions. That was more than fifty years ago. In all that time my temperament has not changed, by even a shade. I have been punished many and many a time, and bitterly, for doing things first and reflecting afterward, but these tortures have been of no value to me; I still do the thing commanded by Circumstance and Temperament, and reflect afterward. Always violently. When I am reflecting, on those occasions, even deaf persons can hear me think.

I went by the way of Cincinnati, and down the Ohio and Mississippi. My idea was to take ship, at New Orleans, for Para. In New Orleans I inquired, and found there was no ship leaving for Para. Also, that there never had *been* one leaving for Para. I reflected. A policeman came and asked me what I was doing, and I told him. He made me move on; and said if he caught me reflecting in the public street again he would run me in.

After a few days I was out of money. Then Circumstance arrived, with another turning point of my life – a new link. On my way down, I had made the acquaintance of a pilot; I begged him to teach me the river, and he consented. I became a pilot.

By and by Circumstance came again – introducing the Civil War, this time, in order to push me ahead a stage or two toward the literary profession. The boats stopped running, my livelihood was gone.

Circumstance came to the rescue with a new turning point and a fresh link. My brother was appointed secretary to the new Territory of Nevada, and he invited me to go with him and help him in his office. I accepted.

In Nevada, Circumstance furnished me the silver fever and I went into the mines to make a fortune and enter the ministry. As I supposed; but that was not the idea. The idea was, to move me another step toward literature. For amusement I scribbled things for the Virginia City *Enterprise*. One isn't a printer ten years without setting up acres of good and bad literature, and learning – unconsciously at first, consciously later – to discriminate between the two, within his mental limitations; and meantime he is unconsciously acquiring what is called a "style." One of my efforts attracted attention, and the *Enterprise* sent for me, and put me on its staff.

And so I became a journalist – another link. By and by Circumstance and the Sacramento *Union* sent me to the Sandwich Islands for five or six months, to write up sugar. I did it; and threw in a good deal of extraneous matter that hadn't anything to do with sugar. But it was this extraneous matter that helped me to another link.

It made me notorious, and San Francisco invited me to lecture. Which I did. And profitably. I had long had a desire to travel and see the world, and now the platform had furnished me the means. So I joined the "Quaker City Excursion."

When I returned to America, Circumstance was waiting on the pier – with the *last* link: I was asked to *write a book*, and I did it, and called it *The Innocents Abroad*. Thus at last I became a member of the literary guild. That was forty-two years ago, and I have been a member ever since. Leaving the Rubicon incident away back where it belongs, I can say with truth that the reason I am in the literary profession is because I had the measles when I was twelve years old.

III

Now what interests me, as regards these details, is not the details themselves, but the fact that none of them was foreseen by me, none of them was planned by me, I was the author of none of them. Circumstance, working in harness with my temperament, created them all and compelled them all. I often offered help, and with the best intentions, but it was rejected: as a rule, uncourteously. I could never plan a thing and get it to come out the way I planned it. It came out some other way – some way I had not counted upon.

And so I do not admire the human being – as an intellectual marvel – as much as I did when I was young, and got him out of books, and did not know him personally. When I used to read that such and such a general did a certain brilliant thing, I believed it. Whereas it was not so. Circumstance did it, by help of his temperament. The circumstances would have failed of effect with a general of another temperament: he might see the chance, but lose the advantage by being by nature too slow or too quick or too doubtful. Once General Grant was asked a question about a matter which had been much debated by the public and the newspapers; he answered the question without any hesitancy: "General, who planned the march through Georgia?" "The enemy!" He added that the enemy usually makes your plans for you. He meant that the enemy, by neglect or through force of circumstances, leaves an opening for you, and you see your chance and take advantage of it.

Circumstances do the planning for us all, no doubt, by help of our temperaments. I see no great difference between a man and a watch, except that the man is conscious and the watch isn't, and the man *tries* to plan things and the watch doesn't. The watch doesn't wind itself, and doesn't regulate itself – these things are done exteriorly. Outside influences, outside circumstances, wind the *man* and regulate him. Left to himself he wouldn't get regulated at all, and the sort of time he would keep would not be valuable. Some rare men are wonderful watches, with gold case, compensation balance, and all those things, and some men are only simple and sweet and humble Waterburys. I am a Waterbury. A Waterbury of that kind, some say.

A nation is only an individual, multiplied. It makes plans, and Circumstance comes and upsets them – or enlarges them. A gang of patriots throws the tea overboard; it destroys a Bastile. The plans stop there; then Circumstance comes in, quite unexpectedly, and turns these modest riots into a revolution.

And there was poor Columbus. He elaborated a deep plan to find a new route to an old country. Circumstance revised his plan for him, and he found a new *world*. And *he* gets the credit of it, to this day. He hadn't anything to do with it.

Necessarily the scene of the real turning point of my life (and of yours) was the Garden of Eden. It was there that the first link was forged of the chain that was ultimately to lead to the emptying of me into the literary guild. Adam's *temperament* was the first command the Deity ever issued to a human being on this planet. And it was the only command Adam would *never* be able to disobey. It said, "Be weak, be water, be characterless, be cheaply persuadable." The later command, to let the fruit alone, was certain to be disobeyed. Not by Adam himself, but by his *temperament* – which he did not create and had no authority over. For the *temperament* is the man; the thing tricked out with clothes and named Man, is merely its Shadow, nothing more. The law of the tiger's temperament is, Thou shalt kill; the law of the sheep's temperament is, Thou shalt not kill. To issue later commands requiring the tiger to let the fat stranger alone, and requiring the sheep to imbue its hands in the blood of the lion is not worth while, for those commands *can't* be obeyed. They would invite to violations of the law of *temperament*, which is supreme, and takes precedence of all other authorities. I cannot help feeling disappointed in Adam and Eve. That is, in their temperaments. Not in *them*, poor helpless young creatures – afflicted with temperaments made out of butter; which butter was commanded to get into contact with fire and *be melted*. What I cannot help wishing is, that Adam and Eve had been postponed, and Martin Luther and Joan of Arc put in their place – that splendid pair equipped with temperaments not made of butter, but

of asbestos. By neither sugary persuasions nor by hellfire could
Satan have beguiled *them* to eat the apple.

There would have been results! Indeed yes. The apple would be
intact to-day: there would be no human race; there would be no
you; there would be no *me*. And the old, old, creation-dawn scheme
of ultimately launching me into the literary guild would have been
defeated.

February 1910

This book is set in BASKERVILLE. John Baskerville of Birmingham formed his ideas of letter-design during his early career as a writing-master and engraver of inscriptions. He retired in middle age, set up a press of his own and produced his first book in 1757.